WEBSTER'S
CONCISE
DICTIONARY

RHR
PRESS

New York

Contents

Pronunciation Key   iv

Abbreviations Key   v

A Dictionary of the English Language   1

Computer & Multimedia Glossary   435

Signs   447

Avoiding Insensitive and Offensive Language   448

Proofreaders' Marks   451

Metric and U.S. Measurements   454

Pronunciation Key

STRESS

Pronunciations are marked for stress to reveal the relative differences in emphasis between syllables. In words of two or more syllables, a primary stress mark (ˊ), as in **mother** (muᵺer), follows the syllable having greatest stress. A secondary stress mark (ˈ), as **grandmother** (grandˊmuᵺˈər), follows a syllable having slightly less stress than primary but more stress than an unmarked syllable.

ENGLISH SOUNDS

a	act, bat, marry		o͝o	book, tour
ā	age, paid, say		o͞o	ooze, fool, too
â(r)	air, dare, Mary		ou	out, loud, cow
ä	ah, part, balm		p	pot, supper, stop
b	back, cabin, cab		r	read, hurry, near
ch	child, beach		s	see, passing, miss
d	do, madder, bed		sh	shoe, fashion, push
e	edge, set, merry		t	ten, matter, bit
ē	equal, bee, pretty		th	thin, ether, path
ēr	ear, mere		ᵺ	that, either, smooth
f	fit, differ, puff		u	up, sun
g	give, trigger, beg		û(r)	urge, burn, cur
h	hit, behave		v	voice, river, live
hw	which, nowhere		w	witch, away
i	if, big, mirror		y	yes, onion
ī	ice, bite, deny		z	zoo, lazy, those
j	just, tragic, fudge		zh	treasure, mirage
k	keep, token, make		ə	used in unaccented syllables
l	low, mellow, bottle (botˊl)			to indicate the sound of the
m	my, summer, him			reduced vowel in alone,
n	now, sinner, button (butˊn)			system, easily, gallop, circus
ng	sing, Washington		ᵊ	used between ī and r and
o	ox, bomb, wasp			between ou and r to show
ō	over, boat, no			triphthongal quality, as in **fire**
ô	order, ball, raw			(fiᵊr), **hour** (ouᵊr)
oi	oil, joint, joy			

NON-ENGLISH SOUNDS

A	as in French **ami** (A mēˊ)		flap in Italian and Spanish
KH	as in Scottish **loch** (lôKH)		and a sound in French and
N	as in French **bon** (bôN) [used		German similar to KH but pro-
	to indicate that the preceding		nounced with voice]
	vowel is nasalized.]	Y	as in French **tu** (tY)
Œ	as in French **feu** (fŒ)	ᵊ	as in French **Bastogne**
R	[a symbol for any non-English		(bAstônˊyᵊ)
	r sound, including a trill or		

ABBREVIATIONS KEY

adj.	adjective
adv.	adverb
aux.	auxiliary
Brit.	British
cap.	capital
conj.	conjunction
def.	definition(s)
esp.	especially
fem.	feminine
interj.	interjection
irreg.	irregular
l.c.	lowercase
n.	noun
pl.	plural
prep.	preposition
pron.	pronoun
pt.	preterit (past tense)
sing.	singular
usu.	usually
v.	verb

A

A, a (ā) *n.* first letter of English alphabet.

a (ə; *when stressed* ā) *adj. or indef. art. before initial consonant sounds.* **1.** some. **2.** one. **3.** any.

a-, prefix indicating: **1.** not, a s *atypical.* **2.** without, as *amorality.*

AA, 1. administrative assistant. **2.** Alcoholics Anonymous. **3.** anti-aircraft.

A.A., Associate in Arts.

AAA 1. Agricultural Adjustment Administration. **2.** Amateur Athletic Association. **3.** American Automobile Association. **4.** antiaircraft artillery. **5.** Automobile Association of America.

AAA *Symbol.* **1.** a proportional shoe width size, narrower than AA. **2.** the highest quality rating for a corporate or municipal bond. **3.** *Electricity.* a battery size for 1.5 volt dry cells: diameter, 0.4 in. (1 cm); length 1.7 in. (4.3 cm).

A.A.A. 1. Amateur Athletic Association. **2.** American Automobile Association. **3.** Automobile Association of America.

A.A.A.L. American Academy of Arts and Letters.

A.A.A.S. American Association for the Advancement of Science. Also, **AAAS**

A.A.E. American Association of Engineers.

A.Ae.E. Associate in Aeronautical Engineering.

A.A.E.E. American Association of Electrical Engineers.

AAES American Association of Engineering Societies.

AAF 1. Allied Air Forces. **2.** (in the U.S., formerly) Army Air Forces. Also, **A.A.F.**

A.Agr. Associate in Agriculture.

AAM air-to-air missile.

a&b assault and battery.

A&E Arts and Entertainment (a cable television station).

a&h *Insurance.* accident and health.

a&i *Insurance.* accident and indemnity.

A&M Agricultural and Mechanical (college). Also, **A and M**

A&R (in the recording industry) artists and repertory. Also, **A. & R., A-and-R**

a&r assault and robbery.

a&s *Insurance.* accident and sickness.

AAP Association of American Publishers.

A.A.P.S.S. American Academy of Political and Social Science.

a.a.r. 1. against all risks. **2.** average annual rainfall.

aard′vark′ (ärd′värk′) *n.* African ant-eating mammal.

AARP (*pronounced as initials or* ärp) American Association of Retired Persons.

A.A.S. 1. Fellow of the American Academy. [from Latin *Academiae Americanae Socius*] **2.** American Academy of Sciences. **3.** Associate in Applied Science.

A.A.U. Amateur Athletic Union. Also, **AAU**

A.A.U.P. 1. American Association of University Professors. **2.** American Association of University Presses. Also, **AAUP**

A.A.U.W. American Association of University Women.

A.B., Bachelor of Arts.

A.B.A., American Bar Association.

a•back′ (ə bak′) *adv.* by surprise.

ab•a•cus (ab′ə kəs) *n.* **1.** calculating device using rows of sliding beads. **2.** slab at top of column.

a•baft′ (ə baft′) *prep. Naut.* **1.** behind. —*adv.* **2.** at the stern.

ab′a•lo′ne (ab′ə lō′nē) *n.* edible mollusk with mother-of-pearl shell.

a•ban′don (ə ban′dən) *v.* **1.** leave completely; forsake. **2.** give up. —*n.* **3.** freedom from constraint. —**a•ban′don•ment,** *n.*

a•ban′doned, *adj.* **1.** forsaken or deserted. **2.** lacking in moral restraint.

a•base′ (ə bās′) *v.,* abased, abasing. lower; degrade. —**a•base′ment,** *n.*

a•bash′ (ə bash′) *v.* to embarrass or shame.

a•bate′ (ə bāt′) *v.,* abated, abating. lessen or subside. —**a•bate′ment,** *n.*

ab•at•toir′ (ab′ə twär′, ab′ə twär′) *n.* slaughterhouse.

ab′bé (a bā′, ab′ā) *n.* abbot; priest.

ab′bess (ab′is) *n.* convent head.

ab′bey (ab′ē) *n.* monastery or convent.

ab′bot (ab′ət) *n.* monastery head.

abbr., abbreviation.

ab•bre′vi•ate′ (ə brē′vē āt′) *v.,* -ated, -ating. shorten. —**ab•bre′vi•a′tion,** *n.*

ABC, *n., pl.* ABC's, ABCs. **1.** alphabet. **2.** (*pl.*) basics.

abcb air-blast circuit breaker.

ABD all but dissertation: applied to a person who has completed all requirements for a doctoral degree except for the writing of a dissertation. Also, **abd.**

abd 1. abdomen. **2.** abdominal.

abd. 1. abdicated. **2.** abdomen. **3.** abdominal.

ab′di•cate′ (ab′di kāt′) *v.,* -cated, -cating. give up (power or office). —**ab′di•ca′tion,** *n.*

ab′do•men (ab′də mən) *n.* part of body between thorax and pelvis; belly. —**ab•dom′i•nal** (ab dom′ə nl) *adj.*

ab•dom′i•nals, *n.pl.* muscles of abdomen. Also, **abs.**

ab•duct′ (ab dukt′) *v.* kidnap. —**ab•duc′tion,** *n.* —**ab•duc′tor,** *n.*

a•beam′ (ə bēm′) *adv. Naut.* across a ship.

a•bed′ (ə bed′) *adv.* in bed.

ab′er•ra′tion (ab′ə rā′shən) *n.* **1.** deviation from normal or right course. **2.** mental lapse.

a•bet′ (ə bet′) *v.*, **abetted, abetting.** encourage in wrongdoing. —**a•bet′tor, a•bet′ter,** *n.*

a•bey′ance (ə bā′əns) *n.* temporary inactivity.

A.B.F.M. American Board of Foreign Missions.

ab•hor′ (ab hôr′) *v.*, **-horred, -horring.** loathe; consider repugnant. —**ab•hor′rence,** *n.* —**ab•hor′rent,** *adj.*

a•bide′ (ə bīd′) *v.*, **abode** (ə bōd′) or **abided, abiding. 1.** remain; stay. **2.** dwell. **3.** wait for. **4.** agree; conform. **5.** *Informal.* tolerate; bear.

a•bid′ing, *adj.* steadfast; lasting.

a•bil′i•ty (ə bil′i tē) *n., pl.* **-ties. 1.** power or talent. **2.** competence.

ab′ject (ab′jekt, ab jekt′) *adj.* **1.** humiliating. **2.** despicable. —**ab′ject•ly,** *adv.* —**ab•jec′-tion,** *n.*

ab•jure′ (ab jŏŏr′) *v.*, **-jured, -juring.** renounce or forswear. —**ab′ju•ra′tion,** *n.*

abl. *Grammar.* ablative.

ab′la•tive (ab′lə tiv) *adj. Gram.* denoting origin, means, etc.

a•blaze′ (ə blāz′) *adj.* **1.** on fire. **2.** gleaming. **3.** excited.

a′ble (ā′bəl) *adj.*, **abler, ablest. 1.** having sufficient power or qualification. **2.** competent. —**a′bly,** *adv.*

-able, suffix indicating: **1.** able to be, as *readable.* **2.** tending to, as *changeable.* **3.** worthy of, as *loveable.*

a′ble-bod′ied, *adj.* physically fit.

A.B.L.S. Bachelor of Arts in Library Science.

ab•lu′tion (ə blōō′shən) *n.* ritual washing.

ABM antiballistic missile.

abn airborne.

ab′ne•gate′ (ab′ni gāt′) *v.*, **-gated, -gating.** deny to oneself. —**ab′ne•ga′tion,** *n.*

ab•nor′mal (ab nôr′məl) *adj.* not normal; not usual or typical. —**ab′nor•mal′i•ty** (-mal′i tē) *n.* —**ab•nor′mal•ly,** *adv.*

ABO *Physiology.* ABO system (of blood classification).

a•board′ (ə bôrd′) *adv.* **1.** on a ship, train, etc. —*prep.* **2.** on.

a•bode′ (ə bōd′) *n.* **1.** home. **2.** stay.

a•bol′ish (ə bol′ish) *v.* end, annul, or make void.

ab′o•li′tion (ab′ə lish′ən) *n.* **1.** act of abolishing. **2.** end of slavery in the U.S. —**ab′o•li′tion•ist,** *n.*

A′-bomb′ (ā′bom′) *n.* atomic bomb.

a•bom′i•na•ble (ə bom′ə nə bəl) *adj.* hateful; loathesome. —**a•bom′i•na•bly,** *adv.*

a•bom′i•nate′ (-nāt′) *v.*, **-nated, -nating.** abhor or hate. —**a•bom′i•na′tion,** *n.*

ab′o•rig′i•nal (ab′ə rij′ə nl) *adj.* **1.** original. —*n.* **2.** aborigine.

ab′o•rig′i•ne (-rij′ə nē) *n.* original inhabitant of a land.

a•bort′ (ə bôrt′) *v.* **1.** have or cause abortion. **2.** end prematurely. —**a•bor′tive,** *adj.*

a•bor′tion, *n.* end of pregnancy by expulsion of fetus before it is viable. —**a•bor′tion•ist,** *n.*

a•bound′ (ə bound′) *v.* be or have plentifully; teem.

a•bout′ (ə bout′) *prep.* **1.** concerning. **2.** near, in, on, or around. **3.** ready. —*adv.* **4.** approximately. **5.** almost. **6.** on all sides. **7.** oppositely. —*adj.* **8.** active.

—**Usage.** Both ON and ABOUT mean "concerning"; ABOUT is used when the information given is general and not too technical: *a novel* ABOUT *the Civil War.* ON is used when the information is particular, as by being scholarly or technical: *an important article* ON *the Civil War.*

a•bout′-face′, *n.* reversal of position.

a•bove′ (ə buv′) *adv.* **1.** higher. **2.** previously. **3.** in or to heaven. —*prep.* **4.** higher or greater than. —*adj.* **5.** foregoing.

a•bove′board′, *adv., adj.* honest; fair.

abp. archbishop.

abr. 1. abridge. **2.** abridged. **3.** abridgment.

ab′ra•ca•dab′ra (ab′rə kə dab′rə) *n.* **1.** word used in magic. **2.** meaningless talk.

a•brade′ (ə brād′) *v.*, **abraded, abrading.** wear or scrape off. —**a•bra′sion,** *n.*

a•bra′sive (ə brā′siv, -ziv) *adj.* **1.** abrading. **2.** annoying. —*n.* **3.** material or substance used to grind or smooth. —**a•bra′sive•ly,** *adv.*

a•breast′ (ə brest′) *adv., adj.* **1.** next to. **2.** informed; aware.

a•bridge′ (ə brij′) *v.*, **abridged, abridging.** shorten. —**a•bridg′ment,** *n.*

a•broad′ (ə brôd′) *adv., adj.* **1.** out of one's own country. **2.** in circulation.

ab′ro•gate′ (ab′rə gāt′) *v.*, **-gated, -gating.** end, annul, or repeal. —**ab′ro•ga′tion,** *n.*

ab•rupt′ (ə brupt′) *adj.* **1.** sudden; unexpected. **2.** steep. —**ab•rupt′ly,** *adv.* —**ab•rupt′ness,** *n.*

ABRV Advanced Ballistic Reentry Vehicle.

abs, *n.pl.* abdominals.

ab′scess (ab′ses) *n.* infected, pus-filled part of the body.

ab•scond′ (ab skond′) *v.* depart suddenly and secretly.

ab′sent *adj.* (ab′sənt) **1.** not present. **2.** lacking. —*v.* (ab sent′) **3.** keep away. —**ab′-sence,** *n.*

ab′sen•tee′ (ab′sən tē′) *n.* absent person.

ab′sent-mind′ed, *adj.* forgetful or preoccupied. —**ab′sent-mind′ed•ly,** *adv.* —**ab′-sent-mind′ed•ness,** *n.*

ab′sinthe (ab′sinth) *n.* bitter green liqueur.

ab′so•lute′ (ab′sə lōōt′) *adj.* **1.** complete;

perfect. **2.** pure. **3.** unrestricted. **4.** despotic. —**ab′so•lute′ly,** *adv.*

absolute pitch, ability to identify exact musical pitch.

absolute zero, temperature ($-273.16°$ C or $-459.69°$ F) at which molecular activity ceases.

ab•solve′ (ab zolv′) *v.,* **-solved, -solving. 1.** release or free. **2.** remit sins of. **3.** forgive. —**ab′so•lu′tion** (ab′sə lōō′shən) *n.*

ab•sorb′ (ab sôrb′, -zôrb′) *v.* **1.** take in. **2.** occupy completely; fascinate. —**ab•sor′bent,** *adj., n.* —**ab•sorp′tion,** *n.* —**ab•sorp′tive,** *adj.*

abs. re. *Law.* in the absence of the defendant. [from Latin *absente reo*]

ab•stain′ (ab stān′) *v.* refrain (from). —**ab•sten′tion** (-sten′shən) *n.*

ab•ste′mi•ous (ab stē′mē əs) *adj.* moderate in eating, drinking, etc.

ab′sti•nence (ab′stə nəns) *n.* forebearance; self-restraint. —**ab′sti•nent,** *adj.*

abstr. 1. abstract. **2.** abstracted.

ab′stract *adj.* (ab strakt′, ab′strakt) **1.** apart from specific matter. **2.** theoretical. **3.** hard to understand. **4.** (of art) not representing natural objects or forms. —*n.* (ab′strakt) **5.** summary. **6.** essence. —*v.* (ab strakt′) **7.** remove or steal. **8.** summarize. —**ab•strac′-tion,** *n.*

ab•tract′ed, *adj.* preoccupied; absent-minded.

ab•struse′ (ab strōōs′) *adj.* hard to understand.

ab•surd′ (ab sûrd′, -zûrd′) *adj.* ridiculous. —**ab•surd′ly,** *adv.* —**ab•surd′i•ty,** *n.*

abt. about.

a•bun′dance (ə bun′dəns) *n.* plentiful supply. —**a•bun′dant,** *adj.* —**a•bun′dant•ly,** *adv.*

a•buse′ *v.,* abused, abusing, *n.* —*v.* (ə-byōōz′) **1.** use or treat wrongly. —*n.* (ə-byōōs′) **2.** wrong use or treatment. **3.** insult. —**a•bu′sive,** *adj.* —**a•bu′sive•ness,** *n.*

a•but′ (ə but′) *v.,* abutted, abutting. be adjacent to.

a•but′ment, *n.* structural part sustaining pressure.

a•buzz′ (ə buz′) *adj.* full of activity or talk.

abv. above.

a•bys′mal (ə biz′məl) *adj.* deep; measureless.

a•byss′ (ə bis′) *n.* **1.** very deep chasm. **2.** hell. Also, **a•bysm′** (ə biz′əm).

Ab′ys•sin′i•an (ab′ə sin′ē ən) *adj.* **1.** from ancient Ethiopia. —*n.* **2.** type of cat.

AC, 1. air conditioning. **2.** Also, **ac., a.c., A.C.** alternating current.

ACA 1. American Camping Association. **2.** American Canoe Association. **3.** American Casting Association.

ACAA Agricultural Conservation and Adjustment Administration.

a•ca′cia (ə kā′shə) *n.* tropical tree or shrub.

acad. academy. Also, **Acad.**

ac′a•dem′ic (ak′ə dem′ik) *adj.* Also, **ac′a•dem′i•cal. 1.** of a school, college, etc. **2.** theoretical. —*n.* **3.** college student or teacher.

a•cad′e•my (ə kad′ə mē) *n., pl.* **-mies. 1.** school. **2.** cultural society.

AC and U Association of Colleges and Universities. Also, **AC&U**

a•can′thus (ə kan′thəs) *n.* Mediterranean plant.

a cap•pel′la (ä′ kə pel′ə) *adv., adj. Music.* without instrumental accompaniment.

acb air circuit breaker.

ACC Atlantic Coast Conference.

acc. 1. accelerate. **2.** acceleration. **3.** accept. **4.** acceptance. **5.** accompanied. **6.** accompaniment. **7.** accordant. **8.** according. **9.** account. **10.** accountant. **11.** accounted. **12.** accusative.

ACCD American Coalition of Citizens with Disabilities.

ac•cede′ (ak sēd′) *v.,* **-ceded, -ceding. 1.** consent. **2.** reach.

accel. *Music.* accelerando.

ac•cel′er•ate′ (ak sel′ə rāt′) *v.,* **-ated, -ating.** speed up; hasten. —**ac•cel′er•a′tion,** *n.*

ac•cel′er•a′tor, *n.* pedal that controls vehicle's speed.

ac′cent *n.* (ak′sent) **1.** emphasis. **2.** characteristic pronunciation. **3.** mark showing stress, etc. —*v.* (ak sent′) **4.** emphasize.

ac•cen′tu•ate′ (ak sen′chōō āt′) *v.,* **-ated, -ating.** stress or emphasize. —**ac•cen′tu•a′-tion,** *n.*

ac•cept′ (ak sept′) *v.* **1.** receive willingly. **2.** agree to. **3.** believe. —**ac•cept′a•ble,** *adj.* —**ac•cept′ed,** *adj.* —**ac•cept′a•bil′i•ty,** *n.* —**ac•cept′a•bly,** *adv.* —**ac•cept′ance,** *n.*

—**Usage.** Because of similarity in pronunciation, ACCEPT and EXCEPT are sometimes confused in writing. ACCEPT is a verb meaning "to receive willingly": *Please accept my gift.* EXCEPT is usually a preposition meaning "other than": *Everybody came except you.* When EXCEPT is used as a verb, it means "to leave out": *Some students were excepted from taking the exam.*

ac′cess (ak′ses) *n.* **1.** right or means of approach. **2.** attack.

ac•ces′si•ble, *adj.* easy to reach or influence. —**ac•ces′si•bil′i•ty,** *n.*

ac•ces′sion (-sesh′ən) *n.* **1.** attainment of an office, etc. **2.** increase.

ac•ces′so•ry (-ses′ə rē) *n., pl.* **-ries. 1.** something added for convenience, decoration, etc. **2.** one who helps another commit a felony.

ac′ci•dence (ak′si dəns) *n.* part of grammar dealing with inflection.

ac′ci•dent (ak′si dənt) *n.* unexpected event, usually unfortunate. —**ac′ci•den′tal,** *adj.* —**ac′ci•den′tal•ly,** *adv.*

ac′ci•dent-prone′, *adj.* inclined to have accidents.

ac•claim′ (ə klām′) *v.* **1.** salute with applause, cheers, etc. —*n.* **2.** applause, cheers, etc. —**ac′cla•ma′tion** (ak′lə mā′shən) *n.*

ac•cli′mate (ak′lə māt′, ə klī′mit) *v.*, **-ated, -ating.** accustom to new conditions. Also, **ac•cli′ma•tize′.**

ac•cliv′i•ty (ə kliv′i tē) *n.*, *pl.* **-ties.** upward slope.

ac′co•lade′ (ak′ə lād′, -läd′) *n.* award, honor, or applause.

accom accommodate.

ac•com′mo•date′ (ə kom′ə dāt′) *v.*, **-dated, -dating. 1.** do a favor for. **2.** supply. **3.** provide with room, food, etc. **4.** adjust.

ac•com′mo•dat′ing, *adj.* helpful; obliging.

ac•com′mo•da′tion, *n.* **1.** act of accommodating. **2.** (*pl.*) space for lodging or travel.

accomp. 1. accompaniment. **2.** accomplishment.

ac•com′pa•ni•ment (ə kum′pə ni mənt, ə kump′ni-) *n.* **1.** something added as decoration, etc. **2.** subsidiary music for performer.

ac•com′pa•ny, *v.*, **-nied, -nying. 1.** go or be with. **2.** provide musical accompaniment for. —**ac•com′pa•nist,** *n.*

ac•com′plice (ə kom′plis) *n.* partner in crime.

ac•com′plish (ə kom′plish) *v.* do or finish.

ac•com′plished, *adj.* **1.** done; finished. **2.** expert.

ac•com′plish•ment, *n.* **1.** completion. **2.** skill or learning.

ac•cord′ (ə kôrd′) *v.* **1.** agree; be in harmony. **2.** cause to agree. **3.** grant; allow. —*n.* **4.** agreement; harmony. —**ac•cord′•ance,** *n.* —**ac•cord′ant,** *adj.*

ac•cord′ing•ly, *adv.* therefore.

according to, 1. in keeping or proportion to. **2.** on authority of.

ac•cor′di•on (ə kôr′dē ən) *n.* bellowslike musical instrument.

ac•cost′ (ə kôst′) *v.* approach or confront.

ac•count′ (ə kount′) *n.* **1.** story; report. **2.** explanation. **3.** reason. **4.** importance. **5.** consideration. **6.** record of business transactions. —*v.* **7.** explain. **8.** report. **9.** consider.

ac•count′a•ble, *adj.* **1.** responsible. **2.** explainable. —**ac•count′a•bly,** *adv.*

ac•count′ant, *n.* person whose profession is accounting.

ac•count′ing, *n.* organization and maintenance of financial records. —**ac•count′an•cy,** *n.*

ac•cou′ter•ments (ə kōō′trə mənts, -tər-) *n.pl.* personal clothing or equipment. Also, **ac•cou′tre•ments.**

accrd. accrued.

ac•cred′it (ə kred′it) *v.* **1.** attribute. **2.** certify with credentials. —**ac•cred′i•ta′tion,** *n.*

ac•cre′tion (ə krē′shən) *n.* increase by growth or addition.

ac•crue′ (ə krōō′) *v.*, **-crued, -cruing.** be added (to). —**ac•cru′al,** *n.*

acct. 1. account. **2.** accountant.

ac•cul′tur•ate′ (ə kul′chə rāt′) *v.*, **-at•ed, -at•ing.** adopt cultural traits of another group. —**ac•cul′tur•a•tion,** *n.*

accum. 1. accumulate. **2.** accumulative.

ac•cu′mu•late′ (ə kyōō′myə lāt′) *v.*, **-lated, -lating.** gather; collect. —**ac•cu′mu•la′tion,** *n.* —**ac•cu′mu•la•tive** (-lə tiv) *adj.* —**ac•cu′mu•la′tor,** *n.*

ac′cu•rate (ak′yər it) *adj.* exact; correct. —**ac′cu•rate•ly,** *adv.* —**ac′cu•ra•cy,** *n.*

ac•curs′ed (ə kûr′sid, ə kûrst′) *adj.* **1.** cursed. **2.** hateful. Also, **ac•curst′.**

accus. accusative.

ac•cu′sa•tive (ə kyōō′zə tiv) *adj. Gram.* denoting verb's direct object.

ac•cuse′ (ə kyōōz′) *v.*, **-cused, -cusing.** blame; charge. —**ac′cu•sa′tion** (ak′yōō zā′shən) *n.* —**ac•cus′er,** *n.* —**ac•cus′a•to′ry,** *adj.*

ac•cus′tom (ə kus′təm) *v.* make used to.

ac•cus′tomed, *adj.* **1.** usual; habitual. **2.** habituated.

ACDA Arms Control and Disarmament Agency.

AC/DC 1. *Electricity.* alternating current or direct current. **2.** *Slang.* sexually responsive to both men and women; bisexual. Also, **A.C./D.C., ac/dc, a-c/d-c, a.c.-d.c.**

acdt accident.

ace (ās) *n.*, *v.* **aced, acing.** —*n.* **1.** playing card with single spot. **2.** expert who excels at something. **3.** *Tennis.* serve opponent cannot touch. —*v.* **4.** score ace against. **5.** do very well on.

a•cer′bic (ə sûr′bik) *adj.* **1.** sour. **2.** sharp or severe. —**a•cer′bi•ty,** *n.*

a•ce′ta•min′o•phen (ə sē′tə min′ə fən) *n.* substance used to reduce pain or fever.

ac′e•tate′ (as′i tāt′) *n.* salt or ester of acetic acid.

a•ce′tic (ə sē′tik) *adj.* of or producing vinegar.

acetic acid, sharp-tasting acid found in vinegar.

ac′e•tone′ (as′i tōn′) *n.* flammable liquid used as a solvent.

a•cet′y•lene′ (ə set′l ēn′) *n.* gas used in welding, etc.

acft aircraft.

ACH automated clearinghouse.

ACh *Biochemistry.* acetylcholine.

ache (āk) *v.*, **ached, aching.** *n.* —*v.* **1.** suffer dull pain. —*n.* **2.** dull pain.

achiev. achievement.

a•chieve′ (ə chēv′) *v.*, **achieved, achieving.** accomplish; bring about. —**a•chieve′ment,** *n.*

A•chil′les heel (ə kil′ēz) vulnerable spot.

ach·ro·mat·ic (ak/rə mat/ik) *adj.* colorless.

ac·id (as/id) *n.* **1.** chemical compound containing hydrogen replaceable by a metal to form a salt. **2.** sour substance. —*adj.* **3.** of acids. **4.** sour or sharp. —**a·cid/i·ty,** *n.*

acid rain, rain containing chemicals from industrial pollution.

a·cid/u·lous (ə sij/ə ləs) *adj.* sour or sharp.

ack. 1. acknowledge. **2.** acknowledgment.

ac·knowl/edge (ak nol/ij) *v.,* **-edged, -edging. 1.** recognize; admit. **2.** show appreciation for. —**ac·knowl/edg·ment,** *n.*

A.C.L.S. American Council of Learned Societies.

ACLU 1. American Civil Liberties Union. **2.** American College of Life Underwriters. Also, **A.C.L.U.**

ACM Association for Computing Machinery.

ac/me (ak/mē) *n.* highest point.

ac/ne (ak/nē) *n.* skin eruption.

ACOC Air Command Operations Center.

ACOG American College of Obstetricians and Gynecologists.

ac/o·lyte/ (ak/ə līt/) *n.* altar attendant.

ac/o·nite/ (ak/ə nīt/) *n.* plant yielding medicine and poison.

a/corn (ā/kôrn, ā/kərn) *n.* fruit or nut of the oak.

acorn squash, dark green acorn-shaped winter squash.

a·cous/tic (ə kōō/stik) *adj.* of sound or hearing. —**a·cous/ti·cal·ly,** *adv.*

a·cous/tics, *n.* **1.** science of sound. **2.** sound qualities.

A.C.P. American College of Physicians.

acpt. acceptance.

acq acquisition.

ac·quaint/ (ə kwānt/) *v.* make known or familiar.

ac·quaint/ance, *n.* **1.** someone personally known. **2.** general knowledge.

ac/qui·esce/ (ak/wē es/) *v.,* **-esced, -escing.** agree or comply. —**ac/qui·es/cence,** *n.* —**ac/qui·es/cent,** *adj.*

ac·quire/ (ə kwīr/) *v.,* **-quired, -quiring.** get; obtain. —**ac·quire/ment,** *n.*

ac/qui·si/tion (ak/wə zish/ən) *n.* **1.** acquiring. **2.** something acquired.

ac·quis/i·tive (ə kwiz/i tiv) *adj.* eager to acquire. —**ac·quis/i·tive·ness,** *n.*

ac·quit/ (ə kwit/) *v.,* **-quitted, -quitting. 1.** free of blame or guilt. **2.** behave or conduct. —**ac·quit/tal,** *n.*

a/cre (ā/kər) *n.* unit of land area (1/640 sq. mi. or 43,560 sq. ft.). —**a/cre·age,** *n.*

ac/rid (ak/rid) *adj.* sharp; biting.

ac/ri·mo·ny (ak/rə mō/nē) *n.* harshness or bitterness of manner or speech. —**ac/ri·mo/ni·ous,** *adj.*

ac/ro·bat/ (ak/rə bat/) *n.* performer on trapeze, tightrope, etc. —**ac/ro·bat/ic,** *adj.*

ac/ro·bat/ics, *n.* (*used with a pl. v.*) **1.** acrobat's feats. **2.** any feats requiring skill.

ac/ro·nym (ak/rə nim) *n.* word formed from successive initials or groups of letters, as NATO, UNICEF.

ac/ro·pho/bi·a (ak/rə fō/bē ə) *n.* fear of heights.

a·cross/ (ə krôs/) *prep.* **1.** from side to side of. **2.** on the other side of. —*adv.* **3.** from one side to another.

across-the-board, *adj.* applying to all members or categories.

a·cryl/ic (ə kril/ik) *n.* chemical used to make textile fibers and paints.

A.C.S. 1. Advanced Communications System. **2.** American Cancer Society. **3.** American Chemical Society. **4.** American College of Surgeons. **5.** autograph card signed. Also, **ACS**

A.C.S.C. Association of Casualty and Surety Companies.

A/cs pay. accounts payable. Also, **a/cs pay.**

A/cs rec. accounts receivable. Also, **a/cs rec.**

acst acoustic.

acsy accessory.

act (akt) *n.* **1.** something done. **2.** law or decree. **3.** part of a play or opera. —*v.* **4.** do something. **5.** behave. **6.** pretend. **7.** perform on stage.

actg. acting.

ACTH *Biochemistry.* a polypeptide hormone that stimulates the cortex of adrenal glands. [*a(dreno)c(ortico)t(ropic) h(ormone)*]

act/ing, *adj.* substitute.

ac/tin·ism (ak/tə niz/əm) *n.* action of radiant energy in causing chemical changes. —**ac·tin/ic** (-tin/ik) *adj.*

ac·tin/i·um (ak tin/ē əm) *n.* radioactive metallic element.

ac/tion (ak/shən) *n.* **1.** process or state of being active. **2.** something done. **3.** behavior. **4.** combat. **5.** lawsuit.

ac/tion·a·ble, *adj.* providing grounds for a lawsuit.

ac/ti·vate/ (ak/tə vāt/) *v.,* **-vated, -vating.** make active; start. —**ac/ti·va/tion,** *n.*

ac/tive (ak/tiv) *adj.* **1.** in action; busy, nimble, or lively. **2.** indicating that the subject performs the action of the verb. —**ac/tive·ly,** *adv.*

ac/tiv·ism, *n.* vigorous action toward social or political goals. —**ac/tiv·ist,** *n.*

ac·tiv/i·ty (ak tiv/i tē) *n., pl.* **-ties. 1.** being active. **2.** busy action. **3.** specific occupation or pursuit.

actl actual.

ac/tor (ak/tər) *n.* performer in play. —**ac/tress,** *n.fem.*

ACTP American College Testing Program.

actr actuator.

ac/tu·al (ak/chōō əl) *adj.* real. —**ac/tu·al·ly** (-al/i tē) *adv.* —**ac/tu·al/i·ty,** *n.*

ac/tu·ar/y (ak/chōō er/ē) *n., pl.* **-aries.** calculator of insurance rates, etc. —**ac/tu·ar/i·al,** *adj.*

ac′tu·ate′ (ak′chōō āt′) *v.*, **-ated, -ating.** cause to act; effect.

actvt activate.

a·cu′i·ty (ə kyōō′i tē) *n.* sharpness of perception.

a·cu′men (ə kyōō′mən) *n.* mental keenness.

ac′u·punc′ture (ak′yōō pungk′chər) *n.* Chinese art of healing by inserting needles into the skin. —**ac′u·punc′tur·ist,** *n.*

a·cute′ (ə kyōōt′) *adj.* **1.** sharp; pointed. **2.** severe. **3.** crucial. **4.** keen, clever. **5.** high-pitched. **6.** (of an angle) less than 90 degrees. —**a·cute′ly,** *adv.* —**a·cute′ness,** *n.*

ACV 1. Also, **A.C.V.** actual cash value. **2.** air cushion vehicle.

ACW *Radio.* alternating continuous waves.

a·cy′clo·vir′ (ā sī′klə vēr′) *n.* drug used to treat genital herpes.

ad (ad) *n. Informal.* advertisement.

A.D., anno Domini: in the year of our Lord.

ADA 1. adenosine deaminase. **2.** American Dental Association. **3.** American Diabetes Association **4.** Americans for Democratic Action.

A.D.A. 1. American Dental Association. **2.** American Diabetes Association. **3.** Americans for Democratic Action.

ADAD (ā′dad), a coded card or other device that when inserted into a telephone allows the user to reach a number without dialing. [*a(utomatic telephone) d(ialing-)a(nnouncing) d(evice)*]

ad′age (ad′ij) *n.* proverb.

a·da′gio (ə dä′jō, -zhē ō′) *adj., adv. Music.* slow.

ad′a·mant′ (ad′ə mənt) *n.* **1.** hard substance. —*adj.* **2.** Also, **ad′a·man′tine.** unyielding.

ADAMHA Alcohol, Drug Abuse, and Mental Health Administration.

Ad′am's ap′ple (ad′əmz) projection of thyroid cartilage in front of neck.

a·dapt′ (ə dapt′) *v.* adjust to new requirements. —**a·dapt′a·ble,** *adj.* —**a·dapt′a·bil′i·ty,** *n.* —**ad′ap·ta′tion** (ad′ap tā′shən) *n.* —**a·dapt′er, a·dap′tor,** *n.*

A.D.B. accidental death benefit. Also, **adb.**

ADC 1. advanced developing countries. **2.** Aid to Dependent Children. **3.** Air Defense Command.

A.D.C. aide-de-camp.

add (ad) *v.* **1.** unite or join. **2.** find the sum (of). **3.** increase.

ad′dend (ad′end, ə dend′) *n.* number to be added to another.

ad·den′dum (ə den′dəm) *n., pl.* **-da** (-də). something to be added.

ad′der (ad′ər) *n.* small venomous snake.

ad′dict, *n.* (ad′ikt) **1.** person habituated to a drug, etc. —*v.* (ə dikt′) **2.** habituate (to). —**ad·dic′tion,** *n.* —**ad·dic′tive,** *adj.*

ad·di′tion (ə dish′ən) *n.* **1.** adding. **2.** anything added. **3. in addition to,** besides.

—**ad·di′tion·al,** *adj.* —**ad·di′tion·al·ly,** *adv.*

ad′di·tive (ad′i tiv) *n.* added ingredient.

ad′dle (ad′l) *v.*, **-dled, -dling. 1.** confuse. **2.** spoil.

addn. addition.

addnl. additional.

ad·dress′ (ə dres′) *n.* **1.** formal speech. **2.** place of residence. **3.** manner of speaking. **4.** skill. —*v.* **5.** speak or write (to). **6.** send. **7.** apply (oneself). —**ad′dress·ee′** (ad′re sē′) *n.*

ad·duce′ (ə dōōs′, ə dyōōs′) *v.*, **-duced, -ducing.** present; cite.

ad′e·noid′ (ad′n oid′) *n.* mass of tissue in upper pharynx.

a·dept′, *adj.* (ə dept′) **1.** skilled. —*n.* (ad′ept, ə dept′) **2.** expert.

ad′e·quate (ad′i kwit) *adj.* sufficient; fit. —**ad′e·quate·ly,** *adv.* —**ad′e·qua·cy,** *n.*

ADF automatic direction finder.

ad fin. to, toward, or at the end. [from Latin *ad finem*]

ADH *Biochemistry.* antidiuretic hormone.

ADHD attention deficit hyperactivity disorder.

ad·here′ (ad hēr′) *v.*, **-hered, -hering. 1.** stick or cling. **2.** be faithful or loyal. —**ad·her′ence,** *n.* —**ad·her′ent,** *n., adj.* —**ad·he′sion** (-hē′zhən) *n.*

ad·he′sive (ad hē′siv, -ziv) *adj.* **1.** coated with a sticky substance. **2.** sticky. —*n.* **3.** adhesive substance or material.

ad hoc (ad hok′, hōk′) for a specified purpose.

ad hom′i·nem (hom′ə nəm, -nem′) attacking an opponent personally instead of answering an argument.

a·dieu′ (ə dōō′, ə dyōō′) *interj., n. French.* good-by; farewell.

ad inf. to infinity; endlessly; without limit. Also, **ad infin.** [from Latin *ad infinitum*]

ad in·fi·ni′tum (ad in′fə nī′təm) to infinity; without end.

ad init. at the beginning. [from Latin *ad initium*]

ad int. in the meantime. [from Latin *ad interim* for the time between]

ad′i·os′ (ad′ē ōs′, ä′dē-) *interj. Spanish.* good-by; farewell.

ad′i·pose′ (ad′ə pōs′) *adj.* fatty.

adj., 1. adjective. **2.** adjustment. **3.** adjutant.

Adj.A. Adjunct in Arts.

ad·ja′cent (ə jā′sənt) *adj.* near; adjoining.

ad′jec·tive (aj′ik tiv) *n.* word describing a noun. —**ad′jec·ti′val** (-tī′vəl) *adj.*

ad·join′ (ə join′) *v.* be next to.

ad·journ′ (ə jûrn′) *v.* suspend (meeting) till another time. —**ad·journ′ment,** *n.*

adjt. adjutant.

ad·judge′ (ə juj′) *v.*, **-judged, -judging. 1.** decree or decide. **2.** award.

ad·ju′di·cate′ (ə jōō′di kāt′) *v.*, **-cated, -cat-**

A

ing. decide on as a judge. —**ad•ju′di•ca′•tion,** *n.*

ad′junct (aj′ungkt) *n.* something added.

ad•jure′ (ə jŏŏr′) *v.,* **-jured, -juring.** request or command, esp. under oath.

ad•just′ (ə just′) *v.* **1.** fit; adapt. **2.** regulate. **3.** settle. —**ad•just′a•ble,** *adj.* —**ad•just′er, ad•jus′tor,** *n.* —**ad•just′ment,** *n.*

ad′ju•tant (aj′ə tənt) *n.* military assistant to commandant.

ADL Anti-Defamation League (of B'nai B'rith). Also, **A.D.L.**

ad-lib′ (ad lib′) *v.,* **-libbed, -libbing.** improvise (speech, music, etc.).

ad loc. at or to the place. [from Latin *ad locum*]

Adm., admiral.

adm. or **admn., 1.** administration. **2.** administrative. **3.** administrator.

ad′man′ (ad′man′, -mən) *n.* advertising professional.

admin. administration.

ad•min′is•ter (ad min′ə stər) *v.* **1.** manage; direct. **2.** dispense or give.

ad•min′is•tra′tion (-ə strā′shən) *n.* **1.** management. **2.** dispensing. **3.** executive officials. —**ad•min′is•tra′tive,** *adj.*

ad•min′is•tra′tor, *n.* manager.

ad′mi•ral (ad′mər əl) *n.* **1.** high-ranking navy officer. **2.** brightly colored type of butterfly.

ad′mi•ral•ty, *n., pl.* **-ties.** navy department.

ad•mire′ (ad mīᵊr′) *v.,* **-mired, -miring.** regard highly. —**ad•mir′er,** *n.* —**ad′mi•ra′tion** (ad′mə rā′shən) *n.* —**ad′mi•ra•ble,** *adj.*

ad•mis′si•ble (ad mis′ə bəl) *adj.* allowable.

ad•mis′sion (-mish′ən) *n.* **1.** act of admitting. **2.** entrance price. **3.** confession or acknowledgment.

ad•mit′ (-mit′) *v.,* **-mitted, -mitting. 1.** allow to enter. **2.** permit. **3.** confess or acknowledge. —**ad•mit′tance,** *n.*

ad•mit′ted•ly, *adv.* without evasion or doubt.

ad•mix′ture (-miks′chər) *n.* thing added. —**ad•mix′,** *v.*

ad•mon′ish (ad mon′ish) *v.* **1.** warn. **2.** reprove. —**ad′mo•ni′tion** (ad′mə nish′ən) *n.* —**ad•mon′i•to′ry,** *adj.*

admov. (in prescriptions) **1.** apply. [from Latin *admovē*] **2.** let it be applied. [from Latin *admoveātur*]

ad nau′se•am (ad nô′zē əm) to a sickening degree.

a•do′ (ə dōō′) *n.* activity; fuss.

a•do′be (ə dō′bē) *n.* sun-dried brick.

ad′o•les′cence (ad′l es′əns) *n.* period between childhood and adulthood. —**ad′o•les′cent,** *adj., n.*

a•dopt′ (ə dopt′) *v.* take or accept as one's own. —**a•dop′tion,** *n.* —**a•dopt′ive,** *adj.*

a•dore′ (ə dôr′) *v.,* adored, adoring. regard

highly; worship. —**a•dor′a•ble,** *adj.* —**ad′o•ra′tion** (ad′ə rā′shən) *n.*

a•dorn′ (ə dôrn′) *v.* decorate. —**a•dorn′•ment,** *n.*

ADP 1. *Biochemistry.* an ester of adenosine and pyrophosphoric acid, $C_{10}H_{12}N_5O_3H_3P_2O_7$, serving to transfer energy during glycolysis. [*a(denosine)* *d(i)p(hosphate)*] **2.** automatic data processing.

ad part. dolent. (in prescriptions) to the painful parts. [from Latin *ad partēs dolentēs*]

adptr adapter.

ad•re′nal (ə drēn′l) *adj.* of a pair of glands near the kidneys.

ad•ren′al•in (ə dren′l in) *n.* glandular secretion that speeds heart, etc.

a•drift′ (ə drift′) *adv., adj.* floating about, esp. helplessly.

a•droit′ (ə droit′) *adj.* expert; deft. —**a•droit′ly,** *adv.* —**a•droit′ness,** *n.*

adrs address.

ADS 1. Alzheimer's Disease Society. **2.** American Dialect Society.

a.d.s. autograph document, signed.

ad•sorb′ (ad sôrb′, -zôrb′) *v.* hold on a surface in a condensed layer.

adst. feb. (in prescriptions) when fever is present. [from Latin *adstante febre*]

ADTS Automated Data and Telecommunications Service.

ad′u•late′ (aj′ə lāt′) *v.,* **-lated, -lating.** flatter excessively. —**ad′u•la′tion,** *n.* —**ad′u•la•to′ry** (-lə tôr′ē) *adj.*

a•dult′ (ə dult′) *adj.* **1.** full-grown; mature. —*n.* **2.** full-grown person. —**a•dult′hood,** *n.*

a•dul′ter•ate′, *v.,* **-ated, -ating.** make impure. —**a•dul′ter•a′tion,** *n.* —**a•dul′ter•ant,** *n.*

a•dul′ter•y, *n., pl.* **-teries.** marital infidelity. —**a•dul′ter•er,** *n.* —**a•dul′ter•ess,** *n.* —**a•dul′ter•ous,** *adj.*

adv., 1. advance. **2.** adverb. **3.** adverbial. **4.** advertisement.

ad val. in proportion to value. [from Latin *ad valorem*]

ad va lo′rem (ad və lôr′əm) fixed at a percentage of the value.

ad•vance′ (ad vans′) *v.,* **-vanced, -vancing. 1.** move forward. **2.** propose. **3.** raise in rank, price, etc. **4.** supply beforehand; lend. —*n.* **5.** forward move. **6.** promotion. **7.** increase. **8.** loan. **9.** friendly gesture. —*adj.* **10.** early. —**ad•vance′ment,** *n.*

ad•vanced′, *adj.* **1.** progressive. **2.** relatively learned, old, etc.

ad•van′tage (ad van′tij) *n.* **1.** more favorable condition. **2.** benefit. —**ad′van•ta′•geous,** *adj.*

ad′vent (ad′vent) *n.* **1.** arrival. **2.** coming of Christ. **3.** (*cap.*) month before Christmas.

ad′ven•ti′tious (ad′vən tish′əs) *adj.* accidentally added.

ad•ven′ture (ad ven′chər) *n., v.,* **-tured, -turing.** —*n.* **1.** risky undertaking. **2.** exciting event. —*v.* **3.** risk or dare. —**ad•ven′tur•er,** *n.* —**ad•ven′tur•ous,** *adj.*

ad′verb (ad′vûrb) *n.* word modifying a verb, verbal noun, or other adverb. —**ad•ver′bi•al,** *adj.*

ad•ver•sar′y (ad′vər ser′ē) *n., pl.* **-saries.** opponent.

ad•verse′ (ad vûrs′) *adj.* opposing; antagonistic. —**ad•verse′ly,** *adv.*

ad•ver′si•ty (-vûr′si tē) *n., pl.* **-ties.** misfortune.

ad•vert′ (ad vûrt′) *v.* refer.

ad′ver•tise′ (ad′vər tīz′) *v.,* **-tised, -tising.** bring to public notice. —**ad′ver•tis′er,** *n.* —**ad′ver•tise′ment,** *n.* —**ad′ver•tis′ing,** *n.*

ad•vice′ (ad vīs′) *n.* **1.** opinion offered. **2.** news.

ad•vis′a•ble (ad vī′zə bəl) *adj.* wise or desirable. —**ad•vis′a•bil′i•ty,** *n.*

ad•vise′ (ad vīz′) *v.* **-vised, -vising. 1.** offer an opinion. **2.** recommend. **3.** consult (with). **4.** give news. —**ad•vis′er, ad•vi′sor,** *n.*

ad•vis′ed•ly, *adv.* after consideration; deliberately.

ad•vi′so•ry, *adj.* **1.** giving advice. —*n.* **2.** report on conditions.

ad′vo•cate′, *v.,* **-cated, -cating,** *n.* —*v.* (ad′və kāt′) **1.** urge; recommend. —*n.* (-kit) **2.** supporter of cause. **3.** lawyer. —**ad′vo•ca•cy,** *n.*

advt. advertisement.

adz (adz) *n.* axlike tool.

AE 1. account executive. **2.** Actors Equity. **3.** American English.

ae. at the age of. [from Latin *aetātis*]

A.E. 1. Agricultural Engineer. **2.** Associate in Education. **3.** Associate in Engineering.

a.e. *Math.* almost everywhere.

A.E.A. 1. Actors' Equity Association. **2.** Also, **AEA** *British.* Atomic Energy Authority.

A.E. and P. Ambassador Extraordinary and Plenipotentiary.

AEC Atomic Energy Commission.

A.E.C. *Insurance.* additional extended coverage.

A.Ed. Associate in Education.

Ae.E. Aeronautical Engineer.

A.E.F. American Expeditionary Forces; American Expeditionary Force. Also, **AEF**

ae′gis (ē′jis) *n.* sponsorship.

A.Eng. Associate in Engineering.

ae′on (ē′ən, ē′on) *n.* eon.

aeq. equal. [from Latin *aequālis*]

aer′ate (âr′āt) *v.,* **-ated, -ating.** expose to air.

aer′i•al (âr′ē əl) *adj.* **1.** of or in air. **2.** lofty. —*n.* **3.** radio antenna.

aer′ie (âr′ē, ēr′ē) *n, pl.* **-ies.** high nest, as of an eagle.

aero-, prefix indicating: **1.** air. **2.** aircraft. Also, **aer-.**

aer•o′bic (â rō′bik) *adj.* **1.** needing oxygen to live. **2.** of aerobics.

aer•o′bics, *n.pl.* exercises designed to strengthen the heart and lungs.

aerodyn aerodynamic.

aer′o•dy•nam′ics (âr′ō dī nam′iks) *n.* science of action of air against solids. —**aer′o•dy•nam′ic,** *adj.*

aeron. aeronautics.

aer′o•naut′ (âr′ə nôt′) *n.* pilot.

aer′o•nau′tics, *n.* science of flight in aircraft. —**aer′o•naut′i•cal,** *adj.*

aer′o•plane′ (âr′ə plān′) *n. Brit.* airplane.

aer′o•sol′ (âr′ə sôl′) *n.* **1.** liquid distributed through a gas. **2.** spray of such liquid.

aer′o•space′ (âr′ō spās′) *n.* **1.** earth's atmosphere and the space beyond. —*adj.* **2.** of missiles, aircraft, and spacecraft.

aes•thet′ic (es thet′ik) *adj.* **1.** of beauty. **2.** appreciating beauty. —**aes′thete** (-thēt) *n.*

aes•thet′ics, *n.* study of beauty.

aet. at the age of. Also, **aetat.** [from Latin *aetātis*]

AF 1. Air Force. **2.** Anglo-French. **3.** Asian Female.

af 1. audiofidelity. **2.** audiofrequency. **3.** autofocus.

Af. 1. Africa. **2.** African.

A.F. 1. Air Force. **2.** Anglo-French. **3.** audio frequency.

a.f. audio frequency.

A.F.A. Associate in Fine Arts.

AFAIK as far as I know.

A.F.A.M. Ancient Free and Accepted Masons.

a•far′ (ə fär′) *adv.* at a distance.

AFB Air Force Base.

A.F.B. American Federation for the Blind.

AFBF American Farm Bureau Federation.

AFC 1. American Football Conference. **2.** American Foxhound Club. **3.** Association Football Club. **4.** automatic flight control. **5.** automatic frequency control.

AFCS automatic flight control system.

AFDC Aid to Families with Dependent Children. Also, **A.F.D.C.**

aff. 1. affairs. **2.** affirmative. **3.** affix.

af′fa•ble (af′ə bəl) *adj.* friendly; cordial. —**af′fa•bil′i•ty,** *n.*

af•fair′ (ə fâr′) *n.* **1.** matter of business. **2.** event. **3.** amorous relationship.

af•fect′ (ə fekt′) *v.* **1.** act on. **2.** impress the feelings of; move. **3.** pretend to possess or feel.

—**Usage.** Because of similarity in pronunciation, AFFECT and EFFECT are sometimes confused in writing. The verb AFFECT means "to act on" or "to move": *His words affected the crowd so deeply that many wept.* The verb EFFECT means "to bring about, accomplish": *The new taxes effected many changes in people's lives.* The noun EFFECT means "result, consequence": *the tragic effect of the hurricane.*

af'fec•ta'tion (af'ek tā'shən) *n.* pretense.

af•fect'ed (ə fek'tid) *adj.* **1.** vain; haughty. **2.** diseased; infected. **—af•fect'ed•ly,** *adv.*

af•fec'tion (ə fek'shən) *n.* **1.** love. **2.** disease.

af•fec'tion•ate, *adj.* fondly tender; loving. **—af•fec'tion•ate•ly,** *adv.*

af•fi'ance (ə fī'əns) *v.* -anced, -ancing. become engaged to.

af'fi•da'vit (af'i dā'vit) *n.* written statement under oath.

af•fil'i•ate', *v.,* -ated, -ating, *n.* —*v.* (ə fil'-ē āt') **1.** join; connect. —*n.* (-ē it) **2.** associate. —af•fil'i•a'tion, *n.*

af•fin'i•ty (ə fin'i tē) *n., pl.* -ties. **1.** attraction. **2.** similarity.

af•firm' (ə fûrm') *v.* **1.** state; assert. **2.** ratify. —af'fir•ma'tion (af'ər mā'shən) *n.*

af•firm'a•tive, *adj.* saying yes; affirming.

affirmative action, policy to increase employment opportunities for women and minorities.

af•fix' *v.* (ə fiks') **1.** attach. —*n.* (af'iks) **2.** added part.

af•flict' (ə flikt') *v.* distress; trouble. —af•flic'tion, *n.*

af'flu•ent (af'lōō ənt) *adj.* rich; abundant. —af'flu•ence, *n.*

af•ford' (ə fôrd') *v.* **1.** have resources enough. **2.** provide.

af•fray' (ə frā') *n.* fight.

af•front' (ə frunt') *n., v.* insult.

afft. affidavit.

AFGE American Federation of Government Employees.

Afgh. Afghanistan. Also, **Afg.**

af'ghan (af'gan) *n.* woolen blanket.

a•field' (ə fēld') *adv.* astray.

a•fire' (ə fīər') *adv., adj.* on fire.

A1c airman, first class.

AFL **1.** American Federation of Labor. **2.** American Football League.

A.F.L. American Federation of Labor. Also, **A.F. of L.**

a•flame' (ə flām') *adv., adj.* in flames.

AFL-CIO, American Federation of Labor and Congress of Industrial Organizations.

a•float' (ə flōt') *adv., adj.* **1.** floating. **2.** in circulation. **3.** out of debt.

AFM **1.** American Federation of Musicians. **2.** audio frequency modulation.

a•foot' (ə fōōt') *adv., adj.* **1.** on foot. **2.** in existence.

a•fore'said' (ə fôr'sed') *adj.* said before. Also, **a•fore'men'tioned** (-men'shənd).

a•foul' (ə foul') *adv., adj.* colliding; entangled; in conflict.

AFP *Biochemistry.* alphafetoprotein.

Afr African.

Afr. **1.** Africa. **2.** African.

A.-Fr. Anglo-French.

a•fraid' (ə frād') *adj.* full of fear.

a•fresh' (ə fresh') *adj.* again.

Af'ri•can (af'ri kən) *n.* native of Africa. —Af'ri•can, *adj.*

Af'ri•can-A•mer'i•can, *n., adj.* black American.

African violet, *n.* hairy-leaved African houseplant with purple, pink, or white flowers.

Af'ri•kaans' (af'ri käns', -känz') *n.* language of South Africa, derived from Dutch.

Af'ri•ka'ner (-kä'nər, -kan'ər) *n.* white South African who speaks Afrikaans.

Af'ro (af'rō) *n.* full, bushy hairstyle.

Af'ro-A•mer'i•can, *n., adj.* African-American.

AFS American Folklore Society.

A.F.S. American Field Service.

AFSCME American Federation of State, County, and Municipal Employees.

aft (aft) *adv. Naut.* at or toward the stern.

af'ter (af'tər) *prep.* **1.** behind. **2.** about. **3.** later than. **4.** next to. **5.** in imitation of. —*adv.* **6.** behind. **7.** later.

af'ter•birth', *n.* placenta and other matter expelled from uterus after childbirth.

af'ter•care', *n.* care of recovering patient.

af'ter•ef•fect', *n.* reaction.

af'ter•glow', *n.* **1.** glow after sunset. **2.** pleasant memory.

af'ter•life', *n.* life after death.

af'ter•math' (-math') *n.* results.

af'ter•noon', *n.* period between noon and evening.

af'ter•taste', *n.* taste remaining in the mouth.

af'ter•thought', *n.* later thought.

af'ter•ward (-wərd) *adv.* later. Also, **af'ter•wards.**

AFTRA (af'trə), American Federation of Television and Radio Artists. Also, **A.F.T.R.A.**

Ag *Symbol, Chemistry.* silver. [from Latin *argentum*]

Ag. August.

ag. **1.** agricultural. **2.** agriculture.

A.G. **1.** Adjutant General. **2.** Attorney General. Also, **AG**

AGA Amateur Gymnastics Association.

AGAC American Guild of Authors and Composers.

a•gain' (ə gen') *adv.* **1.** once more. **2.** besides.

a•gainst' (ə genst') *prep.* **1.** opposed to. **2.** in or into contact with.

a•gape' (ə gāp') *adv., adj.* wide open.

a'gar (ä'gär) *n.* seaweed gel used as food thickener.

ag'ate (ag'it) *n.* **1.** kind of quartz. **2.** child's marble.

a•ga've (ə gä'vē) *n.* thick-leaved desert plant.

AGC **1.** advanced graduate certificate. **2.** automatic gain control. Also, **A.G.C.**

AGCA automatic ground-controlled approach.

AGCL automatic ground-controlled landing.

agcy., agency.

age (āj) *n., v.,* **aged, aging.** —*n.* **1.** length of time in existence. **2.** stage; period. **3.** legal maturity. —*v.* **4.** make or become older.

ag'ed (ā'jid *for 1;* ājd *for 1–3*) *adj.* **1.** having lived long. **2.** matured. —*n.pl.* **3.** elderly persons.

age'ism, *n.* discrimination against elderly persons. —**age'ist**, *n.*

age'less, *adj.* **1.** apparently not aging. **2.** not outdated.

a'gen•cy (ā'jən sē) *n., pl.* **-cies.** **1.** office. **2.** action. **3.** means.

a•gen'da (ə jen'də) *n.* matters to be dealt with.

a'gent (ā'jənt) *n.* **1.** person acting for another. **2.** cause; means. **3.** official.

ag•glom'er•ate', *v.,* -ated, -ating, *adj., n.* —*v.* (ə glom'ə rāt') **1.** collect into a mass. —*adj.* (-ər it) **2.** collected in a mass. —*n.* (-ər it) **3.** such a mass. —**ag•glom'er•a'tion**, *n.*

ag'gran•dize' (ə gran'dīz, ag'rən dīz') *v.,* -dized, -dizing. increase in size, rank, etc. —**ag•gran'dize•ment** (-diz mənt) *n.*

ag'gra•vate' (ag'rə vāt') *v.,* -vated, -vating. **1.** make worse. **2.** annoy. —**ag'gra•va'tion**, *n.*

—**Usage.** In formal speech and writing, the meaning "to annoy" (*Stop aggravating me!*) is sometimes criticized and is used less often than the meaning "to make worse" (*His insulting words aggravated the tense situation*).

ag'gre•gate, *adj., n., v.,* -gated, -gating. —*adj.* (ag'ri git) **1.** combined. —*n.* (-git) **2.** whole amount. —*v.* (-gāt') **3.** collect; gather. —**ag'gre•ga'tion**, *n.*

ag•gres'sion (ə gresh'ən) *n.* hostile act; encroachment. —**ag•gres'sor**, *n.*

ag•gres'sive (ə gres'iv) *adj.* **1.** boldly energetic. **2.** hostile.

ag•grieve' (ə grēv') *v.,* -grieved, -grieving. wrong severely.

Agh. (in Afghanistan) afghani.

a•ghast' (ə gast') *adj.* struck with fear or horror.

AGI **1.** Also, **agi.** adjusted gross income. **2.** American Geological Institute.

ag'ile (aj'əl) *adj.* quick; nimble. —**a•gil'i•ty** (ə jil'i tē) *n.*

agit. (in prescriptions) shake, stir. [from Latin *agitā*]

ag'i•tate' (aj'i tāt') *v.,* -tated, -tating. **1.** shake. **2.** disturb; excite. **3.** discuss. —**ag'i•ta'tion**, *n.* —**ag'i•ta'tor**, *n.*

a•glow' (ə glō') *adj., adv.* glowing.

AGM air-to-ground missile.

AGMA American Guild of Musical Artists. Also, **A.G.M.A.**

ag•nos'tic (ag nos'tik) *n.* one who believes God is beyond human knowledge. —**ag•nos'ti•cism** (-tə siz'əm) *n.*

a•go' (ə gō') *adj., adv.* in the past.

a•gog' (ə gog') *adj.* eagerly excited.

ag'o•nize' (ag'ə nīz') *v.,* -nized, -nizing. **1.** torture. **2.** suffer anxiety.

ag'o•ny (-nē) *n., pl.* -nies. intense pain or suffering.

ag'o•ra•pho'bi•a (ag'ər ə fō'bē ə) *n.* fear of open spaces.

agr. **1.** agricultural. **2.** agriculture.

a•grar'i•an (ə grâr'ē ən) *adj.* of the land.

a•gree' (ə grē') *v.,* **agreed, agreeing. 1.** consent or promise. **2.** be in harmony. **3.** be similar. **4.** be pleasing. —**a•gree'ment**, *n.*

a•gree'a•ble, *adj.* **1.** pleasant. **2.** willing. —**a•gree'a•bly**, *adv.*

ag'ri•busi'ness (ag'rə biz'nis) large-scale business of growing, processing, and distributing farm products.

agric. **1.** agricultural. **2.** agriculture.

ag'ri•cul'ture, *n.* science of farming. —**ag'ri•cul'tur•al**, *adj.*

agron. agronomy.

a•gron'o•my (ə gron'ə mē) *n.* science of farm management and crop production.

a•ground' (ə ground') *adv., adj. Naut.* onto the bottom.

AGS **1.** American Gem Society. **2.** American Geographical Society. **3.** American Geriatrics Society.

A.G.S. Associate in General Studies.

agst. against.

Agt. agent. Also, **agt.**

AGU American Geophysical Union.

a'gue (ā'gyōō) *n.* fever, usu. malarial.

ah (ä) *interj.* (exclamation of pain, surprise, or satisfaction)

AHA American Heart Association.

A.H.A. **1.** American Historical Association. **2.** American Hospital Association.

AHAUS Amateur Hockey Association of the United States.

AHE Association for Higher Education.

A.H.E. Associate in Home Economics.

a•head' (ə hed') *adv.* **1.** in front; forward. **2.** winning.

AHF *Biochemistry.* antihemophilic factor.

AHL **1.** American Heritage Foundation. **2.** American Hockey League.

a•hoy' (ə hoi') *interj. Naut.* (hey there!)

AHQ **1.** Air Headquarters. **2.** Army Headquarters.

AHRA American Hot Rod Association.

AHS American Humane Society.

AHSA American Horse Shows Association.

AI **1.** Amnesty International. **2.** artificial insemination. **3.** artificial intelligence. Also, **A.I.**

A.I.A. **1.** American Institute of Architects. **2.** American Insurance Association.

A.I.C. 1. Army Intelligence Center. **2.** American Institute of Chemists.

AIChE American Institute of Chemical Engineers. Also, **A.I.Ch.E.**

aid (ād) *v., n.* help.

aide (ād) *n.* assistant.

aide-de-camp (ād′də kamp′) *n., pl.* **aides-de-camp.** military assistant.

AIDS (ādz) *n.* acquired immunity deficiency syndrome, a disease making one increasingly susceptible to infections and other diseases.

ail (āl) *v.* **1.** trouble. **2.** be sick.

ai′ler·on′ (ā′lə ron′) *n.* flap on airplane wing.

ail′ment, *n.* illness.

AILS automatic instrument landing system.

aim (ām) *v.* **1.** point or direct. **2.** intend. —*n.* **3.** act of aiming. **4.** target. **5.** purpose. —**aim′less,** *adj.*

A.I.M.E. 1. American Institute of Mining Engineers. **2.** Association of the Institute of Mechanical Engineers.

A.I.M.U. American Institute of Marine Underwriters.

AInd Anglo-Indian.

ain't (ānt) *v. Nonstandard or Dial.* am not; are not; is not.

—**Usage.** AIN'T is more common in uneducated speech, though it occurs with some frequency in the informal speech of the educated: *I ain't going. He ain't so young anymore.* The question form "Ain't I...?" is sometimes substituted for "Aren't I...?", which is usually considered to be ungrammatical. AIN'T also occurs in some humorous or set phrases, and it is sometimes used to give emphasis: *Ain't it the truth! It just ain't so!*

AIP American Institute of Physics.

air (âr) *n.* **1.** mixture of gases forming atmosphere of earth. **2.** appearance; manner. **3.** tune. —*v.* **4.** expose to air. **5.** broadcast.

air bag, bag that inflates automatically to protect passengers in a car collision.

air′borne′, *adj.* carried by air; flying.

air′brush′, *n.* **1.** atomizer for spraying paint. —*v.* **2.** paint with an airbrush.

air conditioning, control of interior air for temperature, humidity, etc. —**air-conditioned,** *adj.*

air′craft′, *n.* vehicle or vehicles for flight.

air′field′, *n.* ground area for airplanes to land on and take off from.

air′ force′, military branch for air operations.

air gun, gun operated by compressed air.

air′head′, *n. Slang.* scatterbrained or stupid person.

air′lift′, *n.* **1.** major transport by air. —*v.* **2.** move by airlift.

air′line′, *n.* air transport company.

air′lin′er, *n.* large passenger airplane operated by airline.

air′mail′, *n.* **1.** system of sending mail by airplane. **2.** mail sent by airmail. Also, **air′mail′.** —**air′mail′,** *v.*

air′man, *n., pl.* **-men.** aviator.

air′plane′, *n.* powered heavier-than-air craft with wings.

air′port′, *n.* airfield for loading, repairs, etc.

air raid, attack by aircraft.

air rifle, air gun with rifled bore.

air′ship′, *n.* lighter-than-air aircraft.

air′sick′ness, *n.* nausea from motion in air travel. —**air′sick′,** *adj.*

air′space′, *n.* space above a nation, city, etc., over which it has jurisdiction or control.

air′tight′, *adj.* **1.** impermeable to air. **2.** perfect; free of error.

air′waves′, *n.pl.* medium of radio and television broadcasting.

air′wor′thy, *adj.,* **-thier, -thiest.** (of an aircraft) safe or fit to fly.

air′y, *adj.,* **-ier, -iest. 1.** of or like air. **2.** delicate. **3.** unrealistic. **4.** well ventilated. **5.** light; gay. —**air′i·ly,** *adv.* —**air′i·ness,** *n.*

AIS administrative and information services.

AISI American Iron and Steel Institute.

aisle (īl) *n.* passageway.

a·jar′ (ə jär′) *adj., adv.* partly opened.

AK, Alaska.

a.k.a., also known as.

A.K.C. American Kennel Club.

a·kim′bo (ə kim′bō) *adj., adv.* with hands at hips.

a·kin′ (ə kin′) *adj.* **1.** related. **2.** alike.

-al, 1. adjective suffix meaning: of or pertaining to, as *tribal;* characterized by, as *typical.* **2.** noun suffix meaning: act or process, as *refusal.*

AL, Alabama.

à la or **a la** (ä′ lä, ä′ lə) *prep.* in the manner or style of.

Ala., Alabama.

al′a·bas′ter (al′ə bas′tər) *n.* white gypsum.

à la carte (ä′ lə kärt′) with each dish separately priced.

a·lac′ri·ty (ə lak′ri tē) *n.* quickness; readiness.

à la mode (ä′ lə mōd′) **1.** in the fashion. **2.** with ice cream.

a·larm′ (ə lärm′) *n.* **1.** fear of danger. **2.** sudden warning. **3.** call to arms. —*v.* **4.** fill with fear.

alarm clock, clock with device to awaken sleeper.

a·larm′ist, *n.* spreader of needless fear; sensationalist.

a·las′ (ə las′) *interj.* (cry of sorrow.)

Alb. 1. Albania. **2.** Albanian. **3.** Albany. **4.** Alberta.

alb. (in prescriptions) white. [from Latin *albus*]

al′ba·core′ (al′bə kôr′) *n.* type of tuna.

al′ba•tross′ (al′bə trôs′) *n.* large white sea bird.

al•be′it (ôl bē′it) *conj.* though.

al•bi′no (al bī′nō) *n., pl.* **-nos.** one lacking in pigmentation.

ALBM air-launched ballistic missile.

al′bum (al′bəm) *n.* **1.** blank book for pictures, stamps, etc. **2.** container with recordings.

al•bu′men (al byōō′mən) *n.* egg white.

al•bu′min (-mən) *n.* water-soluble protein found in egg white, milk, blood, etc.

alc. alcohol.

alcd alcad: aluminum clad.

al′che•my (al′kə mē) *n.* medieval chemistry. **—al′che•mist,** *n.*

ALCM air-launched cruise missile. Also, **A.L. C.M.**

al′co•hol′ (al′kə hôl′) *n.* colorless intoxicating liquid formed by fermentation.

al′co•hol′ic, *adj.* **1.** of alcohol. **—***n.* **2.** one addicted to alcohol.

al′co•hol•ism, *n.* addiction to alcohol.

al′cove (al′kōv) *n.* recessed space.

Ald. alderman. Also, **ald.**

al′der (ôl′dər) *n.* small tree, usually growing in moist places.

al′der•man (ôl′dər mən) *n., pl.* **-men.** representative on city council.

ale (āl) *n.* dark, bitter beer.

a•lert′ (ə lûrt′) *adj.* **1.** vigilant. **—***n.* **2.** air-raid alarm. **—***v.* **3.** warn. **—a•lert′ly,** *adv.* **—a•lert′ness,** *n.*

ale′wife′ (āl′wīf′) *n., pl.* **-wives.** North American shadlike fish.

al•fal′fa (al fal′fə) *n.* forage plant also grown as food.

al•fres′co (al fres′kō) *adv., adj.* in the open air. Also, **al fres′co.**

Alg. 1. Algerian. **2.** Algiers.

alg. algebra.

al′ga (al′gə) *n., pl.* **-gae** (-jē). water plant; seaweed.

al′ge•bra (al′jə brə) *n.* branch of mathematics using symbols rather than specific numbers. **—al′ge•bra′ic** (-jə brā′ik) *adj.*

ALGOL (al′gol) *n.* computer language using mathematical symbols.

Al•gon′qui•an (al gong′kē ən, -kwē ən) *n.* member of a North American Indian people. Also, **Al•gon′ki•an.**

al′go•rithm (al′gə riħ′əm) *n.* set of rules or steps to solve mathematical problem, program computer, etc. **—al′go•rith′mic,** *adj.*

a′li•as (ā′lē əs) *adv.* **1.** otherwise known as. **—***n.* **2.** assumed name.

al′i•bi′ (al′ə bī′) *n.* **1.** defense of accused one as being elsewhere. **2.** excuse.

al′ien (āl′yən) *n.* **1.** foreigner. **—***adj.* **2.** foreign.

al′ien•ate′ (-yə nāt′) *v.,* **-ated, -ating.** lose friendship of; repel. **—al′ien•a′tion,** *n.*

al′ien•ist, *n.* psychiatrist who gives legal testimony.

a•light′ (ə līt′) *v.* **1.** dismount after travel. **2.** descend to perch or sit. **—***adv., adj.* **3.** lighted up.

a•lign′ (ə līn′) *v.* bring into line. **—a•lign′-ment,** *n.*

a•like′ (ə līk′) *adv.* **1.** similarly. **—***adj.* **2.** similar.

al′i•men′ta•ry (al′ə men′tə rē) *adj.* of or for food.

alimentary canal, tube-shaped bodily passage for digestion of food.

al′i•mo′ny (al′ə mō′nē) *n.* money for support of a wife after separation or divorce.

a•live′ (ə līv′) *adj.* **1.** living. **2.** active. **3.** lively. **4.** teeming; swarming.

alk. 1. alkali. **2.** alkaline.

al′ka•li′ (al′kə lī′) *n.* chemical that neutralizes acids to form salts. **—al′ka•line′,** *adj.*

al′ka•loid′ (-loid′) *n.* organic compound in plants, as morphine.

all (ôl) *adj.* **1.** the whole of. **2.** every. **—***n., pron.* **3.** the whole; everything. **—***adv.* **4.** entirely.

Al′lah (al′ə, ä′lə) *n.* Muslim name for God.

All′-Amer′ican, *adj.* **1.** best in the U.S., as in a sport. **2.** typically American. **—***n.* **3.** all-American player or team.

all′-around′, *adj.* **1.** versatile. **2.** having many uses.

al•lay′ (ə lā′) *v.* quiet or lessen.

al•lege′ (ə lej′) *v.,* **-leged, -leging.** declare; state, often without proof. **—al′le•ga′tion** (al′i gā′shən) *n.* **—al•leg′ed•ly** (-lej′id-) *adv.*

al•le′giance (ə lē′jəns) *n.* loyalty.

al′le•go′ry (al′ə gôr′ē) *n., pl.* **-ries.** symbolic story. **—al′le•gor′i•cal,** *adj.*

al•le′gro (ə lā′grō, ə leg′rō) *adv. Music.* fast.

al′le•lu′ia (al′ə lōō′yə). *interj.* (hallelujah.)

al′ler•gen (al′ər jən) *n.* substance that causes allergic reaction. **—al′ler•gen′ic** (-jen′ik) *adj.*

al′ler•gist (-jist) *n.* doctor who treats allergies.

al′ler•gy (-jē) *n., pl.* **-gies.** bodily sensitiveness to certain substances. **—al•ler′gic** (ə-lûr′jik) *adj.*

al•le′vi•ate′ (ə lē′vē āt′) *v.,* **-ated, -ating.** lessen; relieve. **—al•le′vi•a′tion,** *n.*

al′ley (al′ē) *n.* narrow street.

alley cat, stray cat.

al•li′ance (ə lī′əns) *n.* **1.** union; joining. **2.** marriage. **3.** treaty. **4.** parties to treaty.

al•lied′ (ə līd′, al′īd) *adj.* **1.** joined by treaty. **2.** related.

al′li•ga′tor (al′i gā′tər) *n.* broad-snouted type of crocodile.

all′-im•por′tant, *adj.* supremely necessary.

all′-in•clu′sive, *adj.* comprehensive.

al•lit′er•a′tion (ə lit′ə rā′shən) *n.* series of words starting with the same sound.

al′lo•cate′ (al′ə kāt′) *v.*, **-cated, -cating.** allot. —**al′lo•ca′tion,** *n.*

al•lot′ (ə lot′) *v.*, **-lotted, -lotting. 1.** divide; distribute. **2.** assign. —**al•lot′ment,** *n.*

all′-out′, *adj.* total; unrestricted.

al•low′ (ə lou′) *v.* **1.** permit. **2.** give. **3.** admit. —**al•low′a•ble,** *adj.* —**al•low′ance,** *n.*

al′loy, *n.* (al′oi) **1.** mixture of metals. —*v.* (ə loi′) **2.** mix (metals). **3.** adulterate.

all right, 1. yes; I agree. **2.** in a satisfactory way. **3.** safe; sound. **4.** acceptable; satisfactory.

—**Usage.** The one-word spelling ALRIGHT is used in informal writing, probably by analogy with such words as *altogether* and *already.* However, the phrase ALL RIGHT is preferred in formal, edited writing.

All Saints′ Day, church festival Nov. 1 in honor of saints.

all′spice′, *n.* sharp, fragrant spice.

all′-star′, *adj.* **1.** consisting of star performers. —*n.* **2.** member of all-star team or group.

all′-time′, *adj.* never equaled or surpassed.

al•lude′ (ə lōōd′) *v.*, **-luded, -luding.** refer (to) in words. —**al•lu′sion,** *n.*

al•lure′ (ə lŏŏr′) *v.*, **-lured, -luring.** attract; tempt. —**al•lure′ment,** *n.*

al•lu′vi•um (ə lōō′vē əm) *n.* earth deposited by rivers, etc. —**al•lu′vi•al,** *adj.*

al•ly′, *v.*, **-lied, -lying,** *n.*, *pl.* **-lies.** —*v.* (ə lī′) **1.** unite in an alliance. —*n.* (al′ī) **2.** person, nation, etc., bound to another, as by treaty.

ALM audio-lingual method.

al′ma ma′ter (äl′mə mä′tər; al′mə mā′tər) one's school.

al′ma•nac′ (ôl′mə nak′) *n.* calendar showing special events, etc.

al•might′y (ôl mī′tē) *adj.* **1.** having all power. —*n.* **2.** (*cap.*) God.

al′mond (ä′mənd) *n.* edible nut of the almond tree.

al′most (ôl′mōst, ôl mōst′) *adv.* nearly.

alms (ämz) *n.pl.* charity.

al′oe (al′ō) *n.* plant with fleshy leaves.

a•loft′ (ə lôft′) *adv.*, *adj.* high up.

a•lo′ha (ə lō′ə, ä lō′hä) *n.*, *interj.* **1.** (hello). **2.** (farewell.)

a•lone′ (ə lōn′) *adj.*, *adv.* **1.** apart. **2.** by oneself.

a•long′ (ə lông′) *prep.* **1.** through length of. —*adv.* **2.** onward. **3.** together; with one.

a•long′side′, *adv.* **1.** to one's side. —*prep.* **2.** beside.

a•loof′ (ə lōōf′) *adv.* **1.** at a distance. —*adj.* **2.** reserved; indifferent. —**a•loof′ness,** *n.*

a•lot′ (ə lot′) *n.* LOT (def. 5).

—**Usage.** The spelling ALOT, though fairly common in informal writing such as memos and personal letters, is usually considered an error. The two-word spelling A LOT is the accepted form: *He has a lot of money. I like her*

a lot. A LOT is itself considered informal; in formal speech or writing, the phrases "a great number," "a great amount," or "a great deal" are usually substituted for A LOT.

a•loud′ (ə loud′) *adv.* loudly.

Alp. alpine.

A.L.P. American Labor Party. Also, **ALP**

al•pac′a (al pak′ə) *n.* South American sheep with soft, silky wool.

al′pha (al′fə) *n.* first letter of Greek alphabet.

al′pha•bet′ (al′fə bet′, -bit) *n.* letters of a language in order. —**al′pha•bet′i•cal,** *adj.* —**al′pha•bet•ize′,** *v.*

al′pha•nu•mer′ic, *adj.* using both letters and numbers. Also, **al′pha•nu•mer′i•cal.** —**al′pha•nu•mer′i•cal•ly,** *adv.*

al′pine (al′pīn, -pin) *adj.* **1.** of or like a high mountain. **2.** growing or found above the timberline.

al•read′y (ôl red′ē) *adv.* previously.

al•right′ (ôl rīt′) *adv.*, *adj.* ALL RIGHT.

—**Usage.** See ALL RIGHT.

ALS amyotrophic lateral sclerosis.

a.l.s. autograph letter, signed.

al′so (ôl′sō) *adv.* in addition.

alt., 1. alteration. **2.** alternate. **3.** altitude. **4.** alto.

Alta. Alberta.

al′tar (ôl′tər) *n.* **1.** platform for religious rites. **2.** communion table.

al′ter (ôl′tər) *v.* change. —**al′ter•a′tion,** *n.*

al′ter•ca′tion (ôl′tər kā′shən) *n.* dispute.

alter ego, 1. intimate friend. **2.** perfect substitute for oneself. **3.** other side of one's personality.

al′ter•nate′, *v.*, **-nated, -nating,** *adj.*, *n.* —*v.* (-nāt′) **1.** occur or do in turns. —*adj.* (-nit) **2.** being by turns. —*n.* (-nit) **3.** substitute. —**al′ter•na′tion,** *n.*

alternating current, electric current that regularly reverses its direction.

al•ter′na•tive (-tûr′nə tiv) *n.* **1.** other choice. —*adj.* **2.** offering a choice.

al′ter•na′tor (-tər nā′tər) *n.* generator of alternating current.

al•though′ (ôl ƚhō′) *conj.* even though.

al•tim′e•ter (al tim′i tər, al′tə mē′tər) *n.* device for measuring altitude.

al′ti•tude′ (al′ti tōōd′, -tyōōd′) *n.* height.

altm altimeter.

altn alternate.

altntr alternator.

altnv alternative.

al′to (al′tō) *n.*, *pl.* **-tos.** lowest female voice.

al′to•geth′er (ôl′tə geƚh′ər) *adv.* entirely.

altrd altered.

altrn alternation.

al′tru•ism (al′trōō iz/əm) *n.* devotion to others. —**al′tru•ist,** *n.* —**al′tru•is/tic,** *adj.*

ALU *Computers.* arithmetic/logic unit.

al′um (al′əm) *n.* astringent substance, used in medicine, etc.

a•lu′mi•num (ə lōō′mə nəm) *n.* light, silvery metal. Also, *Brit.*, **al′u•min′i•um** (al′yə-min′ē əm).

a•lum′na (ə lum′nə) *n.*, *pl.* **-nae** (-nē). female graduate.

a•lum′nus (-nəs) *n.*, *pl.* **-ni** (-nī). graduate.

al′ways (ôl′wāz, -wēz) *adv.* **1.** all the time. **2.** every time.

Aly. alley.

Alz•hei•mer′s disease (älts′hī mərz, ôlts′-) disease marked by increasing memory loss and mental deterioration, usually in old age.

am (am; *unstressed* əm, m) *v.* 1st pers. sing. pres. indic. of **be**.

Am., **1.** America. **2.** American.

a.m., the period before noon. Also, **A.M.**

A.M.A., American Medical Association.

a•mal′gam (ə mal′gəm) *n.* mixture, esp. one with mercury.

a•mal′ga•mate′ (-gə māt′) *v.*, **-mated,** **-mating.** combine. —**a•mal′ga•ma′tion,** *n.*

a•man′u•en′sis (ə man′yōō en′sis) *n.*, *pl.* **-ses.**. secretary.

am′a•ranth′ (am′ə ranth′) *n.* plant grown as food and for its flowers.

am′a•ret′to (am′ə ret′ō, ä′mə-) almond-flavored liqueur.

am′a•ryl′lis (am′ə ril′is) *n.* plant with large, lilylike flowers.

a•mass′ (ə mas′) *v.* collect.

am′a•teur′ (am′ə chŏŏr′, -chər) *n.* nonprofessional artist, athlete, etc. —**am′a•teur′ish,** *adj.* —**am′a•teur•ism,** *n.*

am′a•to′ry (am′ə tôr′ē) *adj.* of love.

a•maze′ (ə māz′) *v.*, amazed, amazing. awe. —**a•maze′ment,** *n.*

Am′a•zon′ (am′ə zon′, -zən) *n.* **1.** female warrior of Greek legend. **2.** tall, powerful woman.

Amb. Ambassador. Also, **amb.**

am•bas′sa•dor (am bas′ə dər, -dôr′) *n.* diplomat of highest rank.

am′ber (am′bər) *n.* **1.** yellowish fossil resin. —*adj.* **2.** yellowish.

am′ber•gris′ (-grēs′) *n.* gray secretion of sperm whale, used in perfumes.

am′bi•dex′trous (am′bi dek′strəs) *adj.* using both hands equally well.

am′bi•ence (am′bē əns) *n.* surroundings; atmosphere. Also, **am′bi•ance.** —**am′bi•ent,** *adj.*

am•big′u•ous (am big′yōō əs) *adj.* unclear in meaning. —**am′bi•gu′i•ty,** *n.*

am•bi′tion (-bish′ən) *n.* **1.** desire for success, power, etc. **2.** object so desired. —**am•bi′tious,** *adj.*

am•biv′a•lent (-biv′ə lənt) *adj.* with conflicting emotions. —**am•biv′a•lence,** *n.*

am′ble (am′bəl) *v.*, **-bled,** **-bling,** *n.* —*v.* **1.** to go at an easy gait. —*n.* **2.** easy gait.

am•bro′sia (am brō′zhə) *n.* food of Greek and Roman gods.

am′bu•lance (am′byə ləns) *n.* vehicle for sick or wounded.

am′bu•la•to′ry (-lə tôr′ē) *adj.* able to walk.

am′bus•cade′ (am′bə skād′) *n.* ambush.

am′bush (-bŏŏsh) *n.* **1.** concealment for a surprise attack. **2.** surprise attack. **3.** place of such concealment. —*v.* **4.** attack thus.

AMC American Movie Classics (a cable channel).

A.M.D.G. for the greater glory of God: motto of the Jesuits. Also **AMDG** [from Latin *ad majōrem Deī glōriam*]

A.M.E. **1.** Advanced Master of Education. **2.** African Methodist Episcopal.

a•me′ba (ə mē′bə) *n.*, *pl.* **-bas** or **-bae** (-bē). microscopic one-celled animal. Also, **a•moe′-ba.**

AMEDS Army Medical Service. Also, **AMedS**

a•mel′io•rate′ (ə mēl′yə rāt′) *v.*, **-rated,** -rating. improve. —**a•mel′io•ra′tion,** *n.*

a′men′ (ā′men′, ä′men′) *interj.* (so be it!)

a•me′na•ble (ə mē′nə bəl, ə men′ə-) *adj.* willing.

a•mend′ (ə mend′) *v.* **1.** change or correct. **2.** improve. —**a•mend′ment,** *n.*

a•mends′, *n.pl.* reparation.

a•men′i•ty (ə men′i tē) *n.*, *pl.* **-ties.** pleasant feature, etc.

Amer. **1.** America. **2.** Also, **Amer** American.

Am′er•a′sian (am′ə rā′zhən) *n.* person of mixed American and Asian descent.

A•mer′i•can (ə mer′i kən) *n.* **1.** citizen of the U.S. **2.** native of N. or S. America. —*adj.* **3.** of the U.S. or its inhabitants. **4.** of N. or S. America.

American Indian, member of the aboriginal peoples of N. or S. America.

A•mer′i•can•ism (-kə niz′əm) *n.* **1.** devotion to the U.S. **2.** custom, etc., of the U.S.

A•mer′i•can•ize′ (-kə nīz′) *v.*, make or become American in character.

American plan, payment of fixed hotel rate for room, service, and meals.

American Sign Language, visual-gesture language used by deaf people in U.S. and English-speaking parts of Canada.

AmerSp American Spanish.

am′e•thyst (am′ə thist) *n.* violet quartz used in jewelry.

AMEX (am′eks), American Stock Exchange. Also, **Amex**

am/fm (ā′em′ef′em′), (of a radio) able to receive both AM and FM stations. Also, **AM/FM**

AMG Allied Military Government.

ami acute myocardial infarction.

a′mi•a•ble (ā′mē ə bəl) *adj.* pleasantly kind or friendly. —**a′mi•a•bil′i•ty,** *n.* —**a′mi•a•bly,** *adv.*

am′i•ca•ble (am′i kə bəl) *adj.* not hostile. —**am′i•ca•bly,** *adv.*

a•mid′ (ə mid′) *prep.* among. Also, **a•midst′.**
a•mid′ships′ or **-ship′,** *adv.* in or toward the middle part of a ship.
a•mi′go (ə mē′gō, ä mē′-) *n., pl.* **-gos.** *Spanish.* friend.
a•mi′no ac′id (ə mē′nō, am′ə nō) type of organic compound from which proteins are made.
a•miss′ (ə mis′) *adv.* **1.** wrongly. *—adj.* **2.** wrong.
am′i•ty (am′i tē) *n.* friendship.
A.M.L.S. Master of Arts in Library Science.
amm antimissle missle.
am′me•ter (am′mē′tər) *n.* instrument for measuring current in amperes.
am•mo (am′ō) *n. Slang.* ammunition.
am•mo′nia (ə mōn′yə) *n.* colorless, pungent, water-soluble gas.
am′mu•ni′tion (am′yə nish′ən) *n.* bullets, shot, etc., for weapons.
Amn Air Force. airman.
am•ne′sia (am nē′zhə) *n.* loss of memory. —am•ne′si•ac′ (-zhē ak′, -zē-), **am•ne′sic,** *adj., n.* —am•nes′tic (-nes′tik) *adj.*
am′nes•ty (am′nə stē) *n.* pardon for political crimes.
AMNH American Museum of Natural History.
am′ni•o•cen•te′sis (am′nē ō sen tē′sis) *n., pl.* **-ses** (-sēz). surgical procedure of withdrawing fluid from pregnant woman for genetic diagnosis of fetus.
a•mok′ (ə muk′, ə mok′) *adv.* amuck.
a•mong′ (ə mung′) *prep.* **1.** in the midst of. **2.** in the group of. Also, **a•mongst′.**
—Usage. See BETWEEN.
a•mor′al (ā môr′əl) *adj.* indifferent to moral standards. —a′mo•ral′i•ty (ā′mə ral′i tē) *n.*
AMORC Ancient Mystic Order Rosae Crucis.
am′o•rous (am′ər əs) *adj.* inclined to, or showing, love.
a•mor′phous (ə môr′fəs) *adj.* formless.
amort. amortization.
am′or•tize′ (am′ər tīz′, ə môr′tīz) *v.,* **-tized, -tizing.** pay off. —am′or•ti•za′tion, *n.*
a•mount′ (ə mount′) *n.* **1.** sum total. **2.** quantity. *—v.* **3.** add up (to); equal.

—Usage. AMOUNT refers to quantity that cannot be counted (*the amount of paperwork; the amount of energy*), while NUMBER refers to things that can be counted (*a number of songs; a number of days*).

a•mour′ (ə mŏŏr′) *n.* love affair.
AMP Biochemistry. a white, crystalline, water-soluble nucleotide, $C_{10}H_{12}N_5O_3H_2PO_4$, obtained by the partial hydrolysis of ATP or of ribonucleic acid. [*a(denosine) m(ono) p(hosphate)*]
amp. Electricity. **1.** amperage. **2.** ampere; amperes.
AMPAS Academy of Motion Picture Arts and Sciences.

am′per•age (am′pər ij, am pēr′-) *n.* strength of an electric current in amperes.
am′pere (am′pēr) *n.* unit measuring electric current.
am′per•sand′ (am′pər sand′) *n.* sign (&) meaning "and."
am•phet′a•mine (am fet′ə mēn′, -min) *n.* drug stimulating nervous system.
am•phib′i•an (-fib′ē ən) *n.* **1.** animal living both in water and on land. *—adj.* **2.** Also, **am•phib′i•ous.** operating on land or water.
am′phi•the′a•ter (am′fə thē′ə tər, -thē∂′-) *n.* theater with seats tiered around its center.
ampl amplifier.
am′ple (am′pəl) *adj.,* **-pler, -plest. 1.** sufficient. **2.** abundant. —am′ply, *adv.*
am′pli•fy′ (am′plə fī′) *v.,* **-fied, -fying.** make larger or louder. —am′pli•fi′er *n.* —am′pli•fi•ca′tion, *n.*
am′pli•tude′ (-tōōd′, -tyōōd′) *n.* **1.** extent. **2.** abundance.
am′pule (am′pyōōl, -pōōl) *n.* sealed glass or plastic vial containing solution for hypodermic injection. Also, **am′pul, am′poule.**
am′pu•tate′ (am′pyōō tāt′) *v.,* **-tated, -tating.** cut off (a limb). —am′pu•ta′tion, *n.* —am′pu•tee′, *n.*
AMS 1. Agricultural Marketing Service. **2.** American Mathematical Society. **3.** American Meteorological Society. **4.** American Musicological Society.
A.M.S. Army Medical Staff.
A.M.S.W. Master of Arts in Social Work.
AMT alternative minimum tax.
amt. amount.
A.M.T. 1. Associate in Mechanical Technology. **2.** Associate in Medical Technology. **3.** Master of Arts in Teaching.
amu atomic mass unit. Also, **AMU**
a•muck′ (ə muk′) *adv.* murderously insane.
am′u•let (am′yə lit) *n.* magical charm.
A.Mus. Associate in Music.
A.Mus.D. Doctor of Musical Arts.
a•muse′ (ə myōōz′) *v.,* **amused, amusing. 1.** entertain. **2.** cause mirth in. —a•muse′ment, *n.*
amusement park, park with roller coasters or other recreational rides.
AMVETS (am′vets′), an organization of U.S. veterans of World War II and more recent wars. [*Am(erican) Vet(eran)s*]
an (ən; *when stressed* an) *adj.* or *indef. art.* before initial vowel sounds. See **a.**
A.N.A. 1. American Newspaper Association. **2.** American Nurses Association. **3.** Association of National Advertisers. Also, **ANA**
a•nach′ro•nism (ə nak′rə niz′əm) *n.* chronological discrepancy. —a•nach′ro•nis′tic, *adj.*
an′a•con′da (an′ə kon′də) *n.* large South American snake.
an′a•gram′ (an′ə gram′) *n.* word formed from letters of another.

a′nal (ān′l) *adj.* of the anus.

an′al•ge′sic (an′əl jē′zik) *n.* drug for relieving pain.

analog computer, computer that solves problems by using voltages as analogies of numerical variables.

an′a•logue′ (an′l ôg′) *n.* something analogous to something else. Also, **an′a•log′.**

a•nal′o•gy (ə nal′ə jē) *n.*, *pl.* **-gies.** similarity in some respects. —**a•nal′o•gous** (-gəs) *adj.*

a•nal′y•sis (-sis) *n.*, *pl.* **-ses** (-sēz′). **1.** separation into constituent parts. **2.** summary. **3.** psychoanalysis. —**an′a•lyst** (an′l ist) *n.* —**an′a•lyt′ic, an′a•lyt′i•cal,** *adj.* —**an′a•lyze′,** *v.*, **-lyzed, -lyzing.**

analyt. analytical.

an′ar•chy (an′ər kē) *n.* lawless society. —**an′ar•chism,** *n.* —**an′ar•chist,** *n.*

anat. 1. anatomical. **2.** anatomist. **3.** anatomy.

a•nath′e•ma (ə nath′ə mə) *n.* **1.** solemn curse. **2.** thing or person detested.

a•nat′o•my (ə nat′ə mē) *n.*, *pl.* **-mies. 1.** structure of an animal or plant. **2.** science dealing with such structure. —**an′a•tom′i•cal** (an′ə tom′i kəl) *adj.*

ANBS Armed Nuclear Bombardment Satellite.

ANC 1. Also, **A.N.C.** African National Congress. **2.** Army Nurse Corps.

anc automatic noise control.

anc. ancient.

-ance, suffix meaning: action, as *appearance*; state or quality, as *brilliance*; thing or object, as *contrivance*.

an′ces•tor (an′ses tər) *n.* person from whom one is descended. —**an′ces•try,** *n.* —**an•ces′tral,** *adj.*

an′chor (ang′kər) *n.* **1.** heavy device for keeping boats, etc., in place. **2.** main broadcaster who coordinates TV or radio newscast. —*v.* **3.** fasten by an anchor. **4.** serve as anchor for (newscast). —**an′chor•age,** *n.*

an′chor•man′, *n.*, *pl.* **-men.** person who anchors a newscast. Also, *fem.*, **an′chor•wom′an;** *masc.* or *fem.*, **an′chor•per′son.**

an′cho•vy (an′chō vē) *n.*, *pl.* **-vies.** small herringlike fish.

an′cient (ān′shənt) *adj.* **1.** of long ago. **2.** very old. —*n.* **3.** person who lived long ago.

an′cil•lar′y (an′sə ler′ē) *adj.* subordinate; auxiliary.

and (and; *unstressed* ənd, ən, n) *conj.* **1.** with; also. **2.** *Informal.* (used in place of **to** in infinitive): *Try and stop me.*

an•dan′te (än dän′tā) *adv. Music.* at moderate speed.

and′i′rons (and′ī′ərnz) *n.pl.* metal supports for logs in fireplace.

an′dro•gen (an′drə jən) *n.* male sex hormone, as testosterone.

an•drog′y•nous (an droj′ə nəs) *adj.* having both masculine and feminine characteristics.

an′droid (an′droid) *n.* automaton in human form.

andz anodize.

an′ec•dote′ (an′ik dōt′) *n.* short story.

a•ne′mi•a (ə nē′mē ə) *n.* inadequate supply of hemoglobin and red blood cells. —**a•ne′mic,** *adj.*

an′e•mom′e•ter (an′ə mom′i tər) *n.* instrument for measuring wind speed.

a•nem′o•ne′ (ə nem′ə nē′) *n.* buttercuplike plant with colorful flowers.

aner aneroid.

an′es•the′sia (an′əs thē′zhə) *n.* insensibility to pain, usually induced by a drug **(an′es•thet′ic)** (-thet′ik). —**an•es′the•tize′** (ə nes′thə tīz′) *v.*, **-tized, -tizing.**

an′eu•rysm (an′yə riz′əm) *n.* permanent pouch formed in a weakened artery wall. Also, **an′eu•rism.**

a•new′ (ə nōō′, ə nyōō′) *adv.* again.

ANF *Biochemistry.* atrial natriuretic factor.

ANG 1. acute necrotizing gingivitis; trench mouth. **2.** Air National Guard.

ang. 1. angiogram. **2.** angle.

an′gel (ān′jəl) *n.* **1.** spiritual being who is messenger of God. **2.** very kind and helpful person.

angel food cake, light, spongy cake made with egg whites.

an′ger (ang′gər) *n.* **1.** strong displeasure; outrage. —*v.* **2.** cause anger in.

an•gi′na pec′to•ris (an jī′nə pek′tə ris) coronary attack.

Angl. 1. Anglican. **2.** Anglicized.

an′gle (ang′gəl) *n.*, *v.*, **-gled, -gling.** —*n.* **1.** spread between converging lines or surfaces. —*v.* **2.** fish with a hook on a line. **3.** try for something by artful means. **4.** bend in angles. —**an′gler,** *n.*

an′gle•worm′, *n.* worm used in fishing.

An′gli•can (ang′gli kən) *adj.* **1.** of the Church of England. —*n.* **2.** member of this church.

An′gli•cize′ (-sīz′) *v.*, **-cized, -ciz•ing.** make or become English in form or character.

An′glo-Sax′on (ang′glō sak′sən) *n.* **1.** person of English descent. **2.** inhabitant of England before 1066. —*adj.* **3.** of Anglo-Saxons.

anglr angular.

An•go′ra (ang gôr′ə) *n.* **1.** cat, goat, or rabbit with long, silky hair. **2.** (*l.c.*) yarn or fabric from Angora goat or rabbit.

an′gry (ang′grē) *adj.*, **-grier, -griest. 1.** full of anger. **2.** inflamed. —**an′gri•ly,** *adv.*

angst (ängkst) *n.* feeling of dread, anxiety, or anguish.

ang′strom (ang′strəm) *n.* (*often cap.*) unit of measure for wavelengths of light.

an′guish (ang′gwish) *n.* intense pain or grief.

an′gu•lar (ang′gyə lər) *adj.* having angles. —**an•gu•lar′i•ty,** *n.*

anhyd. *Chemistry.* anhydrous.

ani *Telecommunications.* automatic number identification.

an'i•line (an'l in) *n.* oily liquid used in dyes, plastics, etc.

anim. *Music.* animato.

an'i•mad•vert' (an'ə mad vûrt') *v.* criticize. —**an'i•mad•ver'sion** (-vûr'zhən) *n.*

an'i•mal (an'ə məl) *n.* **1.** living thing that is not a plant. **2.** beast. —*adj.* **3.** of animals.

an'i•mate', *v.*, -mated, -mating, *adj.* —*v.* (-māt') **1.** make alive or lively. —*adj.* (-mit) **2.** alive. —**an'i•ma'tion,** *n.*

an'i•mism (-miz'əm) *n.* belief that animals and natural objects have souls. —**an'i•mist,** *n., adj.* —**an'i•mis'tic,** *adj.*

an'i•mos'i•ty (an'ə mos'i tē) *n., pl.* -ties. strong ill will or enmity.

an'i•mus (-məs) *n.* strong dislike; animosity.

an'ise (an'is) *n.* plant yielding aromatic seed (**an'i•seed'**).

an'kle (ang'kəl) *n.* joint between foot and leg.

an'klet (-klit) *n.* **1.** short, ankle-length sock. **2.** ornament for ankle.

anl automatic noise limiter.

anlg analog.

anlr annular.

ann. **1.** annals. **2.** annuity. **3.** years. [from Latin *annī*]

an'nals (an'lz) *n.pl.* historical record of events.

an•neal' (ə nēl') *v.* to toughen or temper.

an•nex', *v.* (ə neks') **1.** add; join. —*n.* (an'-eks) **2.** part, etc., attached. —**an'nex•a'tion,** *n.*

an•ni'hi•late' (ə nī'ə lāt') *v.*, -lated, -lating. destroy completely. —**an•ni'hi•la'tion,** *n.*

an'ni•ver'sa•ry (an'ə vûr'sə rē) *n., pl.* -ries. annual recurrence of the date of a past event.

annot. **1.** annotated. **2.** annotation. **3.** annotator.

an'no•tate' (an'ə tāt') *v.*, -tated, -tating. supply with notes. —**an'no•ta'tion,** *n.*

an•nounce' (ə nouns') *v.*, -nounced, -nouncing. make known. —**an•nounce'ment,** *n.* —**an•nounc'er,** *n.*

an•noy' (ə noi') *v.* irritate or trouble. —**an•noy'ance,** *n.*

an'nu•al (an'yōō əl) *adj.* **1.** yearly. **2.** living only one season. —*n.* **3.** annual plant. **4.** yearbook. —**an'nu•al•ly,** *adv.*

an•nu'i•tant (ə nōō'i tnt, ə nyōō'-) *n.* person who receives an annuity.

an•nu'i•ty, *n., pl.* -ties. income in annual payments.

an•nul' (ə nul') *v.*, -nulled, -nulling. make void. —**an•nul'ment,** *n.*

an'nu•lar (an'yə lər) *adj.* ring-shaped.

An•nun'ci•a'tion (ə nun'sē ā'shən) *n.* announcement to Virgin Mary of incarnation of Christ (March 25).

ano alphanumeric output.

an'ode (an'ōd) *n.* **1.** electrode with positive charge. **2.** negative terminal of a battery.

an'o•dyne' (an'ə dīn') *n.* medication that relieves pain.

a•noint' (ə noint') *v.* to put oil on, as in consecration.

a•nom'a•ly (ə nom'ə lē) *n., pl.* -lies. something irregular or abnormal. —**a•nom'a•lous,** *adj.*

a•non' (ə non') *adv. Archaic.* soon.

anon., anonymous.

a•non'y•mous (ə non'ə məs) *adj.* by someone unnamed. —**an'o•nym'i•ty** (an'ə nim'i tē) *n.* —**a•non'y•mous•ly,** *adv.*

an'o•rak' (an'ə rak') *n.* hooded jacket; parka.

an'o•rex'i•a (an'ə rek'sē ə) *n.* **1.** loss of appetite. **2.** Also, **anorexia ner•vos'a** (nûr vō'sə). eating disorder marked by excessive dieting.

an•oth'er (ə nuth'ər) *adj.* **1.** additional. **2.** different. —*n.* **3.** one more. **4.** different one.

ANPA American Newspaper Publishers Association.

ANRC American National Red Cross.

ANS American Name Society.

ans. answer.

ANSI (an'sē), American National Standards Institute.

an'swer (an'sər) *n.* **1.** reply. **2.** solution. —*v.* **3.** reply to. **4.** suit. **5.** be responsible. **6.** correspond.

an'swer•a•ble, *adj.* **1.** able to be answered. **2.** responsible.

ant (ant) *n.* common small insect.

-ant, suffix meaning: one that performs or promotes, as *pollutant*; performing, promoting, or being, as *pleasant*.

ANTA (an'tə), American National Theatre and Academy.

ant•ac'id (ant as'id) *n.* medicine to counteract acids.

an•tag'o•nism' (an tag'ə niz'əm) *n.* hostility. —**an•tag'o•nist,** *n.* —**an•tag'o•nis'tic,** *adj.* —**an•tag'o•nize',** *v.*, -nized, -nizing.

ant•arc'tic (ant ärk'tik, -är'tik) *adj.* (*often cap.*) of or at the South Pole.

an'te (an'tē) *n.* **1.** (in poker) stake put in pot before cards are dealt. **2.** price or cost of something. —*v.* **3.** (in poker) put (one's ante) into the pot. **4.** produce or pay (one's share).

ante- prefix indicating: **1.** happening before, as *antediluvian.* **2.** in front of, as *anteroom.*

ant'eat'er, *n.* tropical American mammal having long snout and feeding on ants and termites.

an'te•bel'lum (an'tē bel'əm) *adj.* before a war, esp. the American Civil War.

an'te•ced'ent (an'tə sēd'nt) *adj.* **1.** prior. —*n.* **2.** anything that precedes.

an'te•date' (an'ti dāt') *v.*, -dated, -dating. **1.** happen earlier than. **2.** date earlier than true time; predate.

an'te•di•lu'vi•an (an'tē di lōo'vē ən) *adj.* before the Flood.

an'te•lope' (an'tl ōp') *n.* deerlike animal.

an•ten'na (an ten'ə) *n., pl.* -**nae** (-nē), *for 1.* **1.** feeler on the head of an insect, etc. **2.** wires for transmitting radio waves, TV pictures, etc.

an•te'ri•or (an tēr'ē ər) *adj.* **1.** earlier. **2.** frontward.

an'te•room' (an'tē rōōm', -rŏŏm') *n.* room before the main room.

an'them (an'thəm) *n.* patriotic or sacred hymn.

an'ther (an'thər) *n.* pollen-bearing part of stamen.

anthol. anthology.

an•thol'o•gy (an thol'ə jē) *n., pl.* -**gies.** collection of writings.

an'thra•cite' (an'thrə sīt') *n.* hard coal.

an'thrax (an'thraks) *n.* cattle disease.

anthrop. 1. anthropological. **2.** anthropology.

an'thro•poid' (an'thrə poid') *adj.* resembling a human or an ape.

anthropol. anthropology.

an'thro•pol'o•gy (-pol'ə jē) *n.* science of humankind. —**an'thro•pol'o•gist,** *n.*

an'thro•po•mor'phic (-pə môr'fik) *adj.* ascribing human qualities to a nonhuman thing or being. —**an'thro•po•mor'phism** (-fiz əm) *n.*

anti-, prefix indicating: **1.** against or opposed to, as *antisocial.* **2.** acting against, as *antihistamine.*

an'ti•bi•ot'ic (an'ti bī ot'ik) *n.* substance used to destroy microorganisms.

an'ti•bod'y, *n., pl.* -**bodies.** substance in the blood that destroys bacteria.

an'tic (an'tik) *n.* **1.** odd behavior. —*adj.* **2.** playful.

an•tic'i•pate' (an tis'ə pāt') *v.,* -**pated,** -**pating. 1.** expect and prepare for. **2.** foresee. —**an•tic'i•pa'tion,** *n.*

an'ti•cli'max (an'tē klī'maks, an'tī-) *n.* disappointing or undramatic outcome.

an'ti•co•ag'u•lant (an'tē kō ag'yə lənt, an'tī-) *n.* substance that prevents coagulation of blood.

an'ti•de•pres'sant (an'tē di pres'ənt, an'tī-) *n.* drug for relieving depression.

an'ti•dote' (an'ti dōt') *n.* medicine counteracting poison, etc.

an'ti•freeze' (an'ti frēz', an'tē-) *n.* liquid used in engine's radiator to prevent freezing of cooling fluid.

an'ti•gen (an'ti jən, -jen') *n.* substance that stimulates production of antibodies.

an'ti•his'ta•mine' (an'tē his'tə min, -mēn') *n.* substance used esp. against allergic reactions.

an'ti•mat'ter (an'tē mat'ər, an'tī-) *n.* matter with charges opposite to those of common particles.

an'ti•mo'ny (an'tə mō'nē) *n.* brittle white metallic element.

an'ti•ox'i•dant (an'tē ok'si dənt, an'tī-) *n.* organic substance counteracting oxidation damage in animal tissues.

an'ti•pas'to (an'ti pä'stō) *n., pl.* -**pas'tos,** -**pas'ti** (-pä'stē). Italian appetizer.

an•tip'a•thy (an tip'ə thē) *n., pl.* -**thies.** dislike; aversion.

an'ti•per'spi•rant (an'ti pûr'spər ənt) *n.* astringent product for reducing perspiration.

an•tip'o•des (an tip'ə dēz') *n.pl.* places opposite each other on the globe.

antiq. 1. antiquarian. **2.** antiquary. **3.** antiquity.

an'ti•quar'i•an (an'ti kwâr'ē ən) *adj.* **1.** of the study of antiquities. —*n.* **2.** antiquary.

an'ti•quar'y (-kwer'ē) *n., pl.* -**ries.** collector of antiquities.

an'ti•quat'ed (-kwā'tid) *adj.* old or obsolete.

an•tique' (an tēk') *adj.* **1.** old or oldfashioned. —*n.* **2.** valuable old object.

an•tiq'ui•ty (-tik'wi tē) *n., pl.* -**ties. 1.** ancient times. **2.** something ancient.

an'ti-Sem'ite (an'tē sem'īt, an'tī-) *n.* person hostile to Jews. —**an'ti-Se•mit'ic** (-sə mit'ik) *adj.* —**an'ti-Sem'i•tism** (-sem'i tiz'əm) *n.*

an'ti•sep'tic (an'tə sep'tik) *adj.* **1.** destroying certain germs. —*n.* **2.** antiseptic substance.

an'ti•so'cial (an'tē sō'shəl, an'tī-) *adj.* **1.** hostile to society. **2.** not sociable.

an•tith'e•sis (an tith'ə sis) *n., pl.* -**ses.** direct opposite.

an'ti•tox'in (an'ti tok'sin) *n.* substance counteracting germ-produced poisons in the body.

an'ti•trust' (an'tē trust', an'tī-) *adj.* opposing or intended to restrain business trusts or monopolies.

ant'ler (ant'lər) *n.* horn on deer, etc.

an'to•nym (an'tə nim) *n.* word of opposite meaning.

ANTU (an'tōō), *Trademark.* a brand of gray, water-insoluble, poisonous powder, $C_{11}H_{10}N_2S$, used for killing rodents; alphanaphthylthiourea.

a'nus (ā'nəs) *n.* opening at lower end of alimentary canal.

an'vil (an'vil) *n.* iron block on which hot metals are hammered into shape.

anx•i'e•ty (ang zī'i tē) *n., pl.* -**ties. 1.** worried distress. **2.** eagerness. —**anx'ious** (angk'shəs) *adj.* —**anx'ious•ly,** *adv.*

an'y (en'ē) *adj.* **1.** one; some. **2.** every. —*pron.* **3.** any person, etc. —**an'y•bod'y,** **an'y•one',** *pron.* —**an'y•thing',** *pron.* —**Usage.** See SOME.

an'y•how', *adv.* in any way, case, etc. Also, **an'y•way'.**

an'y•place', *adv.* anywhere.

an'y•time', *adv.* at any time.

an'y•where', *adv.* in, at, or to any place.

ANZUS (an'zəs), Australia, New Zealand, and

the United States, especially as associated in the mutual defense treaty **(ANZUS Pact** or **ANZUS Treaty)** of 1952.

A/O 1. account of. **2.** and others. Also, **a/o**

AOA Administration on Aging.

AOH Ancient Order of Hibernians.

aoi angle of incidence.

A′-OK′ (ā′ō kā′) *adj., adv.* OK; perfect. Also, **A′-O•kay′.**

AOL *Computers.* America Online.

A′ one′ (ā′ wun′) *adj.* excellent. Also, **A′ 1′, A′-1′.**

AOR 1. advice of rights. **2.** album-oriented radio. **3.** album-oriented rock.

aor angle of reflection.

a•or′ta (ā ôr′tə) *n., pl.* **-tas, -tae** (-tē). main blood vessel from heart.

AOS 1. American Opera Society. **2.** American Orchid Society.

A.O.U. American Ornithologists' Union.

AP 1. adjective phrase. **2.** *Education.* Advanced Placement. **3.** Air Police. **4.** American plan. **5.** antipersonnel. Also, **A.P.**

Ap. 1. Apostle. **2.** Apothecaries'. **3.** April.

A/P 1. account paid. **2.** accounts payable. **3.** authority to pay or purchase. Also, **a/p**

a-p American plan.

a.p. 1. additional premium. **2.** advanced placement. **3.** as prescribed. **4.** author's proof.

APA 1. American Psychiatric Association. **2.** American Psychological Association.

A.P.A. 1. American Philological Association. **2.** American Protective Association. **3.** American Protestant Association. **4.** American Psychiatric Association. **5.** American Psychological Association. **6.** Associate in Public Administration.

a•pace (ə pās′) *adv.* quickly.

A•pach′e (ə pach′ē) *n., pl.* **A•pach•e, A•pach•es.** member of a group of American Indian peoples of the U.S. Southwest.

a•part′ (ə pärt′) *adv.* **1.** into pieces. **2.** separately.

a•part′heid (-hāt, -hīt) *n.* (formerly, in South Africa) separation of and discrimination against blacks.

a•part′ment (-mənt) *n.* set of rooms in a dwelling.

ap′a•thy (ap′ə thē) *n., pl.* **-thies.** lack of emotion or interest. **—ap′a•thet′ic** (-thet′ik) *adj.*

APB all-points bulletin.

APC 1. Also, **A.P.C.** *Pharmacology.* aspirin, phenacetin, and caffeine: a compound formerly used in colds and cold remedies. **2.** armored personnel carrier.

APCB Air Pollution Control Board.

ape (āp) *n., v.,* **aped, aping.** **—n. 1.** large, tailless monkeylike animal. **—v. 2.** imitate stupidly.

aper. aperture.

a•pé•ri•tif (ə per′i tēf′) *n.* liquor served before meal.

ap′er•ture (ap′ər chər) *n.* opening.

a′pex (ā′peks) *n.* tip; summit.

aph. *Linguistics.* aphetic.

a•pha′sia (ə fā′zhə) *n.* loss of ability to speak or to understand language. **—a•pha′sic** (-zik) *adv.*

a•phe′li•on (ə fē′lē ən, ap hē′-) *n.* point farthest from sun in orbit of planet or comet.

a′phid (ā′fid, af′id) *n.* plant-sucking insect.

APHIS Animal and Plant Health Inspection Service.

aph′o•rism′ (af′ə riz′əm) *n.* brief maxim.

aph′ro•dis′i•ac′ (af′rə dē′ze ak′, -diz′ē ak′) *adj.* **1.** sexually exciting. **—n. 2.** aphrodisiac food, drug, etc.

API American Petroleum Institute. Also, **A.P.I.**

a′pi•ar′y (ā′pē er′ē) *n., pl.* **-ries.** place where bees are kept.

a•piece′ (ə pēs′) *adv.* for each.

APL 1. allowance parts list. **2.** *Computers.* an interactive programming language. [*A P(rogramming) L(anguage)*]

APLA American Patent Law Association.

a•plen′ty (ə plen′tē) *adv., adv.* in generous amounts.

a•plomb (ə plom′, ə plum′) *n.* poise; self-possession.

A.P.O. Army & Air Force Post Office. Also, **APO**

A•poc′a•lypse (ə pok′ə lips) *n.* **1.** revelation of the apostle John. **2.** (*l.c.*) prophetic revelation. **—a•poc′a•lyp′tic,** *adj.*

A•poc′ry•pha (ə pok′rə fə) *n.* uncanonical parts of the Bible.

a•poc′ry•phal, *adj.* not verified; dubious.

ap′o•gee (ap′ə jē′) *n.* remotest point of satellite orbit.

a′po•lit′i•cal (ā′pə lit′i kəl) *adj.* not interested in politics.

a•pol′o•gist (ə pol′ə jist) *n.* advocate; defender.

a•pol′o•gize′, *v.,* **-gized, -gizing.** offer apology.

a•pol′o•gy, *n., pl.* **-gies. 1.** statement of regret for one's act. **2.** stated defense. **—a•pol′o•get′ic** (-jet′ik) *adj.*

ap′o•plex′y (ap′ə plek′sē) *n.* sudden loss of bodily function due to bursting of blood vessel. **—ap/o•plec′tic** (-plek′tik) *adj.*

a•pos′tate (ə pos′tāt, -tit) *n.* deserter of one's faith, cause, etc. **—a•pos′ta•sy** (-tə sē) *n.*

a′ pos•te′ri•o′ri (ā′ po stēr′ē ôr′ī, -ôr′ē) *adj.* **1.** from particular instances to a general principle. **2.** based on observation or experiment.

a•pos′tle (ə pos′əl) *n.* **1.** disciple sent by Jesus to preach gospel. **2.** moral reformer. **—ap′os•tol′ic** (ap′ə stol′ik) *adj.*

a•pos′tro•phe (ə pos′trə fē) *n.* **1.** sign (′) indicating an omitted letter, the possessive, or certain plurals. **2.** words in passing to one person or group. —**a•pos'tro•phize'** (-fīz') *v.*, **-phized, -phizing.**

a•poth'e•car'y (ə poth'ə ker'ē) *n.*, *pl.* **-ries.** druggist.

a•poth'e•o'sis (ə poth'ē ō'sis, ap'ə thē'ə sis) *n.*, *pl.* **-ses** (-sēz, -sēz'). **1.** elevation to the rank of a god. **2.** ideal example; epitome.

app. 1. apparatus. **2.** apparent. **3.** appendix. **4.** *Computers.* application. **5.** applied. **6.** appointed. **7.** approved. **8.** approximate.

ap•pall' (ə pôl') *v.* fill with horror. Also, **ap•pal'.** —**ap•pall'ing,** *adj.*

appar. 1. apparent. **2.** apparently.

ap'pa•ra'tus (ap'ə rat'əs, -rā'təs) *n.* **1.** instruments and machines for some task. **2.** organization.

ap•par'el (ə par'əl) *n.* **1.** clothes. —*v.* **2.** dress.

ap•par'ent (ə par'ənt, ə pâr'-) *adj.* **1.** obvious. **2.** seeming. —**ap•par'ent•ly,** *adv.*

ap'pa•ri'tion (ap'ə rish'ən) *n.* specter.

appd. approved.

ap•peal' (ə pēl') *n.* **1.** call for aid, mercy, etc. **2.** request for corroboration or review. **3.** attractiveness. —*v.* **4.** make an appeal.

ap•pear' (ə pēr') *v.* **1.** come into sight. **2.** seem.

ap•pear'ance (-əns) *n.* **1.** act of appearing. **2.** outward look.

ap•pease' (ə pēz') *v.*, **-peased, -peasing. 1.** placate. **2.** satisfy. —**ap•pease'ment,** *n.*

ap•pel'lant (ə pel'ənt) *n.* one who appeals.

ap•pel'late (ə pel'it) *adj.* dealing with appeals.

ap'pel•la'tion (ap'ə lā'shən) *n.* name or title.

ap•pend' (ə pend') *v.* add; join.

ap•pend'age (ə pen'dij) *n.* subordinate attached part.

ap'pen•dec'to•my (ap'ən dek'tə mē) *n.*, *pl.* **-mies.** removal of the appendix.

ap•pen'di•ci'tis (ə pen'də sī'tis) *n.* inflammation of appendix.

ap•pen'dix (ə pen'diks) *n.*, *pl.* **-dixes, -dices** (-də sēz'). **1.** supplement. **2.** closed tube from the large intestine.

ap'per•tain' (ap'ər tān') *v.* belong or pertain.

ap'pe•tite' (ap'i tīt') *n.* desire, esp. for food.

ap'pe•tiz'er (-tī'zər) *n.* portion of food or drink served before meal to stimulate appetite. —**ap'pe•tiz'ing,** *adj.*

appl. 1. appeal. **2.** applicable. **3.** application. **4.** applied.

ap•plaud' (ə plôd') *v.* praise by clapping, cheers, etc. —**ap•plause'** (ə plôz') *n.*

ap'ple (ap'əl) *n.* common edible fruit.

ap'ple•jack', *n.* brandy made from fermented cider.

ap'ple•sauce', *n.* apples stewed to a pulp.

ap•pli'ance (ə plī'əns) *n.* special device or instrument.

ap'pli•ca•ble (ap'li kə bəl) *adj.* that can be applied.

ap'pli•cant (-kənt) *n.* one who applies.

ap'pli•ca'tion (-kā'shən) *n.* **1.** act of applying. **2.** use to which something is put. **3.** relevance. **4.** petition; request. **5.** form filled out by applicant. **6.** persistent attention.

ap'pli•ca'tor, *n.* device for applying a substance, as medication.

ap'pli•qué' (ap'li kā') *n.*, *v.*, **-quéd, -quéing.** —*n.* **1.** cutout design of one material applied to another. —*v.* **2.** decorate with appliqué.

ap•ply' (ə plī') *v.* **-plied, -plying. 1.** put on. **2.** put into practice. **3.** use or devote. **4.** be relevant. **5.** make request.

appmt. appointment.

ap•point' (ə point') *v.* **1.** choose; name. **2.** furnish. —**ap•point•ee',** *n.* —**ap•poin'tive,** *adj.*

ap•point'ment, *n.* **1.** act of choosing or naming. **2.** prearranged meeting. **3.** equipment.

ap•por'tion (ə pôr'shən) *v.* divide into shares. —**ap•por'tion•ment,** *n.*

ap'po•site (ap'ə zit) *adj.* suitable.

ap•praise' (ə prāz') *v.*, **-praised, -praising.** estimate the value of. —**ap•prais'al,** *n.* —**ap•prais'er,** *n.*

ap•pre'ci•a•ble (ə prē'shē ə bəl) *adj.* noticeable; significant.

ap•pre'ci•ate' (-shē āt') *v.*, **-ated, -ating. 1.** value at true worth. **2.** increase in value. —**ap•pre'ci•a'tion,** *n.* —**ap•pre'cia•tive** (-shə tiv) *adj.*

ap•pre•hend' (ap'ri hend') *v.* **1.** take into custody. **2.** understand.

ap'pre•hen'sion (-hen'shən) *n.* **1.** anxiety. **2.** comprehension. **3.** arrest.

ap'pre•hen'sive (-siv) *adj.* worried; anxious.

ap•pren'tice (ə pren'tis) *n.*, *v.*, **-ticed, -ticing.** —*n.* **1.** assistant learning a trade. —*v.* **2.** bind as such an assistant. —**ap•pren'tice•ship',** *n.*

ap•prise' (ə prīz') *v.*, **-prised, -prising.** notify. Also, **ap•prize'.**

ap•proach' (ə prōch') *v.* **1.** come near to. **2.** make a proposal to. —*n.* **3.** coming near. **4.** access. **5.** method.

ap'pro•ba'tion (ap'rə bā'shən) *n.* approval.

approp. appropriation.

ap•pro'pri•ate', *adj.*, *v.*, **-ated, -ating.** —*adj.* (ə prō'prē it) **1.** suitable; proper. —*v.* (-prē āt') **2.** designate for use. **3.** take possession of. —**ap•pro'pri•ate•ly,** *adv.* —**ap•pro'pri•ate•ness,** *n.* —**ap•pro'pri•a'tion,** *n.*

ap•prove' (ə prōōv') *v.*, **-proved, -proving. 1.** think or speak well of. **2.** confirm. —**ap•prov'al,** *n.*

approx., approximate.

ap•prox'i•mate, *adj.*, *v.*, **-mated, -mating.** —*adj.* (ə prok'sə mit) **1.** near; similar. —*v.*

(-māt′) **2.** come near to. —**ap•prox′i•mate′-ly,** *adv.* —**ap•prox′i•ma′tion,** *n.*

apprp appropriate.

apprx approximate.

appt. 1. appoint. **2.** appointed. **3.** appointment.

apptd. appointed.

ap•pur′te•nance (ə pûr′tn əns) *n.* accessory.

ap•pur′te•nant, *adj.* pertaining.

appx appendix.

Apr., April.

aprch approach.

a′pri•cot′ (ap′ri kot′, ā′pri-) *n.* peachlike fruit.

A′pril (ā′prəl) *n.* fourth month of year.

a′ pri•o′ri (ā′ prē ôr′ī, -ôr′ē) *adj.* **1.** from a general law to a particular instance. **2.** existing in the mind independent of experience.

a′pron (ā′prən) *n.* protective garment for the front of one's clothes.

ap′ro•pos′ (ap′rə pō′) *adv.* **1.** opportunely. **2.** with reference. —*adj.* **3.** timely.

aprt airport.

A.P.S. 1. American Peace Society. **2.** American Philatelic Society. **3.** American Philosophical Society. **4.** American Physical Society. **5.** American Protestant Society.

A.P.S.A. American Political Science Association.

apse (aps) *n.* vaulted recess in a building, as in a church.

apt (apt) *adj.* **1.** prone. **2.** likely. **3.** skilled; able. —**apt′ly,** *adv.* —**apt′ness,** *n.*

apt., apartment.

ap′ti•tude′ (ap′ti tōōd′, -tyōōd′) *n.* skill; talent.

apu auxiliary power unit.

apv approve.

apvd approved.

apvl approval.

apx. appendix.

AQ *Psychology.* achievement quotient.

aq. water. [from Latin *aqua*]

AQAB Air Quality Advisory Board.

aq. bull. (in prescriptions) boiling water. [from Latin *aqua bulliēns*]

aq. comm. (in prescriptions) common water. [from Latin *aqua commūnis*]

aq. dest. (in prescriptions) distilled water. [from Latin *aqua dēstillāta*]

aq. ferv. (in prescriptions) hot water. [from Latin *aqua fervēns*]

AQL acceptable quality level.

aqstn acquisition.

aq′ua•cul′ture (ak′wə kul′chər) *n.* cultivation of aquatic animals or plants.

Aq′ua•lung′, *Trademark.* underwater breathing device using compressed air.

aq′ua•ma•rine′, *n.* **1.** light greenish blue. **2.** beryl of this color.

a•quar′i•um (ə kwâr′ē əm) *n., pl.* **-iums, -ia**

(-ē ə). place for exhibiting aquatic animals and plants.

a•quat′ic (ə kwat′ik, ə kwot′-) *adj.* of or living in water.

aq′ue•duct′ (ak′wi dukt′) *n.* artificial channel for conducting water.

a′que•ous (ā′kwē əs, ak′wē-) *adj.* of or like water.

aq′ui•line′ (ak′wə līn′, -lin) *adj.* (of a nose) curved upward.

AR, Arkansas.

ARA Agricultural Research Administration.

A.R.A. 1. American Railway Association. **2.** Associate of the Royal Academy.

Ar′ab (ar′əb) *n.* **1.** member of a people living or originating in Arabia, a peninsula in SW Asia. —*adj.* **2.** of Arabs. Also, **A•ra′bi•an** (ə-rā′bē ən).

Ar′a•bic (ar′ə bik) *n.* **1.** Semitic language spoken chiefly in S.W. Asia and N. Africa. —*adj.* **2.** of Arabic, Arabia, or Arabs.

Arabic numeral, any of the numerals 0, 1, 2, 3, 4, 5, 6, 7, 8, or 9.

ar′a•ble (ar′ə bəl) *adj.* plowable.

a•rach′nid (ə rak′nid) *n.* small eight-legged arthropod, as the spider.

Aram Aramaic. Also, **Aram.**

A•rap′a•ho′ or **-hoe′** (ə rap′ə hō′) *n., pl.* **-hos** or **-hoes** or **hoe.** member of a North American Indian people.

ar′bit•er (är′bi tər) *n.* judge.

ar′bi•trage′ (-träzh′) *n.* simultaneous sale of security or commodity in different markets to profit from unequal prices. —**ar′bi•trag′er, ar′bi•tra•geur′** (-trä zhûr′) *n.*

ar•bit′ra•ment (är bi′trə mənt) *n.* judgment by an arbiter.

ar′bi•trar′y (är′bi trer′ē) *adj.* **1.** subject to personal judgment. **2.** capricious. **3.** abusing powers. —**ar′bi•trar′i•ly,** *adv.*

ar′bi•trate′ (-trāt′) *v.,* **-trated, -trating.** adjudicate as, or submit to, an arbiter. —**ar′bi•tra′tion,** *n.* —**ar′bi•tra′tor,** *n.*

ar′bor (är′bər) *n.* tree-shaded walk or garden.

ar•bo′re•al (-bôr′ē əl) *adj.* of or living in trees.

ar′bo•re′tum (är′bə rē′təm) *n., pl.* **-tums, -ta** (-tə). parklike area with trees or shrubs for study or display.

ar′bor•vi′tae (är′bər vī′tē) *n.* evergreen tree.

ar•bu′tus (är byōō′təs) *n.* **1.** variety of evergreen shrub. **2.** creeping flowering plant.

arc (ärk) *n.* **1.** part of circle. **2.** luminous current between two electric conductors.

ar•cade′ (är kād′) *n.* **1.** row of archways. **2.** covered passage with stores.

ar•cane′ (är kān′) *adj.* known only to those with special knowledge.

arc cos *Trigonometry.* arc cosine.

arc cot *Trigonometry.* arc cotangent.

arc csc *Trigonometry.* arc cosecant.

arch (ärch) *n*. **1.** upwardly curved structure. —*v*. **2.** cover with an arch. —*adj*. **3.** chief. **4.** roguish.

archaeol. 1. archaeological. **2.** archaeology.

ar′chae•ol′o•gy (är′kē ol′ə jē) *n*. study of past cultures from artifacts. Also, **ar′che•ol′•o•gy**. —ar′chae•o•log′i•cal (-ə loj′i kəl) *adj*. —ar′chae•ol′o•gist, *n*.

ar•cha′ic (är kā′ik) *adj*. **1.** no longer used. **2.** ancient.

arch′an′gel (ärk′ān′jəl) *n*. chief angel.

arch′bish′op (ärch′bish′əp) *n*. bishop of highest rank.

Archbp. Archbishop.

archd. 1. archdeacon. **2.** archduke. Also, **Archd.**

arch′di′o•cese (ärch dī′ə sis, -sēz′, -sēs′) *n*. diocese of archbishop. —arch′di•oc′e•san (-os′ə sən) *adj., n*.

arch′duke′, *n*. royal prince.

Arch. E. Architectural Engineer.

arch′en′e•my, *n., pl*. -mies. chief enemy.

arch′er (är′chər) *n*. one who shoots a bow and arrow. —arch′er•y, *n*.

ar′che•type′ (är′ki tīp′) *n*. original pattern or model.

ar′chi•pel′a•go′ (är′kə pel′ə gō′) *n., pl*. -gos, -goes. **1.** body of water with many islands. **2.** the islands.

ar′chi•tect′ (är′ki tekt′) *n*. designer of buildings. —ar′chi•tec′ture, *n*. —ar′chi•tec′tur•al, *adj*.

ar′chives (är′kīvz) *n.pl*. **1.** documents. **2.** place for documents.

archt. architect.

arch′way′ (ärch′wā′) *n*. entrance covered by arch.

ARCN *Computers*. Attached Resource Computer Network.

A.R.C.S. 1. Associate of the Royal College of Science. **2.** Associate of the Royal College of Surgeons.

arc′tic (ärk′tik, är′tik) *adj*. (*often cap*.) of or at the North Pole.

ard acute respiratory disease.

ar′dent (är′dnt) *adj*. earnest; zealous. —ar′dent•ly, *adv*.

ar′dor (är′dər) *n*. zeal.

ARDS *Pathology*. adult respiratory distress syndrome.

ar′du•ous (är′jōō əs) *adj*. **1.** difficult. **2.** steep. **3.** severe.

are (är; *unstressed* ər) *v*. pres. indic. pl. of **be**.

ar′e•a (âr′ē ə) *n*. **1.** extent of surface; region. **2.** scope.

area code, three-digit number used in long-distance telephone dialing.

a•re′na (ə rē′nə) *n*. open space for contests, shows, etc.

aren't (ärnt, är′ənt) contraction of **are not**.

arf acute respiratory failure.

Arg *Biochemistry*. arginine.

Arg. Argentina.

ar′go•sy (är′gə sē) *n., pl*. -sies. *Poetic*. large merchant ship or fleet.

ar′got (är′gō, -gət) *n*. special vocabulary used by particular group of people.

ar′gue (är′gyōō) *v*., -gued, -guing. **1.** present reasons for or against something. **2.** dispute. **3.** persuade. —ar′gu•ment, *n*. —ar′gu•men•ta′tion, *n*.

ar′gu•men′ta•tive (-men′tə tiv) *adj*. tending to dispute.

argus advanced research on groups under stress.

ar′gyle (är′gīl) *n*. (*often cap*.) diamond-shaped knitting pattern, as of socks.

a′ri•a (är′ē ə) *n*. operatic solo.

-arian, suffix indicating: **1.** one connected with, as *librarian*. **2.** one supporting or practicing, as *vegetarian*.

ar′id (ar′id) *adj*. dry. —a•rid′i•ty (ə rid′i tē) *n*.

a•right′ (ə rīt′) *adv*. rightly.

a•rise′ (ə rīz′) *v*., arose (ə rōz′), arisen (ə-riz′ən), arising. **1.** move or get up. **2.** occur.

ar′is•toc′ra•cy (ar′ə stok′rə sē) *n., pl*. -cies. **1.** state governed by nobility. **2.** nobility. —a•ris′to•crat′ (ə ris′tə krat′) *n*. —a•ris′to•crat′ic, *adj*.

arith. 1. arithmetic. **2.** arithmetical.

a•rith′me•tic (ə rith′mə tik) *n*. computation with figures. —ar′ith•met′i•cal (ar′ith met′i-kəl) *adj*. —ar′ith•met′i•cal•ly, *adv*.

Ariz., Arizona.

ark (ärk) *n. Archaic*. large ship.

Ark. Arkansas.

ARL Association of Research Libraries.

arl average remaining lifetime.

arm (ärm) *n*. **1.** upper limb from hand to shoulder. **2.** weapon. **3.** combat branch. **4.** armlike part. —*v*. **5.** equip with weapons; outfit.

ar•ma′da (är mä′də) *n*. fleet of warships.

ar′ma•dil′lo (är′mə dil′ō) *n*. burrowing mammal covered with plates of bone and horn.

ar′ma•ged′don (är′mə ged′n) *n*. crucial or final conflict.

ar′ma•ment (är′mə mənt) *n*. **1.** military weapons. **2.** arming for war.

arm′chair′, *n*. chair with supports for the arms.

arm′ful, *n., pl*. -fuls. capacity of both arms.

ar′mi•stice (är′mə stis) *n*. truce.

ar′mor (är′mər) *n*. protective covering against weapons.

ar′mor•y (-mə rē) *n., pl*. -ries. **1.** storage place for weapons. **2.** military drill hall.

arm′pit′, *n*. hollow part under arm at shoulder.

ar′my (är′mē) *n., pl*. -mies. **1.** military force for land combat. **2.** large group.

aro *Commerce*. after receipt of order.

a•ro′ma (ə rō′mə) *n*. odor. —ar′o•mat′ic (ar′ə mat′ik) *adj*.

a·ro'ma·ther'a·py, *n.* **1.** use of fragrances to alter a person's mood. **2.** treatment of facial skin with fragrant floral and herbal substances.

a·round' (ə round') *adv., prep.* **1.** on every side of. **2.** somewhere in or near. **3.** about.

a·rouse' (ə rouz') *v.,* aroused, arousing. **1.** awaken. **2.** stir to act. **—a·rous'al,** *n.*

ARP *Stock Exchange.* adjustable-rate preferred.

ar·peg'gi·o' (är pej'ē ō', -pej'ō) *n.* sounding of notes in a chord in succession.

ARR American Right to Read.

arr. 1. arranged. **2.** arrangement. **3.** *Music.* arranger. **4.** arrival. **5.** arrive; arrived; arrives.

ar·raign' (ə rān') *v.* **1.** call to court. **2.** accuse. **—ar·raign'ment,** *n.*

ar·range' (ə rānj') *v.,* -ranged, -ranging. **1.** place in order. **2.** plan or prepare. **—ar·range'ment,** *n.*

ar'rant (ar'ənt) *adj.* downright.

ar·ray' (ə rā') *v.* **1.** arrange. **2.** clothe. **—n. 3.** arrangement, as for battle. **4.** clothes.

ar·rears' (ə rērz') *n.pl.* overdue debt.

ar·rest' (ə rest') *v.* **1.** seize (person) by law. **2.** stop. **—n. 3.** seizure. **4.** stoppage.

ar·rest'ing, *adj.* attracting attention; engaging.

arrgt. arrangement.

ar·rive' (ə rīv') *v.,* -rived, -riving. reach a place. **—ar·riv'al,** *n.*

ar'ro·gant (ar'ə gənt) *adj.* insolently proud. **—ar'ro·gance,** *n.* **—ar'ro·gant·ly,** *adv.*

ar'ro·gate' (-gāt') *v.,* -gated, -gating. claim presumptuously; appropriate. **—ar'ro·ga'tion,** *n.*

ar'row (ar'ō) *n.* pointed stick shot by a bow.

ar'row·head', *n.* pointed tip of arrow.

ar'row·root', *n.* edible starch from tropical plant root.

ar·roy'o (ə roi'ō) *n., pl.* -os. steep, dry gulch.

ARS 1. advanced record system. **2.** Agricultural Research Service. **3.** American Rescue Service. **4.** American Rose Society.

ar'se·nal (är'sə nl) *n.* military storehouse or factory.

ar'se·nic (är'sə nik) *n.* **1.** metallic element. **2.** poisonous powder.

ar'son (är'sən) *n.* malicious burning of a building.

art (ärt) *n.* **1.** production of something beautiful or extraordinary. **2.** skill; ability. **3.** cunning. **—art'ful,** *adj.*

art dec'o (dek'ō) *n.* (*often caps.*) 1920s decorative art with geometric designs.

ar·te'ri·o·scle·ro'sis (är tēr'ē ō sklə rō'sis) *n.* hardening of arteries.

ar'ter·y (är'tə rē) *n., pl.* -ries. **1.** blood vessel from the heart. **2.** main channel. **—ar·te'ri·al** (-tēr'ē əl) *adj.*

ar·te'sian well (-tē'zhən) deep well whose water rises under its own pressure.

ar·thri'tis (är thrī'tis) *n.* inflammation of a joint. **—ar·thrit'ic** (-thrit'ik) *adj.*

ar'thro·pod' (är'thrə pod') *n.* invertebrate with segmented body and jointed legs, as the lobster.

ar'ti·choke' (är'ti chōk') *n.* plant with an edible flower head.

ar'ti·cle (är'ti kəl) *n.* **1.** literary composition. **2.** thing; item. **3.** the words *a, an,* or *the.*

ar·tic'u·late, *adj., v.,* -lated, -lating. **—adj.** (är tik'yə lit) **1.** clear. **2.** able to speak. **3.** jointed. **—v.** (-lāt') **4.** speak, esp. distinctly. **5.** joint. **—ar·tic'u·la'tion,** *n.*

ar'ti·fact' (är'tə fakt') *n.* object made by human being or beings.

ar'ti·fice (är'tə fis) *n.* trick.

ar·tif'i·cer (-tif'ə sər) *n.* craftsperson.

ar'ti·fi'cial (-tə fish'əl) *adj.* **1.** manufactured, esp. as an imitation. **2.** affected. **—ar'ti·fi'cial·ly,** *adv.* **—ar'ti·fi'ci·al'i·ty** (-fish'ē·al'i tē) *n.*

artificial respiration, forcing of air into and out of lungs of a nonbreathing person.

ar·til'ler·y (är til'ə rē) *n.* mounted guns.

ar'ti·san (är'tə zən) *n.* person skilled in a practical art.

art'ist (är'tist) *n.* practitioner of fine art. **—ar·tis'tic,** *adj.* **—art'ist·ry,** *n.*

art'less, *adj.* natural.

art'y, *adj.,* artier, artiest. *Informal,* self-consciously artistic.

ARU *Computers.* audio response unit.

A.R.V. 1. AIDS-related virus. **2.** American Revised Version (of the Bible).

ARVN (är'vin), (in the Vietnam War) a soldier in the army of South Vietnam. [*A(rmy of the) R(epublic of) V(iet) N(am)*]

as (az; *unstressed* əz) *adv.* **1.** to such an extent. **—conj. 2.** in the manner, etc., that. **3.** while. **4.** because. **—pron. 5.** that.

ASA 1. Acoustical Society of America. **2.** American Standards Association. **3.** the numerical exposure index of a photographic film under the system adopted by the American Standards Association.

ASAP (ā'es'ā'pē', ā'sap) **1.** as soon as possible. **2.** without delay. Also, **A.S.A.P., a.s.a.p.**

ASAT (ā'sat'), antisatellite.

as·bes'tos (as bes'təs, az-) *n.* fibrous material formerly used in fireproofing.

ASBM air-to-surface ballistic missile. Also, **A. S.B.M.**

ASC American Society of Cinematographers. Also, **A.S.C.**

ASCAP (as'kap), American Society of Composers, Authors, and Publishers.

ASCE American Society of Civil Engineers.

as·cend' (ə send') *v.* climb. **—as·cent',** *n.*

as·cend'an·cy, *n.* domination; power. **—as·cend'ant,** *adj., n.*

As·cen'sion (ə sen'shən) *n.* bodily passing of Christ to heaven.

as'cer·tain' (as'ər tān') *v.* find out.

as•cet′ic (ə set′ik) *n.* **1.** one who lives austerely. —*adj.* **2.** austere or abstemious. —**as•cet′i•cism** (-ə siz′əm) *n.*

ASCII (as′kē) *n.* standardized code for computer storage and transmission.

ASCM antiship capable missile.

as•cor′bic ac′id (ə skôr′bik) vitamin C.

as′cot (as′kət, -kot) *n.* tie or scarf with broad ends.

ASCP American Society of Clinical Pathologists.

ascr *Electronics.* asymmetrical semiconductor controlled rectifier..

as•cribe′ (ə skrīb′) *v.,* **-cribed, -cribing.** attribute. —**as•crip′tion** (ə skrip′shən) *n.*

ASCS Agricultural Stabilization and Conservation Service.

ASCU Association of State Colleges and Universities.

ASE American Stock Exchange. Also, **A.S.E.**

ASEAN Association of Southeast Asian Nations. Also, **A.S.E.A.N.**

a•sep′sis (a sep′sis, ā sep′-) *n.* absence of certain harmful bacteria. —**a•sep′tic** (-tik) *adj.*

a•sex′u•al (ā sek′shōō əl) *adj.* **1.** without sex; sexless. **2.** having no sex organs.

asgd. assigned.

asgmt. assignment.

asgn assign.

ash (ash) *n.* **1.** (*pl.* **ashes**) residue of burned matter. **2.** a common tree. —**ash′y,** *adj.*

a•shamed′ (ə shāmd′) *adj.* feeling shame.

ASHD arteriosclerotic heart disease.

ash′en (ash′ən) *adj.* pale gray.

a•shore′ (ə shôr′) *adv., adj.* on or to shore.

ash′tray′, *n.* container for tobacco ashes.

ASI 1. *Aeronautics.* airspeed indicator. **2.** American Safety Institute.

A′sian (ā′zhən) *n.* native of Asia. —**Asian,** *adj.*

A′si•at′ic (ā′zhē at′ik) *adj., n. Offensive.* Asian.

a•side′ (ə sīd′) *adv.* **1.** on or to one side. **2.** separate.

as′i•nine′ (as′ə nīn′) *adj.* stupid.

ask (ask) *v.* **1.** put a question to. **2.** request. **3.** invite. **4.** inquire.

a•skance′ (ə skans′) *adv.* with doubt or disapproval.

a•skew′ (ə skyōō′) *adv., adj.* twisted.

ASL 1. American Shuffleboard League. **2.** American Sign Language. **3.** American Soccer League.

ASLA American Society of Landscape Architects.

a•sleep′ (ə slēp′) *adj., adv.* sleeping.

ASM air-to-surface missile.

asm assemble.

ASME American Society of Mechanical Engineers.

ASN Army service number.

Asn *Biochemistry.* asparagine.

ASNE American Society of Newspaper Editors.

a•so′cial (ā sō′shəl) *adj.* **1.** not sociable. **2.** selfish.

asp (asp) *n.* poisonous snake.

as•par′a•gus (ə spar′ə gəs) *n.* plant with edible shoots.

as•par′tame (ə spär′tām, as′pər tām′) *n.* artificial low-calorie sweetener.

A.S.P.C.A. American Society for the Prevention of Cruelty to Animals.

ASPCC American Society for the Prevention of Cruelty to Children.

as′pect (as′pekt) *n.* **1.** appearance. **2.** phase; condition. **3.** direction faced.

as′pen (as′pən) *n.* variety of poplar.

as•per′i•ty (ə sper′i tē) *n., pl.* **-ties.** roughness.

as•per′sion (ə spûr′zhən, -shən) *n.* derogatory criticism.

as′phalt (as′fôlt) *n.* hard, black material used for pavements.

as•phyx′i•ate′ (as fik′sē āt′) *v.,* **-ated, -ating.** affect by a lack of oxygen; choke or smother. —**as•phyx′i•a′tion,** *n.*

as′pic (as′pik) *n.* jelly made from meat, fish, or vegetable stock.

as•pire′ (ə spī⁻r′) *v.,* **-pired, -piring.** long, aim, or seek for. —**as•pir′ant,** *n.* —**as′pi•ra′tion** (as′pə rā′shən) *n.*

as′pi•rin (as′pər in, -prin) *n.* crystalline derivative of salicylic acid, used for relief of headaches and other pains.

ASR 1. airport surveillance radar. **2.** *U.S. Navy.* air-sea rescue.

asr *Teletype.* automatic send-receive.

ass (as) *n.* **1.** donkey. **2.** fool.

as•sail′ (ə sāl′) *v.* attack. —**as•sail′ant,** *n.*

as•sas′sin (ə sas′in) *n.* murderer, esp. of an important person. —**as•sas′si•nate′,** *v.,* **-nated, -nating.** —**as•sas′si•na′tion,** *n.*

as•sault′ (ə sôlt′) *n., v.* attack.

as•say′ (ə sā′) *v.* analyze or evaluate. —**as′say,** *n.* —**as•say′er,** *n.*

as•sem′blage (ə sem′blij) *n.* **1.** group; assembly. **2.** act of assembling.

as•sem′ble (ə sem′bəl) *v.,* **-bled, -bling.** come or bring together.

as•sem′bly, *n., pl.* **-blies. 1.** group gathered together. **2.** legislative body. **3.** putting together of parts.

as•sem′bly•man, *n., pl.* **-men.** member of legislative assembly. Also, *fem.,* **as•sem′bly•wom′an;** *masc.* or *fem.,* **as•sem′bly•per′son.**

as•sent′ (ə sent′) *v.* **1.** agree. —*n.* **2.** agreement.

as•sert′ (ə sûrt′) *v.* **1.** state; declare. **2.** claim. **3.** present (oneself) boldly. —**as•ser′tion,** *n.* —**as•ser′tive,** *adj.* —**as•ser′tive•ly,** *adv.* —**as•ser′tive•ness,** *n.*

as•sess′ (ə ses′) *v.* evaluate, as for taxes. —**as•sess′ment,** *n.* —**as•ses′sor,** *n.*

A

as′set (as′et) *n.* **1.** item of property. **2.** quality.

as·sid′u·ous (ə sij′ŏŏ əs) *adj.* persistent; devoted. —**as·sid′u·ous·ly,** *adv.*

as·sign′ (ə sīn′) *v.* **1.** give. **2.** appoint. **3.** transfer. —*n.* **4.** one to whom something is transferred. —**as·sign′a·ble,** *adj.* —**as·sign·ee′,** *n.* —**as·sign′ment,** *n.*

as′sig·na′tion (as′ig nā′shən) *n.* appointment; rendezvous.

as·sim′i·late′ (ə sim′ə lāt′) *v.,* -lated, -lating. absorb or become absorbed; merge. —**as·sim′i·la′tion,** *n.*

as·sist′ (ə sist′) *v., n.* help; aid. —**as·sist′-ant,** *n., adj.* —**as·sist′ance,** *n.*

assn., association.

assoc. 1. associate. **2.** associated. **3.** association.

as·so′ci·ate′, *v.,* -ated, -ating, *n., adj.* —*v.* (ə sō′shē āt′, -sē-) **1.** connect or join. **2.** keep company. —*n.* (-it) **3.** partner; colleague. —*adj.* (-it) **4.** allied. —**as·so′ci·a′tion,** *n.*

as′so·nance (as′ə nəns) *n.* similarity of sound in words or syllables. —**as′so·nant,** *adj.*

as·sort′ (ə sôrt′) *v.* **1.** classify. **2.** vary. —**as·sort′ed,** *adj.* —**as·sort′ment,** *n.*

ASSR Autonomous Soviet Socialist Republic. Also, **A.S.S.R.**

asst., assistant.

asstd. assorted.

as·suage′ (ə swāj′) *v.,* -suaged, -suaging. lessen (pain, grief, etc.).

as·sume′ (ə sōōm′) *v.,* -sumed, -suming. **1.** take without proof. **2.** undertake. **3.** pretend. **4.** take upon oneself.

as·sump′tion (ə sump′shən) *n.* **1.** unverified belief. **2.** undertaking. **3.** (*cap.*) ascent to heaven of Virgin Mary.

as·sure′ (ə shŏŏr′) *v.,* -sured, -suring. **1.** affirm to. **2.** convince; make sure. **3.** encourage. **4.** insure. —**as·sur′ance,** *n.* —**as·sured′,** *adj., n.*

Assyr. Assyrian.

AST Atlantic Standard Time. Also, **A.S.T., a.s.t.**

astb *Electronics.* astable.

as′ter (as′tər) *n.* plant with many petals around a center disk.

as′ter·isk (as′tə risk) *n.* star (*) symbol used in writing as a reference mark.

—**Pronunciation.** The word ASTERISK is pronounced (as′tə risk). Note that the final syllable is pronounced (-risk), with the (s) before the (k). Both (as′tə riks) and (as′tə rik), although occasionally heard among educated speakers, are considered nonstandard pronunciations.

a·stern′ (ə stûrn′) *adv., adj. Naut.* toward or at the rear.

as′ter·oid (as′tə roid′) *n.* planetlike body beyond Mars.

asth′ma (az′mə) *n.* painful respiratory disorder. —**asth·mat′ic** (az mat′ik) *adj., n.*

a·stig′ma·tism (ə stig′mə tiz′əm) *n.* eye defect resulting in imperfect images. —**as′tig·mat′ic** (as′tig mat′ik) *adj.*

a·stir′ (ə stûr′) *adj., adv.* active.

ASTM American Society for Testing Materials. Also, **A.S.T.M.**

as·ton′ish (ə ston′ish) *v.* surprise greatly; amaze. —**as·ton′ish·ing,** *adj.* —**as·ton′ish·ing·ly,** *adv.* —**as·ton′ish·ment,** *n.*

as·tound′ (ə stound′) *v.* amaze greatly.

a·strad′dle (ə strad′l) *adv., prep.* astride.

as′tral (as′trəl) *adj.* of the stars.

a·stray′ (ə strā′) *adj., adv.* straying.

a·stride′ (ə strīd′) *adv., adj., prep.* straddling.

as·trin′gent (ə strin′jənt) *adj.* causing constriction of skin tissue.

as·trol′o·gy (ə strol′ə jē) *n.* study of stars to determine their influence on human affairs. —**as′tro·log′i·cal** (as′trə loj′i kəl) *adj.* —**as·trol′o·ger,** *n.*

Astronomy. 1. astronomer. **2.** astronomical. **3.** astronomy.

as′tro·naut (as′trə nôt′) *n.* traveler outside earth's atmosphere.

as′tro·nau′tics, *n.* science and technology of space travel. —**as′tro·nau′tic, as′tro·nau′ti·cal,** *adj.*

as′tro·nom′i·cal (-nom′i kəl) *adj.* **1.** of astronomy. **2.** extremely great, high, etc. —**as′-tro·nom′i·cal·ly,** *adv.*

as·tron′o·my (ə stron′ə mē) *n.* science of all the celestial bodies. —**as′tron′o·mer,** *n.*

as′tro·phys′ics (as′trō fiz′iks) *n.* branch of astronomy dealing with physical properties of celestial bodies. —**as′tro·phys′i·cist** (-ə-sist) *n.*

as·tute′ (ə stōōt′, ə styōōt′) *adj.* shrewd; clever. —**as·tute′ly,** *adv.* —**as·tute′ness,** *n.*

ASU American Students Union.

a·sun′der (ə sun′dər) *adv., adj.* apart.

A.S.V. American Standard Version (of the Bible). Also, **ASV**

A.S.W. Association of Scientific Workers.

ASWG American Steel Wire Gauge.

a·sy′lum (ə sī′ləm) *n.* **1.** institution for care of ill or needy persons. **2.** place of refuge; sanctuary.

asym assymmetric.

a·sym′me·try (ā sim′i trē) *n.* lack of symmetry. —**a′sym·met′ric** (ā′sə me′trik), **a′-sym·met′ri·cal,** *adj.*

asymp *Math.* asymptote.

asyn asynchronous.

at (at; *unstressed* ət, it) *prep.* (word used in indicating place, time, etc.)

ATA Air Transport Association.

A.T.A. Associate Technical Aide.

at′a·vism (at′ə viz′əm) *n.* reappearance of ancestral traits. —**at′a·vist,** *n.* —**at′a·vis′tic** (-vis′tik) *adj.*

atb *Telephones.* all trunks busy.

ATC 1. Air Traffic Control. **2.** Air Transport Command.

atch attach.

ate (āt; *Brit.* et) *v.* pt. of **eat.**

at/el•ier/ (at/l yā/) *n.* studio, esp. of an artist.

ATF (Bureau of) Alcohol, Tobacco, and Firearms.

a/the•ism (ā/thē iz/əm) *n.* belief that there is no God. —**a/the•ist,** *n.* —**a/the•is/tic** (-is/-tik) *adj.*

ath/lete (ath/lēt) *n.* one who participates in sports or physical exercises. —**ath•let/ic** (-let/ik) *adj.*

—Pronunciation. The word ATHLETE is normally pronounced as a two-syllable word: (ath/lēt). Similarly, ATHLETIC has only three syllables: (ath let/ik). Pronunciations of these words that add an extra syllable, with a weak vowel sound inserted between the (th) and the (l), are not considered standard.

athlete's foot, ringworm of the feet.

a•thwart/ (ə thwôrt/) *adv., prep.* from side to side of.

ATLA American Trial Lawyers Association.

at/las (at/ləs) *n.* book of maps.

ATM, automated teller machine, which provides certain bank services when an electronic card is inserted.

at/mos•phere/ (at/məs fēr/) *n.* **1.** air surrounding earth. **2.** pervading mood. —**at/-mos•pher/ic** (-fer/ik) *adj.*

at. no. atomic number.

at/oll (at/ôl) *n.* ring-shaped coral island.

at/om (at/əm) *n.* smallest unit making up chemical element. —**a•tom/ic** (ə tom/ik) *adj.* —**a•tom/i•cal•ly,** *adv.*

atomic bomb, bomb whose force is derived from nuclear fission of certain atoms, causing the conversion of some mass to energy (atomic energy). Also, **atom bomb.**

at/om•iz/er (at/ə mī/zər) *n.* device for making a fine spray.

a•ton/al (ā tōn/l) *adj.* lacking tonality. —**a/-to•nal/i•ty** (-nal/i tē) *n.*

a•tone/ (ə tōn/) *v.,* atoned, atoning. make amends (for). —**a•tone/ment,** *n.*

a•top/ (ə top/) *adj., adv., prep.* on or at the top of.

ATP *Biochemistry.* an ester of adenosine and triphosphoric acid, $C_{10}H_{12}N_5O_4H_4P_3O_9$. [*a(denosine) t(ri)p(hosphate)*]

atr antitransmit-receive.

a/tri•um (ā/trē əm) *n., pl.* atria, atriums. **1.** enclosed court in public building. **2.** either of two upper chambers of the heart.

a•tro/cious (ə trō/shəs) *adj.* **1.** wicked. **2.** very bad. —**a•troc/i•ty** (ə tros/i tē) *n.*

at/ro•phy (a/trə fē) *n., v.,* -phied, -phying. —*n.* **1.** wasting away of the body. —*v.* **2.** cause or undergo atrophy.

at/ro•pine/ (a/trə pēn/) *n.* poisonous alkaloid of belladonna.

ATS *British. Military.* Auxiliary Territorial Service.

A.T.S. 1. American Temperance Society. **2.** American Tract Society. **3.** American Transport Service.

att. 1. attached. **2.** attention. **3.** attorney.

at•tach/ (ə tach/) *v.* **1.** fasten or join. **2.** take by legal authority.

at/ta•ché/ (at/ə shā/) *n.* embassy official.

at•tach/ment (ə tach/mənt) *n.* **1.** an attaching. **2.** something fastened on. **3.** affectionate tie.

at•tack/ (ə tak/) *v.* **1.** act against with sudden force **2.** do vigorously. —*n.* **3.** an attacking; onset. —**at•tack/er,** *n.*

at•tain/ (ə tān/) *v.* **1.** reach; arrive at. **2.** accomplish; fulfill. —**at•tain/a•ble,** *adj.* —**at•tain/ment,** *n.*

at/tar (at/ər) *n.* perfume from flowers.

at•tempt/ (ə tempt/) *v., n.* try.

at•tend/ (ə tend/) *v.* **1.** be present at. **2.** go with. **3.** take care of. **4.** give heed to. —**at•tend/ance,** *n.* —**at•tend/ant,** *n., adj.*

at•ten/tion (ə ten/shən) *n.* **1.** act of attending. **2.** careful notice. —**at•ten/tive,** *adj.* —**at•ten/tive•ly,** *adv.*

at•ten/u•ate/ (-yōō āt/) *v.,* -ated, -ating. **1.** make thin. **2.** lessen; abate. —**at•ten/u•a/tion,** *n.*

at•test/ (ə test/) *v.* declare or certify as true, genuine, etc. —**at/tes•ta/tion** (at/e stā/shən) *n.*

att. gen. attorney general.

at/tic (at/ik) *n.* room under the roof.

at•tire/ (ə tīⁱr/) *v.,* -tired, -tiring, *n.* —*v.* **1.** dress; adorn. —*n.* **2.** clothes.

at/ti•tude/ (at/i tōōd/, -tyōōd/) *n.* **1.** feeling or opinion, esp. as expressed. **2.** posture.

attn., attention.

at•tor/ney (ə tûr/nē) *n.* lawyer.

attorney general, *pl.* attorneys general, attorney generals. chief law officer of a country or state.

at•tract/ (ə trakt/) *v.* **1.** draw toward. **2.** invite; allure. —**at•trac/tion,** *n.* —**at•tract/-tive,** *adj.* —**at•trac/tive•ly,** *adv.* —**at•trac/-tive•ness,** *n.*

at•tract/ant, *n.* substance that attracts.

attrib. 1. attribute. **2.** attributive. **3.** attributively.

at•trib/ute, *v.,* -uted, -uting, *n.* —*v.* (ə trib/-yōōt) **1.** ascribe; credit; impute. —*n.* (at/rə-byōōt/) **2.** special quality, aspect. —**at/tri•bu/tion,** *n.*

at•tri/tion (ə trish/ən) *n.* wearing down.

at•tune/ (ə tōōn/, ə tyōōn/) *v.,* -tuned, -tuning. harmonize.

atty., attorney.

Atty. Gen. Attorney General.

ATV, *n.* all-terrain vehicle: small motor vehicle with treads or wheels for nonroad travel.

a•twit′ter (ə twit′ər) *adj.* excited; nervous.

at. wt. atomic weight. Also, **at wt**

a•typ′i•cal (ā tip′i kəl) *adj.* not typical; irregular. —**a•typ′i•cal•ly,** *adv.*

AU astronomical unit.

Au *Symbol, Chemistry.* gold. [from Latin *aurum*]

au. author.

A.U. *Physics.* angstrom unit. Also, **a.u.**

A.U.A. American Unitarian Association.

au′burn (ô′bərn) *adj.* reddish brown.

A.U.C. 1. from the founding of the city (of Rome in 753? B.C.). [from Latin *ab urbe conditā*] **2.** in the year from the founding of the city (of Rome). [from Latin *annō urbis conditae*]

auc′tion (ôk′shən) *n.* **1.** sale of goods to highest bidders. —*v.* **2.** sell by auction. —**auc′tion•eer′,** *n., v.*

aud. 1. audit. **2.** auditor.

au•da′cious (ô dā′shəs) *adj.* bold; daring. —**au•dac′i•ty** (-das′i tē) *n.*

au′di•ble (ô′də bəl) *adj.* that can be heard. —**au′di•bil′i•ty,** *n.* —**au′di•bly,** *adv.*

au′di•ence (ô′dē əns) *n.* **1.** group of hearers or spectators. **2.** formal hearing or interview.

au′di•o′ (ô′dē ō′) *adj.* **1.** of sound reception or reproduction. —*n.* **2.** audible part of TV.

au′di•ol′o•gy (-ol′ə jē) *n.* study and treatment of hearing disorders. —**au′di•ol′o•gist,** *n.*

au′di•om′e•ter (-om′i tər) *n.* instrument for testing hearing.

au′di•o•tape′ (ô′dē ō-) *n.* magnetic tape for recording sound.

au′di•o•vis′u•al, *adj.* using films, TV, and recordings, as for education.

au′dit (ô′dit) *n.* official examination of accounts. —**au′dit,** *v.* —**au′di•tor,** *n.*

au•di′tion (ô dish′ən) *n.* **1.** hearing. —*v.* **2.** give a hearing to.

au′di•to′ri•um (-tôr′ē əm) *n.* large meeting room.

au′di•to′ry, *adj.* of hearing.

Aug., August.

au′ger (ô′gər) *n.* drill.

aught (ôt) *n.* **1.** anything. **2.** zero (0). —*adv.* **3.** at all.

aug•ment′ (ôg ment′) *v.* increase. —**aug′men•ta′tion,** *n.*

au′gur (ô′gər) *v.* predict; bode. —**au′gu•ry** (-gyə-) *n.*

Au′gust (ô′gəst) *n.* eighth month of year.

au•gust′ (ô gust′) *adj.* majestic.

au jus (ō zhōōs′) *adj.* (of meat) served in the natural juices.

auk (ôk) *n.* northern diving bird.

auld lang syne (ōld′ lang zīn′) fondly remembered times.

AUM air-to-underwater missile.

aunt (ant, änt) *n.* **1.** sister of a parent. **2.** wife of an uncle.

au pair (ō pâr′) person, usu. young foreign

visitor, who does household tasks in exchange for room and board.

au′ra (ôr′ə) *n.* **1.** atmosphere, quality, etc. **2.** radiance coming from the body.

au′ral (ôr′əl) *adj.* of or by hearing.

au′re•ole′ (ôr′ē ōl′) *n.* halo.

au′ re•voir′ (ō′ rə vwär′) *French.* good-by.

au′ri•cle (ôr′i kəl) *n.* **1.** outer part of ear. **2.** chamber in heart. —**au•ric′u•lar** (ô rik′yə lər) *adj.*

au•rif′er•ous (ô rif′ər əs) *adj.* containing gold.

au•ror′a (ə rôr′ə) *n.* display of bands of light in the night sky.

AUS Army of the United States. Also, **A.U.S.**

Aus. 1. Austria. **2.** Austrian.

aus′pice (ô′spis) *n.* (*usually pl.*) patronage.

aus•pi′cious (ô spish′əs) *adj.* favorable. —**aus•pi′cious•ly,** *adv.*

Aust. 1. Austria. **2.** Austria-Hungary. **3.** Austrian.

aus•tere′ (ô stēr′) *adj.* **1.** harsh; stern. **2.** severely simple. —**aus•ter′i•ty,** *n.*

Austral Australian.

Austral. 1. Australasia. **2.** Australia. **3.** Australian.

Aus•tral′ian (ô strāl′yən) *n.* native or citizen of Australia. —**Australian,** *adj.*

Aus′tri•an (ô′strē ən) *n.* native of Austria. —**Austrian,** *adj.*

auth. 1. authentic. **2.** author. **3.** authority. **4.** authorized.

au•then′tic (ô then′tik) *adj.* reliable; genuine. —**au•then′ti•cal•ly,** *adv.* —**au′then•tic′i•ty** (-tis′i tē) *n.* —**au•then′ti•cate′,** *v.*

au′thor (ô′thər) *n.* writer or creator. —**au′thor•ship′,** *n.*

au•thor′i•tar′i•an (ə thôr′i târ′ē ən) *adj.* requiring total obedience.

au•thor′i•ta′tive (-tā′tiv) *adj.* to be accepted as true.

au•thor′i•ty, *n., pl.* **-ties. 1.** right to order or decide. **2.** one with such right. **3.** respected source of information.

au′thor•ize′ (ô′thə rīz′) *v.,* **-ized, -izing.** permit officially. —**auth′or•i•za′tion,** *n.*

Auth. Ver. Authorized Version (of the Bible).

au•tism (ô′tiz əm) *n.* disorder characterized by extreme self-absorption and detachment from reality. —**au•tis′tic** (ô tis′tik) *adj.*

au′to (ô′tō) *n.* automobile.

auto-, prefix meaning self or same, as *autograph.*

au′to•bi•og′ra•phy, *n., pl.* **-phies.** story of one's own life.

au•toc′ra•cy (ô tok′rə sē) *n., pl.* **-cies.** absolute political power. —**au′to•crat′** (ô′tə krat′) *n.* —**au′to•crat′ic,** *adj.*

au′to•di′dact (ô′tō dī′dakt) *n.* self-taught person.

AUTODIN (ô′tō din), automatic digital network.

au′to•graph′ (ô′tə graf′) *n.* signature.

au•to•im•mune (ô′tō i myōōn′) *adj.* of or relating to the body's immune response to its own components.

au′to•mat′ (ô′tə mat′) *n.* restaurant with coin-operated service.

au′to•mate (-māt′) *v.*, **-mated, -mating.** make or become automatic.

au′to•mat′ic (-mat′ik) *adj.* **1.** self-acting. **2.** inevitably following. —**au′to•mat′i•cal•ly,** *adv.*

automatic pilot, automatic electronic control system for piloting aircraft.

au′to•ma′tion (-mā′shən) *n.* system of controlling a mechanical process automatically, as by electronic devices.

au•tom′a•ton (ô tom′ə ton′) *n.* mechanical device or figure; robot.

au′to•mo•bile′ (ô′tə mə bēl′) *n.* motorized passenger vehicle.

autonomic nervous system (ô′tə nom′ik) system of nerves controlling involuntary functions such as heartbeat.

au•ton′o•my (ô ton′ə mē) *n.* self-government. —**au′to•nom′ic,** *adj.* —**au•ton′o•mous,** *adj.*

au′top•sy (ô′top sē) *n., pl.* **-sies.** examination of body for causes of death.

autoxfmr autotransformer.

au′tumn (ô′təm) *n.* season before winter; fall. —**au•tum′nal** (ô tum′nl) *adj.*

AUX *Linguistics.* auxiliary verb. Also, **Aux**

aux. auxiliary; auxiliaries. Also, **aux, auxil.**

aux•il′ia•ry (ôg zil′yə rē) *adj., n., pl.* **-ries.** —*adj.* **1.** assisting. **2.** subsidiary. —*n.* **3.** aid. **4.** noncombat naval vessel. **5.** verb preceding other verbs to express tense, etc.

AV 1. arteriovenous. **2.** atrioventricular. **3.** audiovisual.

av. 1. avenue. **2.** average. **3.** avoirdupois weight.

A-V 1. atrioventricular. **2.** audiovisual.

A/V 1. Also, **a.v.** ad valorem. **2.** audiovisual.

A.V. 1. Artillery Volunteers. **2.** audiovisual. **3.** Authorized Version (of the Bible).

a•vail′ (ə vāl′) *v.* **1.** be of use, value, etc. **2.** take to (oneself) advantageously. —*n.* **3.** benefit; advantage.

a•vail′a•ble, *adj.* present for use. —**a•vail′a•bil′i•ty,** *n.*

av′a•lanche′ (av′ə lanch′) *n.* mass of snow, ice, etc., falling down mountain.

a•vant′-garde′ (ə vänt′gärd′, av′änt-) *adj.* progressive, esp. in art.

av′a•rice (av′ər is) *n.* greed. —**av′a•ri′cious** (-rish′əs) *adj.*

A.V.C. 1. American Veterans' Committee. **2.** automatic volume control. Also, **AVC**

avdp. avoirdupois weight.

ave., avenue.

a•venge′ (ə venj′) *v.*, **avenged, avenging.** take vengeance for. —**a•veng′er,** *n.*

av′e•nue′ (av′ə nyōō′) *n.* **1.** broad street. **2.** approach.

a•ver′ (ə vûr′) *v.*, **averred, averring.** affirm; declare.

av′er•age (av′ər ij) *n., adj., v.*, **-aged, -aging.** —*n.* **1.** sum of a series of numbers divided by the number of terms in the series. —*adj.* **2.** of or like an average. **3.** typical. —*v.* **4.** find average of.

a•verse′ (ə vûrs′) *adj.* unwilling. —**a•verse′-ly,** *adv.* —**a•verse′ness,** *n.*

a•ver′sion (ə vûr′zhən) *n.* dislike.

a•vert′ (ə vûrt′) *v.* **1.** turn away. **2.** prevent.

AVF all-volunteer force.

avg., average.

a′vi•ar′y (ā′vē er′ē) *n., pl.* **-aries.** place in which birds are kept.

a′vi•a′tion (ā′vē ā′shən) *n.* science of flying aircraft. —**a′vi•a′tor,** *n.* —**a′vi•a′trix,** *n. fem.*

av′id (av′id) *adj.* eager. —**a•vid′i•ty,** *n.* —**av′id•ly,** *adv.*

avlbl available.

AVMA American Veterinary Medical Association.

avn. aviation.

av′o•ca′do (av′ə kä′dō, ä′və-) *n., pl.* **-dos.** tropical pear-shaped fruit.

av′o•ca′tion (av′ə kā′shən) *n.* hobby.

a•void′ (ə void′) *v.* shun; evade. —**a•void′a•ble,** *adj.* —**a•void′ance,** *n.*

av′oir•du•pois′ (av′ər də poiz′) *n.* system of weights with 16-ounce pounds.

a•vow′ (ə vou′) *v.* declare; confess. —**a•vow′al,** *n.* —**a•vowed′,** *adj.*

avr automatic voltage regulator.

a•vun′cu•lar (ə vung′kyə lər) *adj.* of or like an uncle.

AW Articles of War.

a.w. 1. actual weight. **2.** (in shipping) all water. **3.** atomic weight. Also, **aw**

AWACS (ā′waks), a detection aircraft, fitted with radar and computers, capable of simultaneously tracking and plotting large numbers of low-flying aircraft. [*A(irborne) W(arning) A(nd) C(ontrol) S(ystem)*]

a•wait′ (ə wāt′) *v.* wait for.

a•wake′ (ə wāk′) *v.*, **awoke** (ə wōk′) or **awaked, awaking,** *adj.* —*v.* **1.** Also, **a•wak′en.** rouse from sleep. —*adj.* **2.** not asleep.

a•wak′en, *v.* awake. —**a•wak′en•ing,** *n., adj.*

a•ward′ (ə wôrd′) *v.* **1.** bestow; grant. —*n.* **2.** thing bestowed.

a•ware′ (ə wâr′) *adj.* conscious (of). —**a•ware′ness,** *n.*

a•wash′ (ə wosh′) *adj.* overflowing with water.

a•way′ (ə wā′) *adv.* **1.** from this or that place. **2.** apart. **3.** aside. —*adj.* **4.** absent. **5.** distant.

AWB air waybill.

awe (ô) *n., v.*, **awed, awing.** —*n.* **1.** respectful fear. —*v.* **2.** fill with awe.

awe•some (ô′səm) *adj.* **1.** inspiring or characterized by awe. **2.** *Slang.* very impressive.

awe′struck′, *adj.* filled with awe. Also, **awe′strick′en.**

aw′ful (ô′fəl) *adj.* **1.** fearful. **2.** very bad. **3.** *Informal.* very.

aw′ful•ly, *adv.* **1.** very badly. **2.** *Informal.* very.

AWG American Wire Gauge.

a•while′ (ə hwīl′) *adv.* for a short time.

—**Usage.** The adverb AWHILE is always spelled as one word: *We rested awhile.* A WHILE is a noun phrase (an article and a noun) and is used after a preposition: *We rested for a while.*

AWI Animal Welfare Institute.

AWIS Association of Women in Science.

awk′ward (ôk′wərd) *adj.* **1.** clumsy. **2.** embarrassing. **3.** difficult; risky. —**awk′ward•ly,** *adv.* —**awk′ward•ness,** *n.*

awl (ôl) *n.* small drill.

awn (ôn) *n.* bristlelike part plant.

awn′ing (ô′ning) *n.* canvas overhang.

AWOL (*pronounced as initials or* ā′wôl) *adj., adv.* absent without leave.

a•wry′ (ə rī′) *adv., adj.* **1.** twisted. **2.** wrong.

AWS American Weather Service.

AWSA American Water-Skiing Association.

ax (aks) *n.* small chopping tool. Also, **axe.**

ax′i•om (ak′sē əm) *n.* accepted truth. —**ax′i•o•mat′ic** (-ə mat′ik) *adj.*

ax′is (ak′sis) *n., pl.* **axes** (ak′sēz). line about which something turns. —**ax′i•al,** *adj.*

ax′le (ak′səl) *n.* bar on which a wheel turns.

ay (ā), *adv. Poetic.* always. Also, **aye.**

a′ya•tol′lah (ä′yə tō′lə) *n.* chief Muslim leader.

aye (ī) *adv., n.* yes.

A.Y.H. American Youth Hostels.

AZ Arizona (for use with ZIP code).

az. **1.** azimuth. **2.** azure.

a•zal′ea (ə zāl′yə) *n.* flowering shrub.

AZT, *n.Trademark.* drug used in AIDS treatment.

Az′tec (az′tek) *n.* American Indian people whose Mexican empire was conquered by Spaniards in 1521. —**Az′tec•an,** *adj.*

az′ure (azh′ər) *adj., n.* sky-blue.

B

B, b (bē) *n.* second letter of English alphabet.

B.A., Bachelor of Arts.

B.A.A. Bachelor of Applied Arts.

B.A.A.E. Bachelor of Aeronautical and Astronautical Engineering.

Bab. Babylon; Babylonia.

bab′ble (bab′əl) *v.,* **-bled, -bling. 1.** talk indistinctly or foolishly. **2.** make a murmuring sound. —**bab′ble,** *n.*

babe (bāb) *n.* **1.** baby. **2.** innocent person.

ba·boon′ (ba boon′, bə-) *n.* large monkey of Africa and Arabia.

ba·bush′ka (bə boosh′kə) *n.* woman's head scarf.

ba′by (bā′bē) *n., pl.* **-bies,** *v.,* **-bied, -bying.** —*n.* **1.** infant. **2.** childish person. —*v.* **3.** pamper. —**ba′by·hood′,** *n.* —**ba′by·ish,** *adj.*

baby boom, period of increase in the rate of births. —**baby boomer.**

ba′by-sit′, *v.,* **-sat** (-sat′), **-sitting.** tend another's child for a few hours. —**ba′by-sit′-ter,** *n.*

BAC blood-alcohol concentration: the percentage of alcohol in the bloodstream.

bac′ca·lau′re·ate (bak′ə lôr′ē it) *n.* bachelor's degree.

bac′cha·nal′ (bak′ə nal′) *n.* drunken revelry. —**bac′cha·na′li·an** (-nā′lē ən) *adj., n.*

bach′e·lor (bach′ə lər) *n.* **1.** unmarried man. **2.** person holding first degree at a college. —**bach′e·lor·hood′,** *n.* —**bach′e·lor·ship′,** *n.*

ba·cil′lus (bə sil′əs) *n., pl.* **-cilli** (-sil′ī). type of bacteria.

back (bak) *n.* **1.** hinder part of human and animal body. **2.** rear. **3.** spine. —*v.* **4.** sponsor. **5.** move backward. **6.** bet in favor of. **7.** furnish or form a back. —*adj.* **8.** being behind. **9.** in the past. **10.** overdue. —*adv.* **11.** at or toward the rear. **12.** toward original point or condition. **13.** in return. —**back′er,** *n.* —**back′ing,** *n.*

back′bite′, *v.,* **-bit** (-bit′), **-bitten, -biting.** discuss (someone) maliciously.

back′board′, *n.* in basketball, vertical board behind basket.

back′bone′, *n.* **1.** spine. **2.** strength of character. —**back′boned′,** *adj.*

back′break′ing, *adj.* fatiguing.

back′drop′, *n.* **1.** curtain at the back of a stage. **2.** background of an event; setting.

back′field′, *n.* football players behind the line.

back′fire′, *v.,* **-fired, firing. 1.** (of an engine) ignite prematurely. **2.** bring results opposite to those planned. —**back′fire′,** *n.*

back′gam′mon (-gam′ən) *n.* board game for two persons.

back′ground′, *n.* **1.** parts in the rear. **2.** distant portions in a picture. **3.** origins; antecedents.

back′hand′, *n.* **1.** in tennis and other sports, stroke made with back of hand facing direction of movement. —*adj.* **2.** backhanded. —*adv.* **3.** in a backhanded way. —*v.* **4.** hit with a backhand.

back′hand′ed, *adj.* **1.** with upper part of hand forward. **2.** ambiguous.

back′lash′, *n.* retaliatory reaction.

back′log′, *n.* reserve or accumulation, as of work.

back′pack′, *n.* **1.** knapsack. —*v.* **2.** hike using backpack.

back′-ped′al, *v.,* **-aled, -aling. 1.** slow a bicycle by pressing backward on pedals. **2.** retreat from or reverse a previous stand or opinion.

back′side′, *n.* **1.** rear. **2.** rump.

back′slap′ping, *n.* exaggerated friendliness. —**back′slap′per,** *n.*

back′slide′, *v.,* **-slid** (-slid′), **-slidden** or **-slid, -sliding.** relapse into bad habits. —**back′slid′er,** *n.*

back′stage′, *adv.* **1.** in theater wings or dressing rooms. —*adj.* **2.** of secret activities or private lives.

back′stroke′, *n.* swimming stroke performed while lying on back.

back talk, impertinent talk.

back′track′, *v.* retreat slowly.

back′up′, *n.* **1.** person or thing that supports or reinforces another. **2.** accumulation caused by a stopping, as of traffic. **3.** alternate kept in reserve.

back′ward (-wərd) *adv.* Also, **back′wards. 1.** toward the back or rear. **2.** back foremost. **3.** toward or in the past. —*adj.* **4.** toward the back or past. **5.** behind in time or progress. **6.** bashful. —**back′ward·ly,** *adv.* —**back′-ward·ness,** *n.*

back′wa′ter, *n.* place that is backward or stagnant.

back′woods′, *n.pl.* wooded or unsettled districts. —**back′woods′man,** *n.*

ba′con (bā′kən) *n.* cured back and sides of a hog.

bact. 1. bacterial. **2.** bacteriology. **3.** bacterium.

bac·te′ri·a (bak tēr′ē ə) *n.pl., sing.* **-um** (-əm). group of one-celled organisms, involved in fermentation, infectious disease, etc. —**bac·te′ri·al,** *adj.* —**bac·te′ri·al·ly,** *adv.*

bac·te′ri·ol′o·gy (-ol′ə jē) *n.* science dealing with bacteria. —**bac·te′ri·o·log′i·cal** (-ə loj′i kəl) *adj.* —**bac·te′ri·ol′o·gist,** *n.*

bad (bad) *adj.,* **worse** (wûrs), **worst** (wûrst), *n.* —*adj.* **1.** not good. —*n.* **2.** bad thing, condition, or quality. **—bad/ly,** *adv.* **—bad/-ness,** *n.*

——Usage. The adjective BAD, meaning "unpleasant, unattractive, unfavorable, spoiled, etc.," is the usual form after such verbs as *sound, smell, look,* and *taste: The music sounds bad. The locker room smells bad. You look pretty bad; are you sick? The water tasted bad.* After the verb *feel,* the adjective BADLY may also be used (*She was feeling badly that day*), although BAD is more common in formal writing. BAD as an adverb appears mainly in informal situations: *He wanted to win pretty bad.*

bad blood, hostility.

badge (baj) *n.* emblem or insignia.

badg/er (baj/ər) *n.* **1.** burrowing mammal. **—***v.* **2.** harass.

bad/min•ton (bad/min tn) *n.* game similar to lawn tennis.

bad/-mouth/ (-mouth/, -mouth/) *v.* criticize. Also, **bad/mouth/.**

BAE 1. Bureau of Agricultural Economics. **2.** Bureau of American Ethnology.

B.A.E. 1. Bachelor of Aeronautical Engineering. **2.** Bachelor of Agricultural Engineering. **3.** Bachelor of Architectural Engineering. **4.** Bachelor of Art Education. **5.** Bachelor of Arts in Education.

B.A.Ed. Bachelor of Arts in Education.

B.A.E.E. Bachelor of Arts in Elementary Education.

baf/fle (baf/əl) *v.*, **-fled, -fling,** *n.* **—***v.* **1.** thwart; confuse. **—***n.* **2.** obstacle; obstruction. **—baf/fle•ment,** *n.*

bag (bag) *n.*, *v.*, **bagged, bagging. —***n.* **1.** sack or receptacle of flexible material. **2.** purse. **—***v.* **3.** bulge. **4.** put into a bag. **5.** kill or catch. **—bag/gy,** *adj.* **—bag/gi•ness,** *n.*

bag/a•telle/ (bag/ə tel/) *n.* article of small value.

B.Ag.E. Bachelor of Agricultural Engineering.

ba/gel (bā/gəl) *n.* hard ringlike roll.

bag/gage (bag/ij) *n.* trunks, suitcases, etc., for travel.

bag/pipe/, *n.* (*often pl.*) musical instrument with windbag and two or more pipes. **—bag/pip/er,** *n.*

B.Agr. Bachelor of Agriculture.

B.Ag.Sc. Bachelor of Agricultural Science.

bah (bä, ba) *interj.* (exclamation of contempt or annoyance).

bail (bāl) *n.* **1.** security for the return of a prisoner to custody. **2.** person giving bail. **3.** handle of kettle or pail. **—***v.* **4.** give or obtain liberty by bail. **5.** dip water out of boat. **6. bail out,** make a parachute jump. **—bail/a•ble,** *adj.* **—bail/ee/,** *n.* **—bail/ment,** *n.* **—bail/or,** *n.* **—bail/er,** *n.*

bail/iff (bā/lif) *n.* public officer similar to sheriff or deputy.

bail/i•wick (bā/lə wik/) *n.* **1.** district under

bailiff's jurisdiction. **2.** person's area of authority, skill, etc.

Ba. Is. Bahama Islands.

bait (bāt) *n.* **1.** food used as lure in fishing or hunting. **—***v.* **2.** prepare with bait. **3.** set dogs upon for sport.

B.A.Jour. Bachelor of Arts in Journalism.

bake (bāk) *v.*, **baked, baking. 1.** cook by dry heat, as in oven. **2.** harden by heat. **—bak/-er,** *n.*

baker's dozen, a dozen plus one; 13.

bak/er•y, *n.*, *pl.* **-eries.** place for baking; baker's shop.

BAK file (bak), *Computers.* backup file.

baking powder, white powder used as leavening agent in baking.

baking soda, sodium bicarbonate, white powder used as an antacid and in baking.

BAL 1. *Chemistry.* British Anti-Lewisite: dimercaprol. **2.** *Computers.* Basic Assembly Language.

bal blood alcohol level.

Bal. Baluchistan.

bal. 1. balance. **2.** balancing.

bal/a•lai/ka (bal/ə lī/kə) *n.* musical instrument similar to guitar.

bal/ance (bal/əns) *n.*, *v.*, **-anced, -ancing. —***n.* **1.** instrument for weighing. **2.** equilibrium. **3.** harmonious arrangement. **4.** act of balancing. **5.** remainder, as of money due. **—***v.* **6.** weigh. **7.** set or hold in equilibrium. **8.** be equivalent to. **9.** reckon or adjust accounts. **—bal/anc•er,** *n.*

bal/co•ny (bal/kə nē) *n.*, *pl.* **-nies. 1.** platform projecting from wall of building. **2.** theater gallery.

bald (bôld) *adj.* **1.** lacking hair on scalp. **2.** plain; undisguised. **—bald/ly,** *adv.* **—bald/-ness,** *n.*

bal/der•dash/ (bôl/dər dash/) *n.* nonsense.

bale (bāl) *n.*, *v.*, **baled, baling. —***n.* **1.** large bundle or package. **—***v.* **2.** make into bales. **—bal/er,** *n.*

bale/ful, *adj.* evil; menacing. **—bale/ful•ly,** *adv.* **—bale/ful•ness,** *n.*

balk (bôk) *v.* **1.** stop or stop short. **2.** hinder; thwart. **—***n.* **3.** hindrance. **4.** in baseball, illegal stop in pitcher's motion. **—balk/y,** *adj.*

ball (bôl) *n.* **1.** round or roundish body. **2.** game played with ball. **3.** social assembly for dancing. **4.** *Informal.* good time. **—***v.* **5.** make or form into ball.

bal/lad (bal/əd) *n.* **1.** narrative folk song or poem. **2.** sentimental popular song.

bal/last (bal/əst) *n.* **1.** heavy material carried to ensure stability. **—***v.* **2.** furnish with ballast.

ball bearing, 1. bearing in which a moving part turns on steel balls. **2.** ball so used.

bal/le•ri/na (bal/ə rē/nə) *n.* leading woman ballet dancer.

bal•let/ (ba lā/) *n.* theatrical entertainment by dancers.

B

ballistic missile (bə lis′tik) guided missile completing its trajectory in free fall.

bal•lis′tics, n. study of the motion of projectiles. —**bal•lis′tic,** adj.

bal•loon′ (bə lōōn′) n. **1.** bag filled with a gas lighter than air, designed to float in atmosphere. —v. **2.** go up in balloon. **3.** increase rapidly. —**bal•loon′ist,** n.

bal′lot (bal′ət) n., v., **-loted, -loting.** —n. **1.** paper used in voting. **2.** vote. —v. **3.** vote by ballot.

ball′park′, n. baseball arena.

ball′point′ pen, pen laying down ink with small ball bearing.

ball′room′, n. room for dancing.

bal′ly•hoo′ (bal′ē hōō′) n. **1.** Informal. exaggerated publicity. —v. **2.** tout.

balm (bäm) n. **1.** fragrant, oily substance obtained from tropical trees. **2.** aromatic ointment or fragrance.

balm′y, adj., **balmier, balmiest. 1.** mild; refreshing. **2.** fragrant. —**balm′i•ly,** adv. —**balm′i•ness,** n.

ba•lo′ney (bə lō′nē) n. Informal. **1.** bologna. **2.** false or foolish talk.

bal′sa (bôl′sə, bäl′-) n. tropical tree with light wood.

bal′sam (bôl′səm) n. **1.** fragrant substance exuded from certain trees. **2.** any of these trees. —**bal•sam′ic** (bôl sam′ik) adj.

Balt. Baltic.

balun balanced-to-unbalanced network.

bal′us•ter (bal′ə stər) n. pillarlike support for railing.

bal′us•trade′ (-ə strād′) n. series of balusters supporting a railing.

B.A.M. 1. Bachelor of Applied Mathematics. **2.** Bachelor of Arts in Music.

bam•boo′ (bam bōō′) n., pl. **-boos.** treelike tropical grass having a hollow woody stem.

bam•boo′zle (bam bōō′zəl) v., **-zled, -zling.** Informal. confuse or trick.

B.A.Mus.Ed. Bachelor of Arts in Music Education.

ban (ban) v., **banned, banning,** n. —v. **1.** prohibit. —n. **2.** prohibition.

ba•nal′ (bə nal′, -näl′, bān′l) adj. trite. —**ba•nal′i•ty,** n.

ba•nan′a (bə nan′ə) n. **1.** tropical plant. **2.** fruit of this plant.

band (band) n. **1.** strip of material for binding. **2.** stripe. **3.** company of persons. **4.** group of musicians. —v. **5.** mark with bands. **6.** unite. —**band′mas′ter,** n. —**bands′man,** n.

band′age (ban′dij) n., v., **-aged, -aging.** —n. **1.** strip of cloth for binding wound. —v. **2.** bind with bandage. —**band′ag•er,** n.

Band′-Aid′, n. **1.** Trademark. small adhesive bandage with gauze center. **2.** (often l.c.) makeshift aid or solution.

ban•dan′na (ban dan′ə) n. colored handkerchief with figures. Also, **ban•dan′a.**

B and B 1. Trademark. a brand of liqueur combining Benedictine and brandy. **2.** bed-and-breakfast. Also, **B&B**

B&D bondage and discipline: used in reference to sadomasochistic sexual practices. Also, **B and D**

ban′dit (ban′dit) n. robber; outlaw. —**ban′dit•ry,** n.

B&S Brown and Sharp wire gauge.

band′stand′, n. platform on which band performs.

band′wag′on, n. **1.** large, ornate wagon for carrying band in parade. **2.** cause or movement that appears popular and successful.

ban′dy (ban′dē) v., **-died, -dying,** adj. —v. **1.** strike to and fro. **2.** exchange (words) back and forth. —adj. **3.** bent outward. —**ban′dy-leg′ged** (-leg′id, -legd′) adj.

bane (bān) n. thing causing death or destruction.

bane′ful, adj. destructive. —**bane′ful•ly,** adv. —**bane′ful•ness,** n.

bang (bang) n. **1.** loud, sudden noise. **2.** (often pl.) fringe of hair across forehead. —v. **3.** make loud noise. **4.** strike noisily.

ban′gle (bang′gəl) n. bracelet.

bang′-up′, adj. Informal. excellent.

ban′ish (ban′ish) v. **1.** exile. **2.** drive or put away. —**ban′ish•ment,** n.

ban′is•ter (ban′ə stər) n. **1.** baluster. **2.** (pl.) balustrade.

ban′jo (ban′jō) n., pl. **-jos, -joes.** musical instrument similar to guitar, with circular body. —**ban′jo•ist,** n.

bank (bangk) n. **1.** pile; heap. **2.** slope bordering stream. **3.** place or institution for receiving and lending money. **4.** store of something, such as blood, for future use. —v. **5.** border with or make into bank. **6.** cover fire to make burn slowly. **7.** act as bank. **8.** deposit or keep money in bank. **9.** rely (on). —**bank′er,** n. —**bank′ing,** n.

bank′roll′, n. **1.** money possessed. —v. **2.** pay for; fund.

bank′rupt (-rupt) n. **1.** insolvent person. —adj. **2.** insolvent. **3.** lacking. —v. **4.** make bankrupt. —**bank′rupt•cy,** n.

ban′ner (ban′ər) n. flag.

banns (banz) n.pl. notice of intended marriage. Also, **bans.**

ban′quet (bang′kwit) n. **1.** feast. —v. **2.** dine or entertain at banquet. —**ban′quet•er,** n.

ban′shee (ban′shē) n. female spirit of Irish folklore whose wailing means a loved one is about to die.

ban′tam (ban′təm) n. **1.** breed of small domestic fowl. —adj. **2.** tiny.

ban′ter (ban′tər) n. **1.** good-natured teasing. —v. **2.** address with or use banter. —**ban′ter•er,** n.

ban′yan (ban′yən) n. East Indian fig tree.

ba′o•bab′ (bā′ō bab′, bä′ō-) n. tropical tree with thick trunk and gourdlike fruit.

Bap. Baptist. Also, **Bapt.**

bap. baptized.

B.A.P.C.T. Bachelor of Arts in Practical Christian Training.

B.App.Arts. Bachelor of Applied Arts.

bap′tism (bap′tiz əm) n. immersion in or application of water, esp. as initiatory rite in Christian church. —**bap•tis′mal,** adj.

Bap′tist (-tist) n. Christian who undergoes baptism only after profession of faith.

bap•tize′ (bap tīz′, bap′tīz) v., -tized, -tizing. **1.** administer baptism. **2.** christen. —**bap•tiz′er,** n.

bar (bär) n., v., **barred, barring,** prep. —n. **1.** long, evenly shaped piece of wood or metal. **2.** band; stripe. **3.** long ridge in shallow waters. **4.** obstruction; hindrance. **5.** line marking division between two measures of music. **6.** place where liquors are served. **7.** legal profession or its members. **8.** railing in courtroom between public and court officers. **9.** place in courtroom where prisoners are stationed. —v. **10.** provide or fasten with a bar. **11.** block; hinder. —prep. **12.** except for. —**barred,** adj.

barb (bärb) n. **1.** point projecting backward. —v. **2.** furnish with barb. —**barbed,** adj.

bar•bar′i•an (bär bâr′ē ən) n. **1.** savage or uncivilized person. —adj. **2.** uncivilized. —**bar•bar′i•an•ism,** n. —**bar•bar′ic** (-bar′ik) adj. —**bar•bar′i•cal•ly,** adv.

bar′ba•rism (-bə riz′əm) n. barbarian state or act.

bar•bar′i•ty (-bar′i tē) n., pl. -ties. **1.** cruelty. **2.** crudity.

bar′ba•rous (-bər əs) adj. **1.** barbarian. **2.** harsh; harsh-sounding. —**bar′ba•rous•ly,** adv. —**bar′ba•rous•ness,** n.

bar′be•cue′ (bär′bi kyōō′) n., v., -cued, -cuing. —n. **1.** outdoor meal at which foods are roasted over an open fire. **2.** animal roasted whole. —v. **3.** broil or roast over an open fire. Also, **bar′be•que′.**

bar′ber (bär′bər) n. **1.** one who gives haircuts, shaves, etc. —v. **2.** shave or cut the hair.

bar•bi′tu•rate′ (bär bich′ər it, bär′bi tŏŏr′it, -tyŏŏr′-) n. sedative drug.

B.Arch. Bachelor of Architecture.

B.Arch.E. Bachelor of Architectural Engineering.

bar code, series of lines of different widths placed on item for identification by computer scanner.

bard (bärd) n. **1.** ancient Celtic poet. **2.** any poet. —**bard′ic,** adj.

bare (bâr) adj., barer, barest, v., bared, baring. —adj. **1.** uncovered; unclothed. **2.** unfurnished. **3.** unconcealed. **4.** mere. —v. **5.** make bare. —**bare′ness,** n. —**bare′foot′,** adj., adv.

bare′back′, adv., adj. without a saddle.

bare′faced′, adj. **1.** undisguised. **2.** impudent.

bare′ly, adv. **1.** no more than; only. **2.** nakedly.

bar′gain (bär′gən) n. **1.** agreement. **2.** advantageous purchase. —v. **3.** discuss or arrive at agreement. —**bar′gain•er,** n.

barge (bärj) n., v., **barged, barging.** —n. **1.** unpowered vessel for freight. —v. **2.** carry by barge. **3.** move clumsily. **4.** Informal. intrude. —**barge′man,** n.

barit. baritone.

bar′i•tone′ (bar′i tōn′) n. **1.** male voice or part between tenor and bass. **2.** baritone singer, instrument, etc.

bar′i•um (bâr′ē əm, bar′-) n. metallic element.

bark (bärk) n. **1.** cry of a dog. **2.** external covering of woody plants. **3.** Also, **barque.** three-masted vessel. —v. **4.** sound a bark. **5.** utter with barking sound. **6.** strip off bark of. **7.** rub off the skin of.

bark′er (bär′kər) n. person who stands at the entrance to a show, shouting out its attractions.

bar′ley (bär′lē) n. edible cereal plant.

bar mitz′vah (bär mits′və) Jewish religious ceremony recognizing manhood.

barn (bärn) n. farm building for storage and stabling. —**barn′yard′,** n.

bar′na•cle (bär′nə kəl) n. type of shellfish that clings to ship bottoms, floating timber, etc. —**bar′na•cled,** adj.

barn′storm′, v. tour rural areas giving speeches or performing plays.

baro barometer.

ba•rom′e•ter (bə rom′i tər) n. instrument for measuring atmospheric pressure. —**bar′o•met′ric** (bar′ə me′trik) adj.

bar′on (bar′ən) n. member of lowest nobility. Also, **bar′on•ess.** —**bar′on•age,** n. —**ba•ro′ni•al** (bə rō′ nē əl) adj.

bar′on•et (-ə nit, -net′) n. member of hereditary British commoner order, ranking below baron. —**bar′on•et•cy,** n.

Ba•roque′ (bə rōk′) n. artistic style marked by exuberant decoration and grotesque effects.

barr. barrister.

bar′rack, n. (bar′ək) **1.** (usually pl.) building for lodging soldiers. —v. **2.** lodge in barracks.

bar′ra•cu′da (bar′ə kōō′də) n. edible eellike fish.

bar•rage′ (bə räzh′) n. barrier of concentrated artillery fire.

bar′rel (bar′əl) n., v., -reled, -reling. —n. **1.** wooden cylindrical vessel with bulging sides. **2.** quantity held in such vessel. —v. **3.** put in barrel or barrels.

bar′ren (bar′ən) adj. **1.** sterile; unfruitful. **2.** dull. —**bar′ren•ness,** n.

bar•rette′ (bə ret′) n. clasp for hair.

bar′ri•cade′ (bar′i kād′, bar′i kād′) n., v., -caded, -cading. —n. **1.** defensive barrier. —v. **2.** block or defend with barricade.

bar′ri•er (bar′ē ər) n. obstacle; obstruction.

bar′ring (bär′ing) prep. excepting.

bar'ris•ter (bar'ə stər) *n.* in England, lawyer in higher courts.

bar'room' (bär'-) *n.* room with a bar for serving liquor.

bar'row (bar'ō) *n.* **1.** flat frame for carrying load. **2.** artificial mound, as over a grave.

BART (bärt), Bay Area Rapid Transit.

Bart. Baronet.

bar'tend'er (bär'-) *n.* person mixing and serving drinks at a bar.

bar'ter (bär'tər) *v.* **1.** trade by exchange. —*n.* **2.** act of bartering.

B.A.S. 1. Bachelor of Agricultural Science. **2.** Bachelor of Applied Science.

ba'sal (bā'səl, -zəl) *adj.* basic.

ba•salt' (bə sôlt', bā'sôlt) *n.* dark, hard rock. —**ba•sal'tic,** *adj.*

B.A.Sc. 1. Bachelor of Agricultural Science. **2.** Bachelor of Applied Science.

base (bās) *n., v.,* **based, basing,** *adj.,* **baser, basest.** —*n.* **1.** bottom or foundation of something. **2.** fundamental principle. **3.** starting point. **4.** *Mil.* **a.** protected place from which operations proceed. **b.** supply installation. **5.** chemical compound which unites with an acid to form a salt. —*v.* **6.** make foundation for. —*adj.* **7.** despicable. **8.** inferior. **9.** counterfeit. —**base'ness,** *n.*

base'ball', *n.* **1.** game of ball played by two teams of nine players on diamond-shaped field. **2.** ball used.

base'board', *n.* board or molding at the base of a room's walls.

base'less, *adj.* groundless; unfounded.

base'line', *n.* **1.** line between bases on baseball diamond. **2.** line at each end of tennis court. **3.** basic standard or level; guideline. Also, **base line.**

base'ment, *n.* story of building below the ground floor.

base on balls, *pl.* **bases on balls.** awarding of first base to a batter after four pitches not strikes.

bash (bash) *v.* **1.** hit hard. **2.** attack with blows or words. —*n.* **3.** hard blow. **4.** big, lively party.

bash'ful, *adj.* shy; timid. —**bash'ful•ly,** *adv.* —**bash'ful•ness,** *n.*

ba'sic (bā'sik) *adj.* **1.** rudimentary. **2.** essential. —*n.* **3.** (*pl.*) rudiments. —**ba'si•cal•ly,** *adv.*

BASIC (bā'sik) *n.* computer programming language using English words, punctuation, and algebraic notation.

bas'il (baz'əl, bā'zəl) *n.* mintlike herb.

ba•sil'i•ca (bə sil'i kə) *n.* **1.** ancient church. **2.** Roman Catholic church.

ba'sin (bā'sən) *n.* **1.** circular vessel for liquids. **2.** area drained by river. **3.** area of lower land, not drained to outside.

ba'sis (bā'sis) *n., pl.* **-ses** (-sēz). **1.** base (defs. 1, 2). **2.** principal ingredient.

bask (bask) *v.* lie in or expose to warmth.

bas'ket (bas'kit) *n.* receptacle woven of twigs, strips of wood, etc.

bas'ket•ball', *n.* **1.** game of ball played by two teams of five players on rectangular court. **2.** ball used.

bas•ma'ti (bäs mä'tē) *n.* variety of long-grain rice that is notably fragrant.

bas'-re•lief' (bä'ri lēf') *n.* sculpture in which figures project slightly.

bass *adj., n., pl.* (for 3) **basses, bass.** —*adj.* (bās) **1.** of the lowest musical part or range. —*n.* **2.** (bās) bass part, voice, instrument, etc. **3.** (bas) any of various edible, spiny fishes.

basset hound (bas'it) short-legged hound with drooping ears.

bas'si•net' (bas'ə net') *n.* basket with hood, used as cradle.

bas•soon' (ba sōōn', bə-) *n.* baritone woodwind instrument.

bas'tard (bas'tərd) *n.* **1.** illegitimate child. **2.** *Slang.* mean person. —*adj.* **3.** illegitimate in birth. **4.** not pure or authentic. —**bas'tard•i•za'tion,** *n.* —**bas'tard•ize',** *v.*

baste (bāst) *v.,* **basted, basting. 1.** sew with temporary stitches. **2.** moisten (meat, etc.) while cooking.

bas'tion (bas'chən) *n.* **1.** projecting part of fortification. **2.** fortified place. **3.** something that preserves or protects.

bat (bat) *n., v.,* **batted, batting.** —*n.* **1.** stick or club, esp. as used in ball games. **2.** nocturnal flying mammal. —*v.* **3.** strike with bat. **4.** take turn in batting. **5.** blink; flutter.

batch (bach) *n.* material, esp. bread, prepared in one operation.

bat'ed (bā'tid) *adj.* (of breath) held back in suspense.

BATF Bureau of Alcohol, Tobacco, and Firearms.

bath (bath) *n., pl.* **baths. 1.** washing of entire body. **2.** water used. —**bath'room',** *n.* —**bath'tub',** *n.*

bathe (bāth) *v.,* **bathed, bathing. 1.** take a bath. **2.** immerse in liquid; moisten. —**bath'er,** *n.*

bathing suit, garment worn for swimming; swimsuit.

ba'thos (bā'thos, -thōs) *n.* **1.** ludicrous change in tone from lofty to commonplace. **2.** false pathos; trite sentiment. —**ba•thet'ic** (bə thet'ik) *adj.*

bath'robe', *n.* robe worn going to and from bath.

ba•tik' (bə tēk') *n.* cloth partly waxed to resist dye.

bat mitz'vah (bät mits'və) Jewish religious ceremony for a girl, paralleling the bar mitzvah.

ba•ton' (bə ton', ba-) *n.* staff or rod, esp. one used by orchestral conductor.

batt. 1. battalion. **2.** battery.

bat•tal'ion (bə tal'yən) *n.* military unit of three or more companies.

bat'ten (bat'n) *n.* **1.** strip of wood. —*v.* **2.** fasten or furnish with battens. **3.** fatten or grow fat.

bat'ter (bat'ər) *v.* **1.** beat persistently. **2.** damage by hard usage. —*n.* **3.** semiliquid cooking mixture. **4.** one who bats.

battering ram, heavy beam for beating down walls, gates, etc.

bat'ter•y, *n., pl.* -teries. **1.** device for producing electricity. **2.** combination of artillery pieces. **3.** illegal attack by beating or wounding.

bat'tle (bat'l) *n., v.,* -tled, -tling. —*n.* **1.** hostile encounter. —*v.* **2.** fight. —**bat'tle•field',** *n.* —**bat'tle•ground',** *n.* —**bat'tler,** *n.*

bat'tle•ment, *n.* indented parapet.

bat'tle•ship', *n.* heavily armed warship.

bat'ty (bat'ē) *adj.,* -tier, -tiest. *Slang.* crazy or eccentric.

bau'ble (bô'bəl) *n.* trinket.

baud (bôd) *n.* unit used to measure speed of a signal or data transfer, as in computers.

baux'ite (bôk'sīt, bō'zīt) *n.* principal ore of aluminum.

Bav. 1. Bavaria. **2.** Bavarian.

bawd'y (bô'dē) *adj.,* **bawdier, bawdiest.** obscene. —**bawd'i•ness,** *n.*

bawl (bôl) *v.* **1.** shout out. —*n.* **2.** shout.

bay (bā) *n.* **1.** inlet of sea or lake. **2.** vertical section of window. **3.** compartment or recess in a building. **4.** deep, prolonged bark. **5.** stand made by hunted animal or person. **6.** reddish brown. **7.** laurel tree. —*v.* **8.** bark. **9.** bring to bay (def. 5). —*adj.* **10.** of the color bay.

bay'ber'ry, *n., pl.* -ries. fragrant shrub with berries.

bayc *Electronics.* bayonet candelabra.

bay cand dc *Electronics.* bayonet candelabra double-contact.

bay cand sc *Electronics.* bayonet candelabra single-contact.

bay leaf, dried leaf of the laurel, used in cooking.

bay'o•net (bā'ə net', bā'ə nit) *n., v.,* -neted, -neting. —*n.* **1.** daggerlike instrument attached to rifle muzzle. —*v.* **2.** kill or wound with bayonet.

bay'ou (bī'ōō) *n., pl.* **bayous.** arm of river, etc.

ba•zaar' (bə zär') *n.* marketplace.

ba•zoo'ka (bə zōō'kə) *n.* hand-held rocket launcher.

BB (bē'bē') *n., pl.* **BB's.** small metal shot fired from an air rifle (**BB gun**).

B.B.A. 1. Bachelor of Business Administration. **2.** Big Brothers of America.

BBB Better Business Bureau.

BBB a quality rating for a corporate or municipal bond, lower than A and higher than BB.

B.B.C. British Broadcasting Corporation. Also, **BBC**

bbl., barrel.

bbq barbecue.

bbrg ball bearing.

BBS *Computers.* **1.** bulletin board service. **2.** bulletin board system.

B.C., before Christ.

BCA Boys' Clubs of America.

bcc blind carbon copy.

BCD 1. *Military.* bad conduct discharge. **2.** *Computers.* binary-coded decimal system.

B.C.E., before the Common (or Christian) Era.

B.Cer.E. Bachelor of Ceramic Engineering.

bcfsk binary-coded frequency-shift keying.

bch. bunch.

B.Ch. Bachelor of Chemistry.

B.Ch.E. Bachelor of Chemical Engineering.

bci binary-coded information.

B.C.L. Bachelor of Civil Law.

bcn beacon.

BCNU *Pharmacology.* carmustine. [abbreviation of the chemical name *1,3-bis 2-chloroethyl-1-nitrosourea*]

B.Com.Sc. Bachelor of Commercial Science.

B.C.P. 1. Bachelor of City Planning. **2.** Book of Common Prayer.

B.C.S. 1. Bachelor of Chemical Science. **2.** Bachelor of Commercial Science.

Bd *Symbol.* baud.

BD. (in Bahrain) dinar; dinars.

bd. 1. board. **2.** bond. **3.** bound. **4.** bundle.

B/D 1. bank draft. **2.** bills discounted. **3.** Accounting. brought down.

b/d barrels per day.

B.D. 1. Bachelor of Divinity. **2.** bank draft. **3.** bills discounted.

B.D.A. 1. Bachelor of Domestic Arts. **2.** Bachelor of Dramatic Art.

bdc bottom dead center.

bde *Military.* brigade.

bd elim band elimination.

B.Des. Bachelor of Design.

bd. ft. board foot; board feet.

bdg binding.

bdgh binding head.

bdl. bundle.

bdle. bundle.

bdrm. bedroom.

bdry boundary.

B.D.S. Bachelor of Dental Surgery.

b.d.s. (in prescriptions) twice a day. [from Latin *bis diē sūmendum*]

BDSA Business and Defense Services Administration.

be (bē; *unstressed* bē, bi) *v.* **1.** exist. **2.** occur.

beach (bēch) *n.* **1.** sand or pebbles of seashore. —*v.* **2.** run or pull a ship onto beach.

beach'comb'er, *n.* **1.** person who gathers salable jetsam or refuse on a beach. **2.** vagrant living on a beach.

beach'head', *n.* part of beach landed on and seized by military force.

B

bea'con (bē'kən) *n.* **1.** signal, esp. a fire. —*v.* **2.** serve as beacon.

bead (bēd) *n.* **1.** small ball of glass, pearl, etc., designed to be strung. **2.** (*pl.*) necklace. —*v.* **3.** ornament with beads. —**bead'ing,** *n.* —**bead'y,** *adj.*

bea'gle (bē'gəl) *n.* short-legged hunting dog.

beak (bēk) *n.* **1.** bill of bird. **2.** beaklike object.

beak'er, *n.* large glass.

beam (bēm) *n.* **1.** horizontal support secured at both ends. **2.** breadth of ship. **3.** ray of light or other radiation. —*v.* **4.** emit beams. **5.** smile radiantly. —**beam'ing,** *adj.*

bean (bēn) *n.* **1.** edible seed of certain plants. **2.** plant producing such seed.

bear (bâr) *v.,* **bore** (bôr), **borne** (bôrn), **bearing,** *n.* —*v.* **1.** support. **2.** carry. **3.** undergo; endure. **4.** move; go. **5.** give birth to. —*n.* **6.** large shaggy mammal. **7.** clumsy or rude person. **8.** speculator who counts on falling prices. —**bear'er,** *n.* —**bear'a•ble,** *adj.* —**bear'ish,** *adj.* —**bear'ish•ly,** *adv.*

beard (bērd) *n.* **1.** hair on face of man. **2.** similar growth or part. —*v.* **3.** defy. —**beard'ed,** *adj.* —**beard'less,** *adj.*

bear hug, tight embrace.

bear'ing, *n.* **1.** manner. **2.** reference; relation. **3.** *Mach.* part in which another part moves. **4.** (*often pl.*) position; direction. **5. bearings,** orientation.

bear market, stock market with falling prices.

beast (bēst) *n.* **1.** animal. **2.** coarse or inhuman person.

beast'ly, *adj.,* **-lier, -liest. 1.** brutish. **2.** nasty. —**beast'li•ness,** *n.*

beat (bēt) *v.,* **beat, beaten** or **beat, beating,** *n.* —*v.* **1.** strike repeatedly. **2.** dash against. **3.** mark time in music. **4.** defeat. **5.** throb. —*n.* **6.** blow. **7.** sound of a blow. **8.** habitual rounds. **9.** musical time. —**beat'a•ble,** *adj.* —**beat'en,** *adj.* —**beat'er,** *n.*

be'a•tif'ic (bē'ə tif'ik) *adj.* blissful. —**be'a• tif'i•cal•ly,** *adv.*

be•at'i•tude' (bē at'i tōōd', -tyōōd') *n.* **1.** blessedness. **2.** (*often cap.*) declaration of blessedness made by Christ (Matthew 5).

beat'nik (bēt'nik) *n.* disillusioned, unconventional person, esp. of the 1950s.

beau (bō) *n.,* *pl.* **beaus, beaux. 1.** lover. **2.** fop.

beau'te•ous (byōō'tē əs) *adj.* beautiful. —**beau'te•ous•ly,** *adv.* —**beau'te•ous• ness,** *n.*

beau•ti'cian (-tish'ən) *n.* person who works in beauty parlor.

beau'ti•ful (-tə fəl) *adj.* having beauty. —**beau'ti•ful•ly,** *adv.*

beau'ti•fy' (-fī') *v.,* **-fied, -fying.** make beautiful. —**beau'ti•fi•ca'tion,** *n.*

beau'ty, *n.,* *pl.* **-ties. 1.** quality that excites admiration. **2.** beautiful thing or person.

beauty parlor, salon for women's haircuts and styling. Also, **beauty shop.**

bea'ver (bē'vər) *n.* **1.** amphibious rodent. **2.** its fur.

bec. because.

be•cause' (bi kôz', -koz', -kuz') *conj.* **1.** for the reason that. —*adv.* **2.** by reason (of).

beck (bek) *n.* beckoning gesture.

beck'on (-ən) *v.* signal by gesture. —**beck'- on•er,** *n.*

be•cloud' (bi kloud') *v.* **1.** obscure with clouds. **2.** confuse.

be•come' (bi kum') *v.,* **became** (-kām'), **become, becoming. 1.** come to be. **2.** suit. —**be•com'ing,** *adj.*

bed (bed) *n., v.,* **bedded, bedding.** —*n.* **1.** piece of furniture on or in which a person sleeps. **2.** sleep. **3.** piece of ground for planting. **4.** foundation. —*v.* **5.** plant in bed. —**bed'time',** *n.*

bed'bug', *n.* bloodsucking insect.

bed'ding, *n.* blankets, sheets, etc., for a bed.

be•dev'il (bi dev'əl) *v.,* **-iled, -il•ing. 1.** torment maliciously. **2.** confuse; confound.

bed'fast', *adj.* bedridden.

bed'fel'low, *n.* **1.** sharer of bed. **2.** ally.

bed'lam (bed'ləm) *n.* **1.** scene of loud confusion. **2.** lunatic asylum.

Bed'ou•in (bed'ōō in) *n.* **1.** desert Arab. **2.** nomad.

bed'pan', *n.* shallow pan used as toilet for bedridden person.

be•drag'gled (bi drag'əld) *adj.* soiled and wet.

bed'rid•den', *adj.* confined to bed.

bed'rock', *n.* **1.** continuous solid rock under soil. **2.** firm foundation or basis.

bed'room', *n.* sleeping room.

bed'sore', *n.* skin ulcer caused by long confinement in bed.

bed'spread', *n.* cover for bed.

bed'stead' (-sted', -stid) *n.* frame for bed.

bee (bē) *n.* **1.** four-winged, nectar-gathering insect. **2.** local gathering. —**bee'hive',** *n.* —**bee'keep'er,** *n.*

beech (bēch) *n.* tree bearing small edible nuts (**beech'nuts'**). —**beech'en,** *adj.*

beef (bēf) *n.,* *pl.* **beeves. 1.** bull, cow, or steer. **2.** edible flesh of such an animal. **3.** brawn. —**beef'y,** *adj.* —**beef'i•ness,** *n.* —**beef'steak',** *n.*

bee'line', *n.* direct course.

beep (bēp) *n.* **1.** short tone, usu. high in pitch, as from automobile horn or electronic device. —*v.* **2.** make or cause to make a beep.

beep'er, *n.* small electronic device whose signal notifies person carrying it of telephone message.

beer (bēr) *n.* beverage brewed and fermented from cereals.

beet (bēt) *n.* plant with edible root.

bee'tle (bēt'l) *v.,* **-tled, -tling,** *n.* —*v.* **1.** project. —*n.* **2.** insect with hard, horny forewings.

bef. before.

B.E.F. British Expeditionary Force; British Expeditionary Forces.

be•fall′ (bi fôl′) *v.*, **-fell, -fallen, -falling.** happen; happen to.

be•fit′ (bi fit′) *v.*, **-fitted, -fitting.** be fitting for. —**be•fit′ting,** *adj.*

be•fore′ (bi fôr′) *adv.* **1.** in front. **2.** earlier. —*prep.* **3.** in front of. **4.** previously to. **5.** in future of. **6.** in preference to. **7.** in precedence of. **8.** in presence of. —*conj.* **9.** previously to time when.

be•fore′hand′, *adv.* in advance; ahead of time.

be•friend′ (bi frend′) *v.* act as friend toward.

be•fud′dle (bi fud′l) *v.*, **-dled, -dling.** confuse thoroughly. —**be•fud′dle•ment,** *n.*

beg (beg) *v.*, **begged, begging. 1.** ask for charity. **2.** ask humbly.

be•get′ (bi get′) *v.*, **begot** (bi got′), **begotten** or **begot, begetting.** procreate. —**be•get′ter,** *n.*

beg′gar (beg′ər) *n.* **1.** one who begs alms. **2.** penniless person. —*v.* **3.** reduce to poverty. —**beg′gar•y,** *n.*

beg′gar•ly, *adj.* penurious.

be•gin′ (bi gin′) *v.*, **-gan** (-gan′), **-gun** (-gun′), **-ginning. 1.** start. **2.** originate. —**be•gin′ner,** *n.* —**be•gin′ning,** *n.*

be•gone′ (bi gôn′) *interj.* (depart!)

be•gon′ia (bi gōn′yə) *n.* tropical flowering plant.

be•grudge′ (bi gruj′) *v.*, **-grudged, -grudging. 1.** envy the good fortune or pleasure of. **2.** give or allow reluctantly.

be•guile′ (bi gīl′) *v.*, **-guiled, -guiling. 1.** delude. **2.** charm; divert. —**be•guile′ment,** *n.* —**be•guil′er,** *n.*

be•half′ (bi haf′) *n.* **1.** side; part. **2.** interest; favor.

be•have′ (bi hāv′) *v.*, **-haved, -having. 1.** conduct oneself. **2.** act properly.

be•hav′ior (-yər) *n.* manner of behaving.

be•head′ (bi hed′) *v.* cut off head of.

be•he′moth (bi hē′məth) *n.* any huge or extremely powerful creature or thing.

be•hest′ (bi hest′) *n.* urgent request.

be•hind′ (bi hīnd′) *prep.* **1.** at the back of. **2.** later than. —*adv.* **3.** at the back. **4.** in arrears. —*n.* **5.** *Informal.* buttocks.

be•hold′ (bi hōld′) *v.*, **beheld, beholding,** *interj.* —*v.* **1.** look at; see. —*interj.* **2.** look! —**be•hold′er,** *n.*

be•hold′en, *adj.* obliged.

be•hoove′ (bi hōōv′) *v.*, **-hooved, -hooving.** be necessary for (someone).

beige (bāzh) *n.* light brown.

be′ing (bē′ing) *n.* **1.** existence. **2.** something that exists.

Bel. 1. Belgian. **2.** Belgic. **3.** Belgium.

be•la′bor (bi lā′bər) *v.* **1.** discuss, etc., excessively. **2.** beat.

be•lat′ed (bi lā′tid) *adj.* late. —**be•lat′ed•ly,** *adv.*

belch (belch) *v.* **1.** eject gas from stomach. **2.** emit violently. —*n.* **3.** act of belching.

be•lea′guer (bi lē′gər) *v.* beset with difficulties.

bel′fry (bel′frē) *n., pl.* **-fries.** bell tower.

Belg. 1. Belgian. **2.** Belgium.

be•lie′ (bi lī′) *v.*, **-lied, -lying. 1.** misrepresent. **2.** show to be false. **3.** lie about. —**be•li′er,** *n.*

be•lief′ (bi lēf′) *n.* **1.** thing believed. **2.** conviction. **3.** faith.

be•lieve′ (bi lēv′) *v.*, **-lieved, -lieving. 1.** trust. **2.** accept as true. **3.** regard as likely. —**be•liev′a•ble,** *adj.* —**be•liev′er,** *n.*

be•lit′tle (bi lit′l) *v.*, **-littled, -littling.** disparage.

bell (bel) *n.* **1.** metal instrument producing ringing sound. —*v.* **2.** put bell on. **3.** flare outward. —**bell′-like′,** *adj.*

bel•la•don′na (bel′ə don′ə) *n.* poisonous plant yielding medicinal drug.

belle (bel) *n.* beautiful woman.

bell′hop′, *n.* person who carries luggage and runs errands in a hotel. Also, **bell′boy′.**

bel′li•cose′ (bel′i kōs′) *adj.* warlike.

bel•lig′er•ent (bə lij′ər ənt) *adj.* **1.** warlike. **2.** engaged in war. —*n.* **3.** nation at war. —**bel•lig′er•ence, bel•lig′er•en•cy,** *n.* —**bel•lig′er•ent•ly,** *adv.*

bel′low (bel′ō) *v.* **1.** roar, as a bull. **2.** utter in deep, loud voice. —*n.* **3.** act or sound of bellowing.

bel′lows (bel′ōz, -əz) *n.sing. and pl.* collapsing device producing strong current of air.

bell pepper, plant yielding a mild, bell-shaped pepper.

bell′weth′er (bel′weth′ər) *n.* **1.** male sheep leading a flock. **2.** one that leads or marks a trend.

bel′ly (bel′ē) *n., pl.* **-lies,** *v.*, **-lied, -lying.** —*n.* **1.** abdomen. **2.** inside. **3.** protuberant surface. —*v.* **4.** swell out.

bel′ly•ache′, *n., v.*, **-ached, aching.** —*n.* **1.** pain in the abdomen. —*v.* **2.** *Informal.* complain.

be•long′ (bi lông′) *v.* **1.** be a member of. **2.** belong to, be the property of.

be•long′ings, *n.pl.* possessions; effects.

be•lov′ed (bi luv′id, -luvd′) *adj.* **1.** greatly loved. —*n.* **2.** object of love.

be•low′ (bi lō′) *adv.* **1.** beneath. **2.** in lower rank. —*prep.* **3.** lower than.

belt (belt) *n.* **1.** band for encircling waist. **2.** any flexible band. —*v.* **3.** gird or furnish with belt. —**belt′ing,** *n.*

belt′way′, *n.* highway around perimeter of urban area.

B.E.M. 1. Bachelor of Engineering of Mines. **2.** British Empire Medal.

be•moan′ (bi mōn′) *v.* lament.

B

be•mused′ (bi myōozd′) *adj.* lost in thought; preoccupied.

bench (bench) *n.* **1.** long seat. **2.** judge's seat. **3.** body of judges. **4.** work table.

bench′mark′, *n.* standard against which others can be measured or judged. Also, **bench′ mark′.**

bend (bend) *v.,* **bent, bending,** *n.* —*v.* **1.** curve. **2.** become curved. **3.** cause to submit. **4.** turn or incline. —*n.* **5.** a bending. **6.** something bent.

be•neath′ (bi nēth′) *adj.* **1.** in a lower place, state, etc. —*prep.* **2.** under. **3.** lower than. **4.** unworthy of.

ben′e•dic′tion (ben′i dik′shən) *n.* blessing.

benef. beneficiary.

ben′e•fac′tion (-fak′shən) *n.* **1.** doing of good. **2.** benefit conferred. —**ben′e•fac′tor** (-tər) *n.* —**ben′e•fac′tress,** *n.fem.*

be•nef′i•cent (bə nef′ə sənt) *adj.* doing good. —**be•nef′i•cence,** *n.* —**be•nef′i•cent• ly,** *adv.*

ben•e•fi′cial (ben′ə fish′əl) *adj.* helpful. —**ben′e•fi′cial•ly,** *adv.*

ben′e•fi′ci•ar•y (-fish′ē er′ē, -fish′ə rē) *n., pl.* **-aries.** recipient of benefits.

ben′e•fit (-fit) *n., v.,* **-fited, -fiting.** —*n.* **1.** act of kindness. **2.** entertainment for worthy cause. —*v.* **3.** do good to. **4.** gain advantage.

be•nev′o•lent (bə nev′ə lənt) *adj.* desiring to do good. —**be•nev′o•lence,** *n.*

Beng. 1. Bengal. **2.** Bengali.

B. Engr. Bachelor of Engineering.

be•night′ed (bi nī′tid) *adj.* ignorant.

be•nign′ (bi nīn′) *adj.* **1.** kind. **2.** favorable. —**be•nign′ly,** *adv.*

be•nig′nant (-nig′nənt) *adj.* **1.** kind. **2.** beneficial. —**be•nig′nan•cy,** *n.* —**be•nig′nant• ly,** *adv.* —**be•nig′ni•ty,** *n.*

bent (bent) *adj.* **1.** curved. **2.** determined. —*n.* **3.** curve. **4.** inclination.

be•numb′ (bi num′) *v.* **1.** make numb. **2.** make inactive; stupefy.

ben′zene (ben′zēn, ben zēn′) *n.* inflammable liquid, used as solvent.

ben′zine (-zēn) *n.* liquid used in cleaning and dyeing.

B.E.P. Bachelor of Engineering Physics.

be•queath′ (bi kwēth′, -kwēth′) *v.* dispose of by will. —**be•queath′al,** *n.*

be•quest′ (bi kwest′) *n.* legacy.

ber bit error rate.

be•rate′ (bi rāt′) *v.,* **-rated, -rating.** scold.

be•reave′ (bi rēv′) *v.,* **-reaved** or **-reft, -reaving. 1.** deprive of. **2.** make desolate. —**be•reave′ment,** *n.*

be•ret′ (bə rā′) *n.* cloth cap.

ber′i•ber′i (ber′ē ber′ē) *n.* disease caused by vitamin deficiency.

Ber. Is. Bermuda Islands.

berm (bûrm) *n.* **1.** shoulder of road. **2.** mound of snow or dirt.

ber′ry (ber′ē) *n., pl.* **-ries,** *v.,* **-ried, -rying.**

—*n.* **1.** small juicy fruit. —*v.* **2.** produce or gather berries.

ber•serk′ (bər sûrk′, -zûrk′) *adj.* wild; frenzied.

berth (bûrth) *n.* **1.** sleeping space for traveler. **2.** mooring space for vessel. —*v.* **3.** assign berth.

ber′yl (ber′əl) *n.* green mineral.

B.E.S. Bachelor of Engineering Science.

be•seech′ (bi sēch′) *v.,* **-sought, -seeching.** implore; beg. —**be•seech′ing•ly,** *adv.*

be•set′ (bi set′) *v.,* **-set, -setting. 1.** attack on all sides. **2.** surround.

BEShT *Judaism.* Baal Shem-Tov.

be•side′ (bi sīd′) *prep.* **1.** at the side of. **2.** compared with. **3.** in addition to. —*adv.* **4.** in addition.

be•sides′, *adv.* **1.** moreover. **2.** otherwise. —*prep.* **3.** in addition to. **4.** other than.

be•siege′ (bi sēj′) *v.,* **-sieged, -sieging.** lay siege to. —**be•sieg′er,** *n.*

be•smirch′ (bi smûrch′) *v.* defile.

be•sot′ted (bi sot′id) *adj.* **1.** drunk. **2.** infatuated.

be•speak′ (bi spēk′) *v.,* **-spoke** (-spōk′), **-spoken** or **-spoke, -speaking. 1.** ask for in advance. **2.** imply.

best (best) *adj.* **1.** of highest quality. **2.** most suitable. —*adv.* **3.** most excellently. **4.** most fully. —*n.* **5.** best thing. —*v.* **6.** defeat.

bes′tial (bes′chəl, bēs′-) *adj.* **1.** beastlike. **2.** brutal. —**bes′ti•al′i•ty** (-chē al′i tē) *n.* —**bes′tial•ly,** *adv.*

be•stir′ (bi stûr′) *v.,* **-stirred, -stirring.** stir up.

best man, chief attendant of the bridegroom at a wedding.

be•stow′ (bi stō′) *v.* **1.** present. **2.** apply.

be•strew′ (bi strōō′) *v.,* **-strewed, -strewed** or **-strewn, -strewing. 1.** cover. **2.** scatter.

bet (bet) *v.,* **bet** or **betted, betting,** *n.* —*v.* **1.** risk on a chance result. —*n.* **2.** thing or amount bet. —**bet′ter, bet′tor,** *n.*

be•take′ (bi tāk′) *v.,* **-took** (-tŏŏk′), **-taken, -taking.** betake oneself, **1.** go. **2.** resort (to).

be′tel nut (bēt′l) seed of a palm, often chewed in the tropics.

bête′ noire′ (bāt′ nwär′, bet′) most dreaded person or thing.

be•tide′ (bi tīd′) *v.,* **-tided, -tiding.** happen.

be•to′ken (bi tō′kən) *v.* indicate.

be•tray′ (bi trā′) *v.* **1.** expose by treachery. **2.** be unfaithful to. **3.** reveal. **4.** deceive. **5.** seduce. —**be•tray′al,** *n.* —**be•tray′er,** *n.*

be•troth′ (bi trōth′, -trôth′) *v.* promise to marry. —**be•troth′al,** *n.* —**be•trothed′** (-trōthd) *adj., n.*

bet′ter (bet′ər) *adj.* **1.** of superior quality. **2.** healthier. —*adv.* **3.** in a more excellent way. **4.** more. —*n.* **5.** something better. **6.** one's superior. —*v.* **7.** improve on. —**bet′ter• ment,** *n.*

betw between.

be•tween′ (bi twēn′) *prep.* **1.** in the space separating. **2.** intermediate to. **3.** connecting. **4.** one or the other of. **5.** by the combined effect of. —*adv.* **6.** in the intervening space or time.

—**Usage.** Traditionally, BETWEEN is used to show relationship involving two people or things (*to decide between tea and coffee*), while AMONG expresses more than two (*The four brothers quarrelled among themselves*). BETWEEN, however, is also used to express relationship of persons or things considered individually, no matter how many: *Between holding public office, teaching, and raising a family, she has little free time.*

be•twixt′ (bi twikst′) *prep., adv.* between.

BeV (bev), *Physics.* billion electron-volts. Also, **Bev, bev**

bev′el (bev′əl) *n., v.,* **-eled, -eling.** —*n.* **1.** surface cutting off a corner. **2.** device for drawing angles. —*v.* **3.** cut or slant at a bevel.

bev′er•age (bev′ər ij) *n.* drink.

bev′y (bev′ē) *n., pl.* **-ies. 1.** flock of birds. **2.** group.

BEW Board of Economic Warfare.

be•wail′ (bi wāl′) *v.* lament.

be•ware′ (bi wâr′) *v.,* **-wared, -waring.** be wary (of).

be•wil′der (bi wil′dər) *v.* confuse. —**be•wil′dered,** *adj.* —**be•wil′der•ing,** *adj.* —**be•wil′der•ing•ly,** *adv.* —**be•wil′der•ment,** *n.*

be•witch′ (bi wich′) *v.* enchant. —**be•witch′ing,** *adj.*

be•yond′ (bē ond′) *prep.* **1.** on the farther side of. **2.** farther, more, or later on. —*adv.* **3.** farther on.

BF black female.

bf. *Law.* brief.

B/F *Accounting.* brought forward.

B.F. 1. Bachelor of Finance. **2.** Bachelor of Forestry.

b.f. *Printing.* boldface. Also, **bf**

B.F.A. Bachelor of Fine Arts.

B.F.A.Mus. Bachelor of Fine Arts in Music.

bfo *Electronics.* beat-frequency oscillator.

bfr 1. before. **2.** buffer.

B.F.S. Bachelor of Foreign Service.

BFT biofeedback training. Also, **bft**

B.F.T. Bachelor of Foreign Trade.

bg. 1. background. **2.** bag.

B.G. 1. Birmingham gauge. **2.** brigadier general. Also, **BG**

bge beige.

bGH *Biochemistry, Agriculture.* bovine growth hormone.

Bglr. bugler.

BHA *Chemistry, Pharmacology.* a synthetic antioxidant, $C_{11}H_{16}O_2$. [*b(utylated) h(ydroxy) a(nisole)*]

BHC *Chemistry.* a crystalline, water-soluble,

poisonous solid, $C_6H_6Cl_6$. [*b(enzene) h(exa) c(hloride)*]

bhd. bulkhead.

B.H.L. 1. Bachelor of Hebrew Letters. **2.** Bachelor of Hebrew Literature.

Bhn *Metallurgy.* Brinell hardness number.

bhp brake horsepower. Also, **BHP, B.H.P., b.hp., b.h.p.**

BHT *Chemistry, Pharmacology.* an antioxidant, $C_{15}H_{24}O$. [*b(utylated) h(ydroxy)t(oluene)*]

bi-, prefix meaning twice or two, as *bisect.*

BIA Bureau of Indian Affairs.

BiAF bisexual Asian female.

BiAM bisexual Asian male.

bi•an′nu•al (bī an′yōō əl) *adj.* occurring twice a year. —**bi•an′nu•al•ly,** *adv.*

bi′as (bī′əs) *n.* **1.** slant. **2.** prejudice. —*v.* **3.** prejudice.

bi•ath′lon (bī ath′lon) *n.* athletic contest comprising two consecutive events.

bib (bib) *n.* cloth to protect dress.

BiBF bisexual black female.

Bibl Biblical. Also, **Bibl.**

bibl. 1. biblical. **2.** bibliographical. **3.** bibliography.

Bi′ble (bī′bəl) *n.* Old and New Testaments. —**Bib′li•cal** (bib′li kəl) *adj.* —**Bib′li•cal•ly,** *adv.*

BiblHeb Biblical Hebrew.

bib′li•og′ra•phy (bib′lē og′rə fē) *n., pl.* **-phies.** list of sources.

BiBM bisexual black male.

bib′u•lous (bib′yə ləs) *adj.* fond of or addicted to drink.

bi•cam′er•al (bī kam′ər əl) *adj.* composed of two legislative bodies.

bicarb. 1. bicarbonate. **2.** bicarbonate of soda.

bi•car′bo•nate of soda (bī kär′bə nit, -nāt′) baking soda.

bi•cen•ten′ni•al, *n.* two-hundredth anniversary. Also, **bi′cen•ten′a•ry.**

bi′ceps (-seps) *n.* muscle of upper arm.

bick′er (bik′ər) *v.* squabble.

bi•cus′pid, *n.* tooth having two cusps or points.

bi′cy•cle (bī′si kəl) *n., v.,* **-cled, -cling.** —*n.* **1.** two-wheeled vehicle. —*v.* **2.** ride a bicycle. —**bi′cy•cler, bi′cy•clist,** *n.*

bid (bid) *v.,* **bade** (bad, bād) or **bid** (for 3), **bidden** or **bid, bidding,** *n.* —*v.* **1.** command. **2.** say. **3.** offer. —*n.* **4.** offer. —**bid′der,** *n.* —**bid′ding,** *n.*

bid′a•ble, *adj.* **1.** worth bidding. **2.** *Archaic.* obedient.

bide (bīd) *v.,* **bided, biding. bide one's time,** await opportunity.

bi•det′ (bē dā′) *n.* tub for bathing genital areas.

B.I.E. Bachelor of Industrial Engineering.

bi•en′ni•al (bī en′ē əl) *adj.* occurring every two years. —**bi•en′ni•al•ly,** *adv.*

bier (bēr) *n.* stand for a coffin.

BiF bisexual female.

bi·fo′cal (bī fō′kəl, bī′fō′-) *adj.* **1.** having two focuses. **2.** (of eyeglass lens) having separate areas for near and far vision. —*n.* **3.** (*pl.*) eyeglasses with bifocal lenses.

big (big) *adj.*, **bigger, biggest. 1.** large. **2.** important. —**big′ness,** *n.*

big′a·my (big′ə mē) *n., pl.* -**mies.** crime of marrying again while legally married. —**big′a·mist,** *n.* —**big′a·mous,** *adj.*

big bang theory, theory that universe began with explosion of dense mass of matter and is still expanding.

big′horn′ (big′hôrn′) *n.* wild sheep of western U.S.

bight (bīt) *n.* **1.** loop of rope. **2.** deep bend in seashore.

Big O *Slang.* orgasm.

big′ot (big′ət) *n.* bigoted person. —**big′ot·ry,** *n.*

big′ot·ed, *adj.* intolerant of another's creed, belief, or opinion. —**big′ot·ed·ly,** *adv.*

big shot, *Informal.* important person.

bike (bīk) *n.* **1.** bicycle, motorbike, or motorcycle. —*v.* **2.** ride a bike. —**bik′er,** *n.*

bi·ki′ni (bi kē′nē) *n.* woman's brief two-piece bathing suit.

BIL Braille Institute Library.

bi·lat′er·al (bī lat′ər əl) *adj.* on or affecting two sides.

bile (bīl) *n.* **1.** digestive secretion of the liver. **2.** ill nature.

bilge (bilj) *n., v.,* **bilged, bilging.** —*n.* **1.** outer part of ship bottom. **2.** water in a bilge. **3.** wide part of cask. —*v.* **4.** cause to leak at the bilge.

bi·lin′gual (bī ling′gwəl) speaking or expressed in two languages. —**bi·lin′gual·ly,** *adv.*

bil′ious (bil′yəs) *adj.* **1.** pertaining to bile or excess bile. **2.** peevish.

bilk (bilk) *v.* cheat; defraud.

bill (bil) *n.* **1.** account of money owed. **2.** piece of paper money. **3.** draft of proposed statute. **4.** written list. **5.** horny part of bird's jaw. **6.** poster. —*v.* **7.** charge.

bill′board′, *n.* large outdoor advertising display panel.

bil′let (bil′it) *n., v.,* -**leted, -leting.** —*n.* **1.** lodging for a soldier. —*v.* **2.** provide with lodging.

bil·let-doux′ (bil′ā dōō′) *n., pl.* **billets-doux** (-dōōz′). love letter.

bill′fold′, *n.* wallet.

bil′liards (bil′yərdz) *n.* game played with hard balls (**billiard balls**) on a table. —**bil′liard,** *adj.* —**bil′liard·ist,** *n.*

bil′lion (bil′yən) *n.* thousand million. —**bil′lionth,** *adj., n.*

bil′lion·aire′ (-âr′) *n.* owner of billion dollars or more.

bill of fare, menu.

bill of sale, document transferring personal property from seller to buyer.

bil′low (bil′ō) *n.* **1.** great wave. —*v.* **2.** surge. —**bil′low·y,** *adj.* —**bil′low·i·ness,** *n.*

billy goat, male goat.

BiM bisexual male.

bim′bo (bim′bō) *n., pl.* -**bos, -boes.** *Slang.* **1.** foolish or inept person. **2.** disreputable woman.

bi·month′ly (bī munth′lē) *adv., adj.* every two months.

bin (bin) *n., v.,* **binned, binning.** —*n.* **1.** box for storing grain, coal, etc. —*v.* **2.** store in bin.

bi′na·ry (bī′nə rē) *adj.* **1.** involving two parts, choices, etc. **2.** of a numerical system in which each place of a number is expressed as 0 or 1.

bind (bīnd) *v.,* **bound, binding. 1.** tie or encircle with band. **2.** unite. **3.** oblige. **4.** attach cover to book. —**bind′er,** *n.*

B.Ind.Ed. Bachelor of Industrial Education.

bind′ing, *n.* **1.** something that binds. —*adj.* **2.** obligatory.

binge (binj) *n., v.,* **binged, binging.** —*n.* **1.** bout of excessive indulgence, as in eating. —*v.* **2.** go on binge.

bin′go (bing′gō) *n.* game of chance using cards with numbered squares.

bin′na·cle (bin′ə kəl) *n.* stand for ship's compass.

bin·oc′u·lars (bə nok′yə lərz, bī-) *n.pl.* field glasses.

bio-, prefix meaning life or living organisms, as *biodegradable.*

bi′o·chem′is·try (bī′ō kem′ə strē) *n.* chemistry of living matter. —**bi′o·chem′i·cal** (-i-kəl) *adj.* —**bi·o′chem′i·cal·ly,** *adv.* —**bi′o·chem′ist,** *n.*

bi′o·de·grad′a·ble, *adj.* decaying and being absorbed into environment.

bi′o·en′gi·neer′ing, *n.* **1.** application of engineering principles to problems in biology and medicine. **2.** application of biological principles to manufacturing or engineering processes.

bi′o·eth′ics, *n.* study of ethical implications of medical or biological procedures.

bi′o·feed′back′, *n.* method for achieving self-control through observation of one's brain waves, blood pressure, etc.

biog. **1.** biographer. **2.** biographical. **3.** biography.

bi·og′ra·phy (bī og′rə fē) *n., pl.* -**phies.** written account of person's life. —**bi·og′ra·pher,** *n.* —**bi′o·graph′i·cal** (-ə graf′i kəl) *adj.* —**bi′o·graph′i·cal·ly,** *adv.*

bi′o·haz′ard, *n.* **1.** anything used in or produced in biological research that poses a health hazard. **2.** risk posed by a biohazard.

biol., biology.

biological clock, 1. natural mechanism regulating bodily cycles. **2.** this mechanism seen as the passage of one's child-bearing ability.

biological warfare, use of toxic organisms as weapons.

bi•ol′o•gy (bī ol′ə jē) *n.* science of living matter. —**bi′o•log′i•cal** (-ə loj′i kəl) *adj.* —**bi′o•log′i•cal•ly,** *adv.* —**bi•ol′o•gist,** *n.*

bi•on′ics (bī on′iks) *n.* use of electronic devices to increase human strength or ability. —**bi•on′ic,** *adj.*

bi′op•sy (bī′op sē) *n., pl.* **-sies.** examination of specimen of living tissue.

bi′o•rhythm (bī′ō-) *n.* natural, periodic bodily cycle, as sleeping and waking.

BIOS (bī′ōs, -os), *Computers.* firmware that directs many basic functions of the operating system. [*B(asic) I(nput)/O(utput) S(ystem)*]

bi′o•sphere′ (bī′ə-) *n.* the part of the earth's surface and atmosphere that supports life.

bi′o•tech•nol′o•gy (bī′ō-) *n.* use of living organisms in making drugs or other products or to manage the environment.

bi•par′ti•san (bī pär′tə zən) *adj.* representing two parties. —**bi•par′ti•san•ship′,** *n.*

bi•par′tite (-pär′tīt) *adj.* **1.** having two parts. **2.** shared by two; joint.

bi′ped (-ped) *n.* **1.** two-footed animal. —*adj.* **2.** having two feet.

birch (bûrch) *n.* tree with light bark. —**birch′-en,** *adj.*

bird (bûrd) *n.* vertebrate with feathers and wings.

bird′ie, *n.* score of one under par on a golf hole.

bird′s′-eye′ (bûrdz′ī′) *adj.* seen from above.

birth (bûrth) *n.* **1.** fact of being born. **2.** lineage. **3.** origin. —**birth′day′,** *n.* —**birth′place′,** *n.*

birth control, contraception.

birth′mark′, *n.* blemish on the skin at birth.

birth′rate′, *n.* number of births in given time and place.

birth′right′, *n.* hereditary right.

B.I.S. 1. Bank for International Settlements. **2.** British Information Services.

bis′cuit (bis′kit) *n.* small, soft, raised bread.

bi•sect′ (bī sekt′) *v.* cut into two parts. —**bi•sec′tion,** *n.* —**bi•sec′tion•al,** *adj.* —**bi•sec′-tor,** *n.*

bi•sex′u•al, *adj.* **1.** being both heterosexual and homosexual. —*n.* **2.** bisexual person. —**bi•sex′u•al′i•ty,** *n.*

bish′op (bish′əp) *n.* **1.** overseer of a diocese. **2.** piece in chess.

bish′op•ric (-rik) *n.* diocese or office of bishop.

bi′son (bī′sən) *n., pl.* **bisons, bison.** oxlike mammal.

bisque (bisk) *n.* creamy soup.

bis′tro (bis′trō, bē′strō) *n.* French café.

bit (bit) *n., v.,* **bitted, bitting.** —*n.* **1.** mouthpiece of bridle. **2.** small amount. **3.** drill. **4.** unit of computer information. —*v.* **5.** restrain with a bit.

bitch (bich) *n.* **1.** female dog. **2.** *Slang.* mean woman. —*v.* **3.** *Slang.* complain.

bite (bīt) *v.,* **bit, bitten** or **bit, biting,** *n.* —*v.*

1. cut or grip with teeth. **2.** sting. **3.** corrode. —*n.* **4.** act of biting. **5.** wound made by biting. **6.** sting. **7.** piece bitten off. —**bit′er,** *n.*

bit′ing, *adj.* **1.** harsh to the senses. **2.** severely critical. —**bit′ing•ly,** *adv.*

bit′ter (bit′ər) *adj.* **1.** of harsh taste. **2.** hard to receive or bear. **3.** intensely hostile. —*n.* **4.** something bitter. —**bit′ter•ly,** *adv.* —**bit′-ter•ness,** *n.*

bit′tern (bit′ərn) *n.* type of heron.

bit′ters, *n.pl.* liquor with bitter vegetable ingredients.

bit′ter•sweet′, *adj.* **1.** tasting both bitter and sweet. **2.** being both painful and pleasant.

bi•tu′men (bī tōō′mən, -tyōō′-) *n.* asphalt or asphaltlike substance. —**bi•tu′mi•nous,** *adj.*

bituminous coal, soft coal that burns with a yellow, smoky flame.

bi′valve′, *n.* mollusk with two shells hinged together. —**bi′valve′, bi•val′vular,** *adj.*

biv′ou•ac′ (biv′ōō ak′), *n., v.,* **-acked, -acking.** —*n.* **1.** temporary resting or assembly place for troops. —*v.* **2.** dispose or meet in bivouac.

bi•week′ly (bī-) *adv., adj.* **1.** every two weeks. **2.** twice a week.

BiWF bisexual white female.

BiWM bisexual white male.

bi•zarre′ (bi zär′) *adj.* strange.

B.J. Bachelor of Journalism.

Bk *Symbol, Chemistry.* berkelium.

bk 1. back. **2.** *Baseball.* balk; balks. **3.** black.

bk. 1. bank. **2.** book.

bkbndr. bookbinder.

bkcy. bankruptcy.

bkdn breakdown.

bkg. 1. banking. **2.** bookkeeping. **3.** breakage.

bkgd. background.

bklr. *Printing.* black letter.

bkpg. bookkeeping.

bkpr. bookkeeper.

bkpt. bankrupt.

bks. 1. banks. **2.** barracks. **3.** books.

bkt. 1. basket. **2.** bracket. **3.** bucket.

bl. 1. bale; bales. **2.** barrel; barrels. **3.** black. **4.** block. **5.** blue.

b/l *Commerce.* bill of lading. Also, **B/L**

B.L. 1. Bachelor of Laws. **2.** Bachelor of Letters. **3.** bill of lading.

b.l. 1. bill of lading. **2.** *Military.* breech loading.

B.L.A. 1. Bachelor of Landscape Architecture. **2.** Bachelor of Liberal Arts.

blab (blab) *v.,* **blabbed, blabbing. 1.** talk idly. **2.** reveal secrets.

black (blak) *adj.* **1.** without brightness or color. **2.** having dark skin color. **3.** without light. **4.** gloomy. **5.** wicked. —*n.* **6.** member of a dark-skinned people, esp. of Africa, or African ancestry. **7.** black clothing. **8.** something black. —*v.* **9.** make or become black.

B

—**black′ness,** *n.* —**black′ly,** *adv.* —**black′-ish,** *adj.*

black′-and-blue′, *adj.* discolored, as by bruising.

black′ball′, *n.* **1.** adverse vote. —*v.* **2.** ostracize.

black′ber′ry, *n., pl.* **-ries. 1.** dark-purple fruit. **2.** plant bearing it.

black′bird′, *n.* black-feathered American bird.

black′board′, *n.* dark board for writing on with chalk.

black′en, *v.* **1.** black (def. 9). **2.** defame.

black-eyed Su′san (soo′zən) plant having yellow, daisylike flowers with dark center.

black′guard (blag′ärd, -ərd) *n.* **1.** despicable person. —*v.* **2.** revile.

black′head′ (blak′-) *n.* small fatty mass in a skin follicle.

black hole, area in outer space whose great density prevents radiation of light.

black′jack′, *n.* **1.** short flexible club. **2.** game of cards; twenty-one. —*v.* **3.** strike with a blackjack.

black′list′, *n.* list of persons in disfavor. —**black′list′,** *v.*

black magic, sorcery.

black′mail′, *n.* **1.** extortion by intimidation. —*v.* **2.** extort by blackmail. —**black′mail′·er,** *n.*

black market, illegal buying and selling of goods in violation of laws.

black′out′, *n.* **1.** extinction of lights. **2.** loss of consciousness.

black sheep, person who causes embarrassment or shame to his or her family.

black′smith′, *n.* **1.** person who shoes horses. **2.** person who forges iron objects.

black′thorn′, *n.* thorny shrub with plumlike fruit.

black′top′, *n., v.,* **-topped, -topping.** —*n.* **1.** bituminous paving substance, as asphalt. —*v.* **2.** pave with blacktop.

black widow, poisonous spider.

blad′der (blad′ər) *n.* sac in body holding urine.

blade (blād) *n.* **1.** cutting part of knife, sword, etc. **2.** leaf. **3.** thin, flat part. **4.** dashing young man. —**blad′ed,** *adj.* —**blade′-like′,** *adj.*

blame (blām) *v.,* **blamed, blaming,** *n.* —*v.* **1.** hold responsible for fault. **2.** find fault with. —*n.* **3.** censure. **4.** responsibility for censure. —**blam′a·ble, blame′ful, blame′wor′thy,** *adj.* —**blame′less,** *adj.*

blanch (blanch) *v.* whiten.

bland (bland) *adj.* **1.** not harsh. **2.** not flavorful. —**bland′ly,** *adv.* —**bland′ness,** *n.*

blan′dish (blan′dish) *v.* coax. —**blan′dish·ment,** *n.*

blank (blangk) *adj.* **1.** not written on. **2.** without interest or emotion. **3.** white. **4.** unrhymed. —*n.* **5.** place lacking something. **6.** space to be filled in. **7.** paper with such

space. —*v.* **8.** make blank. —**blank′ly,** *adv.* —**blank′ness,** *n.*

blan′ket (blang′kit) *n.* **1.** warm bed covering. —*v.* **2.** cover.

blare (blâr) *v.,* **blared, blaring,** *n.* —*v.* **1.** sound loudly. —*n.* **2.** loud, raucous noise.

blar′ney (blär′nē) *n.* **1.** wheedling talk. —*v.* **2.** wheedle.

bla·sé′ (blä zā′) *adj.* bored; unimpressed.

blas·pheme′ (blas fēm′) *v.* speak impiously or evilly. —**blas·phem′er,** *n.* —**blas′phe·mous** (blas′fə məs) *adj.* —**blas′phe·my,** *n.*

blast (blast) *n.* **1.** gust of wind. **2.** loud trumpet tone. **3.** stream of air. **4.** explosion. **5.** charge of explosive. —*v.* **6.** blow. **7.** blight; destroy. **8.** explode. —**blast′er,** *n.*

blast furnace, forced-air furnace for smelting iron ore.

blast′off′, *n.* rocket launching.

bla′tant (blāt′nt) *adj.* brazenly obvious. —**bla′tan·cy,** *n.* —**bla′tant·ly,** *adv.*

blaze (blāz) *n., v.,* **blazed, blazing.** —*n.* **1.** bright flame. **2.** bright glow. **3.** brightness. **4.** mark cut on tree. **5.** white spot on animal's face. —*v.* **6.** burn or shine brightly. **7.** mark with blazes (def. 4).

blaz′er, *n.* sports jacket.

bla′zon (blā′zən) *v.* depict or proclaim.

bldg., building.

Bldg.E. Building Engineer.

bldr. builder.

B.L.E. Brotherhood of Locomotive Engineers.

bleach (blēch) *v.* **1.** whiten. —*n.* **2.** bleaching agent.

bleach′ers, *n.pl.* tiers of spectators' seats.

bleak (blēk) *adj.* **1.** bare. **2.** cold. **3.** dreary; depressing. —**bleak′ly,** *adv.* —**bleak′ness,** *n.*

blear (blēr) *v.* **1.** dim, esp. with tears. —*n.* **2.** bleared state. —**blear′y,** *adj.*

bleat (blēt) *v.* **1.** cry, as sheep, goat, etc. —*n.* **2.** such a cry. —**bleat′er,** *n.*

bleed (blēd) *v.,* **bled** (bled), **bleeding.** lose or cause to lose blood.

bleep (blēp) *v.* delete or block (sound, esp. speech) from a recording or broadcast.

blem′ish (blem′ish) *v.* **1.** mar. —*n.* **2.** defect. —**blem′ish·er,** *n.*

blend (blend) *v.* **1.** mix. —*n.* **2.** mixture.

blend′er, *n.* electric appliance that purées or mixes food.

bless (bles) *v.,* **blessed** or **blest, blessing. 1.** consecrate. **2.** request divine favor on. **3.** extol as holy. —**bless′ed** (bles′id, blest) *adj.* —**bless′ing,** *n.*

blight (blīt) *n.* **1.** plant disease. **2.** ruin. —*v.* **3.** wither. **4.** ruin.

blimp (blimp) *n.* small nonrigid airship.

blind (blīnd) *adj.* **1.** sightless. **2.** uncomprehending. **3.** hidden. **4.** without an outlet. **5.** without advance knowledge. —*v.* **6.** make blind. —*n.* **7.** something that blinds. **8.** ruse or disguise. —**blind′ly,** adv. —**blind′ness,** n.

blind date, arranged date between two strangers.

blind′fold′, v. **1.** cover eyes. —n. **2.** covering over eyes. —adj. **3.** with covered eyes.

blind′side′, v., **-sided, -siding.** hit someone unawares.

blink (blingk) v. **1.** wink. **2.** ignore. —n. **3.** act of blinking. **4.** gleam.

blip (blip) n. **1.** point of light on radar screen, indicating an object. **2.** brief interruption or upward turn in a continuity.

bliss (blis) n. **1.** gladness. **2.** supreme happiness. —**bliss′ful,** adj. —**bliss′ful•ly,** adv. —**bliss′ful•ness,** n.

blis′ter (blis′tər) n. **1.** vesicle on the skin. —v. **2.** raise blisters on. —**blis′ter•y,** adj.

B.Lit. Bachelor of Literature.

blithe (blīth, blīth) adj. joyous; cheerful. —**blithe′ly,** adv.

blithe′some, adj. cheerful.

B.Litt. Bachelor of Letters.

blitz (blits) n. Also, **blitz′krieg′** (-krēg′). **1.** swift, violent war, waged by surprise. —v. **2.** attack by blitz.

bliz′zard (bliz′ərd) n. severe snowstorm.

blk. 1. black. **2.** block. **3.** bulk.

blkg 1. blanking. **2.** blocking.

B.LL. Bachelor of Laws.

BLM Bureau of Land Management. Also, **B.L.M.**

blo blower.

bloat (blōt) v. swell.

blob (blob) n. **1.** small lump or drop. **2.** shapeless mass.

bloc (blok) n. political or economic confederation.

block (blok) n. **1.** solid mass. **2.** platform. **3.** obstacle. **4.** single quantity. **5.** unit of city street pattern. —v. **6.** obstruct. **7.** outline roughly. —**block′er,** n.

block•ade′ (blo kād′) n., v., **-aded, -ading.** —n. **1.** shutting-up of place by armed force. **2.** obstruction. —v. **3.** subject to blockade.

block′bust′er, n. highly successful movie, novel, etc.

block′head′, n. stupid person.

block′house′, n. fortified structure.

blond (blond) adj. **1.** light-colored. **2.** having light-colored hair, skin, etc. —n. **3.** blond person. —**blonde,** adj., n.fem.

blood (blud) n. **1.** red fluid in arteries and veins. **2.** bloodshed. **3.** extraction. —**blood′y,** adj. —**blood′i•ness,** n. —**blood′less,** adj.

blood count, number of red and white blood cells in specific volume of blood.

blood′cur′dling, adj. causing terror or horror.

blood′hound′, n. large dog with acute sense of smell.

blood′mo•bile′ (-mə bēl′) n. truck for receiving blood donations.

blood pressure, pressure of blood against inner walls of blood vessels.

blood′shed′, n. slaughter.

blood′shot′, adj. with eye veins conspicuous.

blood′stream′, n. blood flowing through the body's circulatory system.

blood′suck′er, n. **1.** leech. **2.** extortionist.

blood′thirst′y, adj. murderous; savage.

blood vessel, artery, vein, or capillary.

bloom (blōom) n. **1.** flower. **2.** health. **3.** healthy glow. —v. **4.** blossom. **5.** flourish. —**bloom′ing,** adj.

bloom′ers (blōo′mərz) n.pl. loose trousers formerly worn by women.

bloop′er (blōo′pər) n. embarrassing mistake.

blos′som (blos′əm) n. **1.** flower. —v. **2.** produce blossoms. **3.** develop.

blot (blot) n., v., **blotted, blotting.** —n. **1.** spot; stain. —v. **2.** stain; spot. **3.** dry with absorbent material. **4.** destroy.

blotch (bloch) n. **1.** large spot or stain. —v. **2.** stain; spot. —**blotch′y,** adj.

blot′ter, n. **1.** piece of paper for blotting. **2.** book in which events are recorded.

blouse (blous, blouz) n. women's upper garment.

blow (blō) v., **blew** (blōo), **blown, blowing,** n. —v. **1.** (of air) move. **2.** drive by current of air. **3.** sound a wind instrument. **4.** go bad. **5.** explode. **6.** blossom. —n. **7.** blast of air. **8.** sudden stroke. **9.** sudden shock, calamity, etc. **10.** blossoming. —**blow′er,** n. —**blow′y,** adj.

blow′-by-blow′, adj. detailed.

blow′out′, n. rupture of tire.

blow′pipe′, n. pipe used to direct stream of gas.

blow′torch′, n. device producing hot flame.

blow′up′, n. **1.** explosion. **2.** Informal. emotional outbreak. **3.** photographic enlargement.

BLS Bureau of Labor Statistics.

bls. 1. bales. **2.** barrels.

B.L.S. 1. Bachelor of Library Science. **2.** Bureau of Labor Statistics.

BLT a bacon, lettuce, and tomato sandwich. Also, **B.L.T.**

bltin built-in.

blub′ber (blub′ər) n. **1.** fat of whales. —v. **2.** weep.

bludg′eon (bluj′ən) n. **1.** heavy club. —v. **2.** strike with a bludgeon.

blue (blōo) n., adj., **bluer, bluest,** v., **blued, bluing** or **blueing.** —n. **1.** color of sky. —adj. **2.** (of skin) discolored by cold, etc. **3.** melancholy. —v. **4.** make blue. —**blue′ness,** n. —**blu′ish,** adj.

blue′ber′ry, n., pl. **-ries.** edible berry, usually bluish.

blue′bird′, n. small, blue North American bird.

blue blood, aristocrat. —**blue′blood′ed,** *adj.*

blue chip′, high-priced stock yielding regular dividends.

blue′-col′lar, *adj.* of or designating factory workers or other manual laborers.

blue′jay′, *n.* crested North American jay.

blue jeans, trousers of blue denim.

blue law, law against certain practices, as business, on Sunday.

blue′print′, *n.* white-on-blue photocopy of line drawing. —**blue′print′,** *v.*

blue ribbon, highest award.

blues, *n.pl.* **1.** melancholy. **2.** melancholy genre of jazz.

bluff (bluf) *v.* **1.** mislead by show of boldness. —*n.* **2.** act of bluffing. **3.** one who bluffs. **4.** steep cliff or hill. —*adj.* **5.** vigorously frank. **6.** steep. —**bluff′ly,** *adv.* —**bluff′ness,** *n.* —**bluff′er,** *n.*

blu′ing, *n.* bleaching agent. Also, **blue′ing.**

blun′der (blun′dər) *n.* **1.** mistake. —*v.* **2.** err. **3.** move blindly. —**blun′der•er,** *n.*

blunt (blunt) *adj.* **1.** having a dull edge or point. **2.** abrupt in manner. —*v.* **3.** make blunt. —**blunt′ly,** *adv.* —**blunt′ness,** *n.*

blur (blûr) *v.,* **blurred, blurring,** *n.* —*v.* **1.** obscure. **2.** make or become indistinct. —*n.* **3.** smudge. —**blur′ry,** *adj.*

blurb (blûrb) *n.* brief advertisement.

blurt (blûrt) *v.* utter suddenly.

blush (blush) *v.* **1.** redden. **2.** feel shame. —*n.* **3.** reddening. **4.** reddish tinge. —**blush′ful,** *adj.* —**blush′ing•ly,** *adv.*

blus′ter (blus′tər) *v.* **1.** be tumultuous. **2.** be noisy or swaggering. —*n.* **3.** tumult. **4.** noisy talk. —**blus′ter•er,** *n.*

blvd., boulevard.

blw below.

blzd blizzard.

BM 1. basal metabolism. **2.** *Surveying.* bench mark. **3.** black male. **4.** *Informal.* bowel movement.

bm *Electricity.* break-before-make: a relay contact.

B.M. 1. Bachelor of Medicine. **2.** Bachelor of Music. **3.** British Museum.

B.Mar.E. Bachelor of Marine Engineering.

B.M.E. 1. Bachelor of Mechanical Engineering. **2.** Bachelor of Mining Engineering. **3.** Bachelor of Music Education.

B.M.Ed. Bachelor of Music Education.

B.Met. Bachelor of Metallurgy.

B.Met.E. Bachelor of Metallurgical Engineering.

BMEWS (bē myōōz′), *U.S. Military.* Ballistic Missile Early Warning System.

B.Mgt.E. Bachelor of Management Engineering.

BMI Broadcast Music, Inc.

B.Min.E. Bachelor of Mining Engineering.

BMOC big man on campus. Also, **B.M.O.C.**

BMR basal metabolic rate.

B.M.S. Bachelor of Marine Science.

B.M.T. Bachelor of Medical Technology.

B.Mus. Bachelor of Music.

B.M.V. Blessed Mary the Virgin. [from Latin *Beāta Maria Virgō*]

bn brown.

Bn. 1. Baron. **2.** Battalion.

bn. battalion.

B.N. Bachelor of Nursing.

BNA British North America. Also, **B.N.A.**

BND Germany's national intelligence service. [from German *B(undes)n(achrichten)d(ienst)*]

bnls boneless.

bnr burner.

B.N.S. Bachelor of Naval Science.

bnsh burnish.

bnz bronze.

bo 1. blackout. **2.** *Electronics.* blocking oscillator.

B/o *Accounting.* brought over.

B.O. 1. Board of Ordnance. **2.** *Informal.* body odor. **3.** *Theater.* box office.

b.o. 1. back order. **2.** box office. **3.** branch office. **4.** broker's order. **5.** buyer's option.

bo′a (bō′ə) *n.* **1.** large snake. **2.** long scarf of silk or feathers.

boar (bôr) *n.* male of swine.

board (bôrd) *n.* **1.** thin flat piece of timber. **2.** table, esp. for food. **3.** daily meals. **4.** official controlling body. —*v.* **5.** cover or close with boards. **6.** furnish with food. **7.** take meals. **8.** enter (a ship, train, etc.). —**board′er,** *n.*

board′ing•house′, *n.* house where one can get room and board for payment.

board′walk′, *n.* wooden walk along beach.

boast (bōst) *v.* **1.** speak with pride; be proud of. **2.** speak with excessive pride. —*n.* **3.** thing boasted. —**boast′er,** *n.* —**boast′ful,** *adj.*

boat (bōt) *n.* **1.** vessel. —*v.* **2.** go or move in boat. —**boat′house′,** *n.* —**boat′man,** *n.* —**boat′ing,** *n.*

boat′swain (bō′sən) *n.* petty officer on ship.

bob (bob) *n.,* *v.,* **bobbed, bobbing.** —*n.* **1.** short jerky motion. **2.** short haircut. —*v.* **3.** move jerkily. **4.** cut short. —**bob′ber,** *n.*

bob′bin (bob′in) *n.* reel; spool.

bob′by pin, flat metal hairpin.

bob′cat′, *n., pl.* **-cats, -cat.** North American lynx.

bob′o•link′ (-ə lingk′) *n.* meadow-dwelling songbird.

bob′sled′, *n., v.,* **-sledded, -sledding.** —*n.* **1.** long sled with two pairs of runners and a steering mechanism. —*v.* **2.** ride on a bobsled.

bob′tail′, *n.* **1.** short tail. —*v.* **2.** cut short.

bob′white′, *n.* North American quail.

BOD biochemical oxygen demand.

bode (bōd) *v.,* **boded, boding.** portend.

bo•de′ga (bō dä′gə) *n.* (esp. among Spanish-speaking Americans) grocery store.

bod′ice (bod′is) *n.* fitted waist.

bod′y (bod′ē) *n., pl.* **bodies,** *v.,* **bodied, bodying.** —*n.* **1.** animal's physical structure. **2.** corpse. **3.** main mass. **4.** collective group. —*v.* **5.** invest with body. —**bod′i•ly,** *adj., adv.*

bod′y•guard′, *n.* guard for personal safety.

body language, communication through gestures or attitudes.

body piercing, piercing of a body part, as the navel, to insert ornamental ring or stud.

bog (bog) *n., v.,* **bogged, bogging.** —*n.* **1.** swampy ground. —*v.* **2.** sink or catch in a bog. —**bog′gy,** *adj.*

bog′gle (bog′əl) *v.,* **-gled, -gling. 1.** overwhelm or bewilder. **2.** bungle; botch.

bo′gus (bō′gəs) *adj.* counterfeit; fake.

bo′gy (bō′gē, bŏŏg′ē, bŏŏ′gē) *n., pl.* **-gies.** hobgoblin. Also, **bo′gey, bo′gie.**

bo•he′mi•an (bō hē′mē ən) *n.* **1.** person who leads an unconventional life. —*adj.* **2.** of or characteristic of a bohemian.

boil (boil) *v.* **1.** heat to bubbling point. **2.** be agitated. **3.** cook by boiling. —*n.* **4.** act or state of boiling. **5.** inflamed sore. —**boil′er,** *n.*

bois′ter•ous (boi′stər əs) *adj.* rough; noisy. —**bois•ter•ous•ly,** *adv.* —**bois′ter•ous•ness,** *n.*

bok′ choy′ (bok′ choy′) Asian plant whose leaves are used as a vegetable. Also, **bok′ choy′.**

Bol. Bolivia.

bol. (in prescriptions) bolus (larger than a regular pill).

bold (bōld) *adj.* **1.** fearless. **2.** conspicuous. —**bold′ly,** *adv.* —**bold′ness,** *n.*

bo•le′ro (bə lâr′ō, bō-) *n., pl.* **-ros. 1.** lively Spanish dance. **2.** waist-length, open vest.

boll (bōl) *n.* rounded seed vessel or pod of plant.

boll weevil, beetle that attacks bolls of cotton.

bo•lo′gna (bə lō′nē) *n.* beef and pork sausage.

Bol′she•vik (bōl′shə vik) *n., pl.* **-viks, -viki.** Russian communist. Also, **Bol′she•vist** (-vist). —**Bol′she•vism** (-viz′əm) *n.* —**Bol′she•vik, Bol′she•vis′tic,** *adj.*

bol′ster (bōl′stər) *n.* **1.** long pillow. —*v.* **2.** support. —**bol′ster•er,** *n.*

bolt (bōlt) *n.* **1.** bar fastening a door. **2.** similar part in a lock. **3.** threaded metal pin. **4.** sudden flight. **5.** roll of cloth. **6.** thunderbolt. —*v.* **7.** fasten. **8.** swallow hurriedly. **9.** move or leave suddenly. **10.** sift. —**bolt′er,** *n.*

bomb (bom) *n.* **1.** projectile with explosive charge. **2.** *Slang.* total failure. —*v.* **3.** attack with bombs. **4.** *Slang.* fail totally. —**bomb′proof′,** *adj.*

bom•bard′ (bom bärd′) *v.* **1.** attack with artillery or bombs. **2.** assail vigorously.

—**bom′bar•dier′** (-bər dēr′) *n.* —**bom•bard′ment,** *n.*

bom′bast (bom′bast) *n.* pompous words. —**bom•bas′tic, bom•bas′ti•cal,** *adj.*

bomb′er (bom′ər) *n.* **1.** airplane that drops bombs. **2.** one who plants bombs.

bomb′shell′, *n.* something or someone having a sensational effect.

BOMFOG brotherhood of man, fatherhood of God.

bo′na fide′ (bō′nə fīd′) real.

bo•nan′za (bə nan′zə) *n.* **1.** rich mass of ore. **2.** good luck.

bon′bon′ (bon′bon′) *n.* piece of candy.

bond (bond) *n.* **1.** something that binds or unites. **2.** bondsman. **3.** written contractual obligation. **4.** certificate held by creditor. —*v.* **5.** put on or under bond. **6.** mortgage.

bond′age (bon′dij) *n.* slavery.

bond′man, *n., pl.* **-men.** man in bondage; male slave. Also, **bond′wom′an,** *n.fem.*

bonds′man, *n., pl.* **-men.** person who gives surety for another by bond.

bone (bōn) *n., v.,* **boned, boning.** —*n.* **1.** piece of the skeleton. **2.** hard substance composing it. —*v.* **3.** remove bones of. —**bon′y,** *adj.*

bon′er (bō′nər) *n. Slang.* stupid mistake.

bon′fire′ (bon′-) *n.* outdoor fire.

bon′go (bong′gō) *n., pl.* **-gos, -goes.** small hand drum.

bon′kers (bong′kərz) *adj. Slang.* crazy.

bon′net (bon′it) *n.* woman's or child's head covering.

bon′sai (bon sī′, bōn-) *n., pl.* **bonsai.** dwarf tree or shrub.

bo′nus (bō′nəs) *n.* extra payment.

boo (bōō) *interj.* (exclamation used to frighten or express contempt.)

boo′-boo′, *n. Slang.* **1.** stupid mistake. **2.** minor injury.

boo′by (bōō′bē) *n., pl.* **-bies.** *Informal.* fool. Also, **boob.**

booby prize, prize given to worst player in contest.

booby trap, trap set for any person who happens on it.

book (bŏŏk) *n.* **1.** printed or blank sheets bound together. **2.** (*pl.*) accounts. **3.** division of literary work. —*v.* **4.** enter in book. **5.** engage beforehand. —**book′bind′er,** *n.* —**book′case′,** *n.* —**book′keep′er,** *n.* —**book′let,** *n.* —**book′sell′er,** *n.* —**book′store′, book′shop′,** *n.*

book′end′, *n.* prop for books.

book′ie, *n.* bookmaker.

book′ing, *n.* engagement of professional entertainer.

book′ish, *adj.* fond of reading. —**book′ish•ness,** *n.*

book′mak′er, *n.* professional bettor.

book′mark′, *n.* something for marking one's place in a book.

B

book′worm′, *n.* bookish person.

boom (boom) *v.* **1.** make a loud hollow sound. **2.** flourish vigorously. —*n.* **3.** loud hollow sound. **4.** rapid development. **5.** spar extending sail. **6.** beam on derrick.

boom′er•ang′ (boo′mə rang′) *n.* **1.** Australian throwing stick that returns in flight. —*v.* **2.** cause harm to the originator; backfire.

boon (boon) *n.* benefit.

boon′docks′, *n.pl.* **1.** backwoods. **2.** remote rural area.

boon′dog′gle (-dog′əl) *n. Informal.* useless work paid for with public money.

boor (boor) *n.* unmannerly, rude person. —**boor′ish,** *adj.*

boost (boost) *v.* **1.** lift by pushing. **2.** praise; advocate. **3.** increase. —*n.* **4.** upward push. **5.** assistance. —**boost′er,** *n.*

boot (boot) *n.* **1.** covering for foot and leg. **2.** kick. —*v.* **3.** kick. **4.** dismiss or discharge.

booth (booth) *n.* **1.** light structure for exhibiting goods, etc. **2.** small compartment.

boot′leg′, *n., v.,* **-legged, -legging,** *adj.* —*n.* **1.** illicit liquor. —*v.* **2.** deal in illicit goods. —*adj.* **3.** illicit. —**boot′leg′ger,** *n.*

boot′less, *adj.* futile; useless.

boo′ty (boo′tē) *n., pl.* **-ties.** plunder.

booze (booz) *n., v.,* **boozed, boozing.** *Informal.* —*n.* **1.** liquor. —*v.* **2.** drink liquor excessively. —**booz′er,** *n.*

bop (bop) *v.,* **bopped, bopping,** *n. Slang.* —*v.* **1.** hit. —*n.* **2.** a blow.

BOQ *U.S. Military.* bachelor officers' quarters.

bor. borough.

bo′rax (bôr′aks) *n.* white crystalline substance used as cleanser, in glassmaking, etc.

bor•del′lo (bôr del′ō) *n.* brothel.

bor′der (bôr′dər) *n.* **1.** edge; margin. **2.** frontier. —*v.* **3.** make a border. **4.** adjoin. —**bor′der•land′,** *n.* —**bor′der•line′,** *n.*

bore (bôr) *v.,* **bored, boring,** *n.* —*v.* **1.** drill into. **2.** be uninteresting to. —*n.* **3.** bored hole. **4.** inside diameter. **5.** dull person. —**bore′dom,** *n.* —**bor′er,** *n.*

bo′ric acid (bôr′ik) antiseptic acid.

born (bôrn) *adj.* brought forth from the womb by birth.

born′-a•gain′, *adj.* recommitted to faith through an intensely religious experience.

bor′ough (bûr′ō, bur′ō) *n.* **1.** small incorporated municipality. **2.** division of city.

bor′row (bor′ō) *v.* **1.** take or obtain on loan. **2.** adopt.

—**Usage.** Do not confuse BORROW and LEND. One way to keep the meanings distinct is to think of BORROW as "take," while LEND is "give." So you can *borrow* something you don't have, and you can *lend* something you do have.

borscht (bôrsht) *n.* beet soup.

bos′om (booz′əm, boo′zəm) *n.* **1.** breast. —*adj.* **2.** intimate. —**bos′om•y,** *adj.*

boss (bôs) *n.* **1.** employer. **2.** powerful politician. —*v.* **3.** control; manage. **4.** be domineering. —**boss′y,** *adj.*

bot. **1.** botanic; botanical. **2.** botanist. **3.** botany. **4.** bottle.

B.O.T. Board of Trade.

bot′a•ny (bot′n ē) *n.* science of plant life. —**bo•tan′i•cal** (bə tan′i kəl) *adj.* —**bot′a•nist,** *n.*

botch (boch) *v.* **1.** bungle. **2.** do clumsily. —*n.* **3.** botched work. —**botch′y,** *adj.* —**botch′er,** *n.* —**botch′er•y,** *n.*

both (bōth) *adj., pron.* **1.** the two. —*conj.* *adv.* **2.** alike.

both′er (bo*th*′ər) *v.* **1.** annoy. **2.** trouble or inconvenience (oneself). —*n.* **3.** annoying or troublesome thing. —**both′er•some,** *adj.*

bot′tle (bot′l) *n., v.,* **-tled, -tling.** —*n.* **1.** sealed container for liquids. —*v.* **2.** put into bottle. —**bot′tler,** *n.*

bot′tle•neck′, *n.* **1.** narrow passage. **2.** place of impeded progress.

bot′tom (bot′əm) *n.* **1.** lowest or deepest part. **2.** underside. **3.** lowest rank. —*v.* **4.** reach or furnish with bottom.

bot′tom•less, *adj.* **1.** without bottom. **2.** without limit.

bottom line, basic or decisive point.

bot′u•lism′ (boch′ə liz′əm) *n.* disease caused by eating spoiled foods.

bou′doir (boo′dwär, -dwôr) *n.* woman's bedroom.

bouf•fant′ (boo fänt′) *adj.* puffed out, as a hairdo.

bough (bou) *n.* branch of tree.

bouil′la•baisse′ (boo′yə bäs′, bool′-) *n.* fish stew.

bouil′lon (bool′yon, -yən, boo′-) *n.* clear broth.

boul′der (bōl′dər) *n.* large rock.

boul′e•vard′ (bool′ə värd′) *n.* broad avenue.

bounce (bouns) *v.,* **bounced, bouncing,** *n.* —*v.* **1.** spring back. —*n.* **2.** act of bouncing. —**boun′ci•ness,** *n.* —**bounc′y,** *adj.*

bounc′ing, *adj.* healthy.

bound (bound) *adj.* **1.** in bonds. **2.** made into book. **3.** obligated. **4.** going toward. —*v.* **5.** jump. **6.** limit. **7.** adjoin. **8.** name boundaries of. —*n.* **9.** jump. **10.** (*usually pl.*) boundary.

bound′a•ry (boun′də rē, -drē) *n., pl.* **-ries.** borderline; limit.

bound′less, *adj.* unlimited.

boun′te•ous (boun′tē əs) *adj.* **1.** generous. **2.** plentiful. Also, **boun′ti•ful.** —**boun′te•ous•ly,** *adv.* —**boun′te•ous•ness,** *n.*

boun′ty, *n., pl.* **-ties.** **1.** generosity. **2.** gift.

bou•quet′ (bō kā′, boo-) *n.* **1.** bunch of flowers. **2.** aroma.

bour′bon (bûr′bən) *n.* corn whiskey.

bour•geois′ (boor zhwä′) *n., pl.* **-geois. 1.** one of the middle class. —*adj.* **2.** of the middle class.

bour/geoi•sie/ (-zē/) *n.* middle class.
bout (bout) *n.* **1.** contest. **2.** attack.
bou•tique/ (boo̅ tēk/) *n.* small shop with fashionable items.
bo/vine (bō/vīn, -vēn) *adj.* oxlike or cowlike.
bow (bou, *for 1, 2, 3, 5, 9;* bō, *for 4, 6, 7, 8*), *v.* **1.** bend down. **2.** bend in worship, respect, etc. **3.** subdue. **4.** curve. —*n.* **5.** inclination of head or body. **6.** strip of bent wood for shooting arrow. **7.** looped knot. **8.** rod for playing violin. **9.** front of ship. —**bow/man,** *n.*
bowd/ler•ize/ (bōd/lə rīz/, boud/-) *v.,* **-ized, -izing.** to expurgate (a written work) in a prudish manner.
bow/el (bou/əl, boul) *n.* intestine. Also, **bow/els.**
bow/er (bou/ər) *n.* leafy shelter.
bowl (bōl) *n.* **1.** deep round dish. **2.** rounded hollow part. **3.** ball rolled at pins in various games. —*v.* **4.** roll a ball underhand. **5.** play bowling games. —**bowl/ing,** *n.*
bow/leg/ged (bō leg/id) *adj.* having legs curved outward.
box (boks) *n.* **1.** receptacle of wood, metal, etc. **2.** compartment. **3.** blow, as of the hand or fist. **4.** Also, **box/wood/.** evergreen tree or shrub. —*v.* **5.** put into box. **6.** fight with fists. —**box/er,** *n.* —**box/ing,** *n.* —**box/like,** *adj.*
box/car/, *n.* completely enclosed railroad freight car.
box office, office at which tickets are sold.
boy (boi) *n.* male child. —**boy/hood,** *n.* —**boy/ish,** *adj.*
boy/cott (-kot) *v.* **1.** abstain from dealing with or using. —*n.* **2.** instance of boycotting.
boy/friend/, *n.* **1.** male sweetheart or lover. **2.** male friend.
boy scout, member of organization for boys **(Boy Scouts)** promoting self-reliance and service.
boy/sen•ber/ry (boi/zən ber/ē, -sən-) *n., pl.* **-ries.** blackberrylike fruit.
BP 1. beautiful people; beautiful person. **2.** blood pressure.
bp 1. between perpendiculars. **2.** blueprint. **3.** boilerplate.
bp. 1. baptized. **2.** birthplace. **3.** bishop.
B/P *Commerce.* bills payable.
B.P. 1. Bachelor of Pharmacy. **2.** Bachelor of Philosophy. **3.** *Finance.* basis point. **4.** *Archaeology.* before the present: (in radiocarbon dating) in a specified amount of time or at a specified point in time before A.D. 1950. **5.** *Commerce.* bills payable.
b.p. 1. *Finance.* basis point. **2.** below proof. **3.** *Commerce.* bills payable. **4.** *Physics, Chemistry.* boiling point. **5.** the public good [from Latin *bonum publicum*].
bpa bandpass amplifier.
B.P.A. Bachelor of Professional Arts.
BPD barrels per day. Also, **B.P.D.**
B.P.E. Bachelor of Physical Education.

B.Pet.E. Bachelor of Petroleum Engineering.
B.Ph. Bachelor of Philosophy.
B.P.H. Bachelor of Public Health.
B.Pharm. Bachelor of Pharmacy.
B.Phil. Bachelor of Philosophy.
BPI 1. Also, **bpi** *Computers.* **a.** bits per inch. **b.** bytes per inch. **2.** Bureau of Public Inquiries.
bpl. birthplace.
B.P.O.E. Benevolent and Protective Order of Elks.
bps *Computers.* bits per second. Also, **BPS**
BR 1. *Real Estate.* bedroom. **2.** Bureau of Reclamation.
Br *Symbol, Chemistry.* bromine.
Br. 1. branch (in place names). **2.** brick. **3.** Britain. **4.** British.
br. 1. bedroom. **2.** branch. **3.** brass. **4.** brig. **5.** bronze. **6.** brother. **7.** brown.
b.r. *Commerce.* bills receivable. Also, **B.R., B/R**
bra (brä) *n.* brassiere.
brace (brās) *n., v.,* **braced, bracing.** —*n.* **1.** stiffening device. **2.** pair. **3.** character, {or}, used to connect words or lines to be considered together. —*v.* **4.** fasten with brace. **5.** make steady. **6.** stimulate. —**brac/er,** *n.*
brace/let (brās/lit) *n.* ornamental band for the wrist.
brack/et (brak/it) *n.* **1.** armlike support for ledge. **2.** mark, [or], for enclosing parenthetical words. —*v.* **3.** furnish with or place within brackets.
brack/ish (brak/ish) *adj.* salty.
brad (brad) *n.* small wire nail.
brag (brag) *v.,* **bragged, bragging,** *n.* boast. —**brag/ger,** *n.*
brag/gart (-ərt) *n.* boastful person.
braid (brād) *v.* **1.** weave together. —*n.* **2.** something braided.
braille (brāl) *n.* (*often cap.*) alphabet for the blind.
brain (brān) *n.* **1.** soft mass of nerves in cranium. **2.** intelligence. —*v.* **3.** dash out the brains. —**brain/y,** *adj.* —**brain/less,** *adj.*
brain death, complete ending of brain function, used as legal definition of death. —**brain/-dead,** *adj.*
brain drain, loss of trained professional personnel to another company, nation, etc.
brain/storm/, *n.* sudden idea.
brain/wash/, *v.* indoctrinate under stress. —**brain/wash/ing,** *n.*
braise (brāz) *v.,* **braised, braising.** cook slowly in moisture.
brake (brāk) *n., v.,* **braked, braking.** —*n.* **1.** device for arresting motion. **2.** thicket. **3.** large fern. —*v.* **4.** slow or stop with a brake. —**brake/man,** *n.*
bram/ble (bram/bəl) *n.* **1.** rose plant. **2.** prickly shrub. —**bram/bly,** *adj.*
bran (bran) *n.* husk of grain.
branch (branch) *n.* **1.** division of plant's stem or trunk. **2.** limb; offshoot. **3.** local office,

B

store, etc. **4.** division of body, system, family, etc. —v. **5.** put forth or divide into branches.

brand (brand) n. **1.** trademark. **2.** kind; make. **3.** burned mark. **4.** burning piece of wood. —v. **5.** mark with a brand.

brand′ish (bran′dish) v. shake; wave.

brand′-new′ (bran′-, brand′-) adj. extremely new.

bran′dy (bran′dē) n., pl. **-dies.** spirit from fermented grapes.

brash (brash) adj. **1.** impudent; tactless. **2.** rash; impetuous.

brass (bras) n. **1.** alloy of copper and zinc. **2.** musical instrument such as trumpet or horn. **3.** Informal. high-ranking officials. **4.** impudence. —brass′y, adj.

bras·siere′ (brə zēr′) n. undergarment supporting the breasts.

brass tacks, n.pl. basics.

brat (brat) n. spoiled or rude child.

brat′wurst′ (brat′wûrst, -vŏŏrst′, brät′-) n. pork sausage.

bra·va′do (brə vä′dō) n., pl. **-does, -dos.** boasting; swaggering.

brave (brāv) adj., **braver, bravest,** n., v., **braved, braving.** —adj. **1.** courageous. —n. **2.** North American Indian warrior. —v. **3.** meet courageously. **4.** defy. —brave′ly, adv. —brave′ness, brav′er·y, n.

bra′vo (brä′vō, brä vō′) interj. well done!

brawl (brôl) n. **1.** quarrel. —v. **2.** quarrel noisily. —brawl′er, n.

brawn (brôn) n. **1.** muscles. **2.** muscular strength. —brawn′y, adj.

bray (brā) n. **1.** cry of a donkey. —v. **2.** sound a bray. —bray′er, n.

Braz. 1. Brazil. **2.** Brazilian.

braze (brāz) v., **brazed, brazing.** work in brass.

bra′zen (brā′zən) adj. **1.** of or like brass. **2.** shameless; impudent. —v. **3.** face boldly. —bra′zen·ly, adv. —bra′zen·ness, n.

bra′zier (brā′zhər) n. receptacle for burning charcoal.

Bra·zil′ nut (brə zil′) three-sided edible seed of South American tree.

B.R.C.A. Brotherhood of Railway Carmen of America.

B.R.C.S. British Red Cross Society.

brdg bridge.

B.R.E. Bachelor of Religious Education.

breach (brēch) n. **1.** a breaking. **2.** gap in barrier. **3.** infraction; violation. **4.** break in friendship. —v. **5.** make breach.

bread (bred) n. **1.** food of baked dough. **2.** livelihood. **3.** Slang. money. —v. **4.** cover with breadcrumbs.

bread′crumb′, n. (usually pl.) a crumb of bread.

breadth (bredth, bretth) n. width.

bread′win′ner, n. main money earner in family.

break (brāk) v., **broke** (brōk), **broken, breaking,** n. —v. **1.** separate into parts. **2.** violate; dissolve. **3.** fracture. **4.** lacerate. **5.** interrupt. **6.** disclose. **7.** fail; disable. **8.** (pp. broke) ruin financially. **9.** weaken. **10.** tame. —n. **11.** forcible disruption or separation. **12.** gap. **13.** attempt to escape. **14.** marked change. **15.** brief rest. **16.** Informal. opportunity. —break′a·ble, adj. —break′age, n.

break′down′, n. **1.** failure to operate. **2.** nervous crisis. **3.** analysis of figures.

break′er, n. wave breaking on land.

break′fast (brek′fəst) n. **1.** first meal of day. —v. **2.** eat breakfast.

break′-in′ (brāk′-) n. illegal forcible entry into home, office, etc.

break′neck′, adj. reckless or dangerous, esp. because of excessive speed.

break′through′, n. fundamental discovery.

break′up′, n. **1.** dispersal or disintegration. **2.** ending of a personal relationship.

break′wa′ter, n. barrier against the force of waves.

breast (brest) n. **1.** chest. **2.** milk gland. **3.** seat of thoughts and feelings. —v. **4.** oppose boldly.

breast′bone′, n. sternum.

breast′stroke′, n. swimming stroke in which the arms move forward, outward, and rearward while the legs kick.

breath (breth) n. **1.** air inhaled and exhaled. **2.** ability to breathe. **3.** light breeze. —breath′less, adj.

breathe (brēth) v., **breathed, breathing. 1.** inhale and exhale. **2.** blow lightly. **3.** live. **4.** whisper. —breath′a·bil′i·ty, n. —breath′a·ble, adj.

breath′er (brē′thər) n. Informal. short rest.

breath′tak′ing (breth′-) adj. awesome or exciting.

breech′es (brich′iz) n.pl. trousers.

breed (brēd) v., **bred** (bred), **breeding,** n. —v. **1.** produce. **2.** raise. —n. **3.** related animals. **4.** lineage. **5.** sort. —breed′er, n.

breed′ing, n. **1.** ancestry. **2.** training. **3.** manners.

breeze (brēz) n. light current of air. —breez′y, adj.

breeze′way′, n. open-sided roofed passageway joining two buildings.

breth′ren (breth′rin) n. a pl. of **brother.**

bre·vet′ (brə vet′, brev′it) n. **1.** promotion without increase of pay. —v. **2.** appoint by brevet.

bre′vi·ar′y (brē′vē er′ē, brev′ē-) n., pl. **-aries.** book of daily prayers and readings.

brev′i·ty (brev′i tē) n. shortness.

brew (brōō) v. **1.** prepare beverage such as beer or ale. **2.** concoct. —n. **3.** quantity brewed. **4.** act or instance of brewing. —brew′er, n. —brew′er·y, n.

brg bearing.

bri′ar (brī′ər) n. brier.

bribe (brīb) n., v., **bribed, bribing.** —n. **1.**

gift made for corrupt performance of duty. —*v.* **2.** give or influence by bribe. —**brib′er,** *n.* —**brib′er•y,** *n.*

bric′-a-brac′ (brik′ə brak′) *n.* trinkets.

brick (brik) *n.* **1.** building block of baked clay. —*v.* **2.** fill or build with brick. —**brick′-lay′er,** *n.* —**brick′lay′ing,** *n.*

brick′bat′, *n.* **1.** fragment of brick. **2.** caustic criticism.

bride (brīd) *n.* woman newly married or about to be married. —**brid′al,** *adj.*

bride′groom′, *n.* man newly married or about to be married.

brides′maid′, *n.* bride's wedding attendant.

bridge (brij) *n.,* *v.,* bridged, bridging. —*n.* **1.** structure spanning river, road, etc. **2.** card game for four players. **3.** artificial replacement for tooth or teeth. —*v.* **4.** span.

bridge′head′, *n.* military position held on hostile river shore.

bridge′work′, *n.* dental bridges.

bri′dle (brīd′l) *n.,* *v.,* -dled, -dling. —*n.* **1.** harness at horse's head. **2.** anything that restrains. —*v.* **3.** put bridle on. **4.** restrain.

bridle path, wide path for riding horses.

brief (brēf) *adj.* **1.** short. **2.** concise. —*n.* **3.** concise statement. **4.** outline of arguments and facts. —*v.* **5.** instruct in advance. —**brief′ly,** *adv.* —**brief′ness,** *n.*

brief′case′, *n.* flat carrier for business papers, etc.

bri′er (brī′ər) *n.* **1.** prickly plant. **2.** plant with woody root.

brig (brig) *n.* **1.** two-masted square-rigged ship. **2.** ship's jail.

bri•gade′ (bri gād′) *n.,* *v.* -gaded, -gading. —*n.* **1.** large military unit or body of troops. —*v.* **2.** form into brigade.

brig′a•dier′ (brig′ə dēr′) *n.* military officer between colonel and major general. Also, **brigadier general.**

brig′and (brig′ənd) *n.* bandit.

Brig. Gen. brigadier general.

bright (brīt) *adj.* **1.** shining. **2.** filled with light. **3.** brilliant. **4.** clever. —**bright′en,** *v.* —**bright′ly,** *adv.* —**bright′ness,** *n.*

bril′liant (bril′yənt) *adj.* **1.** sparkling. **2.** illustrious. **3.** highly intelligent. —*n.* **4.** brilliant diamond. —**bril′liant•ly,** *adv.* —**bril′-liance,** **bril′lian•cy, bril′liant•ness,** *n.*

brim (brim) *n.,* *v.,* brimmed, brimming. —*n.* **1.** upper edge; rim. —*v.* **2.** fill or be full to brim. —**brim′ful,** *adj.*

brim′stone′, *n.* sulfur.

brin′dle (brin′dl) *n.* brindled coloring or animal.

brin′dled, *adj.* having dark streaks or spots.

brine (brīn) *n.,* *v.,* brined, brining. —*n.* **1.** salt water. **2.** sea. —*v.* **3.** treat with brine. —**brin′y,** *adj.*

bring (bring) *v.,* brought (brôt), bringing. **1.** fetch. **2.** cause to come. **3.** lead.

brink (bringk) *n.* edge.

bri•quette′ (bri ket′) *n.* small block of com-

pressed coal dust or charcoal used as fuel. Also, **bri•quet′.**

brisk (brisk) *adj.* **1.** lively. **2.** stimulating. —**brisk′ly,** *adv.* —**brisk′ness,** *n.*

bris′ket (bris′kit) *n.* animal's breast.

bris′tle (bris′əl) *n.,* *v.,* -tled, -tling. —*n.* **1.** short, stiff, coarse hair. —*v.* **2.** rise stiffly. **3.** show indignation. —**bris′tly,** *adv.*

Brit. 1. Britain. **2.** British.

britch′es (brich′iz) *n.* *(used with a pl. v.)* breeches.

Brit′ish (brit′ish) *adj.* of Great Britain or its inhabitants. —**Brit′ish•er,** *n.*

British thermal unit, amount of heat needed to raise temperature of 1 lb. (0.4 kg) water 1°F. *Abbr.:* Btu, BTU

Brit′on (brit′n) *n.* native of Great Britain.

brit′tle (brit′l) *adj.* breaking readily. —**brit′-tle•ness,** *n.*

brk brake.

brkg breaking.

brkr Electricity. breaker.

brkt bracket.

brng burning.

broach (brōch) *n.* **1.** tool for enlarging hole. —*v.* **2.** use broach. **3.** pierce. **4.** mention for first time.

broad (brôd) *adj.* **1.** wide. **2.** main. **3.** liberal. —**broad′ly,** *adv.*

broad′cast′, *v.,* -cast or -casted, -casting. *n.,* *adj.* —*v.* **1.** send by radio or television. **2.** scatter widely. —*n.* **3.** something broadcasted. **4.** radio or television program. —*adj.* **5.** sent by broadcasting. —**broad′cast′er,** *n.*

broad′cloth′, *n.* fine cotton material.

broad′en, *v.* widen.

broad jump, long jump.

broad′loom′, *n.* carpet woven on wide loom.

broad′-mind′ed, *adj.* tolerant.

broad′side′, *n.,* *adv.,* *v.,* -sided, -siding. —*n.* **1.** simultaneous firing of all guns on one side of warship. **2.** verbal attack. —*adv.* **3.** directly on the side. —*v.* **4.** hit broadside.

broad′-spec′trum, *adj.* (of antibiotics) effective against wide range of organisms.

bro•cade′ (brō kād′) *n.,* *v.,* -caded, -cading. —*n.* **1.** figured woven fabric. —*v.* **2.** weave with figure.

broc′co•li (brok′ə lē) *n.* green plant with edible flower heads.

bro•chure′ (brō shŏŏr′) *n.* pamphlet; booklet.

brogue (brōg) *n.* Irish accent.

broil (broil) *v.* cook by direct heat. —**broil′-er,** *n.*

broke (brōk) *adj.* **1.** without money. **2.** bankrupt.

bro′ken (brō′kən) *v.* **1.** pp. of break. —*adj.* **2.** in fragments. **3.** fractured. **4.** incomplete. **5.** weakened. **6.** imperfectly spoken.

bro′ken•heart′ed, *adj.* sorrowing deeply.

B

bro'ker, *n.* commercial agent. —**bro'ker• age,** *n.*

bro'mide (brō'mīd *or, for 1,* -mid) *n.* **1.** soothing compound. **2.** trite saying.

bro'mine (brō'mēn, -min) *n.* reddish, toxic liquid element.

bron'chi•al (brong'kē əl) *adj.* of the bronchi, two branches of the trachea.

bron•chi'tis (-kī'tis) *n.* inflammation in windpipe and chest. —**bron•chit'ic** (-kit'ik) *adj.*

bron'co (brong'kō) *n., pl.* -cos. pony or small horse of western U.S.

bronze (bronz) *n., v.,* **bronzed, bronzing.** —*n.* **1.** alloy of copper and tin. **2.** brownish color. —*v.* **3.** make bronzelike.

brooch (brōch) *n.* clasp or ornament.

brood (brōod) *n.* **1.** group of animals born at one time. —*v.* **2.** hatch. **3.** think moodily.

brook (brŏok) *n.* **1.** small stream. —*v.* **2.** tolerate.

broom (brōom, brŏom) *n.* **1.** sweeping implement. **2.** shrubby plant.

broom'stick, *n.* handle of a broom.

bros., brothers.

broth (brôth) *n.* thin soup.

broth'el (broth'əl) *n.* house of prostitution.

broth'er (bruŧẖ'ər) *n., pl.* **brothers, brethren. 1.** male child of same parents. **2.** member of same group. —**broth'er•hood',** *n.* —**broth'er•ly,** *adj.*

broth'er-in-law', *n., pl.* **brothers-in-law. 1.** husband's or wife's brother. **2.** sister's husband.

brou'ha•ha' (brōo'hä hä') *n., pl.* -has. uproar.

brow (brou) *n.* **1.** eyebrow. **2.** forehead. **3.** edge of a height.

brow'beat', *v.,* -beat, -beaten, -beating. bully.

brown (broun) *n.* **1.** dark reddish or yellowish color. —*adj.* **2.** of this color. —*v.* **3.** make or become brown.

brown'-bag', *v.,* -bagged, -bagging. bring (one's lunch) to work or school. —**brown'-bag'ger,** *n.*

brown'ie (brou'nē) *n.* **1.** elf who secretly helps with chores. **2.** small, chewy chocolate cake. **3.** (*cap.*) girl scout aged 6 to 8.

brown'out', *n.* reduction of electric power to prevent a blackout.

brown study, deep thought.

browse (brouz) *v.,* **browsed, browsing. 1.** graze; feed. **2.** examine books, etc., at leisure. —**brows'er,** *n.*

brs brass.

Br. Som. British Somaliland.

BR STD British Standard.

brt 1. bright. **2.** brightness.

B.R.T. Brotherhood of Railroad Trainmen.

bru'in (brōo'in) *n.* bear.

bruise (brōoz) *v.,* **bruised, bruising,** *n.* —*v.*

1. injure without breaking. —*n.* **2.** bruised injury.

bruis'er, *n. Informal.* strong, tough man.

bruit (brōot) *v.* rumor.

brunch (brunch) *n.* **1.** meal that serves as both breakfast and lunch. —*v.* **2.** eat brunch.

bru•net' (brōo net') *adj.* dark brown, esp. of skin or hair.

bru•nette' (brōo net') *n.* woman with dark hair and usu. dark skin.

brunt (brunt) *n.* main force.

brush (brush) *n.* **1.** instrument with bristles. **2.** bushy tail. **3.** brief encounter. **4.** dense bushes, shrubs, etc. —*v.* **5.** use brush. **6.** touch lightly.

brush'-off', *n.* abrupt rebuff.

brusque (brusk) *adj.* abrupt; blunt. Also, **brusk.** —**brusque'ly,** *adv.* —**brusque'ness,** *n.*

Brus'sels sprouts (brus'əlz) plant with small, edible heads.

bru'tal•ize' (brōot'l īz') *v.,* -ized, -izing. **1.** make brutal. **2.** treat brutally.

brute (brōot) *n.* **1.** beast. **2.** beastlike person. —*adj.* **3.** not human. **4.** irrational. **5.** like animals. **6.** savage. —**bru'tal,** *adj.* —**bru•tal'i•ty** (brōo tal'i tē) *n.* —**bru'tal•ly,** *adv.* —**brut'ish,** *adj.*

BRV Bravo (a cable television station).

brz braze.

B.S., Bachelor of Science.

B.S.A. 1. Also, **B.S. Agr.** Bachelor of Science in Agriculture. **2.** Bachelor of Scientific Agriculture. **3.** Boy Scouts of America.

B.S.A.A. Bachelor of Science in Applied Arts.

B.S.Adv. Bachelor of Science in Advertising.

B.S.A.E. 1. Also, **B.S.Ae.Eng.** Bachelor of Science in Aeronautical Engineering. **2.** Also, **B. S.Ag.E.** Bachelor of Science in Agricultural Engineering. **3.** Also, **B.S.Arch.E., B.S.Arch. Eng.** Bachelor of Science in Architectural Engineering.

B.S.Arch. Bachelor of Science in Architecture.

B.S.Art.Ed. Bachelor of Science in Art Education.

B.S.B.A. Bachelor of Science in Business Administration.

B.S.Bus. Bachelor of Science in Business.

B.S.Bus.Mgt. Bachelor of Science in Business Management.

B.Sc. Bachelor of Science.

B.S.C. Bachelor of Science in Commerce.

B.S.C.E. Bachelor of Science in Civil Engineering.

B.S.Ch. Bachelor of Science in Chemistry.

B.S.Ch.E. Bachelor of Science in Chemical Engineering.

B.Sch.Music Bachelor of School Music.

B.S.Com. Bachelor of Science in Communications.

B.S.C.P. Brotherhood of Sleeping Car Porters.

B.S.D. Bachelor of Science in Design. Also, **B.S.Des.**

B.S.E. 1. Also, **B.S.Ed.** Bachelor of Science in Education. **2.** Also, **B.S.Eng.** Bachelor of Science in Engineering.

B.S.Ec. Bachelor of Science in Economics.

B.S.E.E. 1. Also, **B.S.E.Engr.** Bachelor of Science in Electrical Engineering. **2.** Bachelor of Science in Elementary Education.

B.S.El.E. Bachelor of Science in Electronic Engineering.

B.S.E.M. Bachelor of Science in Engineering of Mines.

B.S.E.P. Bachelor of Science in Engineering Physics.

B.S.E.S. Bachelor of Science in Engineering Sciences.

B.S.F. Bachelor of Science in Forestry. Also, **B.S.For.**

B.S.F.M. Bachelor of Science in Forest Management.

B.S.F.Mgt. Bachelor of Science in Fisheries Management.

B.S.F.S. Bachelor of Science in Foreign Service.

B.S.F.T. Bachelor of Science in Fuel Technology.

B.S.G.E. Bachelor of Science in General Engineering. Also, **B.S.Gen.Ed.**

B.S.G.Mgt. Bachelor of Science in Game Management.

bsh. bushel; bushels.

B.S.H.A. Bachelor of Science in Hospital Administration.

B.S.H.E. Bachelor of Science in Home Economics. Also, **B.S.H.Ec.**

B.S.H.Ed. Bachelor of Science in Health Education.

bshg bushing.

B.S.Hyg. Bachelor of Science in Hygiene.

B.S.I.E. 1. Also, **B.S.Ind.Ed.** Bachelor of Science in Industrial Education. **2.** Also, **B.S. Ind.Engr.** Bachelor of Science in Industrial Engineering.

B.S.Ind.Mgt. Bachelor of Science in Industrial Management.

B.S.I.R. Bachelor of Science in Industrial Relations.

B.S.I.T. Bachelor of Science in Industrial Technology.

B.S.J. Bachelor of Science in Journalism.

bskt. basket.

Bs/L bills of lading.

B.S.L. 1. Bachelor of Sacred Literature. **2.** Bachelor of Science in Law. **3.** Bachelor of Science in Linguistics.

B.S.L.A. and Nurs. Bachelor of Science in Liberal Arts and Nursing.

B.S.Lab.Rel. Bachelor of Science in Labor Relations.

B.S.L.Arch. Bachelor of Science in Landscape Architecture.

B.S.L.M. Bachelor of Science in Landscape Management.

B.S.L.S. Bachelor of Science in Library Science.

B.S.M. 1. Bachelor of Sacred Music. **2.** Bachelor of Science in Medicine. **3.** Bachelor of Science in Music.

B.S.M.E. 1. Bachelor of Science in Mechanical Engineering. **2.** Bachelor of Science in Mining Engineering. **3.** Also, **B.S.Mus.Ed.** Bachelor of Science in Music Education.

B.S.Met. Bachelor of Science in Metallurgy.

B.S.Met.E. Bachelor of Science in Metallurgical Engineering.

bsmt basement. Also, **Bsmt**

B.S.M.T. Bachelor of Science in Medical Technology. Also, **B.S.Med.Tech.**

B.S.N. Bachelor of Science in Nursing.

B.S.N.A. Bachelor of Science in Nursing Administration.

bsns business

BSO *Astronomy.* blue stellar object.

B.S.Orn.Hort. Bachelor of Science in Ornamental Horticulture.

B.S.O.T. Bachelor of Science in Occupational Therapy.

B.S.P. Bachelor of Science in Pharmacy. Also, **B.S.Phar., B.S.Pharm.**

B.S.P.A. Bachelor of Science in Public Administration.

B.S.P.E. Bachelor of Science in Physical Education.

B.S.P.H. Bachelor of Science in Public Health.

B.S.P.H.N. Bachelor of Science in Public Health Nursing.

B.S.P.T. Bachelor of Science in Physical Therapy. Also, **B.S.Ph.Th.**

B.S.Radio-TV. Bachelor of Science in Radio and Television.

B.S.Ret. Bachelor of Science in Retailing.

B.S.R.T. Bachelor of Science in Radiological Technology.

B.S.S. 1. Bachelor of Secretarial Science. **2.** Bachelor of Social Science.

B.S.S.A. Bachelor of Science in Secretarial Administration.

B.S.S.E. Bachelor of Science in Secondary Education.

B.S.S.S. 1. Bachelor of Science in Secretarial Studies. **2.** Bachelor of Science in Social Science.

B.S.T.&I.E. Bachelor of Science in Trade and Industrial Education.

bstb *Electricity, Electronics.* bistable.

B.S.Trans. Bachelor of Science in Transportation.

Bt. Baronet.

bt. 1. boat. **2.** bought.

B.T. 1. Bachelor of Theology. **2.** board of trade.

B.t. *Biology, Agriculture.* Bacillus thuringiensis.

B.T.Ch. Bachelor of Textile Chemistry.

B.T.E. Bachelor of Textile Engineering.

bth bathroom.

B.Th. Bachelor of Theology.

B

btl. bottle.

btn button.

btn. battalion.

btry. battery.

btry chgr battery charger.

Btu, British thermal unit. Also, **BTU**

bu., bushel.

bub′ble (bub′əl) *n.*, *v.*, **-bled, -bling.** —*n.* **1.** globule of gas, esp. in liquid. **2.** something infirm or unsubstantial. —*v.* **3.** make or give off bubbles. —**bub′bly,** *adj.*

buc′ca•neer′ (buk′ə nēr′) *n.* pirate.

buck (buk) *v.* **1.** leap to unseat a rider. **2.** resist. —*n.* **3.** male of the deer, rabbit, goat, etc.

buck′et (buk′it) *n.* deep, open-topped container; pail.

buck′le (buk′əl) *n.*, *v.*, **-led, -ling.** —*n.* **1.** clasp for two loose ends. —*v.* **2.** fasten with buckle. **3.** bend. **4.** set to work.

buck′ler, *n.* shield.

buck′ram (buk′rəm) *n.* stiff cotton fabric.

buck′shot′, *n.* large lead shot.

buck′skin′, *n.* skin of buck.

buck′tooth′, *n.*, *pl.* **-teeth.** projecting tooth.

buck′wheat′, *n.* plant with edible triangular seeds.

bu•col′ic (byōō kol′ik) *adj.* rustic; rural. —**bu•col′i•cal•ly,** *adv.*

bud (bud) *n.*, *v.*, **budded, budding.** —*n.* **1.** small bulge on plant stem, from which leaves or flowers develop. **2.** small rounded part. —*v.* **3.** produce buds. **4.** begin to grow.

Bud′dhism (bōō′diz əm, bŏŏd′iz-) *n.* Eastern religion based on teachings of Buddha. —**Bud′dhist,** *n.*

bud′dy (bud′ē) *n.*, *pl.* **-dies.** *Informal.* friend; comrade.

budge (buj) *v.*, **budged, budging.** move slightly with effort.

budg′et (buj′it) *n.* **1.** estimate of income and expense. **2.** itemized allotment of funds. —*v.* **3.** plan allotment of. **4.** allot. —**budg′et•ar′-y,** *adv.*

buff (buf) *n.* **1.** thick light-yellow leather. **2.** yellowish brown. —*adj.* **3.** made or colored like buff. —*v.* **4.** polish brightly.

buf′fa•lo′ (buf′ə lō′) *n.*, *pl.* **-loes, -los, -lo.** large bovine mammal.

buff′er, *n.* **1.** cushioning device. **2.** polishing device.

buf′fet *n.* **1.** (buf′it) blow. **2.** (bə fā′) cabinet for china, etc. **3.** (bə fā′) food counter. —*v.* (buf′it) **4.** strike. **5.** struggle.

buf•foon′ (bə fōōn′) *n.* clown. —**buf•foon′-er•y,** *n.* —**buf•foon′ish,** *adj.*

bug (bug) *n.*, *v.*, **bugged, bugging.** —*n.* **1.** insect. **2.** microorganism. **3.** defect or imperfection. **4.** enthusiast. **5.** hidden electronic eavesdropping device. —*v.* **6.** install secret listening device in. **7.** *Informal.* pester.

bug′bear′, *n.* any source, real or imaginary,

of fright or fear. Also, **bug′a•boo′** (bug′ə-bōō′).

bug′gy (bug′ē) *n.*, *pl.* **-gies.** carriage.

bu′gle (byōō′gəl) *n.*, *v.*, **-gled, -gling.** —*n.* **1.** cornetlike wind instrument. —*v.* **2.** sound a bugle. —**bu′gler,** *n.*

build (bild) *v.*, **built, building,** *n.* —*v.* **1.** construct. **2.** form. **3.** develop. —*n.* **4.** manner or form of construction. —**build′er,** *n.*

build′ing, *n.* shelter.

build′up′, *n.* *Informal.* **1.** steady increase. **2.** publicity.

built′-in′, *adj.* **1.** built as part of a structure. **2.** filled in with buildings.

built′-up′, *adj.* **1.** made bigger or higher by addition. **2.** filled in with buildings.

bulb (bulb) *n.* **1.** subterranean bud. **2.** rounded enlarged part. **3.** electric lamp. —**bulb′ar, bulb′ous,** *adj.*

Bulg. 1. Bulgaria. **2.** Bulgarian. Also, **Bulg**

bulge (bulj) *n.*, *v.*, **bulged, bulging.** —*n.* **1.** rounded projection. —*v.* **2.** swell out. —**bulg′y,** *adj.*

bul′gur (bul′gər) *n.* wheat, used in parboiled, cracked, and dried form.

bu•lim′i•a (byōō lim′ē ə, -lē′mē ə, bōō-) *n.* disorder marked by eating binges followed by self-induced vomiting.

bulk (bulk) *n.* **1.** magnitude. **2.** main mass. —*v.* **3.** be of or increase in magnitude.

bulk′head′, *n.* wall-like partition in a ship.

bulk′y, *adj.*, **bulkier, bulkiest.** of great bulk. —**bulk′i•ness,** *n.*

bull (bŏŏl) *n.* **1.** male bovine. **2.** bull-like person. **3.** speculator who depends on rise in prices. **4.** papal document. **5.** *Slang.* lying talk. —*adj.* **6.** male. **7.** marked by rise in prices. —**bull′ish,** *adj.*

bull′dog′, *n.* breed of heavily built dog.

bull′doz′er, *n.* powerful earth-moving tractor.

bul′let (bŏŏl′it) *n.* projectile for firing from small guns.

bul′le•tin (bŏŏl′i tn, -tin) *n.* brief public statement, esp. late news.

bull′fight′, *n.* combat between man and a bull. —**bull′fight′er,** *n.*

bull′finch′, *n.* songbird.

bull′frog′, *n.* large frog.

bull′head′ed, *adj.* stubborn.

bull′horn′, *n.* megaphone.

bul′lion (bŏŏl′yən) *n.* uncoined gold or silver.

bull market, stock market with rising prices.

bull′ock (bŏŏl′ək) *n.* castrated bull.

bull′pen′, *n.* place where relief pitchers warm up.

bull′s′-eye′, *n.* center of target.

bull terrier, dog bred from bulldog and terrier.

bul′ly (bŏŏl′ē) *n.*, *pl.* **-lies,** *v.*, **-lied, -lying.** —*n.* **1.** overbearing person who hurts smaller or weaker people. —*v.* **2.** intimidate.

bul/rush/ (bŏŏl/rush/) *n.* rushlike plant.

bul/wark (bŏŏl/wərk, -wôrk) *n.* **1.** rampart. **2.** protection.

bum (bum) *n. Informal.* **1.** tramp or hobo. **2.** loafer; idler. —*v.* **3.** *Informal.* beg. —*adj.* **4.** of poor quality. **5.** false or misleading. **6.** lame.

bum/ble (bum/bəl) *v.,* -**bled, -bling. 1.** blunder. **2.** bungle; botch.

bum/ble•bee/, *n.* large bee.

bum/mer (bum/ər) *n. Slang.* frustrating or bad experience.

bump (bump) *v.* **1.** strike; collide. —*n.* **2.** act or shock of bumping. **3.** swelling. —**bump/-y,** *adj.*

bump/er, *n.* **1.** device for protection in collisions. **2.** glass filled to brim. —*adj.* **3.** abundant.

bump/kin (bump/kin) *n.* awkward, simple person from rural area.

bun (bun) *n.* kind of bread roll.

bunch (bunch) *n.* **1.** cluster. **2.** group. —*v.* **3.** group; gather.

bun/dle (bun/dl) *n., v.,* -**dled, -dling.** —*n.* **1.** group bound together. **2.** package. —*v.* **3.** wrap in bundle. **4.** dress warmly.

bun/ga•low/ (bung/gə lō/) *n.* cottage.

bun/gle (bung/gəl) *v.,* -**gled, -gling,** *n.* —*v.* **1.** fail to do properly. —*n.* **2.** something bungled. —**bun/gler,** *n.*

bun/ion (bun/yən) *n.* swelling on foot.

bunk (bungk) *n.* **1.** built-in bed. **2.** bunkum.

bunk/er (bung/kər) *n.* **1.** bin. **2.** underground refuge.

bun/kum (bung/kəm) *n.* nonsense. Also, **bunk.**

bun/ny (bun/ē) *n., pl.* -**nies.** *Informal.* rabbit.

bunt (bunt) *v.* push or tap forward.

bun/ting (bun/ting) *n.* **1.** fabric for flags, etc. **2.** flags. **3.** finchlike bird.

buoy (bŏŏ/ē, boi) *n.* **1.** float used as support or navigational marker. —*v.* **2.** support by buoy. **3.** mark with buoy.

buoy/ant (boi/ənt, bŏŏ/yənt) *adj.* **1.** tending to float. **2.** cheerful. —**buoy/an•cy,** *n.* —**buoy/ant•ly,** *adv.*

bur (bûr) *n.* prickly seed case.

bur/den (bûr/dn) *n.* **1.** load. —*v.* **2.** load heavily. —**bur/den•some,** *adj.*

bur/dock (bûr/dok) *n.* prickly plant.

bu/reau (byŏŏr/ō) *n., pl.* -**eaus, -eaux. 1.** chest of drawers. **2.** government department.

bu•reauc/ra•cy (byŏŏ rok/rə sē) *n., pl.* -**cies. 1.** government by bureaus. **2.** bureau officials.

bu/reau•crat/ (byŏŏr/ə krat/) *n.* official of a bureaucracy. —**bu/reau•crat/ic,** *adj.*

burg (bûrg) *n. Informal.* small, quiet city or town.

bur/geon (bûr/jən) *v.* **1.** grow quickly. **2.** begin to grow.

burg/er (bûr/gər) *n.* hamburger.

bur/glar (bûr/glər) *n.* thief who breaks and enters. —**bur/glar•ize/,** *v.* —**bur/gla•ry,** *n.*

Bur/gun•dy (bûr/gən dē) *n., pl.* -**dies.** dry red wine.

bur/i•al (ber/ē əl) *n.* act of burying.

bur/lap (bûr/lap) *n.* coarse fabric of jute, etc.

bur•lesque/ (bər lesk/) *n., v.,* -**lesqued, -lesquing.** —*n.* **1.** artistic travesty. **2.** sexually suggestive entertainment. —*v.* **3.** make a burlesque of.

bur/ly (bûr/lē) *adj.,* -**lier, -liest. 1.** of great size. **2.** brusque.

burn (bûrn) *v.,* **burned** or **burnt, burning,** *n.* —*v.* **1.** be on fire. **2.** consume with fire; be afire. **3.** heat; feel heat. **4.** glow. **5.** feel passion. —*n.* **6.** burned place. —**burn/er,** *n.*

bur/nish (bûr/nish) *v.* **1.** polish. —*n.* **2.** gloss.

burn/out/, *n.* **1.** point at which rocket engine stops because it runs out of fuel. **2.** fatigue and frustration from too much work and stress.

burp (bûrp) *n.* belch. —**burp,** *v.*

burr (bûr) *n.* **1.** cutting or drilling tool. **2.** rough protuberance. **3.** bur.

bur/ro (bûr/ō, bŏŏr/ō, bur/ō) *n., pl.* -**ros.** donkey.

bur/row (bûr/ō, bur/ō) *n.* **1.** animal's hole in ground. —*v.* **2.** make or lodge in burrow. —**bur/row•er,** *n.*

bur/sar (bûr/sər, -sär) *n.* treasurer, esp. of a college.

bur•si/tis (bər sī/tis) *n.* condition in which a bursa (sac containing fluid) becomes inflamed, as in the shoulder or elbow.

burst (bûrst) *v.,* **burst, bursting,** *n.* —*v.* **1.** break open or issue forth violently. **2.** rupture. —*n.* **3.** act or result of bursting. **4.** sudden display.

bur/y (ber/ē) *v.,* **buried, burying. 1.** put into ground and cover. **2.** conceal. —**bur/i•er,** *n.*

bus (bus) *n., pl.* **buses, busses,** *v.,* **bused** or **bussed, busing** or **bussing.** —*n.* **1.** large passenger motor vehicle. —*v.* **2.** move by bus.

bus/boy/, *n.* helper of waiter.

bush (bŏŏsh) *n.* **1.** shrubby plant. **2.** land covered by bushes. —**bush/y,** *adj.* —**bush/i•ness,** *n.*

bushed, *adj. Informal.* exhausted; tired.

bush/el (bŏŏsh/əl) *n.* unit of 4 pecks.

bush league, secondary baseball league. —**bush leaguer.**

busi/ness (biz/nis) *n.* **1.** occupation; profession. **2.** trade. **3.** trading enterprise. **4.** affair; matter. —**busi/ness•man/, busi/ness•wom•an,** *n.*

busi/ness•like/, *adj.* practical and efficient.

bus/ing (bus/ing) *n.* moving of pupils by bus to achieve racially balanced classes. Also, **bus/sing.**

bust (bust) *n.* **1.** sculpture of head and shoulders. **2.** bosom. —*v. Informal.* **3.** burst.

4. become or make bankrupt. **5.** arrest. **6.** hit.

bus′tle (bus′əl) v., **-tled, -tling. 1.** move or act energetically. —n. **2.** energetic activity.

bus′y (biz′ē) adj., **busier, busiest,** v., **busied, busying.** —adj. **1.** actively employed. **2.** full of activity. —v. **3.** make or keep busy. —bus′i•ly, adv. —bus′y•ness, n.

bus′y•bod′y, n., pl. **-bodies.** meddler.

but (but; unstressed bət) conj. **1.** on the contrary. **2.** except. **3.** except that. —prep. **4.** except. —adv. **5.** only.

bu′tane (byōō′tān) n. colorless gas used as fuel.

butch (bŏŏch) adj. Slang. **1.** (of a woman) having traits usu. associated with men. **2.** (of a man) having exaggerated masculine traits.

butch′er (bŏŏch′ər) n. **1.** dealer in meat. **2.** slaughterer. —v. **3.** kill for food. **4.** bungle. —butch′er•y, n.

but′ler (but′lər) n. chief male servant.

butt (but) n. **1.** thick or blunt end. **2.** object of ridicule. **3.** large cask. **4.** cigarette end. **5.** Slang. buttocks. —v. **6.** push with head or horns. **7.** be adjacent; join. **8.** strike with head or horns.

but′ter (but′ər) n. **1.** Also, **but′ter•fat′.** solid fatty part of milk. —v. **2.** put butter on. —but′ter•y, adj.

but′ter•cup′, n. plant with yellow cup-shaped flowers.

but′ter•fin′gers, n., pl. **-gers.** clumsy person.

but′ter•fly′, n., pl. **-flies.** insect with colorful wings.

but′ter•milk′, n. sour liquid remaining after butter has been removed from milk.

but′ter•nut′, n. nut of walnutlike tree.

but′ter•scotch′, n. kind of taffy.

but′tock (but′ək) n. (usually pl.) one of two protuberances forming lower and back part of human trunk.

but′ton (but′n) n. **1.** disk or knob for fastening. **2.** buttonlike object. —v. **3.** fasten with button.

but′ton•down′, adj. **1.** (of a collar) having buttonholes for attachment to shirt. **2.** conventional.

but′ton•hole′, n., v., **-holed, -holing.** —n. **1.** slit through which a button is passed. —v. **2.** accost and detain in conversation.

but′tress (bu′tris) n. **1.** structure steadying wall. —v. **2.** support.

bux′om (buk′səm) adj. (of a woman) attractively plump. —bux′om•ness, n.

buy (bī) v., **bought** (bôt) **buying. 1.** acquire by payment. **2.** bribe. —buy′er, n.

buy′back′, n. repurchase by a company of its own stock.

buy′out′, n. purchase of a majority of shares in a company.

buzz (buz) n. **1.** low humming sound. —v. **2.** make or speak with buzz. —buz′zer, n.

buz′zard (buz′ərd) n. carnivorous bird.

buzz′word′, n. Informal. fashionable cliché used to give specious weight to argument.

B.V. 1. Blessed Virgin. [from Latin Beāta Virgō] **2.** farewell. [from Latin bene valē]

b.v. book value.

B.V.A. Bachelor of Vocational Agriculture.

B.V.D. Trademark. a brand of men's underwear. Also, **BVD′s**

B.V.E. Bachelor of Vocational Education.

bvg beverage.

B.V.I. British Virgin Islands.

bvl bevel.

B.V.M. Blessed Virgin Mary. [from Latin Beāta Virgō Marīa]

bvt. 1. brevet. **2.** brevetted.

BW 1. bacteriological warfare. **2.** biological warfare. **3.** (in television, motion pictures, photography, etc.) black and white.

bw Telecommunications. bandwidth.

BWC Board of War Communications.

BWG Birmingham Wire Gauge.

B.W.I. British West Indies.

bx base exchange. Also, **BX**

bx. box.

by (bī) prep. **1.** near to. **2.** through. **3.** not later than. **4.** past. **5.** using as means or method. —adv. **6.** near. **7.** past.

bye (bī) n. (in a tournament) automatic advancement to the next round.

by′-elec′tion, n. special election to fill vacancy.

by′gone′, adj. **1.** past. —n. **2.** something past.

by′law′, n. standing rule.

by′line′, n. line, as in a newspaper, giving the writer or reporter's name.

BYOB, bring your own booze/beer/bottle.

byp. bypass. Also, **Byp.**

by′pass′, n. **1.** detour. **2.** surgical procedure in which diseased or blocked organ is circumvented. —v. **3.** avoid through bypass.

by′play′, n. action or speech aside from the main action.

by′-prod′uct, n. secondary product.

by′road′, n. side road; byway.

by′stand′er, n. chance looker-on.

byte (bīt) n. unit of computer information, larger than bit.

by′way′, n. little-used road.

by′-word′, n. **1.** catchword. **2.** proverb.

Byz. Byzantine.

Byz′an•tine′ (biz′ən tēn′, -tīn′) adj. (sometimes l.c.) **1.** complex; intricate. **2.** marked by intrigue.

Bz. benzene.

bzr buzzer.

C

C, c (sē) *n.* third letter of English alphabet.

C, Celsius, Centigrade.

C, powerful and flexible computer programming language.

c., **1.** centimeter. **2.** century. **3.** copyright.

CA, California.

ca., circa.

CAA Civil Aeronautics Administration. Also, **C.A.A.**

cab (kab) *n.* **1.** taxicab. **2.** (formerly) one-horse carriage. **3.** part of locomotive, truck, etc., where operator sits.

ca•bal′ (kə bal′) *n.* group of plotters.

ca•ban′a (kə ban′ə, -ban′yə) *n.* small structure for changing clothes at beach or pool.

cab′a•ret′ (kab′ə rā′) *n.* restaurant providing entertainment.

cab′bage (kab′ij) *n.* plant with edible head of leaves.

cab′in (kab′in) *n.* **1.** small house. **2.** room in a ship or plane.

cab′i•net (kab′ə nit) *n.* **1.** advisory council. **2.** piece of furniture with drawers, etc. **—cab′i•net•mak′er,** *n.*

ca′ble (kā′bəl) *n., v.,* **-bled, -bling. —n. 1.** thick, strong rope. **2.** cablegram. **—v. 3.** send cablegram (to).

ca′ble•gram′, *n.* telegram sent by underwater wires.

cable TV, system of distributing television programs to subscribers over coaxial cables.

ca•boose′ (kə bōōs′) *n.* car for the crew at the end of a train.

cab′ri•o•let′ (kab′rē ə lā′) *n.* **1.** type of one-horse carriage. **2.** convertible car.

CAC *Real Estate.* central air conditioning.

C.A.C. Coast Artillery Corps.

ca•ca′o (kə kä′ō) *n., pl.* **-caos.** tropical tree whose seeds yield cocoa, etc.

cache (kash) *n., v.,* **cached, caching. —n. 1.** hiding place for treasure, etc. **—v. 2.** hide.

ca•chet′ (ka shā′) *n.* **1.** official seal or sign. **2.** superior status; prestige.

cack′le (kak′əl) *v.,* **-led, -ling,** *n.* **—v. 1.** utter shrill, broken cry. **—n. 2.** act or sound of cackling.

ca•coph′o•ny (kə kof′ə nē) *n., pl.* **-nies.** harsh, discordant sound.

cac′tus (kak′təs) *n., pl.* **-tuses, -ti** (-tī). leafless, spiny plant.

cad (kad) *n.* ungentlemanly person.

ca•dav′er (kə dav′ər) *n.* corpse. **—ca•dav′er•ous,** *adj.*

CAD/CAM (kad′kam′) *n.* computer-aided design and computer-aided manufacturing.

cad′die (kad′ē) *n., v.,* **-died, -dying. —n. 1.** person who carries one's golf clubs. **—v. 2.** work as caddie. Also, **cad′dy.**

ca′dence (kād′ns) *n.* rhythmic flow or beat.

ca•det′ (kə det′) *n.* military student.

cadge (kaj) *v.,* **cadged, cadging.** obtain by begging.

CADMAT (kad′mat), computer-aided design, manufacture, and test.

cad′mi•um (kad′mē əm) *n.* white metallic element used in plating and alloys.

ca′dre (kä′drā, kad′rē) *n.* highly trained group around which an organization is built.

CAE computer-aided engineering.

Cae•sar′e•an (si zâr′ē ən) *n.* Cesarean.

C.A.F. 1. cost and freight. **2.** cost, assurance, and freight. Also, **c.a.f.**

ca•fé′ (ka fā′) *n.* restaurant.

caf′e•te′ri•a (kaf′i tēr′ē ə) *n.* self-service restaurant.

caf′feine (ka fēn′) *n.* chemical in coffee, etc., used as stimulant. Also, **caf′fein.**

caf′tan (kaf′tan) *n.* long wide-sleeved garment.

cage (kāj) *n., v.,* **caged, caging. —n. 1.** barred box or room. **—v. 2.** put in cage.

cag′ey, *adj.* **-ier, -iest.** shrewd; cautious. Also, **cag′y. —cag′i•ly,** *adv.* **—cag′i•ness,** *n.*

C.A.G.S. Certificate of Advanced Graduate Study.

CAI computer-aided instruction; computer-assisted instruction. Also, **cai**

cais′son (kā′son, -sən) *n.* **1.** ammunition wagon. **2.** airtight underwater chamber.

ca•jole′ (kə jōl′) *v.,* **-joled, -joling.** coax; wheedle. **—ca•jol′er•y,** *n.*

Ca′jun (kā′jən) *n.* Louisianan of Nova Scotia-French origin.

cake (kāk) *n., v.,* **caked, caking. —n. 1.** sweet baked dough. **2.** compact mass. **—v. 3.** form into compact mass.

Cal., California. Also, **Calif.**

cal., 1. caliber. **2.** calorie.

cal′a•bash′ (kal′ə bash′) *n.* kind of gourd.

ca′la•ma′ri (kal′ə mär′ē, kä′lə-) *n.* cooked squid.

cal′a•mine′ (kal′ə mīn′) *n.* powder used in skin lotions.

ca•lam′i•ty (kə lam′i tē) *n., pl.* **-ties.** disaster. **—ca•lam′i•tous,** *adj.*

calc. calculate.

cal′ci•fy′ (kal′sə fī′) *v.* **-fied, -fying.** harden by the deposit of calcium salts. **—cal′ci•fi•ca′tion,** *n.*

cal′ci•mine′ (-mīn′) *n., v.,* **-mined, -mining. —n. 1.** type of paint for ceilings, etc. **—v. 2.** cover with calcimine.

cal′ci•um (kal′sē əm) *n.* white metallic chemical element.

cal′cu•late′ (kal′kyə lāt′) *v.,* **-lated, -lating.**

compute or estimate by mathematics. —**cal/cu•la/tion,** n.

cal/cu•lat/ing, adj. shrewd; scheming.

cal/cu•la/tor, n. small electronic or mechanical device that performs mathematical calculations.

cal/cu•lus (kal/kyə ləs) n. a method of calculation by a system of algebraic notations.

cal/dron (kôl/drən) n. cauldron.

cal/en•dar (kal/ən dər) n. **1.** list of days, weeks, and months of year. **2.** list of events.

cal/en•der (kal/ən dər) n. **1.** press for paper, cloth, etc. —v. **2.** press in such a machine.

calf (kaf) n., pl. **calves. 1.** young of cow, etc. **2.** fleshy part of leg below knee.

cal/i•ber (kal/ə bər) n. **1.** diameter of bullet or gun bore. **2.** quality. Also **cal/i•bre.**

cal/i•brate/ (-brāt/) v., **-brated, -brating.** mark for measuring purposes. —**cal/i•bra/tion,** n.

cal/i•co/ (kal/i kō/) n., pl. **-coes, -cos.** printed cotton cloth.

Calif. California.

cal/i•per (kal/ə pər) n. (usu. pl.) compass for measuring.

ca/liph (kā/lif) n. former title of religious and civil ruler of Islamic world.

cal/is•then/ics (kal/əs then/iks) n.pl. physical exercises.

calk (kôk) v. caulk.

call (kôl) v. **1.** cry out loudly. **2.** announce. **3.** summon. **4.** telephone. **5.** name. **6.** visit briefly. —n. **7.** cry or shout. **8.** summons. **9.** brief visit. **10.** need; demand. —**call/er,** n.

call girl, female prostitute who is called for services.

cal•lig/ra•phy (kə lig/rə fē) n. fancy penmanship; art of beautiful writing. —**cal•lig/ra•pher,** n.

call/ing, n. **1.** trade. **2.** summons.

cal/lous (kal/əs) adj. **1.** unsympathetic. —v. **2.** harden.

cal/low (kal/ō) adj. immature.

cal/lus (kal/əs) n. hardened part of the skin.

calm (käm) adj. **1.** undisturbed. **2.** not windy. —n. **3.** calm state. —v. **4.** make calm. —**calm/ly,** adv. —**calm/ness,** n.

cal/o•mel/ (kal/ə mel/) n. white powder used as cathartic.

ca•lor/ic (kə lôr/ik) adj. **1.** of heat or calories. **2.** high in calories.

cal/o•rie (kal/ə rē) n. measured unit of heat, esp. of fuel or energy value of food.

ca•lum/ni•ate/ (kə lum/nē āt/) v., **-ated, -ating.** slander. —**ca•lum/ni•a/tor,** n. —**cal/um•ny** (kal/əm nē) n.

ca•lyp/so (kə lip/sō) n. **1.** musical style of the West Indies. **2.** song in this style.

ca/lyx (kā/liks) n. small leaflets around flower petals.

cam (kam) n. device for changing circular movement to straight.

CAMA (kam/ə), Telecommunications. centralized automatic message accounting.

ca/ma•ra/de•rie (kä/mə rä/də rē) n. comradeship; fellowship.

Camb. Cambridge.

cam/ber (kam/bər) v. **1.** curve upward slightly. —n. **2.** slight upward curve; convexity.

cam/bric (kām/brik) n. close-woven fabric.

cam/cord/er (kam/kôr/dər) n. hand-held television camera with an incorporated VCR.

cam/el (kam/əl) n. large humped quadruped.

ca•mel/lia (kə mēl/yə) n. shrub with glossy leaves and roselike flowers.

cam/e•o/ (kam/ē ō/) n., pl. **-eos.** carved stone with colored layers.

cam/er•a (kam/ər ə) n. device for making photographs.

camflg camouflage.

cam/i•sole/ (kam/ə sōl/) n. woman's sleeveless undershirt.

cam/o•mile/ (kam/ə mīl/) n. chamomile.

cam/ou•flage/ (kam/ə fläzh/) n., v., **-flaged, -flaging.** —n. **1.** deceptive covering. —v. **2.** hide by camouflage.

camp (kamp) n. **1.** place of temporary lodging, esp. in tents. **2.** faction. **3.** something that amuses by being overdone or tasteless. —adj. **4.** Also, **camp/y.** amusing as camp. —v. **5.** form or live in camp. —**camp/er,** n.

cam•paign/ (kam pān/) n. **1.** military operation. **2.** competition for political office. —v. **3.** engage in campaign. —**cam•paign/er,** n.

cam/phor (kam/fər) n. white crystalline substance used as moth repellent, medicine, etc.

cam/pus (kam/pəs) n. school grounds.

camr camera.

cam/shaft/, n. engine shaft fitted with cams.

can, v., **canned** (**could** for def. 1), **canning** (for def. 2), n. —v. **1.** (kan; unstressed kən) be able or qualified to. **2.** (kan) put in airtight container. —n. **3.** (kan) cylindrical metal container. —**can/ner,** n.

Canad. Canadian.

Ca•na/di•an (kə nā/dē ən) n. citizen of Canada. —**Canadian,** adj.

ca•nal/ (kə nal/) n. **1.** artificial waterway. **2.** tubular passage. —**can/al•ize/** (kan/l īz/) v., **-ized, -izing.**

can/a•pé (kan/ə pē, -pā/) n. morsel of food served as appetizer.

ca•nard/ (kə närd/) n. rumor.

ca•nar/y (kə nâr/ē) n., pl. **-ries.** yellow cage bird.

ca•nas/ta (kə nas/tə) n. rummy played with two decks of cards.

canc. 1. cancel. **2.** canceled. **3.** cancellation.

can/cel (kan/səl) v., **-celed, -celing. 1.** cross out. **2.** make void. —**can/cel•la/tion,** n.

can/cer (kan/sər) n. malignant growth. —**can/cer•ous,** adj.

cand candelabra.

can/de•la/brum (kan/dl ä/brəm) n., pl. **-bra**

(-brə). branched candlestick. Also, **can/de•la/bra,** *pl.* **-bras.**

C. & F. *Commerce.* cost and freight.

C&I 1. commerce and industry. **2.** commercial and industrial.

can/did (kan/did) *adj.* frank or honest. —**can/did•ly,** *adv.* —**can/did•ness,** *n.*

can/di•da (kan/di də) *n.* disease-causing fungus.

can/di•date/ (kan/di dāt/, -dit) *n.* one seeking to be elected or chosen. —**can/di•da•cy,** *n.*

can/di•di/a•sis (-dī/ə sis) *n.* infection caused by candida.

can/dle (kan/dl) *n.* waxy cylinder with wick for burning. —**can/dle•stick/,** *n.*

can/dor (kan/dər) *n.* frankness.

c&sc *Printing.* capitals and small capitals.

cand scr candelabra screw.

C and W country-and-western. Also, **C&W**

can/dy (kan/dē) *n., pl.* **-dies,** *v.,* **-died, -dying.** —*n.* **1.** sweet confection. —*v.* **2.** cook in or cover with sugar.

cane (kān) *n., v.,* **caned, caning.** —*n.* **1.** stick used in walking. **2.** long, woody stem. —*v.* **3.** beat with a cane.

CanF Canadian French.

ca/nine (kā/nīn) *adj.* **1.** of dogs. —*n.* **2.** animal of dog family.

canine tooth, one of the four somewhat pointed teeth next to the incisors.

can/is•ter (kan/ə stər) *n.* small box.

can/ker (kang/kər) *n.* ulcerous sore. —**can/ker•ous,** *adj.*

can/na•bis (kan/ə bis) *n.* **1.** hemp plant; marijuana. **2.** part of hemp plant used as a drug.

canned, *adj.* **1.** put into cans or sealed jars. **2.** *Informal.* recorded.

can/ner•y, *n., pl.* **-ies.** factory where foods are canned.

can/ni•bal (kan/ə bəl) *n.* person who eats human flesh. —**can/ni•bal•ism,** *n.*

can/ni•bal•ize/, *v.,* **ized, -izing.** strip of reusable parts.

can•nol/i (kə nō/lē) *n.* pastry filled with sweet cheese.

can/non (kan/ən) *n.* large mounted gun. —**can/non•eer/,** *n.*

can/non•ade/ (-ə nād/) *n.* long burst of cannon fire.

can/not (kan/ot, ka not/, kə-) *v.* am, are, or is unable to.

can/ny (kan/ē) *adj.,* **-nier, -niest. 1.** careful. **2.** shrewd. —**can/ni•ness,** *n.*

ca•noe/ (kə nōō/) *n.* light boat propelled by paddles. —**ca•noe/,** *v.,* **-noed, -noing.**

can/on (kan/ən) *n.* **1.** rule or law. **2.** recognized books of Bible. **3.** church official. —**ca•non/i•cal** (kə non/i kəl) *adj.*

can/on•ize/, *v.,* **-ized, -izing.** declare as saint. —**can/on•i•za/tion,** *n.*

can/o•py (kan/ə pē) *n., pl.* **-pies.** overhead covering.

cant (kant) *n.* **1.** insincerely virtuous talk. **2.** special jargon.

can't (kant) contraction of **cannot.**

can/ta•loupe/ (kan/tl ōp/) *n.* small melon with orange flesh.

can•tan/ker•ous (kan tang/kər əs) *adj.* ill-natured.

can•ta/ta (kən tä/tə) *n.* dramatic choral composition.

can•teen/ (kan tēn/) *n.* **1.** container for water, etc. **2.** military supply store. **3.** entertainment place for soldiers, etc.

can/ter (kan/tər) *n.* **1.** easy gallop. —*v.* **2.** go at easy gallop.

can/ti•cle (kan/ti kəl) *n.* hymn.

cantil cantilever.

can/ti•le/ver (kan/tl ē/vər) *n.* structure secured at one end only.

can/to (kan/tō) *n., pl.* **-tos.** section of a long poem.

can/ton (kan/tn, kan ton/) *n.* small territorial district, esp. in Switzerland.

can/tor (kan/tər) *n.* synagogue official who sings certain prayers.

canv canvas.

can/vas (kan/vəs) *n.* **1.** cloth used for sails, tents, etc. **2.** sails.

can/vas•back/, *n., pl.* **-backs, -back.** wild duck with a whitish or grayish back.

can/vass (kan/vəs) *v.* **1.** investigate. **2.** solicit votes, etc. —**can/vass•er,** *n.*

can/yon (kan/yən) *n.* narrow valley.

cap (kap) *n., v.,* **capped, capping.** —*n.* **1.** brimless hat. **2.** cover. —*v.* **3.** cover. **4.** surpass.

cap., **1.** capacity. **2.** capital(ize). **3.** capital letter.

ca/pa•ble (kā/pə bəl) *adj.* able; qualified. —**ca/pa•bly,** *adv.* —**ca/pa•bil/i•ty,** *n.*

ca•pa/cious (kə pā/shəs) *adj.* roomy.

ca•pac/i•tor (kə pas/i tər) *n.* device for collecting and holding an electrical charge.

ca•pac/i•ty, *n., pl.* **-ties. 1.** volume. **2.** capability. **3.** role.

cape (kāp) *n.* **1.** sleeveless coat. **2.** projecting point of land.

ca/per (kā/pər) *v.* **1.** leap playfully. —*n.* **2.** playful leap. **3.** bud of shrub, used as seasoning.

cap/il•lar/y (kap/ə ler/ē) *adj., n., pl.* **-laries.** —*adj.* **1.** of or in a thin tube. —*n.* **2.** tiny blood vessel.

cap/i•tal (kap/i tl) *n.* **1.** city in which government is located. **2.** letter different from and larger than its corresponding lowercase letter. **3.** money and property available for business use. **4.** decorative head of structural support. —*adj.* **5.** important or chief. **6.** excellent. **7.** indicating a capital letter; uppercase. **8.** punishable by death.

capital gain, profit from the sale of an asset.

C

capital goods, *n.pl.* machines for production of goods.

cap′i•tal•ism, *n.* system of private investment in and ownership of business. —**cap′i•tal•ist,** *n.* —**cap′i•tal•is′tic** (-is′tik) *adj.*

cap′i•tal•ize′, *v.,* **-ized, -izing. 1.** put in capital letters. **2.** use as capital. **3.** take advantage. —**cap′i•tal•i•za′tion,** *n.*

cap′i•tal•ly, *adv.* well.

cap′i•tol (kap′i tl) *n.* building used by legislature.

ca•pit′u•late′ (kə pich′ə lāt′) *v.,* **-lated, -lating.** surrender. —**ca•pit′u•la′tion,** *n.*

cap′let (kap′lit) *n.* oval-shaped medicinal tablet, coated for easy swallowing.

cap. moll. (in prescriptions) soft capsule. [from Latin *capsula mollis*]

ca′pon (kā′pon, -pən) *n.* castrated rooster.

cap′puc•ci′no (kap′ə chē′nō) *n.* espresso coffee mixed with steamed milk.

ca•price′ (kə prēs′) *n.* whim. —**ca•pri′cious** (-prish′əs, -prē′shəs) *adj.*

caps. 1. capital letters. **2.** (in prescriptions) a capsule [from Latin *capsula*].

cap scr cap screw.

cap′size (kap′sīz) *v.,* **-sized, -sizing.** overturn; upset.

cap′stan (kap′stan, -stan) *n.* device turned to pull cables.

cap′stone, *n.* stone that finishes off a structure.

cap′sule (kap′səl) *n.* small sealed container. —**cap′su•lar,** *adj.*

capt., captain.

cap′tain (kap′tən) *n.* **1.** officer below major or rear admiral. **2.** ship master. —**cap′tain•cy,** *n.*

cap′tion (kap′shən) *n.* heading.

cap′tious (kap′shəs) *adj.* noting trivial faults. —**cap′tious•ly,** *adv.* —**cap′tious•ness,** *n.*

cap′ti•vate′ (kap′tə vāt′) *v.,* **-vated, -vating.** charm. —**cap′ti•va′tion,** *n.* —**cap′ti•va′tor,** *n.*

cap′tive (-tiv) *n.* prisoner. —**cap•tiv′i•ty,** *n.*

cap′ture (-chər) *v.,* **-tured, -turing,** *n.* —*v.* **1.** take prisoner. —*n.* **2.** act or instance of capturing. —**cap′tor,** *n.*

car (kär) *n.* **1.** vehicle, esp. automobile. **2.** cage of elevator.

ca•rafe′ (kə raf′) *n.* broad-mouthed bottle for wine, water, etc.

car′a•mel (kar′ə məl, kär′məl) *n.* confection made of burnt sugar.

car′at (kar′ət) *n.* **1.** unit of weight for gems. **2.** karat.

car′a•van′ (kar′ə van′) *n.* group traveling together, esp. over deserts.

car′a•way (kar′ə wā′) *n.* herb bearing aromatic seeds.

carb carburetor.

car′bide (kär′bīd) *n.* carbon compound.

car′bine (kär′bēn, -bīn) *n.* short rifle.

car′bo•hy′drate (kär′bō hī′drāt, -bə-) *n.* organic compound group including starches and sugars.

car•bol′ic acid (kär bol′ik) brown germicidal liquid.

car′bon (kär′bən) *n.* chemical element occurring as diamonds, charcoal, etc. —**car•bon•if′er•ous,** *adj.*

car′bon•ate′ (kär′bə nāt′) *v.,* **-ated, -ating.** charge with carbon dioxide. —**car′bon•a′tion,** *n.*

carbon dioxide, chemical compound of carbon and oxygen: a gas produced esp. by animal respiration.

carbon monoxide, chemical compound of carbon and oxygen: a poisonous gas produced esp. by automobile engines.

carbon paper, paper coated with a carbon preparation, used to make copies of typed or written material.

Car′bo•run′dum (kär′bə run′dəm) *Trademark.* abrasive material.

car′bun•cle (kär′bung kəl) *n.* painful inflammation under skin.

car′bu•re′tor (kär′bə rā′tər, -byə-) *n.* mechanism that mixes gasoline and air in motor.

car′cass (kär′kəs) *n.* dead body of an animal.

car•cin′o•gen (kär sin′ə jən) *n.* cancer-producing substance. —**car′cin•o•gen′ic** (-sə nə jen′ik) *adj.*

car′ci•no′ma (kär′sə nō′mə) *n., pl.* **-mas, -mata.** malignant tumor.

card (kärd) *n.* **1.** piece of stiff paper, with one's name (**calling card**), marks for game purposes (**playing card**), etc. **2.** comb for wool, flax, etc. —*v.* **3.** dress (wool, etc.) with card. **4.** ask for proof of age.

card′board′, *n.* **1.** thin, stiff pasteboard. —*adj.* **2.** flimsy. **3.** seeming fake.

card′-car′ry•ing, *adj.* **1.** officially enrolled, esp. in the Communist Party. **2.** strongly dedicated.

car′di•ac′ (kär′dē ak′) *adj.* of the heart.

cardiac arrest, abrupt stopping of the heartbeat.

car′di•gan (kär′di gən) *n.* sweater that buttons down the front.

car′di•nal (kär′dn l) *adj.* **1.** main; chief. **2.** (of numbers) used to express quantities or positions in series, e.g., 3, 15, 45. **3.** deep red. —*n.* **4.** red bird. **5.** high official of Roman Catholic Church.

cardio-, prefix meaning heart, as *cardiology.*

car′di•o•graph′ (kär′dē ə graf′) *n.* instrument for recording movements of heart. —**car′di•o•gram′,** *n.*

car′di•ol′o•gy (-ol′ə jē) *n.* study of the heart and its functions. —**car′di•ol•o•gist,** *n.*

car′di•o•pul′mo•nar′y (kär′dē ō-) *adj.* of the heart and lungs.

car′di•o•vas′cu•lar, *adj.* of the heart and blood vessels.

card′sharp′, *n.* person who cheats at card games. Also, **card shark.**

care (kâr) *n.*, *v.*, **cared, caring.** —*n.* **1.** worry. **2.** caution. —*v.* **3.** be concerned or watchful. —**care′free′**, *adj.* —**care′ful**, *adj.* —**care′less**, *adj.*

ca•reen′ (kə rēn′) *v.* tip; sway.

ca•reer′ (kə rēr′) *n.* **1.** profession followed as one's lifework. **2.** course through life. **3.** speed. —*v.* **4.** speed.

care′giv′er, *n.* person who cares for a child or an invalid.

ca•ress′ (kə res′) *v.*, *n.* touch in expressing affection.

car′et (kar′it) *n.* insertion mark (^).

care′tak′er (kâr′-) *n.* **1.** maintenance person. **2.** caregiver.

care′worn′, *adj.* haggard from worry.

car′fare′ (kär′fâr′) *n.* cost of ride.

car′go (kär′gō) *n.*, *pl.* **-goes, -gos.** goods carried by vessel.

car′i•bou′ (kar′ə bōō′) *n.* North American reindeer.

car′i•ca•ture (kar′i kə chər) *n.* mocking portrait. —**car′i•ca•ture**, *v.*, **-tured, -turing.**

Caricom (kar′i kom′, kâr′-), an economic association formed in 1974 by ten Caribbean nations. Also, **CARICOM** [*Cari(bbean) com(-munity)*]

car′ies (kâr′ēz) *n.*, *pl.* **-ies.** tooth decay.

car′il•lon′ (kar′ə lon′, -lən) *n.* musical bells.

car′jack′ing (kär′jak′ing) *n.* theft of car by force. —**car′jack′er**, *n.*

car′mine (-min) *n.*, *adj.* crimson or purplish red.

car′nage (-nij) *n.* massacre.

car′nal (-nl) *adj.* of the body.

car•na′tion (kär nā′shən) *n.* common fragrant flower.

car′ni•val (kär′nə vəl) *n.* **1.** amusement fair. **2.** festival before Lent.

car′ni•vore′ (-vôr′) *n.* flesh-eating mammal. —**car•niv′o•rous** (-niv′ə rəs) *adj.*

car′ob (kar′əb) *n.* **1.** tree bearing long pods. **2.** pulp from the pods, used as chocolate substitute.

car′ol (kar′əl) *n.*, *v.*, **-oled, -oling.** —*n.* **1.** Christmas song. —*v.* **2.** sing joyously. —**car′ol•er**, *n.*

car′om (kar′əm) *v.* **1.** hit and rebound. —*n.* **2.** rebound.

ca•rot′id (kə rot′id) *n.* either of two large arteries in the neck.

ca•rouse′ (kə rouz′) *n.*, *v.*, **-roused, -rousing.** —*n.* **1.** noisy or drunken feast. —*v.* **2.** engage in a carouse. —**ca•rous′al**, *n.*

carp (kärp) *v.* **1.** find fault. —*n.* **2.** large freshwater fish.

car′pal (kär′pəl) *adj.* **1.** of the carpus. —*n.* **2.** wrist bone.

carpal tunnel syndrome, chronic wrist pain associated esp. with repetitive movements, as at a keyboard.

car′pel (kär′pəl) *n.* seed-bearing leaf.

car′pen•ter (pən tər) *n.* builder in wood. —**car′pen•try**, *n.*

car′pet (-pit) *n.* **1.** fabric covering for floors. —*v.* **2.** cover with carpet. —**car′pet•ing**, *n.*

car′pool′, *n.* **1.** group of automobile owners each of whom in turn drives the others along a given route, as in commuting. —*v.* **2.** participate in a carpool.

car′port′, *n.* roof that provides shelter for a car.

car′pus (kär′pəs) *n.*, *pl.* **-pi** (pī). **1.** wrist. **2.** wrist bones as a group.

carr carrier.

carr cur carrier current.

car′rel (kar′əl) *n.* small study space in a library. Also, **car′rell.**

car′riage (-ij) *n.* **1.** wheeled vehicle. **2.** posture. **3.** conveyance.

car′ri•on (-ē ən) *n.* dead flesh.

car′rot (-ət) *n.* plant with orange edible root.

car′rou•sel′ (kar′ə sel′) *n.* merry-go-round.

car′ry (kar′ē) *v.*, **-ried, -rying. 1.** convey; transport. **2.** support; bear. **3.** behave. **4.** win. **5.** extend. **6.** have in stock. **7.** carry out, accomplish. —**car′ri•er**, *n.*

car′ry-out′, *adj.* takeout. —**car′ry-out′**, *n.*

car′sick′ (kär′-) *adj.* nauseated and dizzy from car travel.

cart (kärt) *n.* small wagon. —**cart′age**, *n.*

carte blanche (kärt′ blänch′, blänsh′) unconditional authority.

car•tel′ (kär tel′) *n.* syndicate controlling prices and production.

car′ti•lage (kär′tl ij) *n.* flexible connective body tissue. —**car′ti•lag′i•nous** (-tl aj′ə nəs) *adj.*

car•tog′ra•phy (kär tog′rə fē) *n.* map production. —**car•tog′ra•pher**, *n.*

car′ton (kär′tn) *n.* cardboard box.

car•toon′ (kär tōōn′) *n.* **1.** comic drawing. **2.** design for large art work. —**car•toon′ist**, *n.*

car′tridge (kär′trij) *n.* **1.** case containing bullet and explosive. **2.** container with frequently replaced machine parts.

cart′wheel′, *n.* **1.** sideways handspring. —*v.* **2.** roll forward end over end.

carve (kärv) *v.*, **carved, carving.** cut into form. —**carv′er**, *n.*

CAS collision-avoidance system.

cas 1. calculated airspeed. **2.** castle.

C.A.S. Certificate of Advanced Studies.

ca•sa′ba (kə sä′bə) *n.*, *pl.* **-bas.** melon with yellow rind.

cas•cade′ (kas kād′) *n.* waterfall.

case (kās) *n.*, *v.*, **cased, casing.** —*n.* **1.** example. **2.** situation. **3.** event. **4.** statement of arguments. **5.** medical patient. **6.** lawsuit. **7.** category in inflection of nouns, adjectives, and pronouns. **8. in case**, if. **9.** container. —*v.* **10.** put in case.

ca′sein (kā′sēn) *n.* protein derived from milk, used in making cheese.

case′ment (kās′mənt) *n.* hinged window.

cash (kash) *n.* **1.** money. —*v.* **2.** give or get cash for.

cash′ew (kash′ōō, kə shōō′) *n.* small curved nut.

cash•ier′ (ka shēr′) *n.* **1.** person in charge of money. —*v.* **2.** dismiss in disgrace.

cash′mere (kazh′mēr, kash′-) *n.* soft wool fabric.

cas′ing (kā′sing) *n.* **1.** outer covering. **2.** framework, as of a door. **3.** skin of a sausage.

ca•si′no (kə sē′nō) *n., pl.* **-nos.** amusement or gambling hall.

cask (kask) *n.* barrel for liquids.

cas′ket (kas′kit) *n.* coffin.

cas nut castle nut.

cas•sa′va (kə sä′və) *n.* tropical plant with starchy roots.

cas•se•role′ (kas′ə rōl′) *n.* covered baking dish.

cas•sette′ (kə set′) *n.* compact case that holds film or recording tape.

cas′sock (kas′ək) *n.* long ecclesiastical vestment.

cast (kast) *v.,* **cast, casting,** *n.* —*v.* **1.** throw. **2.** deposit (vote). **3.** pour and mold. **4.** compute. —*n.* **5.** act of casting. **6.** thing cast. **7.** actors in play. **8.** form; mold. **9.** rigid surgical dressing. **10.** tinge. **11.** twist. —**cast′ing,** *n.*

cas•ta•net′ (kas′tə net′) *n.* pieces of bone shell, etc., held in the palm and struck together as musical accompaniment.

cast′a•way′, *n.* shipwrecked person.

caste (kast) *n.* hereditary social division of Hindu society.

cast′er, *n.* small swivel-mounted wheel. Also, **cast′or.**

cas′ti•gate′ (kas′ti gāt′) *v.,* **-gated, -gating.** scold severely. —**cas′ti•ga′tion,** *n.* —**cas′ti•ga′tor,** *n.*

cast′ing, *n.* metal cast in a mold.

cast iron, hard, brittle alloy of carbon, iron, and silicon.

cas′tle (kas′əl) *n., v.,* **-tled, -tling.** —*n.* **1.** royal or noble residence, usually fortified. **2.** chess piece; rook. —*v.* **3.** *Chess.* transpose rook and king.

cas′tor oil (kas′tər) cathartic oil.

cas′trate (kas′trāt) *v.,* **-trated, -trating.** remove testicles of. —**cas•tra′tion,** *n.*

cas′u•al (kazh′ōō əl) *adj.* **1.** accidental; not planned. **2.** not caring.

cas′u•al•ty, *n., pl.* **-ties. 1.** accident injurious to person. **2.** soldier missing in action, killed, wounded, or captured.

cas′u•ist•ry, *n., pl.* **-ries.** adroit, specious argument. —**cas′u•ist,** *n.*

cat (kat) *n.* common domestic animal. —**cat′like′,** *adj.*

cat′a•clysm′ (kat′ə kliz′əm) *n.* upheaval. —**cat′a•clys′mic,** *adj.*

cat′a•comb′ (-kōm′) *n.* underground cemetery.

cat′a•logue′ (kat′l ôg′) *n., v.,* **-logued, -loguing.** —*n.* **1.** organized list. —*v.* **2.** enter in catalogue. Also, **cat′a•log′.**

ca•tal′pa (kə tal′pə) *n.* tree with bell-shaped white flowers.

cat′a•lyst (kat′l ist) *n.* **1.** substance that causes or speeds a chemical reaction without itself being affected. **2.** anything that precipitates an event.

cat′a•ma•ran′ (kat′ə mə ran′) *n.* two-hulled boat.

cat′a•mount′, *n.* wild cat, as the cougar.

cat′a•pult′ (-pult′, -pŏŏlt′) *n.* **1.** device for hurling or launching. —*v.* **2.** hurl.

cat′a•ract′ (-rakt′) *n.* **1.** waterfall. **2.** opacity of eye lens.

ca•tarrh′ (kə tär′) *n.* inflammation of respiratory mucous membranes.

ca•tas′tro•phe (kə tas′trə fē) *n.* great disaster. —**cat′a•stroph′ic** (kat′ə strof′ik) *adj.*

cat′bird′, *n.* songbird with catlike call.

cat′call′, *n.* jeer.

catch (kach) *v.,* **caught** (kôt), **catching,** *n.* —*v.* **1.** capture. **2.** trap or surprise. **3.** hit. **4.** seize and hold. **5.** be in time for. **6.** get or contract. **7.** be entangled. —*n.* **8.** act of catching. **9.** thing that catches. **10.** thing caught. **11.** tricky aspect; snag. —**catch′er,** *n.*

Catch-22 (kach′twen′tē tōō′) *n.* frustrating situation involving contradictions.

catch′ing, *adj.* contagious.

catch′up, *n.* ketchup.

catch′word′, *n.* slogan.

catch′y, *adj.,* **-ier, -iest.** memorable and pleasing.

cate computer-aided test equipment.

cat′e•chism′ (kat′i kiz′əm) *n.* set of questions and answers on religious principles. —**cat′e•chize′** (-kīz) *v.,* **-chized, -chizing.**

cat′e•gor′i•cal (-gôr′i kəl) *adj.* unconditional. —**cat′e•gor′i•cal•ly,** *adv.*

cat′e•go′ry (-gôr′ē) *n., pl.* **-ries.** division; class. —**cat′e•go•rize′** (-gə rīz′) *v.,* **-rized, -rizing.**

ca′ter (kā′tər) *v.* **1.** provide food, etc. **2.** be too accommodating. —**ca′ter•er,** *n.*

cat′er-cor′nered (kat′i-, kat′ē-, kat′ər-) *adj.* **1.** diagonal. —*adv.* **2.** diagonally.

cat′er•pil′lar (kat′ə pil′ər) *n.* **1.** wormlike larva of butterfly. **2.** type of tractor.

cat′er•waul′ (kat′ər wôl′) *v.* **1.** utter long wails, as cats in rut. —*n.* **2.** such a wail.

cat′fish′, *n.* fresh-water fish.

cat′gut′, *n.* string made from animal intestine.

cath *Electricity.* cathode.

Cath. 1. (*often lowercase*) cathedral. **2.** Catholic.

ca•thar′sis (kə thär′sis) *n.* **1.** purging of emotions, as through art. **2.** evacuation of bowels.

ca•thar′tic, *adj.* **1.** effecting a catharsis. **2.**

evacuating the bowels. —*n.* **3.** medicine doing this.

ca•the/dral (kə thē/drəl) *n.* main church of diocese.

cath/e•ter (kath/i tər) *n.* tube inserted into a body passage, as to provide or drain fluids.

cath/ode (kath/ōd) *n.* **1.** electrode with negative charge. **2.** positive terminal of a battery.

cathode ray, beam of electrons coming from a cathode.

cathode-ray tube, vacuum tube generating cathode rays directed at screen, used to display images on receiver or monitor. *Abbr.:* CRT.

Cath/o•lic (kath/ə lik) *adj.* **1.** of or belonging to Roman Catholic Church. **2.** (*l.c.*) universal. —*n.* **3.** member of Roman Catholic Church. —**Ca•thol/i•cism** (kə thol/ə siz/əm) *n.*

cat/kin (kat/kin) *n.* spike of bunched small flowers, as on the willow.

cat/nap/, *n.* **1.** short, light sleep. —*v.* **2.** sleep briefly.

cat/nip, *n.* plant with scented leaves.

CAT scan (kat) **1.** examination using x-rays at various angles to show cross section of body. **2.** image produced by CAT scan. —**CAT scanner**

cat's/-paw/, *n.* person exploited by another.

cat/sup (kat/səp, kech/əp, kach/-) *n.* ketchup.

cat/tail/, *n.* tall spinelike marsh plant.

cat/tle (kat/l) *n.* livestock, esp. cows. —**cat/-tle•man,** *n.*

cat/ty (kat/ē) *adj.,* **-tier, -tiest.** maliciously gossiping.

CATV community antenna television (a cable television system).

cat/walk/, *n.* narrow access walk.

Cau•ca/sian (kô kā/zhən) *adj.* **1.** of or characteristic of one of the racial divisions of humankind, marked by minimum skin pigmentation. —*n.* **2.** Caucasian person. Also, **Cau/-ca•soid/** (-kə soid/).

cau/cus (kô/kəs) *n.* political meeting.

cau/dal (kôd/l) *adj.* of the tail.

caul/dron (kôl/drən) *n.* large kettle.

cau/li•flow/er (kô/lə flou/ər) *n.* plant with an edible head.

caulk (kôk) *v.* **1.** fill or close seams of to keep water or air out. —*n.* **2.** Also, **caulk/ing.** material used to caulk.

caus. causative.

cause (kôz) *n., v.,* **caused, causing.** —*n.* **1.** person or thing producing an effect. **2.** reason. **3.** aim; purpose. —*v.* **4.** bring about; produce. —**caus/al,** *adj.* —**cau•sa/tion,** *n.*

cause cé•lè•bre (kôz/ sə leb/) *n., pl.* **causes cé•lè•bres** (kôz/ sə leb/). controversy attracting great attention.

cause/way/, *n.* raised road.

caus/tic (kô/stik) *adj.,* **1.** corroding. **2.** sharply critical. —**caus/ti•cal•ly,** *adv.*

cau/ter•ize/ (kô/tə rīz/) *v.,* **-ized, -izing.** burn. —**cau/ter•y, cau/ter•i•za/tion,** *n.*

cau/tion (kô/shən) *n.* **1.** carefulness. **2.** warning. —*v.* **3.** warn. —**cau/tious,** *adj.*

cav. 1. cavalier. **2.** cavalry. **3.** cavity.

cav/al•cade/ (kav/əl kād/) *n.* procession, esp. on horseback.

cav/a•lier/ (kav/ə lēr/) *n.* **1.** knight or horseman. **2.** courtly gentleman. —*adj.* **3.** haughty; indifferent. **4.** offhand.

cav/al•ry (kav/əl rē) *n., pl.* **-ries.** troops on horseback or in armored vehicles. —**cav/al•ry•man,** *n.*

cave (kāv) *n., v.,* **caved, caving.** —*n.* **1.** hollow space in the earth. —*v.* **2.** fall or sink.

ca/ve•at/ (kav/ē ät/) *n.* warning.

cave man, 1. Stone Age cave dweller. **2.** rough, brutal man.

cav/ern (kav/ərn) *n.* large cave. —**cav/ern•ous,** *adj.*

cav/i•ar/ (-ē är/) *n.* roe of sturgeon, etc., eaten as a delicacy.

cav/il (-əl) *v.,* **-iled, -iling,** *n.* —*v.* **1.** find trivial faults. —*n.* **2.** trivial objection.

cav/i•ty (-i tē) *n., pl.* **-ties.** a hollow.

ca•vort/ (kə vôrt/) *v.* prance about.

caw (kô) *n.* **1.** harsh call of a crow. —*v.* **2.** make a caw.

cax community automatic exchange.

cay•enne/ (kī en/) *n.* sharp condiment.

cay•use/ (kī yōōs/) *n.* Indian pony.

CB, citizens band: private two-way radio.

cbal counterbalance.

CBAT College Board Achievement Test.

CBC 1. Also, **C.B.C.** Canadian Broadcasting Corporation. —*v.* **2.** *Medicine.* complete blood count.

C.B.D. 1. cash before delivery. **2.** central business district.

C.B.E. Commander of the Order of the British Empire.

C.B.E.L. Cambridge Bibliography of English Literature. Also, **CBEL**

CBI computer-based instruction.

CBO Congressional Budget Office.

cbore counterbore.

cboreo counterbore other side.

CBS Columbia Broadcasting System.

CBT 1. Chicago Board of Trade. **2.** computer-based training.

CBW chemical and biological warfare.

cc, 1. carbon copy. **2.** cubic centimeter.

C.C.A. 1. Chief Clerk of the Admiralty. **2.** Circuit Court of Appeals. **3.** County Court of Appeals.

CCC 1. Civilian Conservation Corps. **2.** Commodity Credit Corporation. **3.** copyright clearance center.

CCD 1. *Electronics.* charge-coupled device. **2.** Confraternity of Christian Doctrine.

ccf hundred cubic feet (used of gas).

ccg *Electricity.* constant-current generator.

C.C.I.A. Consumer Credit Insurance Association.

CCITT Consultative Committee for International Telephony and Telegraphy.

CCK *Physiology.* cholecystokinin.

C.Cls. Court of Claims.

CCM counter-countermeasures.

ccm *Electricity.* constant-current modulation.

ccn contract change notice.

cco crystal-controlled oscillator.

CCP Chinese Communist Party.

C.C.P. **1.** *Law.* Code of Civil Procedure. **2.** Court of Common Pleas.

CCR Commission on Civil Rights.

ccs **1.** *Telephones.* common-channel signaling. **2.** continuous commercial service.

cct *Electricity.* constant-current transformer.

CCTV closed-circuit television.

CCU, coronary-care unit.

ccw counterclockwise.

CD, **1.** certificate of deposit. **2.** Civil Defense. **3.** compact disc.

CDC Centers for Disease Control.

cdc cold-drawn copper.

cdel constant delivery.

cdf *Telephones.* combined distributing frame.

cdg coding.

CD-P compact disc-photographic.

cd pl cadmium plate.

Cdr. Commander. Also, **CDR**

cd rdr card reader.

cdrill counterdrill.

CD-ROM (sē'dē'rom') *n.* compact disc for storing digitized read-only data.

cds cold-drawn steel.

CDT Central daylight time. Also, **C.D.T.**

CDTA Capital District Transportation Authority.

cdx control-differential transmitter.

Ce *Symbol, Chemistry.* cerium.

ce **1.** *Electronics.* common emitter. **2.** communications-electronics.

C.E. **1.** Chemical Engineer. **2.** chief engineer. **3.** Christian Era. **4.** Church of England. **5.** Civil Engineer. **6.** common era. **7.** Corps of Engineers.

c.e. **1.** buyer's risk. [from Latin *cāveat emptor* may the buyer beware] **2.** compass error.

CEA Council of Economic Advisers.

cease (sēs) *v.,* **ceased, ceasing,** *n.* stop; end. —**cease′less,** *adj.*

cease′-fire′, *n.* truce.

ce′dar (sē'dər) *n.* coniferous tree.

cede (sēd) *v.,* **ceded, ceding.** yield or give up.

CEEB College Entrance Examination Board.

C.E.F. Canadian Expeditionary Force.

ceil′ing (sē'ling) *n.* **1.** upper surface of room. **2.** maximum altitude.

cel′e•brate′ (sel'ə brāt') *v.,* **-brated, -brating.** **1.** observe or commemorate. **2.** act re-

joicingly. **3.** perform ritually. **4.** extol. —**cel′e•bra′tion,** *n.* —**cel′e•bra′tor,** *n.*

ce•leb′ri•ty (sə leb'ri tē) *n., pl.* **-ties.** **1.** famous person. **2.** fame.

ce•ler′i•ty (sə ler'i tē) *n.* speed.

cel′er•y (sel'ə rē) *n.* plant with edible leaf stalks.

ce•les′tial (sə les'chəl) *adj.* of heaven or the sky.

cel′i•ba•cy (sel'ə bə sē) *n.* **1.** unmarried state. **2.** sexual abstinence. —**cel′i•bate** (-bit) *n., adj.*

cell (sel) *n.* **1.** a small room or compartment. **2.** microscopic biological structure. **3.** electric battery. **4.** organizational unit. —**cel′lu•lar,** *adj.*

cel′lar (sel'ər) *n.* basement.

cel′lo (chel'ō) *n., pl.* **-los.** large violinlike instrument. —**cel′list,** *n.*

cel′lo•phane′ (sel'ə fān') *n.* transparent wrapping material.

cellular phone, mobile telephone using radio transmission. Also, **cell phone.**

cel′lu•lite′ (sel'yə līt', -lēt') *n.* lumpy fat deposits, esp. in the thighs and buttocks.

cel′lu•loid′ (-loid') *n.* hard, flammable substance.

cel′lu•lose′ (-lōs') *n.* carbohydrate of plant origin, used in making paper, etc.

Cels. Celsius.

Cel′si•us (sel'sē əs) *n.* temperature scale in which water freezes at 0° and boils at 100°.

Celt. Celtic.

CEM communications electronics meteorological.

cem cement.

CEMA Council for Economic Mutual Assistance.

ce•ment′ (si ment') *n.* **1.** clay-lime mixture that hardens into stonelike mass. **2.** binding material. —*v.* **3.** treat with cement. **4.** unite.

cem′e•ter′y (sem'i ter'ē) *n., pl.* **-teries.** burial ground.

cemf counter electromotive force.

cen. **1.** central. **2.** century.

cen′o•taph′ (sen'ə taf') *n.* monument for one buried elsewhere.

Ce′no•zo′ic (sē'nə zō'ik) *adj.* noting the present geologic era.

cen′ser (sen'sər) *n.* incense burner.

cen′sor (sen'sər) *n.* **1.** person eliminating undesirable words, pictures, etc. **2.** official responsible for reforms. —*v.* **3.** deal with as a censor. —**cen′sor•ship′,** *n.*

cen•so′ri•ous (-sôr′ē əs) *adj.* severely critical.

cen′sure (-shər) *n., v.,* **-sured, -suring.** —*n.* **1.** disapproval. —*v.* **2.** rebuke.

cen′sus (sen'səs) *n.* count of inhabitants.

cent (sent) *n.* $\frac{1}{100}$ of a dollar; penny.

cent., century.

cen′taur (sen'tôr) *n.* mythological creature, half horse and half man.

cen•te•nar/i•an (sen′tn âr′ē ən) *n.* person 100 years old.

cen•ten/ar•y (sen ten′ə rē, sen′tn er′ē) *n.*, *pl.* **-aries.** 100th anniversary.

cen•ten/ni•al (-ten′ē əl) *n.* **1.** 100th anniversary. —*adj.* **2.** of 100 years.

cen/ter (sen′tər) *n.* **1.** middle point, part, or person. —*v.* **2.** place or gather at center. **3.** concentrate. Also, **cen/tre.**

cen/ter•fold/, *n.* page that folds out from magazine center.

cen/ter•piece/, *n.* decoration for center of table.

cen/ti•grade/ (sen′ti grād′) *adj.* Celsius.

cen/ti•gram/, *n.* $\frac{1}{100}$ of gram.

cen/ti•li/ter (-lē′tər) *n.* $\frac{1}{100}$ of liter.

cen/ti•me/ter, *n.* $\frac{1}{100}$ of meter.

cen/ti•pede/ (-pēd′) *n.* insect with many legs.

cen/tral (sen′trəl) *adj.* **1.** of or at center. **2.** main. —**cen/tral•ly,** *adv.*

cen/tral•ize/, *v.,* **-ized, -izing. 1.** gather at a center. **2.** concentrate control of. —**cen/tral•i•za/tion,** *n.*

central nervous system, brain and spinal cord.

cen•trif/u•gal (-trif′yə gəl, -ə gəl) *adj.* moving away from center.

cen/tri•fuge/ (-fyōōj′) *n.* high-speed rotating apparatus for separating substances of different densities.

cen•trip/e•tal (-trip′i tl) *adj.* moving toward center.

cen/trist (sen′trist) *n.* **1.** person with political views that are not extreme. —*adj.* **2.** of views that are not extreme.

cen/tu•ry (sen′chə rē) *n.,* *pl.* **-ries.** period of one hundred years.

CEO, chief executive officer.

cephalom. cephalometry.

cer ceramic.

ce•ram/ic (sə ram′ik) *adj.* of clay and similar materials. —**ce•ram/ics,** *n.*

Cer.E. Ceramic Engineer.

ce/re•al (sēr′ē əl) *n.* **1.** plant yielding edible grain. **2.** food from such grain.

cer/e•bel/lum (ser′ə bel′əm) *n.* rear part of brain.

cer/e•bral (ser′ə brəl, sə rē′-) *adj.* **1.** of brain. **2.** intellectual.

cerebral palsy, paralysis due to brain injury.

cer/e•brum (sə rē′brəm, ser′ə-) *n.,* *pl.* **-brums, -bra** (-brə). front, upper part of brain.

cer/e•mo/ny (ser′ə mō′nē) *n.,* *pl.* **-nies.** formal act or ritual. —**cer/e•mo/ni•al,** *adj.,* *n.* —**cer/e•mo/ni•ous,** *adj.*

ce•rise/ (sə rēs′, -rēz′) *adj., n.* medium to deep red.

cermet (sûr′met), ceramic-to-metal: a type of seal.

CERN (sârn, sûrn), European Laboratory for Particle Physics; formerly called European Organization for Nuclear Research. [from French C(onseil) e(uropéen pour la) r(echerche) n(ucléaire)]

cert. 1. certificate. **2.** certification. **3.** certified. **4.** certify.

cer/tain (sûr′tn) *adj.* **1.** without doubt; sure. **2.** agreed upon. **3.** definite but unspecified. —**cer/tain•ly,** *adv.* —**cer/tain•ty,** *n.*

certif. 1. certificate. **2.** certificated.

cer•tif/i•cate (sər tif′i kit) *n.* document of proof.

certificate of deposit, bank receipt showing interest paid for certain period on money deposited.

cer/ti•fy/ (sûr′tə fī′) *v.,* **-fied, -fying. 1.** guarantee as certain. **2.** vouch for in writing. —**cer/ti•fi•ca/tion,** *n.*

cer/ti•tude/ (-tōōd′, -tyōōd′) *n.* sureness.

ce•ru/le•an (sə rōō′lē ən) *adj.* deep blue.

cer/vix (sûr′viks) *n.,* *pl.* **cer•vixes, cer•vices** (sûr′və sēz′, sər vī′sēz). necklike part, esp. lower end of uterus. —**cer/vi•cal** (-vi kəl) *adj.*

Ce•sar/e•an (si zâr′ē ən) *n.* delivery of baby by cutting through abdomen and uterus. Also, **Cesarean section, C-section, Cae•sar/e•an.**

ces•sa/tion (se sā′shən) *n.* stop.

ces/sion (sesh′ən) *n.* ceding.

cess/pool/ (ses′pōōl′) *n.* receptacle for waste, etc., from house.

CETA (sē′tə), Comprehensive Employment and Training Act.

cet. par. other things being equal. [from Latin *ceteris paribus*]

cf., compare.

CFA chartered financial analyst.

CFAE contractor-furnished aircraft equipment.

cfd cubic feet per day.

CFE contractor-furnished equipment.

CFG Camp Fire Girls.

cfh cubic feet per hour.

C.F.I. cost, freight, and insurance. Also, **c.f.i.**

CFL Canadian Football League.

cfm cubic feet per minute.

CFNP Community Food and Nutrition Programs.

CFO chief financial officer. Also, **C.F.O.**

CFP 1. certified financial planner. **2.** contractor-furnished property.

CFR Code of Federal Regulations.

cfr crossfire.

CFS chronic fatigue syndrome.

cfs 1. cold-finished steel. **2.** cubic feet per second.

CFT *Medicine.* complement fixation test.

CFTC Commodity Futures Trading Commission.

cg., centigram.

CGA *Computers.* color graphics adapter.

cgs centimeter-gram-second (system). Also, **CGS, c.g.s.**

ch., 1. chapter. **2.** church.

Cha•blis' (sha blē') n. dry white wine. Also, **cha•blis'**.

chafe (chāf) v., **chafed, chafing.** make sore by rubbing.

chaff (chaf) n. **1.** grain husks. **2.** worthless matter. —v. **3.** tease.

chaf'fer, v. bargain.

chafing dish (chā'fing) device for warming food at table.

cha•grin' (sha grin') n. **1.** shame or disappointment. —v. **2.** cause chagrin to.

chain (chān) n. **1.** connected series of links. **2.** any series. **3.** mountain range. —v. **4.** fasten with chain.

chain reaction, process which automatically continues and spreads.

chain saw, power saw with teeth set on endless chain.

chair (châr) n. **1.** seat with a back and legs. **2.** position of authority. **3.** chairperson. —v. **4.** preside over.

chair'man, n., pl. **-men.** presiding officer. Also, fem., **chair'wom/an;** masc. or fem., **chair'per'son.**

chaise (shāz) n. light, open carriage.

chaise longue (shāz' lông') type of couch.

chal challenge.

Chal. 1. Chaldaic. **2.** Chaldean. **3.** Chaldee.

Chald. 1. Chaldaic. **2.** Chaldean. **3.** Chaldee.

cha•let' (sha lā') n. mountain house.

chal'ice (chal'is) n. cup for ritual wine.

chalk (chôk) n. **1.** soft limestone used to write on chalkboards. —v. **2.** mark with chalk. —**chalk'board/,** n.

chal'lenge (chal'inj) n., v., **-lenged, -lenging.** —n. **1.** call to fight, contest, etc. **2.** demand for identification. **3.** objection to juror. —v. **4.** make challenge to. —**chal'leng•er,** n.

chal'lenged, adj. (used as a euphemism) disabled or deficient.

cham chamfer.

cham'ber (chām'bər) n. **1.** room, esp. bedroom. **2.** assembly hall. **3.** legislative body. **4.** space in gun for ammunition.

cham'ber•maid', n. maid who cleans bedrooms.

chamber music, music for performance by a small ensemble in a room or parlor.

cha•me'le•on (kə mē'lē ən) n. lizard able to change color.

cham'ois (sham'ē) n. **1.** European antelope. **2.** soft leather from its skin.

cham'o•mile' (kam'ə mīl', -mēl') n. plant whose flowers are used in medicine and as a tea. Also, **cam'o•mile/.**

champ, n. (champ). **1.** Informal. champion. —v. (chomp, champ). **2.** bite.

Cham•pagne' (sham pān') n. effervescent white wine. Also, **cham•pagne'.**

cham'pi•on (cham'pē ən) n. **1.** best competitor. **2.** supporter. —v. **3.** advocate. —adj. **4.** best. —**cham'pi•on•ship',** n.

Chan. 1. Chancellor. **2.** Chancery. Also, **Chanc.**

chan. channel.

chanc. 1. chancellor. **2.** chancery.

chance (chans) n., v., **chanced, chancing,** adj. —n. **1.** fate; luck. **2.** possibility. **3.** opportunity. **4.** risk. —v. **5.** occur by chance. **6.** risk. —adj. **7.** accidental.

chan'cel (chan'səl) n. space around church altar.

chan'cel•ler•y (-sə lə rē, -səl rē) n., pl. **-leries.** offices of chancellor.

chan'cel•lor (-sə lər) n. **1.** high government official. **2.** university head.

chan'cer•y (-sə rē) n., pl. **-ceries. 1.** high law court. **2.** helpless position.

chan'cre (shang'kər) n., lesion, as of syphilis.

chanc'y (chan'sē) adj., **-cier, -ciest,** risky; uncertain.

chan'de•lier' (shan'dl ēr') n. hanging lighting fixture.

chan'dler (chand'lər) n. **1.** dealer in candles. **2.** grocer.

change (chānj) v., **changed, changing,** n. —v. **1.** alter in condition, etc. **2.** substitute for. **3.** put on other clothes. —n. **4.** alteration. **5.** substitution. **6.** novelty. **7.** coins of low value. —**chang'er,** n. —**change'a•ble,** adj. —**change'a•bil/i•ty,** n.

change of life, menopause.

change'o'ver, n. change from one system to another.

chan'nel (chan'l) n., v., **-neled, -neling.** —n. **1.** bed of stream. **2.** wide strait. **3.** access; route. **4.** specific frequency band, as in television. —v. **5.** convey or direct in channel.

chant (chant) n. **1.** song; psalm. —v. **2.** sing, esp. slowly. —**chant'er,** n.

chant'ey (shan'tē) n., pl. **-eys, -ies.** sailors' song. Also, **chant'y.**

chan'ti•cleer' (chan'ti klēr') n. rooster.

Cha'nu•kah (кнä'nə kə, hä'-) n. Hanukkah.

cha'os (kā'os) n. utter disorder. —**cha•ot'ic** (-ot'ik) adj.

chap (chap) v., **chapped, chapping.** —v. **1.** roughen and redden. —n. **2.** Informal. fellow.

chap., chapter.

chap'el (chap'əl) n. small church.

chap'er•on' (shap'ə rōn') n., v., **-oned, -oning.** —n. **1.** escort of young unmarried woman for propriety. —v. **2.** older person at young people's social affair. **3.** be a chaperon to or for. Also, **chap'er•one'.**

chap'lain (chap'lin) n. institutional clergyman.

chap'let (chap'lit) n. garland.

chaps (chaps, shaps) n.pl. leather leg protectors worn by cowboys.

chap'ter (chap'tər) n. **1.** division of book. **2.** branch of society.

char (chär) v., **charred, charring.** burn.

char'ac•ter (kar'ik tər) *n.* **1.** personal nature. **2.** reputation. **3.** person in fiction. **4.** written or printed symbol.

char'ac•ter•is'tic (-tə ris'tik) *adj.* **1.** typical. —*n.* **2.** special feature; trait.

char'ac•ter•ize', *v.*, **-ized, -izing. 1.** distinguish. **2.** describe. —**char'ac•ter•i•za'tion,** *n.*

cha•rade' (shə rād') *n.* riddle in pantomime.

char'broil' (chär'-) *v.* broil over charcoal fire.

char'coal', *n.* carbonized wood.

chard (chärd) *n.* plant with edible green leafy stalks.

Char'don•nay' (shär'dn ā') *n.* dry white wine.

charge (chärj) *v.*, **charged, charging,** *n.* —*v.* **1.** load or fill. **2.** put electricity through or into. **3.** command or instruct. **4.** accuse. **5.** ask payment of. **6.** attack. —*n.* **7.** load or contents. **8.** unit of explosive. **9.** care; custody. **10.** command or instruction. **11.** accusation. **12.** expense. **13.** price. **14.** attack. —**charge'a•ble,** *adj.*

charg'er, *n.* battle horse.

char'i•ot (char'ē ət) *n.* ancient two-wheeled carriage. —**char'i•ot•eer',** *n.*

cha•ris'ma (kə riz'mə) *n.* power to charm and inspire people. —**char'is•mat'ic** (kar'iz-mat'ik) *adj.*

char'i•ty (char'i tē) *n., pl.* **-ties. 1.** aid to needy persons. **2.** benevolent institution. —**char'i•ta•ble,** *adj.*

char'la•tan (shär'lə tn) *n.* fraud.

char'ley horse' (chär'lē) cramp or sore muscle, esp. in the leg.

charm (chärm) *n.* **1.** power to attract and please. **2.** magical object, verse, etc. —*v.* **3.** attract; enchant. —**charm'er,** *n.* —**charm'-ing,** *adj.*

char'nel house (chär'nl) place for dead bodies.

chart (chärt) *n.* **1.** sheet exhibiting data. **2.** map. —*v.* **3.** make a chart of.

chart. cerat. (in prescriptions) waxed paper. [from Latin *charta cērāta*]

char'ter, *n.* **1.** document authorizing new corporation. —*v.* **2.** establish by charter. **3.** hire; lease.

charter member, original member of an organization.

char•treuse' (shär trooz') *adj., n.* yellowish green.

char'wom'an (chär'-) *n.* woman who cleans offices, houses, etc.

char'y (châr'ē) *adj.,* **charier, chariest.** careful.

chas chassis.

chase (chās) *v.,* **chased, chasing,** *n.* —*v.* **1.** go after. **2.** drive away. **3.** engrave metal. —*n.* **4.** instance of chasing. —**chas'er,** *n.*

chasm (kaz'əm) *n.* deep cleft in earth.

chas'sis (chas'ē, shas'ē) *n.* frame, wheels, and motor of vehicle.

chaste (chāst) *adj.,* **chaster, chastest. 1.** virtuous. **2.** simple. —**chas'ti•ty** (chas'ti tē) *n.*

chas'ten (chā'sən) *v.* punish to improve.

chas•tise' (chas tīz', chas'tīz) *v.,* **-tised, -tis-ing.** punish; beat.

chat (chat) *v.,* **chatted, chatting,** *n.* —*v.* **1.** talk informally. —*n.* **2.** informal talk.

cha•teau' (sha tō') *n., pl.* **-teaux** (-tōz'). stately residence, esp. in France.

chat'tel (chat'l) *n.* article of property other than real estate.

chat'ter (chat'ər) *v.* **1.** talk rapidly or foolishly. **2.** click or rattle rapidly. —*n.* **3.** rapid or foolish talk.

chat'ter•box', *n.* talkative person.

chat'ty (chat'ē) *adj.,* **-tier, -tiest.** loquacious.

chauf'feur (shō'fər, shō fûr') *n.* hired driver.

chau'vin•ism' (shō'və niz'əm) *n.* **1.** blind patriotism. **2.** fanatic devotion to one's race, gender, etc. —**chau'vin•ist** (-və nist) *n., adj.* —**chau'vin•is'tic,** *adj.*

Ch.B. Bachelor of Surgery. [from Latin *Chīrurgiae Baccalaureus*]

chc choke coil.

chd chord.

Ch.E. Chemical Engineer.

cheap (chēp) *adj.* of low price or value. —**cheap'ly,** *adv.* —**cheap'ness,** *n.* —**cheap'en,** *v.*

cheat (chēt) *v.* **1.** defraud; deceive. —*n.* **2.** fraud. **3.** one who defrauds. —**cheat'er,** *n.*

check (chek) *v.* **1.** stop or restrain. **2.** investigate; verify. **3.** note with a mark. **4.** leave or receive for temporary custody. —*n.* **5.** stop; restraint. **6.** written order for bank to pay money. **7.** bill. **8.** identification tag. **9.** square pattern. **10.** *Chess.* direct attack on king.

check'er, *n.* **1.** piece used in checkers. **2.** (*pl.*) game played by two persons, each with 12 pieces. —*v.* **3.** diversify.

check'er•board', *n.* board with 64 squares on which checkers is played.

check'ered, *adj.* **1.** marked with squares. **2.** varied. **3.** dubious.

check'list', *n.* list of items for comparison, verification, etc.

check'mate' (-māt') *n., v.,* **-mated, -mating.** *Chess.* —*n.* **1.** inescapable check. —*v.* **2.** subject to inescapable check.

check'out', *n.* **1.** act of leaving and paying for hotel room. **2.** counter where customers pay for purchases.

check'point', *n.* place, as at a border, where travelers are stopped for inspection.

check'up', *n.* physical examination.

ched'dar (ched'ər) *n.* sharp cheese.

cheek (chēk) *n.* **1.** soft side of face. **2.** *Informal.* impudence. —**cheek'i•ly,** *adv.* —**cheek'i•ness,** *n.* —**cheek'y,** *adj.*

cheer (chēr) *n.* **1.** shout of support. **2.** gladness. —*v.* **3.** shout encouragement to. **4.** gladden. —**cheer'ful,** *adj.* —**cheer'less,** *adj.* —**cheer'y,** *adj.*

C

cheese (chēz) *n.* solid, edible product from milk.

cheese′burg′er, *n.* hamburger with melted cheese.

cheese′cloth′, *n.* open cotton fabric.

chee′tah (chē′tə) *n.* wild cat resembling leopard.

chef (shef) *n.* chief cook.

Chem. 1. chemical. **2.** chemist. **3.** chemistry.

Chem.E. Chemical Engineer.

chem′i•cal (kem′i kəl) *adj.* **1.** of chemistry. —*n.* **2.** substance in chemistry. —**chem′i•cal•ly,** *adv.*

chemical warfare, warfare with the use of chemicals.

che•mise′ (shə mēz′) *n.* woman's undershirt.

chem′is•try (kem′ə strē) *n.* science of composition of substances. —**chem′ist,** *n.*

che′mo•ther′a•py (kē′mō ther′ə pē) *n.* treatment of disease, esp. cancer, with chemicals.

chem′ur•gy (kem′ûr jē) *n.* chemistry of industrial use of organic substances, as soybeans.

cheque (chek) *n. Brit.* bank check.

cher′ish (cher′ish) *v.* treat as dear.

Cher′o•kee′ (cher′ə kē′) *n., pl.* **-kee, -kees.** member of an American Indian people.

cher′ry (cher′ē) *n., pl.* **-ries.** small red fruit of certain trees.

cher′ub (cher′əb) *n.* **1.** *pl.* **-ubim** (-ə bim). celestial being. **2.** *pl.* **-ubs.** angelic child.

chess (ches) *n.* board game for two, each using 16 pieces.

chest (chest) *n.* **1.** part of body between neck and abdomen. **2.** large box.

chest′nut′ (ches′nut′) *n.* **1.** edible nut of certain trees. **2.** reddish brown. **3.** *Informal.* stale joke.

chev′i•ot (shev′ē ət) *n.* sturdy worsted fabric.

chev′ron (shev′rən) *n.* set of stripes indicating military rank.

chew (chōō) *v.* crush repeatedly with teeth. —**chew′er,** *n.*

chewing gum, flavored preparation for chewing.

chew′y, *adj.,* **-ier, -iest.** not easily chewed.

Chey•enne′ (shī en′, -an′) *n., pl.* **-enne, -ennes.** member of an American Indian people.

chg. 1. change. **2.** charge. Also, **chge.**

chgov changeover.

Chi•an′ti (kē än′tē) *n.* dry red wine. Also, **chi•an′ti.**

chic (shēk) *adj.* stylish.

——**Pronunciation.** The pronunciation (chik) for the word CHIC is considered nonstandard except when used jokingly.

chi•can′er•y (shi kā′nə rē, chi-) *n., pl.* **-ies. 1.** deception; trickery. **2.** trick.

Chi•ca′no (chi kä′nō) *n., pl.* **-nos.** Mexican-American. Also, *n.fem.,* **Chi•ca′na.**

chick (chik) *n.* **1.** young chicken. **2.** *Slang.* young woman.

chick′a•dee′ (chik′ə dē′) *n.* small gray North American bird.

Chick′a•saw′ (chik′ə sô′) *n., pl.* **-saw, -saws.** member of an American Indian people.

chick′en (chik′ən) *n.* common domestic fowl.

chicken pox, viral disease marked by eruption of blisters.

chick′pea′, *n.* **1.** legume with pealike seeds. **2.** its seed.

chic′le (chik′əl) *n.* natural substance used in making chewing gum.

chic′o•ry (-ə rē) *n., pl.* **-ries.** plant with edible leaves and root.

chide (chīd) *v.,* **chided, chiding.** scold. —**chid′er,** *n.*

chief (chēf) *n.* **1.** head; leader. —*adj.* **2.** main; principal. —**chief′ly,** *adv.*

chief′tain (-tən) *n.* leader.

chif•fon′ (shi fon′) *n.* sheer silk or rayon fabric.

chif′fo•nier′ (shif′ə nēr′) *n.* tall chest of drawers.

chig′ger (chig′ər) *n.* larva of certain mites.

chil′blains′ (chil′blānz′) *n.pl.* inflammation caused by overexposure to cold, etc.

child (chīld) *n., pl.* **children** (chil′drən). **1.** baby. **2.** son or daughter. —**child′bear′ing,** *n., adj.* —**child′birth,** *n.* —**child′hood,** *n.* —**child′ish,** *adj.* —**child′less,** *adj.* —**child′like′,** *adj.*

child′bed′, *n.* condition of giving birth.

chil′i (chil′ē) *n., pl.* **-ies. 1.** pungent pod of a red pepper. **2.** dish made with these peppers. Also, **chil′e.**

chill (chil) *n.* **1.** coldness. —*adj.* **2.** cold. **3.** shivering. **4.** not cordial. —*v.* **5.** make or become cool. —**chil′ly,** *adv.*

chime (chīm) *n., v.,* **chimed, chiming.** —*n.* **1.** set of musical tubes, bells, etc. —*v.* **2.** sound harmoniously.

chi•me′ra (ki mēr′ə, kī-) *n.* **1.** (*cap.*) mythical monster with lion's head, goat's body, and serpent's tail. **2.** dream.

chi•mer′i•cal (-mer′i kəl, -mēr′-) *adj.* **1.** unreal; imaginary. **2.** wildly fanciful.

chim′ney (chim′nē) *n.* passage for smoke.

chim′pan•zee′ (chim′pan zē′, chim pan′zē) *n.* large, intelligent African ape.

chin (chin) *n.* part of face below mouth.

chi′na (chī′nə) *n.* ceramic ware.

chin•chil′la (chin chil′ə) *n.* small rodent valued for its fur.

Chi•nese′ (chī nēz′, -nēs′) *n., pl.* **-nese.** native or language of China.

chink (chingk) *n.* **1.** crack. **2.** short ringing sound. —*v.* **3.** make such a sound.

Chi•nook' (shi nŏŏk', -nōōk', chi-) *n., pl.* **-nook** or **nooks.** member of an American Indian people.

chintz (chints) *n.* printed fabric.

chintz'y, *adj.,* **-ler, -iest.** cheap-looking.

chip (chip) *n., v.,* **chipped, chipping.** —*n.* **1.** small flat piece, slice, etc. **2.** broken place. **3.** small plate carrying electric circuit. —*v.* **4.** cut or break off (bits). **5.** dent; mark. **6.** chip in, contribute.

chip'munk (-mungk) *n.* small striped rodent resembling squirrel.

chip'per, *adj. Informal.* lively.

chi•rop'o•dy (ki rop'ə dē, kī-) *n.* treatment of foot ailments. —**chi•rop'o•dist,** *n.*

chi'ro•prac'tor (kī'rə prak'tər) *n.* one who practices therapy based upon adjusting body structures, esp. the spine. —**chi'ro•prac'tic,** *n.*

chirp (chûrp) *n.* **1.** short, sharp sound of birds, etc. —*v.* **2.** make such sound. Also, **chir'rup** (chē'əp, chû'-).

chis'el (chiz'əl) *n.* **1.** tool with broad cutting tip. —*v.* **2.** cut with such tool. **3.** *Informal.* cheat. —**chis'el•er,** *n.*

chit'chat' (chit'chat') *n.* light talk.

chiv'al•ry (shiv'əl rē) *n., pl.* **-ries. 1.** qualities such as courtesy and courage. **2.** knightly way of life. —**chiv'al•ric, chiv'al•rous,** *adj.*

chive (chīv) *n.* (*usually pl.*) onionlike plant with slender leaves.

Ch. J. Chief Justice.

chk check.

chkb check bit.

chld chilled.

chlo'rine (klôr'ēn, -in) *n.* green gaseous element. —**chlo'ric,** *adj.* —**chlor'in•ate'** (-i nāt') *v.,* **-ated. -ating.**

chlo'ro•form' (klôr'ə fôrm') *n.* **1.** liquid used as anesthetic. —*v.* **2.** administer chloroform to.

chlo'ro•phyll (-fil) *n.* green coloring matter of plants.

chm. 1. chairman. **2.** checkmate.

chmbr chamber.

chmn. chairman.

chng change.

choc. chocolate.

chock (chok) *n.* wedge; block.

choc'o•late (chô'kə lit) *n.* **1.** product made from cacao seeds. **2.** dark brown.

Choc'taw (chok'tô) *n., pl.* **taw, -taws.** member of an American Indian people.

choice (chois) *n.* **1.** act or right of choosing. **2.** person or thing chosen. —*adj.* **3.** excellent. —**choice'ness,** *n.*

choir (kwīᵊr) *n.* group of singers.

choke (chōk) *v.,* **choked, choking,** *n.* —*v.* **1.** stop breath of. **2.** obstruct. **3.** be unable to breathe. —*n.* **4.** act of choking.

chol'er•a (kol'ər ə) *n.* acute, often deadly disease.

chol'er•ic (kol'ər ik) *adj.* easily irritated or angered.

cho•les'te•rol' (kə les'tə rôl') *n.* biochemical in many bodily fluids and tissues, sometimes blocking arteries.

chomp (chomp) *v.* chew noisily; champ.

choose (chōōz) *v.,* **chose** (chōz), **chosen, choosing.** take as one thinks best. —**choos'er,** *n.*

choos'y, *adj.,* **-ler, -iest.** hard to please; particular.

C

chop (chop) *v.,* **chopped, chopping,** *n.* —*v.* **1.** cut with blows. **2.** cut in pieces. —*n.* **3.** act of chopping. **4.** slice of meat with rib. **5.** jaw.

chop'per, *n.* **1.** thing that chops. **2.** *Informal.* helicopter.

chop'py, *adj.,* **-pler, -plest.** forming short waves.

chop'sticks', *n.pl.* sticks used in eating, esp. in some Asian countries.

chop su'ey (sōō'ē) Chinese-style vegetable dish.

cho'ral (kôr'əl) *adj.* of or for chorus.

cho•rale' (kə ral', -räl') *n.* **1.** type of hymn. **2.** group singing church music.

chord (kôrd) *n.* **1.** combination of harmonious tones. **2.** straight line across circle.

chore (chôr) *n.* routine job.

cho're•og'ra•phy (kôr'ē og'rə fē) *n.* art of composing dances. —**cho're•o•graph'** (-ə graf') *v.* —**cho're•og'ra•pher,** *n.*

chor'is•ter (kôr'ə stər) *n.* choir singer.

chor'tle (chôr'tl) *v.,* **-tled, -tling,** *n.* chuckle.

cho'rus (kôr'əs) *n.* **1.** group of singers. **2.** recurring melody.

chow (chou) *n. Slang.* food.

chow'der (chou'dər) *n.* vegetable soup usu. containing clams or fish.

chow mein (mān) Chinese-style dish served on fried noodles.

chp 1. chairperson. **2.** chopper.

CHQ Corps Headquarters.

chr chroma.

Chr. 1. Christ. **2.** Christian.

Christ (krīst) *n.* Jesus Christ; (in Christian belief) the Messiah.

chris'ten (kris'ən) *v.* baptize; name.

Chris'ten•dom (kris'ən dəm) *n.* all Christians.

Chris'tian (kris'chən) *adj.* **1.** of Jesus Christ, his teachings, etc. —*n.* **2.** believer in Christianity. —**Chris'tian•ize',** *v.,* **-ized, -izing.**

Chris'ti•an'i•ty (-chē an'i tē) *n.* religion based on teachings of Christ.

Christ'mas (kris'məs) *n.* festival in honor of birth of Christ.

chro•mat'ic (krō mat'ik, krə-) *adj.* **1.** of color. **2.** *Music.* progressing by semitones.

chro'mi•um (krō'mē əm) *n.* lustrous metallic element. Also, **chrome.**

chro/mo•some/ (krō/mə sōm/) *n.* threadlike structure carrying the genes. —**chro/mo•so/mal,** *adj.*

Chron. *Bible.* Chronicles.

chron. **1.** chronicle. **2.** chronograph. **3.** chronological. **4.** chronology.

chron/ic (kron/ik) *adj.* constant; long-lasting; habitual. Also, **chron/i•cal.** —**chron/i•cal•ly,** *adv.*

chron/i•cle (kron/i kəl) *n., v.,* **-cled, -cling.** —*n.* **1.** record of events in order. —*v.* **2.** record in chronicle. —**chron/i•cler,** *n.*

chrono-, prefix meaning time, as *chronometer.*

chro•nol/o•gy (krə nol/ə jē) *n., pl.* **-gies.** historical order of events. —**chron/o•log/i•cal** (kron/l oj/i kəl) *adj.*

chro•nom/e•ter (krə nom/i tər) *n.* very exact clock.

chrst characteristic.

chrys/a•lis (kris/ə lis) *n.* pupa.

chry•san/the•mum (kri san/thə məm) *n.* large, colorful flower of aster family.

chs. chapters.

chub (chub) *n.* fresh-water fish.

chub/by, *adj.,* **-bier, -biest.** plump.

chuck (chuk) *v.* **1.** pat lightly. —*n.* **2.** light pat. **3.** cut of beef.

chuck/le (chuk/əl) *v.,* **-led, -ling,** *n.* —*v.* **1.** laugh softly. —*n.* **2.** soft laugh.

chum (chum) *n.* close friend. —**chum/my,** *adj.,* **-mier, -miest.**

chump (chump) *n. Informal.* fool.

chunk (chungk) *n.* big lump.

chunk/y, *adj.,* **-ier, -iest.** **1.** thick or stout; stocky. **2.** full of chunks.

church (chûrch) *n.* **1.** place of Christian worship. **2.** sect.

churl (chûrl) *n.* **1.** peasant. **2.** boor. —**churl/ish,** *adj.*

churn (chûrn) *n.* **1.** agitator for making butter. —*v.* **2.** agitate.

chute (shōōt) *n.* sloping slide.

chut/ney (chut/nē) *n.* East Indian relish.

chutz/pa (кнŏŏt/spə, hŏŏt/-) *n. Slang.* nerve; impudence; gall. Also, **chutz/pah.**

chw chairwoman.

CI counterintelligence.

Ci curie; curies.

ci **1.** cast iron. **2.** circuit interrupter.

C.I. Channel Islands.

CIA, Central Intelligence Agency.

cib. (in prescriptions) food. [from Latin *cibus*]

C.I.C. **1.** Combat Information Center. **2.** Commander in Chief. **3.** Counterintelligence Corps.

ci•ca/da (si kā/də) *n.* large insect with shrill call.

cid component identification.

C.I.D. Criminal Investigation Department (of Scotland Yard).

c.i.d. *Automotive.* cubic-inch displacement:

the displacement of an engine measured in cubic inches. Also, **cid, CID**

-cide, suffix indicating: **1.** killer, as *pesticide.* **2.** act of killing, as *homicide.*

ci/der (sī/dər) *n.* apple juice.

Cie. Company. Also, **cie.** [from French *Compagnie*]

C.I.F. *Commerce.* cost, insurance, and freight (the price quoted includes the cost of the merchandise, packing, and freight to a specified destination plus insurance charges). Also, **CIF, c.i.f.**

ci•gar/ (si gär/) *n.* roll of tobacco for smoking.

cig/a•rette/ (sig/ə ret/) *n.* roll of smoking tobacco in paper.

CIM **1.** computer input from microfilm. **2.** computer-integrated manufacturing.

C. in C. Commander in Chief. Also, **C-in-C**

cinch (sinch) *n.* **1.** firm hold. **2.** *Informal.* sure or easy thing.

cin/der (sin/dər) *n.* burned piece; ash.

cine cinematographic.

cin/e•ma (sin/ə mə) *n.* **1.** motion pictures. **2.** movie theater.

cin/e•ma•tog/ra•phy (-tog/rə fē) *n.* art or technique of motion-picture photography. —**cin/e•ma•tog/ra•pher,** *n.*

cin/na•mon (sin/ə mən) *n.* brown spice from bark of certain Asian trees.

C.I.O. **1.** chief investment officer. **2.** Congress of Industrial Organizations. Also, **CIO**

CIP Cataloging in Publication: a program in which a partial bibliographic description of a work appears on the verso of its title page.

cip cast-iron pipe.

ci/pher (sī/fər) *n.* **1.** the symbol (0) for zero. **2.** secret writing, using code. —*v.* **3.** calculate.

Cir. circle (approved for postal use).

cir. **1.** about: *cir. 1800.* [from Latin *circā, circiter, circum*] **2.** circle. **3.** circular.

circ (sûrk), circular.

circ. **1.** about: *circ. 1800.* [from Latin *circā, circiter, circum*] **2.** circuit. **3.** circular. **4.** circulation. **5.** circumference.

cir/ca (sûr/kə) *prep.* approximately.

cir/cle (sûr/kəl) *n., v.,* **-cled, -cling.** —*n.* **1.** closed curve of uniform distance from its center. **2.** range; scope. **3.** group of friends or associates. —*v.* **4.** enclose or go in circle.

cir/cuit (-kit) *n.* **1.** set of rounds, esp. in connection with duties. **2.** electrical path or arrangement. —**cir/cuit•ry,** *n.*

circuit breaker, device that interrupts electrical circuit to prevent excessive current.

cir•cu/i•tous (sər kyōō/i təs) *adj.* roundabout. —**cir•cu/i•tous•ly,** *adv.*

cir/cu•lar (-kyə lər) *adj.* **1.** of or in circle. —*n.* **2.** advertisement distributed widely. —**cir/cu•lar•ize/,** *v.,* **-ized, -izing.**

cir/cu•late/ (-lāt/) *v.,* **-lated, -lating.** move or pass around. —**cir/cu•la/tion,** *n.* —**cir/cu•la•to/ry** (-lə tôr/ē) *adj.*

circum-, prefix indicating around or about, as *circumnavigate.*

cir′cum•cise′ (sûr′kəm sīz′) *v.,* **-cised, -cising.** remove foreskin of. **—cir′cum•ci′sion** (-sizh′ən) *n.*

cir•cum′fer•ence (sər kum′fər əns) *n.* **1.** outer boundary of a circle. **2.** length of such a boundary. **—cir•cum′fer•en′tial** (-fə ren′shəl) *adj.*

cir′cum•flex′ (sûr′kəm fleks′) *n.* diacritical mark (^).

cir′cum•lo•cu′tion (-lō kyōō′shən) *n.* roundabout expression.

cir′cum•nav′i•gate′ (-nav′i gāt′) *v.,* **-gated, -gating.** sail around.

cir′cum•scribe′ (-skrīb′) *v.,* **-scribed, -scribing. 1.** encircle. **2.** confine.

cir′cum•spect′ (-spekt′) *adj.* cautious. **—cir′cum•spec′tion** (-spek′shən) *n.*

cir′cum•stance′ (-stans′) *n.* **1.** condition accompanying or affecting event. **2.** detail. **3.** existing condition, esp. with regard to material welfare. **4.** ceremony.

cir′cum•stan′tial (-stan′shəl) *adj.* **1.** of or from circumstances. **2.** detailed. **3.** with definite implications.

cir′cum•vent′ (-vent′) *v.* outwit or evade. **—cir′cum•ven′tion,** *n.*

cir′cus (sûr′kəs) *n.* show with animals, acrobats, etc.

cir•rho′sis (si rō′sis) *n.* chronic liver disease.

cir′rus (sir′əs) *n.* fleecy cloud.

CIS *Computers.* CompuServe Information Services.

C.I.S. Commonwealth of Independent States.

CISC (sisk), complex instruction set computer.

cis′tern (sis′tərn) *n.* reservoir.

cit. 1. citation. **2.** cited. **3.** citizen. **4.** citrate.

C.I.T. counselor in training.

cit′a•del (sit′ə dl, -ə del′) *n.* fortress.

cite (sīt) *v.,* **cited, citing. 1.** mention in proof, etc. **2.** summon. **3.** commend. **—ci•ta′tion,** *n.*

cit′i•zen (sit′ə zən, -sən) *n.* **1.** subject of a country. **2.** inhabitant. **3.** civilian. **—cit′i•zen•ry,** *n.* **—cit′i•zen•ship′,** *n.*

citizens band, CB.

citric acid (si′trik) white powder in citrus fruits.

cit′ron (si′trən) *n.* lemonlike Asian fruit.

cit′ro•nel′la (si′trə nel′ə) *n.* pungent oil used esp. as insect repellent.

cit′rus (si′trəs) *adj.* of the genus including the orange, lemon, etc.

cit′y (sit′ē) *n., pl.* **-ies.** large town.

ciu computer interface unit.

Civ. 1. civil. **2.** civilian.

civ′ic (siv′ik) *adj.* **1.** of cities. **2.** of citizens.

civ′ics, *n.* study of civil affairs and duties of citizens.

civ′il (-əl) *adj.* **1.** of citizens. **2.** civilized. **3.** polite. **—civ′il•ly,** *adv.* **—ci•vil′i•ty** (-vil′i tē) *n.*

ci•vil′ian (si vil′yən) *n.* **1.** nonmilitary or nonpolice person. **—adj. 2.** of such persons.

civ′i•li•za′tion (siv′ə lə zā′shən) *n.* **1.** act of civilizing. **2.** civilized territory.

civ′i•lize (-līz′) *v.,* **-lized, -lizing.** convert from primitive state.

civil liberty, fundamental right guaranteed by law.

civil rights, rights of all people to freedom and equality.

civil servant, employee of civil service.

civil service, branches of governmental administration outside the armed services.

civil war, war between parts of same state.

CJ Chief Justice.

ck. 1. cask. **2.** check. **3.** cook. **4.** cork.

ckb cork base.

ckbd corkboard.

ckpt cockpit.

ckt circuit.

ckt brkr circuit breaker.

ckt cl circuit closing.

ckt op circuit opening.

cl., centiliter.

CLA College Language Association.

claim (klām) *v.* **1.** demand as one's right, property, etc. **2.** assert. **—n. 3.** demand. **4.** assertion. **5.** something claimed. **—claim′ant,** *n.*

clair•voy′ant (klâr voi′ənt), *adj.* seeing beyond physical vision. **—clair•voy′ant,** *n.* **—clair•voy′ance,** *n.*

clam (klam) *n.* common mollusk.

clam′ber (klam′bər, klam′ər) *v.* climb.

clam′my, *adj.,* **-mier, -miest.** cold and moist. **—clam′mi•ness,** *n.*

clam′or (klam′ər) *n.* **1.** loud outcry or noise. **—v. 2.** raise clamor. **—clam′or•ous,** *adj.*

clamp (klamp) *n.* **1.** clasping device. **—v. 2.** fasten with clamp.

clan (klan) *n.* **1.** related families. **2.** clique. **—clan′nish,** *adj.*

clan•des′tine (klan des′tin) *adj.* done in secret.

clang (klang) *v.* **1.** ring harshly. **—n. 2.** Also, **clang′or.** harsh ring.

clank (klangk) *v.* **1.** ring dully. **—n. 2.** dull ringing.

clap (klap) *v.,* **clapped, clapping,** *n.* **—v. 1.** strike together, as hands in applause. **2.** apply suddenly. **—n. 3.** act or sound of clapping. **—clap′per,** *n.*

clap′board (klab′ərd) *n.* overlapping boards on exterior walls.

clap′trap′ (klap′-) *n.* empty speech.

claque (klak) *n.* hired applauders.

clar. clarinet.

clar′et (klar′it) *n.* dry red wine.

clar′i•fy′ (klar′ə fī′) *v.,* **-fied, -fying.** make or become clear. **—clar′i•fi•ca′tion,** *n.*

clar′i•net′ (-ə net′) *n.* musical wind instrument.

clar/i•on (-ē ən) *adj.* clear and loud.

clar/i•ty (-i tē) *n.* clearness.

clash (klash) *v.* **1.** conflict. **2.** collide. —*n.* **3.** collision. **4.** conflict.

clasp (klasp) *n.* **1.** fastening device. **2.** hug. —*v.* **3.** fasten with clasp. **4.** hug.

class (klas) *n.* **1.** group of similar persons or things. **2.** social rank. **3.** group of students ranked together. **4.** division. **5.** *Informal.* elegance, grace, or dignity. —*v.* **6.** place in classes. —**class/mate/**, *n.* —**class/room/**, *n.*

class action, lawsuit on behalf of persons with complaint in common.

clas/sic (klas/ik) *adj.* Also, **clas/si•cal. 1.** of finest or fundamental type. **2.** in Greek or Roman manner. —*n.* **3.** author, book, etc., of acknowledged superiority. —**clas/si•cal•ly,** *adv.* —**clas/si•cism/** (klas/ə siz/əm) *n.*

clas/si•fied/ (klas/ə fīd/) *adj.* limited to authorized persons.

clas/si•fy/, *v.,* **-fied, -fying.** arrange in classes. —**clas/si•fi•ca/tion,** *n.*

class•y, *adj.,* **-ier, -iest.** *Informal.* stylish; elegant. —**class/i•ness,** *n.*

clat/ter (klat/ər) *v., n.* rattle.

clause (klôz) *n.* part of sentence with its own subject and predicate.

claus/tro•pho/bi•a (klô/strə fō/bē ə) *n.* dread of closed places. —**claus/tro•pho/bic,** *adj., n.*

clav/i•chord/ (klav/i kôrd/) *n.* early keyboard instrument.

clav/i•cle (klav/i kəl) *n.* collarbone.

claw (klô) *n.* **1.** sharp, curved nail on animal's foot. —*v.* **2.** tear or scratch roughly.

clay (klā) *n.* soft earth, used in making bricks, pottery, etc. —**clay/ey,** *adj.*

cld. 1. *Stock Exchange.* (of bonds) called. **2.** cleared. **3.** cooled.

cldy cloudy.

clean (klēn) *adj.* **1.** free from dirt, blemish, etc. **2.** trim. **3.** complete. —*adv.* **4.** in clean manner. —*v.* **5.** make clean. —**clean/er,** *n.*

clean/-cut/, *adj.* **1.** neat. **2.** clear-cut.

clean•ly (klen/lē) *adj.* keeping or kept clean. —**clean/li•ness,** *n.*

cleanse (klenz) *v.,* **cleansed, cleansing.** make clean. —**cleans/er,** *n.*

clear (klēr) *adj.* **1.** free from darkness or obscurity. **2.** easily perceived. **3.** evident. **4.** unobstructed. **5.** free of obligations or encumbrances. **6.** blameless. —*adv.* **7.** in a clear manner. —*v.* **8.** make or become clear. **9.** pay in full. **10.** pass beyond. —**clear/ly,** *adv.* —**clear/ness,** *n.*

clear/ance, *n.* **1.** space between objects. **2.** authorization.

clear/-cut/, *adj.* apparent; obvious.

clear/ing, *n.* treeless space.

cleat (klēt) *n.* metal piece to which ropes, etc., are fastened.

cleave (klēv) *v.,* **cleft** (kleft) or **cleaved, cleaving.** split. —**cleav/er,** *n.* —**cleav/age,** *n.*

cleave (klēv) *v.,* **cleaved, cleaving. 1.** cling **2.** remain faithful.

clef (klef) *n.* musical symbol indicating pitch.

cleft (kleft) *n.* split.

cleft palate, birth defect involving fissure in the roof of the mouth.

clem/a•tis (klem/ə tis) *n.* flowering vine.

clem/ent (klem/ənt) *adj.* **1.** lenient. **2.** mild. —**clem/en•cy,** *n.*

clench (klench) *v.* close tightly.

cler/gy (klûr/jē) *n., pl.* **-gies.** religious officials. —**cler/gy•man,** *n.* —**cler/gy•wom•an,** *n.fem.*

cler/ic (kler/ik) *n.* member of the clergy.

cler/i•cal, *adj.* **1.** of clerks. **2.** of clergy.

clerk (klûrk) *n.* **1.** employee who keeps records, etc. **2.** retail sales person.

clev/er (klev/ər) *adj.* bright, witty, or creative. —**clev/er•ly,** *adv.* —**clev/er•ness,** *n.*

clew (kloo) *n.* **1.** ball of yarn, etc. **2.** *Brit.* clue.

clg 1. ceiling. **2.** cooling.

CLI or **cli,** cost-of-living index.

cli•ché/ (klē shā/) *n.* trite expression.

click (klik) *n.* **1.** slight, sharp noise. —*v.* **2.** make a click. **3.** *Slang.* succeed.

cli/ent (klī/ənt) *n.* customer of a professional.

cli/en•tele/ (-ən tel/) *n.* patrons.

cliff (klif) *n.* steep bank.

cliff/-hang/er, *n.* **1.** melodramatic serial in which each part ends in suspense. **2.** suspenseful situation.

cli•mac/ter•ic (klī mak/tər ik) *n.* period of decreasing reproductive capacity.

cli/mate (klī/mit) *n.* weather conditions. —**cli•mat/ic** (-mat/ik) *adj.*

cli/max (klī/maks) *n.* high point; culmination. —**cli•mac/tic** (-mak/tik) *adj.*

climb (klīm) *v.* **1.** ascend; rise. **2. climb down, a.** descend. **b.** *Informal.* retreat; compromise. —*n.* **3.** ascent. —**climb/er,** *n.*

clin. clinical.

clinch (klinch) *v.* **1.** fasten (a nail) by bending the point. **2.** hold tightly. —*n.* **3.** act of clinching. —**clinch/er,** *n.*

cling (kling) *v.,* **clung** (klung), **clinging.** hold firmly to.

clin/ic (klin/ik) *n.* hospital for nonresident or charity patients. —**clin/i•cal,** *adj.*

clink (klingk) *v.* **1.** make light, ringing sound. —*n.* **2.** such a sound.

clink/er (kling/kər) *n.* fused mass of incombustible residue.

clip (klip) *v.,* **clipped, clipping,** *n.* —*v.* **1.** cut with short snips. **2.** hit sharply. —*n.* **3.** act of clipping. **4.** clasp. **5.** cartridge holder. —**clip/-ping,** *n.*

clip/per (klip/ər) *n.* **1.** cutting device. **2.** fast sailing vessel.

clique (klēk) *n.* elitist group.

clit/o•ris (klit/ər is) *n., pl.* **clitorises** or **clitorides** (kli tôr/i dēz/). erectile organ of vulva.

clk. 1. clerk. **2.** clock.

clkg caulking.

clkj caulked joint.

cln clean.

clnc clearance.

clnt coolant.

clo. clothing.

cloak (klōk) *n.* **1.** loose outer garment. —*v.* **2.** cover with cloak. **3.** hide.

cloak′-and-dag′ger, *adj.* of espionage or intrigue.

clob′ber (klob′ər) *v. Informal.* maul.

clock (klok) *n.* device for telling time.

clock′wise′, *adv., adj.* in direction of turning clock hands.

clock′work′, *n.* **1.** mechanism of a clock. **2.** perfectly regular function, like that of a clock.

clod (klod) *n.* piece of earth.

clog (klog) *v.,* **clogged, clogging,** *n.* —*v.* **1.** hamper; obstruct. —*n.* **2.** obstruction, etc. **3.** heavy wooden shoe.

clois′ter (kloi′stər) *n.* **1.** covered walk. **2.** monastery or nunnery.

clone (klōn) *n., v.,* **cloned, cloning.** —*n.* **1.** organism created by asexual reproduction. **2.** *Informal.* duplicate. —*v.* **3.** grow as clone.

clos *Real Estate.* closet.

close, *v.,* **closed, closing,** *adj., closer, closest, adj., n.* —*v.* (klōz) **1.** shut, obstruct, or end. **2.** come to terms. —*adj.* (klōs) **3.** shut. **4.** confined. **5.** lacking fresh air. **6.** secretive. **7.** stingy. **8.** compact. **9.** near. **10.** intimate. —*adv.* (klōs) **11.** in a close manner. —*n.* (klōz) **12.** end. —**close′ly,** *adv.* —**close′ness** (klōs′nəs) *n.* —**clo′sure** (klō′zhər) *n.*

close call (klōs) narrow escape.

closed′-cap′tioned, *adj.* broadcast with captions visible only with decoding device.

closed shop, place where workers must belong to union.

close′out′ (klōz′-) *n.* sale at greatly reduced prices.

clos′et (kloz′it) *n.* **1.** small room or cabinet for clothes, etc. —*adj.* **2.** *Slang.* clandestine.

close′up′ (klōs′-) *n.* **1.** photograph taken at close range. **2.** intimate view.

clot (klot) *n., v.,* **clotted, clotting.** —*n.* **1.** mass, esp. of dried blood. —*v.* **2.** form clot.

cloth (klôth) *n.* fabric of threads.

clothe (klōᵺ) *v.,* **clothed** or **clad** (klad), **clothing.** dress.

clothes (klōz, klōᵺz) *n.pl.* garments; apparel. Also, **cloth′ing.**

cloud (kloud) *n.* **1.** mass of water particles, etc., high in the air. —*v.* **2.** grow dark or gloomy. **3.** lose or deprive of transparency. —**cloud′y,** *adj.* —**cloud′i•ness,** *n.*

clout (klout) *n.* **1.** blow from hand. **2.** influence. —*v.* **3.** strike with hand.

clove (klōv) *n.* **1.** tropical spice. **2.** section of plant bulb.

clo′ver (klō′vər) *n.* three-leaved plant.

clown (kloun) *n.* **1.** comic performer. **2.**

prankster. **3.** fool. —*v.* **4.** act like a clown. —**clown′ish,** *adj.*

cloy (kloi) *v.* weary by excess, as of sweetness.

clp clamp.

clpbd *Real Estate.* clapboard.

clpr clapper.

clp scr clamp screw.

clr. 1. clear. **2.** color. **3.** cooler. **4.** current-limiting resistor.

clrg clearing.

cls classify.

clt cleat.

clthg clothing.

CLU Civil Liberties Union.

C.L.U. Chartered Life Underwriter.

club (klub) *n., v.,* **clubbed, clubbing.** —*n.* **1.** bat. **2.** organized group. **3.** (*pl.*) suit of playing cards. —*v.* **4.** beat with club.

club′foot′, *n.* deformed foot.

club soda, soda water.

cluck (kluk) *n.* **1.** call of hen. —*v.* **2.** utter such call.

clue (klōō) *n.* hint in solving mystery, etc.

clump (klump) *n.* cluster.

clum′sy (klum′zē) *adj., -sier, -siest.* awkward. —**clum′si•ly,** *adv.* —**clum′si•ness,** *n.*

clus′ter (klus′tər) *n.* **1.** group; bunch. —*v.* **2.** gather into cluster.

clutch (kluch) *v.* **1.** seize; snatch. **2.** hold tightly. —*n.* **3.** grasp. **4.** (*pl.*) capture or mastery. **5.** device for engaging or disengaging machinery.

clut′ter (klut′ər) *v., n.* disordered heap or litter.

clws. clockwise.

cm., centimeter.

CMA Canadian Medical Association.

C.M.A. certificate of management accounting.

CMC 1. certified management consultant. **2.** Commandant of the Marine Corps.

cmd *Computers.* core-memory drive.

cmd. command.

cmdg. commanding.

Cmdr. Commander.

Cmdre Commodore.

CME Chicago Mercantile Exchange.

CMEA Council for Mutual Economic Assistance. See **COMECON.**

cmf coherent memory filter.

cmflr cam follower.

C.M.G. Companion of the Order of St. Michael and St. George.

CMI computer-managed instruction. Also, **cmi**

cmil circular Military.

CML current-mode logic.

cml. commercial.

cmnt comment.

CMOS (sē′môs′, -mos′), *Electronics.* complementary metal oxide semiconductor.

CMP *Biochemistry.* cytidine monophosphate.

C

cmpd compound.
cmplm complement.
cmplt complete.
cmpns compensate.
cmpnt component.
cmpr compare.
cmps compass.
cmpsg compensating.
cmpsn composition.
cmpst composite.
cmpt compute.
cmptg computing.
cmptr computer.
cmrlr cam roller.
CMS *Printing.* color management system.
cms current-mode switching.
cmshft camshaft.
cmsn commission.
Cmsr Commissioner.
cmte committee.
CMV *Pathology.* cytomegalovirus.
CMYK *Computers, Printing.* cyan, magenta, yellow, black; used for color mixing for printing.
CN **1.** change notice. **2.** chloroacetophenone: used as a tear gas.
C/N **1.** circular note. **2.** credit note.
cna copper-nickel alloy.
cncl concealed.
cnctrc concentric.
cncv concave.
cnd conduit.
cndct *Electricity.* **1.** conduct. **2.** conductivity. **3.** conductor.
cnds condensate.
cndtn condition.
cnfig configuration.
CNM Certified Nurse Midwife.
CNN Cable News Network (a cable television channel).
CNO Chief of Naval Operations.
CNS central nervous system. Also, **cns**
cnsld consolidate.
cnsltnt consultant.
cnsp conspicuously.
cnstr canister.
cntbd centerboard.
cntd contained.
cntor *Electricity.* contactor.
cnvc convenience.
cnvr conveyor.
cnvt convert.
cnvtb convertible.
cnvtr converter.
cnvx convex.
CO, **1.** Colorado. **2.** Commanding Officer.
co-, prefix indicating: **1.** together, as *cooperate.* **2.** joint or jointly, as *coauthor.*
Co., **1.** Company. **2.** County.
c/o, care of.

COA change of address.
CoA *Biochemistry.* coenzyme A.
coach (kōch) *n.* **1.** enclosed carriage, bus, etc. **2.** adviser, esp. in sports. —*v.* **3.** advise.
co•ag′u•late′ (kō ag′yə lāt′) *v.*, -lated, -lating. thicken, clot, or congeal. —co•ag′u•la′-tion, *n.*
coal (kōl) *n.* **1.** black mineral burned as fuel. —*v.* **2.** get coal.
co′a•lesce′ (kō′ə les′) *v.*, -lesced, -lescing. unite or ally. —co′a•les′cence, *n.*
co′a•li′tion (-lish′ən) *n.* alliance.
coam coaming.
coarse (kôrs) *adj.*, **coarser, coarsest.** **1.** rough or harsh. **2.** vulgar. —coarse′ly, *adv.* —coars′en, *v.* —coarse′ness, *n.*
coast (kōst) *n.* **1.** seashore. —*v.* **2.** drift easily, esp. downhill. **3.** sail along coast. —coast′al, *adj.*
coast′er, *n.* **1.** something that coasts. **2.** object protecting surfaces from moisture.
coast guard, military service that enforces maritime laws, saves lives at sea, etc.
coat (kōt) *n.* **1.** outer garment. **2.** covering, as fur or bark. —*v.* **3.** cover or enclose.
coat′ing, *n.* outer layer.
coat of arms, emblems, motto, etc., of one's family.
co•au′thor (kō ô′thər, kō′ô′-) *n.* one of two or more joint authors. —co•au′thor, *v.*
coax (kōks) *v.* influence by persuasion, flattery, etc. —coax′er, *n.*
co•ax′i•al (kō ak′sē əl) *adj.* having a common axis, as **coaxial cables** for simultaneous long-distance transmission of radio or television signals.
cob (kob) *n.* corncob.
co′balt (kō′bôlt) *n.* silvery metallic element whose compounds provide blue coloring substance.
cob′ble (kob′əl) *v.*, -bled, -bling, *n.* —*v.* **1.** mend (shoes). —*n.* **2.** Also, **cob′ble•stone′.** round stone for paving, etc. —cob′bler, *n.*
COBOL (kō′bôl) *n.* computer language for writing programs to process large files.
co′bra (kō′brə) *n.* venomous snake.
cob′web′ (kob′-) *n.* spider web.
co•caine′ (kō kān′, kō′kān) *n.* narcotic drug.
coch. (in prescriptions) a spoonful. [from Latin *cochlear*]
coch. amp. (in prescriptions) a tablespoonful. [from Latin *cochlear amplum* large spoon(-ful)]
coch. mag. (in prescriptions) a tablespoonful. [from Latin *cochlear magnum* large spoon(-ful)]
coch. med. (in prescriptions) a dessertspoonful. [from Latin *cochlear medium* medium-sized spoon(ful)]
coch. parv. (in prescriptions) a teaspoonful. [from Latin *cochlear parvum* little spoon(ful)]
cock (kok) *n.* **1.** male bird, esp. rooster. **2.**

valve. **3.** hammer in lock of a gun. **4.** pile of hay. —*v.* **5.** set cock of (a gun). **6.** set aslant.

cock•ade' (ko kād') *n.* hat ornament.

cock'a•too' (kok'ə tōō', kok'ə tōō') *n.* colorful crested parrot.

cock'er, *n.* small spaniel.

cock'eyed', *adj.* **1.** having an eye that cannot look straight. **2.** tilted to one side. **3.** absurd. **4.** drunk.

cock'le (kok'əl) *n.* **1.** mollusk with radially ribbed valves. **2.** inmost part.

cock'ney (-nē) *n.* **1.** resident of London, esp. East End. **2.** pronunciation of such persons.

cock'pit', *n.* **1.** space for pilot. **2.** pit where cocks fight.

cock'roach', *n.* common crawling insect.

cock'tail', *n.* **1.** drink containing mixture of liquors. **2.** mixed appetizer.

cock'y, *adj.*, **-ier, -iest.** saucy and arrogant; too sure of oneself. —**cock'i•ness,** *n.*

co'coa (kō'kō) *n.* **1.** powdered seeds of cacao, used esp. in making a beverage. —*adj.* **2.** brown.

co'co•nut' (kō'kə nut', -nət) *n.* large, hardshelled seed of the **co'co palm.**

co•coon' (kə kōōn') *n.* silky larval covering.

cod (kod) *n.* edible Atlantic fish. Also, **cod'fish'.**

C.O.D., cash, or collect, on delivery.

co'da (kō'də) *n.* final passage of a musical movement.

cod'dle (kod'l) *v.*, **-dled, -dling. 1.** pamper. **2.** cook in almost boiling water.

code (kōd) *n.*, *v.*, **coded, coding.** —*n.* **1.** collection of laws or rules. **2.** system of signals or secret words. —*v.* **3.** put in code.

co'deine (kō'dēn) *n.* drug derived from opium.

codg'er (koj'ər) *n.* eccentric man, esp. an old one.

cod'i•cil (kod'ə səl) *n.* supplement, esp. to a will.

cod'i•fy' (kod'ə fī', kō'də-) *v.*, **-fied, -fying.** organize into legal or formal code. —**cod'i•fi•ca'tion,** *n.*

co'ed' (kō'ed', -ed') *n.* female student, esp. in coeducational school.

co'ed•u•ca'tion, *n.* education of both sexes in the same classes. —**co'ed•u•ca'tion•al,** *adj.*

coef coefficient.

co'ef•fi'cient (kō'ə fish'ənt) *n.* number by which another is multiplied.

co•erce' (kō ûrs') *v.*, **-erced, -ercing.** force; compel. —**co•er'cion** (-ûr'shən) *n.* —**co•er'cive,** *adj.*

co•e'val (kō ē'vəl) *adj.* of same period.

co'ex•ist' (kō'ig zist') *v.* **1.** exist simultaneously. **2.** exist together peacefully. —**co'ex•ist'ence,** *n.* —**co'ex•ist'ent,** *adj.*

COFC container-on-flatcar.

C of C Chamber of Commerce.

coff cofferdam.

cof'fee (kô'fē) *n.* **1.** brown seeds of certain tropical trees. **2.** beverage made by roasting and grinding these seeds.

cof'fer (kô'fər) *n.* chest.

cof'fin (kô'fin) *n.* box for a corpse.

C. of S. Chief of Staff.

cog (kog) *n.* tooth on wheel (**cog'wheel'**), connecting with another such wheel.

co'gent (kō'jənt) *adj.* convincing. —**co'gen•cy,** *n.* —**co'gent•ly,** *adv.*

cog'i•tate' (koj'i tāt') *v.*, **-tated, -tating.** ponder. —**cog'i•ta'tion,** *n.* —**cog'i•ta'tor,** *n.*

co'gnac (kōn'yak) *n.* brandy.

cog'nate (kog'nāt) *adj.* **1.** related. —*n.* **2.** a cognate word.

cog•ni'tion (-nish'ən) *n.* knowing.

cog'ni•zance (-nə zəns) *n.* notice, esp. official. —**cog'ni•zant,** *adj.*

cog•no'men (kog nō'mən) *n.* surname.

co'gno•scen'ti (kon'yə shen'tē, kog'nə-), *n.pl., sing.* **-te** (-tā, -tē). those having superior knowledge.

co•hab'it (kō hab'it) *v.* live together, esp. as husband and wife without being married. —**co•hab'i•ta'tion,** *n.*

co•here' (kō hēr') *v.*, **-hered, -hering.** stick together. —**co•he'sion** (-hē'zhən) *n.* —**co•he'sive** (-siv) *adj.*

co•her'ent (-hēr'ənt, -her'-) *adj.* making sense. —**co•her'ence,** *n.*

coho coherent oscillator.

co'hort (kō'hôrt) *n.* **1.** associate; companion. **2.** group, esp. of soldiers.

coif•fure' (kwä fyŏŏr') *n.* arrangement of hair.

coil (koil) *v.* **1.** wind spirally or in rings. —*n.* **2.** ring. **3.** series of spirals.

coin (koin) *n.* **1.** piece of metal issued as money. —*v.* **2.** make metal into money. **3.** invent. —**coin'age,** *n.* —**coin'er,** *n.*

co•in•cide' (kō'in sīd') *v.*, **-cided, -ciding. 1.** occur at same time, place, etc. **2.** match. —**co•in'ci•dence** (-si dəns) *n.* —**co•in'ci•den'tal** (-den'tl) *adj.* —**co•in'ci•den'tal•ly,** *adv.*

co'i•tus (kō'i təs) *n.* sexual intercourse. —**co'i•tal,** *adj.*

coke (kōk) *n.*, *v.*, **coked, coking.** —*n.* **1.** solid carbon produced from coal. **2.** *Slang.* cocaine. —*v.* **3.** convert into coke.

Col., 1. Colonel. **2.** Colorado.

co'la (kō'lə) *n.* soft drink containing extract from kola nuts.

col'an•der (kul'ən dər, kol'-) *n.* large strainer.

colat. (in prescriptions) strained. [from Latin *colātus*]

cold (kōld) *adj.* **1.** without warmth. **2.** not cordial. —*n.* **3.** absence of heat. **4.** common illness marked by runny nose. —**cold'ly,** *adv.* —**cold'ness,** *n.*

cold'-blood'ed, *adj.* **1.** callous; unemotional. **2.** with blood at same temperature as environment.

cold cream, preparation for cleansing or soothing the skin.

cold cuts, *n.pl.* various sliced cold meats and cheeses.

cold feet, *Informal,* lack of courage.

cold shoulder, deliberate show of indifference.

cold turkey, *Informal,* —*n.* **1.** abrupt withdrawal from addictive substance. —*adv.* **2.** impromptu.

cold war, rivalry between nations just short of armed conflict.

colent. (in prescriptions) let them be strained. Also, **colen.** [from Latin *colentur*]

cole′slaw′ (kōl′slô′) *n.* sliced raw cabbage.

colet. (in prescriptions) let it be strained. [from Latin *colētur*]

col′ic (kol′ik) *n.* pain in bowels. —**col′ick•y,** *adj.*

colidar coherent light detection and ranging.

col′i•se′um (kol′i sē′əm) *n.* large stadium.

co•li′tis (kə lī′tis, kō-) *n.* inflammation of the colon.

coll. 1. collateral. **2.** collect. **3.** collection. **4.** collective. **5.** collector. **6.** Also, **Coll.** college. **7.** collegiate. **8.** colloquial. **9.** (in prescriptions) an eyewash. [from Latin *collyrium*]

collab. 1. collaboration. **2.** collaborator.

col•lab′o•rate′ (kə lab′ə rāt′) *v.,* **-rated,** **-rating.** work together. —**col•lab′o•ra′tion,** *n.* —**col•lab′o•ra′tor,** *n.*

col•lage′ (kə läzh′) *n.* work of art made with various materials pasted on a surface.

col•lapse′ (kə laps′) *v.,* **-lapsed, -lapsing,** *n.* —*v.* **1.** fall in or together. **2.** fail abruptly. —*n.* **3.** a falling-in. **4.** sudden failure. —**col•laps′i•ble,** *adj.*

col′lar (kol′ər) *n.* **1.** part of garment around neck. —*v.* **2.** seize by collar.

col′lar•bone′, *n.* slender bone connecting sternum and scapula; clavicle.

col′lard (kol′ərd) *n.* type of kale.

collat. collateral.

col•lat′er•al (kə lat′ər əl) *n.* **1.** security pledged on loan. —*adj.* **2.** additional. **3.** on side.

col′league (kol′ēg) *n.* associate in work, etc.

col•lect′ (kə lekt′) *v.* **1.** gather together. **2.** take payment of. —*adj., adv.* **3.** payable on delivery. —**col•lec′tion,** *n.* —**col•lec′tor,** *n.*

col•lect′i•ble, *n.* **1.** object collected. —*adj.* **2.** able to be collected.

col•lec′tive, *adj.* **1.** joint; by a group. —*n.* **2.** socialist productive group.

collective bargaining, negotiation between union and employer.

col•lec′tiv•ism, *n.* principle of communal control. —**col•lec′tiv•ist,** *n.*

col′lege (kol′ij) *n.* school of higher learning. —**col•le′giate** (kə lē′jit) *adj.*

col•lide′ (kə līd′) *v.,* **-lided, -liding.** come together violently.

col′lie (kol′ē) *n.* kind of large, long-haired dog.

col′lier (kol′yər) *n.* **1.** ship for carrying coal. **2.** coal miner.

col•li′sion (kə lizh′ən) *n.* **1.** crash. **2.** conflict.

colloq. 1. colloquial. **2.** colloquialism. **3.** colloquially.

col•lo′qui•al (kə lō′kwē əl) *adj.* appropriate to casual rather than formal speech or writing. —**col•lo′qui•al•ism,** *n.* —**col•lo′qui•al•ly,** *adv.*

col•lo′qui•um (-kwē əm) *n., pl.* **-quiums, -quia** (-kwē ə). conference of experts.

col′lo•quy (kol′ə kwē) *n., pl.* **-quies.** conversation.

collun. (in prescriptions) a nose wash. [from Latin *collunarium*]

col•lu′sion (kə lōō′zhən) *n.* illicit agreement.

collut. (in prescriptions) a mouthwash. [from Latin *collūtorium*]

collyr. (in prescriptions) an eyewash. [from Latin *collyrium*]

Colo., Colorado.

colog *Math.* cologarithm.

co•logne′ (kə lōn′) *n.* perfumed toilet water.

co′lon (kō′lən) *n.* **1.** mark of punctuation (:). **2.** part of large intestine. —**co•lon′ic** (kə-lon′ik) *adj.*

colo′nel (kûr′nl) *n.* military officer below general. —**colo′nel•cy,** *n.*

co•lo′ni•al•ism (kə lō′nē ə liz′əm) *n.* policy of extending national authority over foreign territories. —**co•lo′ni•al•ist** (-ə list) *n., adj.*

col′on•nade′ (kol′ə nād′) *n.* series of columns.

col′o•ny (kol′ə nē) *n., pl.* **-nies. 1.** group of people settling in another land. **2.** territory subject to outside ruling power. **3.** community. —**co•lo′ni•al** (kə lō′nē əl) *adj., n.* —**col′o•nist,** *n.* —**col′o•nize′,** *v.,* **-nized, -nizing.**

col′or (kul′ər) *n.* **1.** quality of light perceived by human eye. **2.** pigment; dye. **3.** complexion. **4.** vivid description. **5.** (*pl.*) flag. **6.** race. —*v.* **7.** apply color to. **8.** distort in telling. Also, *Brit.,* **col′our.** —**col′or•a′tion,** *n.* —**col′or•ing,** *n.*

col′o•ra•tu′ra (kul′ər ə tŏŏr′ə, -tyŏŏr′ə, kol′-) *n.* soprano specializing in music containing ornamental trills.

col′or-blind′, *adj.* **1.** unable to distinguish certain colors. **2.** without racial bias.

col′ored, *adj. Often Offensive.* belonging to a race other than Caucasian.

col′or•ful, *adj.* **1.** full of color. **2.** vivid; interesting. —**col′or•ful•ly,** *adv.*

col′or•less, *adj.* **1.** without color. **2.** uninteresting. —**col′or•less•ly,** *adv.*

co•los′sal (kə los′əl) *adj.* huge; vast. —**co•los′sal•ly,** *adv.*

co•los′sus (-los′əs) *n.* anything colossal.

colt (kōlt) *n.* young male horse.

col'um•bine' (kol'əm bīn') *n.* branching plant with bright flowers.

col'umn (kol'əm) *n.* **1.** upright shaft or support. **2.** long area of print. **3.** regular journalistic piece. **4.** long group of troops, ships, etc. —**co•lum'nar,** (kə lum'nər) *adj.* —**col'um•nist** (-əm nist) *n.*

com-, prefix indicating: **1.** with or together, as *commingle.* **2.** completely, as *commit.*

co'ma (kō'mə) *n.* unconscious state. —**com'a•tose'** (-tōs') *adj.*

Co•man'che (kə man'chē) *n., pl.* **-che,** **-ches.** member of an American Indian people.

comb (kōm) *n.* **1.** toothed object, for straightening hair or fiber. **2.** growth on a cock's head. **3.** crest. **4.** honeycomb. —*v.* **5.** dress with comb. **6.** search.

com•bat', *v.,* **-bated, -bating,** *n.* —*v.* (kəm bat', kom'bat) **1.** fight. —*n.* (kom'bat) **2.** battle. —**com•bat'ant,** *n.* —**com•bat'ive,** *adj.*

com'bi•na'tion (kom'bə nā'shən) *n.* **1.** act of combining. **2.** mixture. **3.** alliance. **4.** sets of figures dialed to operate a lock.

com•bine', *v.,* **-bined, -bining,** *n.* —*v.* (kəm bīn') **1.** unite; join. —*n.* (kom'bīn) **2.** combination. **3.** machine that cuts and threshes grain.

combl combustible.

com'bo (kom'bō) *n., pl.* **-bos. 1.** *Informal.* small jazz band. **2.** combination.

com•bus'ti•ble (kəm bus'tə bəl) *adj.* **1.** inflammable. —*n.* **2.** inflammable substance.

com•bus'tion (-chən) *n.* burning.

comd. command.

comdg. commanding.

Comdr. commander. Also, **comdr.**

Comdt. commandant. Also, **comdt.**

come (kum) *v.,* **came, come, coming. 1.** approach or arrive. **2.** happen. **3.** emerge.

come'back', *n.* **1.** return to former status. **2.** retort.

COMECON (kom'i kon'), an economic association of Communist countries. Also, **Comecon, CMEA** [*Co(uncil for) M(utual) Econ-(omic Assistance)*]

co•me'di•an (kə mē'dē ən) *n.* humorous actor or performer. —**co•me'di•enne',** *n.fem.*

com'e•dy (kom'i dē) *n., pl.* **-dies. 1.** humorous drama. **2.** drama with happy ending.

come'ly (kum'lē) *adj.,* **-lier, -liest.** attractive. —**come'li•ness,** *n.*

com'er (kum'ər) *n. Informal.* one likely to have great success.

com'et (kom'it) *n.* celestial body orbiting around and lighted by sun, often with misty tail.

COMEX (kō'meks), Commodity Exchange, New York.

com'fort (kum'fərt) *v.* **1.** console or cheer. —*n.* **2.** consolation. **3.** ease. —**com'fort•a•ble,** *adj.* —**com'fort•a•bly,** *adv.*

com'fort•er, *n.* **1.** one who comforts. **2.** warm quilt.

com'ic (kom'ik) *adj.* **1.** of comedy. **2.** Also, **com'i•cal.** funny. —*n.* **3.** comedian. **4.** (*pl.*) comic strips. —**com'i•cal•ly,** *adv.*

comic strip, sequence of drawings relating comic incident or story.

Com. in Chf. Commander in Chief.

coml. commercial.

comm 1. communication. **2.** commutator.

comm. 1. commander. **2.** commerce. **3.** commission. **4.** committee. **5.** commonwealth. Also, **Comm.**

com'ma (kom'ə) *n.* mark of punctuation (,).

com•mand' (kə mand') *v.* **1.** order. **2.** be in control of. **3.** overlook. —*n.* **4.** order. **5.** control. **6.** troops, etc., under commander.

com'man•dant' (kom'ən dant', -dänt') *n.* **1.** local commanding officer. **2.** director of Marine Corps.

com'man•deer' (-dēr') *v.* seize for official use.

com•mand'er, *n.* **1.** chief officer. **2.** *Navy.* officer below captain.

com•mand'ment, *n.* **1.** command. **2.** precept of God.

com•man'do (kə man'dō) *n., pl.* **-dos, -does.** soldier making brief raids against enemy.

com•mem'o•rate' (kə mem'ə rāt') *v.,* **-rated, -rating.** honor memory of. —**com•mem'o•ra'tion,** *n.* —**com•mem'o•ra•tive** (-rə tiv) *adj.*

com•mence' (kə mens') *v.,* **-menced, -mencing.** start.

com•mence'ment, *n.* **1.** beginning. **2.** graduation day or ceremonies.

com•mend' (kə mend') *v.* **1.** praise. **2.** entrust. —**com•mend'a•ble,** *adj.* —**com'men•da'tion** (kom'ən dā'shən) *n.* —**com•mend'a•to'ry,** *adj.*

com•men'su•rate (-men'shə rit, -sə-) *adj.* equal or corresponding. —**com•men'su•rate•ly,** *adv.*

com'ment (kom'ent) *n.* **1.** remark or criticism. —*v.* **2.** make remarks.

com'men•tar'y (-ən ter'ē) *n., pl.* **-taries. 1.** comment. **2.** explanatory essay.

com'men•ta'tor (-tā'tər) *n.* one who discusses news events, etc.

com'merce (kom'ərs) *n.* sale or barter.

com•mer'cial (kə mûr'shəl) *adj.* **1.** of or in commerce. —*n.* **2.** radio or television advertisement. —**com•mer'cial•ly,** *adv.*

com•mer'cial•ize', *v.,* **-ized, -izing.** treat as a business. —**com•mer'cial•i•za'tion,** *n.*

com•min'gle (kə ming'gəl) *v.,* **-gled, -gling.** blend.

com•mis'er•ate' (kə miz'ə rāt') *v.,* **-ated, -ating.** sympathize. —**com•mis'er•a'tion,** *n.*

com'mis•sar'y (kom'ə ser'ē) *n., pl.* **-ies.** store selling food and equipment.

com•mis'sion (kə mish'ən) *n.* **1.** act of committing. **2.** document giving authority. **3.**

group of persons with special task. **4.** usable condition. **5.** fee for agent's services. —*v.* **6.** give commission to. **7.** authorize. **8.** put into service.

com·mis′sion·er, *n.* government official.

com·mit′ (kə mit′) *v.*, **-mitted, -mitting. 1.** give in trust or custody. **2.** refer to committee. **3.** do. **4.** obligate. —**com·mit′ment,** *n.*

com·mit′tee (kə mit′ē) *n.* group assigned to special duties. —**com·mit′tee·man,** *n., pl.* **-men.** —**com·mit′tee·wom′an,** *n., pl.* **-wom·en.**

com·mode′ (kə mōd′) *n.* **1.** chest of drawers. **2.** stand with washbasin. **3.** toilet.

com·mo′di·ous (kə mō′dē əs) *adj.* roomy.

com·mod′i·ty (kə mod′i tē) *n., pl.* **-ties.** article of commerce.

com′mo·dore′ (kom′ə dôr′) *n.* officer below rear admiral.

com′mon (kom′ən) *adj.* **1.** shared by all; joint. **2.** ordinary; usual. **3.** vulgar. —*n.* **4.** area of public land. —**com′mon·ly,** *adv.*

com′mon·er, *n.* one of common people.

common law, system of law based on custom and court decisions.

com′mon·place′, *adj.* **1.** ordinary; trite. —*n.* **2.** commonplace remark.

com′mons, *n.* **1.** (*cap.*) elective house of certain legislatures. **2.** large dining room.

common sense, sound practical judgment. —**com′mon·sense′,** *adj.*

com′mon·weal′ (-wēl′) *n.* public welfare.

com′mon·wealth′ (-welth′) *n.* **1.** democratic state. **2.** people of a state.

com·mo′tion (kə mō′shən) *n.* disturbance.

com·mu′nal (kə myōōn′l, kom′yə nl) *adj.* of or belonging to a community.

com·mune′, *v.*, **-muned, -muning,** *n.* —*v.* (kə myōōn′) **1.** talk together. —*n.* (kom′-yōōn) **1.** small community with shared property. **3.** district.

com·mu′ni·cate′, *v.*, **-cated, -cating. 1.** make known. **2.** transmit. **3.** exchange news, etc. —**com·mu′ni·ca·ble** (-ni kə bəl) *adj.* —**com·mu′ni·ca′tion,** *n.* —**com·mu′ni·ca′tive** (-kā′tiv, -kə-) *adj.* —**com·mu′ni·cant,** *n.*

com·mun′ion (kə myōōn′yən) *n.* **1.** act of sharing. **2.** group with same religion. **3.** sacrament commemorating Jesus' last supper; Eucharist.

com·mu′ni·qué′ (kə myōō′ni kā′) *n.* official bulletin.

com′mu·nism (kom′yə niz′əm) *n.* **1.** social system based on collective ownership of all productive property. **2.** (*cap.*) political doctrine advocating this. —**com′mu·nist** (-nist) *n., adj.* —**com′mu·nis′tic,** *adj.*

com·mu′ni·ty (kə myōō′ni tē) *n., pl.* **-ties. 1.** people with common culture living in one locality. **2.** public.

com·mute′ (kə myōōt′) *v.*, **-muted, -muting. 1.** exchange. **2.** reduce (punishment). **3.** travel between home and work. —**com′mu·**

ta′tion (kom′yə tā′shən) *n.* —**com·mut′er,** *n.*

comp. 1. companion. **2.** comparative. **3.** compare. **4.** compensation. **5.** compilation. **6.** compiled. **7.** compiler. **8.** complement. **9.** complete. **10.** composition. **11.** compositor. **12.** compound. **13.** comprehensive.

com·pact′, *adj.* (kəm pakt′, kom′pakt) **1.** packed together. **2.** pithy. —*v.* (kəm pakt′) **3.** pack together. —*n.* (kom′pakt) **4.** small cosmetic case. **5.** agreement. —**com·pact′ly,** *adv.* —**com·pact′ness,** *n.*

compact disc, optical disc on which music, data, or images are digitally recorded. Also, **CD.**

com·pac′tor (kəm pak′tər, kom′pak-) *n.* appliance that compresses trash into small bundles.

compander *Audio.* compressor-expander.

com·pan′ion (kəm pan′yən) *n.* **1.** associate. **2.** mate. —**com·pan′ion·a·ble,** *adj.* —**com·pan′ion·ate** (-yə nit) *adj.* —**com·pan′ion·ship′,** *n.*

com′pa·ny (kum′pə nē) *n., pl.* **-nies. 1.** persons associated for business or social purposes, etc. **2.** companionship. **3.** guests. **4.** military unit.

compar. comparative.

com·par′a·tive (kəm par′ə tiv) *adj.* **1.** of or based on comparison. —*n.* **2.** *Gram.* intermediate degree of comparison. —**com·par′a·tive·ly,** *adv.*

com·pare′ (kəm pâr′) *v.*, **-pared, -paring. 1.** consider for similarities. **2.** *Gram.* inflect to show degree. —**com′pa·ra·ble** (kom′pər ə·bəl) *adj.* —**com·par′i·son** (kəm par′ə sən) *n.*

com·part′ment (kəm pärt′mənt) *n.* separate room, space, etc. —**com·part·men′tal** (-men′tl) *adj.* —**com·part·men′tal·ize′,** *v.*, **-ized, -izing.**

com′pass (kum′pəs) *n.* **1.** instrument for finding direction. **2.** extent. **3.** tool for making circles.

com·pas′sion (kəm pash′ən) *n.* pity or sympathy. —**com·pas′sion·ate,** *adj.* —**com·pas′sion·ate·ly,** *adv.*

com·pat′i·ble (kəm pat′ə bəl) *adj.* congenial. —**com·pat′i·bil′i·ty,** *n.*

com·pa′tri·ot (kəm pā′trē ət) *n.* person from one's own country.

compd. compound.

com·pel′ (kəm pel′) *v.*, **-pelled, -pelling.** force.

com·pel′ling, *adj.* **1.** forceful. **2.** demanding attention.

com·pen′di·ous (kəm pen′dē əs) *adj.* concise.

com·pen′di·um (-dē əm) *n., pl.*, **-diums, -dia** (-dē ə). **1.** summary. **2.** full list.

com′pen·sate′ (kom′pən sāt′) *v.*, **-sated, -sating. 1.** make up for. **2.** pay. —**com′pen·sa′tion,** *n.* —**com·pen′sa·to′ry** (kəm pen′-sə-) *adj.*

com·pete′ (kəm pēt′) v., -peted, -peting. contend; rival.

com′pe·tent (kom′pi tənt) adj. **1.** able enough. **2.** legally qualified. **3.** sufficient. —**com′pe·tence, com′pe·ten·cy,** n. —**com′pe·tent·ly,** adv.

com′pe·ti′tion (kom′pi tish′ən) n. **1.** contest. **2.** rivalry. —**com·pet′i·tive** (kəm pet′i-tiv) adj. —**com·pet′i·tor,** n.

Comp. Gen. Comptroller General.

com·pile′ (kəm pīl′) v., -piled, -piling. put together; assemble. —**com·pil′er,** n. —**com′-pi·la′tion** (kom′pə lā′shən) n.

compl complete.

com·pla′cen·cy (kəm plā′sən sē) n., pl. -cies. satisfaction, esp. with self. Also, **com·pla′cence.** —**compla′cent,** adj. —**com·pla′-cent·ly,** adv.

com·plain′ (kəm plān′) v. **1.** express pain, dissatisfaction, etc. **2.** accuse. —**com·plain′-er, com·plain′ant,** n. —**com·plaint′,** n.

com·plai′sant (kəm plā′sənt) adj. obliging.

com′ple·ment n. (kom′plə mənt) **1.** that which completes. **2.** full amount. —v. (-ment′) **3.** complete. —**com′ple·men′ta·ry,** adj.

com·plete′ (kəm plēt′) adj., v., -pleted, -pleting, —adj. **1.** entire; perfect. —v. **2.** make complete. —**com·plete′ly,** adv. —**com·plete′ness,** n. —**com·ple′tion,** n.

com·plex′ adj. (kəm pleks′, kom′pleks) **1.** having many parts; intricate. —n. (kom′-pleks) **2.** complex whole. **3.** obsession. —**com·plex′i·ty,** n.

com·plex′ion (kəm plek′shən) n. color of skin.

com′pli·cate′ (kom′pli kāt′) v., -cated, -cat-ing. make complex or difficult. —**com′pli-cat′ed,** adj. —**com′pli·ca′tion,** n.

com·plic′i·ty (kəm plis′i tē) n., pl. -ties. partnership in crime.

com′pli·ment n. (kom′plə mənt) **1.** expres-sion of praise. —v. (-ment′) **2.** express praise.

com′pli·men′ta·ry, adj. **1.** of or being a compliment; praising. **2.** free.

com·ply′ (kəm plī′) v., -plied, -plying. act in accordance. —**com·pli′ance,** n. —**com·pli′-ant, com·pli′a·ble,** adj.

compn compensate.

com·po′nent (kəm pō′nənt) adj. **1.** compos-ing. —n. **2.** part of whole.

com·port′ (kəm pôrt′) v. **1.** conduct (one-self). **2.** suit. —**com·port′ment,** n.

com·pose′ (kəm pōz′) v., -posed, -posing. **1.** make by uniting parts. **2.** constitute. **3.** put in order; calm. **4.** create and write. **5.** set printing type. —**com′po·si′tion** (kom′pə-zish′ən) n.

com·posed′, adj. calm.

com·pos′er, n. writer, esp. of music.

com·pos′ite (kəm poz′it) adj. made of many parts.

com′post (kom′pōst) n. decaying mixture of leaves, etc.

com·po′sure (kəm pō′zhər) n. calm.

com′pote (kom′pōt) n. stewed fruit.

com′pound adj. (kom′pound) **1.** having two or more parts, functions, etc. —n. (kom′-pound) **2.** something made by combining parts. **3.** enclosure with buildings. —v. (kəm pound′) **4.** combine. **5.** condone (crime) for a price. **6.** add to, esp. so as to worsen.

com′pre·hend′ (kom′pri hend′) v. **1.** under-stand. **2.** include. —**com′pre·hen′si·ble,** adj. —**com′pre·hen′sion,** n.

com′pre·hen′sive (-hen′siv) adj. inclusive. —**com′pre·hen′sive·ly,** adv. —**com′pre·hen′sive·ness,** n.

com·press′, v. (kəm pres′) **1.** press together. —n. (kom′pres) **2.** pad applied to affected part of body. —**com·pres′sion,** n. —**com·pres′sor,** n.

com·prise′ (kəm prīz′) v., -prised, -prising. consist of. Also, **com·prize′.** —**com·pris′al,** n.

com′pro·mise′ (kom′prə mīz′) n., v., -mised, -mising. —n. **1.** agreement to mutual concessions. **2.** something intermediate. —v. **3.** settle by compromise. **4.** endanger.

compt. 1. compartment. **2.** Also, **Compt.** comptroller.

comptr comparator.

comp·trol′ler (kən trō′lər) n. controller.

com·pul′sion (kəm pul′shən) n. compelling force. —**com·pul′so·ry** (-sə rē) adj.

com·pul′sive, adj. due to or acting on inner compulsion.

com·punc′tion (kəm pungk′shən) n. re-morse.

com·pute′ (kəm pyo͞ot′) v., -puted, -puting. calculate; figure. —**com′pu·ta′tion** (kom′-) n.

com·put′er, n. electronic apparatus for stor-ing and manipulating data.

com·pu′ter·ize′, v., -ized, -izing. **1.** do by computer. **2.** automate by computer, as a business. —**com·put′er·i·za′tion,** n.

computer virus, virus (def. 3).

Comr. Commissioner.

com′rade (kom′rad) n. companion. —**com′-rade·ship′,** n.

Com·sat (kom′sat′), *Trademark.* a privately owned corporation servicing the global communications satellite system. [*Com(mu-nications) Sat(ellite Corporation)*]

con (kon) adv., n., v., **conned, conning.** —adv. **1.** opposed to a plan, etc. —n. **2.** ar-gument against. —v. **3.** study. **4.** *Informal.* deceive; swindle.

CONAD (kon′ad), Continental Air Defense Command.

conc. 1. concentrate. **2.** concentrated. **3.** con-centration. **4.** concerning. **5.** concrete.

con·cave′ (kon kāv′) adj. curved inward.

—**con•cave′ly**, *adv.* —**con•cav′i•ty** (-kav′i-tē) *n.*

con•ceal′ (kən sēl′) *v.* hide. —**con•ceal′ment**, *n.*

con•cede′ (kən sēd′) *v.*, **-ceded, -ceding. 1.** admit. **2.** yield.

con•ceit′ (kən sēt′) *n.* **1.** excess self-esteem. **2.** fanciful idea. —**con•ceit′ed**, *adj.*

con•ceive′ (kən sēv′) *v.*, **-ceived, -ceiving. 1.** form (plan or idea). **2.** understand. **3.** become pregnant. —**con•ceiv′a•ble**, *adj.* —**con•ceiv′a•bly**, *adv.*

con′cen•trate′ (kon′sən trāt′) *v.*, **-trated, -trating**, —*v.* **1.** bring to one point. **2.** intensify. **3.** give full attention. —*n.* **4.** product of concentration. —**con′cen•tra′tion**, *n.*

concentration camp, guarded compound where political prisoners, minorities, etc., are confined.

con•cen′tric (kən sen′trik) *adj.* having common center.

con′cept (kon′sept) *n.* general notion.

con•cep′tion (kən sep′shən) *n.* **1.** act of conceiving. **2.** idea.

con•cep′tu•a•lize′ (-chōō ə līz′) *v.*, **-lized, -lizing. 1.** form a concept of. **2.** think in concepts. —**con•cep′tu•al•i•za′tion**, *n.*

con•cern′ (kən sûrn′) *v.* **1.** relate to. **2.** involve. **3.** worry. —*n.* **4.** matter that concerns. **5.** business firm.

con•cerned′, *adj.* **1.** interested or affected. **2.** troubled; anxious.

con•cern′ing, *prep.* about.

con′cert (kon′sûrt) *n.* **1.** musical performance. **2.** accord.

con•cert′ed (kən sûr′tid) *adj.* **1.** planned together. **2.** performed together or in cooperation. —**con•cert′ed•ly**, *adv.*

con′cer•ti′na (kon′sər tē′nə) *n.* small accordion.

con•cer′to (kən cher′tō) *n.*, *pl.* **-tos** or **-ti** (-tē). musical piece for principal instruments and orchestra.

con•ces′sion (kən sesh′ən) *n.* **1.** act of conceding. **2.** what is conceded. **3.** grant or franchise conceded by authority.

conch (kongk, konch) *n.* spiral shell.

con•cil′i•ate′ (kən sil′ē āt′) *v.*, **-ated, -ating**. win over; reconcile. —**con•cil′i•a′tion**, *n.* —**con•cil′i•a′tor**, *n.* —**con•cil′i•a•to′ry** (-ə-tôr′ē) *adj.*

con•cise′ (kən sīs′) *adj.* brief; succinct. —**con•cise′ly**, *adv.* —**con•cise′ness**, *n.*

concl conclusion.

con′clave (kon′klāv) *n.* private meeting.

con•clude′ (kən klōōd′) *v.*, **-cluded, -cluding. 1.** finish; settle. **2.** infer. —**con•clu′sion** (-klōō′zhən) *n.* —**con•clu′sive**, *adj.* —**con•clu′sive•ly**, *adv.*

con•coct′ (kon kokt′, kən-) *v.* make by combining. —**con•coc′tion**, *n.*

con•com′i•tant (kon kom′i tənt, kən-) *adj.* **1.** accompanying. —*n.* **2.** anything concomitant. —**con•com′i•tant•ly**, *adv.*

con′cord (kon′kôrd, kong′-) *n.* agreement.

con•cord′ance (kon kôr′dns, kən-) *n.* **1.** concord. **2.** index of key words of book.

con•cor′dat (kon kôr′dat) *n.* agreement, esp. between Pope and a government.

con′course (kon′kôrs, kong′-) *n.* **1.** assemblage. **2.** place for crowds in motion.

concr concrete.

con′crete, *adj.*, *n.*, *v.*, **-creted, -creting.** —*adj.* (kon′krēt, kon krēt′) **1.** real; objective. **2.** made of concrete. —*n.* (kon′krēt) **3.** material of cement and hard matter. —*v.* (konkrēt′) **4.** become solid. —**con•crete′ly**, *adv.* —**con•crete′ness**, *n.* —**con•cre′tion**, *n.*

con′cu•bine′ (kong′kyə bīn′) *n.* woman living with but not married to a man.

con•cu′pis•cent (-kyōō′pi sənt) *adj.* lustful. —**con•cu′pis•cence**, *n.*

con•cur′ (kən kûr′) *v.*, **-curred, -curring. 1.** agree. **2.** coincide. **3.** cooperate. —**con•cur′rence**, *n.* —**con•cur′rent**, *adj.* —**con•cur′rent•ly**, *adv.*

con•cus′sion (kən kush′ən) *n.* injury to brain from blow, etc.

cond. 1. condenser. **2.** condition. **3.** conditional. **4.** conductivity. **5.** conductor.

con•demn′ (kən dem′) *v.* **1.** denounce. **2.** pronounce guilty. **3.** judge unfit. **4.** acquire for public purpose. —**con′dem•na′tion** (kon′dem nā′shən, -dəm-) *n.*

con•dense′ (kən dens′) *v.*, **-densed, -densing. 1.** reduce to denser form. **2.** make or become compact. —**con′den•sa′tion** (kon′den-sā′shən) *n.* —**con•dens′er**, *n.*

condensed milk, thick, sweetened milk.

con′de•scend′ (kon′də send′) *v.* **1.** pretend equality with an inferior. **2.** deign. —**con′de•scen′sion**, *n.*

con′di•ment (kon′də mənt) *n.* seasoning.

con•di′tion (kən dish′ən) *n.* **1.** state of being or health. **2.** fit state. **3.** requirement. —*v.* **4.** put in condition. —**con•di′tion•al**, *adj.* —**con•di′tion•al•ly**, *adv.* —**con•di′tion•er**, *n.*

con•dole′ (kən dōl′) *v.*, **-doled, -doling.** sympathize in sorrow. —**con•do′lence**, *n.*

con′dom (kon′dəm, kun′-) *n.* contraceptive device worn over penis; prophylactic.

con′do•min′i•um (kon′də min′ē əm) *n.* apartment house in which units are individually owned. Also, *Informal,* **con′do** (-dō).

con•done′ (kən dōn′) *v.*, **-doned, -doning.** excuse.

con′dor (kon′dər, -dôr) *n.* vulture.

con•duce′ (kən dōōs′, -dyōōs′) *v.*, **-duced, -ducing.** contribute; lead. —**con•du′cive**, *adj.*

con′duct, *n.* (kon′dukt) **1.** behavior. **2.** management. —*v.* (kən dukt′) **3.** behave. **4.** manage. **5.** lead or carry. **6.** transmit, as electric current. —**con•duc′tion**, *n.* —**con•duc′tive**, *adj.* —**con′duc•tiv′i•ty**, *n.*

con•duct′ance, *n.* ability of conductor to transmit electricity.

con•duc′tor (kən duk′tər) *n.* **1.** guide. **2.** director of an orchestra. **3.** official on trains. **4.** substance that conveys electricity, heat, etc.

con′duit (kon′dwit) *n.* pipe for water, etc.

cone (kōn) *n.* **1.** form tapering from round base to single point. **2.** fruit of fir, pine, etc.

cone′flow′er, *n.* plant having flowers with cone-shaped center disks.

conf. 1. (in prescriptions) a confection. [from Latin *confectiō*] **2.** compare. [from Latin *confer*] **3.** conference. **4.** confessor. **5.** confidential. **6.** conformance.

con′fab (kon′fab) *n.* conversation.

con•fec′tion (kən fek′shən) *n.* candy or other sweet preparation. **—con•fec′tion•er,** *n.* **—con•fec′tion•er′y,** *n.*

confed. 1. confederacy. **2.** confederate. **3.** confederation. Also, **Confed.**

con•fed′er•a•cy (kən fed′ər ə sē) *n., pl.* **-cies. 1.** league. **2.** (*cap.*) Confederate States of America.

con•fed′er•ate, *adj., n., v.,* **-ated, -ating.** —*adj.* (kən fed′ər it) **1.** in league. **2.** (*cap.*) of **Confederate States of America,** separated from U.S. during Civil War. —*n.* (-ər it) **3.** ally. **4.** accomplice. **5.** (*cap.*) citizen of Confederate States of America. —*v.* (-ə rāt′) **6.** be allied. **—con•fed′er•a′tion,** *n.*

con•fer′ (kən fûr′) *v.,* **-ferred, -ferring. 1.** bestow. **2.** consult. **—con′fer•ee′** (kon′fə rē′) *n.* **—con•fer′ment,** *n.* **—con•fer′rer,** *n.*

con′fer•ence (kon′fər əns) *n.* **1.** meeting. **2.** discussion.

con•fess′ (kən fes′) *v.* **1.** admit. **2.** declare one's sins, as to priest. **—con•fes′sion,** *n.*

con•fess′ed•ly (-id lē) *adv.* by confession; admittedly.

con•fes′sion•al, *adj.* **1.** characteristic of confession. —*n.* **2.** place in church set apart for confession.

con•fes′sor, *n.* **1.** one who confesses. **2.** one who hears confessions.

con•fet′ti (kən fet′ē) *n.* bits of colored paper.

con′fi•dant′ (kon′fi dant′, -dänt′) *n.* one to whom secrets are told. **—con′fi•dante′,** *n. fem.*

con•fide′ (kən fīd′) *v.,* **-fided, -fiding. 1.** trust with secret. **2.** entrust.

con′fi•dence (kon′fi dəns) *n.* **1.** full trust. **2.** assurance. **—con′fi•dent,** *adj.* **—con′fi•dent•ly,** *adv.*

confidence game, swindle in which the swindler first gains the victim's confidence.

con′fi•den′tial (-den′shəl) *adj.* **1.** entrusted as secret. **2.** private. **—con′fi•den′tial•ly,** *adv.*

con•fig′u•ra′tion (kən fig′yə rā′shən) *n.* external form.

con•fine′, *v.,* **-fined, -fining,** *n.* —*v.* (kənfīn′) **1.** keep within bounds. **2.** shut or lock up. —*n.* (*pl.*) (kon′fīnz) **3.** boundary.

con•fined′, *adj.* **1.** restricted. **2.** stuffy.

con•fine′ment, *n.* **1.** imprisonment. **2.** childbirth. **3.** period of being confined.

con•firm′ (kən fûrm′) *v.* **1.** make sure. **2.** make valid. **3.** strengthen. **4.** admit into church. **—con′fir•ma′tion** (kon′fər-) *n.*

con•firmed′, *adj.* habitual; inveterate.

con′fis•cate′ (kon′fə skāt′) *v.,* **-cated, -cating.** seize by public authority. **—con′fis•ca′-tion,** *n.*

con′fla•gra′tion (kon′flə grā′shən) *n.* fierce fire.

con•flict′, *v.* (kən flikt′) **1.** oppose; clash. —*n.* (kon′flikt) **2.** battle. **3.** antagonism.

con′flu•ence (kon′flōō əns) *n.* act or place of flowing together. **—con′flu•ent,** *adj.*

con•form′ (kən fôrm′) *v.* **1.** accord; adapt. **2.** make similar. **—con•form′a•ble,** *adj.* **—con•form′ist,** *n.* **—con•form′i•ty,** *n.*

con′for•ma′tion (kon′fôr mā′shən) *n.* form.

con•found′ (kon found′) *v.* **1.** confuse. **2.** perplex.

con•found′ed, *adj.* **1.** bewildered. **2.** damned.

con•front′ (kən frunt′) *v.* **1.** meet or set facing. **2.** challenge openly. **—con′fron•ta′tion** (kon′frən tā′shən) *n.* **—con′fron•ta′tion•al,** *adj.*

con•fuse′ (kən fyōōz′) *v.,* **-fused, -fusing. 1.** throw into disorder. **2.** associate wrongly. **3.** disconcert. **—con•fu′sion,** *n.*

con•fute′ (-fyōōt′) *v.,* **-futed, -futing.** prove to be wrong. **—con′fu•ta′tion,** *n.*

Cong., 1. Congregational. **2.** Congress. **3.** Congressional.

con•geal′ (kən jēl′) *v.* make solid or thick. **—con•geal′ment,** *n.*

con•gen′ial (kən jēn′yəl) *adj.* agreeable; suited. **—con•ge′ni•al′i•ty** (-jē′nē al′i tē) *n.*

con•gen′i•tal (kən jen′i tl) *adj.* innate. **—con•gen′i•tal•ly,** *adv.*

con•gest′ (kən jest′) *v.* fill to excess. **—con•ges′tion,** *n.*

con•glom′er•ate, *n., adj., v.,* **-ated, -ating.** —*n.* (kən glom′ər it) **1.** mixture. **2.** rock formed of pebbles, etc. **3.** company owning variety of other companies. —*adj.* (-ər it) **4.** gathered into a ball. **5.** mixed. —*v.* (-ə rāt′) **6.** gather into round mass. **—con•glom′er•a′tion,** *n.*

congr congruent.

con•grat′u•late′ (kən grach′ə lāt′) *v.,* **-lated, -lating.** express sympathetic joy. **—con•grat′u•la′tion,** *n.* **—con•grat′u•la•to′ry,** *adj.*

con′gre•gate′ (kong′gri gāt′) *v.,* **-gated, -gating.** assemble. **—con′gre•ga′tion,** *n.*

con′gre•ga′tion•al, *adj.* **1.** of congregations. **2.** (*cap.*) denoting church denomination wherein each church acts independently. **—con′gre•ga′tion•al•ism,** *n.* **—con′gre•ga′tion•al•ist,** *n.*

con′gress (kong′gris) *n.* **1.** national legislative body, esp. (*cap.*) of the U.S. **2.** formal meeting. **—con•gres′sion•al** (kəng gresh′ə-nl) *adj.* —**con′gress•man,** *n.* —**con′gress• per′son,** *n.* —**con′gress•wom′an,** *n.fem.*

con′gru•ent (kong′grōō ənt) *adj.* **1.** agreeing. **2.** (of geometric figures) coinciding at all points when superimposed. —**con′gru•ence,** *n.*

con•gru′i•ty (kən grōō′i tē) *n., pl.* **-ties.** agreement. —**con′gru•ous** (kong′grōō əs) *adj.*

coni conical.

con′ic (kon′ik) *adj.* of or like cone. Also, **con′i•cal.**

co′ni•fer (kō′nə fər, kon′ə-) *n.* tree bearing cones. —**co•nif′er•ous** (-nif′ər əs) *adj.*

conj. 1. conjugation. **2.** conjunction. **3.** conjunctive.

con•jec′ture (kən jek′chər) *n., v.,* **-tured, -turing.** guess. —**con•jec′tur•al,** *adj.*

con•join′ (kən join′) *v.* join together.

con′ju•gal (kon′jə gəl) *adj.* of marriage. —**con′ju•gal•ly,** *adv.*

con′ju•gate′ *v.,* **-gated, -gating,** *adj.* —*v.* (kon′jə gāt′) **1.** give inflected forms of (verb) in a fixed order. —*adj.* (-git) **2.** coupled. —**con′ju•ga′tion,** *n.*

con•junc′tion (kən jungk′shən) *n.* **1.** union; combination. **2.** *Gram.* word that joins words, phrases, clauses, or sentences. —**con• junc′tive,** *adj.*

con•junc′ti•vi′tis (kən jungk′tə vī′tis) *n.* inflammation of mucous membrane of the eye.

con′jure (kon′jər, kun′-) *v.,* **-jured, -juring.** invoke or produce by magic. —**con′jur•er,** *n.*

conk (kongk) *v. Slang.* **1.** strike on the head. **2. conk out. a.** break down. **b.** go to sleep. —*n.* **3.** blow on the head.

Conn. Connecticut.

conn diag connection diagram.

con•nect′ (kə nekt′) *v.* join; link. —**con• nec′tion; Brit. con•nex′ion,** *n.* —**con•nec′- tive,** *adj., n.*

con•nive′ (kə nīv′) *v.,* **-nived, -niving.** conspire. —**con•niv′ance,** *n.* —**con•niv′er,** *n.*

con′nois•seur′ (kon′ə sûr′) *n.* skilled judge.

con•note′ (kə nōt′) *v.,* **-noted, -noting.** signify in addition; imply. —**con′no•ta′tion** (kon′ə tā′shən) *n.*

con•nu′bi•al (kə nōō′bē əl, -nyōō′-) *adj.* matrimonial. —**con•nu′bi•al•ly,** *adv.*

con′quer (kong′kər) *v.* **1.** acquire by force. **2.** defeat. —**con′quer•or,** *n.* —**con′quest,** *n.*

con•quis′ta•dor′ (kong kwis′tə dôr′, -kēs′-) *n., pl.* **-quis′ta•dors, -quis′ta•do′res** (-kēs′- tə dôr′ēz, -äz). 16th-century Spanish conqueror of the Americas.

Cons. 1. Conservative. **2.** Constable. **3.** Constitution. **4.** Consul. **5.** Consulting.

cons. 1. consecrated. **2.** conservative. **3.** (in prescriptions) conserve; keep. [from Latin *conservā*] **4.** consolidated. **5.** consonant. **6.** constable. **7.** constitution. **8.** constitutional. **9.** construction. **10.** consul. **11.** consulting.

con′san•guin′e•ous (kon′sang gwin′ē əs) *adj.* related by birth. —**con′san•guin′i•ty,** *n.*

con′science (kon′shəns) *n.* recognition of right or wrong in oneself. —**con′sci•en′tious** (-shē en′shəs) *adj.*

conscientious objector, person who refuses to serve in military for moral reasons.

con′scion•a•ble (-shən-) *adj.* approved by one's conscience.

con′scious (kon′shəs) *adj.* **1.** in possession of one's senses. **2.** aware. **3.** deliberate. —**con′scious•ly,** *adv.* —**con′scious•ness,** *n.*

con′script, *adj.* (kon′skript) **1.** drafted. —*n.* (kon′skript) **2.** one drafted. —*v.* (kən skript′) **3.** draft for military service. —**con• scrip′tion,** *n.*

consec consecutive.

con′se•crate′ (kon′si krāt′) *v.,* **-crated, -crating. 1.** make sacred. **2.** devote. —**con′- se•cra′tion,** *n.*

con•sec′u•tive (kən sek′yə tiv) *adj.* **1.** successive. **2.** logical. —**con•sec′u•tive•ly,** *adv.*

con•sen′sus (kən sen′səs) *n.* agreement.

con•sent′ (kən sent′) *v.* **1.** agree; comply. —*n.* **2.** assent.

con′se•quence′ (kon′si kwens′, -kwəns) *n.* **1.** effect. **2.** importance.

con′se•quent′, *adj.* following; resulting. —**con′se•quen′tial,** *adj.* —**con′se•quent•ly,** *adv.*

con′ser•va′tion (kon′sər vā′shən) *n.* preservation of resources. —**con′ser•va′tion•ism,** *n.* —**con′ser•va′tion•ist,** *n.*

con•serv′a•tive (kən sûr′və tiv) *adj.* **1.** favoring status quo. **2.** cautious. —*n.* **3.** conservative person. —**con•serv′a•tive•ly,** *adv.* —**con•serv′a•tism,** *n.*

con•serv′a•to′ry (-tôr′ē) *n., pl.* **-ries. 1.** school of music or drama. **2.** hothouse.

con•serve′, *v.,* **-served, -serving,** *n.* —*v.* (kən sûrv′) **1.** keep intact. —*n.* (kon′sûrv) **2.** preserves.

con•sid′er (kən sid′ər) *v.* **1.** think over. **2.** deem. **3.** respect. —**con•sid′er•ate,** *adj.* —**con•sid′er•ate•ly,** *adv.*

con•sid′er•a•ble, *adj.* important or sizable. —**con•sid′er•a•bly,** *adv.*

con•sid′er•a′tion (-ə rā′shən) *n.* **1.** thought. **2.** regard. **3.** fee.

con•sid′er•ing, *prep.* in view of.

con•sign′ (kən sīn′) *v.* **1.** deliver. **2.** entrust. **3.** ship. —**con•sign′ment,** *n.*

con•sist′ (kən sist′) *v.* be composed.

con•sist′en•cy (-sis′tən sē) *n., pl.* **-cies. 1.** firmness. **2.** density. **3.** adherence to principles, behavior, etc. —**con•sist′ent,** *adj.* —**con•sist′ent•ly,** *adv.*

con•sis′to•ry (kən sis′tə rē) *n., pl.* **-ries.** church council.

consol. consolidated.

con•sole′, *v.,* **-soled, -soling,** *n.* —*v.* (kən sōl′) **1.** cheer in sorrow. —*n.* (kon′sōl) **2.** control panel. —**con′so•la′tion,** *n.* —**con• sol′a•ble,** *adj.* —**con•sol′er,** *n.*

con•sol′i•date′ (kən sol′i dāt′) *v.*, **-dated, -dating. 1.** make or become firm. **2.** unite. **—con•sol′i•da′tion,** *n.*

con′som•mé′ (kon′sə mā′) *n.* clear soup.

con′so•nant (kon′sə nənt) *n.* **1.** letter for sound made by obstruction of breath. **—adj. 2.** in agreement. **—con′so•nance,** *n.*

con′sort, *n.* (kon′sôrt) **1.** spouse. **—v.** (kən-sôrt′) **2.** associate.

con•sor′ti•um (kən sôr′shē əm, -tē-) *n., pl.* **-tia** (-shē ə, -tē ə). **1.** combination for business purposes. **2.** association.

conspec construction specification.

consperg. (in prescriptions) dust; sprinkle. [from Latin *consperge*]

con•spic′u•ous (kən spik′yōō əs) *adj.* **1.** easily seen. **2.** notable. **—con•spic′u•ous•ly,** *adv.* **—con•spic′u•ous•ness,** *n.*

con•spire′ (kən spīªr′) *v.*, **-spired, -spiring.** plot together. **—con•spir′a•cy** (-spir′ə sē) *n.* **—con•spir′a•tor,** *n.*

Const. Constitution.

const. 1. constable. **2.** constant. **3.** constitution. **4.** constitutional. **5.** construction.

con′sta•ble (kon′stə bəl) *n.* police officer.

con•stab′u•lar′y (kən stab′yə ler′ē) *n., pl.* **-ies.** police.

con′stant (kon′stənt) *adj.* **1.** uniform. **2.** uninterrupted. **3.** faithful. **—n. 4.** something unchanging. **—con′stan•cy,** *n.* **—con′stant•ly,** *adv.*

con′stel•la′tion (kon′stə lā′shən) *n.* group of stars.

con′ster•na′tion (kon′stər nā′shən) *n.* utter dismay.

con′sti•pate′ (kon′stə pāt′) *v.*, **-pated, -pating.** cause difficult evacuation of bowels. **—con′sti•pa′tion,** *n.*

con•stit′u•ent (kən stich′ōō ənt) *adj.* **1.** being part; composing. **—n. 2.** ingredient. **3.** represented voter. **—con•stit′u•en•cy,** *n.*

con′sti•tute′ (kon′sti tōōt′, -tyōōt′) *v.*, **-tuted, -tuting. 1.** compose. **2.** make.

con′sti•tu′tion, *n.* **1.** make-up. **2.** physical condition. **3.** system of governmental principles. **—con′sti•tu′tion•al,** *adj.*

constr. 1. constraint. **2.** construction. **3.** construed.

con•strain′ (kən strān′) *v.* **1.** force or oblige. **2.** confine. **—con•strained′,** *adj.* **—con•straint′,** *n.*

con•strict′ (kən strikt′) *v.* draw together; shrink. **—con•stric′tion,** *n.* **—con•stric′tor,** *n.*

con•struct′ (kən strukt′) *v.* build or devise. **—con•struc′tion,** *n.*

con•struc′tion•ist, *n.* person who interprets laws in specified manner.

con•struc′tive, *adj.* **1.** of construction. **2.** helpful. **—con•struc′tive•ly,** *adv.*

con•strue′ (kən strōō′) *v.*, **-strued, -struing.** interpret.

con′sul (kon′səl) *n.* local diplomatic official. **—con′su•lar,** *adj.* **—con′su•late** (-sə lit) *n.*

con•sult′ (kən sult′) *v.* **1.** ask advice of. **2.** refer to. **3.** confer. **—con•sult′ant,** *n.* **—con′sul•ta′tion,** *n.*

con•sume′ (kən sōōm′) *v.*, **-sumed, -suming. 1.** use up. **2.** devour. **3.** engross.

con•sum′er, *n.* **1.** one that consumes. **2.** purchaser of goods for personal use.

con•sum′er•ism, *n.* policies protecting consumers.

con′sum•mate′, *v.*, **-mated, -mating,** *adj.* **—v.** (kon′sə māt′), *adj.* (kən sum′it, kon′sə-mit). complete or perfect. **—con′sum•ma′-tion,** *n.*

con•sump′tion (kən sump′shən) *n.* **1.** act of consuming. **2.** amount consumed. **3.** wasting disease, esp. tuberculosis of lungs. **—con•sump′tive,** *adj., n.*

cont., continued.

con′tact (kon′takt) *n.* **1.** a touching. **2.** association. **3.** business acquaintance. **—v. 4.** put or bring into contact. **5.** communicate with.

contact lens, corrective lens put directly on eye.

con•ta′gion (kən tā′jən) *n.* spread of disease by contact. **—con•ta′gious,** *adj.*

con•tain′ (kən tān′) *v.* **1.** have within itself. **2.** have space for. **—con•tain′er,** *n.*

con•tam′i•nate′ (kən tam′ə nāt′) *v.*, **-nated, -nating.** make impure. **—con•tam′i•na′tion,** *n.*

contd., continued.

con•temn′ (kən tem′) *v.* scorn.

contemp. contemporary.

con′tem•plate′ (kon′təm plāt′, -tem-) *v.*, **-plated, -plating. 1.** consider. **2.** observe. **3.** intend. **—con′tem•pla′tion,** *n.* **—con•tem′-pla•tive** (kən tem′plə tiv′) *adj.*

con•tem′po•rar′y (kən tem′pə rer′ē) *adj., n., pl.* **-raries.** **—adj. 1.** Also, **con•tem′po•ra′ne•ous** (-rā′nē əs). of same age or period. **—n. 2.** contemporary person.

con•tempt′ (kən tempt′) *n.* **1.** scorn. **2.** disgrace. **3.** disrespect of court. **—con•tempt′i•ble,** *adj.* **—con•temp′tu•ous,** *adj.*

con•tend′ (kən tend′) *v.* **1.** be in struggle. **2.** assert. **—con•tend′er,** *n.*

con•tent′, *adj.* (kən tent′) **1.** Also, **con•tent′ed.** satisfied. **2.** willing. **—v.** (kən tent′) **3.** make content. **—n.** (kən tent′) **4.** Also, **con•tent′ment.** ease of mind. **5.** (kon′tent) (*often pl.*). what is contained. **6.** (kon′tent) capacity. **—con•tent′ed•ly,** *adv.*

con•ten′tion (-shən) *n.* **1.** controversy. **2.** assertion. **—con•ten′tious,** *adj.*

con′test, *n.* (kon′test) **1.** struggle; competition. **—v.** (kən test′) **2.** fight for. **3.** dispute. **—con•test′ant,** *n.*

con′text (kon′tekst) *n.* surrounding words or circumstances. **—con•tex′tu•al** (kən teks′-chōō əl) *adj.*

contg. containing.

con•tig′u•ous (kən tig′yōō əs) *adj.* **1.** touching. **2.** near.

contin. continued.

con′ti•nent (kon′tn ənt) *n.* **1.** major land mass. —*adj.* **2.** characterized by self-restraint. —**con′ti•nen′tal** (-nen′tl) *adj.* —**con′ti•nence,** *n.*

con•tin′gen•cy (kən tin′jən sē) *n., pl.* **-cies.** chance; event.

con•tin′gent, *adj.* **1.** conditional; possible. —*n.* **2.** group. **3.** contingency.

con•tin′u•al (kən tin′yō̅o̅ əl) **1.** happening regularly or frequently. **2.** happening without interruption.

—**Usage.** Use CONTINUAL for actions that occur over and over again (especially actions that are annoying): *The dog's continual barking was driving me crazy.* The word CONTINUOUS is used for actions that keep going and do not stop: *We had continuous electricity during the big storm.*

con•tin′ue, *v.,* -tinued, -tinuing. **1.** go or carry on. **2.** stay. **3.** extend. **4.** carry over. —**con•tin′u•al•ly,** *adv.* —**con•tin′u•ance, con•tin′u•a′tion,** *n.*

con•ti•nu′i•ty (kon′tn ō̅o̅′i tē, -tn yō̅o̅′-) *n., pl.* **-ties. 1.** continuous whole. **2.** script.

con•tin′u•ous (kən tin′yō̅o̅ əs) *adj.* going on without stop; uninterrupted. —**con•tin′u•ous•ly,** *adv.*
—**Usage.** See CONTINUAL.

con•tin′u•um (-yō̅o̅ əm) *n., pl.* **-ua.** continuous extent, series, or whole.

con•tort′ (kən tôrt′) *v.* twist; distort. —**con•tor′tion,** *n.*

con•tor′tion•ist, *n.* person who can twist into unusual positions.

con′tour (kon′tŏo̅r) *n.* outline.

contr. 1. contract. **2.** contracted. **3.** contraction. **4.** contractor. **5.** contralto. **6.** contrary. **7.** contrasted. **8.** control. **9.** controller.

contra-, prefix meaning against, opposite, or opposing, as *contradict.*

con′tra•band (kon′trə band′) *n.* goods prohibited from shipment. —**con′tra•band′, *adj.***

con′tra•cep′tion (-sep′shən) *n.* deliberate prevention of pregnancy. —**con′tra•cep′tive,** *adj., n.*

con′tract, *n.* (kon′trakt) **1.** written agreement. —*v.* (kən trakt′) **2.** draw together; shorten. **3.** acquire. **4.** agree. —**con•trac′tion,** *n.* —**con•trac′tu•al,** *adj.*

con•trac•tor (kon′trak tər) *n.* one who supplies work by contract.

con′tra•dict′ (kon′trə dikt′) *v.* deny as being correct or true. —**con′tra•dic′tion,** *n.* —**con′tra•dic′to•ry,** *adj.*

con•tral′to (kən tral′tō) *n., pl.* **-tos.** lowest female voice.

con•trap′tion (kən trap′shən) *n.* strange machine; gadget.

con′tra•pun′tal (kon′trə pun′tl) *adj.* of or relating to counterpoint.

con′tra•ry (kon′trer ē) *adj., n., pl.* **-ries.** —*adj.* **1.** opposite. **2.** (*also* kən trâr′ē) per-verse. —*n.* **3.** something contrary. —**con′tra•ri•ness,** *n.* —**con′tra•ri•ly,** —**con′tra•ri•wise′,** *adv.*

con•trast′, *v.* (kən trast′) **1.** show unlikeness. **2.** compare. —*n.* (kon′trast) **3.** show of unlikeness. **4.** something unlike.

con′tra•vene′ (kon′trə vēn′) *v.,* -vened, -vening. **1.** oppose. **2.** violate. —**con′tra•ven′tion** (-ven′shən) *n.*

cont. rem. (in prescriptions) let the medicines be continued. [from Latin *continuāntur remedia*]

contrib. 1. contribution. **2.** contributor.

con•trib′ute (kən trib′yō̅o̅t) *v.,* -uted, -uting. give in part; donate. —**con′tri•bu′tion** (kon′trə byō̅o̅′shən) *n.* —**con•trib′u•tor,** *n.* —**con•trib′u•to′ry,** *adj.*

con•trite′ (kən trīt′) *adj.* penitent. —**con•tri′tion** (-trish′ən) *n.*

con•trive′ (kən trīv′) *v.,* -trived, -triving. **1.** plan; devise. **2.** plot. —**con•triv′ance,** *n.*

contro contracting officer.

con•trol′ (kən trōl′) *v.,* -trolled, -trolling, *n.* —*v.* **1.** have direction over. **2.** restrain. —*n.* **3.** power of controlling. **4.** restraint. **5.** regulating device. —**con•trol′la•ble,** *adj.*

con•trol′ler, *n.* **1.** officer who superintends finances. **2.** regulator.

con′tro•ver′sy (kon′trə vûr′sē) *n., pl.* **-sies.** dispute or debate. —**con′tro•ver′sial** (-vûr′shəl) *adj.* —**con′tro•ver′sial•ly,** *adv.*

con′tro•vert′ (kon′trə vûrt′, kon′trə vûrt′) *v.* dispute. —**con′tro•vert′i•ble,** *adj.*

con′tu•ma′cious (kon′tŏo̅ mā′shəs, -tyō̅o̅-) *adj.* stubbornly disobedient. —**con′tu•ma•cy** (-tŏo̅ mə sē, -tyō̅o̅-) *n.*

con′tu•me•ly (kon′tŏo̅ mə lē, -tyō̅o̅-) *n., pl.* **-lies.** contemptuous treatment.

con•tu′sion (kən tō̅o̅′zhən, -tyō̅o̅′-) *n.* bruise.

co•nun′drum (kə nun′drəm) *n.* riddle involving pun.

con′ur•ba′tion (kon′ər bā′shən) *n.* continuous mass of urban settlements.

conv. 1. convention. **2.** conventional. **3.** convertible. **4.** convocation.

con′va•lesce′ (kon′və les′) *v.,* -lesced, -lescing. recover from illness. —**con′va•les′cence,** *n.* —**con′va•les′cent,** *adj., n.*

con•vec′tion (kən vek′shən) *n.* transference of heat by movement of heated matter.

con•vene′ (kən vēn′) *v.,* -vened, -vening. assemble.

con•ven′ient (-vēn′yənt) *adj.* handy or favorable. —**con•ven′ience,** *n.* —**con•ven′ient•ly,** *adv.*

con′vent (kon′vent, -vənt) *n.* community of nuns.

con•ven′tion (kən ven′shən) *n.* **1.** meeting. **2.** accepted usage. —**con•ven′tion•al,** *adj.*

con•verge′ (kən vûrj′) *v.,* -verged, -verging. meet in a point. —**con•ver′gence,** *n.* —**con•ver′gent,** *adj.*

con•ver′sant (kən vûr′sənt) *adj.* acquainted.

con·ver·sa'tion (kon'vər sā'shən) *n.* informal discussion. —**con'ver·sa'tion·al,** *adj.* —**con'ver·sa'tion·al·ist,** *n.*

con·verse', *v.,* -versed, -versing, *adj., n.* —*v.* (kən vûrs') **1.** talk informally. —*adj., n.* (*adj.* kən vûrs'; *n.* kon'vûrs) **2.** opposite. —**con·verse'ly,** *adv.*

con·vert', *v.* (kən vûrt') **1.** change. **2.** persuade to different beliefs. **3.** exchange for something of equivalent value. —*n.* (kon'vûrt) **4.** converted person. —**con·ver'sion,** *n.* —**con·vert'er,** *n.*

con·vert'i·ble, *adj.* **1.** able to be converted. —*n.* **2.** automobile with folding top.

con·vex' (kon veks') *adj.* curved outward. —**con·vex'i·ty,** *n.*

con·vey' (kən vā') *v.* **1.** transport. **2.** transmit. —**con·vey'or, con·vey'er,** *n.*

con·vey'ance, *n.* **1.** act of conveying. **2.** vehicle. **3.** transfer of property.

con·vict', *v.* (kən vikt') **1.** find guilty. —*n.* (kon'vikt) **2.** convicted person.

con·vic'tion, *n.* **1.** a convicting. **2.** firm belief.

con·vince' (kən vins') *v.,* -vinced, -vincing. cause to believe. —**con·vinc'ing,** *adj.* —**con·vinc'ing·ly,** *adv.*

con·viv'i·al (kən viv'ē əl) *adj.* sociable. —**con·viv'i·al'i·ty** (-al'i tē) *n.*

convn convection.

con·voke' (kən vōk') *v.,* -voked, -voking. call together. —**con'vo·ca'tion** (kon'vō kā'shən) *n.*

con'vo·lu'tion (kon'və lōō'shən) *n.* coil. —**con'vo·lut'ed,** *adj.*

con'voy (kon'voi) *v.* **1.** escort for protection. —*n.* **2.** ship, etc., that convoys. **3.** group of ships with convoy.

con·vulse' (kən vuls') *v.,* -vulsed, -vulsing. shake violently. —**con·vul'sion,** *n.* —**con·vul'sive,** *adj.* —**con·vul'sive·ly,** *adv.*

co'ny (kō'nē, kun'ē) *n., pl.* -nies. rabbit fur.

coo (kōō) *v.,* cooed, cooing. murmur softly. —**coo,** *n.*

cook (kōōk) *v.* **1.** prepare by heating. —*n.* **2.** person who cooks. —**cook'book',** *n.* —**cook'er·y,** *n.*

cook'ie, *n.* small sweet cake.

cook'out', *n.* outdoor gathering at which food is cooked and eaten.

cool (kōōl) *adj.* **1.** moderately cold. **2.** calm. **3.** not enthusiastic. **4.** *Slang.* great; excellent. —*v.* **5.** make or become cool. —**cool'ant,** *n.* —**cool'er,** *n.* —**cool'ly,** *adv.* —**cool'ness,** *n.*

coo'lie (kōō'lē) *n.* unskilled laborer, esp. formerly in Far East.

coop (kōōp, kōōp) *n.* **1.** cage for fowls. —*v.* **2.** keep in coop.

coop'er, *n.* barrel maker.

co·op'er·ate' (kō op'ə rāt') *v.,* -ated, -ating. work or act together. Also, **co-op'er·ate'.** —**co·op'er·a'tion,** *n.*

co·op'er·a·tive (-ər ə tiv) *adj.* **1.** involving cooperation. **2.** willing to act with others.

—*n.* **3.** Also, **co-op** (kō'op'). jointly owned apartment house or business.

co-opt' (kō opt') *v.* **1.** choose as fellow member. **2.** win over into larger group.

coord coordinate.

co·or'di·nate', *v.,* -nated, -nating, *adj., n.* —*v.* (kō ôr'dn āt') **1.** put in same or due order. **2.** adjust. —*adj., n.* (-dn it) **3.** equal. Also, **co-or'di·nate.** —**co·or'di·na'tion,** *n.* —**co·or'di·na'tor,** *n.*

coot (kōōt) *n.* aquatic bird.

cop (kop) *n. Slang.* police officer.

co'pay' (kō'pā') *n.* percentage of fee, or fixed amount, paid by patient to health-care provider. Also, **co'pay'ment.**

COPD chronic obstructive pulmonary disease.

cope (kōp) *v.,* coped, coping, *n.* —*v.* **1.** struggle successfully. —*n.* **2.** cloak worn by priests.

cop'i·er (kop'ē ər) *n.* machine for making copies.

co'pi'lot (kō'pī'lət) *n.* aircraft pilot second in command.

cop'ing (kō'ping) *n.* top course of wall.

co'pi·ous (kō'pē əs) *adj.* abundant. —**co'pi·ous·ly,** *adv.*

cop'per (kop'ər) *n.* soft reddish metallic element.

cop'per·head', *n.* venomous snake.

cop pl copper plate.

copse (kops) *n.* thicket. Also, **cop'pice.**

cop'u·late' (kop'yə lāt') *v.,* -lated, -lating. have sexual intercourse. —**cop'u·la'tion,** *n.*

cop'y (kop'ē) *n.; pl.* copies, *v.,* copied, copying. —*n.* **1.** reproduction or imitation. **2.** material to be reproduced. —*v.* **3.** make copy of. —**cop'y·ist,** *n.*

cop'y·cat', *n.* imitator.

cop'y·right', *n.* **1.** exclusive control of book, picture, etc. —*v.* **2.** secure copyright on. —*adj.* **3.** covered by copyright.

co·quette' (kō ket') *n.* female flirt. —**co·quet'tish,** *adj.*

Cor. 1. *Bible.* Corinthians. **2.** Coroner.

cor. 1. corner. **2.** cornet. **3.** coroner. **4.** corpus. **5.** correct. **6.** corrected. **7.** correction. **8.** correlative. **9.** correspondence. **10.** correspondent. **11.** corresponding.

cor'al (kôr'əl) *n.* **1.** substance formed of skeletons of certain marine animals. **2.** reddish yellow.

cord (kôrd) *n.* **1.** small rope. **2.** *Elect.* small insulated cable. **3.** unit of measurement of wood.

cor'dial (kôr'jəl) *adj.* **1.** hearty; friendly. —*n.* **2.** liqueur. —**cor·dial'i·ty** (-jal'i tē, -jē al'-) *n.* —**cor'dial·ly,** *adv.*

cord'less, *adj.* (of electrical appliance) having self-contained power supply.

cor'don (kôr'dn) *n.* **1.** honorary ribbon. **2.** line of sentinels.

cor'do·van (kôr'də vən) *n.* soft leather.

cor'du·roy' (kôr'də roi') *n.* ribbed fabric.

C

core (kôr) *n.*, *v.*, **cored, coring.** —*n.* **1.** central part. —*v.* **2.** remove core of.

co/ri•an/der (kôr/ē an/dər) *n.* herb with pungent leaves and seeds.

cork (kôrk) *n.* **1.** bark of an oak tree. **2.** stopper of cork, rubber, etc. —*v.* **3.** stop with a cork.

cork/screw/, *n.* spiral, pointed instrument for pulling corks.

cor/mo•rant (kôr/mər ənt) *n.* water bird.

corn (kôrn) *n.* **1.** maize. **2.** any edible grain. **3.** single seed. **4.** horny callus, esp. on toe. —*v.* **5.** preserve, esp. in brine.

corn bread, *n.* bread made with cornmeal.

corn/cob/, *n.* core of an ear of corn which holds grains.

cor/ne•a (kôr/nē ə) *n.* transparent part of coat of the eye. —**cor/ne•al**, *adj.*

cor/ner (kôr/nər) *n.* **1.** place or surface where two lines meet. **2.** exclusive control. —*v.* **3.** put in corner. **4.** gain exclusive control of (stock or commodity).

cor/ner•stone/, *n.* **1.** stone representing start of building construction. **2.** something basic; starting point.

cor•net/ (kôr net/) *n.* wind instrument resembling trumpet.

cor/nice (kôr/nis) *n.* horizontal projection at top of a wall.

corn/meal/, *n.* meal made from corn.

corn/starch/, *n.* starchy flour made from corn.

cor/nu•co/pi•a (kôr/nə kō/pē ə, -nyə-) *n.* horn-shaped container of food, etc.; horn of plenty.

corn/y, *adj.*, **-ier, -iest.** trite, sentimental, or old-fashioned.

coroll. corollary. Also, **corol.**

co•rol/la (kə rol/ə, -rō/lə) *n.* petals of a flower.

cor/ol•lar/y (kôr/ə ler/ē) *n.*, *pl.* **-ies.** proposition proved in proving another.

co•ro/na (kə rō/nə) *n.*, *pl.* **-nas, -nae** (-nē). circle of light, esp. around sun or moon.

cor/o•nar/y (kôr/ə ner/ē) *adj.*, *n.*, *pl.* **-naries.** —*adj.* **1.** of arteries supplying heart tissues. —*n.* **2.** heart attack.

cor/o•na/tion (kôr/ə nā/shən) *n.* crowning.

cor/o•ner (kôr/ə nər) *n.* official who investigates deaths not clearly natural.

cor/o•net (kôr/ə net/) *n.* small crown.

corp., corporation.

corpl. corporal. Also, **Corpl.**

corpn. corporation.

cor/po•ral (kôr/pər əl) *adj.* **1.** physical. **2.** *Mil.* officer below sergeant.

cor/po•ra/tion (-rā/shən) *n.* legally formed association for business, etc. —**cor/po•rate** (-pər it, -prit) *adj.*

cor•po/re•al (kôr pôr/ē əl) *adj.* tangible.

corps (kôr) *n.*, *pl.* **corps. 1.** military unit. **2.** any group.

corpse (kôrps) *n.* dead body.

cor/pu•lent (kôr/pyə lənt) *adj.* fat. —**cor/pu•lence**, *n.*

cor/pus (kôr/pəs) *n.*, *pl.* **-pora** (-pər ə). **1.** comprehensive collection of writings. **2.** body, esp. when dead.

cor/pus•cle (kôr/pə səl) *n.* minute body in blood.

corr. 1. correct. **2.** corrected. **3.** correction. **4.** correspond. **5.** correspondence. **6.** correspondent. **7.** corresponding. **8.** corrugated. **9.** corrupt. **10.** corrupted. **11.** corruption.

cor•ral/ (kə ral/) *n.*, *v.*, **-ralled, -ralling.** —*n.* **1.** pen for stock. —*v.* **2.** keep in corral. **3.** corner or capture.

cor•rect/ (kə rekt/) *v.* **1.** mark or remove errors. **2.** rebuke or punish. **3.** counteract. —*adj.* **4.** right. —**cor•rec/tion**, *n.* —**cor•rec/tion•al**, *adj.* —**cor•rec/tive**, *adj.*, *n.* —**cor•rect/ly**, *adv.*

correl. correlative.

cor/re•late/ (kôr/ə lāt/) *v.*, **-lated, -lating.** bring into mutual relation. —**cor/re•la/tion**, *n.* —**cor•rel/a•tive** (kə rel/ə tiv) *adj.*, *n.*

corresp. correspondence.

cor/re•spond/ (kôr/ə spond/) *v.* **1.** conform or be similar. **2.** communicate by letters. —**cor/re•spond/ence**, *n.*

cor/re•spond/ent, *n.* **1.** writer of letters. **2.** reporter in field. —*adj.* **3.** corresponding.

cor/ri•dor (kôr/i dər) *n.* passageway.

cor•rob/o•rate/ (kə rob/ə rāt/) *v.*, **-rated, -rating.** confirm. —**cor•rob/o•ra/tion**, *n.* —**cor•rob/o•ra/tive** (-ə rā/tiv, -ər ə tiv) *adj.*

cor•rode/ (kə rōd/) *v.*, **-roded, -roding. 1.** eat away gradually. **2.** be eaten away. —**cor•ro/sion** (-rō/zhən) *n.* —**cor•ro/sive**, *adj.*, *n.*

cor/ru•gate/ (kôr/ə gāt/) *v.*, **-gated, -gating.** bend into folds. —**cor/ru•ga/tion**, *n.*

cor•rupt/ (kə rupt/) *adj.* **1.** dishonest. **2.** tainted. —*v.* **3.** make or become corrupt. —**cor•rupt/i•ble**, *adj.* —**cor•rup/tion**, **cor•rupt/ness**, *n.*

cor•sage/ (kôr säzh/) *n.* small bouquet to be worn.

cor/sair (kôr/sâr) *n.* pirate.

cor/set (kôr/sit) *n.* undergarment for shaping torso.

corspnd correspond.

cort. (in prescriptions) the bark. [from Latin *cortex*]

cor/tege/ (kôr tezh/) *n.* procession.

cor/tex (kôr/teks) *n.* **1.** bark. **2.** outer covering of brain or other organ. —**cor/ti•cal** (-ti-kəl) *adj.*

cor/ti•sone/ (kôr/tə zōn/, -sōn/) *n.* hormone used esp. in treating inflammatory diseases.

cor•vette/ (kôr vet/) *n.* small fast vessel.

cos *Trigonometry.* cosine.

cos. 1. companies. **2.** consul. **3.** consulship. **4.** counties.

C.O.S. cash on shipment. Also, **c.o.s.**

cosh *Trigonometry.* hyperbolic cosine.

cos•met/ic (koz met/ik) *n.* **1.** product used for beautifying skin, hair, etc. —*adj.* **2.** of cosmetics. **3.** superficial. **—cos′me•tol′o•gist** (-mə tol′ə jist) *n.* **—cos′me•tol′o•gy,** *n.*

cos′mic (koz′mik) *adj.* **1.** of the cosmos. **2.** vast.

cos•mol′o•gy (-mol′ə jē) *n.* study of the origin and structure of the universe. **—cos′mo•log′i•cal** (-mə loj′i kəl) *adj.*

cos′mo•pol′i•tan (koz′mə pol′i tn) *adj.* worldly.

cos′mos (-məs, -mōs) *n.* ordered universe.

cost (kôst) *n.* **1.** price paid. **2.** loss or penalty. **—v. 3.** require as payment. **—cost′ly,** *adj.*

cost′-ef•fec′tive, *adj.* producing optimum results for the expenditure.

cost of living, average amount paid for basic necessities.

cos′tume (kos′tōōm, -tyōōm) *n., v.,* **-tumed, -tuming. —n. 1.** historical or theatrical dress. **—v. 2.** dress or supply with costume.

co′sy (kō′zē) *adj.,* **-sier, -siest.** cozy.

cot (kot) *n.* light bed.

cote (kōt) *n.* shelter for pigeons, sheep, etc.

co′te•rie (kō′tə rē) *n.* group of social acquaintances.

coth *Trigonometry.* hyperbolic cotangent.

co•til′lion (kə til′yən) *n.* **1.** elaborate dance. **2.** formal ball.

cot′tage (kot′ij) *n.* small house.

cottage cheese, soft, mild cheese made from skim milk.

cot′ter (kot′ər) *n.* pin fitting into machinery opening.

cot′ton (kot′n) *n.* downy plant substance made into fabric.

cot′ton-mouth′ (-mouth′) *n.* venomous snake. Also, **water moccasin.**

cot′ton•seed′, *n.* seed of cotton plant, yielding an oil **(cottonseed oil)** used in cooking and medicine.

cot′ton•wood′, *n.* species of poplar.

couch (kouch) *n.* **1.** bed. **—v. 2.** express.

couch potato, *Informal.* person who watches much television.

cou′gar (kōō′gər) *n.* large American wildcat.

cough (kôf) *v.* **1.** expel air from lungs suddenly and loudly. **—n. 2.** act or sound of coughing.

cough drop, lozenge for relieving sore throat, etc.

could (kŏŏd; *unstressed* kəd) *v.* pt. of **can.**

coun′cil (koun′səl) *n.* deliberative or advisory body. **—coun′cil•man,** *n.* **—coun′cil•wo′man,** *n.fem.* **—coun′ci•lor, coun′cil•lor,** *n.*

coun′sel (koun′səl) *n., v.,* **-seled, -seling. —n. 1.** advice. **2.** consultation. **3.** lawyer. **—v. 4.** advise. **—coun′se•lor, coun′sel•lor,** *n.*

count (kount) *v.* **1.** find total number. **2.** name numbers to. **3.** esteem. **4.** rely. **5.** be noticed. **—n. 6.** a counting. **7.** total number.

8. item in indictment. **9.** European nobleman.

count′down′, *n.* backward counting in time units to scheduled event.

coun′te•nance (koun′tn əns) *n., v.,* **-nanced, -nancing. —n. 1.** appearance; face. **2.** encouragement. **—v. 3.** tolerate.

count′er (koun′tər) *n.* **1.** table or display case in store. **2.** one that counts. **3.** anything opposite. **—v. 4.** oppose. **5.** return (blow). **—adv., adj. 6.** contrary.

counter-, prefix indicating: **1.** against, as *counterintelligence.* **2.** in response to, as *counterattack.* **3.** opposiitve, as *counterclockwise.* **4.** complementary, as *counterbalance.*

coun′ter•act′, *v.* act against; neutralize. **—coun′ter•ac′tion,** *n.*

coun′ter•at•tack′, *n., v.* attack in response.

coun′ter•bal′ance, *n., v.,* **-anced, -ancing. —n.** (koun′tər bal′əns) **1.** anything that balances another. **—v.** (koun′tər bal′əns) **2.** offset.

coun′ter•clock′wise′, *adv., adj.* opposite to direction of turning clock hands.

coun′ter•cul′ture, *n.* culture of those opposed to prevailing culture or values.

coun′ter•feit (-fit) *adj.* **1.** fraudulently imitative. **—n. 2.** fraudulent imitation. **—v. 3.** make counterfeits. **4.** feign. **—coun′ter•feit′er,** *n.*

coun′ter•in•tel′li•gence, *n.* thwarting of espionage of a foreign power.

coun′ter•mand′ (-mand′) *v.* revoke (command).

coun′ter•part′, *n.* match or complement.

coun′ter•point′, *n.* combining of melodies.

coun′ter•pro•duc′tive, *adj.* giving contrary results.

coun′ter•sign, *n.* **1.** secret signal. **—v. 2.** sign to confirm another signature.

count′ess (koun′tis) *n.* **1.** wife of count or earl. **2.** woman equal in rank to count or earl.

count′less, *adj.* innumerable.

coun′try (kun′trē) *n., pl.* **-tries. 1.** region. **2.** nation. **3.** rural districts. **—coun′try•man,** *n.* **—coun′try•wom′an,** *n.fem.* **—coun′try•side′,** *n.*

coun′ty (koun′tē) *n., pl.* **-ties.** political unit within state.

coup (kōō) *n., pl.* **coups.** daring and successful stroke.

coup d′é•tat′ (kōō′ dä tä′) *pl.* **coups d′état** (-dä täz′, -tä′). overthrow of a government.

coupe (kōōp) *n.* small, two-door car. Also, **cou•pé′** (kōō pā′).

cou′ple (kup′əl) *n., v.,* **-pled, -pling. —n. 1.** group of two; pair. **—v. 2.** fasten or unite. **—cou′pler,** *n.* **—cou′pling,** *n.*

—Usage. Do not confuse PAIR and COUPLE. Both words have the meaning "a group of two" but are used differently. PAIR is used when two things come as a set, with one not

C

usually used without the other: *a pair of socks, a pair of gloves* or when there is one item that has two parts, as in *a pair of shorts, a pair of scissors.* COUPLE is used for things of the same kind that happen to be two in number: *a couple of books, a couple of chairs.*

cou′plet (kup′lit) *n.* pair of rhyming lines.

cou′pon (kōō′pon, kyōō′-) *n.* certificate entitling holder to a gift or discount.

cour′age (kûr′ij, kur′-) *n.* bravery. —**cou•ra′geous** (kə rā′jəs) *adj.* —**cou•ra′geous•ly,** *adv.*

cour′i•er (kûr′ē ər) *n.* messenger.

course (kôrs) *n., v.,* **coursed, coursing.** —*n.* **1.** continuous passage. **2.** route. **3.** manner. **4.** series of studies. **5.** one part of meal. —*v.* **6.** run.

cours′er, *n.* swift horse.

court (kôrt) *n.* **1.** enclosed space. **2.** level area for certain games. **3.** palace. **4.** assembly held by sovereign. **5.** homage or attention. **6.** place where justice is dealt. **7.** judge or judges. —*v.* **8.** woo. —**court′house,** *n.* —**court′room′,** *n.* —**court′ship,** *n.* —**court′yard′,** *n.*

cour′te•san (kôr′tə zən) *n.* prostitute with noble or wealthy clients.

cour′te•sy (kûr′tə sē) *n., pl.* **-sies. 1.** good manners. **2.** indulgence. —**cour′te•ous** (-tē-əs) *adj.* —**cour′te•ous•ly,** *adv.*

cour′ti•er (kôr′tē ər) *n.* person in attendance at court.

court′ly, *adj.* elegant.

court′-mar′tial, *n., pl.* **courts-martial,** *v.,* **-tialed, -tialing.** —*n.* **1.** military court. —*v.* **2.** try by court-martial.

cous′in (kuz′ən) *n.* child of uncle or aunt.

cou•tu′ri•er (kōō tŏŏr′ē ər, -ē ā′) *n.* designer of stylish, custom-made clothes for women.

cov cutoff valve.

cove (kōv) *n.* recess in shoreline.

cov′en (kuv′ən, kō′vən) *n.* assembly of witches.

cov′e•nant (kuv′ə nənt) *n.* solemn agreement; oath or pact.

cov′er (kuv′ər) *v.* **1.** be or put something over. **2.** include. **3.** have in range. **4.** meet or offset. —*n.* **5.** thing that covers. **6.** concealment. —**cov′er•ing,** *n.*

cov′er•age (-ij) *n.* **1.** protection by insurance. **2.** awareness and reporting of news.

cov′er•let (-lit) *n.* quilt.

covers *Trigonometry.* coversed sine.

cov′ert (kō′vərt) *adj.* secret or covered. —**cov′ert•ly,** *adv.*

cov′er-up′, *n.* concealing of illegal activity, a blunder, etc.

cov′et (kuv′it) *v.* desire greatly or wrongfully. —**cov′et•ous,** *adj.*

cov′ey (kuv′ē) *n., pl.* **-eys.** small flock.

cow (kou) *n.* **1.** female of bovine or other large animal. —*v.* **2.** intimidate.

cow′ard (kou′ərd) *n.* person who lacks courage. —**cow′ard•ice** (-ər dis) *n.* —**cow′ard•ly,** *adj., adv.*

cow′boy′, *n.* cattle herder. Also, **cow′hand′; cow′girl′,** *n. fem.*

cow′er (kou′ər) *v.* crouch in fear.

cowl (koul) *n.* **1.** hooded garment. **2.** hoodlike part.

cow′lick′, *n.* tuft of hair growing in a different direction.

COWPS Council on Wage and Price Stability.

cow′slip′, *n.* plant with yellow flowers.

cox′comb′ (koks′kōm′) *n.* dandy.

cox′swain (kok′sən) *n.* person who steers boat or racing shell. Also, **cox.**

coy (koi) *adj.* affectedly shy. —**coy′ly,** *adv.* —**coy′ness,** *n.*

coy•o′te (kī ō′tē) *n.* wild animal related to wolf.

coz′en (kuz′ən) *v.* cheat or deceive.

co′zy (kō′zē) *adj.,* **-zier, -ziest.** comfortable; snug. —**co′zi•ly,** *adv.* —**co′zi•ness,** *n.*

CP 1. candlepower. **2.** *Pharmacology.* chemically pure.

cP *Physics.* centipoise. Also, **cp**

cp. 1. camp. **2.** center punch. **3.** cerebral palsy. **4.** clock pulse. **5.** command post. **6.** compare. **7.** constant pressure.

C.P. 1. Chief Patriarch. **2.** command post. **3.** Common Pleas. **4.** Common Prayer. **5.** Communist Party.

c.p. 1. chemically pure. **2.** circular pitch. **3.** command post. **4.** common pleas.

CPA, certified public accountant.

CPB Corporation for Public Broadcasting. Also, **C.P.B.**

cpch prop controllable-pitch propeller.

CPCU *Insurance.* Chartered Property and Casualty Underwriter. Also, **C.P.C.U.**

cpd. compound.

CPFF cost plus fixed fee.

CPI, consumer price index.

cpl couple.

cpl. corporal. Also, **Cpl.**

cpld coupled.

cplg coupling.

cplr coupler.

cplry capillary.

CPM 1. *Commerce.* cost per thousand. **2.** Critical Path Method.

cpm 1. card per minute. **2.** *Commerce.* cost per thousand. **3.** critical-path method. **4.** cycles per minute.

CP/M *Trademark.* Control Program/Microprocessors: a microcomputer operating system.

c.p.m. *Music.* common particular meter.

cpntr carpenter.

CPO chief petty officer. Also, **C.P.O., c.p.o.**

CPR, cardiopulmonary resuscitation: a form of lifesaving.

cprs compress.

cprsn compression.

cprsr compressor.

CPS certified professional secretary.

cps 1. *Computers.* characters per second. **2.** cycles per second.

cpse counterpoise.

cpt critical-path technique.

cpt. counterpoint.

CPU, central processing unit, the key component of a computer system.

cpunch counterpunch.

CQ 1. *Radio.* a signal sent at the beginning of radiograms. **2.** *Military.* charge of quarters.

CR 1. conditioned reflex; conditioned response. **2.** consciousness-raising. **3.** critical ratio.

Cr *Symbol, Chemistry.* chromium.

cr 1. cold rolled. **2.** controlled rectifier. **3.** control relay. **4.** crystal rectifier. **5.** current relay.

cr. 1. credit. **2.** creditor. **3.** crown.

C.R. 1. Costa Rica. **2.** *Banking.* credit report.

crab (krab) *n.* crustacean with broad flat body.

crab apple, small tart apple.

crab/by, *adj.,* **-bier, biest.** grouchy. **—crab/-bi•ness,** *n.*

crack (krak) *v.* **1.** make sudden, sharp sound. **2.** break without separating. **—n. 3.** sudden, sharp sound. **4.** break without separation. **5.** smokable form of cocaine.

crack/down/, *n.* stern enforcement of regulations.

crack/er, *n.* **1.** crisp biscuit. **2.** firecracker. **3.** *Disparaging and Offensive.* yokel.

crack/le (krak/əl) *v.,* **-led, -ling,** *n.* **—v. 1.** crack repeatedly. **—n. 2.** crackling sound.

crack/pot/, *n.* person with irrational theories.

crack/up/, *n.* breakdown.

cra/dle (krād/l) *n., v.,* **-dled, -dling. —n. 1.** bed on rockers for baby. **—v. 2.** place in a cradle. **3.** hold protectively.

craft (kraft) *n.* **1.** skill; skilled trade. **2.** cunning. **3.** vessels or aircraft. **—crafts/man,** *n.* **—crafts/wom•an,** *n.fem.* **—crafts/man• ship/,** *n.*

craft/y, *adj.,* **-ier, -iest.** sly. **—craft/i•ly,** *adv.*

crag (krag) *n.* steep rough rock. **—crag/gy,** *adj.*

cram (kram) *v.,* **crammed, cramming. 1.** fill tightly. **2.** study hard.

cramp (kramp) *n.* **1.** involuntary muscular contraction. **—v. 2.** affect with a cramp. **3.** hamper.

cramped (krampt) *adj.* **1.** confined or limited. **2.** (of handwriting) small and crowded.

cran/ber/ry (kran/ber/ē) *n., pl.* **-ries.** red acid edible berry.

crane (krān) *n.* **1.** tall wading bird. **2.** lifting device or machine.

cra/ni•um (krā/nē əm) *n., pl.* **-niums, -nia** (-nē ə). skull. **—cra/ni•al,** *adj.*

crank (krangk) *n.* **1.** right-angled arm for communicating motion. **2.** *Informal.* grouchy person. **—v. 3.** turn with a crank.

crank/y (krang/kē) *adj.,* **-ier, -iest.** ill-tempered. **—crank/i•ness,** *n.*

cran/ny (kran/ē) *n., pl.* **-nies.** cleft.

crap (krap) *n. Slang.* **1.** worthless material. **2.** false or meaningless statements.

crape (krāp) *n.* crepe (defs. 1, 2).

crap/pie (krap/ē) *n.* type of small fish.

craps (kraps) *n.* dice game.

crash (krash) *v.* **1.** strike noisily. **2.** land or fall with damage. **—n. 3.** noise or act of crashing. **4.** collapse. **5.** act or instance of crashing. **6.** rough fabric.

crass (kras) *adj.* unrefined or insensitive; crude. **—crass/ly,** *adv.* **—crass/ness,** *n.*

crate (krāt) *n., v.,* **crated, crating. —n. 1.** box or frame for packing. **—v. 2.** put in crate.

cra/ter, *n.* cup-shaped hole, as in volcano or on moon.

cra•vat/ (krə vat/) *n.* necktie.

crave (krāv) *v.,* **craved, craving.** yearn or beg for.

cra/ven (krā/vən) *adj.* **1.** cowardly. **—n. 2.** coward.

crav/ing, *n.* intense yearning.

craw (krô) *n.* crop of bird.

crawl (krôl) *v.* **1.** move slowly, as on stomach. **—n. 2.** act of crawling. **3.** swimming stroke. **—crawl/er,** *n.*

cray/fish/ (krā/fish/) *n.* crustacean resembling a lobster. Also, **craw/fish/** (krô/-).

cray/on (krā/on) *n.* stick of colored wax or chalk for drawing.

craze (krāz) *v.,* **crazed, crazing,** *n.* **—v. 1.** make insane. **2.** mark with fine cracks, as glaze. **—n. 3.** mania.

cra/zy (krā/zē) *adj.,* **-zier, -ziest.** insane. **—cra/zi•ly,** *adv.* **—cra/zi•ness,** *n.*

CRC Civil Rights Commission.

crc *Computers.* cyclical redundancy check.

crclt circulate.

crcmf circumference.

crctn correction.

cre corrosion-resistant.

creak (krēk) *v.* **1.** squeak sharply. **—n. 2.** creaking sound. **—creak/y,** *adj.*

cream (krēm) *n.* **1.** fatty part of milk. **2.** best part of anything. **—v. 3.** make with cream. **4.** work to a creamy state. **5.** *Informal.* defeat utterly. **—cream/er,** *n.* **—cream/y,** *adj.*

cream/er•y, *n., pl.* **-ies.** producer of dairy goods.

crease (krēs) *n., v.,* **creased, creasing. —n. 1.** mark from folding. **—v. 2.** make creases in.

cre•ate/ (krē āt/) *v.,* **-ated, -ating.** cause to exist. **—cre•a/tion,** *n.* **—cre•a/tive,** *adj.* **—cre•a/tor,** *n.*

crea/ture (krē/chər) *n.* **1.** animate being. **2.** anything created.

cre/dence (krēd/ns) *n.* belief.

C

cre·den'tial (kri den'shəl) n. (usually pl.) verifying document.

cre·den'za (kri den'zə) n. sideboard, esp. one without legs.

cred'i·ble (kred'ə bəl) adj. believable. —cred'i·bil'i·ty, n. —cred'i·bly, adv.

cred'it (kred'it) n. 1. belief. 2. trustworthiness. 3. honor. 4. time allowed for payment. —v. 5. believe. 6. ascribe to.

cred'it·a·ble, adj. worthy. —cred'it·a·bly, adv.

credit card, card entitling holder to charge purchases.

cred'i·tor, n. person owed.

credit union, cooperative group that makes loans to its members at low interest rates.

cred'u·lous (krej'ə ləs) adj. overwilling to believe. —cre·du'li·ty (krə dōō'li tē, -dyōō'- -) n.

creed (krēd) n. formula of belief. Also, cre'do (krē'dō).

creek (krēk, krik) n. brook.

creel (krēl) n. wickerwork basket for carrying fish.

creep (krēp) v., crept (krept) or creeped, creeping, n. —v. 1. move stealthily; crawl. —n. 2. Slang. disagreeable person.

creep'y, adj., -ier, -iest. causing uneasiness.

cre'mate (krē'māt) v., -mated, -mating. burn (corpse) to ashes. —cre·ma'tion, n. —cre'ma·to'ry, adj., n.

Cre'ole (krē'ōl) n. 1. one of French and Spanish blood born in Louisiana. 2. (l.c.) pidgin that has become native language of a group.

cre'o·sote' (krē'ə sōt') n. oily liquid from tar.

crepe (krāp; for 3 also krep) n. 1. light crinkled fabric. 2. Also, crepe paper. thin, wrinkled paper used for decorating. 3. thin, light pancake.

Cres. crescent (in addresses).

cres corrosion-resistant steel.

cre·scen'do (kri shen'dō) n., pl. -dos. Music. gradual increase in loudness.

cres'cent (kres'ənt) n. 1. moon in its first or last quarter. 2. object having this shape.

cress (kres) n. plant with pungent leaves.

crest (krest) n. 1. tuft or plume. 2. figure above coat of arms.

crest'fal'len, adj. abruptly discouraged or depressed.

cre'tin (krēt'n) n. 1. person affected with cretinism, congenital thyroid deficiency. 2. obtuse or boorish person.

cre·tonne' (kri ton') n. heavily printed cotton.

cre·vasse' (krə vas') n. fissure, esp. in glacier.

crev'ice (krev'is) n. fissure.

crew (krōō) n. 1. group of persons working together, as on ship. —v. 2. form crew of.

crew cut, haircut in which the hair is cut close to the head.

crew'el (krōō'əl) n. worsted yarn for embroidery and edging.

CRF Biochemistry. corticotropin releasing factor.

crg carriage.

crib (krib) n., v., cribbed, cribbing. —n. 1. child's bed. 2. rack or bin. —v. 3. put in a crib. 4. plagiarize.

crib'bage (krib'ij) n. card game using scoreboard with pegs.

crick (krik) n. muscular spasm.

crick'et (krik'it) n. 1. leaping, noisy insect. 2. British outdoor ballgame with bats and wickets.

cri'er (krī'ər) n. one who cries or announces.

crim. criminal.

crim. con. Law. criminal conversation.

crime (krīm) n. 1. unlawful act. 2. sin. —crim'i·nal (krim'ə nl) adj., n. —crim'i·nal·ly, adv. —crim'i·nol'o·gist (-nol'ə jist) n. —crim'i·nol'o·gy, n.

criminol. 1. criminologist. 2. criminology.

crimp (krimp) v. 1. make wavy. —n. 2. crimped form.

crim'son (krim'zən) n., adj. deep red.

cringe (krinj) v., cringed, cringing. shrink in fear or servility.

crin'kle (kring'kəl) v., -kled, -kling, n. wrinkle. —crin'kly, adj.

crin'o·line (krin'l in) n. 1. stiff, coarse fabric used as lining. 2. petticoat.

crip'ple (krip'əl) n., v., -pled, -pling. —n. 1. Sometimes Offensive. lame or disabled person or animal. —v. 2. make lame; disable.

cri'sis (krī'sis) n., pl. -ses (-sēz). decisive stage or point.

crisp (krisp) adj. 1. brittle. 2. fresh. 3. brisk. 4. curly. —v. 5. make or become crisp. —crisp'ly, adv. —crisp'ness, n.

criss'cross' (kris'krôs') adj. 1. marked with crossed lines. —n. 2. crisscross pattern. —v. 3. mark with crossed lines.

crit. 1. critic. 2. critical. 3. criticism. 4. criticized.

cri·te'ri·on (krī tēr'ē ən) n., pl. -teria (-tēr'ē ə). standard for judgment.

crit'ic (krit'ik) n. 1. skilled judge. 2. fault-finding person.

crit'i·cal, adj. 1. severe in judgment. 2. involving criticism. 3. crucial. —crit'i·cal·ly, adv.

crit'i·cize' (-sīz') v., -cized, -cizing. 1. discuss as a critic. 2. find fault with. —crit'i·cism (-siz'əm) n.

cri·tique' (kri tēk') n. critical article.

crit'ter (krit'ər) n. Dial. creature.

crk crank.

crkc crankcase.

CRM counter-radar measures.

crn 1. crane. 2. crown.

crnmtr chronometer.

cro cathode-ray oscilloscope.

croak (krōk) v. utter a hoarse cry.

cro•chet′ (krō shā′) v. form thread into designs with hooked needle.

crock (krok) n. earthen jar. —**crock′er•y,** n.

croc′o•dile′ (krok′ə dīl′) n. large aquatic legged reptile with long, powerful jaws and tail.

cro′cus (krō′kəs) n. small bulbous plant blooming in early spring.

crois•sant′ (Fr. krwä sän′; Eng. krə sänt′) n. crescent-shaped roll of flaky pastry.

crone (krōn) n. witchlike old woman.

cro′ny (krō′nē) n., pl. -nies. close friend.

crook (krʊk) n. 1. tight curve. 2. bend. 3. Informal. dishonest person. —v. 4. bend. —**crook′ed,** adj.

croon (krʊn) v. 1. sing softly. —n. 2. such singing. —**croon′er,** n.

crop (krop) n., v., **cropped, cropping.** —n. 1. produce from the soil. 2. short whip. 3. pouch in gullet of bird. —v. 4. remove ends. 5. cut short. 6. reap. 7. **crop up,** show. —**crop′per,** n.

cro•quet′ (krō kā′) n. game with wooden balls and mallets.

cro•quette′ (krō ket′) n. fried or baked piece of chopped food.

cro′sier (krō′zhər) n. staff of bishop.

cross (krôs) n. 1. structure whose basic form has an upright with transverse piece. 2. emblem of Christianity. 3. figure resembling cross. 4. trouble. 5. mixture of breeds. —v. 6. make sign of cross over. 7. put, lie, or pass across. 8. oppose or frustrate. 9. mark (out). 10. mix (breeds). —adj. 11. transverse. 12. ill-humored. —**cross′ly,** adv. —**cross′ness,** n.

cross′bow′ (-bō′) n. weapon consisting of a bow fixed on a stock like that of a rifle.

cross′ breed′, v., -bred, -breeding, n. —v. 1. cross varieties of in breeding; hybridize. —n. 2. hybrid.

cross′-coun′try, adj. 1. proceeding over fields, through woods, etc., rather than on a road or track. 2. from one end of a country to the other. —n. 3. sport of cross-country racing.

cross′-ex•am′ine, v., -ined, -ining. examine closely, as opposing witness. Also, cross′-ques′tion. —cross′-ex•am′in•a′tion, n.

cross′-eye′, n. visual disorder. —cross′-eyed′, adj.

cross reference, reference to another part of book.

cross′road′, n. 1. road that crosses another. 2. (pl.) a. intersection. b. decisive point.

cross section, 1. section made by cutting across something. 2. picture representing such a section. 3. representative sample of a whole.

cross′word puz′zle, puzzle in which words determined from numbered clues are fitted

into pattern of horizontal and vertical squares.

crotch (kroch) n. place where something divides, as the human body between the legs.

crotch′et (kroch′it) n. 1. small hook. 2. whim.

crotch′et•y, adj. grumpy. —crotch′et•i•ness, n.

crouch (krouch) v. 1. stoop or bend low. —n. 2. act or instance of crouching.

croup (krʊp) n. inflammation of throat.

crou′pi•er (krʊ′pē ər, -pē ā′) n. attendant who handles bets and money at gambling table.

crou′ton (krʊ′ton) n. small cube of toasted bread.

crow (krō) v. 1. cry, as cock. 2. boast. —n. 3. cry of cock. 4. black, harsh-voiced bird. 5. (cap.) member of an American Indian people.

crow′bar′, n. iron bar for prying.

crowd (kroud) n. 1. large group of people. —v. 2. throng. 3. press or push. —crowd′ed, adj.

crown (kroun) n. 1. ornate covering for the head of a sovereign. 2. power of a sovereign. 3. top. —v. 4. put crown on. 5. reward or complete.

crow′s′-foot′, n., pl. -feet. (usually pl.) tiny wrinkle at outer corner of the eye.

CRP Biochemistry. C-reactive protein.

crp crimp.

crpt carpet.

crs 1. coarse. 2. cold-rolled steel.

crs. 1. creditors. 2. credits.

crsn corrosion.

crsv corrosive.

crsvr crossover.

CRT, 1. cathode-ray tube. 2. computer monitor that includes cathode-ray tube.

crtg 1. cartridge. 2. crating.

cru′cial (krʊ′shəl) adj. 1. decisive. 2. severe. —cru′cial•ly, adv.

cru′ci•ble (krʊ′sə bəl) n. vessel for melting metals, etc.

cru′ci•fix (krʊ′sə fiks) n. cross with figure of Jesus crucified.

cru′ci•fy′ (-fī′) v., -fied, -fying. put to death on cross. —cru′ci•fix′ion, n.

crude (krʊd) adj., cruder, crudest, n. —adj. 1. unrefined. 2. unfinished. —n. 3. Informal. unrefined petroleum. —crude′ly, adv. —crude′ness, cru•dity, n.

cru′di•tés′ (krʊ′di tā′) n.pl. cut-up raw vegetables served with a dip.

cru′el (krʊ′əl) adj. 1. disposed to inflict pain. 2. causing pain. —cru′el•ly, adv. —cru′el•ness, cru′el•ty, n.

cru′et (krʊ′it) n. stoppered bottle for vinegar, etc.

cruise (krʊz) v., cruised, cruising, n. —v. 1. sail or fly at moderate speed. 2. travel for pleasure. —n. 3. cruising trip.

cruis′er, *n.* **1.** kind of warship. **2.** small pleasure boat.

crul′ler (krul′ər) *n.* doughnutlike cake.

crumb (krum) *n.* small bit of bread, cookie, etc.

crum′ble (krum′bəl) *v.,* **-bled, -bling.** break into fragments; decay.

crum′my (krum′ē) *adj.,* **-mier, -miest.** *Informal,* **1.** shabby. **2.** cheap. **3.** miserable.

crum′ple (krum′pəl) *v.,* **-pled, -pling,** *n.* wrinkle; rumple.

crunch (krunch) *v.* **1.** chew or crush noisily. —*n.* **2.** *Informal.* reduction of resources.

cru•sade′ (krōō sād′) *n., v.,* **-saded, -sading.** —*n.* **1.** Christian expedition to recover Holy Land from Muslims. **2.** campaign for good cause. —*v.* **3.** engage in crusade. —**cru•sad′er,** *n.*

crush (krush) *v.* **1.** bruise or break by pressing. **2.** subdue. —*n.* **3.** dense crowd. **4.** infatuation.

crust (krust) *n.* **1.** hard outer part or covering. **2.** *Informal.* impertinence. —*v.* **3.** cover with crust. —**crust′i•ly,** *adv.* —**crust′i•ness,** *n.* —**crust′y,** *adj.*

crus•ta′cean (kru stā′shən) *n.* sea animal having hard shell. —**crus•ta′cean,** *adj.*

crutch (kruch) *n.* **1.** staff fitting under the armpit for support in walking. **2.** *Informal.* temporary aid or expedient.

crux (kruks) *n., pl.* **cruxes, cruces** (krōō′sēz). vital point.

crv curve.

cry (krī) *v.,* **cried, crying,** *n., pl.* **cries.** —*v.* **1.** make sounds of grief, etc. **2.** utter characteristic sounds. **3.** shout. —*n.* **4.** act or sound of crying.

cryo cryogenic.

cry′o•gen′ics (krī′ə jen′iks) *n.* study or use of extremely low temperatures. —**cry′o•gen′ic,** *adj.*

crypt (kript) *n.* underground chamber.

crypta cryptanalysis.

cryp′tic, *adj.* mysterious. —**cryp′ti•cal•ly,** *adv.*

crypto cryptography.

cryp•tog′ra•phy (krip tog′rə fē) *n.* study or use of code and cipher systems. —**cryp•tog′ra•pher,** *n.*

cryst. 1. crystalline. **2.** crystallized. **3.** crystallography.

crys′tal (kris′tl) *n.* **1.** clear transparent mineral. **2.** body with symmetrical plane faces. **3.** fine glass. **4.** cover of watch face. —**crys′tal•line** (-tl in, -īn′) *adj.*

crys′tal•lize′, *v.,* **-lized, -lizing. 1.** form or cause to form into crystals. **2.** assume or cause to assume definite form. —**crys′tal•li•za′tion,** *n.*

Cs *Symbol, Chemistry.* cesium.

cS *Physics.* centistoke; centistokes. Also, **cs**

cs 1. case; cases. **2.** cast steel. **3.** control switch. **4.** *Computers.* core shift.

C/S cycles per second.

C.S. 1. chief of staff. **2.** Christian Science. **3.** Christian Scientist. **4.** Civil Service. **5.** Confederate States.

c.s. 1. capital stock. **2.** civil service.

CSA Community Services Administration.

C.S.A. Confederate States of America.

CSC Civil Service Commission.

csc *Trigonometry.* cosecant.

CSCE Conference on Security and Cooperation in Europe.

csch *Trigonometry.* hyperbolic cosecant.

csd *Computers.* core-shift drive.

CSEA Civil Service Employees Association.

C/-sec′tion, *n.* Cesarean.

CSF *Physiology.* cerebrospinal fluid.

csg casing.

cshaft crankshaft.

csk. 1. cask. **2.** countersink.

cskh countersunk head.

C.S.O. 1. Chief Signal Officer. **2.** Chief Staff Officer. Also, **CSO**

CSP C-SPAN (a cable channel).

C-SPAN (sē′span′), Cable Satellite Public Affairs Network (a cable channel).

CSR 1. Certified Shorthand Reporter. **2.** customer service representative.

csr customer signature required.

CST, Central Standard Time.

cstl castellate.

CSW Certified Social Worker. Also, **C.S.W.**

Cswy. causeway.

CT, Connecticut.

Ct., 1. Connecticut. **2.** Count.

ct., 1. carat. **2.** cent. **3.** court.

CTA commodities trading adviser.

C.T.A. *Law.* with the will annexed. [from Latin *cum testāmentō annexō*]

CTC 1. centralized traffic control. **2.** Citizens' Training Corps.

ctd coated.

ctf certificate.

ctg. 1. Also, **ctge.** cartage. **2.** cartridge. **3.** coating. **4.** cutting.

CTL 1. *Computers.* complementary transistor logic. **2.** core transistor logic.

ctlry cutlery.

ctlst catalyst.

ct/m count per minute.

ctn *Trigonometry.* cotangent.

ctn. carton.

ctnr container.

c to c center to center.

ctr. 1. center. **2.** contour. **3.** cutter.

ctrfgl centrifugal.

ctrg centering.

ctrl central.

ctrlr controller.

ctrst contrast.

CTS Cleveland Transit System.

cts. 1. centimes. **2.** cents. **3.** certificates.

ct/s count per second.

ctshft countershaft.

CTU centigrade thermal unit. Also, **ctu**

ctwlk catwalk.

ctwt counterweight.

cty county.

cu., cubic.

cub (kub) n. young fox, bear, etc.

cub'by•hole' (kub'ē-) n. small enclosed space.

cube (kyōōb) n., v., **cubed, cubing.** —n. **1.** solid bounded by six squares. **2.** *Math.* third power of a quantity. —v. **3.** make into cubes. **4.** *Math.* raise to third power. —**cu'bic, cu'. bi•cal,** adj.

cu'bi•cle (kyōō'bi kəl) n. small room.

cub'ism, n. artistic style marked by reduction of natural forms to geometric shapes. —**cub'. ist,** adj., n.

cub scout, (*sometimes caps.*) boy scout aged 8 to 10.

cuck'old (kuk'əld) n. husband of unfaithful wife.

cuck'oo (kōō'kōō, kōōk'ōō) n. small bird.

cu'cum•ber (kyōō'kum bər) n. green-skinned cylindrical fruit.

cud (kud) n. food that cow returns to mouth for further chewing.

cud'dle (kud'l) v., **-dled, -dling.** hold tenderly. —**cud'dly,** adj.

cudg'el (kuj'əl) n., v., **-eled, -eling.** —n. **1.** short thick stick. —v. **2.** beat with cudgel.

cue (kyōō) n. **1.** (esp. on stage) something that signals speech or action. **2.** rod for billiards.

cuff (kuf) n. **1.** fold or band at end of sleeve or trouser leg. **2.** slap. —v. **3.** slap.

cu. ft. cubic foot; cubic feet.

cu. in. cubic inch; cubic inches.

cui•sine' (kwi zēn') n. cookery.

cuj. (in prescriptions) of which; of any. [from Latin *cūjus*]

cu'li•nar'y (kyōō'lə ner'ē, kul'ə-) adj. of cooking.

cull (kul) v. select best parts of.

cul'mi•nate' (kul'mə nāt') v., **-nated, -nating.** reach highest point. —**cul'mi•na'tion,** n.

cul'pa•ble (kul'pə bəl) adj. deserving blame. —**cul'pa•bil'i•ty,** n.

cul'prit (kul'prit) n. person arraigned for or guilty of an offense.

cult (kult) n. religious sect or system.

cul'ti•vate' (kul'tə vāt') v., **-vated, -vating. 1.** prepare and care for (land). **2.** develop possibilities of. —**cul'ti•va'tion,** n. —**cul'ti•va'tor,** n.

cul'ti•vat'ed, adj. educated and well-mannered.

cul'ture (kul'chər) n. **1.** raising of plants or animals. **2.** development of mind. **3.** state or form of civilization. —**cul'tur•al,** adj. —**cul'. tur•al•ly,** adv.

culture shock, distress of person exposed to new culture.

culv culvert.

cul'vert (kul'vərt) n. channel under road, etc.

cu m cubic meter.

cum. cumulative.

cum'ber•some (kum'bər səm) adj. clumsy.

cu mm cubic millimeter.

cu'mu•la•tive (kyōō'myə lə tiv) adj. increasing by accumulation.

cu'mu•lus (kyōō'myə ləs) n., pl. **-li.** cloud in form of rounded heaps on flat base. —**cu'. mu•lous,** adj.

cu•ne'i•form' (kyōō nē'ə fôrm') adj. **1.** composed of wedge-shaped elements, as some ancient writing. —n. **2.** cuneiform writing.

cun'ning (kun'ing) n. **1.** skill. **2.** guile. —adj. **3.** clever. **4.** sly.

cuo copper oxide.

cup (kup) n., v., **cupped, cupping.** —n. **1.** small open drinking vessel. —v. **2.** shape like a cup.

cup'board (kub'ərd) n. closet for dishes, etc.

Cu'pid (kyōō'pid) n. Roman god of carnal love.

cu•pid'i•ty (-pid'i tē) n. greed.

cu'po•la (kyōō'pə lə) n. rounded dome.

cu'prous (kyōō'prəs) adj. containing copper.

cur (kûr) n. worthless dog.

cu'rate (kyōōr'it) n. clergyman assisting rector or vicar.

cu•ra'tor (kyōō rā'tər, kyōōr'ā-) n. person in charge of museum collection.

curb (kûrb) n. **1.** strap for restraining horse. **2.** restraint. **3.** edge of sidewalk. —v. **4.** control.

curd (kûrd) n. **1.** substance formed when milk coagulates. —v. **2.** change into curd.

cur'dle (kûr'dl) v., **-dled, -dling.** congeal.

cure (kyōōr) n., v., **cured, curing.** —n. **1.** treatment of disease. **2.** restoration to health. —v. **3.** restore to health. **4.** prepare for use. —**cur'a•ble,** adj. —**cur'a•tive,** adj., n.

cure'-all', n. cure for anything; panacea.

cur'few (kûr'fyōō) n. order to be home or off the streets by a certain time.

cu'ri•o' (kyōōr'ē ō') n., pl. **-rios.** odd valuable article.

cu'ri•os'i•ty (kyōōr'ē os'i tē) n., pl. **-ties. 1.** desire to know. **2.** odd thing.

cu'ri•ous (-əs) adj. **1.** wanting to know. **2.** prying. **3.** strange. —**cu'ri•ous•ly,** adv.

curl (kûrl) v. **1.** form in ringlets. **2.** coil. —n. **3.** ringlet. —**curl'er,** n. —**curl'y,** adj.

cur'lew (kûr'lōō) n. shore bird.

curl'i•cue' (kûr'li kyōō') n. fancy curl.

cur•mudg'eon (kər muj'ən) n. bad-tempered, difficult person.

cur'rant (kûr'ənt) n. **1.** small seedless raisin. **2.** edible acid berry.

cur'ren•cy (kûr'ən sē) n., pl. **-cies. 1.** money

in use in a country. **2.** prevalence. **3.** circulation.

cur′rent (kûr′ənt) *adj.* **1.** present. **2.** generally known or believed. —*n.* **3.** stream; flow. **4.** water, air, etc., moving in one direction. **5.** movement of electricity. —**cur′rent•ly,** *adv.*

cur•ric′u•lum (kə rik′yə ləm) *n., pl.* **-lums, -la** (-lə). course of study.

cur′ry (kûr′ē, kur′ē) *n., pl.* **-ries,** *v.,* **-ried, -rying.** —*n.* **1.** East Indian hot sauce or powder (**curry powder**). —*v.* **2.** prepare with curry. **3.** rub and comb (horse, etc.). **4.** seek (favor) with servility. —**cur′ry•comb′,** *n.*

curse (kûrs) *n., v.,* **cursed** or **curst, cursing.** —*n.* **1.** wish that evil befall another. **2.** evil so invoked. **3.** profane oath. **4.** cause of evil. —*v.* **5.** wish evil upon. **6.** swear. **7.** afflict. —**curs′ed** (kûr′sid, kûrst) *adj.*

cur′sive (kûr′siv) *adj.* (of handwriting) in flowing strokes with letters joined together.

cur′sor (-sər) *n.* movable symbol on computer screen to indicate where data may be input.

cur′so•ry, *adj.* superficial. —**cur′so•ri•ly,** *adv.*

curt (kûrt) *adj.* brief, esp. rudely so. —**curt′-ly,** *adv.*

cur•tail′ (kər tāl′) *v.* cut short. —**cur•tail′-ment,** *n.*

cur′tain (kûr′tn) *n.* **1.** piece of fabric hung to adorn, conceal, etc. —*v.* **2.** cover with curtains.

curt′sy (kûrt′sē) *n., pl.* **-sies,** *v.,* **-sied, -sying.** —*n.* **1.** bow by women. —*v.* **2.** make curtsy.

cur′va•ture (kûr′və chər) *n.* **1.** a curving. **2.** degree of curving.

curve (kûrv) *n., v.,* **curved, curving.** —*n.* **1.** bending line. —*v.* **2.** bend or move in a curve.

cush′ion (koosh′ən) *n.* **1.** soft bag of feathers, air, etc. —*v.* **2.** lessen the effects of.

cush′y (koosh′ē) *adj. Informal.* **1.** easy and profitable. **2.** soft and comfortable.

cusp (kusp) *n.* pointed end.

cus′pid (kus′pid) *n.* canine tooth.

cus•pi•dor′ (-pi dôr′) *n.* receptacle for spit, cigar ash, etc.

cuss (kus) *v. Informal.* curse.

cust. 1. custodian. **2.** custody. **3.** customer.

cus′tard (kus′tərd) *n.* cooked dish of eggs and milk.

cus•to•dy (-tə dē) *n., pl.* **-dies. 1.** keeping; care. **2.** imprisonment. —**cus•to′di•al** (kə-stō′dē əl) *adj.* —**cus•to′di•an,** *n.*

cus′tom (kus′təm) *n.* **1.** usual practice. **2.** set of such practices. **3.** (*pl.*) **a.** duties on imports. **b.** agency collecting these. —*adj.* **4.** made for the individual. —**cus′tom•ar′y,** *adj.* —**cus′tom•ar/i•ly,** *adv.*

cus′tom•er, *n.* **1.** purchaser or prospective purchaser. **2.** *Informal.* person.

cus′tom•ize′, *v.,* **-ized, -iz•ing.** make to individual specifications. —**cus′tom•i•za′tion,** *n.*

cut (kut) *v.,* **cut, cutting,** *n.* —*v.* **1.** sever, as with knife. **2.** wound feelings of. **3.** reap or trim. **4.** shorten by omitting part. **5.** dilute. **6.** move or cross. **7.** be absent from. —*n.* **8.** a cutting. **9.** result of cutting. **10.** straight passage. **11.** engraved plate for printing.

cu•ta′ne•ous (kyoo tā′nē əs) *adj.* of the skin.

cut′back′, *n.* reduction in rate, quantity, etc.

cute (kyoot) *adj.,* **cuter, cutest.** pretty or pleasing.

cu′ti•cle (kyoo′ti kəl) *n.* epidermis, esp. around nails.

cut′lass (kut′ləs) *n.* short curved sword.

cut′ler•y (-lə rē) *n.* knives collectively.

cut′let (-lit) *n.* slice of meat for frying or broiling.

cut′off′, *n.* **1.** point beyond which something is no longer effective or possible. **2.** road that leaves another to make a shortcut.

cut′-rate′, *adj.* offered at reduced prices.

cut′ter, *n.* **1.** one that cuts. **2.** small fast vessel. **3.** sleigh.

cut′throat′, *n.* **1.** murderer. —*adj.* **2.** ruthless.

cut′tle•fish′ (kut′l fish′) *n., pl.* **-fish, -fish-es.** mollusk with ten arms and hard internal shell (**cut′tle•bone′**).

cu yd cubic yard.

CV 1. cardiovascular. **2.** Also, **C.V.** curriculum vitae.

cv 1. continuously variable. **2.** Also, **cvt.** convertible. **3.** counter voltage.

CVA 1. *Pathology.* cerebrovascular accident. **2.** Columbia Valley Authority.

CVD *Commerce.* countervailing duty.

CVJ *Automotive.* constant-velocity joint.

cvntl conventional.

C.V.O. Commander of the Royal Victorian Order.

cvr cover.

cvrsn conversion.

CVT continuously variable transmission.

CW 1. chemical warfare. **2.** *Radio.* continuous wave.

cw 1. clockwise. **2.** continuous wave.

c/w complete with.

CWA 1. Civil Works Administration. **2.** Communications Workers of America.

CWO *Military.* chief warrant officer.

c.w.o. cash with order.

CWPS Council on Wage and Price Stability.

cwt hundredweight; hundredweights.

cx control transmitter.

CY calendar year.

Cy. county.

cy. 1. capacity. **2.** currency. **3.** cycle; cycles.

CYA *Slang* (*sometimes vulgar*). cover your ass.

cy'a•nide' (sī'ə nīd') n. poisonous salt of hydrocyanic acid.

cyber-, prefix meaning computer, as cyberspace.

cy'ber•net'ics (sī'bər net'iks) n. study of organic control and communications systems and mechanical or electronic systems analogous to them, such as robots.

cy'ber•space', n. **1.** realm of electronic communication. **2.** virtual reality.

CYC Biochemistry. cyclophosphamide.

cyc. cyclopedia.

cy'cla•mate' (sī'klə māt') n. artificial sweetening agent.

cy'cle (sī'kəl) n., v., -cled, -cling. —n. **1.** recurring time or process. **2.** complete set. **3.** bicycle, etc. —v. **4.** ride bicycle. —cyc'lic (sik'lik, sī'klik), cyc'li•cal, adj. —cy'clist, n.

cy'clone (sī'klōn) n. **1.** rotary weather system. **2.** tornado. —cy•clon'ic (-klon'ik) adj.

cy'clo•pe'di•a (sī'klə pē'dē ə) n. encyclopedia.

cy'clo•tron' (-tron') n. device used in splitting atoms.

cyg'net (sig'nit) n. young swan.

cyl. 1. cylinder. **2.** cylindrical.

cyl'in•der (sil'in dər) n. **1.** round elongated solid with ends that are equal parallel circles. **2.** machine part or opening in this form. —cy•lin'dri•cal, adj.

Cym. Cymric.

cym'bal (sim'bəl) n. brass plate used in orchestras.

cyn'ic (sin'ik) n. person who doubts or lacks goodness of motive. —cyn'i•cal, adj. —cyn'i•cism (-ə siz'əm) n.

cy'no•sure' (sī'nə shoŏr') n. object that attracts by its brilliance.

CYO Catholic Youth Organization.

cy'press (sī'prəs) n. evergreen tree of pine family.

Cys Biochemistry. cysteine.

cyst (sist) n. sac containing morbid matter formed in live tissue. —cys'tic, adj.

cys'tic fi•bro'sis (sis'tik fī brō'sis) hereditary disease marked by breathing difficulties and growth of excess fibrous tissue.

cytol. 1. cytological. **2.** cytology.

C.Z. Canal Zone. Also, **CZ**

czar (zär) n. former emperor of Russia. Also, tsar.

cza•ri'na (zä rē'nə) n. wife of a czar.

Czech (chɛk) n. native or language of Czech Republic.

D

D, d (dē) *n.* fourth letter of English alphabet.

d. 1. date. **2.** deceased. **3.** degree. **4.** diameter. **5.** dose.

D.A. District Attorney.

dab (dab) *v.*, **dabbed, dabbing. 1.** apply lightly. —*n.* **2.** small moist lump. —**dab′ber,** *n.*

dab′ble (dab′əl) *v.*, **-bled, -bling. 1.** splatter. **2.** play in water. **3.** be interested superficially. —**dab′bler,** *n.*

dachs′hund′ (däks′hŏŏnt′, -hŏŏnd′) *n.* kind of long, short-legged dog.

Da′•cron (dā′kron, dak′ron) *n. Trademark.* strong synthetic fabric.

dad (dad) *n. Informal.* father.

dad′dy (dad′ē) *n.*, *pl.* **-dies.** *Informal.* father.

dad′dy-long′legs′, *n.*, *pl.* **-legs.** spiderlike arachnid with long, slender legs. Also, **dad′-dy long′legs′.**

D.A.E. *Dictionary of American English.* Also, **DAE**

daf′fo•dil (daf′ə dil) *n.* plant with yellow flowers.

daft (daft) *adj.* **1.** insane. **2.** foolish. Also, **daf′fy** (daf′ē). —**daft′ly,** *adv.*

dag dekagram; dekagrams.

dag′ger (dag′ər) *n.* short knifelike weapon.

D.Agr. Doctor of Agriculture.

dahl′ia (dal′yə, däl′-) *n.* showy cultivated flowering plant.

dai′ly (dā′lē) *adj.* **1.** of or occurring each day. —*n.* **2.** daily newspaper.

dain′ty (dān′tē) *adj.*, **-tier, -tiest,** *n.*, *pl.* **-ties.** —*adj.* **1.** delicate. —*n.* **2.** delicacy. —**dain′ti•ly,** *adv.* —**dain′ti•ness,** *n.*

dai′qui•ri (dak′ə rē) *n.*, *pl.* **-ris.** cocktail of rum, lime juice, sugar, and fruit.

dair′y (dâr′ē) *n.*, *pl.* **-ies.** place for making or selling milk, butter, etc. —**dair′y•man,** *n.* —**dair′y•wom•an,** *n. fem.*

da′is (dā′is) *n.* raised platform.

dai′sy (dā′zē) *n.*, *pl.* **-sies.** yellow-and-white flower.

Dak. Dakota.

Da•ko′ta (də kō′tə) *n.*, *pl.* **-ta, -tas.** member of a North American Indian people.

dal dekaliter; dekaliters.

dale (dāl) *n.* valley.

dal′ly (dal′ē) *v.*, **-lied, -lying. 1.** sport; flirt. **2.** delay. —**dal′li•ance,** *n.*

Dal•ma′tian (dal mā′shən) *n.* large white-and-black dog.

dam (dam) *n.*, *v.*, **dammed, damming.** —*n.* **1.** barrier to obstruct water. **2.** female quadruped parent. —*v.* **3.** obstruct with dam.

dam′age (dam′ij) *n.*, *v.*, **-aged, -aging.** —*n.* **1.** injury. **2.** (*pl.*) payment for injury. —*v.* **3.** injure. —**dam′age•a•ble,** *adj.*

dam′ask (dam′əsk) *n.* **1.** woven figured fabric. —*adj.* **2.** pink.

dame (dām) *n.* **1.** woman of rank. **2.** *Slang* (*sometimes offensive*). any woman.

damn (dam) *v.* **1.** declare bad. **2.** condemn to hell. —**dam′na•ble** (-nə bəl) *adj.* —**dam•na′tion,** *n.*

damp (damp) *adj.* **1.** moist. —*n.* **2.** moisture. **3.** noxious vapor. —*v.* Also, **damp′en. 4.** moisten. **5.** depress. **6.** deaden. —**damp′-ness,** *n.*

damp′er, *n.* **1.** control for air or smoke currents. **2.** discouraging influence.

dam′sel (dam′zəl) *n.* maiden.

dam′son (dam′zən, -sən) *n.* small plum.

Dan. 1. *Bible.* Daniel. **2.** Also, **Dan** Danish.

dance (dans) *v.*, **danced, dancing,** *n.* —*v.* **1.** move rhythmically. —*n.* **2.** act of dancing. **3.** gathering or music for dancing. —**danc′er,** *n.* —**dance′a•ble,** *adj.*

D and C *Medicine.* a surgical method for the removal of diseased tissue or an early embryo from the lining of the uterus. [*d(ilation) and c(urettage)*]

D&D drug and disease free.

dan•de•li′on (dan′dl ī′ən) *n.* plant with yellow flowers.

dan′der (-dər) *n.* **1.** loose skin scales from various animals. **2.** *Informal.* anger; temper.

dan′dle (dan′dl) *v.*, **-dled, -dling.** move (a child) lightly up and down.

dan′druff (-drəf) *n.* scaly matter on scalp.

dan′dy (-dē) *n.*, *pl.* **-dies,** *adj.*, **-dier, -diest.** —*n.* **1.** fashionable dresser. —*adj.* **2.** fine.

Dane (dān) *n.* native of Denmark.

dan′ger (dān′jər) *n.* exposure to harm. —**dan′ger•ous,** *adj.* —**dan′ger•ous•ly,** *adv.*

dan′gle (dang′gəl) *v.*, **-gled, -gling.** hang loosely.

Dan′ish (dā′nish) *adj.* **1.** of Denmark, the Danes, or their language. —*n.* **2.** the language of the Danes. **3.** (*sometimes l.c.*) filled pastry.

dank (dangk) *adj.* unpleasantly damp. —**dank′ness,** *n.*

Danl. Daniel.

dap′per (dap′ər) *adj.* neat and well-dressed.

dap′ple (dap′əl) *n.*, *adj.*, *v.*, **-pled, -pling.** —*n.* **1.** mottled marking. —*adj.* **2.** mottled. Also, **dap′pled.** —*v.* **3.** mottle.

DAR Defense Aid Reports.

dar 1. *Military.* defense acquisition radar. **2.** digital audio recording.

D.A.R. Daughters of the American Revolution.

dare (dâr) *v.*, **dared** or **durst** (dûrst), **dared, daring,** *n.* —*v.* **1.** be bold enough. **2.** challenge. —*n.* **3.** challenge. —**dar′ing,** *adj.*, *n.*

dare′dev′il, *n.* **1.** recklessly daring person. —*adj.* **2.** recklessly daring.

dark (därk) *adj.* **1.** lacking light. **2.** blackish. **3.** ignorant. —*n.* **4.** absence of light. —**dark′-en,** *v.* —**dark′ness,** *n.*

Dark Ages, Middle Ages, esp. from A.D. 476 to about 1000.

dark horse, little-known competitor.

dark′room′, *n.* place for developing and printing films.

dar′ling (där′ling) *n.* **1.** loved one. **2.** favorite. —*adv.* **3.** cherished. **4.** charming.

darn (därn) *v.* mend with rows of stitches. —**darn′er,** *n.*

DARPA (där′pə), Defense Advanced Research Projects Agency.

dart (därt) *n.* **1.** slender pointed missile. —*v.* **2.** move swiftly.

dash (dash) *v.* **1.** strike or throw violently. **2.** frustrate. —*n.* **3.** violent blow. **4.** small quantity. **5.** punctuation mark (–) noting abrupt break. **6.** rush.

dash′board′, *n.* instrument board on motor vehicle.

dash′ing, *adj.* **1.** lively. **2.** stylish. —**dash′ing•ly,** *adv.*

das′tard (das′tərd) *n.* coward. —**das′tard•ly,** *adj.*

DAT digital audiotape.

dat. 1. dative. **2.** datum.

da′ta (dā′tə, dat′ə) *n.pl., sing.* **datum** (dā′təm, dat′əm). facts or other information.

da′ta•base′, *n.* collection of data, esp. one accessible by computer.

datacom (dā′tə kom′), data communication.

data processing, high-speed handling of information by computer. —**data processor.**

date (dāt) *n., v.,* **dated, dating.** —*n.* **1.** particular time. **2.** fleshy, edible fruit of date palm. **3.** appointment. **4.** social engagement arranged beforehand, esp. one of a romantic nature. **5.** person with whom one shares such an engagement. —*v.* **6.** exist from particular time. **7.** fix date for or with.

dat′ed, *adj.* **1.** having or showing a date. **2.** out-of-date.

da′tive (dā′tiv) *adj.* denoting verb's indirect object.

dau. daughter.

daub (dôb) *v.* **1.** cover with mud, etc. **2.** paint clumsily. —*n.* **3.** daubed. —**daub′er,** *n.*

daugh′ter (dô′tər) *n.* female child. —**daugh′ter•ly,** *adj.*

daugh′ter-in-law′, *n., pl.* **daughters-in-law.** son's wife.

daunt (dônt, dänt) *v.* **1.** frighten. **2.** dishearten. —**daunt′ing•ly,** *adv.*

daunt′less, *adj.* bold; fearless. —**daunt′less•ly,** *adv.*

D.A.V. Disabled American Veterans. Also, **DAV**

dav′en•port′ (dav′ən pôrt′) *n.* large sofa.

dav′it (dav′it, dā′vit) *n.* crane for boat, etc.

daw′dle (dôd′l) *v.,* **-dled, -dling.** waste time. —**daw′dler,** *n.*

dawn (dôn) *n.* **1.** break of day. —*v.* **2.** begin to grow light. **3.** become apparent.

day (dā) *n.* **1.** period between two nights. **2.** period (24 hours) of earth's rotation on its axis.

day′break′, *n.* first appearance of light; dawn.

day care, supervised care for young children or the elderly, usu. in daytime and at a center outside the home. —**day′-care′,** *adj.*

day′dream′, *n.* **1.** reverie; fancy. —*v.* **2.** indulge in reveries. —**day′dream′er,** *n.*

day′light′, *n.* **1.** light of day. **2.** openness. **3.** (*pl.*) wits; sanity.

daylight-saving time, time one hour later than standard time. Also, Also, **daylight-savings time.**

day′time′, *n.* time from sunrise to sunset.

day′-to-day′, *adj.* **1.** occurring each day. **2.** routine; normal.

daze (dāz) *v.,* **dazed, dazing,** *n.* —*v.* **1.** stun. —*n.* **2.** dazed state.

daz′zle (daz′əl) *v.,* **-zled, -zling.** overwhelm with light.

DB *Radio and Television.* delayed broadcast.

dB *Physics.* decibel; decibels.

D.B. 1. Bachelor of Divinity. **2.** Domesday Book.

d.b. daybook.

dba, doing business as.

D.B.E. Dame Commander of the Order of the British Empire.

D.Bib. Douay Bible.

dbl, 1. decibel. **2.** double.

dblr *Electronics.* doubler.

DBMS *Computers.* Data Base Management System.

DBS *Television.* direct broadcast satellite.

DC, 1. direct current. **2.** District of Columbia.

dcd decode.

dcdr decoder.

DCF divorced Christian female.

D.Ch.E. Doctor of Chemical Engineering.

DCHP *Dictionary of Canadianisms on Historical Principles.*

dckg docking.

dcl door closer.

D.C.L. Doctor of Civil Law.

dclr decelerate.

DCM divorced Christian male.

D.C.M. *British.* Distinguished Conduct Medal.

D.Cn.L. Doctor of Canon Law.

DCPA Defense Civil Preparedness Agency.

D.Crim. Doctor of Criminology.

D.C.S. 1. Deputy Clerk of Sessions. **2.** Doctor of Christian Science. **3.** Doctor of Commercial Science.

DCTL *Computers.* direct-coupled transistor logic.

D.D., Doctor of Divinity.

D

dda digital differential analyzer.

D-day (dē′dā′), **1.** a day set for beginning something. **2.** June 6, 1944, the day the Allies invaded W Europe. Also, **D-Day.**

DDD *Telecommunications.* direct distance dialing.

DDP *Computers.* distributed data processing.

DDR German Democratic Republic. [from German *D(eutsche) D(emokratische) R(epublik)*]

D.D.S., 1. Doctor of Dental Science. **2.** Doctor of Dental Surgery.

D.D.Sc. Doctor of Dental Science.

DDT, strong insecticide, now banned from use.

de-, prefix indicating: **1.** reverse, as *deactivate.* **2.** remove, as *decaffeinate.* **3.** reduce, as *degrade.*

DEA Drug Enforcement Administration.

dea′con (dē′kən) *n.* **1.** cleric inferior to priest. **2.** lay church officer. **—dea′con•ess,** *n.fem.* **—dea′con•ry,** *n.*

de•ac′ti•vate′ (dē ak′tə vāt′) *v.,* **-vated, -vating. 1.** make inactive. **2.** demobilize.

dead (ded) *adj.* **1.** no longer alive or active. **2.** infertile. **3.** complete; absolute **—***n.* **4.** dead person or persons. **—***adv.* **5.** completely. **6.** directly. **—dead′en,** *v.*

dead′beat′, *n.* **1.** person who avoids paying. **2.** sponger.

dead end, 1. street, corridor, etc., that has no exit. **2.** position with no hope of progress. **—dead′-end′,** *adj.*

dead heat, race that finishes in a tie.

dead′line′, *n.* last allowable time.

dead′lock′, *n.* standstill.

dead′ly, *adj.,* **-lier, -liest. 1.** fatal. **2.** dreary. **3.** extremely accurate. **—***adv.* **4.** extremely.

dead′pan′, *adj.* without expression; appearing serious.

dead′wood′, *n.* useless or extraneous persons or things.

deaf (def) *adj.* unable to hear. **—deaf′en,** *v.* **—deaf′ness,** *n.*

deaf′-mute′, *n. Often Offensive.* person unable to hear or speak.

deal (dēl) *v.,* **dealt** (delt), **dealing,** *n.* **—***v.* **1.** conduct oneself toward. **2.** do business. **3.** distribute. **—***n.* **4.** transaction. **5.** quantity. **—deal′er,** *n.*

deal′ing, *n.* (*usually pl.*) transactions or interactions with others.

dean (dēn) *n.* **1.** head of academic faculty. **2.** head of cathedral organization.

dear (dēr) *adj.* **1.** loved. **2.** expensive. **—***n.* **3.** dear one. **—dear′ly,** *adv.*

dearth (dûrth) *n.* scarcity.

death (deth) *n.* end of life. **—death′ly,** *adj.,* *adv.* **—death′bed′,** *n.*

death′less, *adj.* enduring.

de•ba′cle (də bä′kəl, -bak′əl, dā-) *n.* **1.** breakup; rout. **2.** utter failure.

de•bar′ (di bär′) *v.,* **-barred, -barring.** exclude. **—de•bar′ment,** *n.*

de•bark′ (di bärk′) *v.* disembark. **—de′bar•ka′tion,** *n.*

de•base′ (di bās′) *v.,* **-based, -basing.** reduce in quality. **—de•base′ment,** *n.*

de•bate′ (di bāt′) *n., v.,* **-bated, -bating.** **—***n.* **1.** controversial discussion. **—***v.* **2.** argue; discuss. **—de•bat′a•ble,** *adj.* **—de•bat′er,** *n.*

de•bauch′ (di bôch′) *v.* **1.** corrupt; pervert. **—***n.* **2.** period of corrupt indulgence. **—de•bauch′er•y,** *n.*

de•ben′ture (di ben′chər) *n.* short-term, negotiable, interest-producing note representing debt.

de•bil′i•tate′ (di bil′i tāt′) *v.,* **-tated, -tating.** weaken. **—de•bil′i•ta′tion,** *n.*

de•bil′i•ty, *n., pl.* **-ties.** weakness.

deb′it (deb′it) *n.* **1.** recorded debt. **2.** account of debts. **—***v.* **3.** charge as debt.

deb′o•nair′ (deb′ə nâr′) *adj.* **1.** suave; urbane. **2.** relaxed; calm.

de•brief′ (dē brēf′) *v.* gather information from someone about a completed mission.

de•bris′ (də brē′, dā′brē) *n.* rubbish; ruins.

debt (det) *n.* **1.** something owed. **2.** obligation to pay. **—debt′or,** *n.*

de•bug′ (dē bug′) *v.,* **-bugged, -bugging. 1.** remove defects or errors from (computer program). **2.** remove electronic bugs from (room or building).

de•bunk′ (di bungk′) *v.* expose as false.

de•but′ (dā byōō′, di-, dā′byōō) *n.* first public appearance. **—deb′u•tante′,** *n.fem.*

Dec., December.

dec′ade (dek′ād) *n.* 10-year period.

dec′a•dence (dek′ə dəns, di kād′ns) *n.* **1.** decline in quality of power. **2.** decline in morality; corruption. **—dec′a•dent,** *adj.*

decaf. decaffeinated.

de•caf′fein•at•ed (dē kaf′ə nā′təd), *adj.* having the caffeine removed.

dec′a•he′dron (dek′ə hē′drən) *n., pl.* **-drons, -dra** (-drə). solid figure with 10 faces.

de′cal (dē′kal, di kal′) *n.* picture or design on specially prepared paper for transfer to wood, metal, etc.

Dec′a•logue′ (dek′ə lôg′) *n.* Ten Commandments.

de•camp′ (di kamp′) *v.* depart, esp. secretly.

de•cant′ (di kant′) *v.* pour off.

de•cant′er, *n.* bottle.

de•cap′i•tate′ (di kap′i tāt′) *v.,* **-tated, -tating.** behead. **—de•cap′i•ta′tion,** *n.*

de•cath′lon (di kath′lon) *n.* contest of 10 events.

de•cay′ (di kā′) *v., n.* decline in quality, health, etc.

decd. deceased.

de•cease′ (di sēs′) *n., v.,* **-ceased, -ceasing.** **—***n.* **1.** death. **—***v.* **2.** die. **—de•ceased′,** *adj., n.*

de•ce′dent (di sēd′nt) *n. Law.* deceased person.

de•ceit′ (di sēt′) *n.* **1.** fraud. **2.** trick. —**de•ceit′ful,** *adj.*

de•ceive′ (di sēv′) *v.,* **-ceived, -ceiving.** mislead.

de•cel′er•ate′ (dē sel′ə rāt′) *v.* slow down.

De•cem′ber (di sem′bər) *n.* 12th month of year.

de′cen•cy (dē′sən sē) *n., pl.* **-cies. 1.** conformity to standards of morality or behavior. **2.** respectability. **3.** adequacy. **4.** kindness or willingness to help. —**de′cent,** *adj.* —**de′cent•ly,** *adv.*

de•cen′tral•ize′ (dē sen′trə līz′) *v.,* **-ized, -izing.** end central control of. —**de•cen′tral•i•za′tion,** *n.*

de•cep′tion (di sep′shən) *n.* **1.** act of deceiving. **2.** fraud. —**de•cep′tive,** *adj.*

dec′i•bel′ (des′ə bel′, -bəl) *n.* unit of intensity of sound.

de•cide′ (di sīd′) *v.,* **-cided, -ciding.** settle; resolve.

de•cid′ed, *adj.* unambiguous; emphatic. —**de•cid′ed•ly,** *adv.*

de•cid′u•ous (di sij′ōō əs) *adj.* **1.** shedding leaves annually. **2.** falling off at a particular season, as horns.

dec′i•mal (des′ə məl) *adj.* **1.** of tenths. **2.** proceeding by tens. —*n.* **3.** fraction in tenths, hundredths, etc., indicated by dot (**decimal point**) before numerator.

dec′i•mate′ (des′ə māt′) *v.* **-mated, -mating.** kill or destroy large part of.

de•ci′pher (di sī′fər) *v.* find meaning of. —**de•ci′pher•a•ble,** *adj.*

de•ci′sion (di sizh′ən) *n.* **1.** something decided. **2.** firmness of mind.

de•ci′sive (-sī′siv) *adj.* **1.** determining. **2.** resolute. —**de•ci′sive•ly,** *adv.* —**de•ci′sive•ness,** *n.*

deck (dek) *n.* **1.** level on ship. **2.** pack of playing cards. —*v.* **3.** array.

de•claim′ (di klām′) *v.* speak rhetorically. —**de•claim′er,** *n.*

dec′la•ma′tion (dek′lə mā′shən) *n.* oratorical speech. —**de•clam′a•to′ry** (-klam′ə tôr′ē) *adj.*

de•clare′ (di klâr′) *v.,* **-clared, -claring. 1.** make known; proclaim. **2.** affirm. —**dec′la•ra′tion** (dek′lə rā′shən) *n.* —**de•clar′a•tive,** **de•clar′a•to′ry,** *adj.*

de•clen′sion (di klen′shən) *n.* grammatical inflection or set of inflections.

dec′li•na′tion (dek′lə nā′shən) *n.* **1.** slope. **2.** angular height of heavenly body.

de•cline′ (di klīn′) *v.,* **-clined, -clining,** *n.* —*v.* **1.** refuse. **2.** slant down. **3.** give grammatical inflections of; diminish. —*n.* **5.** downward slope. **6.** deterioration.

de•cliv′i•ty (di kliv′i tē) *n., pl.* **-ties.** downward slope.

decn decision.

de•code′ (dē kōd′) *v.,* **-coded, -coding.** decipher from code.

de′com•mis′sion, *v.* retire (vessel) from active service.

decompn decompression.

de′com•pose′ (-kəm pōz′) *v.,* **-posed, -posing. 1.** separate into constituent parts. **2.** rot. —**de′com•po•si′tion,** *n.*

de′con•ges′tant (dē′kən jes′tənt) *adj.* **1.** relieving congestion of the upper respiratory tract. —*n.* **2.** decongestant agent.

de′con•tam′i•nate (-nāt′) *v.,* **-nated, -nating.** make safe by removing or neutralizing harmful contaminants. —**de′con•tam′i•na′tion,** *n.*

decontn decontamination.

dé•cor′ (dā kôr′, di-) *n.* style of decoration, as of a room. Also, **de•cor′.**   **D**

dec′o•rate′ (dek′ə rāt′) *v.,* **-rated, -rating.** furnish with ornament. —**dec′o•ra′tion,** *n.* —**dec′o•ra•tive** (-ər ə tiv) *adj.* —**dec′o•ra′tor,** *n.*

dec′o•rous, *adj.* proper; dignified. —**dec′o•rous•ly,** *adv.*

de•co′rum (di kôr′əm) *n.* propriety.

de•coy′ (*n.* dē′koi, di koi′; *v.* di koi′, dē′koi) *n., v.* lure.

decr decrease.

de•crease′ *v.* **-creased, -creasing,** *n.* —*v.* (di krēs′) **1.** lessen. —*n.* (dē′krēs, di krēs′) **2.** lessening.

de•cree′ (di krē′) *n., v.,* **-creed, -creeing.** —*n.* **1.** published command. —*v.* **2.** proclaim or command.

de•crep′it (di krep′it) *adj.* feeble with age. —**de•crep′i•tude′,** *n.*

de′cre•scen′do (dē′kri shen′dō, dā′-) *adj., adv. Music.* gradually decreasing in loudness.

de•crim′i•nal•ize′ (dē krim′ə nl īz′) *v.,* **-ized, -izing.** cease to treat as a crime. —**de•crim′i•nal•i•za′tion,** *n.*

de•cry′ (di krī′) *v.,* **-cried, -crying.** disparage or denounce.

ded. 1. dedicate. **2.** dedicated. **3.** deduct. **4.** deducted. **5.** deduction.

D.Ed. Doctor of Education.

ded′i•cate′ (ded′i kāt′) *v.,* **-cated, -cating. 1.** set apart. **2.** devote. **3.** inscribe in honor of. —**ded′i•ca′tion,** *n.*

de d in d (in prescriptions) from day to day. [from Latin *dē diē in diem*]

de•duce′ (di dōōs′, -dyōōs′) *v.,* **-duced, -ducing.** derive logically; infer. —**de•duc′i•ble,** *adj.*

de•duct′ (di dukt′) *v.* subtract. —**de•duct′i•ble,** *adj.*

de•duc′tion, *n.* act or result of deducting or deducing. —**de•duc′tive,** *adj.*

deed (dēd) *n.* **1.** act. **2.** written conveyance of property. —*v.* **3.** transfer by deed.

dee′jay′ (dē′jā′) *n.* disc jockey.

deem (dēm) *v.* think; estimate.

de-em′pha•size′ (dē em′fə sīz′) *v.,* **-sized,**

-sizing. place less emphasis on. —de•em′•pha•sis, n.

deep (dēp) adj. 1. extending far down or in. 2. difficult to understand. 3. profound. 4. low in pitch. —n. 5. deep part or space. —adv. 6. at great depth. —deep′en, v. —deep′ly, adv.

deep′-freeze′, v., -froze, -frozen, -freezing, n. —v. 1. freeze rapidly for preservation. —n. 2. refrigerator that deep-freezes.

deep′-fry′, v., -fried, -frying. cook in boiling fat. —deep′-fry′er, n.

deep′-seat′ed, adj. firmly fixed. Also, deep′-root′ed.

deep space, space beyond the solar system.

deer (dēr) n., pl. deer. hoofed, ruminant animal, the male of which usually has antlers.

def. 1. defective. 2. defense. 3. definition. Also, **def**

de•face′ (di fās′) v., -faced, -facing. mar. —de•face′ment, n.

de fac′to (dē fak′tō, dā) 1. in fact; in reality. 2. actually existing, esp. without legal authority.

de•fame′ (di fām′) v., -famed, -faming. attack the reputation of. —def′a•ma′tion (def′ə mā′shən) n. —de•fam′a•to′ry (-fam′ə tôr′ē) adj. —de•fam′er, n.

de•fault′ (di fôlt′) n. 1. failure; neglect. —v. 2. fail to meet obligation.

DEFCON (def′kon), any of several alert statuses for U.S. military forces. [def(ense readiness) con(dition)]

de•feat′ (di fēt′) v., n. overthrow.

de•feat′ism, n. acceptance of defeat too easily. —de•feat′ist, n.

def′e•cate′ (def′i kāt′) v., -cated, -cating. void feces from bowels. —def′e•ca′tion, n.

de′fect n. (dē′fekt, di fekt′) 1. fault; imperfection. —v. (di fekt′) 2. desert a cause, country, etc. —de•fec′tive, adj.

de•fec′tion, n. desertion of a cause, country, etc.

de•fend′ (di fend′) v. 1. protect against attack. 2. uphold. —de•fend′er, n.

de•fend′ant, n. party accused of a crime or sued in court.

de•fense′ (di fens′) n. 1. resistance to attack. 2. defending argument. —de•fense′•less, adj. —de•fen′sive, adj., n.

defense mechanism, unconscious process that protects person from painful ideas or impulses.

de•fer′ (di fûr′) v., -ferred, -ferring. 1. postpone. 2. yield in opinion. 3. show respect. —de•fer′ment, n.

def′er•ence (def′ər əns) n. act of showing respect. —def′er•en′tial (-ə ren′shəl) adj.

de•fi′ance (di fī′əns) n. 1. bold resistance. 2. disregard. —de•fi′ant, adj. —de•fi′ant•ly, adv.

de•fi′cien•cy (di fish′ən sē) n., pl. -cies. lack. —de•fi′cient, adj.

def′i•cit (def′ə sit) n. deficiency of funds.

de•file′ (di fīl′) v., -filed, -filing, n. —v. 1. befoul. 2. desecrate. 3. march in file. —n. 4. narrow pass. —de•file′ment, n.

de•fine′ (di fīn′) v., -fined, -fining. 1. state meaning of. 2. outline or determine precisely. —def′i•ni′tion, n.

def′i•nite (def′ə nit) adj. 1. exact. 2. with fixed limits. —def′i•nite•ly, adv.

de•fin′i•tive (di fin′i tiv) adj. conclusive. —de•fin′i•tive•ly, adv.

defl deflect.

de•flate′ (di flāt′) v., -flated, -flating. release gas from.

de•fla′tion, n. sharp fall in prices. —de•fla′tion•ar′y, adj.

de•flect′ (di flekt′) v. turn from true course. —de•flec′tion, n.

de•fo′li•ate′ (dē fō′lē āt′) v., -ated, -ating. 1. strip of leaves. 2. clear of vegetation, as to expose hidden enemy forces. —de•fo′li•a′tion, n. —de•fo′li•ant (-ənt) n.

de•for′est (di fôr′ist) v. clear of trees or forests. —de•for′es•ta′tion, n.

de•form′, v. mar form of. —de•form′i•ty, n.

de•fraud′, v. cheat. —de•fraud′er, n.

de•fray′, v. pay (expenses).

de•frost′, v. 1. remove frost or ice from. 2. thaw.

defs. definitions.

deft (deft) adj. skillful. —deft′ly, adv. —deft′ness, n.

de•funct′ (di fungkt′) adj. no longer in existence.

de•fuse′ (dē fyōōz′) v. 1. remove detonating fuse from. 2. make less dangerous or tense.

de•fy′ (di fī′) v., -fied, -fying. challenge; resist.

deg. degree; degrees.

de•gen′er•ate′, v., -ated, -ating, adj., n. —v. (di jen′ə rāt′) 1. decline; deteriorate. —adj. (-ər it) 2. having declined 3. corrupt. —n. (-ər it) 4. degenerate person. —de•gen′er•a′tion, n. —de•gen′er•a•cy, n.

deglut. (in prescriptions) may be swallowed; let it be swallowed. [from Latin dēglūtiātur]

de•grade′ (di grād′) v., -graded, -grading. reduce in status. —deg′ra•da′tion (deg′rī•dā′shən) n.

de•gree′ (di grē′) n. 1. stage or extent. 2. 360th part of a complete revolution. 3. unit of temperature. 4. title conferred by college.

de•hu′man•ize′ (dē hyōō′mə nīz′; often -yōō′-) v., -ized, -izing. treat as lacking human qualities or requirements. —de•hu′man•i•za′tion, n.

de′hu•mid′i•fi′er, n. device for removing moisture from air. —de′hu•mid′i•fy, v.

de•hy′drate′, v., -drated, -drating. deprive of water. —de′hy•dra′tion, n.

D.E.I. Dutch East Indies.

de′i•fy′ (dē′ə fī′) v., -fied, -fying. make a god of. —de′i•fi•ca′tion, n.

deign (dān) v. condescend.

de•in'sti•tu'tion•al•ize', *v.*, **-ized, -izing.** release from an institution to community care. —**de•in'sti•tu'tion•al•i•za'tion,** *n.*

de'ism (dē'iz əm) *n.* belief in the existence of a God based on reason and evidence in nature, rather than on divine revelation. —**de'ist,** *n.* —**de•is'tic,** *adj.*

de'i•ty (dē'i tē) *n., pl.* **-ties.** god or goddess.

dé'jà vu' (dā'zhä vōō') feeling of having lived through same moment before.

de•ject'ed (di jek'tid) *adj.* disheartened. —**de•jec'tion,** *n.*

de ju're (di jŏŏr'ē, dā jŏŏr'ā) by right or according to law.

Del. Delaware.

de•lay' (di lā') *v.* **1.** postpone. **2.** hinder. —*n.* **3.** act of delaying. **4.** instance of being delayed. —**de•lay'er,** *n.*

dele delete.

de•lec'ta•ble (di lek'tə bəl) *adj.* delightful. —**de•lec'ta•bly,** *adv.* —**de'lec•ta'tion,** *n.*

del'e•gate *n., v.,* **-gated, -gating.** —*n.* (del'- i git, -gāt') **1.** deputy. **2.** legislator. —*v.* (-gāt') **3.** send as deputy. **4.** commit to another. —**del'e•ga'tion,** *n.*

de•lete' (di lēt') *v.,* **-leted, -leting.** cancel; erase. —**de•le'tion,** *n.*

del'e•te'ri•ous (del'i tēr'ē əs) *adj.* harmful.

del'i (del'ē) *n.* delicatessen.

de•lib'er•ate *adj., v.,* **-ated, -ating.** —*adj.* (di lib'ər it) **1.** intentional. **2.** unhurried. —*v.* (-ə rāt') **3.** consider. **4.** confer. —**de•lib'er•a'tion,** *n.* —**de•lib'er•ate•ly,** *adv.* —**de•lib'er•ate•ness,** *n.* —**de•lib'er•a'tive** (-ə-rā'tiv, -ər ə tiv) *adj.* —**de•lib'er•a'tor,** *n.*

del'i•ca•cy (del'i kə sē) *n., pl.* **-cies. 1.** fineness. **2.** nicety. **3.** choice food.

del'i•cate (-kit) *adj.* **1.** fine. **2.** dainty. **3.** fragile. **4.** tactful. —**del'i•cate•ly,** *adv.*

del•i•ca•tes'sen (del'i kə tes'ən) *n.* store that sells cooked or prepared food.

de•li'cious (di lish'əs) *adj.* pleasing, esp. to taste. —**de•li'cious•ly,** *adv.* —**de•li'cious•ness,** *n.*

de•light' (di līt') *n.* **1.** joy. —*v.* **2.** please highly. **3.** take joy. —**de•light'ed,** *adj.* —**de•light'ful,** *adj.*

de•lim'it (di lim'it) *v.* fix or mark limits of. —**de•lim'i•ta'tion,** *n.*

de•lin'e•ate' (di lin'ē āt') *v.,* **-ated, -ating.** sketch; outline. —**de•lin'e•a'tion,** *n.*

de•lin'quent (di ling'kwənt) *adj.* **1.** neglectful; guilty. —*n.* **2.** delinquent one. —**de•lin'quen•cy,** *n.*

de•lir'i•um (di lēr'ē əm) *n.* mental disorder marked by excitement, visions, etc. —**de•lir'i•ous,** *adj.*

de•liv'er (di liv'ər) *v.* **1.** give up. **2.** carry and turn over. **3.** utter. **4.** direct. **5.** save. **6.** give birth. **7.** assist at birth. —**de•liv'er•ance,** *n.* —**de•liv'er•y,** *n.*

dell (del) *n.* small, wooded valley.

del•phin'i•um (del fin'ē əm) *n., pl.* **-iums, -ia** (-ē ə). blue garden flower.

del'ta (del'tə) *n.* **1.** 4th letter of Greek alphabet. **2.** triangular area between branches of river mouth.

de•lude' (di lōōd') *v.,* **-luded, -luding.** mislead.

del'uge (del'yōōj) *n., v.,* **-uged, -uging.** —*n.* **1.** great flood. —*v.* **2.** flood. **3.** overwhelm.

de•lu'sion (di lōō'zhən) *n.* false opinion or conception. —**de•lu'sive,** *adj.*

de•luxe' (də luks') *adj.* of finest quality.

delve (delv) *v.,* **delved, delving.** search carefully for information. —**delv'er,** *n.*

dely. delivery.

Dem., 1. Democrat. **2.** Democratic.

dem'a•gogue' (dem'ə gog') *n.* unscrupulous popular leader. —**dem'a•gogu'er•y,** *n.*

de•mand' (di mand') *v.* **1.** claim. **2.** require. **3.** ask for in urgent or peremptory manner. —*n.* **4.** claim. **5.** requirement.

de•mar'cate (di mär'kāt, dē'mär kāt') *v.,* **-cated, -cating. 1.** delimit. **2.** set apart. —**de'mar•ca'tion,** *n.*

de•mean' (di mēn') *v.* **1.** conduct (oneself). **2.** lower in dignity.

de•mean'or, *n.* conduct; behavior; deportment.

de•ment'ed (di men'tid) *adj.* crazed.

de•men'tia (-shə, -shē ə) *n.* severe mental impairment.

de•mer'it (di mer'it) *n.* **1.** fault. **2.** rating for misconduct.

demi-, prefix indicating half or lesser, as *demigod.*

dem'i•god' (dem'ē god') *n.* one partly divine and partly human.

de•mil'i•ta•rize' (dē mil'i tə rīz') *v.,* **-rized, -rizing.** free from military influence. —**de•mil'i•ta•ri•za'tion,** *n.*

de•mise' (di mīz') *n., v.,* **-mised, -mising.** —*n.* **1.** death. **2.** transfer of estate. —*v.* **3.** transfer.

dem'i•tasse' (dem'i tas', -täs') *n.* small coffee cup.

dem'o (dem'ō) *n.* product displayed or offered for trial.

de•mo'bi•lize' (dē mō'bə līz') *v.,* **-lized, -lizing.** disband (army). —**de•mo'bi•li•za'tion,** *n.*

de•moc'ra•cy (di mok'rə sē) *n., pl.* **-cies. 1.** government in which the people hold supreme power. **2.** social equality. —**dem'o•crat'** (dem'ə krat') *n.* —**dem'o•crat'ic,** *adj.* —**de•moc'ra•tize',** *v.*

Democratic Party, a major political party in the U.S.

demod (dē'mod), demodulator.

dem'o•graph'ic (dem'ə graf'ik) *adj.* of statistics on population. —**dem'o•graph'i•cal•ly,** *adv.* —**dem'o•graph'ics,** *n.pl.* —**de•mog'ra•phy** (di mog'rə fē) *n.*

de•mol'ish (di mol'ish) *v.* destroy. —**dem'o•li'tion** (dem'ə lish'ən) *n.*

de'mon (dē'mən) *n.* evil spirit.

de•mon'ic (di mon'ik) *adj.* **1.** inspired. **2.**

D

like a demon. Also, **de/mo·ni/a·cal** (dē/mə-nī/ə kəl).

dem/on·strate/ (dem/ən strāt/) v., -strated, -strating. **1.** prove. **2.** describe and explain. **3.** manifest. **4.** parade in support or opposition. —**de·mon/stra·ble** (di mon/strə bəl) adj. —**dem/on·stra/tion,** n. —**dem/on·stra/tor,** n.

de·mon/stra·tive (də mon/strə tiv) adj. **1.** expressive. **2.** explanatory. **3.** conclusive.

de·mor/al·ize/ (di môr/ə līz/) v., -ized, -izing. destroy morale of. —**de·mor/al·i·za/-tion,** n.

de·mote/ (di mōt/) v., -moted, -moting. reduce in rank. —**de·mo/tion,** n.

de·mur/ (di mûr/) v., -murred, -murring, n. —v. **1.** object. —n. **2.** objection. —**de·mur/-ral,** n.

de·mure/ (di myŏŏr/) adj. modest. —**de·mure/ly,** adv.

demux (dē/muks), Telecommunications. demultiplexer.

den (den) n. **1.** cave of wild beast. **2.** squalid place. **3.** room in a home for relaxation.

de·na/ture (dē nā/chər) v., -tured, -turing. make (alcohol) unfit to drink.

deng diesal engine.

D.Eng. Doctor of Engineering.

D.Eng.S. Doctor of Engineering Science.

de·ni/al (di nī/əl) n. **1.** contradiction. **2.** refusal to agree or give.

den/i·grate/ (den/i grāt/) v., -grated, -grating. speak badly of. —**den/i·gra/tion,** n.

den/im (den/əm) n. **1.** heavy cotton fabric. **2.** (pl.) trousers of this.

den/i·zen (den/ə zən) n. inhabitant.

de·nom/i·nate/ (di nom/ə nāt/) v., -nated, -nating. name specifically.

de·nom/i·na/tion, n. **1.** name or designation. **2.** sect. **3.** value of piece of money. —**de·nom/i·na/tion·al,** adj.

de·nom/i·na/tor, n. lower term in fraction.

de·note/ (di nōt/) v., -noted, -noting. **1.** indicate. **2.** mean. —**de/no·ta/tion,** n.

de/noue·ment/ (dā/nŏŏ mäN/) n. **1.** final resolution of plot or story. **2.** outcome of series of events. Also, **dé/noue·ment/.**

de·nounce/ (di nouns/) v., -nounced, -nouncing. **1.** condemn. **2.** inform against. —**de·nounce/ment,** n.

dens density.

dense (dens) adj., denser, densest. **1.** compact. **2.** stupid. —**den/si·ty,** n. —**dense/ly,** adv. —**dense/ness,** n.

dent (dent) n. **1.** hollow. —v. **2.** make a dent.

den/tal (den/tl) adj. of teeth.

den/ti·frice (-tə fris) n. teeth-cleaning substance.

den/tin (-tn, -tin) n. hard tissue that forms most of a tooth. Also, **den/tine** (-tēn).

den/tist (-tist) n. person who prevents and treats oral disease. —**den/tist·ry,** n.

den/ture (-chər, -chŏŏr) n. artificial tooth.

de·nude/ (di nŏŏd/, -nyŏŏd/) v., -nuded, -nuding. make bare; strip. —**den/u·da/tion** (den/yə dā/shən) n.

de·nun/ci·a/tion (di nun/sē ā/shən) n. **1.** condemnation. **2.** accusation.

de·ny/ (di nī/) v., -nied, -nying. **1.** declare not to be true. **2.** refuse to agree or give.

de·o/dor·ant (dē ō/dər ənt) n. agent for destroying odors.

de·o/dor·ize/, v., -ized, -izing. rid of odors. —**de·o/dor·iz/er,** n.

dep. 1. depart. **2.** department. **3.** departs. **4.** departure. **5.** deponent. **6.** deposed. **7.** deposit. **8.** depot. **9.** deputy.

de·part/ (di pärt/) v. **1.** go away. **2.** die. —**de·par/ture,** n.

de·part/ment, n. **1.** part; section. **2.** branch. —**de/part·men/tal,** adj.

de·pend/ (di pend/) v. **1.** rely. **2.** be contingent. —**de·pend/ence,** n. —**de·pend/en·cy,** n. —**de·pend/ent,** adj., n.

de·pend/a·ble, adj. reliable. —**de·pend/a·bil/i·ty,** n. —**de·pend/a·bly,** adv.

de·pict/ (di pikt/) v. **1.** portray. **2.** describe. —**de·pic/tion,** n.

de·pil/a·to/ry (di pil/ə tôr/ē) adj., n., pl. -ries. —adj. **1.** capable of removing hair. —n. **2.** depilatory agent.

de·plete/ (di plēt/) v., -pleted, -pleting. reduce in amount. —**de·ple/tion,** n.

de·plore/, v. (di plôr/ -plōr/) -plored, -ploring. lament. —**de·plor/a·ble,** adj.

de·ploy/ (-ploi/) v. place strategically. —**de·ploy/ment,** n.

de/po·lit/i·cize/ (dē/pə lit/ə sīz/) v., -cized, -cizing. remove from realm of politics.

de·pop/u·late/ (dē pop/yə lāt/) v., -lated, -lating. deprive of inhabitants. —**de·pop/u·la/tion,** n.

de·port/ (di pôrt/) v. **1.** banish. **2.** conduct (oneself). —**de/por·ta/tion** (dē/pôr tā/shən) n.

de·port/ment, n. conduct.

de·pose/ (di pōz/) v., -posed, -posing. **1.** remove from office. **2.** testify. —**dep/o·si/tion** (dep/ə zish/ən) n.

de·pos/it (di poz/it) v. **1.** place. **2.** place for safekeeping. —n. **3.** sediment. **4.** something deposited. —**de·pos/i·tor,** n.

de·pos/i·to/ry (di poz/i tôr/ē) n., pl. -ries. place for safekeeping.

de/pot (dē/pō; Mil. or Brit. dep/ō) n. **1.** station. **2.** storage base.

depr. 1. depreciation. **2.** depression.

de·prave/ (di prāv/) v., -praved, -praving. corrupt. —**de·praved/,** adj. —**de·prav/i·ty** (-prav/i tē) n.

dep/re·cate/ (dep/ri kāt/) v., -cated, -cating. disapprove of. —**dep/re·ca/tion,** n. —**dep/-re·ca·to/ry,** adj.

de·pre/ci·ate/ (di prē/shē āt/) v., -ated, -ating. **1.** reduce or decline in value. **2.** belittle. —**de·pre/ci·a/tion,** n.

dep/re·da/tion (dep/ri dā/shən) n. plunder.

de•press' (di pres') v. **1.** deject. **2.** weaken. **3.** press down. **—de•press'ant,** adj., n. **—de•pressed',** adj.

de•pres'sion, n. **1.** act of depressing. **2.** depressed state. **3.** depressed place. **4.** decline in business. **—de•pres'sive,** adj.

de•prive' (-prīv') v., **-prived, -priving. 1.** divest. **2.** withhold from. **—dep'ri•va'tion,** n.

dept., 1. department. **2.** deputy.

depth (depth) n. **1.** distance down. **2.** profundity. **3.** lowness of pitch. **4.** deep part.

dep'u•ta'tion (dep'yə tā'shən) n. delegation.

dep'u•ty (-tē) n., pl. **-ties.** agent; substitute. **—dep'u•tize'** (-tīz') v., **-tized, -tizing.**

der. 1. derivation. **2.** derivative. **3.** derive. **4.** derived.

de•rail' (dē rāl') v. cause to run off rails. **—de•rail'ment,** n.

de•range' (di rānj') v., **-ranged, -ranging. 1.** disarrange. **2.** make insane. **—de•range'ment,** n.

der'by (dûr'bē; Brit. där'-) n., pl. **-bies. 1.** stiff, rounded hat. **2.** race.

de•reg'u•late' (dē reg'yə lāt') v., **-lated, -lating.** free of regulation. **—de•reg'u•la'tion,** n.

der'e•lict (der'ə likt) adj. **1.** abandoned. **2.** neglectful. **—n. 3.** abandoned. **4.** vagrant.

der'e•lic'tion, n. neglect.

de•ride' (di rīd') v., **-rided, -riding.** mock. **—de•ri'sion** (-rizh'ən) n. **—de•ri'sive** (-rī'siv) adj. **—de•ri'sive•ly,** adv.

deriv. 1. derivation. **2.** derivative. **3.** derive. **4.** derived.

de•rive' (di rīv') v., **-rived, -riving. 1.** get from source. **2.** trace. **3.** deduce. **4.** originate. **—der'i•va'tion** (der'ə vā'shən) n. **—de•riv'a•tive** (di riv'ə tiv) n., adj.

der'ma•ti'tis (dûr'mə tī'tis) n. inflammation of the skin.

der'ma•tol'o•gy (-tol'ə jē) n. medical study and treatment of the skin. **—der'ma•tol'o•gist,** n.

der'o•gate' (der'ə gāt') v., **-gated, -gating.** detract. **—der'o•ga'tion,** n. **—de•rog'a•to'ry** (di rog'ə tôr'ē) adj.

der'rick (der'ik) n. crane with boom pivoted at one end.

der'ri•ère' (der'ē âr') n. buttocks.

DES Pharmacology. diethylstilbestrol.

des designation.

de•scend' (di send') v. **1.** move down. **2.** be descendant. **—de•scent',** n.

de•scend'ant, n. person descended from specific ancestor; offspring.

descr 1. describe. **2.** description.

de•scribe' (di skrīb') v., **-scribed, -scribing. 1.** set forth in words. **2.** trace. **—de•scrib'a•ble,** adj. **—de•scrip'tion** (-skrip'shən) n. **—de•scrip'tive,** adj.

de•scry' (di skrī') v., **-scried, -scrying.** happen to see.

des'e•crate' (des'i krāt') v., **-crated, -crat-**ing. divest of sacredness. **—des'e•cra'tion,** n.

de•seg're•gate' (dē seg'ri gāt') v., **-gated, -gating.** eliminate racial segregation in. **—de•seg're•ga'tion,** n.

de•sen'si•tize' (dē sen'si tīz') v., **-tized, -tizing.** make less sensitive. **—de•sen'si•ti•za'tion,** n.

des'ert n. **1.** (dez'ərt) arid region. **2.** (di zûrt') (often pl.) due reward or punishment. **—v. 3.** (di zûrt') abandon. **—de•sert'er,** n. **—de•ser'tion,** n.

de•serve' (di zûrv') v., **-served, -serving.** be worthy of; merit.

des'ic•cate' (des'i kāt') v., **-cated, -cating.** dry up. **—des'ic•ca'tion,** n.

de•sid'er•a'tum (di sid'ə rā'təm, -rä'-, -zid'-) n., pl. **-ta** (-tə). something wanted.

de•sign' (di zīn') v. **1.** plan. **2.** conceive form of. **—n. 3.** sketch or plan. **4.** art of designing. **5.** scheme. **6.** purpose. **—de•sign'er,** n.

des'ig•nate' (dez'ig nāt') v., **-nated, -nating. 1.** indicate. **2.** name. **—des'ig•na'tion,** n.

designated driver, person who abstains from alcohol at a gathering in order to drive companions home safely.

de•sign'ing, adj. scheming.

de•sire' (di zī°r') v., **-sired, -siring,** n. **—v. 1.** wish for. **2.** request. **—n. 3.** longing. **4.** request. **5.** thing desired. **6.** lust. **—de•sir'a•ble,** adj. **—de•sir'ous,** adj. **—de•sir'a•bil'i•ty,** n.

de•sist' (di zist', -sist') v. stop.

desk (desk) n. **1.** table for writing. **2.** specialized section of organization, esp. newspaper office.

desk'top' publishing, design and production of publications using a microcomputer.

D. ès L. Doctor of Letters. [from French Docteur ès Lettres]

des'o•late adj., v., **-lated, -lating. —adj.** (des'ə lit) **1.** barren. **2.** lonely. **3.** dismal. **—v.** (-ə lāt') **4.** lay waste. **5.** make hopeless. **—des'o•la'tion,** n.

de•spair' (di spâr') n. **1.** hopelessness. **—v. 2.** lose hope.

des'per•a'do (des'pə rä'dō, -rä'-) n., pl. **-does, -dos.** wild outlaw.

des'per•ate (des'pər it) adj. **1.** reckless from despair. **2.** despairing. **—des'per•ate•ly,** adv. **—des'per•a'tion,** n.

des'pi•ca•ble (des'pi kə bəl, di spik'ə-) adj. contemptible. **—des'pi•ca•bly,** adv.

de•spise' (di spīz') v., **-spised, -spising.** scorn.

de•spite' (di spīt') prep. **1.** in spite of. **—n. 2.** insult.

de•spoil' (di spoil') v. plunder.

de•spond' (di spond') v. lose courage or hope. **—de•spond'en•cy,** n. **—de•spond'ent,** adj.

des'pot (des'pət, -pot) *n.* tyrant. —**des•pot'-ic,** *adj.* —**des'pot•ism,** *n.*

D. ès S. Doctor of Sciences. [from French *Docteur ès Sciences*]

des•sert' (di zûrt') *n.* final course of meal, usually sweet.

des'ti•na'tion (des'tə nā'shən) *n.* goal of journey.

des'tine (-tin) *v.,* -tined, -tining. **1.** set apart. **2.** predetermine by fate.

des'ti•ny, *n., pl.* -nies. **1.** predetermined future. **2.** fate.

des'ti•tute' (-tōōt', -tyōōt') *adj.* **1.** without means of support. **2.** deprived. —**des'ti•tu'-tion,** *n.*

destn destination.

de•stroy' (di stroi') *v.* **1.** ruin. **2.** end. **3.** kill.

de•stroy'er, *n.* **1.** one that destroys. **2.** naval vessel.

de•struct' (di strukt') *v.* be destroyed automatically.

de•struc'tion, *n.* **1.** act or means of destroying. **2.** fact of being destroyed. —**de•struct'i•ble,** *adj.* —**de•struc'tive,** *adj.*

des'ue•tude' (des'wi tōōd', -tyōōd') *n.* state of disuse.

des'ul•to'ry (des'əl tôr'ē) *adj.* not methodical. —**des' ul•to'ri•ly,** *adv.*

DET 1. Also, **Det** *Linguistics.* determiner. **2.** *Pharmacology.* diethyltryptamine.

det. 1. 'ntach. **2.** detachment. **3.** detail. **4.** detector. **5.** determine. **6.** (in prescriptions) let it be given [from Latin *dētur*].

de•tach' (di tach') *v.* take off or away. —**de•tach'a•ble,** *adj.*

de•tached', *adj.* **1.** separate. **2.** uninterested.

de•tach'ment, *n.* **1.** act of detaching. **2.** unconcern. **3.** impartiality. **4.** troops for special duty.

de•tail' (di tāl', dē'tāl) *n.* **1.** individual or minute part. **2.** in detail, with all details specified. **3.** troops or group selected for special duty. —*v.* **4.** relate in detail. **5.** assign.

de•tain' (di tān') *v.* **1.** delay. **2.** keep in custody. —**de•ten'tion,** *n.*

de•tect' (di tekt') *v.,* **1.** discover, esp. in or after some act. **2.** perceive. —**de•tec'tion,** *n.* —**de•tec'tor,** *n.*

de•tec'tive, *n.* professional investigator of crimes, etc.

dé•tente (dā tänt') *n.* lessening of international hostility.

de•ter' (di tûr') *v.,* -terred, -terring. discourage or restrain. —**de•ter'ment,** *n.*

de•ter'gent (di tûr'jənt) *adj.* **1.** cleansing. —*n.* **2.** cleansing agent.

de•te'ri•o•rate' (di tēr'ē ə rāt') *v.,* -rated, -rating. make or become worse. —**de•te'ri•o•ra'tion,** *n.*

de•ter'mi•nant' (di tûr'mə nənt) *n.* determining agent or factor.

de•ter'mi•nate (-nit) *adj.* able to be specified.

de•ter'mi•na'tion (-nā'shən) *n.* **1.** act of determining. **2.** firmness of purpose.

de•ter'mine (-min) *v.,* -mined, -mining. **1.** settle; decide. **2.** ascertain. **3.** limit. —**de•ter'mi•na•ble,** *adj.*

de•ter'mined *adj.* resolved.

de•ter'rence (di tûr'əns) *n.* discouragement, as of crime or military aggression. —**de•ter'-rent,** *adj., n.*

de•test' (di test') *v.* hate or despise. —**de•test'a•ble,** *adj.* —**de•test'a•bly,** *adv.* —**de'-tes•ta'tion** (dē'te stā'shən) *n.*

de•throne' (dē thrōn') *v.,* -throned, -throning. remove from a throne.

det'o•nate' (det'n āt') *v.,* -nated, -nating. explode. —**det'o•na'tion,** *n.*

de'tour (dē'tŏōr, di tŏōr') *n.* **1.** roundabout course. —*v.* **2.** make detour.

de'tox *n., v.,* -toxed, -toxing. *Informal.* —*n.* (dē'toks) **1.** detoxification. **2.** hospital unit for patients undergoing detoxification. —*v.* (dē toks') **3.** detoxify.

de•tox'i•fy, *v.,* -fied, -fying. rid of effects of alcohol or drug use. —**de•tox'i•fi•ca'tion,** *n.*

de•tract' (di trakt') *v.* take away quality or reputation. —**de•trac'tion,** *n.* —**de•trac'tor,** *n.*

det'ri•ment (de'trə mənt) *n.* damage or loss. —**det'ri•men'tal** (-men'tl) *adj.*

de•tri'tus (di trī'təs) *n.* **1.** rock particles worn away from a mass. **2.** debris.

deuce (dōōs, dyōōs) *n.* **1.** card or die with two pips. **2.** tie score as in tennis.

Deut. *Bible.* Deuteronomy.

dev. 1. development. **2.** deviation.

de•val'u•ate' (dē val'yōō āt') *v.,* -ated, -ating. reduce in value; depreciate. Also, **de•val'ue.** —**de•val'u•a'tion,** *n.*

dev'as•tate' (dev'ə stāt') *v.,* -tated, -tating. lay waste. —**dev'as•ta'tion,** *n.*

devel. development.

de•vel'op (di vel'əp) *v.* **1.** mature; perfect. **2.** elaborate. **3.** bring into being. **4.** make (images on film) visible. **5.** acquire; gain gradually. —**de•vel'op•ment,** *n.* —**de•vel'op•men'tal,** *adj.* —**de•vel'op•er,** *n.*

de'vi•ate' (dē'vē āt') *v.,* -ated, -ating. **1.** digress. **2.** depart from normal. —**de'vi•a'-tion,** *n.* —**de'vi•ant,** *adj., n.*

de•vice' (di vīs') *n.* **1.** contrivance. **2.** plan. **3.** slogan or emblem.

dev'il (dev'əl) *n.* **1.** Satan. **2.** evil spirit or person. —**dev'il•ish,** *adj.* —**dev'il•try,** *n.*

dev'il-may-care', *adj.* reckless.

devil's advocate, person who takes opposing view for the sake of argument.

devil's food cake, rich chocolate cake.

de'vi•ous (dē'vē əs) *adj.* **1.** circuitous. **2.** not straightforward or sincere. —**de'vi•ous•ly,** *adv.*

de•vise' (di vīz') *v.,* -vised, -vising. **1.** plan; contrive. **2.** bequeath. —**de•vis'er,** *n.*

de·vi′tal·ize′ (dē vīt′l īz′) v., -ized, -izing. remove vitality of. —**de·vi′tal·i·za′tion**, n.

de·void′ (di void′) adj. destitute.

de·volve′ (di volv′) v., -volved, -volving. **1.** transfer or delegate. **2.** fall as a duty.

de·vote′ (di vōt′) v., -voted, -voting. **1.** give up or apply to a certain pursuit, cause, etc. **2.** dedicate.

de·vot′ed, adj. **1.** zealous. **2.** dedicated.

dev′o·tee′ (dev′ə tē′) n. devoted one.

de·vo′tion (di vō′shən) n. **1.** consecration. **2.** attachment or dedication. **3.** (pl.) worship. —**de·vo′tion·al**, adj.

de·vour′ (di vour′) v. consume ravenously.

de·vout′ (di vout′) adj. pious.

dew (dōō, dyōō) n. atmospheric moisture condensed in droplets. —**dew′y**, adj.

dex·ter′i·ty (dek ster′i tē) n. **1.** physical skill. **2.** cleverness. —**dex′ter·ous** (dek′stər-əs, -strəs) adj.

dex′trose (dek′strōs) n. type of sugar.

DF divorced female.

df 1. direction finder. **2.** dissipation factor.

D/F direction finding. Also, **DF**

D.F. 1. Defender of the Faith. [from Latin Dēfēnsor Fideī] **2.** Distrito Federal. **3.** Doctor of Forestry.

D.F.A. Doctor of Fine Arts.

D.F.C. Distinguished Flying Cross.

dfl deflating.

D.F.M. Distinguished Flying Medal.

dfr defrost.

dft drift.

dftg drafting.

dftr deflector.

dftsp draftsperson.

dg decigram; decigrams.

D.G. 1. by the grace of God. [from Latin Deī grātiā] **2.** Director General.

dgr degrease.

dgs degaussing system.

dgt digit.

dgtl digital.

DH 1. Racing. dead heat. **2.** Baseball. designated hitter. Also, **dh**

DH. (in Morocco) dirham; dirhams.

D.H. 1. Doctor of Humanics. **2.** Doctor of Humanities.

DHA Biochemistry. an omega-3 fatty acid present in fish oils. [d(ocosa)h(exaenoic) a(cid)]

D.H.L. 1. Doctor of Hebrew Letters. **2.** Doctor of Hebrew Literature.

dhmy dehumidify.

dhw double-hung window.

dhyr dehydrator.

DI 1. Department of the Interior. **2.** drill instructor.

Di Symbol, Chemistry. didymium.

di. diameter. Also, **dia.**

dia. diameter. Also, **dia**

di′a·be′tes (dī′ə bē′tis, -tēz) n. disease char-

acterized by high levels of glucose in the blood. —**di′a·bet′ic** (-bet′ik) adj., n.

di′a·bol′ic (dī′ə bol′ik) adj. fiendish. Also, **di′a·bol′i·cal.**

di′a·crit′ic (dī′ə krit′ik) n. mark added to a letter to give it a particular phonetic value. Also, **di′a·crit′i·cal** mark.

di′a·dem′ (dī′ə dem′) n. crown.

diag 1. diagonal. **2.** diagram.

di′ag·nose′ (dī′əg nōs′, -nōz′) v., -nosed, -nosing. determine nature of (disease). —**di′ag·no′sis**, n. —**di′ag·nos′tic** (-nos′tik) adj.

di·ag′o·nal (dī ag′ə nl) adj. **1.** connecting two angles. **2.** oblique. —**di·ag′o·nal·ly**, adv.

di′a·gram (dī′ə gram′) n., v., -gramed, -graming. chart or plan. —**di′a·gram·mat′ic** (-grə mat′ik) adj.

di′al (dī′əl, dīl) n., v., -aled, -aling. —n. **1.** numbered face, as on a watch. —v. **2.** select or contact with use of dial.

di′a·lect′ (dī′ə lekt′) n. language of district or class. —**di′a·lec′tal**, adj.

di′a·lec′tic, n. art or practice of debate or conversation by which truth of theory or opinion is arrived at logically. Also, **di′a·lec′tics.** —**di′a·lec′ti·cal**, adj.

di′a·logue′ (dī′ə lôg′) n. conversation between two or more people. Also, **di′a·log′.**

di·al′y·sis (dī al′ə sis) n. process of removing waste products from blood of someone with kidney disease.

di·am′e·ter (dī am′i tər) n. straight line through center of a circle.

di′a·met′ri·cal (-ə me′tri kəl) adj. **1.** of diameters. **2.** completely in contrast.

dia′mond (dī′mənd, dī′ə-) n. **1.** hard, brilliant precious stone. **2.** rhombus or square. **3.** (pl.) suit of playing cards. **4.** baseball field.

dia′mond·back′, n. venomous rattlesnake.

di′a·per (dī′pər, dī′ə pər) n. **1.** infant's underpants. —v. **2.** put diaper on.

diaph diaphragm.

di·aph′a·nous (dī af′ə nəs) adj. very sheer and light.

di′a·phragm′ (dī′ə fram′) n. **1.** wall in body, as between thorax and abdomen. **2.** vibrating membrane. **3.** contraceptive device.

di′ar·rhe′a (dī′ə rē′ə) n. intestinal disorder. Also, **di′ar·rhoe′a.**

di′a·ry (dī′ə rē) n., pl. -ries. personal daily record. —**di′a·rist**, n.

di′a·ther′my (-thûr′mē) n. heating of body by electric currents.

di′a·ton′ic (-ton′ik) adj. Music. made up of the eight notes of the major or minor scale.

di′a·tribe′ (-trīb′) n. denunciation.

dib′ble (dib′əl) n. pointed instrument for planting.

dice (dīs) n.pl., sing. **die**, v., diced, dicing. —n. **1.** small cubes, used in games. —v. **2.** cut into small cubes.

dic′ey (dī′sē) *adj.* **-ier, -iest.** not certain; risky.

di•chot′o•my (dī kot′ə mē) *n., pl.* **-mies.** division into two irreconcilable groups.

dick′er (dik′ər) *v.* bargain.

di•cot′y•le′don (dī kot′l ēd′n, dī′kot l-) *n.* plant having two embryonic seed leaves.

dict. 1. dictation. **2.** dictator. **3.** dictionary.

Dic′ta•phone′ (dik′tə fōn′) *n. Trademark.* brand name for machine that records and plays back dictated speech.

dic′tate (dik′tāt) *v.,* **-tated, -tating,** *n.* —*v.* **1.** say something to be written down. **2.** command. —*n.* **3.** command. —**dic•ta′tion,** *n.*

dic′ta•tor, *n.* absolute ruler. —**dic′ta•to′ri•al** (-tə tôr′ē əl) *adj.* —**dic•ta′tor•ship′,** *n.*

dic′tion (dik′shən) *n.* style of speaking.

dic′tion•ar′y (dik′shə ner′ē) *n., pl.* **-aries.** book on meaning, spelling, pronunciation, etc., of words.

dic′tum (dik′təm) *n., pl.* **-ta, -tums. 1.** authoritative declaration. **2.** saying; maxim.

DID 1. data item description. **2.** *Telecommunications.* direct inward dialing.

di•dac′tic (dī dak′tik) *adj.* instructive.

did′n′t (did′nt) contraction of **did not.**

die (dī) *v.,* **died, dying,** *n., pl.* (for 3) **dies.** —*v.* **1.** cease to be. **2.** lose force; fade. —*n.* **3.** shaping device. **4.** sing. of **dice.**

dieb. alt. (in prescriptions) every other day. [from Latin *diēbus alternīs*]

dieb. secund. (in prescriptions) every second day. [from Latin *diēbus secundīs*]

dieb. tert. (in prescriptions) every third day. [from Latin *diēbus tertius*]

die′hard′, *n.* defender of lost cause.

diel dielectric.

di•er′e•sis (dī er′ə sis) *n., pl.* **-ses.** sign (¨) over a vowel indicating separate pronunciation, as in Noël.

die′sel (dē′zəl, -səl) *n.* **1.** engine using air compression for ignition. **2.** machine powered by such an engine. **3.** fuel consumed by a diesel engine.

di′et (dī′it) *n.* **1.** food. **2.** food specially chosen for health or weight control. **3.** formal assembly. —*v.* **4.** adhere to diet. —**di′e•tar′y** (-i ter′ē) *adj.* —**di′e•tet′ic** (-tet′ik) *adj.* —**di′e•tet′ics,** *n.*

di′e•ti′tian (dī′i tish′ən) *n.* expert in nutrition and dietary requirements. Also, **di′e•ti′cian.**

dif. 1. difference. **2.** different.

diff. 1. difference. **2.** different. **3.** differential.

dif′fer (dif′ər) *v.* **1.** be unlike. **2.** disagree.

dif′fer•ence (dif′ər əns, dif′rəns) *n.* **1.** unlikeness. **2.** disagreement. **3.** amount separating two quantities. —**dif′fer•ent,** *adj.* —**dif′fer•ent•ly,** *adv.*

—**Usage.** DIFFERENT FROM is more common today in introducing a phrase, but DIFFERENT THAN is also used: *New York speech is differ-* ent *from/than that of Chicago.* DIFFERENT THAN is usually used when a clause follows, especially when the word "from" would create an awkward sentence: *The stream followed a different course than the map showed.*

dif′fer•en′ti•ate′ (-en′shē āt′) *v.,* **-ated, -ating. 1.** alter. **2.** distinguish between. —**dif′fer•en′ti•a′tion,** *n.*

dif′fi•cult′ (dif′i kult′, -kəlt) *adj.* **1.** hard to do or understand. **2.** unmanageable.

dif′fi•cul′ty, *n., pl.* **-ties. 1.** condition of being difficult. **2.** embarrassing or difficult situation. **3.** trouble; struggle. **4.** disagreement or dispute.

dif′fi•dent (-dənt) *adj.* timid; shy. —**dif′fi•dence,** *n.*

dif•frac′tion (di frak′shən) *n.* breaking up of rays of light to produce spectrum.

dif•fuse′ *v.,* **-fused, -fusing,** *adj.* —*v.* (difyōōz′) **1.** spread or scatter. —*adj.* (-fyōōs′) **2.** not to the point. **3.** spread or scattered. —**dif•fu′sion,** *n.* —**dif•fu′sive,** *adj.*

dig (dig) *v.,* **dug** (dug) or **digged, digging,** *n.* —*v.* **1.** thrust down. **2.** lift to extract. **3.** form by extraction. **4.** *Slang.* understand or appreciate. —*n.* **5.** sarcastic remark. —**dig′ger,** *n.*

di•gest′ *v.* (di jest′) **1.** prepare (food) for assimilation. **2.** assimilate mentally. —*n.* (dī′jest) **3.** collection or summary, esp. of laws. —**di•ges′tion,** *n.* —**di•gest′ive,** *adj.* —**di•gest′i•ble,** *adj.* —**di•gest′i•bil′i•ty,** *n.*

dig′it (dij′it) *n.* **1.** finger or toe. **2.** any Arabic numeral.

dig′it•al (-i tl) *adj.* of, using, or expressing data in numerals. —**dig′it•al•ly,** *adv.*

dig′i•tal′is (-tal′is, -tā′lis) *n.* medicine derived from the leaves of the foxglove, used to stimulate the heart.

dig′•i•tize′ (-tīz′) *v.,* **-tized, -tizing.** convert (data) to digital form.

dig′ni•fied (dig′nə fīd′) *adj.* marked by dignity; stately.

dig′ni•fy′, *v.,* **-fied, -fying. 1.** honor. **2.** honor more than is deserved.

dig′ni•ta′ry (-ter′ē) *n., pl.* **-ries.** high-ranking person.

dig′ni•ty, *n., pl.* **-ties. 1.** nobility. **2.** worthiness. **3.** high rank, office, or title.

di•gress′ (di gres′, dī-) *v.* wander from main purpose, theme, etc. —**di•gres′sion,** *n.* —**di•gres′sive,** *adj.*

dike (dīk) *n.* **1.** bank for restraining waters. **2.** ditch.

dil 1. dilute. **2.** diluted.

di•lap′i•dat′ed (di lap′i dā′tid) *adj.* decayed.

di•lap′i•da′tion, *n.* ruin; decay.

di•late′ (dī lāt′) *v.,* **-lated, -lating.** expand. —**di•la′tion,** *n.*

dil′a•to′ry (dil′ə tôr′ē) *adj.* delaying; tardy. —**dil′a•to′ri•ness,** *n.*

di•lem′ma (di lem′ə) *n.* predicament.

dil′et·tante′ (dil′i tänt′, dil′i tänt′) *n.* superficial practitioner.

dil′i·gence (dil′i jəns) *n.* earnest effort. —**dil′i·gent,** *adj.*

dill (dil) *n.* plant with aromatic seeds and leaves.

dil′ly-dal′ly (dil′ē dal′ē) *v.,* **-lied, -lying.** waste time, esp. by indecision.

di·lute′ (di lōōt′, dī-) *v.,* **-luted, -luting.** thin, as with water; weaken. —**di·lu′tion,** *n.*

dim (dim) *adj.,* **dimmer, dimmest,** *v.,* **dimmed, dimming.** —*adj.* **1.** not bright. **2.** indistinct. —*v.* **3.** make or become dim. —**dim′ly,** *adv.* —**dim′ness,** *n.*

dime (dīm) *n.* coin worth 10 cents.

di·men′sion (di men′shən, dī-) *n.* **1.** property of space; extension in a given direction. **2.** magnitude. —**di·men′sion·al,** *adj.*

dimin. 1. diminish. **2.** *Music.* diminuendo. **3.** diminutive.

di·min′ish (di min′ish) *v.* lessen; reduce. —**dim·i·nu·tion** (dim′ə nōō′shən, -nyōō′-) *n.*

di·min′u·en′do (dī min′yōō en′dō) *adj., adv. Music.* gradually reducing in loudness.

di·min′u·tive (di min′yə tiv) *adj.* **1.** small. **2.** denoting smallness, etc. —*n.* **3.** diminutive form, as of a word.

dim′i·ty (dim′i tē) *n., pl.* **-ties.** thin cotton fabric.

dim′ple (dim′pəl) *n.* small hollow, esp. in cheek.

dim′wit′, *n. Slang.* stupid person. —**dim′wit′ted,** *adj.*

din (din) *n., v.,* **dinned, dinning.** —*n.* **1.** confused noise. —*v.* **2.** assail with din.

dine (dīn) *v.,* **dined, dining. 1.** eat dinner or another meal. **2.** provide dinner.

din′er, *n.* **1.** person who dines. **2.** railroad dining car. **3.** eatery shaped like such a car.

di·nette′ (-net′) *n.* small area or alcove for dining.

din′ghy (ding′gē) *n., pl.* **-ghies.** small boat.

din′gy (din′jē) *adj.,* **-gier, -giest.** dark; dirty.

din′ner (din′ər) *n.* main meal.

di′no·saur′ (dī′nə sôr′) *n.* any of various extinct reptiles.

d. in p. aeq. (in prescriptions) let it be divided into equal parts. [from Latin *dīvidātur in partēs aequālēs*]

dint (dint) *n.* **1.** force. **2.** dent.

dio diode.

dioc. 1. diocesan. **2.** diocese.

di′o·cese′ (dī′ə sis, -sēz′, -sēs′) *n.* district under a bishop. —**di·oc′e·san** (-os′ə sən) *adj., n.*

diopt *Optics.* diopter.

di′o·ram′a (dī′ə ram′ə, -rä′mə) *n.* miniature three-dimensional scene against painted background.

di·ox′ide (dī ok′sīd, -sid) *n.* oxide with two atoms of oxygen.

di·ox′in (-ok′sin) *n.* toxic by-product of pesticide.

dip (dip) *v.,* **dipped, dipping,** *n.* —*v.* **1.** plunge temporarily in liquid. **2.** bail or scoop. **3.** slope down. —*n.* **4.** act of dipping. **5.** downward slope. **6.** substance into which something is dipped.

diph·the′ri·a (dif thēr′ē ə, dip-) *n.* infectious disease of air passages, esp. throat.

diph′thong (dif′thông, dip′-) *n.* sound containing two vowels.

dipl. 1. diplomat. **2.** diplomatic.

di·plo′ma (di plō′mə) *n.* document of academic qualifications.

di·plo′ma·cy (-sē) *n., pl.* **-cies. 1.** conduct of international relations. **2.** skill in negotiation. —**dip′lo·mat′** (dip′lə mat′) *n.*

dip′lo·mat′ic, *adj.* **1.** of diplomacy. **2.** tactful. —**dip′lo·mat′i·cal·ly,** *adv.*

diplxr *Electronics.* diplexer.

dip′per, *n.* **1.** one that dips. **2.** ladle.

dip′so·ma′ni·a (dip′sə mā′nē ə, -sō-) *n.* morbid craving for alcohol. —**dip′so·ma′ni·ac,** *n.*

dir., director.

dir cplr *Electronics.* directional coupler.

dire (dīər) *adj.,* **direr, direst.** dreadful.

direc. prop. (in prescriptions) with a proper direction. [from Latin *dīrectiōne prōpriā*]

di·rect′ (di rekt′, dī-) *v.* **1.** guide. **2.** command. **3.** manage. **4.** address. —*adj.* **5.** straight. **6.** straightforward. —**di·rect′ly,** *adv.* —**di·rect′ness,** *n.* —**di·rec′tor,** *n.*

direct current, electric current flowing continuously in one direction.

di·rec′tion, *n.* **1.** act of directing. **2.** line along which a thing lies or moves. —**di·rec′tion·al,** *adj.*

di·rec′tive, *n.* order or instruction from authority.

di·rec′to·ry, *n., pl.* **-ries.** guide to locations, telephone numbers, etc.

dire′ful (dīər′fəl) *adj.* dire.

dirge (dûrj) *n.* funeral song.

dir′i·gi·ble (dir′i jə bəl, di rij′ə-) *n.* airship.

dirk (dûrk) *n.* dagger.

dirt (dûrt) *n.* **1.** filth. **2.** earth.

dirt′y, *adj.,* **-ier, -iest,** *v.,* **-ied, -ying.** —*adj.* **1.** soiled. **2.** indecent. —*v.* **3.** soil. —**dirt′i·ness,** *n.*

dis (dis) *v.,* **dissed, dissing,** *n. Slang.* —*v.* **1.** show disrespect for. **2.** disparage. —*n.* **3.** disparagement or criticism.

dis- prefix indicating: **1.** reversal, as *disconnect.* **2.** negation or lack, as *distrust.* **3.** removal, as *disbar.*

dis·a′ble (-ā′bəl) *v.,* **-bled, -bling.** damage capability of. —**dis′a·bil′i·ty,** *n.*

dis·a′bled, *adj.* handicapped; incapacitated.

dis·a·buse′ (-byōōz′) *v.,* **-bused, -busing.** free from deception.

dis′ad·van′tage, *n.* **1.** drawback; handicap. **2.** injury. —**dis′ad·van·ta′geous,** *adj.*

D

dis′ad·van′taged, *adj.* lacking economic and social opportunity.

dis′af·fect′, *v.* alienate. —**dis′af·fec′tion,** *n.*

dis′a·gree′, *v.,* -greed, -greeing. differ in opinion. —**dis′a·gree′ment,** *n.*

dis′a·gree′a·ble, *adj.* unpleasant. —**dis′a·gree′a·bly,** *adv.*

dis′al·low′, *v.* refuse to allow.

dis′ap·pear′, *v.* **1.** vanish. **2.** cease to exist. —**dis′ap·pear′ance,** *n.*

dis′ap·point′, *v.* fail to fulfill hopes or wishes of. —**dis′ap·point′ment,** *n.*

dis′ap·pro·ba′tion, *n.* disapproval.

dis′ap·prove′, *v.,* -proved, -proving. condemn; censure. —**dis′ap·prov′al,** *n.*

dis·arm′, *v.* **1.** deprive of arms. **2.** reduce one's own armed power. —**dis·ar′ma·ment,** *n.*

dis′ar·range′, *v.,* -ranged, -ranging. disorder. —**dis′ar·range′ment,** *n.*

dis′ar·ray′, *n.* lack of order.

disassm disassemble.

dis′as·so′ci·ate (-āt′) *v.,* -ated, -ating. dissociate.

disassy disassembly.

dis·as′ter (di zas′tər) *n.* extreme misfortune. —**dis·as′trous,** *adj.*

dis′a·vow′ (dis′ə vou′) *v.* disown. —**dis′a·vow′al,** *n.* —**dis′a·vow′er,** *n.*

dis·band′, *v.* break up (an organization). —**dis·band′ment,** *n.*

dis·bar′, *v.,* -barred, -barring. expel from law practice. —**dis·bar′ment,** *n.*

dis′be·lieve′, *v.,* -lieved, -lieving. reject as untrue. —**dis′be·lief′,** *n.*

dis·burse′ (dis bûrs′) *v.,* -bursed, -bursing. pay out. —**dis·burse′ment,** *n.*

disc (disk) *n.* **1.** disk. **2.** phonograph record.

dis·card′ *v.* (di skärd′) **1.** reject. —*n.* (dis′kärd) **2.** something discarded. **3.** discarded state.

dis·cern′ (di sûrn′, -zûrn′) *v.* **1.** see. **2.** distinguish. —**dis·cern′ible,** *adj.* —**dis·cern′ing,** *adj.* —**dis·cern′ment,** *n.*

disch discharge.

dis·charge′ *v.,* -charged, -charging, *n.* —*v.* (dis chärj′) **1.** rid of load. **2.** send forth. **3.** shoot. **4.** end employment of. **5.** fulfill. —*n.* (dis′chärj) **6.** act of discharging. **7.** something discharged.

dis·ci′ple (di sī′pəl) *n.* follower.

dis′ci·pline (dis′ə plin) *n., v.,* -plined, -plining. —*n.* **1.** training in rules. **2.** punishment. **3.** subjection to rules. **4.** branch of instruction or learning. —*v.* **5.** train. **6.** punish. —**dis′ci·pli·nar′y,** *adj.* —**dis′ci·pli·nar′i·an,** *n.*

disc jockey, person who plays and comments on recorded music on a radio program. Also, **disk jockey.**

dis·claim′ (dis klām′) *n.* disown.

dis·close′ (di sklōz′) *v.,* -closed, -closing. reveal. —**dis·clo′sure,** *n.*

dis′co (dis′kō) *n., pl.* -cos. **1.** discotheque. **2.** rhythmic style of dance music.

dis·col′or (dis kul′ər) *v.* change in color. —**dis·col′or·a′tion,** *n.*

dis′com·bob′u·late′ (dis′kəm bob′yə lāt′) *v.,* -lated, -lating. confuse or perturb. —**dis′com·bob′u·la′tion,** *n.*

dis·com′fit (dis kum′fit) *v.* **1.** defeat. **2.** thwart. —**dis·com′fi·ture,** *n.*

dis·com′fort (dis kum′fərt) *n.* lack of comfort.

dis′com·mode′ (dis′kə mōd′) *v.,* -moded, -moding. cause inconvenience to.

dis′com·pose′, *v.,* -posed, -posing. **1.** upset the order of. **2.** disturb the composure of. —**dis′com·po′sure,** *n.*

dis′con·cert′ (dis′kən sûrt′) *v.* perturb.

dis′con·nect′, *v.* break connection of.

dis·con′so·late (dis kon′sə lit) *adj.* sad. —**dis·con′so·late·ly,** *adv.*

dis′con·tent′ (-kən tent′) *adj.* Also **dis′con·tent′ed. 1.** not contented. —*n.* **2.** lack of contentment.

dis′con·tin′ue, *v.,* -tinued, -tinuing. end; stop. —**dis′con·tin′u·ance,** *n.* —**dis′con·tin′u·ous,** *adj.*

dis′cord (dis′kôrd) *n.* **1.** lack of harmony. **2.** disagreement; strife. —**dis·cord′ance,** *n.* —**dis·cord′ant,** *adj.*

dis′co·theque′ (dis′kə tek′, dis′kə tek′) *n.* nightclub where recorded dance music is played.

dis′count *v.* (dis′kount, dis kount′) **1.** deduct. **2.** advance money after deduction of interest. **3.** disregard. **4.** allow for exaggeration in. —*n.* (dis′kount) **5.** deduction.

dis·coun′te·nance, *v.,* -nanced, -nancing. **1.** disconcert regularly. **2.** show disapproval of.

dis·cour′age (di skûr′ij, -skur′-) *v.,* -aged, -aging. **1.** deprive of resolution. **2.** hinder. —**dis·cour′age·ment,** *n.*

dis′course, *n., v.,* -coursed, -coursing. —*n.* (dis′kôrs) **1.** talk. **2.** formal discussion. —*v.* (dis kôrs′) **3.** talk.

dis·cour′te·sy, *n., pl.* -sies. **1.** lack of courtesy. **2.** impolite act. —**dis·cour′te·ous,** *adj.*

dis·cov′er (di skuv′ər) *v.* learn or see for first time. —**dis·cov′er·y,** *n.* —**dis·cov′er·a·ble,** *adj.* —**dis·cov′er·er,** *n.*

——**Usage.** Do not confuse DISCOVER and INVENT, two words that deal with something new. DISCOVER is used when the object is an idea or place that existed before, but few people or no one knew about it. In the sentence *Columbus discovered the New World,* the New World clearly existed and was known to the people living there, but not to Columbus and the people of his time. INVENT is used when the object is a device or thing built. In the sentence *Edison invented the light bulb,* the light bulb did not exist before

Edison invented it, and it was not known by anyone.

dis•cred′it, v. **1.** defame. **2.** give no credit to. —n. **3.** lack of belief. **4.** disrepute.

dis•creet′ (di skrēt′) adj. wise; prudent. —dis•creet′ly, adv.

dis•crep′an•cy (di skrep′ən sē) n., pl. -cies. difference; inconsistency. —dis•crep′ant, adj.

dis•crete′ (di skrēt′) adj. separate.

dis•cre′tion (di skresh′ən) n. **1.** freedom of choice. **2.** prudence. —dis•cre′tion•ar′y, adj.

dis•crim′i•nate′, v., -nated, -nating, adj. —v. (di skrim′ə nāt′) **1.** distinguish accurately. **2.** show bias. —adj. (-ə nit) **3.** making distinctions. —dis•crim′i•na′tion, n. —dis•crim′i•na•to′ry, adj.

dis•cur′sive (di skûr′siv) adj. rambling.

dis′cus (dis′kəs) n. disk for throwing in athletic competition.

dis•cuss′ (di skus′) v. talk about. —dis•cus′sion, n.

dis•dain′ (dis dān′, di stān′) v., n. scorn. —dis•dain′ful, adj.

dis•ease′ (di zēz′) n., v., -eased, -easing. —n. **1.** ailment. —v. **2.** affect with disease. —dis•eased′, adj.

dis′em•bark′ (dis′em bärk′) v. leave airplane or ship. —dis•em′bar•ka′tion, n.

dis′em•bod′y, v., -bodied, -bodying. free from the body.

dis′en•chant′, v. free from enchantment or illusion. —dis′en•chant′ment, n.

dis′en•gage′, v., -gaged, -gaging. separate; disconnect. —dis′en•gage′ment, n.

dis•fa′vor, n. **1.** displeasure. **2.** disregard. —v. **3.** regard or treat with disfavor.

dis•fig′ure, v., -ured, -uring. mar. —dis•fig′ure•ment, n.

dis•fran′chise, v., -chised, -chising. deprive of franchise.

dis•gorge′ (dis gôrj′) v., -gorged, -gorging. **1.** vomit forth. **2.** yield up.

dis•grace′ (dis grās′) n., v., -graced, -gracing. —n. **1.** state or cause of dishonor. —v. **2.** bring shame upon. —dis•grace′ful, adj. —dis•grace′ful•ly, adv.

dis•grun′tle (dis grun′tl) v., -tled, -tling. make discontented.

dis•guise′ (dis gīz′, di skīz′) v., -guised, -guising, n. —v. **1.** conceal true identity of. —n. **2.** something that disguises.

dis•gust′ (dis gust′, di skust′) v. **1.** cause loathing in. —n. **2.** loathing. —dis•gust′ed, adj. —dis•gust′ing, adj.

dish (dish) n. **1.** open shallow container. **2.** article of food.

dis′ha•bille′ (dis′ə bēl′, -bē′) n. state of being partially or carelessly dressed.

dis•heart′en, v. discourage.

di•shev′el (di shev′əl) v., -eled, -eling. let hang in disorder.

dis•hon′est, adj. not honest. —dis•hon′est•ly, adv. —dis•hon′es•ty, n.

dis•hon′or, n. **1.** lack of honor. **2.** disgrace. —v. **3.** disgrace. **4.** fail to honor. —dis•hon′or•a•ble, adj.

dish′wash′er, n. person or machine that washes dishes.

dis′il•lu′sion, v. free from illusion. —dis′il•lu′sion•ment, n.

dis′in•cline′, v., -clined, -clining. make or be averse. —dis•in′cli•na′tion, n.

dis•in•fect′, v. destroy disease germs in. —dis′in•fect′ant, n., adj.

dis•in•for•ma′tion, n. false information released by a government to mislead rivals.

dis′in•gen′u•ous, adj. lacking frankness.

dis′in•her′it, v. exclude from inheritance.

dis′in•te•grate′, v., -grated, -grating. separate into parts. —dis•in′te•gra′tion, n.

dis′in•ter′, v., -terred, -terring. take out of the place of interment. —dis′in•ter′ment, n.

dis•in′ter•est, n. indifference.

dis•in′ter•est•ed, adj. **1.** not partial or biased. **2.** not interested. —dis•in′ter•est′ed•ly, adv.

—Usage. Do not confuse DISINTERESTED and UNINTERESTED. DISINTERESTED usually means "able to act fairly; not partial or biased," while UNINTERESTED means "not taking an interest." But the second meaning of DISINTERESTED listed here means the same as UNINTERESTED and many users of English consider this use of DISINTEREST incorrect.

dis•joint′ed, adj. **1.** separated at joints. **2.** incoherent.

disk (disk) n. **1.** flat circular plate. **2.** phonograph record. **3.** plate for storing electronic data. **4.** roundish, flat anatomical part, as in the spine.

disk•ette′ (di sket′) n. floppy disk.

disk jockey, disc jockey.

dis•like′, v., -liked, -liking, n. —v. **1.** regard with displeasure. —n. **2.** distaste.

dis′lo•cate′ (dis′lō kāt′, dis lō′kāt) v., -cated, -cating. **1.** displace. **2.** put out of order. —dis′lo•ca′tion, n.

dis•lodge′, v., -lodged, -lodging. force from place. —dis•lodg′ment, n.

dis•loy′al, adj. not loyal; traitorous. —dis•loy′al•ty, n.

dis′mal (diz′məl) adj. **1.** gloomy. **2.** terrible. —dis′mal•ly, adv.

dis•man′tle (dis man′tl) v., -tled, -tling. **1.** deprive of equipment. **2.** take apart. —dis•man′tle•ment, n.

dis•may′ (dis mā′) v. **1.** dishearten. —n. **2.** disheartenment.

dis•mem′ber (dis mem′bər) v. remove limbs of. —dis•mem′ber•ment, n.

dis•miss′ (dis mis′) v. **1.** direct or allow to go. **2.** discharge. **3.** reject. —dis•mis′sal, n.

D

dis•mount′, v. **1.** get or throw down from saddle. **2.** remove from mounting.

dis•o•be′di•ent, adj. not obedient. —**dis′o•be′di•ence**, n. —**dis′o•bey′**, v.

dis•or′der, n. **1.** lack of order. **2.** illness or disease. —v. **3.** create disorder in. —**dis•or′der•ly**, adj.

dis•or′gan•ize′, v., -ized, -izing. throw into disorder. —**dis•or′gan•i•za′tion**, n.

dis•o′ri•ent′, v. **1.** cause to lose one's way. **2.** confuse. —**dis•o′ri•en•ta′tion**, n.

dis•own′, v. repudiate.

disp 1. dispatcher. **2.** dispenser.

dis•par′age (di spar′ij) v., -aged, -aging. speak slightly of; belittle. —**dis•par′age•ment**, n.

dis•par•ate (dis′pər it, di spar′-) adj. distinct in kind; dissimilar. —**dis•par′i•ty**, n.

dis•pas′sion•ate, adj. impartial; calm. —**dis•pas′sion•ate•ly**, adv.

dis•patch′ (di spach′) v. **1.** send off. **2.** transact quickly. **3.** kill. —n. **4.** act of sending off. **5.** killing. **6.** speed. **7.** message or report. —**dis•patch′er**, n.

dis•pel′ (di spel′) v., -pelled, -pelling. drive off; scatter.

dis•pen′sa•ry (di spen′sə rē) n., pl. -ries. place for dispensing medicines.

dis•pen•sa′tion (dis′pən sā′shən, -pen-) n. **1.** act of dispensing. **2.** divine order. **3.** relaxation of law.

dis•pense′ (di spens′) v., -pensed, -pensing. **1.** distribute. **2.** administer. **3.** forgo. **4.** do away. —**dis•pen′sa•ble**, adj. —**dis•pens′er**, n.

dis•perse′ (di spûrs′) v., -persed, -persing. scatter. —**dis•per′sion, dis•per′sal**, n.

dis•pir′it•ed, adj. downhearted; dejected.

displ displacement.

dis•place′, v., -placed, -placing. **1.** put out of place. **2.** replace. —**dis•place′ment**, n.

dis•play′ (di splā′) v., n. exhibit.

dis•please′, v., -pleased, -pleasing. offend. —**dis•pleas′ure** (-plezh′ər) n.

dis•pose′, v., -posed, -posing. **1.** arrange. **2.** incline. **3.** decide. **4.** get rid. —**dis•pos′a•ble**, adj., n. —**dis•pos′al**, n.

dis′po•si′tion (dis′pə zish′ən) n. **1.** personality or mood. **2.** tendency. **3.** disposal.

dis′pos•sess′, v. deprive of possession. —**dis′pos•ses′sion**, n.

dis′pro•por′tion, n. lack of proportion. —**dis′pro•por′tion•ate**, adj. —**dis′pro•por′tion•ate•ly**, adv.

dis•prove′, v., -proved, -proving. prove false.

dis•pute′ (di spyōot′) v., -puted, -puting, n. —v. **1.** argue or quarrel. —n. **2.** argument; quarrel. —**dis•put′a•ble**, adj. —**dis•pu′tant**, adj., n. —**dis•pu•ta′tion**, n.

dis•qual′i•fy′, v., -fied, -fying. make ineligible. —**dis•qual′i•fi•ca′tion**, n.

dis•qui′et, v. **1.** disturb. —n. **2.** lack of peace.

dis′qui•si′tion (dis′kwə zish′ən) n. formal discourse or treatise.

dis′re•gard′, v. **1.** ignore. —n. **2.** neglect.

dis′re•pair′, n. impaired condition.

dis′re•pute′, n. ill repute. —**dis•rep′u•ta•ble**, adj.

dis′re•spect′, n. lack of respect. —**dis′re•spect′ful**, adj. —**dis′re•spect′ful•ly**, adv.

dis•robe′, v., -robed, -robing. undress.

dis•rupt′ (dis rupt′) v. break up. —**dis•rup′tion**, n. —**dis•rup′tive**, adj.

dis•sat′is•fy′, v., -fied, -fying. make discontented. —**dis′sat•is•fac′tion** (-fak′shən) n.

dis•sect′ (di sekt′, dī-) v. cut apart for examination; analyze in detail. —**dis•sec′tion**, n.

dis•sem′ble (di sem′bəl) v., -bled, -bling. feign. —**dis•sem′bler**, n.

dis•sem′i•nate′ (di sem′ə nāt′) v., -nated, -nating. scatter or spread widely. —**dis•sem′i•na′tion**, n.

dis•sen′sion (di sen′shən) n. **1.** disagreement. **2.** discord.

dis•sent′ (di sent′) v. **1.** disagree. —n. **2.** difference of opinion. —**dis•sent′er**, n.

dis′ser•ta′tion (dis′ər tā′shən) n. formal essay or treatise.

dis•serv′ice, n. harm or injury.

dis′si•dent (dis′i dənt) adj. **1.** refusing to agree or conform. —n. **2.** dissident person. —**dis′si•dence**, n.

dis•sim′i•lar, adj. not similar. —**dis•sim′i•lar′i•ty** (-lar′i tē) n.

dis•sim′u•late′ (di sim′yə lāt′) v., -lated, -lating. disguise; dissemble. —**dis•sim′u•la′tion**, n.

dis′si•pate′ (dis′ə pāt′) v., -pated, -pating. **1.** scatter. **2.** squander. **3.** live dissolutely. —**dis′si•pa′tion**, n.

dis•so′ci•ate′ (di sō′shē āt′, -sē-) v., -ated, -ating. separate.

dis′so•lute′ (dis′ə lōōt′) adj. immoral; licentious. —**dis′so•lute′ly**, adv.

dis•solve′ (di zolv′) v., -solved, -solving. **1.** make solution of. **2.** terminate. **3.** destroy. —**dis′so•lu′tion** (dis′ə lōō′shən) n.

dis′so•nance (dis′ə nəns) n. inharmonious or harsh sound. —**dis′so•nant**, adj.

dis•suade′ (di swād′) v., -suaded, -suading. persuade against.

dist., 1. distance. **2.** district.

dis′taff (dis′taf) n. **1.** staff for holding wool, flax, etc., in spinning. —adj. **2.** of women.

dis′tance (dis′təns) n. **1.** space between. **2.** remoteness. **3.** aloofness.

dis′tant, adj. **1.** remote. **2.** reserved. —**dis′tant•ly**, adv.

dis•taste′, n. dislike; aversion. —**dis•taste′ful**, adj.

Dist. Atty. district attorney.

Dist. Ct. District Court.

dis•tem′per (dis tem′pər) n. infectious disease of dogs and cats.

dis•tend/ (di stend/) *v.* expand abnormally. —**dis•ten/tion,** *n.*

dis•till/ (di stil/) *v.* **1.** obtain by evaporation and condensation. **2.** purify. **3.** fall in drops. —**dis/til•la/tion,** *n.* —**dis•till/er,** *n.* —**dis•till/er•y,** *n.*

dis•tinct/ (di stingkt/) *adj.* **1.** clear. **2.** separate. —**dis•tinct/ly,** *adv.*

dis•tinc/tion, *n.* **1.** act or instance of distinguishing. **2.** discrimination. **3.** difference. **4.** eminence. —**dis•tinc/tive,** *adj.*

dis•tin/guish (di sting/gwish) *v.* **1.** identify as different. **2.** perceive. **3.** make eminent. —**dis•tin/guish•a•ble,** *adj.*

dis•tin/guished, *adj.* dignified or elegant.

distn distortion.

dis•tort/ (di stôrt/) *v.* **1.** twist out of shape. **2.** hide truth or true meaning of. —**dis•tor/tion,** *n.*

distr. 1. distribute. **2.** distribution. **3.** distributor.

dis•tract/ (di strakt/) *v.* **1.** divert attention of. **2.** trouble. —**dis•trac/tion,** *n.*

dis•traught/ (di strôt/) *adj.* crazed with anxiety.

dis•tress/ (di stres/) *n.* **1.** pain or sorrow. **2.** state of emergency. —*v.* **3.** afflict with pain or sorrow.

dis•trib/ute (di strib/yo͞ot) *v.,* **-uted, -uting. 1.** divide in shares. **2.** spread. **3.** sort. —**dis/tri•bu/tion,** *n.* —**dis•trib/u•tor,** *n.*

dis/trict (dis/trikt) *n.* **1.** political division. **2.** region.

district attorney, attorney for the government within a given district, whose job is primarily prosecuting.

dis•trust/, *v.* **1.** suspect. —*n.* **2.** suspicion; doubt. —**dis•trust/ful,** *adj.*

dis•turb/ (di stûrb/) *v.* **1.** interrupt peace of. **2.** unsettle. —**dis•turb/ance,** *n.*

dis•use/ (dis yo͞os/) *n.* absence of use.

ditch (dich) *n.* **1.** trench; channel. —*v.* **2.** *Slang.* get rid of.

dith/er (dith/ər) *n.* **1.** flustered excitement or fear. —*v.* **2.** fail to act resolutely; vacillate.

dit/to (dit/ō) *n., pl.* **-tos,** *adv.* —*n.* **1.** the same. —*adv.* **2.** as stated before.

ditto mark, mark (") indicating repetition.

dit/ty (dit/ē) *n., pl.* **-ties.** simple song.

di/u•ret/ic (dī/ə ret/ik) *adj.* promoting urination. —**di/u•ret/ic,** *n.*

di•ur/nal (dī ûr/nl) *adj.* daily.

div., 1. dividend. **2.** division. **3.** divorced.

di/va (dē/və, -vä) *n.* prima donna (def. 1).

di/van (di van/) *n.* sofa.

dive (dīv) *v.,* **dived** or **dove** (dōv), **dived, diving,** *n.* —*v.* **1.** plunge into water. **2.** plunge deeply. —*n.* **3.** act of diving. —**div/er,** *n.*

di•verge/ (di vûrj/, dī-) *v.,* **-verged, -verging. 1.** move or lie in different directions. **2.** differ. —**di•ver/gence,** *n.* —**di•ver/gent,** *adj.*

di/vers (dī/vərz) *adj.* various.

di•verse/ (di vûrs/, dī-) *adj.* of different kinds or forms. —**di•ver/si•fy/,** *v.,* **-fied, -fying.** —**di•ver/si•ty,** *n.* —**di•ver/si•fi•ca/tion,** *n.*

di•vert/ (di vûrt/, dī-) *v.* **1.** turn aside. **2.** amuse. —**di•ver/sion,** *n.* —**di•ver/sion•ar/y,** *adj.*

di•vest/ (di vest/, dī-) *v.* deprive; dispossess.

di•vide/ (di vīd/) *v.,* **-vided, -viding,** *n.* —*v.* **1.** separate into parts. **2.** apportion. —*n.* **3.** zone separating drainage basins. —**di•vid/a•ble,** *adj.* —**di•vid/er,** *n.*

div/i•dend/ (div/i dend/) *n.* **1.** number to be divided. **2.** share in profits.

di•vine/ (di vīn/) *adj., n., v.,* **-vined, -vining.** —*adj.* **1.** of or from God or a god. **2.** religious. **3.** godlike. —*n.* **4.** theologian or clergyman. —*v.* **5.** prophesy. **6.** perceive. —**div/i•na/tion,** *n.* —**di•vine/ly,** *adv.*

divining rod, forked stick for finding water deposits.

di•vin/i•ty (-vin/i tē) *n., pl.* **-ties. 1.** divine nature. **2.** god.

div. in par. aeq. (in prescriptions) let it be divided into equal parts. [from Latin *dīvidātur in partēs aequālēs*]

di•vi/sion (di vizh/ən) *n.* **1.** act or result of dividing. **2.** thing that divides. **3.** section. **4.** military unit under major general. —**di•vis/i•ble,** *adj.* —**di•vi/sion•al,** *adj.* —**di•vi/sive** (-vī/siv) *adj.*

di•vi/sor (-vī/zər) *n.* number dividing dividend.

di•vorce/ (di vôrs/) *n., v.,* **-vorced, -vorcing.** —*n.* **1.** dissolution of marriage. **2.** separation. —*v.* **3.** separate by divorce. —**di•vor/cee/** (-sē/) *n.fem.*

div/ot (div/ət) *n.* turf gouged out by a golf club stroke.

di•vulge/ (di vulj/, dī-) *v.,* **-vulged, -vulging.** disclose.

Dix/ie (dik/sē) *n.* southern states of the U.S., esp. those that joined Confederacy.

Dix/ie•land/, *n.* style of jazz marked by accented four-four rhythm and improvisation.

DIY *British.* do-it-yourself. Also, **D.I.Y., d.i.y.**

DIYer (dē/ī/wī/ər) *British.* do-it-yourselfer. Also, **DIY'er.**

diz/zy (diz/ē) *adj.,* **-zier, -ziest. 1.** giddy. **2.** confused. **3.** *Informal.* foolish; silly. —**diz/zi•ly,** *adv.* —**diz/zi•ness,** *n.*

D.J. (dē/jā/) disc jockey. Also, **DJ, deejay.**

DJF divorced Jewish female.

DJM divorced Jewish male.

D.Journ. Doctor of Journalism.

D.J.S. Doctor of Juridical Science.

D.J.T. Doctor of Jewish Theology.

DK *Real Estate.* deck.

dk. 1. dark. **2.** deck. **3.** dock.

dkg dekagram; dekagrams.

dkl dekaliter; dekaliters.

dkm dekameter; dekameters.

D

DL diesel.

dl 1. data link. 2. daylight. 3. dead load. 4. deciliter; deciliters. 5. drawing list.

D/L demand loan.

dla data link address.

D. Lit. Doctor of Literature.

D. Litt. Doctor of Letters. [from Latin *Doctor Litterārum*]

D.L.O. dead letter office.

dlr. 1. dealer. 2. Also, **dlr** dollar.

dlrs. dollars. Also, **dlrs**

D.L.S. Doctor of Library Science.

dlvy delivery.

dlx deluxe.

dly 1. delay. 2. dolly.

DM 1. Deutsche mark. 2. divorced male.

dm 1. decimeter; decimeters. 2. demand meter.

DM. direct mail.

Dm. Deutsche mark.

DMA *Computers.* direct memory access.

dmd demodulate.

D.M.D. Doctor of Dental Medicine. [from Latin *Dentāriae Medicīnae Doctor* or *Doctor Medicīnae Dentālis*]

DMDT *Chemistry.* methoxychlor. [*d(i)m(eth-oxy)d(iphenyl)t(richloroethane)*]

D.M.L. Doctor of Modern Languages.

dmm *Electricity.* digital multimeter.

DMN *Chemistry.* dimethylnitrosamine. Also, **DMNA**

dmp *Computers.* dot-matrix printer.

dmpr damper.

dmr dimmer.

D.M.S. 1. Director of Medical Services. 2. Doctor of Medical Science.

DMSO a liquid substance, C_2H_6OS, used in industry as a solvent; proposed as an analgesic and anti-inflammatory. [*d(i)m(ethyl) s(-ulf)o(xide)*]

DMT *Pharmacology.* dimethyltryptamine.

D. Mus. Doctor of Music.

DMV Department of Motor Vehicles.

dmx data multiplex.

DMZ demilitarized zone.

dn. down.

DNA, deoxyribonucleic acid, substance that carries genes along its strands.

DNase (dē′en′ās, -āz), deoxyribonuclease: any of several enzymes that break down the DNA molecule. Also, **DNAase**.

D.N.B. *Dictionary of National Biography.*

DNC Democratic National Committee.

DNR 1. *Medicine.* do not resuscitate (used in hospitals and other health-care facilities). 2. Also, **D.N.R.** do not return.

dntl dental.

do (dō̄; *unstressed* dŏo, də) *v.,* **did, done, doing,** *n.* —*v.* 1. perform; execute. 2. behave. 3. fare. 4. finish. 5. effect. 6. render. 7. suffice. —*n.* 8. *Informal.* social gathering. 9. (dō). first note of musical scale.

DOA, dead on arrival.

DOB date of birth. Also, **D.O.B., d.o.b.**

DOC Department of Commerce.

doc. 1. data output channel. 2. document. 3. Also, **doc** documentation.

do′cent (dō′sənt) *n.* lecturer or guide, esp. in museum.

doc′ile (dos′əl) *adj.* 1. readily taught. 2. tractable. —**do•cil′i•ty,** *n.*

dock (dok) *n.* 1. wharf. 2. place for ship. 3. fleshy part of tail. 4. prisoner's place in courtroom. —*v.* 5. put into dock. 6. cut off end of. 7. deduct from (pay).

dock′et (dok′it) *n.* 1. list of court cases. 2. label.

doc′tor (dok′tər) *n.* 1. medical practitioner. 2. holder of highest academic degree. —*v.* 3. treat medicinally.

doc′tor•ate (-it) *n.* doctor's degree.

doctor's degree, degree of the highest rank awarded by universities.

doc′tri•naire′ (-trə när′) *adj.* orthodox.

doc′trine (-trin) *n.* 1. principle. 2. teachings. —**doc′tri•nal,** *adj.*

doc′u•dra′ma (dok′yə drä′mə, -dram′ə) *n.* fictionalized TV drama depicting actual events.

doc′u•ment, *n.* (-mənt) 1. paper with information or evidence. —*v.* (-ment′) 2. support by documents.

doc′u•men′ta•ry (-men′tə rē) *adj., n., pl.* **-ries.** —*adj.* 1. of or derived from documents. —*n.* 2. film on factual subject.

DOD 1. Department of Defense. 2. *Telecommunications.* direct outward diaing.

dod′der (dod′ər) *v.* shake; tremble; totter. —**dod′der•ing,** *adj.*

dodge (doj) *v.,* **dodged, dodging,** *n.* —*v.* 1. elude. —*n.* 2. act of dodging. 3. trick. —**dodg′er,** *n.*

do′do (dō′dō) *n., pl.* **-dos, -does.** extinct bird.

doe (dō) *n.* female deer, etc. —**doe′skin′,** *n.*

does (duz) *v.* third pers. sing. pres. indic. of **do.**

does′n't (duz′ənt) contraction of **does not.**

doff (dof) *v.* remove.

dog (dôg) *n., v.,* **dogged, dogging.** —*n.* 1. domesticated carnivore. —*v.* 2. follow closely.

dog′-ear′, *n.* folded-down corner of book page. —**dog′-eared′,** *adj.*

dog′ged (dô′gid) *adj.* persistent.

dog′ger•el (dô′gər əl) *n.* bad verse.

dog′house′, *n.* 1. shelter for dog. 2. place of disfavor.

dog′ma (-mə) *n.* system of beliefs; doctrine.

dog•mat′ic (-mat′ik) *adj.* 1. of dogma. 2. opinionated. —**dog•mat′i•cal•ly,** *adv.*

dog′ma•tism′, *n.* aggressive assertion of opinions.

dog′wood′, *n.* flowering tree.

DOHC *Automotive.* double overhead camshaft.

DOI Department of the Interior.

doi′ly (doi′lē) *n.*, *pl.* **-lies.** small napkin.

DOJ Department of Justice.

DOL Department of Labor.

dol. 1. *Music.* dolce. 2. dollar.

Dol′by (dōl′bē) *n. Trademark.* system for reducing high-frequency noise in a tape recording.

dol′drums (dōl′drəmz, dol′-) *n.pl.* 1. flat calms at sea. 2. listless mood.

dole (dōl) *n.*, *v.*, **doled, doling.** —*n.* 1. portion of charitable gift. —*v.* 2. give out sparingly.

dole′ful, *adj.* sorrowful; gloomy. —**dole′ful•ly,** *adv.*

doll (dol) *n.* 1. toy representing baby or other human being. 2. attractive or nice person.

dol′lar (dol′ər) *n.* monetary unit equal to 100 cents.

dol′lop (dol′əp) *n.* lump or blob of soft substance, as whipped cream.

dol′ly (dol′ē) *n.*, *pl.* **-lies.** 1. low cart for moving heavy loads. 2. movable platform for movie or TV camera.

dol′or•ous (dō′lər əs, dol′ər-) *adj.* grievous.

dol′phin (dol′fin) *n.* whalelike animal.

dols. dollars.

dolt (dōlt) *n.* fool. —**dolt′ish,** *adj.*

-dom, suffix indicating: 1. domain, as *kingdom.* 2. rank or station, as *dukedom.* 3. general condition, as *freedom.*

do•main′ (dō mān′) *n.* 1. ownership of land. 2. realm.

dome (dōm) *n.* spherical roof.

do•mes′tic (də mes′tik) *adj.* 1. of or devoted to the home. 2. not foreign. —*n.* 3. household servant. —**do/mes•tic′i•ty** (dō′me stis′-i tē) *n.*

do•mes′ti•cate′ (-kāt′) *v.*, **-cated, -cating.** tame. —**do•mes′ti•ca′tion,** *n.*

domestic partner, unmarried person who cohabits with another.

dom′i•cile′ (dom′ə sīl′, -səl, dō′mə-) *n.* home.

dom′i•nate′ (dom′ə nāt′) *v.*, **-nated, -nating.** 1. rule. 2. tower above. —**dom′i•na′tion,** **dom′i•nance,** *n.* —**dom′i•nant,** *adj.*

dom′i•neer′ (dom′ə nēr′) *v.* rule oppressively. —**dom′i•neer′ing,** *adj.*

do•min′ion (də min′yən) *n.* 1. power of governing. 2. territory governed.

dom′i•no′ (dom′ə nō′) *n.*, *pl.* **-noes.** oblong dotted piece used in game of **dominoes.**

don (don) *v.*, **donned, donning.** put on.

do′nate (dō′nāt, dō nāt′) *v.*, **-nated, -nating.** give. —**do•na′tion,** *n.*

don′key (dong′kē, dông′-, dung′-) *n.* 1. ass. 2. fool.

don′ny•brook′ (don′ē brŏŏk′) *n.* (*often cap.*) brawl; melee.

do′nor (dō′nər) *n.* giver.

doo′dle (dōōd′l) *v.*, **-dled, -dling.** scribble. —**doo′dler,** *n.*

doom (dōōm) *n.* 1. fate. 2. ruin. 3. judgment. —*v.* 4. condemn.

dooms′day′, *n.* day the world ends; Judgment Day.

door (dôr) *n.* 1. movable barrier at entrance. 2. Also, **door′way′.** entrance. —**door′bell′,** *n.* —**door′step′,** *n.*

door′yard′, *n.* yard near front door of house.

D.O.P. *Photography.* developing-out paper.

dope (dōp) *n.* 1. liquid substance used to prepare a surface. 2. *Informal.* narcotic. 3. *Slang.* information; news. 4. *Informal.* stupid person.

dop′ey, *adj.*, **-ier, -iest.** *Informal.* 1. stupid; silly. 2. sluggish or confused, as from drug use. Also, **dop′y.**

Dor. 1. Dorian. 2. Doric.

DORAN (dôr′an, dōr′-), an electronic device for determining range and assisting navigation. [*Do(ppler) r(ange) a(nd) n(avigation)*]

dor′mant (dôr′mənt) *adj.* 1. asleep. 2. inactive. —**dor′man•cy,** *n.*

dor′mer (dôr′mər) *n.* vertical window projecting from sloping roof.

dor′mi•to′ry (dôr′mi tôr′ē) *n.*, *pl.* **-ries.** group sleeping place. Also, **dorm.**

dor′mouse′ (dôr′mous′) *n.*, *pl.* **-mice.** small rodent.

dor′sal (dôr′səl) *adj.* of or on the back.

do′ry (dôr′ē) *n.*, *pl.* **-ries.** flat-bottomed rowboat.

DOS (dôs) *n.* disk operating system for microcomputers.

dose (dōs) *n.*, *v.*, **dosed, dosing.** —*n.* 1. amount of medicine taken at one time. —*v.* 2. give doses to. —**dos′age,** *n.*

dos′si•er′ (dos′ē ā′) *n.* file of documents.

dot (dot) *n.*, *v.*, **dotted, dotting.** —*n.* 1. small spot. —*v.* 2. mark with or make dots.

do′tard (dō′tərd) *n.* senile person.

dote (dōt) *v.*, **doted, doting.** 1. be overfond. 2. be senile. —**dot′age,** *n.*

dou′ble (dub′əl) *adj.*, *n.*, *v.*, **-bled, -bling.** —*adj.* 1. twice as great, etc. 2. of two parts. 3. deceitful. —*n.* 4. double quantity. 5. duplicate. —*v.* 6. make or become double. 7. bend or fold. 8. turn back. —**doub′ly,** *adv.*

double bass (bās) lowest-pitched instrument of violin family.

doub′le-cross′, *v.* cheat or betray. —**doub′-le-cross′er,** *n.*

doub′le-dig′it, *adj.* involving two-digit numbers.

dou′ble en•ten′dre (än tän′drə, -tänd′) *n.*, *pl.* **-ten′dres** (-tän′drəz, -tändz′). saying with two meanings.

dou′ble•head′er, *n.* two games played on the same day in rapid succession.

double play, baseball play in which two players are put out.

double standard, standard that differs for different persons or groups.

double take, delayed response, as to something not immediately recognized.

doub/le-talk/, n. evasive talk.

doubt (dout) v. **1.** be uncertain about. —n. **2.** uncertainty. —doubt/less, adv., adj.

doubt/ful, adj. **1.** having doubts. **2.** causing doubts or suspicion. —doubt/ful•ly, adv.

douche (do͞osh) n., v., **douched, douching.** —n. **1.** jet of liquid applied to a body part or cavity. —v. **2.** apply a douche.

dough (dō) n. mixture of flour, liquid, etc., for baking.

dough/nut (dō/nət, -nut/) n. ringlike cake of fried, sweet dough. —dough/nut•like/, adj.

dour (do͝or, dou°r, dou/ər) adj. sullen.

douse (dous) v., **doused, dousing. 1.** plunge; dip. **2.** extinguish.

DOVAP (dō/vap), Electronics. a system for plotting the trajectory of a missile or other rapidly moving object by means of radio waves bounced off it. [Do(ppler) V(elocity) a(nd) P(osition)]

dove (duv) n. pigeon.

dove/cote/, n. structure for tame pigeons. Also, **dove/cot/.**

dove/tail/, n. **1.** tenon-and-mortise joint. —v. **2.** join by dovetail. **3.** fit together harmoniously.

Dow. dowager.

dow/a•ger (dou/ə jər) n. **1.** titled or wealthy widow. **2.** dignified elderly woman.

dow/dy (dou/dē) adj., **-dier, -diest.** not stylish or attractive.

dow/el (dou/əl) n. wooden pin fitting into hole.

dow/er (dou/ər) n. widow's share of husband's property.

down (doun) adv. **1.** to, at, or in lower place or state. **2.** on or to ground. **3.** on paper. —prep. **4.** in descending direction. —n. **5.** descent. **6.** soft feathers. —v. **7.** subdue. —down/wards, adv. —down/ward, adv., adj. —down/y, adj.

down/cast/, adj. dejected.

down/er, n. Informal. **1.** depressing experience or person. **2.** sedative drug.

down/fall/, n. **1.** ruin. **2.** fall. —down/fall/-en, adj.

down/grade/, v., **-graded, -grading,** n. —v. **1.** reduce in rank, importance, etc. —n. **2.** downward slope.

down/heart/ed, adj. dejected. —down/-heart/ed•ly, adv.

down/hill/ (adv. -hil/; adj. -hil/) adv., adj. in downward direction.

down/play/, v. minimize.

down/pour/, n. heavy rain.

down/right/, adj. **1.** thorough. —adv. **2.** completely.

down/scale/, adj. of or for people at lower end of economic scale.

down/size/, v., **-sized, -sizing. 1.** make smaller version of. **2.** reduce in size or number.

down/stage/ (adv. -stāj/; adj. -stāj/) adv., adj. at or toward front of stage.

down/stairs/ (adv. -stârz/; adj. -stârz/) adv., adj. to or on lower floor.

down/stream/, adv., adj. with current of stream.

Down syndrome, genetic disorder characterized by mental retardation, a wide, flattened skull, and slanting eyes. Also, **Down's syndrome.**

down/-to-earth/, adj. objective; practical.

down/town/, n. **1.** central part of town. —adj. **2.** of this part. —adv. **3.** to or in this part.

down/trod/den, adj. oppressed.

down/turn/, n. downward trend.

dow/ry (dou/rē) n., pl. **-ries.** bride's estate.

dowse (dous) v., **dowsed, dowsing.** use divining rod. —dows/er, n.

dox•ol/o•gy (dok sol/ə jē) n., pl. **-gies.** hymn praising God.

doz., dozen.

doze (dōz) v., **dozed, dozing,** n. —v. **1.** sleep lightly. —n. **2.** light sleep.

doz/en (duz/ən) n., pl. **dozen, dozens.** group of 12.

DP 1. data processing. **2.** displaced person.

dp 1. dashpot: relay. **2.** data processing. **3.** deflection plate. **4.** depth. **5.** dial pulsing. **6.** Baseball. double play; double plays. **7.** Electricity. double-pole. **8.** dripproof.

D/P documents against payment.

D.P. 1. data processing. **2.** displaced person.

d.p. (in prescriptions) with a proper direction. [from Latin dīrēctiōne prōpriā]

D.P.A. Doctor of Public Administration.

DPC Defense Plant Corporation.

dpdt Electricity. double-pole double-throw.

dpg damping.

DPH Department of Public Health.

D. Ph. Doctor of Philosophy.

D.P.H. Doctor of Public Health.

dpi Computers. dots per inch.

DPL diplomat.

D.P.M. Doctor of Podiatric Medicine.

D.P.P. Insurance. deferred payment plan.

D.P.S. Doctor of Public Service.

dpst Electricity. double-pole single-throw.

dpstk dipstick.

DPT diphtheria, pertussis, and tetanus: a mixed vaccine used for primary immunization. Also, **DTP**

dpt. 1. department. **2.** deponent.

D.P.W. Department of Public Works. Also, **DPW**

dpx duplex.

DQ disqualify.

Dr., 1. Doctor. **2.** Drive.

drab (drab) n., adj., **drabber, drabbest.** —n. **1.** dull brownish gray. —adj. **2.** colored drab. **3.** uninteresting. —drab/ness, n.

draft (draft) n. **1.** drawing; sketch. **2.** rough

version. **3.** current of air. **4.** haul. **5.** swallow of liquid. **6.** depth in water of a vessel. **7.** selection for military service. **8.** written request for payment. —*v.* **9.** plan. **10.** write. **11.** enlist by draft. —**draft′y,** *adj.* —**draft•ee′,** *n.*

drafts′man, *n.* person who draws plans, etc.

drag (drag) *v.,* **dragged, dragging,** *n.* —*v.* **1.** draw heavily; haul. **2.** dredge. **3.** trail on ground. **4.** pass slowly. —*n.* **5.** thing used in dragging. **6.** hindrance.

drag′net′, *n.* **1.** net for dragging in water. **2.** system for catching criminal.

drag′on (drag′ən) *n.* fabled reptile.

drag′on•fly′, *n., pl.* **-flies.** large four-winged insect.

dra•goon′ (drə gōōn′) *n.* **1.** heavily armed mounted soldier, formerly common in European armies. —*v.* **2.** force; coerce.

drag race, race with cars accelerating from a standstill.

drain (drān) *v.* **1.** draw or flow off gradually. **2.** empty; dry. **3.** exhaust. —*n.* **4.** channel or pipe for draining. —**drain′er,** *n.* —**drain′-age,** *n.*

drake (drāk) *n.* male duck.

dram (dram) *n.* **1.** apothecaries' weight, equal to ⅛ ounce. **2.** small drink of liquor.

dra′ma (drä′mə, dram′ə) *n.* **1.** story acted on stage. **2.** vivid series of events.

dra•mat′ic (drə mat′ik) *adj.* **1.** of plays or theater. **2.** highly vivid. —**dra•mat′i•cal•ly,** *adv.*

dra•mat′ics, *n.* **1.** theatrical art. **2.** exaggerated conduct or emotion.

dram′a•tist (dram′ə tist, drä′mə-) *n.* playwright.

dram′a•tize′, *v.,* **-tized, -tizing.** put in dramatic form. —**dram′a•ti•za′tion,** *n.*

dram. pers. *Theater.* dramatis personae.

drape (drāp) *v.,* **draped, draping,** *n.* —*v.* **1.** cover with fabric. **2.** arrange in folds. —*n.* **3.** draped hanging. —**dra′per•y,** *n.*

dras′tic (dras′tik) *adj.* extreme. —**dras′ti•cal•ly,** *adv.*

draught (draft) *n. Brit.* draft.

draw (drô) *v.,* **drew** (drōō), **drawn, drawing,** *n.* —*v.* **1.** pull; lead. **2.** take out. **3.** attract. **4.** sketch. **5.** take in. **6.** deduce. **7.** stretch. **8.** make or have as draft. —*n.* **9.** act of drawing. **10.** part that is drawn. **11.** equal score. **12.** *Informal.* attraction to public.

draw′back′, *n.* disadvantage.

draw′bridge′, *n.* bridge that can be drawn up.

draw′er (drôr *for 1, 2;* drô′ər *for 3) n.* **1.** sliding compartment. **2.** (*pl.*) trouserlike undergarment. **3.** person who draws.

draw′ing, *n.* drawn picture.

drawl (drôl) *v.* **1.** speak slowly. —*n.* **2.** drawled utterance.

drawn (drôn) *adj.* tense; haggard.

dray (drā) *n.* low, strong cart. —**dray′man,** *n.*

drch. drachma; drachmas. Also, **dr.**

D.R.E. 1. Director of Religious Education. **2.** Doctor of Religious Education.

dread (dred) *v.* **1.** fear. —*n.* **2.** fear. **3.** awe. —*adj.* **4.** feared. **5.** revered.

dread′ful, *adj.* **1.** very bad. **2.** inspiring dread.

dread′ful•ly, *adv. Informal.* very.

dread′locks′, *n.* hairstyle with many long, ropelike locks.

dream (drēm) *n.* **1.** ideas imagined during sleep. **2.** reverie. —*v.* **3.** have dream (about). **4.** fancy. —**dream′er,** *n.* —**dream′y,** *adj.*

dream team, group of experts associated in some joint action.

drear′y, *adj.,* **drearier, dreariest.** gloomy or boring. —**drear′i•ly,** *adv.* —**drear′i•ness,** *n.*

dredge (drej) *n., v.,* **dredged, dredging.** —*n.* **1.** machine for moving earth at the bottom of river, etc. —*v.* **2.** move with dredge. **3.** sprinkle with flour.

dregs (dregz) *n.pl.* sediment.

drench (drench) *v.* soak.

dress (dres) *n.* **1.** woman's garment. **2.** clothing. —*v.* **3.** clothe. **4.** ornament. **5.** prepare. **6.** treat (wounds). —**dress′mak′er,** *n.* —**dress′mak′ing,** *n.*

dres•sage′ (drə säzh′, dre-) *n.* art of training a horse in obedience and precision of movement.

dress circle, semicircular division of seats in a theater.

dress′er, *n.* **1.** bureau; chest of drawers. **2.** person who dresses another. **3.** person who dresses in a certain way.

dress′ing, *n.* **1.** sauce or stuffing. **2.** application for wound.

dress rehearsal, final rehearsal with costumes.

dress′y, *adj.,* **-ier, -iest.** fancy; formal.

dri dead-reckoning indicator.

drib′ble (drib′əl) *v.,* **-bled, -bling,** *n.* —*v.* **1.** fall in drops. **2.** bounce repeatedly. —*n.* **3.** trickle.

dri′er (drī′ər) *n.* dryer.

drift (drift) *n.* **1.** deviation from set course. **2.** tendency. **3.** something driven, esp. into heap. —*v.* **4.** carry or be carried by currents.

drift′er, *n.* person who moves frequently.

drill (dril) *n.* **1.** boring tool. **2.** methodical training. **3.** furrow for seeds. **4.** sowing machine. **5.** strong twilled cotton. —*v.* **6.** pierce with drill. **7.** train methodically. —**drill′er,** *n.*

drink (dringk) *v.,* **drank** (drangk), **drunk** (drungk), **drinking,** *n.* —*v.* **1.** swallow liquid. **2.** swallow alcoholic liquids. —*n.* **3.** liquid for quenching thirst. **4.** alcoholic beverage. —**drink′er,** *n.*

drip (drip) *v.,* **dripped, dripping. 1.** fall or let fall in drops. —*n.* **2.** act of dripping.

drive (drīv) *v.,* **drove** (drōv), **driven, driving,** *n.* —*v.* **1.** send by force. **2.** control; guide. **3.** convey or travel in vehicle. **4.** impel. —*n.* **5.**

military offensive. **6.** strong effort. **7.** trip in vehicle. **8.** road for driving. **—driv/er,** *n.*

drive/-by/ *n., pl.* **-bys. 1.** action of driving by something specified. **2.** shooting that occurs from vehicle driving by. **—drive/-by/,** *adj.*

drive/-in/, *adj.* **1.** designed for persons in automobiles. **—***n.* **2.** a drive-in bank, movie theater, etc.

driv/el (driv/əl) *v.,* **-eled, -eling,** *n.* **—***v.* **1.** droll. **2.** talk foolishly. **—***n.* **3.** foolish talk.

drive/way/, *n.* road on private property.

driz/zle (driz/əl) *v.,* **-zled, -zling,** *n.* rain in fine drops.

droll (drōl) *adj.* amusingly odd. **—droll/er•y,** *n.*

drom/e•dar/y (drom/i der/ē, drum/-) *n., pl.* **-daries.** one-humped camel.

drone (drōn) *v.,* **droned, droning,** *n.* **—***v.* **1.** make humming sound. **2.** speak dully. **—***n.* **3.** monotonous tone. **4.** male of honeybee.

drool (drōōl) *v.* **1.** salivate. **—***n.* **2.** saliva dripping from the mouth.

droop (drōōp) *v.* **1.** sink or hang down. **2.** lose spirit. **—***n.* **3.** act of drooping. **—droop/-y,** *adj.*

drop (drop) *n., v.,* **dropped, dropping. —***n.* **1.** small mass of liquid. **2.** small quantity. **3.** fall. **4.** steep slope. **—***v.* **5.** fall or let fall. **6.** cease. **7.** visit. **—drop/per,** *n.*

drop kick, kick made by dropping ball to the ground and kicking it as it starts to bounce up. **—drop/kick/,** *v.* **—drop/-kick/er,** *n.*

drop/out/, *n.* student who quits before graduation.

drop/sy (drop/sē) *n.* edema.

dross (drôs) *n.* refuse.

drought (drout) *n.* dry weather.

drove (drōv) *n.* **1.** group of driven cattle. **2.** crowd.

drown (droun) *v.* suffocate by immersion in liquid.

drowse (drouz) *v.,* **drowsed, drowsing.** be sleepy. **—drow/sy,** *adj.* **—drow/si•ness,** *n.*

drsg dressing.

DRTL *Computers.* diode resistor transistor logic.

drub (drub) *v.,* **drubbed, drubbing. 1.** beat. **2.** defeat.

drudge (druj) *n., v.,* **drudged, drudging. —***n.* **1.** person doing tedious work. **—***v.* **2.** do such work. **—drudg/er•y,** *n.*

drug (drug) *n., v.,* **drugged, drugging. —***n.* **1.** therapeutic chemical. **2.** narcotic. **—***v.* **3.** mix or affect with drug. **—drug/store/,** *n.*

drug/gist, *n.* **1.** prepares drugs; pharmacist. **2.** person who owns or operates drugstore.

dru/id (drōō/id) *n.* (*often cap.*) member of a pre-Christian religious order in Europe. **—dru/id•ism,** *n.*

drum (drum) *n., v.,* **drummed, drumming. —***n.* **1.** percussion musical instrument. **2.** eardrum. **—***v.* **3.** beat on or as on drum. **—drum/mer,** *n.*

drum major, leader of marching band.

drum majorette, majorette.

drum/stick/, *n.* **1.** stick for beating a drum. **2.** leg of a cooked fowl.

drunk (drungk) *adj.* intoxicated. Also, **drunk/en.**

drunk/ard (drung/kərd) *n.* habitually drunk person.

D.R.V. (on food labels) Daily Reference Value: the amount of nutrients appropriate for one day.

drvr driver.

dry (drī) *adj.,* **drier, driest,** *v.,* **dried, drying. —***adj.* **1.** not wet. **2.** rainless. **3.** not yielding liquid. **4.** thirsty. **5.** boring. **6.** not expressing emotion. **7.** not sweet. **—***v.* **8.** make or become dry. **—dry/ly,** *adv.* **—dry/ness,** *n.*

dry/ad (drī/əd, -ad) *n.* (*often cap.*) nymph of the woods.

dry/-clean/, *v.* clean with solvents. **—dry/-clean/er,** *n.*

dry/er, *n.* machine for drying.

dry ice, solid carbon dioxide, used esp. as a refrigerant.

dry run, rehearsal or trial.

drzl drizzle.

Ds *Symbol, Chemistry.* (formerly) dysprosium.

ds 1. diode switch. **2.** domestic service.

D.S. 1. *Music.* from the sign. [from Italian *dal segno*] **2.** Doctor of Science.

d.s. 1. daylight saving. **2.** *Commerce.* Also, **D/S** days after sight. **3.** document signed.

DSA *Medicine.* digital subtraction angiography.

dsb *Electronics.* double sideband.

dsbl disable.

DSC 1. The Discovery Channel (a cable channel). **2.** Defense Supplies Corporation.

D.Sc. Doctor of Science.

D.S.C. 1. Distinguished Service Cross. **2.** Doctor of Surgical Chiropody.

dscc dessicant.

dscont discontinue.

dscrm *Electronics.* discriminator.

dsd *Computers.* dual-scan display.

dsdd *Computers.* double-side, double-density.

dsgn design.

dshd *Computers.* double-side, high density.

dsl diesel.

dsltr desalter.

dslv dissolve.

D.S.M. 1. Distinguished Service Medal. **2.** Doctor of Sacred Music.

DSNA Dictionary Society of North America.

D.S.O. Distinguished Service Order.

dsp *Computers.* digital signal processing.

D.S.P. died without issue. [from Latin *dēcessit sine prōle*]

dspec design specification.

dspl display.

dspo disposal.

DSR *Medicine.* dynamic spatial reconstructor.

D.S.S. Doctor of Social Science.

dssd *Computers.* double-side, single-density.

DST, daylight-saving time.

dstlt distillate.

dstng distinguish.

DSU disk storage unit.

D. Surg. Dental Surgeon.

D.S.W. **1.** Doctor of Social Welfare. **2.** Doctor of Social Work.

DT *Slang.* detective. Also, **D.T.**

dt **1.** decay time. **2.** double throw.

dtd dated.

d.t.d. (in prescriptions) give such doses. [from Latin *dentur tālēs dosēs*]

D.Th. Doctor of Theology. Also, **D.Theol.**

DTL *Computers.* diode transistor logic.

dtl detail.

dtmf *Telecommunications.* dual-tone multifrequency.

DTP **1.** desktop publishing. **2.** diphtheria, tetanus, and pertussis. See **DPT.**

dtrbd *Computers.* daughterboard.

dtrs distress.

d.t.'s (dē′tēz′), *Pathology.* delirium tremens.

dtv digital television.

dty cy duty cycle.

Du. **1.** Duke. **2.** Dutch.

du′al (dōo′əl, dyōo′-) *adj.* **1.** of two. **2.** double; twofold. —**du′al•ism,** *n.* —**du•al′i•ty** (-al′i tē) *n.*

dub (dub) *v.,* **dubbed, dubbing.** **1.** name formally. **2.** furnish with new sound track.

du′bi•ous (dōo′bē əs) *adj.* doubtful. —**du′-bi•ous•ly,** *adv.*

du′cal (dōo′kəl, dyōo′-) *adj.* of dukes.

duch′ess (duch′is) *n.* **1.** duke's wife. **2.** woman equal in rank to duke.

duch′y (duch′ē) *n., pl.* **duchies. 1.** territory of duke. **2.** small state.

duck (duk) *v.* **1.** plunge under water. **2.** stoop quickly. **3.** avoid. —*n.* **4.** act of ducking. **5.** type of swimming bird. **6.** heavy cotton fabric. —**duck′ling,** *n.*

duck′bill′, *n.* small, egg-laying mammal.

duct (dukt) *n.* tube or canal in body. —**duct′-less,** *adj.*

duc′tile (duk′tl, -til) *adj.* **1.** readily drawn out; malleable. **2.** compliant. —**duc•til′i•ty,** *n.*

duct tape (duk, dukt) strongly adhesive cloth tape, used in plumbing, household repairs, etc.

dud (dud) *n. Informal.* failure.

dude (dōod, dyōod) *n.* **1.** man excessively concerned with his clothes. **2.** *Slang.* fellow; guy. **3.** urban vacationer on ranch.

dudg′eon (duj′ən) *n.* indignation.

due (dōo, dyōo) *adj.* **1.** payable. **2.** proper. **3.** attributable. **4.** expected. —*n.* **5.** something due. **6.** (*sometimes pl.*). regularly payable fee for membership. —*adv.* **7.** in a straight line.

du′el (dōo′əl, dyōo′-) *n., v.* **-eled, -eling.**

—*n.* **1.** prearranged combat between two persons. —*v.* **2.** fight in duel. —**du′el•er, du′el•ist,** *n.*

du•et′ (dōo et′, dyōo-) *n.* music for two performers.

duf′fel bag′ (duf′əl) cylindrical bag for carrying belongings.

duff′er (duf′ər) *n.* **1.** *Informal.* plodding, incompetent person. **2.** person inept at a specific sport, as golf.

dug′out′, *n.* **1.** boat made by hollowing a log. **2.** roofed structure where baseball players sit when not on the field. **3.** rough shelter dug in the ground, as by soldiers.

DUI driving under the influence.

duke (dōok, dyōok) *n.* **1.** ruler of duchy. **2.** nobleman below prince. —**duke′dom,** *n.*

dulc. (in prescriptions) sweet. [from Latin *dulcis*]

dul′cet (dul′sit) *adj.* melodious.

dul′ci•mer (dul′sə mər) *n.* musical instrument with metal strings.

dull (dul) *adj.* **1.** stupid. **2.** not brisk. **3.** tedious. **4.** not sharp. **5.** dim. —*v.* **6.** make or become dull. —**dul′ly,** *adv.* —**dull′ness, dul′ness,** *n.*

du′ly (dōo′lē, dyōo′-) *adv.* **1.** properly. **2.** punctually.

dumb (dum) *adj.* **1.** temporarily unable to speak. **2.** *Often Offensive.* lacking the power of speech. **3.** *Informal.* stupid.

dumb′bell′, *n.* **1.** weighted bar for exercising. **2.** *Informal.* stupid person.

dumb•found′ (dum found′, dum′found′) *v.* astonish. Also, **dumb•found′.**

dumb′wait′er, *n.* small elevator for moving food, etc.

dum′my, *n., pl.* **-mies,** *adj.* —*n.* **1.** model or copy. **2.** *Informal.* **a.** *Offensive.* mute. **b.** stupid person. —*adj.* **3.** counterfeit.

dump (dump) *v.* **1.** drop heavily. **2.** empty. —*n.* **3.** place for dumping. **4.** *Informal.* dilapidated, dirty place.

dump′ling (-ling) *n.* **1.** mass of steamed dough. **2.** dough wrapper with filling.

dump′y, *adj.,* **-ier, -iest.** short and stout. —**dump′i•ness,** *n.*

dun (dun) *v.,* **dunned, dunning,** *n.* —*v.* **1.** demand payment of. —*n.* **2.** demand for payment. **3.** dull brown.

dunce (duns) *n.* stupid person.

dune (dōon, dyōon) *n.* sand hill formed by wind.

dung (dung) *n.* manure; excrement.

dun′ga•ree′ (dung′gə rē′) *n.* coarse cotton fabric for work clothes (**dungarees**).

dun′geon (dun′jən) *n.* underground cell.

dunk (dungk) *v.* **1.** dip in beverage before eating. **2.** submerge briefly in liquid. **3.** thrust (basketball) downward through basket.

du′o (dōo′ō, dyōo′ō) *n.* **1.** duet. **2.** couple or pair.

du′o•de′num (dōo′ə dē′nəm, dyōo′-; dōo-

D

od'n əm, dyo͞o-) *n.* uppermost part of small intestine.

dupe (do͞op, dyo͞op) *n.*, *v.*, duped, duping. —*n.* 1. deceived person. —*v.* 2. deceive.

dupl duplicate.

du'plex (do͞o'pleks, dyo͞o'-) *n.* 1. apartment with two floors. 2. house for two families.

du'pli•cate, *adj.*, *n.*, *v.*, -cated, -cating. —*adj.* (do͞o'pli kit) 1. exactly like. 2. double. —*n.* (-kit) 3. copy. —*v.* (-kāt') 4. copy. 5. double. —**du'pli•ca'tion,** *n.* —**du'pli•ca'tor,** *n.*

du•plic'i•ty (do͞o plis'i tē, dyo͞o-) *n.*, *pl.* -ties. deceitfulness.

duplxr duplexer.

du'ra•ble (do͝or'ə bəl, dyo͝or'-) *adj.* enduring. —**du'ra•bil'i•ty,** *n.* —**du'ra•bly,** *adv.*

du•ra'tion (do͞o rā'shən, dyo͞o-) *n.* continuance in time.

du•ress' (do͞o res', dyo͞o-, do͝or'is, dyo͝or'-) *n.* compulsion.

dur'ing (do͝or'ing, dyo͝or'-) *prep.* in the course of.

du'rum (do͝or'əm, dyo͝or'-) *n.* kind of wheat flour used in pasta.

dusk (dusk) *n.* twilight. —**dusk'y,** *adj.*

dust (dust) *n.* 1. fine particles of earth, etc. 2. dead body. —*v.* 3. free from dust. 4. sprinkle. —**dust'y,** *adj.*

dut *Electronics.* device under test.

Dutch (duch) *n.* people or language of the Netherlands.

Dutch uncle, mentor who criticizes very frankly.

du'ti•ful (do͞o'tə fəl, dyo͞o'-) *adj.* doing one's duties. Also, **du'te•ous** (do͞o'tē əs, dyo͞o'-). —**du'ti•ful•ly,** *adv.*

du'ty (do͞o'tē, dyo͞o'-) *n.*, *pl.* -ties. 1. moral or legal obligation. 2. function. 3. tax, esp. on imports.

D.V. 1. God willing. [from Latin *D(eo) v(olente)*] 2. Douay Version (of the Bible).

dvc device.

dvl develop.

D.V.M. Doctor of Veterinary Medicine. Also, **DVM**

D.V.M.S. Doctor of Veterinary Medicine and Surgery.

dvr diver.

D.V.S. Doctor of Veterinary Surgery.

dvt deviate.

DW *Real Estate.* dishwasher.

dw 1. dishwasher. 2. distilled water. 3. double weight.

D/W *Law.* dock warrant.

dwarf (dwôrf) *n.* 1. abnormally small person, etc. —*v.* 2. make or make to seem small.

dwell (dwel) *v.*, dwelt or dwelled, dwelling. 1. reside. 2. linger, esp. in words. —**dwell'ing,** *n.*

dwg drawing.

DWI driving while intoxicated.

dwin'dle (dwin'dl) *v.*, -dled, -dling. shrink; lessen.

dwl dowel.

DWM *Slang.* dead white male.

dwn drawn.

dwr drawer.

DWT deadweight tons; deadweight tonnage.

dwt 1. deadweight tons; deadweight tonnage. 2. pennyweight; pennyweights.

d.w.t. deadweight tons; deadweight tonnage.

DX *Radio.* distance. Also, **D.X.**

Dx diagnosis.

dx duplex.

Dy *Symbol, Chemistry.* dysprosium.

dye (dī) *n.*, *v.*, dyed, dyeing. —*n.* 1. coloring material. —*v.* 2. color with dye. —**dye'ing,** *n.* —**dy'er,** *n.*

dyed'-in-the-wool', *adj.* uncompromising.

dyke (dīk) *n.* 1. dike. 2. *Slang (often offensive).* female homosexual; lesbian.

dyn 1. dynamic. 2. *Physics.* dyne; dynes.

dyn. dynamics. Also, **dynam.**

dy•nam'ic (dī nam'ik) *adj.* 1. of force. 2. energetic. Also, **dy•nam'i•cal.** —**dy•nam'i•cal•ly,** *adv.* —**dy•na'mism** (dī'nə miz'əm) *n.*

dy'na•mite' (dī'nə mīt') *n.*, *v.*, -mited, -miting. —*n.* 1. explosive. —*v.* 2. blow up with dynamite.

dy'na•mo' (-mō') *n.*, *pl.* -mos. 1. machine for generating electricity. 2. energetic, forceful person.

dy'nas•ty (dī'nə stē) *n.*, *pl.* -ties. rulers of same family. —**dy•nas'tic** (-nas'tik) *adj.*

dynm dynamotor.

dynmm dynamometer.

dynmt dynamite.

dys-, prefix meaning ill or bad, as *dysfunction*.

dys'en•ter'y (dis'ən ter'ē) *n.* infectious disease of bowels.

dys•func'tion (dis fungk'shən) *n.* ineffective functioning. —**dys•func'tion•al,** *adj.*

dys•lex'i•a (dis lek'sē ə) *n.* impairment of ability to read. —**dys•lex'ic,** *adj.*, *n.*

dys•pep'sia (dis pep'shə, -sē ə) *n.* indigestion. —**dys•pep'tic** (-tik) *adj.*

dz., dozen.

E

E, e (ē) *n.* fifth letter of English alphabet.

E, 1. east, eastern. 2. English.

ea., each.

E.A.A. Engineer in Aeronautics and Astronautics.

each (ēch) *adj., pron.* 1. every one. —*adv.* 2. apiece.

ead. (in prescriptions) the same. [from Latin *eādem*]

ea′ger (ē′gər) *adj.* ardent. —**ea′ger·ly,** *adv.* —**ea′ger·ness,** *n.*

ea′gle (ē′gəl) *n.* large bird of prey.

ea′gle-eyed′, *adj.* having unusually sharp eyesight.

EAM National Liberation Front, a Greek underground resistance movement and political coalition of World War II. [from Modern Greek E(*thnikō*) A(*pelevtherōtikò*) M(*étōpo*)]

EAP employee assistance program.

ear (ēr) *n.* 1. organ of hearing. 2. grain-containing part of cereal plant.

ear′drum′, *n.* sensitive membrane in ear.

earl (ûrl) *n.* nobleman ranking below marquis. —**earl′dom,** *n.*

ear′ly (ûr′lē) *adv.,* -lier, -liest, *adj.* 1. in first part of. 2. before usual time.

ear′mark′ (ēr′märk′) *n.* 1. identifying mark. —*v.* 2. designate.

ear′muffs′, *n.pl.* warm connected coverings for the ears.

earn (ûrn) *v.* gain by labor or merit.

ear′nest (ûr′nist) *adj.* 1. very serious. —*n.* 2. portion given to bind bargain. —**ear′nest·ly,** *adv.*

earn′ings, *n.pl.* profits.

ear′phone′ (ēr′fōn′) *n.* sound receiver held to the ear.

ear′ring′ (ēr′ring′, ēr′ing) *n.* ornament worn on ear lobe.

ear′shot′, *n.* hearing range.

ear′split′ting, *adj.* extremely loud or shrill.

earth (ûrth) *n.* 1. planet we inhabit. 2. dry land. 3. soil.

earth′en, *adj.* made of clay or earth. —**earth′en·ware′,** *n.*

earth′ly, *adj.,* -lier, -liest. of or in this world.

earth′quake′, *n.* vibration of earth's surface.

earth′shak′ing, *adj.* seriously affecting something basic, as a belief.

earth′work′, *n.* 1. fortification formed of moved earth. 2. work of art involving large land area.

earth′worm′, *n.* burrowing worm.

earth′y, *adj.,* -ier, -iest. 1. practical; realistic. 2. coarse; unrefined. —**earth′i·ness,** *n.*

ease (ēz) *n., v.,* eased, easing. —*n.* 1. freedom from work, pain, etc. 2. facility. —*v.* 3. relieve.

ea′sel (ē′zəl) *n.* support stand, as for picture.

ease′ment, *n.* right of one property owner to use land of another for some purpose.

east (ēst) *n.* 1. direction from which sun rises. 2. (*sometimes cap.*) region in this direction. —*adj., adv.* 3. toward, in, or from east. —**east′er·ly,** *adj., adv.* —**east′ern,** *adj.* —**east′ward,** *adv., adj.* —**East′ern·er,** *n.*

East′er (ē′stər) *n.* anniversary of resurrection of Christ.

eas′y (ē′zē) *adj.,* easier, easiest. 1. not difficult. 2. at ease. 3. affording comfort. —**eas′i·ly,** *adv.* —**eas′i·ness,** *n.*

eas′y-go′ing, *adj.* 1. casual; relaxed. 2. lenient.

eat (ēt) *v.,* ate (āt), eating, eaten. 1. take into the mouth and swallow. 2. wear away or dissolve.

eat′er·y, *n., pl.* -eries. *Informal.* restaurant.

eating disorder, disorder characterized by severe disturbances in eating habits.

eaves (ēvz) *n.pl.* overhanging edge of roof.

eaves′drop′, *v.,* -dropped, -dropping. listen secretly. —**eaves′drop′per,** *n.*

eax electronic automatic exchange.

EB Epstein-Barr (syndrome).

ebb (eb) *n.* 1. fall of tide. 2. decline. —*v.* 3. flow back. 4. decline.

EBCDIC (eb′sē dik′), *n. Computers.* a code used for data representation and transfer. [*e(xtended)* *b(inary-)c(oded)* *d(ecimal)* *i(nterchange)* *c(ode)*]

EbN east by north.

eb′on·y (eb′ə nē) *n.* 1. hard black wood. —*adj.* 2. very dark.

EbS east by south.

e·bul′lient (i bul′yənt, i bŏŏl′-) *adj.* full of enthusiasm. —**e·bul′lience,** *n.*

EBV Epstein-Barr virus.

EC European Community.

E.C. 1. Engineering Corps. 2. Established Church.

e.c. for the sake of example. [from Latin *exemplī causā*]

ECA Economic Cooperation Administration. Also, **E.C.A.**

ECC *Computers.* error-correction code.

ecc eccentric.

ec·cen′tric (ik sen′trik) *adj.* 1. odd. 2. off center. —*n.* 3. odd person. —**ec′cen·tric′i·ty** (-tris′i tē) *n.*

Eccl. *Bible.* Ecclesiastes. Also, **Eccles.**

eccl. ecclesiastic; ecclesiastical. Also, **eccles.**

ec·cle′si·as′tic (i klē′zē as′tik) *n.* 1. member of the clergy. —*adj.* 2. Also, **ec·cle′si·as′ti·cal.** of church or clergy.

Ecclus. *Bible.* Ecclesiasticus.

ECCM *Military.* electronic countermeasures.

ecd estimated completion date.

ECF extended-care facility.

ECG 1. electrocardiogram. 2. electrocardiograph.

ech echelon.

ech′e•lon (esh′ə lon′) *n.* level of command.

ech′o (ek′ō) *n., pl.* **echoes,** *v.,* **echoed, echoing.** —*n.* 1. repetition of sound, esp. by reflection. —*v.* 2. emit or repeat as echo.

ECL *Computers.* emitter-coupled logic.

é•clair′ (ā klâr′) *n.* cream- or custard-filled pastry.

é•clat′ (ā klä′) *n.* 1. brilliance, as of success. 2. showy or elaborate display. 3. acclaim.

ec•lec′tic (i klek′tik) *adj.* chosen from various sources.

e•clipse′ (i klips′) *n., v.,* **eclipsed, eclipsing.** —*n.* 1. obscuring of light of sun or moon by passage of body in front of it. 2. oblivion. —*v.* 3. obscure.

e•clip′tic (i klip′tik) *n.* apparent annual path of sun.

ECM 1. electronic countermeasures. 2. European Common Market.

ecn engineering change notice.

eco-, prefix meaning ecology, environment or natural habitat, as *ecocide.*

e′co•cide′ (ek′ə sīd′, ē′kə-) *n.* widespread destruction of natural environment.

ecol. 1. ecological. 2. ecology.

E. co•li (ē′ kō′lī), *Escherichia coli,* an anaerobic bacterium.

e•col′o•gy (i kol′ə jē) *n.* science of relationship between organisms and environment. —**e•col′o•gist,** *n.* —**ec′o•log′i•cal** (ek′ə loj′i kəl, ē′kə-) *adj.*

econ. 1. economic. 2. economics. 3. economy.

e′co•nom′i•cal (ek′ə nom′i kəl, ē′kə-) *adj.* thrifty. —**e′co•nom′i•cal•ly,** *adv.*

ec′o•nom′ics, *n.* production, distribution, and use of wealth. —**ec′o•nom′ic,** *adj.* —**e•con′o•mist** (i kon′ə mist) *n.*

e•con′o•mize′ (i kon′ə mīz′) *v.,* **-mized, -mizing.** save; be thrifty.

e•con′o•my, *n., pl.* **-mies.** 1. thrifty management. 2. system of producing and distributing weath.

ec′o•sys′tem (ek′ō sis′təm, ē′kō-) *n.* distinct ecological system.

ecp engineering change proposal.

ecr engineering change request.

ec′ru (ek′rōō) *n., adj.* light brown; beige. Also, **éc•ru** (ā′krōō).

ec′sta•sy (ek′stə sē) *n., pl.* **-sies.** 1. overpowering emotion. 2. rapture. —**ec•stat′ic** (ek stat′ik) *adj.*

ECT electroconvulsive therapy.

-ectomy, suffix meaning surgical removal of, as *tonsillectomy.*

ECU (ā kōō′ *or, sometimes,* ē′sē′yōō′), a money of account of the European Common Market used in international finance. [*E(uropean) C(urrency) U(nit),* perhaps with play on *écu,* an old French coin]

E.C.U. English Church Union.

ec′u•men′i•cal (ek′yōō men′i kəl) *adj.* 1. universal. 2. of or pertaining to movement for universal Christian unity. —**e•cu′men•ism** (i kyōō′mə niz′əm) *n.*

ec′ze•ma (ek′sə mə, eg′zə-, ig zē′-) *n.* disease of skin.

ED Department of Education.

ED₅₀ *Pharmacology.* effective dose for 50 percent of the group.

ed. 1. edited. 2. edition. 3. editor. 4. education.

E.D. 1. Eastern Department. 2. election district. 3. *Finance.* ex dividend. 4. executive director.

EDA Economic Development Administration.

edac error detection correction.

E′dam (ē′dəm) *n.* mild yellow cheese.

EDB *Chemistry.* a colorless liquid, $C_2H_4Br_2$, used as an organic solvent, gasoline additive, pesticide, and soil fumigant. [*e(thylene) d(i)b(romide)*]

Ed.B. Bachelor of Education.

EDC European Defense Community.

Ed.D. Doctor of Education.

ed′dy (ed′ē) *n., pl.* **-dies,** *v.,* **-died, -dying.** —*n.* 1. current at variance with main current. —*v.* 2. whirl in eddies.

e′del•weiss′ (ād′l vīs′, -wīs′) *n.* small, flowering Alpine plant.

e•de′ma (i dē′mə) *n.* abnormal accumulation of fluid in tissue, cavities, or joints of body.

E′den (ēd′n) *n.* garden where Adam and Eve first lived; paradise.

EDES Hellenic National Democratic army, a Greek resistance coalition in World War II. [from Modern Greek *E(thnikós) D(ēmokratikós) E(llēnikós) S(yndésmos)*]

edge (ej) *n., v.,* **edged, edging.** —*n.* 1. border; brink. 2. cutting side. —*v.* 3. border. 4. move sidewise. —**edge′wise′,** *adv.* —**edg′ing,** *n.*

edg′y, *adj.,* **edgier, edgiest.** nervous or tense.

ed′i•ble (ed′ə bəl) *adj.* fit to be eaten. —**ed′i•bil′i•ty,** *n.*

e′dict (ē′dikt) *n.* official decree.

ed′i•fice (ed′ə fis) *n.* building.

ed′i•fy′, *v.,* **-fied, -fying.** instruct. —**ed′i•fi•ca′tion,** *n.*

ed′it (ed′it) *v.* prepare for or direct publication of. —**ed′i•tor,** *n.*

e•di′tion (i dish′ən) *n.* one of various printings of a book.

ed′i•to′ri•al (ed′i tôr′ē əl) *n.* 1. article in periodical presenting its point of view. —*adj.* 2. of or written by editor. —**ed′i•to′ri•al•ize′,** *v.,* **-ized, -izing.**

Ed.M. Master of Education.

EDP, electronic data processing.

eds. 1. editions. **2.** editors.

Ed.S. Education Specialist.

EDT Eastern daylight time. Also, **E.D.T.**

EDTA *Chemistry., Pharmacology.* a colorless compound, $C_{10}H_{16}N_2O_8$, with a variety of medical and other uses. [*e(thylene)-d(iamine)t(etraacetic) a(cid)*]

edtn edition.

edtr editor.

educ. 1. educated. **2.** education. **3.** educational.

ed′u•cate′ (ej′ŏŏ kāt′) *v.*, **-cated, -cating.** provide with knowledge or instruction. —**ed′u•ca′tion,** *n.* —**ed′u•ca′tion•al,** *adj.* —**ed′u•ca′tor,** *n.*

-ee, suffix denoting person who is the object, beneficiary, or performer of an act, as *addressee; grantee; escapee.*

E.E. & M.P. Envoy Extraordinary and Minister Plenipotentiary.

EEC European Economic Community.

EEG, electroencephalogram.

eel (ēl) *n.* snakelike fish.

EENT *Medicine.* eye, ear, nose, and throat.

EEO equal employment opportunity.

EEOC Equal Employment Opportunity Commission.

eeprom *Electronics.* electronically erasable programmable read-only memory.

e′er (âr) *adv. Poetic.* ever.

ee′rie (ēr′ē) *adj.,* **-rier, -riest.** weird; unsettling. —**ee′ri•ly,** *adv.* —**ee′ri•ness,** *n.*

ef emitter follower.

eff. 1. effect. **2.** effective. **3.** efficiency.

ef•face′ (i fās′) *v.,* **-faced, -facing.** wipe out. —**ef•face′ment,** *n.*

ef•fect′ (i fekt′) *n.* **1.** result; consequence. **2.** power to produce results. **3.** operation. **4.** (*pl.*) personal property. —*v.* **5.** bring about; accomplish. —**Usage.** See AFFECT.

ef•fec′tive, *adj.* **1.** producing intended results. **2.** in force.

ef•fec′tive•ly, *adv.* **1.** in an effective way. **2.** for all practical purposes.

ef•fec′tu•al (-chŏŏ əl) *adj.* **1.** capable; adequate. **2.** valid or binding.

ef•fem′i•nate (i fem′ə nit) *adj.* (of a man) having feminine traits.

ef′fer•vesce′ (ef′ər ves′) *v.,* **-vesced, -vescing.** give off bubbles of gas. —**ef′fer•eves′-cence,** *n.* —**ef′fer•ves′cent,** *adj.*

ef•fete′ (i fēt′) *adj.* worn out.

ef•fi•ca′cious (ef′i kā′shəs) *adj.* effective. —**ef′fi•ca•cy** (-kə sē) *n.*

ef•fi′cient (i fish′ənt) *adj.* acting effectively. —**ef•fi′cien•cy,** *n.* —**ef•fi′cient•ly,** *adv.*

ef′fi•gy (ef′i jē) *n., pl.* **-gies.** visual representation of person.

ef′flu•ent (ef′lŏŏ ənt) *n.* **1.** something that flows out. —*adj.* **2.** flowing out.

ef′fort (ef′ərt) *n.* **1.** exertion of power. **2.** attempt.

ef•fron′ter•y (i frun′tə rē) *n., pl.* **-teries.** impudence.

ef•fu′sion (i fyŏŏ′zhən) *n.* free expression of feelings. —**ef•fu′sive,** *adj.*

EFI electronic fuel injection.

EFL English as a foreign language.

efl 1. effluent. **2.** *Photography.* equivalent focal length.

EFM electronic fetal monitor.

efph equivalent full-power hour.

EFT electronic funds transfer. Also, **EFTS**

EFTA European Free Trade Association.

EFTS electronic funds transfer system.

e.g., for example.

EGA *Computers.* enhanced graphics adapter.

e•gal′i•tar′i•an (i gal′i târ′ē ən) *adj.* having all persons equal in status. —**e•gal′i•tar′i•an•ism,** *n.*

egg (eg) *n.* **1.** reproductive body produced by animals. —*v.* **2.** encourage.

egg′head′, *n. Slang.* impractical intellectual.

egg′nog′ (-nog′) *n.* drink containing eggs, milk, etc.

egg′plant′, *n.* purple, egg-shaped vegetable.

EGmc East Germanic.

e′go (ē′gō) *n.* self.

e′go•cen′tric (-sen′trik) *adj.* self-centered.

e′go•ism, *n.* thinking only in terms of oneself. —**e′go•ist,** *n.* —**e′go•is′tic, e′go•is′ti•cal,** *adj.*

e′go•tism (ē′gə tiz′əm) *n.* vanity. —**e′go•tist,** *n.* —**e′go•tis′tic, e′go•tis′ti•cal,** *adj.*

EGR *Automotive.* exhaust-gas recirculation.

e•gre′gious (i grē′jəs) *adj.* flagrant; glaring. —**e•gre′gious•ly,** *adv.*

e′gress (ē′grcs) *n.* exit.

e′gret (ē′grit) *n.* kind of heron.

E•gyp′tian (i jip′shən) *n.* native or citizen of Egypt. —**E•gyp•tian,** *adj.*

eh (ā, e) *interj.* (exclamation of surprise or doubt).

EHF extremely high frequency. Also, **ehf**

EHS Environmental Health Services.

EHV extra high voltage.

E.I. 1. East Indian. **2.** East Indies.

EIA Electronic Industries Association.

ei′der duck (ī′dər) northern sea duck yielding **eiderdown.**

eight (āt) *n., adj.* seven plus one. —**eighth,** *adj., n.*

eight′een′ (ā′tēn′) *n., adj.* ten plus eight. —**eight•eenth′,** *adj., n.*

eight′y, *n., adj.* ten times eight. —**eight′i•eth,** *adj., n.*

E. Ind. East Indian.

EIR Environmental Impact Report.

EIS Environmental Impact Statement.

EISA *Computers.* extended industry standard architecture.

ei′ther (ē′ᴙər, ī′ᴙər) *adj., pron.* **1.** one or the other of two. —*conj.* **2.** (introducing an alternative) —*adv.* **3.** (after negative clauses

E

joined by **and, or, nor.**)

—Pronunciation. The pronunciations (ē'-*th*ər) for the word EITHER and (nē'*th*ər) for the word NEITHER, with the vowel of *see*, are the usual ones in American English. The pronunciations (ī'*th*ər) and (nī'*th*ər), with the vowel of *sigh*, occur occasionally in the U.S., chiefly in the speech of the educated and in the standard English of radio and television. Since the 19th century, the (ī) has been the more common pronunciation in standard British speech.

EJ (ē'jā'), **1.** electronic journalism. **2.** electronic journalist.

e•jac'u•late' (i jak'yə lāt') *v.,* **-lated, -lating. 1.** exclaim. **2.** eject; discharge. **—e•jac'-u•la'tion,** *n.*

e•ject' (i jekt') *v.* force out. **—e•jec'tion,** *n.* **—e•jec'tor,** *n.*

ejn ejection.

ejtr ejector.

eke (ēk) *v.,* **eked, eking. eke out, 1.** supplement. **2.** make (livelihood) with difficulty.

EKG, 1. electrocardiogram. **2.** electrocardiograph.

el. 1. electroluminescent. **2.** elevation.

e•lab'o•rate, *adj., v.,* **-rated, -rating. —***adj.* (i lab'ər it) **1.** done with care and detail. **—***v.* (-ə rāt') **2.** supply details; work out. **—e•lab'o•ra'tion,** *n.*

é•lan' (ā län', ā län') *n.* lively zeal; dashing spirit.

e•lapse' (i laps') *v.,* **elapsed, elapsing.** (of time) pass; slip by.

E.L.A.S. Hellenic People's Army of Liberation, Greek resistance force in World War II. [from Modern Greek *E(thnikòs) L(aikòs) A(peleutherōtikòs) S(tratós)*]

e•las'tic (i las'tik) *adj.* **1.** springy. **—***n.* **2.** material containing rubber. **—e•las'tic/i•ty** (-tis/i tē) *n.*

e•late' (i lāt') *v.,* **elated, elating.** put in high spirits. **—e•la'tion,** *n.*

elb elbow.

el'bow (el'bō) *n.* **1.** joint between forearm and upper arm. **—***v.* **2.** jostle.

elbow grease, hard work.

el'bow•room', *n.* space to move or work freely.

elctd electrode.

elctlt electrolyte; electrolytic.

elctrn electron.

elctrochem electrochemical.

eld'er (el'dər) *adj.* **1.** older. **—***n.* **2.** older person. **3.** small tree bearing clusters of **el'der•ber'ries.**

el'der•ly, *adj.* rather old.

eld'est (el'dist) *adj.* oldest; first-born.

e•lect' (i lekt') *v.* **1.** select by vote. **—***adj.* **2.** selected. **—***n.* **3.** (*pl.*) persons chosen. **—e•lec'tion,** *n.* **—e•lec'tive,** *adj.*

e•lec'tion•eer', *v.* work for candidate in an election.

e•lec'tor•al college (-tər əl) body of special voters (**electors**) chosen to elect president and vice-president of U.S.

e•lec'tor•ate (-tər it) *n.* voters.

e•lec'tri'cian (i lek trish'ən, ē'lek-) *n.* one who installs or repairs electrical systems.

e•lec'tric'i•ty (-tris'i tē) *n.* **1.** agency producing certain phenomena, as light, heat, attraction, etc. **2.** electric current. **—e•lec'tric, e•lec'tri•cal,** *adj.* **—e•lec'tri•cal•ly,** *adv.* **—e•lec'tri•fy',** *v.,* **-fied, -fying.**

e•lec'tro•car'di•o•gram' (i lek'trō kär'dē-ə gram') *n.* graphic record of heart action.

e•lec'tro•car'di•o•graph', *n.* instrument for making electrocardiograms.

e•lec'tro•cute' (i lek'trə kyōōt') *v.,* **-cuted, -cuting.** kill by electricity. **—e•lec'tro•cu'-tion,** *n.*

e•lec'trode (i lek'trōd) *n.* conductor through which current enters or leaves electric device.

e•lec'tro•en•ceph'a•lo•gram (i lek'trō en-sef'ə lə gram') *n.* graphic record of brain action.

e•lec'tro•en•ceph'a•lo•graph', *n.* instrument for making electroencephalo-grams.

e•lec'trol'o•gist (i lek trol'ə jist) *n.* person trained in electrolysis for removing unwanted hair, moles, etc.

e•lec•trol'y•sis (-ə sis) *n.* **1.** decomposition by electric current. **2.** destruction by electric current.

e•lec'tro•lyte' (-trə līt') *n.* substance that conducts electricity when melted or dissolved. **—e•lec'tro•lyt'ic** (-lit'-) *adj.*

e•lec'tro•mag'net (i lek'trō-) *n.* device with iron or steel core made magnetic by electric current in surrounding coil. **—e•lec'-tro•mag•net'ic,** *adj.* **—e•lec'tro•mag'net•ism,** *n.*

e•lec'tro•mo'tive (i lek'trə-) *adj.* of or producing electric current.

e•lec'tron (i lek'tron) *n.* minute particle supposed to be or contain a unit of negative electricity.

electronic mail, e-mail.

e•lec•tron'ics, *n.* science dealing with development of devices involving flow of electrons. **—e•lec•tron'ic,** *adj.* **—e•lec•tron'i•cal•ly,** *adv.*

el'ee•mos'y•nar'y (el'ə mos'ə ner'ē, -moz'-) *adj.* charitable.

el'e•gant (el'i gənt) *adj.* luxurious or refined. **—el'e•gance,** *n.* **—el'e•gant•ly,** *adv.*

el'e•gy (el'i jē) *n., pl.* **-gies.** poem of mourning. **—el'e•gi'ac** (-jī'ək), *adj.*

elek electronic.

elem. 1. element; elements. **2.** elementary.

el'e•ment (el'ə mənt) *n.* **1.** part of whole. **2.** rudiment. **3.** suitable environment. **4.** (*pl.*) atmospheric forces. **5.** substance that cannot be broken down chemically. **6.** (*pl.*) bread and wine of the Eucharist. —**el′e•men′tal** (-men′tl) *adj.*

el′e•men′ta•ry (-tə rē) *adj.* of or dealing with elements or rudiments.

elementary school, school giving elementary instruction in six or eight grades.

el′e•phant (el′ə fənt) *n.* large mammal with long trunk and tusks.

el′e•phan′tine (el′ə fan′tēn, -tīn) *adj.* **1.** huge. **2.** clumsy.

elev. 1. elevation. **2.** elevator.

el′e•vate′ (el′ə vāt′) *v.,* -vated, -vating. **1.** raise higher. **2.** exalt.

el′e•va′tion, *n.* **1.** elevated place. **2.** height. **3.** measured drawing of vertical face.

el′e•va′tor, *n.* **1.** platform for lifting. **2.** grain storage place.

e•lev′en (i lev′ən) *n., adj.* ten plus one. —**e•lev′enth,** *adj., n.*

elex electronics.

elf (elf) *n., pl.* **elves.** tiny mischievous sprite. —**elf′in,** *adj.*

e•lic′it (i lis′it) *v.* draw forth; evoke.

e•lide′ (i līd′) *v.,* -lided, -liding. **1.** omit in pronunciation. **2.** pass over; ignore. —**e•li′sion** (i lizh′ən) *n.*

el′i•gi•ble (el′i jə bəl) *adj.* fit to be chosen; qualified. —**el′i•gi•bil′i•ty,** *n.*

elim eliminate.

e•lim′i•nate′ (i lim′ə nāt′) *v.,* -nated, -nating. get rid of. —**e•lim′i•na′tion,** *n.*

ELISA (i lī′zə, -sə), **1.** *Medicine.* a diagnostic test for past or current exposure to an infectious agent, as the AIDS virus. **2.** *Biology, Medicine.* any similar test using proteins as a probe for the identification of antibodies or antigens. [*e(nzyme-)l(inked) i(mmuno)s(orbent) a(ssay)*]

e•lite′ (i lēt′, ā lēt′) *adj.* **1.** chosen or regarded as finest. —*n.* **2.** (*sing.* or *pl.*) elite group of persons.

e•lit′ism, *n.* rule by an elite. —**e•lit′ist,** *n., adj.*

elix. (in prescriptions) elixir.

e•lix′ir (i lik′sər) *n.* **1.** preparation supposed to prolong life. **2.** kind of medicine.

Eliz. Elizabethan.

elk (elk) *n.* large deer.

el•lipse′ (i lips′) *n.* closed plane curve forming regular oblong figure. —**el•lip′ti•cal,** *adj.*

el•lip′sis (i lip′sis) *n., pl.* -ses. omission of word or words.

elm (elm) *n.* large shade tree.

elmech electromechanical.

elng elongate.

el′o•cu′tion (el′ə kyōō′shən) *n.* art of speaking in public. —**el′o•cu′tion•ar′y,** *adj.* —**el′o•cu′tion•ist,** *n.*

e. long. east longitude.

e•lon′gate (i lông′gāt) *v.,* -gated, -gating. lengthen. —**e′lon•ga′tion,** *n.*

e•lope′ (i lōp′) *v.,* eloped, eloping. run off with lover to be married. —**e•lope′ment,** *n.*

el′o•quent (el′ə kwənt) *adj.* fluent and forcible. —**el′o•quence,** *n.* —**el′o•quent•ly,** *adv.*

elp elliptical.

elpneu electropneumatic.

else (els) *adv.* **1.** instead. **2.** in addition. **3.** otherwise.

else′where′, *adv.* somewhere else.

e•lu′ci•date′ (i lōō′si dāt′) *v.,* -dated, -dating. explain. —**e•lu′ci•da′tion,** *n.* —**e•lu′ci•da′tor,** *n.*

e•lude′ (i lōōd′) *v.,* eluded, eluding. **1.** avoid cleverly. **2.** baffle. —**e•lu′sive,** *adj.* —**e•lu′sive•ly,** *adv.*

—**Usage.** See ESCAPE.

elvn elevation.

EM 1. electromagnetic. **2.** electromotive. **3.** electronic mail. **4.** electron microscope. **5.** electron microscopy. **6.** end matched. **7.** Engineer of Mines. **8.** enlisted man; enlisted men.

Em *Symbol, Physical Chemistry.* emanation.

em 1. electromagnetic. **2.** enlisted men.

E.M. 1. Earl Marshal. **2.** Engineer of Mines.

e•ma′ci•ate′ (i mā′shē āt′) *v.,* -ated, -ating. make lean. —**e•ma′ci•a′tion,** *n.*

e′-mail′ (ē′māl′) *n.* **1.** system for sending messages between computers. **2.** message sent by e-mail. —*v.* **3.** send message to by e-mail. Also, **E-mail.**

em′a•nate′ (em′ə nāt′) *v.,* -nated, -nating. come forth. —**em′a•na′tion,** *n.*

e•man′ci•pate′ (i man′sə pāt′) *v.,* -pated, -pating. liberate. —**e•man′ci•pa′tion,** *n.* —**e•man′ci•pa′tor,** *n.*

e•mas′cu•late′ (i mas′kyə lāt′) *v.,* -lated, -lating. castrate. —**e•mas′cu•la′tion,** *n.*

emb emboss.

em•balm′ (em bäm′) *v.* treat (dead body) to prevent decay. —**em•balm′ er,** *n.*

em•bank′ment (em bank′mənt) *n.* long earthen mound.

em•bar′go (em bär′gō) *n., pl.* -goes. government restriction of movement of ships or goods.

em•bark′ (em bärk′) *v.* **1.** put or go on board ship. **2.** start. —**em′bar•ka′tion,** *n.*

em•bar′rass (em bar′əs) *v.* **1.** make self-conscious or ashamed. **2.** complicate. —**em•bar′rass•ment,** *n.*

em•bas′sy (em′bə sē) *n., pl.* -sies. **1.** ambassador and staff. **2.** headquarters of ambassador.

em•bat′tled (em bat′ld) *adj.* prepared for, engaged in, or beset by conflict.

em•bed′ (em bed′) *v.,* -bedded, -bedding. fix in surrounding mass.

em•bel′lish (em bel′ish) *v.* decorate. —**em•bel′lish•ment,** *n.*

em′ber (em′bər) *n.* live coal.

em•bez′zle (em bez′əl) *v.,* -zled, -zling. steal (money entrusted). —**em•bez′zle•ment,** *n.* —**em•bez′zler,** *n.*

em•bit′ter (em bit′ər) *v.* make bitter.

E

em·bla′zon (em blā′zən) *v.* decorate, as with heraldic devices or emblems.

em′blem (em′bləm) *n.* symbol. —**em′blem·at′ic,** *adj.*

em·bod′y, *v.,* -bodied, -bodying. 1. put in concrete form. 2. comprise. —**em·bod′i·ment,** *n.*

em′bo·lism (em′bə liz′əm) *n.* closing off of blood vessel, as by gas bubble or fat globule.

em·boss′ (em bôs′) *v.* ornament with raised design.

em·brace′ (em brās′) *v.,* -braced, -bracing, *n.* —*v.* 1. clasp in arms. 2. accept willingly. 3. include. —*n.* 4. act of embracing.

em·broi′der (em broi′dər) *v.* decorate with needlework. —**em·broi′der·y,** *n.*

em·broil′, *v.* involve in strife. —**em·broil′-ment,** *n.*

em′bry·o′ (em′brē ō′) *n., pl.* -bryos. organism in first stages of development. —**em′bry·on′ic,** *adj.*

embryol. embryology.

em′cee′ (em′sē′) *n., v.,* -ceed, -ceeing. —*n.* 1. master of ceremonies; person who conducts an event, as a banquet. —*v.* 2. serve as emcee.

e·mend′ (i mend′) *v.* correct. —**e′men·da′-tion** (ē′mən dā′shən) *n.*

emer emergency.

em′er·ald (em′ər əld) *n.* 1. green gem. —*adj.* 2. of a clear, deep green.

e·merge′ (i mûrj′) *v.,* emerged, emerging. come forth or into notice. —**e·mer′gence,** *n.*

e·mer′gen·cy (i mûr′jən sē) *n., pl.* -cies. urgent occasion for action.

e·mer′i·tus (i mer′i təs) *adj.* retaining title after retirement.

em′er·y (em′ə rē) *n.* mineral used for grinding, etc.

E.Met. Engineer of Metallurgy.

e·met′ic (i met′ik) *n.* medicine that induces vomiting.

emf electromotive force. Also, **EMF, E.M.F., e.m.f.**

EMG 1. electromyogram. 2. electromyograph. 3. electromyography.

emi electromagnetic interference.

em′i·grate′ (em′i grāt′) *v.,* -grated, -grating. leave one's country to settle in another. —**em′i·grant,** *n.* —**em′i·gra′tion,** *n.*

é′mi·gré′ (em′i grā′) *n.* emigrant who flees esp. for political reasons.

em′i·nence (em′ə nəns) *n.* high repute. —**em′i·nent,** *adj.* —**em′i·nent·ly,** *adv.*

eminent domain, power of the state to take private property for public use.

em′is·sar′y (em′ə ser′ē) *n., pl.* -saries. agent on mission.

e·mit′ (i mit′) *v.,* emitted, emitting. send forth. —**e·mis′sion,** —**e·mit′ter,** *n.*

e·mol′lient (i mol′yənt) *adj.* 1. softening; soothing. —*n.* 2. emollient substance.

e·mol′u·ment (i mol′yə mənt) *n.* salary.

e·mote′ (i mōt′) *v.,* emoted, emoting. show emotion in or as if in acting. —**e·mot′er,** *n.*

e·mo′tion (i mō′shən) *n.* state of feeling. —**e·mo′tion·al,** *adj.*

EMP *Physics.* electromagnetic pulse.

Emp. 1. Emperor. 2. Empire. 3. Empress.

emp. (in prescriptions) a plaster. [from Latin *emplastrum*]

e.m.p. (in prescriptions) after the manner prescribed; as directed. [from Latin *ex mōdō praescrīptō*]

em′pa·thy (em′pə thē) *n.* sensitive awareness of another's feelings. —**em′pa·thet′ic** (-thet′ik) *adj.* —**em′pa·thize′,** *v.*

em′per·or (em′pər ər) *n.* ruler of empire. —**em′press,** *n.fem.*

em′pha·sis (em′fə sis) *n., pl.* -ses. greater importance; stress. —**em·phat′ic** (-fat′ik) *adj.* —**em·phat′i·cal·ly,** *adv.* —**em′pha·size′,** *v.*

em′phy·se′ma (em′fə sē′mə) *n.* chronic lung disease.

em′pire (em′pīᵊr) *n.* nations under one ruler.

em·pir′i·cal (em pir′i kəl) *adj.* drawing on experience or observation only.

empl employee.

em·ploy′ (em ploi′) *v.* 1. use or hire. —*n.* 2. employment. —**em·ploy′ee,** *n.* —**em·ploy′-er,** *n.* —**em·ploy′ment,** *n.*

em·po′ri·um (em pôr′ē əm) *n.* large store.

em·pow′er, *v.* 1. authorize to act for one. 2. enable. —**em·pow′er·ment,** *n.*

emp′ty (emp′tē) *adj.,* -tier, -tiest, *v.,* -tied, -tying. —*adj.* 1. containing nothing. —*v.* 2. deprive of contents. 3. become empty. —**emp′ti·ness,** *n.*

empty nest syndrome, depressed state felt by some parents after their children have grown up and left home.

EMS 1. emergency medical service. 2. European Monetary System.

ems electromagnetic surveillance.

emsn emission.

EMT, emergency medical technician.

emtr *Electronics.* emitter.

e′mu (ē′myōō) *n.* large flightless Australian bird.

em′u·late′ (em′yə lāt′) *v.,* -lated, -lating. try to equal or excel. —**em′u·la′tion,** *n.*

emuls. (in prescriptions) an emulsion. [from Latin *ēmulsiō*]

e·mul′si·fy′ (i mul′sə fī′) *v.,* -fied, -fying. make into emulsion.

e·mul′sion (-shən) *n.* 1. milklike mixture of liquids. 2. light-sensitive layer on film.

en-, prefix meaning: 1. put into or on, as *enthrone.* 2. cover or surround with, as *encircle.* 3. make or cause to be, as *enlarge.*

en·a′ble (en ā′bəl) *v.,* -bled, -bling. give power, means, etc., to.

en·act′, *v.* 1. make into law. 2. act the part of. —**en·act′ment,** *n.*

enam enamel.

e•nam′el (i nam′əl) *n., v.,* **-eled, -eling.** *—n.*
1. glassy coating fused to metal, etc. **2.** paint
giving a glossy surface. **3.** surface of teeth.
—v. **4.** apply enamel to. **—en•am′el•ware′,**
n.

en•am′or (i nam′ər) *v.* fill with love.

enbl enable.

enc. 1. enclosed. **2.** enclosure. **3.** encyclopedia.

en•camp′, *v.,* settle in camp. **—en•camp′-
ment,** *n.*

encap encapsulate.

en•cap′su•late′ (en kap′sə lāt′) *v.,* **-lated,
-lating.** place as if in a capsule; summarize;
condense.

en•case′ (en kās′) *v.,* **-cased, -casing.** enclose in or as if in a case.

encd encode.

-ence, suffix meaning: act or fact (*abhor-
rence*); state or quality (*absence*).

en•ceph′a•li′tis (en sef′ə lī′tis) *n.* inflammation of the brain.

en•chant′ (en chant′) *v.* bewitch; beguile;
charm. **—en•chant′ment,** *n.*

en′chi•la′da (en′chə lä′də) *n.* food consisting of a tortilla rolled around a filling, usu.
with a chili-flavored sauce.

en•cir′cle, *v.,* **-cled, -cling.** surround.

encl., 1. enclosed. **2.** enclosure.

en′clave (en′klāv, än′-) *n.* country, etc., surrounded by alien territory.

en•close′ (en klōz′) *v.,* **-closed, -closing. 1.**
close in on all sides. **2.** put in envelope.
—en•clo′sure, *n.*

en•code′, *v.,* **-coded, -coding.** convert into
code.

en•co′mi•um (en kō′mē əm) *n., pl.* **-miums,
-mia.** praise; eulogy.

en•com′pass (en kum′pəs) *v.* **1.** encircle. **2.**
contain.

en′core (äng′kôr, än′-) *interj.* **1.** again!
bravo! *—n.* **2.** additional song, etc.

en•coun′ter (en koun′tər) *v.* **1.** meet, esp.
unexpectedly. *—n.* **2.** casual meeting. **3.**
combat.

en•cour′age (en kûr′ij, -kur′-) *v.,* **-aged,
-aging.** inspire or help. **—en•cour′age•
ment,** *n.*

en•croach′ (en krōch′) *v.* trespass. **—en•
croach′ment,** *n.*

encsd encased.

en•cum′ber (en kum′bər) *v.* impede; burden. **—en•cum′brance,** *n.*

ency. encyclopedia. Also, **encyc., encycl.**

en•cyc′li•cal (en sik′li kəl) *n.* letter from
Pope to bishops.

en•cy′clo•pe′di•a (en sī′klə pē′dē ə) *n.* reference book giving information on many
topics. Also, **en•cy′clo•pae′di•a. —en•cy′-
clo•pe′dic,** *adj.*

end (end) *n.* **1.** extreme or concluding part. **2.**
close. **3.** purpose. **4.** result. *—v.* **5.** bring or
come to an end. **6.** result. **—end′less,** *adj.*

en•dan′ger (en dān′jər) *v.* expose to danger.

en•dear′ (en dēr′) *v.* make beloved. **—en•
dear′ment,** *n.*

en•deav′or (en dev′ər) *v., n.* attempt.

en•dem′ic (en dem′ik) *adj.* belonging or
confined to a particular people or place.

end′ing (en′ding) *n.* close.

en′dive (en′dīv, än dēv′) *n.* plant for salad.

en′do•crine (en′də krin, -krīn′) *adj.* **1.** secreting internally into the blood or lymph. **2.**
of glands involved in such secretion.

en•dorse′ (en dôrs′) *v.,* **-dorsed, -dorsing.
1.** approve or support. **2.** sign on back of (a
check, etc.). **—en•dorse′ment,** *n.*

en•dow′ (en dou′) *v.* **1.** give permanent fund
to. **2.** equip. **—en•dow′ment,** *n.*

en•dure′, (en dŏŏr′, -dyŏŏr′) *v.,* **-dured,
-during. 1.** tolerate. **2.** last. **—en•dur′a•ble,**
adj. **—en•dur′ance,** *n.*

ENE east-northeast. Also, **E.N.E.**

en′e•ma (en′ə mə) *n.* liquid injection into
rectum.

en′em•y (en′ə mē) *n., pl.* **-mies.** adversary;
opponent.

en′er•gize′ (en′ər jīz′) *v.,* **-gized, -gizing.**
give energy to. **—en′er•giz′er,** *n.*

en′er•gy (-jē) *n., pl.* **-gies.** capacity for activity; vigor. **—en•er•get′ic** (-jet′ik) *adj.*

en′er•vate′ (en′ər vāt′) *v.,* **-vated, -vating.**
weaken.

en•fee′ble (en′fē′bəl) *v.,* **-bled, -bling.**
weaken.

en•fold′ (en fōld′) *v.* wrap around.

en•force′ (en fôrs′) *v.* **-forced, -forcing.**
compel obedience to. **—en•force′a•ble,** *adj.*
—en•force′ment, *n.* **—en•forc′er,** *n.*

en•fran′chise (en fran′chīz) *v.,* **-chised,
-chising.** admit to citizenship.

ENG *Television.* electronic news gathering.

Eng. 1. England. **2.** English.

eng. 1. engine. **2.** engineer. **3.** engineering. **4.**
engraved. **5.** engraver. **6.** engraving.

enga engage.

en•gage′ (en gāj′) *v.,* **-gaged, -gaging. 1.**
occupy. **2.** hire. **3.** please. **4.** betroth. **5.** interlock with. **6.** enter into conflict with. **—en•
gaged′,** *adj.* **—en•gage′ment,** *n.*

en•gag′ing, *adj.* attractive; charming. **—en•
gag′ing•ly,** *adv.*

Eng. D. Doctor of Engineering.

en•gen′der (en jen′dər) *v.* cause.

en′gine (en′jən) *n.* **1.** machine for converting
energy into mechanical work. **2.** locomotive.

en′gi•neer′ (en′jə nēr′) *n.* **1.** expert in engineering. **2.** engine operator. *—v.* **3.** contrive.

en′gi•neer′ing, *n.* art of practical application of physics, chemistry, etc.

Eng′lish (ing′glish; *often* -lish) *n.* language of
the people of England, Australia, the U.S.,
etc. **—Eng′lish,** *adj.* **—Eng′lish•man,** *n.,*
—Eng′lish•wom′an, *n.fem.*

en•gorge′ (en gôrj′) *v.,* **-gorged, -gorging.**

E

fill or congest, esp. with blood. —**en•gorge/-ment,** *n.*

engr. 1. engineer. **2.** engraved. **3.** engraver. **4.** engraving.

en•grave/ (en grāv/) *v.,* -graved, -graving. cut into hard surface for printing. —**en•grav/er,** *n.* —**en•grav/ing,** *n.*

engrg engineering.

en•gross/ (en grōs/) *v.* occupy wholly.

engrv engrave.

en•gulf/ (en gulf/) *v.* swallow up.

engy energy.

en•hance/ (en hans/) *v.,* -hanced, -hancing. increase.

en•nig/ma (ə nig/mə) *n.* something puzzling. —**en/ig•mat/ic, en/ig•mat/i•cal,** *adj.*

en•join/ (en join/) *v.* prohibit. —**en•join/-der,** *n.*

en•joy/ (en joi/) *v.* find pleasure in or for. —**en•joy/a•ble,** *adj.* —**en•joy/ment,** *n.*

enl. 1. enlarge. **2.** enlarged. **3.** enlisted.

en•large/ (en lärj/) *v.,* -larged, -larging. make or grow larger. —**en•large/ment,** *n.*

enlg enlarge.

en•light/en (en līt/n) *v.* impart knowledge to. —**en•light/en•ment,** *n.*

en•list/ (en•hist/) *v.* enroll for service. —**en•list/ment,** *n.*

en•liv/en (en līv/vən) *v.* make active.

en masse/ (än mas/, äN) in a mass; all together.

en•mesh/ (en mesh/) *v.* entangle.

en/mi•ty (en/mi tē) *n., pl.* -ties. hatred.

en/nui/ (än wē/) *n.* boredom.

e•nor/mi•ty (i nôr/mi tē) *n., pl.* -ties. **1.** extreme wickedness. **2.** grievous crime; atrocity.

e•nor/mous (-məs) *adj.* huge; gigantic. —**e•nor/mous•ly,** *adv.*

e•nough/ (i nuf/) *adj.* **1.** adequate. —*n.* **2.** adequate amount. —*adv.* **3.** sufficiently.

en•plane/ (en/plān/) *v.,* -planed, -planing. board an airplane.

en•quire/ (en kwīr/) *v.,* -quired, -quiring. inquire. —**en•quir/y,** *n.*

en•rage/ (en rāj/) *v.,* -raged, -raging. make furious.

en•rap/ture (en rap/chər) *v.,* -tured, -turing. delight.

enrgz energize.

en•rich/ (en rich/) *v.* make rich or better. —**en•rich/ment,** *n.*

en•roll/ (en rōl/) *v.* take into group or organization. —**en•roll/ment,** *n.*

en route (än rōōt/) on the way.

Ens. Ensign.

en•sconce/ (en skons/) *v.,* -sconced, -sconcing. settle securely or snugly.

en•sem/ble (än säm/bəl) *n.* assembled whole.

en•shrine/ (en shrīn/) *v.,* -shrined, -shrining. cherish.

en•shroud/ (en shroud/) *v.* conceal.

ensi (en/sē), equivalent-noise-sideband-input.

en/sign (en/sīn; *Mil.* -sən) *n.* **1.** flag. **2.** lowest commissioned naval officer.

en•slave/ (en slāv/) *v.,* -slaved, -slaving. make slave of. —**en•slave/ment,** *n.*

en•snare/ (en snâr/) *v.,* -snared, -snaring. entrap.

en•sue/ (en sōō/) *v.,* -sued, -suing. follow.

en•sure/ (en shōōr/) *v.,* -sured, -suring. make certain; secure.

-ent, suffix equivalent to -*ant,* as *president, insistent.*

en•tail/ (en tāl/) *v.* involve.

en•tan/gle (en tang/gəl) *v.,* -gled, -gling. involve; entrap. —**en•tan/gle•ment,** *n.*

en•tente/ (än tänt/) *n.* **1.** international agreement on policy. **2.** alliance of parties to an entente.

en/ter (en/tər) *v.* **1.** come or go in. **2.** begin. **3.** record.

en/ter•i/tis (en/tə rī/tis) *n.* inflammation of the intestines.

en/ter•prise/ (en/tər prīz/) *n.* **1.** project. **2.** initiative.

en/ter•pris/ing, *adj.* showing initiative.

en/ter•tain/ (en/tər tān/) *v.* **1.** amuse. **2.** treat as guest. **3.** hold in mind. —**en/ter•tain/er,** *n.* —**en/ter•tain/ing,** *adj.* —**en/ter•tain/ment,** *n.*

en•thrall/ (en thrôl/) *v.* **1.** hold by fascination; captivate. **2.** enslave.

en•throne (en thrōn/) *v.,* -throned, -throning. place on or as if on a throne. —**en•throne/ment,** *n.*

en•thuse/ (en thōoz/) *v.,* -thused, -thus•ing. show enthusiasm.

en•thu/si•asm (-thōo/zē az/əm) *n.* lively interest. —**en•thu/si•ast/,** *n.* —**en•thu/si•as/-tic,** *adj.*

en•tice/ (en tīs/) *v.,* -ticed, -ticing. lure. —**en•tice/ment,** *n.*

en•tire/ (en tīr/) *adj.* whole. —**en•tire/ly,** *adv.* —**en•tire/ty,** *n.*

en•ti/tle, *v.,* -tled, -tling. permit (one) to claim something. —**en•ti/tle•ment,** *n.*

en/ti•ty (en/ti tē) *n., pl.* -ties. real or whole thing.

en•tomb/, *v.* bury.

entomol. 1. entomological. **2.** entomology. Also, **entom.**

en/to•mol/o•gy (en/tə mol/ə jē) *n.* study of insects. —**en/to•mol/o•gist,** *n.*

en/tou•rage/ (än/tōō räzh/) *n.* group of personal attendants.

entr 1. enter. **2.** entrance.

en/trails (en/trālz, -trəlz) *n.pl.* internal parts of body, esp. intestines.

en/trance, *n., v.,* -tranced, -trancing. —*n.* (en/trəns) **1.** act of entering. **2.** place for entering. **3.** admission. —*v.* (en trans/) **4.** charm.

en′trant (en′trənt) *n.* person who enters competition or contest.

en•trap′ (en trap′) *v.*, **-trapped, -trapping. 1.** catch in a trap. **2.** entice into guilty situation. —**en•trap′ment,** *n.*

en•treat′ (en trēt′) *v.* implore. —**en•treat′ing•ly,** *adv.*

en•treat′y, *n., pl.* **-ies.** earnest request.

en′tree (än′trā) *n.* **1.** main dish of meal. **2.** access.

en•trench′ (en trench′) *v.* fix in strong position. —**en•trench′ment,** *n.*

en′tre•pre•neur′ (än′trə prə nûr′) *n.* independent business manager. —**en′tre•pre•neur′i•al,** *adj.*

en′tro•py (en′trə pē) *n.* **1.** measure of the amount of energy unavailable for useful work in a thermodynamic process. **2.** tendency toward disorder or disorganization in any system.

en•trust′ (en trust′) *v.* give in trust.

en′try (en′trē) *n., pl.* **-tries. 1.** entrance. **2.** recorded statement, etc. **3.** contestant.

en•twine′ (en twīn′) *v.*, **-twined, -twining.** twine around or together.

enum enumerate, enumeration.

e•nu′mer•ate′ (i nōō′mə rāt′, i nyōō′-) *v.*, **-ated, -ating.** list; count. —**e•nu′mer•a′tion,** *n.*

e•nun′ci•ate′ (i nun′sē āt′) *v.*, **-ated, -ating.** say distinctly. —**e•nun′ci•a′tion,** *n.*

env. envelope.

en•vel′op (en vel′əp) *v.* wrap; surround. —**en•vel′op•ment,** *n.*

en′ve•lope′ (en′və lōp′, än′-) *n.* **1.** covering for letter. **2.** covering; wrapper.

en•vi′ron•ment (en vī′rən mənt, -vī′ərn-) *n.* surrounding things, conditions, etc. —**en•vi′ron•men′tal** (-men′tl) *adj.*

en•vi′ron•men′tal•ist (-men′tl ist) *n.* person working to protect environment from pollution or destruction.

en•vi′rons, *n.pl.* outskirts.

en•vis′age (en viz′ij) *v.*, **-aged, -aging.** form mental picture of. Also, **en•vi′sion.**

en′voy (en′voi, än′-) *n.* **1.** diplomatic agent. **2.** messenger.

envr 1. environment. **2.** environmental.

en′vy (en′vē) *n., pl.* **-vies,** *v.*, **-vied, -vying.** —*n.* **1.** discontent at another's good fortune. **2.** thing coveted. —*v.* **3.** regard with envy. —**en′vi•a•ble,** *adj.* —**en′vi•ous,** *adj.* —**en′vi•ous•ly,** *adv.*

en′zyme (en′zīm) *n.* bodily substance capable of producing chemical change in other substances. —**en′zy•mat′ic,** *adj.*

EO executive order.

e.o. ex officio.

EOB Executive Office Building.

EOE 1. equal-opportunity employer. **2.** *Disparaging.* an employee who is considered to have been hired only to satisfy equal-opportunity regulations.

EOF *Computers.* end-of-file.

EOG electrooculogram.

eolm electrooptical light modulator.

eom end of message.

e.o.m. *Chiefly Commerce.* end of the month. Also, **E.O.M.**

e′on (ē′ən, ē′on) *n.* long period of time.

EOP Executive Office of the President.

eot end of tape.

EP 1. European plan. **2.** extended play (of phonograph records).

Ep. *Bible.* Epistle.

EPA, Environmental Protection Agency.

ep′au•let′ (ep′ə let′, -lit) *n.* shoulder piece worn on uniform. Also, **ep′au•lette′.**

Eph. *Bible.* Ephesians. Also, **Ephes., Ephs.**

e•phem′er•al (i fem′ər əl) *adj.* brief.

ep′ic (ep′ik) *adj.* **1.** describing heroic deeds. —*n.* **2.** epic poem.

ep′i•cen′ter (ep′ə sen′tər) *n.* point directly above center of earthquake.

ep′i•cure′ (ep′i kyŏŏr′) *n.* connoisseur of food and drink. —**ep′i•cu•re′an** (-kyə rē′ən) *adj., n.*

ep′i•dem′ic (ep′i dem′ik) *adj.* **1.** affecting many persons at once. —*n.* **2.** epidemic disease.

ep′i•der′mis, *n.* outer layer of skin. —**ep′i•der′mal, ep′i•der′mic,** *adj.*

ep′i•glot′tis (-glot′is) *n., pl.* **-glottises, -glottides** (-glot′i dēz′). thin structure that covers larynx during swallowing.

ep′i•gram′ (ep′i gram′) *n.* witty statement. —**ep′i•gram•mat′ic** (-grə mat′ik) *adj.*

ep′i•lep′sy (ep′ə lep′sē) *n.* nervous disease often marked by convulsions. —**ep′i•lep′tic,** *adj., n.*

ep′i•logue′ (ep′ə lôg′) *n.* concluding part or speech.

Epiph. Epiphany.

e•piph′a•ny (i pif′ə nē) *n.* **1.** act of showing oneself; appearance. **2.** sudden perception or realization. **3.** (*cap.*) festival, Jan. 6, commemorating the Wise Men's visit to Christ.

Epis. 1. Episcopal. **2.** Episcopalian. **3.** *Bible.* Epistle.

Episc. 1. Episcopal. **2.** Episcopalian.

e•pis′co•pa•cy (i pis′kə pə sē) *n., pl.* **-cies.** church government by bishops.

e•pis′co•pal (-pəl) *adj.* **1.** governed by bishops. **2.** (*cap.*) designating Anglican Church. —**E•pis′co•pa′lian** (-pā′lē ən) *n., adj.*

ep′i•sode′ (ep′ə sōd′) *n.* incident. —**ep′i•sod′ic,** (-sod′ik) *adj.*

Epist. *Bible.* Epistle.

e•pis′tle (i pis′əl) *n.* letter.

epit. 1. epitaph. **2.** epitome.

ep′i•taph′ (ep′i taf′) *n.* inscription on tomb.

ep′i•thet′ (ep′ə thet′) *n.* descriptive term for person or things.

e•pit′o•me (i pit′ə mē) *n.* **1.** summary. **2.** typical specimen. —**e•pit′o•mize′,** *v.*, **-mized, -mizing.**

e plu′ri•bus u′num (e plōō′ri bŏŏs′ ōō′-

E

nŏŏm; *Eng.* ē′ plŏŏr′ə bəs yŏŏ′nəm) *Latin.* out of many, one (motto of the U.S.).

ep′och (ep′ək) *n.* distinctive period of time. —**ep′och•al,** *adj.*

ep•ox′y (i pok′sē) *n., pl.* **-ies.** tough synthetic resin used in glues.

EPROM (ē′prom), *Computers.* a memory chip whose contents can be erased and reprogramed. [*e(rasable) p(rogrammable) r(ead)-o(nly) m(emory)*]

EPS earnings per share.

Ep′som salts (ep′səm) salt used esp. as a cathartic. Also, **Ep′som salt.**

EPT excess-profits tax.

ept external pipe thread.

epu emergency power unit.

EQ educational quotient.

eq. 1. equal. 2. equation. 3. equivalent.

eql equal, equally.

eqlz 1. equalize. 2. equalizer.

eqpt. equipment.

eq′ua•ble (ek′wə bəl) *adj.* even; temperate. —**eq′ua•bly,** *adv.*

e′qual (ē′kwəl) *adj., n., v.,* **equaled, equaling.** —*adj.* 1. alike in quantity, rank, size, etc. 2. uniform. 3. adequate. —*n.* 4. one that is equal to. —*v.* 5. be equal to. —**e•qual′i•ty,** *n.* —**e′qual•ize′,** *v.* —**e′qual•ly,** *adv.*

equal sign, symbol (=) indicating equality between terms. Also, **equals sign.**

e′qua•nim′i•ty (ē′kwə nim′i tē) *n.* calmness.

e•quate′ (i kwāt′) *v.,* **equated, equating.** make or consider as equal.

e•qua′tion (i kwā′zhən) *n.* expression of equality of two quantities.

e•qua′tor (-tər) *n.* imaginary circle around earth midway between poles. —**e′qua•to′ri•al,** *adj.*

e•ques′tri•an (i kwes′trē ən) *adj.* 1. of horse riders or horsemanship. —*n.* 2. Also, *for a woman,* **e•ques′tri•enne′.** horse rider.

e′qui•dis′tant (ē′kwi dis′tənt) *adj.* equally distant.

equil equilibrium.

e′qui•lat′er•al, *adj.* having all sides equal.

e′qui•lib′ri•um (-lib′rē əm) *n., pl.* **-riums, -ria.** balance.

e′quine (ē′kwīn) *adj.* of horses.

e′qui•nox′ (ē′kwə noks′) *n.* time when night and day are of equal length. —**e′qui•noc′tial** (-nok′shəl) *adj., n.*

e•quip′ (i kwip′) *v.,* **equipped, equipping.** furnish; provide. —**e•quip′ment,** *n.*

eq′ui•ta•ble (ek′wi tə bəl) *adj.* just; fair. —**eq′ui•ta•bly,** *adv.*

eq′ui•ty, *n., pl.* **-ties.** 1. fairness. 2. share.

equiv. equivalent.

e•quiv′a•lent (i kwiv′ə lənt) *adj., n.* equal.

e•quiv′o•cal (i kwiv′ə kəl) *adj.* 1. ambiguous. 2. questionable.

e•quiv′o•cate′ (-kāt′) *v.,* **-cated, -cating.** express oneself ambiguously or indecisively.

—**e•quiv′o•ca′tion,** *n.* —**e•quiv′o•ca′tor,** *n.*

ER, emergency room.

-er, suffix meaning: person occupied with or working at something, as *roofer*; resident, as *southerner*; person or thing associated with particular characteristic or circumstance, as *teenager*; one that performs or is used in performing action, as *fertilizer.*

e′ra (ēr′ə, er′ə) *n.* period of time.

ERA, 1. Also, **era.** earned run average. 2. Equal Rights Amendment.

e•rad′i•cate′ (i rad′i kāt′) *v.,* **-cated, -cating.** remove completely. —**e•rad′i•ca′tion,** *n.*

e•rase′ (i rās′) *v.,* **erased, erasing.** rub out. —**e•ras′a•ble,** *adj.* —**e•ras′er,** *n.* —**e•ra′sure,** *n.*

ercg erecting.

erct erection.

ere (âr) *prep., conj. Archaic.* before.

e•rect′ (i rekt′) *adj.* 1. upright. —*v.* 2. build.

e•rec′tion (-shən) *n.* 1. something erected. 2. erect state of an organ, as the penis. —**e•rec′tile** (i rek′tl, -tīl) *adj.*

erg (ûrg) *n.* unit of work or energy.

er′go (ûr′gō, er′gō) *conj., adv.* therefore.

er′go•nom′ics (ûr′gə nom′iks) *n.* applied science that coordinates workplace design and equipment with workers′ needs. —**er′go•nom′ic,** *adj.*

ERIC Educational Resources Information Center.

ERISA (ə ris′ə), Employee Retirement Income Security Act.

er′mine (ûr′min) *n.* kind of weasel.

e•rode′ (i rōd′) *v.,* **eroded, eroding.** wear away. —**e•ro′sion,** *n.*

e•rog′e•nous (i roj′ə nəs) *adj.* sensitive to sexual stimulation.

e•rot′ic (i rot′ik) *adj.* 1. of sexual love. 2. arousing sexual desire. —**e•rot′i•cal•ly,** *adv.* —**e•rot′i•cism** (-ə siz′əm) *n.*

e•rot′i•ca (-i kə) *n.pl.* erotic literature and art.

ERP European Recovery Program. Also, **E.R.P.**

err (ûr, er) *v.* 1. be mistaken. 2. sin.

er′rand (er′ənd) *n.* special trip.

er′rant (er′ənt) *adj.* roving.

er•rat′ic (i rat′ik) *adj.* uncontrolled or irregular.

er•ra′tum (i rä′təm, i rat′əm) *n., pl.* **-ta.** (*usually pl.*) error in printing.

errc error correction.

erron. 1. erroneous. 2. erroneously.

er•ro′ne•ous (ə rō′nē əs, e rō′-) *adj.* incorrect. —**er•ro′ne•ous•ly,** *adv.*

er′ror (er′ər) *n.* 1. mistake. 2. sin.

ERS Emergency Radio Service. Also, **E.R.S.**

ers 1. erase. 2. erased.

er•satz′ (er zäts′) *adj.* substitute; synthetic or artificial.

erst′while′, *adj.* former.

ERT, estrogen replacement therapy.

ERTS Earth Resources Technology Satellite.

er•u•dite′ (er′yŏŏ dīt′) *adj.* learned. —**er′u•di′tion** (-dish′ən) *n.*

e•rupt′ (i rupt′) *v.* burst forth. —**e•rup′tion,** *n.*

E.R.V. English Revised Version (of the Bible).

-ery, suffix meaning: things or people collectively (*machinery; peasantry*); occupation, activity, or condition (*archery*); place for (*winery*); characteristic conduct (*prudery*).

er′y•sip′e•las, *n.* infectious skin disease.

e•ryth′ro•cyte′ (i rith′rə sīt′) *n.* red blood cell.

Es *Symbol, Chemistry.* einsteinium.

es electrostatic.

E.S. Education Specialist.

ESA European Space Agency.

Esc. (in Portugal and several other nations) escudo; escudos.

esc. 1. escape. 2. escrow.

es′ca•late′ (es′kə lāt′) *v.,* **-lated, -lating.** increase in intensity or size. —**es′ca•la′tion,** *n.*

es′ca•la′tor, *n.* moving stairway.

es•cal′lop (e skol′əp, e skal′-) *v.* 1. finish with scallops (def. 2) 2. bake in breadcrumbtopped sauce. —*n.* 3. scallop.

es′ca•pade′ (es′kə pād′) *n.* wild prank.

es•cape′ (i skāp′) *v.,* **-caped, -caping,** *n.* —*v.* 1. get away. 2. avoid; elude. —*n.* 3. act or means of escaping. —**es•cap′ee,** *n.*

—**Usage.** ESCAPE, ELUDE, EVADE mean to keep away from something. To ESCAPE is to manage to keep away from danger, pursuit, observation, etc.: *to escape punishment.* To ELUDE is to slip through an apparently tight net, and implies using skill or cleverness: *The fox eluded the hounds.* To EVADE is to turn aside from or go out of reach of a person or thing, usually by moving or directing attention elsewhere: *We evaded the traffic jam by taking an alternate route.*

es•cape′ment (i skāp′mənt) *n.* part of clock that controls speed.

es•cap′ism, *n.* attempt to forget reality through fantasy. —**es•cap′ist,** *n., adj.*

es′ca•role′ (es′kə rōl′) *n.* broad-leaved endive.

es•carp′ment (i skärp′mənt) *n.* long clifflike ridge.

es•chew′ (es choo′) *v.* avoid.

escl escalator.

es′cort, *n.* (es′kôrt) 1. accompanying person or persons for guidance, courtesy, etc. —*v.* (i skôrt′) 2. accompany as escort.

es′crow (es′krō) *n.* legal contract kept by third person until its provisions are fulfilled.

esct escutcheon.

es•cutch′eon (i skuch′ən) *n.* coat of arms.

Esd. *Bible.* Esdras.

ESDI (es′dē), *Computers.* enhanced small device interface.

ESE east-southeast. Also, **E.S.E.**

esk engineering sketch.

Esk. Eskimo.

Es′ki•mo′ (es′kə mō′) *n.* Arctic North American people or language.

ESL, English as a second language.

ESOL (ē′sôl, es′əl), English for speakers of other languages.

ESOP (ē′sop), a plan under which a company's stock is acquired by its employees or workers. [E(mployee) S(tock) O(wnership) P(lan)]

e•soph′a•gus (i sof′ə gəs) *n., pl.* **-gi** (-jī′). tube connecting mouth and stomach.

es′o•ter′ic (es′ə ter′ik) *adj.* intended for select few.

ESP, extrasensory perception.

esp., especially.

es′pa•drille′ (es′pə dril′) *n.* flat shoe with cloth upper and rope sole.

espec. especially.

es•pe′cial (i spesh′əl) *adj.* special. —**es•pe′cial•ly,** *adv.*

Es′pe•ran′to (es′pə rän′tō, -ran′-) *n.* artificial language based on major European languages.

es′pi•o•nage′ (es′pē ə näzh′, -nij) *n.* work or use of spies.

es′pla•nade′ (es′plə näd′, -nād′) *n.* open level space, as for public walks.

ESPN the Entertainment Sports Network (a cable channel).

es•pouse′ (i spouz′, i spous′) *v.,* **-poused, -pousing.** 1. advocate. 2. marry. —**es•pous′al,** *n.*

es•pres′so (e spres′ō) *n.* strong coffee made with steam.

es•prit′ de corps′ (e sprē′ də kôr′) sense of group unity and common purpose.

es•py′ (i spī′) *v.,* **-pied, -pying.** catch sight of.

Esq. Esquire. Also, **Esqr.**

Es•quire′ (es′kwīᵊr) *n. Brit.* title of respect after man's name., in the U.S. chiefly applied to lawyers. *Abbr.:* Esq.

ESR 1. erythrocyte sedimentation rate: the rate at which red blood cells settle in a column of blood, serving as a diagnostic test. 2. electron spin resonance.

ess electronic switching system.

es′say *n.* (es′ā) 1. short treatise. 2. attempt. —*v.* (e sā′) 3. try.

es′say•ist, *n.* writer of essays.

es′sence (es′əns) *n.* 1. intrinsic nature. 2. concentrated form of substance or thought.

es•sen′tial (ə sen′shəl) *adj.* 1. necessary. —*n.* 2. necessary thing.

es•sen′tial•ly, *adv.* basically; necessarily.

EST, Eastern Standard Time.

est., 1. established. 2. estimate. 3. estimated.

estab. established.

es•tab′lish (i stab′lish) v. **1.** set up permanently. **2.** prove.

es•tab′lish•ment, n. **1.** act of establishing. **2.** institution or business. **3.** (often cap.) group controlling government and social institutions.

es•tate′ (i stāt′) n. **1.** landed property. **2.** one's possessions.

es•teem′ (i stēm′) v. **1.** regard. —n. **2.** opinion.

es′ter (es′tər) n. chemical compound produced by reaction between an acid and an alcohol.

Esth. 1. Bible. Esther. **2.** Esthonia.

es′thete, n. aesthete. —**es•thet′ic,** adj.

es′ti•ma•ble (es′tə mə bəl) adj. worthy of high esteem.

es′ti•mate′ v., -mated, -mating, n. —v. (es′tə māt′) **1.** calculate roughly. —n. (-mit) **2.** rough calculation. **3.** opinion. —**es′ti•ma′-tion,** n.

es•trange′ (i strānj′) v., -tranged, -tranging. alienate. —**es•trange′ment,** n.

es′tro•gen (es′trə jən) n. any of several female sex hormones.

es′tu•ar′y (es′chōō er′ē) n., pl. -aries. part of river affected by sea tides.

esu electrostatic unit.

Et Symbol, Chemistry. ethyl.

E.T. 1. Eastern time. **2.** extraterrestrial. Also, **ET**

e.t. electrical transcription.

ETA, estimated time of arrival.

et al. (et al′, äl′, ôl′) and others.

etc. et cetera.

et cet′er•a (et set′ər ə, se′trə) and so on. Abbr.: etc.

etch (ech) v. cut design into (metal, etc.) with acid. —**etch′ing,** n.

E.T.D. estimated time of departure. Also, **ETD**

e•ter′nal (i tûr′nl) adj. **1.** without beginning or end. —n. **2.** (cap.) God. —**e•ter′ni•ty,** n. —**e•ter′nal•ly,** adv.

Eth. Ethiopia.

eth′ane (eth′ān) n. flammable gas used chiefly as a fuel.

e′ther (ē′thər) n. **1.** colorless liquid used as an anesthetic. **2.** upper part of space.

e•the′re•al (i thēr′ē əl) adj. **1.** delicate. **2.** heavenly.

eth′ics (eth′ə sist) n.pl. principles of conduct. —**eth′i•cal,** adj. —**eth′i•cal•ly,** adv.

eth′nic (eth′nik) adj. **1.** sharing a common culture. —n. **2.** member of minority group. —**eth′ni•cal•ly,** adv.

eth•nic′i•ty (-nis′i tē) n. ethnic traits or association.

ethnog. ethnography.

ethnol. 1. ethnological. **2.** ethnology.

eth•nol′o•gy (eth nol′ə jē) n. branch of anthropology dealing with cultural comparisons. —**eth•nol′o•gist,** n.

ethol. ethology.

e•thol′o•gy (ē thol′ə jē) n. scientific study of animal behavior. —**e•thol′o•gist,** n.

e′thos (ē′thos, eth′ōs) n. distinguishing characteristics of person, group, or culture.

eth′yl (eth′əl) n. fluid containing lead, added to gasoline.

ETI extraterrestrial intelligence.

eti elapsed-time indicator.

e′ti•ol′o•gy (ē′tē ol′ə jē) n., pl. -gies. **1.** study of causes, esp. of diseases. **2.** cause or origin, esp. of a disease.

et′i•quette (et′i kit, -ket′) n. conventions of social behavior.

ETO (in World War II) European Theater of Operations. Also, **E.T.O.**

e to e end to end.

etr estimated time of return.

Etr. Etruscan.

ETS Trademark. Educational Testing Service.

et seq., and the following.

et seqq. and those following. Also, **et sqq.** [from Latin et sequentēs, et sequentia]

é′tude (ā′tōōd, ā′tyōōd) n. musical composition played to improve technique but also for its artistic merit.

et ux. Chiefly Law. and wife. [from Latin et uxor]

ETV educational television.

etvm electrostatic transistorized voltmeter.

ety. etymology.

etym. 1. etymological. **2.** etymology. Also, **etymol.**

et′y•mol′o•gy (et′ə mol′ə jē) n., pl. -gies. history of word or words. —**et′y•mol′o•gist,** n.

eu-, prefix meaning good, as eugenics.

eu′ca•lyp′tus (yōō′kə lip′təs) n., pl. -ti. Australian tree.

Eu′cha•rist (yōō′kə rist) n. Holy Communion.

eu•gen′ics (yōō jen′iks) n. science of improving human race. —**eu•gen′ic,** adj.

eu′lo•gy (yōō′lə jē) n., pl. -gies. formal praise. —**eu′lo•gize′,** v.

eu′nuch (yōō′nək) n. castrated man.

eu′phe•mism (yōō′fə miz′əm) n. substitution of mild expression for blunt one. —**eu′-phe•mis′tic,** adj.

eu′pho•ny (yōō′fə nē) n., pl. -nies. pleasant sound. —**eu•pho′ni•ous** (-fō′nē əs) adj.

eu•pho′ri•a (yōō fôr′ē ə) n. strong feeling of happiness or well-being. —**eu•phor′ic,** adj.

Eur. 1. Europe. **2.** European.

Eur•a′sian (yōō rā′zhən) adj. of or originating in both Europe and Asia, or in the two considered as one continent.

eu•re′ka (yōō rē′kə) interj. (exclamation of triumph at a discovery.)

Eu′ro•pe′an (yōōr′ə pē′ən) n. native of Europe. —**Eu′ro•pe′an,** adj.

European plan, system of paying a fixed hotel rate that covers lodging only.

Eu•sta′chian tube (yŏŏ stā′shən) (*often l.c.*) canal between middle ear and pharynx.

eu′tha•na′sia (yŏŏ′thə nā′zhə) *n.* mercy killing.

eV *Physics.* electron-volt. Also, **ev**

E.V. English Version (of the Bible).

EVA *Aerospace.* extravehicular activity.

evac evacuation.

e•vac′u•ate′ (i vak′yŏŏ āt′) *v.*, **-ated, -ating. 1.** vacate; empty. **2.** remove. **3.** help to flee. —e•vac′u•a′tion, *n.*

e•vade′ (i vād′) *v.*, **evaded, evading.** avoid or escape from by cleverness. —e•va′sion, *n.* —e•va′sive, *adj.* —**Usage.** See ESCAPE.

eval evaluation.

e•val′u•ate′ (i val′yŏŏ āt′) *v.*, **-ated, -ating.** appraise. —e•val′u•a′tion, *n.*

ev′a•nes′cent (ev′ə nes′ənt) *adj.* fading away.

e′van•gel′i•cal (ē′van jel′i kəl, ev′ən-) *adj.* **1.** of or in keeping with Gospel. **2.** of those Protestant churches that stress personal conversion through faith.

e•van′ge•list (i van′jə list) *n.* **1.** preacher. **2.** One of the writers of Gospel. —e•van′ge•lism, *n.* —e•van′ge•lize′, *v.*

evap. 1. evaporate. **2.** evaporation.

e•vap′o•rate′ (i vap′ə rāt′) *v.*, **-rated, -rating.** change into vapor. —e•vap′o•ra′tion, *n.*

eve (ēv) *n.* evening before.

e′ven (ē′vən) *adj.* **1.** smooth. **2.** uniform. **3.** equal. **4.** divisible by 2. **5.** calm. —*adv.* **6.** hardly. **7.** indeed. —*v.* **8.** make even. —e′ven•ly, *adv.* —e′ven•ness, *n.*

e′ven•hand′ed, *adj.* impartial; fair.

eve′ning (ēv′ning) *n.* early part of night; end of day.

evening star, bright planet, esp. Venus, visible around sunset.

e•vent′ (i vent′) *n.* anything that happens. —e•vent′ful, *adj.*

e•ven′tu•al (i ven′chŏŏ əl) *adj.* final. —e•ven′tu•al•ly, *adv.*

e•ven′tu•al′i•ty, *n.*, *pl.* **-ties.** possible event.

ev′er (ev′ər) *adv.* at all times.

ev′er•glade′, *n.* tract of low, swampy ground.

ev′er•green′, *adj.* **1.** having its leaves always green. —*n.* **2.** evergreen plant.

ev′er•last′ing, *adj.* lasting forever or indefinitely.

eve′ry (ev′rē) *adj.* **1.** each. **2.** all possible. —eve′ry•bod′y (-bod′ē, -bud′ē), eve′ry•one′, *pron.* —eve′ry•thing′, *pron.* —eve′ry•where′, *adv.* —eve′ry•day′, *adj.*

evg. evening.

e•vict′ (i vikt′) *v.* legally remove from property. —e•vic′tion, *n.*

e′vi•dence (ev′i dəns) *n.*, *v.*, **-denced, -de-**

ncing. —*n.* **1.** grounds for belief. —*v.* **2.** prove.

ev′i•dent, *adj.* clearly so. —ev′i•dent•ly (ev′i dənt lē, ev′i dent′lē) *adv.*

e′vil (ē′vəl) *adj.* **1.** wicked. **2.** unfortunate. —e′vil•do′er, *n.* —e′vil•ly, *adv.*

evil eye, look thought capable of doing harm.

e•vince′ (i vins′) *v.*, **evinced, evincing. 1.** prove. **2.** show.

e•vis′cer•ate′ (i vis′ə rāt′) *v.*, **-ated, -ating. 1.** remove entrails of. **2.** deprive of vital or essential parts.

evm electronic voltmeter.

e•voke′ (i vōk′) *v.*, **evoked, evoking.** call forth. —ev′o•ca′tion (ev′ə kā′shən) *n.* —e•voc′a•tive (i vok′-) *adj.*

e•volve′ (i volv′) *v.*, **evolved, evolving.** develop gradually. —ev′o•lu′tion, *n.* —ev′o•lu′tion•ar′y, *adj.*

evom electronic voltohmmeter.

EW 1. electronic warfare. **2.** enlisted women.

ewe (yŏŏ) *n.* female sheep.

ew′er (yŏŏ′ər) *n.* wide-mouthed pitcher.

ex-, prefix meaning: **1.** out of or from, as *export.* **2.** utterly or thoroughly, as *exacerbate.* **3.** former, as *ex-governor.*

ex., 1. example. **2.** except. **3.** exception. **4.** exchange.

ex•ac′er•bate′ (ig zas′ər bāt′, ek sas′-) *v.*, **-bated, -bating.** make more severe or violent. —ex•ac′er•ba′tion, *n.*

ex•act′ (ig zakt′) *adj.* **1.** precise; accurate. —*v.* **2.** demand; compel. —ex•act′ly, *adv.*

ex•act′ing, *adj.* severe.

ex•ag′ger•ate′ (ig zaj′ə rāt′) *v.*, **-ated, -ating.** magnify beyond truth. —ex•ag′ger•a′tion, *n.*

ex•alt′ (ig zôlt′) *v.* **1.** elevate. **2.** extol. —ex′al•ta′tion, *n.*

ex•am′ (ig zam′) *n. Informal.* examination.

ex•am′ine (-in) *v.*, **-ined, -ining. 1.** investigate. **2.** test. **3.** interrogate. —ex•am′i•na′tion, *n.* —ex•am′in•er, *n.*

ex•am′ple (ig zam′pəl) *n.* **1.** typical one. **2.** model. **3.** illustration.

ex•as′per•ate′ (ig zas′pə rāt′) *v.*, **-ated, -ating.** make angry. —ex•as′per•a•tion, *n.*

Exc. Excellency.

exc. 1. excellent. **2.** except. **3.** exception. **4.** he or she printed or engraved (this). [from Latin *excudit*] **5.** excursion.

ex′ca•vate′ (eks′kə vāt′) *v.*, **-vated, -vating. 1.** dig out. **2.** unearth. —ex•ca•va′tion, *n.* —ex′ca•va′tor, *n.*

ex•ceed′ (ik sēd′) *v.* go beyond; surpass.

ex•ceed′ing•ly, *adv.* very.

ex•cel′ (ik sel′) *v.*, **-celled, -celling.** be superior (to).

ex′cel•len•cy (ek′sə lən sē) *n.*, *pl.* **-cies. 1.** (*cap.*) title of honor. **2.** excellence.

ex′cel•lent, *adj.* remarkably good. —ex′cellence, *n.*

E

ex•cel′si•or (ik sel′sē ər, ek-) *n.* fine wood shavings.

ex•cept′ (ik sept′) *prep.* **1.** Also, **ex•cept′•ing.** other than; excluding. —*v.* **2.** leave out; exclude. **3.** object. —**ex•cep′tion,** *n.* —Usage. See ACCEPT.

ex•cep′tion•a•ble, *adj.* causing objections.

ex•cep′tion•al, *adj.* unusual. —**ex•cep′tion•al•ly,** *adv.*

ex′cerpt, *n.* (ek′sûrpt) **1.** passage from longer writing. —*v.* (ik sûrpt′, ek′sûrpt) **2.** take (passage) from a book, film, etc.

ex•cess′, *n.* (ik ses′) **1.** amount over that required. —*adj.* (ek′ses) **2.** more than necessary, usual, or desirable.

ex•ces′sive, *adj.* more than desirable. —**ex•ces′sive•ly,** *adv.*

exch. 1. exchange. **2.** exchequer. Also **Exch.**

ex•change′ (iks chānj′) *v.,* **-changed, -changing,** *n.* —*v.* **1.** change for something else. —*n.* **2.** act of exchanging. **3.** thing exchanged. **4.** trading place. —**ex•change′a•ble,** *adj.*

ex•cheq′uer (iks chek′ər) *n.* Brit. treasury.

ex′cise, *n., v.,* **-cised, -cising.** —*n.* (ek′sīz) **1.** tax on certain goods. —*v.* (ik sīz′) **2.** cut out. —**ex•ci′sion,** *n.*

ex•cite′ (ik sīt′) *v.,* **-cited, -citing. 1.** stir up. (emotions, etc.). **2.** cause. —**ex•cit′a•ble,** *adj.* —**ex•cite′ment,** *n.*

excl. 1. exclamation. **2.** excluding. **3.** exclusive.

ex•claim′ (ik sklām′) *v.* cry out. —**ex′cla•ma′tion,** *n.*

exclam. 1. exclamation. **2.** exclamatory.

ex•clude′ (ik sklo̅o̅d′) *v.,* **-cluded, -cluding.** shut out. —**ex•clu′sion,** *n.*

ex•clu′sive (ik sklo̅o̅′siv) *adj.* **1.** belonging or pertaining to one. **2.** excluding others. **3.** stylish; chic. —**ex•clu′sive•ly,** *adv.*

ex′com•mu′ni•cate′ (eks′kə myo̅o̅′ni kāt′) *v.,* **-cated, -cating.** cut off from membership. —**ex′com•mu′ni•ca′tion,** *n.*

ex•co′ri•ate′ (ik skôr′ē āt′) *v.,* **-ated, -ating.** denounce. —**ex•co′ri•a′tion,** *n.*

ex′cre•ment (ek′skrə mənt) *n.* bodily waste.

ex•cres′cence (ik skres′əns) *n.* abnormal growth. —**ex•cres′cent,** *adj.*

ex•crete′ (ik skrēt′) *v.,* **-creted, -creting.** eliminate from body. —**ex•cre′tion,** *n.* —**ex′cre•to′ry,** *adj.*

ex•cru′ci•at′•ing (ik skro̅o̅′shē ā′ting) *adj.* **1.** causing intense suffering. **2.** intense or extreme. —**ex•cru′ci•at•ing•ly,** *adv.*

excsv excessive.

exctr exciter.

excud. he or she printed or engraved (this). [from Latin *excudit*]

ex′cul•pate′ (ek′skul pāt′, ik skul′pāt) *v.,* **-pated, -pating.** free of blame. —**ex′cul•pa′tion,** *n.*

ex•cur′sion (ik skûr′zhən) *n.* short trip.

ex•cuse′, *v.,* **-cused, -cusing,** *n.* —*v.* (ik sky o̅o̅z′) **1.** pardon. **2.** apologize for. **3.** justify. **4.** seek or grant release. —*n.* (ik sky o̅o̅s′) **5.** reason for being excused. —**ex•cus′a•ble,** *adj.*

Ex. Doc. executive document.

exec. 1. executive. **2.** executor.

ex′e•crate′ (ek′si krāt′) *v.,* **-crated, -crating. 1.** abominate. **2.** curse. —**ex′e•cra•ble,** *adj.*

ex′e•cute′ (ek′si kyo̅o̅t′) *v.,* **-cuted, -cuting. 1.** do. **2.** kill legally. —**ex′e•cu′tion,** *n.* —**ex′e•cu′tion•er,** *n.*

ex•ec′u•tive (ig zek′yə tiv) *adj.* **1.** responsible for directing affairs. —*n.* **2.** administrator.

ex•ec′u•tor (-tər) *n.* person named to carry out provisions of a will. —**ex•ec′u•trix′,** *n. fem.*

ex′e•ge′sis (ek′si jē′sis) *n., pl.* **-ses** (-sēz). critical explanation or interpretation, esp. of Scripture.

ex•em′plar (ig zem′plər, -plär) *n.* **1.** model or pattern. **2.** typical example.

ex•em′pla•ry (-plə rē) *adj.* **1.** worthy of imitation. **2.** warning.

ex•em′pli•fy′ (-plə fī′) *v.,* **-fied, -fying.** show or serve as example. —**ex•em′pli•fi•ca′tion,** *n.*

ex•empt′ (ig zempt′) *v., adj.* free from obligation. —**ex•emp′tion,** *n.*

exer exercise.

ex′er•cise′ (ek′sər sīz′) *n., v.,* **-cised, -cising.** —*n.* **1.** action to increase skill or strength. **2.** performance. **3.** (*pl.*) ceremony. —*v.* **4.** put through exercises. **5.** use. —**ex′er•cis′er,** *n.*

ex•ert′ (ig zûrt′) *v.* put into action. —**ex•er′tion,** *n.*

exh 1. exhaust. **2.** exhibit.

ex•hale′ (eks hāl′) *v.,* **-haled, -haling.** breathe out; emit breath. —**ex′ha•la′tion,** *n.*

ex•haust′ (ig zôst′) *v.* **1.** use up. **2.** fatigue greatly. —*n.* **3.** used gases from engine. —**ex•haus′ti•ble,** *adj.* —**ex•haus′tion,** *n.*

ex•haus′tive, *adj.* thorough.

ex•hib′it (ig zib′it) *v., n.* show; display. —**ex′hi•bi′tion** (ek′sə bish′ən) *n.* —**ex•hib′i•tor,** *n.*

ex′hi•bi′tion•ism (-bish′ə niz′əm) *n.* desire or tendency to display onself. —**ex′hi•bi′tion•ist,** *n.*

ex•hil′a•rate′ (ig zil′ə rāt′) *v.,* **-rated, -rating.** cheer; stimulate. —**ex•hil′a•ra′tion,** *n.*

ex•hort′ (ig zôrt′) *v.* advise earnestly. —**ex′hor•ta′tion** (eg′zôr tā′shən) *n.*

ex•hume′ (ig zo̅o̅m′, -zyo̅o̅m′) *v.,* **-humed, -huming.** dig up a dead body, etc.

ex′i•gen•cy (ek′si jən sē) *n., pl.* **-cies.** urgent requirement. —**ex′i•gent,** *adj.*

ex′ile (eg′zīl, ek′sīl) *n., v.,* **-iled, -iling.** —*n.* **1.** enforced absence from one's country or home. **2.** one so absent. —*v.* **3.** send into exile.

ex int. Stock Exchange. ex interest.

ex•ist′ (ig zist′) *v.* be; live. —**ex•ist′ence,** *n.* —**ex•ist′ent,** *adj.*

ex′is•ten′tial (eg′zi sten′shəl, ek′si-) *adj.* of human life; based on experience.

ex′is•ten′tial•ism, *n.* philosophy that stresses personal liberty and responsibility. —**ex′is•ten′tial•ist,** *n., adj.*

ex′it (eg′zit, ek′sit) *n.* **1.** way out. **2.** departure. —*v.* **3.** leave.

ex lib. from the library of. [from Latin *ex libris*]

exo-, prefix meaning outside or outer, as *exosphere.*

ex′o•crine (ek′sə krin, -krīn′) *adj.* **1.** secreting externally through a duct. **2.** of glands involved in such secretion.

Exod. *Bible.* Exodus.

ex′o•dus (ek′sə dəs) *n.* departure.

ex off. by virtue of office or position. [from Latin *ex officio*]

ex of•fi′ci•o′ (eks′ ə fish′ē ō′) because of one's office.

ex•on′er•ate (ig zon′ə rāt′) *v.,* -ated, -ating. free of blame. —**ex•on′er•a′tion,** *n.*

exor. executor.

ex•or′bi•tant (ig zôr′bi tənt) *adj.* excessive, esp. in cost. —**ex•or′bi•tance,** *n.*

ex′or•cise′ (ek′sôr sīz′, -sər-) *v.,* -cised, -cising. expel (evil spirit). —**ex′or•cism,** *n.* —**ex′or•cist,** *n.*

ex′o•sphere′ (ek′sō sfēr′) *n.* highest region of the atmosphere.

ex•ot′ic (ig zot′ik) *adj.* **1.** foreign; alien. **2.** strikingly unusual.

exp 1. expand. **2.** expansion. **3.** experiment. **4.** expose. **5.** expulsion.

exp. 1. expenses. **2.** experience. **3.** expired. **4.** exponential. **5.** export. **6.** exported. **7.** exporter. **8.** express.

ex•pand′ (ik spand′) *v.* increase; spread out. —**ex•pan′sion,** *n.* —**ex•pan′sive,** *adj.*

ex•panse′ (ik spans′) *n.* wide extent.

ex•pa′ti•ate′ (ik spā′shē āt′) *v.,* -ated, -ating. talk or write at length.

ex•pa′tri•ate′, *v.,* -ated, -ating, *n., adj.* —*v.* (eks pā′trē āt′) **1.** exile. **2.** remove (oneself) from homeland. —*n.* (-it) **3.** expatriated person. —*adj.* (-it) **4.** exiled; banished.

ex•pect′ (ik spekt′) *v.* look forward to. —**ex•pect′an•cy,** *n.* —**ex•pect′ant,** *adj.* —**ex′•pec•ta′tion,** *n.*

ex•pec′to•rate′ (-rāt′) *v.,* -rated, -rating. spit. —**ex•pec′to•rant,** *n.*

exped expedite.

ex•pe′di•ent, *adj.* **1.** desirable in given circumstances. **2.** conducive to advantage. —*n.* **3.** expedient means. —**ex•pe′di•en•cy,** *n.*

ex′pe•dite′ (ek′spi dīt′) *v.,* -dited, -diting. speed up. —**ex′pe•dit•er,** *n.*

ex′pe•di′tion (ek′spi dish′ən) *n.* **1.** journey to explore or fight. **2.** promptness. —**ex′pe•di′tion•ar′y,** *adj.*

ex′pe•di′tious, *adj.* prompt. —**ex′pe•di′tious•ly,** *adv.*

ex•pel′ (ik spel′) *v.,* -pelled, -pelling. force out.

expen expendable.

ex•pend′ (ik spend′) *v.* **1.** use up. **2.** spend. —**ex•pend′i•ture,** *n.*

ex•pend′a•ble, *adj.* **1.** available for spending. **2.** that can be sacrificed if necessary.

ex•pense′ (ik spens′) *n.* **1.** cost. **2.** cause of spending.

ex•pen′sive, *adj.* costing much. —**ex•pen′sive•ly,** *adv.*

ex•pe′ri•ence (ik spēr′ē əns) *n., v.,* -enced, -encing. —*n.* **1.** something lived through. **2.** knowledge from such things. —*v.* **3.** have experience of.

ex•pe′ri•enced, *adj.* wise or skillful through experience.

ex•per′i•ment, *n.* (ik sper′ə mənt) **1.** test to discover or check something. —*v.* (-ment′) **2.** perform experiment. —**ex•per′i•men′tal** (-men′tl) *adj.* —**ex•per′i•men•ta′tion,** *n.* —**ex•per′i•ment′er,** *n.*

ex′pert, *n.* (eks′pûrt) **1.** skilled person. —*adj.* (ek′spûrt; *also* ik spûrt′) **2.** skilled. —**ex•pert′ly,** *adv.* —**ex•pert′ness,** *n.*

ex′per•tise′ (ek′spər tēz′) *n.* expert skill.

ex′pi•ate′ (ek′spē āt′) *v.,* -ated, -ating. atone for. —**ex′pi•a′tion,** *n.*

ex•pire′ (ik spīr′) *v.,* -pired, -piring. **1.** end. **2.** die. **3.** breathe out. —**ex′pi•ra′tion,** *n.*

exp jt expansion joint.

expl 1. explain. **2.** explanation.

ex•plain′ (ik splān′) *v.* **1.** make plain. **2.** account for. —**ex′pla•na′tion,** *n.* —**ex•plan′a•to′ry** (ik splan′-) *adj.*

expld explode.

ex′ple•tive (ek′spli tiv) *n.* exclamatory oath, usu. profane.

ex′pli•cate′ (-kāt′) *v.,* -cated, -cating. explain in detail.

ex•plic′it (ik splis′it) *adj.* **1.** clearly stated. **2.** outspoken. **3.** having sexual acts or nudity clearly depicted. —**ex•plic′it•ly,** *adv.*

expln explosion.

ex•plode′ (ik splōd′) *v.,* -ploded, -ploding. **1.** burst violently. **2.** disprove; discredit. —**ex•plo′sion,** *n.* —**ex•plo′sive,** *n., adj.*

ex′ploit, *n.* (eks′ploit) **1.** notable act. —*v.* (ik sploit′) **2.** use, esp. selfishly. —**ex′ploi•ta′tion,** *n.* —**ex•ploit′a•tive,** *adj.* —**ex•ploit′er,** *n.*

ex•plore′ (ik splôr′) *v.,* -plored, -ploring. examine from end to end. —**ex′plo•ra′tion** (ek′splə rā′shən) *n.* —**ex•plor′er,** *n.* —**ex•plor′a•to′ry,** *adj.*

expnt 1. exponent. **2.** exponential.

expo exposition.

ex•po′nent (ik spō′nənt *or, esp. for 3,* ek′-spō nənt) *n.* **1.** person who explains. **2.** symbol; typical example. **3.** *Math.* symbol placed to the upper right of another to indicate the power to which the latter is to be raised.

ex•port′, *v.* (ik spôrt′) **1.** send to other countries. —*n.* (ek′spôrt) **2.** what is sent. —**ex′por•ta′tion,** *n.*

ex•pose′ (ik spōz′) *v.,* -posed, -posing. **1.**

E

lay open to harm, etc. **2.** reveal. **3.** allow light to reach (film). —**ex•po′sure,** *n.*

ex′po•sé′ (ek′spō zā′) *n.* exposure of wrongdoing.

ex′po•si′tion (ek′spə zish′ən) *n.* **1.** public show. **2.** explanation.

ex•pos′i•to′ry (ik spoz′i tôr′ē) *adj.* serving to expound or explain.

ex post facto (eks′ pōst′ fak′tō) *adj.* made or done after the fact; retroactive.

ex•pos′tu•late′ (ik spos′chə lāt′) *v.,* -lated, -lating. protest. —**ex•pos′tu•la′tion,** *n.*

ex•pound′ (ik spound′) *v.* state in detail.

expr express.

ex•press′ (ik spres′) *v.* **1.** convey in words, art, etc. **2.** press out. —*adj.* **3.** definite. —*n.* **4.** fast or direct train, etc. **5.** delivery system. —**ex•pres′sion,** *n.* —**ex•pres′sive,** *adj.* —**ex•press′ly,** *adv.*

ex•press′way′, *n.* road for high-speed traffic.

ex•pro′pri•ate′ (eks prō′prē āt′) *v.,* -ated, -ating. take for public use. —**ex•pro′pri•a′-tion,** *n.* —**ex•pro′pri•a′tor,** *n.*

expsr exposure.

expt. experiment.

exptl. experimental.

ex•pul′sion (ik spul′shən) *n.* act of driving out.

ex•punge′ (ik spunj′) *v.,* -punged, -punging. obliterate.

ex′pur•gate′ (ek′spər gāt′) *v.,* -gated, -gating. remove objectionable parts from. —**ex′-pur•ga′tion,** *n.*

Expy. expressway.

ex′qui•site (ik skwiz′it, ek′skwi zit) *adj.* delicately beautiful. —**ex•quis′ite•ly,** *adv.*

exr. executor.

exstg existing.

ext. 1. extension. **2.** exterior. **3.** external. **4.** extinct. **5.** extinguish. **6.** extra. **7.** extract.

ex′tant (ek′stənt, ik stant′) *adj.* still existing.

extd. 1. extended. **2.** extrude.

ex•tem′po•ra′ne•ous (ik stem′pə rā′nē əs) *adj.* impromptu. —**ex•tem′po•re** (ik stem′-pə rē) *adv.*

ex•tend′ (ik stend′) *v.* **1.** stretch out. **2.** offer. **3.** reach. **4.** increase. —**ex•ten′sion,** *n.*

extended family, family comprising a married couple, their children, and close relatives.

ex•ten′sive (-siv) *adj.* far-reaching; broad. —**ex•ten′sive•ly,** *adv.*

ex•tent′ (ik stent′) *n.* degree; breadth.

ex•ten′u•ate′ (ik sten′yōō āt′) *v.,* -ated, -ating. lessen (fault).

ex•te′ri•or (ik stēr′ē ər) *adj.* **1.** outer. —*n.* **2.** outside.

ex•ter′mi•nate′ (ik stûr′mə nāt′) *v.,* -nated, -nating. destroy. —**ex•ter′mi•na′tion,** *n.* —**ex•ter′mi•na′tor,** *n.*

ex•ter′nal (ik stûr′nl) *adj.* outer.

ex•tinct′ (ik stingkt′) *adj.* no longer existing. —**ex•tinc′tion,** *n.*

ex•tin′guish (ik sting′gwish) *v.* put out; end. —**ex•tin′guish•a•ble,** *adj.* —**ex•tin′-guish•er,** *n.*

ex′tir•pate′ (ek′stər pāt′) *v.,* -pated, -pating. destroy totally.

extm extreme.

extn. 1. extension. **2.** external.

extnr extinguisher.

ex•tol′ (ik stōl′) *v.,* -tolled, -tolling. praise.

ex•tort′ (ik stôrt′) *v.* get by force, threat, etc. —**ex•tor′tion,** *n.* —**ex•tor′tion•ate,** *adj.*

extr. 1. exterior. **2.** extract.

ex′tra (ek′strə) *adj.* additional.

extra-, prefix meaning outside or beyond, as *extrasensory.*

ex•tract′, *v.* (ik strakt′) **1.** draw out. —*n.* (ek′strakt) **2.** something extracted. —**ex•trac′tion,** *n.*

ex′tra•cur•ric′u•lar (ek′strə kə rik′yə lər) *adj.* outside the regular curriculum, as of a school.

ex′tra•dite′ (ek′strə dīt′) *v.,* -dited, -diting. deliver (fugitive) to another state. —**ex′tra•di′tion** (-dish′ən) *n.*

ex′tra•le′gal, *adj.* beyond the authority of law.

ex′tra•mu′ral (-myŏŏr′əl) *adj.* involving members of more than one school.

ex•tra′ne•ous (ik strā′nē əs) *adj.* irrelevant. —**ex•tra′ne•ous•ly,** *adv.*

ex•traor′di•nar′y (ik strôr′dn er′ē, ek′strə-ôr′-) *adj.* unusual or remarkable. —**ex•traor′di•nar′i•ly,** *adv.*

ex′tra•trap′o•late′ (ik strap′ə lāt′) *v.,* -lated, -lating. infer from known data. —**ex•trap′o•la′tion,** *n.*

ex′tra•sen′so•ry (ek′strə sen′sə rē) *adj.* beyond one's physical senses.

ex′tra•ter•res′tri•al, *adj.* **1.** being or from outside the earth's limits. —*n.* **2.** extraterrestrial being.

ex•trav′a•gant (ik strav′ə gənt) *adj.* **1.** spending imprudently. **2.** immoderate. —**ex•trav′a•gance,** *n.* —**ex•trav′a•gant•ly,** *adv.*

ex•trav′a•gan′za (-gan′zə) *n.* lavish production.

ex•treme′ (ik strēm′) *adj.* **1.** farthest from ordinary. **2.** very great. **3.** outermost. —*n.* **4.** utmost degree. —**ex•treme′ly,** *adv.*

ex•trem′ism, *n.* tendency to go to extremes, esp. in politics. —**ex•trem′ist,** *n., adj.*

ex•trem′i•ty (ik strem′i tē) *n., pl.* -ties. **1.** extreme part. **2.** limb of body. **3.** distress.

ex′tri•cate′ (ek′stri kāt′) *v.,* -cated, -cating. disentangle.

ex•trin′sic (ik strin′sik, -zik) *adj.* **1.** not inherent or essential. **2.** being or coming from without; external.

ex′tro•vert′ (ek′strə vûrt′) *n.* outgoing person. —**ex′tro•ver′sion,** *n.* —**ex′tro•vert′-ed,** *adj.*

ex•trude′ (ik strōōd′) *v.,* -truded, -truding.

1. force or press out. **2.** shape by forcing through a die. —**ex•tru′sion**, *n.* —**ex•tru′-sive**, *adj.*

ex•u′ber•ant (ig zōō′bər ənt) *adj.* **1.** joyful; vigorous. **2.** lavish. —**ex•u′ber•ance**, *n.* —**ex•u′ber•ant•ly**, *adv.*

ex•ude′ (ig zōōd′, ik sōōd′) *v.*, **-uded, -ud-ing.** ooze out. —**ex′u•da′tion**, *n.*

ex•ult′ (ig zult′) *v.* rejoice. —**ex•ult′ant**, *adj.* —**ex′ul•ta′tion**, *n.*

eye (ī) *n.*, *v.*, **eyed, eying** or **eyeing.** —*n.* **1.** organ of sight. **2.** power of seeing. **3.** close watch. —*v.* **4.** watch closely. —**eye′ball′**, *n.*, *v.* —**eye′sight′**, *n.*

eye′brow′, *n.* ridge and fringe of hair over eye.

eye′ful (ī′fŏŏl) *n.*, *pl.* **-fuls. 1.** thorough view. **2.** *Informal.* attractive person.

eye′glass′es, *n.pl.* pair of corrective lenses in a frame.

eye′lash′, *n.* short hair at edge of eyelid.

eye′let (ī′lit) *n.* small hole.

eye′lid′, *n.* movable skin covering the eye.

eye′o′pen•er, *n.* something that causes sudden enlightenment or awareness.

eye′sore′, *n.* something unpleasant to look at.

eye′tooth′, *n.* canine tooth in upper jaw.

eye′wash′, *n.* **1.** soothing solution for eyes. **2.** nonsense.

eye′wit′ness, *n.* person who sees event.

eylt eyelet.

eypc eyepiece.

ey′rie (âr′ē, ēr′ē) *n.*, *pl.* **-ies.** aerie.

Ez. *Bible.* Ezra. Also, **Ezr.**

Ezek. *Bible.* Ezekiel.

E

F

F, f (ef) *n.* sixth letter of English alphabet.

F, **1.** Fahrenheit. **2.** female.

f., **1.** feet. **2.** female. **3.** folio. **4.** foot. **5.** franc.

fa **1.** final assembly. **2.** forced air.

FAA, Federal Aviation Administration.

F.A.A.A.S. 1. Fellow of the American Academy of Arts and Sciences. **2.** Fellow of the American Association for the Advancement of Science.

fab fabricate.

fa•ble (fā′bəl) *n.* **1.** short tale with moral. **2.** untrue story.

fab•ric (fab′rik) *n.* cloth.

fab•ri•cate′ (-ri kāt′) *v.,* **-cated, -cating. 1.** construct. **2.** devise (lie). —**fab′ri•ca′tion,** *n.*

fab•u•lous (fab′yə ləs) *adj.* **1.** marvelous. **2.** suggesting fables.

fabx fire alarm box.

fac. 1. facsimile. **2.** factor. **3.** factory. **4.** faculty.

fa•çade′ (fə säd′) **1.** building front. **2.** superficial appearance.

face (fās) *n., v.,* **faced, facing.** —*n.* **1.** front part of head. **2.** surface. **3.** appearance. **4.** dignity. —*v.* **5.** look toward. **6.** confront. —**fa′cial** (fā′shəl) *adj.*

face′less, *adj.* lacking distinction or identity.

face′-lift′, *n.* **1.** surgery to eliminate facial sagging or wrinkling. **2.** renovation to improve appearance, as of a building. Also, **face′-lift′ing.**

face′-sav′ing, *adj.* saving one's prestige or dignity.

fac′et (fas′it) *n.* **1.** surface of cut gem. **2.** aspect.

fa•ce′tious (fə sē′shəs) *adj.* joking, esp. annoyingly so. —**fa•ce′tiously,** *adv.* —**fa•ce′-tious•ness,** *n.*

face value (fās′ val′yoo *for 1;* fās′ val′yoo *for 2*) **1.** value printed on the face of a stock, bond, etc. **2.** apparent value.

facil facility.

fac′ile (fas′il) *adj.* glibly easy.

fa•cil•i•tate′ (fə sil′i tāt′) *v.,* **-tated, -tating.** make easier. —**fa•cil′i•ta′tion,** *n.* —**fa•cil′i•ta′tor,** *n.*

fa•cil′i•ty (-i tē) *n., pl.* **-ties. 1.** thing that makes task easier. **2.** dexterity.

fac′ing (fā′sing) *n.* decorative or protective outer material.

F.A.C.P. Fellow of the American College of Physicians. Also, **FACP**

FACS 1. *Biology.* fluorescence-activated cell sorter. **2.** Also, **F.A.C.S.** Fellow of the American College of Surgeons.

facsim. facsimile.

fac•sim•i•le (fak sim′ə lē) *n., pl.* **-les,** *v.,*
-led, -leing. —*n.* **1.** exact copy. **2.** fax. —*v.* **3.** make facsimile of.

fact (fakt) *n.* truth. —**fac′tu•al,** *adj.*

fac′tion (fak′shən) *n.* competing internal group. —**fac′tion•al,** *adj.* —**fac′tion•al•ism,** *n.*

fac′tious, *adj.* causing strife.

fac′tor (fak′tər) *n.* **1.** element. **2.** one of two numbers multiplied.

fac′to•ry (fak′tə rē) *n., pl.* **-ries.** place where goods are made.

fac′ul•ty (fak′əl tē) *n., pl.* **-ties. 1.** special ability. **2.** power. **3.** body of teachers.

fad (fad) *n.* temporary fashion; craze. —**fad′-dish,** *adj.*

fade (fād) *v.,* **faded, fading. 1.** lose freshness, color, or vitality. **2.** disappear gradually.

FAdm Fleet Admiral.

fag (fag) *v.,* **fagged, fagging,** *n.* —*v.* **1.** exhaust. —*n.* **2.** Also, **fag′got.** *Offensive.* homosexual.

fag′ot (fag′ət) *n.* bundle of firewood.

Fahr. Fahrenheit (thermometer). Also, **Fah.**

Fahr′en•heit′ (far′ən hīt′) *adj.* measuring temperature so that water freezes at 32° and boils at 212°.

fail (fāl) *v.* **1.** be unsuccessful or lacking (in). **2.** become weaker. **3.** cease functioning. —**fail′ure,** *n.*

fail′ing, *n.* **1.** weak point of character. —*prep.* **2.** in the absence of.

faille (fīl, fāl) *n.* ribbed fabric.

fail′-safe′, *adj.* ensured against failure of a mechanical system, etc. or against consequences of its failure.

faint (fānt) *adj.* **1.** lacking strength. —*v.* **2.** lose consciousness briefly. —**faint′ly,** *adv.* —**faint′ness,** *n.*

faint′heart′ed, *adj.* lacking courage.

fair (fâr) *adj.* **1.** behaving justly. **2.** moderately good. **3.** sunny. **4.** light-hued. **5.** attractive. —*n.* **6.** exhibition. —**fair′ly,** *adv.* —**fair′ness,** *n.*

fair shake, just and equal opportunity or treatment.

fair′y (fâr′ē) *n., pl.* **fairies. 1.** tiny supernatural being. **2.** *Offensive.* homosexual. —**fair′y•land′,** *n.*

fairy tale, 1. story, usu. for children, about magical creatures. **2.** misleading account.

faith (fāth) *n.* **1.** confidence. **2.** religious belief. **3.** loyalty. —**faith′less,** *adj.*

faith′ful, *adj.* **1.** loyal. **2.** having religious belief. **3.** copying accurately. —**faith′ful•ly,** *adv.* —**faith′ful•ness,** *n.*

fa•ji′tas (fä hē′təz, fə-) *n.* (*used with a sing. or pl. v.*) thin strips of marinated and grilled meat, served with tortillas.

fake (fāk) v., **faked, faking,** n., adj. Informal.
—v. **1.** counterfeit. —n. **2.** thing faked. —adj.
3. deceptive. —**fak/er,** n.

fa•kir/ (fə kēr/) n. Muslim or Hindu monk.

fa•la/fel (fə lä/fəl), n. fried ball of ground
chickpeas.

fal/con (fôl/kən, fal/-) n. bird of prey. —**fal/•
con•ry,** n.

fall (fôl) v., **fell** (fel), **fallen, falling,** n. —v. **1.**
drop. **2.** happen. —n. **3.** descent. **4.** autumn.

fal/la•cy (fal/ə sē) n., pl. **-cies. 1.** false belief.
2. unsound argument. —**fal•la/cious** (fə lā/-
shəs) adj.

fall guy, Slang. **1.** easy victim. **2.** scapegoat.

fal/li•ble (fal/ə bəl) adj. liable to error.
—**fal/li•bil/i•ty,** n.

fall/ing-out/, n., pl. **fallings-out, falling-
outs.** quarrel or estrangement.

fal•lo/pian tube (fə lō/pē ən) either of pair
of ducts in female abdomen that transport
ova from ovary to uterus. Also, **Fallopian
tube.**

fall/out/, n. **1.** radioactive particles carried
by air. **2.** incidental outcome or product.

fal/low (fal/ō) adj. plowed and not seeded.

fallow deer, Eurasian deer with yellowish
coat that is white-spotted in summer.

F.A.L.N. Armed Forces of National Liberation:
a militant underground organization whose
objective is independence for Puerto Rico.
Also, **FALN** [from Spanish F(uerzas) A(rma-
das de) L(iberación) N(acional)]

false (fôls) adj., **falser, falsest. 1.** not true. **2.**
faithless. **3.** deceptive. —**false/hood,** n.
—**false/ly,** adv. —**false/ness,** n. —**fal/si•fy,**
v., **-fied, -fying.**

fal•set/to (fôl set/ō) n., pl. **-tos.** unnaturally
high voice.

fal/ter (fôl/tər) v. hesitate; waver. —**fal/ter•
ing•ly,** adv.

FAM The Family Channel (a cable television
station).

fam. 1. familiar. **2.** family.

F.A.M. Free and Accepted Masons. Also, **F. &
A.M.**

fame (fām) n. widespread reputation; renown. —**famed,** adj.

fa•mil/iar (fə mil/yər) adj. **1.** commonly
known. **2.** intimate. —**fa•mil/i•ar/i•ty** (-ē-
ar/i tē, -yar/-) n. —**fa•mil/iar•ize/,** v., **-ized,
-izing.** —**fa•mil/iar•ly,** adv.

fam/i•ly (fam/ə lē, fam/lē) n., pl. **-lies. 1.**
parents and their children. **2.** relatives. —**fa•
mil/ial** (fə mil/yəl) adj.

family tree, genealogical chart of a family.

fam/ine (fam/in) n. scarcity of food.

fam/ish (fam/ish) v. starve.

fa/mous (fā/məs) adj. widely known; renowned.

fa/mous•ly, adv. very well.

fan (fan) n., v., **fanned, fanning.** —n. **1.** device for causing current of air. **2.** Informal.
devotee. —v. **3.** blow upon with fan. **4.** stir
up.

fa•nat/ic (fə nat/ik) n. person excessively devoted to cause. —**fa•nat/i•cal,** adj. —**fa•
nat/i•cism** (-ə siz/əm) n.

fan/ci•er (fan/sē ər) n. person interested in
something, as dogs.

fan/cy (fan/sē) n., pl. **-cies,** adj., **-cier, -ciest,**
v., **-cied, -cying.** —n. **1.** imagination. **2.** thing
imagined. **3.** whim. **4.** taste. —adj. **5.** ornamental. —v. **6.** imagine. **7.** crave. —**fan/ci•
ful,** adj. —**fan/ci•ly,** adv. —**fan/ci•ness,** n.

fan/cy-free/, adj. free from emotional ties,
esp. from love.

fan/cy•work/, n. ornamental needlework.

F. & T. Insurance. fire and theft.

fan/fare/, n. **1.** chorus of trumpets. **2.** showy
flourish.

fang (fang) n. long, sharp tooth. —**fanged,**
adj.

fan/ny, n., pl. **-nies.** Informal, buttocks.

fan•ta/sia (fan tā/zhə) n. fanciful musical
work.

fan/ta•size/ (-tə sīz/) v., **-sized, -sizing.**
have fantasies.

fan•tas/tic (-tas/tik) adj. **1.** wonderful and
strange. **2.** fanciful. Also, **fan•tas/ti•cal.**
—**fan•tas/ti•cal•ly,** adv.

fan/ta•sy (-tə sē, -zē) n., pl. **-sies. 1.** imagination. **2.** imagined thing.

FAO Food and Agriculture Organization.

F.A.Q. Australian. fair average quality. Also,
f.a.q.

far (fär) adv., adj., **farther, farthest.** at or to
great distance.

f/a ratio fuel-air ratio.

far/a•way/ (fär/ə wā/) adj. **1.** distant; remote. **2.** preoccupied; detached; dreamy.

farce (färs) n. light comedy. —**far/ci•cal,** adj.

fare (fâr) n., v., **fared, faring.** —n. **1.** price of
passage. **2.** food. —v. **3.** eat. **4.** get along. **5.**
go.

Far East, countries of east and southeast
Asia.

fare/well/ (fâr/wel/) interj., n., adj. good-by.

far/-fetched/, adj. not reasonable or probable.

far/-flung/, adj. **1.** extending over a great
distance or wide area. **2.** widely distributed.

fa•ri/na (fə rē/nə) n. flour or grain cooked as
a cereal. —**far/i•na/ceous** (far/ə nā/shəs)
adj.

farm (färm) n. **1.** tract of land for agriculture.
—v. **2.** cultivate land. —**farm/a•ble,** adj.
—**farm/er,** n. —**farm/house/,** n. —**farm/-
ing,** n. —**farm/yard/,** n.

far/o (fâr/ō) n. gambling game in which players bet on cards.

far/-off/, adj. distant.

far/-out/, adj. Slang. extremely unconventional.

far•ra/go (fə rä/gō, -rā/-) n., pl. **-goes.** confused mixture.

far/-reach/ing, adj. of widespread influence.

F

far'row (far'ō) *n.* **1.** litter of pigs. —*v.* **2.** (of swine) bear.

far'-sight'ed (-sī'tid, -sī'-) *adj.* **1.** seeing distant objects best. **2.** planning for future. —**far'sigh'ed•ness,** *n.*

far'ther (fär'ᵗħər) *compar. of* **far.** *adv.* **1.** at or to a greater distance. —*adj.* **2.** more distant. **3.** additional.

—**Usage.** FARTHER is used to indicate physical distance: *Is it much farther to the hotel?* FURTHER is used to refer to additional time, amount, or abstract ideas: *I would rather not talk about this further.* But both FARTHER and FURTHER are often used for distance of any kind: *Here is the solution; look no farther/further. His study of the novel reaches farther/further than any earlier one.*

far'thest (-ᵗħist) *superl. of* **far.** *adv.* **1.** at or to the greatest distance. —*adj.* **2.** most distant.

FAS 1. fetal alcohol syndrome. **2.** Foreign Agricultural Service.

F.A.S. *Commerce.* free alongside ship: without charge to the buyer for goods delivered alongside ship. Also, **f.a.s., fas**

FASB Financial Accounting Standards Board.

fas'ci•nate' (fas'ə nāt') *v.,* **-nated, -nating.** attract irresistibly. —**fas'ci•na'tion,** *n.*

fas'cism (fash'iz əm) *n.* principle of strong undemocratic government. —**fas'cist,** *n.,* *adj.* —**fa•scis'tic,** *adj.*

fash'ion (fash'ən) *n.* **1.** prevailing style. **2.** manner. —*v.* **3.** make.

fash'ion•a•ble, *adj.* of the latest style. —**fash'ion•a•bly,** *adv.*

fast (fast) *adj.* **1.** quick; swift. **2.** secure. —*adv.* **3.** tightly. **4.** swiftly. —*v.* **5.** abstain from food. —*n.* **6.** such abstinence.

fast'back', *n.* rear of automobile, curved downward.

fas'ten (fas'ən) *v.* **1.** fix securely. **2.** seize. —**fas'ten•er, fas'ten•ing,** *n.*

fast'-food', *adj.* specializing in food that can be prepared and served quickly.

fas•tid'i•ous (fa stid'ē əs, fə-) *adj.* highly critical and demanding. —**fas•tid'i•ous•ly,** *adv.* —**fas•tid'i•ous•ness,** *n.*

fast'ness, *n.* fortified place.

fat (fat) *n., adj.,* **fatter, fattest.** —*n.* **1.** greasy substance. —*adj.* **2.** fleshy. —**fat'ty,** *adj.*

fa'tal (fāt'l) *adj.* causing death or ruin. —**fa'tal•ly,** *adv.*

fa'tal•ism, *n.* belief in unchangeable destiny. —**fa'tal•ist,** *n.* —**fa'tal•is'tic,** *adj.*

fa•tal'i•ty (fā tal'i tē, fə-) *n., pl.* **-ties. 1.** death by a disaster. **2.** fate.

fate (fāt) *n., v.,* **fated, fating.** —*n.* **1.** destiny. **2.** death or ruin. —*v.* **3.** destine.

fat'ed, *adj.* subject to fate; destined.

fate'ful, *adj.* involving important or disastrous events.

fath. fathom.

fa'ther (fä'ᵗħər) *n.* **1.** male parent. **2.** (*cap.*) God. **3.** priest. —**fa'ther•hood',** *n.* —**fa'ther•less,** *adj.* —**fa'ther•ly,** *adj.*

fa'ther-in-law', *n., pl.* **fathers-in-law.** spouse's father.

fa'ther•land', *n.* **1.** one's native country. **2.** land of one's ancestors.

fath'om (faᵗħ'əm) *n.* **1.** nautical measure equal to six feet. —*v.* **2.** understand.

fa•tigue' (fə tēg') *n., v.,* **-tigued, -tiguing.** —*n.* **1.** weariness. **2.** (*pl.*) military work clothes. —*v.* **3.** weary.

fat'ten, *v.* grow fat or wealthy.

fatty acid, organic acid found in animal and vegetable fats.

fat'u•ous (fach'ōō əs) *adj.* **1.** foolish or stupid. **2.** unreal. —**fa•tu'i•ty** (fə tōō'i tē, -tyōō'-) *n.*

fau'cet (fô'sit) *n.* valve for liquids.

fault (fôlt) *n.* defect. —**fault'i•ly,** *adv.* —**fault'i•ness,** *n.* —**faul'ty,** *adj.*

faun (fôn) *n.* Roman deity, part man and part goat.

fau'na (fô'nə) *n., pl.* **-nas, -nae** (-nē). animals or animal life of particular region or period.

faux pas' (fō pä') social error.

fa'vor (fā'vər) *n.* **1.** kind act. **2.** high regard. —*v.* **3.** prefer. **4.** oblige. **5.** resemble. Also, **fa'vour.** —**fa'vor•a•ble,** *adj.* —**fa'vor•ite,** *adj., n.*

fa'vor•it•ism (fā'vər ə tiz'əm) *n.* preference shown toward certain persons.

fawn (fôn) *n.* **1.** young deer. —*v.* **2.** seek favor by servility.

fax (faks) *n.* **1.** method of transmitting written or graphic material by telephone or radio. **2.** item transmitted in this way. —*v.* **3.** send by fax. **4.** communicate by fax.

faze (fāz) *v.,* **fazed, fazing.** *Informal,* daunt.

f.b. 1. freight bill. **2.** *Sports.* fullback.

F.B.A. Fellow of the British Academy.

FBI, Federal Bureau of Investigation.

fbk firebrick.

fbm foot board measure.

FBO for the benefit of. Also, **F/B/O**

fbr fiber.

fbrbd fiberboard.

FC foot-candle; footcandles. Also, **fc**

fc 1. *Computers.* ferrite core. **2.** file cabinet. **3.** fire control.

f.c. 1. *Baseball.* fielder's choice. **2.** *Printing.* follow copy.

FCA Farm Credit Administration.

FCC, Federal Communications Commission.

fcg facing.

FCIA Foreign Credit Insurance Association.

FCIC Federal Crop Insurance Corporation.

fcp. foolscap.

fcr fuse current rating.

fcs. francs.

fcsg focusing.

fcsle forecastle.

fctn function.

fctnl functional.

fcty factory.

fcy. fancy.

fd feed.

F.D. 1. Defender of the Faith. [from Latin *Fidei Defensor*] **2.** fire department. **3.** focal distance.

FDA, Food and Drug Administration.

fdb field dynamic braking.

fdbk feedback.

fdc 1. fire department connection. **2.** *Computers.* floppy-disk controller.

fdd *Computers.* floppy-disk drive.

fddl frequency-division data link.

Fdg *Banking.* funding.

FDIC, Federal Deposit Insurance Corporation.

fdm frequency-division multiplex.

fdn foundation.

fdp *Hardware.* full dog point.

FDR Franklin Delano Roosevelt.

fdr 1. feeder. **2.** finder. **3.** fire door.

fdry foundry.

fd svc food service.

fdx *Telecommunications.* full duplex.

Fe *Symbol, Chemistry.* iron. [from Latin *ferrum*]

fe. he or she has made it. [from Latin *fecit*]

fear (fēr) *n.* **1.** feeling of coming harm. **2.** awe. —*v.* **3.** be afraid of. **4.** hold in awe. —**fear/ful,** *adj.* —**fear/less,** *adj.*

fea•si•ble (fē/zə bəl) *adj.* able to be done. —**fea•si•bil/i•ty,** *n.*

feast (fēst) *n.* **1.** sumptuous meal. **2.** religious celebration. —*v.* **3.** provide with or have feast.

feat (fēt) *n.* remarkable deed.

feath/er (feth/ər) *n.* one of the growths forming bird's plumage. —**feath/er•y,** *adj.*

fea/ture (fē/chər) *n., v.,* **-tured, -turing.** —*n.* **1.** part of face. **2.** special part, article, etc. —*v.* **3.** give prominence to.

Feb., February.

Feb/ru•ar/y (feb/rōō er/ē, feb/yōō-) *n., pl.* **-aries.** second month of year.

—**Pronunciation.** The second pronunciation for FEBRUARY shown above, with the first (r) replaced by (y), occurs because neighboring sounds that are alike tend to become different. This word also conforms to the pattern (-yōō er/ē) by analogy with the pronunciation of the first month of the year, *January.* Although the pronunciation of FEBRUARY with (y) is often criticized, both pronunciations are used by educated speakers and are considered standard.

fe/ces (fē/sēz) *n.pl.* excrement. —**fe/cal** (fē/kəl) *adj.*

feck/less (fek/lis) *adj.* **1.** incompetent. **2.** irresponsible and lazy.

fe/cund (fē/kund) *adj.* productive. —**fe•cun/di•ty,** *n.*

fed., 1. federal. **2.** federated. **3.** federation.

fed/er•al (fed/ər əl) *adj.* **1.** of states in permanent union. **2.** (*sometimes cap.*) of U.S. government. —**fed/er•al•ly,** *adv.*

fed/er•ate/ (fed/ə rāt/) *v.,* **-ated, -ating.** unite in league. —**fed/er•a/tion,** *n.*

fedn. federation.

fe•do/ra (fi dôr/ə) *n.* soft felt hat.

Fed. Res. Bd. Federal Reserve Board.

Fed. Res. Bk. Federal Reserve Bank.

fee (fē) *n.* **1.** payment for services, etc. **2.** ownership.

fee/ble (fē/bəl) *adj.,* **-bler, -blest.** weak. —**fee/bly,** *adv.*

feed (fēd) *v.,* **fed** (fed), **feeding,** *n.* —*v.* **1.** give food to. **2.** eat. —*n.* **3.** food. —**feed/er,** *n.*

feed/back/, *n.* **1.** return of part of output of a process to its input. **2.** informative response.

feel (fēl) *v.,* **felt** (felt), **feeling,** *n.* —*v.* **1.** perceive or examine by touch. **2.** be conscious of. **3.** have emotions. —*n.* **4.** touch. —**feel/ing,** *adj., n.*

feel/er, *n.* **1.** proposal or remark designed to elicit opinion or reaction. **2.** organ of touch, as an antenna.

feign (fān) *v.* pretend.

feint (fānt) *n.* **1.** deceptive move. —*v.* **2.** make feint.

feist/y (fī/stē) *adj.,* **-ier, -iest. 1.** full of energy; spirited. **2.** ready to argue or fight; pugnacious. —**feist/i•ly,** *adv.* —**feist/i•ness,** *n.*

feld/spar/ (feld/spär/, fel/-) *n.* hard crystalline mineral.

fe•lic/i•tate/ (fə lis/i tāt/) *v.,* **-tated, -tating.** congratulate. —**fe•lic/i•ta/tion,** *n.*

fe•lic/i•tous (-təs) *adj.* suitable.

fe•lic/i•ty, *n., pl.* **-ties.** happiness.

fe/line (fē/līn) *adj.* **1.** of or like cats. —*n.* **2.** animal of the cat family.

fell (fel) *v.* cut or strike down.

fel/low (fel/ō) *n.* **1.** man. **2.** companion. **3.** equal. **4.** member of learned or professional group. —**fel/low•ship/,** *n.*

fel/on (fel/ən) *n.* criminal.

fel/o•ny (fə lō/nē əs) *n., pl.* **-nies.** serious crime. —**fe•lo/ni•ous,** *adj.*

felr feeler.

felt (felt) *n.* **1.** matted fabric. —*adj.* **2.** of felt.

FeLV feline leukemia virus.

fem., 1. female. **2.** feminine.

FEMA Federal Emergency Management Agency.

fe/male (fē/māl) *adj.* **1.** belonging to sex that brings forth young. —*n.* **2.** female person or animal.

fem/i•nine (fem/ə nin) *adj.* of women. —**fem/i•nin/i•ty,** *n.*

fem/in•ism (-i niz/əm) *n.* support of equal rights for women. —**fem/in•ist,** *adj., n.*

F

fe′mur (fē′mər) *n.* thigh bone. —**fem′o•ral** (fem′ər əl) *adj.*

fen (fen) *n.* swampy ground; marsh.

fence (fens) *n., v.,* **fenced, fencing.** —*n.* **1.** wall-like enclosure around open area. **2.** person who receives and disposes of stolen goods. —*v.* **3.** fight with sword for sport. **4.** sell to a fence. —**fenc′er,** *n.* —**fenc′ing,** *n.*

fend (fend) *v.* ward off.

fend′er, *n.* metal part over automobile wheel.

fen′nel (fen′l) *n.* plant with seeds used for flavoring.

FEPA Fair Employment Practices Act.

FEPC Fair Employment Practices Commission.

FERA Federal Emergency Relief Administration.

fe′ral (fēr′əl, fer′-) *adj.* **1.** in a wild state; not tamed. **2.** having returned to a wild state.

FERC Federal Energy Regulatory Commission.

fer′ment, *n.* (fûr′ment) **1.** substance causing fermentation. **2.** agitation. —*v.* (fər ment′) **3.** cause or undergo fermentation.

fer′men•ta′tion, *n.* chemical change involving effervescence or decomposition.

fern (fûrn) *n.* nonflowering plant with feathery leaves.

fe•ro′cious (fə rō′shəs) *adj.* savagely fierce. —**fe•ro′cious•ly,** *adv.* —**fe•roc′i•ty** (fə ros′i tē) *n.*

fer′ret (fer′it) *n.* **1.** kind of weasel. —*v.* **2.** search intensively.

Fer′ris wheel (fer′is) amusement ride consisting of large upright wheel with suspended seats.

fer′rous (fer′əs) *adj.* of or containing iron. Also, **fer′ric** (ik).

fer′ry (fer′ē) *n., pl.* **-ries,** *v.,* **-ried, -rying.** —*n.* **1.** Also, **fer′ry•boat′.** boat making short crossings. **2.** place where ferries operate. —*v.* **3.** carry or pass in ferry.

fer′tile (fûr′tl) *adj.* **1.** producing abundantly. **2.** able to bear young. —**fer•til′i•ty,** *n.* —**fer′ti•li•za′tion,** *n.* —**fer′ti•lize′,** *v.,* **-lized, -lizing.** —**fer′ti•liz′er,** *n.*

fer′vent (fûr′vənt) *adj.* ardent; passionate. —**fer′ven•cy, fer′vor,** *n.* —**fer′vent•ly,** *adv.*

fer′vid (-vid) *adj.* vehement. —**fer′vid•ly,** *adv.*

fes′tal (fes′tl) *adj.* of feasts.

fes′ter (fes′tər) *v.* **1.** generate pus. **2.** rankle.

fes′ti•val (fes′tə vəl) *n.* celebration. Also, **fes•tiv′i•ty** (-tiv′i tē). —**fes′tive,** *adj.* —**fes′tive•ly,** *adv.*

fes•toon′ (fe stōōn′) *n.* **1.** garland hung between two points. —*v.* **2.** adorn with festoons.

FET 1. *Banking.* federal estate tax. **2.** *Electronics.* field-effect transistor.

F.E.T. Federal Excise Tax.

fet′a (fet′ə) *n.* Greek cheese usu. from sheep's or goat's milk.

fetch (fech) *v.* go and bring.

fetch′ing, *adj.* captivating. —**fetch′ing•ly,** *adv.*

fete (fāt, fet) *n., v.,* **feted, feting.** —*n.* **1.** festival. **2.** party. —*v.* **3.** honor with a fete.

fet′id (fet′id, fē′tid) *adj.* stinking; rank.

fe′tish (fet′ish, fē′tish) *n.* object worshiped. —**fet′ish•ism,** *n.* —**fet′ish•ist,** *n.* —**fet′ish•ist′ic,** *adj.*

fet′lock (fet′lok′) *n.* **1.** part of horse's leg behind hoof. **2.** tuft of hair on this part.

fet′ter (fet′ər) *n.* **1.** shackle for feet. **2.** (*pl.*) anything that restrains. —*v.* **3.** put fetters on. **4.** restrain from action.

fet′tle (fet′l) *n.* condition.

fe′tus (fē′təs) *n.* unborn offspring. —**fe′tal,** *adj.*

feud (fyōōd) *n.* **1.** lasting hostility. —*v.* **2.** engage in feud.

feu′dal•ism (fyōōd′l iz′əm) *n.* system by which land is held in return for service. —**feu′dal,** *adj.*

fe′ver (fē′vər) *n.* **1.** bodily condition marked by high temperature. **2.** intense nervous excitement. —**fe′ver•ish,** *adj.* —**fe′ver•ish•ly,** *adv.*

few (fyōō) *adj., n.* not many. —**Usage.** See LESS.

fext fire extinguisher.

fey (fā) *adj.* **1.** strange; whimsical. **2.** supernatural; enchanted.

fez (fez) *n., pl.* **fezzes.** felt cap.

ff, 1. folios. **2.** (and the) following (pages, verses, etc.).

FFA Future Farmers of America.

F.F.A. *Commerce.* free from alongside (ship). Also, **f.f.a.**

FFC 1. Foreign Funds Control. **2.** free from chlorine.

F.F.I. free from infection.

ffilh *Hardware.* flat fillister head.

ffrr full frequency-range recording.

F.F.V. First Families of Virginia.

ffwd fast forward.

FG, field goal(s).

fgd forged.

fgn. foreign.

FGP Foster Grandparent Program.

FGT federal gift tax.

fgy foggy.

FH *Pathology.* familial hypercholesterolemia.

fh fire hose.

FHA 1. Farmers' Home Administration. **2.** Federal Housing Administration. **3.** Future Homemakers of America.

FHLB Federal Home Loan Bank.

FHLBA Federal Home Loan Bank Administration.

FHLBB Federal Home Loan Bank Board.

FHLBS Federal Home Loan Bank System.

FHLMC Federal Home Loan Mortgage Corporation.

FHWA Federal Highway Administration.

fhy fire hydrant.

F.I. Falkland Islands.

FIA Federal Insurance Administration.

fi/an•cé/ (fē/än sā/, fē än/sā) *n.* betrothed man. —**fi/an•cée/**, *n.fem.*

fi•as/co (fē as/kō) *n., pl.* **-cos, -coes.** failure.

fi/at (fē/ät, fī/ət) *n.* decree.

fib (fib) *n., v.,* **fibbed, fibbing.** —*n.* **1.** mild lie. —*v.* **2.** tell a fib. —**fib/ber,** *n.*

fi/ber (fī/bər) *n.* **1.** threadlike piece, esp. one that can be worn. **2.** any of the threadlike structures that form plant or animal tissue. **3.** roughage. Also, **fi/bre.** —**fi/brous,** *adj.* —**fi/broid,** *adj.*

fi/ber•glass/, *n.* material composed of fine glass fibers.

fiber optics, technology of sending light and images through glass or plastic fibers. —**fi/ber-op/tic,** *adj.*

fib/ril•la/tion (fib/rə lā/shən, fī/brə-) *n.* abnormally fast and irregular heartbeat. —**fib/ril•late,** *v.*

fi•bro/sis (fī brō/sis) *n.* excess fibrous connective tissue in an organ.

fib/u•la (fib/yə lə) *n., pl.* **-lae** (-lē), **-las.** outer thinner bone from knee to ankle.

FICA (fī/kə, fē/-) Federal Insurance Contributions Act.

fiche (fēsh) *n.* microfiche.

fick/le (fik/əl) *adj.* inconstant; disloyal.

fict. fiction.

fic/tion (fik/shən) *n.* **1.** narrative of imaginary events. **2.** something made up. —**fic/tion•al,** *adj.* —**fic•ti/tious,** *adj.*

fid. fiduciary.

fid/dle (fid/l) *n., v.,* **-dled, -dling.** —*n.* **1.** violin. —*v.* **2.** play folk or popular tunes on violin. **3.** trifle. —**fid/dler,** *n.*

fid/dle•sticks/, *interj.* (exclamation of impatience, disbelief, etc.).

fi•del/i•ty (fi del/i tē, fī-) *n., pl.* **-ties.** faithfulness.

fidg/et (fij/it) *v.* **1.** move restlessly. —*n.* **2.** (*pl.*) restlessness. —**fid/get•y,** *adj.*

FIDO (fī/dō), *Aeronautics.* a system for evaporating the fog above airfield runways. [*f(og) i(nvestigation) d(ispersal) o(perations)*]

fi•du/cial (fi dōō/shəl, -dyōō/-) *adj.* based on trust, as paper money not backed by precious metal.

fi•du/ci•ar/y (-shē er/ē) *adj., n., pl.* **-ies.** —*adj.* **1.** being a trustee. **2.** held in trust. —*n.* **3.** trustee.

field (fēld) *n.* **1.** open ground. **2.** area of interest.

field day, **1.** day for outdoor sports or contests. **2.** chance for unrestricted enjoyment.

fiend (fēnd) *n.* **1.** devil. **2.** cruel person. **3.** *Informal.* addict. —**fiend/ish,** *adj.* —**fiend/ish•ly,** *adv.*

fierce (fērs) *adj.,* **fiercer, fiercest.** wild; violent. —**fierce/ly,** *adv.*

fier/y (fīˀr/ē, fī/ə rē) *adj.,* **-ier, -iest. 1.** of or like fire. **2.** ardent.

fi•es/ta (fē es/tə) *n.* festival.

fife (fīf) *n.* high-pitched flute.

FIFO (fī/fō), *n.* **1.** *Commerce.* first-in, first-out. **2.** *Computers.* a storage and retrieval technique, in which the first item stored is also the first item retrieved.

fif/teen/ (fif/tēn/) *n., adj.* ten plus five. —**fif•teenth/,** *adj., n.*

fifth (fifth) *adj.* **1.** next after fourth. —*n.* **2.** fifth part.

fifth column, traitorous group within a country.

fifth wheel, one that is unnecessary or unwanted.

fif/ty (fif/tē) *n., adj.* ten times five. —**fif/ti•eth,** *adj., n.*

fig (fig) *n.* fruit of semitropical tree.

fig. (fig) **1.** figurative. **2.** figuratively. **3.** figure.

fight (fīt) *n., v.,* **fought, fighting.** battle. —**fight/er,** *n.*

fig/ment (fig/mənt) *n.* imagined story.

fig/ur•a•tive (-yər ə tiv) *adj.* not literal. —**fig/ur•a•tive•ly,** *adv.*

fig/ure, *n., v.,* **-ured, -uring.** —*n.* **1.** written symbol, esp. numerical. **2.** amount. **3.** shape. —*v.* **4.** compute. **5.** be prominent.

fig/ure•head/, *n.* powerless leader.

figure of speech, use of words in nonliteral sense.

fig/ur•ine/ (-yə rēn/) *n.* miniature statue.

FIIG (fig), Federal Item Identification Guide.

fil 1. filament. **2.** *Hardware.* fillister.

fil/a•ment (fil/ə mənt) *n.* fine fiber.

fil/bert (fil/bərt) *n.* kind of nut.

filch (filch) *v.* steal.

file (fīl) *n., v.,* **filed, filing.** —*n.* **1.** storage place for documents. **2.** line of persons, etc. **3.** metal rubbing tool. —*v.* **4.** arrange or keep in file. **5.** march in file. **6.** rub with file. —**fil/er,** *n.*

fi•let/ mi•gnon/ (fi lā/ min yon/, -yôɴ/) *n.* round of beef tenderloin cut thick.

filh *Hardware.* fillister head.

fil/i•al (fil/ē əl) *adj.* befitting sons and daughters.

fil/i•bus/ter (fil/ə bus/tər) *n.* **1.** obstruction of legislation by prolonged speaking. —*v.* **2.** use filibuster to impede legislation. —**fil/i•bus ter•er,** *n.*

fil/i•gree/ (-i grē/) *n.* ornamental work of fine wires.

Fil/i•pi/no (fil/ə pē/nō) *n.* native of the Philippines.

fill (fil) *v.* **1.** make full. **2.** pervade. **3.** supply. —*n.* **4.** full supply. —**fill/ing,** *n.*

fil•let/ (fi lā/) *n.* narrow strip, esp. of meat or fish. Also, **fi/let.**

fil/lip (fil/əp) *n.* thing that excites.

fil/ly (fil/ē) *n., pl.* **-lies.** young female horse.

film (film) *n.* **1.** thin coating. **2.** roll or sheet with photographically sensitive coating. **3.** motion picture. —v. **4.** make motion picture of.

film′strip′, n. length of film containing still pictures for projecting on screen.

film′y, adj., **-ier, -iest. 1.** partly transparent. **2.** blurred. —**film′i•ness,** n.

filt. (in prescriptions) filter. [from Latin *filtrā*]

fil′ter (fil′tər) n. **1.** device for straining substances. —v. **2.** remove by or pass through filter. —**fil•tra′tion,** n.

filth (filth) n. **1.** dirt. **2.** obscenity; offensive indecency. —**filth′y,** adj. —**filth′i•ness,** n.

fin (fin) n. winglike organ on fishes. —**finned,** adj.

fi•na′gle (fi nā′gəl) v., **-gled, -gling.** practice or obtain by trickery. —**fi•na′gler,** n.

fi′nal (fīn′l) adj. last. —**fi′nal•ist,** n. —**fi•nal′i•ty** (fī nal′i tē) n. —**fi′nal•ize′,** v., **-ized, -izing.** —**fi′nal•ly,** adv.

fi•na′le (fi nä′lē) n. last part.

fi•nance′ (fi nans′, fī′nans) n., v., **-nanced, -nancing.** —n. **1.** money matters. **2.** (pl.) funds. —v. **3.** supply with money. —**fi•nan′cial,** adj. —**fi•nan′cial•ly,** adv.

fin•an•cier′ (fin′an sēr′, fī′nən-) n. professional money handler.

finch (finch) n. type of small songbird.

find (fīnd) v., **found** (found), **finding,** n. —v. **1.** come upon. **2.** learn. —n. **3.** discovery.

fine (fīn) adj., **finer, finest,** n., v., **fined, fining.** —adj. **1.** excellent. **2.** delicate; thin. —n. **3.** money exacted as penalty. —v. **4.** subject to fine.

fine art, (usually pl.) painting, sculpture, etc., created primarily for beauty.

fin′er•y, n. showy dress.

fi•nesse′ (fi ness′) n. artful delicacy.

fin′ger (fing′gər) n. one of five terminal parts of hand. —**fin′ger•nail′,** n. —**fin′ger•tip,** n.

fin′ger•print′, n. **1.** impression of markings of surface of finger, used for identification. —v. **2.** take or record fingerprints of.

fin′ick•y (fin′i kē) adj., **-ier, -iest.** fussy. Also, **fin′ic•al.**

fi′nis (fin′is, fē nē′, fī′nis) n. end.

fin′ish (fin′ish) v. **1.** end. **2.** perfect. **3.** give desired surface to. —n. **4.** completion. **5.** surface coating or treatment.

fi′nite (fī′nīt) adj. having bounds or limits. —**fi′nite•ly,** adv.

Finn (fin) n. native of Finland.

fin′nan had′die (fin′ən had′ē) smoked haddock.

Finn′ish (fin′ish) n. **1.** language of Finland. —adj. **2.** of Finland, the Finns, or Finnish.

fin. sec. financial secretary.

F.I.O. *Commerce.* free in and out: a term of contract in which a ship charterer pays for loading and unloading.

fiord (fyôrd, fē ôrd′) n. narrow arm of sea. Also, **fjord.**

fir (fûr) n. cone-bearing evergreen tree.

fire (fīªr) n., v., **fired, firing.** —n. **1.** burning. **2.** ardor. **3.** discharge of firearms. —v. **4.** set on fire. **5.** discharge. **6.** *Informal.* dismiss.

fire′arm′, n. gun.

fire′bomb′, n. **1.** incendiary bomb. —v. **2.** attack with firebombs.

fire′fight′er, n. person who fights destructive fires. —**fire′fight′ing,** n., adj.

fire′fly′, n., pl. **-flies.** nocturnal beetle with light-producing organ.

fire′man (fīr′mən) n., pl. **-men. 1.** firefighter. **2.** person maintaining fires.

fire′place′, n. semiopen place for fire.

fire′plug′, n. hydrant with water for fighting fires.

fire′proof′, adj. safe against fire.

fire′side′, n. area close to fireplace; hearth.

fire′trap′, n. dilapidated building.

fire′works′, n.pl. devices ignited for display of light.

firm (fûrm) adj. **1.** hard or stiff. **2.** fixed. **3.** resolute. —v. **4.** make or become firm. —n. **5.** business organization. —**firm′ly,** adv. —**firm′ness,** n.

fir′ma•ment (fûr′mə mənt) n. sky.

first (fûrst) adj., adv. **1.** before all others. —n. **2.** first thing, etc.

first aid, immediate treatment.

first class, 1. best or highest class or grade. **2.** most expensive class in travel. **3.** class of mail sealed against inspection. —**first′-class′,** adj.

first′hand′, adj., adv. from the first or original source. Also, **first′-hand′.**

first′-rate′, adj. **1.** of the highest quality, rank, etc. —adv. **2.** very well.

fis′cal (fis′kəl) adj. financial.

fish (fish) n., pl. **fish, fishes,** v. —n. **1.** cold-blooded aquatic vertebrate. —v. **2.** try to catch fish. —**fish′er•man,** n. —**fish′er•y,** n.

fish′y, adj., **-ier, -iest. 1.** like a fish, esp. in taste or smell. **2.** questionable; dubious. —**fish′i•ness,** n.

fis′sion (fish′ən) n. division into parts. —**fis′sion•a•ble,** adj.

fis′sure (fish′ər) n. narrow opening caused by break; crack.

fist (fist) n. closed hand.

fist′ful (-fŏŏl) n., pl. **fuls.** handful.

fist′i•cuffs′ (-i kufs′) n.pl. fight with the fists.

fit (fit) adj., **fitter, fittest,** v., **fitted, fitting,** n. —adj. **1.** well suited. **2.** in good condition. —v. **3.** be or make suitable. **4.** equip. —n. **5.** manner of fitting. **6.** sudden attack of illness or emotion. —**fit′ness,** n.

fit′ful, adj. irregular.

fit′ting, adj. **1.** appropriate. —n. **2.** attached part. **3.** trial of new clothes, etc., for fit.

five (fīv) n., adj. four plus one.

fix (fiks) v. **1.** make fast or steady. **2.** repair.

3. prepare. —**fix′a•ble,** *adv.* —**fixed,** *adj.* —**fix′ed•ly,** *adv.* —**fix′er,** *n.*

fix•a′tion (fik sā′shən) *n.* obsession.

fix′ings, *n.pl. Informal.* things accompanying main item.

fix′ture (-chər) *n.* thing fixed in place.

fizz (fiz) *v., n.* hiss.

fiz′zle (fiz′əl) *v.,* **-zled, -zling,** *n.* —*v.* **1.** hiss weakly. **2.** *Informal.* fail. —*n.* **3.** act of fizzling.

fjord (fyôrd, fē ôrd′) *n.* fiord.

fk fork.

FL, Florida.

fl., 1. (he or she) flourished. **2.** fluid.

Fla., Florida.

flab (flab) *n.* loose, excessive flesh.

flab′ber•gast′ (flab′ər gast′) *v. Informal.* astound.

flab′by (flab′ē) *adj.,* **-bier, -biest.** not firm. —**flab′bi•ness,** *n.*

flac′cid (flak′sid, flas′id) *adj.* flabby.

flag (flag) *n., v.,* **flagged, flagging.** —*n.* **1.** cloth with symbolic colors or design. **2.** plant with long narrow leaves. **3.** Also, **flag′stone′.** paving stone. —*v.* **4.** signal with flags (def. 1). **5.** fall off in vigor, energy, etc.

flag′el•late′ (flaj′ə lāt′) *v.,* **-lated, -lating.** whip; flog. —**flag′el•la′tion,** *n.*

flag′on (flag′ən) *n.* large bottle.

fla′grant (flā′grənt) *adj.* glaring. —**fla′gran•cy,** *n.* —**fla′grant•ly,** *adv.*

flag′ship′, *n.* ship of senior naval officer.

flail (flāl) *n.* **1.** hand instrument for threshing. —*v.* **2.** strike or strike at as with flail.

flair (flâr) *n.* aptitude; talent.

flak (flak) *n.* **1.** antiaircraft fire. **2.** critical or hostile reaction.

flake (flāk) *n., v.,* **flaked, flaking.** —*n.* **1.** small thin piece. —*v.* **2.** separate into flakes.

flak′y, *adj.,* **-ier, -iest. 1.** of or like flakes. **2.** lying or coming off in flakes. **3.** *Slang.* eccentric; odd. Also, **flak′ey.** —**flak′i•ness,** *n.*

flam•blé (fläm bā′) *adj.* served in flaming liquor.

flam•boy′ant (flam boi′ənt) *adj.* showy; colorful. —**flam•boy′ance,** *n.* —**flam•boy′ant•ly,** *adv.*

flame (flām) *n., v.,* **flamed, flaming.** blaze.

fla•men′co (flə meng′kō) *n.* Spanish gypsy dance and music style.

fla•min′go (flə ming′gō) *n., pl.* **-gos, -goes.** tall, red, aquatic bird.

flam′ma•ble (flam′ə bəl) easily set on fire. —**flam′ma•bil′i•ty,** *n.*

flange (flanj) *n.* projecting rim.

flank (flangk) *n.* **1.** side. —*v.* **2.** be at side of. **3.** pass around side of.

flan′nel (flan′l) *n.* soft wool fabric.

flap (flap) *v.,* **flapped, flapping,** *n.* —*v.* **1.** swing loosely and noisily. **2.** move up and down. —*n.* **3.** flapping movement. **4.** something hanging loosely. **5.** *Informal.* emotionally agitated state.

flare (flâr) *v.,* **flared, flaring,** *n.* —*v.* **1.** burn with unsteady or sudden flame. **2.** spread outward. —*n.* **3.** signal fire.

flare′up′, *n.* sudden outburst or outbreak.

flash (flash) *n.* **1.** brief light. **2.** instant. **3.** news dispatch. —*v.* **4.** gleam suddenly.

flash′back′, *n.* **1.** earlier event inserted out of order in a story or dramatic work. **2.** sudden recollection of a past event.

flash′bulb′, *n.* bulb giving burst of light for photography.

flash′cube′, *n.* device containing four flashbulbs.

flash′ing, *n.* protective metal for roof joints and angles.

flash′light′, *n.* portable battery-powered light.

flash′y, *adj.,* **-ier, -iest.** showy. —**flash′i•ness,** *n.*

flask (flask) *n.* kind of bottle.

flat (flat) *adj.,* **flatter, flattest,** *n.* —*adj.* **1.** level. **2.** horizontal. **3.** not thick. **4.** staunch. **5.** dull. **6.** below musical pitch. —*n.* **7.** something flat. **8.** apartment. —**flat′ly,** *adv.* —**flat′ness,** *n.* —**flat′ten,** *v.*

flat′bed′, *n.* truck with trailer platform open on all sides.

flat′car′, *n.* railroad car without sides or top.

flat′fish′, *n.* fish with broad, flat body, as flounder.

flat′foot′, *n., pl.* **-feet** for 2, **-foots** for 3. **1.** flattened condition of arch of foot. **2.** feet with flattened arches. **3.** *Slang.* police officer.

flat′-out′, *adj. Informal.* **1.** using full speed, resources, etc. **2.** downright.

flat′ter (flat′ər) *v.* praise insincerely. —**flat′ter•y,** *n.*

flat′u•lent (flach′ə lənt) *adj.* **1.** having an accumulation of gas in the intestines. **2.** inflated and empty; pompous. —**flat′u•ence,** *n.*

flat′ware′, *n.* table utensils and dishes.

flaunt (flônt) *v.* display boldly.

flav. (in prescriptions) yellow. [from Latin *flāvus*]

fla′vor (flā′vər) *n.* **1.** taste. —*v.* **2.** give flavor to. —**fla′vor•ing,** *n.*

flaw (flô) *n.* defect. —**flawed,** *adj.* —**flaw′less,** *adj.* —**flaw′less•ly,** *adv.*

flax (flaks) *n.* linen plant. —**flax′en,** *adj.*

flay (flā) *v.* strip skin from.

F.L.B. Federal Land Bank.

fld. 1. field. **2.** fluid.

fldg folding.

fl dr fluid dram; fluid drams.

fldt floodlight.

fldxt (in prescriptions) fluidextract. [from Latin *fluidextractum*]

flea (flē) *n.* small, bloodsucking insect.

flea market, market, often outdoors, where used articles, antiques, etc., are sold.

fleck (flek) *n.* **1.** speck. —*v.* **2.** spot.

fledg′ling (flej′ling) *n.* young bird.

F

flee (flē) *v.*, **fled** (fled), **fleeing.** run away from.

fleece (flēs) *n.*, *v.*, **fleeced, fleecing.** —*n.* **1.** wool of sheep. —*v.* **2.** swindle. —**fleec′y,** *adj.*

fleet (flēt) *n.* **1.** organized group of ships, aircraft, or road vehicles. —*adj.* **2.** swift.

fleet′ing, *adj.* temporary; not lasting.

flesh (flesh) *n.* **1.** muscle and fat of animal body. **2.** body. **3.** soft part of fruit or vegetable. —**flesh′y,** *adj.*

flesh′ly, *adj.* carnal.

flesh′pot′, *n.* place of unrestrained pleasure.

FLETC Federal Law Enforcement Training Center.

flex (fleks) *v.* bend. —**flex′i•ble,** *adj.* —**flex′i•bil′i•ty,** *n.*

flg **1.** flange. **2.** flooring.

flh flathead.

flick (flik) *n.* **1.** light stroke. —*v.* **2.** strike lightly.

flick′er, *v.* **1.** glow unsteadily. —*n.* **2.** unsteady light.

fli′er (flī′ər) *n.* aviator.

flight (flīt) *n.* **1.** act or power of flying. **2.** trip through air. **3.** steps between two floors. **4.** hasty departure.

flight′less, *adj.* incapable of flying.

flight′y, *adj.*, **-ier, -iest.** capricious. —**flight′i•ness,** *n.*

flim′sy (flim′zē) *adj.*, **-sier, -siest.** weak or thin. —**flim′si•ness,** *n.*

flinch (flinch) *v.* shrink; wince.

fling (fling) *v.*, **flung** (flung), **flinging,** *n.* —*v.* **1.** throw violently. —*n.* **2.** act of flinging.

flint (flint) *n.* hard stone that strikes sparks. —**flint′y,** *adj.*

flip (flip) *v.*, **flipped, flipping,** *n.*, *adj.*, **flipper, flippest.** —*v.* **1.** move, as by snapping finger. **2.** turn over with sudden stroke. —*n.* **3.** such movement. —*adj.* **4.** flippant.

flip′-flop′, *n.* **1.** sudden reversal, as of opinion. **2.** backward somersault.

flip′pant (flip′ənt) *adj.* pert; disrespectful. —**flip′pant•ly,** *adv.* —**flip′pan•cy,** *n.*

flip′per, *n.* broad flat limb.

flirt (flûrt) *v.* **1.** act amorously without serious intentions. —*n.* **2.** person who flirts. —**flir•ta′tion,** *n.* —**flir•ta′tious,** *adj.* —**flir•ta′tious•ly,** *adv.*

flit (flit) *v.*, **flitted, flitting.** move swiftly.

fll frequency-locked loop.

flld full load.

flm flame.

flmb flammable.

flmt flush mount.

fln fuel line.

float (flōt) *v.* **1.** rest or move on or in liquid, air, etc. —*n.* **2.** something that floats. **3.** decorated parade wagon. —**flo•ta′tion,** *n.*

flock (flok) *n.* **1.** group of animals. —*v.* **2.** gather in flock.

floe (flō) *n.* field of floating ice.

flog (flog) *v.*, **flogged, flogging.** beat; whip.

flood (flud) *n.* **1.** overflowing of water. —*v.* **2.** overflow or cover with water, etc.

flood′light′, *n.* artificial light for large area.

floor (flôr) *n.* **1.** bottom surface of room, etc. **2.** level in building. **3.** right to speak. —*v.* **4.** furnish with floor. **5.** knock down.

floor′ing, *n.* floor covering.

flop (flop) *v.*, **flopped, flopping,** *n. Informal.* —*v.* **1.** fall flatly. **2.** fail. **3.** flap. —*n.* **4.** act of flopping.

flop′py, *adj.* **-pier, -piest.** limp. —**flop′pi•ness,** *n.*

floppy disk, thin plastic disk for storing computer data.

FLOPS (flops), *Computers.* floating-point operations per second.

flor. flourished. [from Latin *flōruit*]

flo′ra (flôr′ə) *n.*, *pl.* **floras, florae** (flôr′ē) plants or plant life of a particular region or period.

flo′ral, *adj.* of flowers.

flor′id (flôr′id) *adj.* ruddy. —**flo•rid′i•ty,** *n.*

flo′rist, *n.* dealer in flowers.

floss (flôs) *n.* **1.** silky fiber from certain plants. **2.** thread used to clean between teeth. —*v.* **3.** use dental floss. —**floss′y,** *adj.*

flot flotation.

flo•til′la (flō til′ə) *n.* small fleet.

flot′sam (flot′səm) *n.* floating wreckage.

flounce (flouns) *v.*, **flounced, flouncing,** *n.* —*v.* **1.** go with an angry fling. —*n.* **2.** flouncing movement. **3.** ruffle for trimming.

floun′der (floun′dər) *v.* **1.** struggle clumsily. —*n.* **2.** clumsy effort. **3.** flat edible fish.

flour (flouᵊr, flou′ər) *n.* finely ground meal.

flour′ish (flûr′ish) *v.* **1.** thrive. **2.** brandish. —*n.* **3.** act of brandishing. **4.** decoration.

flout (flout) *v.* mock; scorn.

flow (flō) *v.* **1.** move in stream. —*n.* **2.** act or rate of flowing.

flow chart, chart showing steps in procedure or system.

flow′er (flou′ər) *n.*, *v.* blossom; bloom. —**flow′er•y,** *adj.*

fl. oz. fluid ounce; fluid ounces.

flr **1.** failure. **2.** filler. **3.** floor.

FLRA Federal Labor Relations Authority.

flrt flow rate.

flry flurry.

flt **1.** flashlight. **2.** flight. **3.** float.

fltg floating.

fltr **1.** filter. **2.** flutter.

flu (flōō) *n.* influenza.

flub (flub) *v.*, **flubbed, blubbing.** botch; bungle.

fluc′tu•ate′ (fluk′chōō āt′) *v.*, **-ated, -ating.** vary irregularly. —**fluc′tu•a′tion,** *n.*

flue (flōō) *n.* duct for smoke, etc.

flu′ent (flōō′ənt) *adj.* writing and speaking with ease. —**flu′en•cy,** *n.* —**flu′ent•ly,** *adv.*

fluff (fluf) *n.* downy particles. —**fluff′y,** *adj.*

flu′id (floo′id) *n.* **1.** substance that flows. —*adj.* **2.** liquid or gaseous. —**flu•id′i•ty,** *n.*

fluke (flook) *n.* **1.** lucky chance. **2.** flounder (def. 3).

flume (floom) *n.* channel; trough.

flunk (flungk) *v. Informal.* fail, esp. in a course or examination.

flun′ky, *n., pl.* **-kies.** servant or follower.

fluor fluorescent.

fluo•res′cence (floo res′əns, flô) *n.* emission of light upon exposure to radiation, etc. —**fluo•res′cent,** *adj.*

fluorescent lamp, tubular lamp using phosphors to produce radiation of light.

fluor′i•da′tion (floor′ə dā′shən, flôr′-) *n.* addition of fluorides to drinking water to reduce tooth decay. —**fluor′i•date′,** *v.,* **-dated, -dating.**

fluor•ide′ (-īd) *n.* chemical compound containing fluorine.

fluor′ine (-ēn) *n.* yellowish toxic gaseous element.

fluor′o•scope′ (-ə skōp′) *n.* device for examining the body with x-rays.

flur′ry (flûr′ē) *n., pl.* **-ries. 1.** light snowfall. **2.** agitated state.

flush (flush) *n.* **1.** rosy glow. —*v.* **2.** redden. **3.** wash out with water. —*adj.* **4.** even with surrounding surface. **5.** well supplied.

flusoch fluted socket head.

flus′ter (flus′tər) *v.* confuse.

flute (floot) *n., v.,* **fluted, fluting.** —*n.* **1.** musical wind instrument. **2.** groove. —*v.* **3.** form flutes in. —**flut′ing,** *n.*

flut′ist, *n.* flute player. Also, **flau′tist** (flô′-tist, flou′-).

flut′ter (flut′ər) *v.* **1.** wave in air. —*n.* **2.** agitation. —**flut′tery,** *adj.*

flux (fluks) *n.* **1.** a flowing. **2.** continuous change. **3.** substance that promotes fusion of metals.

flv flush valve.

flw flat washer.

flwp followup.

fly (flī) *v.,* **flew** (floo), **flown** (flōn), **flying,** *n., pl.* **flies.** —*v.* **1.** move or direct through air. **2.** move swiftly. —*n.* **3.** winged insect. —**fly′er,** *n.*

fly′-blown′, *adj.* tainted; spoiled.

fly′-by-night′, *adj.* **1.** unreliable, esp. in business. **2.** not lasting.

flying saucer, disk-shaped missile or plane, thought to come from outer space.

fly′leaf′, *n., pl.* **-leaves.** blank page in front or back of a book.

fly′wheel′, *n.* wheel for equalizing speed of machinery.

flywhl flywheel.

FM 1. Federated States of Micronesia (approved for postal use). **2.** *Electronics.* frequency modulation: a method of impressing a signal on a radio carrier wave. **3.** *Radio.* a system of radio broadcasting by means of frequency modulation.

Fm *Symbol, Chemistry.* fermium.

fm 1. *Symbol, Physics.* femtometer. **2.** field manual.

fm. 1. fathom; fathoms. **2.** from.

f.m. (in prescriptions) make a mixture. [from Latin *fiat mistūra*]

FMB Federal Maritime Board.

FMC Federal Maritime Commission.

FMCS Federal Mediation and Conciliation Service.

fmcw frequency-modulated continuous wave.

F.Mk. finmark; Finnish markka. Also, **FMk**

fmla formula.

fmr former.

fmw *Computers.* firmware.

fn footnote.

fnd found.

FNMA Federal National Mortgage Association.

fnsh finish.

fo. 1. *Electricity.* fast-operate: a type of relay. **2.** foldout. **3.** folio.

F.O. 1. field officer. **2.** foreign office. **3.** *Military.* forward observer.

foal (fōl) *n.* young horse.

foam (fōm) *n.* **1.** mass of tiny bubbles. —*v.* **2.** form foam. —**foam′y,** *adj.*

foam rubber, spongy rubber used esp. in cushions.

fob (fob) *n.* watch chain.

FOBS fractional orbital bombardment system. Also, **F.O.B.S.**

foc focal.

fo′cus (fō′kəs) *n., pl.* **-cuses, -ci** (-sī), *v.,* **-cused, -cusing.** —*n.* **1.** point at which refracted rays meet. **2.** state of sharpness for image from optical device. **3.** central point. —*v.* **4.** bring into focus. —**fo′cal,** *adj.*

fod′der (fod′ər) *n.* livestock food.

foe (fō) *n.* enemy.

fog (fog) *n., v.,* **fogged, fog•ging.** —*n.* **1.** thick mist. **2.** mental confusion. —*v.* **3.** make or become enveloped with fog. —**fog′gy,** *adj.* —**fog′gi•ness,** *n.*

fo′gy (fō′gē) *n., pl.* **-gies.** old-fashioned person.

FOIA Freedom of Information Act.

foi′ble (foi′bəl) *n.* weak point.

foil (foil) *v.* **1.** frustrate. —*n.* **2.** thin metallic sheet. **3.** thing that sets off another by contrast. **4.** thin sword for fencing.

foist (foist) *v.* impose unjustifiably.

fol. 1. folio. **2.** (in prescriptions) a leaf. [from Latin *folium*] **3.** followed. **4.** following.

fold (fōld) *v.* **1.** bend over upon itself. **2.** wrap. **3.** collapse. —*n.* **4.** folded part. **5.** enclosure for sheep.

-fold, suffix meaning: **1.** having so many parts, as *a fourfold plan.* **2.** times as many, as *to increase tenfold.*

F

fold'er, *n.* **1.** folded printed sheet. **2.** outer cover.

fo'li•age (fō'lē ij) *n.* leaves.

folic acid (fō'lik, fol'ik) vitamin used in treating anemia.

fo'li•o' (fō'lē ō') *n.*, *pl.* **-ios. 1.** sheet of paper folded once. **2.** book printed on such sheets.

folk (fōk) *n.*, *pl.* **folk** or **folks. 1.** people. *—adj.* **2.** of or from the common people.

folk'lore', *n.* customs and beliefs of people.

folk'lor•ist, *n.* expert on folklore. **—folk'lor• is'tic,** *adj.*

folk song, 1. song originating among the common people. **2.** song of similar character written by a known composer. **—folk singer.**

folk'sy, *adj.*, **-sier, -siest.** *Informal,* suggesting genial simplicity. **—folk'si•ness,** *n.*

foll. following.

fol'li•cle (fol'i kəl) *n.* **1.** seed vessel. **2.** small cavity, sac, or gland.

fol'low (fol'ō) *v.* **1.** come or go after. **2.** conform to. **3.** work at. **4.** move along. **5.** watch or understand. **6.** result.

fol'low•er, *n.* **1.** person who follows. **2.** disciple.

fol'low•ing, *n.* group of admirers or disciples.

fol'low-through', *n.* **1.** last part of a motion, as after a ball has been struck. **2.** act of continuing a plan, program, etc., to completion.

fol'ly (fol'ē) *n.*, *pl.* **-lies.** foolishness.

fo•ment' (fō ment') *v.* foster. **—fo'men•ta'- tion,** *n.* **—fo•ment'er,** *n.*

fond (fond) *adj.* **1.** having affection. **2.** foolish. **—fond'ly,** *adv.* **—fond'ness,** *n.*

fon'dant (fon'dənt) *n.* sugar paste used in candies.

fon'dle (fon'dl) *v.*, **-dled, -dling.** caress.

fon•due' (fon dōō', -dyōō') *n.* dip of melted cheese, liquor, and seasonings.

font (font) *n.* **1.** receptacle for baptismal water. **2.** printing type style.

food (fōōd) *n.* what is taken in for nourishment.

food processor, appliance for chopping, shredding or otherwise processing food.

fool (fōōl) *n.* **1.** person acting stupidly. *—v.* **2.** trick. **3.** act frivolously. **—fool'ish,** *adj.*

fool'har'dy, *adj.*, **-dier, -diest.** rash.

fool'proof', *adj.* proof against accident.

foot (fōōt) *n.*, *pl.* **feet** (fēt), *v.* *—n.* **1.** part of leg on which body stands. **2.** unit of length equal to 12 inches. **3.** lowest part; base. *—v.* **4.** walk. **—foot'print',** *n.*

foot'ball', *n.* game played with pointed leather ball.

foot'hill', *n.* hill at foot of mountains.

foot'hold', *n.* **1.** secure place for foot to rest. **2.** firm basis for progress.

foot'ing, *n.* **1.** secure position. **2.** basis for relationship.

foot'less, *adj.* **1.** having no basis. **2.** awkward or inefficient.

foot'lights', *n.pl.* **1.** lights at the front of a stage floor. **2.** acting.

foot'lock'er, *n.* small trunk kept at the foot of a bed.

foot'loose', *adj.* free to go or travel about.

foot'man, *n.* male servant.

foot'note', *n.* note at foot of page.

foot'-pound', *n.* work done by force of one pound moving through distance of one foot.

foot'step', *n.* sound of walking.

foot'stool', *n.* low stool for resting the feet.

fop (fop) *n.* haughty, overdressed man. **—fop'pish,** *adj.*

for (fôr; *unstressed* fər) *prep.* **1.** with the purpose of. **2.** in the interest of. **3.** in place of. **4.** in favor of. **5.** during. *—conj.* **6.** seeing that. **7.** because.

for'age (fôr'ij) *n.*, *v.*, **-aged, -aging.** *—n.* **1.** food for stock. *—v.* **2.** search for supplies.

for'ay (fôr'ā) *n.* **1.** raid. **2.** venture.

for•bear' (fôr bâr') *v.*, **-bore** (-bôr'), **-borne** (-bôrn'), **-bearing. 1.** refrain from. **2.** be patient. **—for•bear'ance,** *n.*

for•bid' (fər bid', fôr-) *v.*, **-bade** (-bad', -bād') or **-bad, -bidden** or **-bid, -bidding.** give order against.

for•bid'ding, *adj.* intimidating or discouraging.

force (fôrs) *n.*, *v.*, **forced, forcing.** *—n.* **1.** strength. **2.** coercion. **3.** armed group. **4.** influence. *—v.* **5.** compel. **6.** make yield. **—force'ful,** *adj.*

for'ceps (fôr'səps, -seps) *n.* medical tool for seizing and holding.

for'ci•ble (fôr'sə bəl) *adj.* by means of force. **—for'ci•bly,** *adv.*

ford (fôrd) *n.* **1.** place for crossing water by wading. *—v.* **2.** cross at ford. **—ford'a•ble,** *adj.*

fore (fôr) *adj.*, *adv.* **1.** at the front. **2.** earlier. *—n.* **3.** front.

fore-, prefix meaning: **1.** before, as *forewarn.* **2.** front, as *forehead.* **3.** preceding, as *forefather.* **4.** chief, as *foreman.*

fore'arm', *n.* arm between elbow and wrist.

fore'bear', *n.* ancestor.

fore•bode', *v.*, **-boded, -boding.** portend.

fore'cast', *v.*, **-cast, -casting,** *n.* *—v.* **1.** predict. *—n.* **2.** prediction.

fore'cas•tle (fōk'səl, fōr'kas'əl) *n.* forward part of vessel's upper deck.

fore•close' (-klōz') *v.*, **-closed, -closing.** deprive of the right to redeem (mortgage, etc.). **—fore•clo'sure,** *n.*

fore'fa'ther, *n.* ancestor. **—fore'moth'er,** *n.fem.*

fore'fin'ger, *n.* finger next to thumb.

fore'front', *n.* foremost place.

fore•go'ing, *adj.* previous.

fore'gone' conclusion, inevitable result.

fore'ground', *n.* nearest area.

fore′hand′, *n.* in sports, stroke made with palm of hand facing direction of movement. —**fore′hand′,** *adj.*

fore′head (fôr′id, fôr′hed′) *n.* part of face above eyes.

for′eign (fôr′in) *adj.* **1.** of or from another country. **2.** from outside. —**for′eign•er,** *n.*

fore′man or **-wom′an** or **per′son** *n.*, *pl.* **-men** or **-women** or **-persons.** person in charge of work crew or jury.

fore′most′, *adj.*, *adv.* first.

fore′noon′, *n.* daylight time before noon.

fo•ren′sic (fə ren′sik) *adj.* of or for public discussion or courtroom procedure.

fore′play′, *n.* sexual stimulation leading to intercourse.

fore′run′ner, *n.* predecessor.

fore•see′, *v.*, **-saw, -seen, -seeing.** see beforehand. —**fore′sight′,** *n.*

fore•shad′ow, *v.* indicate beforehand.

fore′skin′, *n.* skin on end of penis.

for′est (fôr′ist) *n.* land covered with trees. —**for′est•er,** *n.* —**for′est•ry,** *n.*

fore•stall′, *v.* thwart by earlier action.

for′est•a′tion (fôr′ə stā′shən) *n.* planting of forests.

forest ranger, officer who supervises care and preservation of forests.

fore•tell′, *v.*, **-told, -telling.** predict.

fore′thought′, *n.* **1.** prudence. **2.** previous calculation.

for•ev′er (fôr ev′ər, fər-) *adv.* always.

fore•warn′, *v.* warn in good time.

fore′word′, *n.* introduction.

for′feit (fôr′fit) *n.* **1.** penalty. —*v.* **2.** lose as forfeit. —*adj.* **3.** forfeited. —**for′fei•ture,** *n.*

for•gath′er, *v.* assemble.

forge (fôrj) *n.*, *v.*, **forged, forging.** —*n.* **1.** place for heating metal before shaping. —*v.* **2.** form by heating and hammering. **3.** imitate fraudulently. **4.** move ahead persistently. —**forg′er,** *n.* —**for′ger•y,** *n.*

for•get′ (fər get′) *v.*, **-got** (-got′), **-gotten, -getting.** fail to remember. —**for•get′ful,** *adj.* —**for•get′ta•ble,** *adj.*

for•get′-me-not′, *n.* small plant with blue flowers.

for•give′ (fər giv′) *v.*, **-gave** (-gāv′), **-given, -giving.** grant pardon. —**for•giv′a•ble,** *adj.* —**for•give′ness,** *n.* —**for•giv′ing,** *adj.*

for•go′ (fôr gō′) *v.*, **-went** (-went′), **-gone** (-gon′), **-going.** do without.

fork (fôrk) *n.* **1.** pronged instrument. **2.** point of division. —*v.* **3.** branch.

fork′lift′, *n.* vehicle with two power-operated prongs for lifting heavy weights.

for•lorn′ (fôr lôrn′) *adj.* abandoned. —**for•lorn′ly,** *adv.*

form (fôrm) *n.* **1.** shape. **2.** mold. **3.** custom; standard practice. **4.** document to be filled in. —*v.* **5.** shape. —**form′less,** *adj.*, —**form′-less•ness,** *n.*

for′mal (fôr′məl) *adj.* **1.** according to custom

or standard practice. **2.** ceremonious. **3.** precisely stated. —**for′mal•ly,** *adv.* —**for′mal•ize′,** *v.*

form•al′de•hyde′ (fôr mal′də hīd′, fər-) *n.* solution used as disinfectant, etc.

for•mal′i•ty (-mal′i tē) *n.*, *pl.* **-ties. 1.** in accordance with custom. **2.** act done as matter of standard practice.

for′mat (fôr′mat) *n.*, *v.*, **-matted, -matting.** —*n.* **1.** general arrangement. —*v.* **2.** prepare (a computer disk) for writing and reading.

for•ma′tion (fôr mā′shən) *n.* **1.** act of forming. **2.** material that forms. **3.** pattern of ships, aircraft, etc., moving together.

form′a•tive (fôr′mə tiv) *adj.* **1.** giving or acquiring form. **2.** relating to formation and development.

for′mer (fôr′mər) *adj.* **1.** earlier. **2.** first-mentioned. —**for′mer•ly,** *adv.*

form′fit′ting, *adj.* snug.

for′mi•da•ble (fôr′mi də bəl) *adj.* awesome. —**for′mi•da•bly,** *adv.*

form letter, standardized letter that can be sent to many people.

for′mu•la (fôr′myə lə) *n.*, *pl.* **-las, -lae** (-lē′). **1.** scientific description in figures and symbols. **2.** set form of words.

for′mu•late′ (fôr′myə lāt′) *v.*, **-lated, -lating.** state systematically. —**for′mu•la′tion,** *n.*

for′ni•cate′ (fôr′ni kāt′) *v.*, **-cated, -cating.** have illicit sexual relations. —**for′ni•ca′tion,** *n.* —**for′ni•ca′tor,** *n.*

for•sake′ (fôr sāk′) *v.*, **-sook** (-sook′), **-saken, -saking.** desert; abandon.

for•swear′, *v.*, **-swore, -sworn, -swearing. 1.** renounce. **2.** perjure.

for•syth′i•a (fôr sith′ē ə, fər-) *n.* shrub bearing yellow flowers.

fort (fôrt) *n.* fortified place.

forte (fôrt, fôr′tā) *n.* **1.** one's strong point. —*adv.* (fôr′tā). **2.** *Music.* loudly.

—**Pronunciation.** In the noun sense (*She draws pretty well, but sculpture is really her forte*), the established, traditional pronunciation of FORTE is with one syllable: (fôrt). However, the two-syllable pronunciation (fôr′tā), which is correct for the adverb (a musical term borrowed from Italian), is increasingly heard for the noun as well, and is now also considered standard.

forth (fôrth) *adv.* **1.** onward. **2.** into view. **3.** abroad.

forth′com′ing, *adj.* about to appear.

forth′right′, *adj.* direct in manner or speech.

forth′with′, *adv.* at once.

for′ti•fi•ca′tion (fôr′tə fi kā′shən) *n.* defensive military construction.

for′ti•fy′ (fôr′tə fī′) *v.*, **-fied, -fying.** strengthen.

F

for•tis′si•mo′ (fôr tis′ə mō′) *adj., adv. Music.* very loud.

for′ti•tude′ (fôr′ti tōōd′, -tyōōd′) *n.* patient courage.

fort′night′, *n.* two weeks.

FORTRAN (fôr′tran) *n.* computer programming language used esp. for solving problems in science and engineering.

for′tress (fôr′tris) *n.* fortified place.

for•tu′i•tous (fôr tōō′i təs, -tyōō′-) *adj.* 1. accidental. 2. lucky. **—for•tu′i•tous•ly,** *adv.* **—for•tu′i•ty,** *n.*

for′tu•nate (fôr′chə nit) *adj.* lucky. **—for′-tu•nate•ly,** *adv.*

for′tune, *n.* 1. wealth. 2. luck.

for′tune-tell′er, *n.* person who claims to read the future. **—for′tune-tell′ing,** *n.*

for′ty (fôr′tē) *n., adj.* ten times four. **—for′-ti•eth,** *adj., n.*

fo′rum (fôr′əm) *n.* assembly for public discussion.

for′ward (fôr′wərd) *adv.* 1. onward. **—***adj.* 2. advanced. 3. bold. **—***v.* 4. send on. **—for′-ward•er,** *n.* **—for′ward•ly,** *adv.* **—for′-ward•ness,** *n.*

F.O.S. *Commerce.* 1. free on station. 2. free on steamer. Also, **f.o.s.**

fos′sil (fos′əl) *n.* petrified remains of animal or plant. **—fos′sil•i•za′tion,** *n.* **—fos′sil•ize′,** *v.*

fos′ter (fô′stər) *v.* 1. promote growth. **—***adj.* 2. reared in a family but not related.

F.O.T. *Commerce.* free on truck. Also, **f.o.t.**

foul (foul) *adj.* 1. filthy; dirty. 2. abominable. 3. unfair. **—***n.* 4. violation of rules in game. **—***v.* 5. make or become foul. 6. entangle. **—foul′ly,** *adv.*

foul′-up′, *n.* mix-up caused esp. by bungling.

found (found) *v.* establish.

foun•da′tion, *n.* 1. base for building, etc. 2. organization endowed for public benefit. 3. act of founding.

foun′der (foun′dər) *v.* 1. fill with water and sink. 2. go lame. **—***n.* 3. person who founds.

found′ling, *n.* abandoned child.

found′ry (foun′drē) *n., pl.* **-ries.** place where molten metal is cast.

foun′tain (foun′tn) *n.* 1. spring of water. 2. source. Also, **fount.**

foun′tain•head′, *n.* source.

foue for official use only.

four (fôr) *n., adj.* three plus one. **—fourth,** *n., adj.*

four′-flush′, *v.* bluff. **—four′flush′er,** *n.*

four′-score′, *adj.* eighty.

four′some (-səm) *n.* 1. set or group of four. 2. golf match between two pairs of players.

four′square′, *adj.* 1. firm; forthright. **—***adv.* 2. firmly; frankly.

four′teen′, *n., adj.* ten plus four. **—four′-teenth′,** *adj., n.*

4WD four-wheel drive.

fowl (foul) *n.* bird, esp. hen or rooster.

fox (foks) *n.* 1. carnivorous animal of dog family. 2. crafty person. **—***v.* 3. trick.

fox′glove′, *n.* tall plant with bell-shaped flowers.

fox′hole′, *n.* small pit used for cover in battle.

fox trot, dance for couples.

fox′y, *adj.,* **-ier, -iest.** 1. cunning. 2. *Slang.* attractive.

foy′er (foi′ər, foi′ā) *n.* lobby.

fp 1. faceplate. 2. *Music.* forte-piano. 3. *Football.* forward pass.

F.P. *Physics.* foot-pound; foot-pounds.

f.p. 1. fireplug. 2. foolscap. 3. foot-pound; foot-pounds. 4. *Music.* forte-piano. 5. freezing point. 6. fully paid.

FPC 1. Federal Power Commission. 2. fish protein concentrate.

FPHA Federal Public Housing Authority.

Fpl *Real Estate.* fireplace.

fpl fire plug.

fpm feet per minute. Also, **ft/min, ft./min.**

FPO 1. field post office. 2. fleet post office.

fprf fireproof.

fps 1. Also, **ft/sec** feet per second. 2. *Physics.* foot-pound-second.

f.p.s. 1. Also, **ft./sec.** feet per second. 2. *Physics.* foot-pound-second. 3. frames per second.

fpsps feet per second per second. Also, **ft/s²**

FPT freight pass-through.

fpt female pipe thread.

Fr., 1. Father. 2. French. 3. Friar. 4. Friday.

frac fractional.

fra′cas (frā′kəs, frak′əs) *n.* tumult.

frac′tion (frak′shən) *n.* part of whole. **—frac′tion•al,** *adj.*

frac′tious (frak′shəs) *adj.* unruly.

frac′ture (frak′chər) *n., v.,* **-tured, -turing.** break or crack.

frag fragment.

frag′ile (fraj′əl) *adj.* easily damaged. **—fra-gil′i•ty** (frə jil′i tē) *n.*

frag′ment, *n.* (frag′mənt) 1. broken part. 2. bit. **—***v.* (frag′ment, frag ment′) 3. break into fragments. **—frag′men•tar′•y,** *adj.* **—frag′men•ta′tion,** *n.*

fra′grance (frā′grəns) *n.* pleasant smell. **—fra′grant,** *adj.*

frail (frāl) *adj.* weak; fragile. **—frail′ty,** *n.*

frame (frām) *n., v.,* **framed, framing. —***n.* 1. enclosing border. 2. skeleton. **—***v.* 3. devise. 4. put in frame. **—frame′work′,** *n.*

frame′-up′, *n.* fraudulent incrimination.

franc (frangk) *n.* French coin.

fran′chise (fran′chīz) *n.* 1. right to vote. 2. right to do business.

frank (frangk) *adj.* 1. candid. **—***v.* 2. mail without charge. **—frank′ly,** *adv.* **—frank′-ness,** *n.*

frank′furt•er (frangk′fər tər) *n.* cooked sausage.

frank/in•cense/ (frang/kin sens/) n. aromatic resin.

fran/tic (fran/tik) adj. wildly excited. —fran/ti•cal•ly, adv.

F.R.A.S. Fellow of the Royal Astronomical Society.

fra•ter/nal (frə tûr/nl) adj. brotherly. —fra•ter/nal•ly, adv.

fra•ter/ni•ty, n., pl. -ties. male society.

frat/er•nize/ (frat/ər nīz/) v., -nized, -nizing. associate fraternally or intimately. —frat/er•ni•za/tion, n.

frat/ri•cide/ (fra/tri sīd/, frā/-) n. 1. act of killing one's brother. 2. person who kills his or her brother. —frat/ri•cid/al, adj.

fraud (frôd) n. trickery. —fraud/u•lent, adj. —fraud/u•lent•ly, adv.

fraught (frôt) adj. full; charged.

fray (frā) n. 1. brawl. —v. 2. ravel.

fraz/zle (fraz/əl) v., -zled, -zling, n. Informal. —v. 1. fray. 2. fatigue. —n. 3. state of fatigue.

FRB 1. Federal Reserve Bank. 2. Federal Reserve Board. Also, **F.R.B.**

frbd freeboard.

FRC Federal Radio Commission.

FRCD Finance. floating-rate certificate of deposit.

F.R.C.P. Fellow of the Royal College of Physicians.

F.R.C.S. Fellow of the Royal College of Surgeons.

freak (frēk) n. abnormal phenomenon, person, or animal. —freak/ish, freak/y, adj.

freck/le (frek/əl) n. small brownish spot on skin. —freck/led, adj.

free (frē) adj., freer, freest, adv., v., freed, freeing. —adj. 1. having personal rights or liberty. 2. independent. 3. open. 4. without charge. —adv. 5. without charge. —v. 6. make free. —free/dom, n. —free/ly, adv.

free/boot/er, n. pirate.

free/-for-all/, n. Informal. brawl; melee.

free/lance/ (-lans/) adj., n., v., -lanced, -lancing. adj. 1. hiring out one's work job by job. —n. 2. Also, **free/lanc/er.** freelance worker. —v. 3. work as freelance.

free/load/, v. Informal. take advantage of the generosity of others. —free/load/er, n.

Free/ma/son, n. member of secret fraternal association for mutual assistance and promotion of brotherly love. —Free/ma/son•ry, n.

free radical, molecule capable of multiplying rapidly and harming the immune system.

free/think/er, n. person with original religious opinions. —free/think/ing, adj., n.

free/way/, n. major highway.

freeze (frēz) v., froze (frōz), frozen, freezing, n. —v. 1. harden into ice. 2. fix (prices, etc.) at a specific level. 3. make unnegotiable. —n. 4. act of freezing. —freez/er, n.

freight (frāt) n. 1. conveyance of goods. 2. goods conveyed. 3. price paid.

freight/er, n. ship carrying mainly freight.

French (french) n. language or people of France. —French, adj. —French/man, n. —French/wom/an, n.fem.

French dressing, 1. salad dressing of oil and vinegar. 2. creamy orange salad dressing.

French fries, strips of potato that have been deep-fried.

French horn, coiled brass wind instrument.

fre•net/ic (frə net/ik) adj. frantic.

fren/zy (fren/zē) n., pl. -zies. wild excitement. —fren/zied, adj.

freq. 1. frequency. 2. frequent. 3. frequentative. 4. frequently.

freqm frequency meter.

frequ frequency.

fre/quen•cy (frē/kwən sē) n., pl. -cies. 1. state of being frequent. 2. rate of recurrence. 3. Physics. number of cycles in a unit of time.

fre/quent adj. (frē/kwənt) 1. occurring often. —v. (fri kwent/) 2. visit often.

fres fire-resistant.

fres/co (fres/kō) n., pl. -coes, -cos. painting on damp plaster.

fresh (fresh) adj. 1. new. 2. not salty, as water. 3. not preserved. 4. not spoiled. 5. Informal. impudent. —fresh/en, v. —fresh/ly, adv. —fresh/ness, n.

fresh/et (fresh/it) n. sudden flooding of a stream.

fresh/man, n., pl. -men. first-year student.

fresh/wa/ter, adj. of or living in water that is not salty.

fret (fret) n., v., fretted, fretting. —n. 1. vexation. 2. interlaced design. 3. metal or wood ridge across strings of an instrument, as a guitar. —v. 4. ornament with fret. 5. worry. —fret/ful, adj. —fret/work/, n.

Freud/i•an (froi/dē ən) adj. 1. of or relating to psychoanalytic theories of Sigmund Freud. —n. 2. person, esp. a psychoanalyst, who follows Freud's theories.

F.R.G. Federal Republic of Germany.

F.R.G.S. Fellow of the Royal Geographical Society.

Fri., Friday.

fri/a•ble (frī/ə bəl) adj. crumbly.

fri/ar (frī/ər) n. member of Roman Catholic monastic order. —fri/ar•y, n.

fric/as•see/ (frik/ə sē/) n. stewed meat or fowl.

frict friction.

fric/tion (frik/shən) n. 1. act or effect of rubbing together. 2. conflict. —fric/tion•al, adj.

Fri/day (frī/dā, -dē) n. sixth day of week.

friend (frend) n. 1. person attached to another by personal regard. 2. (cap.) Quaker; member of Society of Friends, a Christian sect. —friend/ly, adj. —friend/ship, n.

frieze (frēz) n. decorative, often carved band, as around a room.

F

frig′ate (frig′it) *n.* **1.** fast sailing warship. **2.** destroyerlike warship.

fright (frīt) *n.* **1.** sudden fear. **2.** shocking thing. —**fright′en,** *v.* —**fright′en•ing•ly,** *adv.*

fright′ful, *adj.* **1.** causing fright. **2.** *Informal.* ugly; tasteless.

fright′ful•ly, *adv. Informal.* very.

frig′id (frij′id) *adj.* **1.** very cold. **2.** coldly disapproving. **3.** lacking sexual appetite. —**fri•gid′i•ty, frig′id•ness,** *n.*

frill (fril) *n.* **1.** ruffle. **2.** unnecessary feature. —*v.* **3.** ruffle. —**frill′y,** *adj.*

fringe (frinj) *n.* border of lengths of thread, etc.

frip′per•y (frip′ə rē) *n., pl.* **-peries.** cheap finery.

Fris. Frisian. Also, **Fris**

frisk (frisk) *v.* **1.** frolic. **2.** search (person) for concealed weapon, drugs, etc. —**frisk′i•ness,** *n.* —**frisk′y,** *adj.*

frit′ter (frit′ər) *v.* **1.** squander little by little. —*n.* **2.** fried batter cake.

friv′o•lous (friv′ə ləs) *adj.* not serious or appropriate. —**fri•vol′i•ty** (fri vol′i tē) *n.*

frizz (friz) *n., v.,* curl. Also, **friz′zle.** —**friz′-zy,** *adj.*

Frl. Fräulein: the German form of address for an unmarried woman.

frm frame.

FRN *Finance.* floating-rate note.

frnc furnace.

frng fringe.

fro (frō) *adv.* from; back.

frock (frok) *n.* **1.** dress. **2.** loose robe.

frog (frog) *n.* **1.** small, tailless amphibian. **2.** hoarseness.

frol′ic (frol′ik) *n., v.,* **-icked, -icking.** —*n.* **1.** fun; gaiety. —*v.* **2.** play merrily. —**frol′ic•some,** *adj.*

from (frum, from; *unstressed* frəm) *prep.* **1.** out of. **2.** because of. **3.** starting at.

frond (frond) *n.* divided leaf.

front (frunt) *n.* **1.** foremost part. **2.** area of battle. **3.** appearance; pretense. **4.** false operation concealing illegal activity. —*adj.* **5.** of or at the front. —*v.* **6.** face. —**fron′tal,** *adj.*

front′age (frun′tij) *n.* front extent of property.

front burner, condition of top priority.

fron•tier′ (frun tēr′) *n.* **1.** border of a country. **2.** outer edge of civilization. —**fron•tiers′man,** *n.*

fron′tis•piece′ (frun′tis pēs′, fron′-) *n.* picture preceding title page.

front′-run′ner, *n.* person who leads in a competition.

frost (frôst) *n.* **1.** state of freezing. **2.** cover of ice particles. —*v.* **3.** cover with frost or frosting. —**frost′y,** *adj.*

frost′bite′, *n.* gangrenous condition caused by extreme cold. —**frost′-bit′ten,** *adj.*

frost′ing, *n.* **1.** sweet preparation for covering cakes. **2.** lusterless finish for glass, etc.

froth (frôth) *n., v.* foam. —**froth′y,** *adj.*

fro′ward (frō′wərd, frō′ərd) *adj.* perverse.

frown (froun) *v.* **1.** show concentration or displeasure on face. —*n.* **2.** frowning look.

frowz′y (frou′zē) *adj.* **-ier, -iest.** slovenly.

frpl *Real Estate.* fireplace.

FRS Federal Reserve System.

Frs. Frisian.

frs. francs.

F.R.S. Fellow of the Royal Society.

F.R.S.L. Fellow of the Royal Society of Literature.

F.R.S.S. Fellow of the Royal Statistical Society.

frt. **1.** freight. **2.** front.

fruc′ti•fy′ (fruk′tə fī′, frŏŏk′-) *v.,* **-fied, -fy-ing.** **1.** bear fruit. **2.** make productive. —**fruc′ti•fi•ca′tion,** *n.*

fruc′tose (-tōs) *n.* sweet sugar in honey and many fruits.

fru′gal (frŏŏ′gəl) *adj.* thrifty. —**fru•gal′i•ty** (-gal′i tē) *n.* —**fru′gal•ly,** *adv.*

fruit (frŏŏt) *n.* **1.** edible product of a plant. **2.** result.

fruit′ful, *adj.* productive; successful.

fru•i′tion (frŏŏ ish′ən) *n.* attainment.

fruit′less, *adj.* unsuccessful.

frump (frump) *n.* dowdy, unattractive woman. —**frump′y,** *adj.*

frus′trate′ (frus′trāt) *v.,* **-trated, -trating.** thwart. —**frus•tra′tion,** *n.*

frus′tum (frus′təm) *n.* segment of conical solid with parallel top and base.

frwk framework.

fry (frī) *v.,* **fried, frying,** *n., pl.* **fries,** (for 4) fry. —*v.* **1.** cook in fat over direct heat. —*n.* **2.** something fried. **3.** feast of fried things. **4.** young fish.

frz freeze.

frzr freezer.

FS Federal Specification.

fs **1.** field service. **2.** fire station. **3.** functional schematic.

f.s. foot-second; foot-seconds.

FSA Farm Security Administration

fsbl **1.** feasible. **2.** fusible.

fsc full scale.

FSH *Biochemistry.* follicle-stimulating hormone.

fsk frequency-shift keying.

FSLIC Federal Savings and Loan Insurance Corporation.

fsm field-strength meter.

FSN Federal Stock Number.

FSO foreign service officer.

FSR Field Service Regulations.

fssn fission.

fstnr fastener.

fsz full size.

ft., **1.** feet. **2.** foot. **3.** fort.

FTC, Federal Trade Commission.

ftd fitted.

ftg 1. fitting. **2.** footing.

fth. fathom; fathoms. Also, **fthm.**

ft./hr. feet per hour.

fthrd female thread.

ft-L *Optics.* foot-lambert.

ft-lb *Physics.* foot-pound.

ft./min. feet per minute.

FTP *Computers.* File Transfer Protocol.

ft-pdl *Physics.* foot-poundal.

ft./sec. feet per second.

FTZ free-trade zone.

fu fuse.

fuch′sia (fyoo′shə) *n.* **1.** plant with drooping flowers. **2.** bright purplish red color.

fudge (fuj) *n.* kind of candy.

fuel (fyoo′əl) *n., v.,* **fueled, fueling.** —*n.* **1.** substance that maintains fire. —*v.* **2.** supply with or take in fuel.

fu′gi•tive (fyoo′ji tiv) *n.* **1.** fleeing person. —*adj.* **2.** fleeing. **3.** impermanent.

fugue (fyoog) *n.* musical composition in which themes are performed by different voices in turn. —**fu′gal,** *adj.*

fuhld fuseholder.

-ful, suffix meaning: **1.** full of or characterized by, as *beautiful.* **2.** tending to or able to, as *harmful.* **3.** as much as will fill, as *spoonful.*

ful′crum (fool′krəm, ful′-) *n., pl.* **-crums, -cra.** support on which lever turns.

ful•fill′ (fool fil′) *v.* **1.** carry out. **2.** satisfy. —**ful•fill′ment, ful•fil′ment,** *n.*

full (fool) *adj.* **1.** filled. **2.** complete. **3.** abundant. —*adv.* **4.** completely. **5.** very. —**ful′ly,** *adv.* —**full′ness,** *n.*

full′back′, *n.* (in football) running back positioned behind the quarterback.

full′-bod′ied, *adj.* of full strength, flavor, or richness.

full′-fledged′, *adj.* fully developed.

full′-scale′, *adj.* **1.** of exact size as an original. **2.** all-out.

ful′mi•nate′ (ful′mə nāt′) *v.,* **-nated, -nating,** *n.* —*v.* **1.** explode loudly. **2.** issue denunciations. —*n.* **3.** explosive chemical salt. —**ful′mi•na′tion,** *n.*

ful′some (fool′səm, ful′-) *adj.* excessive.

fum′ble (fum′bəl) *v.,* **-bled, -bling,** *n.* —*v.* **1.** grope clumsily. **2.** drop. —*n.* **3.** act of fumbling.

fume (fyoom) *n., v.,* **fumed, fuming.** —*n.* **1.** vapor. —*v.* **2.** emit fumes. **3.** show anger.

fu′mi•gate′ (fyoo′mi gāt′) *v.,* **-gated, -gating.** disinfect with fumes. —**fu′mi•ga′tion,** *n.*

fun (fun) *n.* play; joking.

func′tion (fungk′shən) *n.* **1.** proper activity. **2.** formal social gathering. —*v.* **3.** act; operate. —**func′tion•al,** *adj.*

func′tion•ar′y (-shə ner′ē) *n., pl.* **-aries.** official.

fund (fund) *n.* **1.** stock of money. —*v.* **2.** pay for.

fun′da•men′tal (fun′də men′tl) *adj.* **1.** basic. —*n.* **2.** basic principle. —**fun′da•men′tal•ly,** *adv.*

fun′da•men′tal•ist, *n.* believer in literal interpretation of a religious text, as the Bible. —**fun′da•men′tal•ism,** *n.*

fu′ner•al (fyoo′nər əl) *n.* burial rite. —**fu′-ner•al,** *adj.*

fu•ne′re•al (-nēr′ē əl) *adj.* **1.** mournful. **2.** of funerals.

fun′gus (fung′gəs) *n., pl.* **fungi** (fun′jī). plant of group including mushrooms and molds. —**fun′gous,** *adj.*

funk (fungk) *n. Informal.* depression.

funk′y (fung′kē) *adj.,* **-ier, -iest. 1.** earthy, as blues-based jazz. **2.** *Slang.* offbeat.

funl funnel.

fun′nel (fun′l) *n., v.,* **-neled, -neling.** —*n.* **1.** cone-shaped tube. **2.** smokestack of vessel. —*v.* **3.** channel or focus.

fun′ny (fun′ē) *adj.,* **-nier, -niest. 1.** amusing. **2.** *Informal.* strange.

funny bone, part of elbow that tingles when the nerve is hit.

fur (fûr) *n., v.,* **furred, furring.** —*n.* **1.** thick hairy skin of animal. **2.** garment made of fur. —*v.* **3.** trim with fur. —**fur′ry,** *adj.*

fur′be•low′ (fûr′bə lō′) *n.* showy trimming.

fur′bish (fûr′bish) *v.* polish; renew.

fu′ri•ous (fyoor′ē əs) *adj.* **1.** full of fury. **2.** violent. —**fu′ri•ous•ly,** *adv.*

furl (fûrl) *v.* roll tightly.

fur′long (fûr′lông) *n.* $\frac{1}{8}$ of mile; 220 yards.

fur′lough (fûr′lō) *n.* **1.** leave of absence. **2.** temporary layoff from work. —*v.* **3.** give a furlough to.

furn 1. furnish. **2.** furniture.

fur′nace (fûr′nis) *n.* structure in which to generate heat.

fur′nish (fûr′nish) *v.* **1.** provide. **2.** fit out with furniture.

fur′nish•ing, *n.* **1.** article of furniture, etc. **2.** clothing accessory.

fur′ni•ture (-ni chər) *n.* tables, chairs, beds, etc.

fu′ror (fyoor′ôr, -ər) *n.* general excitement.

fur′ri•er (fûr′ē ər) *n.* dealer in furs.

fur′row (fûr′ō) *n.* **1.** trench made by plow. **2.** wrinkle. —*v.* **3.** make furrows in.

fur′ther (fûr′thər) *adv.* **1.** to a greater distance or extent. **2.** moreover. —*adj.* **3.** more. —*v.* **4.** promote. —**fur′ther•ance,** *n.* —**Usage.** See FARTHER.

fur′ther•more′, *adv.* in addition.

fur′ther•most′, *adj.* most distant.

fur′thest (-thist) *adj.* **1.** most distant or remote. —*adv.* **2.** to greatest distance.

fur′tive (-tiv) *adj.* stealthy. —**fur′tive•ly,** *adv.* —**fur′tive•ness,** *n.*

fu′ry (fyoor′ē) *n., pl.* **-ries. 1.** violent passion, esp. anger. **2.** violence.

furze (fûrz) *n.* low evergreen shrub.

fuse (fyooz) *n., v.,* **fused, fusing.** —*n.* **1.**

F

safety device that breaks an electrical connection under excessive current. **2.** Also, **fuze.** device for igniting explosive. —*v.* **3.** blend, esp. by melting together. —**fu′si•ble,** *adj.* —**fu′sion** (fyoo′zhən) *n.*

fu′se•lage′ (fyoo′sə läzh′, -lij) *n.* framework of an airplane.

fu′sil•lade′ (fyoo′sə lād′, -läd′) *n.* simultaneous gunfire.

fuslg fuselage.

fuss (fus) *n.* **1.** needless concern or activity. —*v.* **2.** make or put into fuss. —**fuss′y,** *adj.*

fus′tian (fus′chən) *n.* **1.** stout fabric of cotton and flax. **2.** turgid writing or speech.

fus′ty (fus′tē) *adj.,* **-tier, -tiest. 1.** moldy; musty. **2.** old fashioned; out-of-date.

fut. future.

fu′tile (fyoot′l, fyoo′tīl) *adj.* useless; unsuccessful. —**fu•til′i•ty** (-til′i tē) *n.*

fu′ton (foo′ton) *n.* thin, quiltlike mattress.

fu′ture (fyoo′chər) *n.* **1.** time to come. —*adj.* **2.** that is to come. —**fu′tur•is′tic,** *adj.* —**fu•tu′ri•ty,** *n.*

fuzz (fuz) *n.* fluff.

fuzz′y, *adj.,* **-ier, -iest. 1.** covered with fuzz. **2.** blurred. —**fuzz′i•ly,** *adv.* —**fuzz′i•ness,** *n.*

fv flux valve.

f.v. on the back of the page. [from Latin *foliō versō*]

FVC *Medicine.* forced vital capacity.

FWA Federal Works Agency.

FWD 1. Also, **4WD** four-wheel drive. **2.** front-wheel drive.

fwd. 1. foreword. **2.** forward.

F.W.I. French West Indies.

fwv full wave.

Fwy. freeway.

FX foreign exchange.

fx. 1. fracture. **2.** fractured.

fxd fixed.

fxtr fixture.

FY fiscal year.

FYI, for your information.

fz fuze.

G

G, g (jē) *n.* seventh letter of English alphabet.

G, motion picture rating: general; suitable for all ages.

g. 1. good. **2.** gram. **3.** gravity.

GA, 1. Gamblers Anonymous. **2.** general of the army. **3.** Georgia.

Ga., Georgia.

G.A.A. Gay Activists' Alliance.

gab (gab) *n., v.,* **gabbed, gabbing.** *Informal.* chatter. —**gab'by,** *adj.*

GABA (gab'ə), *Biochemistry.* a neurotransmitter of the central nervous system that inhibits excitatory responses. [g(amma-)a(mino)b(u-tyric) a(cid)]

gab'ar·dine' (gab'ər dēn') *n.* twill fabric.

gab'ble (gab'əl) *n., v.,* **-bled, -bling.** —*n.* **1.** rapid, unintelligible talk. —*v.* **2.** talk gabble.

ga'ble (gā'bəl) *n.* triangular wall from eaves to roof ridge.

G/A con. *Insurance.* general average contribution.

gad (gad) *v.,* **gadded, gadding.** wander restlessly.

gad'a·bout', *n.* person who flits from one social activity to another.

G/A dep. *Insurance.* general average deposit.

gad'fly', *n., pl.* **-flies.** annoyingly critical person.

gadg'et (gaj'it) *n. Informal.* any ingenious device. —**gad'get·ry,** *n.*

GAE General American English.

gaff (gaf) *n.* **1.** hook for landing fish. **2.** spar on the upper edge of fore-and-aft sail.

gaffe (gaf) *n.* social blunder.

gaf'fer, *n.* **1.** chief electrician on a film or TV show. **2.** *Informal.* old man.

gag (gag) *v.,* **gagged, gagging,** *n.* —*v.* **1.** stop up mouth to keep (person) silent. **2.** suppress statements of. **3.** retch. —*n.* **4.** something that gags. **5.** *Informal.* joke.

gage (gāj) *n., v.,* **gaged, gaging.** —*n.* **1.** token of challenge. **2.** pledge. **3.** gauge. —*v.* **4.** gauge.

gag'gle (gag'əl) *n.* flock of geese.

GAI guaranteed annual income.

gai'e·ty (gā'i tē) *n., pl.* **-ties.** merriment.

gai'ly (gā'lē) *adv.* merrily.

gain (gān) *v.* **1.** obtain. **2.** earn. **3.** improve. **4.** move faster than another. —*n.* **5.** profit. —**gain'ful,** *adj.* —**gain'ful·ly,** *adv.*

gain·say' (gān'sā', gān sā') *v.,* **-said, -saying.** contradict.

gait (gāt) *n.* manner of walking.

gai'ter, *n.* **1.** covering for lower leg, worn over the shoe. **2.** kind of shoe.

gal (gal) *n. Informal.* girl.

gal., gallon.

ga'la (gā'lə, gal'ə; *esp. Brit.* gä'lə) *adj.* **1.** festive. —*n.* **2.** festive occasion.

gal'ax·y (gal'ək sē) *n., pl.* **-axies. 1.** (*often cap.*) Milky Way. **2.** brilliant assemblage. —**ga·lac'tic** (gə lak'tik) *adj.*

gale (gāl) *n.* **1.** strong wind. **2.** noisy outburst, as of laughter.

gal/h *Symbol.* gallons per hour.

gall (gôl) *v.* **1.** chafe. **2.** irritate. —*n.* **3.** sore due to rubbing. **4.** bile. **5.** *Informal.* impudence. **6.** abnormal growth on plants.

gal'lant (gal'ənt; *for also* gə lant', -länt') *adj.* chivalrous. —**gal'lant·ly,** *adv.* —**gal'lant·ry,** *n.*

gall bladder, sac in which bile is stored.

gal'le·on (gal'ē ən, gal'yən) *n.* large sailing vessel.

gal'ler·y (gal'ə rē) *n.* **1.** corridor. **2.** balcony. **3.** place for art exhibits.

gal'ley (gal'ē) *n.* **1.** vessel propelled by many oars. **2.** kitchen of ship.

gal'li·vant' (gal'ə vant') *v.* wander about, seeking pleasure.

gal'lon (gal'ən) *n.* unit of capacity equal to 4 quarts.

gal'lop (gal'əp) *v.* **1.** run at full speed. —*n.* **2.** fast gait.

gal'lows (gal'ōz, -əz) *n.* wooden frame for execution by hanging.

gall'stone', *n.* stone formed in bile passages.

gal/min *Symbol.* gallons per minute.

ga·lore' (gə lôr') *adv.* in abundance.

ga·losh'es (gə losh'iz) *n.pl.* overshoes.

gals. gallons.

gal/s *Symbol.* gallons per second.

galv galvanic.

gal·van'ic (gal van'ik) *adj.* **1.** producing or caused by electric current. **2.** stimulating; exciting.

gal'va·nize' (-və nīz') *v.,* **-nized, -nizing. 1.** stimulate by or as by galvanic current. **2.** coat with zinc.

galvnm galvanometer.

galvs galvanized steel.

galy galley.

GAM 1. graduate in Aerospace Mechanical Engineering. **2.** ground-to-air missile.

gam'bit (gam'bit) *n.* **1.** sacrificial move in chess. **2.** clever tactic.

gam'ble (gam'bəl) *v.,* **-bled, -bling,** *n.* —*v.* **1.** play for stakes at game of chance. **2.** wager; risk. —*n.* **3.** *Informal.* uncertain venture. —**gam'bler,** *n.*

gam'bol (gam'bəl) *v.,* **-boled, -boling,** *n.* frolic.

game (gām) *n.* **1.** pastime or contest. **2.** wild

animals, hunted for sport. —*adj.* **3.** brave and willing. **4.** lame.

game plan, carefully planned strategy or course of action.

gam′ete (gam′ēt) *n.* mature sexual reproductive cell that unites with another to form a new organism.

gam′in (gam′in) *n.* street urchin. —**gam′ine** (-ēn), *n.fem.*

gam′ut (gam′ət) *n.* full range.

gam′y (gā′mē) *adj.,* **-ier, -iest. 1.** having the strong flavor of game, esp. slightly tainted game. **2.** showing pluck; game. **3.** risqué. —**gam′i•ness,** *n.*

G&AE *Accounting.* general and administrative expense.

gan′der (gan′dər) *n.* male goose.

G and T gin and tonic. Also, **g and t**

gang (gang) *n.* **1.** group; band. **2.** work crew. **3.** band of criminals.

gan′gling (gang′gling) *adj.* awkwardly tall and thin.

gan′gli•on (gang′glē ən) *n., pl.* **-glia, -glions.** nerve center.

gang′plank′ (gang′plangk′) *n.* temporary bridge to docked vessel.

gan′grene (gang′grēn, gang grēn′) *n.* death of body tissue. —**gan′gre•nous,** *adj.*

gang′ster, *n.* member of a criminal gang.

gang′way′ *n.* (gang′wā′) **1.** entrance to ship. **2.** narrow passage. —*interj.* (gang′wā′) **3.** (make way!)

gan′try (gan′trē) *n., pl.* **-tries. 1.** spanning framework for traveling crane. **2.** wheeled framework with scaffolds for erecting rocket.

GAO General Accounting Office.

gaol (jāl) *n., v. Brit.* jail.

gap (gap) *n.* **1.** opening; vacant space. **2.** ravine.

gape (gāp, gap) *v.,* **gaped, gaping. 1.** open mouth as in wonder. **2.** open wide.

GAPL Ground-to-Air Data Link.

gar (gär) *n.* long, slim fish.

ga•rage′ (gə räzh′, -räj′) *n.* place where motor vehicles are kept or repaired.

garb (gärb) *n.* **1.** clothes. —*v.* **2.** clothe.

gar′bage (gär′bij) *n.* refuse; trash.

gar•ban′zo (gär bän′zō) *n., pl.* **-zos.** chickpea.

gar′ble (gär′bəl) *v.,* **-bled, -bling.** misquote or mix up.

gar′den (gär′dn) *n.* **1.** area for growing plants. —*v.* **2.** make or tend garden. —**gar′den•er,** *n.*

gar•de′nia (gär dē′nyə, -nē ə) *n.* flowering evergreen shrub.

gar′den-vari′ety, *adj.* common; ordinary.

gar•gan′tu•an (gär gan′choo ən) *adj.* gigantic; colossal.

gar′gle (gär′gəl) *v.,* **-gled, -gling,** *n.* —*v.* **1.** rinse throat. —*n.* **2.** liquid for gargling.

gar′goyle (gär′goil) *n.* grotesquely carved figure.

gar′ish (gâr′ish, gar′-) *adj.* glaring; showy. —**gar′ish•ly,** *adv.* —**gar′ish•ness,** *n.*

gar′land (gär′lənd) *n.* **1.** wreath of flowers, etc. —*v.* **2.** deck with garland.

gar′lic (gär′lik) *n.* plant with edible, pungent bulb. —**gar′lick•y,** *adj.*

gar′ment (gär′mənt) *n.* article of dress.

gar′ner (gär′nər) *v.* gather; acquire.

gar′net (gär′nit) *n.* deep-red gem.

gar′nish (gär′nish) *v.* **1.** adorn. **2.** decorate (food). —*n.* **3.** decoration for food.

gar′nish•ee′ (gär′ni shē′) *v.,* **-nisheed, -nisheeing.** attach (money or property of defendant).

gar′ret (gar′it) *n.* attic.

gar′ri•son (gar′ə sən) *n.* **1.** body of defending troops. —*v.* **2.** provide with garrison.

gar•rote′ (gə rot′, -rōt′) *n., v.,* **-roted, -roting.** —*n.* **1.** strangulation. —*v.* **2.** strangle.

gar′ru•lous (gar′ə ləs, gar′yə-) *adj.* talkative. —**gar•ru′li•ty,** *n.*

gar′ter (gär′tər) *n.* fastening to hold up stocking.

garter snake, common, harmless striped snake.

gas (gas) *n., pl.* **gases,** *v.,* **gassed, gassing.** —*n.* **1.** fluid substance, often burned for light or heat. **2.** gasoline. —*v.* **3.** overcome with gas. —**gas′e•ous,** *adj.*

gash (gash) *n.* **1.** long deep cut. —*v.* **2.** make gash in.

gas′ket (gas′kit) *n.* ring or strip used as packing.

gas′o•hol′ (-hôl′) *n.* fuel mixture of gasoline and alcohol.

gas′o•line′ (gas′ə lēn′, gas′ə lēn′) *n.* inflammable liquid from petroleum, used esp. as motor fuel.

gasp (gasp) *n.* **1.** sudden short breath. —*v.* **2.** breathe in gasps.

gas′tric (gas′trik) *adj.* of stomachs.

gas•tri′tis (ga strī′tis) *n.* inflammation of the stomach.

gas′tro•nom′i•cal (gas′trə nom′i kəl) *adj.* of good eating. Also, **gas′tro•nom′ic.** —**gas• tron′o•my** (gə stron′ə mē) *n.*

GAT 1. *Military.* Ground Attack Tactics. **2.** Ground-to-Air Transmitter.

gate (gāt) *n.* movable hinged barrier.

gate′way′, *n.* passage or entrance.

gath′er (gath′ər) *v.* **1.** bring or come together. **2.** infer. **3.** harvest. —*n.* **4.** pucker. —**gath′er•ing,** *n.*

GATT (gat), General Agreement on Tariffs and Trade.

gauche (gōsh) *adj.* unsophisticated; socially clumsy.

gaud′y (gô′dē) *adj.,* **-ier, -iest.** vulgarly showy. —**gaud′i•ly,** *adv.* —**gaud′i•ness,** *n.*

gauge (gāj) *v.,* **gauged, gauging,** *n.* —*v.* **1.** estimate. **2.** measure. —*n.* **3.** standard of measure. **4.** distance between railroad rails.

gaunt (gônt) *adj.* haggard; bleak.

gaunt'let (gônt'lit, gänt'-) *n.* **1.** large-cuffed glove. **2.** Also, **gant'let** (gant'-). double row of persons beating offender passing between them.

gauze (gôz) *n.* transparent fabric. —**gauz'y**, *adj.*

gav'el (gav'əl) *n.* chairperson's mallet.

G.A.W. guaranteed annual wage.

gawk (gôk) *v.* stare stupidly.

gawk'y, *adj.*, **-ier, -iest.** clumsy. —**gawk'i• ness.** *n.*

gay (gā) *adj.*, **gayer, gayest,** *n.* —*adj.* **1.** joyous. **2.** bright. **3.** *Slang.* homosexual. —*n.* **4.** *Slang.* homosexual. —**gay'ly,** *adv.*

gaz. **1.** gazette. **2.** gazetteer.

gaze (gāz) *v.*, **gazed, gazing,** *n.* —*v.* **1.** look steadily. —*n.* **2.** steady look.

ga•ze'bo (gə zā'bō, -zē'-) *n., pl.* **-bos, -boes.** open structure, as a pavilion, on a site with a pleasant view.

ga•zelle' (gə zel') *n.* small antelope.

ga•zette' (gə zet') *n.* newspaper.

gaz'et•teer' (gaz'i tēr') *n.* geographical dictionary.

gaz•pa'cho (gäz pä'chō) *n.* Spanish chilled vegetable soup.

GB **1.** *Computers.* gigabyte: 1000 megabytes. **2.** *Finance.* Gold Bond. **3.** (on CB radio) goodbye. **4.** Great Britain.

Gb *Electricity.* gilbert.

G.B. Great Britain.

G.B.E. Knight Grand Cross of the British Empire or Dame Grand Cross of the British Empire.

GBF gay black female.

gbg garbage.

GBM gay black male.

GBO *Commerce.* goods in bad order.

GBS *Radiography.* Gall Bladder Series.

Gc **1.** gigacycle; gigacycles. **2.** gigacycles per second.

GCA Girls' Clubs of America.

g-cal gram calorie. Also, **g-cal.**

G.C.B. Grand Cross of the Bath.

GCC Gulf Cooperation Council.

G.C.D. **1.** *Math.* greatest common denominator. **2.** greatest common divisor. Also, **g.c.d.**

GCE *British.* General Certificate of Education.

G.C.F. *Math.* greatest common factor; greatest common divisor. Also, **g.c.f.**

GCG *Military.* Guidance Control Group.

G.C.M. *Math.* greatest common measure. Also, **g.c.m.**

GCPS gigacycles per second. Also, **Gc/s, Gc/sec**

GCR *Military.* ground-controlled radar.

G.C.T. Greenwich Civil Time.

GCU *Aerospace.* Ground Control Unit.

GD **1.** *Real Estate.* garbage disposal. **2.** General Delivery.

Gd *Symbol, Chemistry.* gadolinium.

gd. **1.** good. **2.** guard.

G.D. **1.** Grand Duchess. **2.** Grand Duke.

Gde. (in Haiti) gourde; gourdes.

GDI *Slang.* God Damned Independent.

gdlk grid leak.

Gdn guardian.

gdn garden.

gdnc guidance.

Gdns. gardens.

GDP gross domestic product.

GDR German Democratic Republic. Also, **G.D.R.**

gds. goods.

GE *Medicine.* gastroenterology.

Ge *Symbol, Chemistry.* germanium.

g.e. *Bookbinding.* gilt edges.

gear (gēr) *n.* **1.** toothed wheel that engages with another. **2.** equipment. —*v.* **3.** connect by gears. **4.** adjust.

gear'shift', *n.* gear-changing lever in automotive transmission system.

GEB Guiding Eyes for the Blind.

geb. born. [from German *geboren*]

geck'o (gek'ō) *n., pl.* **-os** or **-oes.** small tropical lizard.

GED, general equivalency diploma.

gee (jē) *interj.* (exclamation of surprise or disappointment.)

gee'zer (gē'zər) *n.* odd or eccentric man, esp. an older one.

GEF **1.** Gauss Error Function. **2.** *Military.* ground equipment failure.

Gei'ger counter (gī'gər) instrument for measuring radioactivity.

gei'sha (gā'shə, gē'-) *n.* Japanese woman trained to provide entertainment and companionship for men.

gel (jel) *n., v.,* **gelled, gel•ling.** —*n.* **1.** jellylike or gluelike substance. —*v.* **2.** become gel.

gel'a•tin (jel'ə tn) *n.* substance from animal skins, etc., used in jellies, glue, etc. —**ge• lat'i•nous** (jə lat'n əs) *adj.*

geld'ing (gel'ding) *n.* castrated male horse. —**geld,** *v.*

gel'id (jel'id) *adj.* icy.

gem (jem) *n.* precious stone.

Gen., General.

gen'darme (zhän'därm) *n.* French police officer.

gen'der (jen'dər) *n.* **1.** *Gram.* set of classes including all nouns, distinguished as masculine, feminine, neuter. **2.** character of being male or female; sex.

gene (jēn) *n.* biological unit that carries inherited traits.

ge•ne•al'o•gy (jē'nē ol'ə jē, -al'-, jen'ē-) *n., pl.* **-gies.** study or account of ancestry. —**ge'• ne•a•log'i•cal** (-ə loj'i kəl) *adj.* —**ge'ne•al'• o•gist,** *n.*

gen'er•al (jen'ər əl) *adj.* **1.** of or including all. **2.** usual. **3.** undetailed. —*n.* **4.** highest-ranking army officer. —**gen'er•al•ly,** *adv.*

G

gen•er•al•i•ty (-al′i tē) *n.*, *pl.* **-ties.** general statement offered as accepted truth.

gen•er•al•ize′, *v.*, **-ized, -izing.** make generalities. **—gen′er•al•i•za′tion,** *n.*

general practitioner, doctor whose practice is not limited to any specific branch of medicine.

gen′er•ate′ (jen′ə rāt′) *v.*, **-ated, -ating.** produce. **—gen′er•a•tive** (-ər ə tiv) *adj.*

gen•er•a′tion, *n.* **1.** all individuals born in one period. **2.** such period (about 30 years). **3.** production. **—gen′er•a′tion•al,** *adj.*

Generation X (eks) the generation born in the U.S. after 1965.

gen′er•a′tor, *n.* device for producing electricity, gas, etc.

ge•ner′ic (jə ner′ik) *adj.* **1.** of entire categories. **2.** (of merchandise) unbranded. **—ge•ner′i•cal•ly,** *adv.*

gen′er•ous (jen′ər əs) *adj.* **1.** giving freely. **2.** abundant. **—gen′er•os′i•ty** (-ə ros′i tē) *n.*

gen′e•sis (-ə sis) *n.* birth or origin.

ge•net′ics (jə net′iks) *n.* science of heredity. **—ge•net′ic,** *adj.* **—ge•net′i•cal•ly,** *adv.* **—ge•net′i•cist,** *n.*

gen., genl., general.

gen′ial (jēn′yəl, jē′nē əl) *adj.* openly friendly. **—ge′ni•al′i•ty** (-al′i tē) *n.* **—gen′ial•ly,** *adv.*

ge′nie (jē′nē) *n.* spirit, often appearing in human form.

genit. genitive.

gen•i•ta•li•a (jen′i tā′lē ə, -tāl′yə) *n.pl.* genitals.

gen′i•tals (-tlz) *n.pl.* sexual organs. **—gen′i•tal,** *adj.*

gen′i•tive (jen′i tiv) *n.* **1.** grammatical case usu. indicating possession, origin, or other close association. **—adj.** **2.** of or relating to this case.

gen′ius (jēn′yəs) *n.* **1.** exceptional natural ability. **2.** person having such ability.

genl general.

Genl. General.

Gen. Mtg. *Banking.* general mortgage.

gen′o•cide′ (jen′ə sīd′) *n.* planned extermination of national or racial group.

gen′re (zhän′rə) *n.* class or category of artistic work.

Gent. gentleman; gentlemen. Also, **gent.**

gen•teel′ (jen tēl′) *adj.* well-bred; refined. **—gen•til′i•ty** (-til′i tē) *n.*

gen′tian (jen′shən) *n.* plant with blue flowers.

gen′tile (jen′tīl) *adj.* (*sometimes cap.*) not Jewish or Mormon. **—gentile,** *n.*

gen′tle (jen′tl) *adj.*, **-tler, -tlest. 1.** mild; kindly. **2.** respectable. **3.** careful in handling things. **—gen′tle•ness,** *n.* **—gen′tly,** *adv.*

gen′tle•man, *n.*, *pl.* **-men. 1.** man of good breeding and manners. **2.** (used as polite term) any man.

gen′tri•fi•ca′tion (jen′trə fi kā′shən) *n.* replacement of existing population by others with more wealth or status. **—gen′tri•fy,** *v.*, **-fied, -fying.**

gen′try, *n.* wellborn people.

gen•u•flect′ (-yo͞o flekt′) *v.* kneel partway in reverence. **—gen′u•flec′tion,** *n.*

gen′u•ine (-yo͞o in *or, sometimes,* -īn′) *adj.* real. **—gen′u•ine•ly,** *adv.* **—gen′u•ine•ness,** *n.*

ge′nus (jē′nəs) *n.*, *pl.* **genera, genuses.** biological group including one or several species.

Gen X (jen′ eks′) Generation X. Also, **GenX.**

geo-, prefix meaning the earth or ground, as *geography.*

geod. 1. geodesy. **2.** geodetic.

ge′ode (jē′ōd) *n.* hollow nodular stone often lined with crystals.

ge′o•des′ic dome (jē′ə des′ik, -dē′sik) dome with framework of straight members that form grid.

geog. 1. geographer. **2.** geographic; geographical. **3.** geography.

ge•og′ra•phy (jē og′rə fē) *n.* study of earth's surface, climate, etc. **—ge•og′ra•pher,** *n.* **—ge′o•graph′i•cal** (-ə graf′i kəl) **ge′o•graph′ic,** *adj.*

geol. 1. geologic; geological. **2.** geologist. **3.** geology.

ge•ol′o•gy (jē ol′ə jē) *n.* science of earth's structure. **—ge′o•log′i•cal** (-ə loj′i kəl) *adj.* **—ge•ol′o•gist,** *n.*

geom. 1. geometric; geometrical. **2.** geometry.

ge′o•mag•net′ic (jē′ō mag net′ik) *adj.* of the earth's magnetism. **—ge′o•mag′net•ism** (-ni tiz′əm) *n.*

ge•om′e•try (jē om′i trē) *n.* branch of mathematics dealing with shapes. **—ge′o•met′ric** (-ə me′trik) **ge′o•met′ri•cal,** *adj.*

ge′o•phys′ics (jē′ō fiz′iks) *n.* science of the physics of the earth and its atmosphere. **—ge′o•phys′i•cal,** *adj.*

ge′o•pol′i•tics, *n.* study of politics in relation to geography. **—ge′o•po•lit′i•cal,** *adj.*

GEOS Geodetic Earth Orbiting Satellite.

ge′o•sta′tion•ar′y, *adj.* of an orbiting satellite remaining in same spot over the earth. Also, **ge′o•syn′chro•nous.**

ge′o•ther′mal, *adj.* of the earth's internal heat.

Ger. 1. German. **2.** Germany.

ger. 1. gerund. **2.** gerundive.

ge•ra′ni•um (ji rā′nē əm) *n.* small plant with showy flowers.

ger′bil (jûr′bəl) *n.* small burrowing rodent, popular as a pet.

ger′i•at′rics (jer′ē a′triks, jer′-) *n.* branch of medicine dealing with aged persons. **—ger′i•at′ric,** *adj.*

germ (jûrm) *n.* **1.** microscopic disease-producing organism. **2.** seed or origin.

Ger′man (jûr′mən) *n.* native or language of Germany. **—German,** *adj.*

ger•mane′ (jər mān′) *adj.* pertinent.

German measles, rubella.

German shepherd, large dog with thick, usually gray or black-and-tan coat.

ger′mi•cide′ (jûr′mə sīd′) *n.* agent that kills germs. —**ger′mi•cid′al,** *adj.*

ger′mi•nate′, *v.,* **-nated, -nating.** begin to grow. —**ger′mi•na′tion,** *n.*

ger′on•tol′o•gy (jer′ən tol′ə jē, jēr′-) *n.* study of aging and problems and care of old people. —**ger′on•tol′o•gist,** *n.*

ger′ry•man′der (jer′i man′dər) *v.* divide into voting districts so as to give one group or area an unequal advantage.

ger′und (jer′and) *n.* noun form of a verb.

Gestapo (gə stä′pō), the German secret police under Hitler. [from German *Ge(heime) Sta(ats)po(lizei)* secret state police]

ges•ta′tion (je stā′shən) *n.* period of being carried in womb.

ges•tic′u•late′ (je stik′yə lāt′) *v.,* **-lated, -lating.** make gestures. —**ges•tic′u•la′tion,** *n.*

ges′ture (jes′chər) *n., v.,* **-tured, -turing.** —*n.* **1.** expressive movement of body, head, etc. **2.** act demonstrating attitude or emotion. —*v.* **3.** make expressive movements.

get (get) *v.,* **got** (got), **got** or **gotten, getting. 1.** obtain. **2.** cause to be or do. **3.** be obliged to. **4.** arrive. **5.** become.

get′a•way, *n.* **1.** escape. **2.** start of race. **3.** place for relaxing, etc.

get′-up, *n. Informal.* costume; outfit.

GeV *Physics.* gigaelectron volt. Also, **Gev**

gew′gaw (gyōō′gô, gōō′-) *n.* gaudy ornament.

gey′ser (gī′zər, -sər) *n.* hot spring that emits jets of water.

GF gay female.

gfci ground-fault circuit interrupter.

GFE government-furnished equipment.

GFR German Federal Republic.

G.F.T.U. General Federation of Trade Unions.

GG 1. gamma globulin. **2.** great gross.

GGR great gross.

GH growth hormone.

GHA Greenwich hour angle.

ghast′ly (gast′lē) *adj.,* **-lier, -liest. 1.** frightful. **2.** deathly pale.

gher′kin (gûr′kin) *n.* **1.** small cucumber. **2.** small pickle.

ghet′to (get′ō) *n., pl.* **-tos, -toes. 1.** (formerly) Jewish part of city. **2.** city area in which mostly poor minorities live. —**ghet′-to•ize,** *v.,* **-ized, -izing.**

GHF gay Hispanic female.

GHM gay Hispanic male.

ghost (gōst) *n.* disembodied soul of dead person. —**ghost′ly,** *adj.*

ghost′writ′er, *n.* person who writes for another who is presumed to be the author. —**ghost′write′,** *v.*

ghoul (gōōl) *n.* **1.** spirit that preys on dead. **2.** person morbidly interested in misfortunes. —**ghoul′ish,** *adj.*

GHz *Physics.* gigahertz; gigahertzes.

G.I. (jē′ī′) *Informal.* enlisted soldier.

gi′ant (jī′ənt) *n.* **1.** being of superhuman size or strength. **2.** person of great accomplishments. —**gi′ant•ess,** *n.fem.*

Gib. Gibraltar.

gib′ber (jib′ər) *v.* speak unintelligibly. —**gib′ber•ish,** *n.*

gib′bet (jib′it) *n.* gallows with projecting arm.

gib′bon (gib′ən) *n.* small, long-armed ape.

gibe (jīb) *v.,* **gibed, gibing,** *n.* jeer.

gib′lets (jib′lits) *n.pl.* heart, liver, and gizzard of a fowl.

gid′dy (gid′ē) *adj.,* **-dier, -diest. 1.** frivolous. **2.** dizzy. —**gid′di•ly,** *adv.* —**gid′di•ness,** *n.*

gift (gift) *n.* **1.** present. **2.** act of giving. **3.** power of giving. **4.** talent.

gift′ed, *adj.* **1.** talented. **2.** highly intelligent.

gig (gig) *n.* **1.** carriage drawn by one horse. **2.** light boat. **3.** *Slang.* engagement, as of musician. **4.** *Slang.* job.

gi•gan′tic (jī gan′tik, ji-) *adj.* befitting a giant. —**gi•gan′ti•cal•ly,** *adv.*

gig′gle (gig′əl) *v.,* **-gled, -gling,** *n.* —*v.* **1.** laugh lightly in a silly way. —*n.* **2.** silly laugh.

GIGO (gī′gō) *n.* axiom that faulty data input to a computer will result in faulty output.

gig′o•lo′ (jig′ə lō′) *n., pl.* **-los. 1.** male professional escort. **2.** man supported by his female lover.

Gi′la monster (hē′lə) large, venomous lizard.

gild (gild) *v.,* **gilded** or **gilt, gilding.** coat with gold.

gill *n.* **1.** (gil) breathing organ on fish. **2.** (jil) unit of liquid measure, ¼ pint (4 fluid ounces).

GILMER guardian of impressive letters and master of excellent replies.

gilt (gilt) *n.* gold used for gilding.

gilt′-edged′, *adj.* of the highest quality. Also, **gilt′-edge′.**

gim′crack′ (jim′krak′) *n.* trifle.

gim′let (gim′lit) *n.* small tool for boring holes.

gim′mick (gim′ik) *n.* device or trick.

gimp′y (gim′pē) *adj.,* **gimpier, gimpiest.** *Slang.* limping or lame.

gin (jin) *n., v.,* **ginned, ginning.** —*n.* **1.** flavored alcoholic drink. **2.** machine for separating cotton from its seeds. **3.** trap. **4.** card game. —*v.* **5.** put (cotton) through gin.

gin′ger (jin′jər) *n.* **1.** plant with spicy root used in cookery. **2.** spirit; animation.

ginger ale, carbonated soft drink flavored with ginger.

gin′ger•bread′, *n.* **1.** cake flavored with ginger and molasses. **2.** elaborate or gaudy architectural ornamentation.

G

gin′ger·ly, *adj.* **1.** wary. —*adv.* **2.** warily.

gin′ger·snap′, *n.* crisp cookie flavored with ginger.

ging′ham (ging′əm) *n.* checked cotton fabric.

gin′gi·vi′tis (jin′jə vī′tis) *n.* inflammation of the gums.

gink′go (ging′kō, jing′-) *n., pl.* **-goes.** shade tree native to China, with fan-shaped leaves. Also, **ging′ko,** *pl.* **-koes.**

gin′seng (jin′seng) *n.* plant with a medicinal root.

gi·raffe′ (jə raf′) *n.* tall, long-necked animal of Africa.

gird (gûrd) *v.,* **girt** or **girded, girding. 1.** encircle with or as with belt. **2.** prepare.

gird′er, *n.* horizontal structural beam.

gir′dle, *n., v.,* **-dled, -dling.** —*n.* **1.** encircling band. **2.** light corset. —*v.* **3.** encircle.

girl (gûrl) *n.* female child. —**girl′hood′,** *n.* —**girl′ish,** *adj.*

girl′friend′, *n.* **1.** frequent or favorite female companion; sweetheart. **2.** female friend.

GIRLS (gûrlz), Generalized Information Retrieval and Listing System.

girl scout, *(sometimes caps.)* member of organization for girls (**Girl Scouts**).

girth (gûrth) *n.* **1.** distance around. —*v.* **2.** gird.

GI's (jē′īz′), **the GI's,** *Slang.* diarrhea. Also, **G.I.'s, G.Is** [probably for *GI shits*]

gis′mo (giz′mō) *n.* gadget. Also, **giz′mo.**

gist (jist) *n.* essential meaning.

give (giv) *v.,* **gave** (gāv), **given, giving,** *n.* —*v.* **1.** bestow. **2.** emit. **3.** present. **4.** yield. —*n.* **5.** elasticity.

give′a·way′, *n. Informal.* **1.** revealing act, remark, etc. **2.** TV show in which contestants compete for prizes.

giv′en, *adj.* **1.** stated; fixed. **2.** inclined; disposed. —*n.* **3.** established fact or condition.

giz′zard (giz′ərd) *n.* muscular stomach of birds.

GJ *Informal.* grapefruit juice.

GJF gay Jewish female.

GJM gay Jewish male.

Gk Greek. Also, **Gk.**

Gl *Symbol, Chemistry.* glucinum.

gl gold.

gl. 1. glass; glasses. **2.** gloss.

g/l grams per liter.

gla′cial (glā′shəl) *adj.* **1.** of glaciers or ice sheets. **2.** bitterly cold.

gla′cier, *n.* mass of ice moving slowly down slope.

glad (glad) *adj.,* **gladder, gladdest. 1.** pleased; happy. **2.** causing joy. —**glad′den,** *v.* —**glad′ness,** *n.*

glade (glād) *n.* open space in forest.

glad′i·a′tor (glad′ē ā′tər) *n.* Roman swordsman fighting for public entertainment.

glad′i·o′lus (-ō′ləs) *n., pl.* **-lus, -li** (-lī),

-luses. plant bearing tall spikes of flowers. Also, **glad′i·o′la.**

glad′ly, *adv.* **1.** with pleasure. **2.** willingly.

glam′or·ize′ (glam′ə rīz′) *v.,* **-ized, -izing.** make glamorous. —**glam′or·i·za′tion,** *n.*

glam′our (glam′ər) *n.* alluring charm. —**glam′or·ous,** *adj.* —**glam′or·ous·ly,** *adv.*

glance (glans) *v.,* **glanced, glancing,** *n.* —*v.* **1.** look briefly. **2.** strike obliquely. —*n.* **3.** brief look.

gland (gland) *n.* body organ that secretes some substance. —**glan′du·lar,** *adj.*

glan′ders, *n.* disease of horses.

glare (glâr) *n., v.,* **glared, glaring.** —*n.* **1.** strong light. **2.** fierce look. **3.** bright, smooth surface. —*v.* **4.** shine with strong light. **5.** stare fiercely.

glar′ing, *adj.* very obvious; conspicuous. —**glar′ing·ly,** *adv.*

glass (glas, gläs) *n.* **1.** hard, brittle, transparent substance. **2.** (*pl.*) eyeglasses. **3.** drinking vessel of glass. **4.** anything made of glass. —*adj.* **5.** of glass. —*v.* **6.** cover with glass. —**glass′ware′,** *n.*

glass ceiling, not generally acknowledged upper limit to professional advancement, esp. for women or minorities.

glass′y, *adj.,* **-ier, -iest. 1.** like glass, as in transparency. **2.** without expression; dull.

glau·co′ma (glô kō′mə, glou-) *n.* condition of elevated fluid pressure within the eyeball, causing increasing loss of vision.

glaze (glāz) *v.,* **glazed, glazing,** *n.* —*v.* **1.** furnish with glass. **2.** put glossy surface on. **3.** make (eyes) expressionless. —*n.* **4.** glossy coating.

gla′zier (glā′zhər) *n.* person who installs glass.

GLB gay, lesbian, bisexual.

glb *Math.* greatest lower bound.

Gld. guilder; guilders.

gleam (glēm) *n.* **1.** flash of light. —*v.* **2.** emit gleams.

glean (glēn) *v.* gather laboriously, as grain left by reapers. —**glean′ing,** *n.*

glee (glē) *n.* joy; mirth. —**glee′ful,** *adj.* —**glee′ful·ly,** *adj.*

glee club, singing club.

glen (glen) *n.* narrow valley.

GLF Gay Liberation Front.

glib (glib) *adj.* suspiciously fluent. —**glib′ly,** *adv.* —**glib′ness,** *n.*

glide (glīd) *v.,* **glided, gliding,** *n.* —*v.* **1.** move smoothly and gradually. —*n.* **2.** gliding movement.

glid′er, *n.* motorless aircraft.

glim′mer (glim′ər) *n.* **1.** faint unsteady light. —*v.* **2.** shine faintly. —**glim′mer·ing,** *n.*

glimpse (glimps) *n., v.,* **glimpsed, glimpsing.** —*n.* **1.** brief view. —*v.* **2.** catch glimpse of.

glint (glint) *n., v.* gleam.

glis′ten (glis′ən) *v., n.* sparkle.

goal

glitch (glich) *n. Informal.* malfunction; hitch.

glit'ter (glit'ər) *v.* **1.** reflect light with a brilliant sparkle. **2.** make a brilliant show. —*n.* **3.** sparkling light or luster. **4.** showy brilliance. **5.** small glittering ornaments. —**glit'ter•y,** *adj.*

glitz'y (glit'sē) *adj.,* **-ier, -iest.** *Informal,* tastelessly showy; flashy and pretentious.

Gln *Biochemistry.* glutamine.

GLO *Slang.* get the lead out.

gloam'ing (glō'ming) *n.* dusk.

gloat (glōt) *v.* gaze or speak with unconcealed triumph.

glob (glob) *n.* rounded lump or mass.

global warming (glō'bəl) increase in the average temperature of the earth's atmosphere, causing changes in climate.

globe (glōb) *n.* **1.** earth; world. **2.** sphere depicting the earth. **3.** any sphere. —**glob'al,** *adj.* —**glob'al•ly,** *adv.*

globe'trot'ter, *n.* one who travels regularly all over the world.

glob'ule (glob'yōōl) *n.* small sphere. —**glob'u•lar,** *adj.*

gloom (glōōm) *n.* **1.** low spirits. **2.** darkness.

gloom'y, *adj.,* **-ier, -iest. 1.** dejected; low-spirited. **2.** depressing. **3.** dark; dismal.

glo'ri•fy' (glôr'ə fī') *v.,* **-fied, -fying. 1.** extol. **2.** make glorious. —**glor'i•fi•ca'tion,** *n.*

glo'ry, *n., pl.* **-ries,** *v.,* **-ried, -rying.** —*n.* **1.** great praise or honor. **2.** magnificence. **3.** heaven. —*v.* **4.** exult. —**glor'i•ous,** *adj.* —**glor'i•ous•ly,** *adv.*

gloss (glos) *n.* **1.** external show. **2.** shine. **3.** explanation of text. —*v.* **4.** put gloss on. **5.** annotate. **6.** explain away. —**glos'sy,** *adj.*

glos'sa•ry (glos'ə rē) *n., pl.* **-ries.** list of key words with definitions.

glot'tis (glot'is) *n.* opening at upper part of larynx. —**glot'tal,** *adj.*

glove (gluv) *n., v.,* **gloved, gloving.** —*n.* **1.** hand covering with sheath for each finger. —*v.* **2.** cover with glove. —**gloved,** *adj.*

glow (glō) *n.* **1.** light emitted by substance. **2.** brightness or warmth. —*v.* **3.** shine.

glow'er (glou'ər) *v.* **1.** frown sullenly. —*n.* **2.** frown.

glow'worm' (glō'wûrm') *n.* kind of firefly.

GLP Gross Lawyer Product.

glpg glowplug.

glsry glossary.

Glu *Biochemistry.* glutamic acid.

glu'cose' (glōō'kōs) *n.* sugar found in fruits and animal tissues.

glue (glōō) *n., v.,* **glued, gluing.** —*n.* **1.** adhesive substance, esp. from gelatin. —*v.* **2.** fasten with glue. —**glue'like',** *adj.* —**glue'y,** *adj.*

glum (glum) *adj.,* **glummer, glummest.** gloomily sullen.

glut (glut) *v.,* **glutted, glutting,** *n.* —*v.* **1.** feed or fill to excess. —*n.* **2.** full supply. **3.** surfeit.

glu'ten (glōōt'n) *n.* substance left in flour after starch is removed.

glu'tin•ous, *adj.* gluelike.

glut'ton (glut'n) *n.* greedy person. —**glut'ton•ous,** *adj.* —**glut'ton•y,** *n.*

glv globe valve.

Gly *Biochemistry.* glycine.

glyc. (in prescriptions) glycerite. [from Latin *glyceritum*]

glyc'er•in (glis'ər in) *n.* thick liquid used as a sweetener, lotion, etc. Also, **glyc'er•ine.**

glyc'er•ol (-ə rôl') *n.* glycerin.

glycn glycerine.

gly'co•gen (glī'kə jən, -jen') *n.* carbohydrate in animal tissues, changed into glucose when needed.

glz glaze.

GM 1. gay male. **2.** General Manager. **3.** General Medicine. **4.** Greenwich Meridian.

gm. 1. gram; grams. **2.** guided missile.

G.M. 1. General Manager. **2.** Grand Marshal. **3.** Grand Master. Also, **GM**

G.M.&S. general, medical, and surgical.

GMAT 1. *Trademark.* Graduate Management Admissions Test. **2.** Greenwich Mean Astronomical Time.

GMB *British.* Grand Master of the Bath.

gmbl gimbal.

Gmc Germanic. Also, **Gmc.**

GMP *Biochemistry.* a ribonucleotide constituent of ribonucleic acid. [*g(uanosine) m(ono)p(hosphate)*]

GMT Greenwich Mean Time. Also, **G.M.T.**

gmtry geometry.

gmv guaranteed minimum value.

GMW gram-molecular weight.

gn green.

G.N. Graduate Nurse.

gnarl (närl) *n.* knot on a tree.

gnarled (närld) *adj.* bent and distorted.

gnash (nash) *v.* grind (the teeth) together, as in rage.

gnat (nat) *n.* small fly.

gnaw (nô) *v.* **1.** wear away by biting. **2.** distress. —**gnaw'ing,** *adj.*

gnd *Electricity.* ground.

GNI *Economics.* Gross National Income.

gnltd granulated.

GNMA Government National Mortgage Association.

gnome (nōm) *n.* dwarf in superstition.

GNP, gross national product.

GnRH gonadotropin releasing hormone.

gnu (nōō, nyōō) *n., pl.* **gnus, gnu.** African antelope.

go (gō) *v.,* **went** (went), **gone** (gôn), **going. 1.** move; depart. **2.** act. **3.** become. **4.** harmonize.

goad (gōd) *n.* **1.** pointed stick. **2.** stimulus. —*v.* **3.** drive with goad. **4.** tease; taunt.

goal (gōl) *n.* **1.** aim. **2.** terminal or target in

G

race or game. **3.** single score in various games.

goal/keep/er, *n.* in sports, player whose chief duty is to prevent opposition from scoring a goal. Also, **goal/tend/er;** *Informal,* **goal/ie.**

goat (gōt) *n.* horned mammal related to sheep.

goat·ee/ (gō tē/) *n.* pointed beard.

goat/herd/, *n.* person who tends goats.

gob (gob) *n.* **1.** mass. **2.** *Slang.* sailor.

gob/ble (gob/əl) *v.,* **-bled, -bling,** *n.* **—v. 1.** eat greedily. **2.** make cry of male turkey. **—n. 3.** this cry.

gob/ble·de·gook/ (-dē gōok/) *n.* meaningless or roundabout speech or writing.

gob/bler, *n.* male turkey.

go/-be·tween/, *n.* intermediary.

gob/let (gob/lit) *n.* stemmed glass.

gob/lin (gob/lin) *n.* elf.

God (god) *n.* **1.** Supreme Being. **2.** (*l.c.*) deity. **—god/dess,** *n.fem.* **—god/like/,** *adj.*

god/ly, *adj.,* **-lier, -liest. 1.** of God or gods. **2.** conforming to religion. **—god/li·ness,** *n.*

god/par/ent, *n.* sponsor of child at baptism. **—god/child/,** *n.* **—god/daugh/ter,** *n.* **—god/fath/er,** *n.* **—god/moth/er,** *n.* **—god/son/,** *n.*

god/send/, *n.* anything unexpected but welcome.

goes (gōz) third pers. sing. pres. indic. of **go.**

go/fer (gō/fər) *n. Slang.* employee who mainly runs errands.

gog/gle (gog/əl) *n., v.,* **-gled, -gling. —n. 1.** (*pl.*) protective eyeglasses. **—v. 2.** stare wtih wide-open eyes.

goi/ter (goi/tər) *n.* enlargement of thyroid gland, causing swelling on neck.

G.O.K. *Medicine.* God Only Knows.

gold (gōld) *n.* **1.** precious yellow metal. **2.** bright yellow. **—gold, gold/en,** *adj.*

gold/brick/, *Slang.* **—n. 1.** Also, **gold/brick/-er.** person who loafs on the job. **—v. 2.** shirk work.

gold/en·rod/, *n.* plant bearing clusters of yellow flowers.

gold/finch/, *n.* yellow-feathered American finch.

gold/fish/, *n.* small, gold-colored fish.

golf (golf) *n.* game played on outdoor course with special clubs and small ball. **—golf/er,** *n.*

go/nad (gō/nad, gon/ad) *n.* ovary or testis. **—go·nad/al,** *adj.*

gon/do·la (gon/dl ə *or, esp. for 1,* gon dō/lə) *n.* **1.** narrow canal boat used in Venice. **2.** low-sided freight car. **—gon/do·lier/** (-lēr/) *n.*

gon/er (gô/nər) *n. Informal.* person or thing that is dying, lost, or past recovery.

gong (gông) *n.* brass or bronze disk sounded with soft hammer.

gon/or·rhe/a (gon/ə rē/ə) *n.* contagious venereal disease.

goo (gōō) *n., pl.* **goos. 1.** thick or sticky substance. **2.** sentimentality. **—goo/ey,** *adj.*

goo/ber (gōō/bər) *n.* peanut.

good (gōōd) *adj.* **1.** morally excellent. **2.** of high or adequate quality. **3.** kind. **4.** skillful. **—n. 5.** benefit. **6.** excellence. **7.** (*pl.*) possessions. **8.** (*pl.*) cloth. **—good/ness,** *n.*

good/-by/, *interj., n., pl.* **-bys.** farewell. Also, **good/-bye/.**

Good Friday, Friday before Easter.

good/ly, *adj.,* **-lier, -liest.** numerous; abundant.

good Sa·mar/i·tan (sə mar/i tn) person who helps those in need.

good/will/, *n.* friendly feelings or intentions.

good/y (gōōd/ē) *n., pl.* **-ies.** food pleasing to eat, as candy.

goof (gōōf) *Informal,* **—n. 1.** fool. **2.** blunder. **—v. 3.** blunder. **—goof/y,** *adj.*

goon (gōōn) *n. Slang.* **1.** hoodlum hired to threaten or commit violence. **2.** stupid, foolish, or awkward person.

goose (gōōs) *n., pl.* **geese.** web-footed water bird.

goose/ber/ry (gōōs/-) *n., pl.* **-ries.** tart, edible acid fruit.

goose flesh, bristling of hair on the skin, as from cold or fear. Also, **goose pimples, goose bumps.**

G.O.P., Grand Old Party (epithet of the Republican Party).

go/pher (gō/fər) *n.* burrowing rodent.

gore (gôr) *n., v.,* **gored, goring. —n. 1.** clotted blood. **2.** triangular insert of cloth. **—v. 3.** pierce with horn or tusk. **4.** finish with gores (def. 2). **—gor/y,** *adj.*

gorge (gôrj) *n., v.,* **gorged, gorging. —n. 1.** narrow rocky cleft. **—v. 2.** stuff with food.

gor/geous (gôr/jəs) *adj.* **1.** splendid. **2.** very beautiful. **—gor/geous·ly,** *adv.*

go·ril/la (gə ril/ə) *n.* large African ape.

gos/ling (goz/ling) *n.* young goose.

gos/pel (gos/pəl) *n.* **1.** teachings of Christ and apostles. **2.** absolute truth.

gos/sa·mer (gos/ə mər) *n.* **1.** filmy cobweb. **—adj. 2.** like gossamer.

gos/sip (gos/əp) *n., v.,* **-siped, -siping. —n. 1.** idle talk, esp. about others. **2.** person given to gossip. **—v. 3.** talk idly about others. **—gos/sip·y,** *adj.*

Goth. Gothic. Also, **Goth, goth.**

Goth/ic (goth/ik) *adj.* **1.** of a style of European architecture from the 12th to 16th centuries. **2.** (*often l.c.*) of a style of literature marked by gloomy settings and sinister events.

Gou/da (gou/də, gōō/-) *n.* mild, yellowish Dutch cheese.

gouge (gouj) *n., v.,* **gouged, gouging. —n. 1.** chisel with hollow blade. **—v. 2.** dig out with gouge. **3.** extract by coercion. **—goug/-er,** *n.*

gou'lash (gōō'läsh, -lash) *n.* seasoned stew.

gourd (gôrd, gŏŏrd) *n.* dried shell of kind of cucumber.

gour•mand' (gŏŏr mänd', gŏŏr'mənd) *n.* enthusiastic or greedy eater.

gour'met (gŏŏr mā', gŏŏr'mā) *n.* lover of fine food.

gout (gout) *n.* painful disease of joints. —**gout'y,** *adj.*

gov., 1. government. **2.** governor.

gov'ern (guv'ərn) *v.* **1.** rule. **2.** influence. **3.** regulate.

gov'ern•ess, *n.* woman who teaches children in their home.

gov'ern•ment (-ərn mənt, -ər mənt) *n.* **1.** system of rule. **2.** political governing body. —**gov'ern•men'tal,** *adj.*

gov'er•nor (-ər nər, -ə nər) *n.* **1.** person who governs, esp. head of a state in the U.S. **2.** device that controls speed.

govt., government.

gown (goun) *n.* **1.** woman's dress. **2.** loose robe.

G.P., General Practitioner.

GPA grade point average.

gpad gallons per acre per day.

gpcd gallons per capita per day.

gpd gallons per day.

gph 1. gallons per hour. **2.** graphite.

gpi ground-position indicator.

gpib *Computers.* general-purpose interface bus.

gpm 1. gallons per mile. **2.** gallons per minute.

G.P.O. 1. general post office. **2.** Government Printing Office. Also, **GPO**

GPRF gay Puerto Rican female.

GPRM gay Puerto Rican male.

GPS *Aerospace, Navigation.* Global Positioning System.

gps gallons per second.

GPU General Postal Union; Universal Postal Union.

GPU (gä'pä'ōō', jē'pē'yōō'), (in the Soviet Union) the secret-police organization (1922–23) functioning under the NKVD. Also, **G.P.U.** [from Russian *G(osudárstvennoe) p(olitícheskoe) u(pravlénie) state political directorate]*

GQ General Quarters.

gr 1. gear. **2.** grain. **3.** gram; grams. **4.** gross.

Gr. 1. Grecian. **2.** Greece. **3.** Greek.

gr. 1. grade. **2.** grain; grains. **3.** gram; grams. **4.** grammar. **5.** gravity. **6.** great. **7.** gross. **8.** group.

G.R. King George. [from Latin *Geōrgius Rēx*]

grab (grab) *v.,* **grabbed, grabbing,** *n.* —*v.* **1.** seize eagerly. —*n.* **2.** act of grabbing.

grace (grās) *n., v.,* **graced, gracing.** —*n.* **1.** beauty of form, movement, etc. **2.** goodwill. **3.** God's love. **4.** prayer said at table. —*v.* **5.** lend grace to; favor. —**grace'ful,** *adj.*

—**grace'ful•ly,** *adv.* —**grace'less,** *adj.* —**grace'less•ly,** *adv.*

gra'cious (grā'shəs) *adj.* kind. —**gra'cious•ly,** *adv.* —**gra'cious•ness,** *n.*

grack'le (grak'əl) *n.* blackbird with iridescent black plumage.

grad. 1. *Math.* gradient. **2.** graduate. **3.** graduated.

gra•da'tion (grā dā'shən) *n.* change in series of stages.

grade (grād) *n., v.,* **graded, grading.** —*n.* **1.** degree in a scale. **2.** scholastic division. **3.** Also, **gra'di•ent.** slope. —*v.* **4.** arrange in grades. **5.** level.

grade crossing, intersection of a railroad track and another track, a road, etc.

grade school, elementary school.

grad'u•al (graj'ōō əl) *adj.* changing, moving, etc., by degrees. —**grad'u•al•ly,** *adv.*

grad'u•ate, *n.* (-it) **1.** recipient of diploma. —*adj.* (-it) **2.** graduated. **3.** of or in academic study beyond the baccalaureate level. —*v.* (-āt') **4.** receive or confer diploma or degree. **5.** mark in measuring degrees. —**grad'u•a'tion,** *n.*

graf•fi'ti (grə fē'tē) *n.pl., sing.* -**to** (-tō) markings written on public surfaces.

graft (graft) *n.* **1.** twig, etc., inserted in another plant to unite with it. **2.** profit through dishonest use of one's position. —*v.* **3.** make graft. **4.** make dishonest profits. —**graft'er,** *n.*

gra'ham (grā'əm, gram) *adj.* made of unsifted whole-wheat flour.

Grail (grāl) *n.* in medieval legend, the cup or chalice used at the last supper of Christ with the apostles.

grain (grān) *n.* **1.** seed of cereal plant. **2.** particle. **3.** pattern of wood fibers. —**grain'y,** *adj.*

gram (gram) *n.* metric unit of weight.

-gram, suffix meaning something written or drawn, as *diagram.*

gram'mar (gram'ər) *n.* **1.** features of a language as a whole. **2.** knowledge or usage of the preferred forms in speaking or writing. —**gram•mar'i•an** (grə mar'ē ən) *n.* —**grammat'i•cal** (-mat'i kəl) *adj.*

gran 1. granite. **2.** granular; granulated.

gran'a•ry (grā'nə rē, gran'ə-) *n., pl.* -**ries.** storehouse for grain.

grand (grand) *adj.* **1.** large; major. **2.** impressive. —*n.* **3.** grand piano. **4.** *Informal.* a thousand dollars. —**grand'ly,** *adv.* —**grand'ness,** *n.*

grand'child' (gran'chīld') *n.* child of one's son or daughter. —**grand'son',** *n.* —**grand'daugh'ter,** *n.fem.*

gran•dee' (gran dē') *n.* nobleman.

gran'deur (gran'jər, -jŏŏr) *n.* imposing greatness.

gran•dil'o•quence (gran dil'ə kwəns) *n.* lofty, often pompous speech. —**gran•dil'o•quent,** *adj.*

G

gran′di•ose′ (gran′dē ōs′) *adj.* grand or pompous.

grand jury, jury designated to determine if a law has been violated and whether the evidence warrants prosecution.

grand′par′ent, *n.* parent of parent. —**grand′fa′ther,** *n.* —**grand′moth′er,** *n. fem.*

grand piano, large piano with a horizontal case on three legs.

grand slam, home run with three runners on base.

grand′stand′ (gran′-, grand′-) *n.* **1.** sloped open-air place for spectators. —*v.* **2.** conduct oneself or perform to impress onlookers.

grange (grānj) *n.* farmers′ organization.

gran′ite (gran′it) *n.* granular rock.

gra•no′la (grə nō′lə) *n.* cereal of dried fruit, grains, nuts, etc.

grant (grant) *v.* **1.** bestow. **2.** admit. —*n.* **3.** thing granted.

gran•tee′ (gran tē′) *n.* grant receiver.

grants′man•ship′, *n.* skill in securing grants, as for research.

gran′u•late′ (gran′yə lāt′) *v.,* -lated, -lating. form into granules. —**gran′u•la′tion,** *n.*

gran′ule (-yōōl) *n.* small grain. —**gran′u•lar,** *adj.*

grape (grāp) *n.* smooth-skinned fruit that grows in clusters.

grape′fruit′, *n.* large yellow citrus fruit.

grape′vine′, *n.* **1.** vine on which grapes grow. **2.** person-to-person route by which gossip or information spreads.

graph (graf) *n.* diagram showing relations by lines, etc.

-graph, suffix meaning: **1.** something written or drawn, as *autograph.* **2.** instrument that writes or records, as *seismograph.*

graph′ic, *adj.* **1.** vivid. **2.** of writing, painting, etc. —**graph′i•cal•ly,** *adv.*

graph′ite (-īt) *n.* soft, dark mineral.

graph•ol′o•gy (gra fol′ə jē) *n.* study of handwriting. —**graph•ol′o•gist,** *n.*

-graphy, suffix meaning: **1.** process or form of writing, printing, recording, or describing, as *biography.* **2.** art or science concerned with these, as *geography.*

grap′nel (grap′nl) *n.* hooked device for grasping.

grap′ple (grap′əl) *n., v.,* -pled, -pling. —*n.* **1.** hook for grasping. —*v.* **2.** try to grasp. **3.** try to cope.

GRAS (gras), generally recognized as safe: a status label assigned by the FDA to a listing of substances not known to be hazardous and thus approved for use in foods.

grasp (grasp) *v.* **1.** seize and hold. **2.** understand. —*n.* **3.** act of gripping. **4.** mastery.

grasp′ing, *adj.* greedy.

grass (gras) *n.* **1.** ground-covering herbage. **2.** cereal plant. —**grass′y,** *adj.*

grass′hop′per, *n.* leaping insect.

grass′land′, *n.* open grass-covered land; prairie.

grass roots, ordinary citizens, as contrasted with leadership or elite. —**grass′-roots′,** *adj.*

grass widow, woman who is separated or divorced.

grate (grāt) *v.,* grated, grating, *n.* —*v.* **1.** irritate. **2.** make harsh sound. **3.** rub into small bits. —*n.* **4.** Also, **grat′ing.** metal framework. —**grat′er,** *n.*

grate′ful, *adj.* **1.** thankful. **2.** welcome as news. —**grate′ful•ly,** *adv.*

grat′i•fy′ (grat′ə fī′) *v.,* -fied, -fying. please. —**grat′i•fi•ca′tion,** *n.*

gra′tis (grat′is, grā′tis) *adv., adj.* free of charge.

grat′i•tude′ (grat′i tōōd′, -tyōōd′) *n.* thankfulness.

gra•tu′i•tous (grə tōō′i təs, -tyōō′-) *adj.* **1.** free of charge. **2.** without reasonable cause.

gra•tu′i•ty, *n., pl.* -ties. tip.

grave (grāv) *n., adj.* graver, gravest. —*n.* **1.** place of or excavation for burial. —*adj.* **2.** solemn. **3.** important. —**grave′yard′,** *n.*

grav′el (grav′əl) *n.* small stones.

grav′el•ly, *adj.* **1.** made up of or like gravel. **2.** harsh-sounding; raspy.

graveyard shift, work shift usu. beginning about midnight.

grav•i•ta′tion (grav′i tā′shən) *n.* force of attraction between bodies. —**grav′i•tate′,** *v.,* -tated, -tating.

grav′i•ty, *n., pl.* -ties. **1.** force attracting bodies to the earth′s center. **2.** seriousness.

gra′vy (grā′vē) *n., pl.* -vies. juices from cooking meat.

gray (grā) *n.* **1.** color between black and white. —*adj.* **2.** of this color. **3.** ambiguous. **4.** vaguely depressing. —**gray′ish,** *adj.* —**gray′ness,** *n.*

gray′beard′, *n.* old man.

gray matter, 1. nerve tissue of brain and spinal cord. **2.** *Informal.* brains; intelligence.

graze (grāz) *v.,* grazed, grazing. **1.** feed on grass. **2.** brush in passing.

Gr. Br. Great Britain. Also, **Gr. Brit.**

grbx gearbox.

grd 1. grind. **2.** guard.

grdl griddle.

grdtn graduation.

GRE Graduate Record Examination.

grease *n., v.,* greased, greasing. —*n.* (grēs) **1.** animal fat. **2.** fatty or oily matter. —*v.* (grēs, grēz) **3.** put grease on or in. —**greas′y,** *adj.*

great (grāt) *adj.* **1.** very large. **2.** important. —**great′ly,** *adv.* —**great′ness,** *n.*

Great Dane, kind of very large dog.

grebe (grēb) *n.* diving bird.

greed (grēd) *n.* excessive desire. —**greed′i•ly,** *adv.* —**greed′y,** *adj.*

Greek (grēk) *n.* native or language of Greece. —**Greek,** *adj.*

green (grēn) *adj.* **1.** of color of vegetation. **2.** unripe. **3.** inexperienced. —*n.* **4.** green color. **5.** grassy land. —**green′ish,** *adj.* —**green′ness,** *n.*

green′back′, *n.* U.S. legal-tender note.

green′belt′, *n.* area of woods, parks, or open land surrounding a community.

green′er•y, *n., pl.* **-eries.** plants; foliage.

green′-eyed′, *adj.* jealous or envious.

green′gro′cer, *n.* retailer of fresh fruit and vegetables.

green′horn′, *n.* **1.** novice. **2.** naive or gullible person.

green′house′, *n.* building where plants are grown.

greenhouse effect, heating of atmosphere resulting from absorption by certain gases of solar radiation.

green′room′, *n.* lounge in theater for use by performers.

green thumb, exceptional skill for growing plants.

greet (grēt) *n.* **1.** address in meeting. **2.** react to; receive. —**greet′ing,** *n.*

gre•gar′i•ous (gri gâr′ē əs) *adj.* fond of company.

grem′lin (grem′lin) *n.* mischievous elf.

gre•nade′ (gri nād′) *n.* hurled explosive.

gren′a•dier′ (gren′ə dēr′) *n. Brit.* member of special infantry regiment.

grey (grā) *n., adj.* gray.

grey′hound′, *n.* slender fleet-footed dog.

GRF growth hormone releasing factor.

GRI Government Reports Index.

grid (grid) *n.* **1.** covering of crossed bars. **2.** system of crossed lines.

grid′dle (grid′l) *n.* shallow frying pan.

grid′i′ron, *n.* **1.** grill. **2.** football field.

grid′lock′, *n.* **1.** complete stoppage of movement in all directions due to traffic. **2.** stoppage of a process, as legislation.

grief (grēf) *n.* keen sorrow.

griev′ance (grē′vəns) *n.* **1.** wrong. **2.** complaint against wrong.

grieve (grēv) *v.,* **grieved, grieving.** feel sorrow; inflict sorrow on.

griev′ous, *adj.* causing grief, pain, etc. —**grie′vous•ly,** *adv.*

grif′fin (grif′in) *n.* monster of fable with head and wings of eagle and body of lion. Also, **gryph′on.**

grill (gril) *n.* **1.** barred utensil for broiling. —*v.* **2.** broil on grill. **3.** question persistently.

grille (gril) *n.* ornamental metal barrier.

grim (grim) *adj.,* **grimmer, grimmest. 1.** stern. **2.** harshly threatening. —**grim′ly,** *adv.* —**grim′ness,** *n.*

gri•mace′ (grim′əs, gri mās′) *n., v.,* **-maced, -macing.** smirk.

grime (grīm) *n.* dirt. —**grim′y,** *adj.*

grin (grin) *v.,* **grinned, grinning,** *n.* —*v.* **1.** smile openly and broadly. —*n.* **2.** broad smile.

grind (grīnd) *v.,* **ground** (ground), **grinding,** *n.* —*v.* **1.** wear, crush, or sharpen by friction. **2.** operate by turning crank. —*n.* **3.** *Informal.* dreary routine. —**grind′stone,** *n.*

grip (grip) *n., v.,* **gripped, gripping.** —*n.* **1.** grasp. **2.** handclasp. **3.** small suitcase. **4.** handle. —*v.* **5.** grasp. —**grip′per,** *n.*

gripe (grīp) *v.,* **griped, griping,** *n.* —*v.* **1.** grasp. **2.** produce pain in bowels. **3.** *Informal.* complain. —*n.* **4.** *Informal.* complaint. —**grip′er,** *n.*

grippe (grip) *n.* influenza.

gris′ly (griz′lē) *adj.,* **-lier, -liest.** gruesome.

grist (grist) *n.* grain to be ground. —**grist′-mill′,** *n.*

gris′tle (gris′əl) *n.* cartilage. —**gris′tly,** *adj.*

grit (grit) *n., v.,* **gritted, gritting.** —*n.* **1.** fine particles. **2.** courage. —*v.* **3.** cause to grind together. —**grit′ty,** *adj.*

grits (grits) *n.pl.* ground grain.

griz′zly (griz′lē) *adj.,* **-zlier, -zliest.** gray, as hair or fur. Also, **griz′zled.**

grizzly bear, large bear of western U.S. and Canada, with coarse, gray-tipped fur.

gro. gross.

groan (grōn) *n.* **1.** moan of pain, derision, etc. —*v.* **2.** utter groans. —**groan′er,** *n.*

gro′cer (grō′sər) *n.* dealer in foods, etc.

gro′cer•y, *n., pl.* **-ies. 1.** store selling food. **2.** (*usually pl.*) food bought at such a store.

grog (grog) *n.* **1.** mixture of rum and water. **2.** any alcoholic drink.

grog′gy, *adj.,* **-gier, -giest.** dizzy. —**grog′gi•ness,** *n.*

groin (groin) *n.* hollow where thigh joins abdomen.

grom grommet.

grom′met (grom′it, grum′-) *n.* eyelet.

groom (grōōm, grŏŏm) *n.* **1.** person in charge of horses or stables. **2.** bridegroom. —*v.* **3.** make neat.

grooms′man, *n., pl.* **-men.** attendant of bridegroom.

groove (grōōv) *n., v.,* **grooved, grooving.** —*n.* **1.** furrow. —*v.* **2.** form groove in.

grope (grōp) *v.,* **groped, groping.** feel blindly.

gros′beak′ (grōs′bēk′) *n.* finch with a thick, conical bill.

gross (grōs) *adj.* **1.** before deductions. **2.** flagrant. —*n.* **3.** amount before deductions. **4.** twelve dozen. —**gross′ly,** *adv.* —**gross′ness,** *n.*

gross national product, total monetary value of all goods and services produced in a country during one year.

gro•tesque′ (grō tesk′) *adj.* **1.** fantastically ugly or absurd. **2.** fantastic.

grot′to (grot′ō) *n., pl.* **-tos, -toes.** cave.

grouch (grouch) *Informal.* —*v.* **1.** sulk. —*n.* **2.** sulky person. **3.** sullen mood. —**grouch′y,** *adj.*

ground (ground) *n.* **1.** earth's solid surface.

G

2. tract of land. **3.** motive. **4.** (*pl.*) dregs. **5.** rational basis. —*adj.* **6.** of or on ground. —*v.* **7.** instruct in elements. **8.** run aground.

ground ball, batted baseball that rolls or bounces along the ground. Also, **ground'er.**

ground'hog', *n.* woodchuck.

ground'less, *adj.* without rational basis.

ground rules, basic rule of conduct in a situation.

ground'swell', *n.* surge of feelings, esp. among the general public.

ground'work', *n.* basic work.

group (grōōp) *n.* **1.** number of persons or things placed or considered together. —*v.* **2.** place in or form group.

group'er (grōō'pər) *n.*, *pl.* **-ers, -er.** large sea bass of warm waters.

group'ie, *n.*, *pl.* **-ies. 1.** young female fan of rock group. **2.** ardent fan of any celebrity.

grouse (grous) *n.* game bird of America and Britain.

grout (grout) *n.* thin, coarse mortar, used between tiles.

grove (grōv) *n.* small wood.

grov'el (grov'əl, gruv'-) *v.*, **-eled, -eling.** humble oneself, esp. by crouching.

grow (grō) *v.*, **grew** (grōō), **grown, growing.** increase in size; develop. —**grow'er,** *n.*

growl (groul) *n.* **1.** guttural, angry sound. —*v.* **2.** utter growls.

grown'up', *n.* adult. —**grown'-up',** *adj.*

growth (grōth) *n.* **1.** act of growing. **2.** something that has grown.

grp group.

grph graphic.

grs grease.

grshft gearshaft.

grtg grating.

grtr grater.

GRU (in the former Soviet Union) the Chief Intelligence Directorate of the Soviet General Staff, a military intelligence organization founded in 1920 and functioning as a complement to the KGB. Also, **G.R.U.** [from Russian *G(lávnoe) r(azvédyvatel'noe) u(pravlénie)*]

grub (grub) *n.*, *v.*, **grubbed, grubbing.** —*n.* **1.** larva. **2.** drudge. **3.** *Informal.* food. —*v.* **4.** dig.

grub'by, *adj.*, **-bier, -biest. 1.** dirty. **2.** sordid. —**grub'bi•ness,** *n.*

grudge (gruj) *n.* *v.*, **grudged, grudging.** —*n.* **1.** lasting malice. —*v.* **2.** begrudge. —**grudg'ing•ly,** *adv.*

gru'el (grōō'əl) *n.* thin cereal.

gru•el•ing (grōō'ə ling, grōō'ling) *adj.* exhausting.

grue'some (grōō'səm) *adj.* causing horror and repugnance. —**grue'some•ly,** *adv.* —**grue'some•ness,** *n.*

gruff (gruf) *adj.* surly. —**gruff'ly,** *adv.* —**gruff'ness,** *n.*

grum'ble (grum'bəl) *v.*, **-bled, -bling.** murmur in discontent. —**grum'bler,** *n.*

grump'y (grum'pē) *adj.*, **grumpier, grumpiest.** surly. —**grump'i•ness,** *n.*

grun'gy (grun'jē) *adj.*, **-gier, -giest.** *Slang.* dirty or run down.

grunt (grunt) *n.* **1.** guttural sound. **2.** *Slang.* foot soldier. **3.** *Slang.* low-ranking worker. —*v.* **4.** utter grunts.

Grv. grove.

grv groove.

gr. wt. gross weight.

gryph'on (grif'ən) *n.* griffin.

GS 1. General Schedule (referring to the Civil Service job classification system). **2.** general staff. **3.** German silver.

gs ground speed.

G.S. 1. general secretary. **2.** general staff. Also, **g.s.**

GSA 1. General Services Administration. **2.** Girl Scouts of America. Also, **G.S.A.**

G.S.C. General Staff Corps.

GSE ground-support equipment.

Gsil German silver.

gskt gasket.

GSL Guaranteed Student Loan.

G spot (jē'spot'), Gräfenberg spot: a patch of tissue in the vagina purportedly excitable and erectile. Also, **G-spot.**

GSR 1. galvanic skin reflex. **2.** galvanic skin response.

gsr glide slope receiver.

GST Greenwich Sidereal Time.

G-suit (jē'sōōt'), *Aerospace.* anti-G suit: a flier's or astronaut's suit. Also, **g-suit.** [*g(ravity) suit*]

GT 1. Game Theory. **2.** gigaton; gigatons. **3.** grand theft **4.** *Automotive.* grand touring: a car type.

gt. 1. gilt. **2.** great. **3.** (in prescriptions) a drop [from Latin *gutta*].

Gt. Br. Great Britain. Also, **Gt. Brit.**

g.t.c. 1. good till canceled. **2.** good till countermanded. Also, **G.T.C.**

gtd. guaranteed.

GTG ground-to-ground.

GTO *Automotive.* Gran Turismo Omologato: a car style (grand touring).

GTP *Biochemistry.* an ester that is an important metabolic cofactor and precursor in the biosynthesis of cyclic GMP. [*g(uanosine) t(ri)p(hosphate)*]

gtrb gas turbine.

GTS gas turbine ship.

gtt. (in prescriptions) drops. [from Latin *guttae*]

GU 1. genitourinary. **2.** Guam (for use with ZIP code).

gua'no (gwä'nō) *n.* manure; excrement of sea birds.

guar., guarantee(d).

guar'an•tee' (gar'ən tē') *n.*, *v.*, **-teed, -teeing.** —*n.* **1.** pledge given as security. —*v.* **2.**

pledge. **3.** assure. Also, **guar′an•ty′.** —**guar′an•tor′** (-tôr′) n.

guard (gärd) v. **1.** watch over. —n. **2.** person who guards. **3.** body of guards. **4.** close watch.

guard′ed, adj. **1.** cautious; prudent. **2.** protected or restrained. —**guard′ed•ly,** adv.

guard′i•an, n. **1.** person who guards. **2.** person entrusted with care of another. —**guard′i•an•ship′,** n.

gua′va (gwä′və) n. large yellow fruit of tropical tree.

gu′ber•na•to′ri•al (gōō′bər nə tôr′ē əl, gyōō′-) adj. of governors.

guer•ril′la (gə ril′ə) n. member of band of soldiers that harasses the enemy.

guess (ges) v. **1.** form opinion on incomplete evidence. **2.** be right in such opinion. —n. **3.** act of guessing. —**guess′er,** n.

guess′work′, n. **1.** act of guessing. **2.** conclusions from guesses.

guest (gest) n. **1.** visitor. **2.** customer at hotel, restaurant, etc.

guf•faw′ (gu fô′, gə-) n. **1.** loud laughter. —v. **2.** laugh loudly.

GUGB the Chief Directorate for State Security: the former Soviet Union's secret police organization (1934–1941) functioning as part of the NKVD. Also, **G.U.G.B.** [from Russian G(l-ávnoe) u(pravlénie) g(osudárstvennoĭ) b(ezopásnosti)]

GUI (gōō′ē), Computers. graphical user interface.

Gui. Guiana.

guid′ance (gīd′ns) n. **1.** act or instance of guiding. **2.** advice over period of time.

guide (gīd) v., **guided, guiding,** n. —v. **1.** show the way. —n. **2.** one that guides. —**guid′er,** n.

guide′book′, n. book of directions, advice, and information, as for tourists.

guided missile, radio-controlled aerial missile.

guide′line′, n. guide or indication of future course of action.

gui′don (gīd′n) n. small flag.

guild (gild) n. commercial organization for common interest.

guile (gīl) n. cunning. —**guile′less,** adj.

guil′lo•tine′ (gil′ə tēn′, gē′ə-) n. machine for beheading.

guilt (gilt) n. fact or feeling of having committed a wrong. —**guilt′i•ly,** adv. —**guilt′y,** adj.

Guin. Guinea.

guin′ea (gin′ē) n., pl. -**eas.** former British coin, worth 21 shillings.

guinea fowl, domesticated fowl. Also, **guinea hen.**

guinea pig, 1. South American rodent. **2.** subject of experiment.

guise (gīz) n. outward appearance.

gui•tar′ (gi tär′) n. stringed musical instrument. —**gui•tar′ist,** n.

gulch (gulch) n. ravine.

gulf (gulf) n. **1.** arm of sea. **2.** abyss.

gull (gul) n. **1.** web-footed sea bird. **2.** dupe. —v. **3.** cheat; trick.

gul′let (gul′it) n. throat.

gul′li•ble (gul′ə bəl) adj. easily deceived. —**gul′li•bil′i•ty,** n.

gul′ly (gul′ē) n., pl. -**lies.** deep channel cut by running water.

gulp (gulp) v. **1.** swallow in large mouthfuls. —n. **2.** act of gulping.

gum (gum) n., v., **gummed, gumming.** —n. **1.** sticky substance from plants. **2.** chewing gum. **3.** tissue around teeth. —v. **4.** smear with gum. —**gum′my,** adj.

gum′bo (gum′bō) n., pl. -**bos.** soup made with okra.

gum′drop′, n. small chewy candy.

gump′tion (gump′shən) n. **1.** initiative; resourcefulness. **2.** courage; spunk.

gum′shoe′, n., pl. -**shoes. 1.** Slang. detective. **2.** rubber overshoe.

gun (gun) n., v., **gunned, gunning.** —n. **1.** tubular weapon which shoots missiles with explosives. —v. **2.** hunt with gun. **3.** cause (an engine) to speed up quickly. —**gun′ner,** n. —**gun′ner•y,** n.

gun′cot′ton, n. explosive made of cotton and acids.

gung′-ho′ (gung′hō′) adj. Informal. thoroughly enthusiastic and loyal.

gunk (gungk) n. Slang. sticky or greasy matter.

gun′man, n., pl. -**men.** armed criminal.

gun′ny, n., pl. -**nies.** coarse material used for sacks.

gun′pow′der, n. explosive mixture.

gun′shot′, n. shot fired from gun.

gun′smith′, n. person who makes or repairs firearms.

gun′wale (gun′l) n. upper edge of vessel's side.

gup′py (gup′ē) n., pl. -**pies.** tiny tropical fish.

gur′gle (gûr′gəl) v., -**gled, -gling,** n. —v. **1.** flow noisily. —n. **2.** sound of gurgling.

gur′ney (gûr′nē) n. wheeled table or stretcher for transporting patients.

gu′ru (gōōr′ōō, gōō rōō′) n. **1.** Hindu spiritual teacher. **2.** any respected leader.

gush (gush) v. **1.** flow or emit suddenly. **2.** talk effusively. —n. **3.** sudden flow. —**gush′y,** adj.

gush′er, n. jet of petroleum from underground.

gus′set (gus′it) n. angular insertion, as in clothing.

gus′sy (gus′ē) v., -**sied, -sying.** dress up or decorate showily.

gust (gust) n. **1.** blast of wind. **2.** outburst. —**gust′y,** adj.

gus′ta•to′ry (gus′tə tôr′ē) adj. of taste.

gus′to (gus′tō) n., pl. -**toes.** keen enjoyment.

G

gut (gut) *n., v.,* **gutted, gutting.** —*n.* **1.** intestine. **2.** (*pl.*) *Informal,* courage. —*v.* **3.** destroy interior of.

gut'less, *adj.* lacking courage.

guts'y, *adj.,* **gutsier, gutsiest.** daring or courageous. —**guts'i•ness,** *n.*

gut'ter (gut'ər) *n.* channel for leading off rainwater.

gut'tur•al (gut'ər əl) *adj.* **1.** of or in throat. —*n.* **2.** guttural sound. —**gut'tur•al•ly,** *adv.*

guy (gī) *n.* **1.** rope, etc., used to guide or steady object. **2.** *Informal.* fellow.

guz'zle (guz'əl) *v.,* **-zled, -zling.** drink greedily. —**guz'zler,** *n.*

g.v. 1. gravimetric volume. **2.** gigavolt; gigavolts.

gvl gravel.

GVW gross vehicle weight; gross vehicular weight.

GW gigawatt; gigawatts. Also, **Gw**

GWF gay white female.

GWh Gigawatt-hour.

GWM gay white male.

Gy *Physics.* gray: a measure of radiation absorption.

gy gray.

gym•na'si•um (jim nā'zē əm) *n., pl.* **-siums, -sia.** place for physical exercise. *Informal,* **gym.**

gym'nast (jim'nəst, -nast) *n.* performer of gymnastics.

gym•nas'tics (-nas'tiks) *n.pl.* physical exercises that demonstrate strength, balance, or agility. —**gym•nas'tic,** *adj.*

GYN 1. gynecological. **2.** gynecologist. **3.** gynecology. Also, **gyn.**

gy'ne•col'o•gy (gī'ni kol'ə jē, jin'i-) *n.* branch of medicine dealing with care of women. —**gy'ne•co•log'ic** (-kə loj'ik), **gy'ne•co•log'i•cal,** *adj.* —**gy'ne•col'o•gist,** *n.*

gyp (jip) *v.,* **gypped, gypping.** *Informal.* cheat.

gyp'sum (jip'səm) *n.* soft common mineral.

Gyp'sy (jip'sē) *n., pl.* **-sies.** member of wandering people.

gy'rate (jī'rāt, jī rāt') *v.,* **-rated, -rating.** whirl. —**gy•ra'tion,** *n.*

gy'ro•scope' (jī'rə skōp') *n.* rotating wheel mounted to maintain absolute direction in space.

GySgt *Marine Corps.* gunnery sergeant.

GZ ground zero.

H

H, h (āch) *n.* eighth letter of English alphabet.

ha (hä) *interj.* (exclamation of surprise, suspicion, etc.).

Hab. *Bible.* Habakkuk.

ha′be•as cor′pus (hā′bē əs kôr′pəs) writ requiring that arrested person be brought before court to determine whether he or she is legally detained.

hab′er•dash′er•y (hab′ər dash′ə rē) *n., pl.* **-eries.** shop selling men's items. —**hab′er•dash′er,** *n.*

hab′it (hab′it) *n.* **1.** customary practice or act. **2.** garb. —**ha•bit′u•al** (hə bich′ōō əl) *adj.* —**ha•bit′u•al•ly,** *adv.* —**ha•bit′u•a′tion,** *n.*

hab′it•a•ble (hab′i tə bəl) *adj.* able to be inhabited. —**hab′it•a•bly,** *adv.*

hab′i•tant, *n.* resident.

hab′i•tat′ (-tat′) *n.* natural dwelling.

hab′i•ta′tion, *n.* abode.

ha•bit′u•ate′ (hə bich′ōō āt′) *v.,* **-ated, -ating.** accustom; make used to. —**ha•bit′u•a′tion,** *n.*

ha•bit′u•é′ (-ōō ā′) *n.* habitual visitor.

HAC House Appropriations Committee.

hack (hak) *v.* **1.** cut or chop roughly. **2.** cough sharply. —*n.* **3.** cut or notch. **4.** artistic drudge. **5.** vehicle for hire. —*adj.* **6.** routine.

hack′er, *n. Slang.* **1.** skilled computer enthusiast. **2.** computer user who tries to gain unauthorized access to systems.

hack′les (hak′əlz) *n.pl.* **1.** hair that can bristle on the back of an animal's neck. **2.** anger.

hack′ney (-nē) *n., pl.* **-neys.** horse or carriage for hire.

hack′neyed, *adj.* trite; common.

hack′saw′, *n.* saw for cutting metal.

had′dock (had′ək) *n.* food fish of northern Atlantic.

Ha′des (hā′dēz) *n.* hell.

haft (haft) *n.* handle.

hag (hag) *n.* repulsive old woman.

hag′gard (hag′ərd) *adj.* gaunt with fatigue.

hag′gle (hag′əl) *v.,* **-gled, -gling.** argue over price.

hai′ku (hī′kōō) *n., pl.* **-ku.** Japanese poem consisting of 3 lines of 5, 7, and 5 syllables, respectively.

hail (hāl) *n.* **1.** ice pellets (**hail′stones′**) **2.** shout. **3.** salutation. —*v.* **4.** pour down hail. **5.** greet. **6.** call out to.

hair (hâr) *n.* **1.** filament on human head, animal body, etc. **2.** hairs collectively. —**hair′y,** *adj.* —**hair′i•ness,** *n.* —**hair′dres′ser,** *n.* —**hair′less,** *adj.* —**hair′pin′,** *n.*

hair′breadth′, *n.* narrow margin of safety. Also, **hairs′breadth′.**

hair′cut′, *n.* **1.** act of cutting hair. **2.** hair style.

hair′do′ (-dōō′) *n., pl.* **-dos.** hair arrangement.

hair′piece′, *n.* toupee or wig.

hair′-rais′ing, *adj.* terrifying.

hair′spray′, *n.* liquid spray for holding the hair in place.

hair′style′, *n.* way of cutting or arranging hair. —**hair′styl′ist,** *n.*

hair′-trig′ger, *adj.* easily activated or set off.

hake (hāk) *n.* codlike marine food fish.

Hal *Chemistry.* halogen.

hal′cy•on (hal′sē ən) *adj.* peaceful; happy; carefree.

hale (hāl) *v.,* **haled, haling,** *adj.* —*v.* **1.** summon forcibly. —*adj.* **2.** healthy.

half (haf) *n., pl.* **halves,** *adj., adv.* —*n.* **1.** one of two equal parts. —*adj.* **2.** being half. **3.** incomplete. —*adv.* **4.** partly.

half′back′, *n.* (in football) one of two backs who line up on each side of the fullback.

half′-baked′, *adj.* **1.** not sufficiently planned or prepared. **2.** foolish.

half′-breed′, *n. Offensive.* offspring of parents of two races.

half brother, brother related through one parent only.

half′-cocked′, *adj.* ill-considered or ill-prepared.

half′-heart′ed, *adj.* unenthusiastic. —**half′-heart′ed•ly,** *adv.* —**half-heart′ed•ness,** *n.*

half′-life′, *n., pl.* **-lives.** time required for one half the atoms of a radioactive substance to decay.

half sister, sister related through one parent only.

half′-truth′, *n.* deceptive statement that is only partly true.

half′way′ (-wā′, -wā′) *adv.* **1.** to the midpoint. **2.** partially or almost. —*adj.* **3.** midway. **4.** partial or inadequate.

halfway house, residence for persons released from hospital, prison, etc., to ease their return to society.

half′-wit′, *n.* stupid or foolish person. —**half′-wit′ted,** *adj.*

hal′i•but (hal′ə bət, hol′-) *n.* large edible fish.

hal′i•to′sis (hal′i tō′sis) *n.* bad breath.

hall (hôl) *n.* **1.** corridor. **2.** large public room.

hal′le•lu′jah (hal′ə lōō′yə) *interj.* Praise ye the Lord! Also, **hal′le•lu′iah.**

hall′mark′ (hôl′-) *n.* **1.** mark or indication of genuineness or quality. **2.** distinguishing characteristic.

hal′low (hal′ō) *v.* consecrate. —**hal′lowed,** *adj.*

Hal'low•een' (hal/ə wēn/, -ō ēn/, hol/-) n. the evening of October 31, observed by dressing in costumes. Also, **Hal/low•e'en/**.

hal•lu/ci•na/tion (hə lōō/sə nā/shən) n. illusory perception. —**hal•luc/ci•nate/**, v. —**hal•lu/ci•na•to/ry** (-nə tôr/ē) adj.

hal•lu/ci•no•gen (-nə jən) n. substance that produces hallucinations. —**hal•lu/ci•no•gen/ic** (-jen/ik) adj.

hall/way/, n. corridor.

ha/lo (hā/lō) n., pl. -los, -loes. radiance surrounding a head.

halt (hôlt) v. 1. falter; limp. 2. stop. —adj. 3. lame. —n. 4. stop. —**halt/ing**, adj. —**halt/ing•ly**, adv.

hal/ter (hôl/tər) n. 1. strap for horse. 2. noose. 3. woman's top tied behind the neck and back.

halve (hav) v., halved, halving. divide in half.

hal/yard (hal/yərd) n. line for hoisting sail or flag.

ham (ham) n., v. hammed, hamming. —n. 1. meat from rear thigh of hog. 2. amateur radio operator. 3. performer who overacts. —v. 4. overact. —**ham/my**, adj.

ham/burg/er (ham/bûr/gər) n. sandwich of ground beef in bun.

ham/let (ham/lit) n. small village.

ham/mer (ham/ər) n. 1. tool for pounding. —v. 2. pound with hammer. —**ham/mer•er**, n.

ham/mock (ham/ək) n. hanging bed of canvas, etc.

ham/per (ham/pər) v. 1. impede. —n. 2. large basket.

ham/ster (ham/stər) n. small burrowing rodent kept as a pet.

ham/string/, n., v., -strung, -stringing. —n. 1. tendon behind the knee. —v. 2. disable by cutting hamstring. 3. make powerless or ineffective.

hand (hand) n. 1. terminal part of arm. 2. worker. 3. side as viewed from certain point. 4. style of handwriting. 5. pledge of marriage. 6. cards held by player. —v. 7. pass by hand.

H&A Health and Accident.

hand/bag/, n. woman's purse.

hand/ball/, n. ball game played against a wall.

hand/bill/, n. small printed notice usu. distributed by hand.

hand/book/, n. small guide or manual.

hand/clasp/, n. handshake.

hand/cuff/, n. 1. shackle for wrist. —v. 2. put handcuff on.

hand/ful (-fŏŏl) n., pl. -fuls. 1. amount hand can hold. 2. difficult person or thing.

hand/gun/, n. pistol.

hand/i•cap/ (han/dē kap/) n., v., -capped, -capping. —n. 1. disadvantage. —v. 2. subject to disadvantage.

hand/i•craft/, n. 1. manual skill. 2. work or products requiring such skill. Also, **hand/craft/**.

hand/i•work/, n. 1. work done by hand. 2. personal work or accomplishment.

hand/ker•chief (hang/kər chif, -chēf/) n. small cloth for wiping face.

han/dle (han/dl) n., v., -dled, -dling. —n. 1. part to be grasped. —v. 2. feel or grasp. 3. manage. 4. Informal. endure. 5. deal in. —**han/dler**, n.

hand/made/, adj. made individually by worker.

hand/out/, n. 1. something given to a beggar. 2. item of publicity.

hand/shake/, n. clasping of hands in greeting or agreement.

hands/-off/, adj. characterized by nonintervention.

hand/some (han/səm) adj. 1. of fine appearance. 2. generous. —**hand/some•ly**, adv.

hands/-on/, adj. characterized by or involving active personal participation.

hand/spring/, n. complete flipping of body, landing first on hands, then on feet.

hand/-to-mouth/, adj. providing bare existence; precarious.

hand/writ/ing, n. writing done by hand. —**hand/writ/ten** (-rit/n) adj.

hand/y (han/dē) adj., -ier, -iest. 1. convenient. 2. dexterous. 3. useful. —**hand/i•ly**, adv.

han/dy•man/, n., pl. -men. worker at miscellaneous physical chores.

hang (hang) v., hung (hung), or hanged, hanging, n. —v. 1. suspend. 2. suspend by neck until dead. —n. 3. manner of hanging. —**hang/ing**, n. —**hang/man**, n. —**hang/er**, n.

hang/ar (hang/ər) n. shed, esp. for aircraft.

hang/dog/, adj. shamefaced or cowed.

hang glider, kitelike glider for soaring through the air from hilltops, etc. (**hang gliding**).

hang/nail/, n. small piece of partially detached skin around fingernail.

hang/o/ver, n. ill feeling from too much alcohol.

hang/up/, n. Informal. obsessive problem.

hank (hangk) n. skein of yarn.

han/ker (hang/kər) v. yearn. —**han/ker•ing**, n.

hank/y-pank/y (hang/kē pang/kē) n. Informal. 1. mischief. 2. illicit sexual relations.

han/som (han/səm) n. two-wheeled covered cab.

Ha/nuk•kah (кнä/nə kə, hä/-) n. annual Jewish festival.

hap/haz/ard (hap haz/ərd) adj. 1. accidental. —adv. 2. by chance. —**hap•haz/ard•ly**, adv.

hap/less, adj. unlucky.

hap/pen (hap/ən) v. occur. —**hap/pen•ing**, n.

hap/pen•stance/ (-stans/) *n.* chance happening or event.

hap/py (hap/ē) *adj.*, **-pier, -piest. 1.** pleased; glad. **2.** pleasurable. **3.** bringing good luck. **—hap/pi•ly,** *adv.* **—hap/pi•ness,** *n.*

ha/ra•ki/ri (här/ə kēr/ē) *n.* Japanese ritual suicide by cutting the abdomen.

ha•rangue/ (hə rang/) *n., v.,* **-rangued, -ranguing. —n. 1.** vehement speech. **—v. 2.** address in harangue.

ha•rass/ (hə ras/, har/əs) *v.* annoy; disturb. **—ha•rass/er,** *n.* **—har•ass/ment,** *n.*

—Pronunciation. HARASS has traditionally been pronounced (har/əs). A newer pronunciation, (hə ras/), which has developed in North American but not British English, is sometimes criticized. However, it is now the more common pronunciation among younger educated U.S. speakers, some of whom are barely familiar with the older form.

har/bin•ger (här/bin jər) *n., v.* herald.

har/bor (här/bər) *n.* **1.** sheltered water for ships. **2.** shelter. **—v. 3.** give shelter.

hard (härd) *adj.* **1.** firm; not soft. **2.** difficult. **3.** severe. **4.** indisputable. **—hard/en,** *v.* **—hard/ness,** *n.*

hard/-bit/ten, *adj.* tough; stubborn.

hard/-boiled/, *adj.* **1.** boiled long enough for yolk and white to solidify. **2.** not sentimental; tough.

hard cider, fermented cider.

hard/-core/, *adj.* **1.** unalterably committed. **2.** graphic; explicit.

hard/hat/, *n.* **1.** worker's helmet. **2.** working-class conservative.

hard/head/ed, *adj.* **1.** practical; realistic; shrewd. **2.** obstinate; willful.

hard/heart/ed, *adj.* unfeeling; pitiless.

hard/-line/, *adj.* uncompromising, as in politics. Also, **hard/line/. —hard/-lin/er,** *n.*

hard/ly, *adv.* barely.

hard/-nosed/, *adj. Informal.* **1.** practical and shrewd. **2.** tough; stubborn. **—hard/nose/,** *n.*

hard/ship, *n.* severe toil, oppression or need.

hard/tack/, *n.* hard biscuit.

hard/ware/, *n.* **1.** metalware. **2.** the machinery of a computer.

hard/wood/, *n.* hard, compact wood of various trees.

har/dy (här/dē) *adj.,* **-dier, -diest. 1.** fitted to endure hardship. **2.** daring. **—har/di•ness,** *n.*

hare (hâr) *n.* mammal resembling rabbit.

hare/brained/, *adj.* foolish.

hare/lip/, *n.* split upper lip.

har/em (hâr/əm, har/-) *n.* **1.** women's section of Muslim palace. **2.** the women there.

hark (härk) *v.* listen. Also, **hark/en.**

har/le•quin (här/lə kwin, -kin) *n.* masked clown in theater and pantomime.

har/lot (här/lət) *n.* prostitute. **—har/lot•ry,** *n.*

harm (härm) *n.* **1.** injury. **2.** evil. **—v. 3.** injure. **—harm/ful,** *adj.*

harm/less, *adj.* **1.** causing no harm. **2.** immune from legal action. **—harm/less•ly,** *adv.* **—harm/less•ness,** *n.*

har•mon/i•ca (här mon/i kə) *n.* musical reed instrument.

har/mo•ny (här/mə nē) *n., pl.* **-nies. 1.** agreement. **2.** combination of agreeable musical sounds. **—har•mon/ic** (-mon/ik) *adj.* **—har•mon/i•cal•ly,** *adv.* **—har/mo•nize/,** *v.,* **-nized, -nizing. —har•mon/i•ous** (-mō/nē əs) *adj.*

har/ness (här/nis) *n.* **1.** horse's working gear. **—v. 2.** put harness on.

harp (härp) *n.* **1.** plucked musical string instrument. **—v. 2.** dwell persistently in one's words. **—harp/ist, harp/er,** *n.*

har•poon/ (här pōōn/) *n.* **1.** spear used against whales. **—v. 2.** strike with harpoon.

harp/si•chord/ (härp/si kôrd/) *n.* keyboard instrument with plucked strings. **—harp/si•chord/ist,** *n.*

har/ri•dan (har/i dn) *n.* scolding, vicious woman.

har/ri•er (har/ē ər) *n.* hunting dog.

har/row (har/ō) *n.* **1.** implement for leveling or breaking up plowed land. **—v. 2.** draw a harrow over. **3.** distress. **—har/row•ing,** *adj.*

har/ry (har/ē) *v.,* **-ried, -rying.** harass.

harsh (härsh) *adj.* **1.** rough. **2.** unpleasant. **3.** highly severe. **—harsh/ly,** *adv.* **—harsh/ness,** *n.*

hart (härt) *n.* male red deer.

har/vest (här/vist) *n.* **1.** gathering of crops. **2.** season for this. **3.** crop. **—v. 4.** reap. **—har/vest•er,** *n.*

has (haz; *unstressed* həz, əz) *v.* third pers. sing. pres. indic. of **have.**

has/-been/, *n.* one that is no longer effective, successful, etc.

hash (hash) *n.* **1.** chopped meat and potatoes. **2.** *Slang.* hashish. **—v. 3.** chop.

hash/ish (hash/ēsh, hä shēsh/) *n.* narcotic of Indian hemp.

hasn't (haz/ənt) contraction of **has not.**

hasp (hasp) *n.* clasp for door, lid, etc.

has/sle (has/əl) *n., v.,* **-sled, -sling.** *Informal,* **—n. 1.** disorderly dispute. **2.** troublesome situation. **—v. 3.** bother; harass.

has/sock (has/ək) *n.* cushion used as footstool, etc.

has/ten (hā/sən) *v.* hurry. **—haste** (hāst), **hast/i•ness,** *n.* **—hast/y,** *adj.* **—hast/i•ly,** *adv.*

hat (hat) *n.* covering for head. **—hat/ter,** *n.*

hatch (hach) *v.* **1.** bring forth young from egg. **2.** be hatched. **—n. 3.** cover for opening. **—hatch/er•y,** *n.*

hatch/et (hach/it) *n.* small ax.

hatchet job, maliciously destructive critique.

H

hatch′way′, *n.* opening in ship's deck.
hate (hāt) *v.*, **hated, hating,** *n.* —*v.* **1.** feel enmity. —*n.* **2.** Also, **hat′red.** strong dislike.
hate′ful, *adj.* **1.** full of hate. **2.** arousing hate. —**hate′ful•ly,** *adv.* —**hate′ful•ness,** *n.*
haugh′ty (hô′tē) *adj.*, **-tier, -tiest.** disdainfully proud. —**haugh′ti•ly,** *adv.* —**haugh′ti•ness,** *n.*
haul (hôl) *v.* **1.** pull; drag. —*n.* **2.** pull. **3.** distance of carrying. **4.** thing hauled. **5.** thing gained.
haunch (hônch, hänch) *n.* hip.
haunt (hônt, hänt) *v.* **1.** visit often, esp. as ghost. —*n.* **2.** place of frequent visits. —**haunt′ed,** *adj.*
haunt′ing, *adj.* lingering in the mind.
haust. (in prescriptions) draught. [from Latin *haustus*]
haute cou•ture′ (ōt′ kōō tōōr′) high fashion.
haute cui•sine′ (ōt′ kwi zēn′) gourmet cooking.
have (hav; *unstressed* həv, əv; *for usually* haf) *v.*, **had, having. 1.** possess; contain. **2.** get. **3.** be forced or obligated. **4.** be affected by. **5.** give birth to.

—**Usage.** See **of.**

ha′ven (hā′vən) *n.* **1.** harbor. **2.** place of shelter.
have′-not′, *n.* (*usually pl.*) individual or group without wealth.
haven't (hav′ənt) contraction of **have not.**
hav′er•sack′ (hav′ər sak′) *n.* bag for rations, etc.
hav′oc (hav′ək) *n.* devastation.
Haw. (hô) Hawaii.
hawk (hôk) *n.* **1.** bird of prey. —*v.* **2.** hunt with hawks. **3.** peddle.
hawk′er, *n.* peddler.
haw′ser (hô′zər, -sər) *n.* cable for mooring or towing ship.
haw′thorn′ (hô′thôrn′) *n.* small tree with thorns and small, bright fruit.
hay (hā) *n.* grass cut and dried for fodder. —**hay′field′,** *n.* —**hay′stack′,** *n.*
hay fever, disorder of eyes and respiratory tract, caused by pollen.
hay′wire′, *adj. Informal.* amiss.
haz hazardous.
haz′ard (haz′ərd) *n., v.* risk. —**haz′ard•ous,** *adj.*
haze (hāz) *v.*, **hazed, hazing,** *n.* —*v.* **1.** play abusive tricks on. —*n.* **2.** fine mist. —**ha′zy,** *adj.*
ha′zel (hā′zəl) *n.* **1.** tree bearing edible nut (**ha′zel•nut′**). **2.** light reddish brown.
Hb *Symbol, Biochemistry.* hemoglobin.
h.b. *Sports.* halfback.
H.B.M. His Britannic Majesty; Her Britannic Majesty.

HBO Home Box Office (a cable television channel).
H′-bomb′, *n.* hydrogen bomb.
HBP high blood pressure.
HBV hepatitis B.
H.C. 1. Holy Communion. **2.** House of Commons.
h.c. for the sake of honor. [from Latin *honōris causā*]
hce human-caused error.
H.C.F. *Math.* highest common factor. Also, **h.c.f.**
hCG human chorionic gonadotropin.
H.C.M. His Catholic Majesty; Her Catholic Majesty.
H. Con. Res. House concurrent resolution.
HCR highway contract route.
hcs high-carbon steel.
hd. 1. hand. **2.** hard. **3.** head.
h.d. 1. heavy duty. **2.** (in prescriptions) at bedtime [from Latin *hōra dēcubitūs*]
hdbk. handbook.
hdcp handicap.
hdd *Computers.* hard-disk drive.
hdg heading.
hdkf. handkerchief.
HDL high-density lipoprotein.
hdl handle.
hdlg handling.
hdlng headlining.
hdn harden.
hdns hardness.
H. Doc. House document.
HDPE high-density polyethylene.
hdqrs., headquarters.
hdr header.
hdshk *Computers.* handshake.
hdst headset.
HDTV high-definition television.
hdw. hardware. Also, **hdwe, hdwr.**
hdwd hardwood.
hdx *Telecommunications.* half duplex.
he (hē; *unstressed* ē) *pron.* **1.** male last mentioned. —*n.* **2.** male.
head (hed) *n.* **1.** part of body joined to trunk by neck. **2.** leader. **3.** top or foremost part. —*adj.* **4.** at the head. **5.** leading or main. —*v.* **6.** lead. **7.** move in certain direction.
head′ache′, *n.* **1.** pain in upper part of head. **2.** worrying problem.
head′dress, *n.* covering or decoration for the head.
head′first′, *adv.* headlong.
head′ing, *n.* caption.
head′light′, *n.* light with reflector at front of vehicle.
head′line′, *n.* title of newspaper article.
head′long′, *adj., adv.* **1.** with the head foremost. **2.** in impulsive manner.
head′-on′, *adj., adv.* with the head or front foremost.

head'phone', *n. (usually pl.)* device worn over the ears for listening to an audiotape, etc.

head'quar'ters, *n.* center of command or operations.

head'stone', *n.* stone marker at head of grave.

head'strong', *adj.* willful.

head'way', *n.* progress.

head'y, *adj.*, **headier, headiest. 1.** impetuous. **2.** intoxicating.

heal (hēl) *v.* **1.** restore to health. **2.** get well.

health (helth) *n.* **1.** soundness of body. **2.** physical condition. —**health'ful**, —**health'y**, *adj.*

HEAO High Energy Astrophysical Observatory.

heap (hēp) *n., v.* pile (defs. 1, 2, 8, 9).

hear (hēr) *v.*, **heard** (hûrd), **hearing. 1.** perceive by ear. **2.** listen. **3.** receive report. —**hear'er**, *n.* —**hear'ing**, *n.*

heark'en (här'kən) *v.* listen.

hear'say', *n.* gossip; indirect report.

hearse (hûrs) *n.* vehicle used to carry coffin.

heart (härt) *n.* **1.** muscular organ keeping blood in circulation. **2.** seat of life or emotion. **3.** compassion. **4.** vital part. **5.** (*pl.*) suit of playing cards. —**heart'less**, *adj.* —**heart'less·ly**, *adv.* —**heart'less·ness**, *n.*

heart'ache', *n.* grief.

heart attack, sudden insufficiency of oxygen supply to heart that results in heart muscle damage.

heart'break', *n.* great sorrow or anguish. —**heart'break'ing**, *adj.* —**heart'bro'ken**, *adj.*

heart'burn', *n.* burning sensation in stomach and esophagus, sometimes caused by rising stomach acid.

heart'en, *v.* encourage.

heart'felt', *adj.* deeply felt.

hearth (härth) *n.* place for fires.

heart'-rend'ing, *adj.* causing sympathetic grief.

heart'sick', *adj.* extremely sad.

heart'-to-heart', *adj.* sincere and intimate.

heart'y, *adj.*, **-ier, -iest. 1.** cordial. **2.** genuine. **3.** vigorous. **4.** substantial. —**heart'i·ly**, *adv.* —**heart'i·ness**, *n.*

heat (hēt) *n.* **1.** warmth. **2.** form of energy raising temperature. **3.** intensity of emotion. **4.** sexual arousal, esp. female. —*v.* **5.** make or become hot. **6.** excite. —**heat'er**, *n.*

heat'ed, *adj.* **1.** supplied with heat. **2.** emotionally charged. —**heat'ed·ly**, *adv.*

heath (hēth) *n.* **1.** Also, **heath'er.** low evergreen shrub. **2.** uncultivated land overgrown with shrubs.

hea'then (hē'ən) *n., adj.* pagan. —**hea'then·ish**, *adj.*

heat'stroke', *n.* headache, fever, etc., caused by too much heat.

heave (hēv) *v.*, **heaved, heaving**, *n.* —*v.* **1.** raise with effort. **2.** lift and throw. **3.** *Slang.*

vomit. **4.** rise and fall. —*n.* **5.** act or instance of heaving.

heav'en (hev'ən) *n.* **1.** abode of God, angels, and spirits of righteous dead. **2.** (*often pl.*) sky. **3.** bliss. —**heav'en·ly**, *adj.*

heav'y (hev'ē) *adj.*, **-ier, -iest. 1.** of great weight. **2.** substantial. **3.** clumsy; indelicate. —**heav'i·ly**, *adv.* —**heav'i·ness**, *n.*

heav'y-du'ty, *adj.* made for hard use.

heav'y-hand'ed, *adj.* tactless; clumsy.

heav'y-heart'ed, *adj.* preoccupied with sorrow or worry. —**heav'y-heart'ed·ness**, *n.*

heav'y-set', *adj.* large in body.

Heb Hebrew.

Heb. 1. Hebrew. **2.** *Bible.* Hebrews. Also, **Hebr.**

He'brew (hē'brōō) *n.* **1.** member of people of ancient Palestine. **2.** their language, now the national language of Israel. —**He'brew**, *adj.*

heck'le (hek'əl) *v.*, **-led, -ling.** harass with comments, etc. —**heck'ler**, *n.*

hec'tare (hek'târ) *n.* 10,000 square meters (2.47 acres).

hec'tic (-tik) *adj.* marked by excitement, passion, etc. —**hec'ti·cal·ly**, *adv.*

hec'tor (-tər) *v., n.* bully.

hedge (hej) *n., v.*, **hedged, hedging.** —*n.* **1.** Also, **hedge'row'.** fence of bushes or small trees. —*v.* **2.** surround with hedge. **3.** offset (risk, bet, etc.).

hedge'hog', *n.* spiny mammal.

he'don·ist (hēd'n ist) *n.* person living for pleasure. —**he'do·nis'tic**, *adj.* —**he'don·ism** (-iz'əm) *n.*

heed (hēd) *v.* **1.** notice. **2.** pay serious attention to. —**heed**, *n.* —**heed'ful**, *adj.* —**heed'less**, *adj.* —**heed'less·ly**, *adv.*

heel (hēl) *n.* **1.** back of foot below ankle. **2.** part of shoe, etc., covering this. —*v.* **3.** furnish with heels. **4.** lean to one side.

heft (heft) *n.* **1.** heaviness. **2.** significance. —*v.* **3.** weigh by lifting.

hef'ty, *adj.*, **-tier, -tiest. 1.** heavy. **2.** sturdy. **3.** substantial. —**heft'i·ness**, *n.*

he·gem'o·ny (hi jem'ə nē, hej'ə mō'-) *n., pl.* **-nies.** domination or leadership.

heif'er (hef'ər) *n.* young cow without issue.

height (hīt) *n.* **1.** state of being high. **2.** altitude. **3.** apex. —**height'en**, *v.*

Heim'lich maneuver (hīm'lik) procedure to aid choking person by applying pressure to upper abdomen.

hei'nous (hā'nəs) *adj.* hateful.

heir (âr) *n.* inheritor. —**heir'ess**, *n.fem.*

heir'loom', *n.* possession long kept in family.

heist (hīst) *Slang.* —*n.* **1.** robbery. —*v.* **2.** rob.

hel'i·cop'ter (hel'i kop'tər, hē'li-) *n.* heavier-than-air craft lifted by horizontal propeller.

he'li·o·trope' (hē'lē ə trōp') *n.* **1.** shrub with fragrant flowers. **2.** light purple color.

he'li·um (hē'lē əm) *n.* light, gaseous element.

he′lix (hē′liks) *n.*, *pl.* **hel′i·ces** (hel′ə sēz′), **helixes.** spiral.

hell (hel) *n.* abode of condemned spirits. —**hell′ish**, *adj.* —**hell′ish·ly**, *adv.*

Hel·len′ic (he len′ik, -lē′nik) *adj.* Greek.

hel·lo′ (he lō′, hə-, hel′ō) *interj.* (exclamation of greeting.)

helm (helm) *n.* **1.** control of rudder. **2.** steering apparatus. —**helms′man**, *n.*

hel′met (hel′mit) *n.* protective head covering.

help (help) *v.* **1.** aid. **2.** save. **3.** relieve. **4.** avoid. —*n.* **5.** aid; relief. **6.** helping person or thing. —**help′er**, *n.* —**help′ful**, *adj.* —**help′ful·ly**, *adv.* —**help′ful·ness**, *n.*

help′ing, *n.* portion of food served.

help′less, *adj.* unable to act for oneself. —**help′less·ly**, *adv.* —**help′less·ness**, *n.*

help′mate′, *n.* companion and helper. Also, **help′meet′.**

hel′ter-skel′ter (hel′tər skel′tər) *adv.* in a disorderly way.

hem (hem) *v.*, **hemmed, hemming,** *n.* —*v.* **1.** confine. **2.** fold and sew down edge of cloth. **3.** make throat-clearing sound. —*n.* **4.** hemmed border.

hem′i·sphere′ (hem′i sfēr′) *n.* **1.** half the earth or sky. **2.** half sphere. —**hem′i·spher′i·cal**, *adj.*

hem′lock (hem′lok′) *n.* **1.** coniferous tree. **2.** poisonous plant.

he′mo·glo′bin (hē′mə glō′bin, hem′ə-) *n.* oxygen-carrying compound in red blood cells.

he′mo·phil′i·a (hē′mə fil′ē ə) *n.* genetic disorder marked by excessive bleeding. —**he′mo·phil′i·ac′**, *n.*

hem′or·rhage (hem′ər ij) *n.* discharge of blood.

hem′or·rhoid′ (hem′ə roid′) *n.* (*usually pl.*) painful dilation of blood vessels in anus. —**hem′or·rhoi′dal**, *adj.*

hemp (hemp) *n.* **1.** herb fiber used for rope. **2.** intoxicating drug made from hemp plant.

hen (hen) *n.* **1.** female domestic fowl **2.** female bird. —**hen′ner·y**, *n.*

hence (hens) *adv.* **1.** therefore. **2.** from now on. **3.** from this place, etc.

hence′forth′ (hens′fôrth′, hens′fôrth′) *adv.* from now on.

hench′man (hench′mən) *n.*, *pl.* **-men. 1.** associate in wrongdoing. **2.** trusted attendant.

hen′na (hen′ə) *n.* red dye.

hen′pecked′, *adj.* nagged or controlled by one's wife.

hep′a·rin (hep′ə rin) *n.* anticoagulant found esp. in liver.

hep′a·ti′tis (hep′ə tī′tis) *n.* inflammation of the liver.

her (hûr; *unstressed* hər, ər) *pron.* **1.** objective case of **she.** —*adj.* **2.** of or belonging to female.

her′ald (her′əld) *n.* **1.** messenger or forerunner. **2.** proclaimer. —*v.* **3.** proclaim. **4.** give promise of.

her′ald·ry, *n.* art of devising and describing coats of arms, tracing genealogies, etc. —**he·ral′dic** (he ral′dik, hə-) *adj.*

herb (ûrb; *esp. Brit.* hûrb) *n.* flowering plant with nonwoody stem. —**her·ba·ceous** (hûr-bā′shəs, ûr-) *adj.* —**herb·al** (ûr′bəl, hûr′-) *adj.*

herb′age (ûr′bij, hûr′-) *n.* **1.** nonwoody plants. **2.** leaves and stems of herbs.

herb′i·cide (hûr′bə sīd′, ûr′-) *n.* substance for killing plants, esp. weeds. —**her′bi·cid′al**, *adj.*

her·biv′o·rous (hûr biv′ər əs, ûr-) *adj.* feeding on plants. —**her′bi·vore′** (hûr′bə vôr′, ûr′-) *n.*

her·cu·le′an (hûr′kyə lē′ən, hûr kyōō′lē-) *adj.* **1.** requiring extraordinary strength or effort. **2.** having extraordinary strength, courage, or size.

herd (hûrd) *n.* **1.** animals feeding or moving together. —*v.* **2.** go in herd. **3.** tend herd. —**herd′er, herds′man,** *n.*

here (hēr) *adv.* **1.** in or to this place. **2.** present.

here′a·bout′ *adv.* in this vicinity. Also, **here′a·bouts′.**

here·af′ter, *adv.* **1.** in the future. —*n.* **2.** future life.

here·by′, *adv.* by this.

he·red′i·tar′y (hə red′i ter′ē) *adj.* **1.** passing from parents to offspring. **2.** of heredity. **3.** by inheritance. —**he·red′i·tar′i·ly**, *adv.*

he·red′i·ty, *n.* transmission of traits from parents to offspring.

here·in′, *adv.* in this place.

her′e·sy (her′ə sē) *n.*, *pl.* **-sies.** unorthodox opinion or doctrine. —**her′e·tic** (her′i tik) *n.* —**he·ret′i·cal**, *adj.*

here·to·fore′, *adv.* before now.

here·with′, *adv.* along with this.

her′it·a·ble (her′i tə bəl) *adj.* capable of being inherited.

her′it·age (her′i tij) *n.* **1.** inheritance. **2.** traditions and history.

her·maph′ro·dite′ (hûr maf′rə dīt′) *n.* animal or plant with reproductive organs of both sexes. —**her·maph′ro·dit′ic** (-dit′ik) *adj.*

her·met′ic (hûr met′ik) *adj.* airtight. Also, **hermet′i·cal.** —**her·met′i·cal·ly**, *adv.*

her′mit (hûr′mit) *n.* recluse.

her′mit·age (-mi tij) *n.* hermit's abode.

her′ni·a (hûr′nē ə) *n.* rupture in abdominal wall, etc.

he′ro (hēr′ō) *n.*, *pl.* **-roes. 1.** man of valor, nobility, etc. **2.** main male character in story. —**her′oine** (her′ō in) *n.fem.* —**he·ro′ic** (hi-rō′ik) *adj.* —**her′o·ism′** (her′ō iz′əm) *n.*

her′o·in (her′ō in) *n.* illegal morphinelike drug.

her′on (her′ən) *n.* long-legged wading bird.

hero sandwich, large sandwich of cold cuts, etc., in long roll.

herp. herpetology. Also, **herpet.**

her/pes (hûr/pēz) *n.* viral disease characterized by blisters on skin or mucous membranes.

herpetol. 1. herpetological. **2.** herpetology.

her/ring (her/ing) *n.* north Atlantic food fish.

her/ring•bone/, *n.* **1.** pattern of slanting lines in vertical rows. **2.** fabric of this.

hers (hûrz) *pron.* **1.** possessive form of **she,** used predicatively. **2.** her belongings or family.

her•self/, *pron.* emphatic or reflexive form of **her.**

hertz (hûrts) *n., pl.* **hertz.** radio frequency of one cycle per second.

hes/i•tate/ (hez/i tāt/) *v.,* **-tated, -tating. 1.** hold back in doubt. **2.** pause. **3.** stammer. **—hes/i•tant** (-tənt) *adj.* **—hes/i•ta/tion, hes/i•tan•cy,** *n.*

het heterodyne.

het/er•o•dox/ (het/ər ə doks/) *adj.* unorthodox. **—het/er•o•dox/y,** *n.*

het/er•o•ge/ne•ous (-jē/nē əs) *adj.* **1.** unlike. **2.** varied.

het/er•o•sex/u•al, *adj.* sexually attracted to opposite sex. **—het/er•o•sex/u•al,** *n.*

HETP *Chemistry.* hexaethyl tetraphosphate.

heu•ris/tic (hyōō ris/tik; *often* yōō-) *adj.* **1.** serving to indicate. **2.** denoting learning esp. by experiment.

hew (hyōō; *often* yōō) *v.,* **hewed, hewed** or **hewn, hewing. 1.** chop or cut. **2.** cut down. **—hew/er,** *n.*

hex (heks) *v.* **1.** cast spell on. **2.** bring bad luck to. **—n. 3.** spell; jinx.

hex/a•gon/ (hek/sə gon/, -gən) *n.* six-sided polygon. **—hex•ag/o•nal** (hek sag/ə nl) *adj.*

hex hd hexagonal head.

hex soch hexagonal socket head.

hey/day/ (hā/dā/) *n.* time of greatest vigor.

HF 1. high frequency. **2.** Hispanic female.

Hf *Symbol, Chemistry.* hafnium.

hf. half.

hf. bd. *Printing.* half-bound.

hfe human-factors engineering.

HG 1. High German. **2.** *British.* Home Guard.

Hg *Symbol, Chemistry.* mercury. [from Latin *hydrargyrum,* from Greek *hydrárgyros* literally, liquid silver]

hg hectogram; hectograms.

H.G. 1. High German. **2.** His Grace; Her Grace.

hGH human growth hormone.

hgr hanger.

hgt., height.

hgwy., highway.

H.H. 1. His Highness; Her Highness. **2.** His Holiness.

hhd hogshead; hogsheads.

HH.D. Doctor of Humanities.

HHFA Housing and Home Finance Agency.

H-hour (āch/ou*r/, -ou/ər), the time, usually unspecified, set for the beginning of a planned attack.

HHS Department of Health and Human Services.

HI, Hawaii.

hi•a/tus (hī ā/təs) *n., pl.* **-tuses, -tus.** break or interruption in a series, action, etc.

hi•ba/chi (hi bä/chē) *n.* small charcoal brazier covered with a grill.

hi/ber•nate/ (hī/bər nāt/) *v.,* **-nated, -nating.** spend winter in dormant state. **—hi/ber•na/tion,** *n.* **—hi/ber•na/tor,** *n.*

hi•bis/cus (hī bis/kəs, hi-) *n.* plant with large flowers.

hic/cup (hik/up, -əp) *n.* **1.** sudden involuntary drawing in of breath. **—v. 2.** have hiccups. Also, **hic/cough** (hik/up).

hick (hik) *n.* provincial, unsophisticated person.

hick/o•ry (hik/ə rē) *n., pl.* **-ries.** tree bearing edible nut (**hickory nut**).

hide (hīd) *v.,* **hid** (hid), **hidden** or **hid, hiding,** *n.* **—v. 1.** conceal or be concealed. **—n. 2.** animal's skin.

hide/a•way, *n.* private retreat.

hide/bound/, *adj.* narrow and rigid in opinion.

hid/e•ous (hid/ē əs) *adj.* **1.** very ugly. **2.** revolting.

hide/-out/, *n.* safe place to hide, esp. from the law.

hie (hī) *v.,* **hied, hieing** or **hying.** *Archaic.* go hastily.

hi/er•ar/chy (hī/ə rär/kē) *n., pl.* **-chies.** graded system of officials. **—hi/er•ar/chi•cal, hi/er•ar/chic,** *adj.* **— hi/er•ar/chi•cal•ly,** *adv.*

hi/er•o•glyph/ic (hī/ər ə glif/ik, hī/rə-) *adj.* **1.** of picture writing, as among ancient Egyptians. **—n. 2.** hieroglyphic symbol. **3.** (*usually pl.*) symbol, sign, etc., difficult to decipher.

HIF human-initiated failure.

hi/-fi/ (hī/fī/) *adj.* of high fidelity. **—hi/-fi/,** *n.*

high (hī) *adj.* **1.** tall. **2.** lofty. **3.** expensive. **4.** shrill. **5.** *Informal.* exuberant with drink or drugs. **6.** greater than normal. **7.** elevated in pitch. **—adv. 8.** at or to high place, rank, etc.

high/ball/, *n.* drink of whiskey mixed with club soda or ginger ale.

high/brow/, *n.* **1.** cultured person. **—adj. 2.** typical of a highbrow.

high fidelity, reproduction of sound without distortion. **—high/ fi•del/i•ty,** *adj.*

high/-flown/, *adj.* **1.** pretentious. **2.** bombastic.

high frequency, radio frequency between 3 and 30 megahertz. **—high/-fre/quen•cy,** *adj.*

high/-hand/ed, *adj.* overbearing.

high/lands (-ləndz) *n.* elevated part of country.

high/light/, *v.* **1.** emphasize. **—n. 2.** impor-

H

tant event, scene, etc. **3.** area of strong reflected light.

high′ly, *adv.* **1.** in high place, etc. **2.** very; extremely.

high′-mind′ed, *adj.* noble in feelings or principles.

high′ness (-nis) *n.* **1.** high state. **2.** (*cap.*) title of royalty.

high′-pres′sure, *adj.,* *v.,* **-sured, -suring.** —*adj.* **1.** stressful. **2.** aggressive. —*v.* **3.** persuade aggressively.

high′rise′, *n.* high building. —**high′rise′,** *adj.*

high′road′, *n.* highway.

high′ school′, *n.* school for grades 9 through 12.

high seas, open ocean, esp. beyond territorial waters.

high′-spir′it•ed, *adj.* lively; vivacious.

high′-strung′, *adj.* nervous.

high′-tech′, *n.* **1.** technology using highly sophisticated and advanced equipment and techniques. —*adj.* **2.** using or suggesting high-tech.

high′-ten′sion, *adj.* of relatively high voltage.

high′way′, *n.* main road.

high′way′man, *n.,* *pl.* **-men.** highway robber.

H.I.H. His Imperial Highness; Her Imperial Highness.

hi′jack′ (hī′jak′) *v.* seize (plane, truck, etc.) by force. —**hi′jack′er,** *n.*

hike (hīk) *v.,* **hiked, hiking,** *n.* —*v.* **1.** walk long distance. —*n.* **2.** long walk. —**hik′er,** *n.*

hi•lar′i•ous (hi lâr′ē əs, -lar′-) *adj.* **1.** very funny. **2.** very cheerful. —**hi•lar′i•ous•ly,** *adv.* —**hi•lar′i•ty,** *n.*

hill (hil) *n.* high piece of land. —**hill′y,** *adj.*

hill′bil′ly (-bil′ē) *n.,* *pl.* **-lies.** *Sometimes Offensive.* **1.** Southern mountaineer. **2.** yokel; rustic.

hill′ock (-ək) *n.* little hill.

hilt (hilt) *n.* sword handle.

him (him) *pron.* objective case of **he.**

him•self′ (him self′; *medially often* im-) *pron.* reflexive or emphatic form of **him.**

hind (hīnd) *adj.* **1.** rear. —*n.* **2.** female red deer.

hin′der (hin′dər) *v.* **1.** retard. **2.** stop. —**hin′drance,** *n.*

hind′most′ (hīnd′-) *adj.* last.

hind′sight′, *n.* keen awareness of how one should have avoided past mistakes.

Hin′du (hin′dōō) *n.* adherent of Hinduism. —**Hindu,** *adj.*

Hin′du•ism, *n.* major religion of India.

hinge (hinj) *n.,* *v.,* **hinged, hinging.** —*n.* **1.** joint on which door, lid, etc., turns. —*v.* **2.** depend. **3.** furnish with hinges.

hint (hint) *n.* **1.** indirect suggestion. —*v.* **2.** give hint.

hin′ter•land′ (hin′tər land′) *n.* area remote from cities.

hip (hip) *n.* **1.** projecting part of each side of body below waist. —*adj. Slang.* **2.** familiar with the latest styles or ideas.

hipar high-power acquisition radar.

hip′-hop′, *n. Slang.* popular subculture as characterized by rap music.

hipot high potential.

hip′pie (hip′ē) *n.* person of 1960s who rejected conventional cultural and moral values.

hip′po (hip′ō) *n.,* *pl.* **-pos.** hippopotamus.

hip′po•drome′ (hip′ə drōm′) *n.* arena, esp. for horse events.

hip′po•pot′a•mus (hip′ə pot′ə məs) *n.,* *pl.* **-muses, -mi** (-mī′). large African water mammal.

hire (hīʳr) *v.,* **hired, hiring,** *n.* —*v.* **1.** purchase services or use of. —*n.* **2.** payment for services or use.

hire′ling (-ling) *n.* person whose loyalty can be bought.

hir′sute (hûr′sōōt, hûr sōōt′) *adj.* hairy. —**hir′sute•ness,** *n.*

his (hiz; *unstressed* iz) *pron.* **1.** possessive form of **he. 2.** his belongings.

His•pan′ic (hi span′ik) *n.* person of Spanish or Latin-American descent. —**Hispanic,** *adj.*

hiss (his) *v.* **1.** make prolonged *s* sound. **2.** express disapproval in this way. —*n.* **3.** hissing sound.

hist. 1. histology. **2.** historian. **3.** historical. **4.** history.

his′ta•mine′ (his′tə mēn′, -min) *n.* organic compound released during allergic reactions.

his•tor′ic (hi stôr′ik) *adj.* **1.** Also, **his•tor′i•cal.** of history. **2.** important in or surviving from the past. —**his•tor′i•cal•ly,** *adv.*

his′to•ry (his′tə rē, -trē) *n.,* *pl.* **-ries. 1.** knowledge, study, or record of past events. **2.** pattern of events determining future. —**his•to′ri•an** (hi stôr′ē ən) *n.*

his′tri•on′ics (his′trē on′iks) *n.pl.* exaggerated, esp. melodramatic, behavior. —**his′tri•on′ic,** *adj.* —**his′tri•on′i•cal•ly,** *adv.*

hit (hit) *v.,* **hit, hitting,** *n.* —*v.* **1.** strike. **2.** collide with. **3.** meet. **4.** guess. —*n.* **5.** collision. **6.** blow. **7.** success. **8.** *Slang.* murder. —**hit′ter,** *n.*

hitch (hich) *v.* **1.** fasten. **2.** harness to cart, etc. **3.** raise or move jerkily. —*n.* **4.** fastening or knot. **5.** obstruction. **6.** jerk.

hitch′hike′, *v.,* **-hiked, -hiking.** beg a ride from a stranger. —**hitch′hik′er,** *n.*

hith′er (hith′ər) *adv.* to this place. —**hith′er•ward,** *adv.*

hith′er•to′, *adv.* until now.

HIV, human immunodeficiency virus, the cause of AIDS.

hive (hīv) *n.* shelter for bees.

hives (hīvz) *n.pl.* eruptive skin condition.

H.J. here lies. [from Latin *hīc jacet*]

H.J. Res. House joint resolution.

H.J.S. here lies buried. [from Latin *hīc jacet sepultus*]

HK Hong Kong.

hksw *Telephones.* hookswitch.

hl 1. haul. 2. hectoliter; hectoliters.

H.L. House of Lords.

HLA *Immunology.* human leukocyte antigen.

HLBB Home Loan Bank Board.

hlcl helical.

hlcptr helicopter.

hldg holding.

hldn holddown.

hldr holder.

hll *Computers.* high-level language.

hlpr helper.

HLTL *Computers.* high-level transistor logic.

HLTTL *Computers.* high-level transistor-transistor logic.

HM Hispanic male.

hm hectometer; hectometers.

H.M. Her Majesty; His Majesty.

hma *Computers.* high-memory area.

HMAS Her Majesty's Australian Ship; His Majesty's Australian Ship.

hmc harmonic.

HMCS Her Majesty's Canadian Ship; His Majesty's Canadian Ship.

hmd humidity.

HMF Her Majesty's Forces; His Majesty's Forces.

HMMV humvee: a military vehicle. Also, **HMMWV.** [*H(igh)-M(obility) M(ultipurpose) W(heeled) V(ehicle)*]

HMO, *pl.* **HMOs, HMO's.** health maintenance organization: health-care plan that provides comprehensive services to subscribers.

hmr hammer.

H.M.S., Her (or His) Majesty's Ship.

hnd cont hand control.

hndrl handrail.

hndst handset.

hndwl handwheel.

hng hinge.

hntg hunting.

HO (hō), (in police use) habitual offender.

Ho *Symbol, Chemistry.* holmium.

ho. house.

H.O. 1. Head Office. 2. Home Office.

hoa'gie (hō'gē) *n.* hero sandwich. Also, **hoa'gy.**

hoard (hôrd) *n.* 1. accumulation for future use. —*v.* 2. accumulate as hoard. —**hoard'-er,** *n.*

hoar'frost' (hôr'frôst') *n.* frost (def. 2).

hoarse (hôrs) *adj.* gruff in tone.

hoary (hôr'ē) *adj.* 1. white with age or frost. 2. old. Also, **hoar.**

hoax (hōks) *n.* 1. mischievous deception. —*v.* 2. deceive; trick.

hob'ble (hob'əl) *v.,* -**bled,** -**bling.** 1. limp. 2. fasten legs to prevent free movement.

hob'by (hob'ē) *n., pl.* -**bies.** favorite avocation or pastime. —**hob'by·ist,** *n.*

hob'by·horse', *n.* 1. rocking toy for riding. 2. favorite subject for discussion.

hob'gob'lin, *n.* something causing superstitious fear.

hob'nob' (-nob') *v.,* -**nobbed, -nobbing.** associate socially.

ho'bo (hō'bō) *n., pl.* -**bos, -boes.** tramp; vagrant.

hock (hok) *n.* 1. joint in hind leg of horse, etc. —*v.* 2. pawn.

hock'ey (hok'ē) *n.* game played with bent clubs (**hockey sticks**) and ball or disk.

hock'shop', *n.* pawnshop.

ho'cus-po'cus (hō'kəs pō'kəs) *n.* 1. sleight of hand. 2. trickery.

hod (hod) *n.* 1. trough for carrying mortar, bricks, etc. 2. coal scuttle.

hodge'podge' (hoj'poj') *n.* mixture; jumble.

hoe (hō) *n., v.,* **hoed, hoeing.** —*n.* 1. tool for breaking ground, etc. —*v.* 2. use hoe on.

hog (hôg) *n., v.,* **hogged, hogging.** —*n.* 1. domesticated swine. 2. greedy or filthy person. —*v.* 3. take greedily. —**hog'gish,** *adj.*

hogs'head', *n.* large cask.

hog'tie', *v.,* -**tied, -tying.** 1. tie with all four feet or arms together. 2. hamper; thwart.

hog'wash', *n.* nonsense; bunk.

hog'-wild', *adj.* wildly enthusiastic.

hoi' pol·loi' (hoi' pə loi') common people; the masses.

hoist (hoist) *v.* 1. lift, esp. by machine. —*n.* 2. hoisting apparatus. 3. act of lifting.

hok'ey (hō'kē) *adj.,* **hokier, hokiest.** 1. mawkish. 2. obviously contrived. —**hok'i·ness,** *n.*

HOLC Home Owners' Loan Corporation. Also, **H.O.L.C.**

hold (hōld) *v.,* **held** (held), **holding,** *n.* —*v.* 1. have in hand. 2. possess. 3. sustain. 4. adhere. 5. celebrate. 6. restrain or detain. 7. believe. 8. consider. —*n.* 9. grasp. 10. influence. 11. cargo space below ship's deck. —**hold'er,** *n.*

hold'ing, *n.* 1. leased land, esp. for farming. 2. (*pl.*) legally owned property, esp. securities.

hold'out', *n.* one who refuses to take part, give in, etc.

hold'o'ver, *n.* one remaining from a former period.

hold'up', *n.* 1. delay. 2. robbery at gunpoint.

hole (hōl) *n., v.,* **holed, holing.** —*n.* 1. opening. 2. cavity. 3. burrow. 4. in golf, one of the cups into which the ball is driven. —*v.* 5. drive into hole.

hol'i·day' (hol'i dā') *n.* 1. day or period without work. —*adj.* 2. festive.

ho'li·ness (hō'lē nis) *n.* holy state or character.

ho·lis'tic (hō lis'tik) *adj.* of or using thera-

H

pies that consider the body and the mind as an integrated whole.

hol'lan·daise' (hol'ən dāz') n. rich egg-based sauce.

hol'low (hol'ō) adj. **1.** empty within. **2.** sunken. **3.** dull. **4.** unreal. —n. **5.** cavity. —v. **6.** make hollow.

hol'ly (hol'ē) n., pl. **-lies.** shrub with bright red berries.

hol'ly·hock' (-hok', -hôk') n. tall flowering plant.

hol'o·caust' (hol'ə kôst', hō'lə-) n. **1.** great destruction, esp. by fire. **2.** (cap.) Nazi killing of Jews during World War II.

ho'lo·gram' (hol'ə gram', hō'lə-) n. three-dimensional image made by a laser.

ho·log'ra·phy (hə log'rə fē) n. process of making holograms.

hol'ster (hōl'stər) n. case for pistol.

ho'ly (hō'lē) adj., **-lier, -liest. 1.** sacred. **2.** dedicated to God.

Holy Ghost, third member of Trinity. Also, **Holy Spirit.**

hom'age (hom'ij, om'-) n. reverence or respect.

home (hōm) n. **1.** residence. **2.** native place or country. —adv. **3.** to or at home. —**home'land',** n. —**home'ward,** adv., adj. —**home'less,** adj. —**home'made',** adj.

home'ly, adj., **-lier, -liest. 1.** plain; not beautiful. **2.** simple; without pretense. —**home'li·ness,** n.

home'mak'er, n. person who manages a home.

ho'me·op'a·thy (hō'mē op'ə thē) n. method of treating disease with small doses of drugs that in a healthy person would cause symptoms like those of the disease. —**ho'me·o·path'ic** (-ə path'ik) adj.

ho'me·o·sta'sis (hō'mē ə stā'sis) n. tendency of a system to maintain internal stability. —**ho'me·o·stat'ic** (-stat'ik) adj.

home'sick', adj. longing for home. —**home'sick'ness,** n.

home'spun', adj. **1.** spun at home. **2.** unpretentious. —n. **3.** cloth made at home.

home'stead (-sted, -stid) n. dwelling with its land and buildings.

home'stretch', n. last part of racetrack, endeavor, etc.

hom'ey (hō'mē) adj., **-ier, -iest.** cozy.

hom'i·cide' (hom'ə sīd', hō'mə-) n. killing of one person by another. —**hom'i·cid'al,** adj.

hom'i·ly (hom'ə lē) n., pl. **-lies.** sermon. —**hom'i·let'ic** (-let'ik) adj.

hom'i·ny (hom'ə nē) n. **1.** hulled corn. **2.** coarse flour from corn.

homo-, prefix meaning same or identical, as homogeneous.

ho'mo·ge'ne·ous (hō'mə jē'nē əs) adj. **1.** unvaried in content. **2.** alike. —**ho'mo·ge·ne'i·ty** (-ji nē'ə tē) n.

ho·mog'e·nize' (hə moj'ə nīz', hō-) v.,

-nized, -nizing. form by mixing and emulsifying. —**ho·mog'e·ni·za'tion,** n.

ho'mo·graph' (hom'ə graf', hō'mə-) n. word spelled the same as another but having a different meaning.

hom'o·nym (hom'ə nim) n. word like another in sound, but not in meaning.

ho'mo·pho'bi·a (hō'mə fō'bē ə) n. unreasoning fear or hatred of homosexuals.

Ho'mo sa'pi·ens (hō'mō sā'pē ənz) human being.

ho'mo·sex'u·al (hō'mə sek'shōō əl) adj. **1.** sexually attracted to same sex. —n. **2.** homosexual person. —**ho'mo·sex'u·al'i·ty** (-al'i·tē) n.

Hon., 1. Honorable. **2.** Honorary.

hon'cho (hon'chō) n., pl. **-chos.** Slang. **1.** leader; boss. **2.** important or influential person.

Hond. Honduras.

hone (hōn) n., v., **honed, honing.** —n. **1.** fine whetstone. —v. **2.** sharpen to fine edge.

hon'est (on'ist) adj. **1.** trustworthy. **2.** sincere. **3.** virtuous. —**hon'est·ly,** adv. —**hon'es·ty,** n.

hon'ey (hun'ē) n. sweet fluid produced by bees (**hon'ey·bees'**).

hon'ey·comb', n. wax structure built by bees to store honey.

hon'ey·dew' melon, sweet muskmelon.

hon'eyed (-ēd) adj. sweet or flattering, as speech.

hon'ey·moon', n. vacation taken by newly married couple. —**hon'ey·moon'er,** n.

hon'ey·suck'le, n. shrub bearing tubular flowers.

honk (hongk) n. **1.** sound of automobile horn. **2.** nasal sound of goose, etc. —v. **3.** make such sound.

hon'or (on'ər) n. **1.** public or official esteem. **2.** something as token of this. **3.** good reputation. **4.** high ethical character. **5.** chastity. —v. **6.** revere. **7.** confer honor. **8.** show regard for. **9.** accept as valid.

hon'or·a·ble, adj. **1.** worthy of honor. **2.** of high principles. —**hon'or·a·bly,** adv.

hon'o·rar'i·um (on'ə râr'ē əm) n., pl. **-iums, -ia** (-ē ə). fee paid for professional services customarily not recompensed.

hon'or·ar'y (-rer'ē) adj. conferred as honor.

hood (hŏŏd) n. **1.** covering for head and neck. **2.** automobile engine cover. **3.** hoodlum. —**hood'ed,** adj.

hood'lum (hŏŏd'ləm, hŏŏd'-) n. violent petty criminal.

hood'wink' (hŏŏd'wingk') v. deceive.

hoof (hŏŏf, hŏŏf) n., pl. **hoofs, hooves** (hŏŏvz, hŏŏvz). horny covering of animal foot. —**hoofed,** adj.

hook (hŏŏk) n. **1.** curved piece of metal for catching, etc. **2.** fishhook. **3.** sharp curve. —v. **4.** seize, etc., with hook.

hook'er, n. Slang. prostitute, esp. one who solicits on the street.

hook′up′, *n.* connection of parts or apparatus into circuit, network, machine, or system.

hoo′li·gan (hōō′li gən) *n.* hoodlum.

hoop (hōōp, hŏŏp) *n.* circular band.

hoop′la (hōōp′lä) *n. Informal.* 1. commotion. 2. sensational publicity.

hoo·ray′ (hŏŏ rā′) *interj., n.* (hurrah.)

hoot (hōōt) *v.* 1. shout in derision. 2. (of owl) utter cry. —*n.* 3. owl′s cry. 4. shout of derision.

hop (hop) *v.*, **hopped, hopping**, *n.* —*v.* 1. leap, esp. on one foot. —*n.* 2. such a leap. 3. plant bearing cones used in brewing. 4. (*pl.*) the cones of this plant.

hope (hōp) *n., v.*, **hoped, hoping.** —*n.* 1. feeling that something desired is possible. 2. object of this. 3. confidence. —*v.* 4. look forward to with hope. —**hope′ful**, *adj.* —**hope′ful·ly**, *adv.* —**hope′less**, *adj.* —**hope′less·ly**, *adv.*

Ho′pi (hō′pē) *n., pl.* **-pi, -pis.** member of an American Indian people of the southwest.

hop′per (hop′ər) *n.* funnel-shaped trough for grain, etc.

hor. 1. horizon. 2. horizontal. 3. horology.

horde (hôrd) *n.* 1. multitude. 2. nomadic group.

hore′hound′ (hôr′hound′) *n.* herb containing bitter juice.

hor. interm. (in prescriptions) at intermediate hours. [from Latin *hōrā intermediīs*]

ho·ri′zon (hə rī′zən) *n.* apparent line between earth and sky.

hor′i·zon′tal (hôr′ə zon′tl) *adj.* 1. at right angles to vertical. 2. level. —*n.* 3. horizontal line, etc.

hor′mone (hôr′mōn) *n.* endocrine gland secretion that activates specific organ, mechanism, etc. —**hor·mo′nal**, *adj.*

horn (hôrn) *n.* 1. hard growth on heads of cattle, goats, etc. 2. hornlike part. 3. musical wind instrument. —**horned**, *adj.* —**horn′y**, *adj.*

hor′net (hôr′nit) *n.* large wasp.

horn′pipe′, *n.* 1. lively dance. 2. music for it.

horol. horology.

hor′o·scope′ (hôr′ə skōp′) *n.* chart of heavens used in astrology.

hor·ren′dous (hə ren′dəs) *adj.* dreadful; horrible. —**hor·ren′dous·ly**, *adv.*

hor′ri·ble (hôr′ə bəl) *adj.* dreadful. —**hor′ri·bly**, *adv.*

hor′rid (-id) *adj.* abominable. —**hor′rid·ly**, *adv.*

hor′ror (hôr′ər) *n.* intense fear or repugnance. —**hor′ri·fy**, *v.*, **-fied, -fying.**

hors-d′oeuvre′ (ôr dûrv′) *n., pl.* **-d′oeuvres** (-dûrv′, -dûrvz′). tidbit served before meal.

horse (hôrs) *n.* 1. large domesticated quadruped. 2. cavalry. 3. frame with legs for bearing work, etc. —**horse′back′**, *n., adv.*

—**horse′man**, *n.* —**horse′wo′man**, *n.fem.* —**horse′hair′**, *n.*

horse′play′, *n.* rough or boisterous play.

horse′pow′er, *n.* unit of power, equal to 550 foot-pounds per second.

horse′rad′ish, *n.* cultivated plant with pungent root.

horse sense, common sense.

horse′shoe′, *n.* 1. H-shaped iron plate nailed to horse′s hoof. 2. arrangement in this form. 3. (*pl.*) game in which horseshoes are tossed.

hor. som. (in prescriptions) at bedtime. [from Latin *hōrā somnī* at the hour of sleep]

hors′y, *adj.*, **-ier, -iest.** 1. of or like a horse. 2. dealing with or interested in horses.

hort. 1. horticultural. 2. horticulture.

hor′ta·to′ry (hôr′tə tôr′ē) *adj.* urging strongly.

hor′ti·cul′ture (hôr′ti kul′chər) *n.* cultivation of gardens. —**hor′ti·cul′tur·al**, *adj.* —**hor′ti·cul′tur·ist**, *n.*

hor. un. spatio (in prescriptions) at the end of one hour. [from Latin *hōrae ūnius spatiō*]

horz horizontal.

Hos. *Bible.* Hosea.

ho·san′na (hō zan′ə) *interj.* (praise the Lord!)

hose (hōz) *n.* 1. stockings. 2. flexible tube for water, etc.

ho′sier·y (hō′zhə rē) *n.* stockings.

hosp. hospital.

hos′pice (hos′pis) *n.* 1. shelter for pilgrims, strangers, etc. 2. facility for supportive care of dying persons.

hos′pi·ta·ble (hos′pi tə bəl, ho spit′ə-) *adj.* showing hospitality. —**hos′pi·ta·bly**, *adv.*

hos′pi·tal (hos′pi tl) *n.* institution for treatment of sick and injured. —**hos′pi·tal·i·za′tion**, *n.* —**hos′pi·tal·ize′**, *v.*, **-ized, -izing.**

hos′pi·tal′i·ty (-tal′i tē) *n., pl.* **-ties.** warm reception of guests, etc.

host (hōst) *n.* 1. entertainer of guests. 2. great number. 3. (*cap.*) bread consecrated in Eucharist. —**host′ess**, *n.fem.*

hos′tage (hos′tij) *n.* person given or held as security.

hos′tel (hos′tl) *n.* inexpensive transient lodging.

hos′tile (hos′tl; *esp. Brit.* -tīl) *adj.* 1. opposed; unfriendly. 2. of enemies. —**hos·til′i·ty** (ho stil′i tē) *n.*

hot (hot) *adj.*, **hotter, hottest.** 1. of high temperature. 2. feeling great heat. 3. sharptasting. 4. ardent. 5. fresh or new. 6. *Informal.* currently popular. 7. *Informal.* performing very well. 8. *Slang.* recently stolen. —**hot′ly**, *adv.* —**hot′ness**, *n.*

hot′bed′, *n.* 1. covered and heated bed of earth for growing plants. 2. place where something thrives and spreads.

hot′-blood′ed, *adj.* excitable.

hot cake, pancake.

H

hot dog, 1. frankfurter. **2.** *Slang.* person who acts flamboyantly; show-off.

ho·tel' (hō tel') *n.* house offering food, lodging, etc.

hot flash, sudden, brief feeling of heat experienced by some menopausal women.

hot'head', *n.* impetuous or rash person. —**hot'head'ed,** *adj.*

hot'house' *n.* greenhouse.

hot line, system for instantaneous communications of major importance.

hot plate, portable electrical appliance for cooking.

hot potato, *Informal.* unpleasant or risky situation or issue.

hot rod, *Slang.* car with speeded-up engine. —**hot rodder.**

hot'shot', *n. Slang.* skillful and often vain person.

hot tub, large tub of hot water big enough for several persons.

hot water, *Informal.* trouble.

hound (hound) *n.* **1.** any of several breeds of hunting dog. —*v.* **2.** hunt or track.

hour (ouᵊr, ou'ər) *n.* period of 60 minutes. —**hour'ly,** *adj., adv.*

hour'glass', *n.* timepiece operating by visible fall of sand.

house *n., v.,* **housed, housing.** —*n.* (hous) **1.** building, esp. for residence, rest, etc. **2.** family. **3.** legislative or deliberative body. **4.** commercial firm. —*v.* (houz) **5.** provide with a house.

house'break'er, *n.* person who breaks into another's house to steal. —**house'break'ing,** *n.*

house'bro'ken, *adj.* trained to excrete outdoors or to behave appropriately indoors.

house'fly', *n., pl.* **-flies.** common insect.

house'hold', *n.* **1.** people of house. —*adj.* **2.** domestic.

house'hold'er, *n.* **1.** person who owns house. **2.** head of household.

house'hus'band, *n.* married man who stays at home to manage the household.

house'keep'er, *n.* person who manages a house. —**house'keeping,** *n.*

house'plant', *n.* ornamental plant grown indoors.

house'warm'ing, *n.* party to celebrate a new home.

house'wife', *n., pl.* **-wives.** woman in charge of the home. —**house'wife'ly,** *adj.*

house'work', *n.* work done in housekeeping.

hous'ing (hou'zing) *n.* **1.** dwellings collectively. **2.** container.

HOV high-occupancy vehicle.

hov'el (huv'əl, hov'-) *n.* small mean dwelling.

hov'er (huv'ər, hov'-) *v.* **1.** stay fluttering or suspended in air. **2.** linger about.

Hov'er·craft', *n. Trademark.* vehicle that can skim over water on cushion of air.

how (hou) *adv.* **1.** in what way. **2.** to, at, or in what extent, price, or condition. **3.** why.

how·ev'er, *conj.* **1.** nevertheless. —*adj.* **2.** to whatever extent.

how'itz·er (hou'it sər) *n.* short-barreled cannon for firing shells at an elevated angle.

howl (houl) *v.* **1.** utter loud long cry. **2.** wail. —*n.* **3.** cry of wolf, etc. **4.** wail.

how'so·ev'er, *adv.* however.

hoy'den (hoid'n) *n.* tomboy. —**hoy'den·ish,** *adj.*

HP, horsepower.

HPER Health, Physical Education, and Recreation.

hpot helical potentiometer.

hps high-pressure steam.

HPV human papilloma virus.

HQ, headquarters.

hr., hour.

H.R. House of Representatives.

HRA Health Resources Administration.

H-R diagram *Astronomy.* Hertzsprung-Russell diagram.

H.R.E. 1. Holy Roman Emperor. **2.** Holy Roman Empire.

H. Rept. House report.

H. Res. House resolution.

hrg hearing.

H.R.H. His Royal Highness; Her Royal Highness.

H.R.I.P. here rests in peace. [from Latin *hīc requiēscit in pāce*]

hrs. 1. hot-rolled steel. **2.** hours.

hrzn horizon.

H.S., High School.

hse house.

hsg housing.

H.S.H. His Serene Highness; Her Serene Highness.

hshld household.

HSI heat stress index.

H.S.M. His Serene Majesty; Her Serene Majesty.

hss high-speed steel.

HST Hawaii Standard Time. Also, **H.S.T., h.s.t.**

hsth hose thread.

HSV-1 herpes simplex virus: usually associated with oral herpes. Also, **HSV-I.**

HSV-2 herpes simplex virus: usually causing genital herpes. Also, **HSV-II.**

ht., height.

htd heated.

htg heating.

HTLV *Pathology.* human T-cell lymphotropic virus.

HTLV-1 *Pathology.* human T-cell lymphotropic virus type 1. Also, **HTLV-I.**

HTLV-2 *Pathology.* human T-cell lymphotropic virus type. Also, **HTLV-II.**

HTLV-3 *Pathology.* human T-cell lymphotropic virus type 3; AIDS virus. Also, **HTLV-III.**

HTML *Computers.* HyperText Markup Language.

htr heater.

Hts. Heights.

ht tr heat-treat.

HUAC (hyōō/ak), House Un-American Activities Committee.

hub (hub) *n.* central part of wheel.

hub/bub (hub/ub) *n.* confused noise.

hu/bris (hyōō/bris, hōō/-) *n.* excessive pride or self-confidence.

huck/le•ber/ry (huk/əl ber/ē) *n., pl.* **-ries.** edible berry of heath shrub.

huck/ster (huk/stər) *n.* **1.** peddler. **2.** aggressive seller or promoter.

HUD (hud) Department of Housing and Urban Development.

hud/dle (hud/l) *v.,* **-dled, -dling,** *n.* —*v.* **1.** crowd together. —*n.* **2.** confused heap or crowd.

hue (hyōō) *n.* **1.** color. **2.** outcry.

huff (huf) *n.* fit of anger. —**huf/fy,** *adj.*

hug (hug) *v.,* **hugged, hugging,** *n.* —*v.* **1.** clasp in arms. **2.** stay close to. —*n.* **3.** tight clasp.

huge (hyōōj; *often* yōōj) *adj.,* **huger, hugest.** very large in size or extent. —**huge/ly,** *adv.* —**huge/ness,** *n.*

hu/la (hōō/lə) *n.* Hawaiian dance with intricate arm movements.

hulk (hulk) *n.* hull remaining from old ship.

hulk/ing, *adj.* bulky; clumsy. Also, **hulk/y.**

hull (hul) *n.* **1.** outer covering of seed or fruit. **2.** body of ship. —*v.* **3.** remove hull of.

hul/la•ba•loo/ (hul/ə bə lōō/) *n., pl.* **-loos.** *Informal,* uproar.

hum (hum) *v.,* **hummed, humming,** *n.* —*v.* **1.** make low droning sound. **2.** sing with closed lips. **3.** be busy or active. —*n.* **4.** indistinct murmur. —**hum/mer,** *n.*

hu/man (hyōō/mən) *adj.* **1.** of or like people or their species. —*n.* **2.** Also, **human being.** a person. —**hu/man•ness,** *n.*

hu•mane/ (-mān/) *adj.* tender; compassionate. —**hu•mane/ly,** *adv.*

hu/man•ism, *n.* system of thought focusing on human interests, values, and dignity. —**hu/man•ist,** *n., adj.* —**hu/man•is/tic,** *adj.*

hu•man/i•tar/i•an (-man/i târ/ē ən) *adj.* **1.** philanthropic. —*n.* **2.** philanthropist.

hu•man/i•ty, *n., pl.* **-ties. 1.** humankind. **2.** human state or quality. **3.** kindness. **4.** (*pl.*) literature, philosophy, etc., as distinguished from the sciences.

hu/man•ize/ (-mə nīz/) *v.,* **-ized, -izing.** make or become human or humane. —**hu/man•i•za/tion,** *n.*

hu/man•kind/, *n.* people collectively.

hu/man•ly, *adv.* by human means.

hum/ble (hum/bəl, um/-) *adj.,* **-bler, -blest,** *v.,* **-bled, -bling.** —*adj.* **1.** low in rank, etc. **2.**

meek. —*v.* **3.** abase. —**hum/ble•ness,** *n.* —**hum/bly,** *adv.*

hum/bug (hum/bug/) *n.* **1.** hoax. **2.** falseness.

hum/drum/ (hum/drum/) *adj.* dull.

hu/mid (hyōō/mid) *adj.* (of air) moist. —**hu•mid/i•fi/er,** *n.* —**hu•mid/i•fy/,** *v.,* **-fied, -fy-ing.** —**hu•mid/i•ty,** *n.*

hu/mi•dor/ (-mi dôr/) *n.* humid box or chamber.

hu•mil/i•ate/ (hyōō mil/ē āt/) *v.,* **-ated, -ating.** lower pride or self-respect of. —**hu•mil/i•a/tion,** *n.*

hu•mil/i•ty, *n.* humbleness.

hum/ming•bird/, *n.* very small American bird.

hum/mock (hum/ək) *n.* hillock or knoll.

hu•mon/gous (hyōō mung/gəs, -mong/-) *adj. Slang.* extraordinarily large.

hu/mor (hyōō/mər) *n.* **1.** funniness. **2.** mental disposition. **3.** whim. —*v.* **4.** indulge mood or whim of. —**hu/mor•ist,** *n.* —**hu/mor•ous,** *adj.* —**hu/mor•ous•ly,** *adv.*

hump (hump) *n.* **1.** rounded protuberance. —*v.* **2.** raise in hump.

hump/back/, *n.* **1.** back with hump. **2.** person with such a back. Also, **hunch/back/.**

hu/mus (hyōō/məs) *n.* dark organic material in soils, produced by decomposing vegetable or animal matter.

hunch (hunch) *v.* **1.** push out or up in a hump. —*n.* **2.** hump. **3.** guess or suspicion.

hun/dred (hun/drid) *n., adj.* ten times ten. —**hun/dredth,** *adj., n.*

Hun•gar/i•an (hung gâr/ē ən) *n.* native or language of Hungary. —**Hun•gar/ian,** *adj.*

hun/ger (hung/gər) *n.* **1.** feeling caused by need of food. —*v.* **2.** be hungry.

hun/gry, *adj.,* **-grier, -griest. 1.** craving food. **2.** desirous. —**hun/gri•ly,** *adv.* —**hung/ri•ness,** *n.*

hunk (hungk) *n.* **1.** large piece. **2.** *Slang.* handsome, muscular man.

hun/ker (hung/kər) *v.* squat down.

hunt (hunt) *v.* **1.** chase to catch or kill. **2.** search for. —*n.* **3.** act of hunting. **4.** search. —**hunt/er,** *n.* —**hunt/ress,** *n.fem.*

hur/dle (hûr/dl) *n., v.,* **-dled, -dling.** —*n.* **1.** barrier in race track. —*v.* **2.** leap over.

huricn hurricane.

hurl (hûrl) *v.* drive or throw forcefully. —**hurl/er,** *n.*

hurl/y-burl/y (hûr/lē bûr/lē) *n.* noisy disorder and confusion.

hur•rah/ (hə rä/, -rô/) *interj., n.* (exclamation of joy, triumph, etc.) Also, **hur•ray/** (-rā/).

hur/ri•cane/ (hûr/i kān/, hur/-) *n.* violent storm.

hur/ry (hûr/ē, hur/ē) *v.,* **-ried, -rying,** *n., pl.* **-ries.** —*v.* **1.** act with haste. —*n.* **2.** need for haste. **3.** haste. —**hur/ried•ly,** *adv.*

hurt (hûrt) *v.,* **hurt, hurting,** *n.* —*v.* **1.** injure or pain. **2.** harm. **3.** offend. —*n.* **4.** injury or damage. —**hurt/ful,** *adj.*

H

hur'tle (hûr'tl) v., -tled, -tling. strike or rush violently.

husb. husbandry.

hus'band (huz'bənd) n. 1. man of married pair. —v. 2. manage prudently.

hus'band•ry, n. farming and raising of livestock.

hush (hush) interj. 1. (command to be silent.) —n. 2. silence.

husk (husk) n. 1. dry covering of fruits and seeds. —v. 2. remove husk.

husk'y, adj., -ier, -iest, n., pl. -ies. —adj. 1. big and strong. 2. hoarse. —n. 3. (sometimes cap.) sturdy sled dog of arctic regions.

hus'sy (hus'ē, huz'ē) n., pl. -sies. 1. ill-behaved girl. 2. lewd woman.

hus'tle (hus'əl) v., -tled, -tling, n. —v. 1. work energetically. 2. force or shove violently. —n. 3. energetic activity. 4. discourteous shoving.

hus'tler, n. Slang. 1. person eager for success. 2. swindler. 3. prostitute.

hut (hut) n. small humble dwelling.

hutch (huch) n. 1. pen for small animals. 2. chestlike cabinet with open shelves above.

H.V. 1. high velocity. 2. Also, **h.v., hv** high voltage. 3. high volume.

HVAC heating, ventilating, and air conditioning.

HVDC high-voltage direct current.

HVP hydrolyzed vegetable protein. Also, **H.V.P.**

hvps high-voltage power supply.

hvy. heavy.

HW 1. half wave. 2. Real Estate. hardwood. 3. high water. 4. hot water (heat).

HWM high-water mark. Also, **H.W.M., h.w.m.**

hwy., highway.

hy. Electricity. (formerly) henry.

hy'a•cinth (hī'ə sinth) n. bulbous flowering plant.

hyb hybrid.

hy'brid (hī'brid) n. offspring of organisms of different breeds, species, etc.

hy'brid•ize, v., -ized, -izing, produce or cause to produce hybrids. —**hy'brid•i•za'-tion,** n.

hyd. 1. hydrant. 2. hydraulics. 3. hydrostatics.

hydm hydrometer.

hydr hydraulic.

hy•dran'gea (hī drān'jə) n. flowering shrub.

hy'drant (hī'drənt) n. water pipe with outlet.

hydraul. hydraulics.

hy•drau'lic (hī drô'lik) adj. 1. of or operated by liquid. 2. of hydraulics.

hy•drau'lics, n. science of moving liquids.

hydrelc hydroelectric.

hydro-, prefix meaning: 1. water. 2. hydrogen.

hy'dro•car'bon (hī'drə kär'bən) n. compound containing only hydrogen and carbon.

hy'dro•e•lec'tric (hī'drō-) adj. of electricity

generated by hydraulic energy. —**hy'dro•e•lec•tric'i•ty,** n.

hy'dro•foil' (hī'drə foil') n. powered vessel that can skim on water.

hy'dro•gen (-jən) n. inflammable gas, lightest of elements.

hy'dro•gen•ate' (hī'drə jə nāt', hī droj'ə-) v., -ated, -ating. combine with or treat with hydrogen. —**hy•drog'e•nat'ed,** adj.

hydrogen bomb, powerful bomb utilizing thermonuclear fusion.

hydrogen peroxide, liquid used as antiseptic and bleach.

HYDROPAC (hī'drə pak'), an urgent warning of navigational dangers in the Pacific Ocean, issued by the U.S. Navy Hydrographic Office.

hy'dro•pho'bi•a (hī'drə fō'bē ə) n. 1. rabies. 2. fear of water.

hy'dro•plane', n. 1. airplane that lands on water. 2. light, high-speed motorboat.

hy'dro•pon'ics (-pon'iks) n. cultivation of plants in liquids rather than in soil. —**hy'-dro•pon'ic,** adj.

hydros. hydrostatics.

hy'dro•ther'a•py, n. use of water externally in the treatment of disease or injury.

hy•e'na (hī ē'nə) n. carnivorous African mammal.

hy'giene (hī'jēn) n. 1. the application of scientific knowledge to the preservation of health. 2. a condition or practice conducive to health, as cleanliness. —**hy'gi•en'ic** (-jē-en'ik, -jen'-, -jē'nik) adj. —**hy•gien'ist** (-jē'nist, -jen'ist) n.

hy•grom'e•ter (hī grom'i tər) n. instrument for measuring humidity.

hy'men (hī'mən) n. fold of mucous membrane partly enclosing the vagina in a virgin.

hymn (him) n. song of praise.

hym'nal (him'nl) n. book of hymns. Also, **hymn'book'.**

hyp. 1. hypotenuse. 2. hypothesis. 3. hypothetical.

hype (hīp) v., hyped, hyping, n. Informal. —v. 1. stimulate or agitate. 2. create interest in by flamboyant or questionable methods. —n. 3. intensive or exaggerated promotion.

hyper-, prefix meaning over, above, or excessive, as hyperactive.

hy'per•ac'tive (hī'pər-) adj. abnormally active. —**hy'per•ac•tiv'i•ty,** n.

hy•per'bo•le' (hī pûr'bə lē) n. exaggeration for rhetorical effect. —**hy'per•bol'ic** (hī'pər-bol'ik) adj.

hy'per•crit'i•cal (hī'pər-) adj. excessively critical.

hy'per•gly•ce'mi•a (-glī sē'mē ə) n. abnormally high level of glucose in the blood. —**hy'per•gly•ce'mic** (-mik) adj.

hy'per•ten'sion, n. abnormally high blood pressure. —**hy'per•ten'sive,** adj., n.

hy'per•ven'ti•la'tion, n. prolonged rapid or deep breathing. —**hy'per•ven'ti•late',** v.

hy'phen (hī'fən) n. short line (-) connecting

parts or syllables of a word. —**hy′phen•ate′**, v. —**hy′phen•a′tion**, n.

hyp•no′sis (hip nō′sis) n., pl. -**ses** (-sēz). artificially produced sleeplike state. —**hyp•not′ic** (-not′ik) adj. —**hyp′no•tism′** (-nə-tiz′əm) n. —**hyp′no•tist**, n. —**hyp′no•tize′**, v.

hy′po (hī′pō) n., pl. -**pos**. hypodermic needle or injection.

hy′po•al′ler•gen′ic, adj. designed to minimize the chance of an allergic reaction.

hy′po•chon′dri•a (hī′pə kon′drē ə) n. morbid fancies of ill health. —**hy′po•chon′dri•ac′**, n., adj.

hy•poc′ri•sy (hi pok′rə sē) n., pl. -**sies**. pretense of virtue, piety, etc.

hyp′o•crite (hip′ə krit) n. person given to hypocrisy. —**hyp′o•crit′i•cal,** adj.

hy′po•der′mic (hī′pə dûr′mik) adj. **1.** introduced under the skin, as needle. **2.** syringe and needle for hypodermic injections.

hy′po•gly•ce′mi•a (hī′pō glī sē′mē ə) n. abnormally low level of glucose in the blood. —**hy′po•gly•ce′mic** (-mik) adj.

hy•pot′e•nuse (hī pot′n ōōs′, -yōōs′) n. side of right triangle opposite right angle.

hypoth. 1. hypothesis. **2.** hypothetical.

hy′po•ther′mi•a (hī′pə thûr′mē ə) n. body temperature below normal.

hy•poth′e•sis (hī poth′ə sis, hi-) n., pl. -**ses** (-sēz′). **1.** proposed explanation. **2.** guess. —**hy′po•thet′i•cal** (-pə thet′i kəl) adj.

hys′ter•ec′to•my (his′tə rek′tə mē) n., pl. -**mies**. removal of uterus.

hys•te′ri•a (hi ster′ē ə, -stēr′-) n. **1.** uncontrollable emotion. **2.** psychological disorder. —**hys•ter′i•cal** (-ster′-) adj. —**hys•ter′i•cal•ly,** adv.

hys•ter′ics (-ster′iks) n.pl. fit of hysteria.

Hz, hertz.

H

I

I, i (ī) *n.* ninth letter of English alphabet.

I (ī) *pron.* subject form of first pers. sing. pronoun.

IA, Iowa. Also, **Ia.**

IAAF International Amateur Athletic Federation.

IAB 1. Industry Advisory Board. 2. Inter-American Bank.

IAC Industry Advisory Commission.

IACA Independent Air Carriers Association.

IACB International Association of Convention Bureaus.

IADB 1. Inter-American Defense Board. 2. Inter-American Development Bank.

IAEA International Atomic Energy Agency.

IAG International Association of Gerontology.

IAIA Institute of American Indian Arts.

IAMAW International Association of Machinists and Aerospace Workers.

IAS 1. *Aeronautics.* indicated air speed. 2. Institute for Advanced Study.

ias indicate airspeed.

IAT international atomic time.

IATA International Air Transport Association.

-iatrics, suffix meaning medical care or treatment, as *geriatrics.*

-iatry, suffix meaning healing or medical practice, as *psychiatry.*

IATSE International Alliance of Theatrical Stage Employees (and Moving Picture Machine Operators of the U.S. and Canada).

iaw in accordance with.

ib. 1. in the same book, chapter, page, etc. [from Latin *ibidem*] 2. instruction book.

IBA 1. Independent Bankers Association. 2. International Bar Association.

IBC 1. International Broadcasting Corporation. 2. international business company.

IBD inflammatory bowel disease.

IBEW International Brotherhood of Electrical Workers.

i'bex (ī'beks) *n.,* *pl.* **i'bex•es, ib'i•ces'** (ib'ə-sēz', ī'bə-), **i'bex.** wild goat with backward-curving horns.

IBF international banking facilities.

ibid. (ib'id) ibidem.

i'bi•dem' (ib'i dəm, i bī'dəm) *adv.* in the same book, chapter, etc., previously cited.

i'bis (ī'bis) *n.* wading bird.

-ible, variant of *-able.*

IBR infectious bovine rhinotracheitis.

I.B.T.C.W.H. International Brotherhood of Teamsters, Chauffeurs, Warehousemen, and Helpers of America.

i'bu•pro'fen (ī'byo͞o prō'fən) *n.* anti-inflammatory drug that reduces pain and swelling.

-ic, 1. adjective suffix meaning: of or pertaining to, as *prophetic*; like or characteristic of, as *idyllic*; containing or made of, as *alcoholic*; produced by or suggestive of, as *Homeric.* 2. noun suffix meaning: person having, as *arthritic*; agent or drug, as *cosmetic*; follower, as *Socratic.*

ICA 1. International Communication Agency (1978–82). 2. International Cooperation Administration.

ICAO International Civil Aviation Organization.

icas intermittent commercial and amateur service.

ICBM intercontinental ballistic missile. Also, **I. C.B.M.**

ICC, Interstate Commerce Commission.

ice (īs) *n.,* *v.,* **iced, icing.** —*n.* 1. water frozen solid. 2. frozen dessert. —*v.* 3. cover with ice or icing. 4. cool with ice. —**iced,** *adj.* —**i'ci•ly,** *adv.* —**i'ci•ness,** *n.* —**i'cy,** *adj.*

ice'berg' (-bûrg) *n.* mass of ice floating at sea.

ice'box', *n.* food chest cooled by ice.

ice cream, frozen dessert made with cream or milk, sweeteners, and flavorings.

Icel. 1. Iceland. 2. Icelandic. Also, **Icel**

ice skate, shoe with metal blade for skating on ice. —**ice-skate,** *v.* —**ice skater.**

ICF *Physics.* inertial confinement fusion: an experimental method for producing controlled thermonuclear energy.

ich'thy•ol'o•gy (ik'thē ol'ə jē) *n.* study of fishes. —**ich'thy•ol•o•gist,** *n.*

i'ci•cle (ī'si kəl) *n.* hanging tapering mass of ice.

ic'ing, *n.* preparation for covering cakes.

ICJ International Court of Justice.

ICM Institute of Computer Management.

icm 1. intercom. 2. intercommunication.

i'con (ī'kon) *n.* sacred image.

i•con'o•clast' (-ə klast') *n.* attacker of cherished beliefs. —**i•con'o•clas'tic,** *adj.*

ICR 1. Institute of Cancer Research. 2. Institute for Cooperative Research.

ICRC International Committee of the Red Cross.

icrm ice cream.

-ics, suffix meaning: 1. art, science, or field, as *physics.* 2. activities or practices of a certain kind, as *acrobatics.*

ICSE International Committee for Sexual Equality.

ICSH *Biochemistry, Pharmacology.* interstitial-cell stimulating hormone.

ICU, intensive care unit.

icw interrupted continuous wave.

id (id) *n.* part of the psyche that is the source of unconscious and instinctive impulses.

ID (ī′dē′) *pl.* **IDs, ID's.** document, card, or other means of identification.

ID, Idaho. Also, **Id., Ida.**

IDA 1. Industrial Development Agency. **2.** Institute for Defense Analysis.

IDB 1. Industrial Development Board. **2.** industrial development bond.

IDE *Computers.* integrated drive electronics: hard-drive interface.

i•de′a (ī dē′ə, ī dēə′) *n.* conception in mind; thought.

i•de′al (ī dē′əl, ī dēl′) *n.* **1.** conception or standard of perfection. —*adj.* **2.** being an ideal. **3.** not real. —**i•de′al•ly,** *adv.* —**i•de′al•ize′,** *v.,* -ized, -izing.

i•de′al•ism′, *n.* belief in or behavior according to ideals. —**i•de′al•ist,** *n.* —**i•de′al•is′tic,** *adj.*

ident 1. identical. **2.** identification.

i•den′ti•cal (ī den′ti kəl, i den′-) *adj.* same. —**i•den′ti•cal•ly,** *adv.*

i•den′ti•fy′, *v.,* -fied, -fying. **1.** recognize as particular person or thing. **2.** regard as or prove to be identical. —**i•den′ti•fi•ca′tion,** *n.*

i•den′ti•ty (-tē) *n., pl.* -ties. **1.** fact of being same. **2.** self.

i′de•ol′o•gy (ī′dē ol′ə jē, id′ē-) *n., pl.* -gies. beliefs of group, esp. political. —**i′de•o•log′i•cal,** *adj.*

idf *Telephones.* intermediate distributing frame.

id′i•om (id′ē əm) *n.* **1.** expression peculiar to a language. **2.** dialect. —**id′i•o•mat′ic** (-mat′ik) *adj.*

id′i•o•path′ic (id′ē ə path′ik) *adj.* of unknown cause, as a disease.

id′i•o•syn′cra•sy (-sing′krə sē, -sin′-) *n., pl.* -sies. unusual individual trait. —**id′i•o•syn•crat′ic,** *adj.*

id′i•ot (id′ē ət) *n.* utterly foolish person. —**id′i•ot′ic** (-ot′ik) *adj.* —**id′i•ot′i•cal•ly,** *adv.* —**id′i•o•cy,** *n.*

i′dle (īd′l) *adj., v.,* **idled, idling.** —*adj.* **1.** doing nothing. **2.** valueless. **3.** groundless. —*v.* **4.** do nothing. —**i′dler,** *n.* —**i′dly,** *adv.*

i′dol (īd′l) *n.* object worshiped or adored. —**i′dol•ize′,** *v.*

i•dol′a•try (ī dol′ə trē) *n., pl.* -tries. worship of idols. —**i•dol′a•ter,** *n.* —**i•dol′a•trous,** *adj.*

IDP 1. integrated data processing. **2.** International Driving Permit.

IDR 1. Institute for Dream Research. **2.** international drawing rights.

idrty indirectly.

idx index.

i′dyll (īd′l) *n.* composition describing pastoral scene. Also, **i′dyl.** —**i•dyl′lic** (ī dil′ik) *adj.*

i.e., that is.

IEC International Electrotechnical Commission.

I.E.E.E. (ī′ trip′əl ē′), Institute of Electrical and Electronics Engineers. Also, **IEEE**

IEP Individualized Educational Program.

IES Illuminating Engineering Society.

if (if) *conj.* **1.** in case that. **2.** whether. **3.** though.

IFA *Medicine.* immunofluorescence assay.

IFALP International Federation of Air Line Pilots Associations.

IFC 1. International Finance Corporation. **2.** International Fisheries Commission **3.** International Freighting Corporation.

IFF 1. *Military.* Identification, Friend or Foe: a system to distinguish between friendly and hostile aircraft. **2.** Institute for the Future.

iff *Math.* if and only if.

if′fy, *adj.,* -fier, -fiest. *Informal,* not resolved; indefinite.

IFIP (if′ip), International Federation for Information Processing.

I.F.L.W.U. International Fur and Leather Workers' Union.

IFN *Biochemistry, Pharmacology.* interferon.

ifr instrument flight rules.

IFS International Foundation for Science.

I.F.S. Irish Free State.

IG *Electronics.* ignitor: an electron device.

Ig *Immunology.* immunoglobulin.

I.G. 1. Indo-Germanic. **2.** Inspector General.

IgA *Immunology.* immunoglobulin A.

IgE *Immunology.* immunoglobulin E.

IGFET insulated-gate field-effect transistor.

IgG *Immunology.* immunoglobulin G.

ig′loo (ig′lōō) *n., pl.* -loos. snow hut.

IgM *Immunology.* immunoglobulin M.

ign. 1. ignition. **2.** unknown [from Latin *ignōtus*].

ig′ne•ous (ig′nē əs) *adj.* **1.** produced by great heat. **2.** of fire.

ig•nite′ (ig nīt′) *v.,* -nited, -niting. set on or catch fire. —**ig•ni′tion** (-nish′ən) *n.*

ig•no′ble (ig nō′bəl) *adj.* **1.** dishonorable. **2.** humble. —**ig•no′bly,** *adv.*

ig′no•min′i•ous (ig′nə min′ē əs) *adj.* **1.** humiliating. **2.** contemptible. —**ig′no•min′y,** *n.*

ig′no•ra′mus (-rā′məs, -ram′əs) *n.* ignorant person.

ig′no•rant (ig′nər ənt) *adj.* **1.** lacking knowledge. **2.** unaware. —**ig′no•rance,** *n.*

ig•nore′ (ig nôr′) *v.,* -nored, -noring. disregard.

igt ingot.

i•gua′na (i gwä′nə) *n.* large tropical lizard.

IGY International Geophysical Year.

IHL International Hockey League.

ihp indicated horsepower. Also, **IHP**

IHS 1. Jesus. [from Latin, from Greek: partial transliteration of the first three letters of *Iēsoûs* Jesus] **2.** Jesus Savior of Men. [from Latin *Iēsus Hominum Salvātor*] **3.** in this sign (the cross) shalt thou conquer. [from Latin *In Hōc Signō Vincēs*] **4.** in this (cross) is salvation. [from Latin *In Hōc Salūs*]

IL, Illinois.

Il-, prefix equivalent to *in-*, as *illogical*.
ILA 1. International Law Association. **2.** International Longshoremen's Association. Also, **I. L.A.**
ILAS Instrument Landing Approach System.
I.L.G.W.U. International Ladies' Garment Workers' Union. Also, **ILGWU**
ilk (ilk) *n.* family or kind.
ill (il) *adj.* **1.** not well; sick. **2.** evil. **3.** unfavorable. *—n.* **4.** evil; harm. **5.** ailment. *—adv.* **6.** badly. **7.** with difficulty.
Ill., Illinois.
ill′-ad•vised′, *adj.* showing bad judgment.
ill′-bred′, *adj.* rude.
il•le′gal (i lē′gəl) *adj.* unlawful. —**il•le′gal•ly**, *adv.*
il•leg′i•ble, *adj.* hard to read. —**il•leg′i•bil′i•ty**, *n.* —**il•leg′i•bly**, *adv.*
il′le•git′i•mate (il′i jit′ə mit) *adj.* **1.** unlawful. **2.** born to unmarried parents. —**il′le•git′i•ma•cy** (-mə sē) *n.*
ill′-fat′ed, *adj.* doomed.
il•lib′er•al, *adj.* **1.** not generous. **2.** narrow in attitudes or beliefs.
il•lic′it, *adj.* unlawful; not allowed.
il•lim′it•a•ble (i lim′i tə bəl) *adj.* boundless.
il•lit′er•ate (i lit′ər it) *adj.* **1.** unable to read and write. *—n.* **2.** illiterate person. —**il•lit′er•a•cy**, *n.*
ill′-man′nered, *adj.* having bad manners.
ill′ness, *n.* **1.** state of being ill. **2.** particular ailment; sickness.
il•log′i•cal (i loj′i kəl) *adj.* not logical. —**il•log′i•cal•ly**, *adv.*
ill′-starred′, *adj.* unlucky; ill-fated.
ill′-treat′, *v.* abuse. —**ill′-treat′ment**, *n.*
illum illuminate.
il•lu′mi•nate′ (i lōō′mə nāt′) *v.*, **-nated, -nating.** supply with light. Also, **il•lu′mine** (-min). —**il•lu′mi•na′tion**, *n.*
illus., **1.** illustrated. **2.** illustration.
ill′-use′ *v.*, **-used, -using**, *n. —v.* (il′yōōz′) **1.** treat badly or unjustly. *—n.* (-yōōs′) **2.** Also, **ill′-us′age**. bad or unjust treatment.
il•lu′sion (i lōō′zhən) *n.* false impression or appearance. —**il•lu′sive** (-siv), **il•lu′so•ry** (-sə rē, -zə-) *adj.*
il′lus•trate′ (il′ə strāt′, i lus′trāt) *v.*, **-trated, -trating. 1.** explain with examples, etc. **2.** furnish with pictures. —**il′lus•tra′tion**, *n.* —**il•lus′tra•tive** (i lus′trə tiv) *adj.* —**il′lus•tra′tor**, *n.*
il•lus′tri•ous (i lus′trē əs) *adj.* **1.** famous. **2.** glorious.
ill will, hostile feeling.
ILO International Labor Organization. Also, **I.L.O.**
I.L.P. Independent Labour Party.
ILS 1. *Aeronautics.* instrument landing system. **2.** Integrated Logistic Support.
ILTF International Lawn Tennis Federation.
I.L.W.U. International Longshoremen's and Warehousemen's Union.

Im-, suffix equivalent to *in-*, as *immature*.
imag imaginary.
im′age (im′ij) *n.* **1.** likeness. **2.** idea. **3.** conception of one's character. *—v.* **4.** mirror.
im′age•ry, *n.*, *pl.* **-ries. 1.** mental images collectively. **2.** use of figures of speech.
im•ag′ine (i maj′in) *v.*, **-ined, -ining. 1.** form mental images. **2.** think; guess. —**im•ag′i•na′tion** (-nā′shən) *n.* —**im•ag′i•na•tive** (-nə tiv) *adj.* —**im•ag′i•na•ble**, *adj.*
i•mam′ (i mäm′) *n.* Muslim religious leader.
im•bal′ance (im bal′əns) *n.* lack of balance.
im′be•cile (im′bə sil) *n.* **1.** *Obsolete.* a retarded person having a mental age of up to eight years. **2.** a foolish or stupid person. —**im′be•cil′ic**, *adj.* —**im′be•cil′i•ty** (-sil′i•tē) *n.*
im•bibe′ (im bīb′) *v.*, **-bibed, -bibing.** drink. —**im•bib′er**, *n.*
im•bro′glio (im brōl′yō) *n.*, *pl.* **-glios.** complicated affair.
im•bue′ (im byōō′) *v.*, **-bued, -buing. 1.** inspire. **2.** saturate.
IMCO Inter-Governmental Maritime Consultive Organization.
imd intermodulation distortion.
IMF International Monetary Fund. Also, **I.M.F.**
imit. 1. Also, **imit** imitation. **2.** imitative.
im′i•tate′ (im′i tāt′) *v.*, **-tated, -tating. 1.** copy. **2.** counterfeit. —**im′i•ta′tive**, *adj.* —**im′i•ta′tor**, *n.* —**im′i•ta′tion**, *n.*
im•mac′u•late (i mak′yə lit) *adj.* **1.** spotlessly clean. **2.** pure.
im′ma•nent (im′ə nənt) *adj.* being within. —**im′ma•nence**, *n.*
im′ma•te′ri•al (im′ə tēr′ē əl) *adj.* **1.** unimportant. **2.** spiritual.
im′ma•ture′, *adj.* not mature. —**im′ma•tu′ri•ty**, *n.*
im•meas′ur•a•ble, *adj.* limitless. —**im•meas′ur•a•bly**, *adv.*
immed immediate.
im•me′di•ate (i mē′dē it) *adj.* **1.** without delay. **2.** nearest. **3.** present. —**im•me′di•a•cy** (-ə sē) *n.* —**im•me′di•ate•ly**, *adv.*
im′me•mo′ri•al, *adj.* beyond memory or record.
im•mense′ (i mens′) *adj.* **1.** vast. **2.** boundless. —**im•men′si•ty**, *n.* —**im•mense′ly**, *adv.*
im•merse′ (i mûrs′) *v.*, **-mersed, -mersing. 1.** plunge into liquid. **2.** absorb, as in study. —**im•mer′sion**, *n.*
im′mi•grant (im′i grənt) *n.* person who immigrates.
im′mi•grate′ (-grāt′) *v.*, **-grated, -grating.** come to new country. —**im′mi•gra′tion**, *n.*
im′mi•nent (im′ə nənt) *adj.* about to happen. —**im′mi•nence**, *n.*
im•mo′bile (i mō′bəl, -bēl) *adj.* not moving. —**im′mo•bil′i•ty**, *n.* —**im•mo′bi•lize′**, *v.*

im·mod'er·ate (-it) *adj.* excessive. **—im·mod'er·ate·ly,** *adv.*

im·mod'est, *adj.* not modest. **—im·mod'es·ty,** *n.*

im'mo·late' (im'ə lāt') *v.,* **-lated, -lating. 1.** sacrifice. **2.** destroy by fire. **—im'mo·la'tion,** *n.*

im·mor'al, *adj.* not moral. **—im'mo·ral'i·ty,** *n.* **—im·mor'al·ly,** *adv.*

im·mor'tal, *adj.* **1.** not subject to death or oblivion. **—n. 2.** immortal being. **—im'mor·tal'i·ty,** *n.* **—im·mor'tal·ize',** *v.*

im·mov'a·ble (i mōō'və bəl) *adj.* **1.** fixed. **2.** unchanging.

im·mune' (i myōōn') *adj.* **1.** protected from disease. **2.** exempt. **—im·mu'ni·ty,** *n.* **—im'·mu·ni·za'tion,** *n.* **—im'mu·nize',** *v.*

Immune system, network of cells and tissues that protects the body from pathogens and foreign substances.

immunol. immunology.

im'mu·nol'o·gy (-nol'ə jē) *n.* branch of science dealing with the immune system. **—im'·mu·nol'o·gist,** *n.*

im·mure' (i myōōr') *v.,* **-mured, -muring.** confine within walls.

im·mu'ta·ble, *adj.* unchangeable. **—im·mu'ta·bil'i·ty,** *n.* **—im·mu'ta·bly,** *adv.*

imp (imp) *n.* **1.** little demon. **2.** mischievous child. **—imp'ish,** *adj.* **—imp'ish·ly,** *adv.*

im'pact *n.* (im'pakt) **1.** collision. **2.** influence; effect. **—v.** (im pakt') **3.** collide with. **4.** have effect.

im·pact'ed, *adj.* (of a tooth) wedged too tightly in its socket to erupt properly.

im·pair' (im pâr') *v.* damage; weaken. **—im·pair'ment,** *n.*

im·pale' (im pāl') *v.,* **-paled, -paling.** fix upon sharp stake, etc.

im·pal'pa·ble, *adj.* that cannot be felt or understood.

im·pan'el, *v.,* **-eled, -eling.** list for jury duty.

im·part', *v.* **1.** tell. **2.** give.

im·par'tial, *adj.* unbiased. **—im'par·ti·al'i·ty** (-shē al'i tē) *n.* **—im·par'tial·ly,** *adv.*

im·pas'sa·ble, *adj.* not able to be passed through or along.

im'passe (im'pas, im pas') *n.* deadlock.

im·pas'sioned, *adj.* full of passion.

im·pas'sive, *adj.* **1.** emotionless. **2.** calm. **—im·pas'sive·ly,** *adv.*

im·pa'tience, lack of patience. **—im·pa'tient,** *adj.* **—im·pa'tient·ly,** *adv.*

impd impedance.

im·peach' (im pēch') *v.* charge with misconduct in office. **—im·peach'ment,** *n.*

im·pec'ca·ble (im pek'ə bəl) *adj.* faultless. **—im·pec'ca·bly,** *adv.*

im'pe·cu'ni·ous (im'pi kyōō'nē əs) *adj.* without money.

im·ped'ance (im pēd'ns) *n.* total opposition to alternating current by an electric circuit.

im·pede' (im pēd') *v.,* **-peded, -peding.** hinder. **—im·ped'i·ment** (-ped'ə mənt) *n.*

im·ped'i·men'ta (-ped'ə men'tə) *n.pl.* baggage, etc., carried with one.

im·pel' (im pel') *v.,* **-pelled, -pelling.** urge forward.

im·pend' (im pend') *v.* be imminent.

im·pen'e·tra·ble, *adj.* that cannot be penetrated. **—im·pen'e·tra·bil'i·ty,** *n.* **—im·pen'e·tra·bly,** *adv.*

imper. imperative.

im·per'a·tive (im per'ə tiv) *adj.* **1.** necessary. **2.** *Gram.* denoting command.

im'per·cep'ti·ble, *adj.* **1.** very slight. **2.** not perceptible. **—im'per·cep'ti·bly,** *adv.*

imperf. imperfect.

im·per'fect, *adj.* **1.** having defect. **2.** not complete. **3.** *Gram.* denoting action in progress. **—im'per·fec'tion,** *n.* **—im·per'fect·ly,** *adv.*

im·pe'ri·al (im pēr'ē əl) *adj.* of an empire or emperor.

im·pe'ri·al·ism', *n.* policy of extending rule over other peoples. **—im·pe'ri·al·ist,** *n., adj.* **—im·pe'ri·al·is'tic,** *adj.*

im·per'il, *v.,* **-iled, -iling.** endanger.

im·pe'ri·ous (im pēr'ē əs) *adj.* domineering. **—im·pe'ri·ous·ly,** *adv.*

im·per'ish·a·ble, *adj.* immortal; not subject to decay. **—im·per'ish·a·bly,** *adv.*

im·per'me·a·ble, *adj.* not permitting penetration. **—im·per'me·a·bil'i·ty,** *n.*

impers. impersonal.

im·per'son·al, *adj.* without personal reference or bias. **—im·per'son·al·ly,** *adv.*

im·per'son·ate' (im pûr'sə nāt') *v.,* **-ated, -ating.** act the part of. **—im·per'son·a'tion,** *n.* **—im·per'son·a'tor,** *n.*

im·per'ti·nence, *n.* **1.** rude presumption. **2.** irrelevance. **—im·per'ti·nent,** *adj.* **—im·per'ti·nent·ly,** *adv.*

im'per·turb'a·ble, *adj.* calm. **—im'per·turb'a·bly,** *adv.*

im·per'vi·ous (im pûr'vē əs) *adj.* **1.** not allowing penetration. **2.** incapable of being affected. **—im·per'vi·ous·ly,** *adv.*

im'pe·ti'go (im'pi tī'gō) *n.* contagious skin infection characterized by pustules.

im·pet'u·ous (im pech'ōō əs) *adj.* rash or hasty. **—im·pet'u·os'i·ty** (-os'i tē) *n.* **—im·pet'u·ous·ly,** *adv.*

im'pe·tus (im'pi təs) *n.* **1.** stimulus. **2.** force of motion.

impf. imperfect.

imp. gal. imperial gallon.

im·pi'e·ty, *n., pl.* **-ties. 1.** lack of piety. **2.** act showing this.

im·pinge' (im pinj') *v.,* **-pinged, -pinging. 1.** strike; collide. **2.** encroach.

im'pi·ous (im'pē əs, im pī'-) *adj.* **1.** irreligious. **2.** disrespectful.

impl implement.

im·pla'ca·ble (im plak'ə bəl, -plā'kə-) *adj.* not to be placated.

im·plant' *v.* (im plant') **1.** instill. —*n.* (im'-plant') **2.** device or material used to repair or replace part of the body.

im·plaus'i·ble, *adj.* not plausible. —**im·plau'si·bil'i·ty,** *n.*

im·ple·ment *n.* (im'plə mənt) **1.** instrument or tool. —*v.* (-ment', -mənt) **2.** put into effect. —**im'ple·men·ta'tion,** *n.*

im'pli·cate' (im'pli kāt') *v.,* -cated, -cating. involve as guilty.

im'pli·ca'tion, *n.* **1.** act of implying. **2.** thing implied. **3.** act of implicating.

im·plic'it (im plis'it) *adj.* **1.** unquestioning; complete. **2.** implied. —**im·plic'it·ly,** *adv.*

im·plode' (im plōd') *v.,* -ploded, -ploding. burst inward. —**im·plo'sion,** *n.*

im·plore' (im plôr') *v.,* -plored, -ploring. urge or beg.

implr impeller.

im·ply' (im plī') *v.,* -plied, -plying. **1.** indicate. **2.** suggest.

im·po·lite', *adj.* rude.

im·pol'i·tic, *adj.* not wise or prudent.

im·pon'der·a·ble, *adj.* that cannot be weighed, measured or evaluated.

im·port' *v.* (im pôrt') **1.** bring in from another country. **2.** matter; signify. —*n.* (im'-pôrt) **3.** anything imported. **4.** significance. —**im'por·ta'tion,** *n.* —**im·port'er,** *n.*

im·por'tant (im pôr'tnt) *adj.* **1.** of some consequence. **2.** prominent. —**im·por'tance,** *n.* —**im·por'tant·ly,** *adv.*

im'por·tune' (im'pôr tōōn', -tyōōn', im pôr'-chən) *v.,* -tuned, -tuning. beg persistently. —**im·por'tu·nate,** *adj.*

im·pose' (im pōz') *v.,* -posed, -posing. **1.** set as obligation. **2.** intrude (oneself). **3.** deceive. —**im'po·si'tion** (-pə zish'shən) *n.*

im·pos'ing, *adj.* impressive.

im·pos'si·ble, *adj.* that cannot be done or exist. —**im·pos'si·bil'i·ty,** *n.* —**im·pos'si·bly,** *adv.*

im'post (im'pōst) *n.* tax or duty.

im·pos'tor (im pos'tər) *n.* person who deceives under false name. Also, **im·pos'ter.** —**im·pos'ture** (-chər) *n.*

im'po·tence (im'pə təns) *n.* **1.** lack of power. **2.** lack of sexual powers. —**im'po·tent,** *adj.*

im·pound', *v.* seize by law.

im·pov'er·ish (im pov'ər ish, -pov'rish) *v.* make poor.

im·prac'ti·ca·ble (im prak'ti kə bəl) *adj.* incapable of being put into practice or use.

im·prac'ti·cal, *adj.* not usable or useful.

im'pre·ca'tion (-pri kā'shən) *n.* curse. —**im'pre·cate,** *v.*

im'pre·cise', *adj.* not precise.

im·preg'na·ble (im preg'nə bəl) *adj.* resistant to or proof against attack.

im·preg'nate (-nāt) *v.,* -nated, -nating. **1.**
make pregnant. **2.** saturate; infuse. —**im'-preg·na'tion,** *n.*

im'pre·sa'ri·o (im'prə sär'ē ō', -sâr'-) *n.* person who organizes or manages entertainment events, as opera.

im·press' *v.* (im pres') **1.** affect with respect, etc. **2.** fix in mind. **3.** stamp. **4.** force into public service. —*n.* (im'pres) **5.** act of impressing. —**im·pres'sive,** *adj.* —**im·pres'sive·ly,** *adv.*

im·pres'sion (im presh'ən) *n.* **1.** effect on mind or feelings. **2.** notion. **3.** printed or stamped mark.

im·pres'sion·a·ble, *adj.* easily influenced, esp. emotionally. —**im·pres'sion·a·bly,** *adv.*

im·pres'sion·ism, *n.* (*often cap.*) style of 19th-century painting characterized by short brush strokes to represent the effect of light on objects. —**im·pres'sion·ist,** *n., adj.* —**im·pres'sion·is'tic,** *adj.*

imprg impregnate.

im'pri·ma'tur (im'pri mä'tər, -mā'-) *n.* **1.** permission to print or publish. **2.** sanction; approval.

im'print (im'print) *n.* **1.** mark made by pressure. **2.** sign of event, etc., making impression.

im·pris'on, *v.* put in prison. —**im·pris'on·ment,** *n.*

imprl imperial.

im·prob'a·ble, *adj.* unlikely. —**im·prob'a·bil'i·ty,** *n.* —**im·prob'a·bly,** *adv.*

im·promp'tu (im promp'tōō, -tyōō) *adj., adv.* without preparation.

im·prop'er, *adj.* not right, suitable, or proper. —**im'pro·pri'e·ty** (im'prə prī'i tē) *n.* —**im·prop'er·ly,** *adv.*

improv **1.** improvement. **2.** improvisation.

im·prove', *v.,* -proved, -proving. make or become better. —**im·prove'ment,** *n.*

im·prov'i·dent, *adj.* not providing for the future. —**im·prov'i·dence,** *n.* —**im·prov'i·dent·ly,** *adv.*

im'pro·vise' (im'prə vīz') *v.,* -vised, -vising. prepare for or perform at short notice. —**im·prov'i·sa'tion** (im prov'ə zā'shən) *n.*

imprsn impression.

im·pru'dent, *adj.* not prudent; unwise.

im'pu·dent (im'pyə dənt) *adj.* shamelessly bold. —**im'pu·dence,** *n.* —**im'pu·dent·ly,** *adv.*

im·pugn' (im pyōōn') *v.* cast doubt on.

im'pulse (im'puls) *n.* **1.** inciting influence. **2.** sudden inclination. —**im·pul'sive,** *adj.* —**im·pul'sive·ly,** *adv.*

im·pu'ni·ty (im pyōō'ni tē) *n.* exemption from punishment.

im·pure', *adj.* **1.** not pure. **2.** immoral. —**im·pu'ri·ty,** *n.*

im·pute' (im pyōōt') *v.,* -puted, -puting. attribute.

impv. imperative.

imrs immersion.

in (in) *prep.* **1.** within. **2.** into. **3.** while; during. **4.** into some place. —*adv.* **5.** inside; within.

IN, Indiana.

in-, prefix meaning not or lacking, as *inexperience.*

in., inch.

INA 1. international normal atmosphere. **2.** Israeli News Agency.

in ab•sen'tia (in ab sen'shə, -shē ə) *adv. Latin.* in absence.

in•ac'ti•vate' (in ak'tə vāt') *v.,* -vated, -vating. make inactive. —**in•ac'ti•va'tion,** *n.*

in'ad•vert'ent (in'əd vûr'tnt) *adj.* **1.** heedless. **2.** unintentional. —**in'ad•vert'ence,** *n.* —**in'ad•vert'ent•ly,** *adv.*

in•al'ien•a•ble, *adj.* not to be taken away or transferred.

in•am'o•ra'ta (in am'ə rä'tə, in'am-) *n.* female lover.

in•ane' (i nān') *adj.* silly; ridiculous. —**in•an'i•ty** (i nan'i tē) *n.*

in'ar•tic'u•late (-lit) *adj.* not clear in expression.

in'as•much' as, **1.** seeing that. **2.** to the extent that.

in•au'gu•rate' (in ô'gyə rāt') *v.,* -rated, -rating. **1.** induct into office. **2.** begin. —**in•au'gu•ral,** *adj., n.* —**in•au'gu•ra'tion,** *n.*

inbd inboard.

in'board', *adj., adv.* **1.** inside a hull or aircraft. **2.** nearer the center, as of an airplane.

in'born', *adj.* present at birth; innate.

in'bound', *adj.* inward bound.

in'breed', *v.* produce by breeding of related individuals. —**in'breed'ing,** *n.* —**in'bred',** *adj.*

inc., **1.** incomplete. **2.** incorporated. **3.** increase.

In'ca (ing'kə) *n., pl.* -cas. member of South American Indian people dominant in Peru before the Spanish conquest. —**In'can,** *adj.*

incand incandescent.

in'can•des'cence (in'kən des'əns) *n.* glow of intense heat. —**in'can•des'cent,** *adj.*

in'can•ta'tion (in'kan tā'shən) *n.* **1.** magic ritual. **2.** spell.

in'ca•pac'i•tate' (in'kə pas'i tāt') *v.,* -tated, -tating. make unfit. —**in'ca•pac'i•ty,** *n.*

in•car'cer•ate' (in kär'sə rāt') *v.,* -ated, -ating. imprison. —**in•car'cer•a'tion,** *n.*

in•car'nate (in kär'nit, -nāt) *adj.* embodied in flesh. —**in'car•na'tion,** *n.*

in•cen'di•ar'y (in sen'dē er'ē) *adj., n., pl.* -aries. —*adj.* **1.** of or for setting fires. **2.** arousing strife. —*n.* **3.** person who maliciously sets fires.

in•cense' *v.,* -censed, -censing, *n.* —*v.* (in-sens') **1.** enrage. —*n.* (in'sens) **2.** substance burned to give a sweet odor.

in•cen'tive (in sen'tiv) *n.* stimulus; motivation.

in•cep'tion (in sep'shən) *n.* beginning.

in•ces'sant (in ses'ənt) *adj.* unceasing; uninterrupted. —**in•ces'sant•ly,** *adv.*

in'cest (in'sest) *n.* sexual relations between close relatives. —**in•ces'tu•ous** (-ses'chōō-əs) *adj.*

inch (inch) *n.* unit of length, $\frac{1}{12}$ foot.

in•cho'ate (in kō'it) *adj.* just begun; incomplete.

inch'worm', *n.* moth larva that moves in looping motion.

in'ci•dence (in'si dəns) *n.* range of occurrence or effect.

in'ci•dent, *n.* **1.** happening. **2.** side event. —*adj.* **3.** likely. **4.** naturally belonging. —**in'ci•den'tal** (-den'tl) *adj., n.* —**in'ci•den'tal•ly,** *adv.*

incin incinerator.

in•cin'er•ate' (in sin'ə rāt') *v.,* -ated, -ating. burn to ashes. —**in•cin'er•a'tor,** *n.*

in•cip'i•ent (in sip'ē ənt) *adj.* beginning. —**in•cip'i•ence,** *n.*

in•cise' (in sīz') *v.,* -cised, -cising. cut into; engrave. —**in•ci'sion,** *n.*

in•ci'sive (-sī'siv) *adj.* **1.** sharp. **2.** uncomfortably sharp.

in•ci'sor (in sī'zər) *n.* cutting tooth.

in•cite' (in sīt') *v.,* -cited, -citing. urge to action. —**in•cite'ment,** *n.*

incl., including.

in•cline' *v.,* -clined, -clining, *n.* —*v.* (in-klīn') **1.** tend. **2.** slant. **3.** dispose. —*n.* (in'-klīn) **4.** slanted surface. —**in'cli•na'tion,** *n.*

incln inclined.

in•close' (in klōz') *v.,* -closed, -closing. enclose.

incls inclosure.

in•clude' (in klōōd') *v.,* -cluded, -cluding. **1.** contain. **2.** have among others. —**in•clu'sion** (-klōō'zhən) *n.* —**in•clu'sive** (-siv) *adj.*

incm incoming.

incmpl incomplete.

incnd incendiary.

incog incognito.

in•cog'ni•to' (in'kog nē'tō, in kog'ni tō') *adj., adv.* using assumed name.

incoh incoherent.

in'com•bus'ti•ble, *adj.* incapable of being burned.

in'come (in'kum) *n.* money received.

in'com'ing, *adj.* coming in.

in'com•mu'ni•ca'do (in'kə myōō'ni kä'dō) *adv., adj.* without means of communicating.

in•com'pa•ra•ble, *adj.* unequaled. —**in•com'pa•ra•bly,** *adv.*

in'con•sid'er•ate, *adj.* thoughtless.

in•con'ti•nent, *adj.* **1.** unable to control bodily discharges. **2.** lacking sexual self-restraint. —**in•con'ti•nence,** *n.*

incor. 1. Also, **incorp.** incorporated. **2.** incorrect.

in•cor'po•rate' (-pə rāt') *v.,* -rated, -rating. **1.** form a corporation. **2.** include as part. —**in•cor'po•ra'tion,** *n.*

I

in•cor•po•re•al, *adj.* not corporeal or material.

incorr. incorrect. Also, **incor.**

in•cor•ri•gi•ble (in kôr′i jə bəl, -kor′-) *adj.* not to be reformed.

incpt intercept.

incr. 1. increase. **2.** increased. **3.** increasing. **4.** increment.

in•crease, *v.,* -creased, -creasing, *n.* —*v.* (in krēs′) **1.** make or become more or greater. —*n.* (in′krēs) **2.** instance of increasing. **3.** growth or addition. —**in•creas′ing•ly,** *adv.*

in•cred/i•ble, *adj.* unbelievable; amazing. —**in•cred′i•bly,** *adv.*

in•cred/u•lous, *adj.* not believing. —**in•cred′u•lous•ly,** *adv.*

in′cre•ment (in′krə mənt, ing′-) *n.* addition; increase. —**in′cre•men′tal** (-men′tl) *adj.*

in•crim/i•nate′ (in krim′ə nāt′) *v.,* -nated, -nating. charge with or involve in a crime. —**in•crim/i•na′tion,** *n.*

incrt increment.

in•crust′, *v.* cover with crust or outer layer. —**in′crus•ta/tion,** *n.*

in′cu•bate′ (in′kyə bāt′, ing′-) *v.,* -bated, -bating. keep warm, as eggs for hatching. —**in′cu•ba/tion,** *n.*

in′cu•ba′tor, *n.* **1.** heated case for incubating. **2.** apparatus in which premature infants are cared for.

in•cul/cate (in kul′kāt, in′kul kāt′) *v.,* -cated, -cating. teach; instill.

in•cum/bent (in kum′bənt) *adj.* **1.** obligatory. —*n.* **2.** office holder. —**in•cum′ben•cy,** *n.*

in•cur′ (in kûr′) *v.,* -curred, -curring. bring upon oneself.

in•cur/sion (in kûr′zhən, -shən) *n.* raid.

Ind., Indiana.

Ind.E. Industrial Engineer.

in•debt/ed, *adj.* obligated by debt. —**in•debt/ed•ness,** *n.*

in′de•ci/pher•a•ble, *adj.* illegible.

in′de•ci/sion, *n.* inability to decide.

in•deed′ (in dēd′) *adv.* **1.** in fact. —*interj.* **2.** (used to express surprise, contempt, etc.)

indef. indefinite.

in′de•fat/i•ga•ble (in′di fat′i gə bəl) *adj.* tireless.

in•del/i•ble (in del′ə bəl) *adj.* unerasable.

in•dem/ni•fy′ (in dem′nə fī′) *v.,* -fied, -fying. compensate for or insure against loss, etc. —**in•dem/ni•ty,** *n.*

in•dent′ (in dent′) *v.* **1.** notch. **2.** set in from margin. —**in′den•ta/tion,** *n.*

in•den/ture (in den′chər) *n., v.,* -tured, -turing. —*n.* **1.** contract binding one to service. —*v.* **2.** bind by indenture.

indep independent.

in′de•pend/ent, *adj.* **1.** free. **2.** not influenced by or dependent on others. —**in′de•pend/ence,** *n.*

in′-depth′, *adj.* intensive; thorough.

in′de•struct/i•ble, *adj.* that cannot be destroyed.

in′dex (in′deks) *n., pl.* -dexes, -dices (-də-sēz′), *v.* —*n.* **1.** list of names, topics, etc. with page references. **2.** indicator. —*v.* **3.** provide with index.

In′di•an (-dē ən) *n.* **1.** native of India. **2.** Also, **Amer′ican In′dian.** member of the aboriginal peoples of N. and S. America. —**In′dian,** *adj.*

Indian summer, period of mild, dry weather in late fall.

Indic. 1. indicating. **2.** indicative. **3.** indicator.

in′di•cate′ (in′di kāt′) *v.,* -cated, -cating. **1.** be a sign of. **2.** point to. —**in′di•ca′tion,** *n.* —**in•dic/a•tive** (-dik′ə tiv) *adj.* —**in′di•ca′tor,** *n.*

in•dict′ (in dīt′) *v.* charge with crime. —**in•dict/ment,** *n.*

in•dif/fer•ent, *adj.* **1.** without interest or concern. **2.** moderate. —**in•dif/fer•ence,** *n.*

in•dig/e•nous (in dij′ə nəs) *adj.* native.

in′di•gent (in′di jənt) *adj.* needy; destitute. —**in′di•gence,** *n.*

in′di•ges/tion, *n.* difficulty in digesting food.

in′dig•na/tion (in′dig nā′shən) *n.* righteous anger. —**in•dig/nant,** *adj.*

in•dig/ni•ty, *n., pl.* -ties. **1.** loss of dignity. **2.** cause of this.

in′di•go′ (in′di gō′) *n., pl.* -gos, -goes. blue dye.

in′dis•crim/i•nate (in′di skrim′ə nit) *adj.* done at random; haphazard

in′dis•pose′, *v.,* -posed, -posing. **1.** make ill. **2.** make unwilling.

in′dis•posed′, *adj.* **1.** mildly ill. **2.** unwilling. —**in′dis•po•si/tion,** *n.*

in′dis•sol/u•ble (in′di sol′yə bəl) *adj.* that cannot be dissolved, decomposed, undone, or destroyed.

in•dite′ (in dīt′) *v.,* -dited, -diting. write.

individ. individual. Also, **indiv.**

in′di•vid/u•al (in′də vij′ōō əl) *adj.* **1.** single; particular. **2.** of or for one only. —*n.* **3.** single person, animal, or thing. —**in′di•vid/u•al/i•ty** (-al′i tē) *n.* —**in′di•vid/u•al•ly,** *adv.*

in′di•vid/u•al•ist, *n.* person dependent only on self. —**in′di•vid/u•al•ism′,** *n.*

indl industrial.

indn induction.

in•doc/tri•nate′ (in dok′trə nāt′) *v.,* -nated, -nating. train to accept doctrine. —**in•doc/tri•na′tion,** *n.*

in′do•lent (in′dl ənt) *adj.* lazy. —**in′do•lence,** *n.*

in•dom/i•ta•ble (in dom′i tə bəl) *adj.* that cannot be conquered or dominated.

in′door′, inside a building. —**in•doors′,** *adv.*

indt indent.

indtry industry.

in•du'bi•ta•ble (in dōō'bi tə bəl, -dyōō'-) *adj.* undoubted. —**in•du'bi•ta•bly,** *adv.*

induc. induction.

in•duce' (in dōōs', -dyōōs') *v.,* -duced, -duc•ing. **1.** persuade; influence. **2.** cause; bring on. —**in•duce'ment,** *n.*

in•duct' (in dukt') *v.* bring into office, military service, etc. —**in'duc•tee',** *n.*

in•duc'tion, *n.* **1.** reasoning from particular facts. **2.** act of inducting. —**in•duc'tive,** *adj.*

in•dulge' (in dulj') *v.,* -dulged, -dulging. **1.** accommodate whims, appetites, etc., of. **2.** accommodate one's own whims, appetites, etc. —**in•dul'gence,** *n.* —**in•dul'gent,** *adj.*

indus. 1. industrial. **2.** industry.

in•dus'tri•al•ist (in dus'trē ə list) *n.* owner of industrial plant.

in•dus'tri•al•ize', *v.,* -ized, -izing. convert to modern industrial methods.

in•dus'tri•ous, *adj.* hard-working. —**in•dus'tri•ous•ly,** *adv.*

in'dus•try (in'də strē) *n., pl.* -tries. **1.** trade or manufacture, esp. with machinery. **2.** diligent work. —**in•dus'tri•al,** *adj.*

indv individual.

in•e'bri•ate' *v.,* -ated, -ating. *n.* —*v.* (in ē'brī āt') **1.** make drunk. —*n.* (-it) **2.** drunken person. —**in•e'bri•a'tion,** *n.*

in•ef'fa•ble (in ef'ə bəl) *adj.* that cannot be described.

in•ef•fec'tu•al, *adj.* futile; unsatisfactory.

in•ept' (in ept', i nept') *adj.* careless; unskilled. —**in•ept'i•tude',** *n.* —**in•ept'ly,** *adv.* —**in•ept'ness,** *n.*

in•eq'ui•ty, *n., pl.* -ties. injustice.

in•ert' (in ûrt', i nûrt') *adj.* **1.** without inherent power to move, resist, or act. **2.** slow-moving. —**in•er'tia,** *n.*

in•ev'i•ta•ble (in ev'i tə bəl) *adj.* not to be avoided. —**in•ev'i•ta•bil'i•ty,** *n.* —**in•ev'i•ta•bly,** *adv.*

in•ex'o•ra•ble (in ek'sər ə bəl) *adj.* unyielding. —**in•ex'o•ra•bly,** *adv.*

in•ex'pert (in eks'pûrt, in'ik spûrt') *adj.* unskilled.

in•ex'pli•ca•ble (in ek'spli kə bəl, in'ik-splik'ə-) *adj.* not to be explained. —**in•ex'pli•ca•bly,** *adv.*

in•ex'tri•ca•ble (in ek'stri kə bəl, in'ik-strik'ə-) *adj.* that cannot be freed or disentangled. —**in•ex'tri•ca•bly,** *adv.*

INF European-based U.S. nuclear weapons that were capable of striking the Soviet Union and Soviet ones that could hit Western Europe. [*I(ntermediate-range) N(uclear) F(orces)*]

inf 1. *Math.* greatest lower bound. [from Latin *infimum*] **2.** infinite. **3.** infinity.

Inf. 1. infantry. **2.** infuse [from Latin *infunde*].

in f. in the end; finally. [from Latin *in fine*]

in•fal'li•ble, *adj.* never failing or making mistakes. —**in•fal'li•bly,** *adv.*

in'fa•my (in'fə mē) *n., pl.* -mies. evil repute. —**in'fa•mous,** *adj.*

in'fant (in'fənt) *n.* very young baby. —**in'fan•cy,** *n.* —**in'fan•tile'** (-fən tīl') *adj.*

in'fan•try (in'fən trē) *n., pl.* -tries. soldiers who fight on foot. —**in'fan•try•man,** *n.*

in•farct' (in' färkt', in färkt') *n.* area of dead or dying tissue, as in the heart. Also, **in•farc'tion.**

in•fat'u•ate' (in fach'ōō āt') *v.,* -ated, -ating. inspire with foolish passion. —**in•fat'u•a'tion,** *n.*

in•fect' (in fekt') *v.* affect, esp. with disease germs. —**in•fec'tion,** *n.*

in•fec'tious, *adj.* spreading readily.

in•fer' (in fûr') *v.,* -ferred, -ferring. conclude or deduce. —**in'fer•ence,** *n.*

in•fe'ri•or (in fēr'ē ər) *adj.* **1.** less good, important, etc. —*n.* **2.** person inferior to others. —**in•fe'ri•or'i•ty** (-ôr'i tē) *n.*

in•fer'nal (in fûr'nl) *adj.* **1.** of hell. **2.** *Informal.* outrageous.

in•fer'no (-nō) *n., pl.* -nos. hell.

in•fest' (in fest') *v.* overrun; trouble. —**in'fes•ta'tion,** *n.*

in'fi•del (in'fi dl, -del') *n.* unbeliever.

in'field', *n.* **1.** area of baseball field inside base lines. **2.** players in infield. —**in'field'er,** *n.*

in'fight'ing, *n.* conflict within group.

in•fil'trate (in fil'trāt, in'fil trāt') *v.,* -trated, -trating. pass in, as by filtering. —**in'fil•tra'tion,** *n.*

infin. infinitive.

in'fi•nite (in'fə nit) *adj.* **1.** vast; endless. —*n.* **2.** that which is infinite. —**in•fin'i•ty** (in fin'i tē) *n.*

in'fin•i•tes'i•mal (in'fin i tes'ə məl) *adj.* immeasurably small. —**in'fin•i•tes'i•mal•ly,** *adv.*

in•fin'i•tive (in fin'i tiv) *n.* simple form of verb.

in•firm' (-fûrm') *adj.* feeble; weak. —**in•fir'mi•ty,** *n.*

in•fir'ma•ry (-fûr'mə rē) *n., pl.* -ries. hospital.

in•flame', *v.,* -flamed, -flaming. **1.** set afire. **2.** redden. **3.** excite. **4.** cause bodily reaction marked by redness, pain, etc. —**in•flam'ma•ble** (-flam'ə bəl) *adj.* —**in•flam'ma•to'ry** (-tô'rē) *adj.* —**in•flam•ma'tion** (-flə mā'shən) *n.*

in•flate' (in flāt') *v.,* -flated, -flating. **1.** swell or expand with air or gas. **2.** increase unduly. —**in•flat'a•ble,** *adj.*

in•fla'tion (-shən) *n.* **1.** rise in prices when currency or credit expands faster than available goods or services. **2.** act of inflating. —**in•fla'tion•ar'y,** *adj.*

in•flect' (in flekt') *v.* **1.** bend. **2.** modulate. **3.** display forms of a word. —**in•flec'tion,** *n.* —**in•flec'tion•al,** *adj.*

in•flict' (in flikt') *v.* impose harmfully. —**in•flic'tion,** *n.*

I

in′flu•ence (in′flōō əns) *n., v.,* **-enced, -enc-
ing.** —*n.* **1.** power to affect another. **2.** something that does this. —*v.* **3.** move, affect, or
sway. —**in′flu•en′tial** (-en′shəl) *adj.*

in′flu•en′za (-en′zə) *n.* contagious disease
caused by virus.

in′flux′, *n.* instance of flowing in.

info (in′fō), information.

in′fo•mer′cial (in′fō mûr′shəl) *n.* program-
length television commercial designed to appear to be standard programming rather than
an advertisement.

in•form′ (in fôrm′) *v.* supply with information. —**in•form′ant,** *n.* —**in•form′er,** *n.*
—**in•form′a•tive,** *adj.*

in′for•ma′tion (-fər mā′shən) *n.* factual
knowledge. —**in′for•ma′tion•al,** *adj.*

Information superhighway, large-scale
communications network linking computers,
television sets, etc.

in′fo•tain′ment (in′fō tān′mənt) *n.* broadcasting or publishing that strives to treat factual matter in an entertaining way, as by
dramatizing or fictionalizing real events.

in•frac′tion (in frak′shən) *n.* violation.

in′fra•red′ (in′frə-) *n.* part of invisible spectrum.

in′fra•struc′ture, *n.* **1.** basic framework of
system or organization. **2.** basic facilities, as
transportation and communications systems.

in•fringe′ (in frinj′) *v.* **-fringed, -fringing.**
violate; encroach. —**in•fringe′ment,** *n.*

in•fu′ri•ate′ (in fyŏŏr′ē āt′) *v.,* **-ated, -ating.**
enrage.

in•fuse′ (in fyōōz′) *v.,* **-fused, -fusing. 1.** instill; fortify. **2.** steep. —**in•fu′sion,** *n.*

in•gen′ious (in jēn′yəs) *adj.* inventive;
clever. —**in•gen′ious•ly,** *adv.* —**in•ge•nu′i•
ty** (in′jə nōō′i tē, -nyōō′-) *n.*

in′ge•nue′ (an′zhə nōō) *n.* **1.** role of an innocent young woman in a play. **2.** actress
who plays this role.

in•gen′u•ous (in jen′yōō əs) *adj.* free from
deceit; innocent. —**in•gen′u•ous•ly,** *adv.*

in•gest′ (in jest′) *v.* take into the body, as
food or liquid. —**in•ges′tion,** *n.*

in′got (ing′gət) *n.* cast mass of metal.

in•grained′, *adj.* fixed firmly.

in′grate (in′grāt) *n.* ungrateful person.

in•gra′ti•ate′ (in grā′shē āt′) *v.,* **-ated, -at-
ing.** get (oneself) into someone's good
graces.

in•gre′di•ent (in grē′dē ənt) *n.* element or
part of mixture.

in′gress (in′gres) *n.* entrance.

INH *Pharmacology, Trademark.* a brand of iso-
niazid.

in•hab′it (in hab′it) *v.* live in. —**in•hab′it•
ant,** *n.*

in•hal′ant (in hā′lənt) *n.* substance inhaled,
as a medicine.

in′ha•la′tor (in′hə lā′tər) *n.* **1.** apparatus to
help one inhale medicine, etc. **2.** respirator.

in•hale′ (in hāl′) *v.,* **-haled, -haling.** breathe
in. —**in′ha•la′tion,** *n.*

in•hal′er, *n.* inhalator.

inher. inheritance.

in•here′ (in hēr′) *v.,* **-hered, -hering.** be inseparable part or element. —**in•her′ent**
(-hēr′ənt, -her′-) *adj.*

in•her′it (in her′it) *v.* become heir to. —**in•
her′it•ance,** *n.*

in. Hg *Meteorology.* inch of mercury.

in•hib′it (in hib′it) *v.* restrain or hinder.
—**in′hi•bi′tion,** *n.*

in•hib′i•tor, *n.* substance that slows or stops
a chemical reaction.

in′house′ (*adj.* in′hous′; *adv.* -hous′) *adj.,
adv.* within or using an organization's own
staff or resources.

in•hu′man, *adj.* **1.** brutal; heartless. **2.** not
human. —**in′hu•man′i•ty,** *n.*

in•im′i•cal (i nim′i kəl) *adj.* **1.** adverse. **2.**
hostile.

in•im′i•ta•ble (i nim′i tə bəl) *adj.* not to be
imitated.

in•iq′ui•ty (i nik′wi tē) *n., pl.* **-ties. 1.**
wicked injustice. **2.** sin. —**in•iq′ui•tous,** *adj.*

init. Also, **init** initial.

in•i′tial (i nish′əl) *adj., n., v.,* **-tialed, -tial-
ing.** —*adj.* **1.** of or at beginning. —*n.* **2.** first
letter of word. —*v.* **3.** sign with initials of
one's name. —**in•i′tial•ly,** *adv.*

in•i′ti•ate′ (i nish′ē āt′) *v.,* **-ated, -ating. 1.**
begin. **2.** admit with ceremony. —**in•i′ti•a′-
tion,** *n.*

in•i′ti•a•tive (i nish′ē ə tiv, i nish′ə-) *n.* **1.**
beginning action. **2.** readiness to proceed.

in•ject′ (in jekt′) *v.* force, as into tissue. —**in•
jec′tion,** *n.* —**in•jec′tor,** *n.*

in•junc′tion (in jungk′shən) *n.* order or ad-
monition.

in′jure (in′jər) *v.,* **-jured, -juring. 1.** hurt. **2.**
do wrong to. —**in•ju′ri•ous** (-jŏŏr′ē əs) *adj.*
—**in•ju′ri•ous•ly,** *adv.* —**in′ju•ry,** *n.*

ink (ingk) *n.* **1.** writing fluid. —*v.* **2.** mark
with ink. —**ink′y,** *adj.*

ink′ling (ingk′ling) *n.* hint.

inl inlet.

in′land (*adj.* in′lənd; *adv., n.* -land′, -lənd)
adj. **1.** of or in the interior of a region. **2.** not
foreign. —*adv.* **3.** of or toward inland area.
—*n.* **4.** inland area.

in′-law′ (in lô′, in′lô′) *n.* relative by marriage.

in•lay′, *v.,* **-laid, -laying,** *n.* —*v.* (in′lā′, in′-
lā′) **1.** ornament with design set in surface.
—*n.* (in′lā′) **2.** inlaid work.

in′let (-let, -lit) *n.* narrow bay.

in-line skate, roller skate with four wheels in
a straight line.

in loc. cit. in the place cited. [from Latin *in
locō citātō*]

in′mate′, *n.* person confined in prison, hospital, etc.

in mem. in memoriam.

in•me•mo′ri•am (in mə môr′ē əm) in memory (of).

in′most′, *adj.* farthest within. Also, **in′ner•most′**.

inn (in) *n.* **1.** hotel. **2.** tavern.

in•nards (in′ərdz) *n.pl.* **1.** internal parts of the body. **2.** internal parts, structure, etc., of something.

in•nate′ (i nāt′, in′āt) *adj.* natural; born into one.

in′ner (in′ər) *adj.* **1.** being farther within. **2.** spiritual.

inner city, central part of city.

in′ner-direct′ed, *adj.* guided by one's own values rather than by external pressures.

in′ning (in′ing) *n. Baseball.* one round of play for both teams.

in′no•cence (in′ə səns) *n.* **1.** freedom from guilt. **2.** lack of worldly knowledge. —**in′no•cent**, *adj., n.*

in•noc′u•ous (i nok′yōō əs) *adj.* harmless.

in′no•vate′ (in′ə vāt′) *v.*, **-vated, -vating.** bring in something new. —**in′no•va′tion**, *n.* —**in′no•va′tor**, *n.* —**in′no•va′tive**, *adj.*

in′nu•en′do (in′yōō en′dō) *n.*, *pl.* **-dos, -does.** hint of wrong.

in•nu′mer•a•ble, *adj.* **1.** very numerous. **2.** that cannot be counted.

in•oc′u•late′ (i nok′yə lāt′) *v.*, **-lated, -lating.** immunize. —**in•oc′u•la′tion**, *n.*

inop inoperative.

in•or′di•nate (in ôr′dn it) *adj.* excessive. —**in•or′di•nate•ly**, *adv.*

inorg. inorganic.

INP International News Photos.

inp input.

in′pa′tient, *n.* patient who stays in hospital while receiving care or treatment.

in′put′, *n., v.*, **-putted** or **-put, putting.** —*n.* **1.** power, etc., supplied to machine. **2.** information given computer. —*v.* **3.** enter (data) into computer. —**in′put′ter**, *n.*

inq inquiry.

in′quest, *n.* legal inquiry, esp. by coroner.

in•quire′ (in kwī°r′) *v.*, **-quired, -quiring. 1.** ask. **2.** make investigation. —**in•quir′y** (in-kwī°r′ē, in′kwə rē) *n.*

in′qui•si′tion (in′kwə zish′ən, ing′-) *n.* probe; investigation. —**in•quis′i•tor**, *n.*

in•quis′i•tive (-kwiz′i tiv) *adj.* having great curiosity.

inr inner.

in re (in rē′, rā′) in the matter of.

I.N.R.I. Jesus of Nazareth, King of the Jews. [from Latin *Iēsūs Nazarēnus, Rēx Iūdaeōrum*]

in′road′, *n.* encroachment.

ins., **1.** inches. **2.** insurance.

in•sane′ (in sān′) *adj.* mentally deranged. —**in•san′i•ty** (-san′i tē) *n.*

in•sa′ti•a•ble (in sā′shə bəl, -shē ə-) *adj.* impossible to satisfy.

in•scribe′ (in skrīb′) *v.*, **-scribed, -scribing.**

1. write or engrave. **2.** dedicate. —**in•scrip′-tion** (-skrip′shən) *n.*

in•scru′ta•ble (in skrōō′tə bəl) *adj.* that cannot be understood. —**in•scru′ta•bil′i•ty**, *n.*

in./sec. inches per second.

in′sect (in′sekt) *n.* small six-legged animal with body in three parts.

in•sec′ti•cide′ (-sek′tə sīd′) *n.* chemical for killing insects.

in•sem′i•nate′ (in sem′ə nāt′) *v.*, **-nated, -nating. 1.** sow seed in. **2.** impregnate. —**in•sem′i•na′tion**, *n.*

in•sen′sate (in sen′sāt, -sit) *adj.* without feeling.

in•sen′si•ble, *adj.* **1.** incapable of feeling or perceiving. **2.** not aware; unconscious. **3.** not perceptible by the senses.

insep. inseparable. Also, **insep**

in•sert′, *v.* (in sûrt′) **1.** put or set in. —*n.* (in′sûrt) **2.** something inserted. —**in•ser′-tion**, *n.*

in′shore′, *adj.* **1.** on or close to the shore. —*adv.* **2.** toward the shore.

in′side′ (in′sīd′, in′sīd′) *prep.*, *adv.* **1.** within. —*n.* **2.** inner part. —*adj.* **3.** inner.

in′sid′er, *n.* **1.** member of certain organization, society, etc. **2.** person who has influence, esp. because privy to confidential information.

in•sid′i•ous (in sid′ē əs) *adj.* artfully treacherous. —**in•sid′i•ous•ly**, *adv.*

in′sight′, *n.* discernment.

in•sig′ni•a (in sig′nē ə) *n.*, *pl.* **-nia** or **-nias.** badge or other symbol of rank, honor, etc.

in•sin′u•ate′ (in sin′yōō āt′) *v.*, **-ated, -ating. 1.** hint slyly. **2.** put into mind. **3.** make one's way artfully. —**in•sin′u•a′tion**, *n.*

in•sip′id (in sip′id) *adj.* without distinctive qualities; vapid. —**in•sip′id•ly**, *adv.*

in•sist′ (in sist′) *v.* be firm or persistent. —**in•sist′ence**, *n.* —**in•sist′ent**, *adj.*

in′so•far′, *adv.* to such extent.

insol. insoluble.

in′sole′, *n.* **1.** inner sole of shoe. **2.** removable inner sole.

in′so•lent (in′sə lənt) *adj.* boldly rude. —**in′so•lence**, *n.*

in•sol′vent, *adj.* without funds to pay one's debts. —**in•sol′ven•cy**, *n.*

in•som′ni•a (in som′nē ə) *n.* sleeplessness.

in′so•much′, *adv.* **1.** to such a degree (that). **2.** inasmuch (as).

in•sou′ci•ant (in sōō′sē ənt) *adj.* free from concern or anxiety. —**in•sou′ci•ance**, *n.*

insp. **1.** inspection. **2.** inspector.

in•spect′ (in spekt′) *v.* view critically or officially. —**in•spec′tion**, *n.*

in•spec′tor, *n.* **1.** person with duty to inspect. **2.** minor police official.

in•spire′ (in spī°r′) *v.*, **-spired, -spiring. 1.** arouse (emotion, etc.). **2.** prompt to extraordinary actions. **3.** inhale. —**in′spi•ra′tion**, (in′spə rā′shən) *n.* —**in′spi•ra′tion•al**, *adj.*

Inst., 1. Institute. 2. Institution.

in•stall′ (in stôl′) *v.* 1. put in position for use. 2. establish. —**in′stal•la′tion,** *n.*

in•stall′ment, *n.* division, as of payment or story. Also, **in•stal′ment.**

installment plan, system for paying in installments.

in′stance (in′stəns) *n., v.,* **-stanced, -stancing.** —*n.* 1. case; example. —*v.* 2. cite.

in′stant, *n.* 1. moment. 2. point of time now present. —*adj.* 3. immediate. —**in′stant•ly,** *adv.*

in′stan•ta′ne•ous (-stən tā′nē əs) *adj.* occurring, etc., in an instant. —**in′stan•ta′ne•ous•ly,** *adv.*

in•stead′ (in sted′) *adv.* in place of.

in′step′, *n.* upper arch of foot.

in′sti•gate′ (in′sti gāt′) *v.,* **-gated, -gating.** incite to action. —**in′sti•ga′tion,** *n.* —**in′sti•ga′tor,** *n.*

in•still′ (in stil′) *v.* introduce slowly. —**in•still′ment,** *n.*

in′stinct (in′stingkt) *n.* natural impulse or talent. —**in•stinc′tive,** *adj.*

in′sti•tute′ (in′sti tōōt′, -tyōōt′) *v.,* **-tuted, -tuting,** *n.* —*v.* 1. establish. 2. put into effect. —*n.* 3. society or organization. 4. established law, custom, etc.

in′sti•tu′tion, *n.* 1. organization with public purpose. 2. established tradition, etc. 3. act of instituting. —**in′sti•tu′tion•al,** *adj.* —**in′sti•tu′tion•al•ize′,** *v.,* **-ized, -izing.**

instl 1. install. 2. installation.

instm instrumentation.

instr. 1. instruct. 2. instructor. 3. instrument. 4. instrumental.

in•struct′ (in strukt′) *v.* 1. order. 2. teach. —**in•struc′tion,** *n.* —**in•struc′tive,** *adj.* —**in•struc′tor,** *n.*

in′stru•ment (in′strə mənt) *n.* 1. tool. 2. device for producing music. 3. means; agent. 4. legal document. —**in′stru•men′tal** (-men′tl) *adj.* —**in′stru•men•tal′i•ty** (-tal′i tē) *n.*

insuf insufficient.

insul 1. insulate. 2. insulation.

in′su•lar (in′sə lər, ins′yə-) *adj.* 1. of islands. 2. narrow in viewpoint. —**in′su•lar′i•ty,** *n.*

in′su•late′ (-lāt′) *v.,* **-lated, -lating.** cover with nonconducting material. —**in′su•la′tion,** *n.* —**in′su•la′tor,** *n.*

in′su•lin (in′sə lin, ins′yə-) *n.* synthetic hormone used to treat diabetes.

in•sult′ *v.* (in sult′) 1. treat with open contempt. —*n.* (in′sult) 2. such treatment.

in•su′per•a•ble (in sōō′pər ə bəl) *adj.* that cannot be overcome.

in•sure′, *v.,* **-sured, -suring.** 1. make certain. 2. guarantee payment in case of harm to or loss of. —**in•sur′ance,** *n.* —**in•sured′,** *n., adj.* —**in•sur′er,** *n.*

in•sur′gent (in sûr′jənt) *n.* 1. rebel. —*adj.* 2. rebellious.

in′sur•rec′tion (in′sə rek′shən) *n.* armed revolt. —**in′sur•rec′tion•ist,** *n.*

int., 1. interest. 2. interior 3. interjection. 4. international. 5. intransitive.

in•tact′ (in takt′) *adj.* undamaged; whole.

in•tagl′io (in tal′yō, -täl′-) *n., pl.* **-taglios, -tagli** (-tal′yē, -täl′-). design carved into rather than projecting from a surface.

in′take′, *n.* 1. point at which something is taken in. 2. what is taken in.

intchg interchangeable.

intcom intercommunication.

intcon interconnection.

integ 1. integral. 2. integrate.

in′te•ger (in′ti jər) *n.* 1. whole number. 2. entity.

in′te•gral (in′ti grəl, in teg′rəl) *adj.* 1. necessary to completeness. 2. entire.

in′te•grate′ (in′ti grāt′) *v.,* **-grated, -grating.** 1. bring into whole. 2. complete. 3. abolish segregation by race. —**in′te•gra′tion,** *n.*

integrg integrating.

in•teg′ri•ty (in teg′ri tē) *n.* 1. soundness of character; honesty. 2. perfect condition.

in•teg′u•ment (in teg′yə mənt) *n.* skin, rind, etc.

intel intelligence.

in′tel•lect′ (in′tl ekt′) *n.* 1. reasoning. 2. mental capacity.

in′tel•lec′tu•al, *adj.* 1. of intellect. 2. devising concepts in dealing with problems. —*n.* 3. person who pursues intellectual interests. —**in′tel•lec′tu•al•ly,** *adv.*

in•tel′li•gence (in tel′i jəns) *n.* 1. ability to learn and understand. 2. news. 3. gathering of secret information. —**in•tel′li•gent,** *adj.*

in•tel′li•gi•ble (-jə bəl) *adj.* understandable. —**in•tel′li•gi•bil′i•ty,** *n.* —**in•tel′li•gi•bly,** *adv.*

INTELSAT (in tel′sat′, in′tel-), International Telecommunications Satellite Consortium.

inten intensity.

in•tend′ (in tend′) *v.* plan; design.

in•tend′ed, *n. Informal.* person one plans to marry.

Intens *Grammar.* intensifier. Also, **intens**

intens. 1. intensifier. 2. intensive.

in•tense′ (in tens′) *adj.* 1. extremely powerful. 2. emotional. —**in•ten′si•fi•ca′tion** (-ten′sə fi kā′shən) *n.* —**in•ten′si•fy′** *v.,* **-fied, -fying.** —**in•ten′si•ty,** *n.*

in•ten′sive, *adj.* thorough.

in•tent′ (in tent′) *n.* 1. purpose. —*adj.* 2. firmly concentrated. 3. firmly purposeful. —**in•tent′ly,** *adv.*

in•ten′tion, *n.* 1. purpose. 2. meaning. —**in•ten′tion•al,** *adj.*

in•ter′ (in tûr′) *v.,* **-terred, -terring.** bury.

inter-, prefix meaning: 1. between or among, as *interdepartmental.* 2. reciprocally, as *interdependent.*

in′ter•act′ (in′tər akt′) *v.* act upon one another. —**in′ter•ac′tion,** *n.* —**in′ter•ac′tive,** *adj.*

in'ter•breed', *v.*, -bred, -breeding. crossbreed (plant or animal).

in'ter•cede' (-sēd') *v.*, -ceded, -ceding. act or plead in behalf. —**in'ter•ces'sion**, *n.*

in'ter•cept' (-sept') *v.* stop or check passage. —**in'ter•cep'tion**, *n.* —**in'ter•cep'tor**, *n.*

in'ter•change', *v.*, -changed, -changing, *n.* —*v.* (in'tər chānj') **1.** exchange. **2.** alternate. —*n.* (in'tər chānj') **3.** act or place of interchanging.

in'ter•con'ti•nen'tal, *adj.* **1.** between or among continents. **2.** capable of traveling between continents.

in'ter•course', *n.* **1.** dealings. **2.** sexual relations.

in'ter•de•nom'i•na'tion•al, *adj.* between or involving different religious denominations.

in'ter•de'part•men'tal, *adj.* involving or existing between two or more departments.

in'ter•de•pend'ent, *adj.* mutually dependent. —**in'ter•de•pend'ence**, *n.*

in'ter•dict' *n.* (in'tər dikt') **1.** decree that prohibits. —*v.* (in'tər dikt') **2.** prohibit. —**in'ter•dic'tion**, *n.*

in'ter•est (in'tər ist, -trist) *n.* **1.** feeling of attention, curiosity, etc. **2.** business or ownership. **3.** benefit. **4.** payment for use of money. —*v.* **5.** excite or hold interest of.

interest group, group acting together because of a common interest, etc.

in'ter•est•ing (-tər ə sting, -trə sting, -təres'ting) *adj.* engaging the attention or curiosity.

in'ter•face', *n.*, -faced, -facing, *v.* —*n.* (in'tər fās') **1.** surface forming common boundary between two spaces. **2.** common boundary between people, concepts, etc. **3.** computer hardware or software that communicates information between entities, as between computer and user. —*v.* (in'tərfās', in'tər fās') **4.** interact or coordinate smoothly.

in'ter•fere' (-fēr') *v.*, -fered, -fering. **1.** hamper. **2.** intervene. **3.** meddle. —**in'ter•fer'ence**, *n.*

in'ter•im (in'tər əm) *n.* **1.** meantime. —*adj.* **2.** temporary.

in•te'ri•or (in tēr'ē ər) *adj.* **1.** inside. **2.** inland. —*n.* **3.** interior part.

interj. interjection.

in'ter•ject' (in'tər jekt') *v.* add or include abruptly.

in'ter•jec'tion (-jek'shən) *n.* **1.** act of interjecting. **2.** something interjected. **3.** interjected word that forms a complete utterance, as *indeed!*

in'ter•lace', *v.*, -laced, -lacing. unite by or as if by weaving together; intertwine.

in'ter•lard', *v.* mix in.

in'ter•lock', *v.*, lock, join, or fit together closely.

in'ter•loc'u•tor (-lok'yə tər) *n.* participant in conversation.

in'ter•loc'u•to'ry (-tôr'ē) *adj.* **1.** of or in conversation. **2.** *Law.* not final.

in'ter•lop'er (-lō'pər) *n.* intruder.

in'ter•lude' (-lood') *n.* **1.** intervening episode, time, etc. **2.** performance in intermission.

in'ter•mar'ry, *v.*, -ried, -rying. **1.** (of groups) become connected by marriage. **2.** marry outside one's religion, ethnic group, etc. —**in'ter•mar'riage**, *n.*

in'ter•me'di•ar'y (-mē'dē er'ē) *adj.*, *n.*, *pl.* -aries. —*adj.* **1.** intermediate. —*n.* **2.** person negotiating between others.

in'ter•me'di•ate (-it) *adj.* being or acting between two others.

in•ter'ment (in tûr'mənt) *n.* burial.

in'ter•mez'zo (in'tər met'sō, -med'zō) *n.*, *pl.* -mezzos, -mezzi (-met'sē, -med'zē). short musical composition, as between divisions of a longer work.

in•ter'mi•na•ble (in tûr'mə nə bəl) *adj.* seeming to be without end; endless. —**in•ter'mi•na•bly**, *adv.*

in'ter•mis'sion (in'tər mish'ən) *n.* interval between acts in drama, etc.

in'ter•mit'tent (-mit'nt) *adj.* alternately ceasing and starting again. —**in'ter•mit'tent•ly**, *adv.*

in•tern' (in tûrn') *v.* **1.** hold within certain limits; confine. —*n.* (in'tûrn) **2.** Also, **in'terne.** resident assistant physician on hospital staff. —**in•tern'ment**, *n.*

in•ter'nal (in tûr'nl) *adj.* **1.** interior; inner. **2.** not foreign; domestic. —**in•ter'nal•ly**, *adv.*

internal medicine, branch of medicine dealing with diagnosis and nonsurgical treatment of diseases.

internat. international.

in'ter•na'tion•al, *adj.* **1.** among nations. **2.** of many nations. —**in'ter•na'tion•al•ly**, *adv.*

in'ter•na'tion•al•ism, *n.* principle of international cooperation. —**in'ter•na'tion•al•ist**, *n.*

in'ter•na'tion•al•ize', *v.*, -ized, -izing. **1.** make international. **2.** bring under international control.

in'ter•ne'cine (-nē'sēn, -sīn, -nes'ēn, -īn) *adj.* **1.** of conflict within a group. **2.** mutually destructive.

In'ter•net', *n.* large computer network linking smaller networks worldwide.

in'tern•ist (in'tûr nist, in tûr'nist) *n.* doctor specializing in internal medicine.

in'ter•per'son•al, *adj.* between persons.

in'ter•plan'e•tar'y, *adj.* between planets.

in'ter•play', *n.* reciprocal action.

Interpol (in'tər pōl'), International Criminal Police Organization.

in•ter'po•late' (in tûr'pə lāt') *v.*, -lated, -lating. insert to alter or clarify meaning. —**in•ter'po•la'tion**, *n.*

in'ter•pose', v., -posed, -posing. **1.** place between things. **2.** intervene.

in•ter'pret (in tûr'prit) v. **1.** explain. **2.** construe. **3.** translate. —**in•ter'pre•ta'tion**, n. —**in•ter'pret•er**, n.

in'ter•ra'cial, adj. of, for, or between persons of different races.

in'ter•re•lat'ed, adj. closely associated.

interrog. 1. interrogation. **2.** interrogative.

in•ter'ro•gate' (in ter'ə gāt') v., -gated, -gating. question. —**in•ter'ro•ga'tion**, n. —**in'ter•rog'a•tive** (in'tə rog'ə tiv) adj. —**in•ter'ro•ga'tor**, n.

in'ter•rupt' (in'tə rupt') v. break in; stop. —**in'ter•rup'tion**, n.

in'ter•scho•las'tic, adj. existing or occurring between schools.

in'ter•sect' (-sekt') v. divide by crossing; cross.

in'ter•sec'tion, n. **1.** place where roads meet. **2.** act of intersecting.

in'ter•sperse' (-spûrs') v., -spersed, -spersing. **1.** scatter at random. **2.** vary with something scattered.

in'ter•state', adj. involving number of states.

in'ter•stel'lar, adj. situated or occurring between the stars.

in•ter'stice (in tûr'stis) n. chink or opening.

in'ter•twine', v., -twined, -twining. unite by twining together.

in'ter•ur'ban, adj. between cities.

in'ter•val (in'tər val) n. **1.** intervening time or space. **2.** difference in musical pitch between two tones.

in'ter•vene' (-vēn') v., -vened, -vening. **1.** come or be between. **2.** mediate. —**in'ter•ven'tion** (-ven'shən) n. —**in'ter•ven'tion•ist**, n.

in'ter•view', n. **1.** conversation to obtain information. **2.** meeting. —v. **3.** have interview with. —**in'ter•view'er**, n.

in•tes'tate (in tes'tāt, -tit) adj. **1.** without having made a will. **2.** not disposed of by will.

in•tes'tine (in tes'tin) n. lower part of alimentary canal. —**in•tes'ti•nal**, adj.

intfc Computers. interface.

in'ti•mate, adj., n., v., -mated, -mating. —adj. (in'tə mit) **1.** close; friendly. **2.** private. **3.** thorough. —n. (-mit) **4.** intimate friend. —v. (-māt') **5.** imply. —**in'ti•ma•cy** (-mə sē) n. —**in'ti•ma'tion**, n. —**in'ti•mate•ly**, adv.

in•tim'i•date' (in tim'i dāt') v., -dated, -dating. make timid; frighten. —**in•tim'i•da'tion**, n.

intk intake.

intl. 1. internal. **2.** Also, **intnl.** international.

intlk interlock.

intlz initialize.

intmd intermediate.

intmt intermittent.

in'to (in'tōō; unstressed -tōō, -tə) prep. to inside of.

in•tone', v., -toned, -toning. **1.** use particular spoken tone. **2.** chant. —**in'to•na'tion**, n.

in to'to (in tō'tō) completely.

in•tox'i•cate' (in tok'si kāt') v., -cated, -cating. affect with or as with alcoholic liquor. —**in•tox'i•ca'tion**, n.

intpr interpret.

intr. 1. interior. **2.** intransitive. **3.** introduce. **4.** introduced. **5.** introducing. **6.** introduction. **7.** introductory.

in•trac'ta•ble, adj. stubborn; unmanageable.

in'tra•mu'ral (in'trə myōōr'əl) adj. within one school.

intrans. intransitive.

in trans. in transit. [from Latin in trānsitū]

in•tran'si•gent (in tran'si jənt) adj. uncompromising. —**in•tran'si•gence**, n.

in•tran'si•tive (-tiv) adj. (of verb) not having a direct object.

in'tra•ve'nous (in'trə vē nəs) adj. within vein.

in•trep'id (in trep'id) adj. fearless. —**in'tre•pid'i•ty** (-tre pid'i tē) n.

Int. Rev. Internal Revenue.

intrf interference.

intrg interrogate.

in'tri•cate (in'tri kit) adj. complicated. —**in'tri•ca•cy** (-kə sē) n. —**in'tri•cate•ly**, adv.

in•trigue', v., -trigued, -triguing, n. —v. (in trēg') **1.** interest by puzzling. **2.** plot. —n. (in trēg', in'trēg) **3.** crafty design or plot.

in•trin'sic (in trin'sik, -zik) adj. inherent; basic. —**in•trin'si•cal•ly**, adv.

intro introduction.

in'tro•duce' (in'trə dōōs', -dyōōs') v., -duced, -ducing. **1.** bring to notice, use, etc. **2.** be preliminary to. **3.** make (person) known to another. —**in'tro•duc'tion** (-duk'shən) n. —**in'tro•duc'to•ry** (-duk'tə rē) adj.

in'tro•spec'tion (in'trə spek'shən) n. examination of one's own thoughts and motives. —**in'tro•spec'tive**, adj.

in'tro•vert' (-vûrt') n. person concerned chiefly with inner thoughts or feelings. —**in'tro•ver'sion** (-vûr'zhən) n. —**in'tro•vert'ed**, adj.

intrpl interpolate.

intrpt interrupt.

in•trude' (in trōōd') v., -truded, -truding. come or bring in without welcome. —**in•trud'er**, n. —**in•tru'sion** (-trōō'zhən) n. —**in•tru'sive** (-siv) adj. —**in•tru'sive•ly**, adv.

intsct intersect.

intstg interstage.

in'tu•i'tion (in'tōō ish'ən, -tyōō-) n. instinctive perception. —**in•tu'i•tive** (-i tiv) adj. —**in•tu'i•tive•ly**, adv.

intvl interval.

in′•un•date′ (ĭn′ən dāt′, -un-) *v.*, **-dated, -dating.** flood. **—in′un•da′tion,** *n.*

in•ure′ (in yŏŏr′, i nŏŏr′) *v.*, **-ured, -uring.** accustom; harden.

inv. 1. he or she invented it. [from Latin *invenit*] **2.** invented. **3.** invention. **4.** inventor. **5.** inventory. **6.** investment. **7.** invoice.

in•vade′ (in vād′) *v.*, **-vaded, -vading.** enter as an enemy. **—in•vad′er,** *n.* **—in•va′sion** (-vā′zhən) *n.*

in′•va•lid, *n.* **1.** (in′və lĭd) sick person. *—adj.* **2.** (in′və lĭd) sick. **3.** (in′və lĭd) for invalids. **4.** (in val′ĭd) not valid. **—in•val′i•date′** *v.*, **-dated, -dating.**

in•val′u•a•ble, *adj.* beyond valuing; priceless.

in•vec′tive (in vek′tĭv) *n.* **1.** censure. **2.** harsh taunts or accusations.

in•veigh′ (in vā′) *v.* attack violently in words.

in•vei′gle (in vā′gəl, -vē′-) *v.* **-gled, -gling.** lure into action. **—in•vei′gler,** *n.*

in•vent′ (in vent′) *v.* devise (something new). **—in•ven′tion,** *n.* **—in•ven′tive,** *adj.* **—in•ven′tor,** *n.*
—**Usage.** See DISCOVER.

in′•ven•to•ry (in′vən tôr′ē) *n.*, *pl.* **-tories.** list or stock of goods.

in•verse′ (in vûrs′, in′vûrs) *adj.* **1.** reversed. **2.** opposite. **3.** inverted. **—in•verse′ly,** *adv.*

in•vert′ (-vûrt′) *v.* **1.** turn upside down. **2.** reverse. **3.** make contrary. **—in•ver′sion,** *n.*

in•ver′te•brate, *adj.* without backbone. *—n.* **2.** invertebrate animal.

in•vest′ (in vest′) *v.* **1.** spend money, esp. so as to get larger amount in return. **2.** give or devote (time, etc.). **3.** furnish with power or authority. **—in•vest′ment,** *n.* **—in•ves′tor,** *n.*

in•ves′ti•gate′ (in ves′ti gāt′) *v.*, **-gated, -gating.** examine in detail. **—in•ves′ti•ga′tion,** *n.* **—in•ves′ti•ga′tive,** *adj.* **—in•ves′ti•ga′tor,** *n.*

in•vet′er•ate (in vet′ər it) *adj.* confirmed in habit.

in•vid′i•ous (in vid′ē əs) *adj.* **1.** likely to arouse envy. **2.** offensively unjust.

in•vig′or•ate′ (in vig′ə rāt′) *v.*, **-ated, -ating.** give vigor to.

in•vin′ci•ble (in vin′sə bəl) *adj.* unconquerable. **—in•vin′ci•bil′i•ty,** *n.*

in•vi′o•la•ble (in vī′ə lə bəl) *adj.* that must not or cannot be violated. **—in•vi′o•la•bil′i•ty,** *n.*

in•vi′o•late (-lit, -lāt′) *adj.* **1.** not hurt or desecrated. **2.** undisturbed.

in•vite′ (-vīt′) *v.*, **-vited, -viting. 1.** ask politely. **2.** act so as to make likely. **3.** attract. **—in′vi•ta′tion** (in′vi tā′shən) *n.*

in•vit′ing, *adj.* attractive or tempting.

in vi′tro (in vē′trō) developed or maintained in a controlled nonliving environment, as a laboratory vessel.

in′•vo•ca′tion (in′və kā′shən) *n.* prayer for aid, guidance, etc.

in′voice (in′vois) *n.*, *v.*, **-voiced, -voicing.** *—n.* **1.** list with prices of goods sent to buyer. *—v.* **2.** list on invoice.

in•voke′ (in vōk′) *v.*, **-voked, -voking. 1.** beg for. **2.** call on in prayer. **3.** cite as authoritative.

in•vol′un•tar′y, *adj.* **1.** not done intentionally. **2.** not under conscious control.

in•volve′ (in volv′) *v.*, **-volved, -volving. 1.** include as necessary. **2.** complicate. **3.** implicate. **4.** engross. **—in•volve′ment,** *n.*

invs inverse.

invt. 1. inventory. **2.** invert.

invtr inverter.

in•vul′ner•a•ble, *adj.* **1.** that cannot be wounded or damaged. **2.** proof against attack.

in′ward (in′wərd) *adv.* **1.** Also, **in′wards.** toward the interior. *—adj.* **2.** toward the interior. **3.** inner. *—n.* **4.** inward part. **—in′ward•ly,** *adv.*

in′-your-face′, *adj.* *Informal.* involving confrontation; defiant; provocative.

Io., Iowa.

I/O, input/output.

IOC International Olympic Committee. Also, **I. O.C.**

i′o•dine′ (ī′ə dīn′, -din; *in Chem. also* -dēn′) *n.* nonmetallic element used in medicine.

I.O.F. Independent Order of Foresters.

IOM interoffice memo.

i′on (ī′ən, ī′on) *n.* electrically charged particle.

-ion, suffix meaning: action or process (*inspection*); result of action (*creation*); state or condition (*depression*).

i′o•nize′ (ī′ə nīz′) *v.*, **-nized, -nizing. 1.** separate or change into ions. **2.** produce ions in. **3.** become ionized. **—i′on•i•za′tion,** *n.*

i•on′o•sphere (ī on′ə sfēr′) *n.* outermost region of earth's atmosphere, consisting of ionized layers.

I.O.O.F. Independent Order of Odd Fellows.

i•o′ta (ī ō′tə) *n.* very small quantity.

IOU, written acknowledgment of debt.

IPA 1. International Phonetic Alphabet. **2.** International Phonetic Association. **3.** International Press Association. Also, **I.P.A.**

IPB illustrated parts breakdown.

ip′e•cac′ (ip′i kak′) *n.* drug from root of South American shrub.

i.p.h. 1. *Printing.* impressions per hour. **2.** inches per hour. Also, **iph**

IPI International Patent Institute.

IPL information processing language. Also, **ipl**

IPM integrated pest management.

ipm inches per minute. Also, **i.p.m.**

IPO initial public offering.

ipr inches per revolution. Also, **i.p.r.**

ips inches per second. Also, **i.p.s.**

ip′so fac′to (ip′sō fak′tō) by the fact itself.

I

IQ, intelligence quotient.

IR 1. information retrieval. **2.** infrared. **3.** intelligence ratio.

Ir Irish.

Ir *Symbol, Chemistry.* iridium.

ir 1. infrared. **2.** insulation resistance.

Ir. 1. Ireland. **2.** Irish.

I.R. 1. immediate reserve. **2.** infantry reserve. **3.** intelligence ratio. **4.** internal revenue.

IRA (*pronounced as initials or* ī′rə) individual retirement account.

I•ra′ni•an (i rā′nē ən, i rä′-) *n.* native of Iran. —**I•ra′ni•an,** *adj.*

I•ra′qi (i rak′ē, i rä′ kē) *n., pl.* **-qis.** native of Iraq. —**I•ra′qi,** *adj.*

i•ras′ci•ble (i ras′ə bəl) *adj.* easily angered.

IRB 1. Industrial Relations Bureau. **2.** industrial revenue bond.

IRBM intermediate range ballistic missile. Also, **I.R.B.M.**

IRC 1. Internal Revenue Code. **2.** International Red Cross.

ire (ī°r) *n.* anger. —**i′rate** (ī rāt′, ī′rāt) *adj.*

ir′i•des′cence (ir′i des′əns) *n.* play of rainbowlike colors. —**ir′i•des′cent,** *adj.*

i′ris (ī′ris) *n.* **1.** colored part of the eye. **2.** perennial plant with showy flowers.

I′rish (ī′rish) *n.* language or people of Ireland. —**Irish,** *adj.*

irk (ûrk) *v.* vex; annoy. —**irk′some,** *adj.*

IRO 1. International Refugee Organization. **2.** International Relief Organization.

i′ron (ī′ərn) *n.* **1.** metallic element. **2.** implement for pressing cloth. **3.** (*pl.*) shackles. —*adj.* **4.** of or like iron. —*v.* **5.** press with iron (def. 2).

i′ron-clad′, *adj.* **1.** iron-plated, as a ship. **2.** very rigid or exacting.

iron curtain, (formerly) barrier between Communist and non-Communist areas.

i′ro•ny (ī′rə nē, ī′ər-) *n., pl.* **-nies. 1.** figure of speech in which meaning is opposite to what is said. **2.** outcome contrary to expectations. —**i•ron′ic** (ī ron′ik), **i•ron′ic•al,** *adj.* —**i•ron′i•cal•ly,** *adv.*

Ir′o•quois′ (ir′ə kwoi′, -kwoiz′) *n., pl.* **-quois.** member of a group of North American Indian peoples.

IRQ *Computers.* interrupt request.

ir•ra′di•ate′ (i rā′dē āt′) *v.,* **-ated, -ating. 1.** illuminate. **2.** expose to radiation. **3.** shine. —**ir•ra′di•a′tion,** *n.*

ir•ra′tion•al (i rash′ə nl) *adj.* without reason or judgment.

ir•rec′on•cil′a•ble (i rek′ən sī′lə bəl) *adj.* **1.** that cannot be brought into agreement. **2.** bitterly opposed.

ir′re•deem′a•ble (ir′i dē′mə bəl) *adj.* that cannot be redeemed.

ir′re•duc′i•ble (ir′i dōō′sə bəl, -dyōō′-) *adj.* that cannot be reduced.

ir•ref′u•ta•ble (i ref′yə tə bəl) *adj.* not refutable.

irreg. 1. irregular. **2.** irregularly.

ir•reg′u•lar (i reg′yə lər) *adj.* **1.** not symmetrical. **2.** not fixed. **3.** not conforming to rule or normality. —**ir•reg′u•lar′i•ty,** *n.*

ir•rel′e•vant (i rel′ə vənt) *adj.* not relevant. —**ir•rel′e•vance,** *n.*

ir′re•li′gious (ir′i lij′əs) *adj.* **1.** not religious. **2.** hostile to religion.

ir•rep′a•ra•ble (i rep′ər ə bəl) *adj.* that cannot be rectified. —**ir•rep′a•ra•bly,** *adv.*

ir′re•press′i•ble (ir′i pres′ə bəl) *adj.* that cannot be repressed. —**ir′re•press′i•bly,** *adv.*

ir′re•proach′a•ble (ir′i prō′chə bəl) *adj.* blameless.

ir′re•sist′i•ble (ir′i zis′tə bəl) *adj.* not to be withstood. —**ir′re•sist′i•bly,** *adv.*

ir•res′o•lute′ (i rez′ə lōōt′) *adj.* undecided.

ir′re•spec′tive, *adj.* without regard to.

ir′re•spon′si•ble (ir′i spon′sə bəl) *adj.* not concerned with responsibilities. —**ir′re•spon′si•bly,** *adv.*

ir′re•triev′a•ble (ir′i trē′və bəl) *adj.* that cannot be recovered.

ir•rev′er•ent (i rev′ər ənt) *adj.* lacking respect. —**ir•rev′er•ent•ly,** *adv.*

ir•rev′o•ca•ble (i rev′ə kə bəl) *adj.* not to be revoked or annulled. —**ir•rev′o•ca•bly,** *adv.*

irrglr irregular.

ir′ri•gate′ (ir′i gāt′) *v.,* **-gated, -gating.** supply with water. —**ir′ri•ga′tion,** *n.*

ir′ri•ta•ble (ir′i tə bəl) *adj.* easily angered. —**ir′ri•ta•bil′i•ty,** *n.* —**ir′ri•ta•bly,** *adv.*

ir′ri•tate′ (-tāt′) *v.,* **-tated, -tating. 1.** anger or vex. **2.** make sensitive. **3.** excite to action. —**ir′ri•tant** (-tnt) *n.* —**ir′ri•ta′tion,** *n.*

ir•rup′tion (i rup′shən) *n.* **1.** bursting in. **2.** invasion.

IRS, Internal Revenue Service.

is (iz) *v.* third pers. sing. pres. indic. of **be.**

ISA Instrument Society of America.

Isa. *Bible.* Isaiah.

ISBA International Seabed Authority.

ISBN International Standard Book Number.

ISDN integrated-services digital network.

isgn insignia.

-ish, suffix meaning: **1.** of or belonging to, as *British.* **2.** like or having characteristics of, as *babyish.* **3.** inclined to, as *bookish.* **4.** near or about, as *fiftyish.* **5.** somewhat, as *reddish.*

i′sin•glass′ (ī′zən glas′, ī′zing-) *n.* **1.** transparent substance from some fish. **2.** mica.

isl. 1. island. **2.** isle. Also, **Isl.**

Is•lam′ (is läm′, is′ləm, iz′-) *n.* religious faith founded by Muhammad (A.D. 570–632). —**Is•lam′ic,** *adj.*

is′land (ī′lənd) *n.* body of land surrounded by water. —**is′land•er,** *n.*

isle (īl) *n.* small island.

is′let (ī′lit) *n.* tiny island.

isln isolation.

isls. islands. Also, **Isls.**

ism (iz′əm) *n.* distinctive doctrine, theory, or system.

-ism, suffix meaning: action or practice (*baptism*); state or condition (*barbarism*); doctrine or principle (*Marxism*); distinctive feature or usage (*witticism*).

ISO 1. incentive stock option. 2. in search of. 3. *Photography.* International Standardization Organization.

iso isometric.

i′so•bar (ī′sə bär′) *n.* line on map connecting points at which barometric pressure is the same.

isol isolate.

i′so•late′ (ī′sə lāt′) *v.,* **-lated, -lating.** set apart. —**i′so•la′tion,** *n.*

i′so•la′tion•ist, *n.* person opposed to participation in world affairs. —**i′so•la′tion•ism,** *n.*

i′so•met′rics, *n.pl.* exercises in which one body part is tensed against another. —**i′so•met′ric,** *adj.*

isos isosceles.

i•sos′ce•les′ (ī sos′ə lēz′) *adj.* (of triangle) having two sides equal.

i′so•tope′ (ī′sə tōp′) *n.* one of two or more forms of an element that vary in atomic weight.

ISR Institute for Sex Research.

Isr. 1. Israel. 2. Israeli.

Is•rae′li (iz rā′lē) *n., pl.* **-lis, -li.** native of Israel. —**Is•rae′li,** *adj.*

iss issue.

ISSN International Standard Serial Number.

is′sue (ish′ōō) *v.,* **-sued, -suing,** *n.* —*v.* 1. send out. 2. publish. 3. distribute. 4. emit. 5. emerge. —*n.* 6. act of issuing. 7. thing issued. 8. point in question. 9. offspring. 10. result. —**is′su•ance,** *n.*

-ist, suffix meaning: 1. one who makes or produces, as *novelist.* 2. one who operates, as *machinist.* 3. advocate, as *socialist.*

Isth. isthmus. Also, **isth.**

isth′mus (is′məs) *n.* strip of land surrounded by water and connecting two larger bodies.

ISV International Scientific Vocabulary.

it (it) *pron.* third pers. sing. neuter pronoun.

I.T.A. Initial Teaching Alphabet. Also, **i.t.a.**

ital., italic.

I•tal′ian (i tal′yən) *n.* native or language of Italy. —**I•tal′ian,** *adj.*

—**Pronunciation.** The pronunciation of ITALIAN with the beginning sound (ī), (pronounced like *eye*) is heard primarily from uneducated speakers. This pronunciation is sometimes used as a joke and sometimes as

an insult, but is considered offensive in either case.

i•tal′ic (i tal′ik, ī tal′-) *n.* printing type that slopes to right. Also, **i•tal′ics.** —**i•tal′i•cize′** (-ə sīz′) *v.,* **-cized, -cizing.** —**i•tal′ic,** *adj.*

ITC 1. International Trade Commission. 2. investment tax credit.

itch (ich) *v.* 1. feel irritation of skin. —*n.* 2. itching sensation. 3. restless desire. —**itch′y,** *adj.*

i′tem (ī′təm) *n.* separate article.

i′tem•ize′, *v.,* **-ized, -izing.** state by items; list. —**i′tem•i•za′tion,** *n.*

it′er•ate′ (it′ə rāt′) *v.,* **-ated, -ating.** say or do repeatedly. —**it′er•a′tion,** *n.*

i•tin′er•ant (ī tin′ər ənt, i tin′-) *adj.* 1. traveling. —*n.* 2. person who goes from place to place.

i•tin′er•ar′y (-ə rer′ē) *n., pl.* **-aries.** 1. route. 2. plan of travel.

-itis, suffix meaning inflammation of a body part, as *tonsillitis.*

ITO International Trade Organization.

its (its) *adj.* possessive form of **it.**

it′s (its) contraction of **it is.**

it•self′, *pron.* reflexive form of **it.**

ITU International Telecommunication Union.

I.T.U. International Typographical Union.

ITV instructional television.

IU 1. immunizing unit. 2. Also, **I.U.** international unit.

IUD intrauterine device.

IUS *Rocketry.* inertial upper stage.

IV (ī′vē′) *n., pl.,* **IVs, IV′s.** apparatus for intravenous delivery of medicines, etc.

I′ve (īv) contraction of *I have.*

-ive, suffix meaning: tending to (*destructive*); of the nature of (*festive*).

IVF in vitro fertilization.

i′vo•ry (ī′və rē, ī′vrē) *n., pl.* **-ries.** 1. hard white substance in tusks. 2. yellowish white.

ivory tower, remoteness or aloofness from wordly affairs.

i′vy (ī′vē) *n., pl.* **ivies.** climbing evergreen vine. —**i′vied,** *adj.*

I.W. Isle of Wight.

i.w. 1. inside width. 2. isotopic weight.

IWC International Whaling Commission.

I.W.W. Industrial Workers of the World. Also, **IWW**

-ize, suffix meaning: 1. engage in, as *economize.* 2. treat in a certain way, as *idolize.* 3. become or form into, as *unionize.* 4. make or cause to be, as *civilize.*

J

J, j (jā) *n.* tenth letter of English alphabet.
JA 1. joint account. **2.** Joint Agent. **3.** Judge Advocate. **4.** Junior Achievement. Also, **J.A.**
Ja. January.
jab (jab) *v.,* **jabbed, jabbing,** *n.* poke; thrust.
jab/ber (jab/ər) *v.* **1.** talk rapidly or indistinctly. —*n.* **2.** such talk.
J.A.C. Junior Association of Commerce.
jack (jak) *n.* **1.** lifting device. **2.** person. **3.** knave in playing cards. **4.** male. **5.** flag; ensign. —*v.* **6.** raise with jack.
jack/al (jak/əl) *n.* wild dog of Asia and Africa.
jack/ass/, *n.* **1.** male donkey. **2.** fool.
jack/et (jak/it) *n.* **1.** short coat. **2.** any covering.
Jack Frost, frost personified.
jack/ham/mer, *n.* compressed-air portable drill for rock, etc.
jack/-in-the-box/, *n., pl.* **-boxes.** toy consisting of box from which figure springs up when the lid is opened.
jack/-in-the-pul/pit, *n., pl.* **-pulpits.** plant with upright spike enclosed by leaflike part.
jack/knife/, *n., pl.* **-knives,** *v.,* **-knifed, -knifing.** —*n.* **1.** large folding pocketknife. **2.** dive in which diver bends over, then straightens out. —*v.* **3.** (of a trailer truck) have or cause to have the cab and trailer swivel into a V.
jack/pot/, *n.* cumulative prize in contest, lottery, etc.
jack rabbit, large rabbit of western America.
Ja•cuz/zi (jə kōō/zē) *n., pl.* **-zis.** *Trademark.* brand name for type of whirlpool bath.
jade (jād) *n., v.,* **jaded, jading.** —*n.* **1.** valuable green stone. **2.** old horse. —*v.* **3.** weary. —**jad/ed,** *adj.*
jag (jag) *n.* **1.** projection; ragged edge. **2.** *Slang.* drunken spree. —**jag/ged,** *adj.*
jag/uar (jag/wär) *n.* large South American wildcat.
jai/ a•lai/ (hī/ lī/, hī/ ə lī/) *n.* game played on three-walled court with basketlike rackets.
jail (jāl) *n.* **1.** prison. —*v.* **2.** put in prison. —**jail/er,** *n.*
Ja/la•pe/ño (hä/lə pān/yō) *n., pl.* **-ños.** Mexican hot pepper.
ja•lop/y (jə lop/ē) *n., pl.* **-pies.** old, decrepit automobile.
jam (jam) *v.,* **jammed, jamming,** *n.* —*v.* **1.** push or squeeze. **2.** make or become unworkable. —*n.* **3.** people or objects jammed together. **4.** *Informal.* difficult situation. **5.** preserve of entire fruit.
jamb (jam) *n.* side post of door or window.
jam/bo•ree/ (jam/bə rē/) *n.* merry gathering.
Jan., January.

jan/gle (jang/gəl) *v.,* **-gled, -gling,** *n.* —*v.* **1.** sound harshly. —*n.* **2.** harsh sound.
jan/i•tor (jan/i tər) *n.* caretaker of building. —**jan/i•to/ri•al** (-tôr/ē əl) *adj.*
Jan/u•ar/y (jan/yōō er/ē) *n.* first month of year.
Jap. 1. Japan. **2.** Japanese.
Jap/a•nese/ (jap/ə nēz/, -nēs/) *n., pl.* **-nese.** native or language of Japan. —**Japanese,** *adj.*
Japn. 1. Japan. **2.** Japanese. Also, **Japn**
jar (jär) *n., v.,* **jarred, jarring.** —*n.* **1.** broadmouthed bottle. **2.** unpleasant sound. **3.** sudden shock or shake. —*v.* **4.** shock or shake. **5.** conflict.
jar/gon (jär/gən, -gon) *n.* language meaningful only to a particular trade, etc.
Jas. *Bible.* James.
jas/mine (jaz/min, jas/-) *n.* fragrant shrub.
jas/per (jas/pər) *n.* precious quartz.
jaun/dice (jôn/dis, jän/-) *n.* illness causing yellowed skin, etc.
jaun/diced, *adj.,* **1.** skeptical. **2.** envious.
jaunt (jônt, jänt) *n.* short trip.
jaun/ty (jôn/tē, jän/-) *adj.* **-tier, -tiest.** sprightly. —**jaun/ti•ly,** *adv.* —**jaun/ti•ness,** *n.*
Jav. Javanese.
jave/lin (jav/lin, jav/ə-) *n.* spear.
jaw (jô) *n.* either of two bones forming mouth.
jaw/bone/, *n., v.,* **-boned, -boning.** —*n.* **1.** bone of the jaw. —*v.* **2.** influence by persuasion, esp. by public appeal.
jaw/break/er, *n.* **1.** word that is hard to pronounce. **2.** very hard candy.
jay (jā) *n.* noisy colorful bird.
jay/walk/, *v.* cross street improperly. —**jay/walk/er,** *n.*
jazz (jaz) *n.* **1.** popular music of black American origin. **2.** *Slang.* insincere talk.
jazz/y, *adj.,* **-ier, -iest. 1.** of or like jazz music. **2.** flashy.
jb junction box.
JC 1. junior college. **2.** juvenile court.
J.C. 1. Jesus Christ. **2.** Julius Caesar. **3.** *Law.* jurisconsult. [from Latin *jūris cōnsultus*]
J.C.B. 1. Bachelor of Canon Law. [from Latin *Jūris Canonicī Baccalaureus*] **2.** Bachelor of Civil Law. [from Latin *Jūris Civilis Baccalaureus*]
J.C.C. Junior Chamber of Commerce.
J.C.D. 1. Doctor of Canon Law. [from Latin *Jūris Canonicī Doctor*] **2.** Doctor of Civil Law. [from Latin *Jūris Civilis Doctor*]
JCI Jaycees International.
JCL *Computers.* job control language.

J.C.L. Licentiate in Canon Law. [from Latin *Jūris Canonicī Licentiātus*]

J.C.S. Joint Chiefs of Staff. Also, **JCS**

jct. junction. Also, **jctn.**

J.D., **1.** Doctor of Jurisprudence; Doctor of Law. **2.** Doctor of Laws. **3.** Justice Department.

JDC Juvenile Detention Center.

JDL Jewish Defense League.

Je. June.

jeal'ous (jel'əs) *adj.* **1.** resentful of another's success, etc.; envious. **2.** vigilant, esp. against rivalry. —**jeal'ous•ly**, *adv.* —**jeal'ous•y**, *n.*

jeans (jēnz) *n.pl.* cotton trousers.

Jeep (jēp) *n. Trademark.* small rugged type of automobile.

jeer (jēr) *v.* **1.** deride. —*n.* **2.** deriding shout.

Je•ho'vah (ji hō'və) *n.* God.

je•june' (ji jōōn') *adj.* **1.** lacking interest or significance; insipid. **2.** lacking maturity; childish.

jell (jel) *v.* **1.** become like jelly in consistency. **2.** become clear or definite.

jel'ly (jel'ē) *n., pl.* **-lies,** *v.,* **-lied, -lying.** —*n.* **1.** soft, semisolid food, as fruit juice boiled down with sugar. —*v.* **2.** make into, or provide with, jelly.

jel'ly•bean', *n.* small, bean-shaped, chewy candy.

jel'ly•fish', *n., pl.* **-fish, -fishes.** marine animal with soft, jellylike body.

jelly roll, thin cake spread with jelly and rolled up.

jen'ny (jen'ē) *n., pl.* **-nies. 1.** spinning machine. **2.** female donkey, wren, etc.

jeop'ard•ize' (jep'ər dīz') *v.,* **-ized, -izing.** risk; endanger. —**jeop'ard•y,** *n.*

Jer. 1. *Bible.* Jeremiah. **2.** Jersey.

jer'e•mi'ad (jer'ə mī'əd, -ad) *n.* prolonged lament; complaint.

jerk (jûrk) *n.* **1.** quick, sharp thrust, pull, etc. **2.** *Slang.* stupid person. —*v.* **3.** give jerk to. —**jerk'y,** *adj.*

jer'kin (jûr'kin) *n.* close-fitting, usu. sleeveless jacket.

jerk'wa'ter, *adj.* insignificant and remote.

jer'ry-built' (jer'ē-) *adj.* flimsily made.

jer'sey (jûr'zē) *n.* type of shirt.

jest (jest) *n., v.* joke; banter. —**jest'er,** *n.*

Je'sus (jē'zəs, -zəz) *n.* founder of Christian religion. Also called **Jesus Christ.**

jet (jet) *n., v.,* **jetted, jetting,** *adj.* —*n.* **1.** stream under pressure. **2.** Also, **jet plane.** plane operated by jet propulsion. —*v.* **3.** spout. —*adj.* **4.** deep black.

jet lag, fatigue after jet flight to different time zone.

jet'lin'er, *n.* jet plane carrying passengers.

jet propulsion, propulsion of plane, etc., by reactive thrust of jet. —**jet' pro•pelled',** *adj.*

jet'sam (jet'səm) *n.* goods thrown overboard to lighten distressed ship.

jet'ti•son (jet'ə sən, -zən) *v.* cast (jetsam) out.

jet'ty (jet'ē) *n., pl.* **-ties.** wharf; pier.

Jew (jōō) *n.* **1.** follower of Judaism. **2.** descendant of Biblical Hebrews. —**Jew'ish,** *adj.*

jew'el (jōō'əl) *n.* precious stone; gem. —**jew'el•er,** *n.* —**jew'el•ry,** *n.*

JFET (jā'fet), junction field-effect transistor.

JFK John Fitzgerald Kennedy.

jg junior grade. Also, **j.g.**

JHS IHS (defs. 1, 2).

J.H.S. junior high school.

jib (jib) *n.* triangular sail on forward mast.

jibe (jīb) *v.,* **jibed, jibing. 1.** gibe. **2.** *Informal.* be consistent.

jif'fy (jif'ē) *n., pl.* **-fies.** short time.

jig (jig) *n., v.,* **jigged, jigging.** —*n.* **1.** lively folk dance. —*v.* **2.** dance a jig.

jig'ger (jig'ər) *n.* glass measure of 1½ oz. (45 ml) for liquors.

jig'gle, *v.,* **-gled, -gling,** *n.* —*v.* **1.** move back and forth, etc. —*n.* **2.** act of jiggling.

jig'saw', *n.* saw with narrow vertical blade for cutting curves, patterns, etc.

jigsaw puzzle, set of irregularly cut flat pieces that form a picture when fitted together.

jilt (jilt) *v.* reject (a previously encouraged suitor).

Jim Crow (jim) (*sometimes l.c.*) discrimination against blacks. —**Jim'-Crow',** *adj.*

jim'my (jim'ē) *n., pl.* **-mies,** *v.,* **-mied, -mying.** —*n.* **1.** short crowbar. —*v.* **2.** force open with or as if with a jimmy.

jim'son•weed' (jim'sən wēd') *n.* coarse weed with poisonous leaves.

jin'gle (jing'gəl) *v.,* **-gled, -gling,** *n.* —*v.* **1.** make repeated clinking sound. —*n.* **2.** clink; tinkle. **3.** very simple verse.

jin'go•ism (jing'gō iz'əm) *n.* chauvinism marked by aggressive foreign policy. —**jin'-go•ist,** *n.* —**jin'go•is'tic,** *adj.*

jin•rik'i•sha (jin rik'shô, -shä) *n.* rickshaw. Also, **jin•rik'sha.**

jinx (jingks) *n.* **1.** cause of bad luck. —*v.* **2.** cause bad luck.

jit'ter•bug' (jit'ər bug') *n.* jazz dance.

jit'ters, *n.pl. Informal.* nervousness. —**jit'ter•y,** *adj.*

jive (jīv) *n., v.,* **jived, jiving.** —*n.* **1.** swing music or early jazz. **2.** deceptive or meaningless talk. —*v.* **3.** *Slang.* fool or kid.

JJ. 1. Judges. **2.** Justices.

jk jack.

jkt jacket.

jl journal.

Jl. 1. Journal. **2.** July.

jn join.

jnr. junior.

jnt. joint.

job (job) *n., v.,* **jobbed, jobbing.** —*n.* **1.**

J

piece of work. **2.** employment. —*v.* **3.** sell wholesale. —**job′less,** *adj.*

job action, work slowdown by employees to win demands.

Jo. Bapt. John the Baptist.

job′ber, *n.* **1.** wholesaler. **2.** dealer in odd lots of merchandise.

job lot, large assortment of goods sold as a single unit.

JOBS (jobz), Job Opportunities in the Business Sector.

jock (jok) *n. Informal.* **1.** athlete. **2.** enthusiast.

jock′ey (jok′ē) *n.* **1.** rider of race horses. —*v.* **2.** maneuver.

jo•cose′ (jō kōs′, jə-) *adj.* jesting; merry. Also, **joc′und** (jok′ənd, jō′kənd). —**jo•cos′i•ty** (-kos′i tē) *n.*

joc′u•lar (jok′yə lər) *adj.* joking. —**joc′u•lar′i•ty** (-lar′i tē) *n.*

jodh′purs (jod′pərz) *n.pl.* riding breeches.

Jo. Div. John the Divine.

Jo. Evang. John the Evangelist.

jog (jog) *v.,* **jogged, jogging,** *n.* —*v.* **1.** nudge; shake. **2.** run at slow, steady pace. —*n.* **3.** nudge. **4.** steady pace. **5.** projection. —**jog′ger,** *n.*

joie de vi′vre (zhwʌdᵊ vēᵊ/vʀᵊ) *n. French.* delight in being alive.

join (join) *v.* **1.** put together. **2.** become member of.

join′er, *n.* **1.** assembler of woodwork. **2.** *Informal.* person who likes to join clubs, etc. —**join′er•y,** *n.*

joint (joint) *n.* **1.** place or part in which things join. **2.** movable section. **3.** cheap, sordid place. **4.** *Slang.* marijuana cigarette. —*adj.* **5.** shared or sharing. —*v.* **6.** join or divide at joint. —**joint′ly,** *adv.*

joist (joist) *n.* floor beam.

joke (jōk) *n., v.,* **joked, joking.** —*n.* **1.** amusing remark, story, etc. —*v.* **2.** make or tell joke. **3.** speak only to amuse. —**jok′er,** *n.* —**jok′ing•ly,** *adv.*

jol′ly (jol′ē) *adj.,* **-lier, -liest,** *v.,* **-lied, -lying,** *adv.* —*adj.* **1.** gay; merry. —*v.* **2.** try to keep (someone) in good humor. —*adv.* **3.** *Brit. Informal.* very. —**jol′li•ness, jol′li•ty,** *n.*

jolt (jōlt) *v., n.* jar; shake.

jon′quil (jong′kwil, jon′-) *n.* fragrant yellow or white narcissus.

josh (josh) *v. Informal.* tease.

jos′tle (jos′əl) *v.,* **-tled, -tling,** *n.* —*v.* **1.** push rudely. —*n.* **2.** rude push.

jot (jot) *n., v.,* **jotted, jotting.** —*n.* **1.** bit. —*v.* **2.** write.

jounce (jouns) *v.,* **jounced, jouncing,** *n.* —*v.* **1.** move joltingly. —*n.* **2.** jouncing movement. —**jounc′y,** *adj.*

jour. 1. journal. **2.** journeyman.

journ. journalism.

jour′nal (jûr′nl) *n.* **1.** daily record. **2.** periodical. **3.** part of shaft in contact with bearing.

jour′nal•ese′ (-ēz′, -ēs′) *n.* writing style typical of newspapers and magazines.

jour′nal•ism (-iz′əm) *n.* newspaper writing. —**jour′nal•ist,** *n.* —**jour′nal•is′tic,** *adj.*

jour′ney (jûr′nē) *n.* **1.** act or course of traveling. —*v.* **2.** travel.

jour′ney•man, *n., pl.* **-men.** hired skilled worker.

joust (joust) *n.* fight between mounted knights.

jo′vi•al (jō′vē əl) *adj.* vigorously cheerful. —**jo′vi•al′i•ty** (-al′i tē) *n.*

jowl (joul) *n.* jaw or cheek.

joy (joi) *n.* gladness; delight. —**joy′ful, joy′ous,** *adj.*

joy′ride′, *n.* ride for pleasure, esp. in recklessly driven vehicle.

joy′stick′, *n.* **1.** *Informal.* control stick of airplane. **2.** lever for controlling cursor or other graphic element.

JP, Justice of the Peace.

JPEG (jā′peg), Joint Photographic Experts Group.

Jpn. 1. Japan. **2.** Japanese. Also, **Jpn**

Jr., junior. Also, **jr.**

JRC Junior Red Cross.

JSC Johnson Space Center.

J.S.D. Doctor of the Science of Law; Doctor of Juristic Science.

jt. joint.

Ju. June.

ju′bi•lant (jōō′bə lənt) *adj.* rejoicing. —**ju′bi•la′tion** (-lā′shən) *n.*

ju′bi•lee′ (jōō′bə lē′) *n.* celebration, esp. of anniversary.

Jud. *Bible.* **1.** Judges. **2.** Judith (Apocrypha).

jud. 1. judge. **2.** judgment. **3.** judicial. **4.** judiciary.

Ju′da•ism′ (-dē iz′əm, -də-) *n.* religion of the Jewish people.

Judg. *Bible.* Judges.

judge (juj) *n., v.,* **judged, judging.** —*n.* **1.** person who decides cases in court of law. **2.** person making authoritative decisions. **3.** discriminating person; connoisseur. —*v.* **4.** decide on. —**judg′er,** *n.*

judg′ment (-mənt) *n.* **1.** decision, as in court of law. **2.** good sense.

judg•men′tal (-men′tl) *adj.* making judgments, esp. on morality.

ju•di′cial (jōō dish′əl) *adj.* **1.** of justice, courts of law, or judges. **2.** thoughtful; wise. —**ju•di′cial•ly,** *adv.*

ju•di′ci•ar′y (-dish′ē er′ē, -dish′ə rē) *n., pl.* **-ies,** *adj.* —*n.* **1.** legal branch of government. —*adj.* **2.** of judges, etc.

ju•di′cious, *adj.* wise; prudent. —**ju•di′cious•ly,** *adv.* —**ju•di′cious•ness,** *n.*

ju′do (jōō′dō) *n.* martial art based on jujitsu.

jug (jug) *n.* **1.** container for liquids. **2.** *Slang.* prison.

jug′ger•naut′ (jug′ər nôt′) *n.* any large, overpowering, irresistible force.

jug'gle (jug'əl) v., **-gled, -gling.** perform tricks by tossing and catching objects. —jug'gler, n.

jug'u•lar (jug'yə lər) adj. **1.** of the neck. —n. **2.** large vein in neck.

juice (jōōs) n. liquid part of plant, fruit, etc. —juic'i•ness, n. —juic'y, adj.

juic'er, n. **1.** appliance for squeezing fruit and vegetable juice. **2.** Slang. heavy drinker.

ju•jit'su (jōō jit'sōō) n. Japanese method of wrestling and self-defense.

ju'jube (jōō'jōōb, jōō'jōō bē') n. chewy fruity lozenge.

juke box (jōōk') coin-operated music player.

Jul., July.

ju'li•enne' (jōō'lē en') adj., v. (of vegetables) cut into thin strips.

Ju•ly' (jōō lī', jə-) n. seventh month of year.

jum'ble (jum'bəl) n., v., **-bled, -bling.** —n. **1.** confused mixture. —v. **2.** make jumble of.

jum'bo (jum'bō) adj. very large.

jump (jump) v. **1.** spring up; leap. **2.** raise. —n. **3.** spring; leap. **4.** rise. **5.** Informal. advantage.

jump'er, n. **1.** one that jumps. **2.** sleeveless dress worn over blouse. **3.** electric cable for starting dead car battery.

jump'-start', n. **1.** starting of car engine with jumpers (def. 3). —v. **2.** give a jump-start to. **3.** enliven or revive.

jump'suit', n. **1.** one-piece suit worn by parachutist. **2.** garment fashioned after it.

jump'y, adj. **-ier, -iest.** nervous. —jump'i•ly, adv. —jump'i•ness, n.

Jun., June.

jun'co (jung'kō) n., pl. **-cos.** small North American finch.

junc'tion (jungk'shən) n. **1.** union. **2.** place of joining.

junc'ture (-chər) n. **1.** point of time. **2.** crisis. **3.** joint.

June (jōōn) n. sixth month of year.

jun'gle (jung'gəl) n. wildly overgrown tropical land.

jun'ior (jōōn'yər) adj. **1.** younger. **2.** lower. —n. **3.** third-year high school or college student.

junior college, two-year college.

junior high school, school usu. encompassing grades 7 through 9.

ju'ni•per (jōō'nə pər) n. coniferous evergreen shrub or tree.

junk (jungk) n. **1.** useless material; rubbish. **2.** type of Chinese ship. **3.** narcotics, esp. heroin. —v. **4.** discard. —junk'y, adj.

junk'er, n. Informal. old vehicle ready to be scrapped.

jun'ket (jung'kit) n. **1.** custard. **2.** pleasure excursion. **3.** trip by government official at public expense. —v. **4.** entertain. —jun'ke•teer', jun'ket•er, n.

junk food, high-calorie food of little nutritional value.

junk'ie, n. Informal. **1.** drug, esp. heroin, addict. **2.** person who craves or is enthusiastic for something.

junk mail, unsolicited commercial material mailed in bulk.

jun'ta (hōōn'tə, jun'-, hun'-) n. military group that seizes power and rules.

—Pronunciation. When the word JUNTA was borrowed into English from Spanish in the early 17th century, its pronunciation was thoroughly Anglicized to (jun'tə). During the 20th century, esp. in North America, the pronunciation (hōōn'tə), which comes from Spanish (hōōn'tä) has come into frequent use, probably through people's renewed awareness of the word's Spanish origins. A hybrid form, combining English and Spanish influence, (hun'tə) is also heard. Any of these pronunciations is perfectly standard.

Ju'pi•ter (jōō'pi tər) n. largest of sun's planets.

Jur. D. Doctor of Law. [from Latin Jūris Doctor]

ju'ris•dic'tion (jōōr'is dik'shən) n. authority, range of control, etc., of judge or the like. —ju'ris•dic'tion•al, adj.

jurisp. jurisprudence. Also, **juris.**

ju'ris•pru'dence (-prōōd'ns) n. science of law.

ju'rist, n. expert in law.

Jur. M. Master of Jurisprudence.

ju'ror (jōōr'ər, -ôr) n. member of jury. Also, ju'ry•man, fem. jur'y•wom'an.

ju'ry (jōōr'ē) n., pl. **-ries.** group of persons selected to make decisions, esp. in law court.

just (just) adj. **1.** fair; right. **2.** legal. **3.** true. —adv. **4.** exactly. **5.** barely. **6.** only. —just'ly, adv.

jus'tice (jus'tis) n. **1.** fairness; rightness. **2.** administration of law. **3.** high judge.

justice of the peace, local public officer who performs marriages, tries minor cases, etc.

jus'ti•fy', v., **-fied, -fying. 1.** show to be true, right, etc. **2.** defend. —jus'ti•fi•ca'tion, n. —jus'ti•fi'a•ble, adj. —jus'ti•fi'a•bly, adv.

jut (jut) v., **jutted, jutting,** n. —v. **1.** project. —n. **2.** projection.

jute (jōōt) n. East Indian plant whose fibers are used for fabrics, etc.

juv. juvenile.

ju've•nile (jōō'və nl, -nīl') adj. **1.** young. —n. **2.** young person. **3.** youthful theatrical role. **4.** book for children.

juvenile delinquency, illegal or antisocial behavior by a minor. —juvenile delinquent.

jux'ta•pose' (juk'stə pōz', juk'stə pōz') v. **-posed, -posing.** place close for comparison. —jux'ta•po•si'tion (-pə zish'ən) n.

JV 1. joint venture. **2.** junior varsity. Also, **J.V.**

Jy. July.

J

K

K, k (kā) *n.* eleventh letter of English alphabet.

K, 1. karat. 2. Kelvin. 3. kilobyte. 4. kilometer. 5. thousand.

k, 1. karat. 2. kilogram.

kA *Electricity.* kiloampere; kiloamperes.

ka•bu′ki (kə boō′kē, kä′boō kē′) *n.* popular drama of Japan.

kai′ser (kī′zər) *n.* German emperor.

kale (kāl) *n.* type of cabbage.

ka•lei′do•scope′ (kə lī′də skōp′) *n.* optical device in which colored bits change patterns continually. —**ka•lei′do•scop′ic** (-skop′ik) *adj.*

Kan. Kansas. Also, **Kans., Kas.**

kan′ga•roo′ (kang′gə roō′) *n., pl.* **-roos, -roo.** Australian marsupial with long hind legs used for leaping.

kangaroo court, self-appointed tribunal disregarding law or human rights.

Kans., Kansas.

ka′o•lin (kā′ə lin) *n.* fine white clay used to make porcelain.

ka′pok (kā′pok) *n.* silky down from seeds of certain trees.

ka•put′ (kä poōt′, -poōt′, kə-) *adj. Informal.* 1. extinct. 2. out of order.

ka′ra•o′ke (kar′ē ō′kē) *n.* act of singing along to music in which original vocals have been eliminated.

kar′at (kar′ət) *n.* $\frac{1}{24}$ part: unit for measuring purity of gold.

ka•ra′te (kə rä′tē) *n.* Japanese technique of unarmed combat.

kar′ma (kär′mə) *n.* fate as the result of one's actions in successive incarnations. —**kar′-mic,** *adj.*

Kas., Kansas.

ka′ty•did (kā′tē did) *n.* large green grasshopper.

kay′ak (kī′ak) *n.* Eskimo canoe, esp. of skin.

ka•zoo′ (kə zoō′) *n.* tubular musical toy that vibrates and buzzes when one hums into it.

KB, kilobyte.

kbar (kā′bär), kilobar; kilobars.

K.B.E. Knight Commander of the British Empire.

KBP *Chess.* king's bishop's pawn.

kc, kilocycle.

K.C.B. Knight Commander of the Bath.

kCi kilocurie; kilocuries.

K.C.M.G. Knight Commander of the Order of St. Michael and St. George.

Kčs. koruna; korunas. [from Czech *k(oruna) č(esko)s(lovenská)*]

kc/s kilocycles per second. Also, **kc/sec**

K.C.S.I. Knight Commander of the Order of the Star of India.

K.C.V.O. Knight Commander of the (Royal) Victorian Order.

KD 1. kiln-dried. 2. Also, **k.d.** *Commerce.* knocked-down.

KD. (in Kuwait) dinar; dinars.

ke•bab′ (kə bob′) *n.* cubes of marinated meat broiled on a skewer. Also, **ke•bob′.**

keel (kēl) *n.* 1. central framing member of ship's bottom. —*v.* 2. fall sideways.

keen (kēn) *adj.* 1. sharp. 2. excellent. 3. intense. 4. eager. —*v.* 5. wail; lament. —**keen′ly,** *adv.* —**keen′ness,** *n.*

keep (kēp) *v.,* **kept** (kept), **keeping,** *n.* —*v.* 1. continue. 2. detain. 3. support. 4. maintain. 5. withhold. 6. observe. 7. last. —*n.* 8. board and lodging. —**keep′er,** *n.*

keep′ing, *n.* 1. conformity. 2. care.

keep′sake′, *n.* souvenir.

keg (keg) *n.* small barrel.

kelp (kelp) *n.* large brown seaweed.

Kel′vin (kel′vin) *adj.* > of or noting an absolute scale of temperature in which 0° equals −273.16° Celsius.

ken (ken) *n.* knowledge.

Ken., Kentucky.

ken′nel (ken′l) *n.* 1. doghouse. 2. establishment where dogs are boarded and cared for.

ker′chief (kûr′chif, -chēf) *n.* cloth head covering.

ker′nel (kûr′nl) *n.* center part of nut.

ker′o•sene′ (ker′ə sēn′) *n.* type of oil.

kes′trel (kes′trəl) *n.* small falcon that hovers as it hunts.

ketch′up (kech′əp, kach′-) *n.* type of thick tomato sauce with spices.

ket′tle (ket′l) *n.* pot for boiling liquids.

ket′tle•drum′, *n.* large drum with round copper bottom.

key (kē) *n.* 1. part for operating lock. 2. explanation. 3. operating lever. 4. musicial tonality. 5. reef. —*adj.* 6. chief. —*v.* 7. intensify; excite.

key′board′, *n.* 1. row of keys on piano, computer, etc. —*v.* 2. insert (data) into computer. —**key′board′er,** *n.*

key′note′, *n.* 1. basic note of a musical piece; tonic. 2. theme of meeting, etc.

key′stone′, *n.* stone forming summit of arch.

kg, kilogram.

KGB Committee for State Security: the intelligence and internal-security agency of the former Soviet Union. Also, **K.G.B.** [from Russian *K(omitét) g(osudárstvennoĭ) b(ezo-pásnosti)*]

kgf kilogram-force.

kg-m kilogram-meter; kilogram-meters.

KGPS kilograms per second. Also, **kgps**

Kh Knoop hardness.

khak′i (kak′ē, kä′kē) *adj., n.* yellowish brown.

khan (kän, kan) *n.* Asian ruler.

Khn Knoop hardness number.

kHz, kilohertz.

Ki. *Bible.* Kings.

KIA, killed in action.

KIAS knot indicated airspeed.

kib•butz′ (ki boots′, -boots′) *n., pl.* **-but′zim.** Israeli collective community.

kib′itz•er (kib′it sər) *n. Informal.* person offering unwanted advice. **—kib′itz,** *v.*

kick (kik) *v.* **1.** strike with foot. **2.** recoil. **3.** *Informal.* complain. **—n. 4.** act or result of kicking. **5.** *Informal.* thrill. **—kick′er,** *n.*

kick′back′, *n.* portion of an income given, often secretly, to someone who made the income possible.

kick′off′, *n.* **1.** kick that begins play in football or soccer. **2.** beginning of anything.

kick′stand′, *n.* pivoting bar for holding cycle upright when not in use.

kid (kid) *n., v.,* **kidded, kidding. —n. 1.** young goat. **2.** leather from its skin. **3.** *Informal.* child. **—v. 4.** *Informal.* fool; tease. **—kid′der,** *n.*

kid′nap (kid′nap) *v.,* **-napped** or **-naped, -napping** or **-naping.** carry off by force, esp. for ransom; abduct. **—kid′nap•per, kid′nap•er,** *n.*

kid′ney (kid′nē) *n.* **1.** gland that secretes urine. **2.** kind.

kidney bean, plant cultivated for its edible seeds.

kidney stone, abnormal stony mass formed in kidney.

kiel•ba′sa (kil bä′sə, kēl-) *n., pl.* **-sas, -sy** (-sē). smoked Polish sausage.

kil. kilometer; kilometers.

kill (kil) *v.* **1.** end life of; murder. **2.** destroy; cancel. **—n. 3.** animal slain. **—kill′er,** *n.*

killer whale, large, predatory, black-and-white dolphin.

kill′ing, *n.* **1.** act of one that kills. **2.** quick, large profit. **—adj. 3.** fatal. **4.** exhausting.

kill′-joy′, *n.* person who spoils pleasure of others.

kiln (kil, kiln) *n.* large furnace for making bricks, etc.

ki′lo (kē′lō, kil′ō) *n., pl.* **-los. 1.** kilogram. **2.** kilometer.

kilo-, prefix meaning thousand, as *kilowatt.*

kil′o•byte (kil′ə bīt′) *n.* **1.** 1024 bytes. **2.** (loosely) 1000 bytes.

kil′o•cy′cle, *n.* kilohertz.

kil′o•gram′, *n.* 1000 grams. Also, **kilo.**

kil′o•hertz′, *n., pl.* **-hertz.** radio frequency of 1000 cycles per second. Also, *formerly,* **kil′o•cy′cle.**

kil′o•li′ter (-lē′-), *n.* 1000 liters.

ki•lom′e•ter (ki lom′i tər, kil′ə mē′-) *n.* 1000 meters.

—Pronunciation. The first pronunciation of KILOMETER is something of a mystery. The usual pronunciation both for *units of measurement* starting with *kilo-* (*kilobyte*) and for *units of length* ending in *-meter* (*centimeter*) gives primary stress to the first syllable and secondary to the third *-me-.* Logically, KILOMETER should follow this pattern, and in fact has been pronounced (kil′ə mē′tər) since the early 1800s. However, another pronunciation of KILOMETER, with stress on the *-om-,* or second syllable, has been around for nearly as long. It is reinforced by words for *instruments* of measurement (rather than *units* of measurement) that also end in *-meter* (*thermometer, barometer*). Although criticized because it does not fit the expected pattern, the pronunciation (ki lom′i tər) is very common in American English and has gained popularity in Britain. Both pronunciations are used by educated speakers, including scientists.

kil′o•watt′, *n.* 1000 watts.

kilt (kilt) *n.* man's skirt, worn in Scotland.

ki•mo′no (kə mō′nə, -nō) *n., pl.* **-nos.** loose dressing gown.

kin (kin) *n.* relatives. Also, **kins′folk′. —kins′man,** *n.* **—kins′wom′an,** *n.fem.*

kind (kīnd) *adj.* **1.** compassionate; friendly. **—n. 2.** type; group. **—kind′ness,** *n.*

kin′der•gar′ten (kin′dər gär′tn, -dn) *n.* school for very young children.

kind′heart′ed (kīnd′-) *adj.* having or showing kindness. **—kind′heart′ed•ly,** *adv.* **—kind′heart′ed•ness,** *n.*

kin′dle (kin′dl) *v.,* **-dled, -dling. 1.** set afire. **2.** rouse.

kin′dling, *n.* material for starting fire.

kind′ly (kīnd′lē) *adj.,* **-lier, -liest,** *adv. —adj.* **1.** kind; gentle. **—adv. 2.** in kind manner. **3.** cordially; favorably. **—kind′li•ness,** *n.*

kin′dred (kin′drid) *adj.* **1.** related; similar. **—n. 2.** relatives.

kin′e•scope′ (kin′ə skōp′) *n.* **1.** television tube. **2.** filmed recording of television show.

ki•net′ic (ki net′ik, kī-) *adj.* of motion.

king (king) *n.* sovereign male ruler. **—king′ly,** *adj.*

king′dom (-dəm) *n.* government ruled by king or queen.

king′fish′er, *n.* colorful, fish-eating bird.

king′-size′, *adj.* extra large.

kink (kingk) *n., v.* twist; curl. **—kink′y,** *adj.,* **-ier, -iest.**

kin′ship, *n.* **1.** family relationship. **2.** affinity; likeness.

ki•osk (kē′osk, kē osk′) *n.* small open structure where newspapers, refreshments, etc., are sold.

kip-ft one thousand foot-pounds.

kip′per (kip′ər) *n.* salted, dried fish.

kis′met (kiz′mit, -met, kis′-) *n.* fate.

kiss (kis) *v.* **1.** touch with lips in affection,

K

etc. —*n.* **2.** act of kissing. **3.** type of candy. —**kiss′a•ble,** *adj.*

kit (kit) *n.* set of supplies, tools, etc.

kitch′en (kich′ən) *n.* room for cooking. —**kitch′en•ware′,** *n.*

kitch′en•ette′ (-ə net′) *n.* small, compact kitchen.

kite (kīt) *n.* **1.** light, paper-covered frame flown in wind on long string. **2.** type of falcon.

kith and kin (kith) friends and relations.

kitsch (kich) *n.* something tawdry designed to appeal to undiscriminating persons.

kit′ten (kit′n) *n.* young cat.

kit′ten•ish, *adj.* playfully coy or cute.

kit′ty-cor′nered, *adj.* cater-cornered. Also, **kit′ty-cor′ner.**

ki′wi (kē′wē) *n.* **1.** flightless bird of New Zealand. **2.** egg-sized brown berry with edible green pulp.

K.J.V. King James Version (of the Bible).

KKK, Ku Klux Klan.

KKt *Chess.* king's knight.

KKtP *Chess.* king's knight's pawn.

kl kiloliter; kiloliters. Also, **kl.**

Klee′nex (klē′neks) *Trademark.* soft paper tissue.

klep′to•ma′ni•a (klep′tə mā′nē ə) *n.* irresistible desire to steal. —**klep′to•ma′ni•ac′,** *n.*

klutz (kluts) *n. Slang.* clumsy person. —**klutz′y,** *adj.* —**klutz′i•ness,** *n.*

km, kilometer.

kMc kilomegacycle; kilomegacycles.

km/sec kilometers per second.

KN *Chess.* king's knight.

kn knot; 1 nautical mile.

kn. (in Germany and Austria) kronen.

knack (nak) *n.* special skill.

knack′wurst (näk′wûrst, -wŏŏrst) *n.* spicy sausage.

knap′sack′ (nap′sak′) *n.* supply bag carried on back.

knave (nāv) *n.* dishonest rascal. —**knav′er•y,** *n.* —**knav′ish,** *adj.*

knead (nēd) *v.* mix (dough).

knee (nē) *n.* middle joint of leg.

knee′cap′, *n.* flat bone at front of knee.

knee′-jerk′, *adj. Informal.* reacting in an automatic, habitual way.

kneel (nēl) *v.,* **knelt** (nelt) or **kneeled, kneeling.** be on one's knees.

knell (nel) *n.* slow, deep sound of bell.

knick′ers (nik′ərz) *n.pl.* type of short breeches.

knick′knack′ (nik′nak′) *n.* trinket.

knife (nīf) *n., pl.* **knives** (nīvz). cutting blade in handle.

knight (nīt) *n.* **1.** chivalrous medieval soldier of noble birth. **2.** holder of honorary rank. **3.** piece in chess. —*v.* **4.** name man a knight. —**knight′hood,** *n.* —**knight′ly,** *adj., adv.*

knit (nit) *v.,* **knitted** or **knit, knitting.** form netlike fabric. —**knit′ting,** *n.*

knob (nob) *n.* rounded handle. —**knob′by,** *adj.*

knock (nok) *v.* **1.** strike hard; pound. **2.** *Informal.* criticize. —*n.* **3.** hard blow, etc. **4.** *Informal.* criticism. —**knock′er,** *n.*

knock′-knee′, *n.* inward curvature of the legs at the knees. —**knock′-kneed′,** *adj.*

knock′out′, *n.* **1.** boxing blow that knocks opponent to the canvas. **2.** *Informal.* one that is extremely attractive.

knock′wurst (nok′wûrst, -wŏŏrst) *n.* knackwurst.

knoll (nōl) *n.* small hill.

knot (not) *n., v.,* **knotted, knotting.** —*n.* **1.** intertwining of cords to bind. **2.** cluster. **3.** lump. **4.** hard mass where branch joins tree trunk. **5.** one nautical mile per hour. —*v.* **6.** tie or tangle. —**knot′ty,** *adj.*

know (nō) *v.,* **knew** (nōō, nyōō), **known, knowing,** *n.* —*v.* **1.** understand, remember, or experience. —*n.* **2.** *Informal.* state of knowledge, esp. of secrets. —**know′a•ble,** *adj.*

know′-how′, *n. Informal.* skill.

know′ing, *adj.* **1.** having knowledge. **2.** shrewd. **3.** deliberate. —**know′ing•ly,** *adv.*

knowl′edge (nol′ij) *n.* facts, etc., known.

know′ledge•a•ble (-i jə bəl) *adj.* well-informed.

KNP *Chess.* king's knight's pawn.

kn sw knife switch.

Knt. Knight.

knuck′le (nuk′əl) *n.* **1.** joint of a finger. —*v.* **2. knuckle down,** apply oneself earnestly. **3. knuckle under,** submit; yield.

knuck′le•head′, *n. Informal.* stupid, inept person.

KO (kā′ō′, kā′ō′) knockout.

ko•al′a (kō ä′lə) *n.* gray, tree-dwelling Australian marsupial.

K. of C. Knights of Columbus.

K. of P. Knights of Pythias.

kohl′ra′bi (kōl rä′bē, -rab′ē) *n., pl.* **-bies.** variety of cabbage.

koi (koi) *n., pl.* **kois, koi.** colorful carp.

ko′la (kō′lə) *n.* tropical African tree grown for its nuts, used to flavor soft drinks.

kook (kōōk) *n. Slang.* eccentric. —**kook′y,** *adj.*

kop. kopeck.

Ko•ran′ (kə rän′, -ran′, kô-) *n.* sacred scripture of Islam.

Ko•re′an (kə rē′ən) *n.* native or language of Korea. —**Ko•re′an,** *adj.*

ko′sher (kō′shər) *adj.* (among Jews) permissible to eat.

kow′tow′ (kou′tou′, -tou′, kō′-) *v.* act obsequiously.

KP *Chess.* king's pawn.

K.P. 1. *Military.* kitchen police. **2.** Knight of

the Order of St. Patrick. **3.** Knights of Pythias.

kpc kiloparsec; kiloparsecs.

kph kilometers per hour. Also, **k.p.h.**

KR *Chess.* king's rook.

Kr *Symbol, Chemistry.* krypton.

Kr. 1. (in Sweden and the Faeroe Islands) krona; kronor. **2.** (in Iceland) króna; krónur. **3.** (in Denmark and Norway) krone; kroner.

kr. 1. (in Germany and Austria) kreutzer. **2.** (in Sweden and the Faeroe Islands) krona; kronor. **3.** (in Iceland) króna; krónur. **4.** (in Denmark and Norway) krone; kroner.

KRP *Chess.* king's rook's pawn.

krs (in Turkey) kurus.

krsn kerosene.

kryp′ton (krip′ton) *n.* inert gas, an element found in very small amounts in the atmosphere.

KS, Kansas.

ksi one thousand pounds per square inch. [k(*ilo*) + s(*quare*) i(*nch*)]

ksr *Telecommunications.* keyboard send and receive.

Kt *Chess.* knight. Also, **Kt.**

Kt. knight.

kt. 1. karat; karats. **2.** kiloton; kilotons. **3.** knot; knots.

K.T. 1. Knights Templars. **2.** Knight of the Order of the Thistle.

Kt. Bach. knight bachelor.

ku′dos (kōō′dōz, -dōs, -dos, kyōō′-) *n.* praise; glory.

kud′zu (kōōd′zōō) *n.* fast-growing vine planted for fodder and to retain soil.

kum′quat (kum′kwot) *n.* small citrus fruit.

kung′ fu′ (kung′ fōō′, kŏŏng′) Chinese technique of unarmed combat.

kV kilovolt; kilovolts. Also, **kv**

K.V. *Music.* Köchel-Verzeichnis, the chronological listing of Mozart's works.

kVA kilovolt-ampere; kilovolt-amperes. Also, **kva**

kVAhm kilovolt-ampere hour meter.

KW, kilowatt. Also, **kw**

kWh kilowatt-hour. Also, **kwhr, K.W.H.**

KWIC (kwik), of or designating an alphabetical concordance of the principal terms in a text showing every occurrence of each term surrounded by a few words of the context. [k(*ey*)-w(*ord*)-i(*n*)-c(*ontext*)]

kwy keyway.

KY, Kentucky. Also, **ky.**

kybd keyboard.

kypd keypad.

K

L

L, l (el) *n.* twelfth letter of English alphabet.

L., 1. lake. 2. large. 3. Latin. 4. left. 5. length. 6. *Brit.* pound. 7. long.

l., 1. left. 2. length. 3. *pl.* **ll.** line. 4. liter.

LA, Louisiana. Also, **La.**

lab (lab) *n.* laboratory.

la/bel (lā/bəl) *n., v.,* **-beled, -beling.** —*n.* 1. tag bearing information. —*v.* 2. put label on.

la/bi·um (lā/bē əm) *n., pl.* **-bia** (-bē ə). folds of skin bordering the vulva. —**la/bi·al,** *adj.*

la/bor (lā/bər) *n.* 1. bodily toil; work. 2. childbirth. 3. workers as a group. —*v.* 4. work. Also, *Brit.,* **la/bour.** —**la/bor·er,** *n.*

lab/o·ra·to/ry (lab/rə tôr/ē, lab/ər ə-) *n., pl.* **-ries.** place for scientific work.

la/bored, *adj.* done with difficulty.

la·bo/ri·ous (lə bôr/ē əs) *adj.* involving much labor.

labor union, organization of workers for mutual aid, esp. by collective bargaining.

la·bur/num (lə bûr/nəm) *n.* poisonous tree with drooping yellow flowers.

lab/y·rinth (lab/ə rinth) *n.* 1. maze. 2. internal ear. —**lab/y·rin/thine** (-rin/thin, -thīn) *adj.*

lac (lak) *n.* resinous secretion of Asian insect.

lace (lās) *n., v.,* **laced, lacing.** —*n.* 1. fancy network of threads. 2. cord. —*v.* 3. fasten with lace. —**lac/y,** *adj.*

lac/er·ate/ (las/ə rāt/) *v.,* **-ated, -ating.** tear; mangle. —**lac/er·a/tion,** *n.*

lach/ry·mal (lak/rə məl) *adj.* of or producing tears.

lach/ry·mose/ (-mōs/) *adj.* tearful.

lack (lak) *n.* 1. deficiency. —*v.* 2. be wanting.

lack/a·dai/si·cal (lak/ə dā/zi kəl) *adj.* listless.

lack/ey (lak/ē) *n.* servile follower.

lack/lus/ter, *adj.* uninteresting.

la·con/ic (lə kon/ik) *adj.* using few words. —**la·con/i·cal·ly,** *adv.*

lac/quer (lak/ər) *n.* 1. kind of varnish. —*v.* 2. coat with lacquer.

la·crosse/ (lə krôs/) *n.* game of ball played with long rackets.

lac/tate (lak/tāt) *v.,* **-tated, -tating.** secrete milk. —**lac·ta/tion,** *n.*

lac/tic (-tik) *adj.* of or from milk.

lac/tose (-tōs) *n.* sweet crystalline substance in milk.

la·cu/na (lə kyōō/nə) *n., pl.* **-nae** (-nē), **-nas.** 1. cavity. 2. gap.

LACW leading aircraftswoman.

lad (lad) *n.* boy.

lad/der (lad/ər) *n.* structure of two sidepieces with steps between.

lad/en (lād/n) *adj.* loaded heavily.

lad/ing (lā/ding) *n.* cargo; freight.

la/dle (lād/l) *n., v.,* **-dled, -dling.** —*n.* 1. large deep-bowled spoon. —*v.* 2. dip with ladle.

la/dy (lā/dē) *n., pl.* **-dies.** 1. refined woman. 2. mistress of household. 3. title of noblewoman.

la/dy·bug/, *n.* small spotted beetle. Also, **la/dy·bird/.**

la/dy·fin/ger, *n.* small oblong cake.

la/dy's-slip/per, *n.* orchid with slipper-shaped flower lips. Also, **la/dy-slip/per.**

LaF Louisiana French.

lag (lag) *v.,* **lagged, lagging,** *n.* —*v.* 1. move slowly or belatedly. —*n.* 2. instance of lagging.

la/ger (lä/gər, lô/-) *n.* kind of beer.

lag/gard (lag/ərd) *adj.* 1. lagging. —*n.* 2. person who lags.

la·gniappe/ (lan yap/, lan/yap) *n.* 1. small gift given with a purchase. 2. gratuity. Also, **la·gnappe/.**

la·goon/ (lə gōōn/) *n.* shallow pond connected with a body of water.

laid/-back/ (lād/-) *adj. Informal.* relaxed; easygoing.

lair (lâr) *n.* den of beast.

lais/sez-faire/ (les/ā fâr/) *adj.* without interfering in trade, others' affairs, etc.

la/i·ty (lā/i tē) *n.* laypersons.

LAK cell *Immunology.* lymphokine-activated killer cell.

lake (lāk) *n.* large body of water enclosed by land.

La·ko/ta (lə kō/tə) *n., pl.* **-tas** or **-ta.** member of a Plains Indian people.

lam (lam) *n., v.,* **lammed, lamming.** *Slang.* —*n.* 1. hasty escape. —*v.* 2. escape; flee. 3. **on the lam,** hiding or fleeing from the police.

la/ma (lä/mə) *n.* Tibetan or Mongolian Buddhist priest.

La·maze/ method (lə mäz/) method by which expectant mother is prepared for birth by classes, exercises, etc.

lamb (lam) *n.* young sheep.

lam·baste/ (lam bāst/, -bast/) *v.,* **-basted, -basting.** *Informal.* 1. beat severely. 2. reprimand harshly.

lam/bent (lam/bənt) *adj.* flickering or glowing lightly. —**lam/ben·cy,** *n.*

lame (lām) *adj.,* **lamer, lamest,** *v.,* **lamed, laming.** —*adj.* 1. crippled. 2. inadequate. —*v.* 3. make lame.

la·mé/ (la mā/, lä-) *n.* ornamental fabric with metallic threads.

lame duck (lām) elected official completing term after election of successor.

la·ment/ (lə ment/) *v.* 1. mourn; regret. —*n.*

2. Also, **lam/en•ta/tion** (lam/ən tā/shən) expression of lament. —**la•ment/a•ble,** *adj.*

lam/i•na (lam/ə nə) *n., pl.* **-nae** (-nē), **-nas.** thin layer.

lam/i•nate/ *v.,* **-nated, -nating,** *adj.* —*v.* (lam/ə nāt/) **1.** split into thin layers. **2.** cover or form with layers. —*adj.* (-nāt/, -nit) **3.** Also, **lam/i•nat/ed.** made of layers. —**lam/i• na/tion,** *n.*

lamp (lamp) *n.* light source. —**lamp/shade/,** *n.* —**lamp/post/,** *n.*

lamp/black/, *n.* pigment from soot.

lam•poon/ (lam pōōn/) *n.* **1.** vicious satire. —*v.* **2.** satirize.

lam/prey (lam/prē) *n.* eellike fish.

LAN (lan), local area network.

lance (lans) *n., v.,* **lanced, lancing.** —*n.* **1.** long spear. —*v.* **2.** open with lancet.

lan/cet (lan/sit) *n.* sharp-pointed surgical tool.

land (land) *n.* **1.** part of the earth's surface above water. **2.** region. —*v.* **3.** bring or come to land. **4.** fall to earth or floor.

lan/dau (lan/dô, -dou) *n.* carriage with folding top.

land/ed, *adj.* **1.** owning land. **2.** consisting of land.

land/fall/, *n.* **1.** approach to or sighting of land. **2.** land sighted or reached.

land/fill/, *n.* **1.** area of land built up from refuse material. **2.** material deposited on landfill.

land/ing, *n.* **1.** act of one that lands. **2.** place for landing persons and goods. **3.** platform between stairs.

land/locked/, *adj.* **1.** shut in completely or almost completely by land. **2.** having no access to sea. **3.** living in waters shut off from sea.

land/lord/, *n.* person who owns and leases property. —**land/la/dy,** *n.fem.*

land/lub/ber (-lub/ər) *n.* person unused to sea.

land/mark/, *n.* **1.** prominent object serving as a guide. **2.** anything prominent of its kind.

land/mass/, *n.* large area of land, as a continent.

land/scape/ (-skāp/) *n., v.,* **-scaped, -scaping.** —*n.* **1.** broad view of rural area. —*v.* **2.** arrange trees, shrubs, etc., for effects. —**land/scap/er,** *n.*

land/slide/, *n.* fall of earth or rock.

lane (lān) *n.* narrow road.

lang. language.

lan/guage (lang/gwij) *n.* **1.** speech. **2.** any means of communication.

lan/guid (lang/gwid) *adj.* without vigor.

lan/guish (-gwish) *v.* **1.** be or become weak. **2.** pine. —**lan/guish•ing,** *adj.* —**lan/guor** (-gər) *n.* —**lan/guor•ous,** *adj.*

lank (langk) *adj.* lean; gaunt. Also, **lank/y.**

lan/o•lin (lan/l in) *n.* fat from wool.

lan/tern (lan/tərn) *n.* case for enclosing light.

lantern jaw, long, thin jaw. —**lan/- tern-jawed/,** *adj.*

lan/yard (lan/yərd) *n.* short rope.

lap (lap) *v.,* **lapped, lapping,** *n.* —*v.* **1.** lay or lie partly over. **2.** wash against. **3.** take up with tongue. —*n.* **4.** overlapping part. **5.** one circuit of racecourse. **6.** part of body of sitting person from waist to knees.

la•pel/ (lə pel/) *n.* folded-back part on front of a garment.

lap/i•dar/y (lap/i der/ē) *n., pl.* **-ries,** *adj.* —*n.* **1.** worker in gems. —*adj.* **2.** meticulous in detail.

lap/in (lap/in) *n.* rabbit.

lap/is laz/u•li (lap/is laz/ŏŏ lē, -lī/, laz/yŏŏ-) **1.** deep blue semiprecious gem. **2.** sky-blue color; azure.

lapse (laps) *n., v.,* **lapsed, lapsing.** —*n.* **1.** slight error; negligence. **2.** slow passing. —*v.* **3.** pass slowly. **4.** make error. **5.** slip downward. **6.** become void.

lap/top/, *n.* portable microcomputer that fits on the lap.

laq lacquer.

lar/ce•ny (lär/sə nē) *n., pl.* **-nies.** theft. —**lar/ce•nist,** *n.* —**lar/ce•nous,** *adj.*

larch (lärch) *n.* tree of pine family.

lard (lärd) *n.* **1.** rendered fat of hogs. —*v.* **2.** apply lard to.

lard/er (lär/dər) *n.* pantry.

large (lärj) *adj.,* **larger, largest. 1.** great in size or number. **2.** at large, **a.** at liberty. **b.** in general. —**large/ness,** *n.*

large/ly, *adv.* **1.** in large way. **2.** generally.

large/-scale/, *adj.* extensive.

lar•gess (lär jes/, lär/jis) *n.* generous giving of gifts, or the gifts themselves. Also, **lar• gesse/.**

lar/go (lär/gō) *adj., adv. Music.* slowly.

lar/i•at (lar/ē ət) *n.* long, noosed rope.

lark (lärk) *n.* **1.** songbird. **2.** frolic.

lark/spur/ (-spûr/) *n.* plant with flowers on tall stalks.

lar/va (lär/və) *n., pl.* **-vae** (-vē). young of insect between egg and pupal stages. —**lar/val,** *adj.*

lar/yn•gi/tis (lar/ən jī/tis) *n.* inflammation of larynx.

lar/ynx (lar/ingks) *n., pl.* **larynges** (lə rin/- jēz), **larynxes.** cavity at upper end of windpipe. —**la•ryn/ge•al** (lə rin/jē əl, lar/ən jē/- əl) *adj.*

la•sa/gna (lə zän/yə, lä-) [*n.* baked dish of wide strips of pasta layered with cheese, tomato sauce, and usu. meat. Also, **la•sa/gne.**

las•civ/i•ous (lə siv/ē əs) *adj.* lewd; wanton. —**las•civ/i•ous•ness,** *n.*

la/ser (lā/zər) *n.* device for amplifying radiation of frequencies of visible light.

lash (lash) *n.* **1.** flexible part of whip. **2.** blow with whip. **3.** eyelash. —*v.* **4.** strike with or as with lash. **5.** bind.

lass (las) *n.* girl.

L

las'si•tude' (las'i tōōd', -tyōōd') n. 1. listlessness. 2. indifference.

las'so (las'ō, la sōō') n., pl. -sos, soes, v., -soed, -soing. —n. 1. lariat. —v. 2. catch with lasso.

last (last) adj. 1. latest. 2. final. —adv. 3. most recently. 4. finally. —n. 5. that which is last. 6. foot-shaped form on which shoes are made. —v. 7. endure. —last'ly, adv.

last'ing, adj. going on or enduring a long time. —last'ing•ly, adv.

lat., latitude.

latch (lach) n. 1. device for fastening door or gate. —v. 2. fasten with latch.

late (lāt) adj., adv., later, latest. 1. after proper time. 2. being or lasting well along in time. 3. recent. 4. deceased.

late'ly, adv. recently.

la'tent (lāt'nt) adj. hidden; dormant. —la'ten•cy, n.

lat'er•al (lat'ər əl) adj. on or from the side. —lat'er•al•ly, adv.

la'tex (lā'teks) n. milky plant juice used esp. in making rubber.

lath (lath) n. 1. narrow wood strip. 2. material for holding plaster. —v. 3. cover with laths.

lathe (lāṯẖ) n. machine for turning wood, etc., against a shaping tool.

lath'er (laṯẖ'ər) n. 1. froth made with soap and water. 2. froth from sweating. —v. 3. form or cover with lather.

Lat'in (lat'n) n. 1. language of ancient Rome. 2. member of any people speaking Latin-based language. —Latin, adj.

Latin America, countries in South and Central America where Spanish or Portuguese is spoken. —Lat'in-A•mer'i•can, adj., n.

La•ti'no (lə tē'nō, la-) n. Hispanic.

lat'i•tude' (lat'i tōōd', -tyōōd') n. 1. distance from equator. 2. freedom.

latl lateral.

la•trine' (lə trēn') n. toilet, esp. in military installation.

lat'ter (lat'ər) n. 1. being second of two. 2. later.

lat'tice (lat'is) n. structure of crossed strips. —lat'tice•work', n.

lau laundry.

laud (lôd) v. praise. —laud'a•ble, adj. —laud'a•to'ry, adj.

lau•da•num (lôd'n əm, lôd'nəm) n. tincture of opium.

laugh (laf) v. 1. express mirth audibly. —n. 2. act or sound of laughing. —laugh'ing•ly, adv. —laugh'ter, n.

laugh'a•ble, adj. ridiculous.

laugh'ing•stock', n. object of ridicule.

launch (lônch, länch) v. 1. set afloat. 2. start. 3. throw. —n. 4. large open motorboat. —launch'er, n.

launch pad, platform for launching rockets. Also, **launch'ing pad.**

laun'der (lôn'dər, län'-) v. wash and iron. —laun'der•er, n. —laun'dress, n.fem.

Laun'dro•mat' (-drə mat') n. Trademark. self-service laundry with coin-operated machines.

laun'dry, n., pl. -dries. 1. clothes to be washed. 2. place where clothes are laundered.

lau're•ate (lôr'ē it) n. person who has been honored in a particular field.

lau'rel (lôr'əl) n. 1. small glossy evergreen tree. 2. (pl.) honors.

LAV lymphadenopathy-associated virus.

lav lavatory.

la'va (lä'və, lav'ə) n. molten rock from volcano.

lav'a•to'ry (lav'ə tôr'ē) n., pl. -ries. 1. bathroom. 2. washbowl.

lave (lāv) v., laved, laving. bathe.

lav'en•der (lav'ən dər) n. 1. pale purple. 2. fragrant shrub yielding **oil of lavender.**

lav'ish (lav'ish) adj. 1. extravagant. —v. 2. expend or give abundantly. —lav'ish•ly, adv.

law (lô) n. 1. rules established by government under which people live. 2. rule. 3. legal action. —law'-a•bid'ing, adj. —law'break'er, n. —law'break'ing, n., adj. —law'less, adj. —law'mak'er, n.

law'ful, adj. permitted by law. —law'ful•ly, adv.

lawn (lôn) n. 1. grass-covered land kept mowed. 2. thin cotton or linen fabric.

law'suit', n. prosecution of claim in court.

law'yer (lô'yər, loi'ər) n. person trained in law.

lax (laks) adj. 1. careless. 2. slack. —lax'i•ty, n.

lax'a•tive (lak'sə tiv) adj. 1. purgative. —n. 2. laxative agent.

lay (lā) v., laid, laying, n., adj. —v. 1. place or put down, esp. in flat position. 2. produce eggs. 3. ascribe. 4. devise. 5. pt. of **lie.** —n. 6. position. 7. song. —adj. 8. not clerical or professional. —lay'man, lay'per•son, n. —lay'wom•an, n.fem.

—**Usage.** For many speakers, the verbs LAY and LIE are confused because both have the meaning of "in a flat position." LAY means "to put down" or "to place, especially in a flat position." A general rule to remember is that if the word "put" or "place" can be substituted in a sentence, then LAY is the verb to use: *Lay (= put, place) the books on the table. She laid (= put, placed) the baby in the cradle.* But the verb LIE means "to be in a flat position" or "to be situated": *Lie down and rest a moment. The baby is lying down.* For many speakers, the problem comes in the past tense for these two verbs, because the past tense of LIE is *lay,* which looks like, but is not, the present tense of LAY: *The dog will want to lie in the shade; yesterday it lay in the grass.* Note that we can LAY an infant down in a crib; he or she will LIE there until picked up.

lay'a•way plan, method of purchasing in which store reserves item until customer has completed a series of payments.

lay'er, *n.* one thickness.

lay•ette' (-et') *n.* outfit for newborn child.

lay'off', *n.* temporary dismissal of employees.

lay'out', *n.* arrangement.

lay'o•ver, *n.* stopover.

laze (lāz) *v.,* **lazed, lazing.** pass (time) lazily.

la'zy (lā'zē) *adj.,* **-zier, -ziest. 1.** unwilling to work. **2.** slow-moving. **—la'zi•ly,** *adv.* **—la'zi•ness,** *n.*

lb., *pl.* **lbs., lb.** pound.

lb. ap. *Pharmacology.* pound apothecary's.

L bar. angle iron. Also, **L beam.**

lb. av. pound avoirdupois.

lbf *Physics.* pound-force.

LBJ Lyndon Baines Johnson.

lbl label.

LBO *Finance.* leveraged buyout.

lbr lumber.

lbry library.

lb. t. pound troy.

lbyr labyrinth.

l.c., lowercase.

l.c.a. lowercase alphabet.

LCD *Electronics.* liquid-crystal display.

L.C.D. *Math.* least common denominator; lowest common denominator. Also, **l.c.d.**

L.C.F. *Math.* lowest common factor. Also, **l.c.f.**

L chain *Immunology.* light chain.

LCI *Military.* a type of landing craft used in World War II. [*L(anding) C(raft) I(nfantry)*]

lcl local.

L.C.L. *Commerce.* less than carload lot. Also, **l.c.l.**

L.C.M. least common multiple; lowest common multiple. Also, **l.c.m.**

LCR inductance-capacitance-resistance.

LCT *Military.* a type of landing craft used in World War II. [*L(anding) C(raft) T(ank)*]

LD 1. praise (be) to God. [from Latin *laus Deō*] **2.** learning disability. **3.** learning-disabled. **4.** lethal dose. **5.** long distance (telephone call). **6.** Low Dutch.

LD. (in Libya) dinar; dinars.

Ld. 1. limited. **2.** Lord.

ld 1. leading. **2.** line drawing.

ld. load.

L.D. Low Dutch.

LD₅₀ *Pharmacology.* median lethal dose.

LDC less developed country. Also, **L.D.C.**

ldg. 1. landing. **2.** loading.

LDH *Biochemistry.* lactate dehydrogenase.

LDL *Biochemistry.* low-density lipoprotein.

ldmk landmark.

Ldp. 1. ladyship. **2.** lordship.

LDPE *Chemistry.* low-density polyethylene.

ldr ladder.

L.D.S. 1. Latter-day Saints. **2.** praise (be) to God forever. [from Latin *laus Deō semper*] **3.** Licentiate in Dental Surgery.

l.e. *Football.* left end.

lea (lē, lā) *n.* meadow.

leach (lēch) *v.* **1.** soak through or in. **2.** dissolve from a material by soaking it.

lead (lēd *for 1–4;* led *for 5–7*), *v.,* **led** (led), **leading,** *n.* **—v. 1.** guide by going before or with. **2.** influence. **3.** afford passage. **—n. 4.** foremost place. **5.** heavy malleable metal. **6.** plummet. **7.** graphite used in pencils. **—lead'en,** *adj.* **—lead'er,** *n.* **—lead'er•ship',** *n.*

leading question (lē'ding) question worded to suggest the desired answer.

lead poisoning (led) toxic condition produced by contact with lead or lead compounds.

lead time (lēd) time between beginning of a process and appearance of results.

leaf (lēf) *n., pl.* **leaves** (lēvz), *v.* **—n. 1.** flat green part on stem of plant. **2.** thin sheet. **—v. 3.** thumb through. **—leaf'y,** *adj.*

leaf'let (-lit) *n.* **1.** pamphlet. **2.** small leaf.

league (lēg) *n., v.,* **leagued, leaguing. —n. 1.** alliance; pact. **2.** unit of distance, about three miles. **—v. 3.** unite in league.

leak (lēk) *n.* **1.** unintended hole. **—v. 2.** pass or let pass through leak. **3.** allow to be known unofficially. **—leak'age,** *n.* **—leak'y,** *adj.*

lean (lēn) *v.,* **leaned** or **leant, leaning,** *n., adj.* **—v. 1.** bend. **2.** depend. **—n. 3.** inclination. **4.** lean flesh. **—adj. 5.** not fat. **—lean'ness,** *n.*

lean'ing, *n.* inclination; tendency.

lean'-to', *n., pl.* **-tos.** structure with single-sloped roof abutting a wall.

leap (lēp) *v.,* **leaped** or **leapt** (lept, lept), **leaping,** *n.* **—v. 1.** spring through air; jump. **—n. 2.** jump.

leap'frog', *n., v.,* **-frogged, -frogging. —n. 1.** game in which players leap over each other's backs. **—v. 2.** jump over as in leapfrog.

leap year, year of 366 days.

learn (lûrn) *v.* acquire knowledge or skill. **—learn'er,** *n.* **—learn'ing,** *n.*

learn'ed (lûr'nid) *adj.* knowing much; scholarly.

learning disability, difficulty in reading, writing, etc., associated with impairment of central nervous system. **—learn'ing-dis•a'bled,** *adj.*

lease (lēs) *n., v.,* **leased, leasing. —n. 1.** contract conveying property for certain time. **—v. 2.** get by means of lease.

leash (lēsh) *n.* line for holding dog.

least (lēst) *adj.* **1.** smallest. **—n. 2.** least amount, etc. **—adv. 3.** to least extent, etc.

L

leath′er (leth′ər) *n*. prepared skin of animals. —**leath′er•y,** *adj*.

leath′er•neck′, *n. Informal.* U.S. marine.

leave (lēv) *v*., **left** (left), **leaving,** *n*. —*v*. **1.** depart from. **2.** let remain or be. **3.** have remaining. **4.** bequeath. —*n*. **5.** permission. **6.** farewell. **7.** furlough.

leav′en (lev′ən) *n*. **1.** Also, **leav′en•ing.** fermenting agency to raise dough. —*v*. **2.** produce fermentation.

lech′er•ous (lech′ər əs) *adj*. lustful. —**lech′-er•y,** *n*. —**lech′er,** *n*.

lec′i•thin (les′ə thin) *n*. fatty substances in nerve tissue and egg yolk.

lect. 1. lecture. **2.** lecturer.

lec′tern (lek′tərn) *n*. stand for speaker's papers.

lec′ture (lek′chər) *n*., *v*., **-tured, -turing.** —*n*. **1.** instructive speech. —*v*. **2.** give lecture; moralize. —**lec′tur•er,** *n*.

LED *Electronics.* light-emitting diode.

ledge (lej) *n*. narrow shelf.

ledg′er (lej′er) *n*. account book.

lee (lē) *n*. **1.** shelter. **2.** side away from the wind. **3.** (*pl.*) dregs. —**lee,** *adj*. —**lee′ward,** *adj*., *adv*., *n*.

leech (lēch) *n*. bloodsucking worm.

leek (lēk) *n*. plant resembling onion.

leer (lēr) *n*. **1.** sly or insinuating glance. —*v*. **2.** look with leer.

leer′y (lēr′ē) *adj*., **-ier, -iest.** wary; suspicious. —**leer′i•ness,** *n*.

lee′way′, *n*. **1.** *Naut.* drift due to wind. **2.** extra time, space, etc.

left (left) *adj*. **1.** on side toward west when facing north. **2.** still present; remaining. —*n*. **3.** left side. **4.** political side favoring liberal or radical reform. —**left′-hand′,** *adj*. —**left′-hand′ed,** *adj*. —**left′ist,** *n*., *adj*.

leg (leg) *n*. **1.** one of limbs supporting a body. **2.** any leglike part.

leg′a•cy (leg′ə sē) *n*., *pl*. **-cies.** anything bequeathed.

le′gal (lē′gəl) *adj*. of or according to law. —**le•gal′i•ty** (-gal′i tē) *n*. —**le′gal•ize′,** *v*.

le′gal•ese′ (-gə lēz′, -lēs′) *n*. excessive legal jargon.

leg′a•tee′ (leg′ə tē′) *n*. person bequeathed legacy.

le•ga′tion (li gā′shən) *n*. **1.** diplomatic minister and staff. **2.** official residence of minister.

le•ga′to (lə gä′tō) *adj*., *adv. Music.* smooth and connected; without breaks.

leg′end (lej′ənd) *n*. **1.** story handed down by tradition. **2.** key; inscription. —**leg′end•ar′-y,** *adj*.

leg′er•de•main′ (lej′ər də mān′) *n*. sleight of hand.

leg′ging, *n*. covering for leg.

leg′i•ble (lej′ə bəl) *adj*. easily read. —**leg′i•bil′i•ty,** *n*. —**leg′i•bly,** *adv*.

le′gion (lē′jən) *n*. **1.** military unit. **2.** multitude. —*adj*. **3.** very great in number. —**le′-gion•naire′,** *n*.

legis. 1. legislation. **2.** legislative. **3.** legislature.

leg′is•late′ (lej′is lāt′) *v*., **-lated, -lating. 1.** make laws. **2.** effect by law. —**leg′is•la′-tion,** *n*. —**leg′is•la′tive,** *adj*. —**leg′is•la′-tor,** *n*.

leg′is•la′ture (-chər) *n*. law-making body.

le•git′i•mate (li jit′ə mit) *adj*. **1.** lawful. **2.** after right or established principles. **3.** born to a married couple. —**le•git′i•ma•cy** (-mə sē) *n*.

le•git′i•mize′, *v*., **-mized, -mizing.** show to be or treat as legitimate.

leg′ume (leg′yo̅o̅m, li gyo̅o̅m′) *n*. plant of group including peas and beans. —**le•gu′mi•nous,** *adj*.

lei (lā) *n*. flower wreath for neck.

lei′sure (lē′zhər, lezh′ər) *n*. **1.** freedom from work. —*adj*. **2.** unoccupied; at rest.

lei′sure•ly, *adj*. unhurried.

leit′mo•tif′ (līt′mō tēf′) *n*. **1.** recurring musical phrase in an opera. **2.** dominant theme or underlying pattern.

LEM (lem), lunar excursion module.

lem′ming (lem′ing) *n*. small rodent noted for periodic mass migrations.

lem′on (lem′ən) *n*. **1.** yellowish fruit of citrus tree. **2.** *Informal.* person or thing that is defective or unsatisfactory.

lem′on•ade′ (-ə nād′) *n*. beverage of lemon juice and water.

le′mur (lē′mər) *n*. small monkeylike animal.

lend (lend) *v*., **lent, lending. 1.** give temporary use of. **2.** give; provide. —**lend′er,** *n*. —**Usage.** See BORROW.

length (lengkth, length, lenth) *n*. size or extent from end to end. —**length′en,** *v*. —**length′wise′,** *adv*., *adj*. —**length′y,** *adj*.

le′ni•ent (lē′nē ənt, lēn′yənt) *adj*. merciful; not severe. —**le′ni•ence, le′ni•en•cy,** *n*.

lens (lenz) *n*., *pl*. **lenses.** glass for changing convergence of light rays.

Lent (lent) *n*. season of fasting before Easter. —**Lent′en,** *adj*.

len′til (len′til, -tl) *n*. pealike plant.

le′o•nine′ (lē′ə nīn′) *adj*. of or like the lion.

leop′ard (lep′ərd) *n*. large fierce spotted feline.

le′o•tard′ (lē′ə tärd′) *n*. tight, flexible, one-piece garment worn by acrobats, dancers, etc.

LEP 1. *Physics.* large electron-positron collider. **2.** limited English proficiency.

lep′er (lep′ər) *n*. person afflicted with leprosy.

lep′re•chaun′ (lep′rə kôn′) *n*. Irish sprite.

lep′ro•sy (lep′rə sē) *n*. disease marked by skin ulcerations.

les′bi•an (lez′bē ən) *n*. **1.** female homosexual. —*adj*. **2.** pertaining to female homosexuals.

lese majesty (lēz′ maj′əs tē) or **lèse maj′·es·té** (lēz′ maj′əs tē) n. **1.** offense against the dignity of a ruler. **2.** attack on a revered custom.

le′sion (lē′zhən) n. **1.** injury. **2.** morbid change in bodily part.

less (les) adv. **1.** to smaller extent. —adj. Also, **les′ser. 2.** smaller. **3.** lower in importance. —n. **4.** Also, **lesser.** smaller amount, etc. —prep. **5.** minus. —**less′en,** v.

—**Usage.** FEWER is the comparative form of FEW. It is properly used before plural nouns that refer to individuals or things that can be counted (fewer words; no fewer than 31 states). LESS is the comparative form of LITTLE. It should modify only singular mass nouns that refer to things that are abstract or cannot be counted (less sugar; less doubt). LESS may be used before plural nouns only when they suggest combination into a unit or group (less than $50; less than three miles).

les·see′ (le sē′) n. one granted a lease.

les′ser, adj. **1.** compar. of **little. 2.** minor.

les′son (les′ən) n. **1.** something to be studied. **2.** reproof. **3.** useful experience.

les′sor (les′ôr, le sôr′) n. granter of lease.

lest (lest) conj. for fear that.

let (let) v., **let, letting,** n. —v. **1.** permit. **2.** rent out. **3.** contract for work. —n. **4.** hindrance.

-let, suffix indicating: **1.** small, as booklet. **2.** article worn on, as anklet.

let′down′, n. **1.** disappointment. **2.** decrease in volume, force, energy, etc.

le′thal (lē′thəl) adj. deadly.

leth′ar·gy (leth′ər jē) n., pl. **-gies.** drowsy dullness. —**le·thar′gic** (lə thar′jik) adj. —**le·thar′gi·cal·ly,** adv.

Lett. Lettish.

let′ter (let′ər) n. **1.** written communication. **2.** written component of word. **3.** actual wording. **4.** (pl.) literature. —v. **5.** write with letters.

let′tered, adj. literate; learned.

let′ter·head′, n. **1.** printed information on stationery. **2.** paper with a letterhead.

let′ter-per′fect, adj. precise in every detail.

let′tuce (let′is) n. plant with large leaves used in salad.

let′up′, n. cessation; pause; relief.

leu·ke′mi·a (lōō kē′mē ə) n. cancerous disease of blood cells.

leu′ko·cyte (lōō′kə sīt′) n. white blood cell.

Lev. Bible. Leviticus.

lev′ee (lev′ē) n. **1.** embankment to prevent floods. **2.** (Also, le vē′) reception.

lev′el (lev′əl) adj., n., v., **-eled, -eling.** —adj. **1.** even. **2.** horizontal. **3.** well-balanced. —n. **4.** height; elevation. **5.** level position. **6.** device for determining horizontal plane. —v. **7.** make or become level. **8.** aim. —**lev′el·er,** n.

lev′el·head′ed, adj. sensible and judicious. —**lev′el·head′ed·ness,** n.

lev′er (lev′ər, lē′vər) n. bar moving on fixed support to exert force.

lev′er·age (-ij) n. power or action of lever.

le·vi′a·than (li vī′ə thən) n. **1.** Biblical sea monster. **2.** something of immense size or power.

Le′vi′s (lē′vīz) n. (used with a pl. v.) Trademark. brand of jeans, esp. blue jeans.

lev′i·tate′ (lev′i tāt′) v., **-tated, -tating.** rise or cause to rise into the air, esp. in apparent defiance of gravity. —**lev′i·ta′tion,** n.

lev′i·ty (lev′i tē) n. lack of seriousness.

lev′y (lev′ē) v., **levied, levying,** n., pl. **levies.** —v. **1.** raise or collect by authority. **2.** make (war). —n. **3.** act of levying. **4.** something levied.

lewd (lōōd) adj. obscene. —**lewd′ly,** adv. —**lewd′ness,** n.

lex. 1. lexical. **2.** lexicon.

lex′i·cog′ra·phy (lek′si kog′rə fē) n. writing of dictionaries. —**lex′i·cog′ra·pher,** n.

lex′i·con′ (-kon′, -kən) n. dictionary.

LF 1. Baseball. left field. **2.** Baseball. left fielder. **3.** low frequency.

lf 1. Baseball. left field. **2.** Baseball. left fielder. **3.** Printing. lightface. **4.** line feed.

l.f. Baseball. **1.** left field. **2.** left fielder.

lfb Sports. left fullback.

lg., 1. large. **2.** long.

lgc logic.

lge. large. Also, **lge**

L. Ger. 1. Low German. **2.** Low Germanic.

LGk Late Greek. Also, **LGk, L.Gk.**

lgsltd legislated.

lgsltr legislature.

lgstcs logistics.

lgth. length.

LH Biochemistry, Physiology. luteinizing hormone.

lh Sports. left halfback.

l.h. 1. left hand; left-handed. **2.** lower half. Also, **L.H.**

l.h.b. Sports. left halfback.

L.H.D. 1. Doctor of Humane Letters. **2.** Doctor of Humanities. [from Latin Litterārum Humāniōrum Doctor]

lhdr left-hand drive.

Li Symbol, Chemistry. lithium.

ll Surveying. link; links.

L.I. 1. British. light infantry. **2.** Long Island.

li′a·bil′i·ty (lī′ə bil′i tē) n., pl. **-ties. 1.** debt. **2.** disadvantage. **3.** state of being liable.

li′a·ble, adj. **1.** likely. **2.** subject to obligation or penalty.

li·ai′son (lē ā′zən, lē′ā zôN′) n. **1.** contact to ensure cooperation. **2.** intimacy; affair.

li′ar (lī′ər) n. person who tells lies.

Lib. Liberal.

lib. 1. book. [from Latin liber] **2.** librarian. **3.** library.

L

li•ba'tion (lī bā'shən) *n.* **1.** pouring out of wine or oil to honor a deity. **2.** the liquid poured. **3.** alcoholic drink.

li'bel (lī'bəl) *n., v.,* **-beled, -beling.** —*n.* **1.** defamation in writing or print. —*v.* **2.** publish libel against. —**li'bel•ous,** *adj.*

lib'er•al (lib'ər əl, lib'rəl) *adj.* **1.** favoring extensive individual liberty. **2.** tolerant. **3.** generous. —*n.* **4.** liberal person. —**lib'er•al•ism,** *n.* —**lib'er•al'i•ty** (-ə ral'i tē) *n.* —**lib'er•al•ize',** *v.*

liberal arts, college courses comprising the arts, humanities, and natural and social sciences.

lib'er•ate' (-ə rāt') *v.,* **-ated, -ating.** set free. —**lib'er•a'tion,** *n.* —**lib'er•a'tor,** *n.*

lib'er•tar'i•an (lib'ər târ'ē ən) *n.* person who advocates liberty in thought or conduct.

lib'er•tine' (-tēn', -tin) *n.* dissolute person.

lib'er•ty, *n., pl.* **-ties. 1.** freedom; independence. **2.** right to use place. **3.** impertinent freedom.

li•bi'do (li bē'dō) *n., pl.* **-dos. 1.** sexual desire. **2.** instinctual energies and drives derived from the id. —**li•bid'i•nal** (-bid'n l) *adj.* —**li•bid'i•nous** (-bid'n əs) *adj.*

li'brar'y (lī'brer'ē, -brə rē, -brē) *n., pl.* **-ries. 1.** place for collection of books, etc. **2.** collection of books, etc. —**li•brar'i•an,** *n.*

—**Pronunciation.** LIBRARY, with two barely separated *r*-sounds, is particularly vulnerable to the tendency for neighboring sounds that are alike to become different, or for one of them to disappear altogether. This can lead to forms like the pronunciation (lī'ber ē), which is likely to be heard from less educated or very young speakers and is often criticized. However, (lī'brē), the third pronunciation shown above, is considered perfectly standard, even though one of the *r*-sounds has been dropped.

li•bret'to (li bret'ō) *n., pl.* **-brettos, -bretti** (-bret'ē). words of musical drama. —**li•bret'tist,** *n.*

lic. 1. license. **2.** licensed.

li'cense (lī'səns) *n., v.,* **-censed, -censing.** —*n.* **1.** formal permission. **2.** undue freedom. —*v.* **3.** grant license to. Also, **li'cence.**

li'cen•see' (-sən sē') *n.* person to whom a license is granted.

li•cen'tious (-sen'shəs) *adj.* lewd; lawless. —**li•cen'tious•ly,** *adv.*

li'chen (lī'kən) *n.* crustlike plant on rocks, trees, etc.

lic'it (lis'it) *adj.* lawful.

lick (lik) *v.* **1.** pass tongue over. **2.** *Informal.* beat or defeat. —*n.* **3.** act of licking. **4.** place where animals lick salt.

lick'e•ty-split' (lik'i tē-) *adv. Informal.* at great speed.

lick'ing, *n. Informal.* **1.** beating or thrashing. **2.** defeat or setback.

lic'o•rice (lik'ər ish, -ə ris) *n.* plant root used in candy, etc.

lid (lid) *n.* **1.** movable cover. **2.** eyelid. —**lid'-ded,** *adj.*

lie (lī) *n., v.,* **lied, lying.** —*n.* **1.** deliberately false statement. —*v.* **2.** tell a lie.

lie (lī) *v.,* **lay** (lā), **lain** (lān), **lying,** *n.* —*v.* **1.** assume or have reclining position. **2.** be or remain. —*n.* **3.** manner of lying. —**Usage.** See LAY.

lie detector, polygraph.

lief (lēf) *adv.* gladly.

liege (lēj, lēzh) *n.* **1.** lord. **2.** vassal.

lien (lēn, lē'ən) *n.* right in another's property as payment on claim.

lieu (lōō) *n.* stead.

Lieut. lieutenant.

Lieut. Col. lieutenant colonel.

Lieut. Comdr. lieutenant commander.

lieu•ten'ant (lōō ten'ənt; *in Brit. use, except in the navy,* lef ten'ənt) *n.* **1.** commissioned officer in army or navy. **2.** aide. —**lieu•ten'an•cy,** *n.*

LIF Lifetime (a cable television channel).

life (līf) *n., pl.* **lives** (līvz). **1.** distinguishing quality of animals and plants. **2.** period of being alive. **3.** living things. **4.** mode of existence. **5.** animation. —**life'long',** *adj.* —**life'time',** *n.* —**life'less,** *adj.* —**life'like',** *adj.*

life'blood' *n.* **1.** blood. **2.** vital element.

life'boat', *n.* boat carried on ship to save passengers in the event of sinking.

life'-care', *adj.* providing the basic needs of elderly residents. Also, **life'care'.**

life'guard', *n.* person employed to protect swimmers, as at a beach.

life preserver, buoyant device to keep a person afloat.

lif'er, *n.* person serving a term of imprisonment for life.

life'sav'er, *n.* person or thing that saves from death or a difficult situation. —**life'sav'ing,** *adj., n.*

life'-size', *adj.* of the actual size of a person, etc.

life'style', person's general pattern of living. Also, **life'-style'.**

life'-sup•port', *adj.* of equipment or techniques that sustain or substitute for essential body functions.

life'work', *n.* complete or principal work of a lifetime.

LIFO (lī'fō), **1.** *Commerce.* last-in, first-out. **2.** *Computers.* a data storage and retrieval technique, in which the last item stored is the first item retrieved. [*l(ast) i(n) f(irst) o(ut)*]

lift (lift) *v.* **1.** move or hold upward. **2.** raise or rise. —*n.* **3.** act of lifting. **4.** help. **5.** ride. **6.** exaltation. **7.** *Brit.* elevator.

lift'-off', *n.* departure from ground by rocket, etc., under own power.

lig'a•ment (lig'ə mənt) *n.* band of tissue.

lig′a•ture (lig′ə chər, -chŏŏr′) *n.* **1.** two or more letters combined, as *fl.* **2.** surgical thread or wire for tying blood vessels.

light (līt) *n., adj., v.,* **lighted** or **lit** (lit), **lighting.** —*n.* **1.** that which makes things visible or gives illumination. **2.** daylight. **3.** aspect. **4.** enlightenment. —*adj.* **5.** not dark. **6.** not heavy. **7.** not serious. —*v.* **8.** ignite. **9.** illuminate. **10.** alight; land. **11.** happen (upon). —**light′ly,** *adv.* —**light′ness,** *n.*

light′en, *v.* **1.** become or make less dark. **2.** lessen in weight. **3.** mitigate. **4.** cheer.

light′er, *n.* **1.** something that lights. **2.** barge.

light′-fin′gered, *adj.* given to pilfering.

light′-head′ed, *adj.* as if about to faint.

light′-heart′ed, *adj.* cheerful; without worry. —**light′-heart′ed•ly,** *adv.* —**light′-heart′ed•ness,** *n.*

light′house′, *n.* tower displaying light to guide mariners.

light′ning (-ning) *n.* flash of light in sky caused by electrical discharge.

lightning bug, firefly.

lightning rod, metal rod to divert lightning from a structure into the ground.

light′-year′, *n.* distance that light travels in one year.

lig′ne•ous (lig′nē əs) *adj.* of the nature of or resembling wood.

lig′nite (lig′nīt) *n.* kind of coal.

like (līk) *v.,* **liked, liking,** *adj., prep., conj., n.* —*v.* **1.** find agreeable. **2.** wish. —*adj.* **3.** resembling; similar to. —*prep.* **4.** in like manner with. —*conj.* **5.** *Informal.* as; as if. —*n.* **6.** like person or thing; match. **7.** preference. —**lik′a•ble, like′a•ble,** *adj.*

-like, suffix indicating: like or characteristic of, as *childlike.*

like′ly, *adj.,* **-lier, -liest,** *adv.* —*adj.* **1.** probable. **2.** suitable; promising. —*adv.* **3.** probably. —**like′li•hood′,** *n.*

lik′en, *v.* compare.

like′ness, *n.* **1.** image; picture. **2.** fact of being like.

like′wise′, *adv.* **1.** also. **2.** in like manner.

li′lac (lī′lək, -läk, -lak) *n.* fragrant flowering shrub.

Lil/li•pu′tian (lil′i pyōō′shən) *adj.* **1.** very small. **2.** trivial.

lilt (lilt) *n.* rhythmic cadence. —**lilt′ing,** *adj.*

lil′y (lil′ē) *n., pl.* **-ies.** plant with erect stems and showy flowers.

lil′y-liv′ered (-liv′ərd) *adj.* cowardly.

lily of the valley, *n., pl.* **lilies of the valley.** plant with spike of bell-shaped flowers.

lim. limit.

li′ma bean (lī′mə) flat, edible bean.

limb (lim) *n.* **1.** jointed part of an animal body. **2.** branch.

lim′ber (lim′bər) *adj.* **1.** flexible; supple. —*v.* **2.** make or become limber.

lim′bo (lim′bō) *n., pl.* **-bos. 1.** region on border of hell or heaven. **2.** state of oblivion. **3.**

midway state or place. **4.** dance involving bending backward to pass under horizontal bar.

Lim′burg′er (lim′bûr′gər) *n.* soft strong cheese.

lime (līm) *n., v.,* **limed, liming.** —*n.* **1.** oxide of calcium, used in mortar, etc. **2.** small, greenish, acid fruit of tropical tree. —*v.* **3.** treat with lime.

lime′light′, *n.* **1.** public notice; fame. **2.** strong light formerly used on stage.

lim′er•ick (lim′ər ik) *n.* humorous five-line verse.

lime′stone′, *n.* rock consisting chiefly of powdered calcium.

lim′it (lim′it) *n.* **1.** farthest extent; boundary. —*v.* **2.** fix or keep within limits. —**lim′i•ta′tion,** *n.* —**lim′it•less,** *adj.*

lim′it•ed, *adj.* **1.** restricted **2.** (of trains, etc.) making few stops. —*n.* **3.** limited train.

limn (lim) *v.* **1.** represent in pictures. **2.** describe.

lim′o (lim′ō) *n., pl.* **-os.** *Informal.* limousine.

lim′ou•sine′ (lim′ə zēn′, lim′ə zēn′) *n.* luxurious automobile for several passengers.

limp (limp) *v.* **1.** walk unevenly. —*n.* **2.** lame movement. —*adj.* **3.** not stiff or firm. —**limp′ly,** *adv.* —**limp′ness,** *n.*

lim′pet (lim′pit) *n.* small cone-shelled marine animal.

lim′pid (-pid) *adj.* clear. —**lim•pid′i•ty, lim′-pid•ness,** *n.* —**lim′pid•ly,** *adv.*

lin. 1. lineal. **2.** linear. **3.** liniment.

linch′pin′ (linch′-) *n.* **1.** pin inserted through end of axle to keep wheel on. **2.** something that holds various parts of a structure together.

lin′den (lin′dən) *n.* tree with heart-shaped leaves.

line (līn) *n., v.,* **lined, lining.** —*n.* **1.** long thin mark. **2.** row; series. **3.** course of action, etc. **4.** boundary. **5.** string, cord, etc. **6.** occupation. —*v.* **7.** form line. **8.** mark with line. **9.** cover inner side of.

lin′e•age (lin′ē ij) *n.* ancestry.

lin′e•al (-əl) *adj.* **1.** of direct descent. **2.** Also, **lin′e•ar** (-ər). in or of a line.

lin′e•a•ment (-ə mənt) *n.* feature, as of face.

line drive, batted baseball that travels low, fast, and straight.

line′man, *n., pl.* **-men.** worker who repairs telephone, telegraph, etc., wires.

lin′en (lin′ən) *n.* **1.** fabric made from flax. **2.** articles of linen or cotton.

lin′er (lī′nər) *n.* **1.** ship or airplane on regular route. **2.** lining.

line′-up′, *n.* order.

lin ft linear foot; linear feet.

-ling, suffix meaning: **1.** person connected with, as *hireling.* **2.** little, as *duckling.*

lin′ger (ling′gər) *v.* **1.** stay on. **2.** persist. **3.** delay. —**lin′ger•ing•ly,** *adv.*

L

lin'ge•rie' (län'zhə rā', -jə-, lan'zhə rē') n. women's undergarments.

lin'go (ling'gō) n., pl. **-goes.** *Informal.* language.

lin'gual (ling'gwəl) adj. **1.** of the tongue. **2.** of languages.

lin•gui'ni (-gwē'nē) n. pl. pasta in slender flat form.

lin'guist (-gwist) n. person skilled in languages.

lin•guis'tics, n. science of language. —**lin•guis'tic,** adj.

lin'i•ment (lin'ə mənt) n. liquid applied to bruises, etc.

lin'ing (lī'ning) n. inner covering.

link (lingk) n. **1.** section of chain. **2.** bond. —v. **3.** unite. —**link'age,** n.

links, n.pl. golf course.

link'up', n. **1.** contact set up between military units. **2.** linking element or system.

lin'net (lin'it) n. small songbird.

li•no'le•um (li nō'lē əm) n. floor covering made of cork, oil, etc.

lin'seed' (lin'sēd') n. seed of flax.

lin'sey-wool'sey (lin'zē wŏŏl'zē) n. fabric of linen and wool.

lint (lint) n. bits of thread. —**lint'y,** adj.

lin'tel (lin'tl) n. beam above door or window.

li'on (lī'ən) n. **1.** large tawny animal of Africa and Asia. **2.** person of note. —**li'on•ess,** n.fem.

li'on•heart'ed, adj. exceptionally courageous.

li'on•ize', v., **-ized, -izing.** treat as a celebrity.

lip (lip) n. **1.** fleshy margin of the mouth. **2.** projecting edge. **3.** *Slang.* impudent talk.

lip'o•suc'tion (lip'ə suk'shən, lī'pə-) n. surgical withdrawal of excess fat from under skin.

lip'read'ing, method of understanding spoken words by interpreting speaker's lip movements. —**lip'read'er,** n.

lip service, insincere profession of friendship, admiration, support, etc.

lip'stick', n. coloring for lips.

liq. 1. liquid. **2.** liquor. **3.** (in prescriptions) solution. [from Latin *liquor*]

liq'ue•fy' (lik'wə fī') v., **-fied, -fying.** become liquid. —**liq'ue•fac'tion** (-fak'shən) n.

li•queur' (li kûr', -kyŏŏr') n. strong sweet alcoholic drink.

liq'uid (lik'wid) n. **1.** fluid of molecules remaining together. —adj. **2.** of or being a liquid. **3.** in or convertible to cash.

liq'ui•date' (-wi dāt') v., **-dated, -dating. 1.** settle, as debts. **2.** convert into cash. **3.** eliminate. —**liq'ui•da'tion,** n. —**liq'ui•da'tor,** n.

liq'uor (lik'ər) n. **1.** alcoholic beverage. **2.** liquid.

lisle (līl) n. strong linen or cotton thread.

lisp (lisp) n. **1.** pronunciation of *s* and *z* like *th.* —v. **2.** speak with lisp. —**lisp'er,** n.

lis'some (lis'əm) adj. **1.** lithe; lithesome. **2.** nimble. Also, **lis'som.**

list (list) n. **1.** series of words, names, etc. **2.** inclination to side. —v. **3.** make list. **4.** incline.

lis'ten (lis'ən) v. attend with ear. —**lis'ten•er,** n.

list'less (list'lis) adj. spiritless. —**list'less•ly,** adv. —**list'less•ness,** n.

list price, retail price.

lit., 1. literally. **2.** literature.

lit'a•ny (lit'n ē) n., pl. **-nies. 1.** form of prayer. **2.** prolonged, tedious account.

Lit.B. Bachelor of Letters; Bachelor of Literature. [from Latin *Lit(t)erārum Baccalaureus*]

Lit.D. Doctor of Letters; Doctor of Literature. [from Latin *Lit(t)erārum Doctor*]

li'ter (lē'tər) n. metric unit of capacity, ▪ **1.** 0567 U.S. quarts. Also, *Brit.,* **li'tre.**

lit'er•al (lit'ər əl) adj. **1.** in accordance with strict meaning of words. **2.** exactly as written or stated. —**lit'er•al•ly,** adv.

lit'er•al-mind'ed, adj. interpreting without imagination.

lit'er•ar'y (-ə rer'ē) adj. of books and writings.

lit'er•ate (-ər it) adj. **1.** able to read and write. **2.** educated. —n. **3.** literate person. —**lit'er•a•cy** (-ər ə sē) n.

lit'e•ra'ti (-ə rä'tē, -rä'-) n.pl. persons of scholarly or literary attainments.

lit'er•a•ture (lit'ər ə chər, -chŏŏr', li'trə-) n. writings, esp. those of notable expression and thought.

Lith. 1. Lithuania. **2.** Also, **Lith** Lithuanian.

lith. 1. lithograph. **2.** lithographic. **3.** lithography.

lithe (līth) adj. limber; supple. Also, **lithe'some** (-səm).

lith'i•um (lith'ē əm) n. soft silver-white metallic element.

lith'o•graph' (-ə graf') n. print made from prepared stone or plate. —**li•thog'ra•pher** (li thog'rə fər) n. —**li•thog'ra•phy** (-rə fē) n.

lithol. lithology.

lith'o•sphere' (-ə sfēr') n. crust and upper mantle of the earth.

lit'i•gant (lit'i gənt) n. person engaged in lawsuit.

lit'i•gate' (-gāt') v., **-gated, -gating.** carry on lawsuit. —**lit'i•ga'tion,** n.

lit'mus (lit'məs) n. blue coloring matter turning red in acid solution.

litmus paper, paper treated with litmus for use as a chemical indicator.

litmus test, use of single issue or factor as basis for judgment.

Litt. B. Bachelor of Letters; Bachelor of Literature. [from Latin *Lit(t)erārum Baccalaureus*]

Litt. D., Doctor of Letters; Doctor of Literature.

lit′ter (lit′ər) *n.* **1.** disordered array. **2.** young from one birth. **3.** stretcher. **4.** bedding for animals. **5.** scattered rubbish, etc. —*v.* **6.** strew in disorder.

lit′ter•bug′, *n.* person who litters public places with trash.

lit′tle (lit′l) *adj.,* **-tler, -tlest. 1.** small. **2.** mean. —*adv.* **3.** not much. —*n.* **4.** small amount.

Litt.M. Master of Letters. [from Latin *Lit(t) erārum Magister*]

lit′tor•al (lit′ər əl) *adj.* of the shore of a lake, sea, or ocean.

lit′ur•gy (lit′ər jē) *n., pl.* **-gies.** form of worship. —**li•tur′gi•cal** (li tûr′ji kəl) *adj.*

liv′able (liv′ə bəl) *adj.* habitable or endurable. —**liv′a•bil′i•ty,** *n.*

live (liv *for 1–5;* līv *for 6–8*), *v.,* **lived, living,** *adj.* —*v.* **1.** be alive. **2.** endure in reputation. **3.** rely for food, etc. **4.** dwell. **5.** pass (life). —*adj.* **6.** alive. **7.** energetic. **8.** effective.

live′li•hood′ (līv′lē hŏŏd′) *n.* means of supporting oneself.

live′long′ (liv′-) *adj.* entire; whole.

live′ly (līv′lē) *adj.,* **-lier, -liest,** *adv.* —*adj.* **1.** active; spirited. —*adv.* **2.** vigorously. —**live′-li•ness,** *n.*

liv′er (liv′ər) *n.* abdominal organ that secretes bile.

liv′er•wurst′ (-wûrst′) *n.* liver sausage.

liv′er•y (liv′ə rē, liv′rē) *n., pl.* **-eries. 1.** uniform of male servants. **2.** keeping of horses for hire.

live′stock′ (līv′stok′) *n.* domestic farm animals.

live wire (līv) *Informal.* energetic, keenly alert person.

liv′id (liv′id) *adj.* **1.** dull blue. **2.** furious.

liv′ing (liv′ing) *adj.* **1.** live. **2.** sufficient for living. —*n.* **3.** condition of life. **4.** livelihood.

living room, room in home used for leisure activities, entertaining, etc.

living will, document stipulating that no extraordinary measures be taken to prolong signer's life during terminal illness.

liz′ard (liz′ərd) *n.* four-legged reptile.

Lk. *Bible.* Luke.

lkd locked.

lkg looking.

lkge linkage.

lknt locknut.

lkr locker.

LL 1. Late Latin. **2.** Low Latin. Also, **L.L.**

ll. 1. lines. **2.** low level.

l.l. 1. in the place quoted. [from Latin *locō laudātō*] **2.** loose-leaf.

lla′ma (lä′mə, yä′-) *n.* South American animal.

L. Lat. 1. Late Latin. **2.** Low Latin.

LL.B., Bachelor of Laws.

LL.D., Doctor of Laws.

LL.M. Master of Laws. [from Latin *Lēgum Magister*]

llti long lead-time item.

LM (*often* lem), lunar module.

lm 1. list of material. **2.** *Optics.* lumen; lumens.

L.M. 1. Licentiate in Medicine. **2.** Licentiate in Midwifery. **3.** Lord Mayor.

lm-hr *Optics.* lumen-hour; lumen-hours.

LMT local mean time.

lmtr limiter.

lm/W *Symbol.* lumen per watt.

Ln. lane.

ln logarithm (natural).

lndry rm *Real Estate.* laundry room.

LNG liquefied natural gas.

lnrty linearity.

lntl lintel.

lo (lō) *interj.* (behold!)

load (lōd) *n.* **1.** cargo; anything carried. **2.** charge of firearm. —*v.* **3.** put load on. **4.** oppress. **5.** charge (firearm). —**load′er,** *n.*

loaf (lōf) *n., pl.* **loaves** (lōvz), *v.* —*n.* **1.** shaped mass of bread, etc. —*v.* **2.** idle. —**loaf′er,** *n.*

loam (lōm) *n.* loose fertile soil. —**loam′y,** *adj.*

loan (lōn) *n.* **1.** act of lending. **2.** something lent. —*v.* **3.** lend.

loan shark, *Informal.* usurer. —**loan′shark′-ing,** *n.*

loan′word′, *n.* word borrowed from another language.

loath (lōth, lōth) *adj.* reluctant.

loathe (lōth) *v.,* **loathed, loathing.** feel disgust at; despise. —**loath′some** (lōth′səm, lōth′-) *adj.*

lob (lob) *v.,* **lobbed, lobbing,** *n.* —*v.* **1.** strike or hurl in a high curve. —*n.* **2.** tennis ball so struck.

lob′by, *n., pl.* **-bies,** *v.,* **-bied, -bying.** —*n.* **1.** vestibule or entrance hall. **2.** group that tries to influence legislators. —*v.* **3.** try to influence legislators. —**lob′by•ist,** *n.*

lobe (lōb) *n.* roundish projection. —**lo′bar** (lō′bər, -bär), **lo′bate** (lō′bāt) *adj.*

lo•bot′o•my (lə bot′ə mē, lō-) *n., pl.* **-mies.** surgical incision of brain lobe to treat mental disorder. —**lo•bot′o•mize′,** *v.,* **-mized, -mizing.**

lob′ster (lob′stər) *n.* edible marine shellfish.

loc. locative.

lo′cal (lō′kəl) *adj.* **1.** of or in particular area. —*n.* **2.** local branch of trade union. **3.** train that makes all stops. —**lo′cal•ly,** *adv.*

lo•cale′ (lō kal′, -käl′) *n.* setting; place.

lo•cal′i•ty (-kal′i tē) *n., pl.* **-ties.** place; area.

lo′cal•ize′ (-kə līz′) *v.,* **-ized, -izing.** confine to particular place. —**lo′cal•i•za′tion,** *n.*

lo′cate (lō′kāt, lō kāt′) *v.,* **-cated, -cating.** find or establish place of.

lo•ca′tion, *n.* **1.** act or instance of locating. **2.** place where something is.

L

loc. cit. (lok′ sit′) in the place cited.

lock (lok) *n.* **1.** fastener preventing unauthorized access. **2.** place in canal, etc., for moving vessels from one water level to another. **3.** part of firearm. **4.** tress of hair. —*v.* **5.** secure with lock. **6.** shut in or out. **7.** join firmly.

lock′er, *n.* closet with lock.

lock′et (-it) *n.* small case worn on necklace.

lock′jaw′, *n.* disease in which jaws become tightly locked; tetanus.

lock′out′, *n.* business closure to force acceptance of employer's terms of work.

lock′smith′, *n.* person who makes or repairs locks.

lock′step′, *n.* **1.** way of marching in close file. **2.** rigidly inflexible pattern or process.

lock′up′, *n.* jail.

lo′co (lō′kō) *adj. Slang.* crazy.

lo′co•mo′tion (lō′kə mō′shən) *n.* act of moving about.

lo′co•mo′tive, *n.* engine that pulls railroad cars.

lo′co•weed′ (lō′kō-) *n.* plant causing a disease in livestock.

lo′cust (lō′kəst) *n.* **1.** kind of grasshopper. **2.** flowering American tree.

lo•cu′tion (lō kyōō′shən) *n.* phrase; expression.

lode (lōd) *n.* veinlike mineral deposit.

lode′star′, *n.* guiding star.

lode′stone′, *n.* magnetic stone. Also, **load′stone′.**

lodge (loj) *n., v.,* **lodged, lodging.** —*n.* **1.** hut or house. **2.** members or meeting place of fraternal organization. —*v.* **3.** live or house temporarily. **4.** fix or put; become fixed. —**lodg′er,** *n.*

lodg′ing, *n.* **1.** temporary housing. **2.** (*pl.*) rooms.

lodg′ment, *n.* **1.** lodging. **2.** something lodged. Also, **lodge′ment.**

loep list of effective pages.

lof local oscillator frequency.

loft (lôft) *n.* attic or gallery.

loft′y, *adj.,* **-ier, -iest. 1.** tall. **2.** exalted or elevated. —**loft′i•ly,** *adv.* —**loft′i•ness,** *n.*

log (lôg) *n., v.,* **logged, logging.** —*n.* **1.** trunk of felled tree. **2.** Also, **log′book′.** record of events. —*v.* **3.** fell and cut up trees. **4.** record in log. **5. log in** or **on,** gain access to secured computer system. —**log′ger,** *n.*

logamp logarithmic amplifier.

lo′gan•ber′ry (lō′gən ber′ē) *n., pl.* **-ries.** dark red acid fruit.

log′a•rithm (lô′gə riŧħ′əm) *n. Math.* symbol of number of times a number must be multiplied by itself to equal a given number.

loge (lōzh) *n.* box in theater.

log′ger•head′ (lô′gər hed′, log′ər-) *n.* **1.** stupid person. **2. at loggerheads,** disputing.

log′ic (loj′ik) *n.* science of reasoning. —**log′-ical,** *adj.* —**log′i•cal•ly,** *adv.* —**lo•gi′cian** (lō jish′shən) *n.*

lo•gis′tics (lō jis′tiks, lə-) *n.* science of military supply. —**lo•gis′tic, lo•gis′ti•cal,** *adj.*

log′jam′ (lôg′-) *n.* **1.** pileup of logs, as in a river. **2.** blockage or impasse.

lo′go (lō′gō) *n.* representation or symbol of company name, trademark, etc. Also, **lo′go•type′.**

log′roll′ing, *n.* exchange of support or favors, esp. in politics.

lo′gy (lō′gē) *adj.,* **-gier, -giest.** heavy; dull.

-logy, suffix meaning science or study of, as *theology.*

loin (loin) *n.* part of body between ribs and hipbone.

loin′cloth′, *n.* cloth worn around the loins or hips.

loi′ter (loi′tər) *v.* linger. —**loi′ter•er,** *n.*

loll (lol) *v.* **1.** recline indolently. **2.** hang loosely.

lol′li•pop′ (lol′ē pop′) *n.* hard candy on stick.

lon. longitude.

Lond. London.

lone (lōn) *adj.* alone.

lone′ly (lōn′lē) *adj.,* **-lier, -liest. 1.** alone. **2.** wishing for company. **3.** isolated. —**lone′li•ness,** *n.*

lon′er, *n.* person who spends much time alone.

lone′some (-səm) *adj.* **1.** depressed by solitude. **2.** lone.

long (lông) *adj.* **1.** of great or specified length. —*adv.* **2.** for long space of time. —*v.* **3.** yearn. —**long′ing,** *n.*

lon•gev′i•ty (lon jev′i tē) *n.* long life.

long′hand′ (lông′-) *n.* ordinary handwriting.

lon′gi•tude′ (lon′ji tōōd′, -tyōōd′) *n.* distance east and west on earth's surface.

lon′gi•tu′di•nal (-tōōd′n l, -tyōōd′-) *adj.* **1.** of longitude. **2.** lengthwise.

long jump, jump for distance.

long′-lived′ (-līvd′, -livd′) *adj.* having a long life or duration.

long′-range′, *adj.* spanning a long distance or time.

long′shore′man, *n.* person who loads and unloads ships. —**long′shore′wom′an,** *n.*

long shot, 1. racehorse, team, etc., with little chance for winning. **2.** undertaking with little chance for success.

long′-term′, *adj.* involving a long time.

long′-wind′ed (-win′did) *adj.* speaking or spoken at excessive length.

look (lŏok) *v.,* **1.** direct the eyes. **2.** seem. **3.** face. **4.** seek. —*n.* **5.** act of looking. **6.** appearance.

looking glass, mirror.

look′out′, *n.* **1.** watch. **2.** person for keeping watch. **3.** place for keeping watch.

loom (lŏom) *n.* **1.** device for weaving fabric.

—v. **2.** weave on loom. **3.** appear as large and indistinct.

loon (lōon) n. diving bird.

loon′y, adj., **-ier, -iest.** Informal, **1.** lunatic; insane. **2.** extremely foolish.

loop (lōop) n. **1.** circular form from length of material or line. —v. **2.** form a loop.

loop′hole′, n. **1.** small opening in wall, etc. **2.** means of evasion.

loose (lōos) adj., **looser, loosest,** v., **loosed, loosing.** —adj. **1.** free; unconfined. **2.** not firm or tight. **3.** not exact. **4.** dissolute. —v. **5.** free. **6.** shoot (missiles). —**loos′en,** v. —**loose′ly,** adv. —**loose′ness,** n.

loot (lōot) n. **1.** spoils. —v. **2.** plunder. —**loot′er,** n.

lop (lop) v., **lopped, lopping.** cut off.

lope (lōp) v., **loped, loping,** n. —v. **1.** move or run with long, easy stride. —n. **2.** long, easy stride.

lop′sid′ed, adj. uneven.

loq. he speaks; she speaks. [from Latin loquitur]

lo•qua′cious (lō kwā′shəs) adj. talkative. —**lo•quac′i•ty** (-kwas′ə tē) n.

loran (lôr′an, lōr′-), Electronics. long-range navigation.

lord (lôrd) n. **1.** master. **2.** British nobleman. **3.** (cap.) God. **4.** (cap.) Jesus Christ. —v. **5.** domineer. —**lord′ly,** adj. —**lord′ship,** n.

lore (lôr) n. learning.

lo-res (lō′rez′), Computers. low-resolution.

lor•gnette′ (lôrn yet′) n. eyeglasses on long handle.

lor′ry (lôr′ē) n., pl. **-ries.** Brit. truck.

lose (lōoz) v., **lost** (lôst), **losing. 1.** fail to keep. **2.** misplace. **3.** be deprived of. **4.** fail to win. —**los′er,** n.

loss (lôs) n. **1.** disadvantage from losing. **2.** thing lost. **3.** waste.

lot (lot) n. **1.** object drawn to decide question by chance. **2.** allotted share. **3.** piece of land. **4.** (often pl.) Informal a great number or amount.

—**Usage.** See ALOT.

Lo•thar′i•o (lō thâr′ē ō′) n., pl. **-os.** (often l.c.) man who obsessively seduces women.

lo′tion (lō′shən) n. medicinal liquid for skin.

lot′ter•y (lot′ə rē) n., pl. **-ies.** sale of tickets on prizes to be awarded by lots.

lot′to (lot′ō) n. **1.** game of chance similar to bingo. **2.** lottery in which players choose numbers that are matched against those of the official drawing.

lo′tus (lō′təs) n. water lily of Egypt and Asia.

loud (loud) adj. **1.** strongly audible. **2.** blatant. —**loud′ly,** adv. —**loud′ness,** n.

loud′-mouth′ (-mouth′) n. a braggart; gossip. —**loud′-mouthed′** (-mouthd′, -moutht′) adj.

loud′speak′er, n. device for increasing volume of sound.

lounge (lounj) v., **lounged, lounging,** n. —v. **1.** pass time idly. **2.** loll. —n. **3.** kind of sofa. **4.** public parlor.

louse (lous) n., pl. **lice** (līs). bloodsucking insect.

lous′y (lou′zē) adj., **-ier, -iest. 1.** Informal. bad; poor. **2.** troubled with lice. —**lous′i•ness,** n.

lout (lout) n. boor. —**lout′ish,** adj.

lou′ver (lōo′vər) n. arrangement of slits for ventilation. —**lou′vered,** adj.

lov′a•ble (luv′ə bəl) adj. attracting love. Also, **love′a•ble.** —**lov′a•bly,** adv.

love (luv) n., v., **loved, loving.** —n. **1.** strong affection. **2.** sweetheart. —v. **3.** have love for. —**lov′er,** n. —**love′less,** adj. —**lov′ing,** adj. —**lov′ing•ly,** adv.

love′lorn′ (-lôrn′) adj. deprived of love or a lover.

love′ly (luv′lē) adj., **-lier, -liest.** charming. —**love′li•ness,** n.

love′sick′, adj. sick from intensity of love.

loving cup, large two-handled drinking cup.

low (lō) adj. **1.** not high or tall. **2.** prostrate. **3.** weak. **4.** humble or inferior. **5.** not loud. —adv. **6.** in low position. **7.** in quiet tone. —n. **8.** thing that is low. **9.** moo. —v. **10.** moo.

low′brow′, n. **1.** uncultured person. —adj. **2.** typical of a lowbrow.

low′-cal′ (lō′kal′, -kal′) adj. with fewer calories than usual.

low′down′ n. (lō′doun′) **1.** real and unadorned facts. —adj. (-doun′) **2.** contemptible; mean.

low′er (lō′ər for 1, 2; lou′ər for 3–5) v. **1.** reduce or diminish. **2.** make or become lower. **3.** be threatening. **4.** frown. —n. **5.** lowering appearance.

low′er•case′ (lō′ər-) adj. **1.** (of a letter) of a form often different from and smaller than its corresponding capital letter. —n. **2.** lowercase letter.

low frequency, radio frequency between 30 and 300 kilohertz. —**low′-fre′quen•cy,** adj.

low′-key′, adj. restrained; understated.

low′life′, n., pl. **-lifes.** disreputable or degenerate person.

low′ly, adj., **-lier, -liest.** humble; meek.

low′-mind′ed, adj. coarse; vulgar.

low profile, deliberately inconspicuous manner.

lox (loks) n. salmon cured in brine.

loy′al (loi′əl) adj. faithful; steadfast. —**loy′al•ly,** adv. —**loy′al•ty,** —**loy′al•ness,** n.

loz′enge (loz′inj) n. **1.** flavored candy, often medicated. **2.** diamond shape.

LP long-playing: a phonograph record played at 33⅓ r.p.m.

L.P. Printing. **1.** long primer. **2.** low pressure. Also, **l.p.**

LPG liquefied petroleum gas. Also called **LP gas.**

LPGA Ladies Professional Golf Association.

L

lphldr lampholder.

lpm *Computers.* lines per minute. Also, **LPM**

LPN, licensed practical nurse.

lprsvr life preserver.

L.P.S. Lord Privy Seal.

lptv low-power television.

lpw lumen per watt.

LQ letter-quality.

lqp *Computers.* letter-quality printer.

LR **1.** *Real Estate.* living room. **2.** long range. **3.** lower right.

Lr *Symbol, Chemistry.* lawrencium.

L.R. Lloyd's Register.

LRAM long-range attack missile.

LRBM long-range ballistic missile.

lrg. large.

LRT light-rail transit.

LS **1.** left side. **2.** letter signed. **3.** library science. **4.** lightship.

ls loudspeaker.

L.S. **1.** Licentiate in Surgery. **2.** Linnaean Society. **3.** Also, **l.s.** the place of the seal, as on a document [from Latin *locus sigillī*].

LSA **1.** Leukemia Society of America. **2.** Linguistic Society of America.

LSAT *Trademark.* Law School Admission Test.

lsb **1.** least significant bit. **2.** lower sideband.

l.s.c. in the place mentioned above. [from Latin *locā suprā citātō*]

LSD, lysergic acid diethylamide, a powerful psychedelic drug.

LSI *Electronics.* large-scale integration.

LSM a type of military landing ship. [*l(anding) s(hip) m(edium)*]

L.S.S. Lifesaving Service.

LST an oceangoing military ship, used for landing troops and heavy equipment on beaches. [*l(anding) s(hip) t(ank)*]

l.s.t. local standard time.

Lt., lieutenant.

LTA (of an aircraft) lighter-than-air.

Lt. Col. Lieutenant Colonel. Also **LTC**

Lt. Comdr. Lieutenant Commander. Also, **Lt. Com.**

Ltd. limited.

ltg lighting.

Lt. Gen. Lieutenant General. Also, **LTG**

Lt. Gov. Lieutenant Governor.

L.Th. Licentiate in Theology.

lthr leather.

Lt. Inf. *Military.* light infantry.

LTJG *U.S. Navy.* Lieutenant Junior Grade.

LTL *Commerce.* less-than-truckload lot.

LTR long-term relationship.

ltr. **1.** letter. **2.** lighter.

ltrprs letterpress.

lt-yr light-year; light-years.

lu'au (lōō'ou) *n., pl.* **-aus.** outdoor Hawaiian feast.

lub *Math.* least upper bound.

lub. **1.** lubricant. **2.** lubricating. **3.** lubrication.

lub'ber (lub'ər) *n.* clumsy person.

lubo lubricating oil.

lu'bri•cant (lōō'bri kənt) *n.* lubricating substance.

lu'bri•cate' (-kāt') *v.,* **-cated, -cating.** oil or grease, esp. to diminish friction. —**lu'bri•ca'tion,** *n.* —**lu'bri•ca'tor,** *n.*

lubt lubricant.

lu'cid (lōō'sid) *adj.* **1.** bright. **2.** clear in thought or expression. **3.** rational. —**lu•cid'i•ty, lu'cid•ness,** *n.* —**lu'cid•ly,** *adv.*

Lu'cite (lōō'sīt) *n. Trademark.* transparent plastic.

luck (luk) *n.* **1.** chance. **2.** good fortune. —**luck'less,** *adj.*

luck'y, *adj.,* **-ier, -iest.** having or due to good luck. —**luck'i•ly,** *adv.*

lu'cra•tive (lōō'krə tiv) *adj.* profitable.

lu'cre (lōō'kər) *n.* gain or money.

lu'di•crous (lōō'di krəs) *adj.* ridiculous. —**lu'di•crous•ly,** *adv.*

luf lowest usable frequency.

luff (luf) *v.* **1.** sail into wind. —*n.* **2.** act of luffing.

lug (lug) *v.,* **lugged, lugging,** *n.* —*v.* **1.** pull or carry with effort. **2.** haul. —*n.* **3.** projecting handle. **4.** *Slang.* awkward, clumsy fellow.

luge (lōōzh) *n., v.,* **luged, luging.** —*n.* **1.** small racing sled for one or two persons. —*v.* **2.** race on a luge.

lug'gage (lug'ij) *n.* baggage.

lug nut, large nut, esp. for attaching a wheel to a vehicle.

lu•gu'bri•ous (lōō gōō'brē əs, -gyōō'-) *adj.* excessively mournful or gloomy. —**lu•gu'bri•ous•ly,** *adv.*

luke•warm' (lōōk'-) *adj.* slightly warm.

LULAC League of United Latin-American Citizens.

lull (lul) *v.* **1.** soothe, esp. to sleep. —*n.* **2.** brief stillness.

lull'a•by (-ə bī') *n., pl.* **-bies.** song to lull baby.

lum luminous.

lum•ba'go (lum bā'gō) *n.* muscular pain in back.

lum'bar (lum'bər, -bär) *adj.* of or close to the loins.

lum'ber (lum'bər) *n.* **1.** timber made into boards, etc. —*v.* **2.** cut and prepare timber. **3.** encumber. **4.** move heavily. —**lum'ber•man,** *n.*

lum'ber•jack', *n.* person who fells trees.

lum'ber•yard', *n.* yard where lumber is stored for sale.

lu'mi•nar'y (lōō'mə ner'ē) *n., pl.* **-ies.** **1.** celestial body. **2.** person who inspires many.

lu'min•es'cent (lōō'mə nes'ənt) *adj.* luminous at relatively low temperatures. —**lu'min•es'cence,** *n.*

lu'mi•nous (-nəs) *adj.* giving or reflecting light. —**lu'mi•nos'i•ty** (-nos'i tē) *n.*

lum′mox (lum′əks) *n. Informal.* clumsy, stupid person.

lump (lump) *n.* **1.** irregular mass. **2.** swelling. **3.** aggregation. —*adj.* **4.** including many. —*v.* **5.** put together. **6.** endure. —**lump′y,** *adj.*

lu′na•cy (lōō′nə sē) *n., pl.* **-cies.** insanity.

lu′nar (-nər) *adj.* **1.** of or according to moon. **2.** Also, **lu′nate** (-nāt). crescent-shaped.

lu′na•tic (-tik) *n.* **1.** insane person. —*adj.* **2.** for the insane. **3.** crazy.

lunch (lunch) *n.* **1.** Also, **lunch′eon** (lun′-chən). midday meal. —*v.* **2.** eat lunch.

lunch′eon•ette′ (lun′chə net′) *n.* restaurant for quick, simple lunches.

lung (lung) *n.* respiratory organ.

lunge (lunj) *n., v.,* **lunged, lunging.** —*n.* **1.** sudden forward movement. —*v.* **2.** make lunge.

lu′pine (lōō′pin) *n.* **1.** plant with tall, dense clusters of flowers. —*adj.* **2.** of or resembling the wolf.

lu′pus (lōō′pəs) *n.* any of several diseases characterized by skin eruptions.

lurch (lûrch) *n.* **1.** sudden lean to one side. **2.** helpless plight. —*v.* **3.** make lurch.

lure (lŏŏr) *n., v.,* **lured, luring.** —*n.* **1.** bait. —*v.* **2.** decoy; entice.

lu′rid (lŏŏr′id) *adj.* **1.** glaringly lighted. **2.** intended to be exciting; sensational. —**lu′rid•ly,** *adv.*

lurk (lûrk) *v.* **1.** loiter furtively. **2.** exist unperceived.

lus′cious (lush′əs) *adj.* delicious. —**lus′cious•ly,** *adv.* —**lus′cious•ness,** *n.*

lush (lush) *adj.* **1.** tender and juicy. **2.** abundant.

lust (lust) *n.* **1.** strong desire. —*v.* **2.** have strong desire. —**lust′ful,** *adj.*

lus′ter (lus′tər) *n.* gloss; radiance. Also, **lus′tre.** —**lus′ter•less,** *adj.* —**lus′trous,** *adj.*

lust′y, *adj.,* **-ier, -iest.** vigorous. —**lust′i•ly,** *adv.*

lute (lōōt) *n.* stringed musical instrument.

Luth. Lutheran.

Lu′ther•an (lōō′thər ən) *adj.* of Protestant sect named for Martin Luther. —**Lu′ther•an•ism,** *n.*

Lux. Luxembourg.

lux•u′ri•ant (lug zhŏŏr′ē ənt, luk shŏŏr′-) *adj.* profuse; abundant. —**lux•u′ri•ance,** *n.*

lux•u′ri•ate′ (-āt′) *v.,* **-ated, -ating.** revel; delight.

lux′u•ry (luk′shə rē, lug′zhə-) *n., pl.* **-ries.** something enjoyable but not necessary. —**lux•u′ri•ous** (lug zhŏŏr′ē əs, luk shŏŏr′-) *adj.* —**lux•u′ri•ous•ly,** *adv.* —**lux•u′ri•ous•ness,** *n.*

LV. (in Bulgaria) lev; leva.

lv. **1.** leave; leaves. **2.** (in France) livre; livres.

lvl level.

LVN licensed vocational nurse.

lvr **1.** lever. **2.** louver.

LW low water.

l/w lumen per watt; lumens per watt.

l.w.m. low water mark.

lwop leave without pay.

lwp leave with pay.

lwr lower.

LWV League of Women Voters. Also, **L.W.V.**

lwyr lawyer.

lx *Optics.* lux.

-ly, suffix meaning: in a specified manner, as *loudly*; according to, as *theoretically*; to or from a specified direction, as *inwardly*; like or characteristic of, as *saintly*; every, as *hourly*.

ly•ce′um (lī sē′əm) *n.* hall for lectures, etc.

lye (lī) *n.* alkali solution.

ly′ing-in′, *adj.* **1.** of or for childbirth. —*n.* **2.** childbirth.

Lyme disease (līm) tick-transmitted disease characterized esp. by joint pains and fatigue.

lymph (limf) *n.* yellowish matter from body tissues. —**lym•phat′ic** (lim fat′ik) *adj.*

lym′pho•cyte′ (lim′fə sīt′) *n.* white blood cell producing antibodies.

lynch (linch) *v.* put to death without legal authority.

lynx (lingks) *n., pl.* **lynxes, lynx.** kind of wild cat.

lyr layer.

lyre (līər) *n.* ancient harplike instrument.

lyr′ic (lir′ik) *adj.* Also, **lyr′i•cal.** **1.** (of poetry) musical. **2.** of or writing such poetry. **3.** ardently expressive. —*n.* **4.** lyric poem. **5.** (*pl.*) words for song. —**lyr′i•cal•ly,** *adv.* —**lyr′i•cism** (-ə siz′m) *n.* —**lyr′i•cist,** *n.*

lyt layout.

LZ landing zone.

L

M

M, m (em) *n.* thirteenth letter of English alphabet.

ma (mä) *n. Informal.* mother.

MA, Massachusetts.

M.A., Master of Arts.

MAA master-at-arms.

ma'am (mam, mäm; *unstressed* məm) *n. Informal.* madam.

M.A.Arch. Master of Arts in Architecture.

MAb *Immunology.* monoclonal antibody.

mac maintenance allocation chart.

Mac. *Bible.* Maccabees.

M.Ac. Master of Accountancy.

ma•ca'bre (mə kä'brə, -käb') *adj.* gruesome.

mac•ad'am (mə kad'əm) *n.* road-making material containing broken stones. —**mac•ad'am•ize',** *v.,* -**ized,** -**izing.**

mac'a•ro'ni (mak'ə rō'nē) *n.* **1.** tube-shaped food made of wheat. **2.** 18th-century fop.

mac'a•roon' (mak'ə rōōn') *n.* small cookie, usually containing almonds.

ma•caw' (mə kô') *n.* tropical parrot.

Macc. *Bible.* Maccabees.

mace (mās) *n.* **1.** spiked war club. **2.** staff of office. **3.** spice from part of nutmeg seed. **4.** (*cap.*) *Trademark.* chemical for subduing rioters, etc.

Maced. Macedonia.

mac'er•ate' (mas'ə rāt') *v.,* -**ated,** -**ating.** soften by steeping in liquid. —**mac'er•a'tion,** *n.*

Mach *Physics.* mach number.

mach. **1.** machine. **2.** machinery. **3.** machinist.

ma•che'te (mə shet'ē, -chet'ē) *n.* heavy knife.

Mach'i•a•vel'li•an (mak'ē ə vel'ē ən) *adj.* unscrupulously wily.

mach'i•na'tion (mak'ə nā'shən) *n.* cunning plan.

ma•chine' (mə shēn') *n.* **1.** apparatus or mechanical device. **2.** group controlling political organization.

machine gun, firearm capable of firing continuous stream of bullets.

ma•chin'er•y, *n., pl.* -**eries.** machines or mechanisms.

ma•chin'ist, *n.* operator of powered tool, ship's engines, etc.

ma•chis'mo (mä chēz'mō) *n.* exaggerated masculinity as basis for code of behavior.

Mach' num'ber (mäk) ratio of speed of object to speed of sound.

ma'cho (mä'chō) *adj.* exaggeratedly virile.

mack'er•el (mak'ər əl) *n.* common food fish.

mack'i•naw' (mak'ə nô') *n.* short, heavy, woolen coat.

mack'in•tosh' (mak'in tosh') *n.* raincoat.

mac'ra•mé' (mak'rə mā') *n.* decorative work of knotted cords.

macro-, prefix meaning large, as *macrocosm.*

mac'ro•bi•ot'ic (mak'rō bi ot'ik) *adj.* of or giving long life.

mac'ro•cosm (mak'rə koz'əm) *n.* universe.

ma'cron (mā'kron, mak'ron) *n.* horizontal line over vowel to show it is long.

mad (mad) *adj.,* **madder, maddest. 1.** insane. **2.** *Informal,* angry. **3.** violent. —**mad'man',** *n.* —**mad'den,** *v.* —**mad'ly,** *adv.* —**mad'ness,** *n.*

mad'am (mad'əm) *n.* **1.** female term of address. **2.** woman in charge of brothel.

mad'ame (mad'əm, mə dam', -däm', ma-) *n., pl.* **mesdames** (mā dam', -däm'). French term of address for a married woman.

mad'cap', *adj.* impulsive; rash.

MADD (mad), Mothers Against Drunk Driving.

mad'e•moi•selle' (mad'ə mə zel', mad'-mwə-, mam zel') *n., pl.* **mademoiselles, mesdemoiselles** (mā'də mə zel', -zelz', mäd'mwə-) French term of address for unmarried woman.

Madm. Madam.

Ma•don'na (mə don'ə) *n.* Virgin Mary.

mad'ras (mad'rəs, mə dras', -dräs') *n.* light cotton fabric.

mad'ri•gal (mad'ri gəl) *n.* song for several voices unaccompanied.

M.A.E. **1.** Master of Aeronautical Engineering. **2.** Master of Art Education. **3.** Master of Arts in Education.

M.A.Ed. Master of Arts in Education.

mael'strom (māl'strəm) *n.* **1.** whirlpool. **2.** confusion.

mae'nad (mē'nad) *n.* female votary of Dionysus.

M.Aero.E. Master of Aeronautical Engineering.

maes'tro (mī'strō) *n., pl.* -**tros.** master, esp. of music.

Ma'fi•a (mä'fē ə, maf'ē ə) *n.* criminal society.

mag. **1.** magazine. **2.** magnet. **3.** magnetic. **4.** magnetism. **5.** magneto. **6.** magnitude. **7.** (in prescriptions) large. [from Latin *magnus*]

magamp magnetic amplifier.

mag'a•zine' (mag'ə zēn') *n.* **1.** periodical publication. **2.** storehouse for ammunition, etc. **3.** cartridge receptacle in repeating weapon.

M.Ag.Ec. Master of Agricultural Economics.

M.Ag.Ed. Master of Agricultural Education.

ma•gen'ta (mə jen'tə) *n.* reddish purple.

mag'got (mag'ət) *n.* larva of fly.

Ma'gi (mā'jī) *n.pl. Bible.* the three wise men.

mag/ic (maj/ik) *n.* **1.** seemingly supernatural production of effects. —*adj.* Also, **mag/i·cal.** **2.** of magic. **3.** enchanting. —**ma·gi/cian** (mə jish/ən) *n.*

mag/is·te/ri·al (maj/ə stēr/ē əl) *adj.* masterlike; authoritative.

mag/is·trate/ (-strāt/, -strit) *n.* civil public official.

mag/ma (mag/mə) *n.* molten material beneath the earth's surface, from which igneous rocks and lava are formed.

magn *Electronics.* magnetron.

mag·nan/i·mous (mag nan/ə məs) *adj.* generous; high-minded. —**mag/na·nim/i·ty** (-nə nim/i tē) *n.*

mag/nate (-nāt, -nit) *n.* business leader.

mag·ne/sia (mag nē/zhə) *n.* magnesium oxide, used as laxative.

mag·ne/si·um (-zē əm, -zhəm) *n.* light, silvery, metallic element.

mag/net (mag/nit) *n.* metal body that attracts iron or steel. —**mag·net/ic** (-net/ik) *adj.*

magnetic field, space near magnet, electric current, moving charged particle in which magnetic force acts.

mag/net·ism/ (mag/ni tiz/əm) *n.* **1.** characteristic property of magnets. **2.** science of magnets. **3.** great personal charm. —**mag/net·ize/,** *v.* -ized, -izing

mag/net·ite/ (mag/ni tīt/) *n.* common black mineral.

mag·ne/to (-nē/tō) *n., pl.* -tos. small electric generator.

mag·nif/i·cence (mag nif/ə səns) *n.* **1.** splendor; grandeur. **2.** nobility. **3.** supreme excellence. —**mag·nif/i·cent,** *adj.*

mag/ni·fy/ (mag/nə fī/) *v.,* -fied, -fying. **1.** increase apparent size. **2.** enlarge. —**mag/ni·fi·ca/tion,** *n.* —**mag/ni·fi/er,** *n.*

mag·nil/o·quent (mag nil/ə kwənt) *adj.* grandiose or pompous in expression. —**mag·nil/o·quence,** *n.*

mag/ni·tude/ (-ni tōōd/, -tyōōd/) *n.* **1.** size or extent. **2.** brightness, as of a star.

mag·no/li·a (mag nōl/yə, -nō/lē ə) *n.* tree with large fragrant flowers.

magnum opus (mag/nəm ō/pəs) chief work of writer, composer, or artist.

mag/pie/ (mag/pī/) *n.* black and white bird that steals.

magtd magnitude.

mah mahogany.

ma/ha·ra/jah (mä/hə rä/jə, -zhə) *n.* (formerly) ruling prince in India. —**ma/ha·ra/nee** (-nē) *n.fem.*

ma·hat/ma (mə hät/mə, -hat/-) *n.* person, esp. in India, held in highest esteem for wisdom and saintliness.

mah/-jongg/ (mä/jông/, -zhông/) *n.* Chinese game.

ma·hog/a·ny (mə hog/ə nē) *n., pl.* -nies. tropical American tree.

Ma·hom/et (mə hom/it) *n.* Muhammad.

maid (mād) *n.* **1.** unmarried woman. **2.** female servant.

maid/en, *n.* **1.** young unmarried woman. —*adj.* **2.** of maidens. **3.** unmarried. **4.** initial. —**maid/en·ly,** *adj.* —**maid/en·li·ness,** *n.*

maid/en·hair/, *n.* fern with finely divided fronds.

mail (māl) *n.* **1.** material delivered by postal system. **2.** postal system. **3.** armor, usually flexible. —*adj.* **4.** of mail. —*v.* **5.** send by mail. —**mail/box/,** *n.* —**mail carrier,** *n.* —**mail/man/,** *n.*

mail/lot/ (mä yō/, ma-) *n.* close-fitting, one-piece bathing suit for women.

maim (mām) *v.* cripple; impair.

main (mān) *adj.* **1.** chief; principal. —*n.* **2.** chief pipe or duct. **3.** strength. **4.** ocean. —**main/ly,** *adv.*

main/frame/, *n.* large computer, often the hub of a system serving many users.

main/land/ (-land/, -lənd) *n.* continental land rather than island.

main/spring/, *n.* chief spring of mechanism.

main/stay/, *n.* chief support.

main/stream/, *n.* customary trend of behavior, opinion, etc.

maint maintenance.

main·tain/ (mān tān/) *v.* **1.** support. **2.** assert. **3.** keep in order. —**main/te·nance** (-tə nəns) *n.*

mai/tre d'hô·tel/ (mā/trə dō tel/) headwaiter. Also, **mai/tre d'/** (mā/tər dē/).

maize (māz) *n.* corn.

Maj. Major.

maj/es·ty (maj/ə stē) *n., pl.* -ties. **1.** regal grandeur. **2.** sovereign. —**mə·jes/tik** (mə-jes/tik) *adj.* —**ma·jes/ti·cal·ly,** *adv.*

Maj. Gen. Major General.

ma·jol/i·ca (mə jol/i kə, mə yol/-) *n.* kind of pottery.

ma/jor (mā/jər) *n.* **1.** army officer above captain. **2.** person of legal age. —*adj.* **3.** larger or more important.

ma/jor-do/mo (-dō/mō) *n.* steward.

ma/jor·ette/ (-jə ret/) *n.* female leader of marchers.

major general, army officer above brigadier general.

ma·jor/i·ty (mə jôr/i tē) *n., pl.* -ties. **1.** greater number. **2.** full legal age.

make (māk) *v.,* made (mād), making, *n.* —*v.* **1.** bring into existence; form. **2.** cause; force. **3.** earn. **4.** accomplish. —*n.* **5.** style. **6.** manufacture. —**mak/er,** *n.*

make/-be·lieve/, *n.* **1.** pretending that fanciful thing is true. —*adj.* **2.** fictitious.

make/shift/, *n., adj.* substitute.

make/up/, *n.* **1.** cosmetics. **2.** organization; composition.

mal-, prefix meaning bad or ill, as *maladjustment.*

mal/a·chite/ (mal/ə kīt/) *n.* green mineral, an ore of copper.

M

mal'ad•just'ment, *n.* **1.** faulty adjustment. **2.** inability to adapt to social conditions. —**mal'ad•just'ed,** *adj.*

mal'ad•min'is•ter, *v.* mismanage.

mal'a•droit' (mal'ə droit') *adj.* awkward.

mal'a•dy (mal'ə dē) *n.,* *pl.* **-dies.** illness.

ma•laise' (ma lāz', -lez', mə-) *n.* **1.** weakness; discomfort. **2.** vague uneasiness.

mal'a•mute' (mal'ə myo͞ot') *n.* Alaskan breed of large dogs.

mal'a•prop•ism (mal'ə prop iz'əm) *n.* ludicrous misuse of similar words.

ma•lar'i•a (mə lâr'ē ə) *n.* mosquito-borne disease. —**ma•lar'i•al,** *adj.*

ma•lar'key (mə lär'kē) *n.* *Informal.* nonsense.

mal'a•thi'on (mal'ə thī'on, -ən) *n.* organic insecticide of low toxicity for mammals.

mal'con•tent' (mal'kən tent') *n.* dissatisfied person.

M.A.L.D. Master of Arts in Law and Diplomacy.

mal de mer (mʌl də meʀ') seasickness.

male (māl) *adj.* **1.** of sex that begets young. —*n.* **2.** male person, etc.

mal'e•dic'tion (mal'i dik'shən) *n.* curse.

mal'e•fac'tor (mal'ə fak'tər) *n.* person who does wrong.

ma•lev'o•lent (mə lev'ə lənt) *adj.* wishing evil. —**ma•lev'o•lence,** *n.*

malf malfunction.

mal•fea'sance (mal fē'zəns) *n.* misconduct in office.

mal•formed', *adj.* badly formed. —**mal'for•ma'tion,** *n.*

mal'ice (mal'is) *n.* evil intent. —**ma•li'cious** (mə lish'shəs) *adj.*

ma•lign' (mə līn') *v.* **1.** speak ill of. —*adj.* **2.** evil.

ma•lig'nan•cy (mə lig'nən sē) *n.,* *pl.* **-cies.** **1.** malignant state. **2.** cancerous growth.

ma•lig'nant (-nənt) *adj.* **1.** causing harm or suffering. **2.** deadly.

ma•lin'ger (mə ling'gər) *v.* feign sickness. —**ma•lin'ger•er,** *n.*

mall (môl) *n.* **1.** shaded walk. **2.** covered shopping center.

mal'lard (mal'ərd) *n.* wild duck.

mal'le•a•ble (mal'ē ə bəl) *adj.* **1.** that may be hammered or rolled into shape. **2.** readily influenced. —**mal'le•a•bil'i•ty, mal'le•a•ble•ness,** *n.*

mal'let (mal'it) *n.* wooden-headed hammer.

mal'nu•tri'tion, *n.* improper nutrition.

mal'oc•clu'sion, *n.* irregular contact between upper and lower teeth.

mal•o'dor•ous, *adj.* smelling bad.

mal•prac'tice, *n.* improper professional behavior.

M.A.L.S. 1. Master of Arts in Liberal Studies. **2.** Master of Arts in Library Science.

malt (môlt) *n.* germinated grain used in liquor-making.

malt'ose (môl'tōs) *n.* sugar formed by action of enzyme on starch.

mal•treat' (mal trēt') *v.* abuse.

mam milliammeter.

ma'ma (mä'mə, mə mä') *n.* *Informal.* mother.

mam'bo (mäm'bō) *n.* Latin-American dance style.

mam'mal (mam'əl) *n.* vertebrate animal whose young are suckled.

mam'ma•ry (mam'ə rē) *adj.* of breasts.

mam'mo•gram' (mam'ə gram') *n.* x-ray photograph of a breast, for detection of tumors.

mam'mon (mam'ən) *n.* **1.** material wealth. **2.** greed for riches.

mam'moth (mam'əth) *n.* **1.** large extinct kind of elephant. —*adj.* **2.** huge.

mam'my (mam'ē) *n.,* *pl.* **-mies.** *Informal.* mother.

man (man) *n.,* *pl.* **men** (men), *v.,* **manned, manning.** —*n.* **1.** male person. **2.** person. **3.** human race. —*v.* **4.** supply with crew. **5.** serve.

man'a•cle (man'ə kəl) *n.,* *v.,* **-cled, -cling.** handcuff.

man'age (man'ij) *v.,* **-aged, -aging. 1.** take care of. **2.** direct. —**man'age•a•ble,** *adj.* —**man'a•ger,** *n.* —**man'a•ge'ri•al** (-i jēr'ē-əl) *adj.*

man'age•ment, *n.* **1.** direction. **2.** persons in charge.

ma•ña'na (mä nyä'nä) *n.* *Spanish.* tomorrow.

man'a•tee' (man'ə tē') *n.* plant-eating aquatic mammal. Also, **sea cow.**

man•da'mus (man dā'məs) *n.,* *pl.* **-mus•es.** *Law.* writ from superior court commanding that a thing be done.

man'da•rin (man'də rin) *n.* **1.** public official in Chinese Empire. **2.** (*cap.*) dialect of Chinese.

man'date (man'dāt) *n.* **1.** authority over territory granted to nation by other nations. **2.** territory under such authority. **3.** command, as to take office. —**man'date,** *v.*

man'da•to'ry (man'də tôr'ē) *adj.* officially required.

man'di•ble (man'də bəl) *n.* bone comprising the lower jaw.

man'do•lin' (man'dl in, man'dl in') *n.* plucked stringed musical instrument.

man'drake (man'drāk, -drik) *n.* narcotic herb.

man'drel (man'drəl) *n.* rod or axle in machinery.

man'drill (man'dril) *n.* kind of baboon.

mane (mān) *n.* long hair at neck of some animals.

ma•nège' (ma nezh', -näzh') *n.* art of training and riding horses.

ma•neu'ver (mə no͞o'vər) *n.* **1.** planned movement, esp. in war. —*v.* **2.** change position by maneuver. **3.** put in certain situation by intrigue. —**ma•neu′ver•a•ble,** *adj.*

manf manifold.

man Friday, *pl.* **men Friday.** reliable male assistant.

man′ful, *adj.* resolute. —**man′ful•ly,** *adv.*

man′ga•nese′ (mang′gə nēs′, -nēz′) *n.* hard metallic element.

mange (mānj) *n.* skin disease of animals. —**man′gy,** *adj.*

man′ger (mān′jər) *n.* trough for feeding livestock.

man′gle (mang′gəl) *v.*, **-gled, -gling,** *n.* —*v.* **1.** disfigure, esp. by crushing. **2.** put through mangle. —*n.* **3.** device with rollers for removing water in washing clothes.

man′go (mang′gō) *n.*, *pl.* **-goes.** fruit of tropical tree.

man′grove (mang′grōv, man′-) *n.* kind of tropical tree.

man′han•dle (man′han′dl) *v.*, **-dled, -dling.** handle roughly.

man•hat′tan (man hat′n, mən-) *n.* cocktail of whiskey and vermouth.

man′hole′, *n.* access hole to sewer, drain, etc.

man′hood, *n.* **1.** manly qualities. **2.** state of being a man.

man′-hour′, *n.* ideal amount of work done by one person in an hour.

man′hunt′, *n.* intensive search for fugitive.

ma′ni•a (mā′nē ə) *n.* **1.** great excitement. **2.** violent insanity.

ma′ni•ac′, *n.* lunatic. —**ma•ni′a•cal** (mə nī′ə kəl) *adj.*

man′ic (man′ik) *adj.* irrationally excited or lively.

man′ic-depress′ive, *adj.* suffering from mental disorder in which mania alternates with depression.

man′i•cure′ (man′i kyŏŏr′) *n.* skilled care of fingernails and hands. —**man′i•cure′,** *v.* —**man′i•cur′ist,** *n.*

man′i•fest′ (man′ə fest′) *adj.* **1.** evident. —*v.* **2.** show plainly. —*n.* **3.** list of cargo and passengers. —**man′i•fes•ta′tion,** *n.*

man′i•fes′to (-fes′tō) *n.*, *pl.* **-toes.** public declaration of philosophy or intentions.

man′i•fold′ (man′ə fōld′) *adj.* **1.** of many kinds or parts. —*v.* **2.** copy.

man′i•kin (man′i kin) *n.* model of human body.

Ma•nil′a paper (mə nil′ə) strong, light brown or buff paper.

man in the street, ordinary person.

ma•nip′u•late′ (mə nip′yə lāt′) *v.*, **-lated, -lating.** handle with skill or cunning. —**ma•nip′u•la′tion,** *n.* —**ma•nip′u•la′tor,** *n.*

man′kind′ (man′kīnd′ *for 1;* man′kīnd′ *for 2*) *n.* **1.** human race. **2.** men.

man′ly, *adj.*, **-lier, -liest.** virile.

man′na (man′ə) *n.* divine food given to Israelites.

man′ne•quin (man′i kin) *n.* model for displaying clothes.

man′ner (man′ər) *n.* **1.** way of doing, acting, etc. **2.** (*pl.*) way of acting in society. **3.** sort.

man′ner•ism, *n.* peculiarity of manner.

man′ner•ly, *adj.* polite.

man′nish, *adj.* like a man.

man′-of-war′, *n.*, *pl.* **men-of-war.** warship.

man′or (man′ər) *n.* large estate. —**ma•no′ri•al** (mə nôr′ē əl) *adj.*

man′pow′er, *n.* available labor force.

man•qué′ (mäng kā′) *adj.* unfulfilled.

man′sard (man′särd) *n.* roof with two slopes of different pitch on all sides.

manse (mans) *n.* house and land of parson.

man′serv′ant, *n.* male servant, as valet.

man′sion (man′shən) *n.* stately house.

man′slaugh′ter, *n.* unlawful killing of person without malice.

man′sue•tude′ (man′swi tŏŏd′, -tyŏŏd′) *n.* mildness.

man′ta (man′tə, män′-) *n.* huge ray with pectoral fins.

man′tel (man′tl) *n.* ornamental structure around fireplace.

man•til′la (man til′ə, -tē′ə) *n.* lace head scarf of Spanish women.

man′tis (man′tis) *n.* kind of carnivorous insect.

man•tis′sa (man tis′ə) *n.* decimal part of common logarithm.

man′tle (man′tl) *n.*, *v.*, **-tled, -tling.** —*n.* **1.** loose cloak. —*v.* **2.** envelop. **3.** blush.

man′tra (man′trə, män′-) *n.* Hindu or Buddhist verbal formula for recitation.

man′u•al (man′yŏŏ əl) *adj.* **1.** of or done with hands. —*n.* **2.** small informational book. **3.** hand powered typewriter. —**man′u•al•ly,** *adv.*

man′u•fac′ture (man′yə fak′chər) *n.*, *v.*, **-tured, -turing.** —*n.* **1.** making of things, esp. in great quantity. **2.** thing made. —*v.* **3.** make. —**man′u•fac′tur•er,** *n.*

man′u•mit′ (man′yə mit′) *v.*, **-mitted, -mitting.** release from slavery. —**man′u•mis′sion,** *n.*

ma•nure′ (mə nŏŏr′, -nyŏŏr′) *n.*, *v.*, **-ured, -uring.** —*n.* **1.** fertilizer, esp. dung. —*v.* **2.** apply manure to.

man′u•script′ (man′yə skript′) *n.* handwritten or typed document.

man′y (men′ē) *adj.* **1.** comprising a large number; numerous. —*n.* **2.** large number.

MAO *Biochemistry.* monoamine oxidase.

MAOI *Biochemistry.* monoamine oxidase inhibitor.

MAO inhibitor *Biochemistry.* monoamine oxidase inhibitor.

Mao′ism (mou′iz əm) *n.* policies of Chinese Communist leader Mao Zedong. —**Mao′ist,** *n.*, *adj.*

map (map) *n.*, *v.*, **mapped, mapping.** —*n.* **1.**

M

flat representation of earth, etc. —*v.* **2.** show by map. **3.** plan.

MAPI *Computers.* Messaging Application Programming Interface.

ma'ple (mā'pəl) *n.* northern tree.

mar (mär) *v.*, **marred, marring.** damage.

Mar., March.

mar'a•bou' (mar'ə bōō') *n., pl.* **-bous.** bareheaded stork.

ma•ra'ca (mə rä'kə, -rak'ə) *n.* gourd-shaped rattle filled with seeds or pebbles, used as rhythm instrument.

mar'a•schi'no (mar'ə skē'nō, -shē'-) *n.* cordial made from fermented juice of wild cherry.

maraschino cherry, cherry preserved in real or imitation maraschino.

mar'a•thon' (mar'ə thon', -thən) *n.* long contest, esp. a foot race of 26 miles, 385 yards.

ma•raud' (mə rôd') *v.* plunder. —**ma•raud'-er,** *n.*

mar'ble (mär'bəl) *n.* **1.** crystalline limestone used in sculpture and building. **2.** small glass ball used in children's game. —*adj.* **3.** of marble.

mar'bling, *n.* intermixture of fat with lean in meat.

MARC (märk), a standardized system developed by the Library of Congress for producing and transmitting records. [*ma(chine) r(eadable) c(atologing)*]

march (märch) *v.* **1.** walk with measured tread. **2.** advance. —*n.* **3.** act of marching. **4.** distance covered in march. **5.** music for marching.

March (märch) *n.* third month of year.

M.Arch.E. Master of Architectural Engineering.

mar'chion•ess (mär'shə nis, -nes') *n.* **1.** wife or widow of marquess. **2.** woman of rank equal to marquess.

Mar'di Gras (mär'dē grä', grä') the day before Lent, often celebrated as a carnival.

mare (mâr) *n.* female horse.

mare's'-nest', *n.* discovery that proves to be delusion.

marg. 1. margin. **2.** marginal.

mar'ga•rine (mär'jər in) *n.* butterlike product made from vegetable oils and water or milk.

mar'gin (mär'jin) *n.* **1.** edge. **2.** amount more than necessary. **3.** difference between cost and selling price. —**mar'gin•al,** *adj.*

mar'gi•na'li•a (-jə nā'lē ə) *n.pl.* marginal notes.

mar'gue•rite' (mär'gə rēt') *n.* daisylike chrysanthemum.

mar'i•gold' (mar'i gōld') *n.* common, yellow-flowered plant.

ma'ri•jua'na (mar'ə wä'nə) *n.* narcotic plant.

ma•rim'ba (mə rim'bə) *n.* xylophone with chambers for resonance.

ma•ri'na (mə rē'nə) *n.* docking area for small boats.

mar'i•nade' (mar'ə nād') *n.* pungent liquid mixture for steeping food.

mar'i•nate', *v.* **-nated, -nating.** season by steeping. —**mar'i•na'tion,** *n.*

ma•rine' (mə rēn') *adj.* **1.** of the sea. —*n.* **2.** member of U.S. Marine Corps. **3.** fleet of ships.

Marine Corps, military branch of U.S. Navy.

mar'i•ner (mar'ə nər) *n.* sailor.

mar'i•o•nette' (mar'ē ə net') *n.* puppet on strings.

mar'i•tal (mar'i tl) *adj.* of marriage. —**mar'i•tal•ly,** *adv.*

mar'i•time' (mar'i tīm') *adj.* of sea or shipping.

mar'jo•ram (mär'jər əm) *n.* herb used as seasoning.

mark (märk) *n.* **1.** any visible sign. **2.** object aimed at. **3.** rating; grade. **4.** lasting effect. **5.** German monetary unit. —*v.* **6.** be feature of. **7.** put mark on, as grade or price. **8.** pay attention to. —**mark'er,** *n.*

mark'down', *n.* price reduction.

marked, *adj.* **1.** conspicuous. **2.** ostentatious. **3.** singled out for revenge. —**mark'ed•ly,** *adv.*

mar'ket (mär'kit) *n.* **1.** place for selling and buying. —*v.* **2.** sell or buy. —**mar'ket•a•ble,** *adj.*

mar'ket•place', *n.* **1.** open area where market is held. **2.** the world of business, trade, and economics.

marks'man, *n., pl.* **-men.** person who shoots well. —**marks'man•ship',** *n.* —**marks'wom'an,** *n.fem.*

mark'up', *n.* price increase by retailer.

marl (märl) *n.* earthy deposit used as fertilizer.

mar'lin (mär'lin) *n.* large game fish.

mar'line•spike' (mär'lin spīk') *n.* iron tool used to separate strands of rope.

mar'ma•lade' (mär'mə lād') *n.* fruit preserve.

Mar.Mech.E. Marine Mechanical Engineer.

mar'mo•set' (mär'mə zet', -set') *n.* small, tropical American monkey.

mar'mot (mär'mət) *n.* bushy-tailed rodent.

ma•roon' (mə rōōn') *n., adj.* **1.** dark brownish-red. —*v.* **2.** abandon ashore.

Marq. 1. Marquess. **2.** Marquis.

mar•quee' (mär kē') *n.* projecting shelter over outer door.

mar'que•try (mär'ki trē) *n.* inlaid work forming pattern.

mar'quis (mär'kwis, mär kē') *n.* rank of nobility below duke. Also, *Brit.* **mar'quess** (-kwis). —**mar•quise'** (-kēz') *n.fem.*

mar'qui•sette' (mär'kə zet', -kwə-) *n.* delicate open fabric.

mar'riage (mar'ij) *n.* **1.** legal union of man

and woman. **2.** wedding. —mar′riage•a•ble, *adj.*

mar′row (mar′ō) *n.* soft inner tissue of bone.

mar′ry (mar′ē) *v.*, -ried, -rying. take, give, or unite in marriage.

Mars (märz) *n.* one of the planets.

marsh (märsh) *n.* low, wet land. —marsh′y, *adj.*

mar′shal (mär′shəl) *n.*, *v.*, -shaled, -shaling. —*n.* **1.** federal officer. —*v.* **2.** rally; organize.

marsh gas, decomposition product of organic matter.

marsh′mal′low (-mel′ō, -mal′ō) *n.* soft confection made from gelatin.

marsh marigold, yellow-flowered plant of buttercup family.

mar•su′pi•al (mär sōō′pē əl) *n.* animal carrying its young in pouch, as the kangaroo. —mar•su′pi•al, *adj.*

mart (märt) *n.* market.

mar′ten (mär′tn) *n.* small, American, furbearing animal.

mar′tial (mär′shəl) *adj.* warlike; military. —mar′tial•ly, *adv.*

martial art, any of various forms of East Asian self-defense or combat.

martial law, law imposed by military forces.

mar′tin (mär′tn) *n.* bird of swallow family.

mar′ti•net′ (mär′tn et′) *n.* disciplinarian.

mar•ti′ni (mär tē′nē) *n.* cocktail of gin and vermouth.

mar′tyr (mär′tər) *n.* **1.** person who willingly dies or suffers for a belief. —*v.* **2.** make martyr of. —mar′tyr•dom, *n.*

mar′vel (mär′vəl) *n.*, *v.*, -veled, -veling. —*n.* **1.** wonderful thing. —*v.* **2.** wonder (at). —mar′vel•ous, *adj.*

Marx′ism (märk′siz əm) *n.* doctrine of classless society; communism. —Marx′ist, *n.*, *adj.*

mar′zi•pan′ (mär′zə pan′) *n.* confection of almond paste and sugar.

mas. masculine.

masc. masculine.

mas•car′a (ma skar′ə) *n.* cosmetic for eyelashes.

mas′cot (mas′kot, -kət) *n.* source of good luck.

mas′cu•line (mas′kyə lin) *adj.* of or like men. —mas′cu•lin′i•ty, *n.*

ma′ser (mā′zər) *n.* device for producing electromagnetic waves.

mash (mash) *n.* **1.** soft pulpy mass. —*v.* **2.** crush.

mash′ie, *n.* golf club.

mask (mask) *n.* **1.** disguise for face. —*v.* **2.** disguise.

mas′och•ism (mas′ə kiz′əm, maz′-) *n.* willful suffering. —mas′och•ist, *n.* —mas′och•is′tic, *adj.*

ma′son (mā′sən) *n.* builder with stone, brick, etc. —ma′son•ry, *n.*

mas. pil. (in prescriptions) a pill mass. [from Latin *massa pilulāris*]

mas′quer•ade′ (mas′kə rād′) *n.*, *v.*, -aded, -ading. —*n.* **1.** disguise. **2.** party at which guests wear disguise. —*v.* **3.** wear disguise. —mas′quer•ad′er, *n.*

mass (mas) *n.* **1.** body of coherent matter. **2.** quantity or size. **3.** weight. **4.** (*cap.*) celebration of the Eucharist. **5.** the masses, common people as a whole. —*v.* **6.** form into a mass. —*adj.* **7.** of or affecting the masses. **8.** done on a large scale.

Mass., Massachusetts.

mas′sa•cre (mas′ə kər) *n.*, *v.*, -cred, -cring. —*n.* **1.** killing of many. —*v.* **2.** slaughter.

mas•sage′ (mə säzh′, -säj′) *v.*, -saged, -saging, *n.* —*v.* **1.** treat body by rubbing or kneading. —*n.* **2.** such treatment. —mas•seur′ (mə sûr′), *n.* —mas•seuse′ (mə sōōs′ -sōōz′) *n.fem.*

mas′sive (mas′iv) *adj.* large; heavy. —mas′sive•ly, *adv.*

mass media, means of communication that reaches large numbers of people.

mass noun, noun referring to indefinitely divisible substance or abstract noun.

mass number, number of nucleons in atomic nucleus.

mass′-produce′, *v.*, -duced, -ducing. produce in large quantities. —mass production.

mast (mast) *n.* upright pole.

mas•tec′to•my (ma stek′tə mē) *n.*, *pl.* -mies. surgical removal of a breast.

mas′ter (mas′tər) *n.* **1.** person in control. **2.** employer or owner. **3.** skilled person. —*adj.* **4.** chief. —*v.* **5.** conquer.

mas′ter•ful, *adj.* asserting power or authority. —mas′ter•ful•ly, *adv.*

mas′ter•ly, *adj.* highly skilled.

mas′ter•mind′, *n.* **1.** supreme planner. —*v.* **2.** plan as mastermind.

master of ceremonies, person who conducts events.

mas′ter•piece′, *n.* work of highest skill.

master's degree, academic degree awarded to student who has completed at least one year of graduate study.

master sergeant, noncommissioned officer of highest rank.

mas′ter•stroke′, *n.* extremely skillful action.

mas′ter•y, *n.*, *pl.* -teries. control; skill.

mast′head′, *n.* box in newspaper, etc., giving names of owners and staff.

mas′ti•cate′ (mas′ti kāt′) *v.*, -cated, -cating. chew. —mas′ti•ca′tion, *n.*

mas′tiff (mas′tif) *n.* powerful dog.

mas′to•don′ (mas′tə don′) *n.* large extinct elephantlike mammal.

mas′toid (mas′toid) *n.* protuberance of bone behind ear.

mas′tur•bate′ (mas′tər bāt′) *v.*, -bated, -bating. practice sexual self-gratification. —mas′tur•ba′tion, *n.*

M

mat (mat) *n., v.,* **matted, matting,** *adj.* —*n.*
1. covering for floor or other surface. **2.** border for picture. **3.** padding. **4.** thick mass. **5.** matte. —*v.* **6.** cover with mat. **7.** form into mat. —*adj.* **8.** matte.

mat•a•dor' (mat'ə dôr') *n.* bullfighter.

match (mach) *n.* **1.** stick chemically tipped to strike fire. **2.** person or thing resembling or equaling another. **3.** game. **4.** marriage. —*v.* **5.** equal. **6.** fit together. **7.** arrange marriage for.

match'less, *adj.* unequaled. —**match'less•ly,** *adv.*

match'mak'er, *n.* arranger of marriages.

mate (māt) *n., v.,* **mated, mating.** —*n.* **1.** one of pair. **2.** officer of merchant ship. **3.** assistant. **4.** female member of couple. —*v.* **5.** join; pair.

ma'té (mä'tā), *n., pl.* **-tés.** tealike South American beverage.

ma•te'ri•al (mə tēr'ē əl) *n.* **1.** substance of which thing is made. **2.** fabric. —*adj.* **3.** physical. **4.** pertinent. —**ma•te'ri•al•ly,** *adv.*

ma•te'ri•al•ism, *n.* **1.** devotion to material objects or wealth. **2.** belief that all reality is material. —**ma•te'ri•al•ist,** *n.* —**ma•te'ri•al•is'tic,** *adj.*

ma•te'ri•al•ize', *v.,* **-ized, -izing.** give or assume material form.

ma•te'ri•el' (mə tēr'ē el') *n.* supplies, esp. military.

ma•ter'ni•ty (mə tûr'ni tē) *n.* motherhood. —**ma•ter'nal,** *adj.*

math 1. mathematical. **2.** mathematics.

math'e•mat'ics (math'ə mat'iks) *n.* science of numbers. —**math'e•mat'i•cal,** *adj.* —**math'e•ma•ti'cian** (-mə tish'ən) *n.*

mat'i•née' (mat'n ā') *n.* afternoon performance.

mat'ins (mat'nz) *n.* morning prayer.

matl material.

ma'tri•arch' (mā'trē ärk') *n.* female ruler. —**ma'tri•ar'chy,** *n.*

mat'ri•cide' (ma'tri sīd', mā'-) *n.* killing one's mother. —**mat'ri•cid'al,** *adj.*

ma•tric'u•late' (mə trik'yə lāt') *v.,* **-lated, -lating.** enroll. —**ma•tric'u•la'tion,** *n.*

mat'ri•mo'ny (ma'trə mō'nē) *n., pl.* **-nies.** marriage. —**mat'ri•mo'ni•al,** *adj.*

ma'trix (mā'triks, ma'-) *n., pl.* **-trices** (-tri-sēz'), **-trixes. 1.** place or point where something originates. **2.** mold; model.

ma'tron (mā'trən) *n.* **1.** married woman, esp. one who is mature and dignified. **2.** female institutional officer. —**ma'tron•ly,** *adj.*

MATS (mats), Military Air Transport Service.

Matt. *Bible.* Matthew.

matte (mat) *adj.* **1.** having a dull surface, without luster. —*n.* **2.** dull surface or finish. Also, **mat.**

mat'ter (mat'ər) *n.* **1.** material. **2.** affair or trouble. **3.** pus. **4.** importance. —*v.* **5.** be of importance.

mat'ter-of-fact', *adj.* objective; realistic.

mat'ting (mat'ing) *n.* mat of rushes.

mat'tock (mat'ək) *n.* digging implement with one broad and one pointed end.

mat'tress (ma'tris) *n.* thick filled case for sleeping on.

ma•ture' (mə tŏŏr', -tyŏŏr', -chŏŏr') *adj.,* **-turer, -turest,** *v.,* **-tured, -turing.** —*adj.* **1.** grown or developed. **2.** adult in manner or thought. **3.** payable. —*v.* **4.** become or make mature. —**ma•tu'ri•ty,** *n.* —**ma•ture'ly,** *adv.* —**mat'u•ra'tion** (mach'ə rā'shən) *n.*

MATV master antenna television system.

mat'zo (mät'sə) *n., pl.* **-zos.** unleavened bread.

maud'lin (môd'lin) *adj.* weakly sentimental.

maul (môl) *v.* handle roughly.

maun'der (môn'dər) *v.* **1.** talk meanderingly. **2.** wander.

mau'so•le'um (mô'sə lē'əm, -zə-) *n., pl.* **-leums, -lea** (-lē'ə). tomb in form of building.

mauve (mōv, môv) *n.* pale purple.

ma'ven (mā'vən) *n.* expert.

mav'er•ick (mav'ər ik) *n.* **1.** unbranded calf. **2.** nonconformist.

maw (mô) *n.* mouth.

mawk'ish (mô'kish) *adj.* sickly sentimental. —**mawk'ish•ly,** *adv.* —**mawk'ish•ness,** *n.*

MAX Cinemax (a cable television channel).

max. maximum.

max'i (mak'sē) *n., pl.* **-is.** ankle-length coat or skirt.

max•il'la (mak sil'ə) *n., pl.* **maxillae.** upper jaw. —**max'il•lar'y** (-sə ler'ē) *adj.*

max'im (mak'sim) *n.* general truth.

max'i•mum (mak'sə məm) *n.* **1.** greatest degree or quantity. —*adj.* **2.** greatest possible.

may (mā) *v., pt.* **might** (mīt). (auxiliary verb of possibility or permission.)

May (mā) *n.* fifth month of year.

may'be, *adv.* perhaps.

May'day', *n.* international radio distress call.

may'flow'er, *n.* plant that blossoms in May.

may'fly', *n., pl.* **-flies.** insect with large transparent forewings.

may'hem (mā'hem, -əm) *n.* random violence.

may'on•naise' (mā'ə nāz') *n.* salad dressing made chiefly of egg yolks, oil, and vinegar. Also, *Informal,* **may'o.**

may'or (mā'ər) *n.* chief officer of city. —**may'or•al•ty,** *n.*

maze (māz) *n.* confusing arrangement of paths.

ma•zur'ka (mə zûr'kə, -zŏŏr'-) *n.* lively Polish dance.

MB 1. Manitoba, Canada (for use with ZIP code). **2.** *Computers.* megabyte; megabytes.

Mb *Computers.* megabit; megabits.

mb *Physics.* **1.** millibar; millibars. **2.** millibarn; millibarns.

M.B. *Chiefly British.* Bachelor of Medicine. [from Latin *Medicinae Baccalaureus*]

M.B.A. Master of Business Administration. Also, **MBA**

mbb *Electricity.* make-before-break.

mbd (of oil) million barrels per day.

MBE Multistate Bar Examination.

M.B.E. Member of the Order of the British Empire.

mbl mobile.

Mbm one thousand feet, board measure.

mbm *Computers.* magnetic bubble memory.

MBO management by objective.

mbr member.

MBTA Massachusetts Bay Transportation Authority.

MByte *Computers.* megabyte: 1 million bytes.

MC **1.** Marine Corps. **2.** master of ceremonies. **3.** Medical Corps. **4.** Member of Congress.

Mc **1.** *Physics, Chemistry.* megacurie; megacuries. **2.** *Electricity.* megacycle.

mC **1.** *Electricity.* millicoulomb; millicoulombs. **2.** *Physics, Chemistry.* millicurie; millicuries.

mc **1.** *Electricity.* megacycle. **2.** *Optics.* metercandle. **3.** *Physics, Chemistry.* millicurie; millicuries. **4.** *Electricity.* momentary contact.

M.C. **1.** Master Commandant. **2.** master of ceremonies. **3.** Medical Corps. **4.** Member of Congress. **5.** Member of Council. **6.** *British.* Military Cross.

MCAT Medical College Admission Test.

M.C.E. Master of Civil Engineering.

Mcf one thousand cubic feet. Also, **mcf, MCF**

Mcfd thousands of cubic feet per day.

M.Ch.E. Master of Chemical Engineering.

MChin Middle Chinese.

mchry machinery.

mCi *Physics, Chemistry.* millicurie; millicuries.

M.C.J. Master of Comparative Jurisprudence.

mcm **1.** *Computers.* magnetic-core memory. **2.** thousand circular mils.

MCP male chauvinist pig.

M.C.P. Master of City Planning.

M.C.R. Master of Comparative Religion.

mcw *Electronics.* modulated continuous wave.

MD, Maryland. Also, **Md.**

M.D., Doctor of Medicine.

MDA *Pharmacology.* an amphetamine derivative, $C_{10}H_{13}NO_2$. [*m(ethylene)* *d(ioxy)a(mphetamine)*]

MDAA Muscular Dystrophy Association of America.

MDAP Mutual Defense Assistance Program.

M.Des. Master of Design.

mdf *Telephones.* main distributing frame.

mdl **1.** middle. **2.** minimum detectable level. **3.** module.

Mdlle. Mademoiselle.

mdm medium.

Mdm. Madam.

MDMA an amphetamine derivative, $C_{11}H_{15}NO_2$. [*m(ethylene)* *d(ioxy)m(eth)a(mphetamine)*]

Mdme. Madame.

mdn median.

mdnt. midnight.

mdnz modernize.

MDR minimum daily requirement.

mdse. merchandise.

MDT **1.** mean downtime. **2.** Also, **M.D.T.** Mountain Daylight Time.

me (mē) *pers. pronoun.* objective case of **I.**

ME, Maine.

mead (mēd) *n.* liquor of fermented honey.

mead′ow (med′ō) *n.* level grassland.

mead′ow•lark′, *n.* common American songbird.

mea′ger (mē′gər) *adj.* poor; scanty. Also, **mea′gre.**

meal (mēl) *n.* **1.** food served or eaten. **2.** coarse grain. —**meal′y,** *adj.*

meal′y-mouthed′, *adj.* avoiding candid speech.

mean (mēn) *v.,* **meant** (ment), **meaning,** *adj., n.* —*v.* **1.** intend (to do or signify). **2.** signify. —*adj.* **3.** poor; shabby. **4.** hostile; malicious. **5.** middle. —*n.* **6.** (*pl.*) method of achieving purpose. **7.** (*pl.*) money or property. **8.** intermediate quantity. —**mean′ness,** *n.*

me•an′der (mē an′dər) *v.* wander aimlessly.

mean′ing, *n.* **1.** significance. —*adj.* **2.** significant. —**mean′ing•ful,** *adj.* —**mean′ing•less,** *adj.* —**mean′ing•ly,** *adv.*

mean′time′, *n.* **1.** time between. —*adv.* Also, **mean′while′. 2.** in time between.

meas. **1.** measurable. **2.** measure. **3.** measurement.

mea′sles (mē′zəlz) *n.* infectious disease marked by small red spots.

mea′sly (mē′zlē) *adj.,* **-slier, -sliest.** *Informal,* miserably small.

meas′ure (mezh′ər) *v.,* **-ured, -uring.** *n.* —*v.* **1.** ascertain size or extent. —*n.* **2.** process of measuring. **3.** dimensions. **4.** instrument or system of measuring. **5.** action. —**meas′ur•a•ble,** *adj.* —**meas′ure•ment,** *n.*

meas′ured, *adj.* in distinct sequence.

meat (mēt) *n.* **1.** flesh of animals used as food. **2.** edible part of fruit, nut, etc. **3.** essential part; gist.

meat′y, *adj.,* **-ier, -iest. 1.** with much meat. **2.** rewarding attention.

Mec′ca (mek′ə) *n.* **1.** city in Saudi Arabia, spiritual center of Islam. **2.** (*often l.c.*) place that attracts many.

mech. **1.** mechanical. **2.** mechanics. **3.** mechanism.

me•chan′ic (mə kan′ik) *n.* skilled worker with machinery.

me•chan′i•cal, *adj.* of or operated by machinery. —**me•chan′i•cal•ly,** *adv.*

me•chan′ics, *n.* science of motion and of action of forces on bodies.

mech′an•ism (mek′ə niz′əm) *n.* **1.** structure of machine. **2.** piece of machinery. —**mech′a•nist,** *n.*

M

mech/a•nis/tic (-nis/tik) *adj.* of or like machinery.

mech/a•nize/, *v.,* **-nized, -nizing.** adapt to machinery. **—mech/a•ni•za/tion,** *n.*

med. 1. medical. **2.** medicine. **3.** medieval. **4.** medium.

M.Ed. Master of Education.

med/al (med/l) *n.* badgelike metal object given for merit.

med/al•ist, *n.* medal winner.

me•dal/lion (mə dal/yən) *n.* large medal or medallike ornament.

med/dle (med/l) *v.,* **-dled, -dling.** interfere; tamper. **—med/dler,** *n.* **—med/dle•some,** *adj.*

me/di•a (mē/dē ə) *n.pl.* the means of mass communication, as radio, television, and newspapers.

me/di•al (mē/dē əl) *adj.* average.

me/di•an (mē/dē ən) *adj., n.* middle.

me/di•ate/ (mē/dē āt/) *v.,* **-ated, -ating.** settle (dispute) between parties. **—me/di•a/tion,** *n.* **—me/di•a/tor,** *n.*

med/ic (med/ik) *n. Informal.* doctor or medical aide.

Med/i•caid/ (med/i kād/) *n.* state- and federal-supported medical care for low-income persons.

med/i•cal, *adj.* **1.** of medicine. **2.** curative. **—med/i•cal•ly,** *adv.*

me•dic/a•ment (mə dik/ə mənt, med/i kə-) *n.* healing substance.

Med/i•care/ (med/i kâr/) *n.* government-supported medical insurance for those 65 years old or more.

med/i•cate/, *v.,* **-cated, -cating.** treat with medicine. **—med/i•ca/tion,** *n.*

me•dic/i•nal (mə dis/ə nl) *adj.* curative; remedial. **—me•dic/i•nal•ly,** *adv.*

med/i•cine (med/ə sin) *n.* **1.** substance used in treating disease. **2.** art of preserving or restoring physical health.

medicine man, among American Indians, person believed to have magical powers.

me/di•e•val (mē/dē ē/vəl, mid ē/-) *adj.* of the Middle Ages. Also, **me/di•ae/val.**

me/di•e/val•ism, *n.* **1.** a characteristic of the Middle Ages. **2.** devotion to medieval ideals, etc.

me/di•e/val•ist, *n.* **1.** expert in medieval history, etc. **2.** one devoted to medieval ideals, etc.

me/di•o/cre (mē/dē ō/kər) *adj.* undistinguished. **—me/di•oc/ri•ty** (-ok/ri tē) *n.*

Medit. Mediterranean.

med/i•tate/ (med/i tāt/) *v.,* **-tated, -tating.** think intensely; consider. **—med/i•ta/tion,** *n.* **—med/i•ta/tive,** *adj.*

me/di•um (mē/dē əm) *n., pl.* **-diums** for 1–5, **-dia** (-dē ə) for 1–3, 5, *adj.* **—n. 1.** something intermediate or moderate. **2.** means of doing. **3.** environment. **4.** person believed able to communicate with dead. **5.** means of mass communication. **—adj. 6.** intermediate.

med/ley (med/lē) *n.* mixture, as of tunes.

Med.Sc.D. Doctor of Medical Science.

me•dul/la (mə dul/ə) *n.* soft, marrowlike center of organ.

meek (mēk) *adj.* submissive.

meer/schaum (mēr/shəm, -shôm) *n.* claylike mineral, used for tobacco pipes.

meet (mēt) *v.,* **met** (met), **meeting,** *n., adj.* **—v. 1.** come into contact with. **2.** make acquaintance of. **3.** satisfy. **—n. 4.** equal. **5.** meeting, esp. for sport. **—adj. 6.** proper.

meet/ing, *n.* **1.** a coming together. **2.** persons gathered.

MEG *Medicine.* magnetoencephalogram.

meg 1. *Electricity.* megacycle. **2.** megohm; megohms.

mega-, *prefix.* **1.** one million. **2.** large.

meg/a•hertz/ (meg/ə hûrts/) *n., pl.* **-hertz.** *Elect.* one million cycles per second.

meg/a•lo•ma/ni•a (meg/ə lō mā/nē ə) *n.* delusion of greatness, riches, etc.

meg/a•lop/o•lis (meg/ə lop/ə lis) *n.* very large urbanized area.

meg/a•phone/ (meg/ə fōn/) *n.* cone-shaped device for magnifying sound.

meg/a•ton/, *n.* one million tons, esp. of TNT, as equivalent in explosive force.

MEGO (mē/gō), my eyes glaze over.

mei•o/sis (mī ō/sis) *n.* part of process of gamete formation.

MEK *Chemistry.* methyl ethyl ketone.

mel/a•mine (mel/ə mēn/) *n.* crystalline solid used in manufacturing resins.

mel/an•cho/li•a (mel/ən kō/lē ə) *n.* mental state of severe depression.

mel/an•chol/y (mel/ən kol/ē) *n., pl.* **-cholies. 1.** low spirits; depression. **—adj. 2.** sad.

mé•lange/ (mā länzh/, -länj/) *n.* mixture.

mel/a•nin (mel/ə nin) *n.* pigment accounting for dark color of skin, hair, etc.

mel/a•nism, *n.* unusually high concentration of melanin in skin, etc.

mel/a•no/ma (-nō/mə) *n.* darkly pigmented skin tumor.

meld (meld) *v.* display combination of cards for a score.

me/lee (mā/lā) *n.* confused, general fight.

mel/io•rate/ (mēl/yə rāt/) *v.,* **-rated, -rating.** improve. **—mel/io•ra/tion,** *n.* **—mel/io•ra/tive,** *adj.*

mel•lif/lu•ous (mə lif/lōō əs) *adj.* soft and sweet in speech.

mel/low (mel/ō) *adj.* **1.** soft and rich. **2.** genial. **—v. 3.** make or become mellow.

me•lo/de•on (mə lō/dē ən) *n.* reed organ.

me•lo/di•ous, *adj.* tuneful.

mel/o•dra/ma (mel/ə drä/mə, -dram/ə) *n.* play emphasizing theatrical effects and strong emotions. **—mel/o•dra•mat/ic,** *adj.*

mel/o•dy (mel/ə dē) *n., pl.* **-dies.** arrangement of musical sounds. **—me•lod/ic** (mə lod/ik) *adj.*

mel'on (mel'ən) *n.* edible fruit of certain annual vines.

melt (melt) *v.,* **melted, melted** or **molten, melting. 1.** make or become liquid, esp. by heat. **2.** soften.

melt'down', *n.* melting of nuclear reactor core, causing escape of radiation.

melting pot, place where blending of peoples, races, or cultures takes place.

mel'ton, *n.* smooth woolen fabric.

mem. 1. member. **2.** memoir. **3.** memorandum. **4.** memorial. **5.** memory.

mem'ber (mem'bər) *n.* **1.** part of structure or body. **2.** one belonging to organization. —**mem'ber•ship',** *n.*

mem'brane (mem'brān) *n.* thin film of tissue in animals and plants.

me•men'to (mə men'tō) *n., pl.* **-tos, -toes.** reminder.

mem'oir (mem'wär, -wôr) *n.* **1.** *(pl.)* personal recollection. **2.** biography.

mem'o•ra•bil'i•a (-ər ə bil'ē ə, -bil'yə) *n.pl.* souvenirs.

mem'o•ra•ble, *adj.* worth remembering. —**mem'o•ra•bly,** *adv.*

mem'o•ran'dum (mem'ə ran'dəm) *n., pl.* **-dums, -da** (-də). written statement or reminder. Also, **mem'o** (mem'ō).

me•mo'ri•al (mə môr'ē əl) *n.* **1.** something honoring memory of a person or event. —*adj.* **2.** serving as memorial.

mem'o•rize' (mem'ə rīz') *v.,* **-rized, -rizing.** commit to memory.

mem'o•ry, *n., pl.* **-ries. 1.** faculty of remembering. **2.** something that is remembered. **3.** length of time of recollection. **4.** reputation after death. **5.** capacity of computer to store data.

men'ace (men'is) *v.,* **-aced, -acing,** *n.* —*v.* **1.** threaten evil to. —*n.* **2.** something that threatens.

mé•nage' (mā näzh') *n.* household.

me•nag'er•ie (mə naj'ə rē, -nazh'-) *n.* collection of animals.

mend (mend) *v.* repair; improve. —**mend'er,** *n.*

men•da'cious (men dā'shəs) *adj.* untruthful. —**men•dac'i•ty** (-das'i tē) *n.*

men'di•cant (men'di kənt) *n.* beggar.

M.Eng. Master of Engineering.

men•ha'den (men hād'n) *n., pl.* **-den.** herringlike Atlantic fish.

me'ni•al (mē'nē əl) *adj.* **1.** humble; servile. —*n.* **2.** servant.

me•nin'ges (mi nin'jēz) *n.pl., sing.* **me'ninx** (mē'ningks). three membranes covering brain and spinal cord.

men'in•gi'tis (men'in jī'tis) *n.* inflammation of meninges.

men'o•pause' (men'ə pôz') *n.* cessation of menses, usually between ages of 45 and 50.

me•nor'ah (mə nôr'ə) *n.* symbolic candelabrum used by Jews during Hanukkah.

men'ses (men'sēz) *n.pl.* monthly discharge of blood from uterus. —**men'stru•al** (-strōō-əl) *adj.* —**men'stru•ate'** (-strōō āt') *v.,* **-ated, -ating.** —**men•stru•a'tion** (-strōō ā'-shən) *n.*

men'sur•a•ble (-shər ə bəl, -sər ə bəl) *adj.* measurable. —**men'su•ra'tion,** *n.*

mens'wear', *n.* clothing for men.

-ment, suffix meaning: action or resulting state, as *abridgment*; product, as *fragment*; means, as *ornament*.

men'tal (men'tl) *adj.* of or in the mind. —**men'tal•ly,** *adv.*

men•tal'i•ty (-tal'i tē) *n., pl.* **-ties. 1.** mental ability. **2.** characteristic mental attitude.

men'thol (men'thôl, -thol) *n.* colorless alcohol from peppermint oil. —**men'thol•at'ed** (-thə lā'tid) *adj.*

men'tion (men'shən) *v.* **1.** speak or write of. —*n.* **2.** reference. —**men'tion•a•ble,** *adj.*

men'tor (men'tôr, -tər) *n.* adviser; teacher.

men'u (men'yōō, mā'nyōō) *n.* list of dishes that can be served.

me•ow' (mē ou', myou) *n.* **1.** sound cat makes. —*v.* **2.** make such sound.

M.E.P. Master of Engineering Physics.

m.e.p. mean effective pressure.

M.E.P.A. Master of Engineering and Public Administration.

mEq milliequivalent.

mer. 1. meridian. **2.** meridional.

merc. 1. mercantile. **2.** mercurial. **3.** mercury.

mer'can•tile' (mûr'kən tēl', -tīl', -til) *adj.* of or engaged in trade.

mer'ce•nar'y (mûr'sə ner'ē) *adj., n., pl.* **-naries.** —*adj.* **1.** acting only for profit. —*n.* **2.** hired soldier.

mer'cer•ize' (mûr'sə rīz') *v.,* **-ized, -izing.** treat (cottons) for greater strength.

mer'chan•dise', *n., v.,* **-dised, -dising.** —*n.* (mûr'chən dīz', -dīs') **1.** goods; wares. —*v.* (-dīz') **2.** buy and sell.

mer'chant (-chənt) *n.* person who buys and sells goods for profit.

mer'chant•man, *n., pl.* **-men.** trading ship.

merchant marine, commercial vessels of nation.

mer•cu'ri•al (mər kyŏŏr'ē əl) *adj.* **1.** of mercury. **2.** sprightly. **3.** changeable in emotion.

mer'cu•ry (mûr'kyə rē) *n.* **1.** heavy metallic element. **2.** *(cap.)* one of the planets.

mer'cy (mûr'sē) *n., pl.* **-cies. 1.** pity; compassion. **2.** act of compassion. —**mer'ci•ful,** *adj.* —**mer'ci•less,** *adj.*

mere (mēr) *adj.* only; simple. —**mere'ly,** *adv.*

mer'e•tri'cious (mer'i trish'əs) *adj.* falsely attractive.

mer•gan'ser (mər gan'sər) *n.* fish-eating diving duck.

merge (mûrj) *v.,* **merged, merging.** combine. —**merg'er,** *n.*

me•rid'i•an (mə rid'ē ən) *n.* circle on earth's surface passing through the poles.

M

me•ringue' (mə rang') *n.* egg whites and sugar beaten together.

me•ri'no (mə rē'nō) *n., pl.* **-nos.** kind of sheep.

mer'it (mer'it) *n.* **1.** excellence or good quality. —*v.* **2.** deserve. —**mer'i•to'ri•ous** (-i•tôr'ē əs) *adj.*

mer'maid' (mûr'mād') *n.* imaginary sea creature, half woman and half fish. —**mer'man'**, *n.masc.*

mer'ry (mer'ē) *adj.*, **-rier, -riest.** gay; joyous. —**mer'ri•ly**, *adv.* —**mer'ri•ment**, *n.*

mer'ry-go-round', *n.* revolving amusement ride.

mer'ry•mak'ing, *n.* festivities; hilarity. —**mer'ry-ma'ker**, *n.*

me'sa (mā'sə) *n.* high, steep-walled plateau.

mé'sal•li'ance (mā'zə lī'əns, -zal yäns') *n.* marriage with social inferior.

mesh (mesh) *n.* **1.** open space of net. **2.** net itself. **3.** engagement of gears. —*v.* **4.** catch in mesh. **5.** engage. **6.** match or interlock.

mes'mer•ize' (mez'mə rīz') *v.*, **-ized, -izing.** hypnotize; spellbind. —**mes'mer•ism** (-mə riz'əm) *n.*

mes'o•sphere' (mez'ə sfēr') *n.* atmospheric region between stratosphere and thermosphere.

Mes'o•zo'ic (mez'ə zō'ik) *adj.* pertaining to geologic era occurring between 230 and 65 million years ago.

mes•quite' (me skēt', mes'kēt) *n.* tree of southwest U.S.

mess (mes) *n.* **1.** dirty or disorderly condition. **2.** group taking meals together regularly. **3.** meals so taken. —*v.* **4.** make dirty or untidy. **5.** eat in company. —**messy'y**, *adj.*

mes'sage (mes'ij) *n.* communication.

mes'sen•ger (mes'ən jər) *n.* bearer of message.

Mes•si'ah (mi sī'ə) *n.* **1.** expected deliverer. **2.** (in Christian theology) Jesus Christ.

Messrs. (mes'ərz), plural of **Mr.**

mes•ti'zo (me stē'zō) *n., pl.* **-zos, -zoes.** person part-Spanish, part-Indian. Also, **mes•ti'za** (-zə) *fem.*

Met *Biochemistry.* methionine.

met. 1. metal. **2.** metallurgical. **3.** metaphor. **4.** metaphysics. **5.** meteorology. **6.** metropolitan.

meta-, prefix meaning: **1.** after or beyond, as *metaphysics.* **2.** behind, as *metacarpus.* **3.** change, as *metamorphosis.*

me•tab'o•lism' (mə tab'ə liz'əm) *n.* biological processes of converting food into matter and matter into energy. —**met'a•bol'ic** (met'ə bol'ik) *adj.*

met'a•car'pus (met'ə kär'pəs) *n., pl.* **-pi.** bones of forelimb between wrist and fingers. —**met'a•car'pal**, *adj., n.*

met'al (met'l) *n.* **1.** elementary substance such as gold or copper. **2.** mettle. —**me•tal'lic** (mə tal'ik) *adj.* —**met'al•ware'**, *n.*

metall. 1. metallurgical. **2.** metallurgy.

met'al•lur'gy (met'l ûr'jē) *n.* science of working with metals. —**met'al•lur'gist**, *n.*

met'a•mor'phose (met'ə môr'fōz, -fōs) *v.*, **-phosed, -phosing.** transform.

met'a•mor'pho•sis (-fə sis) *n., pl.* **-ses** (-sēz'). change.

metaph. 1. metaphysical. **2.** metaphysics.

met'a•phor (met'ə fôr', -fər) *n.* figure of speech using analogy. —**met'a•phor'i•cal**, *adj.*

metaphys. metaphysics.

met'a•phys'ics, *n.* branch of philosophy concerned with ultimate nature of reality. —**met'a•phys'ical**, *adj.* —**met'a•phy•si'cian**, *n.*

me•tas'ta•size' (mə tas'tə sīz') *v.*, **-sized, -sizing.** spread from one to another part of the body. —**me•tas'ta•sis** (-sis) *n.* —**met'a•stat'ic** (met'ə stat'ik) *adj.*

met'a•tar'sus (met'ə tär'səs) *n., pl.* **-si.** bones of hindlimb between tarsus and toes. —**met'a•tar'sal**, *adj., n.*

mete (mēt) *v.*, **meted, meting.** allot.

me'te•or (mē'tē ər, -ôr') *n.* celestial body passing through earth's atmosphere. —**me'te•or'ic** (-ôr'ik) *adj.*

me'te•or•ite' (-ə rīt') *n.* meteor reaching earth.

meteorol. 1. Also, **metrl** meteorological. **2.** meteorology.

me'te•or•ol'o•gy (-ə rol'ə jē) *n.* science of atmospheric phenomena, esp. weather. —**me'te•or•o•log'i•cal** (-ər ə loj'i kəl) *adj.* —**me'te•or•ol'o•gist**, *n.*

me'ter (mē'tər) *n.* **1.** unit of length in metric system, equal to 39.37 inches. **2.** rhythmic arrangement of words. **3.** device for measuring flow. —*v.* **4.** measure. Also, *Brit.*, **me'tre.** —**met'ric** (me'trik), **met'ri•cal**, *adj.*

Meth. Methodist.

meth'a•done' (meth'ə dōn') *n.* synthetic narcotic used in treating heroin addiction.

meth'ane (meth'ān) *n.* colorless, odorless, flammable gas.

meth'a•nol' (meth'ə nôl') *n.* colorless liquid used as solvent, fuel, or antifreeze. Also, **methyl alcohol.**

meth'od (meth'əd) *n.* system of doing. —**me•thod'i•cal** (mə thod'i kəl), **me•thod'ic**, *adj.* —**me•thod'i•cal•ly**, *adv.*

meth'od•ol'o•gy (-ə dol'ə jē) *n., pl.* **-gies.** system of methods and principles.

meth'yl (meth'əl) *n.* univalent group derived from methane.

methyl alcohol, methanol.

me•tic'u•lous (mə tik'yə ləs) *adj.* minutely careful.

mé•tier' (mā'tyā) *n.* field of activity in which one has special ability. Also, **mé'tier.**

met•ric (me'trik) *adj.* of decimal system of weights and measures, based on meter and gram. —**met'ri•cize'** (-trə sīz') *v.*, **-cized, -cizing.** —**met'ri•ca'tion**, *n.*

met′ro•nome′ (me′trə nōm′) n. device for marking tempo.

me•trop′o•lis (mi trop′ə lis) n. great city.

met′ro•pol′i•tan (me′trə pol′i tn) adj. **1.** of or in city. **2.** of cities and urban areas.

met′tle (met′l) n. **1.** spirit. **2.** disposition.

met′tle•some (-səm) adj. spirited; courageous.

MeV (mev), Physics. million electron volts; megaelectron volt. Also, **Mev, mev**

mew (myōō) n. **1.** cry of a cat. —v. **2.** emit a mew.

mews, n. street with dwellings converted from stables.

Mex. 1. Mexican. **2.** Mexico.

Mex′i•can, (mek′si kən) n. native of Mexico. —**Mexican,** adj.

MexSp Mexican Spanish.

mez mezzanine.

mez′za•nine′ (mez′ə nēn′, mez′ə nēn′) n. low story between two main floors; balcony.

mez′zo•so•pran′o (met′sō-, med′zō-) n. voice, musical part, or singer intermediate in range between soprano and contralto.

MF 1. married female. **2.** medium frequency. **3.** Middle French.

mF Electricity. millifarad; millifarads.

mf 1. medium frequency. **2.** microfilm. **3.** Electricity. millifarad; millifarads.

mf. 1. Music. mezzo forte. **2.** Electricity. microfarad.

m/f male or female: used especially in classified ads. Also, **M/F**

M.F. 1. Master of Forestry. **2.** Middle French.

M.F.A., Master of Fine Arts.

mfd. manufactured.

mfg. manufacturing.

m/f/h male, female, handicapped: used especially in classified ads. Also, **M/F/H**

M.F.H. master of foxhounds.

MFlem Middle Flemish.

MFM Computers. modified frequency modulation: hard-drive interface.

M.For. Master of Forestry.

mfr. 1. manufacture. **2.** manufacturer.

M.Fr. Middle French.

M.F.S. 1. Master of Food Science. **2.** Master of Foreign Service. **3.** Master of Foreign Study.

mfsk multiple-frequency shift-keying.

M.F.T. Master of Foreign Trade.

MG 1. machine gun. **2.** major general. **3.** military government. **4.** Pathology. myasthenia gravis.

Mg Music. left hand. [from French main gauche]

Mg Symbol, Chemistry. magnesium.

mg 1. milligram; milligrams. **2.** motor-generator.

mGal milligal; milligals.

MGB the Ministry of State Security in the U.S.S.R. (1946–53). [from Russian, for Ministérstvo gosudárstvennoi bezopásnosti]

mgd millions of gallons per day.

mgf magnify.

MGk. Medieval Greek. Also, **MGk**

mgl mogul.

mgmt management.

mgn 1. magneto. **2.** margin.

MGr. Medieval Greek.

mgr. 1. manager. **2.** Monseigneur. **3.** Monsignor. Also, **Mgr.**

mgt. management.

MGy Sgt master gunnery sergeant.

MH Marshall Islands (approved for postal use).

mH Electricity. millihenry; millihenries. Also, **mh**

M.H. Medal of Honor.

M.H.A. Master in Hospital Administration; Master of Hospital Administration.

MHC Biochemistry. major histocompatibility complex.

MHD Physics. magnetohydrodynamics.

mhd 1. magnetohydrodynamic. **2.** masthead.

M.H.E. Master of Home Economics.

MHG Middle High German. Also, **M.H.G.**

M.H.R. Member of the House of Representatives.

M.H.W. mean high water. Also, **MHW, mhw, m.h.w.**

MHz megahertz. Also, **mhz**

mHz millihertz.

MI, Michigan.

MIA Military. missing in action.

M.I.A. 1. Master of International Affairs. **2.** Military. missing in action.

mi•as′ma (mī az′mə, mē-) n., pl. -mata (-mə tə), -mas. vapors from decaying organic matter.

mic 1. micrometer. **2.** microphone.

Mic. Bible. Micah.

mi′ca (mī′kə) n. shiny mineral occurring in thin layers.

Mich., Michigan.

MICR Electronics. magnetic ink character recognition.

micr microscope.

micro-, prefix meaning: **1.** extremely small. **2.** one millionth.

mi′crobe (mī′krōb) n. microorganism, esp. one causing disease.

mi′cro•brew′er•y, n. small brewery usu. producing exotic or high quality beer.

mi′cro•chip′, n. chip (def. 3).

mi′cro•com•put′er, n. compact computer with less capability than minicomputer.

mi′cro•cosm (mī′krə koz′əm) n. world in miniature.

mi′cro•fiche′ (-fēsh′) n. small sheet of microfilm.

mi′cro•film′, n. **1.** very small photograph of book page, etc. —v. **2.** make microfilm of.

mi•crom′e•ter (mī krom′i tər) n. device for measuring minute distances.

M

mi/cron (mī/kron) *n.* millionth part of a meter.

mi•cro•or/gan•ism/ (mī/krō-) *n.* microscopic organism.

mi/cro•phone/ (mī/krə fōn/) *n.* instrument for changing sound waves into changes in electric current.

mi/cro•proc/es•sor (mī/krō pros/es ər, -ə sər; *esp. Brit.* -prō/ses ər, -sə sər) *n.* computer circuit that performs all functions of CPU.

micros. microscopy.

mi/cro•scope/ (mī/krə skōp/) *n.* instrument for inspecting minute objects.

mi/cro•scop/ic (-skop/ik) *adj.* **1.** of microscopes. **2.** extremely small.

mi/cro•sur/ger•y (mī/krō sûr/jə rē) *n.* surgery performed under magnification.

mi/cro•wave/, *n.* **1.** short radio wave used in radar, cooking, etc. **2.** oven that uses microwaves to generate heat in the food. —*v.* **3.** cook in microwave oven.

mid (mid) *adj.* **1.** middle. —*prep.* **2.** amid.

midar (mī/där), microwave detection and ranging.

mid/day/ (-dā/, -dā/) *n.* noon.

mid/dle (mid/l) *adj.* **1.** equally distant from given limits. **2.** medium. —*n.* **3.** middle part.

Middle Ages, period of European history, about A.D. 476 to 1500.

middle class, class of people intermediate between the poor and the wealthy, usu. educated working people.

Middle East, area including Israel and Arab countries of NE Africa and SW Asia.

Middle English, English language of period c1150–1475.

mid/dle•man/, *n.* merchant who buys direct from producer.

middle-of-the-road, *adj.* moderate.

middle school, school encompassing grades 5 or 6 through 8.

mid/dling, *adj.* **1.** medium. —*n.* **2.** (*pl.*) coarse parts of grain.

mid/dy, *n., pl.* -dies. blouse with square back collar.

midge (mij) *n.* minute fly.

midg/et (mij/it) *n.* very small person or thing.

MIDI (mid/ē), *Electronics.* Musical Instrument Digital Interface.

mid/land (-lənd) *n.* interior of country.

MIDN Midshipman.

Midn. Midshipman.

mid/night/, *n.* 12 o'clock at night.

midnight sun, sun visible at midnight in summer in arctic and antarctic regions.

mid/point/, *n.* point at or near the middle.

mid/riff (-rif) *n.* part of body between the chest and abdomen.

mid/ship/man, *n., pl.* -men. rank of student at U.S. Naval or Coast Guard academy.

midst (midst) *n.* middle.

mid/sum/mer (-sum/ər, -sum/-) *n.* **1.** middle of the summer. **2.** summer solstice, around June 21.

mid/term, *n.* **1.** halfway point of school term. **2.** examination given at midterm.

mid/way/ *adj., adv.* (mid/wā/) **1.** in or to middle. —*n.* (-wā/) **2.** area of games and shows at carnival.

mid/wife/, *n., pl.* -wives. woman who assists at childbirth.

mid/win/ter (-win/tər, -win/-) *n.* **1.** middle of winter. **2.** winter solstice, around December 22.

M.I.E. Master of Industrial Engineering.

mien (mēn) *n.* air; bearing.

miff (mif) *n.* **1.** petty quarrel. —*v.* **2.** offend.

MiG (mig), any of several Russian fighter aircraft. Also, **Mig, MIG** [named after Artem *Mi(koyan)* and Mikhail *G(urevich)*, aircraft designers]

might (mīt) *v.* **1.** pt. of **may.** —*n.* **2.** strength; power.

might/y, *adj.,* -ier, -iest, *adv.* —*adj.* **1.** powerful; huge. —*adv.* **2.** *Informal,* very. —**might/i•ness,** *n.*

mi/gnon•ette/ (min/yə net/) *n.* plant with clusters of small flowers.

mi/graine (mī/grān) *n.* painful headache.

mi/grate (-grāt) *v.,* -grated, -grating. go from one region to another. —**mi•gra/tion,** *n.* —**mi/gra•to/ry** (-grə tôr/ē) *adj.* —**mi/grant,** *adj., n.*

mi•ka/do (mi kä/dō) *n., pl.* -dos. a title of emperor of Japan.

mike (mīk) *n. Informal.* microphone.

mil (mil) *n.* one thousandth of inch.

mi•la/dy (mi lā/dē) *n., pl.* -dies. English noblewoman (often used as term of address).

milch (milch) *adj.* giving milk.

mild (mīld) *adj.* gentle; temperate. —**mild/ly,** *adv.* —**mild/ness,** *n.*

mil/dew/ (mil/dōō/, -dyōō/) *n.* **1.** discoloration caused by fungus. —*v.* **2.** affect with mildew.

mile (mīl) *n.* unit of distance, equal on land to 5280 ft.

mile/age (mī/lij) *n.* **1.** miles traveled. **2.** travel allowance.

mile/stone/, *n.* **1.** marker showing road distance. **2.** important event.

mi•lieu/ (mil yōō/, mēl-; *Fr.* mē lyœ/) *n., pl.* -lieus, -lieux. environment.

milit. military.

mil/i•tant (mil/i tənt) *adj.* warlike; aggressive.

mil/i•ta•rism (-tə riz/əm) *n.* **1.** military spirit. **2.** domination by military. —**mil/i•ta•rist,** *n.* —**mil/i•ta•ris/tic,** *adj.*

mil/i•tar•ize/, *v.,* -ized, -izing. equip with military weapons.

mil/i•tar/y (-ter/ē) *adj., n., pl.* -taries. —*adj.* **1.** of armed forces, esp. on land. —*n.* **2.** armed forces or soldiers collectively.

military police, soldiers who perform police duties within army.

mil′i•tate′ (-tāt′) *v.*, **-tated, -tating.** act (for or against).

mi•li′tia (mi lish′ə) *n.* organization for emergency military service. **—mi•li′tia•man,** *n.*

milk (milk) *n.* **1.** liquid secreted by female mammals to feed their young. **—***v.* **2.** draw milk from. **—milk′y,** *adj.* **—milk′maid′,** *n.* **—milk′man′,** *n.*

milk glass, opaque white glass.

milk′weed′, *n.* plant with milky juice.

Milk′y Way′, *Astron.* galaxy containing sun and earth.

mill (mil) *n.* **1.** place where manufacturing is done. **2.** device for grinding. **3.** one tenth of a cent. **—***v.* **4.** grind or treat with mill. **5.** groove edges of (coin). **6.** move about in confusion. **—mill′er,** *n.*

mil•len′ni•um (mi len′ē əm) *n.*, *pl.* **-niums, -nia** (-nē ə). **1.** period of a thousand years. **2.** future reign of Christ on earth.

mil′let (-it) *n.* cereal grass.

milli-, prefix meaning thousand or thousandth.

mil′liard (mil′yərd, -yärd) *n. Brit.* one billion.

mil′li•gram′ (mil′i gram′) *n.* one thousandth of gram.

mil′li•li′ter, *n.* one thousandth of liter.

mil′li•me′ter, *n.* one thousandth of meter.

mil′li•ner (mil′ə nər) *n.* person who makes or sells women's hats.

mil′li•ner′y (-ner′ē, -nə rē) *n.* **1.** women's hats. **2.** business or trade of a milliner.

mil′lion (mil′yən) *n.*, *adj.* 1000 times 1000. **—mil′lionth,** *adj.*, *n.*

mil′lion•aire′ (mil′yə nâr′) *n.* person having a million dollars or more.

mill′race′, *n.* channel for current of water driving mill wheel.

mill′stone′, *n.* **1.** stone for grinding grain. **2.** heavy mental or emotional burden.

mill′stream′, *n.* stream in millrace.

mill′wright′, *n.* person who designs and installs mill machinery.

milque′toast′ (milk′tōst′) *n.* (*often cap.*) timid person.

M.I.L.R. Master of Industrial and Labor Relations.

MIL-STD military standard.

milt (milt) *n.* male secretion of fish.

mime (mīm, mēm) *n.* pantomimist; clown.

mim′e•o•graph′ (mim′ē ə graf′) *n.* **1.** stencil device for duplicating. **—***v.* **2.** copy with mimeograph.

mim′ic (mim′ik) *v.*, **-icked, -icking,** *n.* **—***v.* **1.** imitate speech or actions of. **—***n.* **2.** person who mimics. **—mim′ic•ry,** *n.*

mi•mo′sa (mi mō′sə, -zə) *n.* semitropical tree or shrub.

min minim; minims.

min. 1. mineralogical. **2.** mineralogy. **3.**

minim. **4.** minimum. **5.** mining. **6.** minor. **7.** minuscule. **8.** minute; minutes.

min′a•ret′ (min′ə ret′) *n.* tower for calling Muslims to prayer.

min′a•to′ry (min′ə tôr′ē) *adj.* threatening.

mince (mins) *v.*, **minced, mincing. 1.** chop fine. **2.** speak, move, or behave with affected elegance. **—minc′ing•ly,** *adv.*

mince′meat′, *n.* cooked mixture of finely chopped meat, raisins, spices, etc., used in pies.

mind (mīnd) *n.* **1.** thinking part of human or animal. **2.** intellect. **3.** inclination. **—***v.* **4.** heed; obey.

mind′-blow′ing, *adj.* **1.** astounding. **2.** producing hallucinogenic effect.

M.Ind.E. Master of Industrial Engineering.

mind′ed, *adj.* **1.** having a certain kind of mind. **2.** inclined.

mind′ful, *adj.* careful.

mind′less, *adj.* **1.** heedless. **2.** without intelligence.

mine (mīn) *pron.*, *n.*, *v.*, **mined, mining. —***pron.* **1.** possessive form of I. **—***n.* **2.** excavation in earth for resources. **3.** stationary explosive device used in war. **4.** abundant source. **5.** dig or work in mine. **—***v.* **6.** lay explosive mines. **—min′er,** *n.*

min′er•al (min′ər əl) *n.* **1.** inorganic substance. **2.** substance obtained by mining. **—***adj.* **3.** of minerals.

min′er•al′o•gy (-ə rol′ə jē, -ral′ə-) *n.* science of minerals. **—min′er•a•log′i•cal** (-ər ə loj′i kəl) *adj.* **—min′er•al′o•gist,** *n.*

mineral water, water containing dissolved mineral salts or gases.

min′e•stro′ne (min′ə strō′nē) *n.* thick vegetable soup.

mine′sweep′er, *n.* ship used to remove explosive mines.

min′gle (ming′gəl) *v.*, **-gled, -gling.** associate; mix.

min′i (min′ē) *n.* small version.

mini-, prefix meaning: **1.** smaller than others of its kind. **2.** very short.

min′i•a•ture (min′ē ə chər, min′ə-) *n.* **1.** greatly reduced form. **2.** tiny painting. **—***adj.* **3.** on small scale.

min′i•a•tur•ize′, *v.*, **-ized, -izing.** make in or reduce to very small size. **—min′i•a•tur•i•za′tion,** *n.*

min′i•com•put′er, *n.* computer with capabilities between those of microcomputer and mainframe.

min′im (min′əm) *n.* smallest unit of liquid measure.

min′i•mal•ism (-mə liz′əm) *n.* style, as in art or music, that is spare and simple.

min′i•mize′ (-mīz′) *v.*, **-mized, -mizing.** make minimum.

min′i•mum (-məm) *n.* **1.** least possible quantity, degree, etc. **—***adj.* **2.** Also, **min′i•mal** (-məl) lowest.

Mining Eng. Mining Engineer.

M

min′ion (min′yən) *n.* servile follower.

min′is•ter (min′ə stər) *n.* **1.** person authorized to conduct worship. **2.** government representative abroad. **3.** head of governmental department. —*v.* **4.** give care. —**min′is•te′ri•al** (-stēr′ē əl) *adj.* —**min′is•tra′tion,** *n.*

min′is•try (-ə strē) *n., pl.* **-tries. 1.** religious calling. **2.** clergy. **3.** duty or office of a department of government. **4.** body of executive officials. **5.** act of ministering.

mink (mingk) *n.* semiaquatic fur-bearing animal.

Minn., Minnesota.

min′ne•sing′er (min′ə sing′ər) *n.* lyric poet of medieval Germany.

min′now (min′ō) *n.* tiny fish.

mi′nor (mī′nər) *adj.* **1.** lesser in size or importance. **2.** under legal age. —*n.* **3.** person under legal age.

mi•nor′i•ty (mi nôr′i tē, mī-) *n., pl.* **-ties. 1.** smaller number or part. **2.** relatively small population group. **3.** state or time of being under legal age.

min•ox′i•dil′ (mi nok′si dil′) *n.* drug used in treating hypertension and baldness.

min′strel (min′strəl) *n.* **1.** musician or singer, esp. in Middle Ages. **2.** comedian in blackface.

mint (mint) *n.* **1.** aromatic herb. **2.** place where money is coined. —*v.* **3.** make coins.

mintr miniature.

min′u•end′ (min′yŏŏ end′) *n.* number from which another is to be subtracted.

min′u•et′ (min′yŏŏ et′) *n.* stately dance.

mi′nus (mī′nəs) *prep.* **1.** less. —*adj.* **2.** less than.

mi′nus•cule′ (min′ə skyŏŏl′, mi nus′kyŏŏl) *adj.* tiny.

min′ute *n.* (min′it) **1.** sixty seconds. **2.** (*pl.*) record of proceedings. —*adj.* (mī nŏŏt′, -nyŏŏt′) **3.** extremely small. **4.** attentive to detail. —**mi•nute′ly,** *adv.*

mi•nu′ti•ae′ (mi nŏŏ′shē ē′) *n.pl.* trifling matters.

minx (mingks) *n.* saucy girl.

MIP monthly investment plan.

MIPS (mips), *Computers.* million instructions per second: a measure of computer speed.

mir mirror.

MIr. Middle Irish. Also, **M.Ir.**

mir′a•cle (mir′ə kəl) *n.* supernatural act or effect. —**mi•rac′u•lous** (mi rak′yə ləs) *adj.*

mi•rage′ (mi räzh′) *n.* atmospheric illusion in which images of far-distant objects are seen.

mire (mī°r) *n., v.,* **mired, miring.** —*n.* **1.** swamp. **2.** deep mud. —*v.* **3.** stick fast in mire. **4.** soil with mire. —**mir′y,** *adj.*

mir′ror (mir′ər) *n.* **1.** reflecting surface. —*v.* **2.** reflect.

mirth (mûrth) *n.* gaiety. —**mirth′ful,** *adj.* —**mirth′less,** *adj.*

MIRV (mûrv), multiple independently targetable reentry vehicle. Also, **M.I.R.V.**

mis-, prefix meaning: **1.** wrong, as *misconduct.* **2.** lack of, as *mistrust.*

mis′ad•ven′ture (mis′əd ven′chər) *n.* mishap.

mis′al•li′ance, *n.* incompatible association.

mis′an•thrope′ (mis′ən thrōp′, miz′-) *n.* hater of humanity. —**mis′an•throp′ic** (-throp′ik) *adj.*

mis′ap•ply′, *v.,* **-plied, -plying.** use wrongly. —**mis′ap•pli•ca′tion,** *n.*

mis′ap•pre•hend′, *v.* misunderstand. —**mis′ap•pre•hen′sion** (-hen′shən) *n.*

mis′ap•pro′pri•ate′ (-āt′) *v.,* **-ated, -ating.** use wrongly as one's own. —**mis′ap•pro′pri•a′tion,** *n.*

mis′be•got′ten, *adj.* ill-conceived.

mis′be•have′, *v.,* **-haved, -having.** behave badly. —**mis′be•hav′ior,** *n.*

misc., miscellaneous.

mis•cal′cu•late′, *v.,* **-lated, -lating.** judge badly. —**mis′cal•cu•la′tion,** *n.*

mis•call′, *v.* call by a wrong name.

mis•car′riage, *n.* **1.** premature birth resulting in death of fetus. **2.** failure.

mis•car′ry (mis kar′ē; *for 1 also* mis′kar′ē) *v.,* **-ried, -rying. 1.** have miscarriage. **2.** go wrong.

mis•cast′, *v.* cast in unsuitable role.

Misc. Doc. miscellaneous document.

mis′ce•ge•na′tion (mi sej′ə nā′shən, mis′i jə-) *n.* sexual union between persons of different races.

mis′cel•la′ne•ous (mis′ə lā′nē əs) *adj.* unclassified; various. —**mis′cel•la′ny** (-ə lā′nē) *n.*

mis•chance′, *n.* bad luck.

mis′chief (mis′chif) *n.* **1.** trouble, caused willfully. **2.** tendency to tease. —**mis′chie•vous** (mis′chə vəs), *adj.*

—Pronunciation. The word MISCHIEVOUS is pronounced with three syllables. The pronunciation (mis chē′vē əs), with four syllables, is usually considered nonstandard. Note that although a spelling *mischievious,* which reflects this nonstandard pronunciation by including an extra *i* after the *v,* was occasionally seen between the 16th and 19th centuries, it is not considered a correct spelling today.

mis′ci•ble (mis′ə bəl) *adj.* capable of being mixed.

mis′con•ceive′, *v.,* **-ceived, -ceiving.** misunderstand. —**mis′con•cep′tion,** *n.*

mis•con′duct (-kon′dukt) *n.* improper or illegal conduct.

mis′con•strue′ (mis′kən strŏŏ′) *v.,* **-strued, -struing.** misinterpret.

mis′cre•ant (mis′krē ənt) *n.* villain.

mis•deed′, *n.* immoral deed.

mis′de•mean′or, *n.* minor offense.

mis•do′ing, *n.* (*often pl.*) wrongful act.

mise-en-scène′ (mē zän sen′) *n., pl.* **-scènes**

(-sens′). **1.** placement of actors, scenery, and properties on stage. **2.** surroundings.

mi′ser (mī′zər) *n.* hoarder of wealth. —**mi′ser•ly,** *adj.*

mis•er•a•ble (miz′ər ə bəl) *adj.* **1.** wretched. **2.** deplorable. **3.** contemptible; despicable. —**mis′er•a•bly,** *adv.*

mis′er•y, *n., pl.* **-eries.** wretched condition.

mis•fea′sance (mis fē′zəns) *n.* wrongful exercise of lawful authority.

mis•fire′ (mis fīᵊr′) *v.,* **-fired, -firing.** fail to fire.

mis•fit′ *n.* **1.** (mis fit′, mis′fit′) poor fit. **2.** (mis′fit′) maladjusted person.

mis•for′tune, *n.* bad luck.

mis•giv′ing, *n.* apprehension; doubt.

mis•guide′, *v.,* **-guided, -guiding.** guide wrongly.

mis•han′dle, *v.,* **-dled, -dling. 1.** handle roughly. **2.** manage badly.

mis′hap (mis′hap, mis hap′) *n.* unlucky accident.

mish′mash (mish′mäsh′, -mash′) *n.* jumble; hodgepodge.

mis•in•form′, *v.* give false information to. —**mis′in•for•ma′tion,** *n.*

mis•in•ter′pret, *v.* interpret wrongly. —**mis′in•ter′pre•ta′tion,** *n.*

mis•judge′, *v.,* **-judged, -judging.** judge wrongly. —**mis•judg′ment,** *n.*

mis•lay′, *v.,* **-laid, -laying. 1.** put in place later forgotten. **2.** misplace.

mis•lead′ (-lēd′) *v.,* **-led, -leading. 1.** lead in wrong direction. **2.** lead into error, as in conduct.

mis•man′age, *v.,* **-aged, -aging.** manage badly. —**mis•man′age•ment,** *n.*

mis•match′ *v.* **1.** (mis mach′) match unsuitably. —*n.* (mis mach′, mis′mach′) **2.** unsuitable match.

mis•no′mer (mis nō′mər) *n.* misapplied name.

mi•sog′a•my (mi sog′ə mē, mī-) *n.* hatred of marriage. —**mi•sog′a•mist,** *n.*

mi•sog′y•ny (mi soj′ə nē, mī-) *n.* hatred of women. —**mi•sog′y•nist,** *n.*

mis•place′, *v.,* **-placed, -placing. 1.** forget location of. **2.** place unwisely.

mis′print′ (mis′print′, mis print′) *n.* error in printing.

mis•pri′sion (mis prizh′ən) *n.* neglect or violation of official duty.

mis′pro•nounce′, *v.,* **-nounced, -nouncing.** pronounce wrongly. —**mis′pro•nun′ci•a′tion,** *n.*

mis•quote′, *v.,* **-quoted, -quoting.** quote incorrectly. —**mis′quo•ta′tion,** *n.*

mis•read′ (-rēd′) *v.,* **-read** (red′), **-reading. 1.** read wrongly. **2.** misinterpret.

mis′rep•re•sent′, *v.* give wrong idea of. —**mis′rep•re•sen•ta′tion,** *n.*

mis•rule′, *n.* bad or unwise rule. —**mis•rule′,** *v.*

miss (mis) *v.* **1.** fail to hit, catch, meet, do, etc. **2.** feel absence of. —*n.* **3.** (*cap.*) title of respect for unmarried woman. **4.** girl. **5.** failure to hit, catch, etc.

Miss., Mississippi.

mis′sal (mis′əl) *n.* book of prayers, etc., for celebrating Mass.

mis•shap′en, *adj.* deformed.

mis′sile (mis′əl; *esp. Brit.* -īl) *n.* object thrown or shot, as lance or bullet.

mis′sion (mish′ən) *n.* **1.** group sent abroad for specific work. **2.** duty. **3.** air operation against enemy. **4.** missionary post.

mis′sion•ar′y (-ə ner′ē) *n., pl.* **-aries,** *adj.* —*n.* **1.** person sent to propagate religious faith. —*adj.* **2.** of religious missions.

mis′sive (mis′iv) *n.* written message.

mis•spell′, *v.* spell wrongly.

mis•spend′, *v.,* **-spent, -spending.** squander.

mis•state′, *v.,* **-stated, -stating.** state wrongly. —**mis′state′ment,** *n.*

mis•step′, *n.* error.

mist (mist) *n.* light, thin fog. —**mist′y,** *adj.*

mis•take′ (mi stāk′) *n., v.,* **-took, -taken, -taking.** —*n.* **1.** error in judgment, action, or belief. —*v.* **2.** take or regard wrongly. **3.** misunderstand. **4.** be in error.

Mis′ter (mis′tər) *n.* title of respect for man. *Abbr.:* **Mr.**

mis′tle•toe′ (mis′əl tō′) *n.* parasitic plant.

mis•treat′, *v.* treat badly. —**mis•treat′ment,** *n.*

mis′tress (mis′tris) *n.* **1.** female head of household. **2.** female owner. **3.** female lover of married man.

mis•tri′al, *n.* trial ended without verdict because of legal error or inability of jury to agree on verdict.

mis•trust′, *n.* lack of trust. —**mis•trust′,** *v.*

mis′un•der•stand′, *v.,* **-stood, -standing.** understand wrongly. —**mis′un•der•stand′ing,** *n.*

mis•use′ *n., v.,* **-used, -using.** —*n.* (-yōos′) **1.** improper use. —*v.* (-yōoz′) **2.** use badly or wrongly. **3.** abuse.

MITC mortgage investment tax credit.

mite (mīt) *n.* **1.** tiny parasitic insect. **2.** small thing or bit.

mi′ter (mī′tər) *v.* **1.** join two pieces on diagonal. —*n.* **2.** such joint. **3.** tall cap worn by bishops. Also, *Brit.,* **mi′tre.**

mit′i•gate′ (mit′i gāt′) *v.,* **-gated, -gating.** make less severe.

mi•to′sis (mī tō′sis) *n.* method of cell division. —**mi•tot′ic** (-tot′ik) *adj.*

mitt (mit) *n.* thick glove.

mit′ten (mit′n) *n.* fingerless glove.

mix (miks) *v.,* **mixed** or **mixt, mixing,** *n.* —*v.* **1.** put together; combine. **2.** associate. **3.** confuse. —*n.* **4.** mixture. **5.** mess. —**mix′ture,** *n.*

M

mixed number, number consisting of whole number and fraction or decimal.

mixt. mixture.

mix'-up', *n.* state of confusion.

miz'zen•mast' (miz'ən mast'; *Naut.* -məst) *n.* third mast from forward on ship.

M.J. Master of Journalism.

mk. **1.** (in Germany) mark. **2.** (in Finland) markka.

mkr marker.

MKS meter-kilogram-second. Also, **mks**

MKSA meter-kilogram-second-ampere. Also, **mksa**

mkt. market.

mktg. marketing.

ml, milliliter.

MLA Modern Language Association.

M.L.A. **1.** Master of Landscape Architecture. **2.** Modern Language Association.

M.L.Arch. Master of Landscape Architecture.

MLB Maritime Labor Board.

MLD **1.** median lethal dose. **2.** minimum lethal dose.

mldg molding.

MLF Multilateral Nuclear Force.

MLG. Middle Low German. Also, **M.L.G.**

Mlle. Mademoiselle. Also, **Mlle**

Mlles. Mesdemoiselles.

MLR minimum lending rate.

MLS *Real Estate.* Multiple Listing Service.

M.L.S. Master of Library Science.

MLU *Psycholinguistics.* mean length of utterance.

MLW mean low water.

mm, millimeter.

MMA Metropolitan Museum of Art.

Mme. Madame.

M.M.E. **1.** Master of Mechanical Engineering. **2.** Master of Mining Engineering. **3.** Master of Music Education.

Mmes. Mesdames.

M.Met.E. Master of Metallurgical Engineering.

mmf *Electricity.* magnetomotive force. Also, **m.m.f.**

M.Mgt.E. Master of Management Engineering.

mm Hg millimeter of mercury. Also, **mmHg**

mmho *Electricity.* millimho; millimhos.

MMPI *Psychology.* Minnesota Multiphasic Personality Inventory.

M.M.Sc. Master of Medical Science.

MMT **1.** *Astronomy.* Multiple Mirror Telescope. **2.** *Chemistry.* $C_9H_7MnO_3$, a gasoline additive. [*m(ethylcyclopentadienyl) m(anganese) t(ricarbonyl)*]

mmu memory-management unit.

M.Mus. Master of Music.

M.Mus.Ed. Master of Music Education.

MN, Minnesota.

M.N.A. Master of Nursing Administration.

M.N.A.S. Member of the National Academy of Sciences.

mncpl municipal.

M.N.E. Master of Nuclear Engineering.

mne•mon'ic (ni mon'ik) *adj.* aiding memory.

mnfrm *Computers.* mainframe.

mng managing.

Mngr. Monsignor.

mngr. manager.

mnl manual.

Mnr. manor.

mnrl mineral.

M.N.S. Master of Nutritional Science.

mnstb *Electronics.* monostable.

M.Nurs. Master of Nursing.

MO, **1.** Also, **Mo.** Missouri. **2.** modus operandi.

moan (mōn) *n.* **1.** low groan. *—v.* **2.** utter moans.

moat (mōt) *n.* deep, water-filled ditch around fortification.

mob (mob) *n., v.,* **mobbed, mobbing.** *—n.* **1.** crowd, esp. disorderly one. *—v.* **2.** attack as a mob.

mo'bile *adj.* (mō'bəl, -bēl) **1.** capable of moving or being moved. *—n.* (-bēl) **2.** abstract sculpture with parts that move, as with breezes. *—***mo•bil'i•ty,** *n.*

mo'bi•lize' (mō'bə līz') *v.,* **-lized, -lizing.** make ready for war. *—***mo'bi•li•za'tion,** *n.*

mob'ster (mob'stər) *n.* member of criminal mob.

moc'ca•sin (mok'ə sin, -zən) *n.* **1.** soft shoe. **2.** poisonous snake.

mo'cha (mō'kə) *n.* **1.** kind of coffee. **2.** flavoring made from coffee and chocolate.

mock (mok) *v.* **1.** mimic or ridicule. *—n.* **2.** derision. *—adj.* **3.** imitation.

mock'er•y, *n., pl.* **-ies.** **1.** derision. **2.** dishonest imitation; travesty.

mock'ing•bird', *n.* songbird with imitative voice.

mock'-up', *n.* scale model.

mod (mod) *adj. Informal.* fashionably up-to-date.

mode (mōd) *n.* prevailing style.

mod'el (mod'l) *n., adj., v.,* **-eled, -eling.** *—n.* **1.** standard for imitation. **2.** person who poses, as for artist or photographer. *—adj.* **3.** serving as model. *—v.* **4.** pattern after model. **5.** wear as model. **6.** form.

mo'dem (mō'dəm, -dem) *n.* device enabling transmission of data from or to a computer via telephone or other communication lines.

mod'er•ate *adj., n., v.,* **-ated, -ating.** *—adj.* (mod'ər it) **1.** not extreme. *—n.* (-ər it) **2.** person having moderate views. *—v.* (-ə rāt') **3.** make or become less violent or intense. **4.** preside over. *—***mod'er•a'tion,** *n.* *—***mod'er•ate•ly,** *adv.*

mod'er•a'tor, *n.* director of group discussion.

mod'ern (mod'ərn) *adj.* of recent time.

—mo•der′ni•ty (-dûr′ni tē) *n.* —mod′ern•ize′, *v.*

Modern English, English language since c1475.

mod′ern•ism, *n.* **1.** modern character or tendencies. **2.** modern usage. **3.** divergence from the past in the arts or literature.

mod′ern•is′tic, *adj.* following modern trends.

mod′est (mod′ist) *adj.* **1.** humble in estimating oneself. **2.** simple; moderate. **3.** decent, moral. —mod′est•ly, *adv.* —mod′es•ty, *n.*

MODFET (mod′fet′), *Electronics.* modulation-doped field effect transistor.

ModGk Modern Greek. Also, **Mod. Gk., Mod. Gr.**

ModHeb Modern Hebrew. Also, **Mod. Heb.**

mod′i•cum (mod′i kəm) *n.* small amount.

modif. modification.

mod′i•fy (mod′ə fī′) *v.,* -fied, -fying. alter or moderate. —mod′i•fi•ca′tion, *n.* —mod′i•fi′er, *n.*

mod′ish (mō′dish) *adj.* fashionable.

mo•diste′ (mō dēst′) *n.fem.* maker of women's attire.

mod. praesc. (in prescriptions) in the manner prescribed; as directed. [from Latin *modō praescrīptō*]

mod′u•late′ (moj′ə lāt′) *v.,* -lated, -lating. **1.** soften. **2.** *Radio.* alter (electric current) in accordance with sound waves. **3.** alter the pitch or key of. —mod′u•la′tion, *n.*

mod′ule (moj′ōol) *n.* **1.** unit of measure. **2.** building unit. **3.** self-contained element of spacecraft. —mod′u•lar, *adj.*

mo′dus op′e•ran′di (mō′dəs op′ə ran′dē, -dī) *n., pl.* mo′di op′e•ran′di (mō′dē, -dī). method of operating.

mo′gul (mō′gəl) *n.* **1.** powerful or influential person. **2.** bump on ski slope.

mo′hair′ (mō′hâr′) *n.* fabric from fleece of the Angora goat.

Moham. Mohammedan.

Mo•ham′med•an•ism (mŏŏ ham′i dn iz′-əm, mō-) *n.* Islam. —Mo•ham′med•an, *n., adj.*

M.O.I. *British.* **1.** Ministry of Information. **2.** Ministry of the Interior.

moi′e•ty (moi′i tē) *n., pl.* -ties. half.

moil (moil) *n., v.* labor.

moi•ré′ (mwä rā′, mô-) *n., pl.* -rés. fabric with watery appearance.

moist (moist) *adj.* damp. —mois′ten (moi′sən) *v.* —mois′ten•er, *n.*

mois′ture (-chər) *n.* dampness; small beads of water.

mol *Chemistry.* mole.

mol. **1.** molecular. **2.** molecule.

mo′lar (mō′lər) *n.* broad back tooth.

mo•las′ses (mə las′iz) *n.* thick, dark syrup produced in refining sugar.

mold (mōld) *n.* **1.** form for shaping molten or plastic material. **2.** thing so formed. **3.** fun-

gus growth on animal or vegetable matter. **4.** loose rich earth. —*v.* **5.** shape or form. **6.** become or make covered with mold (def. 3). —mold′y, *adj.*

mold/board′, *n.* curved metal plate on plow.

mold′er, *v.* **1.** decay. —*n.* **2.** person who molds.

mold′ing, *n.* decorative strip with special cross section.

mole (mōl) *n.* **1.** small congenital spot on skin. **2.** small, furred, underground mammal. **3.** spy who works against government agency he or she is employed by.

mol′e•cule′ (mol′ə kyōol′) *n.* smallest physical unit of a chemical element or compound. —mo•lec′u•lar (mə lek′yə lər) *adj.*

mole′hill′, *n.* **1.** small mound of earth raised by moles. **2.** something small and insignificant.

mole′skin′, *n.* **1.** fur of mole. **2.** heavy cotton fabric with suedelike finish.

mo•lest′ (mə lest′) *v.* **1.** annoy by interfering with. **2.** make indecent sexual advances to. —mo′les•ta′tion, *n.*

moll (mol) *n. Slang.* female companion of gangster.

mol′li•fy′ (mol′ə fī′) *v.,* -fied, -fying. appease in temper.

mol′lusk (mol′əsk) *n.* hard-shelled invertebrate animal. Also, mol′lusc.

mol′ly•cod′dle (mol′ē kod′l) *v.,* -dled, -dling. pamper.

molt (mōlt) *v.* shed skin or feathers.

mol′ten (mōl′tən) *adj.* melted.

mol. wt. molecular weight.

mo•lyb′de•num (mə lib′də nəm) *n.* silver-white metallic element used in alloys.

mom (mom) *n. Informal.* mother.

MOMA (mō′mə), Museum of Modern Art.

mo′ment (mō′mənt) *n.* **1.** short space of time. **2.** importance.

mo′men•tar′y (-mən ter′ē) *adj.* very brief in time. —mo′men•tar′i•ly, *adv.*

mo•men′tous (-men′təs) *adj.* important.

mo•men′tum (-təm) *n., pl.* -ta (-tə), -tums. force of moving body.

mom′my (mom′ē) *n., pl.* -mies. *Informal.* mother.

Mon., Monday.

mon′ad (mon′ad, mō′nad) *n.* one-celled organism.

mon′arch (mon′ərk, -ärk) *n.* hereditary sovereign.

mon′ar•chy, *n., pl.* -chies. **1.** government by monarch. **2.** country governed by monarch. —mon′ar•chism, *n.*

mon′as•ter′y (mon′ə ster′ē) *n., pl.* -teries. residence of monks. —mo•nas′tic (mə nas′-tik) *adj.* —mo•nas′ti•cism (-siz′əm) *n.*

Mon′day (mun′dā, -dē) *n.* second day of week.

M

mon'e•tar'y (mon'i ter'ē, mun'-) *adj.* of money.

mon'ey (mun'ē) *n., pl.* **moneys, monies. 1.** pieces of metal or certificates issued as medium of exchange. **2.** wealth.

mon'eyed (-ēd) *adj.* wealthy.

mon'ger (mung'gər, mong'-) *n.* **1.** person involved with something in a contemptible way. **2.** *Brit.* dealer.

mon'gol•ism (mong'gə liz'əm, mon'-) *n. Offensive.* (earlier term for) Down syndrome.

Mon'gol•oid' (-loid') *adj.* designating division of human race including most peoples of eastern Asia.

mon'goose (mong'gōōs', mon'-) *n., pl.* **-gooses.** carnivorous animal of Asia.

mon'grel (mung'grəl, mong'-) *n.* **1.** animal or plant resulting from crossing of different breeds. —*adj.* **2.** of mixed breeds.

mon'i•ker (mon'i kər) *n. Slang.* name. Also, **mon'ick•er.**

mon'ism (mon'iz əm, mō'niz əm) *n.* theory that reality consists of a single element. —**mon'ist,** *n.* —**mo•nis'tic,** *adj.*

mo•ni'tion (mə nish'ən, mō-) *n.* warning.

mon'i•tor (mon'i tər) *n.* **1.** pupil who assists teacher. —*v.* **2.** check continuously.

mon'i•to'ry (-tôr'ē) *adj.* warning.

monk (mungk) *n.* man who is a member of a religious order.

mon'key (mung'kē) *n.* **1.** mammal strongly resembling a human being. —*v.* **2.** trifle idly.

monkey business, mischievous behavior.

monkey wrench, 1. wrench with adjustable jaws. **2.** something that interferes with process or operation.

mono-, prefix meaning one, single, or lone.

mon'o•chrome (mon'ə krōm') *adj.* of one color. Also, **mon'o•chro•mat'ic.**

mon'o•cle (mon'ə kəl) *n.* eyeglass for one eye.

mon'o•clo'nal (mon'ə klōn'l) *adj.* pertaining to cell products derived from single biological clone.

mon'o•cot'y•le'don (mon'ə kot'l ēd'n) *n.* plant having embryo containing single seed leaf.

mo•noc'u•lar (mə nok'yə lər) *adj.* **1.** having one eye. **2.** for use of only one eye.

mon'o•dy (mon'ə dē) *n., pl.* **-dies.** poem lamenting someone's death.

mo•nog'a•my (mə nog'ə mē) *n.* marriage of one woman with one man. —**mo•nog'a•mous,** *adj.* —**mo•nog'a•mist,** *n.*

mon'o•gram' (mon'ə gram') *n.* design made of one's initials. —**mon'o•grammed,** *adj.*

mon'o•graph' (mon'ə graf') *n.* treatise on one subject.

mon'o•lith (-lith) *n.* structure of single block of stone. —**mon'o•lith'ic,** *adj.*

mon'o•logue' (-lôg') *n.* talk by single speaker. Also, **mon'o•log'.** —**mon'o•log'ist, mon'o•logu'ist,** *n.*

mon'o•ma'ni•a, *n.* obsessive zeal for or interest in single thing. —**mon'o•ma'ni•ac,** *n.*

mon'o•nu'cle•o'sis (-nōō'klē ō'sis, -nyōō'-) *n.* infectious disease characterized by fever, swelling of lymph nodes, etc.

mon'o•plane', *n.* airplane with one wing on each side.

mo•nop'o•ly (mə nop'ə lē) *n., pl.* **-lies. 1.** exclusive control. **2.** thing so controlled. **3.** company having such control. —**mo•nop'o•lis'tic,** *adj.* —**mo•nop'o•lize',** *v.*

mon'o•rail' (mon'ə rāl') *n.* **1.** single rail serving as track for wheeled vehicles. **2.** car or train moving on such a rail.

mon'o•so'di•um glu'ta•mate' (mon'ə sō'dē əm glōō'tə māt') white crystalline powder used to intensify flavor of foods.

mon'o•syl'la•ble, *n.* word of one syllable. —**mon'o•syl•lab'ic,** *adj.*

mon'o•the•ism, *n.* doctrine or belief that there is only one God. —**mon'o•the'ist,** *n.,* *adj.* —**mon'o•the•is'tic,** *adj.*

mon'o•tone', *n.* single tone of unvarying pitch.

mo•not'o•ny (mə not'n ē) *n.* wearisome uniformity. —**mo•not'o•nous,** *adj.*

Mons. Monsieur.

mon•sieur' (mə syœ') *n., pl.* **mes•sieurs'** (me syœ') French term of address for man.

mon•si'gnor (mon sē'nyər, mon'sē nyôr', môn'-) *n., pl.* **-gnors, -gno'ri** (môn'sē nyôr'ē). title of certain dignitaries of Roman Catholic Church.

mon•soon' (mon sōōn') *n.* seasonal wind of Indian Ocean.

mon'ster (mon'stər) *n.* **1.** animal or plant of abnormal form. **2.** wicked creature. **3.** anything huge.

mon'strance (mon'strəns) *n.* receptacle used in churches for display of consecrated Host.

mon•stros'i•ty (mon stros'i tē) *n., pl.* **-ties.** grotesquely abnormal thing.

mon'strous (-strəs) *adj.* **1.** huge. **2.** frightful.

Mont. Montana.

mon•tage' (mon täzh'; *Fr.* môn tAzh') *n.* blending of elements from several pictures into one.

month (munth) *n.* any of twelve parts of calendar year.

month'ly, *adj., n., pl.* **-lies,** *adv.* —*adj.* **1.** occurring, appearing, etc., once a month. **2.** lasting for a month. —*n.* **3.** periodical published once a month. —*adv.* **4.** once a month. **5.** by the month.

mon'u•ment (mon'yə mənt) *n.* memorial structure.

mon'u•men'tal (-men'tl) *adj.* **1.** imposing. **2.** serving as monument.

moo (mōō) *n.* **1.** sound cow makes. —*v.* **2.** utter such sound.

mooch (mōōch) *Slang.* —*v.* **1.** try to get without paying. —*n.* **2.** Also, **mooch'er.** person who mooches.

mood (mo͞od) *n.* frame of mind.

mood'y, *adj.*, **-ier, -iest.** of uncertain mood. **—mood'i•ly**, *adv.*

moon (mo͞on) *n.* **1.** body which revolves around earth monthly. **2.** month. **—v. 3.** gaze dreamily.

moon'light', *n.* **1.** light from moon. **—v. 2.** work at second job after principal one.

moon'shine', *n.* illegally made liquor. **—moon'shin'er**, *n.*

moon'stone', *n.* pearly gem.

moon'struck', *adj.* **1.** mentally deranged. **2.** dreamily bemused.

moor (mo͞or) *v.* **1.** secure (ship), as at a dock. **—n. 2.** *Brit.* open peaty wasteland.

moor'ing, *n.* **1.** *(pl.)* cables, etc., by which ship is moored. **2.** place where ship is moored.

moose (mo͞os) *n., pl.* **moose.** large animal of deer family.

moot (mo͞ot) *adj.* debatable.

mop (mop) *n., v.*, **mopped, mopping. —n. 1.** piece of cloth, etc., fastened to stick, for washing or dusting. **—v. 2.** clean with mop. **3.** *Mil.* **mop up,** destroy final resisting elements.

mope (mōp) *v.*, **moped, moping.** be in low spirits.

mo'ped' (mō'ped') *n.* motorized bicycle.

mop'pet (mop'it) *n.* child.

M.Opt. Master of Optometry.

MOR *Music.* middle-of-the-road.

mor. morocco.

mo•raine' (mə rān') *n.* mass of stone, etc., left by glacier.

mor'al (môr'əl) *adj.* **1.** of or concerned with right conduct. **2.** virtuous. **—n. 3.** *(pl.)* principles of conduct. **4.** moral lesson. **—mor'al•ist**, *n.* **—mor'al•is'tic**, *adj.*

mo•rale' (mə ral') *n.* spirits; mood.

mo•ral'i•ty (mə ral'i tē, mô-) *n.* **1.** conformity to rules of right conduct. **2.** moral quality.

mor'al•ize' (môr'ə līz') *v.*, **-ized, -izing.** think or pronounce on moral questions.

mor'al•ly, *adv.* **1.** according to morals. **2.** in one's honest belief.

mo•rass' (mə ras') *n.* swamp.

mor'a•to'ri•um (môr'ə tôr'ē əm) *n., pl.* **-to•ri•a** (tôr'ē ə), **-to•ri•ums. 1.** legal permission to delay payment of debts. **2.** any temporary cessation.

mo'ray (môr'ā, mô rā') *n.* tropical eel.

mor'bid (môr'bid) *adj.* **1.** unwholesome. **2.** of disease. **—mor•bid'i•ty**, *n.* **—mor'bid•ly**, *adv.*

mor'dant (môr'dnt) *adj.* **1.** sarcastic; biting. **2.** burning; corrosive.

more (môr) *adj.* **1.** in greater amount or degree. **2.** additional. **—n. 3.** additional or greater quantity or degree. **—adv. 4.** in addition.

more dict. (in prescriptions) in the manner

directed. Also, **mor. dict.** [from Latin *mōre dictū*]

mo•rel' (mə rel') *n.* edible mushroom.

more•o'ver, *adv.* besides.

mo'res (môr'āz, -ēz) *n.pl.* social and moral customs of group.

more sol. (in prescriptions) in the usual manner. Also, **mor. sol.** [from Latin *mōre solitō*]

mor'ga•nat'ic (môr'gə nat'ik) *adj.* designating marriage between royal person and commoner.

morgue (môrg) *n.* place where corpses are taken for identification.

mor'i•bund' (môr'ə bund') *adj.* dying.

Mor'mon•ism (môr'mən iz'əm) *n.* religion founded in U.S. in 1830. **—Mor'mon**, *n., adj.*

morn (môrn) *n.* morning.

morn'ing, *n.* **1.** first part of day. **—adj. 2.** done, or occurring, in the morning.

morn'ing-glo'ry, *n., pl.* **-ries.** vine with funnel-shaped flowers.

morning sickness, nausea occurring early in the day during the first months of pregnancy.

morning star, bright planet seen in east immediately before sunrise.

mo•roc'co (mə rok'ō) *n.* fine leather.

mo'ron (môr'on) *n.* stupid person. **—mo•ron'ic** (mə ron'ik) *adj.*

mo•rose' (mə rōs') *adj.* gloomily ill-humored. **—mo•rose'ly**, *adv.* **—mo•rose'ness**, *n.*

mor'pheme (môr'fēm) *n.* minimal grammatical unit. **—mor•phe'mic**, *adj.*

mor'phine (môr'fēn) *n.* narcotic found in opium.

morphol. morphology.

mor•phol'o•gy (môr fol'ə jē) *n.* **1.** branch of biology dealing with form and structure of organisms. **2.** form and structure of an organism.

mor'row (môr'ō) *n. Poetic.* the next day.

Morse code (môrs) *n.* telegraphic code of long and short signals.

mor'sel (môr'səl) *n.* small amount.

mort morse taper.

mor'tal (môr'tl) *adj.* **1.** liable to death. **2.** causing death. **3.** to death. **—n. 4.** human being. **—mor'tal•ly**, *adv.*

mor•tal'i•ty (môr tal'i tē) *n., pl.* **-ties. 1.** mortal nature. **2.** relative death rate.

mor'tar (môr'tər) *n.* **1.** bowl in which drugs, etc., are pulverized. **2.** short cannon. **3.** material used to bind masonry.

mor'tar•board', *n.* **1.** board used to hold mortar. **2.** academic cap with square, flat top and tassel.

mort'gage (môr'gij) *n., v.*, **-gaged, -gaging. —n. 1.** conditional transfer of property as security for debt. **—v. 2.** put mortgage on. **—mort'ga•gee'** (-gə jē') *n.* **—mort'ga•gor**, *n.*

mor•ti'cian (môr tish'ən) *n.* undertaker.

M

mor′ti•fy′ (môr′tə fī′) v., **-fied, -fying. 1.** humiliate or shame. **2.** subject (body) to austerity. **—mor′ti•fi•ca′tion,** n.

mor′tise (môr′tis) n., v., **-tised, -tising. —**n. **1.** slot in wood for tenon. —v. **2.** fasten by mortise.

mor′tu•ar′y (môr′chōō er′ē) n., pl. **-aries.** place where bodies are prepared for burial.

MOS Electronics. metal oxide semiconductor.

mos. 1. months. **2.** mosaic.

mo•sa′ic (mō zā′ik) n. design made of small colored pieces of stone, glass, etc.

mo′sey (mō′zē) v. Informal. stroll.

MOSFET (mos′fet′), Electronics. metal oxide semiconducter field-effect transistor.

mosh (mosh) v. Slang. engage in frenzied, violent dancing.

Mos′lem (moz′ləm, mos′-) n., adj. Muslim.

mosque (mosk) n. Muslim place of prayer.

mos•qui′to (mə skē′tō) n., pl. **-toes, -tos.** common biting insect.

moss (môs) n. **1.** small, leafy-stemmed plant growing on rocks, etc. —v. **2.** cover with moss. **—moss′y,** adj.

moss′back′, n. Informal. person having antiquated ideas.

most (mōst) adj. **1.** in greatest amount. **2.** majority of. —n. **3.** greatest quantity. —adv. **4.** to greatest extent.

most′ly, adv. **1.** in most cases. **2.** in greater part.

mot motor.

mote (mōt) n. small particle.

mo•tel′ (mō tel′) n. roadside hotel for automobile travelers.

mo•tet′ (mō tet′) n. unaccompanied polyphonic choral composition.

moth (môth) n. insect, some of whose larvae eat cloth.

moth′ball′, n. ball of camphor, etc., for repelling moths.

moth′er (muth′ər) n. **1.** female parent. **2.** head of group of nuns. **3.** stringy substance forming on fermenting liquids. —adj. **4.** of, like, or being mother. **5.** native. —v. **6.** act as or like mother to. **—moth′er•hood′,** n. **—moth′er•ly,** adj.

moth′er-in-law′, n., pl. **mothers-in-law.** mother of one's spouse.

moth′er•land′, n. **1.** one's native land. **2.** land of one's ancestors.

moth′er-of-pearl′, n. inner layer of certain shells.

mo•tif′ (mō tēf′) n. recurring subject or theme.

mo′tile (mōt′l, mō′til) adj. Biology. capable of moving spontaneously, as cells and spores. **—mo•til′i•ty,** n.

mo′tion (mō′shən) n. **1.** process of changing position. **2.** action or power of movement. **3.** formal proposal made in meeting. —v. **4.** indicate by gesture. **—mo′tion•less,** adj.

motion picture, series of photographs projected so rapidly that objects seem to be moving.

mo′ti•vate′ (mō′tə vāt′) v., **-vated, -vating.** give motive to. **—mo′ti•va′tion,** n.

mo′tive (-tiv) n. **1.** purpose; goal. —adj. **2.** of or causing motion.

mot′ley (mot′lē) adj. widely, often grotesquely, varied.

mo′to•cross′ (mō′tō krôs′) n. motorcycle race over rough terrain.

mo′tor (mō′tər) n. **1.** small, powerful engine. —adj. **2.** of or causing motion. **3.** of or operated by motor. —v. **4.** travel by automobile.

mo′tor•bike′, n. small motorcycle.

mo′tor•boat′, n. boat run by motor.

mo′tor•cade′ (-kād′) n. procession of automobiles.

mo′tor•car′, n. automobile.

mo′tor•cy′cle, n. heavy motor-driven bicycle.

mo′tor•ist, n. automobile driver.

mo′tor•ize′, v., **-ized, -izing.** furnish with motors or motor-driven vehicles.

mo′tor•man′, n., pl. **-men.** person who drives electrically operated vehicle.

mot′tle (mot′l) v., **-tled, -tling.** mark with spots or blotches.

mot′to (mot′ō) n., pl. **-toes, -tos.** phrase expressing one's guiding principle.

moue (mōō) n., pl. **moues** (mōō) pouting grimace.

mould (mōld) n. mold.

mould′er, v. molder.

moult (mōlt) v., n. molt.

mound (mound) n. heap of earth; hill.

mount (mount) v. **1.** go up; get on; rise. **2.** prepare for use or display. **3.** fix in setting. —n. **4.** act or manner of mounting. **5.** horse for riding. **6.** Also, **mounting.** support, setting, etc. **7.** hill.

moun′tain (moun′tn) n. lofty natural elevation on earth's surface. **—moun′tain•ous,** adj.

mountain ash, small tree of rose family.

mountain bike, bicycle designed for off-road use, usu. having smaller frame and wider tires.

moun′tain•eer′, n. **1.** mountain climber. **2.** dweller in mountains. **—moun′tain•eer′ing,** n.

mountain laurel, shrub bearing rose or white flowers.

mountain lion, cougar.

moun′te•bank′ (moun′tə bangk′) n. charlatan.

mourn (môrn) v. grieve; feel or express sorrow (for). **—mourn′er,** n. **—mourn′ful,** adj. **—mourn′ing,** n.

mouse (n. mous; v. also mouz) n., pl. **mice** (mīs), v., **moused, mousing.** —n. **1.** small rodent. **2.** palm-sized device used to select items on computer screen. —v. (mouz) **3.** hunt for mice.

mousse (mōōs) *n.* **1.** frothy dessert. **2.** foamy preparation used to style hair.

mous•tache' (mus'tash, mə stash') *n.* mustache.

mous'y (mou'sē, -zē) *adj.*, **-ier, -iest.** drably quiet in manner or appearance. **—mous'i•ness,** *n.*

mouth *n.*, *pl.* **mouths,** *v.* **—***n.* (mouth) **1.** opening through which animal takes in food. **2.** any opening. **—***v.* (mouth) **3.** utter pompously or dishonestly. **—mouth'ful',** *n.*

mouth organ, harmonica.

mouth'piece', *n.* **1.** piece at or forming mouth. **2.** person, newspaper, etc., speaking for others.

mouth'wash', *n.* solution for cleaning the mouth.

mouth'-wa'ter•ing, *adj.* appetizing, as in appearance or aroma.

mou'ton (mōō'ton) *n.* sheepskin processed to resemble seal or beaver.

move (mōōv) *v.*, **moved, moving,** *n.* **—***v.* **1.** change place or position. **2.** change one's abode. **3.** advance. **4.** make formal proposal in meeting. **5.** affect emotionally. **—***n.* **6.** act of moving. **7.** purposeful action. **—mov'a•ble,** *adj.*, *n.* **—mov'er,** *n.*

move'ment, *n.* **1.** act or process of moving. **2.** trend in thought. **3.** works of mechanism. **4.** principal division of piece of music.

moving picture, motion picture. Also, **mov'•ie.**

mow, *v.*, **mowed, mowed** or **mown, mowing,** *n.* **—***v.* (mō) **1.** cut (grass, etc.). **2.** kill indiscriminately. **—***n.* (mou) **3.** place in barn where hay, etc., are stored. **—mow'er,** *n.*

moz'za•rel'la (mot'sə rel'lə, mōt'-) *n.* mild, white, semisoft cheese.

MP, 1. a member of Parliament. **2.** Military Police.

M.P.A. 1. Master of Professional Accounting. **2.** Master of Public Administration. **3.** Master of Public Affairs.

MPAA Motion Picture Association of America.

MPB Missing Persons Bureau.

MPC Multimedia PC: a system conforming to specifications covering audio, video, and other multimedia components, and able to run multimedia software.

M.P.E. Master of Physical Education.

MPEG (em'peg), Motion Picture Experts Group.

MPers Middle Persian.

mpg miles per gallon. Also, **mi/gal., m.p.g., M.P.G., MPG**

mph, miles per hour.

M.Pharm. Master of Pharmacy.

mpl maintenance parts list.

mpt male pipe thread.

Mr. (mis'tər) *pl.* **Messrs.** (mes'ərz) mister; title of address for man.

MRA Moral Re-Armament.

MRBM medium-range ballistic missile. Also, **mrbm**

M.R.E. Master of Religious Education.

mrg mooring.

MRI, magnetic resonance imaging: process of producing images of the body using strong magnetic field and low-energy radio waves.

mRNA *Genetics.* messenger RNA.

M.R.P. Master in Regional Planning; Master of Regional Planning.

Mrs. (mis'iz, miz'iz) *pl.* **Mmes.** (mā däm', -dam'). title of address for married woman.

MRV *Military.* multiple reentry vehicle. Also, **M.R.V.**

MS, 1. Also, **ms, ms.** manuscript. **2.** Mississippi. **3.** multiple sclerosis.

Ms., (miz) title of address for woman not to be distinguished as married or unmarried.

M.S., Master of Science.

M.S.A. Master of Science in Agriculture.

M.S.A.E. Master of Science in Aeronautical Engineering.

M.S.A.M. Master of Science in Applied Mechanics.

M.S.Arch. Master of Science in Architecture.

MSAT Minnesota Scholastic Aptitude Test.

M.S.B.A. Master of Science in Business Administration.

M.S.B.C. Master of Science in Building Construction.

M.S.Bus. Master of Science in Business.

MSC Manned Spacecraft Center.

M.Sc. Master of Science.

M.Sc.D. Doctor of Medical Science.

M.S.C.E. Master of Science in Civil Engineering.

M.S.Ch.E. Master of Science in Chemical Engineering.

M.Sc.Med. Master of Medical Science.

M.S.Cons. Master of Science in Conservation.

M.S.C.P. Master of Science in Community Planning.

mscr machine screw.

MSD 1. mean solar day. **2.** *Math.* most significant digit.

M.S.D. 1. Doctor of Medical Science. **2.** Master of Science in Dentistry.

M.S.Dent. Master of Science in Dentistry.

MS DOS (em'es' dôs', -dos'), *Trademark.* a microcomputer operating system. Also, **MS-DOS**

M.S.E. 1. Master of Science in Education. **2.** Master of Science in Engineering.

msec millisecond; milliseconds.

m/sec meter per second; meters per second.

M.S.Ed. Master of Science in Education.

M.S.E.E. Master of Science in Electrical Engineering.

M.S.E.M. 1. Master of Science in Engineering Mechanics. **2.** Master of Science in Engineering of Mines.

M.S.Ent. Master of Science in Entomology.

M.S.F. Master of Science in Forestry.

M

M.S.F.M. Master of Science in Forest Management.

M.S.For. Master of Science in Forestry.

MSG, monosodium glutamate.

M.S.Geol.E. Master of Science in Geological Engineering.

M.S.G.M. Master of Science in Government Management.

M.S.G.Mgt. Master of Science in Game Management.

msgr messenger.

Msgr. 1. Monseigneur. 2. Monsignor.

M.Sgt. master sergeant.

MSH 1. *Biochemistry.* melanocyte-stimulating hormone; melanotropin: a hormone that causes dispersal of the black pigment melanin of melanocytes. 2. *Mineralogy.* Mohs scale.

M.S.H.A. Master of Science in Hospital Administration.

M.S.H.E. Master of Science in Home Economics. Also, **M.S.H.Ec.**

M.S.Hort. Master of Science in Horticulture.

M.S.Hyg. Master of Science in Hygiene.

MSI *Electronics.* medium-scale integration.

M.S.J. Master of Science in Journalism.

mskg masking.

msl missile.

M.S.L. 1. Master of Science in Linguistics. 2. Also, **m.s.l.** mean sea level.

msly mostly.

M.S.M. 1. Master of Sacred Music. 2. Master of Science in Music.

M.S.M.E. Master of Science in Mechanical Engineering.

M.S.Met.E. Master of Science in Metallurgical Engineering.

M.S.Mgt.E. Master of Science in Management Engineering.

M.S.N. Master of Science in Nursing.

msnry masonry.

msp *Printing.* manuscript page.

M.S.P.E. Master of Science in Physical Education.

M.S.P.H. Master of Science in Public Health.

M.S.Phar. Master of Science in Pharmacy. Also, **M.S.Pharm.**

M.S.P.H.E. Master of Science in Public Health Engineering.

M.S.P.H.Ed. Master of Science in Public Health Education.

MSS. manuscripts. Also, **MSS, Mss, mss.**

M.S.S. 1. Master of Social Science. 2. Master of Social Service.

M.S.Sc. Master of Social Science.

M.S.S.E. Master of Science in Sanitary Engineering.

MST 1. mean solar time. 2. Mountain Standard Time.

M.S.T. 1. Master of Science in Teaching. 2. Also, **m.s.t.** Mountain Standard Time.

mstr moisture.

MSTS *U.S. Military.* Military Sea Transportation Service.

M.S.W. 1. Master of Social Welfare. 2. Master of Social Work or Master in Social Work. Also, **MSW**

MT, Montana.

MTA Metropolitan Transit Authority.

MTBF mean time between failures.

MTBI mean time between incidents.

MTCF mean time to catastrophic failure.

mtchd matched.

mtd 1. mean temperature difference. 2. mounted.

mtg. 1. meeting. 2. mortgage. 3. mounting. Also, **mtg**

mtge. mortgage.

M.Th. Master of Theology.

mthbd *Computers.* motherboard.

mthd method.

MTI *Electronics.* moving target indicator. Also, **mti**

mtn 1. motion. 2. mountain.

MTO *Military.* (in World War II) Mediterranean Theater of Operations.

MTR mean time to restore.

mtr 1. magnetic tape recorder. 2. meter (instrument).

Mt. Rev. Most Reverend.

mtrg metering.

MTS *Broadcasting.* multichannel television sound.

Mts. mountains. Also, **mts.**

MTTF mean time to failure.

MTTFF mean time to first failure.

MTTM mean time to maintain.

MTTR mean time to repair.

mtu magnetic tape unit.

MTV Music Television (a cable television channel).

mtx matrix.

much (much) *adj.* 1. in great quantity or degree. —*n.* 2. great quantity. 3. notable thing. —*adv.* 4. greatly. 5. generally.

mu•ci•lage (myoo'sə lij) *n.* gummy adhesive. —**mu•ci•lag/i•nous** (-laj'ə nəs) *adj.*

muck (muk) *n.* 1. filth. 2. moist barn refuse. —**muck/y,** *adj.*

muck/rake/, *v.,* -raked, -raking. expose scandal. —**muck/rak/er,** *n.*

mu/cous (myoo'kəs) *adj.* 1. secreting mucus. 2. of or like mucus.

mucous membrane, membrane lining internal surface of organ.

mu/cus (-kəs) *n.* sticky secretion of mucous membrane.

mud (mud) *n.* 1. wet soft earth. 2. scandalous or malicious statements or information. —**mud/dy,** *adj., v.*

mud/dle (mud/l) *v.,* -dled, -dling, *n.* —*v.* 1. mix up; confuse. —*n.* 2. confusion.

mud/dle•head/ed, *adj.* confused in one's thinking.

mud'sling'ing, *n.* efforts to discredit opponent by malicious remarks.

mu•ez'zin (myoō ez'in, moō-) *n.* crier who summons Muslims to prayer.

MUF material unaccounted for.

muf 1. maximum usable frequency. 2. muffler.

muff (muf) *n.* 1. tubular covering for hands. —*v.* 2. bungle. 3. drop (ball) after catching.

muf'fin (muf'in) *n.* small round bread.

muf'fle (muf'əl) *v.,* -fled, -fling, *n.* —*v.* 1. wrap in scarf, cloak, etc. 2. deaden (sound). —*n.* 3. something that muffles.

muf'fler, *n.* 1. heavy neck scarf. 2. device for deadening sound, as on engine.

muf'ti (muf'tē) *n.* civilian dress.

mug (mug) *n., v.,* **mugged, mugging.** —*n.* 1. drinking cup. 2. *Slang.* face. —*v.* 3. assault, usually with intent to rob. 4. *Slang.* grimace. —**mug'ger,** *n.*

mug'gy, *adj.,* -gier, -giest. hot and humid.

mug shot, photograph of the face of a criminal suspect.

mug'wump' (mug'wump') *n.* person who takes independent position.

Mu•ham'mad (moō ham'əd, -hä'məd) *n.* founder of Islam, A.D. 570–632.

muk'luk (muk'luk) *n.* soft boot worn by Eskimos.

mu•lat'to (mə lat'ō, -lä'tō) *n., pl.* -toes. 1. person with one white and one black parent. 2. person with mixed black and white ancestry.

mul'ber'ry (mul'ber'ē, -bə rē) *n., pl.* -ries. tree, the leaves of some of whose species are used as food by silkworms.

mulch (mulch) *n.* 1. loose covering of leaves, straw, etc., on plants. —*v.* 2. surround with mulch.

mulct (mulkt) *v.* 1. deprive of by trickery. 2. fine.

mule (myoōl) *n.* 1. offspring of donkey and mare. 2. woman's house slipper.

mule deer, deer with large ears and gray coat.

mu'le•teer' (myoō'lə tēr') *n.* mule-driver.

mul'ish (myoō'lish) *adj.* obstinate.

mull (mul) *v.* 1. study or ruminate (over). 2. heat and spice.

mul'lah (mul'ə, moōl'ə, moō'lə) *n.* Muslim religious teacher.

mul'lein (mul'ən) *n.* tall, wooly-leaved weed.

mul'let (mul'it) *n.* common food fish.

mul'li•gan (mul'i gən) *n.* stew of meat and vegetables.

mul'li•ga•taw'ny (-gə tô'nē) *n.* curry-flavored soup.

mul'lion (mul'yən) *n.* vertical member separating lights of window.

mult 1. multiple. 2. multiplication.

multi-, prefix meaning many.

mul'ti•cul'tur•al•ism (mul'tē kul'chər ə-liz'əm, mul'tī-) *n.* recognition of different cultural identities within unified society.

mul'ti•far'i•ous (mul'tə fâr'ē əs) *adj.* many and varied.

mul'ti•me'di•a (mul'tē-, mul'tī-) *n.* (used with sing. v.) combined use of several media or mass media.

mul'ti•na'tion•al, *n.* 1. corporation with operations in many countries. —*adj.* 2. pertaining to several nations or multinationals.

mul'ti•ple (mul'tə pəl) *adj.* 1. consisting of or involving many. —*n.* 2. number evenly divisible by stated other number.

multiple sclerosis, disease marked by destruction of areas of brain and spinal cord.

mul'ti•pli•cand' (-pli kand') *n.* number to be multiplied by another.

mul'ti•plic'i•ty (-plis'i tē) *n., pl.* -ties. great number or variety.

mul'ti•ply' (mul'tə plī') *v.,* -plied, -plying. 1. increase the number of. 2. add (number) to itself a stated number of times. —**mul'ti•pli'er,** *n.* —**mul'ti•pli•ca'tion,** *n.*

mul'ti•tude' (mul'ti toōd', -tyoōd') *n.* great number.

mul'ti•tu'di•nous, *adj.* 1. numerous. 2. having many parts.

multr multiplier.

mum (mum) *adj.* silent.

mum'ble (mum'bəl) *v.,* -bled, -bling, *n.* —*v.* 1. speak quietly and unintelligibly. —*n.* 2. mumbling sound.

mum'ble•ty•peg' (mum'bəl tē peg') *n.* game in which pocketknife is flipped so it sticks in ground. Also, **mum'ble-the-peg'** (thə-).

mum'bo jum'bo (mum'bō jum'bō) 1. strange ritual. 2. senseless language.

mum'mer (mum'ər) *n.* 1. person in festive disguise. 2. actor.

mum'mer•y, *n., pl.* -ies. mere show.

mum'my (mum'ē) *n., pl.* -mies. dead body treated to prevent decay.

mumps (mumps) *n.pl.* disease marked by swelling of salivary glands.

mun. 1. municipal. 2. municipality.

munch (munch) *v.* chew.

mun•dane' (mun dān', mun'dān) *adj.* commonplace.

munic. 1. municipal. 2. municipality.

mu•nic'i•pal (myoō nis'ə pəl) *adj.* of a city.

mu•nic'i•pal'i•ty (-pal'i tē) *n., pl.* -ties. self-governing city.

mu•nif'i•cent (myoō nif'ə sənt) *adj.* extremely generous. —**mu•nif'i•cence,** *n.* —**mu•nif'i•cent•ly,** *adv.*

mu•ni'tions (myoō nish'ənz) *n.pl.* weapons and ammunition used in war.

M.U.P. Master of Urban Planning.

mu'ral (myoōr'əl) *n.* 1. picture painted on wall. —*adj.* 2. of walls.

mur'der (mûr'dər) *n.* 1. unlawful willful killing. —*v.* 2. commit murder. —**mur'der•er,**

M

n. **—mur′der•ess,** *n.fem.* **—mur′der•ous,** *adj.*

murk (mûrk) *n.* darkness.

murk′y, *adj.,* **-ier, -iest.** dark and gloomy. **—murk′i•ness,** *n.*

mur′mur (mûr′mər) *n.* **1.** low, continuous, indistinct sound. **2.** complaint. **—v. 3.** speak softly or indistinctly. **4.** complain.

mur′rain (mûr′in) *n.* disease of cattle.

Mus. Muslim.

mus. 1. museum. **2.** music. **3.** musical. **4.** musician.

Mus.B. Bachelor of Music. Also, **Mus. Bac.** [from Latin *Músicae Baccalaureus*]

mus′ca•dine (mus′kə din, -dīn′) *n.* American grape.

mus′cat (mus′kət, -kat) *n.* sweet grape.

mus′ca•tel′ (mus′kə tel′) *n.* wine made from muscat grapes.

mus′cle (mus′əl) *n., v.,* **-cled, -cling. —n. 1.** bundle of fibers in animal body that contract to produce motion. **2.** brawn. **—v. 3.** *Informal.* force one's way. **—mus′cu•lar** (-kyə lər) *adj.*

mus′cle•bound′, *adj.* having enlarged and inelastic muscles.

muscular dys′tro•phy (dis′trə fē) hereditary disease characterized by gradual wasting of muscles.

Mus.D. Doctor of Music. Also, **Mus.Doc., Mus.Dr.** [from Latin *Músicae Doctor*]

muse (myōōz) *v.,* **mused, musing. 1.** reflect quietly. **2.** say or think meditatively.

Muse (myōōz) *n.* one of nine goddesses of the arts.

mu•se′um (myōō zē′əm) *n.* place for permanent public exhibits.

mush (mush *or, esp. for 2, 3,* mōōsh) *n.* **1.** meal boiled in water until thick, used as food. **2.** anything soft. **3.** *Informal.* maudlin sentiment. **—v. 4.** travel on foot, esp. over snow with dog team. **—mush′y,** *adj.*

mush′room (mush′rōōm, -rōōm) *n.* **1.** fleshy fungus, usu. umbrella-shaped, sometimes edible. **—adj. 2.** growing rapidly. **—v. 3.** grow quickly.

mu′sic (myōō′zik) *n.* **1.** art of arranging sounds for effect by rhythm, melody, etc. **2.** score of musical composition. **—mu•si′cian** (-zish′ən) *n.*

mus′i•cal, *adj.* **1.** of music. **2.** pleasant-sounding. **3.** sensitive to or skilled in music. **—n. 4.** Also, **mus′ical com′edy.** a play with music. **—mus′i•cal•ly,** *adv.*

mu′si•cale′ (-kal′) *n.* social occasion featuring music.

mu′si•col′o•gy (-zi kol′ə jē) *n.* scholarly or scientific study of music. **—mu′si•col′o•gist,** *n.*

music video, videotape featuring dramatized rendition of popular song.

musk (musk) *n.* fragrant animal secretion, used in perfume. **—musk′y,** *adj.*

mus′keg (mus′keg) *n.* bog.

mus′kel•lunge′ (mus′kə lunj′) *n., pl.* **-lunges, -lunge.** large fish of pike family.

mus′ket (mus′kit) *n.* early rifle.

mus′ket•eer′, *n.* soldier armed with musket.

musk′mel′on, *n.* sweet edible melon.

musk′ox′, *n., pl.* **-oxen.** large mammal of arctic regions.

musk′rat′, *n.* large aquatic American rodent.

Mus′lim (muz′lim, mŏŏz′-, mŏŏs′-) *n.* **1.** follower of Islam. **—adj. 2.** of or pertaining to Islam.

mus′lin (muz′lin) *n.* plain-weave cotton fabric.

Mus.M. Master of Music. [from Latin *Músicae Magister*]

muss (mus) *Informal,* **—n. 1.** disorder; mess. **—v. 2.** rumple. **—muss′y,** *adj.*

mus′sel (mus′əl) *n.* bivalve mollusk, sometimes edible.

must (must) *aux. v.* **1.** be obliged to. **2.** may be assumed to. **—adj. 3.** necessary. **—n. 4.** anything necessary. **5.** new wine not yet fermented.

mus′tache (mus′tash, mə stash′) *n.* hair growing on upper lip. Also, **mus•ta′chio** (-shō)

mus′tang (mus′tang) *n.* small wild horse of western U.S.

mus′tard (mus′tərd) *n.* pungent yellow powder made from seeds of mustard plant.

mustard gas, oily liquid with irritating, poisonous properties, used in warfare.

mus′ter (mus′tər) *v.* **1.** assemble, as troops; gather. **—n. 2.** assembly.

mus′ty (mus′tē) *adj.,* **-tier, -tiest. 1.** stale-smelling. **2.** out-dated. **—mus′ti•ness,** *n.*

mut. 1. mutilated. **2.** mutual.

mu′ta•ble (myōō′tə bəl) *adj.* subject to change. **—mu′ta•bil′i•ty,** *n.*

mu′tant (myōōt′nt) *n.* **1.** organism resulting from mutation. **—adj. 2.** resulting from mutation.

mu′tate (myōō′tāt) *v.,* **-tated, -tating.** change or cause to change.

mu•ta′tion, *n.* **1.** sudden change in genetic characteristic. **2.** individual or species characterized by such change. **3.** change.

mute (myōōt) *adj.,* **muter, mutest,** *n., v.,* **muted, muting. —adj. 1.** silent. **2.** incapable of speech. **—n. 3.** person unable to utter words. **4.** device for muffling musical instrument. **—v. 5.** deaden sound of.

mu′ti•late′ (myōōt′l āt′) *v.,* **-lated, -lating.** injure by depriving of or damaging part. **—mu′ti•la′tion,** *n.*

mu′ti•ny (myōōt′n ē) *n., pl.* **-nies,** *v.,* **-nied, -nying.** revolt against lawful authority. **—mu′ti•neer′,** *n.* **—mu′ti•nous,** *adj.*

mutt (mut) *n. Slang.* mongrel dog.

mut′ter (mut′ər) *v.* **1.** speak low and indistinctly; grumble. **—n. 2.** act or sound of muttering.

mut′ton (mut′n) *n.* flesh of sheep, used as food.

mut′ton•chops′, *n.pl.* side whiskers that are narrow at temples and broad and short at jawline.

mu′tu•al (myōō′chōō əl) *adj.* **1.** done, etc., by two or more in relation to each other; reciprocal. **2.** common. —**mu′tu•al•ly,** *adv.*

mutual fund, investment company that invests money of its shareholders.

muu′muu′ (mōō′mōō′) *n.*, *pl.* **-muus.** loose-fitting dress.

muw music wire.

mux (muks), *Electronics.* **1.** multiplex. **2.** multiplexer.

muz′zle (muz′əl) *n.*, *v.*, **-zled, -zling.** —*n.* **1.** mouth of firearm. **2.** mouth part of animal's head. **3.** cage for this. —*v.* **4.** put muzzle on. **5.** silence; gag.

MV 1. main verb. **2.** *Electricity.* megavolt; megavolts. **3.** motor vessel.

Mv *Symbol, Chemistry.* mendelevium.

mV *Electricity.* millivolt; millivolts.

mv 1. mean variation. **2.** *Electronics.* multivibrator.

m.v. 1. market value. **2.** mean variation. **3.** *Music.* mezza voce.

mvbl movable.

M.V.Ed. Master of Vocational Education.

mvg moving.

MVP Most Valuable Player. Also, **M.V.P.**

mvt movement.

MW *Electricity.* megawatt; megawatts.

mW *Electricity.* milliwatt; milliwatts.

mw medium wave.

M.W.A. Modern Woodmen of America.

MWG music wire gauge.

mwo modification work order.

mwp maximum working pressure.

M.W.T. Master of Wood Technology.

mwv maximum working voltage.

MX missile experimental: a ten-warhead U.S. intercontinental ballistic missile.

Mx *Electricity.* maxwell; maxwells.

mxd mixed.

mxg mixing.

mxr mixer.

mxt mixture.

my (mī) *pron.* possessive form of **I** used before noun.

my′as•the′ni•a (mī′əs thē′nē ə) *n.* muscle weakness. —**my′as•then′ic** (-then′ik) *adj.*

mycol. mycology.

my•col′o•gy (mī kol′ə jē) *n.* study of fungi. —**my•col′o•gist,** *n.*

my′e•li′tis (mī′ə lī′tis) *n.* **1.** inflammation of spinal cord. **2.** inflammation of bone marrow.

my′na (mī′nə) *n.* Asiatic bird sometimes taught to talk.

M.Y.O.B. mind your own business.

my•o′pi•a (mī ō′pē ə) *n.* near-sightedness. —**my•op′ic** (-op′ik, -ō′pik) *adj.*

myr′i•ad (mir′ē əd) *n.*, *adj.* **1.** very great number. **2.** ten thousand.

myr′i•a•pod′ (mir′i a pod′) *n.* many-legged worm.

myrrh (mûr) *n.* aromatic substance from certain plants.

myr′tle (mûr′tl) *n.* **1.** evergreen shrub. **2.** periwinkle (def. 2).

my•self′, *pron.*, *pl.* **ourselves. 1.** intensive form of **I** or **me. 2.** reflexive form of **me.**

mys′ter•y (mis′tə rē) *n.*, *pl.* **-teries. 1.** anything secret, unknown, or unexplained. **2.** obscurity. **3.** secret rite. —**mys•te′ri•ous** (mi stēr′ē əs) *adj.* —**mys•te′ri•ous•ly,** *adv.*

mys′tic (mis′tik) *adj.* Also, **mys′ti•cal. 1.** mysterious or occult. **2.** spiritual. —*n.* **3.** believer in mysticism.

mys′ti•cism (-tə siz′əm) *n.* doctrine of direct spiritual intuition of God, truth, etc.

mys′ti•fy′, *v.*, **-fied, -fying.** bewilder purposely. —**mys′ti•fi•ca′tion,** *n.*

mys•tique′ (mi stēk′) *n.* aura of mystery or power.

myth (mith) *n.* **1.** legendary story, person, etc. **2.** false popular belief. —**myth′i•cal, myth′ic,** *adj.* —**myth′i•cal•ly,** *adv.*

mythol. 1. mythological. **2.** mythology.

my•thol′o•gy (mi thol′ə jē) *n.*, *pl.* **-gies.** body of myths. —**myth′o•log′i•cal** (mith′ə loj′i kəl) *adj.*

M

N

N, n (en) *n.* fourteenth letter of English alphabet.

N, north, northern.

NA 1. not applicable. **2.** not available.

Na *Symbol, Chemistry.* sodium. [from Latin *natrium*]

n/a 1. no account. **2.** not applicable.

N.A. 1. National Army. **2.** North America. **3.** not applicable. **4.** *Microscopy.* numerical aperture.

NAA National Aeronautic Association.

NAACP National Association for the Advancement of Colored People. Also, **N.A.A.C.P.**

nab (nab) *v.,* **nabbed, nabbing.** *Informal.* seize; arrest.

na'bob (nā'bob) *n.* wealthy, influential, or powerful person.

NACA National Advisory Committee for Aeronautics. Also, **N.A.C.A.**

na•celle' (nə sel') *n.* enclosed shelter for aircraft engine.

na'cre (nā'kər) *n.* mother-of-pearl. —**na'cre•ous** (-krē əs) *adj.*

NAD *Biochemistry.* a coenzyme, $C_{21}H_{27}N_7O_{14}P_2$, involved in many cellular oxidation-reduction reactions. [*n(icotinamide) a(denine) d(inucleotide)*]

N.A.D. National Academy of Design.

NADH *Biochemistry.* an abbreviation for the reduced form of NAD in electron transport reactions. [NAD + H, for hydrogen]

na'dir (nā'dər, -dēr) *n.* **1.** lowest point. **2.** point of celestial sphere directly below given point.

NADP *Biochemistry.* a coenzyme, $C_{21}H_{28}N_7O_{17}P_3$, similar in function to NAD. [*n(icotinamide) a(denine) d(inucleotide) p(hosphate)*]

NAFTA (naf'tə), North American Free Trade Agreement. Also, **Nafta.**

nag (nag) *v.,* **nagged, nagging,** *n.* —*v.* **1.** scold constantly. —*n.* **2.** person who nags. **3.** old horse.

Nah. *Bible.* Nahum.

NAHB National Association of Home Builders.

nai'ad (nā'ad, -əd, nī'-) *n.* water nymph.

nail (nāl) *n.* **1.** slender piece of metal for holding pieces of wood together. **2.** horny plate at end of finger or toe. —*v.* **3.** fasten with nails. **4.** *Informal.* secure or seize.

na•ive' (nä ēv') *adj.* simple; unsophisticated. Also, **na•ïve'.**

na•ive•té' (nä ēv tā') *n.* artless simplicity. Also, **na•ïve•té'.**

na'ked (nā'kid) *adj.* **1.** without clothing or covering. **2.** (of eye) unassisted in seeing. **3.** plain. —**na'ked•ness,** *n.*

NAM National Association of Manufacturers. Also, **N.A.M.**

name (nām) *n., v.,* **named, naming.** —*n.* **1.** word or words by which a person, place, or thing is designated. **2.** reputation. **3.** behalf or authority. —*v.* **4.** give name to. **5.** specify. **6.** appoint. —**nam'a•ble, name'a•ble,** *adj.* —**nam'er,** *n.*

name'less, *adj.* **1.** having no name. **2.** not referred to by name. **3.** incapable of being described.

name'ly, *adv.* that is to say.

name'sake', *n.* one having same name as another.

nan'ny (nan'ē) *n., pl.* **-nies.** child's nursemaid.

nanny goat, female goat.

nan'o•sec'ond (nan'ə sek'ənd, nā'nə-) *n.* one billionth of a second.

nap (nap) *n., v.,* **napped, napping.** —*n.* **1.** short sleep. **2.** short, fuzzy fibers on the surface of cloth. —*v.* **3.** raise fuzz on. **4.** have short sleep.

na'palm (nā'päm) *n.* **1.** highly incendiary jellylike substance used in bombs, etc. —*v.* **2.** bomb or attack with napalm.

nape (nāp, nap) *n.* back of neck.

naph'tha (naf'thə, nap'-) *n.* petroleum derivative.

naph'tha•lene' (-lēn') *n.* white crystalline substance used in mothballs.

nap'kin (nap'kin) *n.* piece of cloth or paper used at table to wipe lips or fingers.

na•po'le•on (nə pō'lē ən, -pōl'yən) *n.* rich, flaky pastry with cream filling.

nar narrow.

narc. narcotics.

nar'cis•sism (när'sə siz'em) *n.* excessive admiration of oneself. —**nar'cis•sis'tic** (-sis'tik) *adj.*

nar•cis'sus (när sis'əs) *n.* spring-blooming plant, as daffodil or jonquil.

nar•co'sis (när kō'sis) *n.* stupor.

nar•cot'ic (-kot'ik) *adj.* **1.** sleep-inducing. —*n.* **2.** substance that dulls pain, induces sleep, etc. **3.** addictive drug, esp. an illegal one.

nar'rate (nar'āt, na rāt') *v.,* **-rated, -rating.** tell. —**nar•ra'tion,** *n.* —**nar'ra•tor,** *n.*

nar'ra•tive (-ə tiv) *n.* **1.** story of events. —*adj.* **2.** that narrates. **3.** of narration.

nar'row (nar'ō) *adj.* **1.** not broad or wide. **2.** literal or strict in interpreting rules, etc. **3.** minute. —*v.* **4.** make or become narrow. —*n.* **5.** narrow place, thing, etc. —**nar'row-mind'ed,** *adj.*

nar'whal (när'wəl) *n.* Arctic whale.

N.A.S. 1. National Academy of Sciences. **2.** naval air station. Also, **NAS**

NASA (nas'ə) *n.* National Aeronautics and Space Administration.

na′sal (nā′zəl) *adj.* **1.** of noses. **2.** spoken through nose. —*n.* **3.** nasal sound. —**na′sal·ly,** *adv.*

NASCAR (nas′kär), National Association for Stock Car Auto Racing. Also, **N.A.S.C.A.R.**

nas′cent (nas′ənt, nā′sənt) *adj.* beginning to exist or develop. —**nas′cence,** *n.*

NASD National Association of Securities Dealers. Also, **N.A.S.D.**

NASDAQ (nas′dak, naz′-), National Association of Securities Dealers Automated Quotations.

na·stur′tium (nə stûr′shəm, na-) *n.* garden plant with yellow, orange, or red flowers.

nas′ty (nas′tē) *adj.*, **-tier, -tiest. 1.** disgustingly unclean. **2.** objectionable. —**nas′ti·ly,** *adv.* —**nas′ti·ness,** *n.*

nat. 1. national. **2.** native. **3.** natural. **4.** naturalist.

na′tal (nāt′l) *adj.* of one's birth.

na′tion (nā′shən) *n.* **1.** people living in one territory under same government. **2.** people related by tradition or ancestry. —**na′tion·al** (nash′ə nl) *adj.*, *n.* —**na′tion·al·ly,** *adv.*

na′tion·al·ism′ (nash′ə nl iz′əm) *n.* devotion to one's nation. —**na′tion·al·ist,** *n.*, *adj.* —**na′tion·al·is′tic,** *adj.*

na′tion·al′i·ty (nash′ə nal′i tē) *n.*, *pl.* **-ties. 1.** condition of being member of a nation. **2.** nation.

na′tion·al·ize′, *v.*, **-ized, -izing.** bring under national control or ownership. —**na′tion·al·i·za′tion,** *n.*

na′tion·wide′ (nā′shən-) *adj.*, *adv.* across entire nation.

na′tive (nā′tiv) *adj.* **1.** belonging to by birth, nationality, or nature. **2.** of natives. **3.** being the place of origin of a person or thing. —*n.* **4.** person, animal, or plant native to region.

Native American, member of indigenous peoples of N. and S. America.

na·tiv′i·ty (nə tiv′i tē) *n.*, *pl.* **-ties.** birth.

natl. national.

NATO (nā′tō) *n.* North Atlantic Treaty Organization.

nat′ty (nat′ē) *adj.*, **-tier, -tiest.** neat; trim.

nat′u·ral (nach′ər əl) *adj.* **1.** of, existing in, or formed by nature. **2.** to be expected in circumstances. **3.** without affectation. **4.** *Music.* neither sharp nor flat. —**nat′u·ral·ly,** *adv.* —**nat′u·ral·ness,** *n.*

natural childbirth, childbirth without use of drugs.

natural gas, mixture of gaseous hydrocarbons that accumulates in porous sedimentary rocks.

natural history, study of natural objects.

nat′u·ral·ism (-ər ə liz′əm) *n.* artistic or literary style that represents objects or events as they occur in nature or real life. —**nat′u·ral·is′tic,** *adj.*

nat′u·ral·ist, *n.* **1.** student of nature. **2.** adherent of naturalism.

nat′u·ral·ize′, *v.*, **-ized, -izing. 1.** confer cit-

izenship upon. **2.** introduce to region. —**nat′u·ral·i·za′tion,** *n.*

natural resource, source of wealth occurring in nature.

natural selection, process by which life forms having traits that enable them to adapt to the environment will survive in greater numbers.

na′ture (nā′chər) *n.* **1.** material world. **2.** universe. **3.** one's character.

naught (nôt) *n.* zero.

naugh′ty (nô′tē) *adj.*, **-tier, -tiest. 1.** disobedient; bad. **2.** improper. —**naugh′ti·ly,** *adv.* —**naugh′ti·ness,** *n.*

nau′sea (nô′zē ə, -zhə, -sē ə, -shə) *n.* **1.** feeling of impending vomiting. **2.** disgust. —**nau′se·ate′** (-zē āt′, -zhē-, -sē-, -shē-) *v.* —**nau′seous** (-shəs, -zē əs) *adj.*

naut. nautical.

nau′ti·cal (nô′ti kəl) *adj.* of ships, sailors, or navigation.

nautical mile, unit of distance equal to 1.852 kilometers.

nau′ti·lus (nôt′l əs) *n.* mollusk having pearly shell.

nav. 1. naval. **2.** navigable. **3.** navigation.

Nav′a·jo′ (nav′ə hō′, nä′və-) *n.*, *pl.* **-jo, -jos, -joes.** member of an American Indian people of the Southwest.

na′val (nā′vəl) *adj.* of ships or navy.

Nav. Arch. Naval Architect.

nave (nāv) *n.* main lengthwise part of church.

na′vel (nā′vəl) *n.* pit in center surface of belly.

navig. navigation.

nav′i·gate′ (nav′i gāt′) *v.*, **-gated, -gating. 1.** traverse (water or air). **2.** direct on a course. —**nav′i·ga′tion,** *n.* —**nav′i·ga′tor,** *n.* —**nav′i·ga·ble,** *adj.*

NAVSAT (nav′sat′), navigational satellite.

na′vy (nā′vē) *n.*, *pl.* **-vies.** a nation's warships and crews.

navy bean, small white bean.

navy blue, dark blue.

nay (nā) *adv.*, *n.* no.

nay′say′er, *n.* person who is habitually negative.

Na′zi (nät′sē, nat′-) *n.* member of the National Socialist party in Germany, headed by Adolf Hitler. —**Na′zism,** *n.*

NB, nota bene.

NBA 1. National Basketball Association. **2.** Also, **N.B.A.** National Book Award. **3.** National Boxing Association.

nba narrowband amplifier.

NBC National Broadcasting System.

NbE north by east.

NBIOS *Computers.* network basic input-output system.

nbr number.

NBS National Bureau of Standards. Also, **N.B.S.**

NbW north by west.

NC, North Carolina. Also, **N.C.**

NCA 1. National Council on the Aging. **2.** National Council on the Arts.

nca nickel-copper alloy.

NCAA National Collegiate Athletic Association. Also, **N.C.A.A.**

N.C.C. National Council of Churches. Also, **NCC**

NCCJ National Conference of Christians and Jews.

ncd no can do.

N.C.O. Noncommissioned Officer.

NC-17 (en/sē/sev/ən tēn/) *Trademark.* motion-picture rating advising that persons under 17 will not be admitted.

NCTE National Council of Teachers of English.

ND, North Dakota. Also, **N.D.**

NDAC National Defense Advisory Commission.

N.Dak., North Dakota.

nde near-death experience.

ndf *Photography.* neutral-density filter.

ndro nondestructive readout.

NDSL National Direct Student Loan.

ndt nondestructive testing.

NE, 1. Nebraska. **2.** northeast.

N.E.A. 1. National Education Association. **2.** National Endowment for the Arts. Also, **NEA**

Ne·an/der·thal/ man (nē an/dər thôl/) subspecies of humans that lived in Stone Age.

neap tide (nēp) tide having lowest high point.

near (nēr) *adv.* **1.** close by. —*adj.* **2.** close. **3.** intimate. —*v.* **4.** approach. —**near/ness,** *n.*

near/by/, *adj., adv.* close by.

near/ly, *adv.* almost; in close agreement.

near/-sight/ed (-sī/tid, -sī/-) *adj.* seeing distinctly only at short distance. —**near/-sight/ed·ness,** *n.*

neat (nēt) *adj.* **1.** orderly. **2.** skillful. **3.** undiluted. —**neat/ly,** *adv.* —**neat/ness,** *n.*

neb (neb) *n.* bill or beak.

NEbE northeast by east.

NEbN northeast by north.

Nebr., Nebraska.

neb/u·la (neb/yə lə) *n., pl.* **-lae** (-lē/), **-las.** luminous mass of gas or stars. —**neb/u·lar,** *adj.*

neb/u·lous (neb/yə ləs) *adj.* **1.** hazy; vague. **2.** cloudlike.

NEC National Electrical Code.

nec necessary.

n.e.c. not elsewhere classified.

nec/es·sar/y (nes/ə ser/ē) *adj., n., pl.* **-saries.** —*adj.* **1.** that cannot be dispensed with. **2.** required by facts or reason; unavoidable. —*n.* **3.** something necessary. —**nec/es·sar/i·ly,** *adv.*

ne·ces/si·tate/ (nə ses/i tāt/) *v.,* **-tated, -tating.** make necessary.

ne·ces/si·ty, *n., pl.* **-ties. 1.** something necessary. **2.** fact of being necessary. **3.** poverty.

neck (nek) *n.* **1.** part connecting head and trunk. —*v.* **2.** *Slang.* play amorously.

neck/er·chief (nek/ər chif, -chēf/) *n.* cloth worn around neck.

neck/lace (-lis) *n.* ornament of gems, etc., worn around neck.

neck/tie/, *n.* cloth strip worn under collar and tied in front.

ne·crol/o·gy (nə krol/ə jē, ne-) *n., pl.* **-gies.** list of persons who have died.

nec/ro·man/cy (nek/rə man/sē) *n.* magic. —**nec/ro·manc/er,** *n.*

ne·cro/sis (nə krō/sis) *n.* death of tissue or of organ.

nec/tar (nek/tər) *n.* **1.** sweet secretion of flower. **2.** drink of gods.

nec/tar·ine/ (nek/tə rēn/) *n.* downless peach.

N.E.D. *New English Dictionary.* Also, **NED**

nee (nā) *adj.* (of woman) born; having as maiden name. Also, **née.**

need (nēd) *n.* **1.** requirement. **2.** condition marked by necessity. —*v.* **3.** depend absolutely or strongly. **4.** be obliged. —**need/ful,** *adj.* —**need/less,** *adj.*

nee/dle (nēd/l) *n., v.,* **-dled, -dling.** —*n.* **1.** slender pointed implement for sewing, knitting, etc. **2.** anything similar, as indicator or gauge. **3.** hypodermic syringe. —*v.* **4.** prod; tease.

nee/dle·point/, *n.* embroidery on canvas.

nee/dle·work/, *n.* art or product of working with a needle, esp. in embroidery.

needs (nēdz) *adv.* necessarily.

need/y, *adj.,* **-ier, -iest.** very poor. —**need/i·ness,** *n.*

ne/er-do-well/ (nâr/-) *n.* person who habitually fails.

NEF National extra fine (a thread measure).

ne·far/i·ous (ni fâr/ē əs) *adj.* wicked.

neg. 1. Also, **neg** negative. **2.** negatively.

ne·gate/ (ni gāt/, neg/āt) *v.,* **-gated, -gating.** deny; nullify. —**ne·ga/tion,** *n.*

neg/a·tive (neg/ə tiv) *adj.* **1.** expressing denial or refusal. **2.** undistinguished. **3.** *Math.* minus. **4.** *Photog.* having light and shade reversed. —*n.* **5.** negative statement, etc. **6.** *Photog.* negative image. —**neg/a·tive·ly,** *adv.*

ne·glect/ (ni glekt/) *v.* **1.** disregard; fail to do. —*n.* **2.** disregard; negligence. —**ne·glect/ful,** *adj.*

neg/li·gee/ (neg/li zhā/, neg/li zhā/) *n.* woman's house robe.

neg/li·gent (neg/li jənt) *adj.* neglectful. —**neg/li·gence,** *n.*

neg/li·gi·ble (-jə bəl) *adj.* unimportant.

ne·go/ti·a·ble (ni gō/shē ə bəl, -shə bəl) *adj.* transferable, as securities. —**ne·go/ti·a·bil/i·ty,** *n.*

ne·go/ti·ate/ (-shē āt/) *v.,* **-ated, -ating. 1.**

deal with; bargain. **2.** dispose of. **—ne•go′ti•a′tion,** *n.* **—ne•go′ti•a′tor,** *n.*

Ne′gro (nē′grō) *n., pl.* **-groes.** *Sometimes Offensive.* member of racial group having brown to black skin. **—Ne′gro,** *adj.* **—Ne′groid** (-groid) *adj.*

NEH National Endowment for the Humanities.

Neh. *Bible.* Nehemiah.

neigh (nā) *n.* **1.** cry of horse; whinny. **—v. 2.** make cry of horse.

neigh′bor (nā′bər) *n.* **1.** person or thing near another. **—v. 2.** be near. **—neigh′bor•ly,** *adj.*

neigh′bor•hood, *n.* **1.** surrounding area. **2.** district having separate identity.

nei′ther (nē′thər, nī′-) *conj., adj.* not either. **—Pronunciation.** See EITHER.

nem′a•tode (nem′ə tōd′) *n.* unsegmented worm.

nem. con. no one contradicting; unanimously. [from Latin *nemine contradicente*]

nem. diss. no one dissenting; unanimously. [from Latin *nemine dissentiente*]

nem′e•sis (nem′ə sis) *n., pl.* **-ses.** cause of one's downfall.

N. Eng. Northern England.

neo-, prefix meaning new, recent, or revived.

Ne′o•lith′ic (nē′ə lith′ik) *adj.* of the later Stone Age.

ne•ol′o•gism (nē ol′ə jiz′əm) *n.* new word or phrase.

ne′on (nē′on) *n.* gas used in electrical signs.

ne′o•nate′ (nē′ə nāt′) *n.* newborn child. **—ne′o•na′tal,** *adj.*

ne′o•phyte′ (-fīt′) *n.* beginner.

ne′o•plasm (-plaz′əm) *n.* tumor.

NEP (nep), New Economic Policy. Also, **Nep, N.E.P.**

ne•pen′the (ni pen′thē) *n.* anything inducing pleasurable sensation of forgetfulness.

neph′ew (nef′yōō) *n.* son of one's brother or sister.

ne•phri′tis (nə frī′tis) *n.* inflammation of the kidneys. **—ne•phrit′ic** (-frit′ik) *adj.*

ne′plus′ul′tra (nē′ plus′ ul′trə, nā′) highest point.

nep′o•tism (nep′ə tiz′əm) *n.* favoritism based on family relationship.

Nep′tune (nep′tōōn, -tyōōn) *n.* planet eighth from the sun.

nerd (nûrd) *n. Slang.* **1.** dull, ineffectual, or unattractive person. **2.** person devoted to nonsocial pursuit.

nerve (nûrv) *n., v.,* **nerved, nerving. —n. 1.** bundle of fiber that conveys impulses between brain and other parts of body. **2.** courage. **3.** *Informal.* presumption. **4.** (*pl.*) anxiety; unease. **—v. 5.** give courage to.

nerve gas, poison gas that interferes with nerve functions, respiration, etc.

nerv′ous, *adj.* **1.** of nerves. **2.** having or caused by disordered nerves. **3.** anxious; uneasy. **—nerv′ous•ly,** *adv.* **—nerv′ous•ness,** *n.*

nerv′y, *adj.,* **-ier, -iest.** *Informal.* presumptuous.

NES New England Sports Network (a cable television channel).

n.e.s. not elsewhere specified. Also, **N.E.S.**

NESC National Electrical Safety Code.

-ness, suffix meaning: quality or state, as *goodness.*

nest (nest) *n.* **1.** place used by animal for rearing its young. **2.** group of things fitting tightly together. **—v. 3.** settle in nest. **4.** fit one within another.

nest egg, money saved for emergencies, retirement, etc.

nes′tle (nes′əl) *v.,* **-tled, -tling.** lie close and snug.

net (net) *adj., n., v.,* **netted, netting. —adj. 1.** exclusive of loss, expense, etc. **—n. 2.** net profit. **3.** Also, **net′ting.** lacelike fabric of uniform mesh. **4.** bag of such fabric. **—v. 5.** gain as clear profit. **6.** cover with net. **7.** ensnare.

Neth. Netherlands.

neth′er (neth′ər) *adj.* lower. **—neth′er•most′,** *adj.*

n. et m. (in prescriptions) night and morning. [Latin *nocte et mane*]

net′tle (net′l) *n., v.,* **-tled, -tling. —n. 1.** plant with stinging hairs. **—v. 2.** irritate; sting.

net′tle•some (-səm) *adj.* **1.** causing irritation. **2.** easily provoked.

net′work′, *n.* **1.** netlike combination. **2.** group of associated radio or television stations, etc. **3.** any system of interconnected elements. **—v. 4.** share information informally with others who have common interests.

neu′ral (nōōr′əl, nyōōr′-) *adj.* of nerves or nervous system.

neu•ral′gia (nōō ral′jə, nyōō-) *n.* sharp pain along nerve.

neur′as•the′ni•a (nōōr′əs thē′nē ə, nyōōr′-) *n.* pattern of symptoms often linked with depression.

neu•ri′tis (nōō rī′tis, nyōō-) *n.* inflammation of nerve. **—neu•rit′ic** (-rit′ik) *adj.*

neurol. neurology; neurological.

neu•rol′o•gy (-rol′ə jē) *n.* study of nerves. **—neu•rol′o•gist,** *n.* **—neu′ro•log′i•cal** (nōōr′ə loj′i kəl) *adj.*

neu′ron (nōōr′on, nyōōr′-) *n.* cell that is basic to nervous system.

neu•ro′sis (nōō rō′sis, nyōō-) *n., pl.* **-ses.** psychoneurosis. **—neu•rot′ic** (-rot′ik) *adj., n.*

neu′ro•sur′ger•y (nōōr′ō sûr′jə rē, nyōōr′-) *n.* surgery of the brain or other nerve tissue.

neu′ro•trans′mit•ter, *n.* chemical substance that transmits nerve impulses across synapse.

neut. 1. neuter. **2.** neutral.

neu′ter (nōō′tər, nyōō′-) *adj.* **1.** neither male nor female. —*v.* **2.** spay or castrate. —**neu′ter,** *n.*

neu′tral (nōō′trəl, nyōō′-) *adj.* **1.** taking no side in controversy. **2.** not emphatic or positive. —*n.* **3.** neutral person or state. —**neu•tral′i•ty** (-tral′i tē) *n.* —**neu′tral•ize′,** *v.,* -ized, -izing. —**neu′tral•ly,** *adv.* —**neu′tral•i•za′tion,** *n.*

neu′tron (nōō′tron, nyōō′-) *n.* particle in nucleus of atom.

Nev., Nevada.

nev′er (nev′ər) *adv.* not ever.

nev′er•the•less′, *adv.* in spite of what has been said.

new (nōō, nyōō) *adj.* **1.** of recent origin or existence. **2.** unfamiliar. —*adv.* **3.** recently; freshly. —**new′ness,** *n.*

new′el (nōō′əl, nyōō′-) *n.* post at the head or foot of stair.

New England, group of states in northeast U.S.

Newf. Newfoundland.

new′fan′gled (-fang′gəld) *adj.* of a new kind or fashion.

new′ly, *adv.* **1.** recently. **2.** anew.

new′ly•wed′, *n.* newly married person.

news (nōōz, nyōōz) *n.* report of recent event.

news′cast′, *n.* radio or television broadcast of news. —**news′cast′er,** *n.*

news′let′ter, *n.* small informative periodical for specialized group.

news′man′, *n.* journalist. Also, **news′wom′an,** *n.fem.*

news′pa′per (nōōz′-, nyōōz′-) *n.* periodical containing news, etc. —**news′pa′per•man′,** *n.* —**news′pa′per•wom′an,** *n.fem.*

news′print′, *n.* paper on which newspapers are printed.

news′reel′, *n.* motion picture of news events.

news′stand′, *n.* sales booth for periodicals, etc.

news′wor′thy, *adj.* interesting enough to warrant press coverage. —**news′wor′thiness,** *n.*

newt (nōōt, nyōōt) *n.* salamander.

New Testament, portion of Christian Bible recording life and teachings of Christ and His disciples.

new′ton (nōōt′n, nyōōt′n) *n.* unit of force.

new wave, movement that breaks with traditional values, etc.

new year, 1. (*cap.*) first day of year. **2.** year approaching.

next (nekst) *adj.* **1.** nearest after. —*adv.* **2.** in nearest place after. **3.** at first subsequent time.

next′-door′, *adj.* in the next house, apartment, etc.

nex′us (nek′səs) *n., pl.* **nexus.** link or series.

NF 1. National fine (a thread measure). **2.** *Pharmacology.* National Formulary. **3.** New-

foundland, Canada (for use with ZIP code). **4.** no funds. **5.** Norman French.

nf *Telecommunications.* noise figure.

n/f no funds. Also, **N/F**

N.F. 1. no funds. **2.** Norman French.

NFC National Football Conference.

NFD. Newfoundland. Also, **Nfd., Nfld.**

NFL National Football League.

NFS not for sale. Also, **N.F.S.**

NG 1. *Chemistry.* nitroglycerin. **2.** *Anatomy.* nasogastric.

ng nanogram; nanograms.

N.G. 1. National Guard. **2.** New Guinea. **3.** no good.

n.g. no good.

NGC *Astronomy.* New General Catalogue: a catalog of clusters, nebulae, and galaxies published in 1888.

NGF nerve growth factor.

NGk New Greek. Also, **N.Gk.**

NGNP nominal gross national product.

NGS National Geodetic Survey.

NGU *Pathology.* nongonococcal urethritis.

NH, New Hampshire. Also, **N.H.**

NHA National Housing Agency. Also, **N.H.A.**

nha next higher assembly.

N. Heb. New Hebrides.

NHG New High German. Also, **NHG., N.H.G.**

NHI *British.* National Health Insurance.

NHL National Hockey League.

NHS 1. *British.* National Health Service. **2.** National Honor Society.

NHSC National Highway Safety Council.

NHTSA National Highway Traffic Safety Administration.

Ni *Symbol, Chemistry.* nickel.

N.I. Northern Ireland.

NIA 1. National Intelligence Authority. **2.** Newspaper Institute of America.

ni′a•cin (nī′ə sin) *n.* nicotinic acid.

nib (nib) *n.* **1.** beak of bird. **2.** pen point.

nib′ble, *v.,* -bled, -bling, *n.* —*v.* **1.** bite off in small bits. —*n.* **2.** small morsel.

nice (nīs) *adj.,* nicer, nicest. **1.** agreeable. **2.** precise. **3.** fastidious. —**nice′ly,** *adv.*

ni′ce•ty (nī′si tē) *n., pl.* -ties. **1.** subtle point. **2.** refinement.

niche (nich) *n.* **1.** recess in wall. **2.** proper role or vocation.

nick (nik) *n.* **1.** notch or hollow place in surface. **2.** precise or opportune moment. —*v.* **3.** make nick in.

nick′el (nik′əl) *n.* **1.** hard silver-white metal. **2.** five-cent coin.

nick′el•o′de•on (-ə lō′dē ən) *n.* **1.** early motion-picture house. **2.** coin-operated automatic piano.

nick′name′, *n., v.,* -named, -naming. —*n.* **1.** name used informally. —*v.* **2.** give nickname to.

nic′o•tine′ (nik′ə tēn′) *n.* alkaloid found in tobacco.

N

nic′o•tin′ic acid (nik′ə tin′ik, -tē′nik, nik′-ə-) vitamin from nicotine.

niece (nēs) n. daughter of one's brother or sister.

nif′ty (nif′tē) adj., -tier, -tiest. Informal. smart; fine.

nig′gard•ly (nig′ərd lē) adj. 1. stingy. 2. meanly small.

nig′gling (nig′ling) adj. trivial.

nigh (nī) adv., adj. near.

night (nīt) n. period between sunset and sunrise.

night′cap′, n. 1. alcoholic drink taken before bed. 2. cap worn while sleeping.

night′club′, n. establishment open at night, offering food, drink, and entertainment.

night crawler, earthworm.

night′fall′, n. coming of night.

night′gown′, n. gown for sleeping. Also, night′dress/.

night′hawk′, n. nocturnal American bird.

night′in•gale′ (nīt′n gāl′, nī′ting-) n. small European bird noted for song.

night′ly, adj., adv. every night.

night′mare′ (-mâr′) n. 1. bad dream. 2. harrowing event.

night owl, n. person who often stays up late at night.

night′shade′, n. plant sometimes used in medicine.

night′shirt′, n. loose shirtlike garment worn in bed.

night stick, billy club.

NIH National Institutes of Health.

ni′hil•ism (nī′ə liz′əm, nē′-) n. total disbelief in principles. —ni′hil•ist, n. —ni′hil•is′tic, adj.

NIK Nickelodeon (a cable television channel).

nil (nil) n. nothing.

nim′ble (nim′bəl) adj., -bler, -blest. agile; quick. —nim′bly, adv. —nim′ble•ness, n.

nim′bus (nim′bəs) n., pl. -bi (-bī), -buses. 1. halo. 2. rain cloud.

NIMBY (usually nim′bē), not in my backyard. Also, Nimby.

NIMH National Institute of Mental Health.

NiMH Electricity. nickel-metal hydride (battery).

nim′rod (nim′rod) n. hunter.

nin′com•poop′ (nin′kəm pōōp′, ning′-) n. fool.

nine (nīn) n., adj. eight plus one. —ninth, n., adj.

nine′pins′, n.pl. bowling game played with nine wooden pins.

nine′teen′, n., adj. ten plus nine. —nine′teenth′, n., adj.

nine′ty, n., adj. ten times nine. —nine′ti•eth, adj., n.

nin′ny (nin′ē) n., pl. -nies. fool.

ni•o•bi•um (nī ō′bē əm) n. steel-gray metallic element.

nip (nip) v., nipped, nipping, n. —v. 1. pinch or bite. 2. check growth of. 3. affect sharply. 4. sip. —n. 5. pinch. 6. biting quality. 7. sip.

nip′ple, n. 1. milk-discharging protuberance on breast. 2. nipple-shaped object.

nip′py, adj., -pier, -piest. 1. chilly. 2. sharp.

ni. pr. (in prescriptions) unless before. [from Latin nisi prius]

NIRA National Industrial Recovery Act. Also, N.I.R.A.

nir•va′na (nir vä′nə, -van′ə, nər-) n. 1. (in Buddhism) freedom from all passion. 2. state of bliss; salvation.

NIST (nist), National Institute of Standards and Technology.

nit (nit) n. egg of louse.

ni′ter (nī′tər) n. white salt used in gunpowder, etc. Also, ni′tre.

nit′-pick′, v. Informal. argue or find fault pettily.

ni′trate (nī′trāt, -trit) n. 1. salt of nitric acid. 2. fertilizer containing nitrates.

ni′tric acid (nī′trik) caustic liquid used in manufacture of explosives, fertilizers, etc.

ni′tro•gen (nī′trə jən) n. colorless, odorless, tasteless gas, used in explosives, fertilizers, etc.

ni′tro•glyc′er•in (nī′trə glis′ər in) n. colorless, highly explosive oil.

ni′trous (nī′trəs) adj. 1. of niter. 2. Also, ni′tric. containing nitrogen.

nitrous oxide, colorless, sweet-smelling gas.

nit′ty-grit′ty (nit′ē grit′ē) n. Slang. essentials of situation.

nit′wit′, n. simpleton.

nix (niks) adv. Informal. no.

NJ, New Jersey. Also, N.J.

NKGB in the U.S.S.R., a secret-police organization (1941–46). [from Russian N(aródnyĭ) k(omissariát) g(osudárstvennoĭ) b(ezopásnosti) People's Commissariat for State Security]

nkl nickel.

NKVD in the U.S.S.R., a secret-police organization (1934–46). [from Russian N(aródnyĭ) K(omissariát) V(nútrennikh) D(el) People's Commissariat of Internal Affairs]

NL 1. Also, NL. New Latin; Neo-Latin. 2. night letter.

nl nonleaded (of gasoline).

N.L. 1. Baseball. National League. 2. New Latin; Neo-Latin.

n.l. 1. Printing. new line. 2. Law. it is not allowed. [from Latin non licet] 3. Law. it is not clear or evident. [from Latin non liquet]

N. Lat. north latitude. Also, N. lat.

N.L.F. National Liberation Front.

nlnr nonlinear.

NLRB National Labor Relations Board. Also, N.L.R.B.

NM, New Mexico.

nmag nonmagnetic.

N. Mex., New Mexico.

NMI no middle initial. Also, nmi

nmi *Symbol.* nautical mile.

nmlz normalize.

NMN no middle name.

NMR 1. *Physics.* nuclear magnetic resonance. 2. *Medicine.* magnetic resonance imaging.

nmr no maintenance required.

NMSQT National Merit Scholarship Qualifying Test.

NMSS National Multiple Sclerosis Society.

N.M.U. National Maritime Union. Also, **NMU**

NNE north-northeast. Also, **N.N.E.**

NNP net national product.

NNW north-northwest. Also, **N.N.W.**

no (nō) *adv., n., pl.* **noes,** *adj.* —*adv.* 1. word used to express dissent, denial or refusal. —*n.* 2. negative vote. —*adj.* 3. not any.

no., 1. north. 2. number.

NOAA National Oceanic and Atmospheric Administration.

no•bel′i•um (nō bel′ē əm, -bē′lē-) *n.* synthetic radioactive element.

no•bil′i•ty (nō bil′i tē) *n., pl.* **-ties.** 1. noble class. 2. noble quality.

no′ble (nō′bəl) *adj.,* **-bler, -blest,** *n.* —*adj.* 1. of high rank by birth. 2. admirable or magnificent. —*n.* 3. person of noble rank. —*no′·* **ble•man,** *n.* —**no′ble•wom′an,** *n.fem.* —**no′bly,** *adv.*

no•blesse′ o•blige′ (nō bles′ ō blēzh′) moral obligation of the rich to display generous conduct.

no′bod′y (nō′bod′ē, -bud′ē, -bə dē) *n., pl.* **-bodies.** 1. no one. 2. no one of importance.

no′-brain′er, *n. Informal.* something requiring little thought.

N.O.C. *Insurance.* not otherwise classified.

noc•tur′nal (nok tûr′nl) *adj.* 1. of night. 2. occurring or active by night.

noc′turne (-tûrn) *n.* dreamy or pensive musical composition.

nod (nod) *v.,* **nodded, nodding,** *n.* —*v.* 1. incline head sharply. 2. become sleepy. 3. sway gently. 4. be absent-minded. —*n.* 5. brief inclination of head, as in assent.

node (nōd) *n.* 1. protuberance. 2. difficulty. 3. joint in plant stem.

nod′ule (noj′ool) *n.* small knob or lump. —**nod′u•lar,** *adj.*

No•el′ (nō el′) *n.* Christmas.

no′-fault′, *n.* (of auto accident insurance, divorces, etc.) effective without establishing fault.

nog′gin (nog′ən) *n.* 1. small mug. 2. *Informal.* head.

n.o.i.b.n. not otherwise indexed by name.

noise (noiz) *n., v.,* **noised, nois•ing.** —*n.* 1. sound, esp. loud or harsh. —*v.* 2. spread rumors. —**noise′less,** *adj.* —**nois′y,** *adj.* —**nois′i•ly,** *adv.* —**nois′i•ness,** *n.*

noi′some (noi′səm) *adj.* offensive.

nol. pros. *Law.* unwilling to prosecute. [from Latin *nolle prosequi*]

nom. *Grammar.* nominative.

no′mad (nō′mad) *n.* wanderer. —**no•mad′·ic,** *adj.*

no man's land, area between warring armies.

Nom. Cap. *Finance.* nominal capital.

nom de plume (nom′ də ploom′) name assumed by writer.

nomen nomenclature.

no′men•cla′ture (nō′mən klā′chər) *n.* set or system of names.

nom′i•nal (nom′ə nl) *adj.* 1. in name only; so-called. 2. trifling. —**nom′i•nal•ly,** *adv.*

nom′i•nate′ (-nāt′) *v.,* **-nated, -nating.** 1. propose as candidate. 2. appoint. —**nom′i•** na′tion, *n.* —**nom′i•na′tor,** *n.*

nom′i•na•tive (nom′ə nə tiv) *adj.* 1. denoting noun or pronoun used as the subject of a sentence. —*n.* 2. nominative case.

nom′i•nee′, *n.* one nominated.

non-, prefix meaning not.

non′age (non′ij, nō′nij) *n.* period of legal minority.

non′a•ge•nar′i•an (non′ə jə når′ē ən, nō′nə-) *n.* person 90 to 99 years old.

nonce (nons) *n.* present occasion.

non′cha•lant′ (non′shə länt′) *adj.* coolly unconcerned. —**non′cha•lance′,** *n.* —**non′·** **cha•lant′ly,** *adv.*

noncom. noncommissioned.

non′com•bat′ant (non′kəm bat′nt, non-kom′bə tnt) *n.* 1. member of military force who is not a fighter. 2. civilian in wartime.

non′com•mis′sioned, *adj. Mil.* not commissioned.

non′com•mit′tal, *adj.* not committing oneself. —**non′com•mit′tal•ly,** *adv.*

non′ com′pos men′tis (non′ kom′pəs men′tis) *Law.* not of sound mind.

non′con•duc′tor, *n.* substance that does not readily conduct heat, electricity, etc.

non′con•form′ist, *n.* person who refuses to conform.

non′de•script′ (non′di skript′) *adj.* of no particular kind.

none (nun) *pron. sing. and pl.* 1. not one; not any. —*adv.* 2. in no way.

non•en′ti•ty, *n., pl.* **-ties.** 1. unimportant person or thing. 2. nonexistent thing.

none′such′, *n.* person or thing without equal.

none′the•less′, *adv.* nevertheless.

nonflm nonflammable.

no′-no′, *n. Informal.* forbidden thing.

non obst. *Law.* notwithstanding. [from Latin *non obstante*]

non′pa•reil′ (non′pə rel′) *adj.* 1. having no equal. —*n.* 2. person or thing without equal.

non•par′ti•san, *adj.* 1. not taking sides. 2. belonging to no party.

non•plus′ (non plus′, non′plus) *v.* confuse.

non•prof′it, *adj.* not profit motivated.

non pros. *Law.* a judgment against a plaintiff

who does not appear in court. [from Latin *non prosequitur* he does not pursue]

non rep. (in prescriptions) do not repeat. [from Latin *non repetatur* it is not repeated]

non•rep•re•sen•ta′tion•al, *adj.* not resembling any object in nature.

non•re•stric′tive, *adj.* noting word, phrase, or clause describing modified element but not essential to its meaning.

non•sec•tar′i•an, *adj.* of no one sect. —**nonsectarian,** *n.*

non′sense (non′sens, -səns) *n.* **1.** senseless or absurd words or action. **2.** anything useless. —**non•sen′si•cal,** *adj.*

non seq. *Logic.* a conclusion which does not follow from the premises. [from Latin *non sequitur* it does not follow]

non se′qui•tur (non sek′wi tər, -tŏŏr′) statement unrelated to preceding one.

non′stand′ard, *adj.* not conforming to usage considered acceptable by educated native speakers.

nonstd nonstandard.

non′stop′, *adj., adv.* without intermediate stops. Also, **non-stop.**

non′sup•port′, *n.* failure to provide financial support.

nonsyn nonsynchronous.

non•un′ion, *adj.* **1.** not belonging to labor union. **2.** not produced by union workers.

non•vi′o•lence, *n.* policy of refraining from using violence. —**non•vi′o•lent,** *adj.*

noo′dle (nŏŏd′l) *n.* thin strip of dough, cooked in soup, etc.

nook (nŏŏk) *n.* **1.** corner of room. **2.** secluded spot.

noon (nŏŏn) *n.* 12 o'clock in daytime. —**noon′time′, noon′tide′,** *n.*

no one, not anyone.

noose (nŏŏs) *n., v.,* **noosed, noosing.** —*n.* **1.** loop with running knot that pulls tight. —*v.* **2.** catch by noose.

NOP not our publication. Also, **N.O.P.**

nor (nôr; *unstressed* nər) *conj.* or not: used with **neither.**

NORAD (nôr′ad), a joint U.S.-Canadian air force command. [*Nor(th American) A(ir) D(efence Command)*]

Nor′dic (nôr′dik) *n.* person marked by tall stature, blond hair, and blue eyes. —**Nor′dic,** *adj.*

norm (nôrm) *n.* standard.

nor′mal (nôr′məl) *adj.* **1.** of standard type; usual. **2.** at right angles. —*n.* **3.** standard; average. **4.** perpendicular line. —**nor′mal•cy, nor•mal′i•ty** (-mal′i tē) *n.* —**nor′mal•ize′,** *v.,* **-ized, -izing.** —**nor′mal•i•za′tion,** *n.* —**nor′mal•ly,** *adv.*

normal school, school for training teachers.

nor′ma•tive (nôr′mə tiv) *adj.* establishing a norm.

Norse (nôrs) *n.* inhabitants or speech of medieval Scandinavia.

north (nôrth) *n.* **1.** cardinal point of compass,

on one's right facing the setting sun. **2.** territory in or to north. —*adj.* **3.** toward, in, or from north. —*adv.* **4.** toward north. —**north′er•ly,** *adj., adv.* —**north′ern,** *adj.* —**north′ern•er,** *n.* —**north′ward,** *adj., adv.*

north′east′, *n.* point or direction midway between north and east. —**north′east′,** *adj., adv.* —**north′east′ern,** *adj.*

North Star, Polaris.

north′west′, *n.* point or direction midway between north and west. —**north′west′,** *adj., adv.* —**north′west′ern,** *adj.*

Norw. 1. Norway. **2.** Norwegian.

NOS *Computers.* network operating system.

nos. numbers. Also, **Nos.**

n.o.s. not otherwise specified.

nose (nōz) *n., v.,* **nosed, nosing.** —*n.* **1.** part of head containing nostrils. **2.** sense of smell. **3.** projecting part. —*v.* **4.** smell. **5.** pry or head cautiously.

nose′cone′, *n.* forward section of rocket.

nose′dive′, *n.* **1.** downward plunge. —*v.* **2.** go into a nosedive.

nose′gay′, *n.* small bouquet.

nosh (nosh) *Informal.* —*v.* **1.** snack (on). —*n.* **2.** snack.

no′-show′, *n.* person who neither uses nor cancels reservation.

nos•tal′gia (no stal′jə) *n.* yearning for the past. —**nos•tal′gic** (-jik) *adj.*

nos′tril (nos′trəl) *n.* external opening of nose for breathing and smelling.

nos′trum (nos′trəm) *n.* medicine allegedly having special powers.

nos′y (nō′zē) *adj.,* **-ier, -iest.** *Informal.* unduly inquisitive. Also, **nos′ey.**

not (not) *adv.* word expressing negation, denial, or refusal.

NOTA none of the above.

no′ta be′ne (nō′tə ben′ē) *Latin.* note well.

no′ta•ble (nō′tə bəl) *adj.* **1.** worthy of note; important. —*n.* **2.** prominent person. —**no′ta•bly,** *adv.*

no′ta•rize′ (nō′tə rīz′) *v.,* **-rized, -rizing.** authenticate by notary.

no′ta•ry (nō′tə rē) *n., pl.* **-ries.** official authorized to verify documents. Also, **notary public.**

no•ta′tion (nō tā′shən) *n.* **1.** note. **2.** special symbol. —**no•ta′tion•al,** *adj.*

notch (noch) *n.* **1.** angular cut. —*v.* **2.** make notch in.

note (nōt) *n., v.,* **noted, noting.** —*n.* **1.** brief record, comment, etc. **2.** short letter. **3.** importance. **4.** notice. **5.** paper promising payment. **6.** musical sound or written symbols. —*v.* **7.** write down. **8.** notice.

note′book′, *n.* **1.** book with blank pages for writing notes. **2.** laptop computer.

not′ed, *adj.* famous.

note′wor′thy, *adj.* notable.

noth′ing (nuth′ing) *n.* **1.** not anything. **2.** trivial action, thing, etc. —*adv.* **3.** not at all.

noth′ing•ness, *n.* **1.** lack of being. **2.** unconsciousness. **3.** absence of worth.

no′tice (nō′tis) *n., v.,* **-ticed, -ticing. —***n.* **1.** information; warning. **2.** note, etc., that informs or warns. **3.** attention; heed. **—***v.* **4.** pay attention to; perceive. **5.** mention. **—no′-tice•a•ble,** *adj.* **—no′tice•a•bly,** *adv.*

no′ti•fy′, *v.,* **-fied, -fying.** give notice to. **—no′ti•fi•ca′tion,** *n.* **—no′ti•fi′er,** *n.*

no′tion (nō′shən) *n.* **1.** idea; conception. **2.** opinion. **3.** whim. **4.** (*pl.*) small items, as pins or trim.

no•to′ri•ous (nō tôr′ē əs, nə-) *adj.* widely known, esp. unfavorably. **—no′to•ri′e•ty** (-tə rī′i tē) *n.*

not′with•stand′ing, *prep.* **1.** in spite of. **—***adv.* **2.** nevertheless. **—***conj.* **3.** although.

nou′gat (nōō′gət) *n.* pastelike candy with nuts.

nought (nôt) *n.* naught.

noun (noun) *n.* word denoting person, place, or thing.

nour′ish (nûr′ish, nur′-) *v.* sustain with food. **—nour′ish•ment,** *n.*

nou′veau riche′ (nōō′vō rēsh′) *pl.* **nou′-veaux riches** (nōō′vō rēsh′). newly rich person.

nou•velle′ cuisine (nōō vel′) cooking that emphasizes fresh ingredients and light sauces.

Nov., November.

no′va (nō′və) *n., pl.* **-vas, -vae** (-vē). star that suddenly becomes much brighter, then gradually fades.

nov′el (nov′əl) *n.* **1.** long fictitious narrative. **—***adj.* **2.** unfamiliar. **—nov′el•ist,** *n.*

nov′el•ty, *n., pl.* **-ties. 1.** unfamiliarity. **2.** unfamiliar or amusing thing.

No•vem′ber (nō vem′bər) *n.* eleventh month of year.

no•ve′na (nō vē′nə, nə-) *n., pl.* **-nae** (-nē), **-nas.** Roman Catholic devotion occurring on nine consecutive days.

nov′ice (nov′is) *n.* **1.** beginner. **2.** person just received into a religious order.

no•vi′ti•ate (nō vish′ē it, -āt′) *n.* probationary period in religious order.

No′vo•caine′ (nō′və kān′) *n. Trademark.* local anesthetic.

now (nou) *adv.* **1.** at present time. **2.** immediately. **—***conj.* **3.** since. **—***n.* **4.** the present.

now′a•days′ (-ə dāz′) *adv.* in these times.

no′where′, *adv.* not anywhere.

nox′ious (nok′shəs) *adj.* harmful.

noz nozzle.

noz′zle (noz′əl) *n.* projecting spout.

NP 1. National pipe (a thread measure). **2.** noun phrase. **3.** nurse-practitioner.

Np *Physics.* neper; nepers.

Np *Symbol, Chemistry.* neptunium.

N.P. 1. new paragraph. **2.** *Law.* nisi prius. **3.** no protest. **4.** notary public.

n.p. 1. net proceeds. **2.** new paragraph. **3.**

Law. nisi prius. **4.** no pagination. **5.** no place of publication. **6.** no protest. **7.** notary public.

NPK *Horticulture.* nitrogen, phosphorus, and potassium.

npl nameplate.

npn negative-positive-negative (transistor).

n.p. or d. no place or date.

NPR National Public Radio. Also, **N.P.R.**

nprn neoprene.

NPT 1. National (taper) pipe thread. **2.** Nonproliferation Treaty.

n.p.t. normal pressure and temperature. Also, **npt**

nr 1. negative resistance. **2.** nuclear reactor.

NRA 1. National Recovery Administration: a former federal agency (1933–36). **2.** National Recreation Area. **3.** National Rifle Association. Also, **N.R.A.**

NRAB National Railroad Adjustment Board.

NRC 1. National Research Council. **2.** Nuclear Regulatory Commission.

NROTC Naval Reserve Officer Training Corps. Also **N.R.O.T.C.**

NRPB National Resources Planning Board.

NRTA National Retired Teachers Association.

nrtn nonreturn.

nrvsbl nonreversible.

nrz nonreturn-to-zero.

NS 1. not sufficient (funds). **2.** Nova Scotia, Canada (for use with ZIP code). **3.** nuclear ship.

Ns *Meteorology.* nimbostratus.

ns 1. Also, **nsec** nanosecond; nanoseconds. **2.** nonserviceable.

N.S. 1. New Style. **2.** Nova Scotia.

n.s. not specified.

NSA 1. National Security Agency. **2.** National Shipping Authority. **3.** National Standards Association. **4.** National Student Association. Also, **N.S.A.**

NSC 1. National Safety Council. **2.** National Security Council.

NSF 1. National Science Foundation. **2.** not sufficient funds. Also, **N.S.F.**

N/S/F not sufficient funds.

N.S.P.C.A. National Society for the Prevention of Cruelty to Animals.

N.S.P.C.C. National Society for the Prevention of Cruelty to Children.

n.s.p.f. not specifically provided for.

NSU *Pathology.* nonspecific urethritis; nongonococcal urethritis.

N.S.W. New South Wales.

NT 1. New Testament. **2.** Northwest Territories, Canada (for use with ZIP code).

Nt *Symbol, Chemistry.* niton.

nt *Physics.* nit; nits.

N.T. 1. New Testament (of the Bible). **2.** Northern Territory. **3.** Northwest Territories.

ntc negative temperature coefficient.

nth (enth) *adj.* utmost.

NTIA National Telecommunications and Information Administration.

ntp normal temperature and pressure.

nts not to scale.

NTSB National Transportation Safety Board.

ntwk network.

nt. wt. net weight. Also, **ntwt**

nu′ance (nōō′äns, nyōō′-) *n.* shade of expression, etc.

nub (nub) *n.* gist.

nu′bile (nōō′bil, -bīl, nyōō′-) *adj.* (of a young woman) **1.** marriageable. **2.** sexually developed and attractive.

nuc nuclear.

NUCFLASH (nōōk′flash′, nyōōk′-), a report of highest precedence notifying the president or deputies of an accidental or unauthorized nuclear-weapon launch or of a nuclear attack. [*nuc(lear) flash*]

nu′cle•ar (nōō′klē ər, nyōō′-) *adj.* of or forming a nucleus.

nuclear energy, energy released by reactions within atomic nuclei, as in nuclear fission or fusion.

nuclear family, social unit composed of father, mother, and children.

nuclear physics, branch of physics dealing with atoms.

nuclear winter, devastation, darkness, and cold that could result from nuclear war.

nu′cle•on (nōō′klē on′, nyōō′-) *n.* proton or neutron.

nu′cle•us (-klē əs) *n.,* *pl.* **-cle•i** (-klē ī), **-cleuses. 1.** central part about which other parts are grouped. **2.** central body of living cell. **3.** core of atom.

nude (nōōd, nyōōd) *adj.* **1.** naked. —*n.* **2.** naked human figure, esp. in art.

nudge (nuj) *v.,* nudged, nudging, *n.* —*v.* **1.** push slightly. —*n.* **2.** slight push.

nud′ism (nōō′diz əm, nyōō′-) *n.* practice of going naked for health. —**nud′ist,** *n.*

nu′ga•to•ry (nōō′gə tôr′ē, nyōō′-) *adj.* **1.** trifling. **2.** futile.

nug′get (nug′it) *n.* lump.

nui′sance (nōō′səns, nyōō′-) *n.* annoying thing or person.

nuke (nōōk, nyōōk) *n.,* *v.,* nuked, nuking. *Slang.* —*n.* **1.** nuclear weapon or power plant. —*v.* **2.** attack with nuclear weapons.

NUL National Urban League. Also **N.U.L.**

null (nul) *adj.* of no effect.

null′i•fy′, *v.,* -fied, -fying. **1.** make null. **2.** make legally void. —**nul′li•fi•ca′tion,** *n.*

Num. *Bible.* Numbers.

num. 1. number. **2.** numeral; numerals.

numb (num) *adj.* **1.** deprived of feeling or movement. —*v.* **2.** make numb. —**numb′ness,** *n.*

num′ber (num′bər) *n.* **1.** sum of group of units. **2.** numeral. **3.** one of series or group. **4.** large quantity. —*v.* **5.** mark with number.

6. count. **7.** amount to in numbers. —**Usage.** See AMOUNT.

num′ber•less, *adj.* too numerous to count.

nu′mer•al (nōō′mər əl, nyōō′-) *n.* **1.** word or sign expressing number. —*adj.* **2.** of numbers.

nu′mer•ate′ (-mə rāt′) *v.,* -ated, -ating. number; count. —**nu′mer•a′tion,** *n.*

nu′mer•a′tor, *n.* part of fraction written above the line, showing number to be divided.

nu•mer′i•cal (nōō mer′i kəl, nyōō-) *adj.* of, denoting number. —**nu•mer′i•cal•ly,** *adv.*

nu′mer•ol′o•gy (nōō′mə rol′ə jē, nyōō′-) *n.* study of numbers to determine supernatural meaning.

nu′mer•ous (-mər əs) *adj.* very many.

nu′mi•nous (nōō′mə nəs, nyōō′-) *adj.* supernatural.

numis. 1. numismatic. **2.** numismatics. Also, **numism.**

nu′mis•mat′ics (nōō′miz mat′iks, -mis-, nyōō′-) *n.* science of coins and medals.

num′skull′ (num′skul′) *n.* *Informal.* dunce. Also, **numb′skull′.**

nun (nun) *n.* woman living with religious group under vows.

nun′ci•o′ (nun′shē ō′, -sē ō′, nōōn′-) *n.,* *pl.* **-cios.** diplomatic representative of a Pope.

nun′ner•y (nun′ə rē) *n.,* *pl.* **-neries.** convent.

nup′tial (nup′shəl, -chəl) *adj.* **1.** of marriage. —*n.* **2.** (*pl.*) marriage ceremony.

nurse (nûrs) *n.,* *v.,* nursed, nursing. —*n.* **1.** person who cares for sick or children. —*v.* **2.** tend in sickness. **3.** look after carefully. **4.** suckle.

nurs′er•y, *n.,* *pl.* **-eries. 1.** room set apart for young children. **2.** place where young trees or plants are grown.

nursery school, school level below kindergarten age.

nurs′ling (-ling) *n.* nursing infant or young animal.

nur′ture (nûr′chər) *v.,* -tured, -turing, *n.* —*v.* **1.** feed and care for during growth. —*n.* **2.** upbringing. **3.** nourishment.

nut (nut) *n.* **1.** dry fruit consisting of edible kernel in shell. **2.** the kernel. **3.** perforated, threaded metal block used to screw on end of bolt. —**nut′crack′er,** *n.* —**nut′shell′,** *n.*

nut′hatch′, *n.* small songbird that seeks food along tree trunks.

nut′meg (-meg) *n.* aromatic seed of East Indian tree.

nu′tri•a (nōō′trē ə, nyōō′-) *n.* **1.** aquatic rodent. **2.** its fur.

nu′tri•ent (nōō′trē ənt, nyōō′-) *adj.* **1.** nourishing. —*n.* **2.** nutrient substance.

nu′tri•ment (-trə mənt) *n.* nourishment.

nu•tri′tion (-trish′ən) *n.* **1.** process of nourishing or being nourished. **2.** study of dietary requirements. **3.** process by which organism converts food into living tissue. —**nu•tri′-**

tious, nu'tri•tive, *adj.* —nu•tri'tion•al, *adj.*
—nu•tri'tion•ist, *n.*

nuts (nuts) *adj. Informal.* crazy.

nut'ty, *adj.,* **-tier, -tiest. 1.** tasting of or like
nuts. **2.** *Informal.* insane; senseless. —**nut'ti•
ness,** *n.*

N.U.W.W. *British.* National Union of Women
Workers.

nuz'zle (nuz'əl) *v.,* **-zled, -zling. 1.** rub noses
against. **2.** cuddle.

NV, Nevada.

NW, northwest. Also, **N.W.**

NWbW northwest by west.

NWC *Military.* National War College.

NWLB National War Labor Board.

NWS National Weather Service.

nwt nonwatertight.

n. wt. net weight.

N.W.T. Northwest Territories.

NY, New York. Also, **N.Y.**

NYA National Youth Administration. Also, **N.
Y.A.**

N.Y.C. New York City. Also, **NYC**

NYCSCE New York Coffee, Sugar, and Cocoa
Exchange.

nyl nylon.

ny'lon (nī'lon) *n.* **1.** tough, elastic synthetic
substance used for yarn, bristles, etc. **2.** (*pl.*)
stockings of nylon.

NYME New York Mercantile Exchange.

nymph (nimf) *n.* **1.** beautiful goddess living
in woodlands, waters, etc. **2.** beautiful young
woman.

nym'pho•ma'ni•a (nim'fə mā'nē ə) *n.* uncontrollable sexual desire in women. —**nym'-
pho•ma'ni•ac',** *n.*

NYP not yet published. Also, **N.Y.P.**

NYSE New York Stock Exchange. Also, **N.Y.
S.E.**

N.Z. New Zealand. Also, **N. Zeal.**

O

O, o (ō) *n.* fifteenth letter of English alphabet.

O (ō) *interj.* **1.** (expression of surprise, gladness, pain, etc.) **2.** word used before name in archaic form of address.

o' (ə, ō) *prep.* shortened form of **of.**

OA office automation.

oa overall.

o/a 1. on account. **2.** on or about.

oaf (ōf) *n.* clumsy, rude person. —**oaf'ish,** *adj.*

oak (ōk) *n.* tree having hard wood. —**oak'en,** *adj.*

oa'kum (ō'kəm) *n.* loose fiber used in calking seams.

OAO *U. S. Aerospace.* Orbiting Astronomical Observatory.

OAP *British.* old-age pensioner.

OAPC Office of Alien Property Custodian.

oar (ōr) *n.* **1.** flat-bladed shaft for rowing boat. —*v.* **2.** row. —**oars'man,** *n.*

oar'lock', *n.* support on gunwale for oar.

OAS Organization of American States.

O.A.S.I. Old Age and Survivors Insurance.

o•a'sis (ō ā'sis) *n., pl.* **-ses.** fertile place in desert.

oat (ōt) *n.* cereal grass having edible seed.

oath (ōth) *n.* **1.** solemn affirmation; vow. **2.** curse.

oat'meal', *n.* **1.** meal made from oats. **2.** cooked breakfast food made from this.

OAU Organization of African Unity. Also, **O. A.U.**

OB 1. Also, **ob** *Medicine.* **a.** obstetrical. **b.** obstetrician. **c.** obstetrics. **2.** off Broadway. **3.** opening of books. **4.** ordered back. **5.** outward bound.

ob. 1. he died; she died. [from Latin *obiit*] **2.** incidentally. [from Latin *obiter*] **3.** oboe. **4.** *Meteorology.* observation.

O.B. 1. opening of books. **2.** ordered back. Also, **O/B**

obb. *Music.* obbligato.

ob'bli•ga'to (ob'li gä'tō) *n., pl.* **-tos, -ti** (-tē). musical line performed by single instrument accompanying a solo part.

obdt. obedient.

ob'du•rate (ob'dŏō rit, -dyŏō-) *adj.* stubborn; not sorry or penitent. —**ob'du•ra•cy,** *n.*

O.B.E. 1. Officer (of the Order) of the British Empire. **2.** Order of the British Empire.

o•bei'sance (ō bā'səns, ō bē'-) *n.* **1.** bow or curtsy. **2.** homage.

ob'e•lisk (ob'ə lisk) *n.* tapering, four-sided monumental shaft.

o•bese' (ō bēs') *adj.* very fat. —**o•bes'i•ty,** *n.*

o•bey' (ō bā') *v.* **1.** do as ordered by. **2.** respond to, as controls. —**o•be'di•ence** (ō bē'-dē əns) *n.* —**o•be'di•ent,** *adj.* —**o•be'di•ent•ly,** *adv.*

ob•fus'cate (ob'fə skāt', ob fus'kāt) *v.,* **-cated, -cating.** confuse; make unclear. —**ob•fus•ca'tion,** *n.*

OB-GYN *Medicine.* **1.** obstetrician-gynecologist. **2.** obstetrics-gynecology.

obit. obituary.

ob'i•ter dic'tum (ob'i tər dik'təm) *pl.* **ob•iter dicta** (-tə) incidental remark.

o•bit'u•ar'y (ō bich'ŏō er'ē) *n., pl.* **-aries.** notice of death.

obj., 1. object. **2.** objective.

ob'ject (ob'jikt, -jekt) **1.** something solid. **2.** thing or person to which attention is directed. **3.** end; motive. **4.** noun or pronoun that represents goal of action. —*v.* (əb jekt') **5.** make protest. —**ob•jec'tion,** *n.* —**ob•jec'tor,** *n.*

ob•jec'tion•a•ble (əb jek'shə nə bəl) *adj.* causing disapproval; offensive.

ob•jec'tive (-tiv) *n.* **1.** something aimed at. **2.** objective case. —*adj.* **3.** real or factual. **4.** unbiased. **5.** being object of perception or thought. **6.** denoting word used as object of sentence. —**ob•jec'tive•ly,** *adv.* —**ob'jec•tiv'i•ty** (ob'jik tiv'i tē) *n.*

object lesson, practical illustration of principle.

ob•jet d'art (ob'zhā där') *pl.* **objets d'art** (ob'zhā där'). object of artistic worth.

ob'jur•gate' (ob'jər gāt', əb jûr'gāt) *v.,* **-gated, -gating.** scold. —**ob'jur•ga'tion,** *n.* —**ob•jur'ga•to'ry** (-gə tôr'ē) *adj.*

objv objective.

obl. 1. oblique. **2.** oblong.

ob'late (ob'lāt, o blāt') *adj.* (of spheroid) flattened at poles.

ob•la'tion (o blā'shən) *n.* offering; sacrifice.

oblg 1. obligate. **2.** obligation. **3.** oblige.

ob'li•gate' (ob'li gāt') *v.,* **-gated, -gating.** bind morally or legally. —**ob'li•ga'tion,** *n.* —**ob•lig'a•to'ry** (ə blig'ə tôr'ē) *adj.*

o•blige' (ə blīj') *v.,* **obliged, obliging. 1.** require; bind. **2.** place under debt of gratitude.

o•blig'ing, *adj.* willing to help.

ob•lique' (ə blēk', ō blēk') *adj.* **1.** slanting. **2.** indirect. —**ob•lique'ly,** *adv.* —**ob•lique'-ness,** *n.*

ob•lit'er•ate' (ə blit'ə rāt') *v.,* **-ated, -ating.** remove all traces of. —**ob•lit'er•a'tion,** *n.*

ob•liv'i•on (ə bliv'ē ən) *n.* **1.** state of being forgotten. **2.** forgetfulness. —**ob•liv'i•ous,** *adj.* —**ob•liv'i•ous•ness,** *n.*

ob'long (ob'lông) *adj.* **1.** longer than broad. —*n.* **2.** oblong rectangle.

ob'lo•quy (ob'lə kwē) *n., pl.* **-quies.** public disgrace.

ob•nox′ious (əb nok′shəs) *adj.* offensive. —**ob•nox′ious•ly,** *adv.*

o′boe (ō′bō) *n.* wind instrument. —**o′bo•ist,** *n.*

obs., obsolete.

ob•scene′ (əb sēn′) *adj.* offensive to decency. —**ob•scene′ly,** *adv.* —**ob•scen′i•ty,** (-sen′i tē, -sē′ni-) *n.*

ob•scu′rant•ism (əb skyŏŏr′ən tiz′əm, ob′-skyŏŏ ran′tiz əm) *n.* willful obscuring of something presented to public. —**ob•scu′rant•ist,** *n.,* *adj.*

ob•scure′ (əb skyŏŏr′) *adj., v.,* **-scured, -scuring.** —*adj.* **1.** not clear. **2.** not prominent. **3.** dark. —*v.* **4.** make obscure. —**ob′-scu•ra′tion** (ob′skyŏŏ rā′shən) *n.* —**ob•scu′ri•ty,** *n.* —**ob•scure′ly,** *adv.*

ob•se′qui•ous (əb sē′kwē əs) *adj.* servilely deferential.

ob′se•quy (ob′si kwē) *n., pl.* **-quies.** funeral rite.

ob•serv′ance (əb zûr′vəns) *n.* **1.** act of observing or conforming. **2.** due celebration. —**ob•serv′ant,** *adj.*

ob•serv′a•to•ry (əb zûr′və tôr′ē) *n., pl.* **-ries.** place equipped for observing stars.

ob•serve′ (əb zûr′və tôr′ē) *v.,* **-served, -serving. 1.** see; notice; watch. **2.** remark. **3.** pay respect to or perform duly. —**ob•serv′a•ble,** *adj.* —**ob′-ser•va′tion** (ob′zər vā′shən) *n.* —**ob•serv′-er,** *n.*

ob•sess′ (əb ses′) *v.* be constantly in thoughts of. —**ob•ses′sion** (-sesh′ən) *n.* —**ob•ses′sive,** *adj.* —**ob•ses′sive•ly,** *adv.*

ob•sid′i•an (əb sid′ē ən) *n.* dark volcanic glass.

obsl obsolete.

ob′so•les′cent (ob′sə les′ənt) *adj.* becoming obsolete. —**ob′so•les′cence,** *n.*

ob′so•lete′ (-lēt′) *adj.* no longer in use.

ob′sta•cle (ob′stə kəl) *n.* something in the way.

obstet. 1. obstetric. **2.** obstetrics.

ob•stet′rics (əb ste′triks) *n.* branch of medicine concerned with childbirth. —**ob′ste•tri′cian** (ob′sti trish′ən) *n.* —**ob•stet′ric, ob•stet′ri•cal,** *adj.*

ob′sti•nate (ob′stə nit) *adj.* **1.** firm; stubborn. **2.** not yielding to treatment. —**ob′sti-na•cy** (-nə sē) *n.* —**ob′sti•nate•ly,** *adv.*

obstn obstruction.

ob•strep′er•ous (əb strep′ər əs) *adj.* unruly.

ob•struct′ (əb strukt′) *v.* block; hinder. —**ob•struc′tion,** *n.* —**ob•struc′tive,** *adj.*

ob•struc′tion•ism (-shə niz′əm) *n.* perverse desire to be obstructive. —**ob•struc′tion•ist,** *n., adj.*

obsv observation.

ob•tain′ (əb tān′) *v.* **1.** get or acquire. **2.** prevail. —**ob•tain′a•ble,** *adj.*

ob•trude′ (əb trŏŏd′) *v.,* **-truded, -truding.** thrust forward; intrude. —**ob•tru′sion** (-trŏŏ′zhən) *n.* —**ob•tru′sive** (-trŏŏ′siv) *adj.*

ob•tuse′ (əb tŏŏs′, -tyŏŏs′) *adj.* **1.** blunt. **2.** not perceptive. **3.** (of angle) between 90° and 180°.

OBulg. Old Bulgarian. Also, **OBulg**

obv obverse.

ob′verse *n.* (ob′vûrs) **1.** front. **2.** side of coin having principal design. **3.** counterpart. —*adj.* (ob vûrs′, ob′vûrs) **4.** facing. **5.** corresponding.

ob′vi•ate′ (ob′vē āt′) *v.,* **-ated, -ating.** take preventive measures against; avoid. —**ob′vi-a′tion,** *n.*

ob′vi•ous (ob′vē əs) *adj.* **1.** readily perceptible. **2.** not subtle. —**ob′vi•ous•ly,** *adv.* —**ob′vi•ous•ness,** *n.*

oc outside circumference.

Oc. ocean. Also, **oc.**

o/c overcharge.

O.C. *Philately.* original cover.

o.c. 1. *Architecture.* on center. **2.** in the work cited. [from Latin *opere citātō*]

oc′a•ri′na (ok′ə rē′nə) *n.* egg-shaped wind instrument.

occ. 1. occasional. **2.** occasionally. **3.** occident. **4.** occidental. **5.** occupation. **6.** occupy.

occas. 1. occasional. **2.** occasionally.

oc•ca′sion (ə kā′zhən) *n.* **1.** particular time. **2.** important time. **3.** opportunity. **4.** reason. —*v.* **5.** give cause for. —**oc•ca′sion•al,** *adj.* —**oc•ca′sion•al•ly,** *adv.*

Oc′ci•dent (ok′si dənt) *n.* West, esp. Europe and Americas. —**Oc′ci•den′tal** (-den′tl) *adj., n.*

oc•clude′ (ə klŏŏd′) *v.,* **-cluded, -cluding.** close; shut. —**oc•clu′sion** (-klŏŏ′zhən) *n.*

oc•cult′ (ə kult′, ok′ult) *adj.* **1.** outside ordinary knowledge. —*n.* **2.** occult matters.

oc′cu•pa′tion (ok′yə pā′shən) *n.* **1.** trade; calling. **2.** possession. **3.** military seizure. —**oc′cu•pa′tion•al,** *adj.*

occupational therapy, therapy utilizing activities for psychological or physical rehabilitation.

oc′cu•py, *v.,* **-pied, -pying. 1.** inhabit or be in. **2.** require as space. **3.** take possession of. **4.** hold attention of. —**oc′cu•pan•cy,** *n.* —**oc′cu•pant,** *n.*

oc•cur′ (ə kûr′) *v.,* **-curred, -curring. 1.** take place. **2.** appear. **3.** come to mind. —**oc•cur′-rence,** *n.*

OCD Office of Civil Defense.

OCDM Office of Civil and Defense Mobilization.

o′cean (ō′shən) *n.* **1.** large body of salt water covering much of earth. **2.** any of its five main parts. —**o′ce•an′ic** (ō′shē an′ik) *adj.*

o′cea•nog′ra•phy (ō′shə nog′rə fē, ō′shē ə-) *n.* study of oceans. —**o′cea•no-graph′ic** (-nə graf′ik) *adj.* —**o′cea•nog′ra-pher,** *n.*

o′ce•lot′ (os′ə lot′, ō′sə-) *n.* small American wildcat.

o′cher (ō′kər) *n.* yellow-to-red earth used as pigment. Also, **o′chre.**

ocld oil-cooled.

o'clock/ (ə klok/) *adv.* by the clock.

OCR *Computers.* **1.** optical character reader. **2.** optical character recognition.

OCS **1.** *Military.* officer candidate school. **2.** Old Church Slavonic. **3.** outer continental shelf.

ocsnl occasional.

Oct., October.

oc'ta•gon/ (ok/tə gon/, -gən) *n.* plane figure with eight sides and eight angles.

oc'tane (ok/tān) *n.* colorless liquid hydrocarbon found in petroleum.

octane number, designation of quality of gasoline.

oc'tave (ok/tiv, -tāv) *n. Music.* **1.** eighth tone from given tone. **2.** interval between such tones.

oc•ta/vo (ok tā/vō, -tä/-) *n., pl.* **-vos.** book whose pages are printed 16 to a sheet.

oc•tet/ (ok tet/) *n.* group of eight, esp. musicians. Also, **oc•tette/.**

octl octal.

octn octane.

Oc•to/ber (ok tō/bər) *n.* tenth month of year.

oc/to•ge•nar/i•an (ok/tə jə när/ē ən) *n.* person 80 to 89 years old.

oc/to•pus (ok/tə pəs) *n., pl.* **-puses, -pi** (-pī). eight-armed sea mollusk.

oc/u•lar (ok/yə lər) *adj.* of eyes.

oc/u•list (-list) *n.* doctor skilled in treatment of eyes.

OD (ō/dē/) *n., pl.* **ODs** or **OD's**, *v.,* **OD'd** or **ODed, OD'ing.** *Slang.* —*n.* **1.** overdose of a drug, esp. a fatal one. —*v.* **2.** take a drug overdose.

odd (od) *adj.* **1.** eccentric; bizarre. **2.** additional; not part of set. **3.** not evenly divisible by two.

odd/ball/, *n. Informal.* peculiar person or thing.

odd/i•ty, *n., pl.* **-ties.** **1.** queerness. **2.** odd thing.

odds (odz) *n.* **1.** chances; probability for or against. **2.** state of disagreement. > **3.** odd things.

odds and ends, 1. miscellany. **2.** remnants.

odds/-on/, *adj.* most likely.

ode (ōd) *n.* poem of praise.

o/di•ous (ō/dē əs) *adj.* hateful.

o/di•um (-əm) *n.* **1.** discredit; reproach. **2.** hatred.

odom odometer.

o•dom/e•ter (ō dom/i tər) *n.* instrument that measures distance traveled.

o/dor (ō/dər) *n.* quality that affects sense of smell; scent. —**o/dor•ous,** *adj.*

o/dor•if/er•ous (ō/də rif/ər əs) *adj.* having odor, esp. unpleasant.

odpsk oil dipstick.

ODT Office of Defense Transportation.

od/ys•sey (od/ə sē) *n.* long, adventurous journey.

OE Old English. Also, **OE.**

Oe *Electricity.* oersted; oersteds.

O.E. **1.** Old English. **2.** *Commerce.* omissions excepted.

o.e. *Commerce.* omissions excepted. Also, **oe**

OEC Office of Energy Conservation.

OECD Organization for Economic Cooperation and Development.

OED *Oxford English Dictionary.* Also, **O.E.D.**

oed/i•pal (ed/ə pəl, ē/də-) *adj. (often cap.)* resulting from the Oedipus complex.

Oedipus complex, libidinous feelings of son toward mother.

OEEC Organization for European Economic Cooperation.

OEM original equipment manufacturer.

oe•nol/o•gy (ē nol/ə jē) *n.* science of wine-making.

oe/no•phile/ (ē/nə fīl/) *n.* connoisseur of wine.

OEO Office of Economic Opportunity.

o'er (ôr) *prep., adv. Poetic.* over.

OES **1.** Office of Economic Stabilization. **2.** Order of the Eastern Star.

oeu/vre (*Fr.* œ/vrə) *n., pl.* **oeu•vres** (*Fr.* œ/vrə). all the works of a writer, painter, etc.

of (uv, ov; *unstressed* əv or, *esp. before consonants,* ə) *prep.* particle indicating: **1.** being from. **2.** belonging to. —*aux. v.* **3.** *Nonstandard.* have.

—**Usage.** Because the preposition OF, when unstressed (*a piece of cake*), and the unstressed or contracted auxiliary verb HAVE (*could have gone; could've gone*) are both pronounced (əv) or (ə) in connected speech, inexperienced writers commonly confuse the two words, spelling HAVE as OF (*I would of handed in my book report, but the dog ate it*). Professional writers use this spelling deliberately, especially in fiction, to represent the speech of the uneducated: *If he could of went home, he would of.*

ofc office.

ofcl official.

ofcr officer.

off (ôf) *adv.* **1.** up or away. **2.** deviating. **3.** out of operation or effect. —*prep.* **4.** up or away from. —*adj.* **5.** no longer in operation or effect. **6.** in error. **7.** on one's way.

of/fal (ô/fəl) *n.* refuse; garbage; carrion.

off/beat/ *adj. Informal.* unconventional.

off/-col/or, *adj.* **1.** not having the usual color. **2.** of questionable taste; risqué.

of•fend/ (ə fend/) *v.* displease greatly.

of•fend/er, *n.* **1.** person who offends. **2.** crimninal.

of•fense/ *n.* **1.** (ə fens/) wrong; sin. **2.** (ə fens/) displeasure. **3.** (ə fens/) attack. **4.** (ô/fens) attacking side. Also, **of•fence/.** —**of•fen/sive,** *adj., n.*

of'fer (ô'fər) v. **1.** present. **2.** propose; suggest. —n. **3.** proposal; bid. —**of'fer•ing,** n.

of'fer•to'ry (-tôr'ē) n., pl. **-ries. 1.** Rom. Cath. Ch. offering to God of bread and wine during Mass. **2.** collection at religious service.

off'hand', adj. **1.** Also, **off'hand'ed.** done without previous thought; informal. **2.** curt. —**off'hand'ed•ly,** adv.

of'fice (ô'fis) n. **1.** place of business. **2.** position of authority. **3.** duty; task. **4.** religious service.

of'fice•hold'er, n. public official.

of'fi•cer, n. person of rank or authority.

of•fi'cial (ə fish'əl) n. **1.** person who holds office. —adj. **2.** authorized. **3.** pertaining to public office. —**of•fi'cial•ly,** adv.

of•fi'ci•ant (ə fish'ē ənt) n. cleric at religious service.

of•fi'ci•ate (-āt') v., **-ated, -ating.** perform official duties. —**of•fi'ci•a'tor,** n.

of•fi'cious, adj. too forward in offering unwanted help.

off'ing (ô'fing) n. **1.** distant area. **2.** foreseeable future.

off'-key', adj. **1.** not in tune. **2.** somewhat incongruous or abnormal.

off'-lim'its, adj. forbidden to be patronized, used, etc.

off'-put'ting, adj. provoking uneasiness, annoyance, etc.

off'set', v., **-set, -setting.** compensate for.

off'shoot', n. branch.

off'shore', adj., adv. in water and away from shore.

off'spring', n. children or descendants.

off'stage', adv., adj. out of sight of audience.

off'-the-cuff', adj. impromptu.

off'-the-rec'ord, adj. not to be quoted.

off'-the-wall', adj. Informal. bizarre.

off'track', adj. occurring away from racetrack.

off year, 1. year without major election. **2.** year marked by reduced production.

ofl offline.

OFlem Old Flemish. Also, **OFlem.**

ofltr oil filter.

O.F.M. Order of Friars Minor (Franciscan). [from Latin Ōrdō Frātrum Minōrum]

OFr. Old French. Also, **OFr**

OFris. Old Frisian. Also, **OFris**

oft (ôft) adv. Poetic. often.

of'ten (ô'fən, ôf'tən) adv. **1.** frequently. **2.** in many cases.

OG officer of the guard.

O.G. 1. officer of the guard. **2.** Architecture. ogee. **3.** Philately. See **o.g.** (def. 1).

o.g. 1. Also, **O.G.** Philately. original gum: the gum on the back of a stamp when it is issued. **2.** Architecture. ogee.

o'gle (ō'gəl) v., **ogled, ogling,** n. —v. **1.** eye with impertinent familiarity. —n. **2.** ogling glance.

OGO U.S. Aerospace. Orbiting Geophysical Observatory.

OGPU (og'pōō), (in the U.S.S.R.) the government's secret-police organization (1923–1934). Also, **Ogpu.** Cf. **KGB.** [from Russian Ógpu, for Ob"edinënnoe gosudárstvennoe politícheskoe upravlénie Unified State Political Directorate]

ogr Telephones. outgoing repeater.

o'gre (ō'gər) n. **1.** hideous giant who eats human flesh. **2.** barbarous person. —**o'gre•ish,** adj. —**o'gress,** n.fem.

ogt Telephones. outgoing trunk.

oh (ō) interj. (exclamation of surprise, etc.)

OH, Ohio.

OHC Automotive. overhead camshaft.

OHG Old High German. Also, **OHG., O.H.G.**

ohm (ōm) n. unit of electrical resistance.

O.H.M.S. On His Majesty's Service; On Her Majesty's Service.

OI opportunistic infection.

OIC officer in charge.

OIcel Old Icelandic.

-oid, suffix meaning resembling or like.

oil (oil) n. **1.** greasy combustible liquid used for lubricating, heating, etc. —v. **2.** supply with oil. —adj. **3.** of oil. —**oil'er,** n. —**oil'y,** adj.

oil'cloth', n. fabric made waterproof with oil.

oil'skin', n. **1.** fabric made waterproof with oil. **2.** (often pl.) garment made of this.

oint'ment (oint'mənt) n. salve.

OIr Old Irish. Also, **OIr.**

OIt Old Italian.

OJ Informal. orange juice. Also, **O.J., o.j.**

OJT on-the-job training. Also, **O.J.T.**

OK, Oklahoma.

OK (ō'kā') adj., adv., v., **OK'd, OK'ing,** n., pl. **OK's.** —adj., adv. **1.** all right; correct. —v. **2.** approve. —n. **3.** agreement or approval. Also, **O.K., o'kay'.**

Okla., Oklahoma.

o'kra (ō'krə) n. tall garden plant with edible pods.

OL Old Latin. Also, **OL.**

Ol. (in prescriptions) oil. [from Latin oleum]

O.L. 1. Also, **o.l.** (in prescriptions) the left eye. [from Latin oculus laevus] **2.** Old Latin.

old (ōld) adj. **1.** far advanced in years or time. **2.** of age. **3.** Also, **old'en.** former; ancient. **4.** wise. —n. **5.** former time.

Old English, English language before c1150.

old'-fash'ioned, adj. having style, ideas, etc. of an earlier time.

Old Guard, (sometimes l.c.) conservative members of any group.

old hand, person with long experience.

old hat, old-fashioned; dated.

old school, supporters of established custom.

old'ster, *n. Informal.* elder.

Old Test. Old Testament (of the Bible).

Old Testament, complete Bible of the Jews, being first division of Christian Bible.

old'-tim'er, *n. Informal.* elderly person.

Old World, Europe, Asia, and Africa. **—old'-world',** *adj.*

OLE *Computers.* object linking and embedding.

o'le•ag'i•nous (ō'lē aj'ə nəs) *adj.* 1. oily. 2. unctuous; fawning.

o'le•an'der (ō'lē an'dər) *n.* poisonous evergreen flowering shrub.

o'le•o•mar'ga•rine (ō'lē ō'-) *n.* margarine. Also, **o'le•o'.**

ol•fac'to•ry (ol fak'tə rē, ōl-) *adj.* pertaining to sense of smell.

OLG Old Low German. Also, **O.L.G.**

ol'i•garch' (ol'i gärk') *n.* ruler in an oligarchy.

ol'i•gar'chy (-gär'kē) *n., pl.* **-chies.** government by small group. **—ol'i•gar'chic,** *adj.*

ol'ive (ol'iv) *n.* 1. evergreen tree valued for its small, oily fruit. 2. fruit of this tree. 3. yellowish green.

OLLA Office of Lend Lease Administration.

olvl oil level.

Om. (formerly, in East Germany) ostmark.

O.M. *British.* Order of Merit.

OMA orderly marketing agreement.

OMB Office of Management and Budget. Also, **O.M.B.**

OMBE Office of Minority Business Enterprise.

om'buds•man' (om'bədz mən, om bŏŏdz'-) *n., pl.* **-men.** official who investigates private individuals' complaints against government. Also, *fem.* **om'buds•wom'an.**

o•me'ga (ō mē'gə, ō meg'ə) *n.* last letter of Greek alphabet.

om'e•let (om'lit, om'ə-) *n.* eggs beaten and cooked with filling. Also, **om'e•lette.**

o'men (ō'mən) *n.* sign indicative of future.

om'i•nous (om'ə nəs) *adj.* threatening evil. **—om'i•nous•ly,** *adv.*

o•mit' (ō mit') *v.,* **omitted, omitting.** 1. leave out. 2. fail to do, etc. **—o•mis'sion** (ō-mish'ən) *n.*

omn. bih. (in prescriptions) every two hours. [from Latin *omnī bihōriō*]

omn. hor. (in prescriptions) every hour. [from Latin *omnī hōra*]

omni-, prefix meaning all.

om'ni•bus' (om'nə bus', -bəs) *n., pl.* **-buses.** 1. bus. 2. anthology.

om•nip'o•tent (om nip'ə tənt) *adj.* almighty. **—om•nip'o•tence,** *n.*

om'ni•pres'ent (om'nə prez'ənt) *adj.* present everywhere at once.

om•nis'cient (om nish'ənt) *adj.* knowing all things. **—om•nis'cience,** *n.*

om•niv'o•rous (om niv'ər əs) *adj.* eating all kinds of foods.

omn. man. (in prescriptions) every morning. Also, **omn man** [from Latin *omnī māne*]

omn. noct. (in prescriptions) every night. Also, **omn noct** [from Latin *omnī nocte*]

omn. quadr. hor. (in prescriptions) every quarter of an hour. Also, **omn quadr hor** [from Latin *omnī quadrante hōrae*]

on (on) *prep.* particle expressing: 1. position in contact with supporting surface. 2. support; reliance. 3. situation or direction. 4. basis. **—adv.** 5. onto a thing, place, or person. 6. forward. 7. into operation. **—adj.** 8. near. **—Usage.** See ABOUT.

once (wuns) *adv.* 1. formerly. 2. single time. 3. at any time. **—conj.** 4. if ever; whenever.

once'-o'ver, *n. Informal.* quick survey.

on'co•gene' (ong'kə jēn') *n.* gene causing beginning of cancerous growth.

on•col'o•gy (-kol'ə jē) *n.* branch of medical science dealing with tumors and cancer. **—on•col'o•gist,** *n.*

on'com'ing, *adj.* approaching.

one (wun) *adj.* 1. single. 2. some. 3. common to all. **—n.** 4. first and lowest whole number. 5. single person or thing. **—pron.** 6. person or thing.

one'ness, *n.* unity.

on'er•ous (on'ər əs, ō'nər-) *adj.* burdensome.

one•self' (wun self', wunz-) *pron.* person's self. Also, **one's self.**

one'-sid'ed, *adj.* 1. with all advantage on one side. 2. biased.

one'-time', *adj.* being such before; former.

one'-track', *adj. Informal.* obsessed with one subject.

one'-way', *adj.* moving or allowing movement in one direction only.

ONF Old North French.

ONFr. Old North French.

on'go'ing, *adj.* in progress; continuing.

ONI Office of Naval Intelligence.

on'ion (un'yən) *n.* common plant having edible bulb.

on'-line', *adj.* operating under the direct control of, or connected to, a main computer.

on'look'er, *n.* spectator; witness.

on'ly (ōn'lē) *adv.* 1. alone; solely. 2. merely. **—adj.** 3. sole. **—conj.** 4. but.

on'o•mat'o•poe'ia (on'ə mat'ə pē'ə, -mǎ'tə-) *n.* formation of word by imitation of a sound.

ONR Office of Naval Research.

on'rush', *n.* rapid advance.

on'set', *n.* 1. beginning. 2. attack.

on'slaught' (on'slôt') *n.* attack.

Ont. Ontario.

on'to, *prep.* upon; on.

on•tog'e•ny (on toj'ə nē) *n.* development of an individual organism.

on•tol'o•gy (on tol'ə jē) *n.* branch of metaphysics studying existence or being.

o'nus (ō'nəs) *n.* burden.

on'ward (-wərd) *adv.* 1. toward or at point ahead. **—adj.** 2. moving forward.

on'yx (on'iks, ō'niks) *n.* varicolored quartz.

O.O.D. 1. officer of the deck. **2.** officer of the day.

oo'dles (ōōd'lz) *n.pl. Informal.* large quantity.

OOG *Computers.* object-oriented graphics.

OOP *Computers.* object-oriented programming.

OOT out of town. Also, **O.O.T.**

ooze (ōōz) *v.,* **oozed, oozing,** *n.* —*v.* **1.** leak out slowly; exude. —*n.* **2.** something that oozes. **3.** soft mud.

OP observation post. Also, **O.P.**

op (op), a style of abstract art. [from *op(tical)*]

Op. *Music.* opus.

op. 1. opera. **2.** operation. **3.** opposite. **4.** opus.

O.P. 1. observation post. **2.** *British Theater.* opposite prompt. **3.** Order of Preachers (Dominican). [from Latin *Ōrdō Praedicātōrum*] **4.** out of print. **5.** *Distilling.* overproof.

o.p. out of print.

OPA Office of Price Administration: the federal agency (1941–46) charged with regulating rents and the distribution and prices of goods during World War II.

opa opaque.

o•pac'i•ty (ō pas'i tē) *n., pl.* **-ties.** state of being opaque.

o'pal (ō'pəl) *n.* precious stone, often iridescent.

o'pa•les'cent (ō'pə les'ənt) *adj.* with opal-like play of color. —**o'pa•les'cence,** *n.*

o•paque' (ō pāk') *adj.* **1.** not transmitting light. **2.** not shining. **3.** not clear.

op. cit. (op' sit') in the work cited.

OPEC (ō'pek) *n.* Organization of Petroleum Exporting Countries.

Op'-Ed' (op'ed') *n.* newspaper section devoted to signed articles and letters.

o'pen (ō'pən) *adj.* **1.** not shut. **2.** not enclosed or covered. **3.** available; accessible. **4.** candid. —*v.* **5.** make or become open. **6.** begin. **7.** come apart. —*n.* **8.** any open space.

o'pen-and-shut', *adj.* easily solved or decided; obvious.

o'pen-end'ed, *adj.* **1.** unrestricted. **2.** having no fixed answer.

o'pen-hand'ed, *adj.* generous.

o'pen•ing, *n.* **1.** unobstructed or unoccupied place. **2.** gap or hole. **3.** beginning. **4.** opportunity.

o'pen-mind'ed, *adj.* without prejudice. —**o'pen-mind'ed•ness,** *n.*

open shop, business in which union membership is not a condition of employment.

OPer. Old Persian.

op'er•a (op'ər ə, op'rə) *n.* sung drama. —**op'er•at'ic** (-ə rat'ik) *adj.*

op'er•a•ble (op'ər ə bəl) *adj.* **1.** able to be operated. **2.** curable by surgery.

opera glasses, small, low-power binoculars.

op'er•ate' (-ə rāt') *v.,* **-ated, -ating. 1.** work

or run. **2.** exert force or influence. **3.** use surgery. —**op'er•a'tion,** *n.* —**op'er•a'tor,** *n.*

operating system, software that directs computer's operations.

op'er•a'tion•al, *adj.* **1.** concerning operations. **2.** in working order. **3.** in operation.

op'er•a'tive (-ər ə tiv, -ə rā'tiv) *n.* **1.** worker. **2.** detective. **3.** spy. —*adj.* **4.** effective.

op'er•et'ta (op'ə ret'ə) *n.* light opera.

OPers Old Persian.

ophthal. 1. ophthalmologist. **2.** ophthalmology.

oph•thal'mi•a (of thal'mē ə) *n.* inflammation of eye.

oph'thal•mol'o•gy (of'thəl mol'ə jē, -thə-, -thal-, op'-) *n.* branch of medicine dealing with eye. —**oph'thal•mol'o•gist,** *n.*

o'pi•ate (ō'pē it, -āt') *n.* medicine containing opium.

o•pine' (ō pīn') *v.,* **-pined, -pining.** express an opinion.

o•pin'ion (ə pin'yən) *n.* belief or judgment.

o•pin'ion•at•ed (-yə nā'tid) *adj.* stubborn in opinions.

o'pi•um (ō'pē əm) *n.* narcotic juice of poppy.

OPM 1. Office of Personnel Management. **2.** operations per minute. **3.** *Slang.* other people's money.

opn operation.

opnr opener.

o•pos'sum (ə pos'əm, pos'əm) *n.* pouched mammal of southern U.S.

Opp. *Music.* opuses. [from Latin *opera*]

opp. 1. opposed. **2.** opposite.

opp hnd opposite hand.

op•po'nent (ə pō'nənt) *n.* **1.** person on opposite side, as in contest. **2.** person opposed to something.

op'por•tune' (op'ər tōōn', -tyōōn') *adj.* appropriate; timely.

op'por•tun'ism, *n.* unprincipled use of opportunities. —**op'por•tun'ist,** *n.* —**op'por•tun•is'tic,** *adj.*

op'por•tu'ni•ty, *n., pl.* **-ties.** temporary possible advantage.

op•pose' (ə pōz') *v.,* **-posed, -posing. 1.** resist or compete with. **2.** hinder. **3.** set as an obstacle. **4.** cause to disfavor something. —**op'po•si'tion,** *n.*

op'po•site (op'ə zit, -sit) *adj.* **1.** in corresponding position on other side. **2.** completely different. —*n.* **3.** one that is opposite.

op•press' (ə pres') *v.* **1.** weigh down. **2.** treat harshly as a matter of policy. —**op•pres'sion** (ə presh'ən) *n.* —**op•pres'sive,** *adj.* —**op•pres'sor,** *n.*

op•pro'bri•um (ə prō'brē əm) *n.* disgrace and reproach. —**op•pro'bri•ous,** *adj.*

OPr Old Provençal.

opr 1. operate. **2.** operator.

oprg operating.

oprs oil pressure.

OPruss Old Prussian.

OPS Office of Price Stabilization. Also, **O.P.S.**

opt (opt) *v.* make a choice.

op′tic (op′tik) *adj.* of eyes.

op′ti•cal, *adj.* **1.** acting by means of sight and light. **2.** made to assist sight. **3.** visual. **4.** of optics. —**op′ti•cal•ly,** *adv.*

optical disc, disk on which digital data is stored and read by laser.

optical scanner, device for scanning and digitizing printed material.

op•ti′cian (op tish′ən) *n.* eyeglass maker.

op′tics, *n.* branch of science dealing with light and vision.

op′ti•mal, *adj.* optimum.

op′ti•mism′ (op′tə miz′əm) *n.* **1.** disposition to hope for best. **2.** belief that good will prevail over evil. —**op′ti•mist,** *n.* —**op′ti•mis′- tic,** *adj.*

op′ti•mum (-məm) *adj., n.* best.

op′tion (op′shən) *n.* **1.** power of choosing. **2.** choice made. —**op′tion•al,** *adj.*

optl optional.

op•tom′e•try (op tom′i trē) *n.* art of testing eyes for eyeglasses. —**op•tom′e•trist,** *n.*

opty opportunity.

op′u•lent (op′yə lənt) *adj.* wealthy. —**op′u• lence,** *n.*

o′pus (ō′pəs) *n., pl.* **op•er•a** (op′ər ə, op′rə). work, esp. musical, usually numbered.

or (ôr; *unstressed* ər) *conj.* (used to connect alternatives).

OR, 1. operating room. **2.** Oregon.

-or, suffix meaning condition or quality, as *pallor*; person or thing that does something, as *orator*.

or′a•cle (ôr′ə kəl) *n.* **1.** answer by the gods to question. **2.** medium giving the answer. —**o•rac′u•lar** (ô rak′yə lər) *adj.*

o′ral (ôr′əl) *adj.* **1.** spoken. **2.** of mouths. —**o′ral•ly,** *adv.*

or′ange (ôr′inj) *n.* **1.** round, reddish-yellow citrus fruit. **2.** reddish yellow.

or′ange•ade′ (-ād′) *n.* drink with base of orange juice.

o•rang′u•tan′ (ô rang′ŏŏ tan′, ə rang′-) *n.* large, long-armed ape. Also, **o•rang′ou• tang′** (-tang′), **o•rang′.**

o•rate′ (ô rāt′, ôr′āt) *v.,* **-rated, -rating.** deliver an oration.

o•ra′tion, *n.* formal speech.

or′a•tor (ôr′ə tər) *n.* eloquent public speaker.

or′a•to′ri•o (-tôr′ē ō′) *n., pl.* **-rios.** religious work for voices and orchestra in dramatic form.

or′a•to′ry, *n., pl.* **-ries. 1.** eloquent speaking. **2.** small room for prayer. —**or′a•tor′i•cal** (ôr′ə tôr′-) *adj.*

orb (ôrb) *n.* **1.** sphere. **2.** any of heavenly bodies.

or′bit (ôr′bit) *n.* **1.** path of planet, etc., around another body. **2.** cavity in skull for eyeball. —*v.* **3.** travel in or send into orbit. —**or′bit•al,** *adj.*

O.R.C. Officers' Reserve Corps.

orch. orchestra.

or′chard (ôr′chərd) *n.* plot of fruit trees.

or′ches•tra (ôr′kə strə, -kes trə) *n.* **1.** *Music.* large company of instrumental performers. **2.** space in theater for musicians. **3.** main floor of theater. —**or•ches′tral,** *adj.*

or′ches•trate′ (ôr′kə strāt′) *v.,* **-trated, -trating. 1.** arrange music for orchestra. **2.** arrange elements of. —**or′ches•tra′tion,** *n.*

or′chid (ôr′kid) *n.* **1.** tropical plant with oddly shaped blooms. **2.** light purple.

ord. 1. Also, **ord** order. **2.** ordinal. **3.** ordinance. **4.** ordinary. **5.** ordnance.

or•dain′ (ôr dān′) *v.* **1.** invest as a member of the clergy. **2.** appoint or direct.

or•deal′ (ôr dēl′, ôr′dēl) *n.* severe test.

or′der (ôr′dər) *n.* **1.** authoritative command. **2.** harmonious arrangement. **3.** group bound by common religious rules. **4.** list of items desired. —*v.* **5.** give an order. **6.** arrange.

or′der•ly, *adj., adv., n., pl.* **-lies.** —*adj.* **1.** methodical. **2.** well-behaved. —*adv.* **3.** according to rule. —*n.* **4.** hospital attendant. —**or′der•li•ness,** *n.*

or′di•nal (ôr′dn əl) *adj.* **1.** showing position in series, as *first, second,* etc. —*n.* **2.** ordinal number.

or′di•nance (ôr′dn əns) *n.* law.

or′di•nar′y (-dn er′ē) *adj., n., pl.* **-ies.** —*adj.* **1.** usual; normal. —*n.* **2.** ordinary condition, etc. —**or′di•nar′i•ly,** *adv.*

or′di•na′tion (ôr′dn ā′shən) *n.* act or ceremony of ordaining. Also, **or•dain′ment.**

ordn. ordnance.

ord′nance (ôrd′nəns) *n.* military weapons of all kinds.

Or′do•vi′cian (ôr′də vish′ən) *adj.* pertaining to geologic period of Paleozoic era.

or′dure (ôr′jər, -dyŏŏr) *n.* dung.

ore (ôr) *n.* metal-bearing rock.

Ore., Oregon.

Oreg. Oregon.

o•reg′a•no (ə reg′ə nō′) *n.* plant with leaves used as seasoning.

orf orifice.

org. 1. organic. **2.** organization. **3.** organized.

or′gan (ôr′gən) *n.* **1.** large musical keyboard instrument sounded by air forced through pipes, etc. **2.** part of animal or plant with specific function. **3.** means of communication. —**or′gan•ist,** *n.*

or′gan•dy (ôr′gən dē) *n., pl.* **-dies.** thin stiff cotton fabric.

or′gan•elle′ (ôr′gə nel′) *n.* specialized cell structure.

or•gan′ic (ôr gan′ik) *adj.* **1.** of carbon compounds. **2.** of living organisms. **3.** of animals or produce raised or grown without synthetic fertilizers, pesticides, etc. —or•gan/i•cal•ly, *adv.*

or/gan•ism (-gə niz/əm) *n.* anything living or formerly alive.

or/gan•ize/ (-gə nīz) *v.*, -ized, -izing. form into coordinated whole; systematize. —or/•gan•i•za/tion, *n.* —or/gan•iz/er, *n.* —or/•gan•i•za/tion•al, *adj.*

or•gan/za (ôr gan/zə) *n.* sheer fabric of rayon, nylon, or silk.

or/gasm (ôr/gaz əm) *n.* sexual climax.

or/gy (ôr/jē) *n.*, *pl.* -gies. wild revelry. —or/•gi•as/tic (-as/tik) *adj.*

o/ri•el (ôr/ē əl) *n.* bay window.

o/ri•ent *n.* (ôr/ē ənt, -ē ent/) **1.** (*cap.*) countries of Asia. —*v.* (ôr/ē ent/) **2.** set facing certain way. **3.** inform about one's situation. —O/ri•en/tal, *adj.* —o/ri•en•ta/tion, *n.*

o/ri•en•teer/ing (-tēr/ing) *n.* sport of navigating unknown terrain.

or/i•fice (ôr/ə fis) *n.* opening.

orig. **1.** origin. **2.** original. **3.** originally.

o/ri•ga/mi (ôr/i gä/mē) *n.* Japanese art of folding paper into decorative or representational forms.

or/i•gin (ôr/i jin) *n.* **1.** source. **2.** beginning. **3.** circumstances of birth or ancestry.

o•rig/i•nal (ə rij/ə nl) *adj.* **1.** first. **2.** novel. **3.** being new work. **4.** capable of creating something original. —*n.* **5.** primary form. **6.** thing copied. **7.** beginning. —o•rig/i•nal/i•ty (-nal/i tē) *n.*

o•rig/i•nal•ly, *adv.* **1.** at first. **2.** in original manner.

o•rig/i•nate/, *v.*, -nated, -nating. **1.** come to be. **2.** give origin to. —o•rig/i•na/tor, *n.* —o•rig/i•na/tion, *n.*

o/ri•ole/ (ôr/ē ōl/) *n.* bright-colored bird of Europe and America.

or/i•son (ôr/i zən) *n.* prayer.

Or/lon (ôr/lon) *n. Trademark.* synthetic fabric resembling nylon.

or/mo•lu/ (ôr/mə lōō/) *n.*, *pl.* -lus. copper-zinc alloy.

orn orange.

or/na•ment *n.* (ôr/nə mənt) **1.** something added to beautify. —*v.* (-ment/, -mənt) **2.** adorn; decorate. —or/na•men/tal, *adj.* —or/na•men•ta/tion, *n.*

or•nate/ (ôr nāt/) *adj.* lavish. —or•nate/ly, *adv.*

or/ner•y (ôr/nə rē) *adj. Informal.* ill-tempered.

ornith. **1.** ornithological. **2.** ornithology.

ornithol. **1.** ornithological. **2.** ornithology.

or/ni•thol/o•gy (ôr/nə thol/ə jē) *n.* study of birds. —or/ni•thol/o•gist, *n.* —or/ni•tho•log/i•cal (-thə loj/i kəl) *adj.*

o/ro•tund/ (ôr/ə tund/) *adj.* **1.** rich and clear in voice. **2.** pompous; bombastic.

or/phan (ôr/fən) *n.* **1.** child whose parents

are both dead. —*adj.* **2.** of or for orphans. —*v.* **3.** bereave of parents.

or/phan•age (-fə nij) *n.* home for orphans.

or/ris (ôr/is) *n.* kind of iris.

ORT Registered Occupational Therapist.

Orth. Orthodox.

orth. **1.** orthopedic **2.** orthopedics.

or/tho•don/tics (ôr/thə don/tiks) *n.* branch of dentistry dealing with irregular teeth. Also, or/tho•don/tia (-don/shə). —or/tho•don/•tic, *adj.* —or/tho•don/tist, *n.*

or/tho•dox/ (ôr/thə doks/) *adj.* **1.** sound and correct in doctrine. **2.** conventional. **3.** (*cap.*) of Christian churches common in eastern Europe. —or/tho•dox/y, *n.*

or•thog/ra•phy (ôr thog/rə fē) *n.*, *pl.* -phies. spelling. —or/tho•graph/ic (ôr/thə•graf/ik), or/tho•graph/i•cal, *adj.*

or/tho•pe/dics (ôr/thə pē/diks) *n.* branch of medicine dealing with the skeletal system. —or/tho•pe/dist, *n.* —or/tho•pe/dic, *adj.*

ORuss Old Russian.

ORV off-road vehicle.

-ory, suffix meaning: **1.** of, characterized by, or serving to, as *excretory*. **2.** place or instrument for, as *crematory*.

OS **1.** Old Saxon. **2.** *Computers.* operating system.

Os *Symbol, Chemistry.* osmium.

O/S (of the calendar) Old Style.

o/s **1.** (of the calendar) Old Style. **2.** out of stock. **3.** *Banking.* outstanding.

O.S. **1.** (in prescriptions) the left eye. [from Latin *oculus sinister*] **2.** Old Saxon. **3.** Old School. **4.** old series. **5.** (of the calendar) Old Style. **6.** ordinary seaman.

o.s. **1.** (in prescriptions) the left eye. [from Latin *oculus sinister*] **2.** ordinary seaman.

O.S.A. Order of St. Augustine.

O.S.B. Order of St. Benedict.

osc oscillator.

os/cil•late/ (os/ə lāt/) *v.*, -lated, -lating. swing to and fro. —os/cil•la/tion, *n.* —os/•cil•la/tor, *n.*

os•cil/lo•scope/ (ə sil/ə skōp/) *n.* device that uses cathode-ray tube to display changes in electric quantity.

os/cu•late/ (os/kyə lāt/) *v.*, -lated, -lating. kiss. —os/cu•la/tion, *n.* —os/cu•la•to/ry (-lə tôr/ē) *adj.*

OSD Office of the Secretary of Defense.

O.S.D. Order of St. Dominic.

O.S.F. Order of St. Francis.

OSFCW Office of Solid Fuels Coordinator for War.

OSHA (ō/shə, osh/ə), the division of the Department of Labor that sets and enforces occupational health and safety rules. [O(ccupational) S(afety and) H(ealth) A(dministration)]

o/sier (ō/zhər) *n.* tough flexible twig used in wickerwork.

-osis, suffix meaning: **1.** action or condition,

as *osmosis*. **2.** abnormal state, as *tuberculosis*.

osl oil seal.

os'mi•um (oz'mē əm) *n.* hard, heavy metallic element used in alloys.

os•mo'sis (oz mō'sis, os-) *n.* diffusion of liquid through membrane.

osmv *Electronics.* one-shot multivibrator.

OSO *U.S. Aerospace.* Orbiting Solar Observatory.

OSP died without issue. [from Latin *obiit sine prōle*]

OSp Old Spanish.

os'prey (os'prē, -prā) *n.* large hawk.

OSRD Office of Scientific Research and Development.

OSS Office of Strategic Services: a U.S. government intelligence agency during World War II. Also, **O.S.S.**

os'se•ous (os'ē əs) *adj.* of, like, or containing bone.

os'si•fy' (os'ə fī') *v.,* **-fied, -fying.** make or become bone. **—os'si•fi•ca'tion,** *n.*

os•ten'si•ble (o sten'sə bəl) *adj.* merely apparent or pretended. **—os•ten'si•bly,** *adv.*

os'ten•ta'tion (os'ten tā'shən, -tən-) *n.* pretentious display. **—os'ten•ta'tious,** *adj.*

os'te•o•ar•thri'tis (os'tē ō är thrī'tis) *n.* arthritis marked by decay of cartilage in joints.

os'te•op'a•thy (os'tē op'ə thē) *n.* treatment of disease by manipulating affected part. **—os'te•o•path'** (-ə path') *n.* **—os'te•o•path'ic,** *adj.*

os'te•o•po•ro'sis (os'tē ō pə rō'sis) *n.* disorder in which bones become increasingly brittle, porous, and prone to fracture.

os'tra•cize' (os'trə sīz') *v.,* **-cized, -cizing.** exclude from society; banish. **—os'tra•cism** (-siz'əm) *n.*

os'trich (ô'strich) *n.* large, swift-footed, flightless bird.

OT 1. occupational therapist. **2.** occupational therapy. **3.** *Bible.* Old Testament. **4.** overnight telegram. **5.** overtime.

O.T. Old Testament (of the Bible).

o.t. overtime.

OTA Office of Technology Assessment.

OTB offtrack betting.

OTC 1. Also, **O.T.C.** Officers' Training Corps. **2.** over-the-counter.

oth'er (uth'ər) *adj.* **1.** additional. **2.** different. **3.** or remaining. **4.** former. **—pron. 5.** other person or thing.

oth'er•wise', *adv.* **1.** in other ways or circumstances. **—adj. 2.** of other sort.

oth'er•world'ly, *adj.* concerned with spiritual or imaginary world.

o'ti•ose' (ō'shē ōs', ō'tē-) *adj.* **1.** idle. **2.** futile.

OTS Officers' Training School. Also, **O.T.S.**

ot'ter (ot'ər) *n.* aquatic mammal.

ot'to•man (ot'ə mən) *n.* low, cushioned seat.

OU (in prescriptions) **1.** both eyes. [from Latin *oculi uterque*] **2.** each eye. [from Latin *oculus uterque*]

ought (ôt) *aux. v.* **1.** be bound by obligation or reasoning. **—n. 2.** cipher (0).

ounce (ouns) *n.* unit of weight equal to $\frac{1}{16}$ lb. avoirdupois or $\frac{1}{12}$ lb. troy.

our (ou°r, ou'ər; *unstressed* är) *pron.* possessive form of **we,** used before noun.

ours, *pron.* possessive form of **we,** used predicatively.

our•selves', *pron.* **1.** reflexive substitute for **us. 2.** intensive with or substitute for **we** or **us.**

-ous, suffix meaning full of or characterized by.

oust (oust) *v.* eject; force out.

oust'er, *n.* ejection.

out (out) *adv.* **1.** away from some place. **2.** so as to emerge or project. **3.** until conclusion. **4.** to depletion. **5.** so as to be extinguished, etc. **—adj. 6.** away from some place. **7.** extinguished, etc. **—prep. 8.** out from. **9.** away along. **—n. 10.** means of evasion.

out-, prefix meaning: **1.** outward, as *outburst.* **2.** outside, as *outbuilding.* **3.** surpass, as *outlast.*

out'age (ou'tij) *n.* interruption or failure in supply of power.

out'-and-out', *adj.* utter; thorough.

out'back', *n.* remote area.

outbd outboard.

out'board', *adj., adv.* on exterior of ship or boat.

out'bound', *adj.* headed for the open sea.

out'break', *n.* **1.** sudden occurrence. **2.** riot.

out'build'ing, *n.* detached building subordinate to main building.

out'burst', *n.* bursting forth.

out'cast', *n.* exiled or rejected person.

out'class', *v.* outdo in style or excellence.

out'come', *n.* consequence.

out'crop', *n.* emerging stratum at earth's surface.

out'cry', *n., pl.* **-cries.** expression of distress or protest.

out•dat'ed, *adj.* obsolete.

out•dis'tance, *v.,* **-tanced, -tancing.** leave behind, as in racing.

out•do', *v.,* **-did, -done, -doing.** surpass.

out'door', *adj.* done or occurring in open air. **—out'doors',** *adv., n.*

out'er, *adj.* **1.** farther out. **2.** on outside.

out'er•most', *adj.* farthest out.

outer space, 1. space beyond the earth's atmosphere. **2.** space beyond the solar system.

out'er•wear', *n.* garments worn over other clothing.

out'field', *n.* part of baseball field beyond diamond. **—out'field'er,** *n.*

out'fit', *n., v.,* **-fitted, -fitting. —n. 1.** set of articles for any purpose. **2.** organized group of persons. **—v. 3.** equip. **—out'fit'ter,** *n.*

out′flank′, *v.* go beyond flank.

out′fox′, *v.* outsmart.

outg outgoing.

out′go′, *n., pl.* **-goes.** expenditure.

out′go′ing *adj.* **1.** (-gō′ing) departing. **2.** (-gō′ing) retiring from a position or office. **3.** (-gō′ing, -gō′-) friendly; sociable.

out′grow′, *v.,* **-grew, -grown, -growing.** grow too large or mature for.

out′growth′, *n.* **1.** natural result. **2.** offshoot.

out′house′, *n.* separate building serving as toilet.

out′ing, *n.* pleasure trip.

out•land′ish (-lan′dish) *adj.* strange.

out′last′, *v.* endure after.

out′law′, *n.* **1.** habitual criminal, esp. a fugitive. **2.** person excluded from protection of law. **—***v.* **3.** prohibit by law. **4.** deny protection of law to. **—out′law′ry,** *n.*

out′lay′, *n.* expenditure.

out′let (-let, -lit) *n.* **1.** opening or passage out. **2.** market for goods.

out′line′, *n., v.,* **-lined, -lining. —***n.* **1.** line by which object is bounded. **2.** drawing showing only outer contour. **3.** general description. **—***v.* **4.** draw or represent in outline.

out′live′ (-liv′) *v.,* **-lived, -living.** live longer than.

out′look′, *n.* **1.** view from place. **2.** mental view. **3.** prospect.

out′ly′ing, *adj.* remote.

out′mod′ed (-mō′did) *adj.* obsolete.

out•num′ber, *v.* be more numerous than.

out′-of-bod′y, *adj.* characterized by sensation that the mind has left the body.

out′-of-date′, *adj.* obsolete.

out′-of-doors′, *adj.* **1.** outdoor. **—***n.* **2.** outdoors.

out′-of-the-way′, *adj.* **1.** isolated. **2.** unusual.

out′pa′tient, *n.* patient visiting hospital to receive treatment.

out′place′ment, *n.* assistance in finding new job, provided by company for employee being let go.

out′post′, *n.* **1.** sentinel station away from main army. **2.** place away from main area.

out′put′, *n.* **1.** production. **2.** quantity produced.

out′rage, *n., v.,* **-raged, -raging. —***n.* **1.** gross violation. **—***v.* **2.** subject to outrage. **—out•ra′geous** (-rā′jəs) *adj.*

ou•tré′ (ōō trā′) *adj.* unconventional; bizarre.

out′reach′ *v.* (out′rēch′) **1.** exceed. **2.** reach out. **—***n.* (out′rēch′) **3.** act of reaching out. **—***adj.* (out′rēch′) **4.** concerned with extending services.

out′rig′ger (-rig′ər) *n.* framework supporting float extended from side of boat.

out′right′ *adj.* (-rīt′) **1.** utter; thorough.

—*adv.* (-rīt′, -rīt′) **2.** without concealment; completely.

out′run′, *v.,* **-ran, -run, -running. 1.** run faster or farther than. **2.** exceed.

out′sell′, *v.,* **-sold, -selling.** exceed in number of sales.

out′set′, *n.* beginning.

out′shine′, *v.,* **-shone** or -shined, -shining. **1.** shine more brightly than. **2.** surpass in excellence.

out′side′ *n.* (out′sīd′, -sīd′) **1.** outer side, aspect, etc. **2.** space beyond enclosure. **—***adj.* (out′sīd′, out′-) **3.** being, done, etc., on the outside. **—***adv.* (out′sīd′) **4.** on or to the outside. **—***prep.* (out′sīd′, out′sīd′) **5.** at the outside of.

out•sid′er, *n.* person not belonging.

out′skirts′, *n.pl.* bordering parts.

out′smart′, *v.* outwit.

out′spo′ken, *adj.* candid.

out′spread′, *adj.* extended.

out′stand′ing, *adj.* **1.** prominent. **2.** not yet paid.

out′strip′, *v.,* **-stripped, -stripping. 1.** excel. **2.** outdistance.

out′take′, *n.* segment of film or recording edited from published version.

out′ward (-wərd) *adj.* **1.** external. **—***adv.* **2.** Also, **out′wards.** toward the outside. **—out′ward•ly,** *adv.*

out′weigh′, *v.* exceed in importance.

out′wit′, *v.,* **-witted, -witting.** defeat by superior cleverness.

out•worn′, *adj.* **1.** no longer vital or appropriate. **2.** useless because of wear.

ov over.

o′va (ō′və) *n.* pl. of ovum.

o′val (ō′vəl) *adj.* egg-shaped; elliptical.

o′va•ry (ō′və rē) *n., pl.* **-ries.** female reproductive gland. **—o•var′i•an** (ō vâr′ē ən) *adj.*

o′vate (ō′vāt) *adj.* egg-shaped.

o•va′tion (ō vā′shən) *n.* enthusiastic applause.

ovbd overboard.

ov′en (uv′ən) *n.* chamber for baking or drying.

o′ver (ō′vər) *prep.* **1.** above in place, authority, etc. **2.** on. **3.** across; through. **4.** in excess of. **5.** concerning. **6.** during. **—***adv.* **7.** so as to affect whole surface. **8.** above. **9.** again. **—***adj.* **10.** finished. **11.** remaining. **12.** upper. **13.** surplus.

o′ver•a•chieve′, *v.,* **-chieved, -chieving.** perform better than expected, esp. in school. **—o′ver•a•chiev′er,** *n.*

o′ver•act′, *v.* perform in an exaggerated manner.

o′ver•age (ō′vər ij) *n.* **1.** surplus. **—***adj.* (ō′vər āj′) **2.** beyond desirable age.

o′ver•all′ (ō′vər ôl′) *adj.* **1.** including everything. **—***n.* **2.** (*pl.*) loose, stout trousers.

o′ver•awe′, *v.,* **-awed, -awing.** dominate with impressiveness or force.

o'ver·bear'ing, *adj.* arrogant; domineering.

o'ver·bite', *n.* occlusion in which upper incisor teeth overlap lower ones.

o'ver·blown', *adj.* **1.** overdone; excessive. **2.** pretentious.

o'ver·board', *adv.* over side of ship into water.

o'ver·cast' (-kast', -kast') *adj.* **1.** cloudy. **2.** gloomy.

o'ver·charge', *v.,* **-charged, -charging. 1.** charge too high a price. **2.** overload. —*n.* (ō'vər chärj') **3.** charge exceeding fair price. **4.** excessive load.

o'ver·coat', *n.* coat worn over ordinary clothing.

o'ver·come', *v.,* **-came, -come, -coming.** defeat; overpower.

o'ver·do', *v.,* **-did, -done, -doing. 1.** do to excess. **2.** exaggerate.

o'ver·dose', *n., v.,* **-dosed, -dosing.** —*n.* **1.** excessive dose. —*v.* **2.** take such a dose.

o'ver·draw', *v.,* **-drew, -drawn, -drawing.** draw upon in excess of. —**o'ver·draft',** *n.*

o'ver·drive', *n.* arrangement of gears providing propeller speed greater than engine crankshaft speed.

o'ver·due', *adj.* due some time before.

o'ver·flow' *v.,* **-flowed, -flown, -flowing.** *n.* —*v.* (ō'vər flō') **1.** flow or run over; flood. —*n.* (ō'vər flō') **2.** instance of flooding. **3.** something that runs over.

o'ver·grow', *v.,* **-grew, -grown, -growing.** cover with growth.

o'ver·hand', *adv.* with hand above shoulder.

o'ver·hang' *v.,* **-hung, -hanging,** *n.* —*v.* (ō'vər hang') **1.** project over. **2.** threaten. —*n.* (ō'vər hang') **3.** projection.

o'ver·haul' *v.* (ō'vər hôl', ō'vər hôl') **1.** investigate thoroughly, as for repair. **2.** overtake. —*n.* (ō'vər hôl') **3.** complete examination.

o'ver·head' *adv.* (ō'ver hed') **1.** aloft. —*n.* (ō'vər hed') **2.** general business expense.

o'ver·hear', *v.,* **-heard, -hearing.** hear without speaker's intent.

o'ver·joyed' (-joid') *adj.* very happy.

o'ver·kill', *n.* **1.** *Mil.* ability to kill more than is needed for victory. **2.** any greatly excessive amount.

o'ver·land' (-land', -lənd) *adv., adj.* across open country.

o'ver·lap' *v.,* **-lapped, -lapping,** *n.* —*v.* (ō'vər lap') **1.** extend over and beyond. —*n.* (ō'vər lap') **2.** overlapping part.

o'ver·lay', *v.,* **-laid, -laying,** *n.* —*v.* **1.** spread over. —*n.* **2.** something used in overlaying.

o'ver·lie', *v.* **-lay, -lain, -lying.** lie over or on.

o'ver·look', *v.* **1.** fail to notice. **2.** afford view over.

o'ver·ly, *adv. Informal.* excessively.

o'ver·night' *adv.* (-nīt') **1.** during the night.

2. on previous night. —*adj.* (-nīt') **3.** done, made, etc., during the night. **4.** staying for one night.

o'ver·pass', *n.* bridge crossing other traffic.

o'ver·play', *v.* exaggerate.

o'ver·pow'er, *v.* **1.** overwhelm in feeling. **2.** subdue.

o'ver·qual'i·fied', *adj.* having more education or experience than required.

o'ver·rate', *v.,* **-rated, -rating.** esteem too highly.

o'ver·reach', *v.* **1.** extend beyond. **2.** defeat (oneself), as by excessive eagerness.

o'ver·re·act', *v.* react too emotionally. —**o'ver·re·ac'tion,** *n.*

o'ver·ride', *v.,* **-rode, -ridden, -riding.** prevail over; supersede.

o'ver·rule', *v.,* **-ruled, -ruling.** rule against.

o'ver·run', *v.,* **-ran, -run, -running. 1.** swarm over. **2.** overgrow.

o'ver·seas', *adv.* over or across the sea.

o'ver·see', *v.,* **-saw, -seen, -seeing.** supervise. —**o'ver·se'er,** *n.*

o'ver·shad'ow, *v.* be more important than.

o'ver·shoe', *n.* protective shoe worn over another shoe.

o'ver·shoot', *v.,* **-shot, -shooting. 1.** shoot over so as to miss. **2.** go beyond.

o'ver·sight', *n.* **1.** error of neglect. **2.** supervision.

o'ver·sleep', *v.,* **-slept, -sleeping.** sleep beyond desired time.

o'ver·state', *v.,* **-stated, -stating.** exaggerate in describing. —**o'ver·state'ment,** *n.*

o'ver·stay', *v.,* **-stayed, -staying.** stay too long.

o'ver·step', *v.,* **-stepped, -stepping.** exceed.

o'ver·stuffed', *adj.* (of furniture) having the frame padded and covered.

o·vert' (ō vûrt', ō'vûrt) *adj.* **1.** not concealed. **2.** giving perceptible cause or provocation.

o'ver·take', *v.,* **-took, -taken, -taking.** catch up with.

o'ver-the-count'er, *adj.* **1.** not listed on or traded through an organized securities exchange. **2.** sold legally without a prescription.

o'ver·throw' *v.,* **-threw, -thrown, -throwing,** *n.* —*v.* (ō'vər thrō') **1.** defeat; put end to. —*n.* (ō'vər thrō') **2.** act of overthrowing.

o'ver·time', *n.* time worked in addition to regular hours. —**o'ver·time',** *adv., adj.*

o'ver·tone', *n.* **1.** additional meaning. **2.** musical tone added to basic tone.

o'ver·ture (ō'vər chər, -chŏŏr') *n.* **1.** offer. **2.** musical prelude to opera, etc.

o'ver·turn', *v.* **1.** tip off base. **2.** defeat.

o'ver·view', *n.* overall perception or description.

o'ver·ween'ing (-wē'ning) *adj.* **1.** conceited. **2.** excessive.

o'ver·weight', *n.* **1.** excess of weight.

—*adj.* (ō′vər wāt′) **2.** weighing more than is normal.

o′ver•whelm′ (-hwelm′, -welm′) *v.* **1.** weigh upon overpoweringly; crush. **2.** stun.

o′ver•work′, *v.*, **-worked** or **-wrought, -working**, *n.* —*v.* (ō′ver wûrk′) **1.** work too hard. —*n.* (ō′vər wûrk′) **2.** work beyond one's strength.

o′ver•wrought′ (ō′vər rôt′, ō′vər-) *adj.* highly excited.

ovh oval head.

ovhd overhead.

ovhl overhaul.

o′vi•duct′ (ō′vi dukt′) *n.* tube through which ova are transported.

o•vip′a•rous (ō vip′ər əs) *adj.* producing eggs that hatch outside body.

OV language (ō′vē′), *Linguistics.* a type of language that has direct objects preceding the verb. [*O(bject)*-*V(erb)*]

ovld overload.

o′void′ (ō′void) *adj.* egg-shaped.

ovp oval point.

ovrd override.

ovsz oversize.

ovtr overtravel.

ov′u•late (ov′yə lāt′, ō′vyə-) *v.*, **-lated, -lating.** produce and discharge eggs (ova) from ovary. —**ov′u•la′tion**, *n.*

ov′ule (ov′yōol, ō′vyōol) *n.* **1.** structure that develops into seed. **2.** small egg.

o′vum (ō′vəm) *n.*, *pl.* **ova** (ō və). female reproductive cell.

ovv overvoltage.

OW Old Welsh.

owe (ō) *v.*, **owed, owing.** be obligated to pay or give to another.

OWI 1. Office of War Information: the U.S federal agency (1942–45) charged with disseminating information about World War II. **2.** operating (a motor vehicle) while intoxicated.

owl (oul) *n.* nocturnal bird of prey. —**owl′-ish**, *adj.*

owl′et, *n.* small owl.

own (ōn) *adj.* **1.** of or belonging to. —*v.* **2.** possess. **3.** acknowledge. —**own′er**, *n.* —**own′er•ship′**, *n.*

ox (oks) *n.*, *pl.* **oxen.** adult castrated male bovine.

ox′blood′, *n.* deep, dull red color.

ox′ bow′ (-bō′) *n.* U-shaped part of yoke placed under and around neck of ox.

oxd oxidized.

ox′ford (oks′fərd) *n.* low shoe laced over instep.

ox′i•dant (ok′si dənt) *n.* chemical agent that oxidizes.

ox′ide (ok′sīd, -sid) *n.* compound of oxygen and another element.

ox′i•dize′ (ok′si dīz′) *v.*, **-dized, -dizing. 1.** add oxygen to. **2.** rust. —**ox′i•di•za′tion, ox′i•da′tion**, *n.*

Oxon. 1. Oxford. [from Latin *Oxonia*] **2.** of Oxford. [from Latin *Oxoniēnsis*]

ox′y•a•cet′y•lene′ (ok′sē ə set′l ēn′, -in) *adj.* denoting a mixture of oxygen and acetylene used for cutting and welding steel.

ox′y•gen (ok′si jən) *n.* colorless, odorless gas necessary to life and fire.

ox′y•gen•ate′ (-jə nāt′) *v.*, **-ated, -ating.** enrich with oxygen. —**ox′y•gen•a′tion**, *n.*

ox′y•mo′ron (ok′si môr′on) *n.*, *pl.* **-mora.** figure of speech that uses seeming contradictions.

oys′ter (oi′stər) *n.* edible, irregularly shaped mollusk.

oz., ounce.

oz. av. ounce avoirdupois.

o′zone (ō′zōn, ō zōn′) *n.* form of oxygen in upper atmosphere.

ozone hole, part of ozone layer depleted by atmospheric pollution.

ozone layer, layer of upper atmosphere where most ozone is concentrated.

ozs. ounces.

oz. t. ounce troy.

P

P, p (pē) *n.* sixteenth letter of English alphabet.

PA, 1. Also, **Pa.** Pennsylvania. **2.** public-address system.

PABA (pä′bə), *Chemistry, Biochemistry.* a crystalline solid, $C_7H_7NO_2$, used especially in pharmaceuticals. [*p(ara-)a(mino)b(enzoic) a(cid)*]

pab′lum (pab′ləm) *n.* simplistic ideas.

PABX *Telephones.* an automatically operated PBX. Also, **pabx** [*p(rivate) a(utomatic) b(ranch) ex(change)*]

PAC (pak) *n., pl.* **PACs, PAC's.** political action committee.

pace (pās) *n., v.,* **paced, pacing.** —*n.* **1.** rate of movement or progress. **2.** linear measure. **3.** step or gait. —*v.* **4.** set pace for. **5.** step regularly. —**pac′er,** *n.*

pace′mak′er, *n.* **1.** one that sets pace. **2.** electrical device for controlling heartbeat.

pace′set′ter, *n.* leader.

pach′y•derm′ (pak′i dûrm′) *n.* thick-skinned mammal, as the elephant.

pach′y•san′dra (pak′ə san′drə) *n., pl.* -dras. low plant used as ground cover.

pa•cif′ic (pə sif′ik) *adj.* peaceful.

pac′i•fism (pas′ə fiz′əm) *n.* principle of abstention from violence. —**pac′i•fist,** *n.* —**pa′ci•fis′tic,** *adj.*

pac′i•fy′, *v.,* -fied, -fying. **1.** calm. **2.** appease. —**pac′i•fi′er,** *n.* —**pac′i•fi•ca′tion,** *n.*

pack (pak) *n.* **1.** bundle. **2.** group or complete set. —*v.* **3.** make into compact mass. **4.** fill with objects. **5.** cram. —**pack′er,** *n.*

pack′age (-ij) *n., v.,* -aged, -aging. —*n.* **1.** bundle; parcel. **2.** container. —*v.* **3.** put into package.

pack′et *n.* **1.** small package. **2.** passenger boat, esp. with fixed route.

pack rat, 1. rat that carries off shiny articles to its nest. **2.** *Informal.* person who saves useless items.

pacm pulse amplitude code modulation.

pact (pakt) *n.* agreement.

pad (pad) *n., v.,* padded, padding. —*n.* **1.** soft, cushionlike mass. **2.** bound package of writing paper. **3.** dull sound of walking. —*v.* **4.** furnish with padding. **5.** expand with false or useless matter. **6.** walk with dull sound.

pad′ding, *n.* material with which to pad.

pad′dle (pad′l) *n., v.,* -dled, -dling. —*n.* **1.** short oar for two hands. —*v.* **2.** propel with paddle. **3.** play in water.

paddle wheel, wheel for propelling ship.

pad′dock (pad′ək) *n.* field for horses.

pad′dy (pad′ē) *n., pl.* -dies. rice field.

paddy wagon, van for transporting prisoners.

pad′lock′, *n.* **1.** portable lock. —*v.* **2.** lock with padlock. **3.** forbid access to.

pa′dre (pä′drā) *n., pl.* -dres. clergyman.

p. ae. (in prescriptions) equal parts. [from Latin *partēs aequālēs*]

pae′an (pē′ən) *n.* song of praise.

PaG Pennsylvania German.

pa′gan (pā′gən) *n.* **1.** worshiper of idols. —*adj.* **2.** idolatrous; heathen. —**pa′gan•ism,** *n.*

page (pāj) *n., v.,* **paged, paging.** —*n.* **1.** written surface. **2.** boy servant. —*v.* **3.** number pages of. **4.** seek by calling by name.

pag′eant (paj′ənt) *n.* elaborate spectacle. —**pag′eant•ry,** *n.*

pag′i•nate′ (-ə nāt′) *v.,* -nated, -nating. number the pages of (a book, etc.). —**pag′i•na′tion,** *n.*

pa•go′da (pə gō′də) *n.* Far Eastern temple tower, esp. Buddhist.

pail (pāl) *n.* bucket.

pain (pān) *n.* **1.** bodily or mental suffering. **2.** (*pl.*) effort. **3.** penalty. —*v.* **4.** hurt. —**pain′-ful,** *adj.* —**pain′ful•ly,** *adv.* —**pain′less,** *adj.* —**pain′less•ly,** *adv.*

pain′kil′ler, *n.* something, esp. an analgesic, that relieves pain.

pains′tak′ing, *adj.* careful.

paint (pānt) *n.* **1.** liquid coloring matter used as coating. —*v.* **2.** represent in paint. **3.** apply paint to. —**paint′er,** *n.* —**paint′ing,** *n.*

pair (pâr) *n., pl.* **pairs, pair,** *v.* —*n.* **1.** combination of two. —*v.* **2.** arrange in pairs. —Usage. See **couple.**

pais′ley (pāz′lē) *n.* fabric woven in colorful, detailed pattern.

pa•jam′as (pə jä′məz, -jam′əz) *n.pl.* nightclothes.

Pak. Pakistan.

pal (pal) *n. Informal.* comrade.

pal′ace (pal′is) *n.* official residence of sovereign.

pal′a•din (pal′ə din) *n.* heroic champion.

pal′an•quin′ (pal′ən kēn′) *n.* enclosed chair or bed carried on men's shoulders.

pal′at•a•ble (pal′ə tə bəl) *adj.* agreeable to taste.

pal′ate (-it) *n.* **1.** roof of mouth. **2.** sense of taste. —**pal′a•tal,** *adj.*

pa•la′tial (pə lā′shəl) *adj.* splendidly built or furnished. —**pa•la′tial•ly,** *adv.*

pal′a•tine (pal′ə tīn′, -tin) *n.* vassal exercising royal privileges in province. —**pa•lat′i•nate′** (pə lat′n āt′, -it) *n.*

pa•lav′er (pə lav′ər, -lä′vər) *n.* **1.** conference. **2.** flattery. **3.** idle talk.

pale (pāl) *adj.,* paler, palest, *v.,* paled, paling, *n.* —*adj.* **1.** without intensity of color; near-white. **2.** dim. —*v.* **3.** become or make pale. —*n.* **4.** stake; picket. **5.** bounds. **6.** enclosed area.

paleog. paleography.

Pa/le•o•lith/ic (pā/lē ə lith/ik) *adj.* denoting early Stone Age.

paleon. paleontology.

paleontol. paleontology.

pa/le•on•tol/o•gy (-ən tol/ə jē) *n.* science of early life forms, as represented by fossils.

Pa/le•o•zo/ic (-ə zō/ik) *adj.* pertaining to geologic era 570 to 230 million years ago.

pal/ette (pal/it) *n.* board on which painter lays and mixes colors.

pal/frey (pôl/frē) *n., pl.* **-freys.** riding horse.

pal/i•mo/ny (pal/ə mō/nē) *n.* alimony awarded to member of unmarried couple.

pal/imp•sest/ (pal/imp sest/) *n.* manuscript with text erased to make room for other text.

pal/in•drome/ (pal/in drōm/) *n.* word or verse reading the same backward as forward.

pal/ing (pā/ling) *n.* pale fence.

pal/i•sade/ (pal/ə sād/) *n.* **1.** fence of pales. **2.** line of tall cliffs.

pall (pôl) *n.* **1.** cloth spread on coffin. **2.** something gloomy. —*v.* **3.** become wearisome or distasteful.

pall/bear/er, *n.* person who attends the coffin at funeral.

pal/let (pal/it) *n.* **1.** straw mattress. **2.** implement for shaping, used by potters. **3.** projecting lip on pawl.

pal/li•ate/ (pal/ē āt/) *v.,* **-ated, -ating.** mitigate; excuse. —**pal/li•a/tive,** *n., adj.*

pal/lid (pal/id) *adj.* pale.

pal/lor (pal/ər) *n.* paleness.

palm (päm) *n.* **1.** inner surface of hand. **2.** tall, unbranched tropical tree. —*v.* **3.** conceal in palm of hand.

pal•met/to (pal met/ō, päl-, pä-) *n., pl.* **-tos, -toes.** species of palm.

palm/is•try (pä/mə strē) *n.* art of telling fortunes from patters of lines on palms of hands. —**palm/ist,** *n.*

palm/y, *adj.,* **palmier, palmiest.** thriving.

pal/o•mi/no (pal/ə mē/nō) *n., pl.* **-nos.** light-tan horse.

pal/pa•ble (pal/pə bəl) *adj.* obvious; tangible. —**pal/pa•bly,** *adv.*

pal/pate (pal/pāt) *v.,* **-pated, -pating.** examine by touch. —**pal•pa/tion,** *n.*

pal/pi•tate/ (pal/pi tāt/) *v.,* **-tated, -tating.** pulsate with unnatural rapidity. —**pal/pi•ta/tion,** *n.*

pal/sy (pôl/zē) *n., pl.* **-sies,** *v.,* **-sied, -sying.** —*n.* **1.** paralysis. **2.** condition with tremors. —*v.* **3.** afflict with palsy.

pal/try (pôl/trē) *adj.,* **-trier, -triest.** trifling. —**pal/tri•ness,** *n.*

PAM 1. *Aerospace.* payload assist module. **2.** Also, **pam** *Telecommunications.* pulse amplitude modulation.

pam. pamphlet.

pamfm pulse amplitude modulation frequency modulation.

pam/pas (pam/pəz; *attributively* -pəs) *n.* vast South American plains.

pam/per (pam/pər) *v.* indulge; coddle.

pam/phlet (pam/flit) *n.* **1.** thin booklet. **2.** argumentative treatise.

pam/phlet•eer/, *n.* writer of pamphlets.

pan (pan) *n., v.,* **panned, panning.** —*n.* **1.** dish for cooking. —*v.* **2.** wash (gravel, etc.) in seeking gold. **3.** *Informal,* criticize harshly. **4.** film panoramically.

Pan, *n.* Greek god of shepherds.

pan- prefix meaning all.

pan/a•ce/a (pan/ə sē/ə) *n.* cure-all.

pa•nache/ (pə nash/, -näsh/) *n.* grand or flamboyant manner; flair.

pan/cake/, *n.* flat fried batter cake.

pan/chro•mat/ic (pan/krō mat/ik) *adj.* sensitive to all visible colors.

pan/cre•as (pan/krē əs, pang/-) *n.* gland near stomach secreting a digestive fluid. —**pan/cre•at/ic,** *adj.*

pan/da (pan/də) *n.* bearlike animal native to Asia.

pan•dem/ic (pan dem/ik) *adj.* epidemic over large area.

pan/de•mo/ni•um (pan/də mō/nē əm) *n.* uproar.

pan/der (-dər) *n.* **1.** person who caters to base passions of others. —*v.* **2.** act as pander. —**pan/der•er,** *n.*

P. and L. profit and loss. Also, **P. & L,** **p. and l.**

pane (pān) *n.* glass section of window.

pan/e•gyr/ic (pan/i jir/ik, -jī/rik) *n.* eulogy.

pan/el (pan/l) *n., v.,* **-eled, -eling.** —*n.* **1.** bordered section of wall, door, etc. **2.** list of persons called for jury duty. **3.** public discussion group. —*v.* **4.** arrange in or ornament with panels. —**pan/el•ing,** *n.* —**pan/el•ist,** *n.*

pang (pang) *n.* sudden feeling of distress.

pan/han/dle, *v.,* **-dled, -dling.** *Informal,* beg from passersby. —**pan/han/dler,** *n.*

pan/ic (pan/ik) *n.* demoralizing terror. —**pan/ick•y,** *adj.* —**pan/ic-strick/en,** *adj.*

pan/i•cle, *n.* loose flower cluster.

pan/nier (pan/yər, -ē ər) *n.* large basket for carrying goods.

pan/o•ply (pan/ə plē) *n., pl.* **-plies. 1.** impressive display. **2.** suit of armor.

pan/o•ram/a (pan/ə ram/ə, -rä/mə) *n.* **1.** view over wide area. **2.** passing scene. —**pan/o•ram/ic,** *adj.*

pan/sy (pan/zē) *n., pl.* **-sies. 1.** species of violet. **2.** *Brit.* (*Offensive*). homosexual.

pant (pant) *v.* **1.** breathe hard and quickly. **2.** long eagerly.

pan/ta•loons/ (pan/tl ōōnz/) *n.pl. Archaic.* trousers.

pan/the•ism/ (pan/thē iz/əm) *n.* religious belief or philosophical doctrine that identifies

God with the universe. —**pan/the•ist,** *n.*
—**pan/the•is/tic,** *adj.*

pan/the•on (pan/thē on/) *n.* **1.** building with tombs or memorials of a nation's illustrious dead. **2.** heroes of a nation, etc., as a group.

pan/ther (pan/thər) *n.* cougar or leopard.

pan/ties (pan/tēz) *n.pl.* women's underpants. Also, **pan/ty.**

pan/to•graph/ (pan/tə graf/) *n.* instrument for copying traced figures.

pan/to•mime/ (pan/tə mīm/) *n., v.,* **-mimed, -miming.** —*n.* **1.** expression by mute gestures. **2.** play in this form. —*v.* **3.** express in pantomime. —**pan/to•mim/ist,** *n.*

pan/try (pan/trē) *n., pl.* **-tries.** room for kitchen supplies.

pants (pants) *n.pl. Informal.* trousers.

pant/y•hose/, *n.* one-piece stockings plus panties for women.

pant/y•waist, *n.* sissy.

pan/zer (pan/zər) *adj.* **1.** armored. —*n.* **2.** tank or other armored vehicle.

pap (pap) *n.* soft food.

pa/pa (pä/pə, pə pä/) *n. Informal.* father.

pa/pa•cy (pā/pə sē) *n., pl.* **-cies.** office or dignity of the pope.

pa/pal (pā/pəl) *adj.* of the pope.

pa•pa/ya (pə pä/yə) *n.* melonlike tropical American fruit.

pa/per (pā/pər) *n.* **1.** thin fibrous sheet for writing, etc. **2.** document. **3.** treatise. **4.** newspaper. —*v.* **5.** decorate with wallpaper. —*adj.* **6.** of paper. —**pa/per•y,** *adj.*

pa/per•back/, *n.* book cheaply bound in paper.

paper tiger, person or nation that has appearance of power but is actually weak.

paper trail, written record.

pa/per•weight/, *n.* small, heavy object placed on papers to keep them from scattering.

pa/pier-mâ•ché/ (pā/pər mə shā/) *n.* molded paper pulp.

pa•pil/la (pə pil/ə) *n., pl.* **-pil•lae** (-pil/ē). small protuberance on skin. —**pap/il•lar/y** (pap/ə ler/ē) *adj.*

pa/pist (pā/pist) *n., adj. Disparaging.* Roman Catholic. —**pa/pism** (-piz/əm) *n.*

pa•poose/ (pa pōōs/) *n.* North American Indian baby. Also, **pap•poose/.**

pap•ri/ka (pa prē/kə) *n.* spice from pepper plant.

Pap test (pap) test for cancer of the cervix.

pa•py/rus (pə pī/rəs) *n., pl.* **-ri.** tall aquatic plant made into paper by ancient Egyptians.

par (pär) *n.* **1.** equality in value or standing. **2.** average amount, etc. **3.** in golf, standard number of strokes.

para- prefix meaning: **1.** beside, as *paradigm.* **2.** beyond, as *parapsychology.* **3.** auxiliary, as *paralegal.*

par/a•ble (par/ə bəl) *n.* moral allegory.

pa•rab/o•la (pə rab/ə lə) *n.* a U-shaped curve, surface, object, etc. —**par•a•bol/ic** (par/ə bol/ik) *adj.*

par/a•chute/ (par/ə shōōt/) *n., v.,* **-chuted, -chuting.** —*n.* **1.** umbrellalike apparatus used to fall safely through air. —*v.* **2.** drop or fall by parachute. —**par/a•chut/ist,** *n.*

pa•rade/ (pə rād/) *n., v.,* **-raded, -rading.** —*n.* **1.** public procession or assembly for display. —*v.* **2.** march in display. **3.** display ostentatiously. —**pa•rad/er,** *n.*

par/a•digm/ (par/ə dīm/, -dim) *n.* example or pattern. —**par/a•dig•mat/ic** (-dig mat/ik) *adj.*

par/a•dise/ (-dīs/, -dīz/) *n.* **1.** heaven. **2.** garden of Eden. **3.** ideal. —**par/a•di•sa/i•cal,** *adj.*

par/a•dox/ (-doks/) *n.* statement that seems self-contradictory. —**par/a•dox/i•cal,** *adj.*

par. aff. (in prescriptions) to the part affected. [from Latin *pars affecta*]

par/af•fin (-fin) *n.* waxy substance from petroleum, used in candles, etc.

par/a•gon/ (-gon/, -gən) *n.* ideal model.

par/a•graph/ (-graf/) *n.* **1.** unit of written or printed matter, begun on new line. —*v.* **2.** divide into paragraphs.

par/a•keet/ (-kēt/) *n.* small parrot.

par/a•le/gal, *n.* attorney's assistant.

par/al•lax/ (-ə laks/) *n.* apparent displacement of object viewed due to changed position of viewer.

par/al•lel/ (-ə lel/, -ləl) *adj., n., v.,* **-leled, -leling.** —*adj.* **1.** having same direction. **2.** having same characteristics. —*n.* **3.** parallel line or plane. **4.** anything parallel. —*v.* **5.** be parallel to. —**par/al•lel•ism,** *n.*

par/al•lel/o•gram (-lel/ə gram/) *n.* a four-sided figure whose opposite sides are parallel.

pa•ral/y•sis (pə ral/ə sis) *n., pl.* **-ses.** loss of voluntary muscular control. —**par/a•lyt/ic** (par/ə lit/ik) *n., adj.* —**par/a•lyze/,** *v.,* **-lyzed, -lizing.**

par/a•me/ci•um (par/ə mē/shē əm, -sē əm) *n., pl.* **-cia** (-shē ə, -sē ə). protozoan.

par/a•med/ic, *n.* person with paramedical duties.

par/a•med/i•cal, *adj.* of supplementary medicine.

pa•ram/e•ter (pə ram/i tər) *n.* determining factor.

par/a•mil/i•ta•ry (par/ə mil/i ter/ē) *adj.* of organizations operating in place of or in addition to a regular military force.

par/a•mount/ (par/ə mount/) *adj.* greatest; utmost.

par/a•mour/ (par/ə mŏŏr/) *n.* lover of married person.

par/a•noi/a (par/ə noi/ə) *n.* mental disorder marked by systematized delusions ascribing hostile intentions to other persons. —**par/a•noi/ac,** *adj., n.*

par/a•pet (par/ə pit, -pet/) *n.* wall at edge of roof or terrace.

par/a•pher•nal/ia (-fər nãl/yə, -fə-) *n.pl.* **1.** equipment. **2.** belongings.

par/a•phrase/, *v.*, -phrased, -phrasing, *n.* —*v.* **1.** rephrase. —*n.* **2.** such restatement.

par/a•ple/gi•a (-plē/jē ə, -jə) *n.* paralysis of lower part of body. —**par/a•ple/gic** *n.*, *adj.*

par/a•pro•fes/sion•al, *adj.* engaged in profession in partial or secondary capacity. —**par/a•pro•fes/sion•al,** *n.*

par/a•psy•chol/o•gy, *n.* branch of psychology that studies psychic phenomena.

par/a•site/ (par/ə sīt/) *n.* animal or plant that lives on another organism. —**par/a•sit/ic** (-sit/ik) *adj.*

par/a•sol/ (par/ə sôl/) *n.* sun umbrella.

par/a•sym/pa•thet/ic, *adj.* nervous system that functions in opposition to sympathetic system.

par/a•thy/roid gland, small gland that regulates blood levels of calcium and phosphate.

par/a•troops/, *n.* force of soldiers who reach battle by parachuting from planes.

par/boil/ (pär/boil/) *v.* precook.

par/cel (pär/səl) *n.*, *v.*, -celed, -celing. —*n.* **1.** goods wrapped together; bundle. **2.** part. —*v.* **3.** divide.

parch (pärch) *v.* dry by heat.

par•chee/si (pär chē/zē) *n.* game resembling backgammon.

parch/ment (pärch/mənt) *n.* skin of sheep, etc., prepared for writing on.

par/don (pär/dn) *n.* **1.** polite indulgence. **2.** forgiveness. —*v.* **3.** excuse; forgive. —**par/don•a•ble,** *adj.*

pare (pâr) *v.*, pared, paring. cut off outer part of.

par/e•gor/ic (par/i gôr/ik) *n.* soothing medicine.

paren parenthesis.

par/ent (pâr/ənt, par/-) *n.* father or mother. —**pa•ren/tal** (pə ren/tl) *adj.* —**par/ent•hood/,** *n.*

par/ent•age (-ən tij) *n.* descent.

pa•ren/the•sis (pə ren/thə sis) *n.*, *pl.* -ses (-sēz). **1.** upright curves ( ) used to mark off interpolation. **2.** material so interpolated. —**par/en•thet/ic** (par/ən thet/ik), **par/en•thet/i•cal,** *adj.* —**par/en•thet/i•cal•ly,** *adv.*

pa•re/sis (pə rē/sis, par/ə sis) *n.* incomplete paralysis.

par excellence (pär ek/sə läns/) superior.

par•fait/ (pär fā/) *n.* frothy frozen dessert.

pa•ri/ah (pə rī/ə) *n.* outcast.

par/i•mu/tu•el (par/i myōō/chōō əl) *n.* form of betting on races.

par/ish (par/ish) *n.* ecclesiastical district. —**pa•rish/ion•er,** *n.*

par/i•ty (par/i tē) *n.* **1.** equality. **2.** similarity. **3.** guaranteed level of farm prices.

park (pärk) *n.* **1.** tract of land set apart for public. —*v.* **2.** place vehicle.

par/ka (pär/kə) *n.* hooded garment.

Par/kin•son's disease (pär/kin səns) neuro-

logical disease characterized by tremors, esp. of fingers and hands, shuffling, and muscular rigidity.

park/way/, *n.* broad thoroughfare with dividing strip or side strips planted with trees, etc.

Parl. **1.** Parliament. **2.** Parliamentary. Also, **parl.**

par/lance (pär/ləns) *n.* way of speaking.

par/lay (pär/lā, -lē) *v.* reinvest original amount and its earnings.

par/ley (pär/lē) *n.* **1.** conference between combatants. —*v.* **2.** hold parley.

par/lia•ment (pär/lə mənt) *n.* legislative body, esp. (*cap.*) of the United Kingdom.

par/lia•men•tar/ian (-men târ/ē ən, -mən-) *n.* expert in parliamentary rules.

par/lia•men/ta•ry (-men/tə rē) *adj.* **1.** of, by, or having a parliament. **2.** in accordance with rules of debate.

par/lor (pär/lər) *n.* room for receiving guests.

parl. proc. parliamentary procedure.

Par/me•san (pär/mə zän/, -zən) *n.* hard, dry Italian cheese.

par/mi•gia/na (pär/mə zhä/nə, -zhän/) *adj.* cooked with Parmesan cheese.

pa•ro/chi•al (pə rō/kē əl) *adj.* **1.** of a parish. **2.** narrow; provincial. —**pa•ro/chi•al•ism,** *n.*

parochial school, school run by religious organization.

par/o•dy (par/ə dē) *n.*, *pl.* -dies, *v.*, -died, -dying. —*n.* **1.** humorous imitation. —*v.* **2.** satirize.

pa•role/ (pə rōl/) *n.*, *v.*, -roled, -roling. —*n.* **1.** conditional release from prison. —*v.* **2.** put on parole. —**pa•rol/a•ble,** *adj.* —**pa•rol•ee/** (-rō lē/) *n.*

par/ox•ysm (par/ək siz/əm) *n.* outburst. —**par/ox•ys/mal,** *adj.*

par•quet/ (pär kā/) *n.* floor of inlaid design.

par/que•try (-ki trē) *n.* wooden mosaic work.

par/ri•cide/ (par/ə sīd/) *n.* crime of killing one's close relative.

par/rot (par/ət) *n.* **1.** hook-billed, bright-colored bird capable of being taught to talk. —*v.* **2.** repeat senselessly.

par/ry (par/ē) *v.*, -ried, -rying, *n.*, *pl.* -ries. —*v.* **1.** ward off; evade. —*n.* **2.** act of parrying.

parse (pärs) *v.*, parsed, parsing. describe (word or sentence) grammatically.

parsec (pär/sek/), *Astronomy.* parallax second.

par/si•mo/ny (pär/sə mō/nē) *n.* excessive frugality. —**par/si•mo/ni•ous,** *adj.*

pars/ley (pär/slē) *n.* garden herb used in seasoning.

pars/nip (pär/snip) *n.* plant with white edible root.

par/son (pär/sən) *n.* member of clergy.

par/son•age (-sə nij) *n.* house provided for parson.

part (pärt) *n.* **1.** portion of a whole. **2.** share. **3.** (*pl.*) personal qualities. —*v.* **4.** separate.

part. adj. participial adjective.

part. aeq. (in prescriptions) equal parts. [from Latin *partes aequales*]

par•take' (pär täk') *v.*, **-took, -taken, -taking.** have share.

par•terre' (pär târ') *n.* rear section of theater seats under balcony.

par'the•no•gen'e•sis (pär'thə nō jen'ə sis) *n.* development of egg without fertilization.

par'tial (pär'shəl) *adj.* **1.** being part; incomplete. **2.** biased. **3.** especially fond. —**par•tial'i•ty,** *n.* —**par'tial•ly,** *adv.*

par•tic'i•pate' (pär tis'ə pāt') *v.*, **-pated, -pating.** take part; share (in). —**par•tic'i•pant,** *n.* —**par•tic'i•pa'tion,** *n.* —**par•tic'i•pa•to'ry** (-pə tôr'ē) *adj.*

par'ti•ci•ple (pär'tə sip'əl) *n.* adjective derived from verb. —**par'ti•cip'i•al** (-sip'ē əl) *adj.*

par'ti•cle (pär'ti kəl) *n.* **1.** tiny piece. **2.** functional word.

par'ti•col'ored (pär'tē kul'ərd) *adj.* having areas of different colors.

par•tic'u•lar (pər tik'yə lər, pə-) *adj.* **1.** pertaining to a specific. **2.** noteworthy. **3.** attentive to details. —*n.* **4.** detail. —**par•tic'u•lar•ly,** *adv.*

par•tic'u•lar•ize', *v.*, **-ized, -izing.** give details. —**par•tic'u•lar•i•za'tion,** *n.*

par•tic'u•late (-lit, -lāt', pär-) *adj.* composed of particles.

part'ing, *n.* departure or separation.

par'ti•san (pär'tə zən, -sən) *n.* **1.** adherent. **2.** guerrilla.

par•ti'tion (pär tish'ən) *n.* **1.** division into portions. **2.** interior wall. —*v.* **3.** divide into parts.

part'ly, *adv.* not wholly.

part'ner (pärt'nər) *n.* **1.** sharer; associate. **2.** joint owner. —**part'ner•ship',** *n.*

par'tridge (pär'trij) *n.* game bird.

part'-song', *n.* song with parts for several voices.

part'-time', *adj.* (-tīm') **1.** involving or working less than the usual or full time. —*adv.* (-tīm') **2.** on a part-time basis.

par'tu•ri'tion (pär'tŏŏ rish'ən, -tyŏŏ-) *n.* childbirth.

part. vic. (in prescriptions) in divided doses. [from Latin *partibus vicibus*]

par'ty (pär'tē) *n., pl.* **-ties. 1.** group with common purpose. **2.** social gathering. **3.** person concerned.

party line, 1. guiding policy of political party. **2.** telephone line connecting telephones of several subscribers.

par•ve•nu' (pär'və nŏŏ', -nyŏŏ') *n., pl.* **-nus.** person with new wealth but not social acceptance.

pas public address system.

pas'chal (pas'kəl) *adj.* of Passover or Easter.

pa•sha' (pä'shə, pə shä') *n.* (formerly) Turkish official.

pass (pas) *v.*, **passed, passed** or **past, passing,** *n.* —*v.* **1.** go past, by, or through. **2.** omit. **3.** approve. **4.** convey. **5.** proceed. **6.** go by; elapse. **7.** die. **8.** be accepted. **9.** go unchallenged. —*n.* **10.** narrow route through barrier. **11.** permission or license. **12.** free ticket. **13.** state of affairs. —**pass'er,** *n.*

pas'sa•ble, *adj.* adequate. —**pas'sa•bly,** *adv.*

pas'sage (pas'ij) *n.* **1.** section of writing, etc. **2.** freedom to pass. **3.** movement; transportation. **4.** corridor. **5.** lapse. **6.** act of passing. —**pas'sage•way',** *n.*

pass'book', *n.* record of depositor's bank balance.

pas•sé' (pa sā') *adj.* out-of-date.

pas'sel (pas'əl) *n.* large group.

pas'sen•ger (pas'ən jər) *n.* traveler on vehicle or craft.

pass'er•by', *n., pl.* **passersby.** person who passes by.

pas'sim (pas'im) *adv.* here and there.

pass'ing, *adj.* brief; transitory.

pas'sion (pash'ən) *n.* **1.** very strong emotion. **2.** sexual love. **3.** (*cap.*) sufferings of Christ. —**pas'sion•ate,** *adj.* —**pas'sion•ate•ly,** *adv.* —**pas'sion•less,** *adj.*

pas'sive (pas'iv) *adj.* **1.** not in action. **2.** acted upon. **3.** submitting without resistance. **4.** designating voice of verbs indicating subject acted upon. —**pas'sive•ly,** *adv.* —**pas'sive•ness, pas•siv'i•ty,** *n.*

passive resistance, nonviolent opposition.

passive smoking, inhaling of others' smoke.

pass'key', *n.* master key.

Pass'o'ver (pas'ō'vər) *n.* annual Jewish festival.

pass'port, *n.* official document giving permission to travel abroad.

pass'word', *n.* secret word used to gain access.

past (past) *adj.* **1.** gone by, as in time. **2.** of an earlier time. **3.** designating a tense or verb formation showing time gone by. —*n.* **4.** time or events gone by. **5.** past tense. —*adv.* **6.** so as to pass by. —*prep.* **7.** after. **8.** beyond.

pas'ta (pä'stə) *n.* Italian flour-and-egg mixture, as spaghetti or macaroni.

paste (pāst) *n., v.*, **pasted, pasting.** —*n.* **1.** soft, sticky mixture. **2.** glass used for gems. —*v.* **3.** fasten with paste. —**past'y,** *adj.*

paste'board', *n.* firm board made of layers of paper.

pas•tel' (pa stel') *n.* soft color.

pas'tern (pas'tərn) *n.* horse's foot between fetlock and hoof.

pas'teur•ize' (pas'chə rīz') *v.*, **-ized, -izing.** heat (milk, etc.) to destroy certain bacteria. —**pas'teur•i•za'tion,** *n.*

pas•tiche' (pa stēsh') *n.* artistic work made up of borrowed details.

pas•tille′ (pa stēl′), *n.* lozenge.

pas′time′ (pas′tīm′) *n.* diversion.

past master, expert.

pas′tor (pas′tər) *n.* minister.

pas′to•ral, *adj.* **1.** having rural charm. **2.** of shepherds. **3.** of pastors.

pas′to•rale′ (-räl′) *n.* dreamy musical composition.

pas•tra′mi (pə strä′mē) *n.* seasoned smoked or pickled beef.

pas′try (pā′strē) *n., pl.* **-tries.** food made of rich paste, as pies.

pas′tur•age (pas′chər ij) *n.* grazing ground.

pas′ture, *n., v.,* **-tured, -turing.** —*n.* **1.** grassy ground for grazing. —*v.* **2.** graze on pasture.

pat (pat) *v.,* **patted, patting,** *n., adj., adv.* —*v.* **1.** strike gently with flat object, hand, etc. —*n.* **2.** light stroke. **3.** small mass. —*adj.* **4.** apt; to the point. —*adv.* **5.** perfectly. **6.** unwaveringly.

patch (pach) *n.* **1.** piece of material used to mend or protect. **2.** any small piece. —*v.* **3.** mend, esp. with patches. —**patch′work′,** *n.*

patch test, allergy test where patch of material containing allergen is applied to skin.

patch′y, *adj.,* **-ier, -iest.** irregular in surface or quality. —**patch′i•ness,** *n.*

patd. patented.

pate (pāt) *n.* crown of head.

pâ•té′ (pä tā′, pa-) *n.* paste of puréed or chopped meat, liver, etc.

pa•tel′la (pə tel′ə) *n., pl.* **-tellae** (tel′ē). kneecap.

pat′ent (pat′nt) *n.* **1.** exclusive right to invention. —*adj.* **2.** protected by patent. **3.** evident. —*v.* **4.** secure patent on.

patent leather, hard, glossy, smooth leather.

patent medicine, drug protected by trademark.

pa•ter′nal (pə tûr′nl) *adj.* **1.** fatherly. **2.** related through father. —**pa•ter′nal•ly,** *adv.*

pa•ter′nal•ism, *n.* benevolent control. —**pa•ter′nal•is′tic,** *adj.*

pa•ter′ni•ty (-ni tē) *n.* fatherhood.

pa′ter•nos′ter (pä′tər nos′tər) *n.* Lord's Prayer.

path (path) *n.* **1.** Also, **path′way′.** narrow way. **2.** route. **3.** course of action.

pa•thet′ic (pə thet′ik) *adj.* arousing pity. —**pa•thet′i•cal•ly,** *adv.*

path′find′er, *n.* person who finds a path.

path′o•gen (path′ə jən, -jen′) *n.* disease-producing agent. —**path′o•gen′ic,** *adj.*

pathol. 1. Also, **pathol** pathological. **2.** pathology.

path′o•log′i•cal (-loj′i kəl) *adj.* sick; morbid. —**path′o•log′i•cal•ly,** *adv.*

pa•thol′o•gy (pə thol′ə jē) *n.* study of disease. —**pa•thol′o•gist,** *n.*

pa′thos (pā′thos, -thōs) *n.* quality or power of arousing pity.

-pathy, suffix meaning: **1.** feeling, as *antipathy.* **2.** method of treatment, as *osteopathy.*

pa′tient (pā′shənt) *n.* **1.** person under care of a doctor. —*adj.* **2.** enduring calmly. —**pa′tience,** *n.* —**pa′tient•ly,** *adv.*

pat′i•na (pat′n ə, pə tē′nə) *n.* film on old bronze, etc.

pa′ti•o′ (pat′ē ō′) *n., pl.* **-tios.** inner open court.

Pat. Off. Patent Office.

pat′ois (pat′wä) *n.* regional form of a language.

pat. pend. patent pending. Also, **patpend**

pa′tri•arch′ (pā′trē ärk′) *n.* **1.** venerable old man. **2.** male head of family. —**pa′tri•ar′chal,** *adj.*

pa′tri•ar′chy (-är′kē) *n., pl.* **-chies.** family group ruled by a father.

pa•tri′cian (pə trish′ən) *n.* **1.** aristocrat. —*adj.* **2.** aristocratic.

pat′ri•cide′ (pa′trə sīd′) *n.* killing one's father. —**pat′ri•cid′al,** *adj.*

pat′ri•mo′ny (-mō′nē) *n., pl.* **-nies.** inherited estate.

pa′tri•ot (pā′trē ət, -ot′; *esp. Brit.* pa′trē ət) *n.* person who supports country. —**pa′tri•ot′ic,** *adj.* —**pa′tri•ot•ism** (-ə tiz′əm) *n.* —**pa′tri•ot′i•cal•ly,** *adv.*

pa•trol′ (pə trōl′) *v.,* **-trolled, -trolling,** *n.* —*v.* **1.** pass through in guarding. —*n.* **2.** person or group assigned to patrol.

pa•trol′man, *n., pl.* **-men.** police officer who patrols.

pa′tron (pā′trən) *n.* **1.** supporter. **2.** regular customer.

pa′tron•age (pā′trə nij, pa′-) *n.* **1.** support by patron. **2.** political control of appointments to office.

pa′tron•ize′, *v.,* **-ized, -izing. 1.** buy from, esp. regularly. **2.** treat condescendingly.

patron saint, saint regarded as special guardian.

pat′ro•nym′ic (pa′trə nim′ik) *n.* name derived from ancestor.

pat′sy (pat′sē) *n., pl.* **-sies.** *Slang.* person easily manipulated.

pat′ter (pat′ər) *v.* **1.** walk quickly. **2.** speak glibly. —*n.* **3.** pattering sound. **4.** rapid, glib speech.

pat′tern (pat′ərn) *n.* **1.** surface design. **2.** characteristic mode of development, etc. **3.** model for copying. —*v.* **4.** make after pattern.

pat′ty (pat′ē) *n., pl.* **-ties. 1.** thin piece of ground or minced food, as of meat. **2.** wafer.

P.A.U. Pan American Union.

pau′ci•ty (pô′si tē) *n.* scarceness.

paunch (pônch) *n.* belly, esp. when large. —**paunch′y,** *adj.*

pau′per (pô′pər) *n.* poor person.

pause (pôz) *n., v.,* **paused, pausing.** —*n.* **1.** temporary stop. —*v.* **2.** make pause.

pave (pāv) *v.,* **paved, paving. 1.** cover with

solid road surface. **2.** prepare. —**pave′ment,**
n.
pa•vil′ion (pə vil′yən) *n.* **1.** light open shelter. **2.** tent.
paw (pô) *n.* **1.** foot of animal. —*v.* **2.** scrape
with paw.
pawl (pôl) *n.* pivoted bar engaging with teeth
of ratchet wheel.
pawn (pôn) *v.* **1.** deposit as security for loan.
—*n.* **2.** state of being pawned. **3.** piece used
in chess. —**pawn′shop′,** *n.*
pawn′bro′ker, *n.* person who lends money
on pledged articles.
paw′paw′ (pô′pô′, pə pô′) *n.* small tree
bearing purple flowers.
PAX *Telephones.* private automatic exchange.
pay (pā) *v.,* **paid, paying,** *n.* —*v.* **1.** give
money required to. **2.** give as compensation.
3. yield profit. **4.** let out (rope). —*n.* **5.**
wages. **6.** paid employ. —**pay′a•ble,** *adj.*
—**pay•ee′,** *n.* —**pay′er,** *n.* —**pay′ment,** *n.*
pay dirt, 1. profitable soil to mine. **2.** *Informal.* any source of wealth.
PAYE 1. pay as you enter. **2.** pay as you earn.
pay′load′, *n.* **1.** revenue-producing freight,
etc. **2.** contents to be carried.
pay′mas′ter, *n.* person in charge of paying
out wages.
pay′off′, *n.* **1.** *Informal,* final consequence.
2. awaited payment.
pay•o′la (pā ō′lə) *n.* bribery.
pay′roll, *n.* **1.** list of employees to be paid. **2.**
total of these amounts.
PB power brakes.
Pb *Symbol, Chemistry.* lead. [from Latin *plum-
bum*]
pb pushbutton.
P.B. 1. British Pharmacopoeia. [from Latin
Pharmacopoeia Britannica] **2.** Prayer Book.
p.b. *Baseball.* passed ball; passed balls.
PBA 1. Professional Bowlers Association. **2.**
Public Buildings Administration.
P.B.A. Patrolmen's Benevolent Association.
PBB *Chemistry.* any of the highly toxic and
possibly carcinogenic aromatic compounds
consisting of two benzene rings in which
bromine takes the place of two or more hydrogen atoms. [*p(oly)b(rominated) b(iphenyl)*]
pbd pressboard.
PBK Phi Beta Kappa.
pblg publishing.
pblr publisher.
PBS Public Broadcasting Service.
PBX a manually or automatically operated telephone facility that handles communications
within an office, office building, or organization. [*P(rivate) B(ranch) Ex(change)*]
PC, 1. *pl.* **PCs** or **PC's.** personal computer. **2.**
politically correct.
PCB, *pl.* **PCBs, PCB's.** highly toxic compound,
formerly used in industry.
pcf pounds per cubic foot.

pchs purchase.
pchsg purchasing.
pcht parchment.
PCI *Computers.* peripheral component inter-
connect.
pci pounds per cubic inch.
PCL *Computers.* Printer Control Language.
pcl pencil.
PCM 1. *Computers.* plug-compatible manufacturer. **2.** Also, **pcm** *Telecommunications.*
pulse code modulation.
PCMCIA Personal Computer Memory Card International Association.
pcmd pulse code modulation digital.
pcmfm pulse code modulation frequency
modulation.
PCNB *Chemistry.* a crystalline compound,
$C_6Cl_5NO_2$, used as a herbicide and insecticide.
[*p(enta)c(hloro)n(itro)b(enzene)*]
PCP, phencyclidine: drug used as tranquilizer.
pct. percent. Also, **pct**
pctm pulse count modulation.
PCV *Automotive.* positive crankcase ventilation.
pcv pollution-control valve.
Pd *Symbol, Chemistry.* palladium.
pd pitch diameter.
pd. paid.
P.D. 1. per diem. **2.** Police Department. **3.** *Insurance.* property damage.
p.d. 1. per diem. **2.** potential difference.
PDA *Computers.* personal digital assistant.
PDB *Chemistry.* a crystalline solid, $C_6H_4Cl_2$,
used especially as a moth repellent.
[*p(ara-)d(ichloro)b(enzene)*]
Pd.B. Bachelor of Pedagogy.
Pd.D. Doctor of Pedagogy.
pdl 1. *Computers.* page description language.
2. poundal.
pdm pulse duration modulation.
Pd.M. Master of Pedagogy.
pdmfm pulse duration modulation frequency
modulation.
P.D.Q. *Informal.* immediately; at once. Also,
PDQ [*p(retty) d(amn) q(uick)*]
PDR Physicians' Desk Reference.
pdr powder.
PDT Pacific daylight time. Also, **P.D.T.**
PE, physical education.
pea (pē) *n.* round edible seed of legume.
peace (pēs) *n.* freedom from war, trouble, or
disturbance. —**peace′mak′er,** *n.* —**peace′-
time′,** *n.*
peace′ful, *adj.* **1.** at peace. **2.** desiring peace.
Also, **peace′a•ble.** —**peace′ful•ly,** *adv.*
—**peace′ful•ness,** *n.*
peach (pēch) *n.* sweet juicy pinkish fruit.
pea′cock′ (pē′kok′) *n.* male peafowl, having
iridescent tail feathers.
pea′fowl′, *n.* bird of pheasant family.
pea′hen′, *n.* female peafowl.
pea jacket, short heavy coat.

P

peak (pēk) *n.* **1.** pointed top. **2.** highest point.

peaked, *adj.* **1.** (pēkt) having peak. **2.** (pē′kid) sickly, haggard.

peal (pēl) *n.* **1.** prolonged sound, as of bells or thunder. **2.** bells. —*v.* **3.** sound in a peal.

pea′nut′, *n.* pod or edible seed of leguminous plant that ripens underground.

pear (pâr) *n.* elongated edible fruit.

pearl (pûrl) *n.* hard, smooth, near-white gem formed within an oyster. —**pearl′y,** *adj.*

peas′ant (pez′ənt) *n.* farm worker.

peat (pēt) *n.* organic soil dried for fuel. —**peat′y,** *adj.*

peat moss, moss from which peat may form, used as mulch.

peb′ble (peb′əl) *n.* small, rounded stone. —**peb′bly,** *adj.*

pec photoelectric cell.

pe•can′ (pi kän′, -kan′) *n.* smooth-shelled nut.

pec′ca•dil′lo (pek′ə dil′ō) *n., pl.* -loes, -los. trifling sin.

pec′ca•ry (pek′ə rē) *n., pl.* -ries. wild American pig.

peck (pek) *v.* **1.** strike with beak. —*n.* **2.** pecking stroke. **3.** dry measure of eight quarts.

pecking order, hierarchy within group.

pec′tin (pek′tin) *n.* substance in ripe fruit that forms jelly.

pec′to•ral (pek′tər əl) *adj.* **1.** of the chest. —*n.* **2.** pectoral muscle or organ.

pec′u•late′ (pek′yə lāt′) *v.,* -lated, -lating. embezzle. —**pec′u•la′tion,** *n.*

pe•cul′iar (pi kyōol′yər) *adj.* **1.** strange; odd. **2.** uncommon. **3.** exclusive. —**pe•cu′li•ar′i•ty** (-lē ar′i tē) *n.* —**pe•cul′iar•ly,** *adv.*

pe•cu′ni•ar′y (pi kyōo′nē er′ē) *adj.* of money.

ped. 1. pedal. **2.** pedestal. **3.** pedestrian.

ped′a•gogue′ (ped′ə gog′) *n.* teacher. —**ped′a•go′gy** (-gō′jē, -goj′ē) *n.* —**ped′a•gog′ic, ped′a•gog′i•cal,** *adj.* —**ped′a•gog′i•cal•ly,** *adv.*

ped′al (ped′l) *n., v.,* -aled, -aling, *adj.* —*n.* **1.** lever worked by foot. —*v.* **2.** work pedals of. —*adj.* **3.** (pē′dəl) of feet.

ped′ant (ped′nt) *n.* person excessively concerned with details. —**pe•dan′tic,** *adj.* —**ped′ant•ry,** *n.*

Ped.D. Doctor of Pedagogy.

ped′dle (ped′l) *v.,* -dled, -dling. carry about for sale. —**ped′dler,** *n.*

ped′er•as•ty (ped′ə ras′tē, pē′də-) *n.* sexual relations between a man and a boy. —**ped′er•ast′,** *n.*

ped′es•tal (ped′ə stl) *n.* base for object.

pe•des′tri•an (pə des′trē ən) *n.* **1.** walker. —*adj.* **2.** walking. **3.** prosaic.

pe′di•at′rics (pē′dē a′triks) *n.* study of care and diseases of children. —**pe′di•a•tri′cian** (pē′dē ə trish′ən) *n.* —**pe′di•at′ric,** *adj.*

ped′i•cab′ (ped′i kab′) *n.* three-wheeled conveyance cab operated by pedals.

ped′i•cure′ (ped′i kyŏŏr′) *n.* professional care of the feet, as trimming of toenails.

ped′i•gree′ (ped′i grē′) *n.* **1.** certificate of ancestry. **2.** ancestry. —**ped′i•greed′,** *adj.*

ped′i•ment (ped′ə mənt) *n.* gablelike architectural feature.

P.E.Dir. Director of Physical Education.

pe•dom′e•ter (pə dom′i tər) *n.* device that measures distance walked.

pe•dun′cle (pi dung′kəl, pē′dung-) *n.* stalk that supports flower cluster.

peek (pēk) *v., n.* peep (defs. 1–3; 5).

peel (pēl) *v.* **1.** remove or lose skin, bark, etc. —*n.* **2.** skin of fruit, etc.

peen (pēn) *n.* sharp end of hammer head.

peep (pēp) *v.* **1.** look through small opening. **2.** look furtively. **3.** show slightly. **4.** utter shrill little cry. —*n.* **5.** quick look. **6.** weak sound. —**peep′er,** *n.*

peer (pēr) *n.* **1.** equal. **2.** noble. —*v.* **3.** look closely.

peer′age (-ij) *n.* **1.** rank of peer. **2.** list of peers.

peer′less, *adj.* without equal. —**peer′less•ness,** *n.*

peeve (pēv) *n., v.,* peeved, peeving. —*n.* **1.** annoyance. —*v.* **2.** annoy; vex.

peev′ish (pē′vish) *adj.* discontented; cross.

pee•wee (pē′wē′) *n. Informal.* person or thing that is unusually small.

P.E.F. *Insurance.* personal effects floater.

peg (peg) *n., v.,* pegged, pegging. —*n.* **1.** pin of wood, metal, etc. —*v.* **2.** fasten with pegs.

peg leg, wooden leg.

P.E.I. Prince Edward Island.

peign•oir′ (pān wär′, pen-) *n.* woman's loose dressing gown.

pe•jo′ra•tive (pi jôr′ə tiv) *adj.* disparaging; negative.

Pe′king•ese′ (pē′kə nēz′, -nēs′) *n., pl.* -ese. long-haired Chinese dog with flat muzzle.

pe′koe (pē′kō) *n.* black tea.

pe•lag′ic (pə laj′ik) *adj.* of seas.

pelec photoelectric.

pel′i•can (pel′i kən) *n.* large-billed bird.

pel•la′gra (pə lag′rə, -lā′grə, -lä′-) *n.* chronic disease from inadequate diet.

pel′let (pel′it) *n.* little ball.

pell′-mell′ (pel′mel′) *adv.* in disorderly haste.

pel•lu′cid (pə lōō′sid) *adj.* **1.** translucent. **2.** clear.

pelt (pelt) *v.* **1.** throw. **2.** assail. —*n.* **3.** a blow. **4.** skin of beast.

pel′vis (pel′vis) *n.* **1.** cavity in lower body trunk. **2.** bones forming this cavity. —**pel′vic,** *adj.*

pem *Computers.* preemptive multitasking.

pem′mi•can (pem′i kən) *n.* dried food.

pen (pen) *n., v.,* penned or (for 4) pent, pen-

ning. —*n.* **1.** device for writing with ink. **2.** small enclosure. —*v.* **3.** write with pen. **4.** confine in pen.

pe′nal (pēn′l) *adj.* of punishment. —**pe′nal·ize′,** *v.*

pen′al·ty (pen′l tē) *n.*, *pl.* **-ties. 1.** punishment. **2.** disadvantage.

pen′ance (-əns) *n.* punishment as penitence for sin.

pence (pens) *n. Brit. pl.* of **penny.**

pen′chant (pen′chənt) *n.* liking.

pen′cil (pen′səl) *n.* enclosed stick of graphite, etc., for marking.

pend (pend) *v.* remain undecided.

pend′ant (pen′dənt) *n.* **1.** hanging ornament. **2.** match; counterpart.

pend′ent (pen′dənt) *adj.* hanging.

pend′ing, *prep.* **1.** until. —*adj.* **2.** undecided.

pen′du·lous (pen′jə ləs, pen′dyə-) *adj.* hanging.

pen′du·lum (-ləm) *n.* hung weight.

pen′e·trate′ (pen′i trāt′) *v.*, **-trated, -trating. 1.** pierce; permeate. **2.** enter. **3.** understand; have insight. —**pen′e·tra·ble** (-trə-bəl) *adj.* —**pen′e·tra′tion,** *n.*

pen′guin (peng′gwin, pen′-) *n.* flightless aquatic bird.

pen′i·cil′lin (pen′ə sil′in) *n.* antibacterial substance produced in certain molds.

pen·in′su·la (pə nin′sə lə) *n.* piece of land nearly surrounded by water. —**pen·in′su·lar,** *adj.*

pe′nis (pē′nis) *n.* male sex organ. —**pe′nile** (pēn′l) *adj.*

pen′i·tent (pen′i tənt) *adj.* **1.** sorry for sin or fault. —*n.* **2.** penitent person. —**pen′i·tence,** *n.*

pen′i·ten′tia·ry (-ten′shə rē) *n.*, *pl.* **-ries.** prison.

pen′knife′, *n.* small pocket knife.

pen′light′, *n.* flashlight shaped like fountain pen.

pen′man, *n.*, *pl.* **-men.** one who writes. —**pen′man·ship′,** *n.*

Penn., Pennsylvania. Also, **Penna.**

pen name, pseudonym.

pen′nant (pen′ənt) *n.* flag, usually tapered. Also, **pen′non.**

pen′ny (pen′ē) *n.*, *pl.* **-nies,** *Brit.* **pence.** small coin, equal to one cent in the U.S. and Canada, and to $\frac{1}{100}$ pound in United Kingdom. —**pen′ni·less,** *adj.*

penny pincher, stingy person. —**pen′ny-pinch′ing,** *adj.*

pen′ny·weight′, *n.* (in troy weight) 24 grains, or $\frac{1}{20}$ of an ounce.

pe·nol′o·gy (pē nol′ə jē) *n.* science of punishment of crime and management of prisoners. —**pe·nol′o·gist,** *n.*

pen pal, person with whom one exchanges letters.

pen′sion (pen′shən) *n.* **1.** fixed periodic payment for past service, etc. **2.** (pän sē ōn′) (in France) boarding house or school. —*v.* **3.** give pension to.

pen′sion·er, *n.* person receiving pension.

pen′sive (pen′siv) *adj.* gravely thoughtful. —**pen′sive·ly,** *adv.* —**pen′sive·ness,** *n.*

pent (pent) *adj.* confined.

penta-, prefix meaning five.

pen′ta·gon′ (pen′tə gon′) *n.* plane figure having five sides and five angles.

pen′ta·gram′ (-gram′) *n.* five-pointed, star-shaped symbol.

pen·tam′e·ter (pen tam′i tər) *n.* verse or line of five feet.

Pen′ta·teuch′ (pen′tə tōōk′, -tyōōk′) *n. Bible.* first five books of the Old Testament.

pen·tath′lon (pen tath′lən, -lon) *n.* athletic contest of five events.

Pen′te·cost′ (pen′ti kôst′) *n.* Christian festival; Whitsunday.

Pen′te·cos′tal, *adj.* of Christian groups that emphasize the Holy Spirit.

pent′house′ (pent′hous′) *n.* rooftop apartment or dwelling.

pent′-up′, *adj.* restrained; confined.

pe·nu′che (pə nōō′chē) *n.* brown-sugar fudge.

pe′nult (pē′nult) *n.* next to last syllable.

pe·nul′ti·mate (pi nul′tə mit) *adj.* being or occurring next to last.

pe·num′bra (pə num′brə) *n.*, *pl.* **-brae** (-brē), **-bras.** partial shadow outside complete shadow of celestial body in eclipse. —**pe·num′bral,** *adj.*

pe·nu′ri·ous (pə nŏŏr′ē əs, -nyŏŏr′-) *adj.* **1.** meanly stingy. **2.** in great poverty.

pen′u·ry (pen′yə rē) *n.* poverty.

pe′on (pē′ən, -on) *n.* **1.** unskilled worker. **2.** indentured worker.

pe′on·age (-ə nij) *n.* work of peon.

pe′o·ny (pē′ə nē) *n.*, *pl.* **-nies.** perennial plant with large flowers.

peo′ple (pē′pəl) *n.*, *v.* **-pled, -pling.** —*n.* **1.** body of persons constituting nation or ethnic group. **2.** persons in general. **3.** person's relatives. —*v.* **4.** populate.

pep (pep) *n.*, *v.*, **pepped, pepping.** *Informal.* —*n.* **1.** vigor. —*v.* **2.** give vigor to. —**pep′py,** *adj.*

pep′per (pep′ər) *n.* **1.** condiment from dried berries. **2.** edible fruit of certain plants. —*v.* **3.** season with pepper. **4.** pelt with shot. —**pep′per·y,** *adj.*

pep′per·corn′, *n.* dried berry of pepper plant.

pepper mill, device for grinding peppercorns.

pep′per·mint′ (-mint′) *n.* aromatic oil of herb, used as flavoring.

pep′per·o′ni (pep′ə rō′nē) *n.*, *pl.* **-nis.** highly seasoned sausage.

pep′sin (pep′sin) *n.* juice secreted in stomach that digests proteins.

pep′tic (pep′tik) *adj.* digestive.

per (pûr; *unstressed* pər) *prep.* for; by means of.

per′ad•ven′ture, *adv. Archaic.* maybe.

per•am′bu•late′, *v.,* -lated, -lating. walk about or through. —**per•am′bu•la′tion,** *n.*

per•am′bu•la′tor, *n.* baby carriage.

per an. per annum.

per an′num (pər an′əm) yearly.

perc percussion.

per•cale′ (pər kāl′) *n.* smooth, closely woven cotton fabric.

per cap′i•ta (pər kap′i tə) by or for each person.

per•ceive′ (pər sēv′) *v.,* -ceived, -ceiving. **1.** gain knowledge of by seeing, hearing, etc. **2.** understand. —**per•ceiv′a•ble, per•cep′ti•ble** (-sep′tə bəl) *adj.*

per•cent′ (pər sent′) *n.* number of parts in each hundred.

per•cent′age (-sen′tij) *n.* **1.** proportion or rate per hundred. **2.** *Informal.* profit; advantage.

per•cen′tile (-tīl, -til) *n.* value of statistical variable that divides distribution of variable into 100 equal parts.

per′cept (pûr′sept) *n.* result of perceiving.

per•cep′tion, *n.* **1.** act or faculty of perceiving. **2.** intuition; insight. **3.** result or product of perceiving.

per•cep′tive, *adj.* **1.** keen. **2.** showing perception.

per•cep′tu•al (-chōō əl) *adj.* involving perception.

perch (pûrch) *n.* **1.** place for roosting. **2.** linear measure of 5½ yards. **3.** square rod (30¼ sq. yards). **4.** common food fish. —*v.* **5.** set or rest on perch.

per•chance′ (pər chans′) *adv. Poetic.* maybe; by chance.

per′co•late′ (pûr′kə lāt′) *v.,* -lated, -lating. filter through. —**per′co•la′tion,** *n.*

per′co•la′tor, *n.* coffee pot.

per•cus′sion (pər kush′ən) *n.* **1.** violent impact. —*adj.* **2.** sounded by striking. —**per•cus′sion•ist,** *n.* —**per•cus′sive** (-kus′iv) *adj.*

per di′em (pər dē′əm) *adv.* **1.** by the day. —*n.* **2.** daily pay or allowance for expenses. **3.** person paid by the day. —*adj.* **4.** paid by the day.

per•di′tion (pər dish′ən) *n.* ruin; hell.

per•dur′a•ble (-dŏŏr′ə bəl, -dyŏŏr′-) *adj.* very durable.

per′e•gri•nate′ (per′i grə nāt′) *v.,* -nated, -nating. travel on foot. —**per′e•gri•na′tion,** *n.*

per′e•grine falcon (per′i grin, -grēn′) bird of prey.

per•emp′to•ry (pə remp′tə rē) *adj.* permitting no denial or refusal. —**per•emp′to•ri•ly,** *adv.* —**per•emp′to•ri•ness,** *n.*

per•en′ni•al (pə ren′ē əl) *adj.* **1.** lasting indefinitely. **2.** living more than two years. —*n.* **3.** perennial plant. —**per•en′ni•al•ly,** *adv.*

perf. 1. perfect. **2.** perforated. **3.** performance.

per′fect (pûr′fikt) *adj.* **1.** faultless. **2.** designating verb tense indicating action already completed. —*n.* **3.** *Gram.* perfect tense. —*v.* (pər fekt′) **4.** make faultless. —**per•fec′tion** (pər fek′shən) *n.* —**per′fect•ly,** *adv.*

per•fec′tion•ism, *n.* insistence on perfection. —**per•fec′tion•ist,** *n.*

per′fi•dy (pûr′fi dē) *n., pl.* -dies. treachery; faithlessness. —**per•fid′i•ous,** *adj.*

per′fo•rate′ (pûr′fə rāt′) *v.,* -rated, -rating. make holes through. —**per′fo•ra′tion,** *n.*

per•force′ (pər fôrs′) *adv.* of necessity.

per•form′ (-fôrm′) *v.* **1.** carry out; do. **2.** act, as on stage. —**per•for′mance,** *n.* —**per•form′er,** *n.*

performing arts, arts requiring public performance.

perf. part, perfect participle.

per′fume, *n., v.,* -fumed, -fuming. —*n.* (pûr′fyŏŏm, pər fyŏŏm′) **1.** sweet-smelling liquid. **2.** sweet smell. —*v.* (pər fyŏŏm′, pûr′-fyŏŏm) **3.** impart fragrance to. —**per•fum′er•y,** *n.*

per•func′to•ry (pər fungk′tə rē) *adj.* done without care or attention. —**per•func′to•ri•ly,** *adv.* —**per•func′to•ri•ness,** *n.*

perh. perhaps.

per•haps′ (pər haps′) *adv.* maybe.

peri-, prefix meaning around, surrounding, or near.

per′i•car′di•um (per′i kär′dē əm) *n.* membranous sac enclosing the heart.

per′i•gee′ (-jē′) *n.* point nearest earth in orbit of a heavenly body.

per′i•he′li•on (per′ə hē′lē ən) *n.* point nearest sun in orbit of a planet or comet.

per′il (per′əl) *n.* **1.** danger. —*v.* **2.** endanger. —**per′il•ous,** *adj.*

per•im′e•ter (pə rim′i tər) *n.* **1.** outer boundary of plane figure. **2.** length of boundary. —**pe•rim′e•tral, per′i•met′ric** (-me′trik) *adj.*

per′i•ne′um (per′ə nē′əm) *n., pl.* -nea. area between genitals and anus.

pe′ri•od (pēr′ē əd) *n.* **1.** portion of time. **2.** mark (.) ending sentence.

pe′ri•od′ic (-od′ik) *adj.* recurring regularly or intermittently. —**pe′ri•od′i•cal•ly,** *adv.*

pe′ri•od′i•cal, *n.* **1.** publication issued at regular intervals. —*adj.* **2.** periodic.

periodic table, table showing chemical elements in related groups.

per′i•o•don′tal (per′ē ə don′tl) *adj.* of or concerning bone, tissue, and gums surrounding and supporting teeth.

per′i•pa•tet′ic (per′ə pə tet′ik) *adj.* walking or traveling about; itinerant.

pe•riph′er•al (pə rif′ər əl) *adj.* **1.** located on periphery. **2.** only partly relevant.

pe•riph′er•y, *n., pl.* -eries. **1.** external boundary. **2.** external surface.

pe•riph′ra•sis (pə rif′rə sis) *n., pl.* -ses.

(-sēz'). use of roundabout form of expression. **—per'i•phras'tic** (per'ə fras'tik) *adj.*

per'i•scope' (per'ə skōp') *n.* optical instrument consisting of a tube in which mirrors or prisms reflect to give a view from below or behind an obstacle.

per'ish (per'ish) *v.* **1.** die. **2.** decay. **—per'-ish•a•ble,** *adj., n.*

per'i•stal'sis (per'ə stôl'sis, -stal'-) *n., pl.* **-ses** (-sēz). muscle contractions and relaxations that move food along alimentary canal.

per'i•to'ne•um (per'i tn ē'əm, -tō'-) *n.* lining of abdominal cavity. **—per'i•to•ne'al,** *adj.*

per'i•to•ni'tis (-tn ī'tis) *n.* swelling of peritoneum.

per'i•win'kle (per'i wing'kəl) *n.* **1.** edible marine snail. **2.** trailing evergreen plant.

per'jure (pûr'jər) *v.,* **-jured, -juring.** lie under oath. **—per'jur•er,** *n.*

per'ju•ry (pûr'jə rē) *n., pl.* **-ries.** false statement made under oath.

perk (pûrk) *v.* **1.** move or raise jauntily. **2.** become lively. **—n. 3.** perquisite. **—perk'y,** *adj.*

perm 1. permanent. **2.** permission.

per'ma•frost' (pûr'mə frôst') *n.* permanently frozen subsoil.

per'ma•nent (-nənt) *adj.* **1.** lasting indefinitely. **—n. 2.** curl permanently set in hair. **—per'ma•nence, per'ma•nen•cy,** *n.* **—per'ma•nent•ly,** *adv.*

permb permeability.

per'me•ate' (pûr'mē āt') *v.,* **-ated, -ating.** penetrate; pervade. **—per'me•a'tion,** *n.* **—per'me•a•ble,** *adj.*

per•mis'sion (-mish'ən) *n.* authorization. **—per•mis'si•ble,** *adj.* **—per•mis'si•bly,** *adv.*

per•mis'sive (-mis'iv) *adj.* **1.** giving permission. **2.** loose or lax in discipline.

per•mit', *v.,* **-mitted, -mitting,** *n.* **—v.** (pər mit') **1.** allow; agree to. **2.** afford opportunity. **—n.** (pûr'mit, pər mit') **3.** written order giving permission.

per'mu•ta'tion (pûr'myōō tā'shən) *n.* alteration; change in order.

per•ni'cious (pər nish'əs) *adj.* **1.** highly hurtful. **2.** deadly.

per'o•ra'tion (per'ə rā'shən) *n.* concluding part of speech.

per•ox'ide (pə rok'sīd) *n.* **1.** oxide containing large amount of oxygen. **2.** antiseptic liquid.

perp. perpendicular.

per'pen•dic'u•lar (pûr'pən dik'yə lər) *adj.* **1.** upright; vertical. **2.** meeting given line at right angles. **—n. 3.** perpendicular line or position.

per'pe•trate' (pûr'pi trāt') *v.,* **-trated, -trating.** commit (crime, etc.). **—per'pe•tra'-tion,** *n.* **—per'pe•tra'tor,** *n.*

per•pet'u•al (pər pech'ōō əl) *adj.* **1.** lasting forever. **2.** unceasing. **—per•pet'u•ate',** *v.*

per'pe•tu'i•ty (pûr'pi tōō'i tē, -tyōō'-) *n.* forever.

per•plex' (pər pleks') *v.* confuse mentally. **—per•plex'i•ty,** *n.*

per pro. *Law.* by one acting as an agent; by proxy. Also, **per proc.** [from Latin *per procurationem*]

per'qui•site (pûr'kwə zit) *n.* incidental profit in addition to fixed pay.

Pers Persian.

Pers. 1. Persia. **2.** Persian.

pers. 1. person. **2.** personal. **3.** personnel.

per se (pûr sā', sē', pər) by, of, for, or in itself; intrinsically.

per'se•cute' (pûr'si kyōōt') *v.,* **-cuted, -cuting.** oppress persistently, esp. for one's beliefs. **—per'se•cu'tion,** *n.* **—per'se•cu'tor,** *n.*

per'se•vere' (pûr'sə vēr') *v.,* **-vered, -vering.** continue steadfastly. **—per'se•ver'-ance,** *n.*

per'si•flage' (pûr'sə fläzh') *n.* light, bantering talk.

per•sim'mon (pər sim'ən) *n.* soft fruit.

per•sist' (pər sist', -zist') *v.* **1.** continue firmly in spite of opposition. **2.** endure. **—per•sist'ence,** *n.* **—per•sist'ent,** *adj.* **—per•sist'ent•ly,** *adv.*

per•snick'et•y (pər snik'i tē) *adj. Informal.* fussy.

per'son (pûr'sən) *n.* **1.** human being. **2.** individual personality. **3.** body.

per'son•a•ble, *adj.* attractive in appearance and manner.

per'son•age (-sə nij) *n.* distinguished person.

per'son•al (-sə nl) *adj.* **1.** of, by, or relating to a certain person. **2.** *Gram.* denoting class of pronouns that refer to speaker, person addressed, or thing spoken of. **3.** *Law.* of property that is movable. **—per'son•al•ly,** *adv.*

personal computer, microcomputer designed for individual use.

personal effects, belongings.

per'son•al'i•ty (-sə nal'ə tē) *n., pl.* **-ties. 1.** distinctive personal character. **2.** famous person.

per'son•al•ize', *v.,* **-ized, -izing. 1.** make personal. **2.** treat as if human.

per'son•al•ty (-sə nəl tē) *n., pl.* **-ties.** personal property.

per•so'na non gra'ta (pər sō'nə non grä'tə) unwelcome.

per•son'i•fy' (pər son'ə fī') *v.,* **-fied, -fying. 1.** attribute personal character to. **2.** embody; typify. **3.** impersonate. **—per•son'i•fi•ca'-tion,** *n.*

per'son•nel' (pûr'sə nel') *n.* employees.

persp perspective.

per•spec'tive (pər spek'tiv) *n.* **1.** depiction as to show space relationships. **2.** mental view.

per'spi•ca'cious (pûr'spi kā'shəs) *adj.* mentally keen. **—per'spi•cac'i•ty** (-kas'i tē) *n.*

per·spic'u·ous (pər spik'yŏŏ əs) *adj.* clearly expressed or presented. **—per'spi·cu'i·ty** (pûr'-) *n.*

per·spire' (pər spī°r') *v.*, **-spired, -spiring.** sweat. **—per'spi·ra'tion** (pûr'spə rā'shən) *n.*

per·suade' (pər swād') *v.*, **-suaded, -suad-ing. 1.** prevail on to act as suggested. **2.** convince. **—per·sua'sive,** *adj.* **—per·sua'sive·ly,** *adv.*

per·sua'sion (-swā'zhən) *n.* **1.** act or power of persuading. **2.** conviction or belief. **3.** religious system.

pert (pûrt) *adj.* bold; saucy. **—pert'ly,** *adv.* **—pert'ness,** *n.*

per·tain' (pər tān') *v.* belong; have reference.

per'ti·na'cious (pûr'tn ā'shəs) *adj.* holding tenaciously to purpose, opinion, etc.

per'ti·nent (-tn ənt) *adj.* relevant. **—per'ti-nence,** *n.* **—per'ti·nent·ly,** *adv.*

per·turb' (pər tûrb') *v.* disturb greatly. **—per'tur·ba'tion,** *n.*

pe·ruke' (pə rōōk') *n.* man's wig.

pe·ruse' (pə rōōz') *v.*, **-rused, -rusing.** read, esp. with care. **—pe·ru'sal,** *n.*

per·vade' (pər vād') *v.*, **-vaded, -vading.** be present throughout. **—per·va'sive,** *adj.*

per·verse' (pər vûrs') *adj.* **1.** stubbornly contrary. **2.** abnormal. **—per·ver'si·ty,** *n.* **—per·verse'ly,** *adv.*

per·vert', *v.* (pər vûrt') **1.** turn from right or moral course or use. **—***n.* (pûr'vûrt) **2.** perverted person. **—per·ver'sion,** *n.*

pe·se'ta (pə sā'tə) *n.*, *pl.* **-tas.** monetary unit of Spain.

pes'ky (pes'kē) *adj.*, **-kier, -kiest.** annoying; troublesome.

pe'so (pā'sō) *n.* monetary unit and coin in Latin America.

pes'si·mism (pes'ə miz'əm) *n.* **1.** disposition to expect worst. **2.** belief that all things tend to evil. **—pes'si·mist,** *n.* **—pes'si·mis'-tic,** *adj.* **—pes'si·mis'ti·cal·ly,** *adv.*

pest (pest) *n.* troublesome person, animal, or thing.

pes'ter (pes'tər) *v.* annoy; harass.

pes'ti·cide' (pes'tə sīd') *n.* poison used to kill harmful insects or weeds.

pes·tif'er·ous (pe stif'ər əs) *adj.* **1.** bearing disease. **2.** dangerous **3.** troublesome.

pes'ti·lence (pes'tl əns) *n.* epidemic disease. **—pes'ti·lent,** *adj.*

pes'tle (pes'əl, pes'tl) *n.* instrument for pounding or crushing.

pes'to (pes'tō) *n.* sauce of basil, nuts, garlic, olive oil, and cheese.

pet (pet) *n.*, *adj.*, *v.*, **petted, petting. —***n.* **1.** tame animal that is cared for affectionately. **2.** favorite. **3.** tantrum. **—***adj.* **4.** treated as pet. **—***v.* **5.** caress.

pet'al (pet'l) *n.* leaf of blossom.

pe·tard' (pi tärd') *n.* explosive device.

Pet.E. Petroleum Engineer.

pe'ter (pē'tər) *v. Informal.* diminish gradually.

pet'i·ole' (pet'ē ōl') *n.* stalk that attaches leaf to stem.

pet'it (pet'ē) *adj. Law.* petty.

pe·tite' (pə tēt') *adj.* small.

pe·ti'tion (pə tish'ən) *n.* **1.** request, esp. formal one. **—***v.* **2.** present petition. **—pe·ti'-tion·er,** *n.*

PETN *Chemistry, Pharmacology.* a crystalline, explosive solid, $C_5H_8N_4O_{12}$. [*p(enta)e(rythritol) t(etra)n(itrate)*]

pet'rel (pe'trəl) *n.* small oceanic bird.

pet'ri·fy' (pe'trə fī') *v.*, **-fied, -fying. 1.** turn into stone. **2.** paralyze with fear.

petro petroleum.

pet'ro·chem'i·cal (pe'trō kem'i kəl) *n.* chemical from petroleum.

pet'ro·dol'lars, *n.pl.* revenues in dollars accumulated by petroleum-exporting countries.

petrog. petrography.

pet'rol (pe'trəl) *n. Brit.* gasoline.

pet'ro·la'tum (pe'trə lā'təm) *n.* gelatinous mass from petroleum.

pe·tro'le·um (pə trō'lē əm) *n.* oily liquid occurring naturally; source of gasoline, kerosene, paraffin, etc.

pe·trol'o·gy (-trol'ə jē) *n.* study of rocks.

pet'ti·coat' (pet'ē kōt') *n.* underskirt.

pet'ti·fog' (pet'ē fog') *v.*, **-fogged, -fog-ging.** quibble over trifles.

pet'tish (pet'ish) *adj.* petulant.

pet'ty (pet'ē) *adj.*, **-tier, -tiest. 1.** small or trivial. **2.** small-minded. **—pet'ti·ness,** *n.*

petty cash, fund for paying minor expenses.

petty jury, jury in civil or criminal trial.

petty officer, noncommissioned officer in navy or coast guard.

pet'u·lant (pech'ə lənt) *adj.* showing impatient irritation. **—pet'u·lance,** *n.*

pe·tu'ni·a (pi tōō'nyə, -tyōō'-) *n.* plant with funnel-shaped flowers.

pew (pyōō) *n.* enclosed bench or seats in church.

pe'wee (pē'wē) *n.* any of certain small birds.

pew'ter (pyōō'tər) *n.* alloy rich in tin.

pf., (of stock) preferred.

Pfc. *Military.* private first class. Also, **PFC**

PFD personal flotation device.

pfd. preferred. Also, **pfd**

pfg. (in Germany) pfennig.

PFM *Telecommunications.* pulse frequency modulation. Also, **P.F.M.**

PG, motion-picture rating: parental guidance recommended.

PG-13, motion-picture rating: material may be unsuitable for children under 13.

pg., page.

PGA 1. Also, **P.G.A.** Professional Golfers' Association. **2.** *Biochemistry.* folic acid [*p(teroyl)* + *g(lutamic) a(cid)*].

pga *Computers.* pin-grid array.

pgmt pigment.

pH, symbol describing acidity or alkalinity of chemical solution.

PHA Public Housing Administration.

pha′e•ton (fā′i tn, fā′ə tən) *n.* open carriage or automobile.

phag′o•cyte′ (fag′ə sīt′) *n.* cell that ingests foreign particles.

pha•lan′ger (fə lan′jər) *n.* tree-dwelling Australian marsupial.

pha′lanx (fā′langks, fal′angks) *n., pl.* **-lanxes, -langes** (fə lan′jēz). **1.** compact body, as of troops, etc. **2.** any bones of fingers or toes.

phal′lus (fal′əs) *n., pl.* **phal•li** (fal′ī). **1.** penis. **2.** image of penis as symbol of fertility. —**phal′lic,** *adj.*

phan′tasm (fan′taz əm) *n.* apparition.

phan•tas′ma•go′ri•a (-mə gôr′ē ə) *n.* shifting series of illusions.

phan′tom (-təm) *n.* **1.** ghostlike image. —*adj.* **2.** unreal.

Phar. **1.** pharmaceutical. **2.** pharmacology. **3.** pharmacopoeia. **4.** pharmacy. Also, **phar.**

Phar′aoh (fâr′ō) *n.* title of ancient Egyptian kings.

Phar.B. Bachelor of Pharmacy.

Phar.D. Doctor of Pharmacy.

Phar′i•see′ (far′ə sē′) *n.* **1.** member of ancient Jewish sect. **2.** (*l.c.*) self-righteous person.

pharm. **1.** pharmaceutical. **2.** pharmacology. **3.** pharmacopoeia. **4.** pharmacy.

phar′ma•ceu′ti•cal (fär′mə sōō′ti kəl) *adj.* pertaining to pharmacy. Also, **phar′ma•ceu′tic.**

phar′ma•col′o•gy (-kol′ə jē) *n.* study of drugs. —**phar′ma•col′o•gist,** *n.*

phar′ma•co•poe′ia (-kə pē′ə) *n.* book on medicines.

phar′ma•cy (-sē) *n., pl.* **-cies. 1.** art or practice of preparing medicines. **2.** place for dispensing medicines. —**phar′ma•cist,** *n.*

Pharm.D. Doctor of Pharmacy.

Pharm.M. Master of Pharmacy.

phar′ynx (far′ingks) *n., pl.* **pharynges** (fərin′jēz), **pharynxes.** tube connecting mouth and nasal passages with esophagus. —**pha•ryn′ge•al,** *adj.* —**phar′yn•gi′tis** (far′ən jī′-tis) *n.*

phase (fāz) *n.* **1.** stage of change. **2.** aspect of changing thing.

phase′out′, *n.* gradual dismissal or termination.

Ph.B. Bachelor of Philosophy. [from Latin *Philosophiae Baccalaureus*]

Ph. C. Pharmaceutical Chemist.

Ph.D., Doctor of Philosophy.

Phe *Biochemistry.* phenylalanine.

P.H.E. Public Health Engineer.

pheas′ant (fez′ənt) *n.* large, long-tailed, brightly colored bird.

phen phenolic.

phe′no•bar′bi•tal′ (fē′nō bär′bi tôl′, -tal′) *n.* white powder used as sedative.

phe′nol (fē′nôl) *n.* carbolic acid. —**phe•no′-lic,** *adj.*

phe•nom′e•non′ (fi nom′ə non′, -nən) *n., pl.* **-e•na** (-ə nə). **1.** something observable. **2.** extraordinary thing or person. —**phe•nom′e•nal,** *adj.* —**phe•nom′e•nal•ly,** *adv.*

pher′o•mone′ (fer′ə mōn′) *n.* chemical substance released by animal that influences behavior of other members of species.

Ph. G. Graduate in Pharmacy.

phh phillips head.

phi′al (fī′əl) *n.* vial.

phil-, prefix meaning loving, having affinity for.

Phila. Philadelphia.

phi•lan′der (fi lan′dər) *v.* (of a man) have love affairs. —**phi•lan′der•er,** *n.*

phi•lan′thro•py (fi lan′thrə pē) *n., pl.* **-pies. 1.** love of humanity. **2.** benevolent act, work, or institution. —**phil′an•throp′ic** (fil′ən-throp′ik), **phil′an•throp′i•cal,** *adj.* —**phi•lan′thro•pist,** *n.*

phi•lat′e•ly (fi lat′l ē) *n.* collection and study of postage stamps, etc. —**phil′a•tel′ic** (fil′ə tel′ik) *adj.* —**phi•lat′e•list,** *n.*

-phile, suffix meaning one that loves or has strong enthusiasm for.

Philem. *Bible.* Philemon.

phil′har•mon′ic (fil′här mon′ik) *adj.* **1.** music-loving. —*n.* **2.** large orchestra.

Phil. I. Philippine Islands.

phil′is•tine′ (fil′ə stēn′, -stīn′) *n.* person indifferent to culture.

phil′o•den′dron (fil′ə den′drən) *n., pl.* **-drons, -dra.** tropical climbing plant.

philol. **1.** philological. **2.** philology.

phi•lol′o•gy (fi lol′ə jē) *n.* linguistics. —**phi•lol′o•gist,** *n.*

philos. **1.** philosopher. **2.** philosophical. **3.** philosophy.

phi•los′o•pher (fi los′ə fər) *n.* **1.** person versed in philosophy. **2.** person guided by reason. **3.** person who remains calm.

phi•los′o•phy (-fē) *n., pl.* **-phies. 1.** study of truths underlying being and knowledge. **2.** system of philosophical belief. **3.** principles of particular field of knowledge or action. **4.** calmness. —**phil′o•soph′ic** (fil′ə sof′ik), **phil′o•soph′i•cal,** *adj.* —**phi•los′o•phize′,** *v.*

phil′ter (fil′tər) *n.* magic potion.

Ph.L. Licentiate in Philosophy.

phle•bi′tis (flə bī′tis) *n.* inflammation of a vein.

phle•bot′o•my (-bot′ə mē) *n., pl.* **-mies.** *Med.* practice of opening a vein to let blood. —**phle•bot′o•mize′,** *v.,* **-mized, -mizing.**

phlegm (flem) *n.* **1.** thick mucus in the respiratory passages. **2.** apathy.

phleg•mat′ic (fleg mat′ik) *adj.* unemotional or unenthusiastic. —**phleg•mat′i•cal•ly,** *adv.*

phlo′em (flō′em) *n.* tissue in plant through which food passes.

phlox (floks) *n.* garden plant with showy flowers.

phm 1. phantom. **2.** phase modulation.

Ph.M. Master of Philosophy.

-phobe, suffix meaning one who hates or fears.

pho′bi•a (fō′bē ə) *n.* morbid fear.

-phobia, suffix meaning fear or dread.

phoe′be (fē′bē) *n.* small American bird.

phoe′nix (fē′niks) *n.* mythical bird that burns, then rises from its ashes.

phofl photoflash.

phon. phonetics.

phone (fōn) *n., v.,* **phoned, phoning.** *Informal,* telephone.

pho′neme (fō′nēm) *n.* minimal unit of speech sound that distinguishes one word from another.

phonet. phonetics.

pho•net′ics (fə net′iks) *n.* science of speech sounds. —**pho•net′ic,** *adj.* —**pho•net′i•cal•ly,** *adv.*

phon′ics (fon′iks) *n.* method of teaching reading and spelling based on phonetics.

phono-, prefix meaning sound.

pho′no•graph′ (fō′nə graf′) *n.* sound-producing machine using records. —**pho′no•graph′ic,** *adj.*

phonol. phonology.

pho•nol′o•gy (fə nol′ə jē) *n., pl.* **-gies.** study of sound changes in language. —**pho′no•log′i•cal** (fōn′l oj′i kəl) *adj.* —**pho•nol′o•gist,** *n.*

pho′ny (fō′nē) *adj.,* **-nier, -niest,** *n., pl.* **-nies.** *Informal.* —*adj.* **1.** false; fraudulent. —*n.* **2.** something phony. —**pho′ni•ness,** *n.*

phos phosphate.

phos′gene (fos′jēn) *n.* poisonous gas.

phos′phate (fos′fāt) *n.* **1.** salt of phosphoric acid. **2.** fertilizer containing phosphorus.

phos′phor (fos′fər) *n.* substance showing luminescence.

phos′pho•resce′ (-fə res′) *v.,* **-resced, -rescing.** be luminous. —**phos′pho•res′cence,** *n.* —**phos′pho•res′cent,** *adj.*

phos′pho•rus (-fər əs) *n.* solid nonmetallic element present in all forms of life. —**phos•phor′ic** (-fôr′ik), **phos′pho•rous,** *adj.*

phot. 1. photograph. **2.** photographer. **3.** photographic. **4.** photography.

pho′to (fō′tō) *n., pl.* **-tos.** *Informal,* photograph.

photo-, prefix meaning light.

pho′to•cop′y, *n., pl.* **-copies.** photographic copy. —**pho′to•cop′y,** *v.*

pho′to•e•lec′tric, *adj.* of or using electrical effects produced by light.

pho′to•en•grav′ing, *n.* process of obtaining a relief-printing surface by photographic reproduction. —**pho′to•en•grav′er,** *n.*

photo finish, finish of race so close as to re-quire scrutiny of photograph to determine winner.

photog. 1. photographer. **2.** photographic. **3.** photography.

pho′to•gen′ic (fō′tə jen′ik) *adj.* looking attractive in photos.

pho′to•graph′ (-graf′) *n.* **1.** picture produced by photography. —*v.* **2.** take photograph. —**pho•tog′ra•pher** (fə tog′rə fər) *n.*

pho•tog′ra•phy (fə tog′rə fē) *n.* process of obtaining images on sensitized surface by action of light. —**pho′to•graph′ic** (fō′tə graf′ik) *adj.*

photom. photometry.

pho′ton (fō′ton) *n.* quantum of electromagnetic radiation.

pho′to•sen′si•tive, *adj.* sensitive to light.

Pho′to•stat′ (fō′tə stat′) *n.* **1.** *Trademark.* camera for photographing documents, etc. **2.** (*l.c.*) the photograph. —*v.* **3.** (*l.c.*) make photostatic copy. —**pho′to•stat′ic,** *adj.*

pho′to•syn′the•sis, *n.* conversion by plants of carbon dioxide and water into carbohydrates, aided by light and chlorophyll.

phr. phrase.

phrase (frāz) *n., v.,* **phrased, phrasing.** —*n.* **1.** sequence of words used as unit. **2.** minor division of musical composition. —*v.* **3.** express in particular way.

phra′se•ol′o•gy (frā′zē ol′ə jē) *n.* **1.** manner of verbal expression. **2.** expressions.

phren. 1. phrenological. **2.** phrenology.

phre•net′ic (frə net′ik) *adj.* frenetic.

phrenol. 1. phrenological. **2.** phrenology.

phre•nol′o•gy (frə nol′ə jē) *n.* theory that mental powers are shown by shape of skull. —**phre•nol′o•gist,** *n.*

phrm pharmacy.

phrmcol pharmacological.

PHS Public Health Service. Also, **P.H.S.**

phsk phase-shift keying.

phy•lac′ter•y (fi lak′tə rē) *n., pl.* **-teries.** leather cube containing Biblical verses.

phy•log′e•ny (fī loj′ə nē) *n.* development of particular group of organisms.

phy′lum (fī′ləm) *n., pl.* **-la.** primary classification of plants or animals.

phys. 1. physical. **2.** physician. **3.** physics. **4.** physiological. **5.** physiology.

phys. chem. physical chemistry.

phys ed (fiz′ ed′), *Informal.* physical education. Also, **phys. ed.**

phys. geog. physical geography.

phys′ic (fiz′ik) *n.* medicine, esp. one that purges.

phys′i•cal, *adj.* **1.** of the body. **2.** of matter. **3.** of physics. —*n.* **4.** full examination of body. —**phys′i•cal•ly,** *adv.*

physical anthropology, study of evolutionary changes in human body structure.

physical science, science that deals with inanimate matter or energy.

physical therapy, treatment of physical disability or pain by techniques such as exercise.

phy•si′cian (fi zish′ən) *n.* medical doctor.

phys•ics (fiz′iks) *n.* science of matter, motion, energy, and force. **—phys′i•cist,** *n.*

phys′i•og′no•my (fiz′ē og′nə mē, -on′ə-) *n., pl.* **-mies.** face.

phys′i•og′ra•phy (-og′rə fē) *n.* study of earth's surface.

physiol. 1. physiological. **2.** physiologist. **3.** physiology.

phys′i•ol′o•gy (-ol′ə jē) *n.* science dealing with functions of living organisms. **—phys′i•o•log′i•cal** (-ə loj′i kəl) *adj.* **—phys′i•ol′o•gist,** *n.* **—phys′i•o•log′i•cal•ly,** *adv.*

phys′i•o•ther′a•py (fiz′ē ō-) *n.* treatment of disease by massage, exercise, etc.

phy•sique′ (fi zēk′) *n.* physical structure.

pi (pī) *n.* the Greek letter, used as symbol for ratio of circumference to diameter.

pi′a•nis′si•mo (pē′ə nis′ə mō′, pyä-) *adv. Music.* very softly.

pi•an′o (pē an′ō) *n., pl.* **-anos,** *adv.* **—n. 1.** Also, **pi•an′o•for′te** (-fōr′tā). musical keyboard instrument in which hammers strike upon metal strings. **—adv.** (pē ä′nō) **2.** *Music.* softly. **—pi•an′ist** (pē an′ist, pē′ə nist) *n.*

pias. (in Turkey and other countries) piaster.

pi•az′za (pē az′ə *or, for 1,* -ät′sə) *n.* **1.** open public square, esp. in Italy. **2.** veranda.

pi′ca (pī′kə) *n.* **1.** size of printing type. **2.** unit of measure in printing.

pic′a•resque′ (pik′ə resk′) *adj.* of a form of fiction that describes adventures of roguish hero.

pic′a•yune′ (pik′ē yōōn′, pik′ə-) *adj.* insignificant; petty.

pic′ca•lil′li (pik′ə lil′ē) *n.* spiced vegetable relish.

pic′co•lo′ (pik′ə lō′) *n., pl.* **-los.** small shrill flute.

pick (pik) *v.* **1.** choose. **2.** pluck. **3.** dig or break into, esp. with pointed instrument. **4.** nibble listlessly. **—n. 5.** choice. **6.** right to choose. **7.** Also, **pick′ax′, pick′axe′.** sharppointed tool for breaking rock, etc. **—pick′er,** *n.*

pick′er•el (pik′ər əl) *n.* small pike.

pick′et (pik′it) *n.* **1.** pointed stake. **2.** demonstration by labor union in front of workplace. **3.** troops posted to warn of enemy attack. **—v. 4.** enclose with pickets. **5.** put pickets in front of.

picket line, line of strikers or other pickets.

pick′le (pik′əl) *n., v.,* **-led, -ling. —n. 1.** cucumber, etc. preserved in spiced vinegar. **2.** predicament. **—v. 3.** preserve in vinegar or brine.

pick′pock′et, *n.* person who steals from others' pockets.

pick′up′, *n.* **1.** ability to accelerate rapidly. **2.** small open-body truck.

pick′y, *adj.,* **-ier, -iest.** extremely fussy or finicky.

pic′nic (pik′nik) *n., v.,* **-nicked, -nicking. —n. 1.** outing and meal in the open. **—v. 2.** have picnic. **—pic′nick•er,** *n.*

pi′cot (pē′kō) *n.* decorative loop along edge of lace, ribbon, etc.

pic′ture (pik′chər) *n., v.,* **-tured, -turing. —n. 1.** painting or photograph. **2.** motion picture. **—v. 3.** represent in picture. **4.** imagine. **—pic•to′ri•al,** *adj.*

pic′tur•esque′ (-chə resk′) *adj.* visually charming or quaint.

PID *Pathology.* pelvic inflammatory disease.

pid′dle (pid′l) *v.,* **-dled, -dling.** waste.

pid′dling, *adj.* trivial; negligible.

pidg′in (pij′ən) *n.* language developed to allow speakers of two different languages to communicate, primarily a simplified form of one of the languages.

pidgin English, English trade jargon used in other countries.

pie (pī) *n.* baked dish of fruit, meat, etc., in pastry crust.

pie′bald′ (pī′bôld′) *adj.* having patches of different colors.

piece (pēs) *n., v.,* **pieced, piecing. —n. 1.** limited or single portion. **2.** one part of a whole. **3.** artistic work. **4.** rifle or cannon. **—v. 5.** make or enlarge by joining pieces.

pièce de ré•sis•tance′ (pyes də Rä zē stäns′) *n., pl.* **pièces de résistance** (pyes-). **1.** principal dish of meal. **2.** principal item of series.

piece goods, goods sold at retail by linear measure.

piece′meal′, *adv.* **1.** gradually. **2.** into fragments.

piece′work′, *n.* work done and paid for by the piece.

pie chart, graph in which sectors of circle represent quantities.

pied (pīd) *adj.* many-colored.

pied′-à-terre′ (pyä′də târ′) *n., pl.* **pieds′-à-terre′** (pyä′-). apartment for part-time use.

pie′-eyed′, *adj. Slang.* drunk.

pie′plant′, *n.* rhubarb.

pier (pēr) *n.* **1.** structure at which vessels are moored. **2.** masonry support.

pierce (pērs) *v.,* **pierced, piercing. 1.** make hole or way through. **2.** make (hole) in.

pi′e•ty (pī′i tē) *n.* piousness.

pif′fle (pif′əl) *n. Informal.* nonsense. **—pif′fling,** *adj.*

pig (pig) *n.* **1.** swine. **2.** bar of metal. **—pig′gish,** *adj.*

pi′geon (pij′ən) *n.* short-legged bird with compact body.

pi′geon•hole′, *n., v.,* **-holed, -holing. —n. 1.** small compartment, as in desk, etc. **—v. 2.** classify. **3.** put aside and ignore.

pi′geon-toed′, *adj.* having toes or feet turned inward.

P

pig′gy·back′, *adv.* **1.** on the back or shoulders. —*adj.* **2.** astride the back. **3.** attached to something else. **4.** of the carrying of truck trailers on trains.

pig′head′ed, *adj.* perversely stubborn.

pig iron, crude iron from furnace.

pig′ment (-mənt) *n.* coloring matter. —**pig′men·tar′y,** *adj.*

pig′men·ta′tion, *n.* coloration.

pig′my (-mē) *n., pl.* **-mies.** pygmy.

pig′pen′, *n.* **1.** stall for pigs. **2.** filthy or untidy place. Also, **pig′sty′.**

pig′tail′, *n.* hanging braid at back of head.

PIK payment in kind. Also, **p.i.k.**

pike (pīk) *n.* **1.** large fresh-water fish. **2.** metal-headed shaft. **3.** highway.

pik′er, *n. Slang.* person who does things cheaply or meanly.

pil. (in prescriptions) pill. [from Latin *pilula*]

pi′laf (pē′läf, pi läf′) *n.* Middle Eastern rice dish.

pi·las′ter (pi las′tər) *n.* shallow decorative imitation of column.

pil′chard (pil′chərd) *n.* marine fish.

pile (pīl) *n., v.,* **piled, piling.** —*n.* **1.** group of things lying one on another. **2.** large amount of anything. **3.** device for producing energy by nuclear reaction. **4.** Also, **pil′ing.** upright driven into ground as foundation member or to retain earth. **5.** hair; down; wool; fur. **6.** nap (def. 2). **7.** *pl.* hemorrhoids. —*v.* **8.** lay in pile. **9.** accumulate.

pil′fer (pil′fər) *v.* steal, esp. from storage. —**pil′fer·age,** *n.*

pil′grim (pil′grim, -grəm) *n.* **1.** traveler, esp. to sacred place. **2.** (*cap.*) early Puritan settler. —**pil′grim·age,** *n.*

pill (pil) *n.* small mass of medicine to be swallowed.

pil′lage (pil′ij) *v.,* **-laged, -laging,** *n.* plunder.

pil′lar (pil′ər) *n.* upright shaft of masonry.

pill′box′, *n.* **1.** small fort. **2.** box for pills.

pil′lo·ry (pil′ə rē) *n., pl.* **-ries,** *v.,* **-ried, -rying.** —*n.* **1.** wooden framework used to confine and expose offenders. —*v.* **2.** put in pillory. **3.** expose to public contempt.

pil′low (pil′ō) *n.* bag of feathers, etc., used as support for head. —**pil′low·case′,** *n.*

pi′lot (pī′lət) *n.* **1.** operator of aircraft. **2.** expert navigator. —*v.* **3.** steer. —*adj.* **4.** experimental.

pi′lot·house′, *n.* enclosed structure on deck of ship.

pilot light, small flame used to relight main burners.

PIM personal information manager.

pim pulse-interval modulation.

pi·men′to (pi men′tō) *n., pl.* **-tos.** dried fruit of tropical tree; allspice.

pi·mien′to (-myen′tō, -men′-) *n., pl.* **-tos.** variety of garden pepper.

pimp (pimp) *n., v.* —*n.* **1.** manager of prostitutes. —*v.* **2.** act as pimp.

pim′per·nel′ (pim′pər nel′, -nl) *n.* variety of primrose.

pim′ple (pim′pəl) *n.* small swelling of skin. —**pim′ply,** *adj.*

pin (pin) *n., v.,* **pinned, pinning.** —*n.* **1.** slender pointed piece of metal, wood, etc., for fastening. —*v.* **2.** fasten with pin. **3.** hold fast; bind.

PIN (pin) personal identification number.

pin′a·fore′ (pin′ə fôr′) *n.* **1.** child's apron. **2.** sleeveless dress.

pin′ball′, *n.* game in which spring-driven ball rolls against pins on sloping board.

pince′-nez′ (pans′nā′, pins′-) *n., pl.* **pince-nez.** eyeglasses supported by pinching nose.

pin′cers (pin′sərz) *n.* gripping tool with two pivoted limbs.

pinch (pinch) *v.* **1.** squeeze, as between finger and thumb. **2.** cramp or affect sharply. **3.** economize. —*n.* **4.** act of pinching. **5.** tiny amount. **6.** distress; emergency. —**pinch′er,** *n.*

pinch′-hit′, *v.,* **-hit, -hitting.** substitute.

pine (pīn) *v.,* **pined, pining,** *n.* —*v.* **1.** long painfully. **2.** fail in health from grief, etc. —*n.* **3.** evergreen tree with needle-shaped leaves. —**pin′y,** *adj.*

pin′e·al gland (pin′ē əl) organ involved in biorhythms and gonadal development.

pine′ap′ple (pīn′ap′əl) *n.* tropical fruit.

pin′feath′er, *n.* undeveloped feather.

ping (ping) *v.* **1.** produce sharp sound like bullet striking metal. —*n.* **2.** pinging sound.

Ping′-Pong′ (ping′pong′) *n. Trademark.* table tennis.

pin′head′, *n.* **1.** head of pin. **2.** stupid person.

pin′ion (pin′yən) *n.* **1.** feather or wing. **2.** small cogwheel. —*v.* **3.** bind (the arms).

pink (pingk) *n.* **1.** pale red. **2.** fragrant garden flower. **3.** highest degree. —**pink,** *adj.*

pink′eye′, *n.* contagious inflammation of membrane covering eye.

pinking shears, shears with notched blades.

pin money, small sum set aside.

pin′na·cle (pin′ə kəl) *n.* lofty peak or position.

pin′nate (pin′āt, -it) *adj.* having leaflets on each side of common stalk.

pi′noch·le (pē′nuk əl, -nok-) *n.* game using 48 cards.

pin′point′, *v.* identify.

PINS (pinz), a person of less than 16 years of age placed under the jurisdiction of a juvenile court. [*P(erson) I(n) N(eed of) S(upervision)*]

pin′stripe′, *n.* very thin stripe in fabric. —**pin′striped′,** *adj.*

pint (pīnt) *n.* liquid and dry measure equal to one-half quart.

pin'tle (pin'tl) *n.* pin or bolt.

pin'to (pin'tō, pĕn'-) *adj.*, *n.*, *pl.* **-tos.** —*adj.*
1. piebald. —*n.* **2.** piebald horse.

pinto bean, bean with pinkish mottled seeds.

pin'up', *n.* large photograph of sexually attractive person.

pin'wheel', *n.* windmill-like toy that spins on stick.

pin'yin' (pin'yin') *n.* system for transliterating Chinese into Latin alphabet.

PIO *U.S. Military.* **1.** public information office. **2.** public information officer.

pi'o•neer' (pī'ə nēr') *n.* **1.** early arrival in new territory. **2.** first one in any effort. —*v.* **3.** act as pioneer.

pi'ous (pī'əs) *adj.* **1.** reverential; devout. **2.** sacred. —**pi'ous•ly,** *adv.* —**pi'ous•ness,** *n.*

pip (pip) *n.* **1.** small fruit seed. **2.** spot on playing card, domino, etc. **3.** disease of fowls.

pipe (pīp) *n.*, *v.*, **piped, piping.** —*n.* **1.** tube for conveying fluid. **2.** tube for smoking tobacco. **3.** tube used as musical instrument. —*v.* **4.** play on pipe. **5.** convey by pipe. —**pip'er,** *n.* —**pipe'line',** *n.*

pipe dream, unrealistic hope.

pipe'line', *n.* **1.** linked pipes for transporting oil, water, etc. **2.** route for supplies. **3.** channel.

pip'ing, *n.* **1.** pipes. **2.** sound of pipes. **3.** kind of trimming.

pip'pin (pip'in) *n.* kind of apple.

pip'squeak' (pip'skwēk') *n. Informal.* small or unimportant person.

pi'quant (pē'kənt, -känt) *adj.* agreeably sharp. —**pi'quan•cy,** *n.*

pique (pēk) *v.*, **piqued, piquing,** *n.* —*v.* **1.** arouse resentment in. **2.** excite (curiosity, etc.). —*n.* **3.** irritated feeling.

pi•qué' (pi kā') *n.* corded cotton fabric.

pi'ra•cy (pī'rə sē) *n.*, *pl.* **-cies. 1.** robbery at sea. **2.** illegal use of material. —**pi'rate,** *n.*, *v.*

pi•ra'nha (pi rän'yə, -ran'-, -rä'nə, -ran'ə) *n.*, *pl.* **-nhas, -nha.** small, fiercely predatory fish.

PIRG Public Interest Research Group.

pir'ou•ette' (pir'ŏŏ et') *v.*, **-etted, -etting,** *n.* —*v.* **1.** whirl about on the toes. —*n.* **2.** such whirling.

pis'ca•to'ri•al (pis'kə tôr'ē əl) *adj.* of fishing.

pis'mire (pis'mī³r', piz'-) *n.* ant.

pis•ta'chi•o' (pi stash'ē ō') *n.*, *pl.* **-chios.** edible nut.

pis'til (pis'tl) *n.* seed-bearing organ of flower. —**pis'til•late** (-tl it, -āt') *adj.*

pis'tol (pis'tl) *n.* short hand-held gun.

pis'tol-whip', *v.*, **-whipped, -whipping.** beat with pistol.

pis'ton (pis'tən) *n.* part moving back and forth in cylinder.

pit (pit) *n.*, *v.*, **pitted, pitting.** —*n.* **1.** hole in ground or other surface. **2.** hollow in body. **3.** part of main floor of theater. **4.** stone of fruit. —*v.* **5.** mark with pits. **6.** set in enmity or opposition. **7.** remove pit.

pi'ta (pē'tə) *n.* round, flat bread with pocket.

pitch (pich) *v.* **1.** throw. **2.** set at certain point. **3.** fall forward. **4.** drop and rise, as ship. —*n.* **5.** relative point or degree. **6.** musical tone. **7.** slope. **8.** sticky dark substance from coal tar. **9.** sap.

pitch'-black', *adj.* extremely black.

pitch'blende' (-blend') *n.* principal ore of uranium and radium.

pitch'-dark', *adj.* very dark.

pitched, *adj.* fought with all available troops.

pitch'er (pich'ər) *n.* **1.** container with spout for liquids. **2.** person who pitches.

pitcher plant, insectivorous plant.

pitch'fork', *n.* sharp-tined fork for handling hay.

pitch'man, *n.*, *pl.* **-men.** person who makes sales pitch.

pitch pipe, small pipe producing pitches.

pit'e•ous (pit'ē əs) *adj.* pathetic. —**pit'e•ous•ly,** *adv.*

pit'fall', *n.* trap; hazard.

pith (pith) *n.* **1.** spongy tissue. **2.** essence. **3.** strength. —**pith'y,** *adj.* —**pith'i•ness,** *n.*

pit'i•a•ble (pit'ē ə bəl) *adj.* **1.** deserving pity. **2.** contemptible. —**pit'i•a•bly,** *adv.*

pit'i•ful (-i fəl) *adj.* **1.** deserving pity. **2.** exciting contempt. **3.** full of pity. —**pit'i•ful•ly,** *adv.* —**pit'i•ful•ness,** *n.*

pit'tance (pit'ns) *n.* meager income.

pi•tu'i•tar'y (pi tŏŏ'ə ter'ē, -tyŏŏ-) *adj.* denoting gland at base of brain.

pit'y (pit'ē) *n.*, *pl.* **-ies,** *v.*, **-ied, pitying.** —*n.* **1.** sympathetic sorrow. **2.** cause for regret. —*v.* **3.** feel pity for. —**pit'i•less,** *adj.* —**pit'i•less•ly,** *adv.*

piv peak inverse voltage.

piv'ot (piv'ət) *n.* **1.** shaft on which something turns. —*v.* **2.** turn on pivot. —**piv'ot•al,** *adj.*

pix'el (pik'səl, -sel) *n.* smallest element of image in video display system.

pix'y (pik'sē) *n.*, *pl.* **pixies.** fairy. Also, **pix'ie.**

pi•zazz' (pə zaz') *n. Informal.* **1.** energy; vigor. **2.** dash; flair. Also, **piz•zazz'.**

pizz. *Music.* pizzicato.

piz'za (pēt'sə) *n.* dish of cheese, tomato sauce, etc., on baked crust.

piz'zer•i'a (pēt'sə rē'ə) *n.* restaurant serving mainly pizza.

piz'zi•ca'to (pit'si kä'tō) *adj. Music.* played by plucking strings with fingers.

p.j.'s (pē'jāz'), *Informal.* pajamas. Also, **P.J.'s**

pjtr projector.

PK 1. personal knowledge **2.** psychokinesis.

pk. 1. pack. **2.** park. **3.** Also, **pk** peak. **4.** peck; pecks.

pkg., package.

P

pkt. 1. packet. **2.** pocket.

PKU *Pathology.* phenylketonuria.

pkwy., parkway.

pl., 1. place. **2.** plural.

PLA People's Liberation Army.

plac•a•ble (plak′ə bəl, plā′kə-) *adj.* forgiving.

plac′ard (plak′ärd, -ərd) *n.* public notice.

pla′cate (plā′kāt, plak′āt) *v.,* **-cated, -cating.** appease. **—pla•ca′tion,** *n.*

place (plās) *n., v.,* **placed, placing. —n. 1.** particular portion of space. **2.** function. **3.** social standing. **4.** stead. **—v. 5.** put in place. **6.** identify from memory. **—place′ment,** *n.*

pla•ce′bo (plə sē′bō) *n., pl.* **-bos, -boes.** pill, etc., containing no medication, given to reassure patient or as control in testing drug.

pla•cen′ta (plə sen′tə) *n.* organ in uterus which attaches to and nourishes fetus.

plac′er (plas′ər) *n.* surface gravel containing gold particles.

plac′id (plas′id) *adj.* serene. **—pla•cid′i•ty,** *n.* **—plac′id•ly,** *adv.*

plack′et (plak′it) *n.* slit at neck, waist, or wrist of garment.

pla′gia•rize′ (plā′jə rīz′) *v.,* **-rized, -rizing.** copy and claim as one's own work. **—pla′-gia•rism,** *n.* **—pla′gia•rist,** *n.*

plague (plāg) *n., v.,* **plagued, plaguing. —n. 1.** often fatal epidemic disease. **2.** affliction or vexation. **—v. 3.** trouble; annoy.

plaid (plad) *n.* **1.** fabric woven in many-colored cross bars. **—adj. 2.** having such pattern.

plain (plān) *adj.* **1.** distinct. **2.** evident. **3.** candid. **4.** ordinary; unpretentious. **5.** bare. **6.** flat. **—adv. 7.** clearly. **8.** candidly. **—n. 9.** level area. **—plain′ly,** *adv.* **—plain′ness,** *n.*

plain′clothes′man, *n., pl.* **-men.** police officer who wears civilian clothes on duty.

plain′song′, *n.* ancient unisonal music of early Christian Church.

plaint (plānt) *n.* complaint.

plain′tiff (plān′tif) *n.* one who brings suit in court.

plain′tive (plān′tiv) *adj.* melancholy. **—plain′tive•ly,** *adv.* **—plain′tive•ness,** *n.*

plait (plāt, plat) *n., v.* **1.** braid. **2.** pleat.

PLAM price-level adjusted mortgage.

plan (plan) *n., v.,* **planned, planning. —n. 1.** scheme of action or arrangement. **2.** drawing of projected structure. **—v. 3.** make plan. **—plan′ner,** *n.*

plane (plān) *n., adj., v.,* **planed, planing. —n. 1.** flat surface. **2.** level. **3.** airplane. **4.** tool for smoothing. **—adj. 5.** flat. **—v. 6.** glide. **7.** smooth with plane.

plan′et (plan′it) *n.* solid heavenly body revolving about sun. **—plan′e•tar′y,** *adj.*

plan′e•tar′i•um (-i târ′ē əm) *n., pl.* **-iums, -ia. 1.** optical device that projects a representation of heavens on a dome. **2.** museum with such device.

plane tree, large, spreading shade tree.

plan′gent (plan′jənt) *adj.* resounding loudly.

plank (plangk) *n.* **1.** long flat piece of timber. **2.** point in political platform. **—plank′ing,** *n.*

plank′ton (plangk′tən) *n.* microscopic organisms floating in water.

plant (plant) *n.* **1.** any member of vegetable group. **2.** equipment for business or process; factory. **—v. 3.** set in ground for growth. **4.** furnish with plants. **—plant′er,** *n.* **—plant′-like′,** *adj.*

plan′tain (plan′tin) *n.* **1.** tropical bananalike plant. **2.** common flat-leaved weed.

plan′tar (plan′tər) *adj.* of the soles of the feet.

plan•ta′tion (plan tā′shən) *n.* large farm, esp. with one crop.

plaque (plak) *n.* **1.** monumental tablet. **2.** sticky, whitish film formed on tooth surfaces.

plash (plash) *n.* **1.** gentle splash. **—v. 2.** splash gently.

plas′ma (plaz′mə) *n.* clear liquid part of blood or lymph.

plas′ter (plas′tər) *n.* **1.** pasty mixture for covering walls, etc. **2.** medicinal preparation spread on cloth and applied to body. **—v. 3.** cover or treat with plaster.

plas′ter•board′, *n.* material for insulating or covering walls.

plaster of Par′is (par′is) form of gypsum in powdery form, used in making plasters and casts.

plas′tic (plas′tik) *adj.* **1.** of or produced by molding. **2.** moldable. **3.** three-dimensional. **—n. 4.** organic material that is hardened after shaping. **—plas•tic′i•ty** (-tis′ə tē) *n.*

plastic surgery, branch of surgery dealing with repair, replacement, or reshaping of parts of body.

plat. 1. plateau. **2.** platinum. **3.** platoon.

plate (plāt) *n., v.,* **plated, plating. —n. 1.** shallow round dish for food. **2.** gold or silver ware. **3.** sheet of metal used in printing. **4.** shaped holder for false teeth. **—v. 5.** coat with metal. **—plat′er,** *n.*

pla•teau′ (pla tō′) *n., pl.* **-teaus, -teaux** (-tōz′, -tōz). raised plain.

plate glass, smooth glass.

plat′en (plat′n) *n.* plate in printing press that presses paper against inked surface.

plat′form (plat′fôrm) *n.* **1.** raised flooring or structure. **2.** set of announced political principles.

plat′i•num (plat′n əm) *n.* precious, malleable metallic element.

plat′i•tude′ (plat′i tōōd′, -tyōōd′) *n.* trite remark. **—plat′i•tud′i•nous,** *adj.*

pla•ton′ic (plə ton′ik) *adj.* without sexual involvement.

pla•toon′ (plə tōōn′) *n.* small military or police unit.

plat′ter (plat′ər) *n.* large serving dish.

plat′y•fish′ (plat′ē-) *n., pl.* **-fish, -fishes.** freshwater fish common in aquariums.

plat′y•pus (plat′i pəs) *n., pl.* **-puses, -pi** (-pī′). duckbill.

plau′dit (plô′dit) *n.* (*usu. pl.*) applause.

plau′si•ble (plô′zə bəl) *adj.* apparently true, reasonable, or trustworthy. —**plau′si•bil′i•ty,** *n.* —**plau′si•bly,** *adv.*

play (plā) *n.* **1.** dramatic work. **2.** recreation. **3.** fun. **4.** change. **5.** movement. —*v.* **6.** act in a play. **7.** engage in game. **8.** perform on musical instrument. **9.** amuse oneself. **10.** move about lightly. —**play′er,** *n.* —**play′ful,** *adj.* —**play′ful•ly,** *adv.* —**play′ful•ness,** *n.* —**play′go′er,** *n.* —**play′mate′,** *n.*

play′back′, *n.* **1.** reproduction of a recording. **2.** apparatus used in producing playbacks.

play′bill′, *n.* program or announcement of play.

play′boy′, *n.* man who pursues life of pleasure without responsibilities or attachments.

play′ground′, *n.* area used, esp. by children, for outdoor recreation.

play′house′, *n.* **1.** theater. **2.** small house for children to play in.

play′-off′, *n.* extra game played to break a tie.

play on words, pun.

play′pen′, *n.* small enclosure in which baby can play.

play′thing′, *n.* toy.

play′wright′ (-rīt′) *n.* writer of plays.

pla′za (plä′zə, plaz′ə) *n.* public square, esp. in Spanish-speaking countries.

PLC *British.* public limited company.

plc power-line carrier.

pld payload.

plea (plē) *n.* **1.** defense; justification. **2.** entreaty.

plea bargain, agreement in which criminal defendant pleads guilty to lesser charge.

plead (plēd) *v.,* **pleaded** or **pled** (pled), **pleading. 1.** make earnest entreaty. **2.** allege formally in court. **3.** argue (case at law). **4.** allege in justification. —**plead′er,** *n.*

pleas′ant (plez′ənt) *adj.* agreeable; pleasing. —**pleas′ant•ly,** *adv.*

pleas′ant•ry, *n., pl.* **-ries.** good-humored remark.

please (plēz) *v.,* **pleased, pleasing.** be or act to pleasure of; seem good. —**pleas′ing•ly,** *adv.*

pleas′ur•a•ble (plezh′ər ə bəl) *adj.* enjoyable.

pleas′ure, *n.* **1.** enjoyment. **2.** person's will or desire.

pleat (plēt) *n.* **1.** double fold of cloth. —*v.* **2.** fold in pleats.

ple•be′ian (pli bē′ən) *adj.* of common people.

pleb′i•scite′ (pleb′ə sīt′) *n.* direct vote by citizens on public question.

plec′trum (plek′trəm) *n., pl.* **-tra** (-trə), **-trums.** object for picking strings of musical instrument.

pledge (plej) *n., v.,* **pledged, pledging.** —*n.* **1.** solemn promise. **2.** property delivered as security on a loan. **3.** toast. —*v.* **4.** bind by pledge. **5.** promise. **6.** deliver as pledge.

Pleis′to•cene′ (plī′stə sēn′) *adj.* pertaining to geologic epoch forming earlier half of Quaternary Period.

ple′na•ry (plē′nə rē, plen′ə-) *adj.* full; complete.

plen′i•po•ten′ti•ar′y (plen′ə pə ten′shē er′ē, -shə rē) *n., pl.* **-aries,** *adj.* —*n.* **1.** diplomat with full authority. —*adj.* **2.** having full authority.

plen′i•tude′ (plen′i tōōd′, -tyōōd′) *n.* abundance.

plen′ty (plen′tē) *n.* **1.** abundant supply. —*adv. Informal.* **2.** very. —**plen′te•ous** (-tē əs), **plen′ti•ful,** *adj.*

pleth′o•ra (pleth′ər ə) *n.* superabundance.

pleu′ra (plŏŏr′ə) *n., pl.* **pleur•ae** (plŏŏr′ē). membrane that covers lung and lines chest wall.

pleu′ri•sy (plŏŏr′ə sē) *n.* inflammation of pleura.

Plex′i•glas′ (plek′si glas′) *n. Trademark.* light, durable transparent plastic.

plex′us (plek′səs) *n., pl.* **-uses, -us.** network.

plf pounds per linear foot.

plf. plaintiff. Also, **plff.**

pli′a•ble (plī′ə bəl) *adj.* easily bent or influenced. —**pli′a•bil′i•ty,** *n.* —**pli′a•bly,** *adv.*

pli′ant (-ənt) *adj.* pliable. —**pli′an•cy,** *n.*

pli′ers (plī′ərz) *n.pl.* small pincers.

plight (plīt) *n.* **1.** distressing condition. —*v.* **2.** promise.

plk *Machinery.* pillowblock.

pll 1. pallet. **2.** *Electronics.* phase-locked loop.

plmg plumbing.

plmr plumber.

pln plane.

plnm plenum.

plnr planar.

plnt planet.

plnty planetary.

PLO, Palestine Liberation Organization.

plod (plod) *v.,* **plodded, plodding. 1.** walk heavily. **2.** work laboriously. —**plod′der,** *n.*

PL/1 *Computers.* programming language one.

plop (plop) *v.,* **plopped, plopping,** *n.* —*v.* **1.** drop with sound like that of object hitting water. **2.** drop with direct impact. —*n.* **3.** plopping sound or fall.

plot (plot) *n., v.,* **plotted, plotting.** —*n.* **1.** secret scheme. **2.** main story of fictional work. **3.** small area of ground. —*v.* **4.** plan secretly. **5.** mark (chart course) on. **6.** divide into plots. —**plot′ter,** *n.*

plov′er (pluv′ər, plō′vər) *n.* shore bird.

plow (plou) *n.* **1.** implement for cutting and turning soil. **2.** similar implement for removing snow. —*v.* **3.** cut or turn with plow. **4.** force way, as through water. Also, **plough.** —**plow′man,** *n.*

P

plow′share′, *n.* blade of plow.

ploy (ploi) *n.* maneuver to gain advantage; stratagem; ruse.

plq plaque.

PLR Public Lending Right.

plr 1. pillar. **2.** pliers. **3.** puller.

plrs *Navigation.* pelorus.

plrt polarity.

pls. 1. please. **2.** pulse.

PLSS portable life support system.

plstc plastic.

plt 1. pilot. **2.** plant.

pltf platform.

pltg 1. planting. **2.** plating.

PLU price lookup.

plu. plural.

pluck (pluk) *v.* **1.** pull out from fixed position. **2.** sound (strings of musical instrument). —*n.* **3.** pull or tug. **4.** courage.

pluck′y, *adj.,* **-ier, -iest.** courageous. —**pluck′i•ness,** *n.*

plug (plug) *n., v.,* **plugged, plugging.** —*n.* **1.** object for stopping hole. **2.** device on electrical cord that establishes contact in socket. **3.** *Slang.* advertisement; favorable mention. —*v.* **4.** stop with or insert plug. **5.** *Slang.* mention favorably. **6.** work steadily. —**plug′ger,** *n.*

plum (plum) *n.* **1.** oval juicy fruit. **2.** deep purple. **3.** *Informal,* favor widely desired.

plumb (plum) *n.* **1.** plummet. —*adj.* **2.** perpendicular. —*adv.* **3.** vertically. **4.** exactly. **5.** *Informal,* completely. —*v.* **6.** make vertical. **7.** measure depth of.

plumb′ing, *n.* system of water pipes, etc. —**plumb′er,** *n.*

plume (ploom) *n., v.,* **plumed, pluming.** —*n.* **1.** feather, esp. large one. **2.** ornamental tuft. —*v.* **3.** preen. **4.** furnish with plumes. —**plum′age** (ploo′mij) *n.*

plum′met (plum′it) *n.* **1.** weight on line for sounding or establishing verticals. —*v.* **2.** plunge.

plump (plump) *adj.* **1.** somewhat fat or thick. —*v.* **2.** make or become plump. **3.** drop heavily. —*n.* **4.** heavy fall. —*adv.* **5.** directly. **6.** heavily. —**plump′ness,** *n.*

plun′der (plun′dər) *v.* **1.** rob. —*n.* **2.** act of plundering. **3.** loot.

plunge (plunj) *v.,* **plunged, plunging.** *n.* —*v.* **1.** dip. **2.** rush. **3.** pitch forward. —*n.* **4.** dive.

plung′er, *n.* **1.** pistonlike part moving within the cylinder of certain machines. **2.** device with handle and suction cup, used to unclog drains.

plunk (plungk) *v.* **1.** drop heavily. **2.** give forth twanging sound. —*n.* **3.** sound of plunking.

plupf. pluperfect. Also, **plup., pluperf.**

plur. 1. plural. **2.** plurality.

plu′ral (ploor′əl) *adj.* **1.** of, being, or containing more than one. —*n.* **2.** plural form. —**plur′al•ize′,** *v.,* **-ized, -izing.**

plu′ral•ism, *n.* condition in which minority groups participate in society, yet maintain their distinctions. —**plu′ral•is′tic,** *adj.*

plu•ral′i•ty (ploo ral′i tē) *n., pl.* **-ties. 1.** in election with three or more candidates, the excess of votes given leading candidate over next candidate. **2.** majority.

plus (plus) *prep.* **1.** increased by. —*adj.* **2.** involving addition. **3.** positive. —*n.* **4.** something additional.

plush (plush) *n.* long-piled fabric.

Plu′to (ploo′tō) *n.* planet ninth in order from the sun.

plu′to•crat′ (ploo′tə krat′) *n.* **1.** wealthy person. **2.** member of wealthy governing class. —**plu•toc′ra•cy** (-tok′rə sē) *n.* —**plu′to•crat′ic,** *adj.*

plu•to′ni•um (ploo tō′nē əm) *n.* radioactive element.

plu•vi•al (ploo′vē əl) *adj.* of rain.

ply (plī) *v.,* **plied, plying,** *n., pl.* **plies.** —*v.* **1.** work with by hand. **2.** carry on, as trade. **3.** supply or offer something repeatedly. **4.** travel regularly. —*n.* **5.** fold; thickness.

plywd plywood.

ply′wood′, *n.* sheets of wood.

Plz. plaza.

plzd polarized.

p.m., after noon. Also, **P.M.**

pmflt pamphlet.

P.M.G. 1. Paymaster General. **2.** Postmaster General. **3.** Provost Marshal General.

pmk. postmark.

P.M.L. *Insurance.* probable maximum loss.

PMLA Publications of the Modern Language Association of America. Also, **P.M.L.A.**

PMS, premenstrual syndrome.

PMT premenstrual tension.

pmt. payment.

PN 1. please note. **2.** promissory note. **3.** psychoneurotic.

pn 1. part number. **2.** please note. **3.** promissory note.

P/N promissory note. Also, **p.n.**

pneum. 1. Also, **pneu** pneumatic. **2.** pneumatics.

pneu•mat′ic (noo mat′ik, nyoo-) *adj.* **1.** of gases. **2.** operated by air. —**pneu•mat′i•cal•ly,** *adv.*

pneu•mo′ni•a (noo mōn′yə, nyoo-) *n.* inflammation of lungs.

pnh pan head.

pnl panel.

pnld paneled.

pnlg paneling.

pnnt pennant.

pnp positive-negative-positive transistor.

pnt paint.

pntgn pentagon.

pnxt. he or she painted it. [from Latin *pinxit*]

P.O., post office.

POA primary optical area.

poach (pōch) *v.* **1.** hunt illegally. **2.** cook (eggs, fruit, etc.) in hot water. **—poach′er,** *n.*

POB post-office box. Also, **P.O.B.**

POC port of call.

pock′et (pok′it) *n.* **1.** small bag sewed into garment. **2.** pouch; cavity. **—***adj.* **3.** small. **—***v.* **4.** put into one's pocket. **5.** take as profit. **6.** suppress.

pock′et•book′, *n.* purse.

pock′et•knife′, *n.* small folding knife.

pock′mark′ (pok′märk′) *n.* acne scar.

pocul. (in prescriptions) a cup. [from Latin *pōculum*]

pod (pod) *n., v.,* **podded, podding. —***n.* **1.** seed covering. **—***v.* **2.** produce pod.

po•di′a•try (pə dī′ə trē) *n.* diagnosis and treatment of foot disorders. **—po•di′a•trist,** *n.*

po′di•um (pō′dē əm) *n., pl.* **-diums, -dia** (-dē ə). small raised platform.

POE 1. port of embarkation. **2.** port of entry. Also, **P.O.E.**

po′em (pō′əm) *n.* composition in verse. **—po′et** (pō′it) *n.*

po′e•sy (-ə sē) *n., pl.* **-sies.** poetry.

poet. 1. poetic; poetical. **2.** poetry.

po′et•as′ter (-as′tər) *n.* inferior poet.

poetic justice, fitting rewards and punishments.

poetic license, liberty taken by writer in deviating from fact to produce desired effect.

po′et•ry (-i trē) *n.* rhythmical composition of words. **—po•et′ic** (pō et′ik), **po•et′i•cal,** *adj.*

POGO (pō′gō), Polar Orbiting Geophysical Observatory.

po•grom′ (pə grum′, -grom′) *n.* organized massacre, esp. of Jews.

poign′ant (poin′yənt) *adj.* keenly distressing. **—poign′an•cy,** *n.*

poin′ci•an′a (poin′sē an′ə) *n., pl.* **-as.** tropical tree.

poin•set′ti•a (poin set′ē ə, -set′ə) *n.* tropical plant with scarlet flowers.

point (point) *n.* **1.** sharp end. **2.** projecting part. **3.** dot. **4.** definite position or time. **5.** compass direction. **6.** basic reason, assertion, etc. **7.** detail. **8.** unit of printing measure. **—***v.* **9.** indicate. **10.** direct. **—point′less,** *adj.*

point′-blank′, *adj.* **1.** direct; plain. **—***adv.* **2.** directly.

point′ed, *adj.* **1.** having a point. **2.** sharp. **3.** aimed at a particular person. **4.** emphasized.

point′er, *n.* **1.** one that points. **2.** long stick for pointing. **3.** breed of hunting dog.

poin′til•lism (pwan′tl iz′əm) *n.* technique in painting of using dots of pure color that are optically mixed into resulting hue by viewer.

poise (poiz) *n., v.,* **poised, poising. —***n.* **1.** balance. **2.** composure. **—***v.* **3.** balance. **4.** be in position for action.

poi′son (poi′zən) *n.* **1.** substance that kills or harms seriously. **—***v.* **2.** harm with poison. **—poi′son•er,** *n.* **—poi′son•ous,** *adj.*

poison ivy, 1. vine or shrub having shiny leaves with three leaflets. **2.** rash caused by touching poison ivy.

poke (pōk) *v.,* **poked, poking,** *n.* thrust.

pok′er (pō′kər) *n.* **1.** rod for poking fires. **2.** card game.

pok′er-faced′, *adj.* showing no emotion or intention.

pok′y (pō′kē) *adj.,* **-ier, -lest.** *Informal,* slow; dull. Also, **poke′y. —pok′i•ness,** *n.*

POL petroleum, oil, and lubricants.

Pol. 1. Poland. **2.** Also, **Pol** Polish.

pol. 1. political. **2.** politics.

po′lar (pō′lər) *adj.* **1.** arctic or antarctic. **2.** in opposition or contrast. **3.** of magnetic poles. **—po•lar′i•ty,** *n.*

polar bear, large white arctic bear.

Po•lar′is (pō lâr′is, -lar′-, pə-) *n.* bright star close to North Pole.

po′lar•i•za′tion (-lər ə zā′shən) *n.* **1.** division of group into opposing factions. **2.** state in which rays of light exhibit different properties in different directions. **—po′lar•ize′,** *v.,* **-ized, -izing.**

pole (pōl) *n., v.,* **poled, poling. —***n.* **1.** long slender rod. **2.** unit of length equal to 16½ ft.; rod. **3.** square rod, 30¼ sq. yards. **4.** each end of axis. **5.** each end showing strongest opposite force. **6.** (*cap.*) native or citizen of Poland. **—***v.* **7.** propel with a pole.

pole′cat′, *n.* small bad-smelling mammal.

po•lem′ics (pə lem′iks) *n.* art or practice of argument. **—po•lem′ic,** *n., adj.* **—po•lem′i•cist,** *n.*

pole vault, athletic event in which vault over horizontal bar is performed with aid of long pole.

po•lice′ (pə lēs′) *n., v.,* **-liced, -licing. —***n.* **1.** organized civil force for enforcing law. **—***v.* **2.** keep in order. **—po•lice′man,** *n.* **—po•lice′wom′an,** *n.*

pol′i•cy (pol′ə sē) *n., pl.* **-cies. 1.** definite course of action. **2.** insurance contract.

pol′i•o•my′e•li′tis (pol′ē ō mī′ə lī′tis) *n.* infantile paralysis. Also, **po′li•o′.**

pol′ish (pol′ish) *v.* **1.** make glossy. **—***n.* **2.** polishing substance. **3.** gloss. **4.** refinement.

Pol′ish (pō′lish) *n.* **1.** language or people of Poland. **—***adj.* **2.** of Poland.

po•lite′ (pə līt′) *adj.* showing good manners; refined. **—po•lite′ly,** *adv.* **—po•lite′ness,** *n.*

polit. econ. political economy.

pol′i•tesse′ (pol′i tes′, pô′lē-) *n.* politeness.

pol′i•tic (pol′i tik) *adj.* **1.** prudent; expedient. **2.** political.

politically correct, marked by progressive attitude on issues of race, gender, etc. **—political correctness.**

political science, social science dealing with political institutions and government.

po•lit/i•cize/ (pə lit/ə sīz/) *v.*, **-cized, -cizing.** give a political bias to.

pol/i•tick/ing (pol/i tik/ing) *n.* political self-aggrandizement.

pol/i•tics (pol/i tiks) *n.* **1.** science or conduct of government. **2.** political affairs, methods, or principles. **—po•lit/i•cal** (pə lit/i kəl) *adj.* **—pol/i•ti/cian,** *n.* **—po•lit/i•cal•ly,** *adv.*

pol/ka (pōl/kə, pō/kə) *n.* lively dance.

polka dot, pattern of dots.

poll (pōl) *n.* **1.** voting or votes at election. **2.** list of individuals, as for voting. **3.** (*pl.*) place of voting. **4.** analysis of public opinion. **—v.** **5.** receive votes. **6.** vote. **7.** ask opinions of.

pol/len (pol/ən) *n.* powdery fertilizing element of flowers. **—pol/li•nate/,** *v.* **—pol/li•na/tion,** *n.*

pol/li•wog/ (pol/ē wog/) *n.* tadpole.

poll/ster (pōl/stər) *n.* person who takes public-opinion polls.

pol•lute/ (pə lōot/) *v.,* **-luted, -luting.** contaminate or make foul. **—pol•lu/tion,** *n.* **—pol•lut/ant,** *n.* **—pol•lut/er,** *n.*

po/lo (pō/lō) *n., pl.* **-los.** game played on horseback.

pol•o•naise/ (pol/ə nāz/, pō/lə-) *n.* slow dance.

pol. sci. political science.

polstr polystyrene.

pol/ter•geist/ (pōl/tər gīst/) *n.* boisterous, often destructive ghost.

polthn polyethylene.

pol•troon/ (pol trōōn/) *n.* coward.

poly-, prefix meaning many.

pol/y•an/dry (pol/ē an/drē) *n.* practice of having more than one husband at a time.

pol/y•es/ter (pol/ē es/tər) *n.* artificial material for plastics and synthetics.

pol/y•eth/yl•ene/ (-eth/ə lēn/) *n.* plastic polymer used esp. for containers, electrical insulation, and packaging.

po•lyg/a•my (pə lig/ə mē) *n.* practice of having many spouses, esp. wives, at one time. **—po•lyg/a•mist,** *n.* **—po•lyg/a•mous,** *adj.*

pol/y•glot/ (pol/ē glot/) *adj.* able to speak, read, or write several languages.

pol/y•gon/ (pol/ē gon/) *n.* figure having three or more straight sides. **—po•lyg/o•nal,** *adj.*

pol/y•graph/ (pol/i graf/) *n.* instrument recording variations in certain body activities, sometimes used to detect lying in response to questions.

pol/y•he/dron (pol/ē hē/drən) *n., pl.* **-drons, -dra** (-drə). solid figure having four or more sides.

pol/y•math/ (pol/ē math/) *n.* person of great learning in several fields.

pol/y•mer (pol/ə mər) *n.* compound formed by the combination of various molecules with water or alcohol eliminated. **—pol/y•mer•i•za/tion,** *n.*

pol/y•no/mi•al (pol/ə nō/mē əl) *n.* algebraic expression consisting of two or more terms.

pol/yp (pol/ip) *n.* **1.** projecting growth from mucous surface. **2.** simple, sedentary aquatic animal form.

po•lyph/o•ny (pə lif/ə nē) *n.* music with two or more melodic lines in equitable juxtaposition. **—pol/y•phon/ic** (pol/ē fon/ik) *adj.*

pol/y•sty/rene (pol/ē stī/rēn, -stēr/ēn) *n.* polymer used in molded objects and as insulator.

pol/y•syl•lab/ic, *adj.* consisting of many syllables.

pol/y•tech/nic (-tek/nik) *adj.* offering instruction in variety of technical subjects.

pol/y•the/ism, *n.* belief in more than one god. **—pol/y•the/ist,** *n., adj.* **—pol/y•the•ist/ic,** *adj.*

pol/y•un•sat/u•rat/ed, *adj.* of a class of animal or vegetable fats associated with low cholesterol content.

po•made/ (po mād/, -mäd/) *n.* hair ointment.

pome/gran/ate (pom/gran/it, pom/i-) *n.* red, many-seeded fruit of Asiatic tree.

pom/mel (pum/əl, pom/-) *n., v.,* **-meled, -meling. —n. 1.** knob. **—v. 2.** strike; beat.

pomp (pomp) *n.* stately display.

pom/pa•dour/ (pom/pə dôr/, -dōōr/) *n.* arrangement of hair brushed up high from forehead.

pom/pa•no/ (pom/pə nō/) *n., pl.* **-nos, -no.** fish inhabiting waters off the S. Atlantic and Gulf states.

pom/pom (pom/pom/) *n.* ornamental tuft.

pomp/ous (pom/pəs) *adj.* affectedly dignified or serious. **—pom•pos/i•ty** (-pos/i tē), **pomp/ous•ness,** *n.* **—pomp/ous•ly,** *adv.*

pon/cho (pon/chō) *n., pl.* **-chos.** blanketlike cloak.

pond (pond) *n.* small lake.

pon/der (pon/dər) *v.* meditate.

pon/der•ous, *adj.* heavy; not graceful.

pone (pōn) *n.* unleavened corn bread.

pon•gee/ (pon jē/) *n.* silk fabric.

pon/iard (pon/yərd) *n.* dagger.

pon/tiff (pon/tif) *n.* **1.** pope. **2.** chief priest; bishop. **—pon•tif/i•cal,** *adj.*

pon•tif/i•cate/ (pon tif/i kāt/) *v.,* **-cated, -cating.** speak with affected air of authority.

pon•toon/ (pon tōōn/) *n.* floating support.

po/ny (pō/nē) *n., pl.* **-nies.** small horse.

po/ny•tail/, *n.* hair gathered and fastened at the back of the head so as to hang freely.

poo/dle (pōōd/l) *n.* kind of dog with thick, curly hair.

pool (pōōl) *n.* **1.** body of still water. **2.** group of persons or things available for use. **3.** game resembling billiards. **—v. 4.** put into common fund.

poop (pōōp) *n.* upper deck on afterpart of a ship.

poor (pŏŏr) *adj.* **1.** having little wealth. **2.** wanting. **3.** inferior. **4.** unfortunate. —*n.* **5.** poor persons. —**poor′ly,** *adv.* —**poor′ness,** *n.*

poor′-mouth′, *v. Informal.* complain about poverty, usu. as an excuse.

pop (pop) *v.,* **popped, popping,** *n., adv.* —*v.* **1.** make or burst with a short, quick sound. **2.** shoot. —*n.* **3.** short, quick sound. **4.** effervescent soft drink. —*adv.* **5.** suddenly.

pop′corn′, *n.* kind of corn whose kernels burst in dry heat.

pope (pōp) *n.* (*often cap.*) head of Roman Catholic Church.

pop′in·jay′ (pop′in jā′) *n.* vain, shallow person.

pop′lar (pop′lər) *n.* any of certain fast-growing trees.

pop′lin (pop′lin) *n.* corded fabric.

pop′o′ver, *n.* very light muffin.

pop′py (pop′ē) *n., pl.* **-pies.** showy-flowered herbs, one species of which yields opium.

pop′py·cock′, *n.* nonsense.

pop′u·lace (pop′yə ləs) *n.* population.

pop′u·lar (-lər) *adj.* **1.** generally liked and approved. **2.** of the people. **3.** prevalent. —**pop′u·lar′i·ty** (-lar′i tē) *n.* —**pop′u·lar·ize′,** *v.,* **-ized, -izing.** —**pop′u·lar·ly,** *adv.*

pop′u·late′ (-lāt′) *v.,* **-lated, -lating.** inhabit.

pop′u·la′tion, *n.* **1.** total number of persons inhabiting given area. **2.** body of inhabitants.

pop′u·lism, *n.* political philosophy or movement promoting the interests of the common people. —**pop′u·list,** *n., adj.*

pop′u·lous, *adj.* with many inhabitants.

p.o.r. pay on return.

por′ce·lain (pôr′sə lin, pôrs′lin) *n.* glassy ceramic ware; china.

porch (pôrch) *n.* exterior shelter on building.

por′cine (pôr′sīn) *adj.* of or like swine.

por′cu·pine′ (pôr′kyə pīn′) *n.* rodent with stout quills.

pore (pôr) *v.,* **pored, poring,** *n.* —*v.* **1.** ponder or read intently. —*n.* **2.** minute opening in skin.

por′gy (pôr′gē) *n., pl.* **-gies.** fleshy salt-water food fish.

pork (pôrk) *n.* flesh of hogs as food.

pork barrel, government funds available for popular local improvements.

por·nog′ra·phy (pôr nog′rə fē) *n.* obscene literature or art. —**por′no·graph′ic** (-nə-graf′ik) *adj.* —**por·nog′ra·pher,** *n.*

po′rous (pôr′əs) *adj.* permeable by water, air, etc. —**po′rous·ness,** *n.*

por′phy·ry (pôr′fə rē) *n., pl.* **-ries.** hard purplish red rock.

por′poise (pôr′pəs) *n.* gregarious aquatic mammal.

por′ridge (pôr′ij, por′-) *n.* boiled cereal.

por′rin·ger (pôr′in jər, por′-) *n.* round dish for soup, etc.

port (pôrt) *n.* **1.** place where ships load and unload. **2.** harbor. **3.** left side of vessel, facing forward. **4.** sweet red wine. —**port,** *adj.*

port′a·ble, *adj.* readily carried. —**port′a·bil′i·ty,** *n.*

por′tage (pôr′tij, pôr täzh′) *n.* **1.** overland route between navigable streams. **2.** act of carrying.

por′tal (pôr′tl) *n.* door or gate, esp. a large one.

port·cul′lis (pôrt kul′is) *n.* heavy iron grating at gateway of castle.

por·tend′ (pôr tend′) *v.* indicate beforehand.

por′tent (-tent) *n.* **1.** omen. **2.** ominous significance. —**por·ten′tous,** *adj.*

por′ter (pôr′tər) *n.* **1.** railroad attendant in parlor or sleeping car. **2.** baggage carrier. **3.** person who cleans or maintains building, store, etc.

por′ter·house′, *n.* choice cut of beefsteak.

port·fo′li·o′ (pôrt fō′lē ō′) *n., pl.* **-lios.** **1.** portable case for papers, etc. **2.** cabinet post.

port′hole′, *n.* opening in ship's side.

por′ti·co′ (pôr′ti kō′) *n., pl.* **-coes, -cos.** roof supported by columns.

por·tiere′ (pôr tyâr′, -têr′) *n.* curtain hung in doorway. Also, **por·tière′.**

por′tion (pôr′shən) *n.* **1.** part of a whole. **2.** share. —*v.* **3.** divide into shares.

port′ly (pôrt′lē) *adj.,* **-lier, -liest.** **1.** fat. **2.** stately. —**port′li·ness,** *n.*

port·man′teau (pôrt man′tō) *n., pl.* **-teaus, -teaux** (-tōz, tō). leather trunk.

por′trait (pôr′trit, -trāt) *n.* picture, sculpture, etc., showing specific person. —**por′trai·ture** (-tri chər) *n.*

por′trait·ist, *n.* person who makes portraits.

por·tray′ (pôr trā′) *v.* represent faithfully, as in picture. —**por·tray′al,** *n.*

Por′tu·guese′ (-chə gēz′, -gēs′) *n., pl.* **-guese.** native or language of Portugal. —**Portuguese,** *adj.*

Portuguese man-of-war, poisonous marine animal.

por′tu·lac′a (pôr′chə lak′ə) *n.* low-growing garden plant.

pos. 1. position. **2.** positive. **3.** possession. **4.** possessive.

P.O.S. point-of-sale; point-of-sales. Also, **POS**

pose (pōz) *v.,* **posed, posing,** *n.* —*v.* **1.** assume or feign physical position, attitude, or character. **2.** take or give specific position. **3.** ask (question). —*n.* **4.** position or character assumed.

po′ser, *n.* **1.** person who poses, as for artist. **2.** difficult question.

po·seur′ (pō zûr′) *n.* affected person.

posh (posh) *adj.* elegant; luxurious.

pos′it (poz′it) *v.* lay down or assume as a fact or principle; postulate.

po·si′tion (pə zish′ən) *n.* **1.** place or attitude. **2.** belief or argument on question. **3.** social or organizational standing. **4.** job. —*v.* **5.** place.

pos·i·tive (poz′i tiv) *adj.* **1.** explicit; not denying or questioning. **2.** emphatic. **3.** confident. **4.** showing lights and shades of original. **5.** *Gram.* denoting first degree of comparison. **6.** denoting more than zero. **7.** deficient in electrons. **8.** revealing presence of thing tested for. —*n.* **9.** something positive. **10.** photographic image. —**pos′i·tive·ly,** *adv.* —**pos′i·tive·ness,** *n.*

pos·i·tron′ (poz′i tron′) *n.* particle with same mass as electron but with positive charge.

posn position.

poss. 1. possession. **2.** possessive. **3.** possible. **4.** possibly.

pos·se (pos′ē) *n.* body of persons assisting sheriff.

pos·sess′ (pə zes′) *v.* **1.** have under ownership or domination. **2.** have as quality. **3.** obsess. —**pos·ses′sor,** *n.* —**pos·ses′sion** (-zesh′ən) *n.*

pos·sessed′, *adj.* controlled by strong feeling or supernatural power.

pos·ses′sive, *adj.* **1.** denoting possession. **2.** obsessed with dominating another.

pos′si·ble (pos′ə bəl) *adj.* that may be, happen, etc. —**pos′si·bil′i·ty,** *n.* —**pos′si·bly,** *adv.*

POSSLQ (pos′əl kyōō′), either of two persons, one of each sex, who share living quarters but are not related by blood, marriage, or adoption: a categorization used by the U.S. Census Bureau. [*p(erson of the) o(pposite) s(ex) s(haring) l(iving) q(uarters)*]

pos′sum (pos′əm) *n.* opossum.

post (pōst) *n.* **1.** upright support. **2.** position of duty or trust. **3.** station for soldiers or traders. **4.** *Chiefly Brit.* mail. —*v.* **5.** put up. **6.** station at post. **7.** *Chiefly Brit.* mail. **8.** enter in ledger. **9.** hasten. **10.** inform. —*adv.* **11.** with speed.

post-, prefix meaning after or behind.

post′age (pō′stij) *n.* charge for mailing.

post′al (pōs′tl) *adj.* concerning mail.

post·bel′lum (-bel′əm) *adj.* after war, esp. U.S. Civil War.

post′card′, *n.* small notecard usu. having picture on one side and space for stamp, address, and message on the other.

post·date′ (pōst dāt′, pōst′-) *v.,* -dated, -dating. **1.** mark with date later than actual date. **2.** follow in time.

post′er (pō′stər) *n.* large public notice.

pos·te′ri·or (po stēr′ē ər, pō-) *adj.* **1.** situated behind. **2.** later. —*n.* **3.** buttocks.

pos·ter′i·ty (po ster′i tē) *n.* descendants.

post exchange, retail store on military base.

post·grad′u·ate (pōst graj′ōō it, -āt′) *adj.* **1.** of postgraduates. —*n.* **2.** student taking advanced work after graduation.

post′haste′, *adv.* speedily.

post′hu·mous (pos′chə məs, -chōō-) *adj.* **1.** arising after one's death. **2.** born after father's death. —**post′hu·mous·ly,** *adv.*

pos·til′ion (pō stil′yən, po-) *n.* person who rides leading left horse of those pulling carriage.

post′man, *n.* mail carrier.

post′mark′, *n.* official mark on mail showing place and time of mailing. —**post′mark′,** *v.*

post′mas′ter, *n.* official in charge of post office.

post me·rid′i·em′ (mə rid′ē əm, -em′) afternoon.

post′mis′tress, *n.* woman in charge of post office.

post·mod′ern, *adj.* pertaining to late 20th century artistic movement that developed in reaction to modernism.

post·mor′tem (-môr′təm) *adj.* **1.** following death. —*n.* **2.** examination of dead body.

post·nat′al (-nāt′l) *adj.* after childbirth.

post office, government office responsible for postal service.

postop (pōst′op′), postoperative. Also, post-op.

post′paid′, *adv., adj.* with postage paid in advance.

post·par′tum (-pär′təm) *adj.* following childbirth.

post·pone′ (pōst pōn′, pōs-) *v.,* -poned, -poning. delay till later. —**post·pone′ment,** *n.*

post·pran′di·al (-pran′dē əl) *adj.* after a meal.

post′script′, *n.* note added to letter after signature.

pos′tu·late′, *v.,* -lated, -lating, *n.* —*v.* (pos′chə lāt′) **1.** require. **2.** assume. —*n.* (-lit) **3.** something postulated.

pos′ture (pos′chər) *n., v.,* -tured, -turing. —*n.* **1.** position of the body. —*v.* **2.** place in particular position. **3.** behave affectedly; pose.

post′war′, *adj.* after a war.

po′sy (pō′zē) *n., pl.* -sies. flower or bouquet.

pot (pot) *n., v.,* **potted, potting.** —*n.* **1.** round deep container for cooking, etc. **2.** total stakes at cards. **3.** *Slang.* marijuana. —*v.* **4.** put into pot.

po′ta·ble (pō′tə bəl) *adj.* drinkable.

pot′ash′ (pot′ash′) *n.* potassium carbonate, esp. from wood ashes.

po·tas′si·um (pə tas′ē əm) *n.* light metallic element.

po·ta′tion (pō tā′shən) *n.* drink.

po·ta′to (pə tā′tō, -tə) *n., pl.* -toes. edible tuber of common garden plant.

pot′bel′ly, *n., pl.* -lies. belly that sticks out. —**pot′bel′lied,** *adj.*

pot′boil′er, *n.* mediocre work of literature or art produced merely for financial gain.

po′tent (pōt′nt) *adj.* **1.** powerful. **2.** (of a

male) capable of sexual intercourse. **—po′-tence,** po/ten•cy, *n.* **—po′tent•ly,** *adv.*

po′ten•tate′ (-tāt′) *n.* powerful person, as a sovereign.

po•ten′tial (pə ten/shəl) *adj.* **1.** possible. **2.** latent. *—n.* **3.** possibility. **—po•ten/ti•al/i•ty,** *n.* **—po•ten/tial•ly,** *adv.*

poth′er (po*th*/ər) *n.*, *v.* fuss.

pot′hole′, *n.* hole formed in pavement.

po′tion (pō/shən) *n.* drink.

pot′luck′, *n.* **1.** meal to which participants bring food to be shared. **2.** whatever happens to be available.

pot′pour•ri′ (pō/pŏŏ rē′) *n.* **1.** fragrant mixture of dried flowers and spices. **2.** miscellany.

POTS (pots), *Telecommunications.* plain old telephone service.

pot′sherd′ (pot/shûrd′) *n.* pottery fragment.

pot′shot′, *n.* **1.** casual or aimless shot. **2.** random or incidental criticism.

pot′tage (pot/ij) *n.* thick soup.

pot′ted, *adj.* **1.** grown in a pot. **2.** *Slang.* drunk.

pot′ter (pot/ər) *n.* **1.** person who makes earthen pots. *—v.* **2.** putter (def. 1).

potter's field, burial ground for the poor.

pot′ter•y, *n.*, *pl.* **-teries.** ware made of clay and baked.

pouch (pouch) *n.* **1.** bag or sack. **2.** baglike sac.

poul′tice (pōl/tis) *n.* soft moist mass applied as medicine.

poul′try (pōl/trē) *n.* domestic fowls.

pounce (pouns) *v.,* **pounced, pouncing,** *n.* *—v.* **1.** swoop down or spring suddenly. **2.** seize eagerly. *—n.* **3.** sudden swoop.

pound (pound) *n.*, *pl.* **pounds, pound,** *v.* *—n.* **1.** unit of weight: in U.S., **pound avoirdupois** (16 ounces) and **pound troy** (12 ounces). **2.** British monetary unit. **3.** enclosure for stray animals. *—v.* **4.** strike repeatedly and heavily. **5.** crush by pounding.

pound cake, rich, sweet cake.

pour (pôr) *v.* **1.** cause to flow; flow. *—n.* **2.** abundant flow.

pout (pout) *v.* **1.** look sullen. *—n.* **2.** sullen look or mood.

POV *Motion Pictures.* point of view: used especially in describing a method of shooting a scene or film.

pov′er•ty (pov/ər tē) *n.* **1.** poorness. **2.** lack.

POW, *pl.* **POWs, POW's.** prisoner of war.

pow′der (pou/dər) *n.* **1.** solid substance crushed to fine loose particles. *—v.* **2.** reduce to powder. **3.** apply powder to. **—pow′der•y,** *adj.*

powder keg, 1. container for gunpowder. **2.** explosive situation.

pow′er (pou/ər) *n.* **1.** ability to act; strength. **2.** faculty. **3.** authority; control. **4.** person, nation, etc., having great influence. **5.** mechanical energy. **6.** product of repeated multiplications of number by itself. **7.** magnify-

ing capacity of an optical instrument. **—pow′er•ful,** *adj.* **—pow′er•ful•ly,** *adv.* **—pow′er•less,** *adj.* **—pow′er•less•ly,** *adv.*

pow′er•house′, *n.* **1.** building where electricity is generated. **2.** person or group with great potential for success.

power of attorney, written legal authorization for another person to act in one's place.

pow′wow′ (pou/wou′) *n.* *Informal.* conference.

pox (poks) *n.* disease marked by skin eruptions.

pp., 1. pages. **2.** past participle.

PPA *Pharmacology.* a substance, $C_9H_{13}NO$, used as an appetite suppressant. [*p(henyl)p(ropanol)a(mine)*]

PPB 1. Also, **P.P.B.** *Publishing.* paper, printing, and binding. **2.** provisioning parts breakdown.

ppb *Publishing.* **1.** paper, printing, and binding. **2.** parts per billion. Also, **p.p.b.**

ppd., 1. postpaid. **2.** prepaid.

p.p.d.o. per person, double occupancy.

PPE *British.* philosophy, politics, and economics.

P.P.F. *Insurance.* personal property floater.

PPH paid personal holidays. Also, **P.P.H.**

pph. pamphlet.

PPI *Pharmacology.* **1.** patient package insert. **2.** Also, **ppi** *Electronics.* plan position indicator. **3.** producer price index.

ppl. participle.

ppll programmable phase-locked loop.

PPLO *Pathology.* pleuropneumonialike organism.

PPM 1. *Computers.* pages per minute. **2.** Also, **ppm** *Telecommunications.* pulse position modulation.

ppm 1. *Computers.* pages per minute: a measure of the speed of a page printer. **2.** parts per million. **3.** pulse per minute.

p.p.m. parts per million. Also, **P.P.M., ppm, PPM**

PPO preferred-provider organization.

ppp 1. peak pulse power. **2.** *Music.* pianississimo; double pianissimo.

ppr. 1. paper. **2.** Also, **p.pr.** present participle.

P.P.S., additional postscript. Also, **p.p.s.**

ppt. *Chemistry.* precipitate. Also, **ppt**

ppv *Television.* pay-per-view. Also, **p.p.v., PPV, P.P.V.**

PQ Quebec, Canada (for use with ZIP code).

p.q. previous question.

PR, public relations.

PRA Public Roads Administration.

prac′ti•ca•ble (prak/ti kə bal) *adj.* able to be put into practice; feasible.

prac′ti•cal, *adj.* **1.** of or from practice. **2.** useful. **3.** level-headed. **4.** concerned with everyday affairs. **5.** virtual. **—prac′ti•cal/i•ty,** *n.* **—prac′ti•cal•ly,** *adv.*

prac′tice (-tis) *n.*, *v.*, **-ticed, -ticing.** *—n.* **1.** habit; custom. **2.** action carried out. **3.** re-

P

peated performance in learning. **4.** professional activity. —*v.* Also, *Brit.*, **prac′tise. 5.** do habitually or as profession. **6.** to repeat to acquire skill. —**prac′ticed,** *adj.*

prac′ti•cum (-ti kəm) *n.* course of study devoted to practical experience in a field.

prac•ti′tion•er (-tish′ə nər) *n.* person engaged in a profession.

prag•mat′ic (prag mat′ik) *adj.* concerned with practical values and results. —**prag′ma•tism,** *n.* —**prag′ma•tist,** *n.* —**prag•mat′i•cal•ly,** *adv.*

prai′rie (prâr′ē) *n.* broad, flat, treeless grassland.

prairie dog, burrowing squirrel of western North America.

prairie schooner, covered wagon.

praise (prāz) *n.*, *v.*, **praised, praising.** —*n.* **1.** words of admiration or strong approval. **2.** grateful homage. —*v.* **3.** give praise to. **4.** worship. —**praise′wor′thy,** *adj.* —**prais′er,** *n.*

pra′line (prā′lēn, prä′-) *n.* confection of caramelized nuts and sugar.

pram (pram) *n. Brit. Informal.* baby carriage.

prance (prans) *v.*, **pranced, prancing,** *n.* —*v.* **1.** step about gaily or proudly. —*n.* **2.** act of prancing. —**pranc′er,** *n.*

prand. (in prescriptions) dinner. [from Latin *prandium*]

prank (prangk) *n.* playful trick. —**prank′ster,** *n.*

prate (prāt) *v.*, **prated, prating.** talk foolishly.

prat′fall′ (prat′fôl′) *n.* fall on the buttocks.

prat′tle (prat′l) *v.*, **-tled, -tling,** *n.* —*v.* **1.** chatter foolishly or childishly. —*n.* **2.** chatter. —**prat′tler,** *n.*

prawn (prôn) *n.* large shrimplike shellfish.

pray (prā) *v.* make prayer.

prayer (prâr) *n.* **1.** devout petition to or spiritual communication with God. **2.** petition. —**prayer′ful,** *adj.*

prblc parabolic.

PRC 1. Also, **P.R.C.** People's Republic of China. **2.** Postal Rate Commission.

prcht parachute.

prcs process.

prcsr processor.

prcst precast.

prdn production.

prdr producer.

pre-, prefix meaning before.

preach (prēch) *v.* **1.** advocate. **2.** deliver (sermon). —**preach′er,** *n.* —**preach′y,** *adj.*

pre′am′ble (prē′am′bəl, prē am′-) *n.* introductory declaration.

prec. 1. preceded. **2.** preceding.

Pre•cam′bri•an (prē kam′brē ən, -kām′-) *adj.* pertaining to earliest era of earth history.

pre•can′cer•ous, *adj.* showing pathological changes that may be preliminary to malignancy.

pre•car′i•ous (pri kâr′ē əs) *adj.* uncertain; dangerous. —**pre•car′i•ous•ly,** *adv.*

pre•cau′tion (pri kô′shən) *n.* prudent advance measure. —**pre•cau′tion•ar′y,** *adj.*

precdg preceding.

pre•cede′ (pri sēd′) *v.*, **-ceded, -ceding.** go before. —**prec′e•dence** (pres′i dens) *n.*

prec′e•dent (pres′i dənt) *n.* past case used as example or guide.

pre′cept (prē′sept) *n.* rule of conduct.

pre•cep′tor (pri sep′tər, prē′sep-) *n.* teacher.

pre′cinct (prē′singkt) *n.* bounded or defined area.

pre•ci•os′i•ty (presh′ē os′i tē) *n.*, *pl.* **-ties.** fastidious refinement.

pre′cious (presh′əs) *adj.* **1.** valuable. **2.** beloved. **3.** affectedly refined. —**pre′cious•ly,** *adv.*

prec′i•pice (pres′ə pis) *n.* sharp cliff.

pre•cip′i•tate′, *v.*, **-tated, -tating,** *adj.*, *n.* —*v.* (pri sip′i tāt′) **1.** hasten occurrence of. **2.** separate (solid from solution). **3.** condense (as vapor into rain). **4.** fling down. —*adj.* (-tit) **5.** rash or impetuous; hasty. —*n.* (-tit) **6.** substance precipitated. **7.** condensed moisture. —**pre•cip′i•tate•ly,** *adv.* —**pre•cip′i•ta′tion,** *n.*

pre•cip′i•tous, *adj.* **1.** like a precipice. **2.** precipitate.

pré•cis′ (prā sē′, prā′sē) *n.* summary.

pre•cise′ (pri sīs′) *adj.* **1.** definite; exact. **2.** distinct. **3.** strict. —**pre•ci′sion** (-sizh′ən), **pre•cise′ness,** *n.* —**pre•cise′ly,** *adv.*

pre•clude′ (pri klōōd′) *v.*, **-cluded, -cluding.** prevent. —**pre•clu′sion** (-klōō′zhən) *n.* —**pre•clu′sive,** *adj.*

pre•co′cious (pri kō′shəs) *adj.* forward in development. —**pre•coc′i•ty** (-kos′ə tē) *n.*

pre′cog•ni′tion (prē′kog nish′ən) *n.* knowledge of future event through extrasensory means.

pre′-Co•lum′bi•an, *adj.* of the period before the arrival of Columbus in the Americas.

pre•con•ceive′, *v.*, **-ceived, -ceiving.** form an opinion beforehand. —**pre′con•cep′tion,** *n.*

pre′con•di′tion, *n.* something necessary for subsequent result.

precp precipitation.

pre•cur′sor (pri kûr′sər, prē′kûr-) *n.* **1.** predecessor. **2.** harbinger.

pred. predicate.

pre•da′cious (pri dā′shəs) *adj.* predatory. Also, **pre•da′ceous.**

pred′a•tor (pred′ə tər) *n.* preying animal.

pred′a•tor′y, *adj.* **1.** plundering. **2.** feeding on other animals.

pred′e•ces′sor (-ses′ər) *n.* one who precedes another.

pre•des′ti•na′tion (pri des′tə nā′shən) *n.* **1.** determination beforehand. **2.** destiny. —**pre•des′tine,** *v.*

pre•de•ter′mine (prē′di tûr′min) *v.*,

-mined, mining. 1. decide in advance. **2.** predestine. —**pre/de•ter/mi•na/tion,** *n.*

pre•dic/a•ment (pri dik/ə mənt) *n.* trying or dangerous situation.

pred/i•cate, *v.,* **-cated, -cating,** *adj., n.* —*v.* (pred/i kāt/) **1.** declare. **2.** find basis for. —*adj.* (-kit) **3.** *Gram.* belonging to predicate. —*n.* (-kit) **4.** *Gram.* part of sentence that expresses what is said of subject. —**pred/i•ca/tion,** *n.*

pre•dict/ (pri dikt/) *v.* tell beforehand. —**pre•dic/tion,** *n.* —**pre•dict/a•ble,** *adj.* —**pre•dic/tor,** *n.*

pre/di•lec/tion (pred/l ek/shən, prēd/-) *n.* preference.

pre/dis•pose/ (prē/di spōz/) *v.,* **-posed, -posing. 1.** make susceptible. **2.** incline. —**pre•dis/po•si/tion,** *n.*

pre•dom/i•nate/ (pri dom/ə nāt/) *v.,* **-nated, -nating. 1.** be more powerful or common. **2.** control. —**pre•dom/i•nance,** *n.* —**pre•dom/i•nant,** *adj.* —**pre•dom/i•nant•ly,** *adv.*

pre•em/i•nent (prē em/ə nənt) *adj.* superior; outstanding. —**pre•em/i•nence,** *n.* —**pre•em/i•nent•ly,** *adv.*

pre•empt/ (prē empt/) *v.* **1.** acquire or reserve before others. **2.** occupy to establish prior right to buy. Also, **pre-empt/.** —**pre•emp/tion,** *n.* —**pre•emp/tive,** *adj.*

preen (prēn) *v.* **1.** trim or clean (feathers or fur). **2.** dress (oneself) carefully.

pref. 1. preface. **2.** prefaced. **3.** prefatory. **4.** preference. **5.** preferred. **6.** prefix. **7.** prefixed. Also, **pref**

prefab prefabricated.

pre•fab/ri•cate/, *v.,* **-cated, -cating.** build in parts for quick assembly. —**pre/fab•ri•ca/tion,** *n.* —**pre/fab,** *n. Informal.*

pref/ace (pref/is) *n., v.,* **-aced, -acing.** —*n.* **1.** preliminary statement. —*v.* **2.** provide with or serve as preface. —**pref/a•to/ry** (-ə tôr/ē) *adj.*

pre/fect (prē/fekt) *n.* magistrate. —**pre/fec•ture** (-fek shər) *n.*

pre•fer/ (pri fûr/) *v.,* **-ferred, -ferring. 1.** like better. **2.** put forward; present (criminal charge, etc).

pref/er•a•ble (pref/ər ə bəl) *adj.* more desirable. —**pref/er•a•bly,** *adv.*

pref/er•ence (-əns) *n.* **1.** liking of one above others. **2.** person or thing preferred. **3.** granting of advantage to one. —**pref/er•en/tial** (-ə ren/shəl) *adj.*

pre•fer/ment (pri fûr/mənt) *n.* promotion.

pre•fig/ure (prē fig/yər) *v.,* **-ured, -uring.** foreshadow.

pre/fix, *n.* (prē/fiks) **1.** syllable or syllables put before word to qualify its meaning. —*v.* (*also* prē fiks/) **2.** put before.

preg/nant (preg/nənt) *adj.* **1.** being with child. **2.** filled; fraught. **3.** momentous. —**preg/nan•cy,** *n.*

pre•hen/sile (pri hen/sil, -sīl) *adj.* adapted for grasping.

pre/his•tor/ic, *adj.* of time before recorded history.

pre•judge/, *v.,* **-judged, -judging.** judge prematurely.

prej/u•dice (prej/ə dis) *n., v.,* **-diced, -dicing.** —*n.* **1.** opinion formed without specific evidence. **2.** disadvantage. —*v.* **3.** affect with prejudice. —**prej/u•di/cial** (-dish/əl) *adj.* —**prej/u•di/cial•ly,** *adv.*

prel/ate (prel/it) *n.* high church official.

prelim. preliminary.

pre•lim/i•nar/y (pri lim/ə ner/ē) *adj., n., pl.* **-naries.** —*adj.* **1.** introductory. —*n.* **2.** preliminary stage or action.

pre•lit/er•ate (prē lit/ər it) *adj.* lacking a written language.

prel/ude (prel/yōōd, prā/lōōd) *n.* **1.** *Music.* **a.** preliminary to a more important work. **b.** brief composition, esp. for piano. **2.** preliminary to major action or event.

prem. premium.

pre•mar/i•tal (prē mar/i tl) *adj.* before marriage.

pre/ma•ture/, *adj.* **1.** born, maturing, or occurring too soon. **2.** overhasty. —**pre/ma•ture/ly,** *adv.* —**pre/ma•ture/ness,** *n.* —**pre/ma•tu/ri•ty,** *n.*

pre•med/i•tate/, *v.,* **-tated, -tating.** plan in advance. —**pre/med•i•ta/tion,** *n.*

pre•mier/ (pri mēr/, -myēr/) *n.* **1.** prime minister. —*adj.* **2.** chief.

pre•miere/ (pri mēr/, -myâr/) *n.* first public performance.

prem/ise (prem/is) *n.* **1.** (*pl.*) building with its grounds. **2.** statement from which a conclusion is drawn.

pre/mi•um (prē/mē əm) *n.* **1.** contest prize. **2.** bonus. **3.** periodic insurance payment.

pre/mo•ni/tion (prem/ə nish/ən, prē/mə-) *n.* foreboding. —**pre•mon/i•to/ry** (pri mon/i-tôr/ē) *adj.*

pre•na/tal (prē nāt/l) *adj.* before birth or before giving birth.

pre•oc/cu•py/, *v.,* **-pied, -pying.** engross completely. —**pre•oc/cu•pa/tion,** *n.*

pre•op (prē/op/), preoperative; preoperatively. Also, **pre/-op/.**

pre/or•dain/, *v.* decree in advance.

prep (prep) *v.,* **prepped, prepping. 1.** get ready; prepare. **2.** attend preparatory school.

prep/ar•a•tor/y school (prep/ər ə tôr/ē) private secondary school preparing students for college. Also, **prep school.**

pre•pare/ (pri pâr/) *v.,* **-pared, -paring. 1.** make or get ready. **2.** manufacture. —**prep/-a•ra/tion** (prep/ə rā/shən) *n.* —**pre•par/a•to/ry,** *adj.* —**pre•par/ed•ness,** *n.*

pre•pay/ (prē pā/) *v.,* **-paid, -paying.** pay beforehand.

pre•pon/der•ant (pri pon/dər ənt) *adj.* superior in force or numbers. —**pre•pon/der•ance,** *n.*

P

prep'o·si'tion (prep/ə zish/ən) *n.* word placed before noun or adjective to indicate relationship of space, time, means, etc. —**prep'o·si'tion·al,** *adj.*

pre'pos·sess'ing (prē/-) *adj.* impressing favorably.

pre·pos'ter·ous (pri pos/tər əs) *adj.* absurd.

prep'py (prep/ē) *n., pl.* **-pies,** *adj.,* **-pier, -piest.** —*n.* **1.** student or graduate of a preparatory school. **2.** person who acts or dresses like a preppy. —*adj.* **3.** of or characteristic of a preppy.

pre'puce (prē/pyōōs) *n.* skin covering head of penis.

pre'quel (prē/kwəl) *n.* sequel to film, play, etc., that prefigures the original.

pre·req'ui·site (pri rek/wə zit, prē-) *adj.* **1.** required in advance. —*n.* **2.** something prerequisite.

pre·rog'a·tive (pri rog/ə tiv, pə rog/-) *n.* special right or privilege.

pres., **1.** present. **2.** president.

pres'age (pres/ij) *v.,* **-aged, -aging. 1.** portend. **2.** predict.

Presb. Presbyterian.

pres'by·o'pi·a (prez/bē ō/pē ə, pres/-) *n.* farsightedness.

Presbyt. Presbyterian.

pres'by·ter (prez/bi tər, pres/-) *n.* **1.** priest. **2.** elder.

pres'by·te'ri·an (-bi tēr/ē ən) *adj.* **1.** (of religious group) governed by presbytery. **2.** (*cap.*) designating Protestant church so governed. —*n.* **3.** (*cap.*) member of Presbyterian Church.

pres'by·ter'y, *n., pl.* **-ies.** body of church elders and (in Presbyterian churches) ministers.

pre'school', *adj.* (prē/skōōl/) **1.** of or for children between infancy and kindergarten age. —*n.* (-skōōl/) **2.** school or nursery for preschool children.

pre'sci·ence (presh/əns, -ē əns) *n.* foresight. —**pre'sci·ent,** *adj.*

prescr prescription.

pre·scribe' (pri skrīb/) *v.,* **-scribed, -scribing. 1.** order for use, as medicine. **2.** order. —**pre·scrip'tion** (-skrip/shən) *n.* —**pre·scrip'tive** (-skrip/tiv) *adj.*

pres'ence (prez/əns) *n.* **1.** fact of being present. **2.** vicinity. **3.** impressive personal quality.

presence of mind, ability to think clearly and act appropriately, as during a crisis.

pres'ent, *adj.* (prez/ənt) **1.** being or occurring now. **2.** being at particular place. **3.** *Gram.* denoting action or state now in progress. —*n.* (prez/ənt) **4.** present time. **5.** *Gram.* present tense. **6.** thing bestowed as gift. —*v.* (pri zent/) **7.** give, bring, or offer. **8.** exhibit. —**pres'en·ta'tion,** *n.*

pre·sent'a·ble (pri zen/tə bəl) *adj.* suitable in looks, dress, etc. —**pre·sent'a·bly,** *adv.*

pre·sen'ti·ment (-mənt) *n.* feeling of something impending, esp. evil.

pres'ent·ly (prez/ənt lē) *adv.* **1.** at present. **2.** soon.

pre·sent'ment (pri zent/mənt) *n.* presentation.

pre·serve' (pri zûrv/) *v.,* **-served, -serving.** *n.* —*v.* **1.** keep alive. **2.** keep safe. **3.** maintain. **4.** prepare (food) for long keeping. —*n.* **5.** (*pl.*) preserved fruit. **6.** place where game is protected. —**pres'er·va'tion** (prez/ər vā/shən) *n.* —**pres'er·va'tion·ist,** *n.* —**pre·serv'a·tive,** *n., adj.* —**pre·serv'er,** *n.*

pre·side' (pri zīd/) *v.,* **-sided, -siding.** act as chairman.

pres'i·dent (prez/i dənt) *n.* **1.** highest executive of republic. **2.** chief officer. —**pres'i·den·cy,** *n.*

pre·sid'i·um (pri sid/ē əm) *n., pl.* **-iums, -ia.** executive committee.

pres. part. present participle.

press (pres) *v.* **1.** act upon with weight or force. **2.** oppress; harass. **3.** insist upon. **4.** urge to hurry or comply. —*n.* **5.** newspapers, etc., collectively. **6.** device for pressing or printing. **7.** crowd. **8.** urgency. —**press'er,** *n.*

press agent, person employed to obtain favorable publicity.

press conference, interview with reporters.

press'ing, *adj.* urgent.

press release, statement distributed to the press.

pres'sure (presh/ər) *n.* **1.** exertion of force by one body upon another. **2.** harassment. **3.** urgency.

pressure cooker, pot for cooking quickly by steam under pressure.

pressure group, group that tries to influence legislation in a particular way.

pres'sur·ize', *v.,* **-ized, -izing.** produce normal air pressure at high altitudes. —**pres'sur·i·za'tion,** *n.*

pres'ti·dig'i·ta'tion (pres/ti dij/i tā/shən) *n.* sleight of hand. —**pres'ti·dig'i·ta'tor,** *n.*

pres·tige' (pre stēzh/, -stēj/) *n.* distinguished reputation. —**pres'tig'ious** (-stij/əs) *adj.*

pres'to (pres/tō) *adv. Music.* quickly.

pre·sume' (pri zōōm/) *v.,* **-sumed, -suming. 1.** take for granted. **2.** act with unjustified boldness. —**pre·sum'a·ble,** *adj.* —**pre·sum'a·bly,** *adv.* —**pre·sump'tion** (-zump/shən) *n.* —**pre·sump'tive,** *adj.* —**pre·sump'tu·ous** (-zump/chōō əs) *adj.*

pre'sup·pose' (prē/sə pōz/) *v.,* **-posed, -posing.** assume. —**pre·sup'po·si'tion,** *n.*

pret. *Grammar.* preterit.

pre·teen', *n.* **1.** child between 10 and 13 years old. —*adj.* **2.** of or for preteens.

pre·tend' (pri tend/) *v.* **1.** make false appearance or claim. **2.** make believe. **3.** claim, as sovereignty. —**pre·tend'er,** *n.* —**pre·tense',** *n.*

pre•ten′sion (pri ten′shən) *n.* **1.** ostentation. **2.** act of pretending. —**pre•ten′tious,** *adj.* —**pre•ten′tious•ly,** *adv.* —**pre•ten′tious•ness,** *n.*

pret′er•it (pret′ər it) *Gram.* —*adj.* **1.** denoting action in past. —*n.* **2.** preterit tense.

pre′ter•nat′u•ral (prē′tər nach′ər əl) *adj.* supernatural.

pre′text (prē′tekst) *n.* ostensible reason; excuse.

pret′ty (prit′ē) *adj.,* -**tier,** -**tiest,** *adv.* —*adj.* **1.** pleasingly attractive. —*adv.* **2.** moderately. **3.** very. —**pret′ti•fy′,** *v.* —**pret′ti•ly,** *adv.* —**pret′ti•ness,** *n.*

pret′zel (pret′səl) *n.* crisp elongated or knotted biscuit.

prev. 1. previous. **2.** previously.

pre•vail′ (pri vāl′) *v.* **1.** be widespread. **2.** exercise persuasion. **3.** gain victory.

pre•vail′ing, *adj.* **1.** most common. **2.** having superior influence.

prev′a•lent (prev′ə lənt) *adj.* widespread; general. —**prev′a•lence,** *n.*

pre•var′i•cate′ (pri var′i kāt′) *v.,* -**cated,** -**cating.** speak evasively; lie. —**pre•var′i•ca′tion,** *n.* —**pre•var′i•ca′tor,** *n.*

pre•vent′ (pri vent′) *n.* hinder; stop. —**pre•vent′a•ble, pre•vent′i•ble,** *adj.* —**pre•ven′tion,** *n.* —**pre•ven′tive, pre•vent′a•tive,** *adj., n.*

pre′view′ (prē′vyōō′) *n., v.* view or show in advance.

pre′vi•ous (prē′vē əs) *adj.* occurring earlier. —**pre′vi•ous•ly,** *adv.*

prey (prā) *n.* **1.** animal hunted as food by another animal. **2.** victim. —*v.* **3.** seize prey. **4.** victimize another. **5.** be obsessive.

PRF 1. Puerto Rican female. **2.** Also, **prf** *Telecommunications.* pulse repetition frequency.

prf. proof. Also, **prf**

prfm performance.

prfrd *Printing.* proofread.

prfrdg *Printing.* proofreading.

prfrdr proofreader.

prft press fit.

prfx prefix.

prgm program.

prgmg *Computers.* programming.

prgmr *Computers.* programmer.

pri primary.

pri•ap′ic (prī ap′ik) *adj.* resembling a phallus.

price (prīs) *n., v.,* **priced, pricing.** —*n.* **1.** amount for which thing is sold. **2.** value. —*v.* **3.** set price on. **4.** *Informal,* ask the price of.

price′less, *adj.* too valuable to set price on.

pric′ey, *adj.,* -**ier,** -**iest.** *Informal,* highpriced. —**pric′i•ness,** *n.*

prick (prik) *n.* **1.** puncture by pointed object. —*v.* **2.** pierce. **3.** point.

prick′le, *n.* sharp point. —**prick′ly,** *adj.*

prickly heat, rash caused by inflammation of sweat glands.

pride (prīd) *n., v.,* **prided, priding.** —*n.* **1.** high opinion of worth of oneself or that associated with oneself. **2.** self-respect. **3.** that which one is proud of. **4.** group of lions. —*v.* **5.** feel pride. —**pride′ful,** *adj.*

priest (prēst) *n.* person authorized to perform religious rites; member of clergy. —**priest′ess,** *n.fem.* —**priest′hood,** *n.*

prig (prig) *n.* self-righteous person. —**prig′gish,** *adj.*

prim (prim) *adj.* stiffly proper. —**prim′ly,** *adv.* —**prim′ness,** *n.*

pri′ma•cy (prī′mə sē) *n., pl.* -**cies.** supremacy.

pri′ma don′na (prē′mə don′ə, prim′ə) *n.* **1.** principal female opera singer. **2.** temperamental person.

pri′ma fa′ci•e (prī′mə fā′shē ē′, fā′shē) *adj. Law.* sufficient to establish a fact unless rebutted.

pri′mal (prī′məl) *adj.* **1.** first; original. **2.** most important.

pri•ma′ri•ly (prī mâr′ə lē, -mer′-) *adv.* **1.** chiefly. **2.** originally.

pri′ma•ry (prī′mer ē, -mə rē) *adj., n., pl.* -**ries.** —*adj.* **1.** first in importance or in order. **2.** earliest. —*n.* **3.** preliminary election for choosing party candidates.

pri′mate (prī′māt *or, esp. for 1,* -mit) *n.* **1.** high church official. **2.** mammal of order including humans, apes, and monkeys.

prime (prīm) *adj., n., v.,* **primed, priming.** —*adj.* **1.** first in importance or quality. **2.** original. —*n.* **3.** best stage or part. —*v.* **4.** prepare for special purpose or function.

prime meridian, meridian running through Greenwich, England, from which longitude east and west is reckoned.

prime minister, chief minister in some governments.

prim′er (prim′ər; *esp. Brit.* prī′mər) *n.* elementary book, esp. for reading.

prime rate, minimum interest rate charged by banks to best-rated customers.

prime time, hours considered to have largest television audience.

pri•me′val (prī mē′vəl) *adj.* of earliest time.

prim′i•tive (prim′i tiv) *adj.* **1.** earliest. **2.** simple; unrefined. —**prim′i•tive•ly,** *adv.* —**prim′i•tive•ness,** *n.*

pri′mo•gen′i•ture (prī′mə jen′i chər) *n.* **1.** state of being firstborn. **2.** inheritance by eldest son.

pri•mor′di•al (prī môr′dē əl) *adj.* existing at or from the very beginning.

primp (primp) *v.* dress fussily.

prim′rose′ (prim′rōz′) *n.* early-flowering garden perennial.

prin. 1. principal. **2.** principally. **3.** principle.

prince (prins) *n.* high-ranking male member of royalty. —**prin′cess,** *n.fem.*

prince′ly, *adj.* lavish.

P

prin′ci•pal (prin′sə pəl) *adj.* **1.** chief. —*n.* **2.** chief; leader. **3.** head of school. **4.** person authorizing another to act for him. **5.** capital sum, distinguished from interest. —**prin′ci•pal•ly**, *adv.*

prin′ci•pal′i•ty (-pal′i tē) *n.*, *pl.* **-ties.** state ruled by prince.

prin′ci•ple (prin′sə pəl) *n.* **1.** rule of conduct or action. **2.** fundamental truth or doctrine. **3.** fundamental cause or factor.

print (print) *v.* **1.** reproduce from inked types, plates, etc. **2.** write in letters like those of print. **3.** produce (photograph) from negative. —*n.* **4.** printed state. **5.** (of book) present availability for sale. **6.** print lettering. **7.** anything printed. —**print′er**, *n.* —**print′a•ble**, *adj.*

print′out′, *n.* printed output of computer.

pri′or (prī′ər) *adj.* **1.** earlier. —*adv.* **2.** previously. —*n.* **3.** officer in religious house. —**pri′or•ess**, *n.fem.* —**pri′o•ry**, *n.*

pri•or′i•tize′ (prī ôr′i tīz′) *v.*, **-tized, -tizing.** arrange in order of priority.

pri•or′i•ty, *n.*, *pl.* **-ties.** **1.** state of being earlier. **2.** precedence.

prism (priz′əm) *n.* transparent body for dividing light into its spectrum. —**pris•mat′ic** (-mat′ik) *adj.*

pris′on (priz′ən) *n.* building for confinement of criminals. —**pris′on•er**, *n.*

pris′sy (pris′ē) *adj.*, **-sier, -siest.** excessively or affectedly proper. —**pris′si•ness**, *n.*

pris′tine (pris′tēn, pri stēn′) *adj.* original; pure.

priv. 1. private. **2.** *Grammar.* privative.

pri′vate (prī′vit) *adj.* **1.** belonging to particular person or group. **2.** free of outside knowledge or intrusion. —*n.* **3.** soldier of lowest rank. —**pri′va•cy**, *n.* —**pri′vate•ly**, *adv.*

pri′va•teer′ (prī′və tēr′) *n.* privately owned vessel commissioned to fight. —**pri′va•teer′ing**, *n.*

private eye, *Informal*, private detective.

pri•va′tion (prī vā′shən) *n.* lack; need.

priv′et (priv′it) *n.* evergreen shrub.

priv′i•lege (priv′ə lij, priv′lij) *n.*, *v.*, **-leged, -leging.** —*n.* **1.** special advantage. —*v.* **2.** grant privilege to.

priv. pr. privately printed.

priv′y (priv′ē) *adj.*, *n.*, *pl.* **privies.** —*adj.* **1.** participating in shared secret. **2.** private. —*n.* **3.** outdoor toilet.

privy council, board of personal advisors.

prize (prīz) *n.*, *v.*, **prized, prizing.** —*n.* **1.** reward for victory, superiority, etc. **2.** thing worth striving for. —*v.* **3.** esteem highly.

prl parallel.

PRM Puerto Rican male.

prm pulse rate modulation.

prm. premium.

prmtr parameter.

prn pseudorandom noise.

p.r.n. (in prescriptions) as the occasion arises; as needed. [from Latin *prō rē nāta*]

prntg printing.

pro (prō) *n.*, *pl.* **pros,** *adv.* —*n.* **1.** argument in favor of something. **2.** *Informal.* professional. —*adv.* **3.** in favor of a plan, etc.

pro-, prefix meaning: **1.** favoring or supporting, as *prowar*. **2.** before or in front of, as *prognosis*.

prob. 1. probable. **2.** probably. **3.** problem.

prob′a•ble (prob′ə bəl) *adj.* **1.** likely to occur, etc. **2.** affording ground for belief. —**prob′a•bil′i•ty**, *n.* —**prob′a•bly**, *adv.*

pro′bate (prō′bāt) *n.*, *adj.*, *v.*, **-bated, -bating.** —*n.* **1.** authentication of will. —*adj.* **2.** of probate. —*v.* **3.** establish will's validity.

pro•ba′tion, *n.* **1.** act of testing. **2.** period of such testing. **3.** conditional release, as from prison. **4.** period in which to redeem past failures or mistakes. —**pro•ba′tion•er**, *n.* —**pro•ba′tion•ar′y**, *adj.*

prob cse probable cause.

probe (prōb) *v.*, **probed, probing,** *n.* —*v.* **1.** examine thoroughly. —*n.* **2.** device for exploring wounds, etc. —**prob′er**, *n.*

pro′bi•ty (prō′bi tē, prob′i-) *n.* honesty.

prob′lem (prob′ləm) *n.* matter involving uncertainty or difficulty. —**prob′lem•at′ic, prob′lem•at′i•cal**, *adj.*

pro•bos′cis (prō bos′is, -kis) *n.*, *pl.* **-cises.** flexible snout, as elephant's trunk.

proc. 1. procedure. **2.** proceedings. **3.** process. **4.** proclamation. **5.** proctor.

pro•ced′ure (prə sē′jər) *n.* course of action. —**pro•ced′ur•al**, *adj.*

pro•ceed′ *v.* (prə sēd′) **1.** go forward. **2.** carry on action. **3.** issue forth. —*n.* (prō′sēd) **4.** (*pl.*). sum derived from sale, etc.

pro•ceed′ing, *n.* **1.** action or conduct. **2.** (*pl.*) **a.** records of society. **b.** legal action.

proc′ess (pros′es; *esp. Brit.* prō′ses) *n.* **1.** series of actions toward given end. **2.** continuous action. **3.** legal summons. **4.** projecting growth. —*v.* **5.** treat by particular process.

pro•ces′sion (prə sesh′ən) *n.* ceremonial movement; parade.

pro•ces′sion•al, *n.* **1.** hymn sung during procession. **2.** hymnal.

pro-choice′ (prō chois′) *adj.* supporting the right to legalized abortion.

pro•claim′ (prō klām′, prə-) *v.* announce publicly. —**proc′la•ma′tion** (prok′lə mā′shən) *n.*

pro•cliv′i•ty (prō kliv′i tē) *n.*, *pl.* **-ties.** natural tendency.

pro•cras′ti•nate′ (prō kras′tə nāt′, prə-) *v.*, **-nated, -nating.** delay from temperamental causes. —**pro•cras′ti•na′tion**, *n.* —**pro•cras′ti•na′tor**, *n.*

pro′cre•ate′ (prō′krē āt′) *v.* **-ated, -ating.** produce or have offspring. —**pro′cre•a′tion**, *n.*

proc•tol′o•gy (prok tol′ə jē) *n.* branch of medicine dealing with rectum. —**proc•tol′o•gist**, *n.*

proc′tor (prok′tər) *n.* **1.** person who watches

over students at examinations. —*v.* **2.** supervise or monitor.

pro•cure′ (prō kyo͝or′, prə-) *v.* **-cured, -curing. 1.** get; obtain. **2.** cause. **3.** hire prostitutes. —**pro•cur′a•ble,** *adj.* —**pro•cure′ment,** *n.*

pro•cur′er, *n.* **1.** one that procures. **2.** Also, **pro•cur′ess,** *fem.* person who arranges for prostitution.

prod (prod) *v.*, **prodded, prodding,** *n.* —*v.* **1.** poke. **2.** incite; goad. —*n.* **3.** poke. **4.** goading instrument.

prod′i•gal (prod′i gəl) *adj.* **1.** wastefully extravagant. **2.** lavish. —*n.* **3.** spendthrift.

prod′i•gal′i•ty (-gal′ə tē) *n.*, *pl.* **-ties.** extravagance; lavishness.

pro•di′gious (prə dij′əs) *adj.* huge; wonderful. —**pro•di′gious•ly,** *adv.*

prod′i•gy (prod′i jē) *n.*, *pl.* **-gies. 1.** very gifted person. **2.** wonderful thing.

pro•duce′, *v.*, **-duced, -ducing,** *n.* —*v.* (prə-do͞os′, -dyo͞os′) **1.** bring into existence; create. **2.** bear, as young, fruit. **3.** exhibit. —*n.* (prod′o͞os, -yo͞os, prō′do͞os, -dyo͞os) **4.** product. **5.** agricultural products. —**pro•duc′er,** *n.* —**pro•duc′tion** (prə duk′shən) *n.* —**pro•duc′tive,** *adj.* —**pro′duc•tiv′i•ty** (prō′duk tiv′i tē, prod′ək-) *n.*

prod′uct (prod′əkt) *n.* **1.** thing produced; result. **2.** result obtained by multiplying.

Prof. Professor.

pro•fane′ (prə fān′, prō-) *adj.*, *v.*, **-faned, -faning.** —*adj.* **1.** irreverent toward sacred things. **2.** secular. —*v.* **3.** defile. **4.** treat (sacred thing) with contempt. —**prof′a•na′tion** (prof′ə nā′shən) *n.*

pro•fan′i•ty (-fan′i tē) *n.*, *pl.* **-ties. 1.** profane quality. **2.** blasphemous or vulgar language.

Prof. Eng. Professional Engineer.

pro•fess′ (prə fes′) *v.* **1.** declare. **2.** affirm faith in. **3.** claim. —**pro•fessed′,** *adj.*

pro•fes′sion, *n.* **1.** learned vocation. **2.** declaration; assertion.

pro•fes′sion•al, *adj.* **1.** following occupation for gain. **2.** of or engaged in profession. —*n.* **3.** professional person. —**pro•fes′sion•al•ism,** *n.* —**pro•fes′sion•al•ly,** *adv.*

pro•fes′sor (prə fes′ər) *n.* college teacher of highest rank. —**pro′fes•so′ri•al** (prō′fə sôr′ē əl, prof′ə-) *adj.*

prof′fer (prof′ər) *v.*, *n.* offer.

pro•fi′cient (prə fish′ənt) *adj.* expert. —**pro•fi′cien•cy,** *n.* —**pro•fi′cient•ly,** *adv.*

pro′file (prō′fīl) *n.* **1.** side view. **2.** informal biographical sketch.

prof′it (prof′it) *n.* **1.** pecuniary gain from business transaction. **2.** net gain after costs. **3.** benefit. —*v.* **4.** gain advantage. **5.** make profit. —**prof′it•a•ble,** *adj.* —**prof′it•a•bly,** *adv.* —**prof′it•less,** *adj.*

prof′it•eer′, *n.* **1.** person who makes unfair profit. —*v.* **2.** act as profiteer.

prof′li•gate (prof′li git, -gāt′) *adj.* **1.** im-

moral. **2.** extravagant. —**prof′li•gate,** *n.* —**prof′li•ga•cy,** *n.*

pro for′ma (prō fôr′mə) done as a matter of form or for the sake of form.

pro•found′ (prə found′) *adj.* **1.** thinking deeply. **2.** intense. **3.** deep. —**pro•found′ly,** *adv.* —**pro•fun′di•ty** (-fun′di tē) *n.*

pro•fuse′ (-fyo͞os′) *adj.* extravagant; abundant. —**pro•fuse′ly,** *adv.* —**pro•fu′sion** (-fyo͞o′zhən) *n.*

Prog. Progressive.

prog. 1. progress. **2.** progressive.

pro•gen′i•tor (prō jen′i tər) *n.* ancestor.

prog′e•ny (proj′ə nē) *n.pl.* children; offspring.

pro•ges′ter•one (prō jes′tə rōn′) *n.* female hormone that prepares uterus for fertilized ovum.

prog′na•thous (prog′nə thəs) *adj.* having protrusive jaws.

prog•no′sis (prog nō′sis) *n.*, *pl.* **-noses** (-nō′sēz). medical forecast.

prog•nos′ti•cate′ (-nos′ti kāt′) *v.*, **-cated, -cating.** predict. —**prog•nos′ti•ca′tion,** *n.*

pro′gram (prō′gram, -grəm) *n.*, *v.*, **-grammed, -gramming.** —*n.* **1.** plan of things to do. **2.** schedule of entertainments. **3.** television or radio show. **4.** plan for computerized problem solving. —*v.* **5.** make program for or including. —**pro′gram•ma•ble,** *adj.* —**pro′gram•mat′ic** (-grə mat′ik) *adj.* —**pro′gram•mer,** *n.*

prog′ress, *n.* (prog′res, -rəs; *esp. Brit.* prō′gres) **1.** advancement. **2.** permanent improvement. **3.** growth. —*v.* (prə gres′) **4.** make progress. —**pro•gres′sion,** *n.* —**pro•gres′sive,** *adj.*, *n.* —**pro•gres′sive•ly,** *adv.*

pro•hib′it (prō hib′it) *v.* forbid; prevent.

pro′hi•bi′tion (prō′ə bish′ən) *n.* **1.** act of prohibiting. **2.** (*cap.*) period, 1920–33, when manufacture and sale of alcoholic drinks was forbidden in U.S. —**pro′hi•bi′tion•ist,** *n.*

pro•hib′i•tive (-hib′ə tiv) *adj.* **1.** serving to prohibit. **2.** too expensive.

proj project.

proj′ect, *n.* (proj′ekt, -ikt; *esp. Brit.* prō′jekt) **1.** something planned. —*v.* (prə jekt′) **2.** plan; contemplate. **3.** impel forward. **4.** display upon surface, as motion picture or map. **5.** extend out; protrude. —**pro•jec′tion,** *n.* —**pro•jec′tor,** *n.*

pro•jec′tile (prə jek′til, -tīl) *n.* object fired with explosive force.

pro•jec′tion•ist (-shə nist) *n.* operator of motion-picture projector.

pro′le•tar′i•at (prō′li târ′ē ət) *n.* working or impoverished class. —**pro′le•tar′i•an,** *adj.*, *n.*

pro-life′, *adj.* opposed to legalized abortion.

pro•lif′er•ate′ (prə lif′ə rāt′) *v.*, **-ated, -ating.** spread rapidly. —**pro•lif′er•a′tion,** *n.*

pro•lif′ic (-ik) *adj.* productive.

pro•lix′ (prō liks′, prō′liks) *adj.* tediously long and wordy. —**pro•lix′i•ty,** *n.*

P

pro′logue (prō′lôg) *n.* introductory part of novel, play, etc.

pro•long′ (prə lông′) *v.* lengthen. —**pro′lon•ga′tion** (prō′-) *n.*

prom (prom) *n.* formal dance at high school or college.

prom′e•nade′ (prom′ə nād′, -näd′) *n., v.,* -naded, -nading. —*n.* 1. leisurely walk. 2. space for such walk. —*v.* 3. stroll.

prom′i•nent (prom′ə nənt) *adj.* 1. conspicuous. 2. projecting. 3. well-known. —**prom′i•nence,** *n.* —**prom′i•nent•ly,** *adv.*

pro•mis′cu•ous (prə mis′kyŏŏ əs) *adj.* 1. having numerous sexual partners on a casual basis. 2. indiscriminate. —**prom′is•cu′i•ty,** (prom′i skyŏŏ′i tē) *n.* —**pro•mis′cu•ous•ly,** *adv.*

prom′ise (prom′is) *n., v.,* -ised, -ising. —*n.* 1. assurance that one will act as specified. 2. indication of future excellence. —*v.* 3. assure by promise. 4. afford ground for expectation. —**prom′is•ing,** *adj.*

prom′is•so′ry (prom′ə sôr′ē) *adj.* containing promise, esp. of payment.

prom′on•to′ry (prom′ən tôr′ē) *n., pl.* -ries. high peak projecting into sea or overlooking low land.

pro•mote′ (prə mōt′) *v.,* -moted, -moting. 1. further progress of. 2. advance. 3. organize. —**pro•mot′er,** *n.* —**pro•mo′tion,** *n.*

prompt (prompt) *adj.* 1. ready to act. 2. done at once. —*v.* 3. incite to action. 4. suggest (action, etc.). —**prompt′er,** *n.* —**prompt′ly,** *adv.* —**prompt′ness, promp′ti•tude′,** *n.*

prom′ul•gate (prom′əl gāt′, prō mul′gāt) *v.,* -gated, -gating. proclaim formally. —**prom′ul•ga′tion,** *n.* —**prom′ul•ga′tor,** *n.*

pron. 1. *Grammar.* pronominal. 2. pronoun. 3. pronounced. 4. pronunciation.

prone (prōn) *adj.* 1. likely; inclined. 2. lying flat, esp. face downward.

prong (prông) *n.* point.

pro′noun (prō′noun′) *n.* word used as substitute for noun. —**pro•nom′i•nal** (-nom′ə-nl) *adj.*

pro•nounce′ (prə nouns′) *v.,* -nounced, -nouncing. 1. utter, esp. precisely. 2. declare to be. 3. announce. —**pro•nounce′ment,** *n.*

pro•nounced′ *adj.* 1. strongly marked. 2. decided.

pron′to (pron′tō) *adv.* promptly; quickly.

pro•nun′ci•a′tion (prə nun′sē ā′shən) *n.* production of sounds of speech.

proof (prŏŏf) *n.* 1. evidence establishing fact. 2. standard strength, as of liquors. 3. trial printing. —*adj.* 4. resisting perfectly.

-proof, suffix meaning resistant.

proof′read′ (-rēd′) *v.,* -read (red′), -reading. read (printers' proofs, etc.) to mark errors. —**proof′read′er,** *n.*

prop (prop) *n., v.,* propped, propping. —*n.* 1. rigid support. 2. propeller. —*v.* 3. support with prop.

prop′a•gan′da (prop′ə gan′də) *n.* doctrines disseminated by organization. —**prop′a•gan′dist,** *n.* —**prop′a•gan′dize,** *v.,* -dized, -dizing.

prop′a•gate′ (prop′ə gāt′) *v.,* -gated, -gating. 1. reproduce; cause to reproduce. 2. transmit (doctrine, etc.). —**prop′a•ga′tion,** *n.*

pro′pane (prō′pān) *n.* colorless flammable gas, used esp. as fuel.

pro•pel′ (prə pel′) *v.,* -pelled, -pelling. drive forward. —**pro•pel′lant, pro•pel′lent,** *n.*

pro•pel′ler, *n.* screwlike propelling device.

pro•pen′si•ty (prə pen′si tē) *n., pl.* -ties. inclination.

prop′er (prop′ər) *adj.* 1. suitable; fitting. 2. correct. 3. designating particular person, place, or thing. —**prop′er•ly,** *adv.*

prop′er•ty, *n., pl.* -ties. 1. that which one owns. 2. attribute.

proph′e•sy (prof′ə sī′) *v.,* -sied, -sying. foretell; predict. —**proph′e•cy** (-sē) *n.*

proph′et (-it) *n.* 1. person who speaks for God. 2. inspired leader. 3. person who predicts. —**pro•phet′ic** (prə fet′ik) *adj.* —**pro•phet′i•cal•ly,** *adv.*

pro′phy•lax′is (prō′fə lak′sis) *n.* protection from or prevention of disease. —**pro′phy•lac′tic,** *adj., n.*

pro•pin′qui•ty (prō ping′kwi tē) *n.* nearness.

pro•pi′ti•ate′ (prə pish′ē āt′) *v.,* -ated, -ating. appease.

pro•pi′tious (-pish′əs) *adj.* favorable. —**pro•pi′tious•ly,** *adv.*

pro•po′nent (prə pō′nənt) *n.* advocate; supporter.

pro•por′tion (prə pôr′shən) *n.* 1. comparative or proper relation of dimensions or quantities. 2. symmetry. 3. (*pl.*) dimensions. —*v.* 4. adjust in proper relation. —**pro•por′tion•al,** *adj.*

pro•por′tion•ate (-shə nit) *adj.* being in due proportion. —**pro•por′tion•ate•ly,** *adv.*

pro•pos′al (prə pō′zəl) *n.* 1. proposition. 2. offer of marriage.

pro•pose′ (prə pōz′) *v.,* -posed, -posing. 1. suggest. 2. intend. 3. offer marriage.

prop′o•si′tion (prop′ə zish′ən) *n.* 1. proposed plan. 2. statement that affirms or denies. 3. proposal of sex. —*v.* 4. make proposition to.

pro•pound′ (prə pound′) *v.* offer for consideration.

propr. proprietor.

pro•pri′e•tor (prə prī′ə tər) *n.* owner or manager. —**pro•pri′e•tar′y,** *adj.*

pro•pri′e•ty, *n., pl.* -ties. 1. appropriateness. 2. (*pl.*) morality; correctness.

pro•pul′sion (prə pul′shən) *n.* propelling force. —**pro•pul′sive** (-siv) *adj.*

pro•rate′ (prō rāt′, prō′rāt′) *v.,* -rated, -rating. divide proportionately.

pros. 1. *Theater.* proscenium. 2. prosody.

pro•sa'ic (prō zā'ik) *adj.* commonplace. —**pro•sa'i•cal•ly,** *adv.*

Pros. Atty. prosecuting attorney.

pro•sce'ni•um (prō sē'nē əm, prə-) *n., pl.* **-niums, -nia** (-nē ə). arch separating stage from auditorium. Also, **proscenium arch.**

pro•scribe' (prō skrīb') *v.* **-scribed, -scribing.** prohibit. —**pro•scrip'tion** (-skrip'shən) *n.*

prose (prōz) *n.* not verse; ordinary language.

pros'e•cute' (pros'i kyōōt') *v.*, **-cuted, -cuting. 1.** begin legal proceedings against. **2.** go on with (task, etc.). —**pros'e•cu'tion,** *n.* —**pros'e•cu'tor,** *n.*

pros'e•lyte' (pros'ə līt') *n., v.*, **-lyted, -lyting.** convert. —**pros'e•lyt•ize'** (-lə tīz') *v.,* **-ized, -izing.**

pros'o•dy (pros'ə dē) *n., pl.* **-dies.** study of poetic meters and versification.

pros'pect (pros'pekt) *n.* **1.** likelihood of success. **2.** outlook; view. **3.** potential customer. —*v.* **4.** search. —**pro•spec'tive** (prə spek'tiv) *adj.* —**pros'pec•tor,** *n.*

pro•spec'tus (prə spek'təs) *n.* description of new investment or purchase.

pros'per (pros'pər) *v.* be successful. —**pros•per'i•ty** (-per'ə tē) *n.* —**pros'per•ous,** *adj.* —**pros'per•ous•ly,** *adv.*

pros'tate (pros'tāt) *n.* gland in males at base of bladder.

pros•the'sis (pros thē'sis) *n., pl.* **-ses** (-sēz). device that substitutes for or supplements missing or defective body part. —**pros•thet'ic** (-thet'ik) *adj.*

pros'ti•tute' (pros'ti tōōt', -tyōōt') *n., v.,* **-tuted, -tuting.** —*n.* **1.** person who engages in sexual intercourse for money. —*v.* **2.** put to base use. —**pros'ti•tu'tion,** *n.*

pros'trate (pros'trāt) *v.,* **-trated, -trating,** *adj.* —*v.* **1.** lay (oneself) face downward, esp. in humility. **2.** exhaust. —*adj.* **3.** lying flat. **4.** helpless. **5.** weak or exhausted. —**pros•tra'tion,** *n.*

pros'y (prō'zē) *adj.,* **prosier, prosiest.** dull.

prot protective.

Prot. Protestant.

pro•tag'o•nist (prō tag'ə nist) *n.* main character.

pro•te•an (prō'tē ən, prō tē'-) *adj.* assuming different forms.

pro•tect' (prə tekt') *v.* shield; defend, as from attack. —**pro•tec'tion,** *n.* —**pro•tec'tive,** *adj.* —**pro•tec'tive•ly,** *adv.* —**pro•tec'tor,** *n.*

pro•tec'tion•ism (-shə niz'əm) *n.* practice of protecting domestic industries from foreign competition by imposing import duties.

pro•tec'tor•ate (-tər it) *n.* **1.** relation by which strong state partly controls weaker state. **2.** such weaker state.

pro'té•gé' (prō'tə zhā') *n.* one under friendly patronage of another. —**pro'té•gée',** *n.fem.*

pro'tein (prō'tēn, -tē in) *n.* nitrogenous compound.

pro tem. for the time being. [from Latin *pro tempore*]

pro tem•por•e (prō' tem'pə rē', -rā') temporarily.

pro'test, *n.* (prō'test) **1.** objection. —*v.* (prətest', prō'test) **2.** express objection. **3.** declare. —**prot'es•ta'tion,** *n.* —**pro•test'er,** *n.*

Prot'es•tant (prot'ə stənt) *n.* Christian who belongs to a church that began by breaking away from the Roman Catholic Church in the 16th century. —**Prot'es•tant•ism',** *n.*

proto-, prefix meaning earliest or foremost.

pro'to•col' (prō'tə kôl') *n.* diplomatic etiquette.

pro'ton (prō'ton) *n.* part of atom bearing positive charge.

pro'to•plasm' (prō'tə plaz'əm) *n.* basis of living matter.

pro'to•type', *n.* model; first or typical version. —**pro'to•typ'i•cal,** *adj.*

pro'to•zo'an (-zō'ən) *n., pl.* **-zoans, -zoa** (-zō'ə). any of various one-celled organisms that obtain nourishment by ingesting food rather than by photosynthesis. —**pro'to•zo'ic,** *adj.*

pro•tract' (prō trakt', prə-) *v.* lengthen. —**pro•trac'tion,** *n.*

pro•trac'tor, *n.* instrument for measuring angles.

pro•trude' (prō trōōd', prə-) *v.,* **-truded, -truding.** project; extend. —**pro•tru'sion** (-trōō'zhən) *n.* —**pro•tru'sive** (-trōō'siv) *adj.*

pro•tu'ber•ant (prō tōō'bər ənt) *adj.* bulging out. —**pro•tu'ber•ance,** *n.*

proud (proud) *adj.* **1.** having pride. **2.** arrogant. **3.** magnificent. —**proud'ly,** *adv.*

Prov. 1. Provençal. **2.** Provence. **3.** *Bible.* Proverbs. **4.** Province. **5.** Provost.

prov. 1. province. **2.** provincial. **3.** provisional. **4.** provost.

prove (prōōv) *v.,* **proved, proving. 1.** establish as fact. **2.** test. **3.** be or become ultimately. —**prov'a•ble,** *adj.*

prov'e•nance (prov'ə nəns, -näns') *n.* place or source of origin.

prov'en•der (prov'ən dər) *n.* fodder.

prov'erb (prov'ərb) *n.* wise, long-current saying. —**pro•ver'bi•al** (prə vûr'bē əl) *adj.*

pro•vide' (prə vīd') *v.,* **-vided, -viding. 1.** supply. **2.** yield. **3.** prepare beforehand. —**pro•vid'er,** *n.*

pro•vid'ed, *conj.* if.

prov'i•dence (prov'i dəns) *n.* **1.** God's care. **2.** economy.

prov'i•dent (-dənt) *adj.* showing foresight; prudent.

prov'i•den'tial (-den'shəl) *adj.* coming as godsend.

prov'ince (prov'ins) *n.* **1.** administrative unit of country. **2.** sphere.

pro·vin'cial (prə vin'shəl) *adj.* **1.** of province. **2.** narrow-minded; unsophisticated.

pro·vi'sion (prə vizh'ən) *n.* **1.** something stated as necessary or binding. **2.** act of providing. **3.** what is provided. **4.** arrangement beforehand. **5.** (*pl.*) food supply. —*v.* **6.** supply with provisions.

pro·vi'sion·al, *adj.* temporary.

pro·vi'so (prə vī'zō) *n., pl.* **-sos, -soes.** something required in an agreement; stipulation.

pro·vo'ca·teur' (prə vok'ə tûr', -tŏŏr'), *n.* person who provokes trouble, esp. as an agent for the police or a foreign power.

pro·voke' (-vōk') *v.,* **-voked, -voking. 1.** exasperate. **2.** arouse. —**prov'o·ca'tion** (prov'ə kā'shən) *n.* —**pro·voc'a·tive** (prə vok'ətiv) *adj.* —**pro·voc'a·tive·ly,** *adv.*

pro'vost (prō'vōst) *n.* **1.** superintendent. **2.** high-ranking university administrator.

pro'vost marshal (prō'vō) *Mil.* head of police.

prow (prou) *n.* front part of ship or aircraft.

prow'ess (prou'is) *n.* **1.** exceptional ability. **2.** bravery.

prowl (proul) *v.* roam or search stealthily. —**prowl'er,** *n.*

prox. the next month. [from Latin *proximo*]

prox·im'i·ty (prok sim'i tē) *n.* nearness.

prox'y (prok'sē) *n., pl.* **proxies.** agent.

prp. **1.** present participle. **2.** purpose.

prphl peripheral.

prpsl proposal.

prs. pairs.

prsrz pressurize.

PRT personal rapid transit.

prt print.

prtg printing.

prtl partial.

prtr printer.

prude (prŏŏd) *n.* person overly concerned with proprieties. —**prud'er·y,** *n.* —**prud'·ish,** *adj.*

pru'dence, *n.* practical wisdom; caution. —**pru'dent, pru·den'tial** (-den'shəl) *adj.* —**pru'dent·ly,** *adv.*

prune (prŏŏn) *v.,* **pruned, pruning,** *n.* —*v.* **1.** cut off (branches, etc.). —*n.* **2.** kind of plum, often dried.

pru'ri·ent (prŏŏr'ē ənt) *adj.* having lewd thoughts. —**pru'ri·ence,** *n.*

Prus. 1. Prussia. **2.** Prussian. Also, **Pruss., Pruss**

prv peak reverse voltage.

prvw preview.

prx prefix.

pry (prī) *v.,* **pried, prying,** *n.* —*v.* **1.** look or inquire too curiously. **2.** move with lever. —*n.* **3.** act of prying. **4.** prying person. **5.** lever.

P.S., 1. Also, **p.s.** postscript. **2.** Public School.

PSA 1. *Medicine.* prostatic specific antigen. **2.** public service announcement.

Psa. *Bible.* Psalms.

psalm (säm) *n.* sacred song.

p's and q's manners; behavior; conduct. [perhaps from some children's difficulty in distinguishing the two letters]

PSAT Preliminary Scholastic Aptitude Test.

PSB *Printing.* prepress service bureau.

PSC Public Service Commission.

PSD prevention of significant deterioration: used as a standard of measurement by the U.S. Environmental Protection Agency.

PSE Pidgin Sign English.

psec picosecond; picoseconds. Also, **ps**

pseud. 1. pseudonym. **2.** pseudonymous.

pseu'do (sŏŏ'dō) *adj.* false; imitation.

pseu'do·nym (sŏŏd'n im) *n.* false name used by writer. —**pseu·don'y·mous** (sŏŏdon'ə məs) *adj.*

psf pounds per square foot. Also, **p.s.f.**

PSG 1. platoon sergeant. **2.** *Medicine.* polysomnogram.

psgr passenger.

psi pounds per square inch. Also, **p.s.i.**

psia pounds per square inch, absolute.

psid pounds per square inch, differential.

psig pounds per square inch, gauge.

psit'ta·co'sis (sit'ə kō'sis) *n.* disease affecting birds and transmissible to humans.

psiv passive.

psm prism.

psnl personal.

pso·ri'a·sis (sə rī'ə sis) *n.* chronic, inflammatory skin disease characterized by scaly patches.

PSRO Professional Standards Review Organization. Also, **P.S.R.O.**

P.SS. postscripts. Also, **p.ss.** [from Latin *postscrīpta*]

PST Pacific Standard Time. Also, **P.S.T., p.s.t.**

pst paste.

pstl pistol.

pstn piston.

psvt *Metallurgy.* passivate.

psvtn preservation.

psych (sīk) *v. Informal.* **1.** intimidate. **2.** prepare psychologically.

psy'che (sī'kē) *n.* human soul or mind.

psy'che·del'ic (sī'ki del'ik) *adj.* noting a mental state of distorted sense perceptions and hallucinations.

psy·chi'a·try (si kī'ə trē, sī-) *n.* science of mental diseases. —**psy'chi·at'ric** (sī'kē a'trik) *adj.* —**psy·chi'a·trist,** *n.*

psy'chic (sī'kik) *adj.* **1.** of the psyche. **2.** pertaining to an apparently nonphysical force or agency. —*n.* **3.** person sensitive to psychic influences.

psy'cho·ac'tive (sī'kō-) *adj.* affecting mental state.

psychoanal. psychoanalysis.

psy'cho·a·nal'y·sis *n.* **1.** study of conscious and unconscious psychological proc-

esses. **2.** treatment according to such study.
—**psy′cho•an′a•lyst,** *n.* —**psy′cho•an′a•lyze′,** *v.*

psy′cho•gen′ic (sī′kə jen′ik) *adj.* originating in mental process or condition.

psychol. 1. psychological. **2.** psychologist. **3.** psychology.

psy•chol′o•gy (sī kol′ə jē) *n.* science of mental states and behavior. —**psy′cho•log′i•cal** (-kə loj′i kəl) *adj.* —**psy′cho•log′i•cal•ly,** *adv.* —**psy•chol′o•gist,** *n.*

psy′cho•neu•ro′sis (sī′kō nŏŏ rō′sis, -nyŏŏ-) *n., pl.* **-ses.** emotional disorder. —**psy′cho•neu•rot′ic** (-rot′ik) *adj., n.*

psy•chop′a•thy (-kop′ə thē) *n., pl.* **-thies.** mental disease. —**psy′cho•path′** (sī′kə path′) *n.* —**psy′cho•path′ic,** *adj.*

psy•cho′sis (-kō′sis) *n., pl.* **-ses** (-sēz). severe mental disease. —**psy•chot′ic** (-kot′ik) *adj., n.*

psy′cho•so•mat′ic (-sə mat′ik) *adj.* (of physical disorder) caused by one's emotional state.

psy′cho•ther′a•py, *n., pl.* **-pies.** treatment of mental disorders. —**psy′cho•ther′a•pist,** *n.*

psy′cho•tro′pic (-trō′pik) *adj.* affecting mental activity.

pt., 1. part. **2.** pint. **3.** point.

PTA 1. Also, **P.T.A.** Parent-Teacher Association. **2.** Philadelphia Transportation Authority.

Pta. peseta.

ptar′mi•gan (tär′mi gən) *n.* species of mountain grouse.

PTC *Biochemistry.* phenylthiocarbamide.

pter′o•dac′tyl (ter′ə dak′til) *n.* extinct flying reptile.

ptfe polytetrafluoroethylene.

ptg. printing.

ptl patrol.

ptly partly.

PTM *Telecommunications.* pulse time modulation. Also, **ptm**

ptn 1. partition. **2.** pattern.

PTO 1. Parent-Teacher Organization. **2.** Patent and Trademark Office. **3.** *Machinery.* power takeoff.

P.T.O. 1. Parent-Teacher Organization. **2.** Also, **p.t.o.** please turn over (a page or leaf).

pto′maine (tō′mān) *n.* substance produced during decay of plant and animal matter.

pts. points.

PTSD posttraumatic stress disorder.

PTT Post, Telegraph, and Telephone (the government-operated system, as in France or Turkey).

ptt push-to-talk.

PTV public television.

Pty *Australian.* proprietary.

pty party.

Pu *Symbol, Chemistry.* plutonium.

pu 1. Also, **p/u** pick up. **2.** power unit. **3.** purple.

pub (pub) *n. Brit. Informal.* tavern.

pu′ber•ty (pyōō′bər tē) *n.* sexual maturity. —**pu′ber•tal,** *adj.*

pu•bes′cent (-bes′ənt) *adj.* arriving at puberty. —**pu•bes′cence,** *n.*

pu′bic (pyōō′bik) *adj.* of or near the genitals.

publ. 1. public. **2.** publication. **3.** publicity. **4.** published. **5.** publisher.

pub′lic (pub′lik) *adj.* **1.** of or for people generally. **2.** open to view or knowledge of all. —*n.* **3.** people. —**pub′lic•ly,** *adv.*

pub′li•ca′tion, *n.* **1.** publishing of book, etc. **2.** item published.

public defender, lawyer who represents indigent clients at public expense.

public domain, legal status of material not protected by copyright or patent.

pub•lic′i•ty (pu blis′i tē) *n.* **1.** public attention. **2.** material promoting this.

pub′li•cize′, *v.,* **-cized, -cizing.** bring to public notice. —**pub′li•cist,** *n.*

public relations, actions of organization in promoting goodwill with the public.

pub′lish (pub′lish) *v.* **1.** issue (book, paper, etc.) for general distribution. **2.** announce publicly. —**pub′lish•er,** *n.*

pubn publication.

PUC Public Utilities Commission. Also, **P.U.C.**

puck (puk) *n.* black rubber disk hit into goal in hockey.

puck′er (puk′ər) *v., n.* wrinkle.

puck′ish (puk′ish) *adj.* mischievous.

P.U.D. pickup and delivery.

pud′ding (pŏŏd′ing) *n.* soft, creamy dish, usually dessert.

pud′dle (pud′l) *n., v.,* **-dled, -dling.** —*n.* **1.** small pool of water, esp. dirty water. —*v.* **2.** fill with puddles.

pudg′y (puj′ē) *adj.,* **-ier, -iest.** short and fat. —**pudg′i•ness,** *n.*

pueb′lo (pweb′lō) *n., pl.* **-los.** village of certain Southwestern Indians.

pu′er•ile (pyōō′ər il, -ə rīl′) *adj.* childish. —**pu′er•il′i•ty,** *n.*

puff (puf) *n.* **1.** short blast of wind. **2.** inflated part. **3.** anything soft and light. —*v.* **4.** blow with puffs. **5.** breathe hard and fast. **6.** inflate. —**puff′i•ness,** *n.* —**puff′y,** *adj.*

puf′fin (puf′in) *n.* sea bird.

pug (pug) *n.* kind of dog.

pu′gil•ism (pyōō′jə liz′əm) *n.* boxing. —**pu′gil•ist,** *n.* —**pu′gi•lis′tic,** *adj.*

pug•na′cious (pug nā′shəs) *adj.* fond of fighting. —**pug•nac′i•ty** (-nas′ə tē) *n.*

pug nose, short, broad, somewhat turned-up nose.

puke (pyōōk) *v.,* **puked, puking,** *n. Slang.* vomit.

pul pulley.

pul′chri•tude′ (pul′kri tōōd′, -tyōōd′) *n.* beauty.

P

pule (pyōōl) *v.*, **puled, puling.** whine.
pull (pŏŏl) *v.* **1.** draw; haul. **2.** tear. **3.** move with force. —*n.* **4.** act of pulling. **5.** force. **6.** handle. **7.** *Informal.* influence in politics, etc.
pul′let (pŏŏl′it) *n.* young hen.
pul′ley (pŏŏl′ē) *n.* wheel for guiding rope.
Pull′man (pŏŏl′mən) *n.* sleeping car on railroad.
pull′out′, *n.* **1.** withdrawal. **2.** section of publication that can be pulled out.
pull′o′ver, *adj.* **1.** put on by being drawn over the head. —*n.* **2.** pullover garment.
pul′mo·nar′y (pul′mə ner′ē, pŏŏl′-) *adj.* of lungs.
pulp (pulp) *n.* **1.** soft fleshy part, as of fruit or tooth. **2.** any soft mass. —*v.* **3.** make or become pulp. —**pulp′y,** *adj.*
pul′pit (pŏŏl′pit, pul′-) *n.* platform in church from which service is conducted or sermon is preached.
pul′sar (pul′sär) *n.* source of pulsating radio energy among stars.
pul′sate (pul′sāt) *v.*, **-sated, -sating.** throb. —**pul·sa′tion,** *n.*
pulse (puls) *n.*, *v.*, **pulsed, pulsing.** —*n.* **1.** heartbeat. —*v.* **2.** pulsate.
pulv. (in prescriptions) powder. [from Latin *pulvis*]
pul′ver·ize′ (pul′və rīz′) *v.*, **-ized, -izing.** reduce to powder. —**pul′ver·i·za′tion,** *n.*
pu′ma (pyōō′mə, pōō′-) *n.* cougar.
pum′ice (pum′is) *n.* porous volcanic glass used as abrasive.
pum′mel (pum′əl) *v.*, **-meled, -meling.** strike; beat.
pump (pump) *n.* **1.** apparatus for raising or driving fluids. **2.** women's shoe. —*v.* **3.** raise or drive with pump. **4.** *Informal,* try to get information from.
pum′per·nick′el (pum′pər nik′əl) *n.* hard, sour rye bread.
pump′kin (pump′kin *or,* *commonly,* pung′-kin) *n.* large orange squash of garden vine.
pun (pun) *n.*, *v.*, **punned, punning.** —*n.* **1.** play with words alike in sound but different in meaning. —*v.* **2.** make pun. —**pun′ster,** *n.*
punc. punctuation.
punch (punch) *n.* **1.** thrusting blow. **2.** tool for piercing material. **3.** sweetened beverage. —*v.* **4.** hit with thrusting blow. **5.** drive (cattle). **6.** cut or indent with punch. —**punch′-er,** *n.*
punch′-drunk′, *adj.* **1.** showing symptoms of cerebral injury. **2.** dazed.
pun′cheon (pun′chən) *n.* large cask.
punch line, climactic phrase in a joke.
punch′y, *adj.*, **-ier, -iest. 1.** befuddled; dazed, as if having been punched. **2.** vigorously effective; forceful.
punc·til′i·ous (pungk til′ē əs) *adj.* exact or careful in conduct.
punc′tu·al (pungk′chōō əl) *adj.* on time. —**punc′tu·al′i·ty,** *n.* —**punc′tu·al·ly,** *adv.*

punc′tu·ate′ (-āt′) *v.*, **-ated, -ating. 1.** mark with punctuation. **2.** accent periodically.
punc′tu·a′tion, *n.* use of commas, semicolons, etc.
punc′ture (pungk′chər) *n.*, *v.*, **-tured, -turing.** —*n.* **1.** perforation. —*v.* **2.** perforate with pointed object.
pun′dit (pun′dit) *n.* learned person.
pun′gent (pun′jənt) *adj.* **1.** sharp in taste. **2.** biting. —**pun′gen·cy,** *n.* —**pun′gent·ly,** *adv.*
pun′ish (pun′ish) *v.* subject to pain, confinement, loss, etc., for offense. —**pun′ish·a·ble,** *adj.* —**pun′ish·ment,** *n.*
pu′ni·tive (pyōō′ni tiv) *adj.* punishing.
punk (pungk) *n.* **1.** substance that will smolder, used esp. to light fires. **2.** *Slang.* something or someone worthless or unimportant. **3.** *Slang.* young hoodlum. **4.** Also, **punk rock.** rock music marked by loudness and aggressive lyrics. **5.** style of clothing, etc., suggesting defiance of social norms. —*adj.* **6.** *Informal.* poor in quality. **7.** of punk rock or punk style.
punt (punt) *n.* **1.** kick in football. **2.** shallow flat-bottomed boat. —*v.* **3.** kick (dropped ball) before it touches ground. **4.** propel (boat) with pole.
pu′ny (pyōō′nē) *adj.*, **-nier, -niest.** small and weak.
pup (pup) *n.* young dog.
pu′pa (pyōō′pə) *n.*, *pl.* **-pae** (-pē) **-pas.** insect in stage between larva and winged adult. —**pu′pal,** *adj.*
pu′pil (pyōō′pəl) *n.* **1.** person being taught. **2.** opening in iris of eye.
pup′pet (pup′it) *n.* **1.** doll or figure manipulated by hand or strings. **2.** person, government, etc., whose actions are controlled by another. —**pup′pet·ry,** *n.*
pup′pet·eer′, *n.* person who manipulates puppets.
pup′py (pup′ē) *n.*, *pl.* **-pies.** young dog.
pup tent, small tent.
pur′blind (pûr′blīnd′) *adj.* **1.** partially blind. **2.** lacking understanding.
pur′chase (pûr′chəs) *v.*, **-chased, -chasing,** *n.* —*v.* **1.** buy. —*n.* **2.** acquisition by payment. **3.** what is purchased. **4.** leverage. —**pur′chas·er,** *n.*
pure (pyŏŏr) *adj.*, **purer, purest. 1.** free of pollutants. **2.** abstract. **3.** absolute. **4.** chaste. —**pure′ly,** *adv.* —**pure′ness,** *n.*
pure′bred, *adj.* (pyŏŏr′bred′) **1.** having ancestors over many generations from a recognized breed. —*n.* (pyŏŏr′bred′) **2.** purebred animal.
pu·rée′ (pyŏŏ rā′, -rē′) *n.*, *v.*, **-réed, -réeing.** —*n.* **1.** cooked food that has been sieved or blended. —*v.* **2.** make purée of.
pur′ga·to·ry (pûr′gə tôr′ē) *n.*, *pl.* **-ries. 1.** *Rom. Cath. Theol.* condition or place of purification, after death, from venial sins. **2.** any condition or place of temporary punishment.

purge (pûrj) *v.*, purged, purging, *n.* —*v.* **1.** cleanse; purify. **2.** rid. **3.** clear by causing evacuation. —*n.* **4.** act or means of purging. —**pur•ga′tion** (-gā′shən) *n.* —**pur′ga•tive** (gə tiv) *adj., n.*

pu′ri•fy′ (pyōōr′ə fī′) *v.*, **-fied, -fying.** make or become pure. —**pu′ri•fi•ca′tion,** *n.*

Pu′rim (pŏōr′im) *n.* Jewish commemorative festival.

pur′ism (pyōōr′iz əm) *n.* insistence on purity in language, style, etc. —**pur′ist,** *n.*

Pu′ri•tan (pyōōr′i tn) *n.* **1.** member of strict Protestant group originating in 16th-century England. **2.** (*l.c.*) person of strict moral views. —**pu′ri•tan′i•cal,** *adj.*

pu′ri•ty (pyōōr′i tē) *n.* condition of being pure.

purl (pûrl) *v.* knit with inverted stitch.

pur′lieu (pûr′lōō, pûrl′yōō) *n., pl.* **-lieus. 1.** (*pl.*) neighborhood. **2.** outlying district.

pur•loin′ (pər loin′, pûr′loin) *v.* steal.

pur′ple (pûr′pəl) *n.* **1.** color blended of red and blue. —*adj.* **2.** of or like purple.

pur•port′, *v.* (pər pôrt′) **1.** claim. **2.** imply. —*n.* (pûr′pôrt) **3.** meaning.

pur′pose (pûr′pəs) *n., v.*, **-posed, -posing.** —*n.* **1.** object; aim; intention. —*v.* **2.** intend. —**pur′pose•ful,** *adj.* —**pur′pose•less,** *adj.*

purr (pûr) *n.* **1.** low continuous sound made by cat. —*v.* **2.** make this sound.

purse (pûrs) *n., v.*, **pursed, pursing.** —*n.* **1.** small case for carrying money. **2.** sum of money offered as prize. —*v.* **3.** pucker.

purs′er, *n.* financial officer.

pur•su′ant (pər sōō′ənt) *adv.* according.

pur•sue′, *v.*, **-sued, -suing. 1.** follow to catch. **2.** carry on (studies, etc.). —**pur•su′-ance,** *n.* —**pur•su′er,** *n.*

pur•suit′ (-sōōt′) *n.* **1.** act of pursuing. **2.** quest. **3.** occupation.

pu′ru•lent (pyōōr′ə lənt, pyōōr′yə-) *adj.* full of pus. —**pu′ru•lence,** *n.*

pur•vey′ (pər vā′) *v.* provide; supply. —**pur•vey′ance,** *n.* —**pur•vey′or,** *n.*

pur′view (pûr′vyōō) *n.* **1.** range of operation, authority, or concern. **2.** range of vision, insight, or understanding.

pus (pus) *n.* liquid matter found in sores, etc.

push (pŏŏsh) *v.* **1.** exert force on to send away. **2.** urge. —*n.* **3.** act of pushing. **4.** strong effort. —**push′er,** *n.*

push′o′ver, *n. Informal.* one easily victimized or overcome.

push′y, *adj.*, **-ier, -iest.** obnoxiously self-assertive. —**push′i•ness,** *n.*

pu′sil•lan′i•mous (pyōō′sə lan′ə məs) *adj.* cowardly.

puss′y (pŏŏs′ē) *n., pl.* **pussies.** cat. Also, **puss.**

puss′y•foot′, *v.* **1.** go stealthily. **2.** act timidly or irresolutely.

pussy willow, small American willow.

pus′tule (pus′chōōl) *n.* pimple containing pus.

put (pŏŏt) *v.*, **put, putting,** *n.* —*v.* **1.** move or place. **2.** set, as to task. **3.** express. **4.** apply. **5.** impose. **6.** throw. —*n.* **7.** throw.

pu′ta•tive (pyōō′tə tiv) *adj.* reputed.

put′-down′, *n. Informal.* snubbing remark.

pu′tre•fy′ (pyōō′trə fī′) *v.*, **-fied, -fying.** rot. —**pu′tre•fac′tion** (-fak′shən) *n.*

pu•tres′cent (-tres′ənt) *adj.* becoming putrid. —**pu•tres′cence,** *n.*

pu′trid (-trid) *adj.* rotten.

putsch (pŏŏch) *n.* sudden political revolt or uprising.

putt (put) *v.* **1.** strike (golf ball) gently. —*n.* **2.** such strike.

put′ter (put′ər) *v.* **1.** busy oneself ineffectively. —*n.* **2.** club for putting.

put′ty (put′ē) *n., v.*, **-tied, -tying.** —*n.* **1.** cement of whiting and oil. —*v.* **2.** secure with putty.

puz′zle (puz′əl) *n., v.*, **-zled, -zling.** —*n.* **1.** device or question offering difficulties. —*v.* **2.** perplex. —**puz′zle•ment,** *n.*

pv 1. *Finance.* par value. **2.** plan view.

PVA polyvinyl acetate.

PVC polyvinyl chloride. Also, **pvc**

Pvt., Private.

PW Palau (approved for postal use).

PWA 1. person with AIDS. **2.** Also, **P.W.A.** Public Works Administration.

P wave a longitudinal earthquake wave that is usually the first to be recorded by a seismograph. [*p(rimary) wave*]

pwb printed-wiring board.

P.W.D. Public Works Department. Also, **PWD**

pwm pulse-width modulation.

pwr power.

pwt pennyweight. Also, **pwt.**

PX, post exchange.

pxt. he or she painted it. [from Latin *pinxit*]

pyg′my (pig′mē) *n., pl.* **-mies.** dwarf.

py′lon (pī′lon) *n.* tall thin structure.

py•lo′rus (pī lôr′əs, pi-) *n., pl.* **-lori** (-lôr′ī). opening between stomach and intestine. —**py•lor′ic,** *adj.*

pymt. payment.

PYO pick your own.

py′or•rhe′a (pī′ə rē′ə) *n.* gum disease.

pyr′a•mid (pir′ə mid) *n.* **1.** solid with triangular sides meeting in point. —*v.* **2.** increase gradually. —**py•ram′i•dal** (pə ram′ə dl) *adj.*

pyre (pīr) *n.* heap of wood, esp. for burning corpse.

py′rite (pī′rīt) *n.* common yellow mineral of low value.

py′ro•ma′ni•a (pī′rə mā′nē ə) *n.* mania for setting fires. —**py′ro•ma′ni•ac′,** *n.*

py′ro•tech′nics (-tek′niks) *n.* fireworks. —**py′ro•tech′nic,** *adj.*

py′thon (pī′thon) *n.* large snake that kills by constriction.

pyx (piks) *n.* container in which Eucharist is kept.

P

Q

Q, q (kyōō) *n.* seventeenth letter of English alphabet.

QA quality assurance.

Q and A (kyōō′ ən ā′, ənd), *Informal.* an exchange of questions and answers. Also, **Q&A**

QB 1. *Football.* quarterback. **2.** *Chess.* queen's bishop.

Q.B. *British Law.* Queen's Bench.

q.b. *Football.* quarterback.

QBP *Chess.* queen's bishop's pawn.

Q.C. 1. quality control. **2.** Quartermaster Corps. **3.** Queen's Counsel. Also, **QC**

QCD *Physics.* quantum chromodynamics.

q.d. (in prescriptions) every day. [from Latin *quāque diē*]

qdisc quick disconnect.

qdrnt quadrant.

qdrtr quadrature.

q.e. which is. [from Latin *quod est*]

Q.E.D., which was to be shown or demonstrated.

Q.E.F. which was to be done. [from Latin *quod erat faciendum*]

Q.F. quick-firing.

Q fever *Pathology.* an acute, influenzalike disease caused by rickettsia. [abbreviation of *query*]

q.h. (in prescriptions) each hour; every hour. [from Latin *quāque hōrā*]

q.i.d. (in prescriptions) four times a day. [from Latin *quater in diē*]

QKt *Chess.* queen's knight.

QKtP *Chess.* queen's knight's pawn.

ql. quintal.

q.l. (in prescriptions) as much as is desired. [from Latin *quantum libet*]

QLI quality-of-life index. Also, **qli**

qlty. quality.

QM 1. Also, **Q.M.** Quartermaster. **2.** *Physics.* quantum mechanics.

q.m. (in prescriptions) every morning. [from Latin *quoque matutino*]

QMC *Military.* Quartermaster Corps. Also, **Q. M.C.**

QMG Quartermaster-General. Also, **Q.M.G., Q. M.Gen.**

QN *Chess.* queen's knight.

q.n. (in prescriptions) every night. [from Latin *quoque nocte*]

QNP *Chess.* queen's knight's pawn.

QP *Chess.* queen's pawn.

q.p. (in prescriptions) as much as you please. Also, **q. pl.** [from Latin *quantum placet*]

Qq. *Bookbinding.* quartos.

qq. questions.

qq. v. (in formal writing) which (words, things, etc.) see. [from Latin *quae vidē*]

QR *Chess.* queen's rook.

qr. 1. farthing. [from Latin *quadrāns*] **2.** quarter. **3.** *Bookbinding.* quire.

QRP *Chess.* queen's rook's pawn.

qry quarry.

q.s. 1. (in prescriptions) as much as is sufficient; enough. [from Latin *quantum sufficit*] **2.** quarter section.

QSO *Astronomy.* quasi-stellar object.

QSS *Astronomy.* quasi-stellar radio source.

qstn question.

qt., *pl.* **qt., qts.** quart.

qto. *Bookbinding.* quarto.

qtr. 1. quarter. **2.** quarterly.

qty., quantity.

qu. 1. quart. **2.** quarter. **3.** quarterly. **4.** queen. **5.** query. **6.** question.

quack (kwak) *n.* **1.** pretender to medical skill. **2.** sound that duck makes. —**quack′er•y,** *n.*

quad (kwod) *n.* **1.** quadrangle. **2.** quadruplet.

quadr quadruple.

quad′ran′gle (-rang′gəl) *n.* **1.** plane figure with four angles and four sides. **2.** Also, *Informal,* **quad.** enclosed four-sided area. —**quad•ran′gu•lar** (kwo drang′gyə lər) *adj.*

quad′rant (-rənt) *n.* **1.** arc of 90°. **2.** instrument for measuring altitudes.

quad′ra•phon′ic (-rə fon′ik) *adj.* of sound reproduced through four recording tracks.

quad•ren′ni•al (kwo dren′ē əl) *adj.* occurring every four years.

quad′ri•cen•ten′ni•al (kwod′rə sen ten′ē-əl) *n.* **1.** 400th anniversary. —*adj.* **2.** of 400 years.

quad′ri•lat′er•al (-lat′ər əl) *adj.* **1.** four-sided. —*n.* **2.** four-sided plane figure.

qua•drille′ (kwo dril′, kwə-) *n.* square dance for four couples.

quad′ri•ple′gi•a (kwod′rə plē′jē ə, -jə) *n.* paralysis of the entire body below the neck. —**quad′ri•ple′gic,** *n., adj.*

quad′ru•ped′ (-rōō ped′) *n.* four-footed animal.

quad•ru′ple (kwo drōō′pəl, -drup′əl) *adj., n., v.,* **-pled, -pling.** —*adj.* **1.** of four parts. **2.** four times as great. —*n.* **3.** number, etc., four times as great as another. —*v.* **4.** increase fourfold.

quad•ru′plet (-drup′lit, -drōō′plit) *n.* one of four children born at one birth.

quad•ru′pli•cate (-drōō′pli kit) *n.* group of four copies.

quaff (kwof, kwaf) *v.* drink heartily.

quag′mire′ (kwag′mīᵊr′, kwog′-) *n.* boggy ground.

qua′hog (kwô′hog, kō′-) *n.* edible American clam.

quail (kwāl) *n., pl.* **quails, quail,** *v.* —*n.* **1.**

game bird resembling domestic fowls. —*v.* **2.** lose courage; show fear.

quaint (kwānt) *adj.* pleasingly odd. —**quaint′ly,** *adv.* —**quaint′ness,** *n.*

quake (kwāk) *v.,* quaked, quaking, *n.* —*v.* **1.** tremble. —*n.* **2.** earthquake.

Quak′er (kwā′kər) *n.* member of Society of Friends.

qual. 1. qualification. qualify. **2.** qualitative; quality.

qual′i•fy′ (kwol′ə fī′) *v.,* -fied, -fying. **1.** make proper or fit. **2.** modify. **3.** mitigate. **4.** show oneself fit. —**qual′i•fi•ca′tion,** *n.*

qual′i•ty, (-i tē) *n., pl.* -ties. **1.** characteristic. **2.** relative merit. **3.** excellence. —**qual′i•ta′- tive** (-tā′tiv) *adj.*

quality time, time devoted exclusively to nurturing cherished person or activity.

qualm (kwäm), *n.* **1.** misgiving; scruple. **2.** feeling of illness.

quan′da•ry (kwon′də rē, -drē) *n., pl.* -ries. dilemma.

quant. quantitative.

quan′ti•fy′ (kwon′tə fī′) *v.,* -fied, -fying. indicate quantity of.

quan′ti•ty (-ti tē) *n., pl.* -ties. **1.** amount; measure. **2.** *Math.* something having magnitude. —**quan′ti•ta′tive,** *adj.*

quan′tum (-təm) *n., pl.* -ta, *adj.* —*n.* **1.** quantity or amount. **2.** *Physics.* very small, indivisible quantity of energy. —*adj.* **3.** sudden and significant.

quar. 1. quarter. **2.** quarterly.

quar′an•tine′ (kwôr′ən tēn′) *n., v.,* -tined, -tining. —*n.* **1.** strict isolation to prevent spread of disease. —*v.* **2.** put in quarantine.

quark (kwôrk, kwärk) *n.* subatomic particle having fractional electric charge and thought to form basis of all matters.

quar′rel (kwôr′əl) *n., v.,* -reled, -reling. —*n.* **1.** angry dispute. —*v.* **2.** disagree angrily. —**quar′rel•some,** *adj.*

quar′ry (kwôr′ē) *n., pl.* -ries, *v.,* -ried, -rying. —*n.* **1.** pit from which stone is taken. **2.** object of pursuit. —*v.* **3.** get from quarry.

quart (kwôrt) *n.* measure of capacity: in liquid measure, ¼ gallon; in dry measure, ⅛ peck.

quar′ter, *n.* **1.** one of four equal parts. **2.** coin worth 25 cents. **3.** (*pl.*) place of residence. **4.** mercy. —*v.* **5.** divide into quarters. **6.** lodge. —*adj.* **7.** being a quarter.

quar′ter•back′, *n.* position in football.

quar′ter•deck′, *n.* rear part of ship's weather deck.

quarter horse, horse capable of great sprints of speed.

quar′ter•ly, *adj., n., pl.* -lies, *adv.* —*adj.* **1.** occurring, etc., each quarter year. —*n.* **2.** quarterly publication. —*adv.* **3.** once each quarter year.

quar′ter•mas′ter, *n.* **1.** military officer in charge of supplies, etc. **2.** naval officer in charge of signals, etc.

quar•tet′ (kwôr tet′) *n.* group of four. Also, **quar•tette′.**

quar′to (kwôr′tō) *n., pl.* -tos. book page of sheets folded twice.

quartz (kwôrts) *n.* crystalline mineral.

qua′sar (kwā′zär, -zər) *n.* astronomical source of powerful radio energy.

quash (kwosh) *v.* subdue; suppress.

qua′si (kwā′zī, -sī, kwä′sē, -zē) *adj.* resembling; to be regarded as if.

quasi-, prefix meaning somewhat.

quat. (in prescriptions) four. [from Latin *quattuor*]

Quat′er•nar′y (kwot′ər ner′ē, kwə tûr′nə- rē) *adj.* pertaining to present geologic period forming latter part of Cenozoic Era.

quat′rain (kwo′trān) *n.* four-line stanza.

qua′ver (kwā′vər) *v.* **1.** quiver. **2.** speak tremulously. —*n.* **3.** quavering tone.

quay (kē) *n.* landing beside water.

Que. Quebec.

quea′sy (kwē′zē) *adj.,* -sier, -siest. **1.** nauseated. **2.** uneasy.

queen (kwēn) *n.* **1.** wife of king. **2.** female sovereign. **3.** fertile female of bees, ants, etc. —*v.* **4.** reign as queen.

queer (kwēr) *adj.* **1.** strange; odd. —*n.* **2.** *Offensive.* homosexual. —*v.* **3.** *Slang.* ruin; impair. —**queer′ly,** *adv.* —**queer′ness,** *n.*

quell (kwel) *v.* suppress.

quench (kwench) *v.* slake or extinguish.

quer′u•lous (kwer′ə ləs, kwer′yə-) *adj.* peevish.

que′ry (kwēr′ē) *n., pl.* -ries, *v.,* -ried, -rying. question.

ques. question.

quest (kwest) *n., v.* search.

ques′tion (kwes′chən) *n.* **1.** sentence put in a form to elicit information. **2.** problem for discussion or dispute. —*v.* **3.** ask a question. **4.** doubt. —**ques′tion•a•ble,** *adj.* —**ques′- tion•er,** *n.*

ques′tion•naire′ (-chə nâr′) *n.* list of questions.

queue (kyōō) *n., v.,* queued, queuing. —*n.* **1.** line of persons. **2.** braid of hair hanging down the back. —*v.* **3.** form in a line.

quib′ble (kwib′əl) *v.,* -bled, -bling, *n.* —*v.* **1.** speak ambiguously in evasion. **2.** make petty objections. —*n.* **3.** act of quibbling. —**quib′- bler,** *n.*

quiche (kēsh) *n.* pielike dish of cheese, onion, etc.

quick (kwik) *adj.* **1.** prompt; done promptly. **2.** swift. **3.** alert. —*n.* **4.** living persons. **5.** sensitive flesh. —*adv.* **6.** quickly. —**quick′ly,** *adv.* —**quick′ness,** *n.*

quick bread, bread made with leavening that permits immediate baking.

quick′en, *v.* **1.** hasten. **2.** rouse. **3.** become alive.

quick′ie, *n.* something done or enjoyed in only a short time.

Q

quick′lime′, *n.* untreated lime.

quick′sand′, *n.* soft sand yielding easily to weight.

quick′sil′ver, *n.* mercury.

quid (kwid) *n.* **1.** portion for chewing. **2.** *Brit. Informal.* one pound sterling.

quid pro quo (kwid′ prō kwō′) *pl.* **quid pro quos, quids pro quo.** something given or taken for something else.

qui•es′cent (kwē es′ənt, kwī-) *adj.* inactive. —**qui•es′cence,** *n.*

qui′et (kwī′it) *adj.* **1.** being at rest. **2.** peaceful. **3.** silent. **4.** restrained. —*v.* **5.** make or become quiet. **6.** tranquillity. —**qui′et•ly,** *adv.* —**qui′et•ness, qui′e•tude′,** *n.*

qui•e′tus (kwī ē′təs) *n.* **1.** final settlement. **2.** release from life.

quill (kwil) *n.* large feather.

quilt (kwilt) *n.* padded and lined bed covering. —**quilt′ed,** *adj.* —**quilt′er,** *n.* —**quilt′ing,** *n.*

quin quintuple.

quince (kwins) *n.* yellowish acid fruit.

qui′nine (kwī′nīn) *n.* bitter substance used esp. in treating malaria.

quinq. (in prescriptions) five. [from Latin *quīnque*]

quint (kwint) *n.* quintuplet.

quin•tes′sence (kwin tes′əns) *n.* essential substance. —**quin′tes•sen′tial** (-tə sen′shəl) *adj.*

quin•tet′ (kwin tet′) *n.* group of five. Also, **quin•tette′.**

quin•tu′plet (-tup′lit, -tōō′plit, -tyōō′-) *n.* one of five children born at one birth.

quip (kwip) *n.,* *v.,* **quipped, quipping.** —*n.* **1.** witty or sarcastic remark. —*v.* **2.** make quip.

quire (kwī°r) *n.* set of 24 uniform sheets of paper.

quirk (kwûrk) *n.* peculiarity. —**quirk′y,** *adj.,* -**i•er,** -**i•est.** —**quirk′i•ness,** *n.*

quirt (kwûrt) *n.* short riding whip.

quis′ling (kwiz′ling) *n.* traitor.

quit (kwit) *v.,* **quitted, quitting. 1.** stop. **2.** leave. **3.** relinquish. —**quit′ter,** *n.*

quit′claim′, *n.* **1.** transfer of one's interest. —*v.* **2.** give up claim to.

quite (kwīt) *adv.* **1.** completely. **2.** really.

quits (kwits) *adj.* with no further payment or revenge due.

quit′tance (kwit′ns) *n.* **1.** requital. **2.** discharge from debt.

quiv′er (kwiv′ər) *v.* **1.** tremble. —*n.* **2.** trembling. **3.** case for arrows.

quix•ot′ic (kwik sot′ik) *adj.* extravagantly idealistic; impractical.

quiz (kwiz) *v.,* **quizzed, quizzing,** *n.,* *pl.* **quizzes.** —*v.* **1.** question. —*n.* **2.** informal questioning.

quiz′zi•cal, *adj.* **1.** comical. **2.** puzzled. —**quiz′zi•cal•ly,** *adv.*

quoin (koin, kwoin) *n.* **1.** external solid angle. **2.** cornerstone. **3.** wedge for securing type.

quoit (kwoit, koit) *n.* flat ring thrown to encircle peg in game of **quoits.**

quon′dam (kwon′dəm, -dam) *adj.* former.

Quon′set hut (kwon′sit) *n.* *Trademark.* semicylindrical metal shelter with end walls.

quor. (in prescriptions) of which. [from Latin *quōrum*]

quo′rum (kwôr′əm) *n.* number of members needed to transact business legally.

quot. 1. quotation. **2.** quotient. Also, **quot**

quo′ta (kwō′tə) *n.* proportional share due.

quote (kwōt) *v.,* **quoted, quoting,** *n.* —*v.* **1.** repeat verbatim. **2.** cite. **3.** state (price of). —*n.* **4.** *Informal,* quotation. —**quo•ta′tion,** *n.* —**quot′a•ble,** *adj.*

quoth (kwōth) *v.* *Archaic.* said.

quotid. (in prescriptions) daily. [from Latin *quotīdiē*]

quo•tid′i•an (kwō tid′ē ən) *adj.* **1.** daily; everyday. **2.** ordinary.

quo′tient (kwō′shənt) *n.* *Math.* number of times one quantity is contained in another.

q.v. 1. (in prescriptions) as much as you wish. [from Latin *quantum vīs*] **2.** *plural* **qq.v.** (in formal writing) which see. [from Latin *quod vidē*]

QWERTY (kwûr′tē, kwer′-), of or pertaining to a keyboard having the keys in traditional typewriter arrangement, with the letters *q, w, e, r, t,* and *y* being the first six of the top row of alphabetic characters, starting from the left side.

R

R, r (är) *n.* eighteenth letter of English alphabet.

R, motion-picture rating: those less than 17 years old must be accompanied by adult.

RA regular army.

Ra *Symbol, Chemistry.* radium.

R.A. 1. rear admiral. 2. regular army. 3. *Astronomy.* right ascension. 4. royal academician. 5. Royal Academy.

R.A.A.F. Royal Australian Air Force.

rab rabbet.

rab′bi (rab′ī) *n.* Jewish religious leader. —rab•bin′ic (rə bin′ik), rab•bin′i•cal, *adj.*

rab′bin•ate (rab′ə nit, -nāt′) *n.* 1. office of a rabbi. 2. rabbis collectively.

rab′bit (rab′it) *n.* small, long-eared mammal.

rab′ble (rab′əl) *n.* mob.

rab′ble-rous′er (-rou′zər) *n.* demagogue.

rab′id (rab′id) *adj.* 1. irrationally intense. 2. having rabies. —rab′id•ly, *adv.*

ra′bies (rā′bēz) *n.* fatal disease transmitted by bite of infected animal.

rac•coon′ (ra kōōn′) *n.* small nocturnal carnivorous mammal.

race (rās) *n., v.,* **raced, racing.** —*n.* 1. contest of speed. 2. onward course or flow. 3. group of persons of common origin. 4. any class or kind. —*v.* 5. engage in race. 6. move swiftly. —rac′er, *n.* —ra′cial (rā′shəl) *adj.*

ra•ceme′ (rā sēm′, rə-) *n.* cluster of flowers along stem.

rac′ism (rā′siz əm) *n.* hatred of or prejudice against another race.

rack (rak) *n.* 1. structure for storage. 2. toothed bar engaging with teeth of pinion. 3. torture device. 4. destruction. —*v.* 5. torture. 6. strain.

rack′et (rak′it) *n.* 1. noise. 2. illegal or dishonest business. 3. Also, **rac′quet.** framed network used as bat in tennis, etc.

rack′e•teer′, *n.* criminal engaged in racket.

rac′on•teur′ (rak′ôn tûr′, -tōōr′, -ən-) *n.* skilled storyteller.

ra•coon′ (ra kōōn′) *n.* raccoon.

rac′quet•ball (rak′it-) *n.* game similar to handball, played with rackets on four-walled court.

rac′y (rā′sē) *adj.,* **-ier, -iest.** 1. lively. 2. risqué. —rac′i•ly, *adv.* —rac′i•ness, *n.*

rad 1. *Math.* radian; radians. 2. radiation absorbed dose. 3. radio. 4. radius.

rad. 1. *Math.* radical. 2. Also, **rd** *Chemistry.* radium. 3. radius. 4. radix.

ra′dar (rā′där) *n.* electronic device capable of locating unseen objects by radio wave.

ra′di•al (-dē əl) *adj.* of rays or radii.

ra′di•ant (-ənt) *adj.* 1. emitting rays of light. 2. bright; exultant. 3. emitted in rays, as heat. —ra′di•ance, *n.* —ra′di•ant•ly, *adv.*

ra′di•ate′ (-āt′) *v.,* **-ated, -ating.** 1. spread like rays from center. 2. emit or issue in rays. —ra′di•a′tion, *n.*

ra′di•a′tor, *n.* heating device.

rad′i•cal (rad′i kəl) *adj.* 1. fundamental. 2. favoring drastic reforms. —*n.* 3. person with radical ideas. 4. atom or group of atoms behaving as unit in chemical reaction. —rad′i•cal•ism, *n.* —rad′i•cal•ly, *adv.*

RADINT radar intelligence.

ra′di•o′ (rā′dē ō′) *n., pl.* **-dios.** 1. way of transmitting sound by electromagnetic waves, without wires. 2. apparatus for sending or receiving such waves.

ra′di•o•ac′tive, *adj.* emitting radiation from the atomic nucleus, as radium, for example, does. —ra′di•o•ac•tiv′i•ty, *n.*

ra′di•o•car′bon, *n.* radioactive isotope of carbon, used in dating organic materials.

ra′di•ol′o•gy (-ol′ə jē) *n.* use of radiation, as x-rays, for medical diagnosis and treatment. —ra′di•ol′o•gist, *n.*

rad′ish (rad′ish) *n.* crisp root of garden plant, eaten raw.

ra′di•um (rā′dē əm) *n.* radioactive metallic element.

ra′di•us (-əs) *n., pl.* **-dii** (-dē ī), **-diuses.** 1. straight line from center of a circle to circumference. 2. one of the bones of the forearm.

RAdm rear admiral. Also, **RADM**

radn radiation.

ra′don (rā′don) *n.* inert gaseous element produced by decay of radium.

rad opr radio operator.

RAF, Royal Air Force.

raf′fi•a (raf′ē ə) *n.* fiber made from leafstalks of palm tree.

raff′ish (raf′ish) *adj.* 1. jaunty; rakish. 2. gaudily vulgar or cheap; tawdry.

raf′fle (raf′əl) *n., v.,* **-fled, -fling.** —*n.* 1. lottery in which chances are sold. —*v.* 2. dispose of by raffle.

raft (raft) *n.* floating platform of logs.

raft′er (raf′tər) *n.* framing member of roof.

rag (rag) *n.* worthless bit of cloth, esp. one torn. —rag′ged (rag′id) *adj.*

ra′ga (rä′gə) *n., pl.* **-gas.** traditional melodic formula of Hindu music.

rag′a•muf′fin (rag′ə muf′in) *n.* ragged child.

rage (rāj) *n., v.,* **raged, raging.** —*n.* 1. violent anger. 2. object of popular enthusiasm. —*v.* 3. be violently angry. 4. prevail violently.

rag′lan (rag′lən) *n.* loose garment with sleeves continuing to collar.

raglan sleeve, set-in sleeve with slanting seam from neckline to armhole.

ra•gout′ (ra gōō′) *n.* stew.

rag′time′, *n.* style of jazz.

rag′weed′, *n.* plant whose pollen causes hay fever.

raid (rād) *n.* **1.** sudden assault or attack. —*v.* **2.** attack suddenly. —**raid′er**, *n.*

rail (rāl) *n.* **1.** horizontal bar used as barrier, support, etc. **2.** one of pair of railroad tracks. **3.** railroad as means of transport. **4.** wading bird. —*v.* **5.** complain bitterly.

rail′ing, *n.* barrier of rails and posts.

rail′ler•y (rā′lə rē) *n.* banter.

rail′road′, *n.* **1.** road with fixed rails on which trains run. —*v.* **2.** transport by means of a railroad. **3.** coerce into hasty action or decision.

rail′way′, *n. Chiefly Brit.* railroad.

rai′ment (rā′mənt) *n.* clothing.

rain (rān) *n.* **1.** water falling from sky in drops. **2.** rainfall. —*v.* **3.** fall or send down as rain. —**rain′y**, *adj.*

rain′bow′ (-bō′) *n.* arc of colors sometimes seen in sky opposite sun during rain. —**rain′-bow•like′**, *adj.*

rain check, 1. postponement of invitation. **2.** ticket for future admission to event postponed by rain.

rain′coat′, *n.* waterproof coat.

rain′fall′, *n.* amount of rain.

rain forest, tropical forest in area of high annual rainfall.

rain′mak′er, *n.* one who induces rain by artificial means.

raise (rāz) *v.*, **raised, raising**, *n.* —*v.* **1.** lift up. **2.** set upright. **3.** cause to appear. **4.** grow. **5.** collect. **6.** rear. **7.** cause (dough) to expand. **8.** end (siege). —*n.* **9.** increase, esp. in pay.

rai′sin (rā′zin) *n.* dried sweet grape.

rai′son d′ê′tre (rā′zōn de′trə) *n., pl.* **rai′sons d′ê′tre.** reason for existence.

ra′jah (rä′jə) *n.* (formerly) Indian king or prince.

rake (rāk) *n., v.*, **raked, raking.** —*n.* **1.** long-handled tool with teeth for gathering or smoothing ground. **2.** dissolute person. **3.** slope. —*v.* **4.** gather or smooth with rake. **5.** fire guns the length of (target).

rake′-off′, *n.* amount received, esp. illicitly.

rak′ish (rā′kish) *adj.* **1.** jaunty. **2.** dissolute.

rall. *Music.* rallentando.

ral′ly (ral′ē) *v.*, **-lied, -lying**, *n., pl.* **-lies.** —*v.* **1.** bring into order again. **2.** call or come together. **3.** revive. **4.** come to aid. —*n.* **5.** renewed order. **6.** renewal of strength. **7.** mass meeting.

ram (ram) *n., v.*, **rammed, ramming.** —*n.* **1.** male sheep. **2.** device for battering, forcing, etc. —*v.* **3.** strike forcibly.

RAM (ram) random-access memory: computer memory available for creating, loading, and running programs and temporarily storing data.

ram′ble, *v.*, **-bled, -bling.** —*v.* **1.** stroll idly. **2.** talk vaguely. —*n.* **3.** leisurely stroll. —**ram′bler**, *n.*

ram•bunc′tious (-bungk′shəs) *adj.* difficult to control or handle; wildly boisterous.

ram′i•fy′ (-ə fī′) *v.*, **-fied, -fying.** divide into branches. —**ram′i•fi•ca′tion**, *n.*

ramp (ramp) *n.* sloping surface between two levels.

ram′page, *n., v.*, **-paged, -paging.** —*n.* (ram′pāj) **1.** violent behavior. —*v.* (ram-pāj′) **2.** move furiously about.

ramp′ant (ram′pənt) *adj.* **1.** vigorous; unrestrained. **2.** standing on hind legs.

ram′part (-pärt, -pərt) *n.* mound of earth raised for defense.

ram′rod′, *n.* rod for cleaning or loading gun.

ram′shack′le, *adj.* rickety.

ranch (ranch) *n.* large farm, esp. for raising stock. —**ranch′er**, *n.*

ran′cid (ran′sid) *adj.* stale. —**ran•cid′i•ty**, *n.*

ran′cor (rang′kər) *n.* lasting resentment. —**ran′cor•ous**, *adj.*

rand (rand) *n., pl.* **rand.** monetary unit of South Africa.

R&B rhythm-and-blues. Also, **r&b, R and B**

R&D research and development. Also, **R and D**

R&E research and engineering.

R. & I. 1. king and emperor. [from Latin *Rēx et Imperātor*] **2.** queen and empress. [from Latin *Rēgīna et Imperātrīx*]

ran′dom (ran′dəm) *adj.* without aim or consistency. —**ran′dom•ly**, *adv.*

R and R 1. rest and recreation. **2.** rest and recuperation. **3.** rest and rehabilitation. **4.** rock-′n′-roll. Also, **R&R**

rand′y (ran′dē) *adj.*, **-ier, -iest.** sexually aroused; lustful.

range (rānj) *n., v.*, **ranged, ranging.** —*n.* **1.** limits; extent. **2.** place for target shooting. **3.** distance between gun and target. **4.** row. **5.** mountain chain. **6.** grazing area. **7.** cooking stove. —*v.* **8.** arrange. **9.** pass over (area). **10.** vary.

rang′er (rān′jər) *n.* **1.** warden of forest tract. **2.** civil officer who patrols large area.

rang′y (rān′jē) *adj.*, **-ier, -iest.** slender and long-limbed.

rank (rangk) *n.* **1.** class, group, or standing. **2.** high position. **3.** row. **4.** (*pl.*) enlisted personnel. —*v.* **5.** arrange. **6.** put or be in particular rank. **7.** be senior in rank. —*adj.* **8.** growing excessively. **9.** offensively strong in smell. **10.** utter. **11.** grossly vulgar. —**rank′-ly**, *adv.* —**rank′ness**, *n.*

rank and file, 1. members apart from leaders. **2.** enlisted soldiers.

rank′ing, *adj.* **1.** senior. **2.** renowned.

ran′kle (rang′kəl) *v.*, **-kled, -kling.** irk.

ran′sack′ (ran′sak) *v.* search thoroughly.

ran′som (ran′səm) *n.* **1.** sum demanded for prisoner. —*v.* **2.** pay ransom for.

rant (rant) *v.* **1.** speak wildly. —*n.* **2.** violent speech. —**rant′er**, *n.*

rap (rap) v., **rapped, rapping,** n. —v. **1.** strike quickly and sharply. —n. **2.** sharp blow. **3.** popular music marked by rhythmical intoning of rhymed verses over repetitive beat. —**rap′per,** n.

ra·pa′cious (rə pā′shəs) adj. plundering; greedy.

rape (rāp) n., v., **raped, raping.** —n. **1.** forcing of sexual intercourse on someone. **2.** abduction or seizure. —v. **3.** commit rape on. **4.** abduct or seize. —**rap′ist,** n.

rap′id (rap′id) adj. **1.** swift. —n. **2.** (pl.) swift-moving part of river. —**ra·pid′i·ty, rap′id·ness,** n. —**rap′id·ly,** adv.

ra′pi·er (rā′pē ər) n. slender sword.

rap′ine (rap′in) n. plunder.

rap·port′ (ra pôr′) n. sympathetic relationship.

rap′proche·ment′ (rap′rōsh män′) n. establishment of harmonious relations.

rap·scal′lion (rap skal′yən) n. rascal.

rap sheet, Slang. record of person's arrests and convictions.

rapt (rapt) adj. engrossed. —**rapt′ly,** adv. —**rapt′ness,** n.

rap′ture (rap′chər) n. ecstatic joy. —**rap′tur·ous,** adj.

ra′ra a′vis (râr′ə ā′vis) n., pl. **ra′rae a′ves** (râr′ē ē′vēz). rare person or thing.

rare (râr) adj., **rarer, rarest. 1.** unusual. **2.** thin, as air. **3.** (of meat) not thoroughly cooked. —**rar′i·ty,** n. —**rare′ly,** adv. —**rare′ness,** n.

rare′bit (râr′bit) n. dish of melted cheese.

rar′e·fy′ (râr′ə fī′) v., **-fied, -fying.** make or become thin, as air.

rar′ing, adj. very eager or anxious.

ras′cal (ras′kəl) n. dishonest person. —**ras·cal′i·ty,** n.

raser (rā′zər), radio-frequency amplification by stimulated emission of radiation.

rash (rash) adj. **1.** thoughtlessly hasty. —n. **2.** skin eruption. —**rash′ly,** adv. —**rash′ness,** n.

rash′er, n. thin slice of bacon or ham.

rasp (rasp) v. **1.** scrape, as with file. **2.** irritate. **3.** speak gratingly. —n. **4.** coarse file. **5.** rasping sound. —**rasp′y,** adj.

rasp′ber′ry (raz′ber′ē, -bə rē) n., pl. **-ries.** small juicy red or black fruit.

rat (rat) n. rodent larger than a mouse.

ratch′et (rach′it) n. wheel or bar having teeth that catch pawl to control motion.

rate (rāt) n., v., **rated, rating.** —n. **1.** charge in proportion to something that varies. **2.** degree of speed, etc. —v. **3.** estimate or fix rate. **4.** consider; judge.

rath′er (rath′ər) adv. **1.** somewhat. **2.** in preference. **3.** on the contrary.

raths′kel·ler (rät′skel′ər, rat′-) n. restaurant or bar below street level.

rat′i·fy′ (rat′ə fī′) v., **-fied, -fying.** confirm formally. —**rat′i·fi·ca′tion,** n.

ra′tio (rā′shō, -shē ō′) n., pl. **-tios.** relative number or extent; proportion.

ra′ti·oc′i·na′tion (rash′ē os′ə nā′shən) n. reasoning.

ra′tion (rash′ən, rā′shən) n. **1.** fixed allowance. —v. **2.** apportion. **3.** put on ration.

ra′tion·al (rash′ə nl) adj. **1.** sensible. **2.** sane. —**ra′tion·al·ly,** adv. —**ra′tion·al′i·ty,** n.

ra′tion·ale′ (-nal′) n. reasonable basis for action.

ra′tion·al·ism, n. advocacy of precise reasoning as source of truth. —**ra′tion·al·ist,** n. —**ra′tion·al·is′tic,** adj.

ra′tion·al·ize′, v., **-ized, -izing. 1.** find reason for one's behavior or attitude. **2.** make rational. —**ra′tion·al·i·za′tion,** n.

RATO (rā′tō), Aeronautics. rocket-assisted takeoff.

rat race, exhausting, competitive routine activity.

rat·tan′ (ra tan′, rə-) n. hollow stem of climbing palm.

rat′tle (rat′l) v., **-tled, -tling,** n. —v. **1.** make series of short sharp sounds. **2.** chatter. **3.** Informal, disconcert. —n. **4.** sound of rattling. **5.** child's toy that rattles.

rat′tle·snake′, n. venomous American snake.

rat′ty, adj., **-tier, -tiest. 1.** of rats. **2.** shabby.

rau′cous (rô′kəs) adj. **1.** hoarse; harsh. **2.** rowdy; disorderly. —**rau′cous·ly,** adv. —**rau′cous·ness,** n.

raun′chy (rôn′chē, rän′-) adj. **-chier, -chiest. 1.** vulgar; smutty. **2.** lecherous. **3.** dirty; slovenly.

rav′age (rav′ij) n., v., **-aged, -aging.** ruin. —**rav′ag·er,** n.

rave (rāv) v., **raved, raving.** talk wildly.

rav′el (rav′əl) v. **1.** disengage threads. **2.** tangle. **3.** make clear. —n. **4.** tangle. **5.** disengaged thread.

ra′ven (rā′vən) n. large shiny black bird.

rav′en·ing (rav′ə ning) adj. greedy for prey.

rav′en·ous, adj. very hungry; greedy. —**rav′en·ous·ly,** adv.

ra·vine′ (rə vēn′) n. deep, narrow valley.

ra′vi·o′li (rav′ē ō′lē) n. small pockets of pasta filled esp. with cheese or meat.

rav′ish (rav′ish) v. **1.** fill with joy. **2.** rape. —**rav′ish·er,** n. —**rav′ish·ment,** n.

rav′ish·ing, adj. extremely beautiful.

raw (rô) adj. **1.** in the natural state. **2.** uncooked. **3.** open. **4.** untrained. —n. **5.** raw condition or substance. —**raw′ness,** n.

raw′boned′, adj. lean and bony.

raw′hide′, n. untanned hide, as of cattle.

ray (rā) n. **1.** narrow beam of light. **2.** trace. **3.** line outward from center. **4.** flat-bodied deep-sea fish.

ray′on (rā′on) n. silklike synthetic fabric.

raze (rāz) v., **razed, razing.** demolish.

R

ra′zor (rā′zər) *n.* sharp-edged instrument for shaving.

razz (raz) *v.* make fun of; mock.

RB 1. *Sports.* right back. **2.** *Football.* right fullback. **3.** *Football.* running back.

Rb *Symbol, Chemistry.* rubidium.

RBC red blood cell.

R.B.I. *Baseball.* run batted in; runs batted in. Also, **RBI, rbi, r.b.i.**

rbr rubber.

R.C. Roman Catholic.

R.C.A.F. Royal Canadian Air Force. Also, **RCAF**

RCB 1. Retail Credit Bureau. **2.** *Football.* right cornerback.

RCC Rape Crisis Center.

R.C.Ch. Roman Catholic Church.

rcd. received.

rcdr recorder.

rcht ratchet.

rcl recall.

rclm reclaim.

R.C.M.P. Royal Canadian Mounted Police. Also, **RCMP**

rcn recreation.

R.C.N. Royal Canadian Navy. Also, **RCN**

rcndt recondition.

R.C.P. Royal College of Physicians.

rcpt. 1. receipt. **2.** receptacle.

rcptn reception.

R.C.S. Royal College of Surgeons.

Rct 1. receipt. **2.** *Military.* recruit. Also, **rct**

RCTL resistor-capacitor-transistor logic.

rcv receive.

rcvd received.

rcvg receiving.

rcvr receiver.

rd., road.

RDA 1. (not in technical use) recommended daily allowance. Compare **U.S. RDA. 2.** recommended dietary allowance. Also, **R.D.A.**

RdAc *Symbol, Chemistry.* radioactinium.

RD&D research, development, and demonstration.

RD&E research, development, and engineering.

rdc reduce.

rdcr reducer.

RDD *Marketing.* random digit dialing.

RDF 1. Also, **rdf** radio direction finder. **2.** rapid deployment force.

rdg 1. reading. **2.** rounding.

rdh round head.

rdl radial.

rdm recording demand meter.

rdout readout.

rdr 1. radar. **2.** reader.

RDS *Pathology.* respiratory distress syndrome.

rdsd roadside.

RDT&E research, development, testing, and engineering.

rdtr radiator.

RDX a white, crystalline explosive, $C_3H_6N_6O_6$. [*R(esearch) D(epartment) (E)x(plosive)*, referring to such a department in Woolwich, England]

re, *n.* (rā) **1.** *Music.* second tone of scale. —*prep.* (rē) **2.** with reference to.

re-, prefix indicating; **1.** repetition, as *reprint, rearm.* **2.** withdrawal.

REA Rural Electrification Administration. Also, **R.E.A.**

reach (rēch) *v.* **1.** come to. **2.** be able to touch. **3.** extend. —*n.* **4.** act of reaching. **5.** extent.

re•act′ (rē akt′) *v.* **1.** act upon each other. **2.** respond.

re•ac′tant (-ak′tənt) *n.* substance that undergoes change in chemical reaction.

re•ac′tion, *n.* **1.** extreme political conservatism. **2.** responsive action. **3.** chemical change. —**re•ac′tion•ar′y,** *n., adj.*

re•ac′tor, *n.* **1.** one that reacts. **2.** apparatus for producing useful nuclear energy.

read (rēd) *v.,* **read** (red), **reading. 1.** observe and understand (printed matter, etc.). **2.** register. **3.** utter aloud (something written or printed). **4.** obtain and store, as in computer memory. —**read′a•ble,** *adj.* —**read′er,** *n.* —**read′er•ship′,** *n.*

read′ing (rē′ding) *n.* **1.** amount read at one time. **2.** interpretation of written or musical work.

read′-on′ly (rēd) *adj.* noting computer files or memory that can be read but not changed.

read′y (red′ē) *adj.,* **readier, readiest,** *v.,* **readied, readying,** *n.* —*adj.* **1.** fully prepared. **2.** willing. **3.** apt. —*v.* **4.** make ready. —*n.* **5.** state of being ready. —**read′i•ly,** *adv.* —**read′i•ness,** *n.*

read′y-made′, *adj.* ready for use when bought.

re•a′gent (rē ā′jənt) *n.* chemical used in analysis and synthesis.

re′al (rē′əl, rēl) *adj.* **1.** actual. **2.** genuine. **3.** denoting immovable property. —**re•al′i•ty** (-al′i tē), **re′al•ness,** *n.* —**re′al•ly,** *adv.*

real estate, land with buildings, etc., on it. Also, **re′al•ty.**

re′al•ism, *n.* **1.** tendency to see things as they really are. **2.** representation of things as they really are. —**re′al•ist,** *n.* —**re′al•is′tic,** *adj.* —**re′al•is′ti•cal•ly,** *adv.*

re′al•ize′, *v.,* **-ized, -izing. 1.** understand clearly. **2.** make real. **3.** get as profit. —**re′al•i•za′tion,** *n.*

realm (relm) *n.* **1.** kingdom. **2.** special field.

ream (rēm) *n.* **1.** twenty quires of paper. —*v.* **2.** enlarge (hole) with a **ream′er.**

reap (rēp) *v.* harvest. —**reap′er,** *n.*

rear (rēr) *n.* **1.** back part. —*adj.* **2.** of or at rear. —*v.* **3.** care for to maturity. **4.** raise; erect. **5.** rise on hind legs.

Rear Adm. Rear Admiral.

rear admiral, naval officer above captain.

re·arm' (rē ärm') v. arm again. —**re·arm'a·ment,** n.

rear'most', adj. farthest back.

rear'ward (-wərd) adv. **1.** Also, **rear'wards.** toward the rear. —adj. **2.** located in the rear.

reasm reassemble.

rea'son (rē'zən) n. **1.** cause for belief, act, etc. **2.** sound judgment. **3.** sanity. —v. **4.** think or argue logically. **5.** infer. —**rea'son·ing,** n. —**rea'son·er,** n.

rea'son·a·ble (rē'zə nə bəl, rēz'nə-) adj. showing sound judgment. —**rea'son·a·bly,** adv.

re·as·sure' (rē'ə shŏŏr', -shûr') v., **-sured, -suring.** restore confidence of. —**re·as·sur'ance,** n.

reassy reassembly.

Réaum. Réaumur (temperature).

reb. Basketball. rebounds.

re'bate, v., **-bated, -bating,** n. —v. (rē'bāt, also ri bāt') **1.** return (part of amount paid). —n. (rē'bāt) **2.** amount rebated.

re·bel', v., **-belled, -belling,** n. —v. (ri bel') **1.** rise in arms against one's government. **2.** resist any authority. —n. (reb'əl) **3.** one who rebels. —**re·bel'lion,** n. —**re·bel'lious,** adj. —**re·bel'lious·ly,** adv. —**re·bel'lious·ness,** n.

re·bound', v. (ri bound') **1.** bound back after impact. —n. (rē'bound) **2.** act of rebounding.

re·buff' (ri buf') n. **1.** blunt check or refusal. —v. **2.** check; repel.

re·buke' (ri byōōk') v., **-buked, -buking,** n. reprimand.

re'bus (rē'bəs) n. puzzle in which pictures and symbols combine to represent a word.

re·but' (ri but') v., **-butted, -butting.** refute. —**re·but'tal,** n.

rec. 1. receipt. **2.** (in prescriptions) fresh. [from Latin recēns] **3.** recipe. **4.** record. **5.** recorder. **6.** recording. **7.** recreation.

recalc recalculate.

re·cal'ci·trant (ri kal'si trənt) adj. resisting control. —**re·cal'ci·trance,** n.

re·call', v. (ri kôl') **1.** remember. **2.** call back. **3.** withdraw. —n. (rē'kôl) **4.** act of recalling.

re·cant' (ri kant') v. retract.

re'cap' (rē'kap') n., v., **-capped, -capping.** —n. **1.** recapitulation. **2.** tire reconditioned by adding strip of new rubber. —v. **3.** recapitulate. **4.** recondition a tire.

re'ca·pit'u·late (rē'kə pich'ə lāt') v., **-lated, -lating.** review; sum up. —**re'ca·pit'u·la'tion,** n.

re·cap'ture, v., **-tured, -turing,** n. —v. **1.** capture again. **2.** experience again. —n. **3.** recovery by capture.

recd. or **rec'd.,** received.

re·cede' (ri sēd') v., **-ceded, -ceding.** move or appear to move back.

re·ceipt' (ri sēt') n. **1.** written acknowledg-

ment of receiving. **2.** (pl.) amount received. **3.** act of receiving.

re·ceiv'a·ble (ri sē'və bəl) adj. still to be paid.

re·ceive', v., **-ceived, -ceiving. 1.** take (something offered or delivered). **2.** experience. **3.** welcome (guests). **4.** accept.

re·ceiv'er, n. **1.** one that receives. **2.** device that receives electricl signals and converts them. **3.** person put in charge of property in litigation. —**re·ceiv'er·ship',** n.

re'cent (rē'sənt) adj. happening, etc., lately. —**re'cent·ly,** adv.

re·cep'ta·cle (ri sep'tə kəl) n. container.

re·cep'tion (ri sep'shən) n. **1.** act of receiving. **2.** fact or manner of being received. **3.** social function.

re·cep'tion·ist, n. person who receives callers in an office.

re·cep'tive (-tiv) adj. quick to understand and consider ideas.

re·cep'tor (-tər) n. nerve ending that is sensitive to stimuli.

re·cess' (ri ses', rē'ses) n. **1.** temporary cessation of work. **2.** alcove. **3.** (pl.) inner part. —v. **4.** take or make recess.

re·ces'sion (-sesh'ən) n. **1.** withdrawal. **2.** economic decline.

re·ces'sion·al, n. music played at end of church service.

re·ces'sive (-ses'iv) adj. **1.** receding. **2.** noting one of pair of hereditary traits that is masked by the other when both are present.

re·cher'ché (rə shâr'shā, rə shâr shā') adj. **1.** very rare or choice. **2.** affectedly refined.

re·cid'i·vism (ri sid'ə viz'əm) repeated or habitual relapse, as into crime. —**re·cid'i·vist,** n., adj.

recip. 1. reciprocal. **2.** reciprocity.

rec'i·pe' (res'ə pē) n. formula, esp. in cookery.

re·cip'i·ent (ri sip'ē ənt) n. **1.** receiver. —adj. **2.** receiving.

re·cip'ro·cal (ri sip'rə kəl) adj. **1.** mutual. —n. **2.** thing in reciprocal position. —**re·cip'ro·cal·ly,** adv.

re·cip'ro·cate' (-kāt') v., **-cated, -cating. 1.** give, feel, etc., in return. **2.** move alternately backward and forward. —**re·cip'ro·ca'tion,** n.

rec'i·proc'i·ty (res'ə pros'i tē) n. interchange.

recirc recirculate.

recit. Music. recitative.

re·cit'al (ri sīt'l) n. musical entertainment.

rec'i·ta·tive' (res'i tə tēv') n. style of vocal music intermediate between speaking and singing.

re·cite' (ri sīt') v., **-cited, -citing. 1.** repeat from memory. **2.** narrate. —**rec'i·ta'tion** (res'i tā'shən) n.

reck'less (rek'lis) adj. careless. —**reck'less·ly,** adv. —**reck'less·ness,** n.

reck'on (rek'ən) v. **1.** calculate. **2.** regard as;

R

esteem. **3.** *Informal.* suppose. **4.** deal (with). **—reck′on•er,** *n.*

reck′on•ing, *n.* **1.** settling of accounts. **2.** navigational calculation.

recl reclose.

re•claim′ (rē klām′) *v.* make usable, as land. **—rec′la•ma′tion** (rek′lə mā′shən) *n.*

re•cline′ (ri klīn′) *v.,* **-clined, -clining.** lean back.

re•clin′er, *n.* chair with adjustable back and footrest.

rec′luse (rek′lōōs, ri klōōs′) *n.* person living in seclusion.

recm recommend.

recog recognition.

re•cog′ni•zance (ri kog′nə zəns, -kon′ə-) *n.* bond pledging one to do a particular act.

rec′og•nize′ (rek′əg nīz′) *v.,* **-nized, -nizing. 1.** identify or perceive from previous knowledge. **2.** acknowledge formally. **3.** greet. **—rec′og•ni′tion** (-nish′ən) *n.* **—rec′og•niz′a•ble,** *adj.*

re•coil′ (rē koil′) *v.* **1.** shrink back. **2.** spring back. **—***n.* **3.** act of recoiling.

rec′ol•lect′ (rek′ə lekt′) *v.* remember. **—rec′ol•lec′tion,** *n.*

rec′om•mend′ (rek′ə mend′) *v.* **1.** commend as worthy. **2.** advise. **—rec′om•men•da′tion,** *n.*

rec′om•pense′ (rek′əm pens′) *v.,* **-pensed, -pensing.** **—***v.* **1.** repay or reward for services, injury, etc. **—***n.* **2.** such compensation.

recon reconnaissance.

rec′on•cile′ (rek′ən sīl′) *v.,* **-ciled, -ciling. 1.** bring into agreement. **2.** restore to friendliness. **—rec′on•cil′i•a′tion** (-sil′ē ā′shən) *n.* **—rec′on•cil′a•ble,** *adj.*

rec′on•dite (rek′ən dīt′) *adj.* **1.** very profound, difficult, or abstruse. **2.** known by a few; esoteric.

re′con•noi′ter (rē′kə noi′tər, rek′ə-) *v.* search area, esp. for military information. **—re•con′nais•sance** (ri kon′ə səns) *n.*

re•cord′ *v.* (ri kôrd′) **1.** set down in writing. **2.** register for mechanical reproduction. **—***n.* (rek′ərd) **3.** what is recorded. **4.** object from which sound is reproduced. **5.** best rate, etc., yet attained. **—***adj.* (rek′ərd) **6.** making or being a record. **—re•cord′ing,** *n.*

re•cord′er, *n.* **1.** person who records. **2.** recording device. **3.** flute with mouthpiece like a whistle and eight finger holes.

re•count′ *v.* (rē kount′) **1.** narrate. **2.** count again. **—***n.* (rē′kount′) **3.** a second count.

re•coup′ (ri kōōp′) *v.* recover; make up.

re′course (rē′kôrs, ri kôrs′) *n.* resort for help.

re•cov′er (ri kuv′ər) *v.* **1.** get back. **2.** reclaim. **3.** regain health. **—re•cov′er•a•ble,** *adj.* **—recov′er•y,** *n.*

recpt receipt.

rec′re•ant (rek′rē ənt) *adj.* **1.** cowardly. **2.** disloyal. **—***n.* **3.** cowardly or disloyal person.

re′-cre•ate′ (rē′krē āt′) *v.,* **-ated, -ating.** create anew.

rec′re•ate′ (rek′rē-) *v.,* **-ated, -ating.** refresh physically or mentally.

rec′re•a′tion, *n.* refreshing enjoyment. **—rec′re•a′tion•al,** *adj.*

re•crim′i•nate′ (ri krim′ə nāt′) *v.,* **-nated, -nating.** accuse in return. **—re•crim′i•na′tion,** *n.*

re′cru•des′cence (rē′krōō des′əns) *n.* breaking out again after inactivity. **—re′cru•des′-cent,** *adj.*

re•cruit′ (ri krōōt′) *n.* **1.** new member of military or other group. **—***v.* **2.** enlist. **—re•cruit′er,** *n.* **—re•cruit′ment,** *n.*

Rec. Sec. Recording Secretary. Also, **rec. sec.**

rect. 1. receipt. **2.** rectangle. **3.** rectangular. **4.** (in prescriptions) rectified. [from Latin *rēctificātus*] **5.** rectifier. **6.** rector. **7.** rectory.

rec′tan′gle (rek′tang′gəl) *n.* parallelogram with four right angles. **—rec•tan′gu•lar** (-tang′gyə lər) *adj.*

rec′ti•fy′ (rek′tə fī′) *v.,* **-fied, -fying.** correct. **—rec′ti•fi•a•ble,** *adj.* **—rec′ti•fi′er,** *n.*

rec′ti•lin′e•ar (rek′tl in′ē ər) *adj.* **1.** forming straight line. **2.** formed by straight lines.

rec′ti•tude′ (rek′ti tōōd′, -tyōōd′) *n.* rightness.

rec′to (rek′tō) *n., pl.* **-tos.** right-hand page of book.

rec′tor (rek′tər) *n.* **1.** member of clergy in charge of parish, etc. **2.** head of university, etc.

rec′to•ry, *n., pl.* **-ries.** parsonage.

rec′tum (rek′təm) *n.* lowest part of intestine. **—rec′tal,** *adj.*

re•cum′bent (ri kum′bənt) *adj.* lying down. **—re•cum′ben•cy,** *n.*

re•cu′per•ate′ (ri kōō′pə rāt′) *v.,* **-ated, -ating.** regain health. **—re•cu′per•a′tion,** *n.*

re•cur′ (ri kûr′) *v.,* **-curred, -curring. 1.** occur again. **2.** return in thought, etc. **—re•cur′rence,** *n.* **—re•cur′rent,** *adj.* **—re•cur′rent•ly,** *adv.*

re•cy′cle (rē sī′kəl) *v.* **-cled, -cling.** treat (refuse) to extract reusable material.

red (red) *n., adj.,* **redder, reddest.** **—***n.* **1.** color of blood. **2.** leftist radical in politics. **—***adj.* **3.** of or like red. **4.** radically to left in politics. **—red′den,** *v.* **—red′dish,** *adj.* **—red′ness,** *n.*

re•dact′ (ri dakt′) *v.* edit.

red blood cell, blood cell that contains hemoglobin and carries oxygen to cells and tissues.

red′cap′, *n.* baggage porter.

re•deem′ (ri dēm′) *v.* **1.** pay off. **2.** recover. **3.** fulfill. **4.** deliver from sin by sacrifice. **—re•deem′er,** *n.* **—re•deem′a•ble,** *adj.* **—re•demp′tion** (-demp′shən) *n.*

red′-hand′ed, *adj., adv.* in the act of wrongdoing.

red′head′, *n.* person with red hair. **—red′-head′ed,** *adj.*

red herring, something intended to distract attention from the real problem or issue.

red'-hot', *adj.* **1.** red with heat. **2.** violent; furious. **3.** very fresh or new.

red'-let'ter, *adj.* memorable.

red'lin'ing, *n.* refusal by banks to grant mortgages in specified urban areas.

red'o•lent (red'l ənt) *adj.* **1.** odorous. **2.** suggestive. —**red'o•lence,** *n.*

re•doubt' (ri dout') *n.* small isolated fort.

re•doubt'a•ble, *adj.* **1.** evoking fear; formidable. **2.** commanding respect.

re•dound' (ri dound') *v.* occur as result.

re•dress', *v.* (ri dress') **1.** set right (a wrong). —*n.* (rē'dres) **2.** act of redressing.

red tape, excessive attention to prescribed procedure.

re•duce' (ri dōōs', -dyōōs') *v.*, -**duced, -ducing. 1.** make less in size, rank, etc. **2.** put into simpler form or state. **3.** remove weight. —**re•duc'er,** *n.* —**re•duc'i•ble,** *adj.* —**re•duc'tion** (-duk'shən) *n.* —**re•duc'tive,** *adj.*

re•dun'dant (ri dun'dənt) *adj.* **1.** excess. **2.** wordy. —**re•dun'dance, re•dun'dan•cy,** *n.* —**re•dun'dant•ly,** *adv.*

redupl. reduplication.

red'wood' (red'wŏŏd') *n.* huge evergreen tree of California.

reed (rēd) *n.* **1.** tall marsh grass. **2.** musical pipe made of hollow stalk. **3.** small piece of cane or metal at mouth of wind instrument. —**reed'y,** *adj.*

reef (rēf) *n.* **1.** narrow ridge near the surface of water. **2.** *Naut.* part of sail rolled or folded to reduce area. —*v.* **3.** shorten (sail) by rolling or folding.

reef'er, *n.* **1.** short heavy coat. **2.** *Slang.* marijuana cigarette.

reek (rēk) *v.* **1.** smell strongly and unpleasantly. —*n.* **2.** such smell.

reel (rēl) *n.* **1.** turning object for wound cord, film, etc. **2.** lively dance. —*v.* **3.** wind on reel. **4.** tell easily and at length. **5.** sway or stagger. **6.** whirl.

re•en'try (rē en'trē) *n.*, *pl.* -tries. **1.** second entry. **2.** return into earth's atmosphere.

reeve (rēv) *v.*, **reeved** or **rove** (rōv), **reeved** or **roven, reeving.** pass (rope) through hole.

ref (ref) *n.*, *v.* referee.

Ref. Ch. Reformed Church.

ref des reference designation.

re•fec'to•ry (ri fek'tə rē) *n.*, *pl.* -ries. dining hall.

re•fer' (ri fûr') *v.*, -**ferred, -ferring. 1.** direct attention. **2.** direct or go for information. **3.** apply. —**re•fer'ral,** *n.*

ref'er•ee' (ref'ə rē') *n.* **1.** judge. —*v.* **2.** act as referee.

ref'er•ence (ref'ər əns) *n.* **1.** act or fact of referring. **2.** something referred to. **3.** person from whom one seeks recommendation. **4.** testimonial.

ref'er•en'dum (ref'ə ren'dəm) *n.*, *pl.* -**dums, -da.** submission to popular vote of law passed by legislature.

ref'er•ent (ref'ər ənt) *n.* something referred to.

re•fill' *v.* (rē fil') **1.** fill again. —*n.* (rē'fil') **2.** second filling.

re•fine' (ri fīn') *v.*, -**fined, -fining. 1.** free from impurities or error. **2.** teach good manners, taste, etc. —**re•fin'er,** *n.* —**re•fine'ment,** *n.*

re•fin'er•y, *n.*, *pl.* -**eries.** establishment for refining, esp. petroleum.

refl. 1. reflection. **2.** reflective. **3.** reflex. **4.** reflexive.

re•flect' (ri flekt') *v.* **1.** cast back. **2.** show; mirror. **3.** bring (credit or discredit) on one. **4.** think. —**re•flec'tion,** *n.* —**re•flec'tive,** *adj.* —**re•flec'tor,** *n.*

re'flex (rē'fleks) *adj.* **1.** denoting involuntary action. **2.** bent. —*n.* **3.** involuntary movement.

re•flex'ive, *adj.* **1.** (of verb) having same subject and object. **2.** (of pronoun) showing identity with subject. —**re•flex'ive•ly,** *adv.*

re•for'est (rē fôr'ist) *v.* replant with forest trees. —**re'for•est•a'tion,** *n.*

re•form' (rē fôrm') *n.* **1.** correction of what is wrong. —*v.* **2.** change for better. —**re•form'er,** *n.* —**ref'or•ma'tion** (ref'ər mā'shən) *n.*

re•form'a•to•ry (ri fôr'mə tôr'ē) *n.*, *pl.* -**ries.** prison for young offenders.

Ref. Pres. Reformed Presbyterian.

refr 1. refrigerate. **2.** refrigerator.

re•frac'tion (ri frak'shən) *n.* change of direction of light or heat rays in passing to another medium. —**re•fract',** *v.* —**re•frac'tive,** *adj.* —**re•frac'tor,** *n.*

re•frac'to•ry, *adj.* stubborn.

re•frain' (ri frān') *v.* **1.** keep oneself (from). —*n.* **2.** recurring passage in song, etc.

re•fresh' (ri fresh') *v.* **1.** reinvigorate. **2.** stimulate. —**re•fresh'ment,** *n.* —**re•fresh'er,** *adj.*, *n.* —**re•fresh'ing,** *adj.*

re•frig'er•ate' (ri frij'ə rāt') *v.*, -**ated, -ating.** make or keep cold. —**re•frig'er•ant** (-ə-rənt) *adj.*, *n.* —**re•frig'er•a'tion,** *n.*

re•frig'er•a'tor, *n.* cabinet for keeping food cold.

Ref. Sp. reformed spelling.

refs. req. references required.

ref'uge (ref'yōōj) *n.* shelter from danger.

ref'u•gee' (ref'yŏŏ jē') *n.* person who flees for safety.

re•ful'gent (ri ful'jənt) *adj.* shining brightly; radiant. —**re•ful'gence,** *n.*

re•fund', *v.* (ri fund') **1.** give back (money). —*n.* (rē'fund) **2.** repayment. —**re•fund'a•ble,** *adj.*

re•fur'bish (rē fûr'bish) *v.* renovate. —**re•fur'bish•ment,** *n.*

re•fuse', *v.*, -**fused, -fusing,** *n.* —*v.* (ri fyōōz') **1.** decline to accept. **2.** deny (re-

R

quest). —*n.* (ref′yŏos) **3.** rubbish. —**re•fus′- al,** *n.*

re•fute′ (ri fyŏot′) *v.,* **-futed, -futing.** prove false or wrong. —**ref′u•ta•ble** (ref′yə tə bəl) *adj.* —**ref′u•ta′tion,** *n.*

Reg. 1. regiment. **2.** queen [from Latin *rēgīna*].

reg. 1. regent. **2.** regiment. **3.** region. **4.** register. **5.** registered. **6.** registrar. **7.** registry. **8.** regular. **9.** regularly. **10.** regulation. **11.** regulator.

re•gain′ (rē gān′) *v.* get again.

re′gal (rē′gəl) *adj.* royal. —**re′gal•ly,** *adv.*

re•gale′ (ri gāl′) *v.,* **-galed, -galing. 1.** entertain grandly. **2.** feast.

re•ga′lia (-gāl′yə) *n.pl.* emblems of royalty, office, etc.

re•gard′ (-gärd′) *v.* **1.** look upon with particular feeling. **2.** respect. **3.** look at. **4.** concern. —*n.* **5.** reference. **6.** attention. **7.** respect and liking.

re•gard′ing, *prep.* concerning.

re•gard′less, *adv.* **1.** without regard; in spite of. —*adj.* **2.** heedless.

re•gat′ta (ri gat′ə, -gä′tə) *n.* **1.** boat race. **2.** organized series of boat races.

regd. registered.

regen regenerate.

re•gen′er•ate′, *v.,* **-ated, -ating,** *adj.* —*v.* (ri jen′ə rāt′) **1.** make over for the better. **2.** form anew. —*adj.* (-ər it) **3.** regenerated. —**re•gen′er•a′tion,** *n.* —**re•gen′er•a′tive,** *adj.*

re′gent (rē′jənt) *n.* **1.** person ruling in place of sovereign. **2.** university governor. —**re′gen•cy,** *n.*

reg′gae (reg′ā) *n.* Jamaican music blending blues, calypso, and rock.

reg′i•cide (rej′ə sīd′) *n.* killing of king.

re•gime′ (rə zhēm′, rā-) *n.* system of rule.

reg′i•men (rej′ə mən) *n.* **1.** course of diet, etc., for health. **2.** rule.

reg′i•ment, *n.* (rej′ə mənt) **1.** infantry unit. —*v.* (rej′ə ment′) **2.** subject to strict, uniform discipline. —**reg′i•men′tal,** *adj.* —**reg′i•men•ta′tion,** *n.*

re′gion (rē′jən) *n.* area; district. —**re′gion•al,** *adj.* —**re′gion•al•ly,** *adv.*

re′gion•al•ism, *n.* feature peculiar to geographical region.

reg′is•ter (rej′ə stər) *n.* **1.** written list; record. **2.** range of voice or instrument. **3.** device for controlling passage of warm air. —*v.* **4.** enter in register. **5.** show. **6.** enter oneself on list of voters. —**reg′is•tra′tion** (-strā′shən) *n.*

reg′is•trar′ (-strär′) *n.* official recorder.

reg′is•try, *n., pl.* **-tries. 1.** registration. **2.** place where register is kept. **3.** register.

reg′nant (reg′nənt) *adj.* **1.** ruling. **2.** widespread.

regr. registrar.

re•gress′ (ri gres′) *v.* return to previous, in-

ferior state. —**re•gres′sion,** *n.* —**re•gres′- sive,** *adj.*

re•gret′ (ri gret′) *v.,* **-gretted, -gretting,** *n.* —*v.* **1.** feel sorry about. —*n.* **2.** feeling of loss or sorrow. —**re•gret′ta•ble,** *adj.* —**re•gret′- ful,** *adj.*

re•group′ (rē grŏop′) *v.* form into new group.

regt. 1. regent. **2.** regiment.

reg′u•lar (reg′yə lər) *adj.* **1.** usual. **2.** symmetrical. **3.** recurring at fixed times. **4.** orderly. **5.** denoting permanent army. —*n.* **6.** regular soldier. —**reg′u•lar′i•ty,** *n.* —**reg′u• lar•ize′,** *v.,* **-ized, -izing.** —**reg′u•lar•ly,** *adv.*

reg′u•late′ (-lāt′) *v.,* **-lated, -lating. 1.** control by rule, method, etc. **2.** adjust. —**reg′u• la′tion,** *n.* —**reg′u•la•to′ry** (-lə tôr′ē) *adj.* —**reg′u•la′tor,** *n.*

re•gur′gi•tate′ (ri gûr′ji tāt′) *v.,* **-tated, -tating.** cast or surge back, esp. from stomach. —**re•gur′gi•ta′tion,** *n.*

re′ha•bil′i•tate′ (rē′hə bil′i tāt′, rē′ə-) *v.,* **-tated, -tating.** restore to good condition. —**re′ha•bil′i•ta′tion,** *n.*

re•hash′, *v.* (rē hash′) **1.** rework or reuse in new form without significant change. —*n.* (rē′hash′) **2.** act of rehashing. **3.** something rehashed.

re•hearse′ (ri hûrs′) *v.,* **-hearsed, -hearsing. 1.** act or direct in practice for performance. **2.** recount in detail. —**re•hears′al,** *n.*

reign (rān) *n.* **1.** royal rule. —*v.* **2.** have sovereign power or title.

re′im•burse′ (rē′im bûrs′) *v.,* **-bursed, -bursing.** repay, as for expenses. —**re′im•burse′- ment,** *n.*

rein (rān) *n.* narrow strap fastened to bridle or bit for controlling animal.

re′in•car•na′tion (rē′in kär nā′shən) *n.* continuation of soul after death in new body.

rein′deer′ (rān′dēr′) *n.* large arctic deer.

reinf reinforce.

re′in•force′ (rē′in fôrs′) *v.,* **-forced, -forcing.** strengthen with support, troops, etc. —**re′in•force′ment,** *n.*

re′in•state′ (rē′in stāt′) *v.,* **-stated, -stating.** put back into former position or state. —**re′- in•state′ment,** *n.*

REIT (rēt), real-estate investment trust.

re•it′er•ate′ (rē it′ə rāt′) *v.,* **-ated, -ating.** repeat. —**re•it′er•a′tion,** *n.* —**re•it′er•a′- tive,** *adj.*

rej reject.

re•ject′, *v.* (ri jekt′) **1.** refuse or discard. —*n.* (rē′jekt) **2.** something rejected. —**re•jec′- tion,** *n.*

re•joice′ (ri jois′) *v.,* **-joiced, -joicing.** be or make glad.

re•join′ (-join′) *v.* answer.

re•join′der (-dər) *n.* response.

re•ju′ve•nate′ (ri jŏo′və nāt′) *v.,* **-nated, -nating.** make young and vigorous again. —**re•ju′ve•na′tion,** *n.*

rel. 1. relating. **2.** relative. **3.** relatively. **4.** released. **5.** religion. **6.** religious.

re•lapse′, v., **-lapsed, -lapsing.** —v. (rilaps′) **1.** fall back into former state or practice. —n. (ri laps′, rē′laps) **2.** act or instance of relapsing.

re•late′ (ri lāt′) v., **-lated, -lating. 1.** tell. **2.** establish or have relation.

re•lat′ed, adj. **1.** associated. **2.** connected by blood or marriage.

re•la′tion, n. **1.** connection. **2.** relative. **3.** narrative. —**re•la′tion•ship′,** n.

rel′a•tive (rel′ə tiv) n. **1.** person connected with another by blood or marriage. —adj. **2.** comparative. **3.** designating word that introduces subordinate clause. —**rel′a•tive•ly,** adv.

relative humidity, ratio of water vapor in the air at a given temperature to the amount the air could hold.

rel′a•tiv′i•ty, n. principle that time, mass, etc. are relative, not absolute concepts.

re•lax′ (ri laks′) v. **1.** make or become less tense, firm, etc. **2.** slacken. —**re′lax•a′tion** (rē′lak sā′shən) n.

re′lay (rē′lā) n. **1.** fresh supply of persons, etc., to relieve others. —v. **2.** carry forward by relays.

re•lease′ (ri lēs′) v., **-leased, -leasing,** n. —v. **1.** let go; discharge. —n. **2.** act or instance of releasing.

rel′e•gate′ (rel′i gāt′) v., **-gated, -gating. 1.** consign. **2.** turn over. —**rel′e•ga′tion,** n.

re•lent′ (ri lent′) v. become more mild or forgiving. —**re•lent′less,** adj.

rel′e•vant (rel′ə vənt) adj. having to do with matter in question. —**rel′e•vance,** n.

re•li′a•ble (ri lī′ə bəl) adj. trustworthy. —**re•li′a•bil′i•ty,** n. —**re•li′a•bly,** adv.

re•li′ance (-əns) n. **1.** trust. **2.** confidence. —**re•li′ant,** adj.

rel′ic (rel′ik) n. **1.** object surviving from past. **2.** personal memorial of sacred person.

re•lief′ (ri lēf′) n. **1.** alleviation of pain, distress, etc. **2.** help. **3.** pleasant change. **4.** projection.

re•lieve′ (ri lēv′) v., **-lieved, -lieving. 1.** ease; alleviate. **2.** break sameness of. **3.** release or discharge from duty.

relig. religion.

re•li′gion (ri lij′ən) n. **1.** spiritual recognition and worship. **2.** particular system of religious belief. —**re•li′gious,** adj. —**re•li′gious•ly,** adv. —**re•li′gious•ness,** n.

re•lin′quish (ri ling′kwish) v. give up; surrender. —**re•lin′quish•ment,** n.

rel′i•quar′y (rel′i kwer′ē) n., pl. **-ies.** receptacle for religious relics.

rel′ish (rel′ish) n. **1.** enjoyment. **2.** chopped pickles, etc. —v. **3.** take enjoyment in.

re•live′ (rē liv′) v., **-lived, -living.** experience again.

re•lo′cate, v., **-cated, cating.** move. —**re′lo•ca′tion,** n.

rel. pron. relative pronoun.

re•luc′tant (ri luk′tənt) adj. unwilling. —**re•luc′tance,** n. —**re•luc′tant•ly,** adv.

re•ly′ (ri lī′) v., **-lied, -lying.** put trust in.

REM (rem) n. quick, darting movement of eyes during sleep.

re•main′ (ri mān′) v. **1.** continue to be. **2.** stay; be left. —n.pl. **3.** that which remains. **4.** corpse.

re•main′der (-dər) n. that which remains.

re•mand′ (ri mand′) v. send back, as to jail or lower court of law. —**re•mand′ment,** n.

re•mark′ (ri märk′) v. **1.** say casually. **2.** perceive; observe. —n. **3.** casual comment. **4.** notice.

re•mark′a•ble, adj. extraordinary. —**re•mark′a•bly,** adv.

rem′e•dy (rem′i dē) v., **-died, -dying,** n., pl. **-dies.** —v. **1.** cure or alleviate. **2.** correct. —n. **3.** something that remedies. —**re•me′di•al,** adj.

re•mem′ber (ri mem′bər) v. **1.** recall to or retain in memory. **2.** mention as sending greetings. —**re•mem′brance** (-brəns) n.

re•mind′ (ri mīnd′) v. cause to remember. —**re•mind′er,** n.

rem′i•nisce′ (rem′ə nis′) v., **-nisced, -niscing.** recall past experiences. —**rem′i•nis′cence,** n. —**rem′i•nis′cent,** adj.

re•miss′ (ri mis′) adj. negligent.

re•mit′ (-mit′) v., **-mitted, -mitting. 1.** send money. **2.** pardon. **3.** abate. —**re•mis′sion,** n.

remitt. remittance.

re•mit′tance, n. money, etc., sent.

re•mit′tent, adj. (of illness) less severe at times.

rem′nant (rem′nənt) n. **1.** small remaining part. **2.** trace.

re•mod′el (rē mod′l) v., **-eled, -eling.** renovate.

re•mon′strate (ri mon′strāt) v., **-strated, -strating.** protest; plead in protest. —**re′mon•stra′tion** (rē′-), **re•mon′strance,** n.

re•morse′ (ri môrs′) n. regret for wrongdoing. —**re•morse′ful,** adj. —**re•morse′less,** adj.

re•mote′ (ri mōt′) adj. **1.** far distant. **2.** faint. —n. **3.** remote control.(def. 2). —**re•mote′ly,** adv. —**re•mote′ness,** n.

remote control, 1. control of an apparatus from a distance, as by radio signals. **2.** Also, **remote.** device used for such control.

re•move′ (ri moov′) v., **-moved, -moving,** n. —v. **1.** take away or off. **2.** move to another place. —n. **3.** distance of separation. —**re•mov′al,** n. —**re•mov′a•ble,** adj.

re•mu′ner•ate′ (ri myoo′nə rāt′) v., **-ated, -ating.** pay for work, etc. —**re•mu′ner•a′tion,** n. —**re•mu′ner•a′tive,** adj.

ren′ais•sance′ (ren′ə säns′) n. **1.** revival. **2.** (cap.) cultural period of the 14th-17th century marked by interest in culture of antiquity.

re′nal (rēn′l) *adj.* of or near the kidneys.

re•nas′cent (ri nā′sənt) *adj.* being reborn; springing again into being or vigor.

rend (rend) *v.* **1.** tear apart. **2.** disturb with noise. **3.** distress.

ren′der, *v.* **1.** cause to be. **2.** do, show, or furnish. **3.** deliver officially. **4.** perform. **5.** give back. **6.** melt (fat). **—ren•di′tion** (-dish′ən) *n.*

ren′dez•vous′ (rän′də vōō′, -dā-) *n., pl.* **-vous.** appointment or place to meet.

ren′e•gade′ (ren′i gād′) *n.* deserter.

re•nege′ (ri nig′, -neg′) *v.,* **-neged, -neging.** *Informal,* break promise.

re•new′ (ri nōō′, -nyōō′) *v.* **1.** begin or do again. **2.** make like new; replenish. **—re•new′a•ble,** *adj.* **—re•new′al,** *n.*

ren′net (ren′it) *n.* **1.** membrane lining stomach of calf or other animal. **2.** preparation of this used in making cheese.

re•nounce′ (ri nouns′) *v.,* **-nounced, -nouncing.** give up voluntarily. **—re•nounce′ment,** *n.*

ren′o•vate′ (ren′ə vāt′) *v.,* **-vated, -vating.** repair; refurbish. **—ren′o•va′tion,** *n.*

re•nown′ (ri noun′) *n.* fame. **—re•nowned′,** *adj.*

rent (rent) *n.* **1.** Also, **rent′al.** payment for use of property. **2.** tear; violent break. **—v. 3.** grant or have use of in return for rent. **—rent′er,** *n.*

rent′al, *n.* **1.** amount given or received as rent. **2.** act of renting. **3.** property rented.

re•nun′ci•a′tion (ri nun′sē ā′shən, -shē-) *n.* act of renouncing.

Rep., 1. Representative. **2.** Republic. **3.** Republican.

re•pair′ (ri pâr′) *v.* **1.** restore to good condition. **2.** go. **—n. 3.** work of repairing. **4.** good condition. **—rep′a•ra•ble** (rep′ər ə bəl) *adj.*

rep′a•ra′tion (rep′ə rā′shən) *n.* amends for injury.

rep′ar•tee′ (rep′ər tē′, -tā′, -är-) *n.* exchange of wit; banter.

re•past′ (ri past′) *n.* meal.

re•pa′tri•ate′ (rē pā′trē āt′) *v.,* **-ated, -ating.** send back to one's native country. **—re•pa′tri•a′tion,** *n.*

re•pay (ri pā′) *v.,* **-paid, -paying.** pay back. **—re•pay′ment,** *n.*

re•peal′ (ri pēl′) *v.* **1.** revoke officially. **—n. 2.** revocation.

re•peat′ (ri pēt′) *v.* **1.** say, tell, or do again. **—n. 2.** act of repeating. **3.** musical passage to be repeated.

re•peat′ed, *adj.* said or done again and again. **—re•peat′ed•ly,** *adv.*

re•peat′er, *n.* **1.** one that repeats. **2.** gun firing several shots in rapid succession.

re•pel′ (ri pel′) *v.,* **-pelled, -pelling. 1.** drive back; thrust away. **2.** excite disgust or suspicion. **—re•pel′lent,** *adj., n.*

re•pent′ (ri pent′) *v.* feel contrition. **—re•**

pent′ance, *n.* **—re•pent′ant,** *adj.* **—re•pent′ant•ly,** *adv.*

re′per•cus′sion (rē′pər kush′ən) *n.* **1.** indirect result. **2.** echo.

rep′er•toire′ (rep′ər twär′, -twôr′, rep′ə-) *n.* group of works that performer or company can perform. Also, **rep′er•to′ry.**

rep′e•ti′tion (rep′ə tish′ən) *n.* repeated action, utterance, etc. **—rep′e•ti′tious,** *adj.* **—re•pet′i•tive** (ri pet′ə tiv) *adj.*

re•pine′ (ri pīn′) *v.,* **-pined, -pining. 1.** complain. **2.** yearn.

repl. 1. replace. **2.** replacement.

re•place′ (ri plās′) *v.,* **-placed, -placing. 1.** take place of. **2.** provide substitute for. **—re•place′ment,** *n.* **—re•place′a•ble,** *adj.*

re•play′, *v.,* **-played, -playing. —v.** (rē plā′) **1.** play again. **—n.** (rē′ plā) **2.** act of replaying. **3.** something replayed.

re•plen′ish (ri plen′ish) *v.* make full again. **—re•plen′ish•ment,** *n.*

re•plete′ (ri plēt′) *adj.* abundantly filled. **—re•ple′tion,** *n.*

rep′li•ca (rep′li kə) *n.* copy.

rep′li•cate (-kāt′) *v.,* **-cated, -cating.** duplicate or reproduce.

rep′li•ca′tion, *n.* **1.** reply. **2.** replica. **3.** act of replicating.

re•ply′ (ri plī′) *v.,* **-plied, -plying,** *n., pl.* **-plies.** answer.

re•port′ (ri pôrt′) *n.* **1.** statement of events or findings. **2.** rumor. **3.** loud noise. **—v. 4.** tell of. **5.** present oneself. **6.** inform against. **7.** write about for newspaper. **—re•port′er,** *n.*

re•port′age (ri pôr′tij, rep′ôr täzh′) *n.* **1.** act of reporting news. **2.** reported news.

re•pose′ (ri pōz′) *n., v.,* **-posed, -posing. —n. 1.** rest or sleep. **2.** tranquillity. **—v. 3.** rest or sleep. **4.** put, as trust. **—re•pose′ful,** *adj.*

re•pos′i•tor′y (ri poz′i tôr′ē) *n., pl.* **-tories.** place where things are stored.

re•pos•sess′ (rē′pə zes′) *v.* take back.

repr. 1. represented. **2.** representing. **3.** reprint. **4.** reprinted.

rep′re•hen′si•ble (rep′rə hen′sə bəl) *adj.* blameworthy. **—rep′re•hen′si•bly,** *adv.*

rep′re•sent′ (rep′ri zent′) *v.* **1.** express; signify. **2.** act or speak for. **3.** portray. **—rep′re•sen•ta′tion,** *n.* **—rep′re•sen•ta′tion•al,** *adj.*

rep′re•sent′a•tive (-zen′tə tiv) *n.* **1.** one that represents another or others. **2.** member of legislative body. **—adj. 3.** representing. **4.** typical.

re•press′ (ri pres′) *v.* **1.** inhibit. **2.** suppress. **—re•pres′sive,** *adj.* **—re•pres′sion,** *n.*

re•prieve′ (ri prēv′) *v.,* **-prieved, -prieving,** *n.* respite.

rep′ri•mand′ (rep′rə mand′) *n.* **1.** severe reproof. **—v. 2.** reprove severely.

re•pris′al (ri prī′zəl) *n.* infliction of injuries in retaliation.

repro 1. reproduce. **2.** reproduction.

re•proach′ (ri prōch′) *v.* **1.** blame; upbraid. —*n.* **2.** blame; discredit. —**re•proach′ful,** *adj.*

rep′ro•bate′ (rep′rə bāt′) *n., adj., v.,* -bated, -bating. —*n.* **1.** hopelessly bad person. —*adj.* **2.** depraved. —*v.* **3.** condemn. —**rep′ro•ba′tion,** *n.*

re′pro•duce′ (rē′prə dōōs′, -dyōōs′) *v.,* -duced, -ducing. **1.** copy or duplicate. **2.** produce by propagation. —**re′pro•duc′tion** (-duk′shən) *n.* —**re′pro•duc′tive,** *adj.*

re•proof′ (ri prōōf′) *n.* censure.

re•prove′ (-prōōv′) *v.,* -proved, -proving. blame.

rept. report.

rep′tile (rep′til, -tīl) *n.* creeping animal, as lizard or snake.

Repub. 1. Republic. **2.** Republican.

re•pub′lic (ri pub′lik) *n.* state governed by representatives elected by citizens.

re•pub′li•can, *adj.* **1.** of or favoring republic. **2.** (*cap.*) of **Republican Party,** one of two major political parties of U.S. —*n.* **3.** (*cap.*) member of Republican Party.

re•pu′di•ate′ (ri pyōō′dē āt′) *v.,* -ated, -ating. reject as worthless, not binding, or false. —**re•pu′di•a′tion,** *n.*

re•pug′nant (ri pug′nənt) *adj.* distasteful. —**re•pug′nance,** *n.*

re•pulse′ (ri puls′) *v.,* -pulsed, -pulsing, *n.* —*v.* **1.** drive back with force. —*n.* **2.** act of repulsing. **3.** rejection. —**re•pul′sion,** *n.*

re•pul′sive, *adj.* disgusting.

rep′u•ta•ble (rep′yə tə bəl) *adj.* of good reputation. —**rep′u•ta•bly,** *adv.*

rep′u•ta′tion (-tā′shən) *n.* **1.** public estimation of character. **2.** good name.

re•pute′ (ri pyōōt′) *n., v.,* -puted, -puting. —*n.* **1.** reputation. —*v.* **2.** give reputation to. —**re•put′ed•ly,** *adv.*

req. 1. Also, **req** request. **2.** require. **3.** Also, **reqd** required. **4.** requisition.

reqn requisition.

reqt requirement.

re•quest′ (ri kwest′) *v.* **1.** ask for. —*n.* **2.** act of requesting. **3.** what is requested.

Req′ui•em (rek′wē əm) *n. Rom. Cath. Ch.* mass for dead.

re•quire′ (ri kwīᵊr′) *v.,* -quired, -quiring. **1.** need. **2.** demand. —**re•quire′ment,** *n.*

req′ui•site (rek′wə zit) *adj.* **1.** necessary. —*n.* **2.** necessary thing.

req′ui•si′tion (-zish′ən) *n.* **1.** formal order or demand. —*v.* **2.** take for official use.

re•quite′ (ri kwīt′) *v.,* -quited, -quiting. make return to or for. —**re•quit′al** (-kwī′təl) *n.*

re′run′ (rē′run′) *n.* **1.** showing of motion picture or television program after its initial run. **2.** the program shown.

RES *Immunology.* reticuloendothelial system.

res 1. resistance. **2.** resistor. **3.** resume.

res. 1. research. **2.** reserve. **3.** residence. **4.**

resident; residents. **5.** residue. **6.** resigned. **7.** resolution.

resc rescind.

re•scind′ (ri sind′) *v.* annul; revoke. —**re•scis′sion,** *n.*

res′cue (res′kyōō) *v.,* -cued, -cuing, *n.* —*v.* **1.** free from danger, capture, etc. —*n.* **2.** act of rescuing. —**res′cu•er,** *n.*

re•search′ (ri sûrch′, rē′sûrch) *n.* **1.** diligent investigation. —*v.* **2.** investigate carefully. —**re•search′er,** *n.*

re•sec′tion (ri sek′shən) *n.* surgical removal of part of organ.

re•sem′ble (ri zem′bəl) *v.,* -bled, -bling. be similar to. —**re•sem′blance,** *n.*

re•sent′ (ri zent′) *v.* feel indignant or injured at. —**re•sent′ful,** *adj.* —**re•sent′ment,** *n.*

res′er•va′tion (rez′ər vā′shən) *n.* **1.** act of withholding or setting apart. **2.** particular doubt or misgiving. **3.** advance assurance of accommodations. **4.** land for use of an Indian tribe.

re•serve′ (ri zûrv′) *v.,* -served, -serving, *n., adj.* —*v.* **1.** keep back; set apart. —*n.* **2.** something reserved. **3.** part of military force held in readiness to support active forces. **4.** reticence; aloofness. —*adj.* **5.** kept in reserve.

re•served′, *adj.* **1.** held for future use. **2.** self-restrained. —**re•serv′ed•ly,** *adv.*

re•serv′ist, *n.* member of military reserves.

res′er•voir′ (rez′ər vwär′, -vwôr′, rez′ə-) *n.* **1.** place where water is stored for use. **2.** supply.

resid residual.

re•side′ (ri zīd′) *v.,* -sided, -siding. **1.** dwell. **2.** be vested, as powers.

res′i•dence (rez′i dəns) *n.* **1.** dwelling place. **2.** act or fact of residing. —**res′i•dent,** *n.* —**res′i•den′tial** (-den′shəl) *adj.*

res′i•den•cy, *n., pl.* -cies. **1.** residence (def. 2). **2.** period of advanced medical training.

res′i•due′ (-dōō′, -dyōō′) *n.* remainder. —**re•sid′u•al** (ri zij′ōō əl) *adj.*

re•sign′ (ri zīn′) *v.* **1.** give up (job, office, etc.), esp. formally. **2.** submit, as to fate or force. —**res′ig•na′tion** (rez′ig nā′shən) *n.*

re•signed′, *adj.* acquiescent.

re•sil′i•ent (ri zil′yənt) *adj.* **1.** springing back. **2.** recovering readily from adversity. —**re•sil′i•ence,** *n.*

res′in (rez′in) *n.* exudation from some plants, used in medicines, etc. —**res′in•ous,** *adj.*

re•sist′ (ri zist′) *v.* withstand; offer opposition to. —**re•sist′ant,** *adj.* —**re•sist′ance,** *n.* —**re•sist′er,** *n.*

re•sis′tor, *n.* device that introduces resistance into electrical circuit.

resin resolution.

resn resonant.

res′o•lute′ (rez′ə lōōt′) *adj.* determined on action or result. —**res′o•lute′ly,** *adv.* —**res′o•lute′ness,** *n.*

res′o•lu′tion, *n.* **1.** formal expression of

R

group opinion. **2.** determination. **3.** solution of problem.

re·solve' (ri zolv') v., **-solved, -solving,** n. —v. **1.** decide firmly. **2.** state formally. **3.** clear away. **4.** solve. —n. **5.** resolution.

res'o·nant (rez'ə nənt) adj. **1.** resounding. **2.** rich in sound. —**res'o·nance,** n. —**res'o·nant·ly,** adv.

res'o·nate (-nāt') v., **-nated, -nating. 1.** resound. **2.** produce resonance.

re·sort' (ri zôrt') v. **1.** apply or turn (to) for use, help, etc. **2.** go often. —n. **3.** place much frequented, esp. for recreation. **4.** recourse.

re·sound' (ri zound') v. echo.

re·sound'ing, adj. impressively thorough or complete. —**re·sound'ing·ly,** adv.

re'source (rē'sôrs, ri sôrs') n. **1.** source of aid or supply. **2.** (pl.) wealth.

re·source'ful, adj. clever. —**re·source'ful·ly,** adv. —**re·source'ful·ness,** n.

resp. 1. respective. **2.** respectively. **3.** respelled; respelling. **4.** respondent.

re·spect' (ri spekt') n. **1.** detail; point. **2.** reference. **3.** esteem. —v. **4.** hold in esteem. **5.** refer to; concern. —**re·spect'er,** n.

re·spect'a·ble, adj. **1.** worthy of respect. **2.** decent. —**re·spect'a·bil'i·ty,** n. —**re·spect'a·bly,** adv.

re·spect'ful, adj. showing respect. —**re·spect'ful·ly,** adv. —**re·spect'ful·ness,** n.

re·spect'ing, prep. concerning.

re·spec'tive, adj. in order previously named. —**re·spec'tive·ly,** adv.

Res. Phys. Resident Physician.

res'pi·ra·tor (res'pə rā'tər) n. apparatus to produce artificial breathing.

re·spire' (ri spīᵊr') v., **-spired, -spiring.** breathe. —**res'pi·ra'tion** (res'pə rā'shən) n. —**res'pi·ra·to'ry,** adj.

res'pite (res'pit) n., v., **-pited, -piting.** —n. **1.** temporary relief or delay. —v. **2.** relieve or cease temporarily.

re·splend'ent (ri splen'dənt) adj. gleaming. —**re·splend'ence,** n.

re·spond' (ri spond') v. answer.

re·spond'ent, adj. **1.** answering. —n. **2.** Law. defendant.

re·sponse' (-spons') n. reply. —**re·spon'sive,** adj. —**re·spon'sive·ly,** adv. —**re·spon'sive·ness,** n.

re·spon'si·bil'i·ty, n., pl. **-ties. 1.** state of being responsible. **2.** obligation. **3.** initiative.

re·spon'si·ble, adj. **1.** causing or allowing things to happen. **2.** capable of rational thought. **3.** reliable. —**re·spon'si·bly,** adv.

rest (rest) n. **1.** refreshing quiet. **2.** cessation from motion, work, etc. **3.** support. **4.** Music. interval of silence. **5.** remainder; others. —v. **6.** be quiet or at ease. **7.** cease from motion. **8.** lie or lay. **9.** be based. **10.** rely. **11.** continue to be. —**rest'ful,** adj. —**rest'ful·ly,** adv. —**rest'ful·ness,** n. —**rest'less,** adj. —**rest'less·ly,** adv. —**rest'less·ness,** n.

res'tau·rant (res'tər ənt, -tə ränt') n. public eating place.

res'tau·ra·teur' (-tər ə tûr') n. restaurant owner.

res'ti·tu'tion (res'ti tōō'shən, -tyōō'-) n. **1.** reparation. **2.** return of rights, etc.

res'tive (res'tiv) adj. restless. —**res'tive·ly,** adv.

re·store' (ri stôr') v., **-stored, -storing. 1.** bring back, as to use or good condition. **2.** give back. —**res'to·ra'tion,** n. —**re·stor'a·tive,** adj., n.

restr. 1. restaurant. **2.** restorer.

re·strain' (ri strān') v. **1.** hold back. **2.** confine.

re·straint' (-strānt') n. **1.** restraining influence. **2.** confinement. **3.** constraint.

re·strict' (ri strikt') v. confine; limit. —**re·stric'tion,** n. —**re·stric'tive,** adj.

rest room, room in public building with washbowls and toilets.

re·sult' (ri zult') n. **1.** outcome; consequence. —v. **2.** occur as result. **3.** end. —**re·sult'ant,** adj., n.

re·sume' (ri zōōm') v., **-sumed, -suming. 1.** go on with again. **2.** take again. —**re·sump'tion** (-zump'shən) n.

ré'su·mé' (rez'ōō mā') n. summary, esp. of education and work.

re·sur'face (rē sûr'fis) v., **-faced, -facing. 1.** give new surface to. **2.** come to the surface again.

re·sur'gent (ri sûr'jənt) adj. rising again. —**re·sur'gence,** n.

res'ur·rect' (rez'ə rekt') v. bring to life again. —**res'ur·rec'tion,** n.

re·sus'ci·tate' (ri sus'i tāt') v. revive. —**re·sus'ci·ta'tion,** n.

ret. 1. retain. **2.** retired. **3.** return. **4.** returned.

re'tail (rē'tāl) n. **1.** sale of goods to consumer. —v. **2.** sell at retail. —**re'tail·er,** n.

re·tain' (ri tān') v. **1.** keep or hold. **2.** engage. —**re·tain'a·ble,** adj.

re·tain'er, n. **1.** fee paid to secure services. **2.** old servant.

re·take' v., **-took, -taken, -taking.** (rē tāk') **1.** take again. **2.** photograph again. —n. (rē' tāk) **3.** picture photographed again.

re·tal'i·ate' (ri tal'ē āt') v., **-ated, -ating.** return like for like, esp. evil. —**re·tal'i·a'tion,** n. —**re·tal'i·a·to'ry** (-ə tôr'ē) adj.

re·tard' (ri tärd') v. delay; hinder. —**re'tar·da'tion,** n.

re·tard'ant, n. substance slowing chemical reaction.

re·tard'ed, adj. **1.** slow or weak in mental development. —n.pl. **2.** retarded persons.

retch (rech) v. try to vomit.

retd. 1. retained. **2.** retired. **3.** returned.

re·ten'tion (ri ten'shən) n. **1.** retaining. **2.** power of retaining. **3.** memory. —**re·ten'tive,** adj.

ret'i·cent (ret'ə sənt) adj. saying little. —**ret'i·cence,** n. —**ret'i·cent·ly,** adv.

ret′i•na (ret′n ə) *n.* coating on back part of eyeball that receives images. **—ret′i•nal,** *adj.*

ret′i•nue′ (ret′n ōō′, -yōō′) *n.* train of attendants.

re•tire′ (ri tī°r′) *v.,* **-tired, -tiring. 1.** withdraw. **2.** go to bed. **3.** end working life. **4.** put out (a batter, etc.) **—re•tire′ment,** *n.*

re•tired′, *adj.* **1.** withdrawn from office, occupation, etc. **2.** secluded.

re•tir′ee′, *n.* person who has retired.

re•tir′ing, *adj.* shy.

retn retain.

re•tool′ (rē tōōl′) *v.* replace tools and machinery of.

re•tort′ (ri tôrt′) *v.* **1.** reply smartly. **—***n.* **2.** sharp or witty reply. **3.** long-necked vessel used in distilling.

re•touch′ (rē tuch′) *v.* touch up.

retr retract.

re•trace′ (rē trās′) *v.,* **-traced, -tracing.** go back over.

re•tract′ (ri trakt′) *v.* withdraw. **—re•trac′-tion,** *n.* **—re•tract′a•ble,** *adj.*

re′tread (rē tred′) *n.* **1.** tire that has had new tread added. **2.** *Informal.* person returned to former position or occupation. **3.** reviving or reworking of old or familiar idea, story, etc.

re•treat′ (ri trēt′) *n.* **1.** forced withdrawal. **2.** private place. **—***v.* **3.** make a retreat. **4.** withdraw.

re•trench′ (ri trench′) *v.* reduce expenses. **—re•trench′ment,** *n.*

ret′ri•bu′tion (re′trə byōō′shən) *n.* requital according to merits, esp. for evil. **—re•trib′-u•tive** (ri trib′yə tiv) *adj.*

re•trieve′ (ri trēv′) *v.,* **-trieved, -trieving,** *n.* **—***v.* **1.** regain or restore. **2.** make amends for. **3.** recover (killed game). **—***n.* **4.** recovery. **—re•triev′er,** *n.*

retro 1. retroactive. **2.** retrograde.

ret′ro•ac′tive (re′trō ak′tiv) *adj.* applying also to past. **—ret′ro•ac′tive•ly,** *adv.*

ret′ro•fit′, *v.,* **-fitted, -fitting.** refit with newly developed equipment.

ret′ro•grade′ (re′trə-) *adj., v.,* **-graded, -grading.** **—***adj.* **1.** moving backward. **—***v.* **2.** move backward. **3.** degenerate.

ret′ro•gress′ (re′trə gres′) *v.* return to earlier or more primitive condition. **—ret′ro•gres′sion,** *n.* **—ret′ro•gres′sive,** *adj.*

ret′ro•spect′ (re′trə spekt′) *n.* occasion of looking back. **—ret′ro•spec′tive,** *adj.* **—ret′-ro•spec′tion,** *n.*

re•turn′ (ri tûrn′) *v.* **1.** go or come back to former place or condition. **2.** put or bring back. **3.** reply. **—***n.* **4.** act or fact of returning. **5.** recurrence. **6.** requital. **7.** reply. **8.** (often *pl.*) profit. **9.** report. **—re•turn′a•ble,** *adj.*

re•turn′ee (ri tûr nē′, -tûr′nē) *n., pl.* **-ees.** person who has returned.

re′u•nite′ (rē′yə nīt′) *v.,* **-nited, -niting.** unite after separation. **—re•un′ion,** *n.*

rev (rev) *n., v.,* **revved, revving.** *Informal,*

—*n.* **1.** revolution (in machinery). **—***v.* **2.** increase speed of (motor).

Rev., Reverend.

re•vamp′ (rē vamp′) *v.* renovate.

re•veal′ (ri vēl′) *v.* disclose.

rev•eil•le (rev′ə lē) *n.* Mil. signal for awakening.

rev′el (rev′əl) *v.,* **-eled, -eling. 1.** enjoy greatly. **2.** make merry. **—***n.* **3.** merrymaking. **—rev′e•ler,** *n.* **—rev′el•ry,** *n.*

rev′e•la′tion, *n.* disclosure.

re•venge′ (ri venj′) *n., v.,* **-venged, -venging.** **—***n.* **1.** harm in return for harm; retaliation. **2.** vindictiveness. **—***v.* **3.** take revenge. **—re•venge′ful,** *adj.* **—re•veng′er,** *n.*

rev′e•nue′ (rev′ən yōō′, -ə nōō′) *n.* income, esp. of government or business.

re•ver′ber•ate′ (ri vûr′bə rāt′) *v.,* **-ated, -ating. 1.** echo back. **2.** reflect. **—re•ver′ber•a′tion,** *n.*

re•vere′ (ri vēr′) *v.,* **-vered, -vering.** hold in deep respect.

rev′er•ence (rev′ər əns) *n., v.,* **-enced, -encing.** **—***n.* **1.** deep respect and awe. **—***v.* **2.** regard with reverence. **—rev′er•ent, rev′er•en′tial** (-ə ren′shəl) *adj.* **—rev′er•ent•ly,** *adv.*

Rev′er•end, *adj.* title used with name of member of the clergy.

rev′er•ie (rev′ə rē) *n.* fanciful musing. Also, **rev′er•y.**

re•verse′ (ri vûrs′) *adj., n., v.,* **-versed, -versing.** **—***adj.* **1.** opposite in position, action, etc. **2.** of or for backward motion. **—***n.* **3.** reverse part, position, etc. **4.** misfortune. **—***v.* **5.** turn in the opposite position, direction, or condition. **—re•ver′sal,** *n.* **—re•vers′i•ble,** *adj.*

re•vert′ (-vûrt′) *v.* go back to earlier state, topic, etc. **—re•ver′sion,** *n.*

re•view′, *n.* **1.** critical article. **2.** repeated viewing. **3.** inspection. **—***v.* **4.** view again. **5.** inspect. **6.** survey. **7.** write a review of. **—re•view′er,** *n.*

re•vile′ (ri vīl′) *v.,* **-viled, -viling.** speak abusively to or about. **—re•vile′ment,** *n.*

re•vise′ (ri vīz′) *v.,* **-vised, -vising.** change or amend content of. **—re•vi′sion,** *n.* **—re•vis′er,** *n.*

re•vi′sion•ism (ri vizh′ə niz′əm) *n.* departure from accepted doctrine. **—re•vi′sion•ist,** *n., adj.*

re•vi′tal•ize′ (rē vīt′l īz′) *v.,* **-ized, -izing.** bring new vitality to. **—re•vi′tal•i•za′tion,** *n.*

re•viv′al (ri vī′vəl) *n.* **1.** restoration to life, use, etc. **2.** religious awakening. **—re•viv′al•ist,** *n.*

re•vive′, *v.,* **-vived, -viving.** bring back to life. **—re•viv′a•ble,** *adj.* **—re•viv′er,** *n.*

re•viv′i•fy′ (ri viv′əfī′) *v.,* **-fied, -fying.** bring back to life. **—re•viv′i•fi•ca′tion,** *n.*

re•voke′ (ri vōk′) *v.,* **-voked, -voking.** annul

R

or repeal. —**rev′o•ca•ble** (rev′ə kə bəl) *adj.*
—**rev′o•ca′tion,** *n.*

re•volt′ (ri vōlt′) *v.* **1.** rebel. **2.** feel disgust.
3. fill with disgust. —*n.* **4.** rebellion. **5.** loathing. —**re•volt′ing,** *adj.*

rev′o•lu′tion (rev′ə lōō′shən) *n.* **1.** overthrow of established government. **2.** fundamental change. **3.** rotation. —**rev′o•lu′tion•**
ar′y, *adj.*, *n.* —**rev′o•lu′tion•ist,** *n.*

rev′o•lu′tion•ize′, *v.*, -ized, -izing. cause
fundamental change in.

re•volve′ (ri volv′) *v.*, -volved, -volving. **1.**
turn round, as on axis. **2.** consider.

re•volv′er, *n.* pistol with revolving cylinder
holding cartridges.

Rev. Stat. Revised Statutes.

re•vue′ (ri vyōō′) *n.* theatrical show.

re•vul′sion (ri vul′shən) *n.* violent change of
feeling, esp. to disgust.

Rev. Ver. Revised Version (of the Bible).

rew rewind.

re•ward′ (ri wôrd′) *n.* **1.** recompense for
merit, service, etc. —*v.* **2.** give reward.

re•ward′ing, *adj.* giving satisfaction.

re•word′ (rē wûrd′) *v.* put into other words.

re•write′, *v.*, -wrote, -written, -writing. **1.**
revise. **2.** write again.

RF 1. radiofrequency. **2.** *Baseball.* right field;
right fielder.

rf *Baseball.* right field; right fielder.

R.F. Reserve Force.

r.f. 1. range finder. **2.** rapid-fire. **3.** reducing
flame. **4.** *Baseball.* right field; right fielder.

R.F.A. Royal Field Artillery.

r.f.b. *Sports.* right fullback. Also, **R.F.B.**

RFC Reconstruction Finance Corporation.

rfc radio-frequency choke.

RFD, rural free delivery.

RFE Radio Free Europe. Also, **R.F.E.**

rfgt refrigerant.

RFI radio frequency interference.

RFLP (rif′lip′), restriction fragment length pol-
ymorphism: a fragment of DNA used to trace
family relationships. Also called **riflip.**

rflx reflex.

RFQ *Commerce.* request for quotation.

r.g. *Football.* right guard.

RGB *Television.* red-green-blue.

rgd rigid.

rglr regular.

rglt regulate.

rgltd regulated.

rgltr regulator.

RGNP real gross national product.

rgtr register.

RH *Meteorology.* relative humidity. Also, **rh**

Rh 1. *Physiology.* Rh factor. **2.** *Metallurgy.*
Rockwell hardness.

Rh *Symbol, Chemistry.* rhodium.

R.H. Royal Highness.

r.h. right hand. right-handed.

rhap′so•dize′ (rap′sə dīz′) *v.*, -dized, -diz-
ing. talk with extravagant enthusiasm.

rhap′so•dy (-sə dē) *n.*, *pl.* -dies. **1.** exaggerated expression of enthusiasm. **2.** irregular
musical composition.

r.h.b. *Football.* right halfback. Also, **RHB,**
R.H.B.

rhd railhead.

rheo rheostat.

rhe′o•stat′ (rē′ə stat′) *n.* device for regulating electric current.

rhe′sus (rē′səs) *n.* kind of monkey.

rhet′o•ric (ret′ər ik) *n.* **1.** skillful use of language. **2.** exaggerated speech. —**rhe•tor′i•**
cal (ri tôr′i kəl) *adj.*

rhetorical question, question asked for effect, not answer.

rheum (rōōm) *n.* thin discharge of mucous
membranes.

rheu′ma•tism′ (rōō′mə tiz′əm) *n.* disease
affecting joints or muscles. —**rheu•mat′ic**
(rōō mat′ik) *adj.*, *n.*

Rh factor, antigen in blood that may cause
severe reaction in individual lacking the substance.

rhine′stone′ (rīn′stōn′) *n.* artificial dia-
mondlike gem.

rhi•ni′tis (rī nī′tis) *n.* inflammation of the
nose.

rhi•noc′er•os (rī nos′ər əs) *n.* large thick-
skinned mammal with horned snout.

RHIP rank has its privileges.

rhi′zome (rī′zōm) *n.* rootlike stem.

Rhn *Metallurgy.* Rockwell hardness number.

Rho. Rhodesia. Also, **Rhod.**

rho′do•den′dron (rō′də den′drən) *n.* flov·
ering evergreen shrub.

rhomb 1. rhombic. **2.** rhomboid.

rhom′boid (rom′boid) *n.* oblique-angled parallelogram with only the opposite sides
equal.

rhom′bus (-bəs) *n.*, *pl.* -buses, -bi (-bī).
oblique-angled parallelogram with all sides
equal.

rhu′barb (rōō′bärb) *n.* garden plant with edible leaf stalks.

rhyme (rīm) *n.*, *v.*, rhymed, rhyming. —*n.* **1.**
agreement in end sounds of lines or words.
2. verse with such correspondence. —*v.* **3.**
make or form rhyme.

rhythm (riᵺ′əm) *n.* movement with uni-
formly recurring beat. —**rhyth′mic, rhyth′-**
mi•cal, *adj.* —**rhyth′mi•cal•ly,** *adv.*

RI, Rhode Island. Also, **R.I.**

rib (rib) *n.*, *v.*, ribbed, ribbing. —*n.* **1.** one of
the slender curved bones enclosing chest. **2.**
riblike part. —*v.* **3.** furnish with ribs. **4.** *Informal,* tease.

R.I.B.A. Royal Institute of British Architects.

rib′ald (rib′əld; *spelling pron.* rī′bəld) *adj.*
bawdy in speech. —**rib′ald•ry,** *n.*

rib′bon (rib′ən) *n.* strip of silk, rayon, etc.

ri•bo•fla′vin (rī′bō flā′vin, -bə-) important vitamin in milk, fresh meat, eggs, etc.

rice (rīs) *n.* edible starchy grain.

rich (rich) *adj.* **1.** having great possessions. **2.** abounding; fertile. **3.** costly. **4.** containing butter, eggs, cream, etc. **5.** strong; vivid. **6.** mellow. —*n.* **7.** rich people. —**rich′ly**, *adv.* —**rich′ness**, *n.*

rich′es, *n.pl.* wealth.

Rich′ter scale (rik′tər) scale for indicating intensity of earthquake.

rick (rik) *n.* stack of hay, etc.

rick′ets (rik′its) *n.* childhood disease often marked by bone deformities.

rick•et•y (rik′i tē) *adj.*, **-ier**, **-iest**. shaky.

rick′shaw (rik′shô, -shä) *n.* two-wheeled passenger vehicle pulled by person.

RICO (rē′kō), Racketeer Influenced and Corrupt Organizations Act.

ric′o•chet′ (rik′ə shā′) *v.*, **-cheted** (-shād′), **-cheting** (-shā′ing), *n.* —*v.* **1.** rebound from a flat surface. —*n.* **2.** such a movement.

ri•cot′ta (ri kot′ə, -kô′tə) *n.* soft Italian cheese.

rid (rid) *v.*, **rid** or **ridded**, **ridding**. clear or free of. —**rid′dance**, *n.*

rid′dle (rid′l) *n.*, *v.*, **-dled**, **-dling**. —*n.* **1.** puzzling question or matter. **2.** coarse sieve. —*v.* **3.** speak perplexingly. **4.** pierce with many holes. **5.** put through sieve.

ride (rīd) *v.*, **rode** (rōd), **ridden**, **riding**, *n.* —*v.* **1.** be carried in traveling. **2.** sit on and manage (horse, etc.). **3.** rest on something. —*n.* **4.** journey on a horse, etc. **5.** vehicle or device in which people ride for amusement.

rid′er, *n.* **1.** person that rides. **2.** clause attached to legislative bill before passage.

ridge (rij) *n.*, *v.*, **ridged**, **ridging**. —*n.* **1.** long narrow elevation. —*v.* **2.** form with ridge.

ridge′pole′, *n.* horizontal beam on roof to which rafters are attached.

rid′i•cule′ (rid′i kyool′) *n.*, *v.*, **-culed**, **-culing**. —*n.* **1.** derision. —*v.* **2.** deride.

ri•dic′u•lous (ri dik′yə ləs) *adj.* absurd. —**ri•dic′u•lous•ly**, *adv.*

RIF (rif), **1.** *Military.* a reduction in the personnel of an armed service or unit. **2.** a reduction in the number of persons employed, especially for budgetary reasons. [*R(eduction) I(n) F(orce)*]

rife (rīf) *adj.* **1.** widespread. **2.** abounding.

riff (rif) *n.* **1.** repeated phrase in jazz or rock music. **2.** variation or improvisation, as on an idea. —*v.* **3.** perform a riff.

riff′raff′ (rif′raf′) *n.* rabble.

ri′fle (rī′fəl) *n.*, *v.*, **-fled**, **-fling**. —*n.* **1.** shoulder firearm with spirally grooved barrel. —*v.* **2.** cut spiral grooves in (gun barrel). **3.** search through to rob. **4.** steal. —**ri′fle•man**, *n.*

rift (rift) *n.* split.

rig (rig) *v.*, **rigged**, **rigging**, *n.* —*v.* **1.** fit with tackle and other parts. **2.** put together as makeshift. **3.** manipulate fraudulently or artificially. —*n.* **4.** arrangement of masts, booms, tackle, etc. **5.** equipment. —**rig′ger**, *n.*

rig′ging, *n.* ropes and chains that support and work masts, sails, etc.

right (rīt) *adj.* **1.** just or good. **2.** correct. **3.** in good condition. **4.** on side that is toward the east when one faces north. **5.** straight. —*n.* **6.** that which is right. **7.** right side. **8.** that justly due one. **9.** conservative side in politics. —*adv.* **10.** directly; completely. **11.** set correctly. **12.** in right position. **13.** correct. —**right′ly**, *adv.* —**right′ness**, *n.* —**right′ist**, *adj.*, *n.*

right angle, 90-degree angle.

right′eous (rī′chəs) *adj.* virtuous. —**right′eous•ly**, *adv.* —**right′eous•ness**, *n.*

right′ful, *adj.* belonging by or having just claim. —**right′ful•ly**, *adv.*

right′-hand′ed, *adj.* **1.** using the right hand more easily. **2.** for the right hand. —**right′-hand′edness**, *n.*

right of way, **1.** right of one vehicle to proceed ahead of another. **2.** path or route that may lawfully be used. **3.** strip of land acquired for use, as by railroad.

right′-to-life′, *adj.* advocating laws making abortion illegal. —**right′-to-lif′er**, *n.*

right wing, conservative element in organization. —**right′-wing′**, *adj.* —**right′-wing′er**, *n.*

rig′id (rij′id) *adj.* **1.** stiff; inflexible. **2.** rigorous. —**ri•gid′i•ty**, *n.* —**rig′id•ly**, *adv.*

rig′ma•role′ (rig′mə rōl′) *n.* confused talk.

rig′or (rig′ər) *n.* **1.** strictness. **2.** hardship. —**rig′or•ous**, *adj.* —**rig′or•ous•ly**, *adv.*

ri′gor mor′tis (rig′ər môr′tis) stiffening of body after death.

R.I.I.A. Royal Institute of International Affairs.

rile (rīl) *v.*, **riled**, **riling**. *Informal*, vex.

rill (ril) *n.* small brook.

rim (rim) *n.*, *v.*, **rimmed**, **rimming**. —*n.* **1.** outer edge. —*v.* **2.** furnish with rim.

rime (rīm) *n.*, *v.*, **rimed**, **riming**. —*n.* **1.** rhyme. **2.** rough white frost. —*v.* **3.** cover with rime.

rind (rīnd) *n.* firm covering, as of fruit or cheese.

ring (ring) *n.*, *v.*, **rang** (rang), **rung** (rung) (for 11, **ringed**), **ringing**. —*n.* **1.** round band for a finger. **2.** any circular band. **3.** enclosed area. **4.** group cooperating for selfish purpose. **5.** ringing sound. **6.** telephone call. —*v.* **7.** sound clearly and resonantly. **8.** seem; appear. **9.** be filled with sound. **10.** signal by bell. **11.** form ring around.

ring′er, *n.* **1.** person or thing that closely resembles another. **2.** athlete entered in competition in violation of eligibility rules.

ring′lead′er, *n.* leader in mischief.

ring′let (-lit) *n.* curl of hair.

ring′mas′ter, *n.* person in charge of performances in circus ring.

ring′worm′, *n.* contagious skin disease.

rink (ringk) *n.* floor or sheet of ice for skating on.

rinse (rins) *v.*, **rinsed, rinsing,** *n.* —*v.* **1.** wash lightly. —*n.* **2.** rinsing act. **3.** preparation for rinsing.

ri'ot (rī'ət) *n.* **1.** disturbance by mob. **2.** wild disorder. —*v.* **3.** take part in riot. —**ri'ot•ous,** *adj.*

rip (rip) *v.*, **ripped, ripping,** *n.* tear. —**rip'per,** *n.*

R.I.P., may he, she, or they rest in peace.

rip cord, cord that opens parachute.

ripe (rīp) *adj.*, **riper, ripest. 1.** fully developed; mature. **2.** ready. —**rip'en,** *v.* —**ripe'ness,** *n.*

rip'off', *n. Slang.* theft or exploitation.

ri•poste' (ri pōst') *n.* quick, sharp reply or reaction.

rip'ple (rip'əl) *v.*, **-pled, -pling,** *n.* —*v.* **1.** form small waves. —*n.* **2.** pattern of small waves.

ripple effect, spreading effect.

rip'-roar'ing, *adj.* boisterously exciting.

rip'saw', *n.* saw for cutting wood with the grain.

rip'tide', *n.* tide that opposes other tides.

RISC (risk), *Computers.* reduced instruction set computer.

rise (rīz) *v.*, **rose** (rōz), **ris•en** (riz'ən), **rising,** *n.* —*v.* **1.** get up. **2.** revolt. **3.** appear. **4.** originate. **5.** move upward. **6.** increase. **7.** (of dough) expand. —*n.* **8.** upward movement. **9.** origin. **10.** upward slope. —**ris'er,** *n.*

ris'i•ble (riz'ə bəl) *adj.* causing laughter.

risk (risk) *n.* **1.** dangerous chance. —*v.* **2.** expose to risk. **3.** take risk of. —**risk'y,** *adj.*

ris•qué' (ri skā') *adj.* bawdy.

rit. *Music.* ritardando. Also, **ritard.**

rite (rīt) *n.* ceremonial act.

rite of passage, event marking passage from one stage of life to another.

rit'u•al (rich'ōō əl) *n.* system of religious or other rites. —**rit'u•al•ism** (-ə liz'əm) *n.* —**rit'u•al•is'tic,** *adj.*

riv. river.

ri'val (rī'vəl) *n.*, *adj.*, *v.*, **-valed, -valing.** —*n.* **1.** competitor. **2.** equal. —*adj.* **3.** being a rival. —*v.* **4.** compete with. **5.** match. —**ri'val•ry,** *n.*

rive (rīv) *v.*, **rived, rived** or **riv•en** (riv'ən), **riving.** split.

riv'er (riv'ər) *n.* large natural stream.

riv'et (riv'it) *n.*, *v.*, **-eted, -eting.** —*n.* **1.** metal bolt hammered after insertion. —*v.* **2.** fasten with rivets.

riv'u•let (riv'yə lit) *n.* small stream.

RJ *Military.* road junction.

rkt rocket.

RL resistance-inductance.

RLB *Football.* right linebacker.

RLC resistance, inductance, capacitance.

rlct *Electricity.* reluctance.

rld rolled.

R.L.D. retail liquor dealer.

rlf relief.

RLL *Computers.* run-length limited.

R.L.O. returned letter office.

rloc relocate.

rlr roller.

rlse release.

rlt relate.

rltn relation.

rltv relative.

rlv relieve.

rlxn relaxation.

rly relay.

RM (in Germany) reichsmark.

rm range marks.

rm. 1. ream. **2.** room.

r.m. (in Germany) reichsmark.

R.M.A. *British.* **1.** Royal Marine Artillery. **2.** Royal Military Academy.

R.M.C. *British.* Royal Military College.

rmd remedy.

rmdr remainder.

rms *Math.* root mean square. Also, **r.m.s.**

R.M.S. 1. Railway Mail Service. **2.** *British.* Royal Mail Service. **3.** *British.* Royal Mail Steamship.

rmt remote.

rmv remove.

rmvbl removable.

RN, registered nurse.

RNA *Genetics.* ribonucleic acid.

R.N.A.S. *British.* Royal Naval Air Service.

RNase (är'en'ās, -āz), *Biochemistry.* ribonuclease. Also, **RNAase** (är'en'ā'ās, -āz).

RNC Republican National Committee.

rnd. round.

rndm random.

rng range.

rnge range.

rngg ringing.

rngr *Telephones.* ringer.

rnl renewal.

RNP *Biochemistry.* a nucleoprotein containing RNA. [*r(ibo)n(ucleo)p(rotein)*]

R.N.R. *British.* Royal Naval Reserve.

rnwbl renewable.

R.N.W.M.P. *Canadian.* Royal Northwest Mounted Police.

rnwy runway.

rny rainy.

RO. (in Oman) rial omani.

ro. 1. *Bookbinding.* recto. **2.** roan. **3.** rood.

R.O. 1. Receiving Office. **2.** Receiving Officer. **3.** Regimental Order. **4.** *British.* Royal Observatory.

ROA *Accounting.* return on assets.

roach (rōch) *n.* cockroach.

road (rōd) *n.* **1.** open way for travel. **2.** Also, **road'stead'.** anchorage near shore.

road'block', *n.* **1.** obstruction placed across road to halt traffic. **2.** obstacle to progress.

road'run'ner, *n.* terrestrial cuckoo of western U.S.

road show, show, as a play, performed by touring actors.

roam (rōm) *v.* wander; rove.

roan (rōn) *adj.* **1.** horse with gray or white spots. —*n.* **2.** roan horse.

roar (rôr) *v.* **1.** make loud, deep sound. —*n.* **2.** loud, deep sound. **3.** loud laughter.

roast (rōst) *v.* **1.** cook by dry heat. —*n.* **2.** roasted meat. —**roast'er**, *n.*

rob (rob) *v.*, **robbed, robbing.** deprive of unlawfully. —**rob'ber**, *n.* —**rob'ber•y**, *n.*

robe (rōb) *n.*, *v.*, **robed, robing.** —*n.* **1.** long loose garment. **2.** wrap or covering. —*v.* **3.** clothe.

rob'in (rob'in) *n.* red-breasted bird.

ro'bot (rō'bət, -bot) *n.* **1.** humanlike machine that performs tasks. **2.** person who acts in mechanical manner.

ro•bot'ics, *n.* technology of computer-controlled robots.

ro•bust' (rō bust', rō'bust) *adj.* healthy.

rock (rok) *n.* **1.** mass of stone. **2.** Also, **rock-'n'-roll.** popular music with steady, insistent rhythm. —*v.* **3.** move back and forth. —**rock'y**, *adj.*

rock bottom, lowest level.

rock'er, *n.* curved support of cradle or **rock'-ing chair.**

rock'et (rok'it) *n.* tube propelled by discharge of gases from it.

rock'et•ry, *n.* science of rocket design.

rock'-ribbed', *adj.* **1.** having ridges of rock. **2.** unyielding.

rock salt, salt occurring in rocklike masses.

ro•co'co (rə kō'kō, rō'kə kō') *n.* elaborate decorative style of many curves. —**ro•co'co,** *adj.*

rod (rod) *n.* **1.** slender shaft. **2.** linear measure of 5½ yards.

ro'dent (rōd'nt) *n.* small gnawing or nibbling mammal.

ro'de•o' (rō'dē ō', rō dā'ō) *n.*, *pl.* **-deos.** exhibition of cowboy skills.

roe (rō) *n.*, *pl.* **roes, roe. 1.** small deer. **2.** fish eggs or spawn.

roent•gen (rent'gən, -jən) *n.* unit for measuring radiation dosage.

R.O.G. *Commerce.* receipt of goods. Also, **ROG, r.o.g.**

rog'er (roj'ər) *interj.* (message) received.

rogue (rōg) *n.* rascal. —**ro'guish,** *adj.* —**ro'guer•y,** *n.*

ROI return on investment. Also, **R.O.I.**

roil (roil) *v.* **1.** make muddy. **2.** vex. —**roil'y,** *adj.*

roist'er (roi'stər) *v.* **1.** swagger. **2.** carouse. —**roist'er•er,** *n.*

ROK Republic of Korea.

role (rōl) *n.* part of function, as of character in play. Also, **rôle.**

role model, person imitated by others.

roll (rōl) *v.* **1.** move by turning. **2.** rock. **3.** have deep, loud sound. **4.** flatten with roller. **5.** form into roll or ball. —*n.* **6.** list; register. **7.** anything cylindrical. **8.** small cake. **9.** deep long sound. —**roll'er,** *n.*

roll'back', *n.* return to lower level.

roll call, calling of names for checking attendance.

Roll'er•blade', *n.*, *v.*, **-blad•ed, -blad•ing.** —*n.* **1.** *Trademark.* brand of in-line skates. —*v.* **2.** (*often l.c.*) skate on in-line skates.

roller coaster, 1. small railroad that moves along winding route with steep inclines. **2.** experience with sharp ups and downs.

roller skate, skate with four wheels. —**roller-skate,** *v.*

rol'lick•ing (rol'i king) *adj.* jolly.

rolling pin, cylinder for rolling out dough.

roll'o'ver, *n.* reinvestment of funds.

roll'-top desk, desk with flexible sliding cover.

ro'ly-po'ly (rō'lē pō'lē, -pō'lē) *adj.* short and round.

ROM (rom) read-only memory: nonmodifiable part of computer memory containing instructions to system.

ro•maine' (rō mān', rə-) *n.* kind of lettuce.

Ro'man (rō'mən) **1.** native or citizen of Rome or Roman Empire. **2.** (*l.c.*) upright style of printing type. —**Ro'man,** *adj.*

Roman candle, kind of firework.

Roman Catholic Church, Christian Church of which pope (Bishop of Rome) is head. —**Roman Catholic.**

ro•mance' (rō mans') *n.*, *v.*, **-manced, -mancing.** —*n.* **1.** colorful, imaginative tale. **2.** colorful, fanciful quality. **3.** love affair. —*v.* **4.** act romantically. **5.** tell fanciful, false story.

Roman numerals, system of numbers using letters as symbols: I = 1, V = 5, X = 10, L = 50, C = 100, D = 500, M = 1,000.

ro•man'tic (rō man'tik) *adj.* **1.** of romance. **2.** impractical or unrealistic. **3.** imbued with idealism. **4.** preoccupied with love. **5.** passionate; fervent. **6.** of a style of art stressing imagination and emotion. —*n.* **7.** romantic person. —**ro•man'ti•cal•ly,** *adv.*

ro•man'ti•cism (-tə siz'əm) *n.* (*often cap.*) romantic spirit or artistic style or movement. —**ro•man'ti•cist,** *n.*

ro•man'ti•cize', *v.*, **-cized, -cizing.** invest with romantic character.

Rom. Cath. Roman Catholic.

Rom. Cath. Ch. Roman Catholic Church.

romp (romp) *v.*, *n.* frolic.

romp'ers, *n.pl.* child's loose outer garment.

RONA *Accounting.* return on net assets.

rood (rōōd) *n.* **1.** crucifix. **2.** one-quarter of an acre.

roof (rōōf, rŏŏf) *n.*, *pl.* **roofs. 1.** upper cover-

R

ing of building. —*v.* **2.** provide with roof. —roof′er, *n.* —roof′ing, *n.*

rook (rŏŏk) *n.* **1.** European crow. **2.** chess piece; castle. —*v.* **3.** cheat.

rook′ie, *n. Slang.* recruit or beginner.

room (rŏŏm, rŏŏm) *n.* **1.** separate space within building. **2.** space. —*v.* **3.** lodge. —room′er, *n.* —room′mate′, *n.* —room′y, *adj.*

roost (rŏŏst) *n.* **1.** perch where fowls rest. —*v.* **2.** sit on roost.

roost′er, *n.* male chicken.

root (rŏŏt, rŏŏt) *n.* **1.** part of plant growing underground. **2.** embedded part. **3.** origin. **4.** quantity that, when multiplied by itself so many times, produces given quantity. —*v.* **5.** establish roots. **6.** implant. **7. root out,** exterminate. **8.** dig with snout. **9.** *Informal,* cheer encouragingly. —root′er, *n.*

root beer, soft drink flavored with extracts of roots, barks, and herbs.

root canal, root portion of the pulp cavity of a tooth.

R.O.P. run-of-paper: a designation specifying that the position of a newspaper or magazine advertisement is to be determined by the publisher.

rope (rōp) *n., v.,* **roped, roping.** —*n.* **1.** strong twisted cord. —*v.* **2.** fasten or catch with rope.

Roque′fort (rōk′fərt) *n. Trademark.* strong cheese veined with mold, made from sheep's milk.

R.O.R. *Law.* released on own recognizance.

Ror′schach test (rôr′shäk) diagnostic test of personality based on interpretations of inkblot designs.

ROS *Computers.* read only storage.

ro′sa•ry (rō′zə rē) *n., pl.* **-ries.** *Rom. Cath. Ch.* **1.** series of prayers. **2.** string of beads counted in saying rosary.

rose (rōz) *n.* thorny plant having showy, fragrant flowers.

ro•sé (rō zā′) *n.* pink wine.

ro′se•ate (rō′zē it, -āt′) *adj.* **1.** rosy. **2.** promising; bright.

rose′mar′y (rōz′mâr′ē, -mə rē) *n.* aromatic shrub used for seasoning.

ro•sette′ (rō zet′) *n.* rose-shaped ornament.

Rosh′ Ha•sha′na (rōsh′ hä shä′nə) Jewish New Year.

ros′in (roz′in) *n.* solid left after distilling pine resin.

ros′ter (ros′tər) *n.* list of persons, groups, events, etc.

ros′trum (ros′trəm) *n., pl.* **-trums, -tra** (-trə). speakers' platform.

ros′y (rō′zē) *adj.,* **-ier, -iest. 1.** pink or pinkish-red. **2.** cheerful; optimistic. **3.** bright. —ros′i•ly, *adv.* —ros′i•ness, *n.*

rot (rot) *v.,* **rotted, rotting,** *n.* —*v.* **1.** decay. —*n.* **2.** decay. **3.** decay of tissue.

ro′tate (rō′tāt) *v.,* **-tated, -tating.** turn on or as on axis. —ro′ta•ry (-tə rē) *adj.* —rota′-tion, *n.* —ro′ta•tor, *n.*

ROTC (är′ō tē sē′, rot′sē) Reserve Officers Training Corps.

rote (rōt) *n.* **1.** routine way. **2. by rote,** from memory in mechanical way.

ro•tis′ser•ie (rō tis′ə rē) *n.* rotating machine for roasting.

ro′tor (rō′tər) *n.* rotating part.

ro′to•till′er (rō′tə til′ər) *n.* motorized device with spinning blades for tilling soil.

rotr rotator.

rot′ten (rot′n) *adj.* **1.** decaying. **2.** corrupt. —rot′ten•ly, *adv.* —rot′ten•ness, *n.*

ro•tund′ (rō tund′) *adj.* round. —ro•tun′di•ty, *n.*

ro•tun′da (rō tun′də) *n.* round room.

rou•é′ (rŏŏ ā′) *n.* dissolute man; rake.

rouge (rŏŏzh) *n., v.,* **rouged, rouging.** —*n.* **1.** red cosmetic for cheeks and lips. **2.** red polishing agent for metal. —*v.* **3.** color with rouge.

rough (ruf) *adj.* **1.** not smooth. **2.** violent in action or motion. **3.** harsh. **4.** crude. —*n.* **5.** rough thing or part. —*v.* **6.** make rough. —rough′ly, *adv.* —rough′ness, *n.*

rough′age (-ij) *n.* coarse or fibrous material in food.

rough′en, *v.* make or become rough.

rou•lette′ (rŏŏ let′) *n.* gambling game based on spinning disk.

Roum. 1. Roumania. **2.** Roumanian.

round (round) *adj.* **1.** circular, curved, or spherical. **2.** complete. **3.** expressed as approximate number. **4.** sonorous. —*n.* **5.** something round. **6.** complete course, series, etc. **7.** part of beef thigh between rump and leg. **8.** song in which voices enter at intervals. **9.** stage of competition, as in tournament. —*adv.* **10.** in or as in a circle. **11.** in circumference. —*prep.* **12.** around. —*v.* **13.** make round. **14.** complete. **15.** bring together. —round′ness, *n.*

round′a•bout′, *adj.* indirect.

roun′de•lay (roun′dl ā′) *n.* song in which phrase is staggered and repeated.

round′house′, *n.* building for servicing locomotives.

round′ly, *adv.* unsparingly.

round table, group gathered for conference.

round trip, trip to and back.

round′up′, *n.* **1.** bringing together. **2.** summary.

round′worm′, *n.* nematode that infests intestines of mammals.

rouse (rouz) *v.,* **roused, rousing.** stir up; arouse.

roust′a•bout′ (roust′ə bout′) *n.* laborer.

rout (rout) *n.* **1.** defeat ending in disorderly flight. —*v.* **2.** force to flee in disorder.

route (rŏŏt, rout) *n., v.,* **routed, routing.** —*n.* **1.** course of travel. —*v.* **2.** send by route.

rou•tine′ (rōō tēn′) *n.* **1.** regular order of action. —*adj.* **2.** like or by routine. **3.** ordinary. —**rou•tine′ly,** *adv.*

rove (rōv) *v.,* **roved, roving.** wander aimlessly. —**rov′er,** *n.*

row (rō) *v.* **1.** propel by oars. **2.** (rou) dispute noisily. —*n.* **3.** trip in rowboat. **4.** persons or things in line. **5.** (rou) noisy dispute. —**row′boat′,** *n.*

row′dy (rou′dē) *adj.,* **-dier, -diest,** *n., pl.* **-dies.** —*adj.* **1.** rough and disorderly. —*n.* **2.** rowdy person. —**row′di•ness,** *n.*

roy′al (roi′əl) *adj.* of kings or queens. —**roy′al•ly,** *adv.*

roy′al•ist, *n.* person favoring royal government. —**royalist,** *adj.* —**roy′al•ism,** *n.*

roy′al•ty, *n., pl.* **-ties. 1.** royal persons. **2.** royal power. **3.** share of proceeds, paid to an author, inventor, etc.

RP 1. *Linguistics.* Received Pronunciation. **2.** repurchase agreement. **3.** *Pathology.* retinitis pigmentosa.

Rp. (in Indonesia) rupiah; rupiahs.

R.P. 1. Reformed Presbyterian. **2.** Regius Professor.

RPG role-playing game.

rpg *Basketball.* rebounds per game.

rplr repeller.

rplsn repulsion.

rplt repellent.

rpm, revolutions per minute.

R.P.O. Railway Post Office. Also, **RPO**

RPQ request for price quotation.

rpr repair.

rprt report.

rps revolutions per second. Also, **r.p.s., r/s**

rpt. 1. repeat. **2.** report.

rptn repetition.

rptr repeater.

RPV *Military.* remotely piloted vehicle.

rpvntv rust preventive.

R.Q. *Physiology.* respiratory quotient.

RR, 1. railroad. **2.** rural route.

RRM renegotiable-rate mortgage.

rRNA *Biochemistry.* ribosomal RNA.

R.R.R. return receipt requested (used in registered mail). Also, **RRR**

RRT rail rapid transit.

R.R.T. registered respiratory therapist.

Rs. 1. (in Portugal) reis. **2.** (in India, Pakistan, and other countries) rupees.

R.S. 1. Recording Secretary. **2.** Reformed Spelling. **3.** Revised Statutes. **4.** Royal Society.

r.s. right side.

RSA Republic of South Africa.

rsc rescue.

rsch research.

RSE Received Standard English.

RSFSR Russian Soviet Federated Socialist Republic. Also, **R.S.F.S.R.**

rslvr resolver.

rspd respond.

rsps response.

rspsb responsible.

rspv 1. respective. **2.** responsive.

rsrc resource.

rss root sum square.

rst restore.

rstg roasting.

rstr 1. *Electronics.* raster. **2.** restrain. **3.** restrict.

RSV Revised Standard Version (of the Bible).

rsv reserve.

RSVP, please reply.

rsvr reservoir.

RSWC right side up with care.

RT radiotelephone.

rt. 1. rate. **2.** right.

r.t. *Football.* right tackle.

rtcl reticle.

rte. route. Also, **Rte.**

RTF *Genetics.* resistance transfer factor; R factor.

rtf *Computers.* rich-text format.

rtg rating.

Rt. Hon. Right Honorable.

RTL resistor-transistor logic.

rtn return.

rtng retaining.

rtnr retainer.

rtr rotor.

rtrv retrieve.

rtry rotary.

Rts. *Finance.* rights.

rtty radio teletypewriter.

rtw ready-to-wear.

rtz return-to-zero.

Ru *Symbol, Chemistry.* ruthenium.

rub (rub) *v.,* **rubbed, rubbing,** *n.* —*v.* **1.** apply pressure to in cleaning, smoothing, etc. **2.** press against with friction. —*n.* **3.** act of rubbing. **4.** difficulty.

rub′ber (rub′ər) *n.* **1.** elastic material from a tropical tree. **2.** *pl.* overshoes. —**rub′ber•ize′,** *v.,* **-ized, -izing.** —**rub′ber•y,** *adj.*

rubber band, band of rubber used for holding things together.

rubber cement, adhesive.

rub′ber•neck′, *Informal.* —*v.* **1.** stare curiously. —*n.* **2.** curious onlooker. **3.** sightseer.

rubber stamp, stamp with rubber printing surface.

rub′bish (rub′ish) *n.* **1.** waste. **2.** nonsense.

rub′ble (rub′əl) *n.* broken stone.

rub′down′, *n.* massage.

ru•bel′la (rōō bel′ə) *n.* usu. mild viral infection. Also, **German measles.**

ru′bi•cund′ (rōō′bi kund′) *adj.* red.

ru′ble (rōō′bəl) *n.* monetary unit of Russia and of some former Soviet states.

ru′bric (rōō′brik) *n.* **1.** title or heading. **2.** class or category.

ru′by (rōō′bē) *n., pl.* **-bies.** red gem.

R

ruck′sack′ (ruk′sak′, rŏŏk′-) *n.* knapsack.

ruck′us (ruk′əs) *n.* noisy commotion.

rud′der (rud′ər) *n.* turning flat piece for steering vessel or aircraft.

rud′dy (rud′ē) *adj.*, **-dier, -diest.** having healthy red color.

rude (rŏŏd) *adj.*, **ruder, rudest. 1.** discourteous. **2.** unrefined; crude. **—rude′ly,** *adv.* **—rude′ness,** *n.*

ru′di•ment (rŏŏ′də mənt) *n.* basic thing to learn. **—ru′di•men′ta•ry** (-men′tə rē) *adj.*

rue (rŏŏ) *v.*, **rued, ruing,** *n.* regret. **—rue′ful,** *adj.*

ruff (ruf) *n.* deep full collar.

ruf′fi•an (ruf′ē ən) *n.* rough or lawless person.

ruf′fle (ruf′əl) *v.*, **-fled, -fling,** *n.* **—v. 1.** make uneven. **2.** disturb. **3.** gather in folds. **4.** beat (drum) softly and steadily. **—n. 5.** break in evenness. **6.** band of cloth, etc., gathered on one edge. **7.** soft steady beat.

rug (rug) *n.* floor covering.

Rug′by (rug′bē) *n.* English form of football.

rug′ged (rug′id) *adj.* **1.** roughly irregular. **2.** severe. **—rug′ged•ly,** *adv.* **—rug′ged•ness,** *n.*

ru′in (rŏŏ′in) *n.* **1.** destruction. **2.** (*pl.*) remains of fallen building, etc. **—v. 3.** bring or come to ruin or ruins. **—ru′in•a′tion,** *n.* **—ru′in•ous,** *adj.*

rule (rŏŏl) *n.*, *v.*, **ruled, ruling. —n. 1.** principle; regulation. **2.** control. **3.** ruler (def. 2). **—v. 4.** control. **5.** decide in the manner of a judge. **6.** mark with ruler. **—rul′ing,** *n.*, *adj.*

rul′er, *n.* **1.** person who rules. **2.** straight-edged strip for measuring, drawing lines, etc.

rum (rum) *n.* alcoholic liquor.

rum′ba (rum′bə, rŏŏm′-) *n.* Cuban dance.

rum′ble (rum′bəl) *v.*, **-bled, -bling,** *n.* **—v. 1.** make long, deep, heavy sound. **—n. 2.** such sound.

ru′mi•nant (rŏŏ′mə nənt) *n.* **1.** cud-chewing mammal, as cows. **—adj. 2.** cud-chewing.

ru′mi•nate′ (-nāt′) *v.*, **-nated, -nating. 1.** chew cud. **2.** meditate. **—ru′mi•na′tion,** *n.* **—ru′mi•na′tive,** *adj.*

rum′mage (rum′ij) *v.*, **-maged, -maging.** search.

rum′my (rum′ē) *n.*, *pl.* **-mies. 1.** card game. **2.** *Slang.* drunkard.

ru′mor (rŏŏ′mər) *n.* **1.** unconfirmed but widely repeated story. **—v. 2.** tell as rumor.

rump (rump) *n.* **1.** hind part of animal's body. **2.** the buttocks.

rum′pus (rum′pəs) *n.* *Informal.* noise.

run (run) *v.*, **ran** (ran), **run, running,** *n.* **—v. 1.** advance quickly. **2.** be candidate. **3.** flow; melt. **4.** extend. **5.** operate. **6.** be exposed to. **7.** manage. **—n. 8.** act or period of running. **9.** raveled line in knitting. **10.** freedom of action. **11.** scoring unit in baseball.

run′a•round′, *n.* *Informal.* evasive treatment.

run′a•way′, *n.* **1.** fugitive; deserter. **2.** something that has broken away from control. **—adj. 3.** escaped; fugitive. **4.** uncontrolled.

run′-down′, *adj.* **1.** fatigued; weary. **2.** fallen into disrepair. **3.** not running because of not being wound.

run′down′, *n.* short summary.

rune (rŏŏn) *n.* ancient Germanic alphabet character. **—ru′nic,** *adj.*

rung (rung) *n.* **1.** ladder step. **2.** bar between chair legs.

run′-in′, *n.* confrontation.

run′ner, *n.* **1.** one that runs. **2.** messenger. **3.** blade of skate. **4.** strip of fabric, carpet, etc.

run′ner-up′, *n.* competitor finishing in second place.

run′off′, *n.* final contest held to break tie.

run′-of-the-mill′, *adj.* mediocre.

run′-on′, *adj.* **1.** of something that is added. **—n. 2.** run-on matter.

runt (runt) *n.* undersized thing.

run′way′, *n.* strip where airplanes take off and land.

rup′ture (rup′chər) *n.*, *v.*, **-tured, -turing. —n. 1.** break. **2.** hernia. **—v. 3.** break. **4.** cause breach of.

ru′ral (rŏŏr′əl) *adj.* of or in the country.

Rus. 1. Russia. **2.** Russian.

ruse (rŏŏz) *n.* trick.

rush (rush) *v.* **1.** move with speed or violence. **—n. 2.** act of rushing. **3.** hostile attack. **4.** grasslike herb growing in marshes. **—adj. 5.** requiring or marked by haste.

rusk (rusk) *n.* sweet raised bread dried and baked again.

Russ. 1. Russia. **2.** Russian. Also, **Russ**

rus′set (rus′it) *n.* reddish brown.

Rus′sian (rush′ən) *n.* native or language of Russia. **—Russian,** *adj.*

rust (rust) *n.* **1.** red-orange coating that forms on iron and steel exposed to air and moisture. **2.** plant disease. **—v. 3.** make or become rusty. **—rust′y,** *adj.*

rus′tic (rus′tik) *adj.* **1.** rural. **2.** simple. **—n. 3.** country person.

rus′ti•cate′ (-ti kāt′) *v.*, **-cated, -cating.** go to or live in the country.

rus′tle (rus′əl) *v.*, **-tled, -tling,** *n.* **—v. 1.** make small soft sounds. **2.** steal (cattle, etc.). **—n. 3.** rustling sound. **—rus′tler,** *n.*

rut (rut) *n.*, *v.*, **rutted, rutting. —n. 1.** furrow or groove worn in the ground. **2.** period of sexual excitement in male deer, goats, etc. **—v. 3.** make ruts in. **4.** be in rut. **—rut′ty,** *adj.*

ru′ta•ba′ga (rŏŏ′tə bā′gə) *n.* yellow turnip.

ruth′less (rŏŏth′lis) *adj.* pitiless. **—ruth′less•ness,** *n.*

RV, recreational vehicle.

rvam reactive volt-ampere meter.

rvlg revolving.

rvlv revolve.

rvm reactive voltmeter.

RVN Republic of Vietnam.

rvrb reverberation.

rvs 1. reverse. **2.** revise.

rvsbl reversible.

rvs cur reverse current.

rvsn revision.

RVSVP (used on invitations) please reply quickly. Also, **R.V.S.V.P., rvsvp, r.v.s.v.p.** [from French r*(épondez) v(ite) s('il) v(ous) p(laît)*]

rvw review.

R/W right of way.

r/w read/write. Also, **r-w**

R.W. 1. Right Worshipful. **2.** Right Worthy.

Rwy. Railway.

Rx, prescription.

Ry. Railway.

rye (rī) *n.* cereal grass used for flour, feed, and whiskey.

R

S

S, s (es) *n.* nineteenth letter of English alphabet.

S, south, southern.

Sa *Symbol, Chemistry.* (formerly) samarium.

Sa. Saturday.

S/A *Banking.* survivorship agreement.

S.A. 1. Salvation Army. **2.** seaman apprentice. **3.** South Africa. **4.** South America. **5.** South Australia. **6.** corporation [from French *société anonyme* or Spanish *sociedad anónima*].

s.a. 1. semiannual. **2.** sex appeal. **3.** without year or date. [from Latin *sine annō*] **4.** subject to approval.

S.A.A. Speech Association of America.

Sab. Sabbath.

Sab′bath (sab′əth) *n.* day of religious observance and rest, observed on Saturday by Jews and on Sunday by most Christians.

sab·bat′i·cal (sə bat′i kəl) *n.* **1.** paid leave of absence for study. —*adj.* **2.** (*cap.*) of the Sabbath.

sa′ber (sā′bər) *n.* one-edged sword. Also, **sa′bre.**

saber saw, portable electric jigsaw.

sa′ble (sā′bəl) *n.* small mammal with dark-brown fur.

sab′o·tage′ (sab′ə täzh′) *n., v.,* **-taged, -taging.** —*n.* **1.** willful injury to equipment, etc. —*v.* **2.** attack by sabotage. —**sab′o·teur′** (-tûr′) *n.*

sac (sak) *n.* baglike part.

sac′cha·rin (sak′ər in) *n.* sweet substance used as sugar substitute.

sac′cha·rine (-ər in, -ə rēn′)· *adj.* overly sweet.

sac′er·do′tal (sas′ər dōt′l) *adj.* priestly.

sa·chet′ (sa shā′) *n.* small bag of perfumed powder.

sack (sak) *n.* **1.** large stout bag. **2.** bag. **3.** *Slang.* dismissal. **4.** plundering. —*v.* **5.** put into a sack. **6.** *Slang.* dismiss. **7.** plunder; loot. —**sack′ing,** *n.*

sack′cloth′, *n.* coarse cloth worn for penance or mourning.

sac′ra·ment (sak′rə mənt) *n.* **1.** rite in Christian church. **2.** (*cap.*) Eucharist. —**sac′ra·men′tal** (-men′tl) *adj.*

sa′cred (sā′krid) *adj.* **1.** holy. **2.** secured against violation. —**sa′cred·ness,** *n.*

sac′ri·fice′ (sak′rə fīs′) *n., v.,* **-ficed, -ficing.** —*n.* **1.** offer of life, treasure, etc., to deity. **2.** surrender of something for purpose. —*v.* **3.** give as sacrifice. —**sac′ri·fi′cial** (-fish′əl) *adj.*

sac′ri·lege (-lij) *n.* profanation of anything sacred. —**sac′ri·le′gious** (-lij′əs, -lē′jəs) *adj.*

sac′ris·tan (sak′ri stən) *n.* sexton.

sac′ris·ty (-ri stē) *n., pl.* **-ties.** room in church, etc., where sacred objects are kept.

sac′ro·il′i·ac′ (sak′rō il′ē ak′, sā′krō-) *n.* joint in lower back.

sac′ro·sanct′ (sak′rō sangkt′) *adj.* sacred.

sac′rum (sak′rəm, sā′krəm) *n., pl.* **sacra.** bone forming rear wall of pelvis.

sad (sad) *adj.,* **sadder, saddest.** sorrowful. —**sad′den,** *v.* —**sad′ly,** *adv.* —**sad′ness,** *n.*

SADD Students Against Drunk Drivers.

sad′dle (sad′l) *n., v.,* **-dled, -dling.** —*n.* **1.** seat for rider on horse, etc. **2.** anything resembling saddle. —*v.* **3.** put saddle on. **4.** burden.

sad′dle·bag′, *n.* pouch laid over back of horse or mounted over rear wheel of bicycle or motorcycle.

sad′ism (sā′diz əm, sad′iz-) *n.* sexual or other enjoyment in causing pain. —**sad′ist,** *n.* —**sa·dis′tic** (sə dis′tik) *adj.*

sa′do·mas′o·chism (sā′dō mas′ə kiz′əm) *n.* sexual or other enjoyment in causing or experiencing pain. —**sa′do·mas′o·chist′,** *n.* —**sa′do·mas′o·chis′tic,** *adj.*

S.A.E. 1. self-addressed envelope. **2.** Society of Automotive Engineers. **3.** stamped addressed envelope. Also, **SAE; s.a.e.** (for defs. 1, 3).

SAF single Asian female.

saf safety.

sa·fa′ri (sə fär′ē) *n.* (in E. Africa) journey; hunting expedition.

safe (sāf) *adj.,* **safer, safest,** *n.* —*adj.* **1.** secure or free from danger. **2.** dependable. —*n.* **3.** stout box for valuables. —**safe′ty,** *n.* —**safe′ly,** *adv.* —**safe′keep′ing,** *n.*

safe′-con′duct, *n.* document authorizing safe passage.

safe′-de·pos′it, *adj.* providing safekeeping for valuables.

safe′guard′, *n.* **1.** something that ensures safety. —*v.* **2.** protect.

safe sex, sexual activity in which precautions are taken to avoid sexually transmitted diseases.

safety glass, shatter-resistant glass.

safety match, match that ignites only when struck on special surface.

safety pin, pin bent back on itself with guard to cover point.

safety razor, razor with blade guard.

saf′flow·er (saf′lou′ər) *n.* thistle-like plant whose seeds yield cooking oil.

saf′fron (saf′rən) *n.* bright yellow seasoning.

S. Afr. 1. South Africa. **2.** South African.

S. Afr. D. South African Dutch. Also, **SAfrD**

sag (sag) *v.,* **sagged, sagging,** *n.* —*v.* **1.** bend, esp. in middle, from weight or pressure. **2.** hang loosely. —*n.* **3.** sagging place.

sa′ga (sä′gə) *n.* heroic tale.

sa·ga'cious (sə gā'shəs) *adj.* shrewd and practical. —**sa·gac'i·ty** (-gas'ə tē) *n.*

sage (sāj) *n., adj.,* **sager, sagest.** —*n.* **1.** wise person. **2.** herb used in seasoning. —*adj.* **3.** wise; prudent. —**sage'ly,** *adv.* —**sage'ness,** *n.*

sage'brush', *n.* sagelike, bushy plant of dry plains of western U.S.

sa'go (sā'gō) *n.* starchy substance from some palms.

sa'hib (sä'ib) *n.* (in colonial India) term of respect for European.

said (sed) *adj.* named before.

sail (sāl) *n.* **1.** sheet spread to catch wind to propel vessel or windmill. **2.** trip on sailing vessel. —*v.* **3.** move by action of wind. **4.** travel over water. —**sail'or,** *n.*

sail'cloth', *n.* fabric used for boat sails or tents.

sail'fish', *n.* large fish with upright fin.

saint (sānt) *n.* holy person. —**saint'hood,** *n.* —**saint'ly,** *adj.* —**saint'li·ness,** *n.*

sake (sāk) *n.* **1.** benefit. **2.** purpose. **3.** (sä'kē) rice wine.

sa·laam (sə läm') *n.* **1.** Islamic salutation. **2.** low bow with hand on forehead.

sal'a·ble (sā'lə bəl) *adj.* subject to or fit for sale. Also, **sale'a·ble.**

sa·la'cious (sə lā'shəs) *adj.* lewd.

sal'ad (sal'əd) *n.* dish esp. of raw vegetables or fruit.

sal'a·man·der (sal'ə man'dər) *n.* small amphibian.

sa·la'mi (sə lä'mē) *n.* kind of sausage.

sal'a·ry (sal'ə rē) *n., pl.* **-ries.** fixed payment for regular work. —**sal'a·ried,** *adj.*

sale (sāl) *n.* **1.** act of selling. **2.** opportunity to sell. **3.** occasion of selling at reduced prices. —**sales'man,** *n.* —**sales'la'dy, sales'wom'-an,** *n.fem.* —**sales'per'son,** *n.* —**sales'-people,** *n.pl.* —**sales'room',** *n.*

sales'man·ship', *n.* skill of selling a product or idea.

sal. hist. salary history.

sal'i·cyl'ic acid (sal'ə sil'ik) substance used in aspirin.

sa'li·ent (sā'lē ənt) *adj.* **1.** conspicuous. **2.** projecting. —*n.* **3.** projecting part. —**sa'li·ence,** *n.* —**sa'li·ent·ly,** *adv.*

sa'line (sā'lēn, -līn) *adj.* salty. —**sa·lin'i·ty** (sə lin'ə tē) *n.*

sa·li'va (sə lī'və) *n.* fluid secreted into mouth by glands. —**sal'i·var'y** (sal'ə ver'ē) *adj.* —**sal'i·vate'** (-vāt') *v.* —**sal'i·va'tion,** *n.*

Salk vaccine (sôk) vaccine against poliomyelitis.

sal'low (sal'ō) *adj.* having sickly complexion.

sal'ly (sal'ē) *n., pl.* **-lies,** *v.,* **-lied, -lying.** —*n.* **1.** sudden attack by besieged troops. **2.** outward burst or rush. **3.** witty remark. —*v.* **4.** make sally.

salm'on (sam'ən) *n.* pink-fleshed food fish of northern waters.

sal'mo·nel'la (sal'mə nel'ə) *n., pl.* **-nellae** (-nel'ē), **-nellas.** bacillus that causes various diseases, including food poisoning.

sa·lon' (sə lon'; *Fr.* sA lôN') *n.* **1.** drawing room. **2.** art gallery.

sa·loon' (sə lōōn') *n.* **1.** place where intoxicating liquors are sold and drunk. **2.** public room.

sal'sa (säl'sə, -sä) *n.* **1.** Latin-American music with elements of jazz, rock, and soul. **2.** sauce, esp. hot sauce containing chilies.

salt (sôlt) *n.* **1.** sodium chloride, occurring as mineral, in sea water, etc. **2.** chemical compound derived from acid and base. **3.** wit. **4.** *Informal,* sailor. —*v.* **5.** season or preserve with salt. —**salt'y,** *adj.* —**salt'i·ness,** *n.*

SALT (sôlt) *n.* Strategic Arms Limitation Talks.

salt'cel'lar, *n.* shaker or dish for salt.

sal·tine' (sôl tēn') *n.* crisp, salted cracker.

salt lick, place where animals lick salt deposits.

salt of the earth, someone thought to embody the best human qualities.

salt'pe'ter (-pē'tər) *n.* potassium nitrate.

sa·lu'bri·ous (sə lōō'brē əs) *adj.* healthful. —**sa·lu'bri·ous·ly,** *adv.* —**sa·lub'ri·ty,** *n.*

sal'u·tar'y (sal'yə ter'ē) *adj.* healthful; beneficial.

sal'u·ta'tion (sal'yə tā'shən) *n.* **1.** greeting. **2.** formal opening of letter.

sa·lute' (sə lōōt') *v.,* **-luted, -luting,** *n.* —*v.* **1.** express respect or goodwill, esp. in greeting. —*n.* **2.** act of saluting.

Salv. Salvador.

sal'vage (sal'vij) *n., v.,* **-vaged, -vaging.** —*n.* **1.** act of saving ship or cargo at sea. **2.** property saved. —*v.* **3.** save from destruction.

sal·va'tion (-vā'shən) *n.* **1.** deliverance. **2.** deliverance from sin.

salve (sav) *n., v.,* **salved, salving.** —*n.* **1.** ointment for sores. —*v.* **2.** apply salve to.

sal'ver (sal'vər) *n.* tray.

sal'vi·a (sal'vē ə) *n.* plant of mint family.

sal'vo (sal'vō) *n., pl.* **-vos, -voes.** discharge of guns, bombs, etc., in rapid series.

SAM, (sam), **1.** shared-appreciation mortgage. **2.** single Asian male. **3.** surface-to-air missile. **4.** Space Available Mail: a special air service for sending parcels to overseas members of the armed forces.

Sam. *Bible.* Samuel.

S. Am. 1. South America. **2.** South American.

sam'ba (sam'bə, säm'-) *n., v.,* **-baed, -baing.** —*n.* **1.** Brazilian dance of African origin. —*v.* **2.** dance the samba.

same (sām) *adj.* **1.** identical or corresponding. **2.** unchanged. **3.** just mentioned. —*n.* **4.** same person or thing. —**same'ness,** *n.*

S. Amer. 1. South America. **2.** South American.

S

Saml. Samuel.

sam'o•var' (sam'ə vär') *n.* metal urn.

sam'pan (sam'pan) *v.* small Far Eastern boat.

sam'ple (sam'pəl) *n., adj., v.,* **-pled, -pling.** —*n.* **1.** small amount to show nature or quality. —*adj.* **2.** as sample. —*v.* **3.** test by sample.

sam'pler, *n.* needlework done to show skill.

sam'u•rai' (sam'ŏŏ rī') *n., pl.* **-rai.** member of hereditary warrior class in feudal Japan.

san sanitary.

san'a•to'ri•um (san'ə tôr'ē əm) *n., pl.* **-toriums, -toria** (-tôr'ē ə). sanitarium.

sanc'ti•fy' (sangk'tə fī') *v.,* **-fied, -fying. 1.** make holy. **2.** give sanction to. —**sanc'ti•fi•ca'tion,** *n.*

sanc'ti•mo'ny (-mō'nē) *n.* hypocritical devoutness. —**sanc'ti•mo'ni•ous,** *adj.*

sanc'tion (sangk'shən) *n.* **1.** permission or support. **2.** legal action by one state against another. —*v.* **3.** authorize; approve.

sanc'ti•ty (sangk'ti tē) *n., pl.* **-ties. 1.** holiness. **2.** sacred character.

sanc'tu•ar'y (-chŏŏ er'ē) *n., pl.* **-ies. 1.** holy place. **2.** area around altar. **3.** place of immunity from arrest or harm.

sanc'tum (-təm) *n., pl.* **-tums, -ta.** private place.

sand (sand) *n.* **1.** fine grains of rock. **2.** (*pl.*) sandy region. —*v.* **3.** smooth with sandpaper. —**sand'er,** *n.* —**sand'y,** *adj.*

san'dal (san'dl) *n.* shoe consisting of sole and straps.

san'dal•wood', *n.* fragrant wood.

sand'bag', *n.* sand-filled bag used as fortification, ballast, or weapon.

sand'bank', *n.* large mass of sand.

sand bar, bar of sand formed by tidal action.

sand'blast', *v.* clean with blast of air or steam laden with sand.

sand'box', *n.* receptacle holding sand for children to play in.

sand dollar, disklike sea animal.

S.&F. *Insurance.* stock and fixtures.

S and H shipping and handling (charges). Also, **S&H**

S&L *Banking.* savings and loan association. Also, **S and L**

sand'lot', *n.* **1.** vacant lot used by youngsters for games. —*adj.* **2.** played in a sandlot.

S and M sadomasochism; sadism and masochism. Also, **S&M, s&m**

S.&M. *Insurance.* stock and machinery.

sand'man', *n.* figure in folklore who puts sand in children's eyes to make them sleepy.

S&P Standard & Poor's.

sand'pa'per, *n.* **1.** paper coated with sand. —*v.* **2.** smooth with sandpaper.

sand'pip'er (-pī'pər) *n.* small shore bird.

s. & s.c. (of paper) sized and supercalendered.

sand'stone', *n.* rock formed chiefly of sand.

sand'storm', *n.* windstorm with clouds of sand.

sand'wich (sand'wich, san'-) *n.* **1.** two slices of bread with meat, etc., between. —*v.* **2.** insert.

sane (sān) *adj.,* **saner, sanest.** free from mental disorder; rational. —**sane'ly,** *adv.*

sang-froid' (*Fr.* sän frwa') *n.* composure.

san•gri'a (sang grē'ə, san-) *n.* iced drink of red wine, sugar, fruit, and soda water.

san'gui•nar'y (sang'gwə ner'ē) *adj.* **1.** bloody. **2.** bloodthirsty.

san'guine (-gwin) *adj.* **1.** hopeful. **2.** red.

san'i•tar'i•um (san'i târ'ē əm) *n., pl.* **-iums, -ia** (-ē ə). place for treatment of invalids and convalescents.

san'i•tar'y (-ter'ē) *adj.* of health. —**san'i•tar'i•ly,** *adv.*

sanitary napkin, pad worn to absorb menstrual flow.

san'i•ta'tion, *n.* application of sanitary measures.

san'i•tize' (-ə-) *v.,* **-tized, -tizing. 1.** free from dirt. **2.** make less offensive by removing objectionable elements.

san'i•ty, *n.* **1.** soundness of mind. **2.** good judgment.

Sans. Sanskrit.

Sansk. Sanskrit.

San'skrit (san'skrit) *n.* extinct language of India.

sap (sap) *n., v.,* **sapped, sapping.** —*n.* **1.** trench dug to approach enemy's position. **2.** juice of woody plant. **3.** *Slang.* fool. —*v.* **4.** weaken; undermine. —**sap'per,** *n.*

sa'pi•ent (sā'pē ənt) *adj.* wise. —**sa'pi•ence,** *n.*

sap'ling (sap'ling) *n.* young tree.

sap'phire (saf'īᵉr) *n.* deep-blue gem.

sap'suck'er, *n.* kind of woodpecker.

Sar. Sardinia.

S.A.R. 1. South African Republic. **2.** Sons of the American Revolution.

sar'casm (sär'kaz əm) *n.* **1.** harsh derision. **2.** ironical gibe. —**sar•cas'tic,** *adj.* —**sar•cas'ti•cal•ly,** *adv.*

sar•co'ma (sär kō'mə) *n., pl.* **-mas, -mata** (-mə tə). type of malignant tumor.

sar•coph'a•gus (sär kof'ə gəs) *n., pl.* **-gi.** stone coffin.

sar•dine' (sär dēn') *n.* small fish.

sar•don'ic (sär don'ik) *adj.* sarcastic. —**sar•don'i•cal•ly,** *adv.*

sa'ri (sär'ē) *n.* length of cloth used as dress in India.

sa•rong' (sə rông') *n.* skirtlike garment.

sar'sa•pa•ril'la (sas'pə ril'ə) *n.* **1.** tropical American plant. **2.** soft drink flavored with roots of this plant.

sar•to'ri•al (sär tôr'ē əl) *adj.* of tailors or tailoring.

SASE, self-addressed stamped envelope.

sash (sash) *n.* **1.** band of cloth usually worn

as belt. **2.** framework for panes of window, etc.

Sask. Saskatchewan.

sass (sas) *Informal.* —*n.* **1.** impudent back talk. —*v.* **2.** answer back impudently. —**sas/sy**, *adj.*

sas/sa•fras/ (sas/ə fras/) *n.* American tree with aromatic root bark.

SAT *Trademark.* Scholastic Aptitude Test.

Sat. 1. Saturday. **2.** Saturn.

sat. 1. satellite. **2.** saturate. **3.** saturated.

Sa/tan (sāt/n) *n.* chief evil spirit; devil. —**sa•tan/ic** (sə tan/ik) *adj.*

SATB *Music.* soprano, alto, tenor, bass.

satch/el (sach/əl) *n.* handbag.

satcom communications satellite.

sate (sāt) *v.*, **sated**, **sating**. satisfy or surfeit.

sa•teen/ (sa tēn/) *n.* glossy fabric.

sat/el•lite/ (sat/l īt/) *n.* **1.** body that revolves around planet. **2.** subservient follower.

satellite dish, dish-shaped reflector, used esp. for receiving satellite and microwave signals.

sa/ti•ate/ (sā/shē āt/) *v.*, **-ated**, **-ating**. surfeit. —**sa/ti•a/tion**, **sa•ti/e•ty** (sə tī/ə tē) *n.*

sat/in (sat/n) *n.* glossy silk or rayon fabric. —**sat/in•y**, *adj.*

sat/ire (sat/īʳr) *n.* use of irony or ridicule in exposing vice, folly, etc. —**sa•tir/i•cal** (sə-tir/i kəl), **sa•tir/ic**, *adj.* —**sa•tir/i•cal•ly**, *adv.* —**sat/i•rist** (sat/ər ist) *n.*

sat/i•rize/ (sat/ə rīz/) *v.*, **-rized**, **-rizing**. subject to satire.

sat/is•fy/ (sat/is fī/) *v.*, **-fied**, **-fying**. **1.** fulfill desire, need, etc. **2.** convince. **3.** pay. —**sat/is•fac/tion** (-fak/shən) *n.* —**sat/is•fac/to•ry**, *adj.* —**sat/is•fac/to•ri•ly**, *adv.*

sa/trap (sā/trap, sa/-) *n.* subordinate ruler, often despotic.

sat/u•rate/ (sach/ə rāt/) *v.*, **-rated**, **-rating**. soak completely. —**sat/u•ra/tion**, *n.*

Sat/ur•day (sat/ər dā/, -dē) *n.* seventh day of week.

Sat/urn (-ərn) *n.* major planet.

sat/ur•nine/ (-ər nīn/) *adj.* gloomy.

sa/tyr (sā/tər, sat/ər) *n.* **1.** woodland deity, part man and part goat. **2.** lecherous person.

sauce (sôs) *n.* **1.** liquid or soft relish. **2.** stewed fruit.

sauce/pan/, *n.* cooking pan with handle.

sau/cer, *n.* small shallow dish.

sau/cy, *adj.*, **-cier**, **-ciest**. impertinent. —**sau/ci•ly**, *adv.* —**sau/ci•ness**, *n.*

sauer/kraut/ (souʳr/krout/, sou/ər-) *n.* chopped fermented cabbage.

sau/na (sô/nə) *n.* bath heated by steam.

saun/ter (sôn/tər) *v.*, *n.* stroll.

sau/ri•an (sôr/ē ən) *adj.* of or resembling a lizard.

sau/ro•pod/ (sôr/ə pod/) *n.* huge dinosaur with small head and long neck and tail.

sau/sage (sô/sij) *n.* minced seasoned meat, often in casing.

sau•té/ (sō tā/, sô-) *v.*, **-téed**, **-téeing**. cook in a little fat.

sau•terne/ (sō tûrn/) *n.* sweet white wine.

sav/age (sav/ij) *adj.* **1.** wild; uncivilized. **2.** ferocious. —*n.* **3.** uncivilized person. —**sav/age•ly**, *adv.* —**sav/age•ry**, *n.*

sa•van/na (sə van/ə) *n.* grassy plain with scattered trees. Also, **sa•van/nah.**

sa•vant/ (sa vänt/) *n.* learned person.

save (sāv) *v.*, **saved**, **saving**, *prep.*, *conj.* —*v.* **1.** rescue or keep safe. **2.** reserve. —*prep.*, *conj.* **3.** except.

sav/ing, *adj.* **1.** rescuing; redeeming. **2.** economical. —*n.* **3.** economy. **4.** (*pl.*) money put by. —*prep.* **5.** except. **6.** respecting.

sav/ior (sāv/yər) *n.* **1.** one who rescues. **2.** (*cap.*) Christ. Also, **sav/iour.**

sa/voir-faire/ (sav/wär fâr/) *n.* competence in social matters.

sa/vor (sā/vər) *n.*, *v.* taste or smell.

sa/vor•y, *adj.*, *n.*, *pl.*, **-ories.** —*adj.* **1.** pleasing in taste or smell. —*n.* **2.** aromatic plant.

sav/vy (sav/ē) *n.*, *adj.*, **-vier**, **-viest.** —*n.* **1.** practical understanding. —*adj.* **2.** shrewd and well-informed.

saw (sô) *n.* **1.** toothed metal blade. —*v.* **2.** cut with saw. —**saw/mill**, *n.* —**saw/yer** (sô/-yər) *n.*

saw/buck/, *n.* **1.** sawhorse. **2.** *Slang.* ten-dollar bill.

saw/dust/, *n.* fine particles of wood produced in sawing.

saw/horse/, *n.* movable frame for supporting wood while it's being sawed.

sax (saks) *n.* saxophone.

Sax/on (sak/sən) *n.* member of Germanic people who invaded Britain in the 5th–6th centuries.

sax/o•phone/ (sak/sə fōn/) *n.* musical wind instrument.

say (sā) *v.*, **said** (sed), **saying**, *n.* —*v.* **1.** speak; declare; utter. **2.** declare as truth. —*n.* **3.** *Informal.* right to speak or choose.

say/ing, *n.* proverb.

say/-so/, *n.*, *pl.* **-sos**. *Informal.* personal assurance; word.

Sb *Symbol*, *Chemistry.* antimony. [from Latin *stibium*]

sb 1. service bulletin. **2.** sideband. **3.** *Optics.* stilb. **4.** stove bolt.

sb. *Grammar.* substantive.

S.B. 1. Bachelor of Science. [from Latin *Scientiae Baccalaureus*] **2.** South Britain (England and Wales).

s.b. *Baseball.* stolen base; stolen bases.

SBA Small Business Administration. Also, **S.B.A.**

SbE south by east.

SBF single black female.

SBIC Small Business Investment Company.

SBLI Savings Bank Life Insurance.

SBM single black male.

SBN *Publishing.* Standard Book Number.

S

sbstr *Electronics.* substrate.

SbW south by west.

SC, South Carolina. Also, **S.C.**

scab (skab) *n., v.,* **scabbed, scabbing.** —*n.* **1.** crust forming over sore. **2.** worker who takes striker's place. —*v.* **3.** form scab. —**scab′by,** *adj.*

scab′bard (skab′ərd) *n.* sheath for sword blade, etc.

sca′bies (skā′bēz, -bē ēz′) *n.* infectious skin disease.

scab′rous (skab′rəs) *adj.* **1.** having a rough surface. **2.** indecent; obscene.

scad (skad) *n. (usually pl.)* great quantity.

scaf′fold (skaf′əld, -ōld) *n.* **1.** Also, **scaf′fold·ing.** temporary framework used in construction. **2.** platform on which criminal is executed.

scal′a·wag′ (skal′ə wag′) *n.* rascal.

scald (skôld) *v.* **1.** burn with hot liquid or steam. **2.** heat just below boiling. —*n.* **3.** burn caused by scalding.

scale (skāl) *n., v.,* **scaled, scaling.** —*n.* **1.** one of flat hard plates covering fish, etc. **2.** flake. **3.** device for weighing. **4.** series of measuring units. **5.** relative measure. **6.** succession of musical tones. —*v.* **7.** remove or shed scales. **8.** weigh. **9.** climb with effort. **10.** reduce proportionately. —**scal′y,** *adj.* —**scal′i·ness,** *n.*

scal′lion (skal′yən) *n.* small green onion.

scal′lop (skol′əp, skal′-) *n.* **1.** bivalve mollusk. **2.** one of series of curves on a border. —*v.* **3.** finish with scallops.

scalp (skalp) *n.* **1.** skin and hair of top of head. —*v.* **2.** cut scalp from. **3.** buy and resell at unofficial price. —**scalp′er,** *n.*

scal′pel (skal′pəl) *n.* small surgical knife.

scam (skam) *n., v.,* **scammed, scamming.** —*n.* **1.** fraudulent scheme; swindle. —*v.* **2.** cheat; defraud.

scamp (skamp) *n.* rascal.

scam′per, *v.* **1.** go quickly. —*n.* **2.** quick run.

scam′pi (skam′pē, skäm′-) *n., pl.* **-pi. 1.** large shrimp. **2.** dish of scampi.

scan (skan) *v.,* **scanned, scanning. 1.** examine closely. **2.** glance at. **3.** analyze verse meter.

Scand Scandinavian.

Scand. 1. Scandinavia. **2.** Scandinavian.

scan′dal (skan′dl) *n.* **1.** disgraceful act; disgrace. **2.** malicious gossip. —**scan′dal·ous,** *adj.* —**scan′dal·mon′ger,** *n.*

scan′dal·ize′, *v.,* **-ized, -izing.** offend; shock.

scan′ner, *n.* **1.** person or thing that scans. **2.** device that monitors selected radio frequencies and reproduces any signal detected. **3.** device that optically scans bar codes, etc., and identifies data.

scan′sion (skan′shən) *n.* metrical analysis of verse.

scant (skant) *adj.* barely adequate. Also,

scant′y. —**scant′i·ly,** *adv.* —**scant′i·ness,** *n.*

scape′goat′ (skāp′gōt′) *n.* one made to bear blame for others.

scape′grace′, *n.* scamp; rascal.

s. caps. *Printing.* small capitals.

scar (skär) *n., v.,* **scarred, scarring.** —*n.* **1.** mark left by wound, etc. —*v.* **2.** mark with scar.

scar′ab (skar′əb) *n.* beetle.

scarce (skârs) *adj.,* **scarcer, scarcest. 1.** insufficient. **2.** rare. —**scar′ci·ty, scarce′ness,** *n.*

scarce′ly, *adv.* **1.** barely. **2.** definitely not.

scare (skâr) *v.,* **scared, scaring,** *n.* —*v.* **1.** frighten. —*n.* **2.** sudden fright.

scare′crow′, *n.* object set up to frighten birds away from planted seed.

scarf (skärf) *n., pl.* **scarfs, scarves** (skärvz). band of cloth esp. for neck.

scar′i·fy′ (skar′ə fī′) *v.,* **-fied, -fying. 1.** scratch (skin, etc.). **2.** loosen (soil).

scar′let (skär′lit) *n.* bright red.

scarlet fever, disease marked by fever and rash.

scar′y (skâr′ē) *adj.* **-ier, -iest.** causing fear.

scat (skat) *v.,* **scatted, scatting.** run off.

scathe (skāth) *v.,* **scathed, scathing.** criticize harshly.

scat′o·log′i·cal (skat′l oj′i kəl) *adj.* concerned with excrement or obscenity. —**sca·tol′o·gy** (skə tol′ə jē) *n.*

scat′ter (skat′ər) *v.* throw loosely about.

scat′ter·brain′, *n.* person incapable of coherent thought. —**scat′ter-brained′,** *adj.*

scatter rug, small rug.

scav scavenge.

scav′enge (skav′inj) *v.,* **-enged, -enging. 1.** search for food. **2.** cleanse. —**scav′en·ger,** *n.*

Sc.B. Bachelor of Science. [from Latin *Scientiae Baccalaureus*]

Sc.B.C. Bachelor of Science in Chemistry.

Sc.B.E. Bachelor of Science in Engineering.

scd specification control drawing.

Sc.D. Doctor of Science. [from Latin *Scientiae Doctor*]

Sc.D.Hyg. Doctor of Science in Hygiene.

Sc.D.Med. Doctor of Medical Science.

scdr screwdriver.

sce source.

sce·nar′i·o′ (si när′ē ō′, -när′-) *n., pl.* **-ios.** plot outline.

scene (sēn) *n.* **1.** location of action. **2.** view. **3.** subdivision of play. **4.** display of emotion. —**sce′nic,** *adj.*

scen′er·y (sē′nə rē) *n.* **1.** features of landscape. **2.** stage set.

scent (sent) *n.* **1.** distinctive odor. **2.** trail marked by this. **3.** sense of smell. —*v.* **4.** smell. **5.** perfume.

scep′ter (sep′tər) *n.* rod carried as emblem of royal power. Also, **scep′tre.**

scep'tic (skep'tik) *n.* skeptic.

SCF single Christian female.

scf standard cubic foot.

scfh standard cubic feet per hour

scfm standard cubic feet per minute.

sch socket head.

Sch. (in Austria) schilling; schillings.

sch. 1. schedule. **2.** school. **3.** schooner.

SCHDM schematic diagram.

sched. schedule.

sched'ule (skej'ool, -ool; *Brit.* shed'yool, shej'ool) *n., v.,* **-uled, -uling.** —*n.* **1.** timetable or list. —*v.* **2.** enter on schedule.

schem schematic.

scheme (skēm) *n., v.,* **schemed, scheming.** —*n.* **1.** plan; design. **2.** intrigue. —*v.* **3.** plan or plot. —**schem'er,** *n.* —**sche•mat'ic** (skimat'ik) *adj.*

scher'zo (skert'sō) *n., pl.* **-zos, -zi** (-sē). playful musical movement.

Schick test (shik) diphtheria test.

schil'ling (shil'ing) *n.* monetary unit of Austria.

schism (siz'əm, skiz'-) *n.* division within church, etc.; disunion. —**schis•mat'ic** (-mat'ik) *adj., n.*

schist (shist) *n.* layered crystalline rock.

schiz'oid (skit'soid) *adj.* having personality disorder marked by depression, withdrawal, etc.

schiz'o•phre'ni•a (skit'sə frē'nē ə) *n.* kind of mental disorder. —**schiz'o•phren'ic** (-fren'ik) *adj., n.*

schle•miel' (shlə mēl') *n. Slang.* awkward and unlucky person.

schlep (shlep) *v.,* **schlepped, schlepping,** *n. Slang.* —*v.* **1.** carry with great effort. —*n.* **2.** slow or awkward person. **3.** tedious journey.

schlock (shlok) *n. Informal.* inferior merchandise. —**schlock'y,** *adj.*

schmaltz (shmälts, shmôlts) *n. Informal.* sentimental art, esp. music. —**schmaltz'y,** *adj.*

Sch.Mus.B. Bachelor of School Music.

schnapps (shnäps, shnaps) *n.* strong alcoholic liquor.

schol'ar (skol'ər) *n.* **1.** learned person. **2.** pupil. —**schol'ar•ly,** *adj.*

schol'ar•ship', *n.* **1.** learning. **2.** aid granted to promising student.

scho•las'tic (skə las'tik) *adj.* of schools or scholars. —**scho•las'ti•cal•ly,** *adv.*

school (skool) *n.* **1.** place for instruction. **2.** regular meetings of teacher and pupils. **3.** believers in doctrine or theory. **4.** group of fish, whales, etc. —*v.* **5.** educate; train. —**school'house',** *n.* —**school'room',** *n.* —**school'teach'er,** *n.*

schoon'er (skoo'nər) *n.* kind of sailing vessel.

schuss (shoos, shoos) *n.* straight downhill ski run at high speed.

schwa (shwä) *n.* vowel sound in certain unstressed syllables, as *a* in *sofa;* usually represented by ə.

sci. 1. science. **2.** scientific.

sci•at'i•ca (sī at'i kə) *n.* neuralgia in hip and thigh. —**sci•at'ic,** *adj.*

SCID *Pathology.* severe combined immune deficiency.

sci'ence (sī'əns) *n.* systematic knowledge, esp. of physical world. —**sci'en•tif'ic** (-tif'ik) *adj.* —**sci'en•tif'i•cal•ly,** *adv.* —**sci'en•tist,** *n.*

science fiction, fiction dealing with space travel, robots, etc.

sci-fi (sī'fī') *n., adj. Informal.* science fiction.

scil. to wit; namely. [from Latin *scilicet*]

scim'i•tar (sim'i tər) *n.* curved sword.

scin•til'la (sin til'ə) *n.* particle, esp. of evidence.

scin'til•late' (-tl āt') *v.,* **-lated, -lating.** sparkle. —**scin'til•la'tion,** *n.*

sci'on (sī'ən) *n.* **1.** descendant. **2.** shoot cut for grafting.

scis'sors (siz'ərz) *n.* cutting instrument with two pivoted blades.

SCLC Southern Christian Leadership Conference. Also, **S.C.L.C.**

scle•ro'sis (skli rō'sis) *n.* hardening, as of tissue. —**scle•rot'ic** (-rot'ik) *adj.*

sclr scaler.

SCM single Christian male.

Sc.M. Master of Science. [from Latin *Scientiae Magister*]

scn specification change notice.

scng scanning.

scnr scanner.

scoff (skôf) *v.* **1.** jeer. —*n.* **2.** derision. —**scoff'er,** *n.*

scoff'law', *n.* person who flouts the law, as by ignoring traffic tickets.

scold (skōld) *v.* **1.** find fault; reprove. —*n.* **2.** scolding person.

sco'li•o•sis (skō'lē ō'sis) *n.* lateral curvature of the spine.

sconce (skons) *n.* wall bracket for candles, etc.

scone (skōn, skon) *n.* small flat cake.

S. Con. Res. Senate concurrent resolution.

scoop (skoop) *n.* **1.** small deep shovel. **2.** bucket of steam shovel, etc. **3.** act of scooping. **4.** quantity taken up. **5.** *Informal,* earliest news report. —*v.* **6.** take up with scoop. **7.** *Informal,* best (competing news media) with scoop (def. 5).

scoot (skoot) *v.* go swiftly.

scoot'er, *n.* low two-wheeled vehicle.

scope (skōp) *n.* extent.

scorch (skôrch) *v.* **1.** burn slightly. —*n.* **2.** superficial burn.

score (skôr) *n., pl.* **scores,** (for 3) **score,** *v.,* **scored, scoring.** —*n.* **1.** points made in game, etc. **2.** notch. **3.** group of twenty. **4.** account; reason. **5.** written piece of music.

S

—*v.* **6.** earn points in game. **7.** notch or cut. **8.** criticize. —**scor′er,** *n.*

scorn (skôrn) *n.* **1.** contempt. **2.** mockery. —*v.* **3.** regard or refuse with scorn. —**scorn′-ful,** *adj.* —**scorn′ful•ly,** *adv.*

scor′pi•on (skôr′pē ən) *n.* small venomous spiderlike animal.

Scot (skot) *n.* native or inhabitant of Scotland. —**Scot′tish,** *adj., n.pl.*

scotch (skoch) *v.* **1.** make harmless. **2.** put an end to.

Scotch, *adj.* **1.** (loosely) Scottish. —*n.* **2.** (*pl.*) (loosely) Scottish people. **3.** whiskey made in Scotland.

scot′-free′, *adj.* avoiding punishment or obligation.

ScotGael Scots Gaelic.

Scots (skots) *n.* English spoken in Scotland.

SCOTUS Supreme Court of the United States. Also, **SCUS**

scoun′drel (skoun′drəl) *n.* rascal.

scour (skou^ər) *v.* **1.** clean by rubbing. **2.** range in searching.

scourge (skûrj) *n., v.,* **scourged, scourging.** —*n.* **1.** whip. **2.** cause of affliction. —*v.* **3.** whip.

scout (skout) *n.* **1.** person sent ahead to examine conditions. —*v.* **2.** examine as scout. **3.** reject with scorn.

scow (skou) *n.* flat-bottomed, flat-ended boat.

scowl (skoul) *n.* **1.** fierce frown. —*v.* **2.** frown fiercely.

SCR *Electronics.* semiconductor controlled rectifier.

scr. **1.** screw. **2.** scruple.

scrab′ble (skrab′əl) *v.,* **-bled, -bling. 1.** scratch with hands, etc. **2.** scrawl.

scrag (skrag) *n.* scrawny creature. —**scrag′-gy,** *adj.*

scrag′gly, *adj.,* **-glier, -gliest.** shaggy.

scram (skram) *v.,* **scrammed, scramming.** *Informal,* go away quickly.

scram′ble (skram′bəl) *v.,* **-bled, -bling,** *n.* —*v.* **1.** move with difficulty, using feet and hands. **2.** mix together. —*n.* **3.** scrambling progression. **4.** struggle for possession.

scrap (skrap) *n., adj., v.,* **scrapped, scrapping.** —*n.* **1.** small piece. **2.** discarded material. **3.** *Informal,* fight. —*adj.* **4.** discarded. **5.** in scraps or as scraps. —*v.* **6.** break up; discard. —**scrap′py,** *adj.*

scrap′book′, *n.* blank book for clippings, etc.

scrape (skrāp) *v.,* **scraped, scraping,** *n.* —*v.* **1.** rub harshly. **2.** remove by scraping. **3.** collect laboriously. —*n.* **4.** act or sound of scraping. **5.** scraped place. **6.** predicament. —**scrap′er,** *n.*

scrap′ple (skrap′əl) *n.* sausagelike food of pork, corn meal, and seasonings.

scratch (skrach) *v.* **1.** mark, tear, or rub with something sharp. **2.** strike out. —*n.* **3.** mark from scratching. **4.** standard. —**scratch′y,** *adj.*

scrawl (skrôl) *v.* **1.** write carelessly or awkwardly. —*n.* **2.** such handwriting.

scraw′ny (skrô′nē) *adj.,* **-nier, -niest.** thin. —**scraw′ni•ness,** *n.*

scream (skrēm) *n.* **1.** loud sharp cry. —*v.* **2.** utter screams.

screech (skrēch) *n.* **1.** harsh shrill cry. —*v.* **2.** utter screeches.

screen (skrēn) *n.* **1.** covered frame. **2.** anything that shelters or conceals. **3.** wire mesh. **4.** surface for displaying motion pictures. —*v.* **5.** shelter with screen. **6.** sift through screen.

screen′play′, *n.* outline or full script of motion picture.

screw (skrōō) *n.* **1.** machine part or fastener driving or driven by twisting. **2.** propeller. **3.** coercion. —*v.* **4.** hold with screw. **5.** turn as screw.

screw′ball′, *Slang.* —*n.* **1.** eccentric or wildly whimsical person. —*adj.* **2.** eccentric.

screw′driv′er, *n.* tool for turning screws.

screw′y, *adj.,* **-ier, -iest.** *Slang.* **1.** crazy. **2.** absurd. —**screw′i•ness,** *n.*

scrib′ble (skrib′əl) *v.,* **-bled, -bling,** *n.* —*v.* **1.** write hastily or meaninglessly. —*n.* **2.** piece of such writing.

scribe (skrīb) *n.* professional copyist.

scrim (skrim) *n.* fabric of open weave.

scrim′mage (skrim′ij) *n., v.,* **-maged, -maging.** —*n.* **1.** rough struggle. **2.** play in football. —*v.* **3.** engage in scrimmage.

scrimp (skrimp) *v.* economize.

scrim′shaw′ (skrim′shô′) *n.* carved articles, esp. of whalebone.

scrip (skrip) *n.* certificate, paper money, etc.

script (skript) *n.* **1.** handwriting. **2.** manuscript.

Scrip′ture (skrip′chər) *n.* **1.** Bible. **2.** (*l.c.*) sacred or religious writing or book. —**scrip′-tur•al,** *adj.*

scrive′ner (skriv′nər) *n.* scribe.

scrn screen.

scrod (skrod) *n.* young codfish or haddock.

scrof′u•la (skrof′yə lə) *n.* tuberculous disease, esp. of lymphatic glands. —**scrof′u•lous,** *adj.*

scroll (skrōl) *n.* roll of inscribed paper.

scro′tum (skrō′təm) *n., pl.* **-ta** (-tə), **-tums.** pouch of skin containing testicles. —**scro′tal,** *adj.*

scrounge (skrounj) *v.,* **scrounged, scrounging.** *Informal,* **1.** beg or mooch. **2.** search. —**scroung′er,** *n.*

scrub (skrub) *v.,* **scrubbed, scrubbing,** *n., adj.* —*v.* **1.** clean by rubbing. —*n.* **2.** low trees or shrubs. **3.** anything small or poor. —*adj.* **4.** small or poor. —**scrub′by,** *adj.*

scruff (skruf) *n.* nape.

scruff′y (skruf′ē) *adj.,* **scruffier, scruffiest.** untidy.

scrump′tious (skrump′shəs) *adj.* extremely pleasing.

scru'ple (skrōō'pəl) *n.* restraint from conscience.

scru'pu·lous (-pyə ləs) *adj.* **1.** having scruples. **2.** careful. **—scru'pu·lous·ly,** *adv.*

scru'ti·nize' (skrōōt'n īz') *v.,* **-nized, -nizing.** examine closely. **—scru'ti·ny,** *n.*

SCS Soil Conservation Service.

SCSI (skuz'ē), a standard for computer interface ports. [*s(mall) c(omputer) s(ystem) i(nterface)*]

sctd scattered.

sctrd scattered.

scty security.

SCU Special Care Unit.

scu'ba (skōō'bə) *n.* self-contained breathing device for swimmers.

scud (skud) *v.,* **scudded, scudding.** move quickly.

scuff (skuf) *v.* **1.** shuffle. **2.** mar by hard use.

scuf'fle, *n., v.,* **-fled, -fling. —n. 1.** rough, confused fight. **—v. 2.** engage in scuffle.

scull (skul) *n.* **1.** oar used over stern. **2.** light racing boat. **—v. 3.** propel with scull.

scul'ler·y (skul'ə rē) *n., pl.* **-leries.** workroom off kitchen.

scul'lion (-yən) *n.* kitchen servant.

sculp. 1. sculptor. **2.** sculptural. **3.** sculpture. Also, **sculpt.**

sculp'ture (skulp'chər) *n.* **1.** three-dimensional art of wood, marble, etc. **2.** piece of such work. **—sculp'tor** (-tər) *n.* **—sculp'tress** (-tris) *n.fem.*

scum (skum) *n.* **1.** film on top of liquid. **2.** worthless persons. **—scum'my,** *adj.*

scup'per (skup'ər) *n.* opening in ship's side to drain off water.

scurf (skûrf) *n.* **1.** loose scales of skin. **2.** scaly matter on a surface. **—scurf'y,** *adj.*

scur'ril·ous (skûr'ə ləs) *adj.* coarsely abusive or derisive. **—scur'ril·ous·ly,** *adv.* **—scur·ril'i·ty** (skə ril'ə tē), **scur'ril·ous·ness,** *n.*

scur'ry (skûr'ē, skur'ē) *v.,* **-ried, -rying,** *n., pl.* **-ries.** hurry.

scur'vy (skûr'vē) *n., adj.,* **-vier, -viest. —n. 1.** disease from inadequate diet. **—adj. 2.** contemptible.

scut'tle (skut'l) *n., v.,* **-tled, -tling. —n. 1.** covered opening, esp. on flat roof. **2.** coal bucket. **—v. 3.** sink intentionally. **4.** scurry.

scut'tle·butt' (-but') *n. Informal.* rumor; gossip.

scythe (sīth) *n.* curved, handled blade for mowing by hand.

SD, South Dakota. Also, **S.D.**

S.D.A. Seventh Day Adventists.

S. Dak., South Dakota.

sdg siding.

SDI Strategic Defense Initiative.

sdl saddle.

sdn sedan.

S. Doc. Senate document.

SDR *Banking.* special drawing rights. Also, **S.D.R.**

sdr sender.

SDS Students for a Democratic Society.

SE, southeast.

sea (sē) *n.* **1.** ocean. **2.** body of salt water smaller than ocean. **3.** turbulence of water. **—sea'board', sea'shore',** *n.* **—sea'coast',** *n.* **—sea'port',** *n.* **—sea'go'ing,** *adj.*

sea anemone, solitary marine polyp.

sea bass (bas) marine food fish.

sea'bed', *n.* ocean floor.

sea cow, manatee.

sea'far'ing, *adj.* traveling by or working at sea. **—sea'far'er,** *n.*

sea'food', *n.* edible marine fish or shellfish.

sea gull, gull.

sea horse, small fish with beaked head.

seal (sēl) *n., pl.* **seals,** (also for 3) **seal,** *v.* **—n. 1.** imprinted device affixed to document. **2.** means of closing. **3.** marine animal with large flippers. **—v. 4.** affix seal to. **5.** close by seal. **—seal'ant,** *n.*

sea legs, ability to adjust balance to motion of ship.

sea level, position of the sea's surface at mean level between low and high tides.

sea lion, large seal.

seam (sēm) *n.* **1.** line formed in sewing two pieces together. **—v. 2.** join with seam.

sea'man, *n., pl.* **-men.** sailor. **—sea'manship',** *n.*

seam'stress (-stris) *n.* woman who sews.

seam'y, *adj.,* **-ier, -iest. 1.** sordid. **2.** having seams. **—seam'i·ness,** *n.*

sé'ance (sā'äns) *n.* meeting to attempt communication with spirits.

sea'plane', *n.* airplane equipped with floats.

sea'port', *n.* port for seagoing vessels.

sear (sēr) *v.* **1.** burn. **2.** dry up.

search (sûrch) *v.* **1.** examine, as in looking for something. **2.** investigate. **—n. 3.** examination or investigation. **—search'er,** *n.*

search'light', *n.* device for throwing strong beam of light.

sea'shell', *n.* shell of marine mollusk.

sea'sick'ness, *n.* nausea from motion of ship. **—sea'sick',** *adj.*

sea'son (sē'zən) *n.* **1.** any of four distinct periods of year. **2.** best or usual time. **—v. 3.** flavor with salt, spices, etc. **—sea'son·al,** *adj.*

sea'son·a·ble, *adj.* appropriate to time of year.

sea'son·ing, *n.* flavoring, as salt, spices, or herbs.

seat (sēt) *n.* **1.** place for sitting. **2.** right to sit, as in Congress. **3.** site; location. **4.** established center. **—v. 5.** place on seat. **6.** find seats for. **7.** install.

seat belt, strap to keep passenger secure in vehicle.

S

seat/ing, *n.* **1.** arrangement of seats. **2.** material for seats.

SEATO (sē/tō), Southeast Asia Treaty Organization (1954–1977).

sea urchin, small, round sea animal with spiny shell.

sea/way/, *n.* waterway giving oceangoing ships access to inland port.

sea/weed/, *n.* plant growing in sea.

sea/wor/thy, *adj.,* -thier, -thiest. fit for sea travel.

se·ba/ceous (si bā/shəs) *adj.* of, resembling, or secreting a fatty substance.

SEbE southeast by east.

seb/or·rhe/a (seb/ə rē/ə) *n.* abnormally heavy discharge from sebaceous glands.

SEbS southeast by south.

SEC Securities and Exchange Commission. Also, **S.E.C.**

sec 1. *Trigonometry.* secant. **2.** second. **3.** section.

sec⁻¹ *Symbol, Trigonometry.* arc secant.

sec. 1. second. **2.** secondary. **3.** secretary. **4.** section. **5.** sector. **6.** according to [from Latin *secundum*].

se·cede/ (si sēd/) *v.,* -ceded, -ceding. withdraw from nation, alliance, etc. —se·ces/sion (-sesh/ən) *n.* —se·ces/sion·ist, *n.*

sech *Math.* hyperbolic secant.

sec. leg. according to law. [from Latin *secundum lēgem*]

se·clude/ (si klōōd/) *v.,* -cluded, -cluding. locate in solitude. —se·clu/sion, *n.*

sec/ond (sek/ənd) *adj.* **1.** next after first. **2.** another. —*n.* **3.** one that is second. **4.** person who aids another. **5.** (*pl.*) imperfect goods. **6.** sixtieth part of minute of time or degree. —*v.* **7.** support; further. —*adv.* **8.** in second place. —sec/ond·ly, *adv.*

sec/ond·ar/y (-ən der/ē) *adj.* **1.** next after first. **2.** of second rank or stage. **3.** less important. —sec/ond·ar/i·ly, *adv.*

sec/ond-guess/, *v.* use hindsight in criticizing or correcting.

sec/ond-hand/, *adj.* **1.** not new. **2.** not original.

second nature, deeply ingrained habit or tendency.

sec/ond-rate/, *adj.* of lesser or minor quality or importance.

second string, squad of players available to replace those who start a game.

second wind (wind) energy for renewed effort.

se/cret (sē/krit) *adj.* **1.** kept from knowledge of others. —*n.* **2.** something secret or hidden. —se/cre·cy, *n.* —se/cret·ly, *adv.*

sec/re·tar/i·at (sek/ri târ/ē ət) *n.* group of administrative officials.

sec/re·tar/y (-ter/ē) *n., pl.* -taries. **1.** office assistant. **2.** head of department of government. **3.** tall writing desk. —sec/re·tar/i·al, *adj.*

se·crete/ (si krēt/) *v.,* -creted, -creting. **1.** hide. **2.** discharge or release by secretion.

se·cre/tion (-krē/shən) *n.* **1.** glandular function of secreting, as bile or milk. **2.** product secreted. —se·cre/to·ry, *adj.*

se·cre/tive (sē/kri tiv, si krē/-) *adj.* **1.** disposed to keep things secret. **2.** secretory. —se·cre/tive·ly, *adv.* —se·cre/tive·ness, *n.*

secs. 1. seconds. **2.** sections.

sect (sekt) *n.* group with common religious faith. —sec·tar/i·an, *adj., n.*

sec/tion (sek/shən) *n.* **1.** separate or distinct part. —*v.* **2.** divide. —sec/tion·al, *adj.*

sec/tor (sek/tər) *n.* **1.** plane figure bounded by two radii and an arc. **2.** part of combat area.

sec/u·lar (sek/yə lər) *adj.* worldly; not religious. —sec/u·lar·ism, *n.* —sec/u·lar·ize/ *v.,* -ized, -izing.

se·cure/ (si kyŏŏr/) *adj., v.,* -cured, -curing. —*adj.* **1.** safe. **2.** firmly in place. **3.** certain. —*v.* **4.** get. **5.** make secure. —se·cure/ly, *adv.*

se·cu/ri·ty (-kyŏŏr/i tē) *n., pl.* -ties. **1.** safety. **2.** protection. **3.** pledge given on loan. **4.** certificate of stock, etc.

security blanket, something that gives feeling of security.

secy secretary. Also, **sec/y**

se·dan/ (si dan/) *n.* closed automobile for four or more.

se·date/ (si dāt/) *adj.* **1.** quiet; sober. —*v.* **2.** give sedative to. —se·date/ly, *adv.* —se·date/ness, *n.*

sed/a·tive (sed/ə tiv) *adj.* **1.** soothing. **2.** relieving pain or excitement. —*n.* **3.** sedative medicine.

sed/en·tar/y (sed/n ter/ē) *adj.* characterized by sitting.

Se/der (sā/dər) *n.* ceremonial dinner at Passover.

sedge (sej) *n.* grasslike marsh plant.

sed/i·ment (sed/ə mənt) *n.* matter settling to bottom of liquid. —sed/i·men/ta·ry, *adj.*

se·di/tion (si dish/ən) *n.* incitement to rebellion. —se·di/tious, *adj.*

se·duce/ (si dōōs/, -dyōōs/) *v.,* -duced, -ducing. **1.** corrupt; tempt. **2.** induce to have sexual intercourse. —se·duc/er, *n.* —se·duc/tion** (-duk/shən) *n.* —se·duc/tive, *adj.*

sed/u·lous (sej/ə ləs) *adj.* diligent.

see (sē) *v.,* saw (sô), seen, seeing, *n.* —*v.* **1.** perceive with the eyes. **2.** find out. **3.** make sure. **4.** escort. —*n.* **5.** office or jurisdiction of bishop.

seed (sēd) *n.* **1.** propagating part of plant. **2.** offspring. —*v.* **3.** sow seed. **4.** remove seed from. —seed/less, *adj.*

seed/ling, *n.* plant grown from seed.

seed money, capital for beginning an enterprise.

seed/y, *adj.,* seedier, seediest. **1.** having many seeds. **2.** shabby. —seed/i·ness, *n.*

see/ing, *conj.* inasmuch as.

seek (sēk) *v.*, **sought, seeking. 1.** search for. **2.** try; attempt. —**seek′er**, *n.*

seem (sēm) *v.* appear (to be or do).

seem′ing, *adj.* apparent. —**seem′ing·ly**, *adv.*

seem′ly, *adj.*, **-lier, -liest.** decorous. —**seem′li·ness**, *n.*

seep (sēp) *v.* ooze; pass gradually. —**seep′age**, *n.*

seer (sēr) *n.* **1.** person who sees. **2.** prophet. —**seer′ess**, *n.*

seer′suck′er (sēr′suk′ər) *n.* crinkled cotton fabric.

see′saw′ (sē′sô′) *n.* **1.** children's sport played on balancing plank. —*v.* **2.** alternate, waver, etc.

seethe (sēᵬ) *v.*, **seethed, seething.** boil; foam.

see′-through′, *adj.* transparent.

seg segment.

seg′ment (seg′mənt) *n.* **1.** part; section. —*v.* **2.** divide into segments. —**seg′men·ta′tion**, *n.* —**seg·men′ta·ry** (-men′tə rē) *adj.*

seg′re·gate′ (seg′ri gāt′) *v.*, **-gated, -gating.** separate from others. —**seg′re·ga′tion**, *n.* —**seg′re·ga′tion·ist**, *n.*

se′gue (sā′gwā, seg′wā) *v.*, **segued, segueing,** *n.* —*v.* **1.** continue at once with the next section, as in piece of music. **2.** make smooth transition. —*n.* **3.** smooth transition.

sei′gnior (sēn′yər, sān′-) *n.* lord. —**seignio′ri·al, sei·gno′ri·al** (sēn yôr′ē əl) *adj.*

seine (sān) *n.*, *v.*, **seined, seining.** —*n.* **1.** kind of fishing net. —*v.* **2.** fish with seine.

seis′mic (sīz′mik, sīs′-) *adj.* of or caused by earthquakes.

seis′mo·graph′ (-mə graf′) *n.* instrument for recording earthquakes. —**seis·mog′ra·phy**, *n.*

seismol. 1. seismological. **2.** seismology.

seis·mol′o·gy (-mol′ə jē) *n.* science of earthquakes. —**seis′mo·log′ic, seis′mo·log′i·cal**, *adj.* —**seis·mol′o·gist**, *n.*

SEIU Service Employees International Union.

seize (sēz) *v.*, **seized, seizing. 1.** take by force or authority. **2.** understand.

seiz′ure (sē′zhər) *n.* **1.** act of seizing. **2.** attack of illness.

sel. 1. select. **2.** selected. **3.** selection; selections. **4.** selectivity. **5.** selector.

sel′dom (sel′dəm) *adv.* not often.

se·lect′ (si lekt′) *v.* **1.** choose. —*adj.* **2.** selected. **3.** choice. —**se·lec′tion**, *n.* —**se·lec′tive**, *adj.* —**se·lec·tiv′i·ty**, *n.*

se·lect′man, *n.*, *pl.* **-men.** town officer in New England.

self (self) *n.*, *pl.* **selves** (selvz), *adj.* —*n.* **1.** person's own nature. **2.** personal advantage or interests. —*adj.* **3.** identical.

self′-ad·dressed′, *adj.* addressed for return to sender.

self′-as·ser′tion, *n.* expression of one's own importance, etc. —**self′-as·ser′tive**, *adj.*

self′-as·sur′ance, *n.* confidence in one's ability or rightness. —**self′as·sured′**, *adj.*

self′-cen′tered, *adj.* interested only in oneself.

self′-con′fi·dence, *n.* faith in one's own judgment, ability, etc. —**self′con′fi·dent**, *adj.*

self′-con′scious, *adj.* excessively aware of being observed by others; embarrassed or uneasy. —**self′-con′scious·ly**, *adv.* —**self′-con′scious·ness**, *n.*

self′-con·tained′, *adj.* **1.** containing within itself all that is necessary. **2.** reserved in behavior.

self′-con·trol′, *n.* restraint of one's actions. —**self′-con·trolled′**, *adj.*

self′-de·fense′, *n.* **1.** act of defending oneself or one's property. **2.** plea that use of force was necessary in defending one's person.

self′-de·ni′al, *n.* sacrifice of one's desires.

self′-de·ter′mi·na′tion, *n.* right or ability to choose government or actions.

self′-ef·fac′ing, *adj.* keeping oneself in the background.

self′-ev′i·dent, *adj.* obvious.

self′-im′age, *n.* conception or evaluation of oneself.

self′-im·por′tant, *adj.* having or showing exaggerated sense of one's own importance.

self′-in′ter·est, *n.* one's personal benefit.

self′ish (sel′fish) *adj.* caring only for oneself. —**self′ish·ly**, *adv.* —**self′ish·ness**, *n.*

self′less, *adj.* having little concern for oneself; unselfish.

self′-made′, *adj.* owing success entirely to one's own efforts.

self′-pos·sessed′, *adj.* calm; poised. —**self′-pos·ses′sion**, *n.*

self′-pres·er·va′tion, *n.* instinctive desire to guard one's safety.

self′-re·spect′, *n.* proper esteem for oneself. —**self′-re·spect′ing**, *adj.*

self′-re·straint′, *n.* self-control.

self′-right′eous, *adj.* convinced one is morally right. —**self′-right′eous·ly**, *adv.* —**self′-right′eous·ness**, *n.*

self′same′, *adj.* identical.

self′-sat′is·fied′, *adj.* complacent. —**self′-sat·is·fac′tion**, *n.*

self′-seek′ing, *n.* **1.** selfish seeking of one's own interests or ends. —*adj.* **2.** given to or characterized by self-seeking.

self′-serv′ice, *adj.* **1.** of a commercial establishment in which customers serve themselves. **2.** designed to be used without the aid of an attendant.

self′-serv′ing, *adj.* serving to further one's own interests.

self′-styled′, *adj.* so called only by oneself.

self′-suf·fi′cient, *adj.* able to supply one's own needs without external assistance. —**self′-suf·fi′ciency**, *n.*

self′-willed′, *adj.* obstinate.

S

sell (sel) *v.*, **sold** (sōld), **selling**. **1.** part with for payment. **2.** betray. **3.** be for sale. **—sell′-er,** *n.*

selsyn self-synchronous.

selt′zer (selt′sər) *n.* effervescent mineral water.

sel′vage (sel′vij) *n.* finished edge on fabric.

SEM 1. *Optics.* scanning electron microscope. **2.** shared equity mortgage.

Sem. 1. Seminary. **2.** Semitic. Also, **Sem**

sem. 1. semicolon. **2.** seminar. **3.** seminary.

se•man′tics (si man′tiks) *n.* study of meanings of words.

sem′a•phore′ (sem′ə fôr′) *n.* apparatus for signaling.

sem′blance (sem′bləns) *n.* **1.** appearance. **2.** copy.

se′men (sē′mən) *n.* male reproductive fluid.

se•mes′ter (si mes′tər) *n.* half school year.

semi-, prefix meaning half or partly.

sem′i•an′nu•al (sem′ē an′yōō əl, sem′ī-) *adj.* occurring every half-year. **—sem′i•an′-nu•al•ly,** *adv.*

sem′i•cir′cle, *n.* half circle. **—sem′i•cir′cu•lar,** *adj.*

semicnd semiconductor.

sem′i•co′lon, *n.* mark of punctuation (;) between parts of sentence.

sem′i•con•duc′tor, *n.* substance, as silicon, with electrical conductivity between that of an insulator and a conductor.

sem′i•fi′nal, *adj.* **1.** of the next to last round in a tournament. **—***n.* **2.** semifinal round or bout.

semih. (in prescriptions) half an hour. [from Latin *sēmihōra*]

sem′i•nal (sem′ə nl) *adj.* **1.** of or consisting of semen. **2.** influencing future development.

sem′i•nar′ (-när′) *n.* class of advanced students.

sem′i•nar′y (-ner′ē) *n.*, *pl.* **-ies.** school, esp. for young women or for divinity students.

Sem′i•nole (-nōl′) *n.*, *pl.* **-nole, -noles.** member of American Indian people of Florida and Oklahoma.

sem′i•pre′cious (sem′ē-, sem′ī-) *adj.* of moderate value.

Se•mit′ic (sə mit′ik) *n.* **1.** language family of Africa and Asia, including Hebrew and Arabic. **—***adj.* **2.** of Semitic languages or their speakers.

sem′i•tone′ (sem′ē-, sem′ī-) *n.* musical pitch halfway between two whole tones.

sem′o•li′na (sem′ə lē′nə) *n.* ground durum.

sen. 1. senate. **2.** senator. **3.** senior. Also, **sen**

sen′ate (sen′it) *n.* legislative body, esp. (*cap.*) upper house of legislatures of United States, Canada, etc. **—sen′a•tor** (-i tər) *n.* **—sen′a•to′ri•al** (-tôr′ē əl) *adj.*

send (send) *v.*, **sent, sending. 1.** cause to go. **2.** have conveyed. **3.** emit. **—send′er,** *n.*

send′-off′, *n.* farewell demonstration of good wishes.

se•nes′cent (si nes′ənt) *adj.* aging. **—se•nes′cence,** *n.*

se′nile (sē′nīl) *adj.* feeble, esp. because of old age. **—se•nil′i•ty** (si nil′ə tē) *n.*

sen′ior (sēn′yər) *adj.* **1.** older. **2.** of higher rank. **3.** denoting last year in school. **—***n.* **4.** senior person.

senior citizen, person 65 years of age or more.

sen•ior′i•ty (sēn yôr′i tē) *n.*, *pl.* **-ties.** status conferred by length of service.

se•ñor′ (se nyôr′) *n.*, *pl.* **-ño•res** (-nyôr′es). *Spanish.* **1.** gentleman. **2.** Mr. or sir. **—se•ño′ra,** *n.*

se•ño•ri′ta (se′nyô rē′tä) *n. Spanish.* **1.** Miss. **2.** young lady.

sens 1. sensitive. **2.** sensitivity.

sen•sa′tion (sen sā′shən) *n.* **1.** operation of senses. **2.** mental condition from such operation. **3.** cause of excited interest.

sen•sa′tion•al, *adj.* **1.** startling; exciting. **2.** of senses or sensation. **—sen•sa′tion•al•ly,** *adv.*

sen•sa′tion•al•ism, *n.* use of sensational subject matter.

sense (sens) *n.*, *v.*, **sensed, sensing. —***n.* **1.** faculty for perceiving physical things (sight, hearing, smell, etc.). **2.** feeling so produced. **3.** (*pl.*) consciousness. **4.** (*often pl.*) rationality; prudence. **5.** meaning. **—***v.* **6.** perceive by senses. **—sense′less,** *adj.*

sen′si•bil′i•ty (sen′sə bil′i tē) *n.*, *pl.* **-ties.** capacity for sensation. **2.** (*often pl.*) sensitive feeling.

sen′si•ble, *adj.* **1.** wise or practical. **2.** aware. **—sen′si•bly,** *adv.*

sen′si•tive, *adj.* **1.** having sensation. **2.** easily affected. **—sen′si•tiv′i•ty,** *n.*

sen′si•tize′ (-tīz′) *v.*, **-tized, -tizing.** make sensitive.

sen′sor (sen′sôr, -sər) *n.* device sensitive to light, temperature, or radiation level that transmits signal to another instrument.

sen′so•ry (-sə rē) *adj.* of sensation or senses.

sen′su•al (sen′shōō əl) *adj.* **1.** inclined to pleasures of the senses. **2.** lewd. **—sen′su•al•ist,** *n.* **—sen′su•al•ism, sen′su•al′i•ty** (-al′i tē) *n.* **—sen′su•al•ly,** *adv.*

sen′su•ous, *adj.* **1.** of or affected by senses. **2.** giving or seeking enjoyment through senses. **—sen′su•ous•ly,** *adv.* **—sen′su•ous•ness,** *n.*

sen′tence (sen′tns) *n.*, *v.*, **-tenced, -tencing. —***n.* **1.** group of words expressing complete thought. **2.** judgment; opinion. **3.** assignment of punishment. **—***v.* **4.** pronounce sentence upon.

sen•ten′tious (sen ten′shəs) *adj.* **1.** using maxims. **2.** affectedly judicious. **3.** pithy.

sen′tient (sen′shənt) *adj.* having feeling. **—sen′tience,** *n.*

sen′ti•ment (-tə mənt) *n.* **1.** opinion. **2.** emotion. **3.** expression of belief or emotion.

sen′ti•men′tal (-men′tl) *adj.* expressing or

showing tender emotion. —**sen'ti•men'tal•ist,** *n.* —**sen'ti•men'tal•ism,** *n.* —**sen'ti•men•tal'i•ty** (-tal'i tē) *n.* —**sen'ti•men'tal•ly,** *adv.*

sen'ti•nel (sen'tn l, -tə nl) *n.* guard.

sen'try (sen'trē) *n., pl.* -**tries.** soldier on watch.

SEP simplified employee pension.

Sep. 1. September. **2.** *Bible.* Septuagint.

sep. 1. *Botany.* sepal. **2.** separable. **3.** separate. **4.** separated. **5.** separation.

se'pal (sē'pəl) *n.* leaflike part of flower.

sep'a•rate', *v.,* -**rated,** -**rating,** *adj.* —*v.* (sep'ə rāt') **1.** keep, put, or come apart. —*adj.* (-rit) **2.** not connected; being apart. —**sep'a•ra'tion,** *n.* —**sep'a•ra•ble,** *adj.* —**sep'a•rate•ly,** *adv.*

sep'a•ra•tist (-ər ə tist, -ə rā'-) *n.* advocate of separation. —**sep'a•ra•tism,** *n.*

sep'a•ra'tor, *n.* apparatus for separating ingredients.

se'pi•a (sē'pē ə) *n.* **1.** brown pigment. **2.** dark brown.

sep'sis (sep'sis) *n.* infection in blood. —**sep'•tic** (-tik) *adj.*

Sept., September.

Sep•tem'ber (sep tem'bər) *n.* ninth month of year.

sep•tet' (sep tet') *n.* group of seven. Also, **sep•tette'.**

sep'ti•ce'mi•a (sep'tə sē'mē ə) *n.* blood poisoning.

septic tank, tank for decomposition of sewage.

sep'tu•a•ge•nar'i•an (sep'chŏŏ ə jə när'ē•ən) *n.* person 70 to 79 years old.

Sep'tu•a•gint (-jint) *n.* oldest Greek version of Old Testament.

sep'tum (sep'təm) *n., pl.* -**ta.** dividing wall in plant or animal structure.

sep'ul•cher (sep'əl kər) *n.* burial place. Also, **sep'ul•chre.** —**se•pul'chral** (sə pul'krəl) *adj.*

seq., 1. sequel. **2.** the following.

seqq. the following (ones). [from Latin *sequentia*]

se'quel (sē'kwəl) *n.* **1.** subsequent event. **2.** literary work, film, etc., continuing earlier one.

se'quence (-kwəns) *n.* **1.** succession; series. **2.** result. —**se•quen'tial** (si kwen'shəl) *adj.*

se•ques'ter (si kwes'tər) *v.* **1.** seclude. **2.** seize and hold. —**se'ques•tra'tion** (sē'-kwes trā'shən) *n.*

se'quin (sē'kwin) *n.* small spangle.

se•quoi'a (si kwoi'ə) *n.* very large tree of northwest U.S.

Ser *Biochemistry.* serine.

ser. 1. serial. **2.** series. **3.** sermon.

se•ra'glio (si ral'yō, -räl'-) *n., pl.* -**glios.** harem.

se•ra'pe (sə rä'pē) *n.* wrap used in Mexico.

ser'aph (ser'əf) *n., pl.* -**aphs, -aphim** (-ə-

fim). angel of highest order. —**se•raph'ic** (sə raf'ik) *adj.*

Serb. 1. Serbia. **2.** Serbian.

sere (sēr) *adj.* withered.

ser'e•nade' (ser'ə nād') *n., v.,* -**naded,** -**nading.** —*n.* **1.** music performed as compliment outside at night. —*v.* **2.** compliment with serenade.

ser'en•dip'i•ty (ser'ən dip'i tē) *n.* luck in making discoveries.

se•rene' (sə rēn') *adj.* **1.** calm. **2.** fair. —**se•ren'i•ty** (-ren'ə tē) *n.* —**se•rene'ly,** *adv.*

serf (sûrf) *n.* **1.** person in feudal servitude. **2.** slave. —**serf'dom,** *n.*

serge (sûrj) *n.* stout twilled fabric.

ser'geant (sär'jənt) *n.* noncommissioned officer above corporal.

sergeant at arms, officer whose chief duty is to preserve order.

se'ri•al (sēr'ē əl) *n.* **1.** story, etc., appearing in installments. —*adj.* **2.** of serial. **3.** of or in series. —**se'ri•al•ly,** *adv.*

se'ries (sēr'ēz) *n.* things in succession.

ser'if (ser'if) *n.* smaller line used to finish off main stroke of letter.

ser'i•graph' (ser'i graf') *n.* silkscreen print.

se'ri•ous (sēr'ē əs) *adj.* **1.** solemn. **2.** important.

ser'mon (sûr'mən) *n.* religious discourse.

serno serial number.

ser'pent (sûr'pənt) *n.* snake. —**ser'pen•tine'** (-pən tēn') *adj.*

serr serrate.

ser'rat•ed (ser'ā tid) *adj.* toothed; notched. Also, **ser'rate** (ser'it).

se'rum (sēr'əm) *n., pl.* **serums, sera** (sēr'ə). **1.** pale-yellow liquid in blood. **2.** such liquid from animal immune to certain disease.

serv. service.

serv'ant (sûr'vənt) *n.* person employed at domestic work.

serve (sûrv) *v.,* **served, serving. 1.** act as servant. **2.** help. **3.** do official duty. **4.** suffice. **5.** undergo (imprisonment, etc.). **6.** deliver.

serv'ice (sûr'vis) *n., v.,* -**iced, -icing.** —*n.* **1.** helpful activity. **2.** domestic employment. **3.** armed forces. **4.** act of public worship. **5.** set of dishes, etc. —*v.* **6.** keep in repair.

serv'ice•a•ble, *adj.* usable.

serv'ice•man, *n., pl.* -**men. 1.** person in armed forces. **2.** gasoline station attendant.

ser'vile (sûr'vil, -vīl) *adj.* slavishly obsequious. —**ser•vil'i•ty** (-vil'ə tē) *n.*

ser'vi•tor (sûr'vi tər) *n.* servant.

ser'vi•tude' (-tōōd', -tyōōd') *n.* bondage.

SES socioeconomic status.

ses'a•me (ses'ə mē) *n.* small edible seed of tropical plant.

ses'qui•cen•ten'ni•al (ses'kwi sen ten'ē əl) *n.* 150th anniversary. —**ses'qui•cen•ten'ni•al,** *adj.*

sess. session.

S

ses′sion (sesh′ən) *n.* sitting, as of a court or class.

set (set) *v.*, **set, setting,** *n.*, *adj.* —*v.* **1.** put or place. **2.** put (broken bone) in position. **3.** arrange (printing type). **4.** pass below horizon. **5.** become firm. —*n.* **6.** group; complete collection. **7.** radio or television receiver. **8.** represented setting of action in drama. —*adj.* **9.** prearranged. **10.** fixed. **11.** resolved.

set′back′, *n.* return to worse condition.

setg setting.

SETI search for extraterrestrial intelligence.

setlg settling.

set•tee′ (se tē′) *n.* small sofa.

set′ter (set′ər) *n.* kind of hunting dog.

set′ting, *n.* **1.** surroundings. **2.** music for certain words.

set′tle (set′l) *v.*, **-tled, -tling. 1.** agree. **2.** pay. **3.** take up residence. **4.** colonize. **5.** quiet. **6.** come to rest. **7.** deposit dregs. —**set′tle•ment,** *n.* —**set′tler,** *n.*

set′-to′ (-tōō′) *n.*, *pl.* **-tos.** brief, sharp fight.

set′up′, *n.* *Informal.* situation in detail.

sev′en (sev′ən) *n.*, *adj.* six plus one. —**sev′enth,** *adj.*, *n.*

sev′en•teen′, *n.*, *adj.* sixteen plus one. —**sev′en•teenth′,** *adj.*, *n.*

seventh heaven, bliss.

sev′en•ty, *n.*, *adj.* ten times seven. —**sev′en•ti′eth,** *adj.*, *n.*

sev′er (sev′ər) *v.* separate; break off. —**sev′er•ance,** *n.*

sev′er•al (sev′ər əl) *adj.* **1.** some, but not many. **2.** respective. **3.** various. —*n.* **4.** some. —**sev′er•al•ly,** *adv.*

se•vere′ (sə vēr′) *adj.*, **-verer, -verest. 1.** harsh. **2.** serious. **3.** plain. **4.** violent or hard. —**se•ver′i•ty** (-ver′i tē) *n.* —**se•vere′ly,** *adv.*

sew (sō) *v.*, **sewed, sewed** or **sewn, sewing.** join or make with thread and needle. —**sew′er,** *n.*

sew′age (sōō′ij) *n.* wastes carried by sewers.

sew′er (sōō′ər) *n.* conduit for waste water, refuse, etc.

sex (seks) *n.* **1.** character of being male or female. **2.** sexual intercourse. —**sex′less,** *adj.* —**sex′u•al** (sek′shōō əl) *adj.* —**sex′u•al•ly,** *adv.* —**sex′u•al′i•ty,** *n.*

sex′a•ge•nar′i•an (sek′sə jə nâr′ē ən) *n.* person 60 to 69 years old.

sex chromosome, chromosome that determines individual's sex.

sex′ism, *n.* bias because of sex, esp. against women. —**sex′ist,** *n.*, *adj.*

sex′tant (sek′stənt) *n.* astronomical instrument for finding position.

sex•tet′ (seks tet′) *n.* group of six. Also, **sex•tette′.**

sex′ton (sek′stən) *n.* church caretaker.

sex′tu•ple (seks tōō′pəl, -tyōō′-, -tup′əl) *adj.* sixfold.

sexual harassment, unwelcome sexual advances, esp. by a superior.

sexual intercourse, genital contact between individuals, esp. penetration of penis into vagina.

sexually transmitted disease, disease transmitted by sexual contact.

sex′y, *adj.*, **-ier, -iest.** sexually interesting or exciting; erotic.

SF 1. *Baseball.* sacrifice fly. **2.** science fiction. **3.** single female. **4.** *Finance.* sinking fund.

sf 1. science fiction. **2.** *Music.* sforzando.

s-f science fiction.

S.F. 1. San Francisco. **2.** senior fellow.

Sfc *Military.* sergeant first class.

sfm surface feet per minute.

SFr. (in Switzerland) franc; francs. Also, **Sfr.**

sft shaft.

sftw software.

sfx suffix.

sfz *Music.* sforzando.

SG 1. senior grade. **2.** Secretary General. **3.** Solicitor General. **4.** Surgeon General.

sg *Grammar.* singular. Also, **sg.**

s.g. specific gravity.

sgd. signed.

sgl single.

SGML *Computers.* Standard Generalized Markup Language.

SGO Surgeon General's Office.

Sgt., Sergeant.

Sgt. Maj. Sergeant Major.

sh 1. sheet. **2.** shower. **3.** shunt.

s/h 1. shipping/handling. **2.** shorthand.

SHA *Navigation.* sidereal hour angle.

shab′by (shab′ē) *adj.*, **-bier, -biest. 1.** worn; wearing worn clothes. **2.** mean. —**shab′bi•ly,** *adv.* —**shab′bi•ness,** *n.*

shack (shak) *n.* rough cabin.

shack′le (shak′əl) *n.*, *v.*, **-led, -ling.** —*n.* **1.** iron bond for wrist, ankle, etc. **2.** U-shaped bolt of padlock. —*v.* **3.** restrain.

shad (shad) *n.* kind of herring.

shade (shād) *n.*, *v.*, **shaded, shading.** —*n.* **1.** slightly dark, cool place. **2.** ghost. **3.** degree of color. **4.** slight amount. —*v.* **5.** protect from light.

shad′ow (shad′ō) *n.* **1.** dark image made by body intercepting light. **2.** shade. **3.** trace. —*v.* **4.** shade. **5.** follow secretly. —**shad′ow•y,** *adj.*

shad′ow•box′, *v.* go through motions of boxing without an opponent, as in training.

shad′y, *adj.*, **-ier, -iest. 1.** in shade. **2.** arousing suspicion. —**shad′i•ness,** *n.*

shaft (shaft) *n.* **1.** long slender rod. **2.** beam. **3.** revolving bar in engine. **4.** vertical space.

shag (shag) *n.* **1.** matted wool, hair, etc. **2.** napped cloth. —**shag′gy,** *adj.*

shah (shä) *n.* (formerly) ruler of Persia (now Iran).

Shak. Shakespeare.

shake (shāk) v., **shook** (shŏŏk), **shaken, shaking,** n. —v. **1.** move with quick irregular motions. **2.** tremble. **3.** agitate. —n. **4.** act of shaking. **5.** tremor. —**shak′er,** n.

shake′down′, n. **1.** extortion, as by blackmail. **2.** thorough search.

shake′up′, n. Informal. organizational reform.

Shaks. Shakespeare.

shak′y, adj., **-ier, -iest. 1.** not firm; insecure. **2.** quavering. **3.** affected by fright. —**shak′i•ly,** adv. —**shak′i•ness,** n.

shale (shāl) n. kind of layered rock.

shall (shal; unstressed shəl) v. **1.** am (is, are) going to. **2.** am (is, are) obliged or commanded to.

shal•lot′ (shal′ət) n. small onionlike plant.

shal•low (shal′ō) adj. not deep.

sham (sham) n. adj., v., **shammed, shamming.** —n. **1.** pretense or imitation. —adj. **2.** pretended. —v. **3.** pretend.

sham′ble, v., **-bled, -bling,** n. —v. **1.** walk awkwardly. —n. **2.** shambling gait. **3.** (pl.) scene of confusion.

shame (shām) n., v., **shamed, shaming.** —n. **1.** painful feeling from wrong or foolish act or circumstance. **2.** disgrace. —v. **3.** cause to feel shame. —**shame′ful,** adj. —**shame′less,** adj.

shame′faced′ (-fāst′) adj. **1.** bashful. **2.** showing shame.

sham•poo′ (sham pōō′) v. **1.** wash (hair, rugs, or upholstery). —n. **2.** act of shampooing. **3.** soap, etc., for shampooing.

sham′rock (sham′rok) n. plant with three-part leaf.

shang′hai (shang′hī) v., **-haied, -haiing.** (formerly) abduct for service as sailor.

shank (shangk) n. part of leg between knee and ankle.

shan′tung′ (shan′tung′) n. silk.

shan′ty (shan′tē) n., pl. **-ties.** rough hut.

shape (shāp) n., v., **shaped, shaping.** —n. **1.** form. **2.** nature. —v. **3.** give form to; take form. **4.** adapt. —**shape′less,** adj.

shape′ly, adj., **-lier, -liest.** handsome in shape. —**shape′li•ness,** n.

shard (shärd) n. fragment, esp. of broken earthenware.

share (shâr) n., v., **shared, sharing.** —n. **1.** due individual portion. **2.** portion of corporate stock. —v. **3.** distribute. **4.** use, enjoy, etc., jointly. —**shar′er,** n. —**share′hold′er,** n.

share′crop′per, n. tenant farmer who pays as rent part of the crop.

shark (shärk) n. **1.** marine fish, often ferocious. **2.** person who victimizes.

shark′skin′, n. smooth, silky fabric with dull surface.

sharp (shärp) adj. **1.** having thin cutting edge or fine point. **2.** abrupt. **3.** keen. **4.** shrewd. **5.** raised in musical pitch. —adv. **6.** punctually. —n. **7.** musical tone one half step above

given tone. —**sharp′en,** v. —**sharp′en•er,** n. —**sharp′ly,** adv. —**sharp′ness,** n.

sharp′er, n. swindler.

sharp′-eyed′, adj. having keen sight.

sharp′shoot′er, n. skilled shooter.

sharp′-tongued′, adj. harsh in speech.

shat′ter (shat′ər) v. break in pieces.

shat′ter•proof′, adj. made to resist shattering.

shave (shāv) v., **shaved, shaved** or **shaven, shaving,** n. —v. **1.** remove hair with razor. **2.** cut thin slices. —n. **3.** act of shaving.

shav′ings, n.pl. thin slices of wood.

shawl (shôl) n. long covering for head and shoulders.

shcr shipping container.

she (shē) pron. **1.** female last mentioned. —n. **2.** female.

sheaf (shēf) n., pl. **sheaves.** bundle.

shear (shēr) v., **sheared, sheared** or **shorn, shearing.** clip, as wool.

shears, n.pl. large scissors.

sheath (shēth) n. **1.** case for sword blade. **2.** any similar covering.

sheathe (shēth) v., **sheathed, sheathing.** put into or enclose in sheath.

she•bang′ (shə bang′) n. Informal. organization or contrivance.

shed (shed) v., **shed, shedding,** n. —v. **1.** pour forth. **2.** cast (light). **3.** throw off. —n. **4.** simple enclosed shelter.

sheen (shēn) n. brightness.

sheep (shēp) n., pl. **sheep.** mammal valued for fleece and flesh.

sheep dog, dog trained to herd sheep.

sheep′fold′, n. enclosure for sheep.

sheep′ish, adj. embarrassed or timid.

sheer (shēr) adj. **1.** very thin. **2.** complete. **3.** steep. —v., n. **4.** swerve.

sheet (shēt) n. **1.** large piece of cloth used as bedding. **2.** broad thin mass or piece. **3.** rope or chain to control sail.

sheik (shēk) n. (Arab) chief. —**sheik′dom,** n.

shek′el (shek′əl) n. ancient Hebrew and modern Israeli monetary unit.

shelf (shelf) n., pl. **shelves** (shelvz). **1.** horizontal slab on wall, etc., for holding objects. **2.** ledge.

shelf life, period during which commodity remains fit for use.

shell (shel) n. **1.** hard outer covering. **2.** shotgun cartridge. **3.** explosive missile from cannon. **4.** light racing boat. —v. **5.** remove shell from. **6.** take from shell. **7.** bombard with shells.

shel•lac′ (shə lak′) n., v., **-lacked, -lacking.** —n. **1.** substance used in varnish. **2.** varnish. —v. **3.** coat with shellac.

shell′fish′, n. aquatic animal having shell.

shell shock, combat fatigue.

shel′ter (shel′tər) n. **1.** place of protection. —v. **2.** protect.

shelve (shelv) v., **shelved, shelving. 1.** put

S

on shelf. **2.** lay aside. **3.** furnish with shelves. **4.** slope.

she·nan'i·gans (shə nan'ĭ gənz) *n.pl. Informal.* mischief.

shep'herd (shep'ərd) *n.* **1.** person who tends sheep. —*v.* **2.** guide while guarding. —**shep'-herd·ess,** *n.*

sher'bet (shûr'bĭt) *n.* frozen fruit-flavored dessert.

sher'iff (sher'ĭf) *n.* county law-enforcement officer.

sher'ry (sher'ē) *n., pl.* **-ries.** strong wine served as cocktail.

SHF 1. single Hispanic female. **2.** Also, **shf** superhigh frequency.

shib'bo·leth (shĭb'ə lĭth) *n.* **1.** peculiarity of pronunciation or usage that distinguishes a group. **2.** slogan; catchword.

shield (shēld) *n.* **1.** plate of armor carried on arm. —*v.* **2.** protect.

shift (shift) *v.* **1.** move about. **2.** change positions. —*n.* **3.** act of shifting. **4.** period of work.

shift'less, *adj.* resourceless or lazy.

shift'y, *adj.,* **-ier, -iest.** tricky; devious. —**shift'i·ly,** *adv.* —**shift'i·ness,** *n.*

shill (shil) *n.* person who poses as a customer to lure others.

shil·le'lagh (shə lā'lē, -lə) *n.* rough Irish walking stick or cudgel.

shil'ling (shĭl'ing) *n.* former British coin, 20th part of pound.

shil'ly-shal'ly (shĭl'ē shal'ē) *v.,* **-lied, -lying.** be irresolute.

shim'mer (shĭm'ər) *v.* **1.** glow faintly; flicker. —*n.* **2.** faint glow. —**shim'mer·y,** *adj.*

shim'my (shĭm'ē) *n., pl.* **-mies,** *v.,* **-mied, -mying.** *Informal.* —*n.* **1.** vibration. —*v.* **2.** vibrate.

shin (shin) *n.* front of leg from knee to ankle.

shin'bone', *n.* tibia.

shin'dig' (shin'dig') *n. Informal.* elaborate and usu. large party.

shine (shīn) *v.,* **shone** (shōn) or (for 4) **shined, shining,** *n.* —*v.* **1.** give forth light. **2.** sparkle. **3.** excel. **4.** polish. —*n.* **5.** radiance. **6.** polish. —**shin'y,** *adj.*

shin'er, *n. Informal.* black eye.

shin'gle (shing'gəl) *n., v.,* **-gled, -gling.** —*n.* **1.** thin slab used in overlapping rows as covering. **2.** close haircut. **3.** (*pl.*) viral skin disease marked by blisters. —*v.* **4.** cover with shingles. **5.** cut (hair) short.

shin'ny, *n.* form of hockey.

shin splints, painful condition of shins associated with strenuous activity.

Shin'to (shin'tō) *n.* native religion of Japan.

ship (ship) *n., v.,* **shipped, shipping.** —*n.* **1.** vessel for use on water. —*v.* **2.** send as freight. **3.** engage to serve on ship. **4.** send away. —**ship'board',** *n.* —**ship'mate',** *n.* —**ship'ment,** *n.* —**ship'per,** *n.*

-ship, suffix meaning: **1.** state or quality, as *friendship.* **2.** position or rank, as *lordship.* **3.** skill or art, as *horsemanship.*

ship'shape', *adj., adv.* in good order.

ship'wreck', *n.* destruction of ship.

ship'wright', *n.* carpenter in ship repair or construction.

ship'yard', *n.* place where ships are built or repaired.

shire (shīᵊr) *n. Brit.* county.

shirk (shûrk) *v.* **1.** evade (obligation). —*n.* **2.** Also, **shirk'er.** person who shirks.

shirr (shûr) *v.* **1.** gather (cloth) on parallel threads. **2.** bake (eggs).

shirt (shûrt) *n.* garment for upper body.

shirt'ing, *n.* fabric used to make shirts.

shirt'tail', *n.* part of shirt below waistline.

shirt'waist', *n.* tailored blouse.

shish' ke·bab' (shish' kə bob') cubes of meat broiled on a skewer.

shiv'er (shiv'ər) *v.* **1.** tremble as with cold. **2.** splinter. —*n.* **3.** quiver. **4.** splinter. —**shiv'er·y,** *adj.*

shl shellac.

shld shield.

shldr shoulder.

shltr shelter.

SHM single Hispanic male.

S.H.M. *Physics.* simple harmonic motion. Also, **s.h.m.**

SHO Showtime (a cable channel).

shoal (shōl) *n.* **1.** shallow part of stream. **2.** large number, esp. of fish.

shoat (shōt) *n.* young pig.

shock (shok) *n.* **1.** violent blow, impact, etc. **2.** anything emotionally upsetting. **3.** state of nervous collapse. **4.** group of sheaves of grain. **5.** bushy mass of hair, etc. —*v.* **6.** strike with force, horror, etc.

shock absorber, device for damping sudden rapid motion.

shock'er, *n.* **1.** something that shocks. **2.** sensational novel, play, etc.

shock therapy, treatment for mental disorders in which drug or electricity is used to induce convulsions.

shod'dy (shod'ē) *adj.,* **-dier, -diest.** of poor quality. —**shod'di·ly,** *adv.* —**shod'di·ness,** *n.*

shoe (shoō) *n., v.,* **shod** (shod), **shoeing.** —*n.* **1.** external covering for foot. **2.** shoelike machine part. —*v.* **3.** provide with shoes.

shoe'horn', *n.* shaped object to assist in slipping into shoe.

shoe'mak'er, *n.* person who makes or mends shoes.

shoe'string', *n.* **1.** lace or string for tying shoes. **2.** very small amount of money.

shoe'tree', *n.* device placed in shoe to hold its shape.

sho'gun (shō'gən) *n.* chief military commander of Japan from 8th to 12th centuries.

shoo (shoō) *v.,* **shooed, shooing.** drive away by shouting "shoo."

shoo′-in′, n. one regarded as certain to win.

shoot (shoot) v. **1.** hit or kill with bullet, etc. **2.** discharge (firearm, bow, etc.). **3.** pass or send rapidly along. **4.** emit. **5.** grow; come forth. —n. **6.** shooting contest. **7.** young twig, etc. —**shoot′er,** n.

shooting star, meteor.

shop (shop) n., v., **shopped, shopping.** —n. **1.** store. **2.** workshop. —v. **3.** inspect or purchase goods. —**shop′per,** n.

shop′lift′er, n. person who steals from shops while posing as customer.

shop′talk′, n. conversation about one's work or occupation.

shop′worn′, adj. worn-out.

shore (shôr) v., **shored, shoring,** n. —v. **1.** prop. —n. **2.** prop. **3.** land beside water. **4.** land or country.

shorn (shôrn) v. pp. of **shear.**

short (shôrt) adj. **1.** not long or tall. **2.** rudely brief. **3.** scanty. **4.** inferior. **5.** crumbly, as pastry. —adv. **6.** abruptly. —n. **7.** anything short. **8.** (pl.) short, loose trousers. **9.** short circuit. —**short′en,** v. —**short′ness,** n.

short′age (shôr′tij) n. scarcity.

short′bread′, n. rich butter cookie.

short′cake′, n. rich biscuit topped with fruit and cream.

short′change′, v., **-changed, -changing. 1.** give less than the correct change to. **2.** cheat; defraud.

short circuit, Elect. abnormal connection between two points in circuit.

short′com′ing, n. defect.

short′cut′, n. shorter way to goal.

short′en•ing (shôrt′ning) n. **1.** butter or other fat used to make pastry short. **2.** act of making or becoming short.

short′hand′, n. system of swift handwriting.

short′-hand′ed, adj. not having enough workers.

short′-lived′ (-līvd, -livd) adj. lasting but short time.

short′ly, adv. in short time.

short shrift, little attention or consideration.

short′•sight′ed, adj. lacking foresight.

short′stop′, n. Baseball. player or position between second and third base.

short′-tem′pered, adj. irascible.

short′wave′, n. radio frequencies used for long-distance transmission.

Sho•sho′ne (shō shō′nē) n., pl. **-ne, -nes.** member of an American Indian people.

shot (shot) n., pl. **shots** or (for 3), **shot. 1.** discharge of firearm, bow, etc. **2.** range of fire. **3.** (often pl.) lead pellets. **4.** act or instance of shooting. **5.** person who shoots. **6.** heavy metal ball.

shot′gun′, n. kind of smoothbore gun.

shot put, competition in which heavy metal ball is thrown for distance. —**shot′-put′ter,** n.

should (shŏŏd) v. pt. of **shall.**

shoul′der (shōl′dər) n. **1.** part of body from neck to upper joint of arm or foreleg. **2.** unpaved edge of road. —v. **3.** push as with shoulder. **4.** take up, as burden.

shout (shout) v. **1.** call or speak loudly. —n. **2.** loud cry.

shove (shuv) v., **shoved, shoving,** n. —v. **1.** push hard. —n. **2.** hard push.

shov′el, n., v., **-eled, -eling.** —n. **1.** implement with broad scoop and handle. —v. **2.** dig or clear with shovel. —**shov′el•er,** n.

show (shō) v., **showed, shown** or **showed, showing,** n. —v. **1.** display. **2.** guide. **3.** explain. **4.** prove. **5.** be visible. —n. **6.** exhibition. **7.** acted entertainment. **8.** appearance.

show′boat′, n. boat used as traveling theater.

show′case′, n., v., **-cased, -casing.** —n. **1.** setting for displaying something. —v. **2.** exhibit to best advantage.

show′down′, n. decisive confrontation.

show′er (shou′ər) n. **1.** short fall of rain. **2.** any similar fall. **3.** bath in which water falls from above. —v. **4.** rain briefly. **5.** give liberally. —**show′er•y,** adj.

show′-off′ (shō′-) n. person who seeks attention.

show′piece′, n. something worthy of being exhibited.

show′place′, n. place notable for its beauty or historical interest.

show′y, adj., **-ier, -iest.** conspicuous; ostentatious.

shp shaft horsepower. Also, **SHP, S.H.P., s.hp., s.h.p.**

shpng shipping.

shpt. shipment.

shrap′nel (shrap′nl) n. shell filled with missiles.

shred (shred) n., v., **shredded** or **shred, shredding.** —n. **1.** torn piece or strip. **2.** bit. —v. **3.** reduce to shreds.

shrew (shroo) n. **1.** quarrelsome woman. **2.** small mouselike mammal. —**shrew′ish,** adj.

shrewd (shrood) adj. astute. —**shrewd•ly,** adv. —**shrewd′ness,** n.

shriek (shrēk) n. **1.** loud shrill cry. —v. **2.** utter shrieks.

shrike (shrīk) n. predatory bird.

shrill (shril) adj. **1.** high-pitched; piercing. —v. **2.** cry shrilly. —**shril′ly,** adv. —**shrill′ness,** n.

shrimp (shrimp) n. small long-tailed edible shellfish.

shrine (shrīn) n. place for sacred relics.

shrink (shringk) v., **shrank** (shrangk) or **shrunk** (shrungk), **shrunk** or **shrunken, shrinking. 1.** draw back. **2.** become smaller.

shrink′age (shring′kij) n. **1.** act of shrinking. **2.** amount of shrinking.

shrinking violet, shy person.

shrink′-wrap′, v., **-wrapped, -wrapping,** n. —v. **1.** seal in plastic film that when exposed

S

to heat shrinks tightly around object. —*n.* **2.** plastic used to shrink-wrap.

shrive (shrīv) *v.*, **shrove** (shrōv) or **shrived, shriven** (shriv′ən) or **shrived, shriving. 1.** impose penance on. **2.** grant absolution to.

shriv′el (shriv′əl) *v.*, **-eled, -eling.** wrinkle in drying.

shroud (shroud) *n.* **1.** burial gown or cloth. **2.** (*pl.*) set of ropes supporting masts of vessel. —*v.* **3.** wrap; cover.

shrub (shrub) *n.* woody perennial plant. —**shrub′ber•y,** *n.*

shrug (shrug) *v.*, **shrugged, shrugging,** *n.* —*v.* **1.** move shoulders to show ignorance, indifference, etc. —*n.* **2.** this movement.

sht. sheet.

shtc short time constant.

shtdn shutdown.

shtg. shortage.

shthg sheathing.

shtick (shtik) *n. Slang.* **1.** show-business routine. **2.** special interest, talent, etc. Also, **shtik.**

shuck (shuk) *n.* **1.** husk. **2.** shell. —*v.* **3.** remove shucks from.

shud′der (shud′ər) *v.* **1.** tremble, as from horror. —*n.* **2.** this movement.

shuf′fle (shuf′əl) *v.*, **-fled, -fling,** *n.* —*v.* **1.** drag feet in walking. **2.** mix (playing cards). **3.** shift. —*n.* **4.** shuffling gait. **5.** act of shuffling cards.

shuf′fle•board′, *n.* game played on marked floor surface.

shun (shun) *v.*, **shunned, shunning.** avoid.

shunt (shunt) *v.* divert; sidetrack.

shut (shut) *v.*, **shut, shutting,** *adj.* —*v.* **1.** close. **2.** confine. **3.** exclude. —*adj.* **4.** closed.

shut′-in′, *n.* person confined, as by illness, to the house, a hospital, etc.

shut′out′, *n.* game in which one side does not score.

shut′ter, *n.* **1.** cover for window. **2.** device for opening and closing camera lens.

shut′ter•bug′, *n.* amateur photographer.

shut′tle (shut′l) *n.*, *v.*, **-tled, -tling.** —*n.* **1.** device for moving thread back and forth in weaving. **2.** bus, plane, etc., moving between two destinations. —*v.* **3.** move quickly back and forth.

shut′tle•cock′, *n.* feathered object hit back and forth in badminton.

shv sheave.

shwr shower.

shy (shī) *adj.*, **shyer** or **shier, shyest** or **shiest,** *v.*, **shied, shying,** *n.*, *pl.* **shies.** —*adj.* **1.** bashful. **2.** wary. **3.** short. —*v.* **4.** start aside, as in fear. **5.** throw suddenly. —*n.* **6.** shying movement. **7.** sudden throw. —**shy′ly,** *adv.* —**shy′ness,** *n.*

shy′ster (shī′stər) *n. Informal.* unscrupulous lawyer.

SI International System of Units. [from French *S(ystème) I(nternationale d'unités)*]

Si *Symbol, Chemistry.* silicon.

S.I. Staten Island.

Si•a•mese′ twins (sī′ə mēz′, -mēs′) twins joined together by body part.

sib′i•lant (sib′ə lənt) *adj.* **1.** hissing. —*n.* **2.** hissing sound. —**sib′i•lance,** *n.*

sib′ling (sib′ling) *n.* brother or sister.

sib′yl (sib′əl) *n.* female prophet. —**sib′yl•line,** *adj.*

sic (sik) *v.*, **sicked, sicking,** *adv.* —*v.* **1.** urge to attack. —*adv.* **2.** *Latin.* so (it reads).

sick (sik) *adj.* **1.** ill; not well. **2.** of sickness. **3.** nauseated. —*n.pl.* **4.** sick people. —**sick′ness,** *n.* —**sick′en,** *v.*

sick′le (sik′əl) *n.* reaping implement with curved blade.

sick′ly, *adj.*, **-lier, -liest,** *adv.* **1.** ailing. **2.** faint; weak. —*adv.* **3.** in sick manner.

side (sīd) *n.*, *adj.*, *v.*, **sided, siding.** —*n.* **1.** edge. **2.** surface. **3.** part other than front, back, top, or bottom. **4.** aspect. **5.** region. **6.** faction. —*adj.* **7.** at, from, or toward side. **8.** subordinate. —*v.* **9.** align oneself.

side′bar′, *n.* short news feature highlighting longer story.

side′board′, *n.* dining-room cupboard.

side′burns′, *n.pl.* short whiskers in front of ears.

side effect, *n.* often adverse secondary effect.

side′kick′, *n.* **1.** close friend. **2.** confederate or assistant.

side′light′, *n.* item of incidental information.

side′line′, *n.*, *v.*, **-lined, -lining.** —*n.* **1.** business or activity in addition to one's primary business. **2.** additional line of goods. **3.** line defining the side of an athletic field. —*v.* **4.** remove from action.

side′long′, *adj.*, *adv.* to or toward the side.

si•de′re•al (sī dēr′ē əl) *adj.* of or determined by stars.

side′sad′dle, *adv.* with both legs on one side of a saddle.

side′show′, *n.* **1.** minor show connected with principal one, as at circus. **2.** subordinate event or spectacle.

side′split′ting, *adj.* extremely funny.

side′-step′, *v.*, **-stepped, -stepping.** avoid, as by stepping aside.

side′swipe′, *v.*, **-swiped, -swiping.** strike along side.

side′track′, *v.* divert.

side′walk′, *n.* paved walk along street.

side′ward (-wərd) *adj.* toward one side. —**side′ward, side′wards,** *adv.*

side′ways′, *adj.*, *adv.* **1.** with side foremost. **2.** toward or from a side. Also, **side′wise′.**

sid′ing, *n.* short railroad track for halted cars.

si′dle (sīd′l) *v.*, **-dled, -dling.** move sideways or furtively.

SIDS (sidz) sudden infant death syndrome.

siege (sēj) *n.* surrounding of place to force surrender.

si•en′na (sē en′ə) *n.* yellowish- or reddish-brown pigment.

si•er′ra (sē er′ə) *n.* chain of hills or mountains whose peaks suggest the teeth of a saw.

si•es′ta (sē es′tə) *n.* midday nap or rest.

sieve (siv) *n., v.,* **sieved, sieving.** —*n.* **1.** meshed implement for separating coarse and fine loose matter. —*v.* **2.** sift.

sift (sift) *v.* separate with sieve. —**sift′er,** *n.*

SIG special-interest group.

Sig. 1. (in prescriptions) write; mark; label: indicating directions to be written on a package or label for the use of the patient. [from Latin *signā*] **2.** let it be written. [from Latin *signētur*] **3.** Signore; Signori: the Italian form of address for a man.

sig. 1. signal. **2.** signature. **3.** signore; signori: an Italian form of address for a man.

sigh (sī) *v.* **1.** exhale audibly in grief, weariness, etc. **2.** yearn. —*n.* **3.** act or sound of sighing.

sight (sīt) *n.* **1.** power of seeing. **2.** glimpse; view. **3.** range of vision. **4.** device for guiding aim. **5.** interesting place. —*v.* **6.** get sight of. **7.** aim by sights. —**sight′less,** *adj.*

sight′ed, *adj.* not blind.

sight′ly, *adj.,* **-lier, -liest.** pleasing to sight. —**sight′li•ness,** *n.*

sight′read′ (rēd) *v.,* **-read** (-red′), **-reading.** perform without previous study.

sight′see′ing, *n.* visiting new places and things of interest. —**sight′se′er,** *n.* —**sight′see′,** *v.*

sign (sīn) *n.* **1.** indication. **2.** conventional mark, figure, etc. **3.** advertising board. **4.** trace. **5.** omen. —*v.* **6.** put signature to. —**sign′er,** *n.*

sig′nal (sig′nl) *n., adj., v.,* **-naled, -naling.** —*n.* **1.** symbolic communication. —*adj.* **2.** serving as signal. **3.** notable. —*v.* **4.** communicate by symbols. —**sig′nal•er,** *n.*

sig′nal•ize′, *v.,* **-ized, -izing.** make notable.

sig′nal•ly, *adv.* notably.

sig′na•to′ry (sig′nə tôr′ē) *n., pl.* **-ries.** signer.

sig′na•ture (-nə chər) *n.* **1.** person's name in own handwriting. **2.** *Music.* sign indicating key or time of piece.

sig′net (sig′nit) *n.* small seal.

sig•nif′i•cance (sig nif′i kəns) *n.* **1.** importance. **2.** meaning. —**sig•nif′i•cant,** *adj.*

significant other, spouse or cohabiting lover.

sig′ni•fy′, *v.,* **-fied, -fying. 1.** make known. **2.** mean. —**sig′ni•fi•ca′tion,** *n.*

Sikh (sēk) *n.* member of religion of India that rejects Hindu caste system. —**Sikh′ism,** *n.*

sil silence.

si′lage (sī′lij) *n.* fodder preserved in silo.

si′lence (sī′ləns) *n., v.,* **-lenced, -lencing.** —*n.* **1.** absence of sound. **2.** muteness. —*v.*

3. bring to silence. —**si′lent,** *adj.* —**si′lent•ly,** *adv.*

si′lenc•er, *n.* device for deadening report of a firearm.

sil′hou•ette′ (sil′ōo et′) *n., v.,* **-etted, -etting.** —*n.* **1.** filled-in outline. —*v.* **2.** show in silhouette.

sil′i•ca (sil′i kə) *n.* silicon dioxide, appearing as quartz, sand, flint, etc.

sil′i•cate (-kit, -kāt′) *n.* mineral consisting of silicon and oxygen with a metal.

sil′i•con (-kən, -kon′) *n.* abundant nonmetallic element.

sil′i•cone′ (-kōn′) *n.* polymer with silicon and oxygen atoms, used in adhesives, lubricants, etc.

sil′i•co′sis (-kō′sis) *n.* lung disease caused by inhaling silica.

silk (silk) *n.* **1.** fine soft fiber produced by silkworms. **2.** thread or cloth made of it. —*adj.* **3.** Also, **silk′en, silk′y.** of silk.

silk′worm′, *n.* caterpillar that spins silk to make its cocoon.

sill (sil) *n.* horizontal piece beneath window, door, or wall.

sil′ly (sil′ē) *adj.,* **-lier, -liest. 1.** stupid. **2.** absurd. —**sil′li•ness,** *n.*

si′lo (sī′lō) *n., pl.* **-los.** airtight structure to hold green fodder.

sils silver solder.

silt (silt) *n.* **1.** earth, etc., carried and deposited by a stream. —*v.* **2.** fill with silt.

Si•lu′ri•an (si lŏŏr′ē ən) *adj.* pertaining to the third period of the Paleozoic Era.

sil′ver (sil′vər) *n.* **1.** valuable white metallic element. **2.** coins, utensils, etc., of silver. **3.** whitish gray. —*adj.* **4.** of or plated with silver. **5.** eloquent. **6.** indicating 25th anniversary. —**sil′ver•y,** *adj.*

sil′ver•fish′, *n.* wingless, silvery-gray insect that damages books, etc.

silver lining, prospect of hope or comfort.

silver nitrate, poisonous powder used in photography and as astringent.

sil′ver-tongued′, *adj.* eloquent.

sil′ver•ware′, *n.* eating and serving utensils of silver or other metal.

sim. 1. similar. **2.** simile. **3.** simulator.

sim′i•an (sim′ē ən) *n.* **1.** ape or monkey. —*adj.* **2.** of apes or monkeys.

sim′i•lar (sim′ə lər) *adj.* with general likeness. —**sim′i•lar′i•ty** (-lar′i tē) *n.* —**sim′i•lar•ly,** *adv.*

sim′i•le′ (-ə lē) *n.* phrase expressing resemblance.

si•mil′i•tude′ (si mil′i tōōd′, -tyōōd′) *n.* **1.** likeness. **2.** comparison.

simlt simultaneous.

SIMM (sim), *Computers.* single inline memory module.

sim′mer (sim′ər) *v.* remain or keep near boiling.

S

si′mo•ny (sī′mə nē) *n.* buying or selling of ecclesiastical preferments.

sim•pa′ti•co′ (sim pä′ti kō′) *adj.* like-minded.

sim′per (sim′pər) *v.* **1.** smile affectedly. —*n.* **2.** affected smile.

sim′ple (sim′pəl) *adj.*, **-pler, -plest. 1.** easy to grasp, use, etc. **2.** plain. **3.** mentally weak. —**sim•plic′i•ty** (-plis′i tē) *n.* —**sim′ply,** *adv.*

simple interest, interest payable only on the principle.

sim′ple-mind′ed, *adj.* **1.** unsophisticated. **2.** mentally deficient.

sim′ple•ton (-tən) *n.* fool.

sim′pli•fy′ (-plə fī′) *v.*, **-fied, -fying.** make simpler. —**sim′pli•fi•ca′tion,** *n.*

sim•plis′tic (-plis′tik) *adj.* foolishly or na-ïvely simple. —**sim•plis′ti•cal•ly,** *adv.*

sim′u•late′ (sim′yə lāt′) *v.*, **-lated, -lating.** feign; imitate. —**sim′u•la′tion,** *n.* —**sim′u•la′tive,** *adj.*

si′mul•cast′ (sī′məl kast′) *n.*, *v.*, **-cast, -casted, -casting.** —*n.* **1.** program broadcast simultaneously on radio and television. —*v.* **2.** broadcast a simulcast.

si′mul•ta′ne•ous (-tā′nē əs) *adj.* occurring at the same time. —**si′mul•ta′ne•ous•ly,** *adv.* —**si′mul•ta•ne′i•ty** (-tə nē′i tē) *n.*

sin (sin) *n.*, *v.*, **sinned, sinning.** —*n.* **1.** offense, esp. against divine law. —*v.* **2.** commit sin. —**sin′ner,** *n.* —**sin′ful,** *adj.* —**sin′ful•ly,** *adv.* —**sin′ful•ness,** *n.*

since (sins) *adv.* **1.** from then till now. **2.** subsequently. —*conj.* **3.** from time when. **4.** because.

sin•cere′ (sin sēr′) *adj.*, **-cerer, -cerest.** honest; genuine. —**sin•cer′i•ty** (-ser′i tē) *n.* —**sin•cere′ly,** *adv.*

si′ne•cure′ (sī′ni kyŏŏr′) *n.* job without real responsibilities.

si′ne di′e (sī′nē dī′ē), without fixing a day for future action.

si′ne qua non′ (sin′ā kwä nōn′) indispensable condition or element.

sin′ew (sin′yōō) *n.* **1.** tendon. **2.** strength. —**sin′ew•y,** *adj.*

sing (sing) *v.*, **sang** (sang) or **sung** (sung), **sung, singing. 1.** utter words to music. **2.** make musical sounds. **3.** acclaim. —**sing′er,** *n.*

singe (sinj) *v.*, **singed, singeing.** *n.* scorch.

sin′gle (sing′gəl) *adj.*, *v.*, **-gled, -gling,** *n.* —*adj.* **1.** one only. **2.** unmarried. —*v.* **3.** select. —*n.* **4.** something single. **5.** unmarried person.

single file, line of persons or things one behind the other.

sin′gle-hand′ed, *adj.* **1.** accomplished by one person. **2.** by one's own effort; unaided. —*adv.* **3.** by one person alone. —**sin′-gle-hand′ed•ly,** *adv.*

sin′gle-mind′ed, *adj.* having or showing a single aim or purpose.

sin′gly, *adv.* **1.** separately. **2.** one at a time. **3.** single-handed.

sing′song′, *adj.* monotonous in rhythm.

sin′gu•lar (sing′gyə lər) *adj.* **1.** extraordinary. **2.** separate. **3.** denoting one person or thing. —*n.* **4.** singular number or form. —**sin′gu•lar′i•ty** (-lar′i tē) *n.* —**sin′gu•lar•ly,** *adv.*

sinh *Math.* hyperbolic sine.

sin′is•ter (sin′ə stər) *adj.* threatening evil.

sink (singk) *v.*, **sank** (sangk) or **sunk** (sungk), **sunk** or **sunken, sinking,** *n.* —*v.* **1.** descend or drop. **2.** deteriorate gradually. **3.** submerge. **4.** dig (a hole, etc.). **5.** bury (pipe, etc.). —*n.* **6.** basin connected with drain. —**sink′er,** *n.*

sink′hole′, *n.* **1.** hole in rock through which surface water drains into underground passage. **2.** depressed area in which drainage collects.

sinking fund, fund for extinguishing indebtedness.

SINS (sinz), *Navigation.* a gyroscopic device indicating the exact speed and position of a vessel. [*s(hip's) i(nertial) n(avigation) s(ystem)*]

sin′u•ous (sin′yŏŏ əs) *adj.* winding.

si′nus (sī′nəs) *n.* cavity or passage, esp. one in the skull connecting with the nasal cavities.

SIOP (sī′op), (formerly) the secret U.S. contingency plan for waging a nuclear war with the Soviet Union. [*s(ingle) i(ntegrated) o(perations) p(lan)*]

sip (sip) *v.*, **sipped, sipping,** *n.* —*v.* **1.** drink little at a time. —*n.* **2.** act of sipping. **3.** amount taken in sip.

si′phon (sī′fən) *n.* **1.** tube for drawing liquids by gravity and suction to another container. —*v.* **2.** move by siphon.

sir (sûr) *n.* **1.** formal term of address to man. **2.** title of knight or baronet.

sire (sī°r) *n.*, *v.*, **sired, siring.** —*n.* **1.** male parent. —*v.* **2.** beget.

si′ren (sī′rən) *n.* **1.** mythical, alluring sea nymph. **2.** noise-making device used on emergency vehicles.

sir′loin (sûr′loin) *n.* cut of beef from the loin.

si′sal (sī′səl, sis′əl) *n.* fiber used in ropes.

sis′sy (sis′ē) *n.*, *pl.* **-sies. 1.** effeminate boy or man. **2.** timid or cowardly person.

sis′ter (sis′tər) *n.* **1.** daughter of one's parents. **2.** nun. —**sis′ter•hood′,** *n.* —**sis′ter•ly,** *adj.*

sis′ter-in-law′, *n.*, *pl.* **sisters-in-law. 1.** sister of one's spouse. **2.** wife of one's brother.

sit (sit) *v.*, **sat** (sat), **sitting. 1.** rest on lower part of trunk of body. **2.** be situated. **3.** pose. **4.** be in session. **5.** seat. —**sit′ter,** *n.*

si•tar′ (si tär′) *n.* Indian lute.

sit′-down′, *n.* strike in which workers occupy their place of employment and refuse to work.

site (sīt) *n.* position; location.

sit'-in', *n.* protest by demonstrators who occupy premises refused to them.

sitting duck, easy target.

sit'u•ate' (sich'ōō āt') *v.*, -ated, -ating. settle; locate.

sit'u•a'tion (-ā'shən) *n.* 1. location. 2. condition. 3. job.

sitz bath (sits) bath in which only the thighs and hips are immersed.

SI units International System of Units.

six (siks) *n.*, *adj.* five plus one. —**sixth**, *adj.*, *n.*

six'teen', *n.*, *adj.* ten plus six. —**six• teenth'**, *adj.*, *n.*

sixth sense, power of intuition.

six'ty, *n.*, *adj.* ten times six. —**six'ti•eth**, *adj.*, *n.*

siz'a•ble (sī'zə bəl) *adj.* fairly large. Also, **size'a•ble.**

size (sīz) *n.*, *v.*, **sized, sizing.** —*n.* 1. dimensions or extent. 2. great magnitude. 3. Also, **sizing.** coating for paper, cloth, etc. —*v.* 4. sort according to size. 5. treat with sizing.

siz'zle (siz'əl) *v.*, -zled, -zling, *n.* —*v.* 1. make hissing sound, as in frying. —*n.* 2. sizzling sound.

S.J. Society of Jesus.

S.J.D. Doctor of Juridical Science. [from Latin *Scientiae Jūridicae Doctor*]

SJF single Jewish female.

SJM single Jewish male.

S.J. Res. Senate joint resolution.

SK Saskatchewan, Canada (for use with ZIP code).

sk. 1. sack. 2. sink. 3. sketch.

skate (skāt) *n.*, *pl.* **skates** or (for 3) **skate,** *v.*, **skated, skating.** —*n.* 1. steel runner fitted to shoe for gliding on ice. 2. roller skate. 3. flat-bodied marine fish; ray. —*v.* 4. glide on skates. —**skat'er, n.**

skate'board', *n.* oblong board on roller-skate wheels.

ske•dad'dle (ski dad'l) *v.*, -dled, -dling. *Informal.* run away hurriedly.

skeet (skēt) *n.* sport of shooting at clay targets hurled to simulate flight of game birds.

skein (skān) *n.* coil of yarn or thread.

skel'e•ton (skel'i tn) *n.* bony framework of human or animal. —**skel'e•tal,** *adj.*

skeleton key, key that opens various simple locks.

skep'tic (skep'tik) *n.* person who doubts or questions. —**skep'ti•cal•ly,** *adv.* —**skep'ti-cal,** *adj.* —**skep'ti•cism** (-siz'əm) *n.*

sketch (skech) *n.* 1. simple hasty drawing. 2. rough plan. —*v.* 3. make sketch (of).

sketch'y, *adj.*, -ier, -iest. vague; approximate. —**sketch'i•ly,** *adv.*

skew (skyōō) *v.* turn aside; swerve or slant.

skew'er, *n.* 1. pin for holding meat, etc., while cooking. —*v.* 2. fasten with skewer.

ski (skē) *n.* 1. slender board fastened to shoe for traveling over snow. —*v.* 2. travel by skis. —**ski'er, n.**

skid (skid) *n.*, *v.*, **skidded, skidding.** —*n.* 1. surface on which to support or slide heavy object. 2. act of skidding. —*v.* 3. slide on skids. 4. slip.

skid row (rō) run-down urban area frequented by vagrants.

skiff (skif) *n.* small boat.

skill (skil) *n.* expertness; dexterity. —**skilled,** *adj.* —**skill'ful,** *adj.* —**skill'ful•ly,** *adv.*

skil'let (skil'it) *n.* frying pan.

skim (skim) *v.*, **skimmed, skimming.** 1. remove from surface of liquid. 2. move lightly on surface.

skim milk, milk from which cream has been removed. Also, **skimmed milk.**

skimp (skimp) *v.* scrimp.

skimp'y, *adj.*, -ier, -iest. scant. —**skimp'i-ness,** *n.*

skin (skin) *n.*, *v.*, **skinned, skinning.** —*n.* 1. outer covering, as of body. —*v.* 2. strip of skin. —**skin'ner, n.**

skin diving, underwater swimming with flippers and face mask, sometimes with scuba gear. —**skin diver,** *n.*

skin'flint', *n.* stingy person.

skin'ny, *adj.*, -nier, -niest. very thin.

skin'ny-dip', *v.*, -dipped, -dipping, *n. Informal.* swim in the nude.

skip (skip) *v.*, **skipped, skipping,** *n.* —*v.* 1. spring; leap. 2. omit; disregard. —*n.* 3. light jump.

skip'per (skip'ər) *n.* 1. master of ship. —*v.* 2. act as skipper of.

skir'mish (skûr'mish) *n.* 1. brief fight between small forces. —*v.* 2. engage in skirmish. —**skir'mish•er, n.**

skirt (skûrt) *n.* 1. part of gown, etc., below waist. 2. woman's garment extending down from waist. 3. (*pl.*) outskirts. —*v.* 4. pass around edge of. 5. border.

skit (skit) *n.* short comedy.

skit'ter (skit'ər) *v.* go or glide rapidly.

skit'tish, *adj.* apt to shy; restless.

skiv'vy (skiv'ē) *n.*, *pl.* -vies. 1. man's cotton T-shirt. 2. (*pl.*) men's underwear consisting of T-shirt and shorts.

sklt skylight.

sks seeks.

Skt Sanskrit. Also, **Skt., Skr., Srkt.**

skt 1. skirt. 2. socket.

sktd skirted.

skul•dug'ger•y (skul dug'ə rē) *n.*, *pl.* -ge-ries. trickery.

skulk (skulk) *v.* sneak about; lie hidden. —**skulk'er, n.**

skull (skul) *n.* bony framework around brain.

skull'cap', *n.* brimless, close-fitting cap.

skunk (skungk) *n.* 1. small, striped, fur-bearing mammal that sprays acrid fluid to defend itself. 2. contemptible person.

S

sky (skī) *n.*, *pl.* **skies.** region well above earth. **—sky′ward′**, *adv.*, *adj.*

sky′cap′, *n.* airport porter.

sky′dive′, *v.*, **-dived, -diving.** make parachute jump with longest free fall possible. **—sky′div′er**, *n.*

sky′jack′, *v. Informal.* seize (aircraft) while in flight. **—sky′jack′er**, *n.*

sky′light′ (-lit′) *n.* window in roof, ceiling, etc.

sky′line′, *n.* **1.** outline against sky. **2.** apparent horizon.

sky′rock′et, *n.* firework that rises into air before exploding.

sky′scrap′er, *n.* building with many stories.

sky′writ′ing, *n.* writing in sky formed by smoke released from airplane.

SL source language.

sl sliding.

s.l. 1. Also, **sl.** salvage loss. **2.** *Bibliography.* without place (of publication). [from Latin *sine locō*]

SLA Special Libraries Association.

slab (slab) *n.* broad flat piece of material.

slack (slak) *adj.* **1.** loose. **2.** inactive. **3.** slackly. **—n. 4.** slack part. **5.** inactive period. **—v. 6.** slacken. **—slack′ly**, *adv.* **—slack′ness**, *n.*

slack′en, *v.* **1.** make or become slack. **2.** weaken.

slack′er, *n.* person who evades work.

slacks, *n.pl.* loose trousers.

slag (slag) *n.* refuse matter from smelting metal from ore.

slake (slāk) *v.*, **slaked, slaking. 1.** allay (thirst, etc.). **2.** treat (lime) with water.

sla′lom (slä′ləm) *n.* downhill ski race over winding course, around numerous barriers.

slam (slam) *v.*, **slammed, slamming**, *n.* **—v. 1.** shut noisily. **—n. 2.** this sound.

slam′mer, *n. Slang.* prison.

slan′der (slan′dər) *n.* **1.** false, defamatory spoken statement. **—v. 2.** utter slander against. **—slan′der•ous**, *adj.*

slang (slang) *n.* markedly informal language. **—slang′y**, *adj.*

slant (slant) *v.* **1.** slope. **—n. 2.** slope. **3.** opinion.

slap (slap) *v.*, **slapped, slapping**, *n.* **—v. 1.** strike, esp. with open hand. **—n. 2.** such blow.

slap′dash′, *adj.* hasty and careless.

slap′hap′py, *adj.*, **-pier, -piest. 1.** befuddled. **2.** agreeably foolish.

slap′stick′, *n.* boisterous comedy with broad farce and horseplay.

slash (slash) *v.* **1.** cut, esp. violently and at random. **—n. 2.** such cut. **—slash′er**, *n.*

slat (slat) *n.*, *v.*, **slatted, slatting. —n. 1.** thin narrow strip. **—v. 2.** furnish with slats.

slate (slāt) *n.*, *v.*, **slated, slating. —n. 1.** kind of layered rock. **2.** dark bluish gray. **3.** list of

nominees. **—v. 4.** put in line for appointment.

slath′er (slath′ər) *v.* spread thickly.

slat′tern (slat′ərn) *n.* untidy woman. **—slat′tern•ly**, *adj.*

slaugh′ter (slô′tər) *n.* **1.** killing of animals, esp. for food. **2.** brutal killing of people, esp. in great numbers. **—v. 3.** kill for food. **4.** massacre. **—slaugh′ter•house′**, *n.*

Slav Slavic. Also, **Slav.**

slave (slāv) *n.*, *v.*, **slaved, slaving. —n. 1.** person owned by another. **—v. 2.** drudge. **—slav′er•y**, *n.*

slav′er (sla′vər) *v.* **1.** let saliva run from mouth. **—n. 2.** saliva coming from mouth.

Slav′ic (slä′vik, slav′ik) *n.* **1.** language family that includes Russian, Polish, Czech, etc. **—adj. 2.** of these languages or their speakers.

slav′ish (slā′vish) *adj.* **1.** without originality. **2.** servile. **—slav′ish•ly**, *adv.*

slaw (slô) *n.* chopped seasoned raw cabbage.

slay (slā) *v.*, **slew** (slōō), **slain, slaying.** kill. **—slay′er**, *n.*

slbl soluble.

SLBM 1. sea-launched ballistic missile. **2.** submarine-launched ballistic missile. Also, **S.L.B.M.**

slc slice.

SLCM sea-launched cruise missile. Also, **S.L.C.M.**

sld *Electricity.* single-line diagram.

sld. 1. sailed. **2.** Also, **sld** sealed.

sldr solder.

SLE *Pathology.* systemic lupus erythematosus.

slea′zy (slē′zē) *adj.*, **-zier, -ziest.** shoddy.

sled (sled) *n.*, *v.*, **sledded, sledding. —n. 1.** vehicle traveling on snow. **—v. 2.** ride on sled.

sledge (slej) *n.*, *v.*, **sledged, sledging. —n. 1.** heavy sledlike vehicle. **2.** Also, **sledge′ham′mer.** large heavy hammer. **—v. 3.** travel by sledge.

sleek (slēk) *adj.* **1.** smooth; glossy. **—v. 2.** smooth. **—sleek′ly**, *adv.* **—sleek′ness**, *n.*

sleep (slēp) *v.*, **slept** (slept), **sleeping**, *n.* **—v. 1.** rest during natural suspension of consciousness. **—n. 2.** state or period of sleeping. **—sleep′less**, *adj.* **—sleep′y**, *adj.* **—sleep′i•ly**, *adv.*

sleep′er, *n.* **1.** person who sleeps. **2.** railroad car equipped for sleeping. **3.** raillike foundation member. **4.** unexpected success.

sleeping bag, warmly lined bag in which a person can sleep.

sleeping car, railroad car with sleeping accommodations.

sleeping sickness, infectious disease of Africa, characterized by lethargy.

sleet (slēt) *n.* hard frozen rain.

sleeve (slēv) *n.* part of garment covering arm. **—sleeve′less**, *adj.*

sleigh (slā) *n.* light sled.

sleight of hand (slīt) skill in conjuring or juggling.

slen'der (slen'dər) *adj.* **1.** small in circumference. **2.** scanty or weak. —**slen'der•ize'**, *v.*, -ized, -izing. —**slen'der•ness**, *n.*

sleuth (slōōth) *n.* detective.

slew (slōō) pt. of **slay.**

slfcl self-closing.

slfcln self-cleaning.

slfcntd self-contained.

slfprop self-propelled.

slftpg self-tapping.

SLIC (Federal) Savings and Loan Insurance Corporation. Also, **S.L.I.C.**

slice (slīs) *n.*, *v.*, **sliced, slicing.** —*n.* **1.** broad flat piece. —*v.* **2.** cut into slices. —**slic'er**, *n.*

slick (slik) *adj.* **1.** sleek. **2.** sly. **3.** slippery. —*n.* **4.** oil-covered area. —*v.* **5.** smooth. —**slick'ness**, *n.*

slick'er, *n.* raincoat.

slide (slīd) *v.*, **slid, sliding,** *n.* —*v.* **1.** move easily; glide. —*n.* **2.** act of sliding. **3.** area for sliding. **4.** landslide. **5.** glass plate used in microscope. **6.** transparent picture.

sliding scale, scale, as of prices, that varies with such conditions as the ability of individuals to pay.

slight (slīt) *adj.* **1.** trifling; small. **2.** slim. —*v.* **3.** treat as unimportant. —*n.* **4.** such treatment; snub. —**slight'ness**, *n.*

slight'ly, *adv.* barely; partly.

sli'ly, *adv.* slyly.

slim (slim) *adj.*, **slimmer, slimmest. 1.** slender. **2.** poor. —*v.* **3.** make or become slim. —**slim'ly**, *adv.* —**slim'ness**, *n.*

slime (slīm) *n.* **1.** thin sticky mud. **2.** sticky secretion of plants or animals. —**slim'y**, *adj.*

sling (sling) *n.*, *v.*, **slung** (slung), **slinging.** —*n.* **1.** straplike device for hurling stones. **2.** looped rope, bandage, etc., as support. —*v.* **3.** hurl. **4.** hang loosely.

sling'shot', *n.* Y-shaped stick with elastic strip between prongs, for shooting small missiles.

slink (slingk) *v.*, **slunk** (slink), **slinking.** go furtively. —**slink'y**, *adj.*

slip (slip) *v.*, **slipped, slipping,** *n.* —*v.* **1.** move or go easily. **2.** slide accidentally. **3.** escape. **4.** make mistake. —*n.* **5.** act of slipping. **6.** mistake. **7.** undergarment. **8.** space between piers for vessel. **9.** twig for propagating. —**slip'page**, *n.*

slip case, box open at one end for a book.

slip cover, easily removable cover for piece of furniture.

slip'knot', *n.* knot that slips easily along cord.

slipped disk, abnormal protrusion of spinal disk between vertebrae.

slip'per, *n.* light shoe.

slip'per•y, *adj.* **1.** causing slipping. **2.** tending to slip.

slip'shod' (-shod') *adj.* careless.

slip'-up', *n.* mistake.

slit (slit) *v.*, **slit, slitting,** *n.* —*v.* **1.** cut apart or in strips. —*n.* **2.** narrow opening.

slith'er (sli*th*'ər) *v.* slide. —**slith'er•y**, *adj.*

sliv'er (sliv'ər) *n.*, *v.* splinter.

SLMA Student Loan Marketing Association.

slob (slob) *n.* slovenly or boorish person.

slob'ber, *v.*, *n.* slaver.

sloe (slō) *n.* small sour fruit of blackthorn.

sloe'-eyed', *adj.* **1.** having very dark eyes. **2.** having slanted eyes.

slog (slog) *v.*, **slogged, slogging.** plod heavily. —**slog'ger**, *n.*

slo'gan (slō'gən) *n.* motto.

sloop (slōōp) *n.* kind of sailing vessel.

slop (slop) *v.*, **slopped, slopping,** *n.* —*v.* **1.** spill liquid. —*n.* **2.** spilled liquid. **3.** swill.

slope (slōp) *v.*, **sloped, sloping,** *n.* —*v.* **1.** incline; slant. —*n.* **2.** amount of inclination. **3.** sloping surface.

slop'py, *adj.* -pier, -piest. **1.** untidy. **2.** careless. —**slop'pi•ly**, *adv.* —**slop'pi•ness**, *n.*

slosh (slosh) *v.* splash.

slot (slot) *n.* narrow opening.

sloth (slôth) *n.* **1.** laziness. **2.** tree-living South American mammal. —**sloth'ful**, *adj.* —**sloth'ful•ness**, *n.*

slot machine, gambling machine.

slouch (slouch) *v.* **1.** move or rest droopingly. —*n.* **2.** drooping posture. —**slouch'y**, *adj.*

slough, *n.* **1.** (slou) muddy area. **2.** (slōō) marshy pond or inlet. **3.** (sluf) cast-off skin or dead tissue. —*v.* (sluf) **4.** be shed. **5.** cast off.

slov'en (sluv'ən) *n.* untidy or careless person. —**slov'en•li•ness**, *n.* —**slov'en•ly**, *adj.*, *adv.*

slow (slō) *adj.* **1.** not fast. **2.** not intelligent or perceptive. **3.** running behind time. —*adv.* **4.** slowly. —*v.* **5.** make or become slow. —**slow'ly**, *adv.*

slow burn, *Informal,* gradual build-up of anger.

slow'down', *n.* slackening of pace or speed.

slow motion, process of projecting or replaying film or television sequence so that action appears to be slowed down.

slow'poke', *n. Informal.* person who moves, works, or acts very slowly.

slow'-wit'ted, *adj.* slow in comprehension.

slp slope.

S.L.P. Socialist Labor Party.

SLR *Photography.* single-lens reflex camera.

sls sales.

slt sleet.

sltd slotted.

sludge (sluj) *n.* mud.

slue (slōō) *v.*, **slued, sluing.** turn round.

slug (slug) *v.*, **slugged, slugging,** *n.* —*v.* **1.** hit with fists. —*n.* **2.** slimy, crawling mollusk having no shell. **3.** billet. **4.** counterfeit coin. **5.** hard blow, esp. with fist. —**slug'ger**, *n.*

S

slug′gard (slug′ərd) *n.* lazy person.

slug′gish, *adj.* inactive; slow. —**slug′gish‑ly,** *adv.* —**slug′gish•ness,** *n.*

sluice (slōōs) *n.* channel with gate to control flow.

slum (slum) *n.* squalid, overcrowded residence or neighborhood.

slum′ber (slum′bər) *v., n.* sleep.

slum′lord′, *n.* landlord who charges exorbitant rents in slums.

slump (slump) *v.* **1.** drop heavily or suddenly. —*n.* **2.** act of slumping.

slur (slûr) *v.* **slurred, slurring,** *n.* —*v.* **1.** say indistinctly. **2.** disparage. —*n.* **3.** slurred sound. **4.** disparaging remark.

slurp (slûrp) *v.* eat or drink with loud sucking noises.

slush (slush) *n.* partly melted snow. —**slush′y,** *adj.*

slush fund, money used for illicit political purposes.

slut (slut) *n.* slatternly woman.

slv sleeve.

slvg 1. salvage. **2.** sleeving.

slvt solvent.

sly (slī) *adj.,* **slyer, slyest** or **slier, sliest. 1.** cunning. **2.** stealthy. —**sly′ly,** *adv.* —**sly′ness,** *n.*

SM 1. service mark. **2.** single male.

Sm *Symbol, Chemistry.* samarium.

sm some.

sm. small.

S‑M 1. Also, **S and M.** sadomasochism. **2.** sadomasochistic. Also, **s‑m, S/M, s/m**

S.M. 1. Master of Science. [from Latin *Scientiae Magister*] **2.** sergeant major. **3.** State Militia.

SMA Surplus Marketing Administration.

smack (smak) *v.* **1.** separate (lips) noisily. **2.** slap. **3.** have taste or trace. —*n.* **4.** smacking of lips. **5.** loud kiss. **6.** slap. **7.** taste. **8.** trace. **9.** small fishing boat. **10.** *Slang.* heroin.

s‑mail (es′māl′), snail mail.

small (smôl) *adj.* **1.** not big; little. **2.** not great in importance, value, etc. **3.** ungenerous. —*adv.* **4.** in small pieces. —*n.* **5.** small part, as of back. —**small′ness,** *n.*

small fry, 1. young children. **2.** unimportant people.

small′-mind′ed, *adj.* petty or selfish.

small′pox′, *n.* contagious disease marked by fever and pustules.

small′-scale′, *adj.* **1.** of limited scope. **2.** being a small version of an original.

small talk, light conversation.

small′-time′, *adj.* of little importance.

smart (smärt) *v.* **1.** cause or feel sharp superficial pain. —*adj.* **2.** sharp; severe. **3.** clever. **4.** stylish. —*n.* **5.** sharp local pain. —**smart′ly,** *adv.*

smart al′eck (al′ik) *Informal,* obnoxiously

conceited and impertinent person. Also, **smart al′ec.**

smart bomb, air-to-surface missile guided by laser beam.

smart′en, *v.* improve in appearance.

smash (smash) *v.* **1.** break to pieces. —*n.* **2.** act of smashing; destruction.

smat see me about this.

smat′ter•ing (smat′ər ing) *n.* slight knowledge.

S.M.B. Bachelor of Sacred Music.

sm. c. small capital; small capitals. Also, **sm. cap.** or **sm. caps**

SMD *Pathology.* senile macular degeneration.

S.M.D. Doctor of Sacred Music.

smear (smēr) *v.* **1.** rub with dirt, grease, etc. **2.** sully. —*n.* **3.** smeared spot. **4.** slanderous attack.

smell (smel) *v.* **1.** perceive with nose. **2.** have odor. —*n.* **3.** faculty of smelling. **4.** odor. —**smell′y,** *adj.,* **-ier, -iest.**

smelling salts, preparation used as restorative.

smelt (smelt) *n., pl.* **smelts, smelt,** *v.* —*n.* **1.** small edible fish. —*v.* **2.** melt (ore or metal). —**smelt′er,** *n.*

smid′gen (smij′ən) *n.* very small amount. Also, **smid′gin, smid′geon.**

smi′lax (smī′laks) *n.* delicate twining plant.

smile (smīl) *v.,* **smiled, smiling,** *n.* —*v.* **1.** assume look of pleasure, etc. **2.** look favorably. —*n.* **3.** smiling look.

smirch (smûrch) *v.* **1.** soil or sully. —*n.* **2.** stain.

smirk (smûrk) *v.* **1.** smile smugly or affectedly. —*n.* **2.** such a smile.

smite (smīt) *v.,* **smote** (smōt), **smit•ten** (smit′n) or **smit, smiting. 1.** strike. **2.** charm.

smith (smith) *n.* worker in metal.

smith′er•eens′ (smith′ə rēnz′) *n.pl.* fragments.

smith′y (smith′ē, smith′ē) *n., pl.* **smithies.** blacksmith's shop.

smk smoke.

sml small.

smls seamless.

S.M.M. Master of Sacred Music.

smock (smok) *n.* long, loose overgarment.

smog (smog) *n.* smoke and fog.

smoke (smōk) *n., v.,* **smoked, smoking.** —*n.* **1.** visible vapor from burning. —*v.* **2.** emit smoke. **3.** draw into mouth and puff out tobacco smoke. **4.** treat with smoke. —**smok′er,** *n.* —**smoke′less,** *adj.* —**smok′y,** *adj.*

smoke detector, alarm activated by presence of smoke.

smoke′house′, *n.* building in which meat or fish is cured with smoke.

smoke screen, 1. mass of dense smoke for concealment from enemy. **2.** something intended to deceive.

smoke′stack′, *n.* **1.** pipe for escape of

smoke, combustion gases, etc. —*adj.* **2.** engaged in heavy industry, as steelmaking.

smol'der (smōl'dər) *v.* **1.** burn without flame. **2.** exist suppressed. Also, **smoul'der.**

S.M.O.M. Sovereign and Military Order of Malta.

smooch (smōōch) *n., v. Informal.* kiss.

smooth (smōōth) *adj.* **1.** even in surface. **2.** easy; tranquil. —*v.* **3.** make smooth. —*n.* **4.** smooth place. —**smooth'ly,** *adv.* —**smooth'ness,** *n.*

smooth'bore', *adj.* (of gun) not rifled.

smor'gas•bord' (smôr'gəs bôrd'; *often* shmôr'-) *n.* table of assorted foods.

smoth'er (smuth'ər) *v.* suffocate.

SMPTE Society of Motion Picture and Television Engineers.

SMS Synchronous Meteorological Satellite.

SMSA Standard Metropolitan Statistical Area.

smudge (smuj) *n., v.,* **smudged, smudging.** —*n.* **1.** dirty smear. **2.** smoky fire. —*v.* **3.** soil.

smug (smug) *adj.* **1.** self-satisfied. **2.** trim. —**smug'ly,** *adv.* —**smug'ness,** *n.*

smug'gle, *v.,* **-gled, -gling. 1.** import or export secretly and illegally. **2.** bring or take secretly. —**smug'gler,** *n.*

smut (smut) *n.* **1.** soot. **2.** smudge. **3.** obscenity. **4.** plant disease. —**smut'ty,** *adj.*

smy summary.

SN 1. Secretary of the Navy. **2.** serial number.

Sn *Symbol, Chemistry.* tin. [from Latin *stannum*]

snack (snak) *n.* light meal.

snaf'fle (snaf'əl) *n.* kind of bit used on bridle.

sna•fu (sna fōō', snaf'ōō), situation normal, all fouled up.

snag (snag) *n., v.,* **snagged, snagging.** —*n.* **1.** sharp projection. **2.** obstacle. —*v.* **3.** catch on snag.

snail (snāl) *n.* crawling, spiral-shelled mollusk.

snake (snāk) *n., v.,* **snaked, snaking.** —*n.* **1.** scaly limbless reptile. —*v.* **2.** move like snake. **3.** drag. —**snak'y,** *adj.*

snap (snap) *v.,* **snapped, snapping,** *n., adj.* —*v.* **1.** make sudden sharp sound. **2.** break abruptly. **3.** bite (at). **4.** photograph. —*n.* **5.** snapping sound. **6.** kind of fastener. **7.** *Informal,* easy thing. —*adj.* **8.** unconsidered.

snap'drag'on, *n.* plant with spikes of flowers.

snap'pish, *adj.* cross.

snap'py, *adj.* **-pier, -piest. 1.** quick. **2.** smart; stylish.

snap'shot', *n.* unposed photograph.

snare (snâr) *n., v.,* **snared, snaring.** —*n.* **1.** kind of trap. **2.** strand across skin of small drum. —*v.* **3.** entrap.

snarl (snärl) *v., n.* **1.** growl. **2.** tangle.

snatch (snach) *v.* **1.** grab. —*n.* **2.** grabbing motion. **3.** scrap of melody, etc. —**snatch'er,** *n.*

SNCC (snik), a U.S. civil-rights organization formed by students and active especially during the 1960s. [*S(tudent) N(onviolent) C(oordinating) C(ommittee)*]

snd sound.

sneak (snēk) *v.* **1.** go or act furtively. —*n.* **2.** person who sneaks. —**sneak'y,** *adj.*

sneak'er, *n.* rubber-soled shoe.

sneak preview, preview of a motion picture, often shown in addition to an announced film.

sneer (snēr) *v.* **1.** show contempt. —*n.* **2.** contemptuous look or remark.

sneeze (snēz) *v.,* **sneezed, sneezing,** *n.* —*v.* **1.** emit breath suddenly and forcibly from nose. —*n.* **2.** act of sneezing.

SNG synthetic natural gas.

snick'er (snik'ər) *n.* derisive, stifled laugh. —**snick'er,** *v.* Also, **snig'ger.**

snide (snīd) *adj.,* **snider, snidest.** derogatory in nasty, insinuating way.

sniff (snif) *v.* **1.** inhale quickly and audibly. —*n.* **2.** such an inhalation. Also, **snif'fle.**

snif'ter (snif'tər) *n.* pear-shaped glass for brandy.

snip (snip) *v.,* **snipped, snipping,** *n.* —*v.* **1.** cut with small, quick strokes. —*n.* **2.** small piece cut off. **3.** cut. **4.** (*pl.*) large scissors.

snipe (snīp) *n., v.,* **sniped, sniping.** —*n.* **1.** shore bird. —*v.* **2.** shoot from concealment. —**snip'er,** *n.*

snip'pet (snip'it) *n.* small bit, scrap, or fragment.

snip'py, *adj.,* **-pier, -piest.** sharp or curt, esp. in haughty or contemptuous way.

snit (snit) *n.* agitated state.

snitch (snich) *Informal,* —*v.* **1.** steal; pilfer. **2.** turn informer; tattle. —*n.* **3.** informer.

sniv'el (sniv'əl) *v.* **1.** weep weakly. **2.** run at the nose.

snkl snorkel.

snl standard nomenclature list.

sno 1. snow. **2.** stock number.

snob (snob) *n.* person overconcerned with position, wealth, etc. —**snob'bish,** *adj.* —**snob'ber•y,** *n.*

snood (snōōd) *n.* band or net for hair.

snoop (snōōp) *Informal,* —*v.* **1.** prowl or pry. —*n.* **2.** Also, **snoop'er.** person who snoops.

snoot'y (snōō'tē) *adj.,* **-ier, -iest.** *Informal,* snobbish; condescending. —**snoot'i•ness,** *n.*

snooze (snōōz) *v.,* **snoozed, snoozing,** *n. Informal.* nap.

snore (snôr) *v.,* **snored, snoring,** *n.* —*v.* **1.** breathe audibly in sleep. —*n.* **2.** sound of snoring. —**snor'er,** *n.*

snor'kel (snôr'kəl) *n.* **1.** tube through which swimmer can breathe while underwater. **2.** ventilating device for submarines.

snort (snôrt) *v.* **1.** exhale loudly and harshly. —*n.* **2.** sound of snorting.

S

snot (snot) *n. Informal.* **1.** nasal mucus. **2.** impudently disagreeable young person. —**snot′ty,** *adj.* **-tier, -tiest.**

snout (snout) *n.* projecting nose and jaw.

snow (snō) *n.* **1.** white crystalline flakes that fall to earth. —*v.* **2.** fall as snow. —**snow′drift′,** *n.* —**snow′fall′,** *n.* —**snow′flake′,** *n.* —**snow′storm′,** *n.* —**snow′y,** *adj.*

snow′ball′, *n.* **1.** ball of snow. **2.** flowering shrub. —*v.* **3.** grow rapidly.

snow′board′, *n.* board for gliding on snow, resembling a wide ski.

snow′bound′, *adj.* immobilized by snow.

snow′drop′, *n.* early-blooming plant with white flowers.

snow′man′, *n.* figure of person made of packed snow.

snow′mo•bile′ (-mə bēl′) *n.* motor vehicle for travel on snow.

snow′shoe′, *n.* racketlike shoe for walking on snow.

snow′suit′, *n.* child's warmly insulated outer garment.

snow tire, tire with deep tread.

snr 1. signal-to-noise ratio. **2.** sonar.

sns sense.

snsr sensor.

sntr *Metallurgy.* sintered.

sntzd sensitized.

snub (snub) *v.*, **snubbed, snubbing,** *n., adj.* —*v.* **1.** treat with scorn. **2.** check or stop. —*n.* **3.** rebuke or slight. —*adj.* **4.** (of nose) short and turned up.

snuff (snuf) *v.* **1.** inhale. **2.** smell. **3.** extinguish. —*n.* **4.** powdered tobacco.

snuf′fle, *v.*, **-fled, -fling,** *n.* sniff.

snug (snug) *adj.*, **snugger, snuggest. 1.** cozy. **2.** trim; neat. —**snug′ly,** *adv.*

snug′gle, *v.*, **-gled, -gling.** nestle.

sny sunny.

so (sō) *adv.* **1.** in this or that way. **2.** to such degree. **3.** as stated. —*conj.* **4.** consequently. **5.** in order that.

soak (sōk) *v.* **1.** wet thoroughly. **2.** absorb. —**soak′er,** *n.*

so′-and-so′, *n., pl.* **so-and-sos.** person or thing not definitely named.

soap (sōp) *n.* **1.** substance used for washing. —*v.* **2.** rub with soap. —**soap′y,** *adj.*

soap′box′, *n.* improvised platform on which speaker stands.

soap′stone′, *n.* variety of talc.

soar (sôr) *v.* fly upward.

sob (sob) *v.*, **sobbed, sobbing,** *n.* —*v.* **1.** weep convulsively. —*n.* **2.** convulsive breath.

so′ber (sō′bər) *adj.* **1.** not drunk. **2.** quiet; grave. —*v.* **3.** make or become sober. —**so•bri′e•ty** (sə brī′i tē), **so′ber•ness,** *n.* —**so′ber•ly,** *adv.*

so′bri•quet′ (sō′bri kā′, -ket′) *n.* nickname.

Soc. 1. socialist. **2.** (*often lowercase*) society. **3.** sociology.

so′-called′, *adj.* called thus.

soc′cer (sok′ər) *n.* game resembling football.

socd source control drawing.

so′cia•ble (sō′shə bəl) *adj.* friendly. —**so′cia•bly,** *adv.* —**so′cia•bil′i•ty,** *n.*

so′cial (sō′shəl) *adj.* **1.** devoted to companionship. **2.** of human society. —**so′cial•ly,** *adv.*

so′cial•ism (-shə liz′əm) *n.* theory advocating community ownership of means of production, etc. —**so′cial•ist,** *n.* —**so′cial•is′tic,** *adj.*

so′cial•ite′ (-shə līt′) *n.* socially prominent person.

so′cial•ize′, *v.*, **-ized, -izing. 1.** associate with others. **2.** put on socialistic basis.

socialized medicine, system to provide nation with complete medical care through government subsidization.

social security, (*often caps.*) federal program of old age, unemployment, health, disability, and survivors' insurance.

social work, services or activities designed to improve social conditions among poor, sick, or troubled persons.

so•ci′e•ty (sə sī′i tē) *n., pl.* **-ties. 1.** group of persons with common interests. **2.** human beings generally. **3.** fashionable people. —**so•ci′e•tal,** *adj.*

Society of Friends, Christian sect founded 1650; Quakers.

so′ci•o•ec•o•nom′ic (sō′sē ō-, sō′shē ō-) *adj.* pertaining to a combination of social and economic factors.

sociol. 1. sociological. **2.** sociology.

so′ci•ol•o•gy (sō′sē ol′ə jē, sō′shē-) *n.* science of social relations and institutions. —**so′ci•o•log′i•cal** (-ə loj′i kəl) *adj.* —**so′ci•ol•o•gist,** *n.*

sock (sok) *n.* short stocking.

sock′et (sok′it) *n.* holelike part for holding another part.

socn source control number.

sod (sod) *n.* grass with its roots.

so′da (sō′də) *n.* **1.** drink made with soda water. **2.** preparation containing sodium.

soda cracker, crisp cracker.

soda fountain, counter at which ice cream, sodas, etc., are served.

so•dal′i•ty (-dal′i tē) *n., pl.* **-ties.** association.

soda water, water charged with carbon dioxide.

sod′den (sod′n) *adj.* **1.** soaked. **2.** stupid. —**sod′den•ness,** *n.*

so′di•um (sō′dē əm) *n.* soft whitish metallic element.

sodium bicarbonate, baking soda.

sodium chloride, salt.

sod′o•my (sod′ə mē) *n.* anal or oral copulation.

SOF sound on a film.

so′fa (sō′fə) *n.* couch with back and arms.

S. of Sol. *Bible.* Song of Solomon.

soft (sôft) *adj.* **1.** yielding readily. **2.** gentle; pleasant. **3.** not strong. **4.** (of water) free from mineral salts. **5.** without alcohol. —**sof′ten,** *v.* —**soft′ly,** *adv.*

soft′ball′, *n.* **1.** form of baseball played with larger, softer ball. **2.** the ball used.

soft′-boiled′, *adj.* boiled only until the egg's yolk is partially set.

soft′-core′, *adj.* sexually provocative without being explicit.

soft drink, nonalcoholic drink, often carbonated.

soft′-heart′ed, *adj.* very sympathetic.

soft′-ped′al, *v.,* **-aled, -aling.** make less obvious.

soft sell, quietly persuasive method of selling.

soft soap, persuasive talk.

soft′ware′, *n.* programs for use with a computer.

sog′gy (sog′ē) *adj.,* **-gier, -giest. 1.** soaked. **2.** damp and heavy. —**sog′gi•ness,** *n.*

soi•gné′ (swän yā′; *Fr.* swA nyä′) *adj.* elegant. Also, **soi•gnée′.**

soil (soil) *v.* **1.** dirty; smudge. —*n.* **2.** spot or stain. **3.** sewage. **4.** earth; ground.

soi•rée′ (swä rā′) *n.* evening party.

so′journ *v.* (sō′jûrn, sō jûrn′) **1.** dwell briefly. —*n.* (sō′jûrn) **2.** short stay.

sol 1. solenoid. **2.** solid.

Sol. 1. Solicitor. **2.** Song of Solomon.

sol. 1. soluble. **2.** solution.

S.O.L. *Slang.* **1.** strictly out (of) luck. **2.** *Vulgar.* shit out (of) luck. Also, **SOL**

sol′ace (sol′is) *n., v.* comfort in grief.

so′lar (sō′lər) *adj.* of the sun.

solar cell, cell that converts sunlight into electricity.

so•lar′i•um (sə lâr′ē əm, sō-) *n., pl.* **-iums, -i•a** (-ē ə). glass-enclosed room for enjoying sunlight.

solar plexus, point on stomach wall just below sternum.

solar system, sun and all the celestial bodies revolving around it.

sol′der (sod′ər) *n.* **1.** fusible alloy for joining metal. —*v.* **2.** join with solder.

sol′dier (sōl′jər) *n.* **1.** member of army. —*v.* **2.** serve as soldier. —**sol′dier•ly,** *adj.* —**sol′-dier•y,** *n.*

sole (sōl) *n., v.,* **soled, soling,** *adj.* —*n.* **1.** bottom of foot or shoe. **2.** edible flatfish. —*v.* **3.** put sole on. —*adj.* **4.** only. —**sole′ly,** *adv.*

sol′e•cism (sol′ə siz′əm, sō′lə-) *n.* **1.** nonstandard usage. **2.** breach of etiquette.

sol′emn (sol′əm) *adj.* **1.** grave; serious. **2.** sacred. —**so•lem′ni•ty** (sə lem′ni tē) *n.* —**sol′emn•ly,** *adv.*

sol′em•nize′ (-nīz′) *v.,* **-nized, -nizing.** observe with ceremonies. —**sol′em•ni•za′tion,** *n.*

so•lic′it (sə lis′it) *v.* **1.** entreat; request. **2.** lure; entice, as to a prostitute. **3.** solicit trade or sex. —**so•lic′i•ta′tion,** *n.*

so•lic′i•tor (-i tər) *n.* **1.** person who solicits. **2.** *Brit.* lawyer.

so•lic′it•ous, *adj.* anxious; concerned. —**so•lic′it•ous•ly,** *adv.* —**so•lic′i•tude′,** *n.*

sol′id (sol′id) *adj.* **1.** having length, breadth, and thickness. **2.** not hollow. **3.** dense. **4.** substantial. **5.** entire. —*n.* **6.** solid body. —**so•lid′i•fy′,** *v.* —**so•lid′i•ty,** *n.*

sol′i•dar′i•ty (-i dar′i tē) *n., pl.* **-ties.** unanimity of attitude or purpose.

sol′id•ly, *adv.* **1.** so as to be solid. **2.** wholeheartedly; fully.

so•lil′o•quy (sə lil′ə kwē) *n., pl.* **-quies.** speech when alone. —**so•lil′o•quize′** (-kwīz′) *v.,* **-quized, -quizing.**

sol′i•taire′ (sol′i târ′) *n.* **1.** card game for one person. **2.** gem set alone.

sol′i•tar′y (sol′i ter′ē) *adj.* **1.** alone. **2.** single. **3.** secluded. —**sol′i•tude′,** *n.*

soln solution.

so′lo (sō′lō) *n., pl.* **-los.** performance by one person. —**so′lo•ist,** *n.*

sol′stice (sol′stis, sōl′-) *n.* time in summer (June 21) or winter (Dec. 21) when sun is at its farthest from equator.

sol′u•ble (sol′yə bəl) *adj.* able to be dissolved. —**sol′u•bil′i•ty,** *n.*

sol′ute (sol′yoōt, sō′loōt) *n.* dissolved substance.

so•lu′tion (sə loō′shən) *n.* **1.** explanation or answer. **2.** dispersion of one substance in another. **3.** resulting substance.

solve (solv) *v.,* **solved, solving.** find explanation of. —**solv′a•ble,** *adj.* —**solv′er,** *n.*

sol′vent (sol′vənt) *adj.* **1.** able to pay one's debts. **2.** causing dissolving. —*n.* **3.** agent that dissolves. —**sol′ven•cy,** *n.*

som start of message.

so•mat′ic (sō mat′ik, sə-) *adj.* of or affecting the body.

som′ber (som′bər) *adj.* gloomy; dark. —**som′ber•ly,** *adv.*

som•bre′ro (som brâr′ō) *n., pl.* **-ros.** tall, broad-brimmed hat.

some (sum; *unstressed* səm) *adj.* **1.** being an unspecified one or number. **2.** certain. —*pron.* **3.** unspecified number or amount.

—**Usage.** some is used in sentences that are affirmative: *I'd like some milk.* any is used instead of some with negative phrases or in questions: *I don't want any milk. I never see any of my friends these days. Do you have any milk?* But some can be used in questions when the answer is expected to be "yes": *Can I have some milk, please?*

some′bod′y (sum′bod′ē, -bud′ē, -bə dē) *pron.* some person. Also, **some′one′.**

some′day′, *adv.* at some distant time.

some′how′, *adv.* in some way.

S

som•er•sault' (sum'ər sôlt') *n.* heels-over-head turn of body.

some'thing', *n.* unspecified thing.

some'time', *adv.* **1.** at indefinite time. —*adj.* **2.** former.

some'times', *adv.* at times.

some'what', *adv.* to some extent.

some'where', *adv.* in, at, or to unspecified place.

som•nam'bu•lism (som nam'byə liz'əm, səm-) *n.* sleep-walking. —**som•nam'bu•list,** *n.*

som'no•lent (som'nə lənt) *adj.* sleepy. —**som'no•lence,** *n.*

son (sun) *n.* male offspring.

so'nar (sō'när) *n.* method or apparatus for detecting objects in water by means of sound waves.

so•na'ta (sə nä'tə) *n.* instrumental composition.

song (sông) *n.* music or verse for singing. —**song'ster,** *n.* —**song'stress,** *n.fem.*

son'ic (son'ik) *adj.* of sound.

sonic boom, loud noise caused by aircraft moving at supersonic speed.

son'-in-law', *n., pl.* **sons-in-law.** husband of one's daughter.

son'net (son'it) *n.* fourteen-line poem in fixed form.

so•no'rous (sə nôr'əs, son'ər əs) *adj.* **1.** resonant. **2.** grandiose in expression. —**so•nor'-i•ty,** *n.* —**so•no'rous•ly,** *adv.*

soon (sōōn) *adv.* in short time.

soot (sŏŏt, sōōt) *n.* black substance in smoke. —**soot'y,** *adj.*

soothe (sōōth) *v.*, **soothed, soothing.** calm; allay.

sooth'say'er (sōōth'sā'ər) *n.* person who predicts.

sop (sop) *n., v.*, **sopped, sopping.** —*n.* **1.** food dipped in liquid. **2.** something given to pacify. —*v.* **3.** soak (food). **4.** absorb.

soph'ism (sof'iz əm) *n.* specious but plausible argument. —**soph'ist,** *n.*

so•phis'ti•cat'ed (sə fis'ti kā'tid) *adj.* worldly; not simple. —**so•phis'ti•cate** (-kit) *n.* —**so•phis'ti•ca'tion,** *n.*

soph'ist•ry (sof'ə strē) *n., pl.* **-ries.** clever but unsound reasoning.

soph'o•more' (sof'ə môr') *n.* second-year high school or college student.

soph'o•mor'ic (-môr'ik) *adj.* intellectually immature.

so'po•rif'ic (sop'ə rif'ik) *adj.* **1.** causing sleep. —*n.* **2.** soporific agent.

sop'py (sop'ē) *adj.*, **-pier, -piest. 1.** drenched. **2.** sentimental.

so•pran'o (sə pran'ō) *n., pl.* **-pranos. 1.** highest singing voice. **2.** singer with such voice.

sor•bet' (sôr bā', sôr'bit) *n.* fruit or vegetable ice.

sor'cer•er (-sər ər) *n.* magician; wizard. Also, *fem.* **sor'cer•ess.** —**sor'cer•y,** *n.*

sor'did (sôr'did) *adj.* **1.** dirty. **2.** ignoble.

sore (sôr) *adj.*, **sorer, sorest,** *n.* —*adj.* **1.** painful or tender. **2.** grieved. **3.** causing misery. **4.** *Informal.* annoyed. —*n.* **5.** sore spot. —**sore'ly,** *adv.* —**sore'ness,** *n.*

sore'head', *n. Informal.* disgruntled person.

sor'ghum (sôr'gəm) *n.* cereal used in making syrup, etc.

so•ror'i•ty (sə rôr'i tē) *n., pl.* **-ties.** club of women or girls.

sor'rel (sôr'əl) *n.* **1.** reddish brown. **2.** sorrel horse. **3.** salad plant.

sor'row (sor'ō) *n.* **1.** grief; regret; misfortune. —*v.* **2.** feel sorrow. —**sor'row•ful,** *adj.* —**sor'row•ful•ly,** *adv.* —**sor'row•ful•ness,** *n.*

sor'ry (sor'ē) *adj.* **1.** feeling regret or pity. **2.** wretched.

sort (sôrt) *n.* **1.** kind or class. **2.** character. **3.** manner. —*v.* **4.** separate; classify. —**sort'er,** *n.*

sor'tie (sôr'tē) *n.* **1.** attack by defending troops. **2.** combat mission.

SOS (es'ō'es') call for help.

so'-so', *adj.* **1.** neither good nor bad. —*adv.* **2.** tolerably.

sot (sot) *n.* drunkard.

sot'to vo'ce (sot'ō vō'chē) *adv.* in a low voice; softly.

sou•brette' (sōō bret') *n.* coquettish maidservant in play or opera.

souf•fle' (sōō flā') *n.* fluffy baked dish.

sough (sou, suf) *v.* **1.** rustle or murmur, as wind. —*n.* **2.** act of soughing.

sought (sôt) pt. and pp. of **seek.**

soul (sōl) *n.* **1.** human spiritual quality. **2.** essential quality. **3.** person. **4.** Also, **soul music.** black popular music drawing on church influences. —*adj.* **5.** of black customs and culture. —**soul'ful,** *adj.* —**soul'less,** *adj.*

sound (sound) *n.* **1.** sensation affecting organs of hearing, produced by vibrations (**sound waves**). **2.** special tone. **3.** noise. **4.** inlet or passage of sea. —*v.* **5.** make sound. **6.** say. **7.** give certain impression. **8.** measure depth of. **9.** examine; question. —*adj.* **10.** healthy; strong. **11.** reliable. **12.** valid. —**sound'proof',** *adj.* —**sound'ly,** *adv.* —**sound'ness,** *n.*

sound barrier, abrupt increase in drag experienced by aircraft approaching speed of sound.

sound bite, brief, memorable statement excerpted for broadcast news.

sounding board, 1. thin board placed in musical instrument to enhance resonance. **2.** person whose reactions reveal acceptability of an idea.

sound'proof', *adj.* **1.** impervious to sound. —*v.* **2.** make soundproof.

sound'track', *n.* band on motion-picture film on which sound is recorded.

soup (soop) *n.* liquid food of meat, vegetables, etc.

soup•çon (soop sôn′) *n.* slight trace.

soup′y, *adj.*, -ier, -iest. 1. resembling soup in consistency. 2. dense. 3. overly sentimental.

sour (sou³r) *adj.* 1. acid in taste; tart. 2. spoiled. 3. disagreeable. —*v.* 4. turn sour. —**sour′ly**, *adv.* —**sour′ness**, *n.*

source (sôrs) *n.* origin.

sour′dough′, *n.* fermented dough used as leavening agent.

sour grapes, *n.* pretended disdain for something unattainable.

souse (sous) *v.*, **soused, sousing**, *n.* —*v.* 1. immerse; drench. 2. pickle. —*n.* 3. act of sousing. 4. pickled food. 5. *Slang.* drunkard.

south (south) *n.* 1. point of compass opposite north. 2. this direction. 3. territory in this direction. —*adj., adv.* 4. toward, in, or from south. —**south′er•ly** (suth′ər lē) *adj., adv.* —**south′ern** (suth′-) *adj.* —**south′ern•er**, *n.* —**south′ward**, *adj., adv.*

south′east′, *n.*, point or direction midway between south and east. —**south′east′**, *adj., adv.*

south′paw′, *n. Informal.* left-handed person.

south′west′, *n.* point or direction midway between south and west. —**south′west′**, *adj., adv.*

sou′ve•nir′ (soo′və nēr′) *n.* memento.

sov′er•eign (sov′rin, -ər in) *n.* 1. monarch. 2. (formerly) British gold coin worth one pound. —*adj.* 3. of a sovereign; supreme. —**sov′er•eign•ty**, *n.*

so′vi•et′ (sō′vē et′, -it) *n.* 1. (in the former USSR) governing body. —*adj.* 2. (*cap.*) of the former USSR.

SOV language *Linguistics.* a type of language that has basic subject-object-verb order.

Sov. Un. Soviet Union.

sow, *v.* (sō) 1. plant seed. —*n.* (sou) 2. female hog. —**sow′er**, *n.*

soy′bean′ (soi′-) *n.* nutritious seed of leguminous plant.

soy sauce, salty sauce made from soybeans.

SP 1. Shore Patrol. 2. Specialist. 3. Submarine Patrol.

sp 1. spare. 2. special-purpose. 3. speed

Sp. 1. Spain. 2. Spaniard. 3. Also, **Sp** Spanish.

sp. 1. space. 2. special. 3. species. 4. specific. 5. specimen. 6. spelling. 7. spirit.

S.P. 1. Shore Patrol. 2. Socialist party. 3. Submarine Patrol.

s.p. without issue; childless. [from Latin *sine prōle*]

spa (spä) *n.* resort at mineral spring.

space (spās) *n., v.*, **spaced, spacing**. —*n.* 1. unlimited expanse. 2. particular part of this. 3. linear distance. 4. interval of time. —*v.* 5. divide into space. 6. set at intervals.

space′craft′, *n., pl.* **-craft.** vehicle for traveling in outer space.

spaced′-out′, *adj. Slang.* dazed by or as if by drugs.

space heater, device for heating small area.

space′ship′, *n.* rocket vehicle for travel between planets.

space shuttle, reusable spacecraft.

space station, manned spacecraft orbiting the earth and serving as base for research.

spa′cious (spā′shəs) *adj.* large; vast. —**spa′cious•ly**, *adv.* —**spa′cious•ness**, *n.*

Spack′le (spak′əl) *n. Trademark.* brand of plasterlike material for patching cracks.

spade (spād) *n., v.*, **spaded, spading**. —*n.* 1. tool with blade for digging. 2. (*pl.*) suit of playing cards. —*v.* 3. dig with spade.

spa•ghet′ti (spə get′ē) *n.* pasta in form of long strings.

Sp. Am. 1. Spanish America. 2. Spanish American.

span (span) *n., v.*, **spanned, spanning**. —*n.* 1. distance between extended thumb and little finger. 2. space between two supports. 3. full extent. 4. team of animals. —*v.* 5. extend over.

span′dex (span′deks) *n.* elastic synthetic fiber.

span′gle (spang′gəl) *n., v.*, **-gled, -gling**. —*n.* 1. small bright ornament. —*v.* 2. decorate with spangles.

span′iel (span′yəl) *n.* kind of dog.

Span′ish (span′ish) *n.* language or people of Spain. —**Spanish**, *adj.*

Spanish fly, preparation of powdered green European beetles once used as aphrodisiac.

Spanish moss, plant that grows in long strands over trees.

spank (spangk) *v.* 1. strike on buttocks. —*n.* 2. such a blow.

spank′ing, *adj.* brisk; vigorous.

spar (spär) *v.*, **sparred, sparring**, *n.* —*v.* 1. box. 2. bandy words. —*n.* 3. *Naut.* mast, yard, etc. 4. bright crystalline mineral.

spare (spâr) *v.*, **spared, sparing**, *adj.*, **sparer, sparest**. —*v.* 1. deal gently with. 2. part with easily. —*adj.* 3. kept in reserve. 4. extra. 5. lean.

spare′rib′, *n.* cut of pork ribs.

spark (spärk) *n.* 1. burning particle. 2. flash of electricity. 3. trace.

spar′kle, *v.*, **-kled, -kling**, *n.* —*v.* 1. emit sparks. 2. glitter. 3. produce little bubbles. —*n.* 4. little spark. 5. brightness.

spark plug, device in internal-combustion engine that ignites fuel.

spar′row (spar′ō) *n.* small, common, hardy bird.

sparse, *adj.*, **sparser, sparsest**. thinly distributed. —**spar′si•ty**, **sparse′ness**, *n.* —**sparse′ly**, *adv.*

Spar′tan, *adj.* austere.

spasm (spaz′əm) *n.* sudden involuntary muscular contraction.

spas•mod′ic (spaz mod′ik) *adj.* 1. of

S

spasms. **2.** intermittent. **—spas•mod/i•cal•ly,** *adv.*

spas/tic (spas/tik) *adj.* of or marked by spasms.

spat (spat) *n.* petty quarrel.

spate (spāt) *n.* sudden outpouring.

spa/tial (spā/shəl) *adj.* of or in space.

spat/ter (spat/ər) *v., n.* sprinkle in many fine drops.

spat/u•la (spach/ə lə) *n.* broad-bladed implement.

spav/in (spav/in) *n.* disease of hock joint in horses.

spawn (spôn) *n.* **1.** eggs of fish, mollusks, etc. **—v. 2.** produce spawn.

spay (spā) *v.* neuter (female dog, cat, etc.).

S.P.C.A. Society for the Prevention of Cruelty to Animals.

S.P.C.C. Society for the Prevention of Cruelty to Children.

spchg supercharge.

spcl special.

spcr spacer.

SPDA single-premium deferred annuity.

sp. del. special delivery.

spdl spindle.

spdom speedometer.

spdt sw single-pole double-throw switch.

speak (spēk) *v.,* **spoke** (spōk), **spoken,** **speaking. 1.** talk; say. **2.** deliver speech.

speak/eas/y, *n., pl.* **-easies.** place selling alcoholic beverages illegally.

speak/er, *n.* **1.** person who speaks. **2.** presiding officer.

spear (spēr) *n.* **1.** long staff bearing sharp head. **—v. 2.** pierce with spear.

spear/head/, *n.* **1.** head of spear. **2.** leader. **—v. 3.** lead.

spear/mint/, *n.* aromatic herb.

spec. 1. special. **2.** specially. **3.** specifically. **4.** specification. **5.** specimen.

spe/cial (spesh/əl) *adj.* **1.** particular in nature or purpose. **2.** unusual. **—n. 3.** special thing or person. **—spe/cial•ly,** *adv.*

spe/cial•ize/, *v.,* **-ized, -izing.** study of work in special field. **—spe/cial•ist,** *n.* **—spe/cial•i•za/tion,** *n.*

spe/cial•ty, *n., pl.* **-ties.** field of special interest or competence.

spe/cie (spē/shē, -sē) *n.* coined money.

spe/cies (spē/shēz, -sēz) *n.* class of related individuals.

specif. 1. specific. **2.** specifically.

spe•cif/ic (spi sif/ik) *adj.* definite. **—spe•cif/i•cal•ly,** *adv.*

spec/i•fi•ca/tion (spes/ə fi kā/shən) *n.* **1.** act of specifying. **2.** detailed requirement.

specific gravity, ratio of density of substance to density of standard substance, water being the standard.

spec/i•fy/, *v.,* **-fied, -fying.** mention or require specifically.

spec/i•men (spes/ə mən) *n.* anything typical of its kind.

spe/cious (spē/shəs) *adj.* plausible but deceptive. **—spe/cious•ly,** *adv.* **—spe/cious•ness,** *n.*

speck (spek) *n.* **1.** spot or particle. **—v. 2.** spot.

speck/le, *n., v.,* **-led, -ling. —n. 1.** small spot. **—v. 2.** mark with speckles.

specs (speks) *n.pl. Informal.* **1.** spectacles; eyeglasses. **2.** specifications (def. 2).

SPECT (spekt), *Medicine.* single photon emission computed tomography.

spec/ta•cle (spek/tə kəl) *n.* **1.** anything presented to sight. **2.** public display. **3.** *(pl.)* eyeglasses.

spec•tac/u•lar (-tak/yə lər) *adj.* dramatic; thrilling. **—spec•tac/u•lar•ly,** *adv.*

spec/ta•tor (spek/tā tər) *n.* observer.

spec/ter (spek/tər) *n.* ghost. Also, **spec/tre.** **—spec/tral** (-trəl) *adj.*

spec/tro•scope/ (spek/trə skōp/) *n.* instrument for producing and examining spectra.

spec/trum (-trəm) *n., pl.* **-tra** (-trə), **-trums.** band of colors formed when light ray is dispersed.

spec/u•late/ (spek/yə lāt/) *v.,* **-lated, -lating. 1.** think; conjecture. **2.** invest at some risk. **—spec/u•la/tion,** *n.* **—spec/u•la/tive** (-lā/tiv, -lə tiv) *adj.* **—spec/u•la/tor,** *n.*

Sp.Ed. Specialist in Education.

speech (spēch) *n.* **1.** power of speaking. **2.** utterance. **3.** talk before audience. **4.** language. **—speech/less,** *adj.*

speed (spēd) *n., v.,* **sped** (sped) or **speeded, speeding. —n. 1.** swiftness. **2.** rate of motion **—v. 3.** increase speed of. **4.** move swiftly. **—speed/er,** *n.* **—speed/y,** *adj.* **—speed/i•ly,** *adv.*

speed•om/e•ter (spē dom/i tər, spi-) *n.* device for indicating speed.

speed/well/, *n.* plant having spikes of small flowers.

spe/le•ol/o•gy (spē/lē ol/ə jē) *n.* exploration and study of caves. **—spe/le•ol/o•gist,** *n.*

spell (spel) *v.,* **spelled** or **spelt, spelling,** *n.* **—v. 1.** give letters of in order. **2.** (of letters) form. **3.** signify. **4.** relieve at work. **—n. 5.** enchantment. **6.** brief period. **—spell/er,** *n.*

spell/bound/, *adj.* fascinated.

spe•lunk/er (spi lung/kər) *n.* person who explores caves. **—spe•lunk/ing,** *n.*

spend (spend) *v.,* **spent, spending. 1.** pay out. **2.** pass (time). **3.** use up. **—spend/er,** *n.*

spend/thrift/, *n.* extravagant spender.

sperm (spûrm) *n.* male reproductive cell. **—sper•mat/ic** (-mat/ik) *adj.*

sper/ma•cet/i (spûr/mə set/ē) *n.* waxy substance from large square-headed whale (sperm whale).

sper•mat/o•zo/on (spûr mat/ə zō/ən, -on) *n., pl.* **-zoa** (-zō/ə). mature male reproductive cell.

sper'mi•cide' (-mə sīd') *n.* sperm-killing agent.

spew (spyōō) *v.* **1.** vomit. **2.** gush or pour out. —*n.* **3.** something spewed.

SPF sun protection factor.

spg spring.

sp. gr. specific gravity. Also, **spg.**

spher spherical.

sphere (sfēr) *n.* **1.** round ball. **2.** particular field of influence or competence. —**spher'i•cal,** *adj.*

sphe'roid (sfēr'oid) *n.* body approximately spherical.

sphinc'ter (sfingk'tər) *n.* muscle closing anus or other body opening. —**sphinc'ter•al,** *adj.*

sphinx (sfingks) *n.* figure of creature with human head and lion's body.

sp.ht. *Physics.* specific heat.

spice (spīs) *n., v.,* **spiced, spicing.** —*n.* **1.** aromatic plant substance used as seasoning. —*v.* **2.** season with spice. —**spic'y,** *adj.*

spick'-and-span' (spik'ən span') *adj.* **1.** spotlessly clean. **2.** perfectly new.

spic'ule (spik'yōōl) *n.* small, needlelike part or process.

spi'der (spī'dər) *n.* wingless, web-spinning insectlike animal. —**spi'der•y,** *adj.*

spiel (spēl, shpēl) *n. Slang.* high-pressure sales talk.

spiff'y (spif'ē) *adj.,* **-ier, -iest.** *Informal.* smart; fine.

spig'ot (spig'ət) *n.* faucet.

spike (spīk) *n., v.,* **spiked, spiking.** —*n.* **1.** large strong nail. **2.** stiff, pointed part. **3.** ear of grain. **4.** stalk of flowers. —*v.* **5.** fasten with spikes. **6.** frustrate or stop. —**spik'y,** *adj.,* **-ier, -iest.**

spill (spil) *v.,* **spilled** or **spilt, spilling. 1.** run or let run over. **2.** shed (blood). —**spil'lage,** *n.*

spill'way', *n.* overflow passage.

spin (spin) *v.,* **spun** (spun), **spinning,** *n.* —*v.* **1.** make yarn or thread from fiber. **2.** secrete filament. **3.** whirl. —*n.* **4.** spinning motion. **5.** short ride. **6.** *Slang.* particular viewpoint or bias. —**spin'ner,** *n.*

spin'ach (spin'ich) *n.* plant with edible leaves.

spinal column, series of vertebrae forming axis of skeleton.

spinal cord, cord of nerve tissue extending through spinal column.

spin control, *Slang.* attempt to give a bias to news coverage.

spin'dle (spin'dl) *n.* **1.** tapered rod. **2.** any shaft or axis.

spin'dling, *adj.* tall and thin. Also, **spin'dly.**

spin doctor, *Slang.* press agent or spokesperson skilled at spin control.

spine (spīn) *n.* **1.** Also, **spinal column.** connected series of bones down back. **2.** any spinelike part. **3.** stiff bristle or thorn. —**spi'nal,** *adj.* —**spin'y,** *adj.*

spine'less, *adj.* weak in character.

spin'et (spin'it) *n.* small piano.

spin'na•ker (spin'ə kər) *n.* large sail.

spinning wheel, device for spinning yarn or thread.

spin'-off', *n.* by-product or secondary development from primary effort or product.

spin'ster (spin'stər) *n. Usually Offensive.* unmarried woman, esp. elderly.

spi'ra•cle (spī'rə kəl, spir'ə-) *n.* blowhole.

spi'ral (spī'rəl) *n., adj., v.,* **-raled, -raling.** —*n.* **1.** curve made by circling a point while approaching or receding from it. —*adj.* **2.** like or of spiral. —*v.* **3.** move spirally. —**spi'ral•ly,** *adv.*

spire (spīr) *n.* tall tapering structure, esp. on tower or roof.

spi•re'a (spī rē'ə) *n.* common garden shrub. Also, **spiraea.**

spir'it (spir'it) *n.* **1.** vital principle in humanity; soul. **2.** supernatural being. **3.** feelings. **4.** vigor. **5.** intent. **6.** (*pl.*) alcoholic liquor. **7.** (*cap.*) Holy Ghost. —*v.* **8.** carry off secretly. —**spir'it•ed,** *adj.* —**spir'it•less,** *adj.*

spir'it•u•al (-chōō əl) *adj.* **1.** of or in spirit; ethereal. **2.** religious. —*n.* **3.** religious song. —**spir'it•u•al•ly,** *adv.* —**spir'it•u•al'i•ty** (-al'i tē) *n.*

spir'it•u•al•ism, *n.* belief that spirits of dead communicate with living. —**spir'it•u•al•ist,** *n., adj.*

spir'it•u•ous, *adj.* **1.** alcoholic. **2.** distilled.

spi'ro•chete' (spī'rə kēt') *n.* mobile, spiral bacteria.

spit (spit) *v.,* **spat** (spat) or **spit** (for 2 **spitted**), **spitting,** *n.* —*v.* **1.** eject from mouth. **2.** pierce. —*n.* **3.** saliva. **4.** *Informal,* image. **5.** rod for roasting meat. **6.** point of land.

spite (spīt) *n., v.,* **spited, spiting.** —*n.* **1.** malice; grudge. —*v.* **2.** annoy out of spite. —**spite'ful,** *adj.* —**spite'ful•ly,** *adv.* —**spite'ful•ness,** *n.*

spit'fire', *n.* person with fiery temper.

spit'tle, *n.* saliva.

spit•toon' (spi tōōn') *n.* cuspidor.

spkl sprinkler.

spkr speaker.

spkt sprocket.

splash (splash) *v.* **1.** dash water, etc. —*n.* **2.** act or sound of splashing. **3.** spot. —**splash'y,** *adj.*

splash'down', *n.* landing of space vehicle in ocean.

splat (splat) *n.* **1.** broad piece forming part of chair back. **2.** sound made by splattering.

splat'ter, *v.* splash widely.

splay (splā) *v., adj.* spread out.

splc splice.

spleen (splēn) *n.* **1.** ductless organ near stomach. **2.** ill humor.

splen'did (splen'did) *adj.* gorgeous; superb; fine. —**splen'did•ly,** *adv.* —**splen'dor,** *n.*

S

sple•net′ic (spli net′ik) *adj.* **1.** of the spleen. **2.** irritable or spiteful.

splice (splīs) *v.*, **spliced, splicing,** *n.* —*v.* **1.** join, as ropes or boards. —*n.* **2.** union made by splicing.

splint (splint) *n.* **1.** brace for broken part of body. **2.** strip of wood for weaving. —*v.* **3.** brace with splints.

splin′ter, *n.* **1.** thin sharp fragment. —*v.* **2.** break into splinters.

split (split) *v.*, **split, splitting,** *n.*, *adj.* —*v.* **1.** separate; divide. **2.** burst. —*n.* **3.** crack or breach. —*adj.* **4.** cleft; divided.

split′-lev′el, *adj.* **1.** having rooms on levels a half story apart. —*n.* **2.** split-level house.

split pea, dried green pea.

split personality, mental disorder in which person acquires several personalities that function independently.

splotch (sploch) *n.*, *v.*, blot; stain. —**splotch′y,** *adj.*

splt spotlight.

spltr splitter.

splurge (splûrj) *n.*, *v.*, **splurged, splurging.** —*n.* **1.** big display or expenditure. —*v.* **2.** make splurge; be extravagant.

splut′ter (splut′ər) *v.* **1.** talk vehemently and incoherently. —*n.* **2.** spluttering talk.

sply supply.

spmkt supermarket.

spnr spanner.

spoil (spoil) *v.*, **spoiled** or **spoilt, spoiling,** *n.* —*v.* **1.** damage; ruin. **2.** become tainted. —*n.* **3.** (*pl.*) booty. **4.** waste material. —**spoil′-age,** *n.* —**spoil′er,** *n.*

spoil′sport′, *n.* person who spoils the pleasure of others.

spoils system, practice of filling nonelective public offices with supporters of victorious party.

spoke (spōk) *n.* bar between hub and rim of wheel.

spokes′man, *n.*, *pl.* **-men.** person speaking for others. Also, *fem.*, **spokes′wom′an;** *masc.* or *fem.*, **spokes′per′son.**

spo/li•a′tion (spō′lē ā′shən) *n.* act of plundering.

sponge (spunj) *n.*, *v.*, **sponged, sponging.** —*n.* **1.** marine animal. **2.** its light skeleton or an imitation, used to absorb liquids. —*v.* **3.** clean with sponge. **4.** impose or live on another. —**spong′er,** *n.* —**spon′gy,** *adj.*

sponge cake, light cake without shortening.

spon′sor (spon′sər) *n.* **1.** one that recommends or supports. **2.** godparent. **3.** advertiser on radio or television. —*v.* **4.** act as sponsor for. —**spon′sor•ship′,** *n.*

spon•ta′ne•ous (spon tā′nē əs) *adj.* **1.** arising without outside cause. **2.** impulsive. —**spon•ta′ne•ous•ly,** *adv.* —**spon′ta•ne′i•ty,** *n.*

spontaneous combustion, ignition of a substance without heat from external source.

spoof (spōōf) *n.* **1.** parody. **2.** prank. —*v.* **3.** make fun of lightly.

spook (spōōk) *Informal,* —*n.* **1.** ghost. —*v.* **2.** frighten. —**spook′y,** *adj.*

spool (spōōl) *n.* cylinder on which something is wound.

spoon (spōōn) *n.* **1.** utensil for stirring or taking up food. —*v.* **2.** lift in spoon. —**spoon′-ful,** *n.*

spoon′bill′, *n.* large wading bird.

spoon′er•ism (spōō′nə riz′əm) *n.* inadvertent transposition of initial sounds of words.

spoon′-feed′, *v.*, **-fed, -feeding. 1.** feed with a spoon. **2.** provide information in a simplified way.

spoor (spōōr) *n.* trail of wild animal.

spo•rad′ic (spə rad′ik) *adj.* occasional; scattered. —**spo•rad′i•cal•ly,** *adv.*

spore (spôr) *n.* seed, as of ferns.

sport (spôrt) *n.* **1.** athletic pastime. **2.** diversion. **3.** abnormally formed plant or animal. —*adj.* **4.** of or for sport. —*v.* **5.** play. —**sports′man,** *n.* —**sports′man•ly,** *adj.* —**sports′man•ship′,** *n.* —**sports′wear′,** *n.*

spor′tive, *adj.* playful. —**spor′tive•ly,** *adv.*

sports car, small, high-powered car.

sport′y, *adj.*, **-ier, -iest.** flashy or showy.

spot (spot) *n.*, *v.*, **spotted, spotting,** *adj.* —*n.* **1.** blot; speck. **2.** locality. —*v.* **3.** stain with spots. **4.** notice. —*adj.* **5.** made, done, etc., at once. —**spot′less,** *adj.* —**spot′ter,** *n.* —**spot′ty,** *adj.*

spot check, random sampling or investigation. —**spot′-check′,** *v.*

spot′light′, *n.* **1.** intense light focused on person or thing, as on stage. **2.** intense public attention.

spouse (spous) *n.* husband or wife.

spout (spout) *v.* **1.** discharge (liquid, etc.) with force. **2.** utter insincerely. —*n.* **3.** pipe or lip on container.

spp. species.

sp/ph split/phase.

sppl spark plug.

S.P.Q.R. the Senate and People of Rome. Also, **SPQR** [from Latin *Senātus Populusque Rōmānus*]

spr spring.

S.P.R. Society for Psychical Research.

sprain (sprān) *v.* **1.** injure by wrenching. —*n.* **2.** such injury.

sprat (sprat) *n.* herringlike fish.

sprawl (sprôl) *v.* **1.** stretch out ungracefully. —*n.* **2.** sprawling position.

spray (sprā) *n.* **1.** liquid in fine particles. **2.** appliance for producing spray. **3.** branch of flowers, etc. —*v.* **4.** scatter as spray. **5.** apply spray to. —**spray′er,** *n.*

sprdr spreader.

spread (spred) *v.*, **spread, spreading,** *n.* —*v.* **1.** stretch out. **2.** extend. **3.** scatter. —*n.* **4.** extent. **5.** diffusion. **6.** cloth cover. **7.** preparation for eating on bread. —**spread'a·ble,** *adj.* —**spread'er,** *n.*

spread'-ea'gle, *adj., v.,* -**gled, -gling.** —*adj.* **1.** suggesting form of eagle with outstretched wings. —*v.* **2.** stretch out in this position.

spread'sheet', *n.* **1.** outsize ledger sheet used by accountants. **2.** such a sheet simulated electronically by computer software.

spree (sprē) *n.* frolic.

SPRF single Puerto Rican female.

sprig (sprig) *n.* twig or shoot.

spright'ly (sprīt'lē) *adj.,* -**lier, -liest.** lively. —**spright'li·ness,** *n.*

spring (spring) *v.,* **sprang** (sprang) or **sprung** (sprung), **sprung, springing,** *n., adj.* —*v.* **1.** leap. **2.** grow or proceed. **3.** disclose. —*n.* **4.** leap; jump. **5.** natural fountain. **6.** season after winter. **7.** elastic device. —*adj.* **8.** of or for spring (def. 6). —**spring'time',** *n.* —**spring'y,** *adj.*

spring'board', *n.* **1.** flexible board used in diving and gymnastics. **2.** starting point.

spring fever, restless feeling associated with spring.

sprin'kle (spring'kəl) *v.,* -**kled, -kling,** *n.* —*v.* **1.** scatter in drops. **2.** rain slightly. —*n.* **3.** instance of sprinkling. **4.** something sprinkled. —**sprin'kler,** *n.*

sprint (sprint) *v.* **1.** run fast. —*n.* **2.** short fast run. —**sprint'er,** *n.*

sprite (sprīt) *n.* elf; fairy.

spritz (sprits, shprits) *v.* **1.** spray briefly. —*n.* **2.** squirt.

sprl spiral.

SPRM single Puerto Rican male.

sprock'et (sprok'it) *n.* tooth on wheel for engaging with chain.

sprout (sprout) *v.* **1.** begin to grow; bud. —*n.* **2.** plant shoot.

sprt support.

spruce (sprōōs) *adj.,* **sprucer, sprucest,** *v., n.* —*adj.* **1.** trim; neat. —*v.* **2.** make spruce. —*n.* **3.** cone-bearing evergreen tree.

spry (sprī) *adj.,* **spryer** or **sprier, spryest** or **spriest.** nimble. —**spry'ly,** *adv.* —**spry'ness,** *n.*

spst sw single-pole single-throw switch.

spt. seaport.

spud (spud) *n.* **1.** spadelike tool. **2.** *Informal,* potato.

spume (spyōōm) *n.* foam.

spu·mo'ni (spə mō'nē) *n.* variously flavored ice cream containing fruit and nuts.

spunk (spungk) *n. Informal.* courage; spirit. —**spunk'y,** *adj.*

spur (spûr) *n., v.,* **spurred, spurring.** —*n.* **1.** sharp device worn on heel to goad horse. **2.** spurlike part. —*v.* **3.** prick with spur. **4.** urge.

spu'ri·ous (spyŏŏr'ē əs) *adj.* not genuine. —**spu'ri·ous·ly,** *adv.* —**spu'ri·ous·ness,** *n.*

spurn (spûrn) *v.* scorn; reject.

spurt (spûrt) *v.* **1.** gush or eject in jet. **2.**

speed up briefly. —*n.* **3.** forceful gush. **4.** brief increase of effort.

sput'nik (spŏŏt'nik, sput'-) *n.* first earth-orbiting satellite, launched by USSR in 1957.

sput'ter (sput'ər) *v.* **1.** emit violently in drops. **2.** splutter. —*n.* **3.** act or sound of sputtering.

spu'tum (spyōō'təm) *n.* spittle, esp. mixed with mucus.

spvn supervision.

spy (spī) *n., pl.* **spies,** *v.,* **spied, spying.** —*n.* **1.** secret observer, esp. one employed by government. —*v.* **2.** watch secretly. **3.** sight.

spy glass, small telescope.

Sq. 1. Squadron. **2.** Square (of a city or town).

sq. 1. sequence. **2.** the following; the following one. [from Latin *sequēns*] **3.** squadron. **4.** square.

sqdn squadron.

sq. ft. square foot; square feet.

sq. in. square inch; square inches.

sq. km square kilometer; square kilometers.

SQL *Computers.* structured query language.

sq. m square meter; square meters.

sq. mi. square mile; square miles.

sq. mm square millimeter; square millimeters.

sqq. the following; the following ones. [from Latin *sequentia*]

sq. r. square rod; square rods.

sq. rt. square root.

squab (skwob) *n.* young pigeon.

squab'ble (skwob'əl) *n., v.,* -**bled, -bling.** —*n.* **1.** petty quarrel. —*v.* **2.** have squabble.

squad (skwod) *n.* small group.

squad car, police car.

squad'ron (-rən) *n.* unit in Navy, Air Force, etc.

squal'id (skwol'id) *adj.* dirty or wretched. —**squal'id·ly,** *adv.* —**squal'id·ness,** *n.*

squall (skwôl) *n.* **1.** strong gust of wind, etc. **2.** loud cry. —*v.* **3.** cry loudly. —**squall'y,** *adj.*

squal'or (skwol'ər) *n.* squalid state.

squan'der (skwon'dər) *v.* use or spend wastefully.

square (skwâr) *n., v.,* **squared, squaring,** *adj.,* **squarer, squarest,** *adv.* —*n.* **1.** plane figure with four equal sides and four right angles. **2.** anything square. **3.** tool for checking right angles. **4.** product of number multiplied by itself. **5.** *Slang.* conventional, conservative, unimaginative person. —*v.* **6.** make square. **7.** adjust; agree. **8.** multiply by itself. —*adj.* **9.** being a square. **10.** level. **11.** honest. —*adv.* **12.** directly. —**square'ly,** *adv.*

square dance, dance by sets of four couples arranged in squares.

square'-rigged', having square sails.

square root, quantity of which a given quantity is the square.

squash (skwosh) *v.* **1.** crush; suppress. —*n.* **2.** game resembling tennis. **3.** fruit of vinelike plant.

S

squat (skwot) *v.*, **squatted** or **squat**, **squatting**, *adj.*, *n.* —*v.* **1.** sit with legs close under body. **2.** settle on land illegally or to acquire title. —*adj.* **3.** Also, **squat′ty.** stocky. —*n.* **4.** squatting position. —**squat′ter,** *n.*

squaw (skwô) *n. Often Offensive.* American Indian woman.

squawk (skwôk) *v.* **1.** loud harsh cry. —*v.* **2.** utter squawks. —**squawk′er,** *n.*

squeak (skwēk) *n.* **1.** small shrill sound. —*v.* **2.** emit squeaks. —**squeak′y,** *adj.* —**squeak′er,** *n.* —**squeak′i•ness,** *n.*

squeal (skwēl) *n.* **1.** long shrill cry. —*v.* **2.** utter squeals. —**squeal′er,** *n.*

squeam′ish (skwē′mish) *adj.* **1.** prudish. **2.** overfastidious. —**squeam′ish•ly,** *adv.* —**squeam′ish•ness,** *n.*

squee′gee (skwē′jē) *n.* implement for cleaning glass surfaces.

squeeze (skwēz) *v.*, **squeezed, squeezing,** *n.* —*v.* **1.** press together. **2.** cram. —*n.* **3.** act of squeezing. **4.** hug.

squelch (skwelch) *v.* **1.** crush. **2.** silence. —*n.* **3.** crushing retort.

squib (skwib) *n.* **1.** short witty item. **2.** hissing firecracker.

squid (skwid) *n.* marine mollusk.

squig′gle (skwig′əl) *n.* short, irregular curve or twist. —**squig′gly,** *adj.*

squint (skwint) *v.* **1.** look with eyes partly closed. **2.** be cross-eyed. —*n.* **3.** squinting look. **4.** cross-eyed condition.

squire (skwīᵊr) *n.*, *v.*, **squired, squiring.** —*n.* **1.** country gentleman. **2.** escort. —*v.* **3.** escort.

squirm (skwûrm) *v.*, *n.* wriggle.

squir′rel (skwûr′əl) *n.* bushy-tailed, tree-living rodent.

squirt (skwûrt) *v.* **1.** gush; cause to gush. —*n.* **2.** jet of liquid.

squish (skwish) *v.* **1.** make gushing sound when squeezed. **2.** squash (def. 1). —*n.* **3.** squishing sound.

sq. yd. square yard; square yards.

Sr., **1.** Senior. **2.** Sister.

Sra. 1. Senhora: a Portuguese form of address for a woman. **2.** Señora: a Spanish form of address for a woman.

SRAM short-range attack missile.

SRB solid rocket booster.

SRBM short-range ballistic missile.

srch search.

S. Rept. Senate report.

S. Res. Senate resolution.

srng syringe.

SRO, **1.** single-room occupancy. **2.** standing room only.

SRS air bag. [*s(upplemental) r(estraint) s(ystem)*]

Srta. 1. Senhorita: a Portuguese form of address for a girl or unmarried woman. **2.** Señorita: a Spanish form of address for a girl or unmarried woman.

srvln surveillance.

SS, social security.

SSA 1. Social Security Act. **2.** Social Security Administration.

SSAE stamped self-addressed envelope.

SSB 1. Selective Service Board. **2.** Social Security Board.

ssb single sideband.

SSBN the U.S. Navy designation for the fleet ballistic missile submarine. [*S(trategic) S(ubmarine) B(allistic) N(uclear)*]

SSC *Banking.* small-saver certificate.

S.Sc.D. Doctor of Social Science.

sscr setscrew.

SS.D. Most Holy Lord: a title of the pope. [from Latin *Sānctissimus Dominus*]

S.S.D. Doctor of Sacred Scripture. [from Latin *Sacrae Scrīptūrae Doctor*]

ssdd *Computers.* single-side, double-density.

SSE south-southeast. Also, **S.S.E., s.s.e.**

sse solid-state electronics.

ssf saybolt second furol.

ssfm single-sideband frequency modulation.

sshd *Computers.* single-side, high-density.

SSI 1. *Electronics.* small-scale integration: the technology for concentrating semiconductor devices in a single integrated circuit. **2.** Supplemental Security Income.

S sleep slow-wave sleep.

SSM surface-to-surface missile.

ssm 1. single-sideband modulation. **2.** solid-state materials.

SSN Social Security number.

SSPE *Pathology.* subacute sclerosing panencephalitis.

SSR Soviet Socialist Republic. Also, **S.S.R.**

ssr solid-state relay.

SSS Selective Service System.

sssd *Computers.* single-side, single-density.

SST, supersonic transport.

ssu saybolt second universal.

SSW south-southwest. Also, **S.S.W., s.s.w.**

St., **1.** Saint. **2.** Street.

Sta. 1. Saint. [from Italian or Spanish *Santa*] **2.** Station.

sta. 1. station. **2.** stationary.

stab (stab) *v.*, **stabbed, stabbing,** *n.* —*v.* **1.** pierce with pointed weapon. —*n.* **2.** thrust with or wound from pointed weapon.

sta′bi•lize′ (stā′bə līz′) *v.*, **-lized, -lizing.** make or keep stable. —**sta′bi•li•za′tion,** *n.* —**sta′bi•liz′er,** *n.*

sta′ble (stā′bəl) *n.*, *v.*, **-bled, -bling,** *adj.* —*n.* **1.** building for horses, etc. —*v.* **2.** keep in stable. —*adj.* **3.** steady; steadfast. —**stab′-ly,** *adv.* —**sta•bil′i•ty,** *n.*

stacc. *Music.* with disconnected notes. [from Italian *staccato*]

stac•ca′to (stə kä′tō) *adj. Music.* disconnected; detached.

stack (stak) *n.* **1.** orderly heap. **2.** (*often pl.*)

book storage area. **3.** funnel for smoke. —*v.*
4. pile in stack. **5.** arrange unfairly.

sta′di•um (stā′dē əm) *n., pl.* **-diums, -dia**
(-ə). large open structure for games.

staff (staf) *n., pl.* **staves** (stāvz) or **staffs** (for
1, 3); **staffs** (for 2); *v.* —*n.* **1.** stick carried as
support, weapon, etc. **2.** body of administra-
tors or assitants. **3.** set of five lines on which
music is written. —*v.* **4.** provide with staff.

staff′er, *n.* member of a staff.

stag (stag) *n.* **1.** adult male deer. —*adj.* **2.** for
men only. —*adv.* **3.** without a date.

stage (stāj) *n., v.,* **staged, staging.** —*n.* **1.**
single step or degree. **2.** raised platform. **3.**
theater. —*v.* **4.** exhibit on stage.

stage′coach′, *n.* horse-drawn public coach
that traveled over fixed route.

stage′hand′, *n.* worker in theater who deals
with properties and scenery.

stage′struck′, *adj.* obsessed with desire to
act.

stag′ger (stag′ər) *v.* **1.** move unsteadily. **2.**
cause to reel. **3.** arrange at intervals. —*n.* **4.**
staggering movement. **5.** (*pl.*) disease of
horses, etc. —**stag′ger•ing,** *adj.*

stag′ing (stā′jing) *n.* scaffolding.

stag′nant (stag′nənt) *adj.* **1.** not flowing;
foul. **2.** inactive. —**stag′nate** (-nāt) *v.,*
-nated, -nating. —**stag•na′tion,** *n.*

staid (stād) *adj.* sedate. —**staid′ly,** *adv.*
—**staid′ness,** *n.*

stain (stān) *n.* **1.** discolored patch. **2.** kind of
dye. —*v.* **3.** mark with stains. **4.** color with
stain.

stain′less, *adj.* **1.** unstained. **2.** not liable to
rusting.

stainless steel, steel allied with chromium to
resist rust.

stair (stâr) *n.* series of steps between levels.
—**stair′case′, stair′way′,** *n.*

stair′well′, *n.* vertical shaft containing stairs.

stake (stāk) *n., v.,* **staked, staking.** —*n.* **1.**
pointed post. **2.** something wagered. **3.** (*pl.*)
prize. **4.** hazard. —*v.* **5.** mark off with
stakes. **6.** wager.

stake′out′, *n.* surveillance by police.

sta•lac′tite (stə lak′tīt) *n.* icicle-shaped formation hanging from cave roof.

sta•lag′mite (stə lag′mīt) *n.* cone-shaped
deposit on cave floor.

stale (stāl) *adj.,* **staler, stalest,** *v.,* **staled,**
staling. —*adj.* **1.** not fresh. —*v.* **2.** make or
become stale. —**stale′ness,** *n.*

stale′mate′ (-māt′) *n., v.,* **-mated, -mating.**
—*n.* **1.** deadlocked position, orig. in chess.
—*v.* **2.** bring to stalemate.

stalk (stôk) *v.* **1.** pursue stealthily. **2.** walk in
haughty or menacing way. —*n.* **3.** plant
stem. —**stalk′er,** *n.*

stall (stôl) *n.* **1.** compartment for one animal.
2. sales booth. **3.** (of airplane) loss of air
speed. **4.** *Slang.* pretext for delay. —*v.* **5.**
keep in stall. **6.** stop; become stopped. **7.**
lose necessary air speed. **8.** *Slang.* delay.

stal′lion (stal′yən) *n.* male horse.

stal′wart (stôl′wərt) *adj.* **1.** robust. **2.** brave.
3. steadfast. —*v.* **4.** stalwart person.

sta′men (stā′mən) *n.* pollen-bearing organ of
flower.

stam′i•na (stam′ə nə) *n.* endurance.

stam′mer (stam′ər) *v.* **1.** speak with involuntary breaks or repetitions. —*n.* **2.** such
speech. —**stam′mer•er,** *n.*

stamp (stamp) *v.* **1.** trample. **2.** mark. **3.** put
paper stamp on. —*n.* **4.** act of stamping. **5.**
marking device. **6.** adhesive paper affixed to
show payment of fees.

stam•pede′ (stam pēd′) *n., v.,* **-peded,**
-peding. —*n.* **1.** panicky flight. —*v.* **2.** flee in
stampede.

stamping ground, favorite haunt.

stance (stans) *n.* position of feet.

stanch (stônch, stanch) *adj.* **1.** staunch. —*v.*
2. stop flow, esp. of blood. —**stanch′ly,** *adv.*
—**stanch′ness,** *n.*

stan′chion (stan′shən) *n.* upright post.

stand (stand) *v.,* **stood** (stŏŏd), **standing,** *n.*
—*v.* **1.** rise or be upright. **2.** remain firm. **3.**
be located. **4.** be candidate. **5.** endure. —*n.*
6. firm attitude. **7.** place of standing. **8.** platform. **9.** support for small articles. **10.** outdoor salesplace. **11.** area of trees. **12.** stop.

stand′ard (stan′dərd) *n.* **1.** approved model
or rule. **2.** flag. **3.** upright support. —*adj.* **4.**
being model or basis for comparison.

stan′dard-bear′er, *n.* leader of a cause.

stand′ard•ize′, *v.,* **-ized, -izing.** make standard. —**stand′ard•i•za′tion,** *n.*

standard time, civil time officially adopted
for a region.

stand′•by′, *n., pl.* **-bys,** *adj.* —*n.* **1.** chief
support. —*adj.* **2.** substitute.

stand′-in′, *n.* substitute.

stand′ing, *n.* **1.** status or reputation. **2.** duration. —*adj.* **3.** upright. **4.** stagnant. **5.** lasting;
fixed.

stand′off′, *n.* tie or draw; situation in which
neither side has advantage.

stand′off′ish, *adj.* tending to be aloof.

stand′out′, *n.* one that is conspicuously superior.

stand′pipe′, *n.* vertical pipe into which water is pumped to obtain required pressure.

stand′point′, *n.* point of view.

stand′still′, *n.* complete halt.

stand′-up′, *adj.* **1.** erect. **2.** performing a
comic monologue while standing alone be-
fore audience.

stan′za (stan′zə) *n.* division of poem.

staph′y•lo•coc′cus (staf′ə lə kok′əs) *n., pl.*
-ci (-sī, -sē). any of several spherical bacteria
occurring in clusters.

sta′ple (stā′pəl) *n., v.,* **-pled, -pling,** *adj.*
—*n.* **1.** bent wire fastener. **2.** chief commodity. **3.** textile fiber. —*v.* **4.** fasten with staple.
—*adj.* **5.** basic. —**sta′pler,** *n.*

star (stär) *n., adj., v.,* **starred, starring.** —*n.*
1. heavenly body luminous at night. **2.** figure

S

with five or six points. **3.** asterisk. **4.** principal performer. **5.** famous performer. —*adj.* **6.** principal. —*v.* **7.** mark with star. **8.** have leading part. —**star′ry,** *adj.* —**star′dom,** *n.*

star′board′ (-bərd, -bôrd′) *n.* right-hand side of vessel, facing forward. —**star′board′,** *adj., adv.*

starch (stärch) *n.* **1.** white tasteless substance used as food and as a stiffening agent. **2.** preparation from starch. —*v.* **3.** stiffen with starch. —**starch′y,** *adj.*

stare (stâr) *v.,* **stared, staring,** *n.* —*v.* **1.** gaze fixedly. —*n.* **2.** fixed look.

star′fish′, *n.* star-shaped marine animal.

star′gaze′, *v.,* **-gazed, -gazing. 1.** gaze at stars. **2.** daydream. —**star′gaz′er,** *n.*

stark (stärk) *adj.* **1.** utter; sheer. **2.** stiff. **3.** bleak. **4.** blunt; harsh. —*adv.* **5.** utterly. —**stark′ly,** *adv.* —**stark′ness,** *n.*

star′let (-lit) *n.* young movie actress.

star′light′, *n.* light emanating from the stars. —**star′lit′,** *adj.*

star′ling (-ling) *n.* small bird.

star′ry-eyed′, *adj.* overly romantic or idealistic.

start (stärt) *v.* **1.** begin. **2.** move suddenly. **3.** establish. —*n.* **4.** beginning. **5.** startled movement. **6.** lead. —**start′er,** *n.*

star′tle, *v.,* **-tled, -tling.** disturb suddenly.

starve (stärv) *v.,* **starved, starving. 1.** die or suffer severely from hunger. **2.** kill or weaken by hunger. —**star•va′tion,** *n.*

stash (stash) *v.* **1.** hide away. —*n.* **2.** something hidden away. **3.** hiding place.

stat (stat) *n.* statistic.

state (stāt) *n., adj., v.,* **stated, stating.** —*n.* **1.** condition. **2.** pomp. **3.** nation. **4.** commonwealth of a federal union. **5.** civil government. —*adj.* **6.** ceremonious. —*v.* **7.** declare. —**state′hood,** *n.* —**state′house,** *n.*

state′craft′, *n.* art of government.

state′less, *adj.* lacking nationality.

state′ly, *adj.,* **-lier, -liest.** dignified. —**state′li•ness,** *n.*

state′ment, *n.* **1.** declaration. **2.** report on business account.

state of the art, most advanced stage.

state′room′, *n.* quarters on ship, etc.

states′man, *n.* leader in government. —**states′man•ship′,** *n.*

stat′ic (stat′ik) *adj.* **1.** fixed; at rest. —*n.* **2.** atmospheric electricity. **3.** interference caused by it.

sta′tion (stā′shən) *n.* **1.** place of duty. **2.** depot for trains, buses, etc. **3.** status. **4.** place for sending or receiving radio or television broadcasts. —*v.* **5.** assign place to.

sta′tion•ar•y (-shə ner′ē) *adj.* not moving; not movable; fixed.

sta′tion•er, *n.* dealer in stationery.

sta′tion•er•y (-shə ner′ē) *n.* writing materials.

sta•tis′tics (stə tis′tiks) *n.* science of collecting, classifying, and using numerical facts.

—**sta•tis′ti•cal,** *adj.* —**sta•tis′ti•cal•ly,** *adv.* —**stat′is•ti′cian** (stat′ə stish′ən) *n.*

stat′u•ar′y (stach′ōō er′ē) *n.* statues.

stat′ue (stach′ōō) *n.* carved, molded, or cast figure.

stat′u•esque′ (-esk′) *adj.* like statue; of imposing figure.

stat′u•ette′ (-et′) *n.* little statue.

stat′ure (-ər) *n.* **1.** height. **2.** achievement.

sta′tus (stā′təs, stat′əs) *n.* **1.** social standing. **2.** present condition.

status quo (kwō) existing state.

status symbol, possession believed to indicate high social status.

stat′ute (stach′ōōt) *n.* law enacted by legislature. —**stat′u•to′ry** (-ōō tôr′ē) *adj.*

statute of limitations, statute defining period within which legal action may be taken.

staunch (stônch) *adj.* **1.** firm; steadfast; strong. —*v.* **2.** stanch. —**staunch′ly,** *adv.* —**staunch′ness,** *n.*

stave (stāv) *n., v.,* **staved** or (for 3) **stove** (stōv), **staving.** —*n.* **1.** one of curved vertical strips of barrel, etc. **2.** *Music.* staff. —*v.* **3.** break hole in. **4.** ward (off).

stay (stā) *v.* **1.** remain; continue. **2.** stop or restrain. **3.** support. —*n.* **4.** period at one place. **5.** stop; pause. **6.** support; prop. **7.** rope supporting mast.

staying power, endurance.

S.T.B. 1. Bachelor of Sacred Theology. [from Latin *Sacrae Theologiae Baccalaureus*] **2.** Bachelor of Theology. [from Latin *Scientiae Theologicae Baccalaureus*]

stbd. starboard.

stbln stabilization.

stby standby.

STC Society for Technical Communication.

stc sensitivity time control.

stch stitch.

STD, sexually transmitted disease.

std., standard.

stdy steady.

stdzn standardization.

Ste. (referring to a woman) Saint. [from French *Sainte*]

stead (sted) *n.* **1.** place taken by another. **2.** advantage.

stead′fast′, *adj.* **1.** fixed. **2.** firm or loyal. —**stead′fast′ly,** *adv.* —**stead′fast′ness,** *n.*

stead′y, *adj.,* **-ier, -iest,** *v.,* **steadied, steadying.** —*adj.* **1.** firmly fixed. **2.** uniform; regular. **3.** steadfast. —*v.* **4.** make or become steady. —**stead′i•ly,** *adv.* —**stead′i•ness,** *n.*

steak (stāk) *n.* slice of meat or fish.

steal (stēl) *v.,* **stole** (stōl), **stolen, stealing. 1.** take wrongfully. **2.** move very quietly.

stealth (stelth) *n.* secret procedure. —**stealth′y,** *adj.* —**stealth′i•ly,** *adv.*

steam (stēm) *n.* **1.** water in form of gas or vapor. —*v.* **2.** pass off as or give off steam. **3.** treat with steam, as in cooking. —*adj.* **4.**

operated by steam. **5.** conducting steam. —**steam/boat/, steam/ship/,** n.

steam/er, n. **1.** vessel moved by steam. **2.** device for cooking, treating, etc., with steam.

steam/roll/er, n. **1.** heavy vehicle with roller used for paving roads. —v. **2.** crush, flatten, or overwhelm as if with steamroller.

steam shovel, machine for excavating.

steed (stēd) n. horse, esp. for riding.

steel (stēl) n. **1.** iron modified with carbon. —adj. **2.** of or like steel. —v. **3.** make resolute. —**steel/y,** adj.

steel wool, mass of stringlike woven steel, used esp. for scouring and smoothing.

steel/yard/ (stēl/yärd/, stil/yərd) n. kind of scale.

steep (stēp) adj. **1.** sloping sharply. **2.** exorbitant. —v. **3.** soak. **4.** absorb. —**steep/ly,** adv.

stee/ple (stē/pəl) n. **1.** lofty tower on church, etc. **2.** spire.

stee/ple·chase/, n. horse race over obstacle course.

stee/ple·jack/, n. person who builds steeples.

steer (stēr) v. **1.** guide; direct. —n. **2.** ox.

steer/age (-ij) n. part of ship for passengers paying cheapest rate.

steg/o·saur/ (steg/ə sôr/) n. plant-eating dinosaur with bony plates along back.

stein (stīn) n. mug, esp. for beer.

stel/lar (stel/ər) adj. of or like stars.

stem (stem) n., v., **stemmed, stemming.** —n. **1.** supporting stalk of plant or of leaf, flower, or fruit. **2.** ancestry. **3.** part of word not changed by inflection. **4.** Naut. bow. —v. **5.** remove stem of. **6.** originate. **7.** stop or check. **8.** make headway against.

stem/ware/, n. glassware with footed stems.

sten stencil.

stench (stench) n. bad odor.

sten/cil (sten/səl) n., v., **-ciled, -ciling.** —n. **1.** sheet cut to pass design through when colored over. —v. **2.** print with stencil.

steno. 1. stenographer. **2.** stenographic. **3.** stenography. Also, **stenog.**

ste·nog/ra·pher (stə nog/rə fər) n. person skilled at shorthand and typing.

ste·nog/ra·phy (-rə fē) n. writing in shorthand. —**sten/o·graph/ic** (sten/ə graf/ik) adj. —**sten/o·graph/i·cal·ly,** adv.

sten·to/ri·an (sten tôr/ē ən) adj. very loud.

step (step) n., v., **stepped, stepping.** —n. **1.** movement of foot in walking. **2.** distance of such movement. **3.** pace. **4.** footprint. **5.** stage in process. **6.** level on stair or ladder. —v. **7.** move by steps. **8.** press with foot.

step-, prefix showing relation by remarriage of parent. —**step/child,** n. —**step/son/,** n. —**step/daugh/ter,** n. —**step/par/ent,** n. —**step/fath/er,** n. —**step/moth/er,** n. —**step/broth/er,** n. —**step/sis/ter,** n.

step/lad/der, n. ladder with flat treads.

steppe (step) n. vast plain.

-ster, suffix meaning one who is, one who is associated with, or one who makes or does.

ster/e·o (ster/ē ō/, stēr/-) n., pl. **-eos.** stereophonic sound or equipment.

ster/e·o·phon/ic (ster/ē ə fon/ik, stēr/-) adj. (of recorded sound) played through two or more speakers.

ster/e·op/ti·con (-op/ti kən) n. projector for slides, etc.

ster/e·o·scope/ (-skōp/) n. device for viewing two pictures at once to give impression of depth. —**ster/e·o·scop/ic** (-skop/ik) adj.

ster/e·o·type/, n., v., **-typed, -typing.** —n. **1.** process of making printing plates from mold taken from composed type. **2.** idea, etc., without originality. **3.** simplified image of person, group, etc. —v. **4.** make stereotype of. **5.** give fixed, trite form to.

ster/ile (ster/il; esp. Brit. -īl) adj. **1.** free from living germs. **2.** unable to produce offspring; barren. —**ste·ril/i·ty** (stə ril/i tē) n.

ster/i·lize/, v., **-lized, -lizing.** make sterile. —**ster/i·li·za/tion,** n. —**ster/i·liz/er,** n.

ster/ling (stûr/ling) adj. **1.** containing 92.5% silver. **2.** of British money. **3.** excellent.

stern (stûrn) adj. **1.** strict; harsh; grim. —n. **2.** hind part of vessel. —**stern/ly,** adv. —**stern/ness,** n.

ster/num (stûr/nəm) n., pl. **-na, -nums.** flat bone in chest connecting with clavicle and ribs.

ste/roid (stēr/oid, ster/-) n. any of a group of fat-soluble organic compounds.

stet (stet) v., **stetted, stetting. 1.** let it stand (direction to retain material previously deleted). **2.** mark with word "stet."

steth/o·scope/ (steth/ə skōp/) n. medical instrument for listening to sounds in body.

ste/ve·dore/ (stē/vi dôr/) n. person who loads and unloads ships.

stew (stōō, styōō) v. **1.** cook by simmering. —n. **2.** food so cooked.

stew/ard (stōō/ərd, styōō/-) n. **1.** person who manages another's affairs, property, etc. **2.** person in charge of food, supplies, etc., for ship, club, etc. **3.** domestic employee on ship or airplane. —**stew/ard·ship/,** n.

St. Ex. Stock Exchange.

stg. 1. stage. **2.** sterling.

stge. storage.

stick (stik) v., **stuck** (stuk), **sticking,** n. —v. **1.** pierce; stab. **2.** thrust. **3.** cause to adhere. **4.** adhere. **5.** persist. **6.** extend. —n. **7.** small length of wood, etc.

stick/er, n. **1.** one that sticks. **2.** adhesive label. **3.** thorn.

stick/-in-the-mud/, n. person who avoids change.

stick/le, v., **-led, -ling. 1.** argue over trifles. **2.** insist on correctness. —**stick/ler,** n.

stick/pin/, n. ornamental pin.

stick shift, manual transmission.

stick/y, adj., **-ier, -iest. 1.** adhering. **2.** humid. —**stick/i·ness,** n.

S

stif stiffener.

stiff (stif) *adj.* **1.** rigid. **2.** not moving easily. **3.** formal. —**stiff′en,** *v.* —**stiff′ly,** *adv.* —**stiff′ness,** *n.*

stiff′-necked′, *adj.* obstinate.

sti′fle (stī′fəl) *v.,* **-fled, -fling. 1.** smother. **2.** repress.

stig′ma (stig′mə) *n., pl.* **stig•ma•ta** (stig-mä′tə, -mə-), **-mas. 1.** mark of disgrace. **2.** pollen-receiving part of pistil. —**stig′ma•tize′,** *v.*

stile (stīl) *n.* set of steps over fence, wall, etc.

sti•let′to (sti let′ō) *n., pl.* **-tos, -toes.** dagger.

still (stil) *adj.* **1.** motionless. **2.** silent. **3.** tranquil. —*adv.* **4.** as previously. **5.** until now. **6.** yet. —*conj.* **7.** nevertheless. —*v.* **8.** make or become still. —*n.* **9.** distilling apparatus. —**still′ness,** *n.*

still′born′, *adj.* born dead.

still life, picture of inanimate objects.

stilt (stilt) *n.* one of two poles enabling user to walk above the ground.

stilt′ed, *adj.* stiffly dignified.

stim′u•lant (stim′yə lənt) *n.* food, medicine, etc., that stimulates briefly.

stim′u•late′ (-lāt′) *v.,* **-lated, -lating. 1.** rouse to action. **2.** invigorate. —**stim′u•la′tion,** *n.* —**stim′u•la′tive,** *adj.*

stim′u•lus (-ləs) *n., pl.* **-li.** something that stimulates.

sting (sting) *v.,* **stung** (stung), **stinging,** *n.* —*v.* **1.** wound with pointed organ, as bees do. **2.** pain sharply. **3.** goad. —*n.* **4.** wound caused by stinging. **5.** sharp-pointed organ. —**sting′er,** *n.*

sting′ray′, *n.* ray with flexible tail armed with bony spine.

stin′gy (stin′jē) *adj.,* **-gier, -giest. 1.** miserly. **2.** scanty. —**stin′gi•ness,** *n.*

stink (stingk) *v.,* **stank** (stangk) or **stunk** (stungk), **stunk, stinking,** *n.* —*v.* **1.** emit bad odor. —*n.* **2.** bad odor.

stint (stint) *v.* **1.** limit. **2.** limit oneself. —*n.* **3.** limitation. **4.** allotted task. —**stint′ing,** *adj.*

sti′pend (stī′pend) *n.* regular pay.

stip′ple (stip′əl) *v.,* **-pled, -pling,** *n.* —*v.* **1.** paint or cover with tiny dots. —*n.* **2.** such painting.

stip′u•late′ (stip′yə lāt′) *v.,* **-lated, -lating.** require as condition of agreement. —**stip′u•la′tion,** *n.* —**stip′u•la•to′ry** (-lə tôr′ē) *adj.*

stir (stûr) *v.,* **stirred, stirring,** *n.* —*v.* **1.** mix or agitate (liquid, etc.), esp. with circular motion. **2.** move. **3.** rouse; excite. —*n.* **4.** movement; commotion. **5.** *Slang.* prison.

stir′-cra′zy, *adj. Slang.* restless from long confinement.

stir′-fry′, *v.,* **-fried, -frying.** fry quickly while stirring constantly over high heat.

stir′rup (stûr′əp, stir′-) *n.* looplike support for foot, suspended from saddle.

stitch (stich) *n.* **1.** complete movement of needle in sewing, knitting, etc. **2.** sudden pain. —*v.* **3.** sew.

stk. stock.

stl 1. steel. **2.** studio-transmitter link.

S.T.L. Licentiate in Sacred Theology.

STM scanning tunneling microscope.

stm 1. steam. **2.** storm.

S.T.M. Master of Sacred Theology.

stmt statement.

stmy stormy.

stng sustaining.

stock (stok) *n.* **1.** goods on hand. **2.** livestock. **3.** stem or trunk. **4.** line of descent. **5.** meat broth. **6.** part of gun supporting barrel. **7.** (*pl.*) framework in which prisoners were publicly confined. **8.** capital or shares of company. —*adj.* **9.** standard; common. **10.** of stock. —*v.* **11.** supply. **12.** store. —**stock′-brok′er,** *n.* —**stock′hold′er,** *n.*

stock•ade′ (sto kād′) *n., v.,* **-aded, -ading.** —*n.* **1.** barrier of upright posts. —*v.* **2.** protect with stockade.

stock company, theatrical company acting repertoire of plays.

stock exchange, place where securities are bought and sold. Also, **stock market.**

stock′i•nette′ (stok′ə net′) *n.* stretchy fabric.

stock′ing, *n.* close-fitting covering for foot and leg.

stocking cap, conical knitted cap with tassel or pompom.

stock′pile′, *n., v.,* **-piled, -piling.** —*n.* **1.** stock of goods. —*v.* **2.** accumulate for eventual use.

stock′-still′, *adj.* motionless.

stock′y, *adj.,* **-ier, -iest.** sturdily built. —**stock′i•ly,** *adv.* —**stock′i•ness,** *n.*

stock′yard′, *n.* enclosure for livestock about to be slaughtered.

stodg′y (stoj′ē) *adj.,* **-ier, -iest.** pompous and uninteresting. —**stodg′i•ly,** *adv.* —**stodg′i•ness,** *n.*

sto′gy (stō′gē) *n., pl.* **-gies.** long, slender, cheap cigar.

sto′ic (stō′ik) *adj.* **1.** Also, **sto′i•cal.** not reacting to pain. —*n.* **2.** person who represses emotion. —**sto′i•cal•ly,** *adv.* —**sto′i•cism** (-siz′əm) *n.*

stoke (stōk) *v.,* **stoked, stoking.** tend (fire). —**stok′er,** *n.*

STOL (es′tôl′), a convertiplane that can become airborne after a short takeoff run and has forward speeds comparable to those of conventional aircraft. [*s(hort) t(ake)o(ff and) l(anding)*]

stole (stōl) *n.* scarf or narrow strip worn over shoulders.

stol′id (stol′id) *adj.* unemotional; not easily moved. —**sto•lid′i•ty,** *n.* —**stol′id•ly,** *adv.*

stom′ach (stum′ək) *n.* **1.** organ of food storage and digestion. **2.** appetite; desire. —*v.* **3.** take into stomach. **4.** tolerate.

stomp (stomp) *v.* tread or tread on heavily.

stone (stōn) *n.*, *pl.* **stones** or (for 4) **stone**, *adj.*, *v.*, **stoned, stoning**, *adv.* —*n.* **1.** hard, nonmetallic mineral substance. **2.** small rock. **3.** gem. **4.** *Brit.* unit of weight = 14 pounds. **5.** stonelike seed. **6.** concretion formed in body. —*adj.* **7.** of stone. —*v.* **8.** throw stones at. **9.** remove stones from. —*adv.* **10.** entirely. —**ston′y,** *adj.* —**ston′i•ly,** *adv.*

Stone Age, prehistoric period before use of metals.

stone′wall′, *v.* be evasive or uncooperative.

stooge (stōōj) *n.* **1.** assistant to comedian. **2.** person acting in obsequious obedience.

stool (stōol) *n.* seat without arms or back.

stool pigeon, *Slang.* decoy or informer.

stoop (stōōp) *v.* **1.** bend forward. **2.** condescend. —*n.* **3.** stooping posture. **4.** small doorway or porch.

stop (stop) *v.*, **stopped, stopping,** *n.* —*v.* **1.** cease; halt. **2.** prevent. **3.** close up. **4.** stay. —*n.* **5.** act, instance, or place of stopping. **6.** hindrance. **7.** device on musical instrument to control tone. —**stop′page,** *n.*

stop′gap′, *n.*, *adj.* makeshift.

stop′o′ver, *n.* temporary stop on journey.

stop′per, *n.* **1.** plug. —*v.* **2.** close with stopper. Also, **stop′ple.**

stop′watch′, *n.* watch with hand that can be stopped or started instantly.

stor storage.

stor′age (stôr′ij) *n.* **1.** place for storing. **2.** act of storing. **3.** state of being stored. **4.** fee for storing.

store (stôr) *n.*, *v.*, **stored, storing.** —*n.* **1.** place where merchandise is kept for sale. **2.** supply. —*v.* **3.** lay up; accumulate. **4.** put in secure place. —**store′keep′er,** *n.*

store′front′, *n.* small, street-level store.

store′house′, *n.* building for storage. —**store′room′,** *n.*

sto′ried (stôr′ēd) *adj.* famed in history or story.

stork (stôrk) *n.* wading bird with long legs and bill.

storm (stôrm) *n.* **1.** heavy rain, snow, etc., with strong winds. **2.** violent assault. —*v.* **3.** blow, rain, etc., strongly. **4.** rage. **5.** attack. —**storm′y,** *adj.* —**storm′i•ly,** *adv.*

sto′ry (stôr′ē) *n.*, *pl.* **-ries. 1.** fictitious tale. **2.** plot. **3.** newspaper report. **4.** *Informal,* lie. **5.** horizontal section of building.

stoup (stōōp) *n.* basin for holy water.

stout (stout) *adj.* **1.** solidly built. **2.** strong. **3.** firm. —*n.* **4.** dark, sweet ale. —**stout′ly,** *adv.* —**stout′ness,** *n.*

stout′-heart′ed, *adj.* brave and resolute.

stove (stōv) *n.* apparatus for giving heat.

stow (stō) *v.* **1.** put away, as cargo. **2.** **stow away,** hide on ship, etc., to get free trip. —**stow′age,** *n.* —**stow′a•way′,** *n.*

STP 1. standard temperature and pressure. **2.** *Slang.* a potent long-acting hallucinogen. [def. 2 probably after *STP,* trademark of a motor-oil additive]

stp stamp.

stpd stripped.

stpg stepping.

stpr *Telephones.* stepper.

str 1. straight. **2.** strength.

str. 1. steamer. **2.** strait. **3.** *Music.* string; strings.

stra•bis′mus (strə biz′məs) *n.* visual defect; cross-eye.

strad′dle (strad′l) *v.*, **-dled, -dling,** *n.* —*v.* **1.** have one leg on either side of. —*n.* **2.** straddling stance.

strafe (strāf, strǎf) *v.*, **strafed, strafing.** shoot from airplanes.

strag′gle (strag′əl) *v.*, **-gled, -gling.** stray from course; ramble. —**strag′gler,** *n.*

straight (strāt) *adj.* **1.** direct. **2.** even. **3.** honest. **4.** right. **5.** *Informal.* heterosexual. —*adv.* **6.** directly. **7.** in straight line. **8.** honestly. —*n.* **9.** five-card consecutive sequence in poker. —**straight′en,** *v.*

straight′-arm′, *v.* deflect an opponent by pushing away with the arm held straight.

straight arrow, often righteously conventional person.

straight′a•way, *adv.* at once. Also, **straight′way′.**

straight′edge′, *n.* bar with straight edge for use in drawing or testing lines.

straight face, expression that conceals feelings, as when keeping a secret.

straight′for′ward, *adj.* direct; frank.

straight man, entertainer who acts as foil for comedian.

strain (strān) *v.* **1.** exert to utmost. **2.** injure by stretching. **3.** sieve; filter. **4.** constrain. —*n.* **5.** great effort. **6.** injury from straining. **7.** severe pressure. **8.** melody. **9.** descendants. **10.** ancestry. **11.** hereditary trait. —**strain′er,** *n.*

strained, *adj.* not natural.

strait (strāt) *n.* **1.** narrow waterway. **2.** (*pl.*) distress.

strait′en, *v.* **1.** put into financial troubles. **2.** restrict.

strait′jack′et, *n.* **1.** garment of strong material designed to bind arms and restrain violent person. **2.** anything that severely confines or hinders.

strait′-laced′, *adj.* excessively strict in conduct or morality.

strand (strand) *v.* **1.** run aground. —*n.* **2.** shore. **3.** twisted component of rope. **4.** tress. **5.** string, as of beads.

strange (strānj) *adj.*, **stranger, strangest. 1.** unusual; odd. **2.** unfamiliar. —**strange′ly,** *adv.*

stran′ger (strān′jər) *n.* person not known or acquainted.

stran′gle (strang′gəl) *v.*, **-gled, -gling. 1.** kill by choking. **2.** choke. —**stran′gler,** *n.* —**stran′gu•la′tion** (-gyə lā′shən) *n.*

stran′gle•hold′, *n.* **1.** illegal wrestling hold

S

in which opponent is choked. **2.** restrictive force.

stran′gu·late′ (-gyə lāt′) v., **-lated, -lating.** constrict. **—stran′gu·la′tion,** n.

strap (strap) n., v., **strapped, strapping.** —n. **1.** narrow strip or band. —v. **2.** fasten with strap.

strapped, adj. needing money.

strat strategic.

strat′a·gem (strat′ə jəm) n. plan; trick.

strat′e·gy (strat′i jē) n., pl. **-gies. 1.** planning and direction of military operations. **2.** plan for achieving goal. **—stra·te′gic** (strə tē′jik) adj. **—stra·te′gi·cal·ly,** adv. **—strat′e·gist,** n.

strat′i·fy′ (strat′ə fī′) v., **-fied, -fying.** form in layers. **—strat′i·fi·ca′tion,** n.

stratig. stratigraphy.

strato stratosphere.

strat′o·sphere′ (-ə sfēr′) n. upper region of atmosphere. **—strat′o·spher′ic** (-sfer′ik, -sfē′-) adj.

stra′tum (strā′təm, strat′əm) n., pl. **-ta** (-tə), **-tums.** layer of material.

straw (strô) n. **1.** stalk of cereal grass. **2.** mass of dried stalks.

straw′ber′ry (-ber′ē, -bə rē) n., pl. **-ries.** fleshy fruit of stemless herb.

straw boss, assistant foreman.

straw vote, unofficial vote taken to determine general trend of opinion.

stray (strā) v. **1.** ramble; go from one's course or rightful place. —adj. **2.** straying. —n. **3.** stray creature.

streak (strēk) n. **1.** long mark or smear. **2.** vein; stratum. —v. **3.** mark with streaks. **4.** flash rapidly. **—streak′y,** adj., **-ier, -iest.**

stream (strēm) n. **1.** flowing body of water. **2.** steady flow. —v. **3.** move in stream. **4.** wave.

stream′er, n. long narrow flag.

stream′line′, adj., n., v., **-lined, -lining.** —adj. **1.** having shape past which fluids move easily. —n. **2.** streamline shape. —v. **3.** shape with streamline. **4.** reorganize efficiently.

street (strēt) n. public city road.

street′car′, n. public conveyance running on rails.

street smarts, shrewd awareness of how to survive in urban environment. **—street′-smart′,** adj.

street′walk′er, n. prostitute who solicits on the streets.

street′wise′, adj. possessing street smarts.

strength (strengkth, strength, strenth) n. **1.** power of body, mind, position, etc. **2.** intensity.

strength′en, v. make or grow stronger.

stren′u·ous (stren′yo͞o əs) adj. vigorous; active. **—stren′u·ous·ly,** adv.

strep throat (strep) acute sore throat caused by streptococci.

strep′to·coc′cus (strep′tə kok′əs) n., pl. **-ci** (-sī, -sē). one of group of disease-producing bacteria. **—strep′to·coc′cal,** adj.

strep′to·my′cin (-mī′sin) n. antibiotic drug.

stress (stres) v. **1.** emphasize. —n. **2.** emphasis. **3.** physical, mental, or emotional strain.

stretch (strech) v. **1.** extend; spread. **2.** distend. **3.** draw tight. —n. **4.** act of stretching. **5.** extension; expansion. **6.** continuous length.

stretch′er, n. **1.** canvas-covered frame for carrying sick, etc. **2.** device for stretching.

strew (stro͞o) v., **strewed, strewed** or **strewn, strewing.** scatter; sprinkle.

strg **1.** steering. **2.** strong.

stri′at·ed (strī′ā tid) adj. furrowed; streaked. **—stri·a′tion** (-ā′shən) n.

strick′en (strik′ən) adj. **1.** wounded. **2.** afflicted, as by disease or sorrow.

strict (strikt) adj. **1.** exacting; severe. **2.** precise. **3.** careful. **4.** absolute. **—strict′ly,** adv. **—strict′ness,** n.

stric′ture (strik′chər) n. **1.** adverse criticism. **2.** morbid contraction of body passage.

stride (strīd) v., **strode** (strōd), **stridden** (strid′n), **striding,** n. —v. **1.** walk with long steps. **2.** straddle. —n. **3.** long step. **4.** steady pace.

stri′dent (strīd′nt) adj. harsh in sound. **—stri′dent·ly,** adv. **—stri′den·cy,** n.

strife (strīf) n. conflict or quarrel.

strike (strīk) v., **struck** (struk), **struck** or **strick·en** (strik′ən), **striking,** n. —v. **1.** deal a blow. **2.** hit forcibly. **3.** cause to ignite. **4.** impress. **5.** efface; mark out. **6.** afflict or affect. **7.** sound by percussion. **8.** discover in ground. **9.** encounter. **10.** (of workers) stop work to compel agreement to demands. **11. strike out,** Baseball. put or be put out on three strikes. —n. **12.** act of striking. **13.** Baseball. failure of batter to hit pitched ball; anything ruled equivalent. **14.** Bowling. knocking-down of all pins with first bowl. **—strik′er,** n.

strik′ing, adj. **1.** conspicuously attractive or impressive. **2.** noticeable; conspicuous.

string (string) n., v., **strung** (strung), **stringing.** —n. **1.** cord, thread, etc. **2.** series or set. **3.** cord on musical instrument. **4.** plant fiber. —v. **5.** furnish with strings. **6.** arrange in row. **7.** mount on string. **—stringed,** adj. **—string′y,** adj.

string bean, bean with edible pod.

strin′gent (strin′jənt) adj. **1.** very strict. **2.** urgent. **—strin′gen·cy,** n. **—strin′gent·ly,** adv.

string′er (string′-) n. **1.** horizontal timber connecting upright posts. **2.** part-time news reporter.

strip (strip) v., **stripped, stripping,** n. —v. **1.** remove covering or clothing. **2.** rob. **3.** cut into strips. —n. **4.** long narrow piece.

stripe (strīp) n., v., **striped, striping.** —n. **1.** band of different color, etc. **2.** welt from whipping. —v. **3.** mark with stripes.

strip'ling (strip'ling) *n.* youth.

strip mine, mine in open pit. —**strip'-mine',** *v.,* -**mined, -mining.**

strip'tease', *n.* act, as in burlesque, in which performer gradually removes clothing. —**strip'per,** *n.*

strive (strīv) *v.,* **strove** (strōv), **striv•en** (striv'ən), **striving.** try hard; struggle.

strk stroke.

strl structural.

strln streamline.

strm 1. storeroom. **2.** stream.

strn strainer.

strobe (strōb) *n.* electronic flash producing rapid bursts of light. Also, **strobe light.**

stroke (strōk) *v.,* **stroked, stroking,** *n.* —*v.* **1.** rub gently. —*n.* **2.** act of stroking. **3.** blow. **4.** blockage or hemorrhage of blood vessel leading to brain. **5.** one complete movement. **6.** piece of luck, work, etc. **7.** method of swimming.

stroll (strōl) *v.* **1.** walk idly. **2.** roam.

stroll'er, *n.* chairlike carriage in which young children are pushed.

strong (strông) *adj.* **1.** vigorous; powerful; able. **2.** intense; distinct. —**strong'ly,** *adv.*

strong'-arm', *adj.* **1.** involving physical force. —*v.* **2.** use physical force.

strong'box', *n.* strongly made box for money.

strong'hold', *n.* fortress.

strong'-mind'ed, *adj.* **1.** having vigorous mental powers. **2.** determined.

stron'ti•um (stron'shē əm, -shəm, -tē əm) *n.* metallic chemical element.

strop (strop) *n.,* *v.,* **stropped, stropping.** —*n.* **1.** flexible strap. —*v.* **2.** sharpen on strop.

struc'ture (struk'chər) *n.* **1.** form of building or arrangement. **2.** something built. —**struc'-tur•al,** *adj.* —**struc'tur•al•ly,** *adv.*

stru'del (strōod'l; *Ger.* shtRōod'l) *n.* fruit-filled pastry.

strug'gle (strug'əl) *v.,* -**gled, -gling,** *n.* —*v.* **1.** contend; strive. —*n.* **2.** strong effort. **3.** combat.

strum (strum) *v.,* **strummed, strumming.** play carelessly on (stringed instrument).

strum'pet (strum'pit) *n.* prostitute.

strut (strut) *v.,* **strutted, strutting,** *n.* —*v.* **1.** walk in vain, pompous manner. —*n.* **2.** strutting walk. **3.** prop; truss.

strych'nine (strik'nin, -nēn, -nīn) *n.* colorless poison.

sttg starting.

sttr stator.

stub (stub) *n.,* *v.,* **stubbed, stubbing.** —*n.* **1.** short remaining piece. **2.** stump. —*v.* **3.** strike (one's toe) against something. —**stub'by,** *adj.*

stub'ble (stub'əl) *n.* **1.** short stumps, as of grain stalks. **2.** short growth of beard. —**stub'bly,** *adj.*

stub'born (stub'ərn) *adj.* **1.** unreasonably obstinate. **2.** persistent. —**stub'born•ly,** *adv.* —**stub'born•ness,** *n.*

stuc'co (stuk'ō) *n., pl.* -**coes, -cos,** *v.,* -**coed, -coing.** —*n.* **1.** plaster for exteriors. —*v.* **2.** cover with stucco.

stuck'-up', *adj. Informal.* snobbishly conceited.

stud (stud) *n.,* *v.,* **studded, studding.** —*n.* **1.** projecting knob, pin, etc. **2.** upright prop. **3.** detachable button. **4.** collection of horses or other animals for breeding. **5.** stallion. —*v.* **6.** set or scatter with studs.

stu'dent (stōōd'nt, styōōd'-) *n.* person who studies.

stud'ied (stud'ēd) *adj.* deliberate.

stu'di•o' (stōō'dē ō', styōō'-) *n., pl.* -**dios. 1.** artist's workroom. **2.** place equipped for radio or television broadcasting.

stud'y (stud'ē) *n., pl.* **studies,** *v.,* **studied, studying.** —*n.* **1.** effort to learn. **2.** object of study. **3.** deep thought. **4.** room for studying, writing, etc. —*v.* **5.** make study of —**stu'di•ous** (stōō'dē əs, styōō'-) *adj.* —**stu'di•ous•ly,** *adv.* —**stu'di•ous•ness,** *n.*

stuff (stuf) *n.* **1.** material. **2.** worthless matter. —*v.* **3.** cram full; pack.

stuffed shirt, pompous, self-satisfied person.

stuff'ing, *n.* material stuffed in something.

stuff'y, *adj.,* -**ier, -iest. 1.** lacking fresh air. **2.** pompous; pedantic. —**stuff'i•ness,** *n.*

stul'ti•fy' (stul'tə fī') *v.,* -**fied, -fying. 1.** cause to look foolish **2.** make futile.

stum'ble (stum'bəl) *v.,* -**bled, -bling. 1.** lose balance. **2.** come unexpectedly upon.

stumbling block, obstacle.

stump (stump) *n.* **1.** lower end of tree after top is gone. **2.** any short remaining part. —*v.* **3.** baffle. **4.** campaign politically. **5.** walk heavily.

stun (stun) *v.,* **stunned, stunning. 1.** render unconscious. **2.** amaze.

stun'ning, *adj.* strikingly attractive.

stunt (stunt) *v.* **1.** check growth. **2.** do stunts. —*n.* **3.** performance to show skill, etc.

stu'pe•fy' (stōō'pə fī', styōō'-) *v.,* -**fied, -fying. 1.** put into stupor. **2.** stun. —**stu'pe•fac'tion** (-fak'shən) *n.*

stu•pen'dous (stōō pen'dəs, styōō-) *adj.* **1.** amazing; marvelous. **2.** immense.

stu'pid (stōō'pid, styōō'-) *adj.* having or showing little intelligence. —**stu•pid'i•ty,** *n.* —**stu'pid•ly,** *adv.*

stu'por (-pər) *n.* dazed or insensible state.

stur'dy (stûr'dē) *adj.,* -**dier, -diest. 1.** strongly built. **2.** firm. —**stur'di•ly,** *adv.* —**stur'di•ness,** *n.*

stur'geon (stûr'jən) *n.* large fish of fresh and salt water.

stut'ter (stut'ər) *v.,* *n.* stammer. —**stut'ter•er,** *n.*

STV subscription television; pay television.

stv satellite television.

S

sty (stī) *n.*, *pl.* **sties. 1.** pig pen. **2.** inflamed swelling on eyelid.

style (stīl) *n.*, *v.*, **styled, styling.** —*n.* **1.** particular kind. **2.** mode of fashion. **3.** elegance. **4.** distinct way of writing or speaking. **5.** pointed instrument. —*v.* **6.** name; give title to. —**sty•lis'tic**, *adj.*

styl'ish, *adj.* fashionable. —**styl'ish•ly**, *adv.*

styl'ist, *n.* person who cultivates distinctive style.

styl'ize, *v.*, **-ized, -izing.** cause to conform to conventionalized style.

sty'lus (stī'ləs) *n.* pointed tool for writing, etc.

sty'mie (stī'mē) *v.*, **-mied, -mying.** hinder or obstruct, as in golf.

styp'tic (stip'tik) *adj.* **1.** checking bleeding. —*n.* **2.** styptic substance. —**styp'sis,** *n.*

Sty'ro•foam' (stī'rə fōm') *n. Trademark.* lightweight plastic.

Su. Sunday.

sua'sion (swā'zhən) *n.* persuasion.

suave (swäv) *adj.* smoothly agreeable. —**suave'ly**, *adv.* —**suav'i•ty, suave'ness,** *n.*

sub-, prefix meaning under; below; beneath; less than.

sub•al'tern (sub ôl'tərn) *n. Brit.* low-ranking officer.

subassy subassembly.

sub'a•tom'ic, *adj.* of particles within an atom.

subch. subchapter.

sub'com•mit•tee, *n.* committee appointed out of main committee.

sub•con'scious, *adj.* **1.** existing beneath consciousness. —*n.* **2.** ideas, feelings, etc., of which one is unaware. —**sub•con'scious•ly,** *adv.*

sub•con'ti•nent (sub kon'tn ənt, sub'kon/-) *n.* large subdivision of continent.

sub'cul'ture, *n.* group with social, economic, or other traits distinguishing it from others within larger society.

sub'cu•ta'ne•ous, *adj.* beneath the skin.

sub'di•vide' (sub'di vīd', sub'di vīd') *v.*, **-vided, -viding.** divide into parts. —**sub'di•vi'sion,** *n.*

sub•due' (səb dōō', -dyōō') *v.*, **-dued, -duing. 1.** overcome. **2.** soften.

sub•fam'i•ly (sub fam'ə lē, sub'fam'ə lē) *n.*, *pl.* **-lies. 1.** category of related organisms within a family. **2.** group of related languages within a family.

sub'head', *n.* **1.** heading of a subdivision. **2.** subordinate division of a title.

subj. 1. subject. **2.** subjective. **3.** subjectively. **4.** subjunctive.

sub'ject, *n.* (sub'jikt) **1.** matter of thought, concern, etc. **2.** person under rule of government. **3.** noun or pronoun that performs action of predicate. **4.** one undergoing action, etc. —*adj.* (sub'jikt) **5.** being a subject. **6.** liable; exposed. —*v.* (səb jekt') **7.** cause to

experience. **8.** make liable. —**sub•jec'tion,** *n.*

sub•jec'tive, *adj.* **1.** personal. **2.** existing in mind. —**sub'jec•tiv'i•ty,** *n.* —**sub•jec'tive•ly,** *adv.*

sub•join' (səb join') *v.* append.

sub•ju•gate' (sub'jə gāt') *v.*, **-gated, -gating.** subdue; conquer. —**sub'ju•ga'tion,** *n.* —**sub'ju•ga'tor,** *n.*

sub•junc'tive (səb jungk'tiv) *adj.* **1.** designating verb mode of condition, impression, etc. —*n.* **2.** subjunctive mode.

sub'lease', *n.*, *v.*, **-leased, -leasing.** —*n.* (sub'lēs') **1.** lease granted by tenant. —*v.* (sub lēs') **2.** rent by sublease.

sub•let' (sub let', sub'let') *v.*, **-let, -letting.** (of lessee) let to another person.

sub'li•mate', *v.*, **-mated, -mating,** *n.* —*v.* (sub'lə māt') **1.** deflect (biological energies) to other channels. **2.** sublime. —*n.* (-mit, -māt') **3.** substance obtained in subliming. —**sub'li•ma'tion,** *n.*

sub•lime' (sə blīm') *adj.*, *n.*, *v.*, **-limed, -liming.** —*adj.* **1.** lofty; noble. —*n.* **2.** that which is sublime. —*v.* **3.** heat (substance) to vapor that condenses to solid on cooling. —**sub•lim'i•ty** (sə blim'i tē) *n.* —**sub•lime'ly,** *adv.*

sub•lim'i•nal (sub lim'ə nl) *adj.* below threshold of consciousness. —**sub•lim'i•nal•ly,** *adv.*

sub'ma•chine' gun, automatic weapon.

sub•ma•rine', *n.* (sub'mə rēn', sub'mə rēn') **1.** vessel that can navigate under water. —*adj.* (sub'mə rēn') **2.** of submarines. **3.** being under sea.

sub•merge' (səb mûrj') *v.*, **-merged, -merging.** plunge under water. —**sub•mer'gence,** *n.*

sub•merse' (-mûrs') *v.*, **-mersed, -mersing.** submerge. —**sub•mer'sion,** *n.* —**sub•mers'•i•ble,** *adj.*

submin subminiature.

sub•mis'sive, *adj.* yielding or obeying readily. —**sub•mis'sive•ly,** *adv.* —**sub•mis'sive•ness,** *n.*

sub•mit' (səb mit') *v.*, **-mitted, -mitting. 1.** yield; surrender. **2.** offer for consideration. —**sub•mis'sion** (-mish'ən) *n.*

sub•nor'mal (sub nôr'məl) *adj.* of less than normal intelligence.

sub•or'bit•al, *adj.* making less than a complete orbit.

sub•or'di•nate, *adj.*, *n.*, *v.*, **-nated, -nating.** —*adj.* (sə bôr'dn it) **1.** of lower rank or importance. —*n.* (sə bôr'dn it) **2.** subordinate person or thing. —*v.* (-dn āt') **3.** treat as subordinate. —**sub•or'di•na'tion,** *n.*

sub•orn' (sə bôrn') *v.* bribe or incite to crime, esp. to perjury.

sub'plot' (sub'plot') *n.* secondary plot.

sub•poe'na (sə pē'nə, səb-) *n.*, *v.*, **-naed, -naing.** —*n.* **1.** summons to appear in court. —*v.* **2.** serve with subpoena.

subq subsequent.

sub ro′sa (sub rō′zə) secretly.

subsc subscription.

sub·scribe′ (səb skrīb′) v., -scribed, -scribing. 1. promise contribution. 2. agree; sign in agreement. 3. contract to receive periodical regularly. —**sub·scrib′er**, n. —**sub·scrip′tion** (-skrip′shən) n.

sub′script (sub′skript) n. letter, number, etc. written low on line.

sub′se·quent (sub′si kwənt) adj. later; following. —**sub′se·quent·ly**, adv.

sub·serve′, v., -served, -serving. promote; assist.

sub·ser′vi·ent (səb sûr′vē ənt) adj. 1. servile; submissive. 2. useful. —**sub·ser′vi·ence**, n. —**sub·ser′vi·ent·ly**, adv.

sub·side′ (səb sīd′) v., -sided, -siding. 1. sink; settle. 2. abate. —**sub·sid′ence**, n.

sub·sid′i·ar′y (-sid′ē er′ē) adj., n., pl. -aries. —adj. 1. auxiliary. 2. subordinate. —n. 3. anything subsidiary.

sub′si·dy (-si dē) n., pl. -dies. direct pecuniary aid, esp. by government. —**sub′si·dize′**, v., -dized, -dizing.

sub·sist′ (səb sist′) v. 1. exist. 2. live (as on food). —**sub·sist′ence**, n.

sub′soil′ (sub′soil′) n. layer of earth immediately underneath surface soil.

sub·son′ic, adj. of a speed below the speed of sound.

subst. 1. Grammar. substantive. 2. substantively. 3. substitute.

substa substation.

sub′stance (sub′stəns) n. 1. matter or material. 2. density. 3. meaning. 4. likelihood.

sub·stand′ard, adj. below standard; not good enough.

sub·stan′tial (səb stan′shəl) adj. 1. actual. 2. fairly large. 3. strong. 4. of substance. 5. prosperous. —**sub·stan′tial·ly**, adv.

sub·stan′ti·ate′ (-shē āt′) v., -ated, -ating. support with evidence. —**sub·stan′ti·a′tion**, n.

sub′stan·tive (sub′stən tiv) n. 1. noun, pronoun, or word used as noun. —adj. 2. of or denoting substantive. 3. independent. 4. essential.

sub′sti·tute′ (sub′sti tōōt′, -tyōōt′) v., -tuted, -tuting, n. —v. 1. put or serve in place of another. —n. 2. substitute person or thing. —**sub′sti·tu′tion**, n.

sub′struc·ture (sub struk′chər, sub′struk′-) n. structure forming a foundation.

sub·sume′ (səb sōōm′) v., -sumed, -suming. consider or include as part of something larger.

sub′ter·fuge′ (sub′tər fyōōj′) n. means used to evade or conceal.

sub′ter·ra·ne·an (-tə rā′nē ən) adj. underground.

sub′text, n. underlying or implicit meaning.

sub′tile (sut′l) adj. subtle.

sub′ti·tle, n., v., -tled, -tling. —n. 1. secondary or subordinate title, as of book. 2. text of dialogue, etc., appearing at bottom of motion picture screen, etc. —v. 3. give subtitles to.

sub′tle (sut′l) adj., -tler, -tlest. 1. delicate; faint. 2. discerning. 3. crafty. —**sub′tle·ty**, n. —**sub′tly**, adv.

sub′to·tal (sub′tōt′l, sub tōt′-) n., v., -totaled, -totaling. —n. 1. total of part of a group of figures. —v. 2. determine subtotal for.

subtr subtract.

sub·tract′ (səb trakt′) v. take from another; deduct. —**sub·trac′tion**, n.

sub′tra·hend′ (sub′trə hend′) n. number subtracted from another number.

sub·trop′i·cal, adj. bordering on tropics.

sub′urb (sub′ûrb) n. district just outside city. —**sub·ur′ban**, adj. —**sub·ur′ban·ite**, n.

sub·ur′bi·a (-bē ə) n. 1. suburbs or suburbanites collectively. 2. life in the suburbs.

sub·ven′tion (səb ven′shən) n. grant of money.

sub·vert′ (-vûrt′) v. overthrow; destroy. —**sub·ver′sion**, n. —**sub·ver′sive**, adj., n.

sub′way′ (sub′wā′) n. underground electric railway.

sub·ze′ro, adj. indicating lower than zero on some scale.

suc 1. succeeding. 2. successor.

suc·ceed′ (sək sēd′) v. 1. end or accomplish successfully. 2. follow and replace.

suc·cess′ (-ses′) n. 1. favorable achievement. 2. good fortune. 3. successful thing or person. —**suc·cess′ful**, adj. —**suc·cess′ful·ly**, adv.

suc·ces′sion (-sesh′ən) n. 1. act of following in sequence. 2. sequence of persons or things. 3. right or process of succeeding another. —**suc·ces′sive**, adj. —**suc·ces′sive·ly**, adv.

suc·ces′sor, n. one that succeeds another.

suc·cinct′ (sək singkt′) adj. without useless words; concise. —**suc·cinct′ly**, adv. —**suc·cinct′ness**, n.

suc′cor (suk′ər) n., v. help; aid.

suc′co·tash′ (suk′ə tash′) n. corn and beans cooked together.

suc′cu·lent (suk′yə lənt) adj. juicy. —**suc′cu·lence**, n.

suc·cumb′ (sə kum′) v. 1. yield. 2. die.

such (such) adj. 1. of that kind, extent, etc. —n. 2. such person or thing.

suck (suk) v. 1. draw in by using lips and tongue. 2. absorb. —n. 3. act of sucking.

suck′er, n. 1. one that sucks. 2. fresh-water fish. 3. Informal, lollipop. 4. shoot from underground stem or root. 5. Informal, gullible person.

suck′le, v., -led, -ling. nurse at breast.

suck′ling (-ling) n. 1. infant. 2. unweaned animal.

su′crose (sōō′krōs) n. sugar obtained esp. from sugar cane or sugar beet.

suct suction.

S

suc'tion (suk'shən) *n.* tendency to draw substance into vacuum.

sud'den (sud'n) *adj.* abrupt; quick; unexpected. —**sud'den•ly,** *adv.* —**sud'den•ness,** *n.*

sudden death, overtime period in which tied contest is won after one contestant scores.

suds (sudz) *n.pl.* **1.** lather. **2.** soapy water. —**suds'y,** *adj.*

sue (soo) *v.,* **sued, suing. 1.** take legal action. **2.** appeal.

suede (swād) *n.* soft, napped leather.

su'et (soo'it) *n.* hard fat about kidneys, etc., esp. of cattle.

suf sufficient.

suf. suffix. Also, **suff.**

Suff. 1. Suffolk. **2.** *Ecclesiastical.* suffragan.

suff. 1. sufficient. **2.** suffix.

suf'fer (suf'ər) *v.* **1.** undergo (pain or unpleasantness). **2.** tolerate. —**suf'fer•er,** *n.*

suf'fer•ance (-əns) *n.* **1.** tolerance. **2.** endurance.

suf•fice' (sə fīs') *v.,* **-ficed, -ficing.** be enough.

suf•fi'cient (-fish'ənt) *adj.* enough. —**suf•fi'cien•cy,** *n.* —**suf•fi'cient•ly,** *adv.*

suf'fix (suf'iks) *n.* element added to end of word to form another word.

suf'fo•cate' (suf'ə kāt') *v.,* **-cated, -cating.** kill or choke by cutting off air to lungs. —**suf'fo•ca'tion,** *n.*

Suffr. *Ecclesiastical.* suffragan.

suf'fra•gan (suf'rə gən) *n.* assistant bishop.

suf'frage (suf'rij) *n.* right to vote. —**suf'fra•gist,** *n.*

suf•fuse' (sə fyooz') *v.* overspread.

sug'ar (shŏog'ər) *n.* **1.** sweet substance, esp. from sugar cane or sugar beet. —*v.* **2.** sweeten with sugar. —**sug'ar•less,** *adj.* —**sug'ar•y,** *adj.*

sugar beet, beet with white root having high sugar content.

sugar cane, tall grass that is the chief source of sugar.

sug'ar•coat', *v.* make more pleasant or acceptable.

sugar maple, maple with sweet sap.

sugar plum, candy.

sug•gest' (səg jest', sə-) *v.* **1.** offer for consideration or action. **2.** imply. —**sug•ges'tion,** *n.*

sug•gest'i•ble, *adj.* easily led or influenced. —**sug•gest'i•bil'i•ty,** *n.*

sug•ges'tive, *adj.* suggesting, esp. something improper. —**sug•ges'tive•ly,** *adv.* —**sug•ges'tive•ness,** *n.*

su'i•cide' (soo'ə sīd') *n.* **1.** intentional killing of oneself. **2.** person who commits suicide. —**su'i•cid'al,** *adj.*

su'i ge'ne•ris (soo'ē jen'ər is, soo'ī) being one of a kind.

suit (soot) *n.* **1.** set of clothes. **2.** legal action.

3. division of playing cards. **4.** petition. **5.** wooing. —*v.* **6.** clothe. **7.** adapt. **8.** please.

suit'a•ble, *adj.* appropriate; fitting. —**suit'a•bly,** *adv.*

suit'case', *n.* oblong valise.

suite (swēt) *n.* **1.** series or set, as of rooms. **2.** retinue.

suit'ing (soo'ting) *n.* fabric for making suits.

suit'or (soo'tər) *n.* wooer.

su'ki•ya'ki (soo'kē yä'kē, sook'ē-, skē-) *n.* Japanese dish of meat and vegetables cooked in soy sauce.

sul'fa drugs (sul'fə) group of antibacterial substances used to treat diseases, wounds, etc.

sul'fate (-fāt) *n.* salt of sulfuric acid.

sul'fide (-fīd, -fid) *n.* sulfur compound.

sul'fur (-fər) *n.* yellow nonmetallic element.

sul•fur'ic (-fyoor'ik) *adj.* of or containing sulfur. Also, **sul'fur•ous.**

sulfuric acid, corrosive liquid used in fertilizers, chemicals, and explosives.

sulk (sulk) *v.* **1.** hold sullenly aloof. —*n.* **2.** fit of sulking.

sulk'y, *adj.,* **-ier, -iest.** *n.* —*adj.* **1.** sullen; illhumored. —*n.* **2.** two-wheeled racing carriage for one person. —**sulk'i•ly,** *adv.* —**sulk'i•ness,** *n.*

sul'len (sul'ən) *adj.* **1.** silently ill-humored. **2.** gloomy. —**sul'len•ly,** *adv.* —**sul'len•ness,** *n.*

sul'ly (sul'ē) *v.,* **-lied, -lying.** soil; defile.

sul'phur (-fər) *n.* sulfur.

sul'tan (sul'tn) *n.* ruler of Muslim country. —**sul'tan•ate',** *n.*

sul•tan'a (-tan'ə) *n.* raisin.

sul'try (-trē) *adj.,* **-trier, -triest.** hot and close. —**sul'tri•ness,** *n.*

sum (sum) *n., v.,* **summed, summing.** —*n.* **1.** aggregate of two or more numbers, etc. **2.** total amount. **3.** gist. —*v.* **4.** total. **5.** summarize.

su'mac (soo'mak, shoo'-) *n.* small tree with long pinnate leaves.

sum'ma•rize' (sum'ə rīz') *v.,* **-rized, -rizing.** make or be summary of.

sum'ma•ry (-rē) *n., pl.* **-ries,** *adj.* —*n.* **1.** concise presentation of main points. —*adj.* **2.** concise. **3.** prompt. —**sum•mar'i•ly** (sə-mâr'ə lē) *adv.*

sum•ma'tion (sə mā'shən) *n.* **1.** act of summing up. **2.** total.

sum'mer (sum'ər) *n.* **1.** season between spring and fall. —*adj.* **2.** of, like, or for summer. —*v.* **3.** spend summer. —**sum'mer•y,** *adj.*

sum'mer•house, *n.* structure in garden to provide shade.

sum'mit (sum'it) *n.* highest point.

sum'mon (sum'ən) *v.* order to appear.

sum'mons, *n.* message that summons.

su'mo (soo'mō) *n.* Japanese form of wrestling featuring extremely heavy contestants.

sump (sump) *n.* pit for collecting water, etc.

sump/tu•ous (sump/chōō əs) *adj.* revealing great expense; luxurious. —**sump/tu•ous•ly**, *adv.* —**sump/tu•ous•ness**, *n.*

sun (sun) *n., v.,* **sunned, sunning.** —*n.* **1.** heat- and light-giving body of solar system. **2.** sunshine. —*v.* **3.** expose to sunshine. —**sun/beam/**, *n.*

Sun., Sunday.

sun/bathe/, *v.,* **-bathed, -bathing.** expose body to sunlight.

Sun/belt/, *n. Informal.* southern and southwestern U.S. Also, **Sun Belt.**

sun/block/, *n.* substance, as a cream, to protect skin from sunburn. Also, **sun/screen/**.

sun/burn/, *n., v.,* **-burned** or **-burnt, -burning.** —*n.* **1.** superficial burn from sun's rays. —*v.* **2.** affect with sunburn.

sun/dae (sun/dā, -dē) *n.* ice cream topped with fruit, etc.

Sun/day (sun/dā, -dē) *n.* first day of week.

sun/der (sun/dər) *v.* separate.

sun/di/al, *n.* outdoor instrument for telling time by shadow.

sun/dry (sun/drē) *adj., n., pl.* **-dries.** —*adj.* **1.** various. —*n.* **2.** (*pl.*) small items of merchandise.

sun/fish/, *n.* fresh-water fish.

sun/flow/er, *n.* tall plant with yellow flowers.

sun/glass/es, *n.pl.* eyeglasses with tinted lenses to permit vision in bright sun.

sun/light/, *n.* light from sun.

sun/lit/, *adj.* lighted by the sun.

sun/ny, *adj.,* **-nier, -niest. 1.** with much sunlight. **2.** cheerful; jolly. —**sun/ni•ly**, *adv.* —**sun/ni•ness**, *n.*

sun/rise/, *n.* ascent of sun above horizon. Also, **sun/up/**.

sun/roof/, *n.* section of automobile roof that can be opened.

sun/screen/, *n.* substance that protects skin from ultraviolet rays of sun.

sun/set/, *n.* descent of sun below horizon. Also, **sun/down/**.

sun/shine/, *n.* light of sun.

sun/spot/, *n.* dark spot on face of sun.

sun/stroke/, *n.* illness from overexposure to sun's rays.

sun/tan/, *n.* darkening of skin caused by exposure to sun.

sup (sup) *v.,* **supped, supping.** eat supper.

su/per (sōō/pər) *n.* **1.** superintendent. —*adj.* **2.** very good; first-rate.

su/per-, prefix meaning above or over; exceeding; larger or more.

su/per•a•bun/dant, *adj.* exceedingly abundant. —**su/per•a•bun/dance**, *n.*

su/per•an/nu•at/ed (-an/yōō ā/tid) *adj.* **1.** retired. **2.** too old for work or use. **3.** antiquated; obsolete.

su•perb/ (sōō pûrb/, sə-) *adj.* very fine. —**su•perb/ly**, *adv.*

su/per•charge/, *v.,* **-charged, -charging. 1.** charge with abundant or excess energy, etc. **2.** supply air to (engine) at high pressure. —**su/per•charg/er**, *n.*

su/per•cil/i•ous (sōō/pər sil/ē əs) *adj.* haughtily disdainful. —**su/per•cil/i•ous•ly**, *adv.* —**su/per•cil/i•ous•ness**, *n.*

su/per•con•duc•tiv/i•ty, *n.* disappearance of electrical resistance in certain metals at extremely low temperatures. —**su/per•con/duct/or**, *n.*

su/per•e/go, *n.* part of personality representing conscience.

su/per•fi/cial (-fish/əl) *adj.* **1.** of, on, or near surface. **2.** shallow, obvious, or insignificant. —**su/per•fi/ci•al/i•ty** (-fish/ē al/i tē) *n.* —**su/per•fi/cial•ly**, *adv.*

su•per/flu•ous (sōō pûr/flōō əs) *adj.* **1.** being more than is necessary. **2.** unnecessary. —**su/per•flu/i•ty** (-flōō/i tē) *n.* —**su•per/flu•ous•ly**, *adv.*

su/per•high/way (sōō/pər hī/wā, sōō/pər-hī/wā/) *n.* highway for travel at high speeds.

su/per•hu/man, *adj.* **1.** beyond what is human. **2.** exceeding human strength.

su/per•im•pose/, *v.,* **-posed, -posing.** place over something else.

su/per•in•tend/ (sōō/pər in tend/, sōō/prin-) *v.* oversee and direct. —**su/per•in•tend/ence**, **su/per•in•tend/en•cy**, *n.* —**su/per•in•tend/ent**, *n., adj.*

su•pe/ri•or (sə pēr/ē ər, sōō-) *adj.* **1.** above average; better. **2.** upper. **3.** arrogant. —*n.* **4.** superior person. **5.** head of convent, etc. —**su•pe/ri•or/i•ty**, *n.*

superl. superlative.

su•per/la•tive (sə pûr/lə tiv, sōō-) *adj.* **1.** of highest kind; best. **2.** highest in comparison. —*n.* **3.** anything superlative. —**su•per/la•tive•ly**, *adv.*

su/per•man/ (sōō/pər-) *n., pl.* **-men.** person of extraordinary or superhuman powers.

su/per•mar/ket, *n.* self-service food store with large variety.

su/per•nat/u•ral, *adj.* **1.** outside the laws of nature; ghostly. —*n.* **2.** realm of supernatural beings or things.

su/per•no/va, *n., pl.* **-vas, -vae** (-vē). nova millions of times brighter than the sun.

su/per•nu/mer•ar/y (-nōō/mə rer/ē, -nyōō/-) *adj., n., pl.* **-aries.** —*adj.* **1.** extra. —*n.* **2.** extra person or thing. **3.** actor with no lines.

su/per•pow/er, *n.* large, powerful nation greatly influencing world affairs.

su/per•script/, *n.* letter, number, or symbol written high on line of text.

su/per•sede/ (-sēd/) *v.,* **-seded, -seding.** replace in power, use, etc.

su/per•son/ic, *adj.* faster than speed of sound.

su/per•star/, *n.* entertainer or sports figure of world renown.

su/per•sti/tion (-stish/ən) *n.* irrational belief in ominous significance of particular thing,

S

event, etc. —**su′per•sti′tious,** *adj.* —**su′per•sti′tious•ly,** *adv.*

su′per•store′, *n.* very large store that stocks wide variety of merchandise.

su′per•struc′ture, *n.* upper part of building or vessel.

su′per•vene′ (-vēn′) *v.,* **-vened, -vening. 1.** come as something extra. **2.** ensue. —**su′per•ven′tion** (-ven′shən) *n.*

su′per•vise′ (-vīz′) *v.,* **-vised, -vising.** direct and inspect. —**su′per•vi′sion** (-vizh′ən) *n.* —**su′per•vi′sor,** *n.* —**su′per•vi′so•ry,** *adj.*

su′per•wom′an, *n., pl.* **-women. 1.** woman of extraordinary or superhuman powers. **2.** woman who copes successfully with demands of career, marriage, and motherhood.

su•pine′ (sōō pīn′) *adj.* **1.** lying on back. **2.** passive. —**su•pine′ly,** *adv.*

supp. 1. supplement. **2.** supplementary. Also, **suppl.**

sup′per (sup′ər) *n.* evening meal.

sup•plant′ (sə plant′) *v.* supersede.

sup′ple (sup′əl) *adj.,* **-pler, -plest.** flexible; limber. —**sup′ple•ly,** *adv.* —**sup′ple•ness,** *n.*

sup′ple•ment *n.* (sup′lə mənt) **1.** something added to complete or improve. —*v.* (-ment′) **2.** add to or complete. —**sup′ple•men′tal** (-men′tl), **sup′ple•men′ta•ry,** *adj.*

sup′pli•cate′ (sup′li kāt′) *v.,* **-cated, -cating.** beg humbly. —**sup′pli•ant** (sup′lē ənt), **sup′pli•cant,** *n., adj.* —**sup′pli•ca′tion,** *n.*

sup•ply′ (sə plī′) *v.,* **-plied, -plying,** *n., pl.* **-plies.** —*v.* **1.** furnish; provide. **2.** fill (a lack). —*n.* **3.** act of supplying. **4.** that supplied. **5.** stock. —**sup•pli′er,** *n.*

supply′-side′, *adj.* of economic theory that reduced taxes will stimulate economic growth.

sup•port′ (sə pôrt′) *v.* **1.** hold up; bear. **2.** provide living for. **3.** uphold; advocate. **4.** corroborate. —*n.* **5.** act of supporting. **6.** maintenance; livelihood. **7.** thing or person that supports. —**sup•port′a•ble,** *adj.* —**sup•port′ive,** *adj.*

support group, group of people who meet regularly to support each other by discussing shared problems.

sup•pose′ (sə pōz′) *v.,* **-posed, -posing. 1.** assume; consider. **2.** take for granted. —**sup•pos′ed•ly** (-pō′zid lē) *adv.* —**sup′po•si′tion** (sup′ə zish′ən) *n.* —**sup′po•si′tion•al,** *adj.*

sup•pos′i•to′ry (sə poz′i tôr′ē) *n., pl.* **-ries.** solid mass of medication that melts on insertion into rectum or vagina.

sup•press′ (sə pres′) *v.* **1.** end forcibly; subdue. **2.** repress. **3.** withhold from circulation. —**sup•pres′sant,** *n.* —**sup•pres′sion** (-presh′ən) *n.* —**sup•pres′si•ble,** *adj.*

Supp. Rev. Stat. Supplement to the Revised Statutes.

sup′pu•rate′ (sup′yə rāt′) *v.,* **-rated, -rating.** form or discharge pus. —**sup′pu•ra′tion,** *n.* —**sup′pu•ra′tive,** *adj.*

supr. 1. superior. **2.** suppress. **3.** supreme.

su′pra (sōō′prə) *adv.* above, esp. in text.

supra cit. cited above. [from Latin *supra citato*]

su•prem′a•cist (sə prem′ə sist, sōō-) *n.* person who advocates supremacy of particular group.

su•preme′ (sə prēm′, sōō-) *adj.* chief; greatest. —**su•prem′a•cy** (-prem′ə sē) *n.* —**su•preme′ly,** *adv.*

supsd supersede.

Supt. superintendent. Also, **supt.**

supv supervise.

supvr. supervisor.

sur•cease′ (sûr sēs′) *n.* end.

sur′charge′, *n., v.,* **-charged, -charging.** —*n.* (sûr′chärj′) **1.** extra or excessive charge, load, etc. —*v.* (sûr chärj′, sûr′chärj′) **2.** put surcharge on. **3.** overburden.

sur′cin′gle (sûr′sing′gəl) *n.* girth that passes around horse's belly.

sure (shōōr, shûr) *adj.,* **surer, surest. 1.** certain; positive. **2.** reliable. **3.** firm. —**sure′ly,** *adv.* —**sure′ness,** *n.*

sure′fire′, *adj. Informal.* certain to succeed.

sure′foot′ed, *adj.* not likely to stumble.

sure′ty (shōōr′i tē, shōōr′tē, shûr′-) *n., pl.* **-ties. 1.** security against loss, etc. **2.** person who accepts responsibility for another.

surf (sûrf) *n.* **1.** waves breaking on shore. —*v.* **2.** ride on crest of wave while standing or lying on surfboard. —**surf′er,** *n.*

sur′face (sûr′fis) *n., adj., v.,* **-faced, -facing.** —*n.* **1.** outer face; outside. —*adj.* **2.** superficial. —*v.* **3.** finish surface of. **4.** come to surface.

surf′board′, *n.* board on which person rides in surfing.

sur′feit (sûr′fit) *n.* **1.** excess, esp. of food or drink. **2.** disgust at excess. —*v.* **3.** overeat; satiate.

surf′ing, *n.* sport of riding the surf, usu. on a **surf′board′.**

surg. 1. surgeon. **2.** surgery. **3.** surgical.

surge (sûrj) *n., v.,* **surged, surging.** —*n.* **1.** swelling or rolling movement or body. —*v.* **2.** rise and fall.

sur′geon (sûr′jən) *n.* person skilled in surgery.

surge protector, device to protect computer, etc., from damage by high-voltage electrical surges.

sur′ger•y (-jə rē) *n., pl.* **-geries. 1.** treatment of disease, etc., by cutting and other manipulations. **2.** room for surgical operations. —**sur′gi•cal** (-ji kəl) *adj.* —**sur′gi•cal•ly,** *adv.*

sur′ly (sûr′lē) *adj.,* **-lier, -liest.** rude; churlish. —**sur′li•ness,** *n.*

sur•mise′ *v.,* (sər mīz′) **-mised, -mising,** *n.* (sər mīz′, sûr′mīz) guess.

sur•mount′ (sər mount′) *v.* **1.** get over or on top of. **2.** overcome. —**sur•mount′a•ble,** *adj.*

sur'name' (sûr'nām') *n.* family name.

sur•pass' (sər pas') *v.* **1.** exceed. **2.** transcend. **—sur•pass'ing,** *adj.*

sur'plice (sûr'plis) *n.* white, loose-fitting robe worn over cassock.

sur'plus (sûr'plus, -pləs) *n.* **1.** amount beyond that needed; excess. *—adj.* **2.** being a surplus.

sur•prise' (sər prīz', sə-) *v.,* **-prised, -prising,** *n.* *—v.* **1.** come upon unexpectedly; astonish. *—n.* **2.** act of surprising. **3.** something that surprises. **4.** feeling of being surprised.

sur•re'al•ism (sə rē'ə liz'əm) *n.* art attempting to express the subconscious. **—sur•re'al•ist,** *n., adj.* **—sur•re'al•is'tic,** *adj.*

sur•ren'der (sə ren'dər) *v.* **1.** yield. *—n.* **2.** act of yielding.

sur'rep•ti'tious (sûr'əp tish'əs) *adj.* stealthy; secret. **—sur'rep•ti'tious•ly,** *adv.*

sur'rey (sûr'ē, sur'ē) *n.* light carriage.

sur'ro•gate' (sûr'ə gāt', -git, sur'-) *n.* **1.** substitute. **2.** judge concerned with wills, estates, etc.

surrogate mother, woman who bears child for another couple.

sur•round' (sə round') *v.* encircle; enclose.

sur•round'ings, *n.pl.* environment.

sur'tax' (sûr'taks') *n.* additional tax, esp. on high incomes.

surv. 1. survey. **2.** surveying. **3.** surveyor.

sur•veil'lance (sər vā'ləns) *n.* close watch.

sur•vey', *v.* (sər vā') **1.** view. **2.** measure or determine dimensions or nature of. *—n.* (sûr'vā) **3.** methodical investigation. **4.** description from surveying.

sur•vey'ing, *n.* science of making land surveys. **—sur•vey'or,** *n.*

sur•vive' (sər vīv') *v.,* **-vived, -viving. 1.** remain alive. **2.** outlive. **—sur•viv'a•ble,** *adj.* **—sur•viv'al,** *n.* **—sur•vi'vor,** *n.*

sus•cep'ti•ble (sə sep'tə bəl) *adj.* apt to be affected; liable. **—sus•cep'ti•bil'i•ty,** *n.* **—sus•cep'ti•bly,** *adv.*

su'shi (soo'shē) *n.* Japanese dish of rice cakes with raw fish, vegetables, etc.

susp suspend.

sus•pect', *v.* (sə spekt') **1.** imagine to be guilty, false, etc. **2.** surmise. *—n.* (sus'pekt) **3.** one suspected. *—adj.* (sus'pekt) **4.** liable to doubt.

sus•pend' (sə spend') *v.* **1.** hang. **2.** keep temporarily inactive. **3.** refuse work to temporarily.

sus•pend'ers, *n.pl.* straps for holding up trousers.

sus•pense' (sə spens') *n.* uncertainty; anxiety. **—sus•pense'ful,** *adj.*

sus•pen'sion, *n.* **1.** act of suspending. **2.** temporary inactivity. **3.** state in which undissolved particles are dispersed in fluid.

suspension bridge, bridge with deck suspended from cables.

sus•pi'cion (sə spish'ən) *n.* **1.** act or instance of suspecting. **2.** trace.

sus•pi'cious, *adj.* **1.** having suspicions. **2.** causing suspicion. **—sus•pi'cious•ly,** *adv.*

sus•tain' (sə stān') *v.* support; maintain. **—sus•tain'er,** *n.*

sus'te•nance (sus'tə nəns) *n.* **1.** food. **2.** maintenance.

su'ture (soo'chər) *n., v.,* **-tured, -turing.** *—n.* **1.** closing of wound. **2.** stitch used to close wound. **3.** line joining two bones, esp. of the skull. *—v.* **4.** join by suture.

su'ze•rain•ty (soo'zə rin tē), *n., pl.* **-ties.** sovereignty of one state over another.

Sv *Physics.* sievert; sieverts.

S.V. Holy Virgin. [from Latin *Sāncta Virgō*]

s.v. 1. under the word (or heading). [from Latin *sub verbo*] **2.** under the word. [from Latin *sub voce*]

SV 40 *Microbiology.* simian virus 40. Also, **SV-40, SV40**

svc. service. Also, **svce.**

svelte (svelt, sfelt) *adj.* slender.

SVGA *Computers.* super video graphics adapter.

svgs. savings.

SVO language *Linguistics.* a type of language that has basic subject-verb-object word order.

svr (of weather) severe.

S.V.R. (in prescriptions) rectified spirit of wine (alcohol). [from Latin *spīritus vīnī rēctificātus*]

SVS still-camera video system.

SW, southwest.

S.W.A. South West Africa.

swab (swob) *n., v.,* **swabbed, swabbing.** *—n.* **1.** bit of cloth, etc., esp. on stick. *—v.* **2.** clean with swab.

swad'dle (swod'l) *v.,* **-dled, -dling.** bind with strips of cloth.

swag (swag) *n.* something fastened at each end and hanging down in the middle.

swag'ger, *v.* **1.** walk with insolent air. *—n.* **2.** swaggering gait.

Swa•hi'li (swä hē'lē) *n.* Bantu language of Africa.

swain (swān) *n.* **1.** country lad. **2.** male admirer or lover.

S.W.A.K. sealed with a kiss. Also, **SWAK** (swak).

swal'low (swol'ō) *v.* **1.** take into stomach through throat. **2.** assimilate. **3.** suppress. *—n.* **4.** act of swallowing. **5.** small graceful migratory bird.

swal'low•tail', *n.* **1.** deeply forked tail like that of swallow. **2.** kind of butterfly.

swa'mi (swä'mē) *n.* Hindu religious teacher.

swamp (swomp) *n.* **1.** marshy ground. *—v.* **2.** drench with water. **3.** overwhelm. **—swamp'y,** *adj.*

swan (swon) *n.* large long-necked swimming bird.

swank (swangk) *adj.,* **swanker, swankest. 1.**

stylish or elegant. **2.** pretentiously stylish. Also, **swank′y.**

swan song, final act or farewell appearance.

swap (swop) *v.,* **swapped, swapping,** *n.* trade.

sward (swôrd) *n.* turf.

swarm (swôrm) *n.* **1.** group of bees. —*v.* **2.** fly off to start new colony. **3.** cluster; throng.

swarth′y (swôr′thē, -thē) *adj.,* **-ier, -iest.** (esp. of skin) dark. —**swarth′i•ness,** *n.*

swash′buck′ler (swosh′buk′lər) *n.* swaggering fellow. —**swash′buck′ling,** *adj., n.*

swas′ti•ka (swos′ti kə) *n.* **1.** kind of cross used as symbol and ornament. **2.** emblem of Nazi Party.

swat (swot) *v.,* **swatted, swatting,** *n. Informal.* —*v.* **1.** strike. —*n.* **2.** sharp blow. —**swat′ter,** *n.*

swatch (swoch) *n.* sample of material or finish.

swath (swoth) *n.* long cut made by scythe or mowing machine.

swathe (swoth, swāth) *v.,* **swathed, swathing,** *n.* —*v.* **1.** wrap closely. —*n.* **2.** bandage.

sway (swā) *v.* **1.** swing to and fro. **2.** influence or incline. —*n.* **3.** act of swaying. **4.** rule.

sway′back′, *n.* excessive downward curvature of the back, esp. of horses. —**sway′backed′,** *adj.*

Swazil. Swaziland.

swbd switchboard.

SWbS southwest by south.

SWbW southwest by west.

SWC Southwest Conference.

swear (swâr) *v.,* **swore** (swôr), **sworn, swearing. 1.** affirm on oath; vow. **2.** use profane language. **3.** bind by oath.

sweat (swet) *v.,* **sweat** or **sweated, sweating,** *n.* —*v.* **1.** excrete moisture through pores. **2.** gather moisture. —*n.* **3.** secretion of sweat glands. **4.** process of sweating. —**sweat′y,** *adj.*

sweat′er, *n.* knitted jacket.

sweat gland, tubular gland in skin that secretes sweat.

sweat′pants′, *n.* pants of absorbent fabric.

sweat′shirt′, *n.* loose pullover of absorbent fabric.

sweat′shop′, *n.* manufacturing establishment employing workers at low wages, for long hours, under poor conditions.

Swed. 1. Sweden. **2.** Swedish.

Swed′ish (swē′dish) *n.* language or people of Sweden. —**Swedish,** *adj.*

sweep (swēp) *v.,* **swept** (swept), **sweeping,** *n.* —*v.* **1.** move or clear with broom, etc. **2.** clear or pass over with forceful, rapid movement. —*n.* **3.** act of sweeping. **4.** extent; range.

sweep′ing, *adj.* of wide range or scope.

sweep′stakes′, *n.* **1.** race for stakes put up by competitors. **2.** lottery.

sweet (swēt) *adj.* **1.** having taste of sugar. **2.** fragrant. **3.** fresh. **4.** pleasant in sound. **5.** amiable. —*n.* **6.** anything sweet. —**sweet′en,** *v.* —**sweet′ly,** *adv.* —**sweet′ness,** *n.*

sweet′bread′, *n.* thymus or pancreas, esp. of calf or lamb, used for food.

sweet′bri′er, *n.* fragrant wild rose.

sweet′en•er, *n.* substance, esp. a substitute for sugar, to sweeten food or drink.

sweet′heart′, *n.* beloved.

sweet′meat′, *n.* confection.

sweet pea, annual vine with fragrant blooms.

sweet pepper, mild-flavored bell-shaped pepper.

sweet potato, plant with sweet edible root.

sweet′-talk′, *v.* cajole; flatter.

sweet tooth, liking or craving for sweets.

sweet′ wil′liam (wil′yəm) low plant with dense flower clusters.

swell (swel) *v.,* **swelled, swelled** or **swollen, swelling,** *n., adj.* —*v.* **1.** grow in degree, force, etc. —*n.* **2.** act of swelling. **3.** wave. —*adj.* **4.** *Informal.* excellent.

swel′ter (swel′tər) *v.* perspire or suffer from heat.

swel′ter•ing, *adj.* **1.** suffering from heat. **2.** oppressively hot.

swerve (swûrv) *v.,* **swerved, swerving,** *n.* —*v.* **1.** turn aside. —*n.* **2.** act of swerving.

SWF single white female.

swg sewage.

S.W.G. standard wire gauge.

swgr switchgear.

swift (swift) *adj.* **1.** moving with speed. **2.** prompt or quick. —*n.* **3.** small bird. —**swift′ly,** *adv.* —**swift′ness,** *n.*

swig (swig) *n., v.,* **swigged, swigging.** *Informal.* —*n.* **1.** deep drink. —*v.* **2.** drink heartily.

swill (swil) *n.* **1.** moist garbage fed to hogs. —*v.* **2.** guzzle.

swim (swim) *v.,* **swam** (swam), **swum** (swum), **swimming,** *n.* —*v.* **1.** move in water by action of limbs, etc. **2.** be immersed. **3.** be dizzy. —*n.* **4.** period of swimming. —**swim′mer,** *n.*

swimming hole, place with water deep enough for swimming.

swim′suit′, *n.* bathing suit.

swin′dle (swin′dl) *v.,* **-dled, -dling,** *n.* —*v.* **1.** cheat; defraud. —*n.* **2.** act of swindling; fraud. —**swin′dler,** *n.*

swine (swīn) *n., pl.* **swine.** hog.

swing (swing) *v.,* **swung** (swung), **swinging,** *n.* —*v.* **1.** move to and fro around point. **2.** brandish. —*n.* **3.** act, way, or extent of swinging. **4.** operation. **5.** scope. **6.** suspended seat for swinging. **7.** style or quality in jazz marked by smooth beat and flowing phrasing.

swing′er, *n. Slang.* **1.** person with modern attitudes. **2.** sexually uninhibited person.

swing shift, work shift from midafternoon until midnight.

swipe (swīp) *n., v.,* **swiped, swiping.** —*n.* **1.** sweeping blow. —*v.* **2.** deal such blow. **3.** *Informal.* steal.

swirl (swûrl) *v., n.* whirl; eddy.

swish (swish) *v.* **1.** rustle. —*n.* **2.** swishing sound.

Swiss cheese (swis) firm, pale yellow cheese with holes.

Swit. Switzerland.

switch (swich) *n.* **1.** flexible rod. **2.** device for turning electric current on or off. **3.** device for moving trains from one track to another. **4.** change. —*v.* **5.** whip with switch. **6.** shift; divert. **7.** turn (electric current) on or off.

switch'back', *n.* zigzag highway or railroad track arrangement for climbing steep grade.

switch'blade', *n.* pocketknife with blade released by spring.

switch'board', *n.* panel for controlling electric circuits.

Switz. Switzerland.

swiv'el (swiv'əl) *n., v.,* **-eled, -eling.** —*n.* **1.** device permitting rotation of thing mounted on it. —*v.* **2.** rotate.

swiz'zle stick (swiz'əl) small wand for stirring mixed drinks.

SWM single white male.

swol'len (swō'lən) pp. of **swell.**

swoon (swoon) *v., n.* faint.

swoop (swoop) *v.* **1.** sweep down upon. —*n.* **2.** sweeping descent.

sword (sôrd) *n.* weapon with blade fixed in hilt or handle. —**sword'play',** *n.* —**swords'man,** *n.*

sword'fish', *n.* marine fish with swordlike upper jaw.

SWP Socialist Workers Party.

swp sweep.

swr *Electronics.* standing-wave ratio.

Swtz. Switzerland.

swvl swivel.

sxs *Telephones.* step-by-step: switching system.

syb'a•rite' (sib'ə rīt') *n.* person devoted to pleasure. —**syb'a•rit'ic** (-rit'ik) *adj.*

syc'a•more' (sik'ə môr') *n.* plane tree.

syc'o•phant (sik'ə fənt, -fant', sī'kə-) *n.* flatterer; parasite. —**syc'o•phan•cy,** *n.*

syll. 1. syllable. **2.** syllabus.

syl•lab'i•cate' (si lab'i kāt') *v.,* **-cated, -cating.** divide into syllables. Also, **syl•lab'i•fy'** (-fī'). —**syl•lab'i•ca'tion,** *n.*

syl'la•ble (sil'ə bəl) *n.* single unit of speech. —**syl•lab'ic** (si lab'ik) *adj.*

syl'la•bus (sil'ə bəs) *n., pl.* **-buses, -bi** (-bī'). outline of course of study.

syl'lo•gism (sil'ə jiz'əm) *n.* three-part chain of logical reasoning.

sylph (silf) *n.* **1.** graceful woman. **2.** imaginary being supposed to inhabit the air.

syl'van (sil'vən) *adj.* **1.** of forests. **2.** wooded.

sym. 1. symbol. **2.** *Chemistry.* symmetrical. **3.** symphony. **4.** symptom.

sym'bi•o'sis (sim'bē ō'sis, -bī-) *n., pl.* **-ses** (-sēz). living together of two dissimilar organisms. —**sym'bi•ot'ic** (-ot'ik) *adj.*

sym'bol (sim'bəl) *n.* **1.** emblem; token; sign. **2.** thing that represents something else. —**sym•bol'ic** (-bol'ik), **sym•bol'i•cal,** *adj.* —**sym'bol•ize',** *v.,* **-ized, -izing.**

sym'bol•ism, *n.* **1.** representing things by symbols. **2.** symbolic meaning of a character.

symm symmetrical.

sym'me•try (sim'i trē) *n., pl.* **-tries.** pleasing balance or proportion. —**sym•met'ri•cal** (si me'tri kəl) *adj.* —**sym•met'ri•cal•ly,** *adv.*

symp symposium.

sym'pa•thet'ic nervous system (sim'pə thet'ik) that part of autonomic nervous system that regulates involuntary reactions to stress.

sym'pa•thize' (-thīz') *v.,* **-thized, -thizing. 1.** be in sympathy. **2.** feel or express sympathy. —**sym'pa•thiz'er,** *n.*

sym'pa•thy (-thē) *n., pl.* **-thies. 1.** agreement in feeling; accord. **2.** compassion. —**sym'pa•thet'ic** (-thet'ik) *adj.* —**sym•pa•thet'i•cal•ly,** *adv.*

sym'pho•ny (sim'fə nē) *n., pl.* **-nies. 1.** composition for orchestra. **2.** harmonious combination. —**sym•phon'ic** (-fon'ik) *adj.*

sym•po'si•um (sim pō'zē əm) *n., pl.* **-siums, -sia** (-zē ə). meeting to present essays on one subject.

symp'tom (simp'təm) *n.* sign or indication, esp. of disease. —**symp'to•mat'ic** (-mat'ik) *adj.*

syn. 1. synonym. **2.** synonymous. **3.** synonymy. **4.** synthetic.

syn'a•gogue' (sin'ə gog') *n.* **1.** assembly of Jews for worship. **2.** place of such assembly.

syn'apse (sin'aps, si naps') *n.* region where nerve impulses are transmitted from axon terminal to adjacent structure. —**syn•ap'tic,** *adj.*

sync (singk) *n., v.,* **synced, syncing.** —*n.* **1.** synchronization. **2.** harmonious relationship. —*v.* **3.** synchronize.

syn'chro•nize' (sing'krə nīz') *v.,* **-nized, -nizing. 1.** occur at same time. **2.** show or set to show same time. —**syn'chro•ni•za'tion,** *n.* —**syn'chro•nous,** *adj.*

syn'co•pate' (sing'kə pāt', sin'-) *v.,* **-pated, -pating. 1.** *Music.* play by accenting notes normally unaccented. **2.** *Gram.* omit middle sound in (word). —**syn'co•pa'tion,** *n.*

synd. 1. syndicate. **2.** syndicated.

syn'di•cate, *n., v.,* **-cated, -cating.** —*n.* (sin'də kit) **1.** combination of persons or companies for large joint enterprise. **2.** agency dealing in news stories, etc. —*v.* (sin'di kāt') **3.** publish as syndicate. —**syn'di•ca'tion,** *n.*

S

syn′drome (sin′drōm, -drəm) *n.* characteristic group of symptoms.

syn′er•gism (sin′ər jiz′əm) *n.* joint action of agents so that their combined effect is greater than sum of individual effects.

syn′fu′el (sin′fyōō′əl) *n.* synthetic fuel.

syn′od (sin′əd) *n.* meeting of church delegates.

syn′o•nym (sin′ə nim) *n.* word meaning same as another. —**syn•on′y•mous** (si non′-ə məs) *adj.* —**syn•on′y•mous•ly,** *adv.*

synop. synopsis.

syn•op′sis (si nop′sis) *n., pl.* **-ses** (-sēz). brief summary.

syn′tax (sin′taks) *n.* arrangement of words into sentences, etc.

synth synthetic.

syn′the•sis (sin′thə sis) *n., pl.* **-ses** (-sēz). **1.** combination of parts into whole. **2.** such whole.

syn′the•size′ (-sīz′) *v.,* **-sized, -sizing.** make by combining parts.

syn′the•siz′er, *n.* electronic, usu. computerized device for creating or modifying musical sounds.

syn•thet′ic (sin thet′ik) *adj.* **1.** produced artificially rather than by nature. **2.** of synthesis. —**syn•thet′i•cal•ly,** *adv.*

synthetic fuel, fuel made esp. from coal or shale.

synthzr synthesizer.

syph′i•lis (sif′ə lis) *n.* infectious venereal disease. —**syph•i•lit′ic** (-lit′ik) *adj., n.*

syr *Pharmacology.* syrup.

Syr. 1. Syria. **2.** Syriac. **3.** Syrian.

sy•rin′ga (sə ring′gə), *n.* shrub with fragrant flowers, as lilac.

syr•inge′ (sə rinj′, sir′inj) *n.* device for drawing in and ejecting fluids.

syr′up (sir′əp, sûr′-) *n.* sweet thick liquid. —**syr′up•y,** *adj.*

SYSOP (sis′op′), systems operator.

syst. system. Also, **sys**

sys′tem (sis′təm) *n.* **1.** orderly assemblage of facts, parts, etc. **2.** plan. **3.** organization of body. —**sys′tem•at′ic** (-tə mat′ik) *adj.* —**sys′tem•at′i•cal•ly,** *adv.*

sys′tem•a•tize′ (-tə mə tīz′) *v.,* **-tized, -tiz-ing.** arrange in or by system.

sys•tem′ic (si stem′ik) *adj.* affecting entire body.

systems analysis, study of data-processing needs of project.

sys′to•le′ (sis′tə lē′) *n.* regular contraction of the heart. —**sys•tol′ic** (si stol′ik) *adj.*

sz. size.

T

T, t (tē) *n.* twentieth letter of English alphabet.

TA 1. transactional analysis. **2.** transit authority.

Ta *Symbol, Chemistry.* tantalum.

t-a *Immunology.* toxin-antitoxin.

tab (tab) *n., v.,* **tabbed, tabbing.** —*n.* **1.** small flap. **2.** tag. —*v.* **3.** furnish with tab.

Ta•bas′co (tə bas′kō) *n. Trademark.* pungent condiment sauce.

tab′by (tab′ē) *n., pl.* -bies, *adj.* —*n.* **1.** striped or brindled cat. **2.** silk fabric. —*adj.* **3.** striped.

tab′er•nac′le (tab′ər nak′əl) *n.* **1.** temporary temple, esp. Jewish. **2.** church for large congregation. **3.** receptacle for Eucharist.

ta′ble (tā′bəl) *n., v.,* **-bled, -bling.** —*n.* **1.** piece of furniture consisting of level part on legs. **2.** food. **3.** company at table. **4.** compact arrangement of information in parallel columns. —*v.* **5.** place on or enter in table. **6.** postpone deliberation on. —**ta′ble•cloth′,** *n.*

tab•leau′ (ta blō′, tab′lō) *n., pl.* -leaux (ta-blōz′). picture.

ta′ble d'hôte′ (tā′bəl dōt′, tab′əl) meal fixed in courses and price.

ta′ble•land′, *n.* elevated, level region of considerable extent.

ta′ble•spoon′, *n.* **1.** large spoon in table service. **2.** tablespoonful.

ta′ble•spoon•ful′, *n., pl.* -fuls. quantity tablespoon holds, about ½ fluid ounce or 3 teaspoonfuls.

tab′let (tab′lit) *n.* **1.** pad of writing paper. **2.** small slab. **3.** pill.

table tennis, game resembling tennis, played on table with paddles and small hollow ball.

ta′ble•ware′, *n.* dishes, etc., used at table.

tab′loid (tab′loid) *n.* newspaper about half ordinary size.

ta•boo′ (tə bōō′, ta-) *adj., n., pl.* -boos, *v.* —*adj.* **1.** forbidden. —*n.* **2.** prohibition. —*v.* **3.** prohibit.

ta′bor (tā′bər) *n.* small drum.

tab′u•late′ (tab′yə lāt′) *v.,* -lated, -lating. arrange in table. —**tab′u•lar,** *adj.* —**tab′u•la′tion,** *n.* —**tab′u•la′tor,** *n.*

tac tactical.

TACAN (tə kan′), tactical air navigation.

tach tachometer.

ta•chom′e•ter (ta kom′i tər, tə-) *n.* instrument for measuring velocity.

tach′y•car′di•a (tak′i kär′dē ə) *n.* excessively rapid heartbeat.

tac′it (tas′it) *adj.* **1.** silent. **2.** implied. **3.** unspoken. —**tac′it•ly,** *adv.*

tac′i•turn′ (tas′i tûrn′) *adj.* inclined to silence. —**tac′i•tur′ni•ty,** *n.* —**tac′i•turn•ly,** *adv.*

tack (tak) *n.* **1.** short nail with flat head. **2.** straight windward run of sailing ship. —*v.* **3.** fasten by tack. **4.** navigate by tacks.

tack′le, *n., v.,* **-led, -ling.** —*n.* **1.** fishing equipment. **2.** hoisting apparatus. —*v.* **3.** undertake to deal with. —**tack′ler,** *n.*

tack′y, *adj.,* -ier, -iest. **1.** *Informal.* shabby; dowdy. **2.** slightly sticky. **3.** in poor taste. —**tack′i•ness,** *n.*

ta′co (tä′kō) *n.* fried tortilla folded and filled with chopped meat, cheese, lettuce, etc.

tact (takt) *n.* skill in handling delicate situations. —**tact′ful,** *adj.* —**tact′ful•ly,** *adv.* —**tact′less,** *adj.* —**tact′less•ly,** *adv.*

tac•ti′cian (tak tish′ən) *n.* person versed in tactics.

tac′tics (tak′tiks) *n.* **1.** maneuvering of armed forces. **2.** methods for attaining success. —**tac′ti•cal,** *adj.* —**tac′ti•cal•ly,** *adv.*

tac′tile (tak′til, -tīl) *adj.* of sense of touch. —**tac•til′i•ty** (-til′i tē) *n.*

tad (tad) *n. Informal.* **1.** small child. **2.** small amount or degree.

tad′pole (tad′pōl) *n.* immature form of frogs, toads, etc.

taf•fe•ta (taf′i tə) *n.* lustrous silk or rayon fabric.

taf′fy (taf′ē) *n., pl.* -fies. molasses candy.

tag (tag) *n., v.,* **tagged, tagging.** —*n.* **1.** small paper, etc., attached as mark or label. **2.** game in which players chase and touch each other. —*v.* **3.** furnish with tag. **4.** touch in playing tag.

T/Agt transfer agent. Also, **T. Agt.**

t'ai chi ch'uan (tī′ jē′ chwän′, chē′) *n.* Chinese system of meditative exercises. Also, **tai′ chi′.**

tail (tāl) *n.* **1.** appendage at rear of animal's body. **2.** something resembling this. **3.** bottom or end part. —*v.* **4.** follow.

tail′bone′, *n.* coccyx.

tail′gate′, *n., v.,* **-gated, -gating.** —*n.* **1.** hinged board at back of vehicle. —*v.* **2.** drive too closely behind.

tail′light′, *n.* light at the rear of automobile, train, etc.

tai′lor (tā′lər) *n.* maker or mender of outer garments.

tail′piece′, *n.* piece, design, etc., added at end; appendage.

tail′pipe′, *n.* exhaust pipe at rear of motor vehicle.

tail′spin′, *n.* descent of airplane in steep spiral course.

tail′wind′ (-wind′) *n.* wind from directly behind.

taint (tānt) *n.* **1.** unfavorable trace. —*v.* **2.** contaminate.

take (tāk) *v.,* **took** (tŏŏk), **taken, taking. 1.**

seize, catch, or embrace. **2.** receive; obtain. **3.** select. **4.** remove. **5.** deduct. **6.** conduct. **7.** travel by. **8.** occupy. **9.** assume. **10.** require.

take′off′, *n.* **1.** leaving of ground in leaping or flying. **2.** place at which one takes off. **3.** *Informal,* piece of mimicry.

take′out′, *adj.* intended to be taken from restaurant and eaten elsewhere.

take′o′ver, *n.* **1.** act of seizing authority or control. **2.** acquisition of corporation through purchase of stock.

tal. (in prescriptions) such; like this. [from Latin *tālis*]

talc (talk) *n.* soft mineral, used for lubricants, etc. Also, **tal′cum.**

tal′cum powder (tal′kəm) powder for the skin made of purified talc.

tale (tāl) *n.* story or lie.

tale′bear′er, *n.* gossip.

tal′ent (tal′ənt) *n.* natural ability. —**tal′ent‑ed,** *adj.*

tal′is‑man (tal′is mən, -iz-) *n.* amulet.

talk (tôk) *v.* **1.** speak; converse. **2.** gossip. —*n.* **3.** speech; conversation. **4.** conference. **5.** gossip. —**talk′a‑tive,** *adj.* —**talk′er,** *n.*

talk′ing-to′, *n., pl.* -tos. scolding.

talk′y, *adj.,* -ier, -iest. **1.** containing too much talk, dialogue, etc. **2.** talkative. —**talk′i‑ness,** *n.*

tall (tôl) *adj.* high.

tal′low (tal′ō) *n.* **1.** suet. **2.** hardened fat for soap, etc.

tal′ly (tal′ē) *n., pl.* -lies, *v.,* -lied, -lying. —*n.* **1.** notched stock indicating amount. **2.** mark on tally. **3.** record of amounts. —*v.* **4.** record.

tal′ly‑ho′ (-hō′) *interj.* cry in hunting on catching sight of fox.

Tal′mud (täl′mŏŏd, tal′məd) *n.* collection of Jewish laws. —**Tal‑mud′ic,** *adj.*

tal′on (tal′ən) *n.* claw.

tal′us (tā′ləs) *n., pl.* -li. anklebone.

tam (tam) *n.* tam-o′-shanter.

ta‑ma′le (tə mä′lē) *n.* Mexican dish of corn-meal, meat, red peppers, etc.

tam′a‑rack′ (tam′ə rak′) *n.* N American larch.

tam′a‑rind (-ə rind) *n.* tropical fruit.

tam′bou‑rine′ (-bə rēn′) *n.* small drum with metal disks in frame.

tame (tām) *adj.,* tamer, tamest, *v.,* tamed, taming. —*adj.* **1.** not wild; domesticated. **2.** uninterestingly conventional. —*v.* **3.** domesticate. —**tam′a‑ble, tame′a‑ble,** *adj.* —**tame′ly,** *adv.* —**tame′ness,** *n.* —**tam′er,** *n.*

tam′-o′-shan′ter (tam′ə shan′tər) *n.* cap with flat crown.

tamp (tamp) *v.* force down or in. —**tamp′er,** *n.*

tam′per, *v.* meddle.

tam′pon (tam′pon) *n.* plug of cotton or the

like for insertion into wound or body cavity to absorb blood.

tan (tan) *v.,* tanned, tanning, *n., adj.* —*v.* **1.** convert into leather. **2.** make or become brown by exposure to sun. —*n.* **3.** light brown. **4.** Also, **tan′bark′.** bark used in tanning hides. —*adj.* **5.** light brown. —**tan′ner,** *n.* —**tan′ner‑y,** *n.*

tan′a‑ger (tan′ə jər) *n.* small, brightly colored bird.

T&A 1. *Slang.* tits and ass. **2.** tonsillectomy and adenoidectomy. Also, **T and A**

t&a tonsils and adenoids.

T&E travel and entertainment. Also, **T and E**

tan′dem (tan′dəm) *adv.* **1.** one behind another. —*adj.* **2.** having one following behind another. —*n.* **3.** team of horses so harnessed.

tang (tang) *n.* strong flavor.

tan′ge‑lo′ (tan′jə lō′) *n., pl.* -los. fruit that is a cross between grapefruit and tangerine.

tan′gent (tan′jənt) *adj.* **1.** touching. —*n.* **2.** tangent line, etc. **3.** sudden change of course, thought, etc. —**tan′gen‑cy,** *n.*

tan‑gen′tial (-jen′shəl) *adj.* **1.** being tangent; touching. **2.** not relevant. —**tan‑gen′tial‑ly,** *adv.*

tan′ge‑rine′ (tan′jə rēn′) *n.* loose-skinned fruit similar to orange.

tan′gi‑ble (tan′jə bəl) *adj.* **1.** discernible by touch. **2.** real. **3.** definite. —**tan′gi‑bil′i‑ty,** *n.* —**tan′gi‑bly,** *adv.*

tan′gle (tang′gəl) *v.,* -gled, -gling, *n.* —*v.* **1.** come or bring together in confused mass. **2.** involve. **3.** snare. **4.** *Informal.* come into conflict. —*n.* **5.** tangled state or mass.

tan′go (tang′gō) *n., pl.* -gos, *v.,* -goed, -going. —*n.* **1.** Spanish-American dance. —*v.* **2.** dance the tango.

tanh *Math.* hyperbolic tangent.

tank (tangk) *n.* **1.** large receptacle. **2.** armored combat vehicle on caterpillar treads.

tank′ard (tang′kərd) *n.* large cup.

tank′er, *n.* ship, truck, or airplane for transporting liquid bulk cargo.

tank top, sleeveless shirt.

tan′nin (tan′in) *n.* astringent compound used in tanning. Also, **tan′nic ac′id.**

tan′ta‑lize′ (tan′tl īz′) *v.,* -lized, -lizing. torment by prospect of something desired. —**tan′ta‑liz′ing‑ly,** *adv.*

tan′ta‑mount′ (tan′tə mount′) *adj.* equivalent.

tan′trum (tan′trəm) *n.* noisy outburst of ill-humor.

tap (tap) *n., v.,* tapped, tapping. —*n.* **1.** plug or faucet through which liquid is drawn. **2.** light blow. —*v.* **3.** draw liquid from. **4.** reach or pierce to draw something off. **5.** strike lightly.

tap dance, dance in which rhythm is audibly tapped out by toe or heel. —**tap′-dance′,** *v.* —**tap′-danc′er,** *n.*

tape (tāp) *n., v.,* taped, taping. —*n.* **1.** narrow strip of flexible material. —*v.* **2.** furnish or tie with tape. **3.** record on tape.

tape deck, audio system component for playing tapes.

tape measure, tape marked for measuring. Also, **tape/line/.**

ta/per (tā/pər) *v.* **1.** make or become narrower toward end. —*n.* **2.** gradual decrease. **3.** small candle.

tape recorder, electrical device for recording or playing back sound recorded on magnetic tape.

tap/es•try (tap/ə strē) *n., pl.* **-tries.** woven, figured fabric for wall hanging, etc.

tape/worm/, *n.* parasitic worm in alimentary canal.

tap/i•o/ca (tap/ē ō/kə) *n.* granular food from starch of tuberous plants.

ta/pir (tā/pər, tə pēr/) *n.* tropical swinelike animal.

tap/room/, *n.* barroom.

tap/root/, *n.* main, central root pointing downward and giving off small lateral roots.

taps, *n.* bugle signal sounded at night as order to extinguish lights, and sometimes at military funerals.

tar (tär) *n., v.,* **tarred, tarring.** —*n.* **1.** dark viscid product made from coal, wood, etc. **2.** sailor. —*v.* **3.** cover with tar. —**tar/ry** (tär/ē) *adj.*

tar/an•tel/la (tar/ən tel/ə) *n.* rapid, whirling southern Italian dance.

ta•ran/tu•la (tə ran/chə lə) *n.* large hairy spider.

tar/dy (tär/dē) *adj.,* **-dier, -diest.** late. —**tar/di•ly,** *adv.* —**tar/di•ness,** *n.*

tare (târ) *n.* **1.** weed. **2.** weight of a wrapping or receptacle.

tar/get (tär/git) *n.* something aimed at.

tar/iff (tar/if) *n.* **1.** list of export or import duties. **2.** one such duty.

tar/nish (tär/nish) *v.* **1.** lose luster. **2.** sully. —*n.* **3.** tarnished coating or state.

ta/ro (tär/ō, târ/ō, tar/ō) *n.* tropical plant cultivated for edible tuber.

ta/rot (tar/ō, ta rō/) *n.* any of set of 22 playing cards used for fortune-telling.

tar•pau/lin (tär pô/lin, tär/pə lin) *n.* waterproof covering of canvas, etc.

tar/pon (tär/pən) *n.* large game fish.

tar/ra•gon/ (tar/ə gon/, -gən) *n.* plant with aromatic leaves used as seasoning.

tar/ry (tar/ē) *v.,* **-ried, -rying. 1.** stay. **2.** linger.

tar/sus (tär/səs) *n., pl.* **-si.** bones forming ankle joint.

tart (tärt) *adj.* **1.** sour; acid. **2.** caustic. —*n.* **3.** pastry shell filled with fruit, etc. —**tart/ly,** *adv.* —**tart/ness,** *n.*

tar/tan (tär/tn) *n.* cloth worn by natives of N Scotland, having crisscross pattern.

tar/tar (tär/tər) *n.* **1.** hard deposit on teeth. **2.** savage, intractable person. —**tar•tar/ic** (-tar/ik, -tär/-) *adj.*

tartar sauce, mayonnaise sauce containing chopped pickles, onions, etc.

tas true airspeed.

task (task) *n.* **1.** assigned piece of work. —*v.* **2.** put strain on.

task force, 1. temporary group of armed units for carrying out specific mission. **2.** temporary committee for solving specific problem.

task/mas/ter, *n.* assigner of tasks.

Tasm. Tasmania.

tas/sel (tas/əl) *n.* fringed ornament hanging from roundish knot.

taste (tāst) *v.,* **tasted, tasting,** *n.* —*v.* **1.** try flavor by taking in mouth. **2.** eat or drink a little of. **3.** perceive flavor. **4.** have particular flavor. —*n.* **5.** act of tasting. **6.** sense by which flavor is perceived. **7.** flavor. **8.** sense of fitness or beauty. —**taste/ful,** *adj.* —**taste/less,** *adj.* —**tast/er,** *n.*

taste bud, one of numerous small bodies, chiefly in tongue, that are organs for sense of taste.

tast/y *adj.,* **-ier, -iest. 1.** savory. **2.** tasting good. —**tast/i•ness,** *n.*

tat (tat) *v.,* **tatted, tatting.** to do, or make by, tatting.

tat/ter (tat/ər) *n.* **1.** torn piece. **2.** (*pl.*) ragged clothing.

tat/ting, *n.* **1.** the making of a kind of knotted lace with a shuttle. **2.** such lace.

tat/tle (tat/l) *v.,* **-tled, -tling,** *n.* —*v.* **1.** tell another's secrets. —*n.* **2.** chatter; gossip. —**tat/tler, tat/tle•tale/,** *n.*

tat•too/ (ta tōō/) *n.* **1.** indelible marking on skin by puncturing and dyeing. **2.** design so made. **3.** military signal on drum, bugle, etc., to go to quarters. —*v.* **4.** mark by tattoo.

taunt (tônt, tänt) *v.* **1.** reproach insultingly or sarcastically. —*n.* **2.** insulting or sarcastic gibe.

taupe (tōp) *n.* dark gray usually tinged with brown, purple, yellow, or green.

taut (tôt) *adj.* tight; tense. —**taut/ly,** *adv.* —**taut/ness,** *n.*

tau•tol/o•gy (tô tol/ə jē) *n., pl.* **-gies.** needless repetition. —**tau/to•log/i•cal** (-tl oj/i-kəl) *adj.*

tav/ern (tav/ərn) *n.* **1.** saloon. **2.** inn.

taw (tô) *n.* **1.** choice playing marble with which to shoot. **2.** game of marbles.

taw/dry (tô/drē) *adj.,* **-drier, -driest.** gaudy; cheap. —**taw/dri•ly,** *adv.* —**taw/dri•ness,** *n.*

taw/ny (tô/nē) *adj.,* **-nier, -niest,** *n.* —*adj.* **1.** of a dark-yellow or yellow-brown color. —*n.* **2.** tawny color.

tax (taks) *n.* **1.** money regularly paid to government. **2.** burdensome duty, etc. —*v.* **3.** impose tax. **4.** burden. **5.** accuse. —**tax/a•ble,** *adj.* —**tax•a/tion,** *n.*

tax/i (tak/sē) *n., v.,* **taxied, taxiing.** —*n.* **1.** taxicab. —*v.* **2.** go in taxicab. **3.** (of airplane)

T

move on ground or water under its own power.

tax'i•cab', *n.* automobile carrying paying passengers.

tax'i•der'my (tak'si dûr'mē) *n.* art of preserving and mounting skins of animals. —**tax'i•der'•mist**, *n.*

tax•on'o•my (tak son'ə mē) *n.*, *pl.* -**mies.** classification, esp. in relation to principles or laws.

tax'pay'er, *n.* person who pays tax.

tax shelter, financial arrangement that reduces or eliminates taxes due.

TB, tuberculosis. Also, **T.B.**

T.B.A. to be announced. Also, **TBA, t.b.a.**

TBD to be determined.

TBI *Automotive.* throttle-body injection.

T-bill (tē'bil'), a U.S. Treasury bill.

tblr tumbler.

tblsht troubleshoot.

T.B.O. *Theater.* total blackout.

T-bond (tē'bond'), a U.S. Treasury bond.

tbs., tablespoon. Also, **tbsp.**

TC 1. Teachers College. 2. technical circular. 3. Trusteeship Council (of the United Nations).

Tc *Symbol, Chemistry.* technetium.

tc 1. thermocouple. 2. time constant.

TCA *Chemistry.* trichloroacetic acid.

TCB taking care of business.

TCBM transcontinental ballistic missile.

TCDD *Pharmacology.* dioxin.

TCE *Chemistry.* trichloroethylene.

T cell, cell involved in regulating immune system's response to infected or malignant cells.

tchr. teacher.

tci terrain-clearance indicator.

TCL transistor-coupled logic.

TCP/IP *Computers.* Transfer Control Protocol/Internet Protocol.

TCS traffic control station.

TCTO time-compliance technical order.

TD 1. technical directive. 2. *Football.* touchdown; touchdowns. 3. trust deed.

td time delay.

T/D *Banking.* time deposit.

T.D. 1. Traffic Director. 2. Treasury Department.

tdc 1. *Electricity.* time-delay closing (of contacts). 2. top dead center.

TDD telecommunications device for the deaf.

tdg twist drill gauge.

TDI temporary disability insurance.

TDL tunnel-diode logic.

TDM *Telecommunications.* time-division multiplex. Also, **tdm**

tdm tandem.

TDN totally digestible nutrients. Also, **t.d.n.**

tdo *Electricity.* time-delay opening (of contacts).

TDOS tape disk operating system.

TDRS Tracking and Data Relay Satellite.

t.d.s. (in prescriptions) to be taken three times a day. [from Latin *ter die sumendum*]

TDTL tunnel-diode transistor logic.

TDY temporary duty.

TE *Football.* tight end.

Te *Symbol, Chemistry.* tellurium.

te thermoelectric.

T/E table of equipment.

tea (tē) *n.* 1. dried aromatic leaves of Oriental shrub. 2. beverage made by infusion of these leaves in hot water. 3. similar beverage made by steeping leaves or flowers of other plants. 4. afternoon meal or reception. —**tea'cup'**, *n.* —**tea'ket'tle**, *n.* —**tea'pot'**, *n.*

teach (tēch) *v.*, **taught, teaching.** impart knowledge to. —**teach'er**, *n.* —**teach'a•ble**, *adj.*

teak (tēk) *n.* East Indian tree with hard wood.

teal (tēl) *n.* 1. any of certain small freshwater ducks. 2. greenish blue.

team (tēm) *n.* 1. persons, etc., associated in joint action. —*v.* 2. join in team. —**team'mate'**, *n.* —**team'work'**, *n.*

team'ster (-stər) *n.* driver of team.

tear (târ) *v.*, **tore** (tôr), **torn, tearing**, *n.* —*v.* 1. pull apart by force. 2. distress. 3. divide. 4. lacerate. 5. rend. —*n.* 6. act of tearing. 7. torn place. 8. (tēr) Also, **tear'drop'.** drop of fluid secreted by eye duct. —**tear'ful** (tēr'-) *adj.*

tear gas (tēr) gas that makes eyes smart and water.

tear'jerk•er (tēr'jûr'kər) *n. Informal.* sentimental story, etc.

tease (tēz) *v.*, **teased, teasing**, *n.* —*v.* 1. annoy by raillery. —*n.* 2. person who teases. —**teas'er**, *n.*

tea'sel (tē'zəl) *n.* plant with prickly leaves and flower heads.

tea'spoon', *n.* small spoon. —**tea'spoon•ful'**, *n.*, *pl.* -**fuls.**

teat (tēt, tit) *n.* nipple.

tech. 1. technic. 2. technical. 3. technology.

tech'ni•cal (tek'ni kəl) *adj.* 1. pertaining to skilled activity. 2. considered in strict sense. —**tech'ni•cal•ly**, *adv.*

tech'ni•cal'i•ty (-kal'i tē) *n.*, *pl.* -**ties.** 1. technical point or detail. 2. technical character.

Tech'ni•col'or, *n. Trademark.* system of making color motion pictures.

tech•nique' (-nēk') *n.* skilled method. Also, **tech•nic'.**

tech•noc'ra•cy (-nok'rə sē) *n.*, *pl.* -**cies.** government by technological experts. —**tech'no•crat'** (-nə krat') *n.*

technol. technology.

tech•nol'o•gy (-nol'ə jē) *n.*, *pl.* -**gies.** 1. practical application of science. 2. technological invention or method. —**tech•no•log'i•cal** (-nə loj'i kəl) *adj.* —**tech•nol'o•gist**, *n.*

tech'no•thrill'er (tek'nō thril'ər) *n.* suspense novel in which sophisticated technology is prominent.

tech. sgt. technical sergeant.

tec•ton′ic (tek ton′ik) *adj.* **1.** of building or construction. **2.** of the structure and movements of the earth's crust.

ted′dy bear (ted′ē) stuffed toy bear.

Te De′um (tā dā′əm) hymn of praise and thanksgiving.

te′di•ous (tē′dē əs, tē′jəs) *adj.* long and tiresome. —**te′di•um,** *n.* —**te′di•ous•ly,** *adv.* —**te′di•ous•ness,** *n.*

tee (tē) *n., v.,* **teed, teeing.** *Golf.* —*n.* **1.** hard mound of earth at beginning of play for each hole. **2.** object from which ball is driven. —*v.* **3.** place on tee. **4.** strike from tee.

teem (tēm) *v.* abound; swarm.

teens (tēnz) *n.pl.* years (13–19) of ages ending in *-teen.* —**teen′ag′er, teen,** *n.* —**teen′age′, teen′aged′,** *adj.*

tee′ter (tē′tər) *Informal.* —*v.* **1.** seesaw. **2.** walk unsteadily. —*n.* **3.** seesaw.

teethe (tēth) *v.,* **teethed, teething.** grow or cut teeth.

tee•to′tal•er (tē tōt′l ər, tē′tōt′-) *n.* person who does not drink alcoholic beverages.

TEFL teaching English as a foreign language.

Tef′lon (tef′lon) *n. Trademark.* **1.** polymer with nonsticking properties, used to coat cookware. —*adj.* **2.** impervious to blame or criticisms.

tel., **1.** telegram. **2.** telegraph. **3.** telephone.

tel′e•cast′ (tel′i kast′) *v.,* **-cast** or **-casted, -casting,** *n.* —*v.* **1.** broadcast by television. —*n.* **2.** television broadcast.

telecom telecommunications.

tel′e•com•mu′ni•ca′tions, *n.* science and technology of transmitting information in the form of electromagnetic signals.

tel′e•con′fer•ence, *n.* conference of participants in different locations via telecommunications equipment.

teleg. **1.** telegram. **2.** telegraph. **3.** telegraphy.

tel′e•gen′ic (-jen′ik) *adj.* having physical qualities that televise well.

tel′e•graph′ (-graf′) *n.* **1.** electrical apparatus or process for sending message (**tel′e•gram′**). —*v.* **2.** send by telegraph. —**te•leg′ra•pher** (tə leg′rə fər) *n.* —**tel′e•graph′ic,** *adj.* —**te•leg′ra•phy** (tə leg′rə fē) *n.*

tel′e•mar′ket•ing, *n.* selling or advertising by telephone.

te•lep′a•thy (tə lep′ə thē) *n.* communication between minds without physical means. —**te•lep′a•thist,** *n.* —**tel′e•path′ic** (tel′ə path′ik) *adj.* —**tel′e•path′i•cal•ly,** *adv.*

teleph. telephony.

tel′e•phone′ (tel′ə fōn′) *n., v.,* **-phoned, -phoning.** —*n.* **1.** electrical apparatus or process for transmitting sound or speech. —*v.* **2.** speak to or transmit by telephone. —**tel′e•phon′ic** (-fon′ik) *adj.* —**tel′e•phon′i•cal•ly,** *adv.* —**te•leph′o•ny** (tə lef′ ə nē) *n.*

tel′e•pho′to, *adj.* of a lens producing large image of small or distant object.

telesat (tel′ə sat′), telecommunications satellite.

tel′e•scope′, *n., v.,* **-scoped, -scoping.** —*n.* **1.** optical instrument for enlarging image of distant objects. —*v.* **2.** force or slide one object into another. —**tel′e•scop′ic** (-skop′ik) *adj.*

tel′e•thon′ (-thon′) *n.* lengthy television broadcast, usu. to raise money for charity.

Tel′e•type′ (tel′i tīp′) *n. Trademark.* teletypewriter.

tel′e•type′writ′er, *n.* telegraphic apparatus with typewriter terminals.

tel′e•van•ge•list (tel′i van′jə list) *n.* evangelist who conducts religious services on television. —**tel′e•van′ge•lism** (-liz′əm) *n.*

tel′e•view′, *v.* view with a television receiver. —**tel′e•view′er,** *n.*

tel′e•vise′ (-vīz′) *v.,* **-vised, -vising.** send or receive by television.

tel′e•vi′sion, *n.* radio or electrical transmission of images.

Tel′ex (tel′eks) *n. Trademark.* two-way teletypewriter system.

tell (tel) *v.,* **told** (tōld), **telling.** **1.** relate. **2.** communicate. **3.** say positively. **4.** distinguish. **5.** inform. **6.** divulge. **7.** order. **8.** produce marked effect. —**tell′ing,** *adj.*

tell′-all′, *adj.* thoroughly revealing.

tell′er, *n.* bank cashier.

tell′tale′, *n.* **1.** divulger of secrets. —*adj.* **2.** revealing.

te•mer′i•ty (tə mer′i tē) *n.* rash boldness.

temp (temp) *n.* temporary worker.

tem′per, *n.* **1.** state or habit of mind. **2.** heat or passion. **3.** control of one's anger. **4.** state of metal after tempering. —*v.* **5.** moderate. **6.** heat and cool metal to obtain proper hardness, etc.

tem′per•a (tem′pər ə) *n.* technique of painting using media containing egg.

tem′per•a•ment (tem′pər ə mənt, -prə-mənt) *n.* mental disposition.

tem′per•a•men′tal (-men′tl) *adj.* **1.** moody or sensitive. **2.** of one's personality. —**tem′per•a•men′tal•ly,** *adv.*

tem′per•ance (tem′pər əns) *n.* **1.** moderation. **2.** total abstinence from alcohol.

tem′per•ate (-pər it) *adj.* moderate. —**tem′per•ate•ly,** *adv.* —**tem′per•ate•ness,** *n.*

Temperate Zone, part of earth's surface lying between either tropic and nearest polar circle.

tem′per•a•ture (-pər ə chər, -prə-) *n.* degree of warmth or coldness.

tem′pest (tem′pist) *n.* violent storm, commotion, or disturbance. —**tem•pes′tu•ous** (-pes′chōō əs) *adj.* —**tem•pes′tu•ous•ly,** *adv.*

tem′plate (tem′plit) *n.* pattern, mold, etc., serving as gauge or guide in mechanical work.

T

tem′ple (tem′pəl) *n.* **1.** place dedicated to worship. **2.** flat region at side of forehead.

tem′po (tem′pō) *n., pl.* **-pos, -pi** (-pē). **1.** rate of speed of musical work. **2.** any characteristic rate or rhythm.

tem′po·ral (tem′pər əl) *adj.* **1.** of time. **2.** worldly. —**tem′po·ral·ly,** *adv.*

tem′po·rar′y (-pə rer′ē) *adj.* not permanent. —**tem′po·rar′i·ly,** *adv.*

tem′po·rize′ (-rīz′) *v.,* **-rized, -rizing. 1.** delay by evasion or indecision. **2.** compromise. —**tem′po·ri·za′tion,** *n.* —**tem′po·ri′zer,** *n.*

tempt (tempt) *v.* **1.** entice. **2.** appeal strongly. —**temp·ta′tion,** *n.* —**tempt′er,** *n.* —**tempt′ress,** *n.fem.*

tem·pur′a (tem pŏŏr′ə) *n.* Japanese deep-fried dish of vegetables or seafood.

ten (ten) *n., adj.* nine plus one.

ten′a·ble (ten′ə bəl) *adj.* defensible in argument. —**ten′a·bil′i·ty,** *n.* —**ten′a·bly,** *adv.*

te·na′cious (tə nā′shəs) *adj.* **1.** holding fast. **2.** retentive. **3.** obstinate. **4.** sticky. —**te·na′cious·ly,** *adv.* —**te·nac′i·ty** (-nas′i tē) **te·na′cious·ness,** *n.*

ten′an·cy (ten′ən sē) *n., pl.* **-cies.** holding; tenure.

ten′ant (-ənt) *n.* **1.** one renting from landlord. **2.** occupant.

Ten Commandments, precepts spoken by God to Israel (Exodus 20, Deut. 10) or delivered to Moses (Exodus 24:12, 34) on Mount Sinai.

tend (tend) *v.* **1.** incline in action or effect. **2.** lead. **3.** take care of.

tend′en·cy (ten′dən sē) *n., pl.* **-cies. 1.** disposition to behave or act in certain way. **2.** predisposition; preference.

ten·den′tious (-den′shəs) *adj.* having or showing bias. —**ten·den′tious·ly,** *adv.*

ten′der, *adj.* **1.** soft; delicate; weak. **2.** immature. **3.** soft-hearted. **4.** kind. **5.** loving. **6.** sensitive. —*v.* **7.** present formally. **8.** offer. —*n.* **9.** something offered. **10.** person who tends. **11.** auxiliary vehicle or vessel. —**ten′der·er,** *n.* —**ten′der·ly,** *adv.* —**ten′der·ness,** *n.* —**ten′der·ize′,** *v.,* **-ized, -izing.**

ten′der·foot′, *n., pl.* **-foots, -feet.** *Informal.* **1.** inexperienced person; novice. **2.** *Western U.S.* newcomer to ranching and mining regions.

ten′der-heart′ed, *adj.* soft-hearted; sympathetic. —**ten′der-heart′ed·ness,** *n.*

ten′der·loin′, *n.* **1.** tender meat on loin of beef, pork, etc. **2.** brothel district of city.

ten′di·ni′tis (ten′də nī′tis) *n.* inflammation of tendon.

ten′don (-dən) *n.* band of fibrous tissue connecting muscle to bone or part.

ten′dril (-dril) *n.* clinging threadlike organ of climbing plants.

ten′e·ment (-ə mənt) *n.* **1.** dwelling place. **2.** Also, **tenement house.** cheap apartment house.

ten′et (-it) *n.* principle, doctrine, dogma, etc.

Tenn., Tennessee.

ten′nis (-is) *n.* game of ball played with rackets (**tennis rackets**) on rectangular court (**tennis court**).

ten′on (-ən) *n.* projection inserted into cavity (**mortise**) to form joint.

ten′or (-ər) *n.* **1.** continuous course or progress. **2.** perceived meaning or intention. **3.** male voice between bass and alto. **4.** singer with this voice.

ten′pins′, *n.* bowling game played with ten pins.

TENS (tenz), *Medicine.* a self-operated portable device used to treat chronic pain by sending electrical impulses through electrodes placed over the painful area. [t(*ranscutaneous*) e(*lectrical*) n(*erve*) s(*timulator*)]

tense (tens) *adj.,* **tenser, tensest,** *v.,* **tensed, tensing,** *n.* —*adj.* **1.** taut; rigid. **2.** emotionally strained. —*v.* **3.** make or become tense. —*n.* **4.** verb inflection indicating time of action or state. —**tense′ly,** *adv.* —**tense′ness,** *n.*

ten′sile (ten′səl, -sil, -sīl) *adj.* **1.** of tension. **2.** ductile.

ten′sion (-shən) *n.* **1.** stretching or being stretched. **2.** strain. **3.** strained relations.

tent (tent) *n.* portable shelter, usually canvas.

ten′ta·cle (ten′tə kəl) *n.* slender, flexible organ for feeling, etc. —**ten′ta·cled,** *adj.*

ten′ta·tive (-tə tiv) *adj.* in trial; experimental. —**ten′ta·tive·ly,** *adv.*

ten′ter·hook′ (-tər hŏŏk′) *n.* **1.** hook to hold cloth stretched on frame. **2. on tenterhooks,** in suspense.

tenth (tenth) *adj., n.* next after ninth.

ten′u·ous (ten′yŏŏ əs) *adj.* **1.** lacking a sound base. **2.** thin, slender. **3.** rarefied. —**ten′u·ous·ly,** *adv.* —**ten′u·ous·ness,** *n.*

ten′ure (-yər) *n.* **1.** holding of something. **2.** assurance of permanent work.

te′pee (tē′pē) *n.* American Indian tent.

tep′id (tep′id) *adj.* lukewarm. —**te·pid′i·ty, tep′id·ness,** *n.* —**tep′id·ly,** *adv.*

TEPP *Chemistry.* tetraethyl pyrophosphate.

te·qui′la (tə kē′lə) *n.* Mexican liquor.

ter tertiary.

ter′cen·ten′ni·al (tûr′-) *n.* 300th anniversary or its celebration. Also, **ter′cen·ten′a·ry.**

term (tûrm) *n.* **1.** name for something. **2.** period, as of school instruction. **3.** (*pl.*) conditions of agreement or bargain. —*v.* **4.** name; designate.

ter′ma·gant (tûr′mə gənt) *n.* shrew (def. 1).

ter′mi·nal (-mə nl) *adj.* **1.** at end; concluding. **2.** leading to death. —*n.* **3.** end or extremity. **4.** terminating point for trains, buses, etc. **5.** point of electrical connection. **6.** device for entering information into or receiving information from computer. —**ter′mi·nal·ly,** *adv.*

ter′mi·nate′ (-nāt′) *v.,* **-nated, -nating. 1.**

end or cease. **2.** occur at end. **—ter′mi·na· ble** (-nə bəl) *adj.* **—ter′mi·na·bly,** *adv.* **—ter′mi·na′tion,** *n.*

ter′mi·nol′o·gy (-nol′ə jē) *n., pl.* **-gies.** terms of technical subject.

ter′mi·nus (-nəs) *n.* **1.** terminal. **2.** goal. **3.** limit.

ter′mite (tûr′mīt) *n.* destructive woodeating insect.

tern (tûrn) *n.* gull-like aquatic bird.

ter′na·ry (tûr′nə rē) *adj.* consisting of or involving three.

terp·si·cho·re′an (tûrp′si kə rē′ən, -kôr′ē- ən) *adj.* of dancing.

terr. 1. Also, **Ter** terrace. **2.** territorial. **3.** territory.

ter′race (ter′əs) *n., v.,* **-raced, -racing. —***n.* **1.** raised level with abrupt drop at front. **2.** flat roof. **3.** open area connected with house. **—***v.* **4.** make or furnish as or with terrace.

ter′ra cot′ta (ter′ə kot′ə) **1.** hard, usually unglazed earthenware. **2.** brownish red.

ter′ra fir′ma (fûr′mə) solid land.

ter·rain′ (tə rān′) *n.* area of land of specified nature.

ter′ra·pin (ter′ə pin) *n.* edible North American turtle.

ter·rar′i·um (tə râr′ē əm) *n., pl.* **-iums, -ia** (-ē ə). glass tank for raising plants or land animals.

ter·raz′zo (tə rä′tsō, -raz′ō) *n.* mosaic flooring composed of stone chips and cement.

ter·res′tri·al (tə res′trē əl) *adj.* of or living on earth.

ter′ri·ble (ter′ə bəl) *adj.* **1.** dreadful. **2.** severe. **—ter′ri·ble·ness,** *n.* **—ter′ri·bly,** *adv.*

ter′ri·er (ter′ē ər) *n.* hunting dog.

ter·rif′ic (tə rif′ik) *adj.* **1.** excellent. **2.** terrifying. **—ter·rif′i·cal·ly,** *adv.*

ter′ri·fy′ (ter′ə fī′) *v.,* **-fied, -fying.** fill with terror. **—ter′ri·fy′ing·ly,** *adv.*

ter′ri·to·ry (ter′i tôr′ē) *n., pl.* **-ries. 1.** region. **2.** land and waters of state. **3.** region not a state but having elected legislature and appointed officials. **—ter′ri·to′ri·al,** *adj.* **—ter′ri·to′ri·al·ly,** *adv.*

ter′ror (ter′ər) *n.* intense fear.

ter′ror·ism, *n.* use of violence and threats to obtain political demands. **—ter′ror·ist,** *n., adj.*

ter′ror·ize′, *v.,* **-ized, -izing.** fill with terror. **—ter′ror·i·za′tion,** *n.*

ter′ry (ter′ē) *n., pl.* **-ries.** pile fabric with loops on both sides. Also, **terry cloth.**

terse (tûrs) *adj.* **1.** concise. **2.** curt; brusque. **—terse′ly,** *adv.* **—terse′ness,** *n.*

ter′ti·ar′y (tûr′shē er′ē) *adj.* of third rank or stage.

terz terrazzo.

TESL teaching English as a second language.

TESOL (tē′sôl, tes′əl), **1.** teaching English to speakers of other languages. **2.** Teachers of English to Speakers of Other Languages.

tes′sel·late′ (tes′ə lāt′) *v.,* **-lated, -lating.** form mosaic pattern from small squares.

test (test) *n.* **1.** trial of or substance used to try quality, content, etc. **2.** examination to evaluate student or class. **—***v.* **3.** subject to test.

tes′ta·ment (tes′tə mənt) *n.* legal will. **—tes′ta·men′ta·ry** (-men′tə rē) *adj.*

tes′tate (-tāt) *adj.* having left a valid will. **—tes′ta·tor,** *n.*

tes′ti·cle (-ti kəl) *n.* either of two male sex glands located in scrotum. Also, **tes·tis** (tes′- tis).

tes′ti·fy′ (-tə fī′) *v.,* **-fied, -fying. 1.** give evidence. **2.** give testimony.

tes′ti·mo′ni·al (-mō′nē əl) *n.* writing certifying character, etc.

tes′ti·mo′ny, *n., pl.* **-nies. 1.** statement of witness under oath. **2.** proof.

tes·tos′ter·one (tes tos′tə rōn′) *n.* male sex hormone.

test tube, small cylindrical glass container used in laboratories.

tes′ty (tes′tē) *adj.,* **-tier, -tiest.** irritable. **—tes′ti·ly,** *adv.* **—tes′ti·ness,** *n.*

tet′a·nus (tet′n əs) *n.* infectious disease marked by muscular rigidity.

tête′-à-tête′ (tāt′ə tāt′, tet′ə tet′) *n.* private conversation.

tetfleyne tetrafluoroethylene.

teth′er (teth′ər) *n.* **1.** rope, chain, etc., for fastening animal to stake. **—***v.* **2.** fasten with tether.

tet′ra (te′trə) *n., pl.* **-ras.** small, brightly colored fish of tropical American waters.

tet′ra·cy′cline (-sī′klēn, klin) *n.* antibiotic.

tet′ra·he′dron (-hē′drən) *n., pl.* **-drons, -dra.** solid contained by four plane faces.

te·tram′e·ter (te tram′i tər) *n.* verse of four feet.

Teut. 1. Teuton. **2.** Teutonic.

TeV *Physics.* trillion electron-volts. Also, **Tev, tev.**

Tex., Texas.

text (tekst) *n.* **1.** main body of matter in book or manuscript. **2.** quotation from Scripture, esp. as subject of sermon, etc. **—tex′tu·al** (-chōō əl) *adj.* **—tex′tu·al·ly,** *adv.*

text′book′, *n.* student's book of study.

tex′tile (teks′tīl, -til) *n.* **1.** woven material. **—***adj.* **2.** woven. **3.** of weaving.

tex′ture (teks′chər) *n.* characteristic surface or composition. **—tex′tur·al,** *adj.*

t/f true/false.

TFE *Chemistry.* tetrafluoroethylene; Teflon.

TFN till further notice.

tfr. transfer.

TFT thin-film transistor.

TFX *Military.* (in designations of aircraft) tactical fighter experimental.

TG 1. transformational-generative (grammar). **2.** transformational grammar.

tg *Trigonometry.* tangent.

T

t.g. *Biology.* type genus.

TGG transformational-generative grammar.

TGIF *Informal.* thank God it's Friday. Also, **T.G.I.F.**

tgl toggle.

tgn *Trigonometry.* tangent.

tgt target.

TGV a high-speed French passenger train. [from French *t(rain à) g(rande) v(itesse)* high-speed train]

Th. Thursday.

T.H. Territory of Hawaii.

Th 227 *Symbol, Chemistry.* radioactinium. Also, **Th-227**

Thai. Thailand.

thal′a•mus (thal′ə məs) *n.* part of brain that transmits and integrates sensory impulses.

tha•lid′o•mide′ (thə lid′ə mīd′) *n.* drug formerly used as sedative, found to cause fetal abnormalities.

thal′li•um (thal′ē əm) *n.* rare metallic element.

than (*th*an, *th*en; *unstressed th*ən, ən) *conj.* particle introducing second member of comparison.

thank (thangk) *v.* **1.** express gratitude for. —*n.* **2.** (*usually pl.*) expression of gratitude. —**thank′ful,** *adj.* —**thank′less,** *adj.* —**thanks′giv′ing,** *n.*

Thanksgiving Day, festival in acknowledgment of divine favor, celebrated in U.S. on fourth Thursday of November and in Canada on second Monday of October.

that (*th*at; *unstressed th*ət) *pron., pl.* **those** (*th*ōz), *adj., adv., conj.* —*pron., adj.* **1.** demonstrative word indicating **a.** the person, thing, etc., more remote. **b.** one of two persons, etc., pointed out or mentioned before (opposed to **this**). **2.** relative pronoun used as: **a.** subject or object of relative clause. **b.** object of preposition. —*adv.* **3.** to that extent. —*conj.* **4.** word used to introduce dependent clause or one expressing reason, result, etc.

thatch (thach) *n.* **1.** rushes, leaves, etc., for covering roofs. —*v.* **2.** cover with thatch.

thaw (thô) *v.* **1.** melt. **2.** remove ice or frost from. —*n.* **3.** act or instance of thawing.

Th.B. Bachelor of Theology. [from Latin *Theologicae Baccalaureus*]

THC *Pharmacology.* a compound, $C_{21}H_{30}O_2$, the active component in cannabis preparations. [*t(etra)h(ydro)c(annabinol)*]

thd 1. thread. **2.** total harmonic distortion.

Th.D. Doctor of Theology. [from Latin *Theologicae Doctor*]

the (*stressed th*ē; *unstressed before a consonant th*ə, *unstressed before a vowel th*ē) *def. article.* **1.** word used, esp. before nouns, with specifying effect. —*adv.* **2.** word used to modify comparative or superlative form of adjective or adverb.

theat. 1. theater. **2.** theatrical.

the′a•ter (thē′ə tər, thē′ə′-) *n.* **1.** building for dramatic presentations, etc. **2.** dramatic art.

3. place of action. Also, **the′a•tre.** —**the•at′-ri•cal** (-ə′tri kəl) *adj.* —**the•at′ri•cal•ly,** *adv.*

thee (thē) *pron. Archaic.* you.

theft (theft) *n.* act or instance of stealing.

their (thâr; *unstressed th*ər) *pron.* **1.** possessive form of **they** used before noun. **2.** (*pl.*) that which belongs to them.

the′ism (thē′iz əm) *n.* belief in one God. —**the′ist,** *n.* —**the•is′tic** (-is′tik) *adj.*

them (*th*em; *unstressed th*əm, əm) *pron.* objective case of **they.**

theme (thēm) *n.* **1.** subject of discourse, etc. **2.** short essay. **3.** melody. —**the•mat′ic** (-mat′ik) *adj.*

them•selves′ (*th*əm selvz′, *th*em′-) *pron.* emphatic or reflexive form of **them.**

then (*th*en) *adv.* **1.** at that time. **2.** soon afterward. **3.** at another time. **4.** besides. **5.** in that case. —*adj.* **6.** being such at that time.

thence (*th*ens) *adv.* **1.** from that place or time. **2.** therefore.

thence′forth′ (*th*ens′fôrth′, *th*ens′fôrth′) *adv.* from that place or time on. Also, **thence′for′ward.**

the•oc′ra•cy (thē ok′rə sē) *n., pl.* **-cies. 1.** government in which authorities claim to carry out divine law. **2.** government by priests. —**the′o•crat′ic** (-ə krat′ik) *adj.*

theol. 1. theologian. **2.** theological. **3.** theology.

the•ol′o•gy (-ol′ə jē) *n.* study of God and of God's relations to the universe. —**the′o•lo′gian** (-ə lō′jən, -jē ən) *n.* —**the′o•log′i•cal** (-loj′i kəl) *adj.*

theor. 1. theorem. **2.** theoretical.

the′o•rem (thē′ər əm, thēr′əm) *n.* **1.** *Math.* statement embodying something to be proved. **2.** rule or law, esp. one expressed by equation or formula.

the′o•ret′i•cal (thē′ə ret′i kəl) *adj.* **1.** in theory. **2.** not practical. **3.** speculative. —**the′o•ret′i•cal•ly,** *adv.*

the′o•ry (thē′ə rē, thēr′ē) *n., pl.* **-ries. 1.** proposition used to explain class of phenomena. **2.** proposed explanation. **3.** principles. —**the′o•rist,** *n.* —**the′o•rize′,** *v.*

theos. 1. theosophical. **2.** theosophy.

the•os′o•phy (thē os′ə fē) *n.* any of various forms of thought based on mystical insight into the divine nature.

ther′a•py (ther′ə pē) *n., pl.* **-pies. 1.** treatment of disease. **2.** psychotherapy. —**ther′a•pist** (-pist) *n.* —**ther′a•peu′tic** (-pyōō′tik) *adj.* —**ther′a•peu′ti•cal•ly,** *adv.* —**ther′a•peu′tics,** *n.*

there (thâr; *unstressed th*ər) *adv.* **1.** in or at that place, point, matter, respect, etc. **2.** to that place. —**there′a•bout′,** **there′a•bouts′,** *adv.* —**there′af′ter,** *adv.* —**there•by′,** *adv.* —**there•for′,** *adv.* —**there•from′,** *adv.* —**there•in′,** *adv.* —**there•in′to,** *adv.* —**there•to′,** *adv.* —**there•un′der,** *adv.*

there′fore′, *adv.* consequently.

there•of′, *adv.* of or from that.

there•on′, *adv.* **1.** on that. **2.** immediately after that.

there′•up•on′, *adv.* **1.** immediately after that. **2.** because of that. **3.** with reference to that.

there•with′, *adv.* with or in addition to that.

therm. thermometer.

ther′mal (thûr′məl) *adj.* of heat.

thermodynam. thermodynamics.

ther′mo•dy•nam′ics (thûr′mō dī nam′iks) *n.* science concerned with relations between heat and mechanical energy or work.

ther•mom′e•ter (thər mom′i tər) *n.* instrument for measuring temperature. —**ther′mo•met′•ric** (thûr′mə me′trik) *adj.*

ther′mo•nu′cle•ar (thûr′mō-) *adj.* of nuclear-fusion reactions at extremely high temperatures.

ther′mo•plas′tic (thûr′mə-) *adj.* **1.** soft and pliable whenever heated, as some plastics, without change of inherent properties. —*n.* **2.** such plastic.

Ther′mos (thûr′məs) *n. Trademark.* container with vacuum between double walls for heat insulation.

ther′mo•sphere′, *n.* region of upper atmosphere in which temperature increases continually with altitude.

ther′mo•stat′ (-mə stat′) *n.* device regulating temperature of heating system, etc. —**ther′mo•stat′ic**, *adj.*

Thes. *Bible.* Thessalonians. Also, **Thess.**

the•sau′rus (thi sôr′əs) *n., pl.* **-sauruses, -sauri** (-sôr′ī). book of synonyms and antonyms.

these (thēz) *pron.* pl. of **this.**

the′sis (thē′sis) *n., pl.* **-ses** (-sēz). **1.** proposition to be proved. **2.** essay based on research.

thes′pi•an (thes′pē ən) *adj.* **1.** of dramatic art. —*n.* **2.** actor or actress.

they (thā) *pron.* nominative plural of **he, she,** and **it.**

T.H.I. temperature-humidity index. Also, **thi**

thi′a•mine (thī′ə min, -mēn′) *n.* vitamin B1. Also, **thi′a•min.**

thick (thik) *adj.* **1.** not thin. **2.** in depth. **3.** compact. **4.** numerous. **5.** dense. **6.** husky. **7.** slow-witted. —*adv.* **8.** so as to be thick. —*n.* **9.** something thick. —**thick′en,** *v.* —**thick′en•er,** *n.* —**thick′en•ing,** *n.* —**thick′ly,** *adv.* —**thick′ness,** *n.*

thick′et, *n.* thick growth of shrubs, bushes, etc.

thick′set′, *adj.* **1.** set thickly; dense. **2.** with heavy or solid body.

thick′-skinned′, *adj.* **1.** having thick skin. **2.** not sensitive to criticism or contempt.

thief (thēf) *n., pl.* **thieves** (thēvz). person who steals. —**thieve,** *v.,* **thieved, thieving.** —**thiev′er•y** (thē′və rē) *n.*

thigh (thī) *n.* part of leg between hip and knee.

thigh′bone′, *n.* femur.

thim′ble (thim′bəl) *n.* cap to protect finger while sewing.

thin (thin) *adj.,* **thinner, thinnest,** *v.,* **thinned, thinning.** —*adj.* **1.** having little extent between opposite sides; slender. **2.** lean. **3.** scanty. **4.** rarefied; diluted. **5.** flimsy. **6.** weak. —*v.* **7.** make or become thinner. —**thin•ner,** *n.* —**thin′ly,** *adv.* —**thin•ness,** *n.*

thing (thing) *n.* **1.** inanimate object. **2.** entity. **3.** matter. **4.** item.

think (thingk) *v.,* **thought** (thôt), **thinking. 1.** conceive in mind. **2.** meditate. **3.** believe. —**think′er,** *n.* —**think′a•ble,** *adj.*

think tank, research organization employed to analyze problems and plan future developments.

thin′-skinned′, *adj.* **1.** having thin skin. **2.** sensitive to criticism or contempt.

third (thûrd) *adj.* **1.** next after second. —*n.* **2.** next after the second. **3.** any of three equal parts.

third′-class′, *adj.* of the lowest class or quality.

third degree, *Chiefly U.S.* use of brutal measures by police (or others) in extorting information or confession.

third dimension, 1. thickness or depth. **2.** aspect that heightens reality.

third party, 1. party to case or quarrel who is incidentally involved. **2.** in two-party political system, usu. temporary party composed of independents.

third′-rate′, *adj.* distinctly inferior.

Third World, developing countries of Asia, Africa, and Latin America.

thirst (thûrst) *n.* **1.** sensation caused by need of drink. —*v.* **2.** be thirsty. —**thirst′y,** *adj.* —**thirst′i•ly,** *adv.* —**thirst′i•ness,** *n.*

thir′teen′ (thûr′tēn′) *n., adj.* ten plus three. —**thir•teenth′,** *adj., n.*

thir′ty (thûr′tē) *n., adj.* ten times three. —**thir′ti•eth,** *adj., n.*

this (this) *pron., pl.* **these** (thēz). *adj., adv.* —*pron., adj.* **1.** demonstrative word indicating something as just mentioned, present, near, etc. —*adv.* **2.** to the indicated extent.

this′tle (this′əl) *n.* prickly plant.

thith′er (thith′ər, thith′-) *adv.* to that place, point, etc.

thkf *Electronics.* thick film.

thkns thickness.

thm *Physics.* therm.

Th.M. Master of Theology.

thml thermal.

thmom thermometer.

thms *Electronics.* thermistor.

thnf *Electronics.* thin film.

thnr thinner.

tho (thō) *conj., adv. Informal.* though.

thong (thông) *n.* **1.** strip of leather. **2.** sandal with strip of leather, etc., passing through first two toes.

T

tho′rax (thôr′aks) *n., pl.* **thoraxes, thoraces** (thôr′ə sēz′). part of trunk between neck and abdomen. **—tho•rac′ic** (thô ras′ik) *adj.*

thor′i•um (thôr′ē əm) *n.* grayish-white radioactive metallic element.

thorn (thôrn) *n.* sharp spine on plant. **—thorn′y,** *adj.*

thor′ough (thûr′ō, thur′ō) *adj.* complete. **—thor′ough•ly,** *adv.* **—thor′ough•ness,** *n.*

thor′ough•bred′ (-ō bred′, -ə bred′) *adj.* **1.** of pure breed. **2.** well-bred. **—***n.* **3.** thoroughbred animal or person.

thor′ough•fare′, *n.* road, street, etc., open at both ends.

thor′ough•go•ing, *adj.* doing things thoroughly.

those (*ħ*ōz) *pron., adj.* pl. of **that.**

thou (*ħ*ou) *pron.* you (now little used except provincially, archaically, in poetry or elevated prose, in addressing God, and by the Friends).

though (*ħ*ō) *conj.* **1.** notwithstanding that. **2.** even if. **3.** nevertheless. **—***adv.* **4.** however.

thought (thôt) *n.* **1.** mental activity. **2.** idea. **3.** purpose. **4.** regard.

thought′ful, *adj.* **1.** meditative. **2.** heedful. **3.** considerate. **—thought′ful•ly,** *adv.* **—thought′ful•ness,** *n.*

thought′less, *adj.* **1.** showing lack of thought. **2.** careless; inconsiderate. **—thought′less•ly,** *adv.*

thou′sand (thou′zənd) *n., adj.* ten times one hundred. **—thou′sandth,** *adj., n.*

Thr *Biochemistry.* threonine.

thr threshold.

thrall (thrôl) *n.* **1.** person in bondage; slave. **2.** slavery; bondage. **—thrall′dom, thral′-dom,** *n.*

thrash (thrash) *v.* **1.** beat thoroughly. **2.** toss wildly. **—thrash′er,** *n.*

thread (thred) *n.* **1.** fine spun cord of flax, cotton, etc. **2.** filament. **3.** helical ridge of screw. **4.** connected sequence. **—***v.* **5.** pass end of thread through needle's eye. **6.** fix beads, etc., on thread.

thread′bare′, *adj.* shabby.

threat (thret) *n.* menace. **—threat′en,** *v.* **—threat′en•er,** *n.*

three (thrē) *n., adj.* two plus one.

3b *Baseball.* **1.** third base. **2.** triple (3-base hit).

three′-di•men′sion•al, *adj.* having or seeming to have depth as well as width and height.

three′fold′, *adj.* **1.** having three parts. **2.** three times as great.

three R's, reading, writing, and arithmetic.

three score, *adj.* sixty.

thren′o•dy (thren′ə dē) *n., pl.* **-dies.** song of lamentation.

thresh (thresh) *v.* separate grain or seeds from a plant. **—thresh′er,** *n.*

thresh′old (thresh′ōld, -hōld) *n.* **1.** doorway sill. **2.** entrance. **3.** beginning; border.

thrice (thrīs) *adv.* three times.

thrift (thrift) *n.* frugality. **—thrift′less,** *adj.*

thrift shop, store that sells secondhand goods.

thrift′y, *adj.,* **-ier, -iest.** saving; frugal. **—thrift′i•ly,** *adv.* **—thrift′i•ness,** *n.*

thrill (thril) *v.* **1.** affect with sudden keen emotion. **2.** vibrate. **—***n.* **3.** sudden wave of keen emotion or excitement.

thrill′er, *n.* suspenseful play or story.

thrive (thrīv) *v.,* **thrived, thriving.** flourish.

thrmo thermostat.

throat (thrōt) *n.* passage from mouth to stomach or lungs.

throat′y, *adj.,* **-ier, -iest.** (of sound) husky; hoarse.

throb (throb) *v.,* **throbbed, throbbing,** *n.* **—***v.* **1.** beat violently or rapidly. **2.** vibrate. **—***n.* **3.** act of throbbing.

throe (thrō) *n.* **1.** spasm. **2.** (*pl.*) pangs.

throm•bo′sis (throm bō′sis) *n.* clotting of blood in circulatory system.

throm′bus (-bəs) *n., pl.* **-bi** (-bī). clot formed in thrombosis.

throne (thrōn) *n.* official chair of sovereign, bishop, etc.

throng (thrông) *n., v.* crowd.

throt throttle.

throt′tle (throt′l) *n., v.,* **-tled, -tling. —***n.* **1.** device controlling flow of fuel. **—***v.* **2.** choke. **3.** check.

through (thrōō) *prep.* **1.** in at one end and out at other. **2.** during all of. **3.** having finished. **4.** by means or reason of. **—***adv.* **5.** in at one end and out at other. **6.** all the way. **7.** to the end. **8.** finished. **—***adj.* **9.** passing through.

through•out′, *prep.* **1.** in all parts of. **—***adv.* **2.** in every part, etc.

throw (thrō) *v.,* **threw** (thrōō), **thrown, throwing,** *n.* **—***v.* **1.** propel or cast. **2.** fell in wrestling. **3.** host. **4.** confuse. **—***n.* **5.** act of throwing. **—throw′er,** *n.*

throw′a•way′, *adj.* **1.** to be discarded after use. **—***n.* **2.** notice distributed free.

throw′back′, *n.* **1.** setback or check. **2.** reversion to ancestral type.

thrt throat.

thru (thrōō) *prep., adv., adj. Informal.* through.

thrum (thrum) *v.,* **thrummed, thrumming,** *n.* **—***v.* **1.** to play on stringed instrument, as guitar, by plucking strings. **2.** to tap with fingers. **—***n.* **3.** act or sound of thrumming. **—thrum′mer,** *n.*

thrush (thrush) *n.* **1.** migratory singing bird. **2.** fungal disease of mouth.

thrust (thrust) *v.,* **thrust, thrusting,** *n.* **—***v.* **1.** push; shove. **2.** stab. **—***n.* **3.** push; lunge. **4.** stab.

thru′way′ (thrōō′wā′) *n.* expressway providing direct route between distant areas.

thstm thunderstorm.

Thu. Thursday.

thud (thud) *n., v.,* **thudded, thudding.** —*n.* **1.** dull striking sound. —*v.* **2.** make thudding sound.

thug (thug) *n.* violent criminal.

thumb (thum) *n.* **1.** short, thick finger next to the forefinger. —*v.* **2.** manipulate with thumb.

thumb'nail', *n.* **1.** nail of thumb. —*adj.* **2.** brief and concise.

thumb'screw', *n.* **1.** instrument of torture that compresses thumbs. **2.** screw turned by thumb and finger.

thumb'tack', *n.* **1.** tack with large, flat head. —*v.* **2.** secure with thumbtack.

thump (thump) *n.* **1.** blow from something thick and heavy. —*v.* **2.** pound.

thump'ing, *adj.* **1.** exceptional. **2.** of or like a thump.

thun'der (thun'dər) *n.* **1.** loud noise accompanying lightning. —*v.* **2.** give forth thunder. **3.** speak loudly. —**thun'der•ous,** *adj.* —**thun'der•storm',** *n.* —**thun'der•show'-er,** *n.*

thun'der•bolt', *n.* flash of lightning with thunder.

thun'der•clap', *n.* crash of thunder.

thun'der•cloud', *n.* electrically charged cloud producing lightning and thunder.

thun'der•head', *n.* mass of cumulus clouds warning of thunderstorms.

thun'der•struck', *adj.* astonished.

Thurs., Thursday.

Thurs'day (thûrz'dā, -dē) *n.* fifth day of week.

thus (thus) *adv.* **1.** in this way. **2.** consequently. **3.** to this extent.

thwack (thwak) *v.* **1.** strike hard with something flat. —*n.* **2.** thwacking blow.

thwart (thwôrt) *v.* **1.** frustrate; prevent. —*n.* **2.** seat across a boat.

thwr thrower.

thy (thī) *adj. Archaic.* your.

thyme (tīm; *spelling pron.* thīm) *n.* plant of mint family.

thy'mus (thī'məs) *n.* gland at base of neck that aids in production of T cells.

thyr *Electronics.* thyristor.

thy'roid (thī'roid) *adj.* of thyroid gland.

thyroid gland, ductless gland near windpipe, involved in controlling metabolism and growth.

thy•self' (thī self') *pron.* **1.** emphatic appositive to **thou** or **thee. 2.** substitute for reflexive **thee.**

THz terahertz.

Ti *Symbol, Chemistry.* titanium.

TIA *Medicine.* transient ischemic attack.

TIAA Teachers Insurance and Annuity Association of America.

ti•ar'a (tē ar'ə, -är'ə, -âr'ə) *n.* woman's ornamental coronet.

Ti•bet'an (ti bet'n) *n.* native or language of Tibet. —**Tibetan,** *adj.*

tib'i•a (tib'ē ə) *n., pl.* **-iae** (-ē ē'), **-ias.** bone from knee to ankle. —**tib'i•al,** *adj.*

tic (tik) *n.* sudden twitch.

tick (tik) *n.* **1.** soft, recurring click. **2.** blood-sucking mitelike animal. **3.** cloth case of mattress, pillow, etc. —*v.* **4.** produce tick (def. 1).

tick'er, *n.* **1.** one that ticks. **2.** telegraphic instrument that prints stock prices and market reports, etc., on tape (**ticker tape**). **3.** *Slang.* heart.

tick'et (-it) *n.* **1.** slip indicating right to admission, transportation, etc. **2.** tag. **3.** summons for traffic or parking violation. —*v.* **4.** attach ticket to.

tick'ing, *n.* cotton fabric for ticks (def. 3).

tick'le, *v.,* **-led, -ling,** *n.* —*v.* **1.** touch lightly so as to make tingle or itch. **2.** gratify. **3.** amuse. —*n.* **4.** act of tickling. —**tick'lish,** *adj.* —**tick'lish•ly,** *adv.*

tickler file, file for reminding user at appropriate times of matters needing attention.

tick'-tack-toe' (tik'tak tō') *n.* game for two players, each trying to complete row of three X's or three O's on nine-square grid.

t.i.d. (in prescriptions) three times a day. [from Latin *ter in diē*]

tidal wave, large, destructive ocean wave produced by earthquake or the like.

tid'bit' (tid'bit') *n.* choice bit.

tid'dly•winks' (tid'lē wingks') *n.* game in which small disks are snapped with larger disks into cup.

tide (tīd) *n., v.,* **tided, tiding.** —*n.* **1.** periodic rise and fall of ocean waters. **2.** stream. —*v.* **3.** help over difficulty. —**tid'al,** *adj.*

tide'land', *n.* land alternately exposed and covered by tide.

tide'wa'ter, *n.* **1.** water affected by tide. —*adj.* **2.** of lowland near sea.

ti'dings (tī'dingz) *n.pl.* news.

ti'dy (tī'dē) *adj.,* **-dier, -diest,** *v.,* **-died, -dy-ing.** —*adj.* **1.** neat; orderly. **2.** fairly large. —*v.* **3.** make tidy. —**ti'di•ly,** *adv.* —**ti'di-ness,** *n.*

tie (tī) *v.,* **tied, tying,** *n.* —*v.* **1.** bind with cord, etc. **2.** confine. **3.** equal or be equal. —*n.* **4.** something used to tie or join. **5.** necktie. **6.** equality in scores, votes, etc. **7.** contest in which this occurs. **8.** bond of kinship, affection, etc.

tie'-dye'ing, *n.* method of dyeing with sections of garment bound so as not to receive dye. —**tie'-dyed',** *adj.*

tie'-in', *n.* link, association, or relationship.

tier (tēr) *n.* row or rank.

tie'-up', *n.* **1.** undesired stoppage of business, traffic, etc. **2.** connection.

tif telephone interference factor.

tiff (tif) *n.* petty quarrel.

ti'ger (tī'gər) *n.* large striped Asian feline. —**ti'gress,** *n.fem.*

tiger lily, lily with flowers of dull-orange color spotted with black.

tight (tīt) *adj.* **1.** firmly in place. **2.** taut. **3.** fitting closely. **4.** impervious to fluids. **5.** stingy. —**tight′en,** *v.* —**tight′ly,** *adv.* —**tight′ness,** *n.*

tight′-fist′ed, *adj.* stingy.

tight′-lipped′, *adj.* reluctant to speak.

tight′rope′, *n.* taut wire or cable on which acrobats perform.

tights, *n.pl.* close-fitting pants, worn esp. by acrobats, etc.

tight′wad′, *n. Slang.* stingy person.

til′de (til′də) *n.* diacritical mark (˜) placed over letter.

tile (tīl) *n., v.,* **tiled, tiling.** —*n.* **1.** thin piece of baked clay, etc., used as covering. —*v.* **2.** cover with tiles.

til′ing, *n.* **1.** operation of covering with tiles. **2.** tiles collectively.

till (til) *prep., conj.* **1.** until. —*v.* **2.** labor on to raise crops. **3.** plow. —*n.* **4.** drawer in back of counter for money. —**till′a•ble,** *adj.* —**till′age,** *n.*

—**Usage.** TILL and UNTIL are used interchangeably in speech and writing: *It rained till/until nearly midnight.* TILL is not a shortened form of UNTIL and is not spelled *'till.* 'TIL is usually considered a spelling error, though commonly used in business and advertising: *open 'til ten.*

till′er *n.* **1.** one that tills. **2.** handle on head of rudder.

tilt (tilt) *v.* **1.** lean; slant. **2.** charge or engage in joust. —*n.* **3.** act of tilting. **4.** slant.

Tim. *Bible.* Timothy.

tim′bale (tim′bəl) *n.* **1.** a preparation of minced meat, etc., cooked in mold. **2.** this mold, usually of paste, and sometimes fried.

tim′ber (tim′bər) *n.* **1.** wood of growing trees. **2.** trees. **3.** wood for building. **4.** wooden beam, etc. —*v.* **5.** furnish or support with timber. —**tim′bered,** *adj.*

tim′ber•line′, *n.* altitude or latitude at which timber ceases to grow.

timber wolf, large brindled wolf of forested Canada and northern United States.

tim′bre (tam′bər, tim′-) *n.* characteristic quality of a sound.

time (tīm) *n., v.,* **timed, timing.** —*n.* **1.** duration. **2.** period of time. **3.** occasion. **4.** point in time. **5.** appointed or proper time. **6.** meter of music. **7.** rate. —*v.* **8.** determine or record time. —**tim′er,** *n.*

time clock, clock with attachment that records times of arrival and departure of employees.

time′-hon′ored, *adj.* long valued or used; traditional.

time′keep′er, *n.* **1.** person who keeps time. **2.** timepiece, esp. as regards accuracy.

time′less, *adj.* **1.** eternal. **2.** referring to no particular time.

time line, 1. linear representation of events in the order in which they occurred. **2.** schedule.

time′ly, *adj.,* **-lier, -liest,** *adv.* —*adj.* **1.** opportune. —*adv.* **2.** opportunely.

time′-out′, *n.* brief suspension of activity, as in sports contest.

time′piece′, *n.* clock; watch.

times, *prep.* multiplied by.

time′-shar′ing, *n.* **1.** plan in which several people share cost of vacation home. **2.** system in which users at different terminals simultaneously use a single computer.

time′ta′ble, *n.* schedule of times of departures, work completion, etc.

time′worn′, *adj.* **1.** impaired by time. **2.** trite.

time zone, one of 24 divisions of globe coinciding with meridians at successive hours from observatory at Greenwich, England.

tim′id (tim′id) *adj.* **1.** easily alarmed. **2.** shy. —**tim′id•ly,** *adv.* —**ti•mid′i•ty, tim′id•ness,** *n.*

tim′ing (tī′ming) *n.* control of speed or occasion of an action, event, etc., so that it occurs at the proper moment.

tim′or•ous (tim′ər əs) *adj.* **1.** fearful. **2.** timid. —**tim′or•ous•ly,** *adv.* —**tim′or•ous•ness,** *n.*

tim′o•thy (tim′ə thē) *n., pl.* **-thies.** coarse fodder grass.

tim′pa•ni (tim′pə nē) *n.pl.* kettledrums. —**tim′pa•nist,** *n.*

tin (tin) *n., v.,* **tinned, tinning.** —*n.* **1.** malleable metallic element. —*v.* **2.** cover with tin. —**tin′ny,** *adj.*

tinct. *Pharmacology.* tincture.

tinc′ture (tingk′chər) *n.* medicinal solution in alcohol.

tin′der (tin′dər) *n.* inflammable substance. —**tin′der•box′,** *n.*

tine (tīn) *n.* prong of fork.

tin′foil′, *n.* tin or alloy in thin sheet, used as wrapping.

tinge (tinj) *v.,* **tinged, tingeing** or **tinging,** *n.* —*v.* **1.** impart trace of color, taste, etc., to. —*n.* **2.** slight trace.

tin′gle (ting′gəl) *v.,* **-gled, -gling,** *n.* —*v.* **1.** feel or cause slight stings. —*n.* **2.** tingling sensation.

tink′er (ting′kər) *n.* **1.** mender of pots, kettles, pans, etc. —*v.* **2.** do the work of a tinker. **3.** work or repair unskillfully or clumsily.

tin′kle (ting′kəl) *v.,* **-kled, -kling,** *n.* —*v.* **1.** make light ringing sounds. —*n.* **2.** tinkling sound.

tin plate, thin iron or steel sheet coated with tin.

tin′sel (tin′səl) *n.* **1.** glittering metal in strips, etc. **2.** anything showy and worthless.

tint (tint) *n.* **1.** color or hue. —*v.* **2.** apply tint to.

tin·tin·nab·u·la·tion (tin'ti nab'yə lā'shən) *n.* ringing or sound of bells.

tin·type', *n.* old type of positive photograph made on sensitized sheet of iron or tin.

ti·ny (tī'nē) *adj.*, **-nier, -niest.** very small.

-tion, suffix meaning action or process, result of action, or state or condition.

tip (tip) *n.*, *v.*, **tipped, tipping.** —*n.* **1.** small gift of money. **2.** piece of private information. **3.** useful hint. **4.** tap. **5.** slender or pointed end. **6.** top. —*v.* **7.** give tip to. **8.** furnish with tip. **9.** tilt. **10.** overturn. **11.** tap. —**tip'per,** *n.*

tip'-off', *n.* *Slang.* hint or warning.

tip'pet, *n.* scarf.

tip'ple, *v.*, **-pled, -pling.** drink alcoholic liquor. —**tip'pler,** *n.*

tip'ster (-stər) *n.* person who sells tips.

tip'sy, *adj.*, **-sier, -siest.** slightly intoxicated. —**tip'si·ly,** *adv.* —**tip'si·ness,** *n.*

tip'toe', *n.*, *v.*, **-toed, -toeing.** —*n.* **1.** tip of toe. —*v.* **2.** move on tiptoes.

tip'top' (-top', -top') *n.* **1.** extreme top. —*adj.* **2.** situated at very top. **3.** *Informal.* of highest excellence.

ti·rade (tī'rād, tī rād') *n.* long denunciation or speech.

ti·ra·mi·su (tir'ə mē'sŏŏ) *n.* Italian dessert.

tire (tīᵊr) *v.*, **tired, tiring,** *n.* —*v.* **1.** exhaust strength, interest, patience, etc. —*n.* **2.** hoop of metal, rubber, etc., around wheel. —**tire'less,** *adj.* —**tire'some,** *adj.*

tired (tīᵊrd) *adj.* **1.** exhausted; fatigued. **2.** weary. —**tired'ly,** *adv.* —**tired'ness,** *n.*

TIROS (tī'rōs), television and infrared observation satellite.

tis'sue (tish'ŏŏ) *n.* **1.** substance composing organism. **2.** light, gauzy fabric.

tissue paper, very thin paper.

Tit. *Bible.* Titus.

tit. title.

ti'tan (tīt'n) *n.* person or thing of great size or power. —**ti·tan'ic** (tī tan'ik) *adj.*

ti·tan'i·um (tī tā'nē əm) *n.* corrosion-resistant metallic element, used to toughen steel.

tit for tat (tit' fər tat') equivalent given in retaliation, repartee, etc.

tithe (tīth) *n.* tenth part.

ti'tian (tish'ən) *n.*, *adj.* yellowish or golden brown.

tit'il·late' (tit'l āt') *v.*, **-lated, -lating.** **1.** tickle. **2.** excite agreeably. —**tit'il·la'tion,** *n.*

tit'i·vate' (-ə vāt') *v.*, **-vated, -vating.** make smart or spruce. —**tit'i·va'tion,** *n.*

ti'tle (tīt'l) *n.*, *v.*, **-tled, -tling.** —*n.* **1.** name of book, picture, etc. **2.** caption. **3.** appellation, esp. of rank. **4.** championship. **5.** right to something. **6.** document showing this. —*v.* **7.** furnish with title.

tit'mouse' (tit'mous') *n.*, *pl.* **-mice.** small bird having crest and conical bill.

tit'ter (tit'ər) *n.* **1.** restrained laugh. —*v.* **2.** laugh in this way.

tit'tle (tit'l) *n.* very small thing.

tit'u·lar (tich'ə lər, tit'yə-) *adj.* **1.** of or having a title. **2.** being so in title only. —**tit'u·lar·ly,** *adv.*

tiz'zy (tiz'ē) *n.*, *pl.*·**-zies.** *Slang.* dither.

TKO *Boxing.* technical knockout. Also, **T.K.O.**

tkt. ticket.

TL 1. target language. **2.** trade-last. **3.** truckload.

Tl *Symbol, Chemistry.* thallium.

TL. (in Turkey) lira; liras.

T/L time loan.

T.L. 1. Also, **t.l.** trade-last. **2.** *Publishing.* trade list.

TLC tender loving care. Also, **T.L.C., t.l.c.**

tlg telegraph.

tlld total load.

tlmy telemetry.

t.l.o. *Insurance.* total loss only.

TLR *Photography.* twin-lens reflex camera.

tlscp telescope.

TM 1. technical manual. **2.** trademark. **3.** Transcendental Meditation.

Tm *Symbol, Chemistry.* thulium.

t.m. true mean.

tmbr timber.

TMC The Movie Channel (a cable television channel).

tmd timed.

TMF The Menninger Foundation.

tmfl time of flight.

tmg timing.

TMI Three Mile Island.

TMJ *Anatomy.* temporomandibular joint.

TML 1. *Chemistry.* tetramethyllead. **2.** three-mile limit.

TMO telegraph money order.

tmpl template.

TMV tobacco mosaic virus.

TN, Tennessee.

TNB *Chemistry.* trinitrobenzene, especially the 1,3,5- isomer.

TNF *Biochemistry.* tumor necrosis factor.

tng 1. tongue. **2.** training.

tnk trunk.

tnl tunnel.

TNN The Nashville Network (a cable television channel).

tnpk. turnpike.

tnsl tensile.

tnsn tension.

TNT, trinitrotoluene.

tntv tentative.

to (tŏŏ; *unstressed* tŏŏ, tə) *prep.* **1.** particle specifying point reached. **2.** sign of the infinitive. —*adv.* **3.** toward. **4. to and fro,** to and from place or thing.

T

TOA time of arrival.

toad (tōd) *n.* tailless, froglike amphibian.

toad'stool', *n.* fungus with umbrellalike cap.

toad'y, *n.*, *pl.* **toadies**, *v.*, **toadied**, **toadying.** —*n.* **1.** fawning flatterer. —*v.* **2.** be toady.

toast (tōst) *n.* **1.** words said before drinking to a person or event. **2.** sliced bread browned by heat. —*v.* **3.** propose as toast. **4.** make toast.

toast'er, *n.* appliance for toasting bread.

toast'mas'ter, *n.* person who introduces the after-dinner speakers or proposes toasts. —**toast'mis'tress,** *n.fem.*

toast'y, *adj.*, **toastier, toastiest.** cozily warm.

Tob. *Bible.* Tobit.

to•bac'co (tə bak'ō) *n.*, *pl.* **-cos, -coes. 1.** plant with leaves prepared for smoking or chewing. **2.** the prepared leaves.

to•bac'co•nist (-bak'ə nist) *n.* dealer in or manufacturer of tobacco.

to•bog'gan (tə bog'ən) *n.* **1.** long, narrow, flat-bottomed sled. —*v.* **2.** coast on toboggan.

toc•ca'ta (tə kä'tə) *n. Music.* keyboard composition in style of improvisation.

toc'sin (tok'sin) *n.* signal, esp. of alarm.

to•day' (tə dā') *n.* **1.** this day, time, or period. —*adv.* **2.** on this day. **3.** at this period.

tod'dle (tod'l) *v.*, **-dled, -dling.** go with short, unsteady steps. —**tod'dler,** *n.*

tod'dy (tod'ē) *n.*, *pl.* **-dies.** drink made of alcoholic liquor and hot water, sweetened and sometimes spiced.

to-do' (tə dōō') *n.*, *pl.* **-dos.** *Informal.* fuss.

toe (tō) *n.* **1.** terminal digit of foot. **2.** part covering toes. —**toe'nail',** *n.*

TOEFL (tō'fəl), Test of English as a Foreign Language.

toe'hold', *n.* **1.** small niche that supports the toes. **2.** any slight advantage.

TOFC trailer-on-flatcar.

tof'fee (tô'fē) *n.* taffy.

to'fu (tō'fōō) *n.* soft cheeselike food made from curdled soybean milk.

to'ga (tō'gə) *n.* ancient Roman outer garment.

to•geth'er (tə geth'ər) *adv.* **1.** into or in proximity, association, or single mass. **2.** at same time. **3.** in cooperation.

to•geth'er•ness, *n.* warm fellowship.

togs, *n.pl. Informal.* clothes.

toil (toil) *n.* **1.** hard, exhausting work. —*v.* **2.** work hard. —**toil'er,** *n.*

toi'let (toi'lit) *n.* **1.** receptacle for excretion. **2.** bathroom. **3.** Also, **toi•lette'.** act or process of dressing.

toi'let•ry, *n.*, *pl.* **-ries.** article or preparation used in grooming oneself.

toilet water, scented liquid used as light perfume.

toil'some (-səm) *adj.* laborious or fatiguing. —**toil'some•ly,** *adv.* —**toil'some•ness,** *n.*

to•kay' (tō kā') *n.* **1.** rich, sweet, aromatic wine. **2.** the variety of grape from which it is made.

toke (tōk) *n.*, *v.*, **toked, toking.** *Slang.* —*n.* **1.** puff on marijuana cigarette. —*v.* **2.** puff or smoke (marijuana).

to'ken (tō'kən) *n.* **1.** thing expressing or representing something else. **2.** metal disk used as ticket, etc. —*adj.* **3.** being merely a token; minimal.

to'ken•ism, *n.* minimal conformity to law or social pressure.

tol tolerance.

tole (tōl) *n.* enameled or lacquered metal.

tol'er•a•ble (tol'ər ə bəl) *adj.* **1.** endurable. **2.** fairly good. —**tol'er•a•bly,** *adv.*

tol'er•ance (-əns) *n.* fairness toward different opinions, etc. —**tol'er•ant,** *adj.* —**tol'er•ant•ly,** *adv.*

tol'er•ate' (-ə rāt') *v.*, **-ated, -ating. 1.** allow. **2.** put up with. —**tol'er•a'tion,** *n.*

toll (tōl) *v.* **1.** sound bell slowly and repeatedly. —*n.* **2.** payment, as for right to travel. **3.** payment for long-distance telephone call.

toll'booth', *n.* booth where toll is collected.

tol'u•ene' (tol'yōō ēn') *n.* flammable liquid.

tom (tom) *n.* male of various animals.

tom'a•hawk' (tom'ə hôk') *n.* light ax used by North American Indians.

Tom and Jer'ry (jer'ē) hot drink of rum, milk, and beaten eggs.

to•ma'to (tə mā'tō) *n.*, *pl.* **-toes.** cultivated plant with pulpy, edible fruit.

tomb (tōōm) *n.* burial place for dead body; grave. —**tomb'stone',** *n.*

tom'boy' (tom'-) *n.* boisterous, romping girl. —**tom'boy'ish,** *adj.*

tom'cat', *n.* male cat.

Tom Col'lins (kol'inz) tall iced drink containing gin, lemon or lime juice, and carbonated water.

tome (tōm) *n.* large book.

tom'fool'er•y (tom'fōō'lə rē) *n.*, *pl.* **-eries.** foolish or silly behavior.

Tommy gun, *Slang.* type of submachine gun.

tom'my•rot', *n. Slang.* nonsense.

to•mog'ra•phy (tə mog'rə fē) *n.* method of making x-rays of selected plane of the body.

to•mor'row (tə môr'ō) *n.* **1.** day after this day. —*adv.* **2.** on day after this day.

tom'-tom', *n.* primitive drum.

ton (tun) *n.* **1.** unit of weight, equal to 2000 pounds (**short ton**) in U.S. and 2240 pounds (**long ton**) in Great Britain. **2.** *Naut.* unit of volume, equal to 100 cubic feet.

to•nal'i•ty (tō nal'i tē) *n.*, *pl.* **-ties. 1.** relation between tones of musical scales. **2.** the tones.

tone (tōn) *n.*, *v.*, **toned, toning.** —*n.* **1.** sound. **2.** quality of sound. **3.** quality, etc., of voice. **4.** firmness. **5.** expressive quality.

6. elegance; amenity. —*v.* **7.** give proper tone to. —**ton′al,** *adj.* —**ton′al·ly,** *adv.*

tone′-deaf′, *adj.* unable to distinguish differences in musical pitch.

tongs (tôngz) *n.pl.* two-armed implement for grasping.

tongue (tung) *n.* **1.** organ on floor of mouth, used for tasting, etc. **2.** language. **3.** tongue-like thing.

tongue′-lash′ing, *n.* severe scolding.

tongue′-tied′, *adj.* unable to speak, as from shyness.

tongue twister, sequence of words difficult to pronounce rapidly.

ton′ic (ton′ik) *n.* **1.** invigorating medicine. —*adj.* **2.** invigorating.

to·night′ (tə nīt′) *n.* **1.** this night. —*adv.* **2.** on this night.

tonn. tonnage.

ton′nage (tun′ij) *n.* **1.** carrying capacity or total volume of vessel. **2.** duty on cargo or tonnage. **3.** ships.

ton·neau′ (tu nō′) *n.*, *pl.* **-neaus, -neaux** (-nōz′). rear compartment of automobile with seats for passengers.

ton′sil (ton′səl) *n.* oval mass of tissue in throat.

ton·sil·lec′to·my (-sə lek′tə mē) *n.*, *pl.* **-mies.** removal of tonsils.

ton′sil·li′tis (-lī′tis) *n.* inflammation of tonsils.

ton·so′ri·al (ton sôr′ē əl) *adj.* of barbers.

ton′sure (ton′shər) *n.* **1.** shaving of head. **2.** shaved part of cleric's head.

to′ny (tō′nē) *adj.*, **-ier, -iest.** swank.

too (tōō) *adv.* **1.** also. **2.** excessively.

tool (tōōl) *n.* **1.** mechanical instrument, as hammer or saw. **2.** exploited person; dupe. —*v.* **3.** decorate with tool.

toot (tōōt) *v.* sound horn.

tooth (tōōth) *n.*, *pl.* **teeth** (tēth). **1.** hard body attached to jaw, used in chewing, etc. **2.** projection. **3.** taste, relish, etc. —**tooth′-ache′,** *n.* —**tooth′brush′,** *n.* —**tooth′-paste′,** *n.* —**tooth′pick′,** *n.*

tooth and nail, with all one's resources and energy.

tooth′some (-səm) *adj.* tasty.

tooth′y (tōō′thē, -thē) *adj.*, **toothier, toothi-est.** having or displaying conspicuous teeth.

top (top) *n.*, *v.*, **topped, topping.** —*n.* **1.** highest point, part, rank, etc. **2.** lid. **3.** child's spinning toy. **4.** separable upper part of clothing. —*v.* **5.** put top on. **6.** be top of. **7.** surpass.

to′paz (tō′paz) *n.* colored crystalline gem.

top brass, high-ranking officials.

top′coat′, *n.* light overcoat.

top′er (tō′pər) *n.* drunkard.

top′flight′ (top′-) *adj.* excellent.

top hat, man's tall silk hat.

top′-heav′y, *adj.* disproportionately heavy at top.

top′ic (top′ik) *n.* subject of discussion or writing.

top′i·cal, *adj.* **1.** of or dealing with matters of current interest. **2.** of topics. **3.** applied to local area. —**top′i·cal·ly,** *adv.*

top kick, *Mil. Slang.* first sergeant.

top′mast′, *n.* mast next above lower mast on sailing ship.

top′most, *adj.* highest.

top′notch′, *adj. Informal.* first-rate.

topog. 1. topographical. **2.** topography.

to·pog′ra·phy (tə pog′rə fē) *n.*, *pl.* **-phies.** description of features of geographical area. —**to·pog′ra·pher,** *n.* —**top′o·graph′ic** (top′ə graf′ik) **top′o·graph′i·cal,** *adj.*

top′per, *n.* **1.** one that tops. **2.** *Slang.* top hat. **3.** short coat worn by women.

top′ping, *n.* sauce or garnish placed on food.

top′ple, *v.*, **-pled, -pling.** fall; tumble.

top′sail′ (-sāl′; *Naut.* -səl) *n.* square sail next above lowest or chief sail.

top′-se′cret, *adj.* extremely secret.

top′soil′, *n.* fertile upper soil.

top′sy-tur′vy (top′sē tûr′vē) *adv., adj.* **1.** upside down. **2.** in confusion.

toque (tōk) *n.* hat with little or no brim.

tor (tôr) *n.* hill.

To′rah (tōr′ə, tôr′ə) *n.* **1.** five books of Moses; Pentateuch. **2.** (*also l.c.*) whole Jewish Scripture. Also, **To′ra.**

torch (tôrch) *n.* light carried in hand.

torch′bear′er, *n.* **1.** person who carries torch. **2.** leader in movement.

tor′e·a·dor′ (tôr′ē ə dôr′) *n.* bullfighter.

torenti torrential.

tor·ment′ *v.* (tôr ment′) **1.** afflict with great suffering. —*n.* (tôr′ment) **2.** agony. —**tor-men′tor, tor·ment′er,** *n.*

tor·na′do (tôr nā′dō) *n.*, *pl.* **-does, -dos.** destructive storm.

torndo tornado.

tor·pe′do (tôr pē′dō) *n.*, *pl.* **-does,** *v.*, **-doed, -doing.** —*n.* **1.** self-propelled missile launched in water and exploding on impact. —*v.* **2.** strike with torpedo.

torpedo boat, small fast warship used to launch torpedoes.

tor′pid (tôr′pid) *adj.* **1.** inactive; sluggish. **2.** dull; apathetic; lethargic. —**tor·pid′i·ty,** *n.* —**tor′pid·ly,** *adv.*

tor′por (-pər) *n.* **1.** suspension of physical activity. **2.** apathy.

torque (tôrk) *n.* rotating force.

tor′rent (tôr′ənt) *n.* rapid, violent stream. —**tor·ren′tial** (tô ren′shəl, tə-) *adj.* —**tor·ren′tial·ly,** *adv.*

tor′rid (tôr′id) *adj.* **1.** very hot. **2.** passionate.

Torrid Zone, part of earth's surface between tropics.

tor′sion (tôr′shən) *n.* **1.** act of twisting. **2.** twisting by two opposite torques. —**tor′sion·al,** *adj.*

T

tor'so (tôr'sō) *n., pl.* **-sos, -si.** trunk of body.

tort (tôrt) *n. Law.* civil wrong (other than breach of contract or trust) for which law requires damages.

torte (tôrt) *n., pl.* **tortes.** rich cake, made with eggs, nuts, and usu. no flour.

tor'tel•li'ni (tôr'tl ē'nē) *n. (used with sing. or pl. v.)* small ring-shaped pieces of pasta filled with meat or cheese.

tor•til'la (tôr tē'ə) *n.* flat, round bread of Mexico, made from cornmeal or wheat flour.

tor'toise (tôr'təs) *n.* turtle.

tor'toise•shell', *n.* **1.** horny brown and yellow shell of certain turtles, used for making combs, etc. **2.** synthetic tortoiseshell. —*adj.* **3.** colored like tortoiseshell.

tor'tu•ous (tôr'chōō əs) *adj.* **1.** twisting; winding. **2.** indirect. —**tor'tu•ous•ly**, *adv.* —**tor'tu•ous•ness**, *n.*

tor'ture (tôr'chər) *n., v.,* **-tured, -turing.** —*n.* **1.** infliction of great pain. —*v.* **2.** subject to torture. —**tor'tur•er**, *n.* —**tor'tur•ous**, *adj.*

To'ry (tôr'ē) *n., pl.* **-ries. 1.** (*also l.c.*) conservative. **2.** American supporter of Great Britain during Revolutionary period. —**To'ry•ism**, *n.*

TOS tape operating system.

toss (tôs) *v.* **1.** throw or pitch. **2.** pitch about. **3.** throw upward. —*n.* **4.** throw or pitch.

toss'up', *n.* **1.** tossing of coin to decide something by its fall. **2.** *Informal.* even chance.

tot (tot) *n.* small child.

to'tal (tōt'l) *adj., n., v.,* **-taled, -taling.** —*adj.* **1.** entire. **2.** utter; outright. —*n.* **3.** total amount. —*v.* **4.** add up. —**to•tal'i•ty** (-tal'i tē) *n.* —**to'tal•ly**, *adv.*

to•tal'i•tar'i•an (tō tal'i târ'ē ən) *adj.* of centralized government under sole control of one party. —**to•tal'i•tar'i•an•ism**, *n.*

tote (tōt) *v.,* **toted, toting**, *n. Informal.* —*v.* **1.** carry or bear, as burden. —*n.* **2.** act or course of toting. **3.** that which is toted. **4.** tote bag.

tote bag, open handbag.

to'tem (tō'təm) *n.* object in nature assumed as emblem of clan, family, or related group. —**to•tem'ic** (-tem'ik) *adj.*

totem pole, pole with totemic figures, erected by Indians of northwest coast of North America.

tot'ter (tot'ər) *v.* **1.** falter. **2.** sway as if about to fall.

tou'can (tōō'kan, -kän) *n.* large-beaked tropical American bird.

touch (tuch) *v.* **1.** put hand, finger, etc., in contact with something. **2.** come or be in contact. **3.** reach. **4.** affect with sympathy. **5.** refer to. —*n.* **6.** act or instance of touching. **7.** perception of things through contact. **8.** contact. —**touch'a•ble**, *adj.* —**touch'ing,** *adj.*

touch' and go', precarious condition.

touch'down', *n. Football.* act of player in touching ball down to ground behind opponent's goal line.

tou•ché' (tōō shā') *interj.* (used to acknowledge telling remark or rejoinder).

touched, *adj.* **1.** moved; stirred. **2.** slightly crazy; unbalanced.

touch'-me-not', *n.* yellow-flowered plant whose ripe seed vessels burst open when touched.

touch'stone', *n.* **1.** stone used to test purity of gold and silver by color produced when it is rubbed with them. **2.** any criterion.

touch'y, *adj.,* **-ier, -iest. 1.** irritable. **2.** requiring tact. —**touch'i•ness**, *n.*

tough (tuf) *adj.* **1.** not easily broken. **2.** difficult to chew. **3.** sturdy. **4.** pugnacious. **5.** trying. —*n.* **6.** ruffian. —**tough'en**, *v.* —**tough'ly**, *adv.* —**tough'ness**, *n.*

tou•pee' (tōō pā') *n.* wig or patch of false hair worn to cover bald spot.

tour (tōōr) *v.* **1.** travel or travel through, esp. for pleasure. —*n.* **2.** trip. **3.** period of duty. —**tour'ist**, *n.* —**tour'ism**, *n.*

tour'de force' (tōōr' də fôrs') *n., pl.* **tours de force.** exceptional achievement.

tour'ma•line' (tōōr'mə lin, -lēn') *n.* mineral occurring in various gems.

tour'na•ment (tōōr'nə mənt, tûr'-) *n.* **1.** meeting for contests. **2.** contest between mounted knights. **3.** competition involving number of rounds. Also, **tour'ney.**

tour'ni•quet (tûr'ni kit, tōōr'-) *n.* bandlike device for arresting bleeding by compressing blood vessels.

tou'sle (tou'zəl, -səl) *v.,* **-sled, -sling.** dishevel.

tout (tout) *Informal.* —*v.* **1.** solicit (business, votes, etc.) importunately. **2.** proclaim; advertise. **3.** give tip on (race horse, etc.). —*n.* **4.** person who touts. —**tout'er**, *n.*

tow (tō) *v.* **1.** drag by rope or chain. —*n.* **2.** act of towing. **3.** thing towed.

to•ward' (tôrd, twôrd) *prep.* Also, **to•wards'. 1.** in direction of. **2.** with respect to. **3.** nearly.

tow'boat', *n.* boat for pushing barges.

tow'el (tou'əl, toul) *n.* cloth or paper for wiping.

tow'el•ing, *n.* fabric of cotton or linen used for towels.

tow'er (tou'ər) *n.* **1.** tall structure. —*v.* **2.** rise high.

tow'er•ing, *adj.* **1.** very high or great. **2.** violent; furious.

tow'head' (tō'hed') *n.* **1.** head of light-colored hair. **2.** person with such hair. —**tow'-head'ed**, *adj.*

tow'line' (tō'līn') *n.* cable for towing.

town (toun) *n.* **1.** small city. **2.** center of city. —**towns'man**, *n.* —**towns'wom'an**, *n.fem.* —**towns'peo'ple, towns'folk'**, *n.pl.*

town house, one of group of similar houses joined by common side walls.

town meeting, meeting of voters of town.

town/ship, *n.* **1.** division of county. **2.** (in U.S. surveys) district 6 miles square.

tow/path/ (tō/path/) *n.* path along bank of canal or river.

tox. toxicology.

tox•e/mi•a (tok sē/mē ə) *n.* blood poisoning resulting from presence of toxins in blood. —tox•e/mic, *adj.*

tox/ic (tok/sik) *adj.* **1.** of toxin. **2.** poisonous. —tox•ic/i•ty, *n.*

tox/i•col/o•gy (-si kol/ə jē) *n.* science of poisons. —tox/i•col/o•gist, *n.*

toxic shock syndrome, rapidly developing toxemia.

tox/in (tok/sin) *n.* poisonous product of microorganism, plant, or animal.

toy (toi) *n.* **1.** plaything. —*v.* **2.** play.

tp. 1. telephone. **2.** test point. **3.** township. **4.** troop.

t.p. 1. title page. **2.** *Surveying.* turning point.

TPA *Biochemistry.* tissue plasminogen activator.

TPC The Peace Corps.

tpd 1. tapped. **2.** tons per day.

tpg tapping.

tph tons per hour.

tpi 1. teeth per inch. **2.** turns per inch.

tpk. turnpike. Also, **Tpk**

tpl triple.

tpm tons per minute.

TPN *Medicine.* total parenteral nutrition.

TPR *Medicine.* temperature, pulse, respiration.

tpr 1. taper. **2.** teleprinter.

tptg tuned-plate tuned-grid.

t quark *Physics.* top quark.

TR technical report.

tr. 1. *Commerce.* tare. **2.** tincture. **3.** trace. **4.** train. **5.** transaction. **6.** *Grammar.* transitive. **7.** translated. **8.** translation. **9.** translator. **10.** transpose. **11.** transposition. **12.** treasurer. **13.** *Music.* trill. **14.** troop. **15.** trust. **16.** trustee.

T.R. 1. in the time of the king. [from Latin *tempore rēgis*] **2.** Theodore Roosevelt. **3.** tons registered. **4.** trust receipt.

TRA Thoroughbred Racing Association.

trace (trās) *n.*, *v.*, **traced, tracing.** —*n.* **1.** mark or track left by something. **2.** small amount. **3.** pulling part of harness. —*v.* **4.** follow trace of. **5.** find out. **6.** draw. —trace/a•ble, *adj.* —trac/er, *n.*

trac/er•y, *n.*, *pl.* **-eries.** ornamental pattern of interlacing lines, etc.

tra/che•a (trā/kē ə) *n.*, *pl.* **-cheae** (-kē ē/). air-conveying tube from larynx to bronchi.

tra/che•ot/o•my (-ot/ə mē) *n.*, *pl.* **-mies.** operation of cutting into trachea, usu. to relieve difficulty in breathing.

track (trak) *n.* **1.** parallel rails for railroad. **2.** wheel rut. **3.** footprint or other mark left. **4.** path. **5.** course. —*v.* **6.** follow; pursue.

track/ball/, *n.* computer input device for controlling pointer on screen by rotating ball set inside case.

track record, record of achievements or performance.

TRACON (trā/kon), terminal radar approach control.

tract (trakt) *n.* **1.** region. **2.** brief treatise.

trac/ta•ble (trak/tə bəl) *adj.* easily managed. —trac/ta•bil/i•ty, *n.* —trac/ta•bly, *adv.*

trac/tion (-shən) *n.* **1.** act or instance of pulling. **2.** adhesive friction.

trac/tor (-tər) *n.* self-propelled vehicle for pulling farm machinery, etc.

trad. tradition; traditional.

trade (trād) *n.*, *v.*, **traded, trading.** —*n.* **1.** buying, selling, or exchange of commodities; commerce. **2.** exchange. **3.** occupation. —*v.* **4.** buy and sell. **5.** exchange. —trad/er, *n.* —trades/man, *n.*

trade/-in/, *n.* goods given in whole or part payment for purchase.

trade/mark/, *n.* name, symbol, etc., identifying brand or source of things for sale.

trade name, word or phrase whereby particular class of goods is designated.

trade/-off/, *n.* exchange of one thing for another.

trade union, labor union.

trade wind (wind) sea wind blowing toward equator from latitudes up to 30° away.

tra•di/tion (trə dish/ən) *n.* **1.** handing down of beliefs, customs, etc., through generations. **2.** something so handed down. —tra•di/tion•al, *adj.* —tra•di/tion•al•ly, *adv.* —tra•di/tion•al•ist, *n.*, *adj.* —tra•di/tion•al•ism, *n.*

tra•duce/ (trə dōōs/, -dyōōs/) *v.*, **-duced, -ducing.** slander.

traf/fic (traf/ik) *n.*, *v.*, **-ficked, -ficking.** —*n.* **1.** traveling persons and things. **2.** trade. —*v.* **3.** trade. —traf/fick•er, *n.*

traffic circle, circular roadway at multiple intersection.

traffic light, set of signal lights at intersection.

tra•ge/di•an (trə jē/dē ən) *n.* actor or writer of tragedy. —tra•ge/di•enne/, *n.fem.*

trag/e•dy (traj/i dē) *n.*, *pl.* **-dies. 1.** serious drama with unhappy ending. **2.** sad event. —trag/ic, *adj.* —trag/i•cal•ly, *adv.*

trail (trāl) *v.* **1.** draw or drag. **2.** be drawn or dragged. **3.** track. —*n.* **4.** path. **5.** track, scent, etc., left.

trail/blaz/er, *n.* pioneer.

trail/er, *n.* **1.** van attached to truck for hauling freight, etc. **2.** vehicle attached to car or truck with accommodations for living, working, etc.

train (trān) *n.* **1.** railroad locomotive with cars. **2.** moving line of persons, vehicles, etc. **3.** series of events, ideas, etc. **4.** trailing part. **5.** retinue. —*v.* **6.** instruct or undergo instruction. **7.** make fit. **8.** aim; direct. —train/a•ble, *adj.* —train•ee/, *n.* —train/er, *n.*

T

train'man, *n., pl.* **-men.** member of crew of railroad train.

traipse (trāps) *v.,* **traipsed, traipsing.** *Informal.* walk aimlessly.

trait (trāt) *n.* characteristic.

trai'tor (trā'tər) *n.* **1.** betrayer of trust. **2.** person guilty of treason. —**trai'tor•ous,** *adj.*

traj trajectory.

tra•jec'to•ry (trə jek'tə rē) *n., pl.* **-ries.** curve described by projectile in flight.

tram (tram) *n. Brit.* streetcar or trolley car.

tram'mel (tram'əl) *n., v.* **-meled, -meling.** —*n.* **1.** impediment to action. —*v.* **2.** hamper.

tramp (tramp) *v.* **1.** tread or walk firmly. **2.** march. —*n.* **3.** firm, heavy tread. **4.** hike. **5.** vagabond.

tram'ple, *v.,* **-pled, -pling.** step roughly on.

tram'po•line' (tram'pə lēn', -lin) *n.* cloth springboard for tumblers.

trance (trans) *n.* half-conscious or hypnotic state.

tranfd. transferred.

tran'quil (trang'kwil) *adj.* peaceful; quiet. —**tran'quil•ly,** *adv.* —**tran•quil'li•ty,** *n.* —**tran'quil•ize',** *v.*

tran'quil•iz'er (-kwi lī'zər) *n.* drug to reduce tension.

trans-, prefix meaning across; through; on the other side; changing thoroughly; beyond or surpassing.

transa transaction.

trans•act' (tran sakt', -zakt') *v.* carry on business. —**trans•ac'tion,** *n.* —**trans•ac'tor,** *n.*

trans•at•lan'tic (trans'ət lan'tik, tranz'-) *adj.* **1.** passing across Atlantic. **2.** on other side of Atlantic.

trans•ceiv'er (tran sē'vər) *n.* radio transmitter and receiver combined in one.

tran•scend' (tran send') *v.* **1.** go or be beyond. **2.** excel.

tran•scend'ent, *adj.* **1.** extraordinary. **2.** superior; supreme.

tran'scen•den'tal (tran'sen den'tl, -sən-) *adj.* beyond ordinary human experience. —**tran'scen•den'tal•ly,** *adv.*

trans'con•ti•nen'tal (trans'kon tn en'tl) *adj.* across a continent.

tran•scribe' (tran skrīb') *v.,* **-scribed, -scribing. 1.** copy. **2.** make recording of. —**tran•scrip'tion** (-skrip'shən), **tran'script,** *n.* —**tran•scrib'er,** *n.*

trans•duc'er (trans dōō'sər, -dyōō'-, tranz-) *n.* device that converts signal from one form of energy to another.

tran'sept (tran'sept) *n.* transverse portion of cross-shaped church.

trans•fer', *v.,* **-ferred, -ferring,** *n.* —*v.* (trans fûr', trans'fər) **1.** convey, hand over, or transport. **2.** be transferred. —*n.* (trans'fər) **3.** means or act of transferring. —**trans•fer'a•ble,** *adj.* —**trans•fer'al,** *n.* —**trans•fer'ence,** *n.*

trans•fig'ure, *v.,* **-ured, -uring. 1.** transform. **2.** glorify. —**trans'fig•u•ra'tion,** *n.*

trans•fix', *v.* **1.** pierce. **2.** paralyze with terror, etc.

trans•form', *v.* change in form, nature, etc. —**trans'for•ma'tion,** *n.*

trans•form'er, *n.* device for converting electrical currents.

trans•fuse' (-fyōōz') *v.,* **-fused, -fusing. 1.** transmit, as by pouring. **2.** transfer blood from one person to another. —**trans•fu'sion,** *n.*

trans•gress' (trans gres', tranz-) *v.* **1.** go beyond limit. **2.** violate law, etc. —**trans•gres'sion** (-gresh'ən) *n.* —**trans•gres'sor,** *n.*

tran'sient (tran'shənt, -zhənt, -zē ənt) *adj.* **1.** lasting or staying only a short time; transitory. —*n.* **2.** transient person. —**tran'sient•ly,** *adv.*

tran•sis'tor (tran zis'tər) *n.* small electronic device replacing vacuum tube.

trans'it (tran'sit, -zit) *n.* passage or conveyance.

tran•si'tion (tran zish'ən, -sish'-) *n.* passage from one condition, etc., to another. —**tran•si'tion•al,** *adj.* —**tran•si'tion•al•ly,** *adv.*

tran'si•tive (tran'si tiv, -zi-) *adj.* (of verb) regularly accompanied by direct object. —**tran'si•tive•ly,** *adv.*

tran'si•to•ry (tran'si tôr'ē, -zi-) *adj.* **1.** not enduring. **2.** brief. —**tran'si•to/ri•ness,** *n.*

transl. **1.** translated. **2.** translation. **3.** translator.

trans•late' (trans lāt', tranz-, trans'lāt, tranz'-) *v.,* **-lated, -lating.** change from one language into another. —**trans•la'tion,** *n.* —**trans•lat'a•ble,** *adj.* —**trans•lat'or,** *n.*

trans•lit'er•ate' (-lit'ə rāt') *v.,* **-ated, -ating.** change into corresponding characters of another alphabet or language. —**trans'lit•er•a'tion,** *n.*

trans•lu'cent (-lōō'sənt) *adj.* transmitting light diffusely. —**trans•lu'cence, trans•lu'cen•cy,** *n.*

trans•mi•gra'tion, *n.* passage of soul into another body.

trans•mis'sion (-mish'ən) *n.* **1.** act or process of transmitting. **2.** something transmitted. **3.** set of gears to transfer force between mechanisms, as in automobile. **4.** broadcast.

trans•mit' (-mit') *v.,* **-mitted, -mitting. 1.** send over or along. **2.** communicate. **3.** hand down. **4.** cause or permit light, heat, etc., to pass through. **5.** emit radio waves. —**trans•mis'si•ble** (-mis'ə bəl), **trans•mit'ta•ble,** *adj.* —**trans•mit'tal,** *n.* —**trans•mit'ter,** *n.*

trans•mog'ri•fy' (-mog'rə fī') *v.,* **-fied, -fying.** change in appearance or form; transform. —**trans•mog'ri•fi•ca'tion,** *n.*

trans•mute' (-myōōt') *v.,* **-muted, -muting.** change from one nature or form to another. —**trans•mut'a•ble,** *adj.* —**trans•mu•ta'tion,** *n.*

trans•na'tion•al, *adj.* going beyond national boundaries or interests.

trans'o•ce•an'ic, *adj.* across or beyond ocean.

tran'som (tran'səm) *n.* **1.** window above door. **2.** crosspiece separating door from window, etc.

tran•son'ic (tran son'ik) *adj.* close to speed of sound; moving 700–780 miles per hour.

transp transparent.

trans'pa•cif'ic (trans'-) *adj.* **1.** passing across Pacific. **2.** on other side of Pacific.

trans•par'ent (-pâr'ənt) *adj.* **1.** allowing objects to be seen clearly through it. **2.** frank. **3.** obvious. —**trans•par'en•cy,** *n.* —**trans•par'ent•ly,** *adv.*

tran•spire' (tran spīᵊr') *v.,* -spired, -spiring. **1.** occur. **2.** give off waste matter, etc., from surface.

trans•plant' *v.* (trans plant') **1.** remove and put or plant in another place. —*n.* **2.** (trans'-plant') act of transplanting. **3.** something transplanted. —**trans'plan•ta'tion,** *n.*

trans•port' *v.* (trans pôrt') **1.** convey from one place to another. **2.** enrapture. —*n.* (trans'pôrt) **3.** something that transports. —**trans'por•ta'tion,** *n.* —**trans•port'er,** *n.*

trans•pose' (-pōz') *v.,* -posed, -posing. alter relative position, order, musical key, etc. —**trans'po•si'tion,** *n.*

trans•sex'u•al, *n.* **1.** person with sex surgically altered. **2.** person feeling identity with opposite sex.

trans•ship', *v.,* -shipped, -shipping. transfer from one conveyance to another. —**trans•ship'ment,** *n.*

trans'sub•stan'ti•a'tion, *n.* (in the Eucharist) conversion of whole substance of bread and wine into body and blood of Christ.

trans•verse' (trans vûrs', tranz-; trans'vûrs, tranz'-) *adj.* **1.** lying across. —*n.* **2.** something transverse. —**trans•verse'ly,** *adv.*

trans•ves'tite (trans ves'tīt, tranz-) *n.* person who dresses like opposite sex.

trap (trap) *n., v.,* **trapped, trapping.** —*n.* **1.** device for catching animals. **2.** scheme for catching a person unawares. **3.** U-shaped section in pipe to prevent escape of air or gases. —*v.* **4.** catch in or set traps. —**trap'per,** *n.*

tra•peze' (tra pēz', trə-) *n.* suspended bar used in gymnastics.

trap'e•zoid' (trap'ə zoid') *n.* four-sided figure with two parallel sides.

trap'pings, *n.pl.* equipment or dress.

trap'shoot•ing, *n.* sport of shooting at clay pigeons hurled from trap.

trash (trash) *n.* rubbish. —**trash'y,** *adj.*

trau'ma (trou'mə, trô'-) *n., pl.* -mata, -mas. **1.** externally produced injury. **2.** experience causing permanent psychological harm. —**trau•mat'ic** (-mat'ik) *adj.*

trav. **1.** traveler. **2.** travels.

tra•vail' (trə vāl', trav'āl) *n.* **1.** toil. **2.** labor pains.

trav'el (trav'əl) *v.,* -eled, -eling, *n.* —*v.* **1.**

journey. **2.** move. —*n.* **3.** journeying. —**trav'el•er,** *n.*

trav'e•logue' (-lôg') *n.* lecture describing travel, usually illustrated. Also, **trav'e•log'.**

trav'erse, *v.,* -ersed, -ersing, *n.* —*v.* (trə-vûrs', trav'ərs) **1.** pass over or through. —*n.* (trav'ərs, trə vûrs') **2.** act of traversing.

trav'es•ty (trav'ə stē) *n., pl.* -ties, *v.,* -tied, -tying. —*n.* **1.** literary burlesque. **2.** debased likeness. —*v.* **3.** make travesty on.

trawl (trôl) *n.* **1.** fishing net dragged on bottom of water. —*v.* **2.** fish with trawl. —**trawl'er,** *n.*

tray (trā) *n.* flat, shallow receptacle or container.

trb treble.

trd tread.

treach'er•y (trech'ə rē) *n., pl.* -eries. betrayal; treason. —**treach'er•ous,** *adj.* —**treach'er•ous•ly,** *adv.* —**treach'er•ous•ness,** *n.*

tread (tred) *v.,* **trod** (trod), **trodden** or **trod,** **treading,** *n.* —*v.* **1.** step, walk, or trample. **2.** crush. —*n.* **3.** manner of walking. **4.** surface meeting road or rail. **5.** horizontal surface of step. —**tread'er,** *n.*

trea'dle (tred'l) *n.* lever, etc., worked by foot to drive machine.

tread'mill', *n.* apparatus worked by treading on moving steps, as for exercise.

treas. **1.** treasurer. **2.** treasury. Also, **Treas.**

trea'son (trē'zən) *n.* violation of allegiance to sovereign or state. —**trea'son•a•ble,** **trea'son•ous,** *adj.*

treasr. treasurer.

treas'ure (trezh'ər) *n., v.,* -ured, -uring. —*n.* **1.** accumulated wealth. **2.** thing greatly valued. —*v.* **3.** prize. **4.** put away for future use.

treas'ure-trove' (-trōv') *n.* **1.** anything valuable that one finds. **2.** treasure of unknown ownership, found hidden.

treas'ur•y, *n., pl.* -uries. **1.** place for keeping public or private funds. **2.** the funds. **3.** (*cap.*) government department that handles funds. —**treas'ur•er,** *n.*

treat (trēt) *v.* **1.** behave toward. **2.** deal with. **3.** relieve or cure. **4.** discuss. **5.** entertain. —*n.* **6.** entertainment. —**treat'ment,** *n.* —**treat'a•ble,** *adj.*

trea'tise (trē'tis) *n.* writing on particular subject.

trea'ty (trē'tē) *n., pl.* -ties. formal agreement between states.

tre'ble (treb'əl) *adj., n., v.,* -bled, -bling. —*adj.* **1.** triple. **2.** of highest pitch or range. **3.** shrill. —*n.* **4.** treble part, singer, instrument, etc. —*v.* **5.** triple. —**tre'bly,** *adv.*

tree (trē) *n., v.,* **treed, treeing.** —*n.* **1.** plant with permanent, woody, usually branched trunk. —*v.* **2.** drive up tree.

tre'foil (trē'foil, tref'oil) *n.* **1.** herb with leaf divided in three parts. **2.** ornament based on this leaf.

T

trek (trek) v., **trekked, trekking,** n. journey.

trel′lis (trel′is) n. lattice.

trem′a•tode′ (trem′ə tōd′, trē′mə-) n. parasitic flatworm.

trem′ble (trem′bəl) v., -bled, -bling, n. —v. 1. quiver. —n. 2. act or state of trembling.

tre•men′dous (tri men′dəs) adj. extraordinarily great. —tre•men′dous•ly, adv.

trem′o•lo (trem′ə lō′) n., pl. -los. vibrating effect on instrument or in voice.

trem′or (trem′ər, trē′mər) n. 1. involuntary shaking. 2. vibration.

trem′u•lous (trem′yə ləs) adj. 1. trembling. 2. fearful. —trem′u•lous•ly, adv.

trench (trench) n. ditch or cut.

trench′ant (tren′chənt) adj. 1. incisive. 2. vigorous. —trench′ant•ly, adv.

trench coat, belted raincoat with epaulets.

trench′er, n. flat piece of wood on which meat is served or carved.

trench′er•man, n., pl. -men. person with hearty appetite.

trench foot, disease of feet due to prolonged exposure to cold and moisture.

trench mouth, acute ulcerating infection of gums and teeth.

trend (trend) n. 1. tendency. 2. increasingly popular fashion.

trend′y, adj., -ier, -iest. Informal. following current fads. —trend′i•ly, adv. —trend′i•ness, n.

trep′i•da′tion (trep′i dā′shən) n. tremulous alarm.

tres′pass (tres′pəs, -pas) v. 1. enter property illicitly. 2. sin. —n. 3. act of trespassing. —tres′pass•er, n.

tress (tres) n. braid of hair.

tres′tle (tres′əl) n. supporting frame or framework.

trey (trā) n. Cards or Dice. three.

TRF Biochemistry. thyrotropin-releasing factor.

trf 1. transfer. 2. tuned radio frequency.

trfc traffic.

TRH Biochemistry. thyrotropin-releasing hormone.

trh truss head.

tri-, prefix meaning three.

tri′ad (trī′ad, -əd) n. group of three.

tri•age′ (trē äzh′) n. sorting victims to determine priority of medical treatment.

tri′al (trī′əl) n. 1. examination before judicial tribunal. 2. test. 3. attempt. 4. state of being tested. 5. source of suffering.

tri′an′gle (trī′ang′gəl) n. figure of three straight sides and three angles. —tri•an′gu•lar, adj.

tri•an′gu•late (-gyə lāt′) v., -lated, -lating. 1. survey by using trigonometric principles. 2. divide into triangles. —tri•an′gu•la′tion, n.

Tri•as′sic (trī as′ik) adj. pertaining to period of Mesozoic Era.

trib. tributary.

tribe (trīb) n. people united by common descent, etc. —trib′al, adj.

tribes′man, n., pl. -men. man belonging to tribe. —tribes′wom′an, n.fem.

trib′u•la′tion (trib′yə lā′shən) n. 1. trouble. 2. affliction.

tri•bu′nal (trī byōōn′l, tri-) n. 1. court of justice. 2. place of judgment.

trib′une (trib′yōōn, tri byōōn′) n. 1. person who defends rights of the people. 2. rostrum.

trib′u•tar′y (trib′yə ter′ē) n., pl. -taries, adj. —n. 1. stream flowing into larger body of water. 2. payer of tribute. —adj. 3. flowing as tributary.

trib′ute (trib′yōōt) n. 1. personal offering, etc. 2. sum paid for peace, etc.

trice (trīs) n. instant.

tri′cen•ten′ni•al (trī′sen ten′ē əl) n. tercentennial.

tri′ceps (trī′seps) n. muscle at back of upper arm.

trich′i•no′sis (trik′ə nō′sis) n. disease due to parasitic worm.

trick (trik) n. 1. artifice or stratagem. 2. prank. 3. knack. 4. cards won in one round. —v. 5. deceive or cheat by tricks. —trick′er•y, n. —trick′ster, n. —trick′y, adj.

trick′le (trik′əl) v., -led, -ling, n. —v. 1. flow in small amounts. —n. 2. trickling flow.

tri′col′or (trī′kul′ər) adj. 1. of three colors. —n. 2. three-colored flag, esp. of France.

tri•cus′pid, adj. having three cusps or points, as tooth.

tri′cy•cle (trī′si kəl, -sik′əl) n. child's vehicle with large front wheel and two smaller rear wheels.

trid. (in prescriptions) three days. [from Latin trīduum]

tri′dent (trīd′nt) n. three-pronged spear.

tried (trīd) adj. tested; proved.

tri•en′ni•al (trī en′ē əl) adj. 1. lasting three years. 2. occurring every three years. —n. 3. period of three years. 4. third anniversary.

tri′fle (trī′fəl) n., v., -fled, -fling. —n. 1. article of small value. 2. trivial matter or amount. —v. 3. deal without due respect. 4. act idly or frivolously. —tri′fler, n. —tri′fling, adj.

tri•fo′li•ate (trī fō′lē it, -āt) adj. having three leaves or leaflike parts.

trig. 1. trigger. 2. trigonometric. 3. trigonometrical. 4. trigonometry.

trig′ger (trig′ər) n. 1. projecting tongue pressed to fire gun. 2. device to release spring. —v. 3. precipitate.

tri•glyc′er•ide′ (trī glis′ə rīd′, -ər id) n. ester forming much of fats and oils stored in tissues.

tri′go•nom′e•try (trig′ə nom′i trē) n. mathematical study of relations between sides and angles of triangles. —trig′o•no•met′ric (-nə-me′trik) adj.

trill (tril) v. 1. sing or play with vibratory effect. —n. 2. act or sound of trilling.

tril′lion (tril′yən) *n.*, *adj.* 1 followed by 12 zeroes.

tril′li•um (tril′ē əm) *n.* plant of lily family.

tril′o•gy (tril′ə jē) *n.*, *pl.* **-gies.** group of three plays, operas, etc., on related theme.

trim (trim) *v.*, **trimmed, trimming,** *n.*, *adj.*, **trimmer, trimmest.** —*v.* **1.** make neat by clipping, paring, etc. **2.** adjust (sails or yards). **3.** dress or ornament. —*n.* **4.** proper condition. **5.** adjustment of sails, etc. **6.** dress or equipment. **7.** trimming. —*adj.* **8.** neat. **9.** in good condition. —**trim′ly,** *adv.* —**trim′mer,** *n.* —**trim′ness,** *n.*

tri•ma•ran′ (trī′mə ran′) *n.* boat with three hulls.

tri•mes′ter (trī mes′tər, trī′mes-) *n.* **1.** period of three months. **2.** one of three divisions of academic year.

trim′ming (trim′ing) *n.* something used to trim.

tri•ni•tro•tol′u•ene′ (trī nī′trō tol′yoo ēn′) *n.* high explosive, known as TNT.

Trin′i•ty (trin′i tē) *n.* unity of Father, Son, and Holy Ghost.

trin′ket (tring′kit) *n.* **1.** bit of jewelry, etc. **2.** trifle.

tri′o (trē′ō) *n.*, *pl.* **trios.** group of three.

trip (trip) *n.*, *v.*, **tripped, tripping.** —*n.* **1.** journey. **2.** stumble. **3.** *Slang.* drug-induced event. *v.* **4.** stumble or cause to stumble. **5.** slip. **6.** tread quickly. —**trip′per,** *n.*

tri•par′tite (trī pär′tīt) *adj.* **1.** divided into or consisting of three parts. **2.** participated in by three parties.

tripe (trīp) *n.* **1.** ruminant's stomach, used as food. **2.** *Slang.* worthless statements or writing.

tri′ple (trip′əl) *adj.*, *n.*, *v.*, **-pled, -pling.** —*adj.* **1.** of three parts. **2.** three times as great. —*n.* **3.** *Baseball.* hit allowing batter to reach third base. —*v.* **4.** make or become triple. —**tri′ply,** *adv.*

tri′plet (trip′lit) *n.* one of three children (**triplets**) born at a single birth.

trip′li•cate (-li kit, -kāt′) *adj.* **1.** triple. —*n.* **2.** set of three copies.

tri′pod (trī′pod) *n.* three-legged stool, support, etc.

trip′tych (trip′tik) *n.* set of three panels side by side, with pictures or carvings.

trit. *Pharmacology.* triturate.

trite (trīt) *adj.*, **triter, tritest.** commonplace; hackneyed. —**trite′ly,** *adv.* —**trite′ness,** *n.*

trit′u•rate′ (trich′ə rāt′) *v.*, **-rated, -rating,** *n.* —*v.* **1.** to reduce to fine particles or powder; pulverize. —*n.* (-ər it) **2.** triturated substance. —**trit′u•ra′tion,** *n.*

tri′umph (trī′əmf, -umf) *n.* **1.** victory. **2.** joy over victory. —*v.* **3.** be victorious or successful. **4.** rejoice over this. —**tri•um′phal,** *adj.* —**tri•um′phant,** *adj.*

tri•um′vir (trī um′vər) *n.*, *pl.* **-virs, -viri** (-və rī′). *Rom. Hist.* any of three magistrates exercising same public function. —**tri•um′vi•ral,** *adj.*

tri•um′vi•rate (-vər it, -və rāt′) *n.* **1.** *Rom. Hist.* the office of triumvir. **2.** government of three joint magistrates. **3.** association of three, as in office.

triv′et (triv′it) *n.* device protecting table top from hot objects.

triv′i•a (triv′ē ə) *n.* things that are very unimportant.

triv′i•al, *adj.* trifling. —**triv′i•al′i•ty,** *n.* —**triv′i•al•ly,** *adv.*

trk **1.** track. **2.** truck.

trkg tracking.

Trl. (used in addresses) trail.

trlg trailing.

trlr trailer.

trly trolley.

TRM trademark.

trm training manual.

trmr trimmer.

trn train.

tRNA *Genetics.* transfer RNA.

trnbkl turnbuckle.

trnd turned.

trngl triangle.

trnr trainer.

trnspn transportation.

trntbl turntable.

TRO *Law.* temporary restraining order.

troch. (in prescriptions) troche; tablet or lozenge.

tro′che (trō′kē) *n.* small tablet of medicinal substance.

tro′chee (trō′kē) *n.* verse foot of two syllables, long followed by short. —**tro•cha′ic** (-kā′ik) *adj.*

trog′lo•dyte′ (trog′lə dīt′) *n.* **1.** cave dweller. **2.** person living in seclusion. **3.** person unacquainted with affairs of the world.

troi′ka (troi′kə) *n.* **1.** Russian vehicle drawn by three horses. **2.** ruling group of three.

troll (trōl) *v.* **1.** sing in rolling voice. **2.** sing as round. **3.** fish with moving line. —*n.* **4.** *Music.* round. **5.** underground monster.

trol′ley (trol′ē) *n.* **1.** trolley car. **2.** pulley on overhead track or wire.

trolley bus, bus drawing power from overhead wires.

trolley car, electric streetcar receiving current from a trolley.

trol′lop (trol′əp) *n.* **1.** untidy or slovenly woman; slattern. **2.** prostitute.

trom•bone′ (trom bōn′, trom′bōn) *n.* brass wind instrument with long bent tube. —**trom•bon′ist,** *n.*

troop (troop) *n.* **1.** assemblage. **2.** cavalry unit. **3.** body of police, etc. —*v.* **4.** gather or move in numbers. **5.** walk, as if in a march. —**troop′er,** *n.*

troop′ship′, *n.* ship for conveyance of military troops; transport.

trop. **1.** tropic. **2.** tropical.

T

trope (trōp) *n.* figure of speech.

tro'phy (trō'fē) *n., pl.* **-phies. 1.** memento taken in hunting, war, etc. **2.** silver cup, etc., given as prize.

trop'ic (trop'ik) *n.* **1.** either of two latitudes (**tropic of Cancer** and **tropic of Capricorn**) bounding torrid zone. **2.** (*pl.*) region between these latitudes. —**trop'i•cal,** *adj.* —**trop'i•cal•ly,** *adv.*

tro'pism (trō'piz əm) *n.* response of plant or animal, as in growth, to influence of external stimuli. —**tro•pis'tic** (-pis'tik) *adj.*

tropo troposphere.

trop'o•sphere' (trop'ə sfēr', trō'pə-) *n.* lowest layer of atmosphere.

trot (trot) *v.,* **trotted, trotting,** *n.* —*v.* **1.** go at gait between walk and run. **2.** go briskly. **3.** ride at trot. —*n.* **4.** trotting gait. —**trot'-ter,** *n.*

troth (trôth, trōth) *n.* **1.** fidelity. **2.** promise.

trou'ba•dour' (trōō'bə dôr') *n.* medieval lyric poet of W Mediterranean area who wrote on love and gallantry.

trou'ble (trub'əl) *v.,* **-bled, -bling,** *n.* —*v.* **1.** distress. **2.** put to or cause inconvenience. **3.** bother. —*n.* **4.** annoyance or difficulty. **5.** disturbance. **6.** inconvenience. —**trou'bler,** *n.* —**trou'ble•some,** *adj.*

trou'bled, *adj.* **1.** emotionally or mentally distressed. **2.** economically or socially distressed.

trou'ble•mak'er, *n.* person who causes trouble.

troub'le•shoot'er, *n.* expert in eliminating causes of trouble.

trough (trôf) *n.* **1.** open boxlike container. **2.** long hollow or channel.

trounce (trouns) *v.,* **trounced, trouncing.** beat severely.

troupe (trōōp) *n.* company of performers. —**troup'er,** *n.*

trou'sers (trou'zərz) *n.pl.* outer garment divided into two separate leg coverings.

trous'seau (trōō'sō, trōō sō') *n., pl.* **-seaux, -seaus** (-sōz). bride's outfit.

trout (trout) *n.* freshwater game fish.

trow'el (trou'əl) *n.* **1.** tool for spreading or smoothing. **2.** small digging tool.

troy (troi) *adj.* expressed in troy weight.

troy weight, system of weights for precious metals and gems.

Trp *Biochemistry.* tryptophan.

trp *Military.* troop.

trq torque.

trsbr transcriber.

trscb transcribe.

trtd treated.

trtmt treatment.

tru'ant (trōō'ənt) *n.* **1.** student absent from school without leave. —*adj.* **2.** absent from school without leave. —**tru'an•cy,** *n.*

truce (trōōs) *n.* suspension of military hostilities.

truck (truk) *n.* **1.** hand or motor vehicle for carrying heavy loads. **2.** vegetables raised for market. **3.** miscellaneous articles. —*v.* **4.** transport by or drive a truck. **5.** trade. —**truck'er,** *n.*

truck farm, farm on which vegetables are grown for market.

truck'le, *v.,* **-led, -ling.** submit humbly.

truckle bed, trundle bed.

truc'u•lent (truk'yə lənt, trōō'kyə-) *adj.* fierce. —**truc'u•lence,** *n.* —**truc'u•lent•ly,** *adv.*

trudge (truj) *v.,* **trudged, trudging,** *n.* —*v.* **1.** walk, esp. wearily. —*n.* **2.** tiring walk. —**trudg'er,** *n.*

true (trōō) *adj.,* **truer, truest. 1.** conforming to fact. **2.** real. **3.** sincere. **4.** loyal. **5.** correct. —**tru'ly,** *adv.* —**true'ness,** *n.*

true'-blue', *adj.* staunch; true.

truf'fle (truf'əl) *n.* **1.** edible fungus. **2.** chocolate confection resembling truffle.

tru'ism (trōō'iz əm) *n.* obvious truth.

trump (trump) *n.* **1.** playing card of suit outranking other suits. **2.** the suit. —*v.* **3.** take with or play trump. **4.** fabricate.

trump'er•y, *n., pl.* **-eries. 1.** something without use or value. **2.** nonsense; twaddle.

trum'pet (trum'pit) *n.* **1.** brass wind instrument with powerful, penetrating tone. —*v.* **2.** blow trumpet. **3.** proclaim. —**trum'pet•er,** *n.*

trun trunnion.

trun'cate (trung'kāt) *v.,* **-cated, -cating.** shorten by cutting. —**trun•ca'tion,** *n.*

trun'cheon (trun'chən) *n.* club.

trun'dle (trun'dl) *v.,* **-dled, -dling,** *n.* —*v.* **1.** roll, as on wheels. —*n.* **2.** small roller, wheel, etc.

trundle bed, low bed on casters, usually pushed under another bed when not in use. Also, **truckle bed.**

trunk (trungk) *n.* **1.** main stem of tree. **2.** box for clothes, etc. **3.** body of person or animal, excepting head and limbs. **4.** main body of anything. **5.** elephant's long flexible nasal appendage.

trunk line, 1. major long-distance transportation line. **2.** telephone line between two switching devices.

truss (trus) *v.* **1.** bind or fasten. **2.** furnish or support with a truss. —*n.* **3.** rigid supporting framework. **4.** apparatus for confining hernia. **5.** bundle.

trust (trust) *n.* **1.** reliance on person's integrity, justice, etc. **2.** confident hope. **3.** credit. **4.** responsibility. **5.** care. **6.** something entrusted. **7.** holding of legal title for another's benefit. **8.** combination of companies, often monopolistic, controlled by central board. —*v.* **9.** place confidence in. **10.** rely on. **11.** hope. **12.** believe. **13.** give credit. —**trust'-ful,** *adj.* —**trust'wor'thy,** *adj.*

trus•tee', *n.* **1.** administrator of company, etc. **2.** holder of trust (def. 7).

trus•tee'ship, *n.* **1.** office of trustee. **2.** control of territory granted by United Nations. **3.** the territory.

trust fund, money, etc., held in trust.

trust territory, territory which United Nations has placed under administrative control of a country.

trust'y, *adj.,* **-ier, -iest,** *n., pl.* **trusties.** —*adj.* **1.** reliable. —*n.* **2.** trusted one. **3.** trustworthy convict given special privileges. —**trust'i•ly,** *adv.* —**trust'i•ness,** *n.*

truth (trōōth) *n.* **1.** true facts. **2.** conformity with fact. **3.** established fact, principle, etc. —**truth'ful,** *adj.* —**truth'ful•ly,** *adv.* —**truth'ful•ness,** *n.*

trx triplex.

try (trī) *v.,* **tried, trying. 1.** attempt. **2.** test. **3.** examine judicially. **4.** strain endurance, patience, etc., of.

try'ing, *adj.* annoying; irksome.

try'out', *n. Informal.* trial or test to ascertain fitness for some purpose.

tryst (trist, trīst) *n.* **1.** appointment, as of lovers, to meet. **2.** the meeting. **3.** place of meeting. —*v.* **4.** meet.

TS 1. tool shed. **2.** top secret. **3.** Also, **t.s.** *Slang* (*vulgar*). tough shit. **4.** transsexual. Also, **T.S.**

tsar (zär, tsär) *n.* czar.

tset'se fly (tset'sē, tsē'tsē) African fly transmitting disease.

T.Sgt. technical sergeant.

TSH *Biochemistry.* thyroid-stimulating hormone.

T'-shirt', *n.* short-sleeved knitted undershirt. Also, **tee'-shirt'.**

tsi tons per square inch.

TSO time-sharing option.

tsp., teaspoon.

T square, T-shaped ruler used in mechanical drawing.

TSR a computer program with any of several ancillary functions, usually held resident in RAM for instant activation while one is using another program. [*t*(*erminate and*) *s*(*tay*) *r*(*esident*)]

TSS *Pathology.* toxic shock syndrome.

tsteq test equipment.

tstg testing.

tstr tester.

tstrz transistorize.

tsu•na'•mi (tsōō nä'mē) *n.* huge wave caused by undersea earthquake or volcano.

TSWG Television and Screen Writers' Guild.

TT Trust Territories.

TTL transistor-transistor logic.

ttl total.

TTL meter *Photography.* through-the-lens meter.

TTS teletypesetter.

TTY teletypewriter.

Tu *Chemistry.* (formerly) thulium.

Tu. Tuesday.

T.U. 1. thermal unit. **2.** toxic unit. **3.** Trade Union. **4.** Training Unit.

t.u. trade union.

tub (tub) *n.* **1.** bathtub. **2.** deep, open-topped container.

tu'ba (tōō'bə, tyōō'-) *n.* low-pitched brass wind instrument.

tub'by (tub'ē) *adj.,* **-bier, -biest.** short of fat.

tube (tōōb, tyōōb) *n.* **1.** hollow pipe for fluids, etc. **2.** compressible container for toothpaste, etc. **3.** railroad or vehicular tunnel. —**tu'bu•lar** (-byə lər) *adj.* —**tub'ing,** *n.*

tu'ber (tōō'bər, tyōō'-) *n.* fleshy thickening of underground stem or shoot. —**tu'ber•ous,** *adj.*

tu'ber•cle (-kəl) *n.* small roundish projection, nodule, or swelling.

tu•ber'cu•lin (tōō bûr'kyə lin, tyōō-) *n.* liquid prepared from tuberculosis bacillus, used in test for tuberculosis.

tu•ber'cu•lo'sis (-lō'sis) *n.* infectious disease marked by formation of tubercles. —**tu•ber'cu•lar, tu•ber'cu•lous,** *adj.*

tube'rose' (tōōb'-, tyōōb'-) *n.* cultivated flowering plant.

tu'bule (-byōōl) *n.* small tube.

tuck (tuk) *v.* **1.** thrust into narrow space or retainer. **2.** cover snugly. **3.** draw up in folds. —*n.* **4.** tucked piece or part.

tuck'er, *n.* **1.** piece of cloth formerly worn by women about neck and shoulders. —*v.* **2.** *Informal.* tire; exhaust.

Tue. Tuesday.

Tues., Tuesday. Also, **Tue.**

Tues'day (tōōz'dā, -dē, tyōōz'-) *n.* third day of week.

tuft (tuft) *n.* **1.** bunch of feathers, hairs, etc., fixed at base. **2.** clump of bushes, etc., —*v.* **3.** arrange in or form tufts. —**tuft'ed,** *adj.*

tug (tug) *v.,* **tugged, tugging,** *n.* —*v.* **1.** drag; haul. —*n.* **2.** act of tugging. **3.** tugboat.

tug'boat', *n.* powerful vessel used for towing.

tug of war, 1. contest between teams pulling opposite ends of rope. **2.** struggle for supremacy.

tu•i'tion (tōō ish'ən, tyōō-) *n.* charge for instruction.

tu'lip (tōō'lip, tyōō'-) *n.* plant bearing showy, cup-shaped flowers.

tulle (tōōl) *n.* thin silk or rayon net.

tum'ble (tum'bəl) *v.,* **-bled, -bling,** *n.* —*v.* **1.** fall over or down. **2.** perform gymnastic feats. **3.** roll about; toss. —*n.* **4.** act of tumbling.

tum'ble-down', *adj.* dilapidated; rundown.

tum'bler, *n.* **1.** drinking glass. **2.** performer of tumbling feats. **3.** lock part engaging bolt.

tum'ble•weed', *n.* plant whose upper part becomes detached and is driven about by wind.

tum'brel (tum'brəl) *n.* farmer's cart that can be tilted to discharge its load. Also, **tum'bril.**

T

tu'mid (tōō'mid, tyōō-) *adj.* **1.** swollen. **2.** turgid; bombastic. —**tu•mid'i•ty,** *n.* —**tu•mes'cent** (-mes'ənt) *adj.*

tum'my (tum'ē) *n., pl.* -**mies.** *Informal.* stomach or abdomen.

tu'mor (tōō'mər, tyōō'-) *n.* abnormal swelling of cells in part of body. —**tu'mor•ous,** *adj.*

tu'mult (tōō'mult, -məlt, tyōō'-) *n.* disturbance, commotion, or uproar. —**tu•mul'tu•ous** (-mul'chōō əs) *adj.*

tun (tun) *n.* large cask.

tu'na (tōō'nə, tyōō'-) *n.* **1.** large oceanic fish. **2.** tunny. Also, **tuna fish.**

tun'dra (tun'drə, tōōn'-) *n.* vast, treeless, arctic plain.

tune (tōōn, tyōōn) *n., v.,* **tuned, tuning.** —*n.* **1.** melody. **2.** state of proper pitch, frequency, or condition. **3.** harmony. —*v.* **4.** adjust to correct pitch. **5.** adjust to receive radio or television signals. —**tune'ful,** *adj.* —**tun'a•ble, tune'a•ble,** *adj.* —**tune'less,** *adj.* —**tun'er,** *n.*

tune'-up', *n.* adjustment, as of motor, to improve working condition.

tung tungsten.

tung'sten (tung'stən) *n.* metallic element used for electric-lamp filaments, etc.

tu'nic (tōō'nik, tyōō'-) *n.* **1.** coat of uniform. **2.** ancient Greek and Roman garment. **3.** woman's upper garment.

tun'ing fork, steel instrument struck to produce pure tone of constant pitch.

tun'nel (tun'l) *n., v.,* -**neled, -neling.** —*n.* **1.** underground passage. —*v.* **2.** make tunnel.

tun'ny, *n., pl.* -**ny, -nies.** large mackerellike fish.

tur turret.

turb turbine.

tur'ban (tûr'bən) *n.* head covering made of scarf wound round head.

tur'bid (tûr'bid) *adj.* **1.** muddy. **2.** dense. **3.** confused. —**tur•bid'i•ty,** *n.*

tur'bine (tûr'bin, -bīn) *n.* motor producing torque by pressure of fluid.

turbo alt turbine alternator.

turbo gen turbine generator.

tur'bo•jet' (tûr'bō-) *n.* **1.** jet engine that compresses air by turbine. **2.** airplane with such engines.

tur'bo•prop' (-prop') *n.* **1.** turbojet with turbine-driven propeller. **2.** airplane with such engines.

tur'bot (tûr'bət) *n.* flatfish.

tur'bu•lent (tûr'byə lənt) *adj.* **1.** disorderly. **2.** tumultuous. —**tur'bu•lence,** *n.* —**tur'bu•lent•ly,** *adv.*

tu•reen' (tōō rēn', tyōō-) *n.* large covered dish for soup, etc.

turf (tûrf) *n.* **1.** covering of grass and roots. **2.** familiar area, as of residence or expertise. —**turf'y,** *adj.*

tur'gid (tûr'jid) *adj.* **1.** swollen. **2.** pompous

or bombastic. —**tur•gid'i•ty, tur'gid•ness,** *n.* —**tur'gid•ly,** *adv.*

Turk. **1.** Turkey. **2.** Also, **Turk** Turkish.

tur'key (tûr'kē) *n.* large, edible American bird.

turkey vulture, blackish brown New World vulture.

tur'mer•ic (tûr'mər ik) *n.* aromatic powder prepared from Asian plant, used as condiment.

tur'moil (tûr'moil) *n.* tumult.

turn (tûrn) *v.* **1.** rotate. **2.** reverse. **3.** divert; deflect. **4.** depend. **5.** sour; ferment. **6.** nauseate. **7.** alter. **8.** become. **9.** use. **10.** pass. **11.** direct. **12.** curve. —*n.* **13.** rotation. **14.** change or point of change. **15.** one's due time or opportunity. **16.** trend. **17.** short walk, ride, etc. **18.** inclination or aptitude. **19.** service or disservice.

turn'a•bout', *n.* change of opinion, loyalty, etc.

turn'buck'le, *n.* link used to couple or tighten two parts.

turn'coat', *n.* renegade.

turning point, point at which decisive change takes place.

tur'nip (tûr'nip) *n.* **1.** fleshy, edible root of cabbagelike plant. **2.** the plant.

turn'key, *n.* keeper of prison keys.

turn'off', *n.* small road that branches off from larger one.

turn'out', *n.* **1.** attendance at meeting, show, etc. **2.** output.

turn'o'ver, *n.* **1.** rate of replacement, investment, trade, etc. **2.** small pastry with filling.

turn'pike' (-pīk') *n.* **1.** barrier across road (**turnpike road**) where toll is paid. **2.** turnpike road.

turn'stile', *n.* horizontal crossed bars in gateway.

turn'ta'ble, *n.* rotating platform.

tur'pen•tine' (tûr'pən tīn') *n.* **1.** type of resin from coniferous trees. **2.** oil yielded by this.

tur'pi•tude' (tûr'pi tōōd', -tyōōd') *n.* depravity.

tur'quoise (tûr'koiz, -kwoiz) *n.* **1.** greenish-blue mineral used in jewelry. **2.** bluish green.

tur'ret (tûr'it, tur'-) *n.* **1.** small tower. **2.** towerlike gun shelter.

tur'tle (tûr'tl) *n.* marine reptile with shell-encased body.

tur'tle•dove' (-duv') *n.* small Old World dove.

tur'tle•neck', *n.* **1.** high, close-fitting collar. **2.** garment with turtleneck.

tusk (tusk) *n.* very long tooth, as of elephant or walrus.

tus'sle (tus'əl) *v.,* -**sled, -sling.** fight; scuffle.

tus'sock (tus'ək) *n.* tuft of growing grass.

tu'te•lage (tōōt'l ij, tyōōt'-) *n.* **1.** guardianship. **2.** instruction. —**tu'te•lar'y** (-er'ē), **tu'te•lar,** *adj.*

tu′tor (tōō′tər, tyōō′-) n. **1.** private instructor. **2.** college teacher (below instructor). —v. **3.** teach. —**tu•to′ri•al** (-tôr′ē əl) adj.

tut′ti-frut′ti (tōō′tē frōō′tē) n. confection, esp. ice cream, flavored with variety of fruits.

tu′tu′ (tōō′tōō′) n. short, full skirt worn by ballerina.

tux (tuks) n. Informal. tuxedo.

tux•e′do (tuk sē′dō) n., pl. -dos. semiformal jacket or suit for men.

TV, television.

TVA 1. tax on value added: a sales tax imposed by member nations of the Common Market on imports from other countries. **2.** Tennessee Valley Authority.

tvi television interference.

tvl travel.

tvlg traveling.

tvlr traveler.

tvm transistor voltmeter.

TVP Trademark. a brand of textured soy protein.

tw typewriter.

twad′dle (twod′l) n. nonsense.

twain (twān) adj., n. Archaic. two.

twang (twang) v. **1.** sound sharply and ringingly. **2.** have nasal tone. —n. **3.** twanging sound.

tweak (twēk) v. **1.** seize and pull or twist. —n. **2.** sharp pull and twist.

tweed (twēd) n. coarse, colored wool cloth.

tweet (twēt) n. **1.** chirping sound. —v. **2.** chirp.

tweet′er, n. small loudspeaker reproducing high-frequency sounds.

tweez′ers (twē′zərz) n.pl. small pincers.

twelve (twelv) n., adj. ten plus two. —**twelfth,** adj., n.

Twelve Step, of or based on program for recovery from addiction that provides 12 progressive levels toward attainment.

twen′ty (twen′tē) n., adj. ten times two. —**twen′ti•eth,** adj., n.

twerp (twûrp) n. Slang. insignificant or despicable person.

twice (twīs) adv. **1.** two times. **2.** doubly.

twid′dle (twid′l) v., -dled, -dling. **1.** turn round and round, esp. with the fingers. **2.** twirl (one's fingers) about each other.

twig (twig) n. slender shoot on tree.

twi′light′ (twī′līt′) n. light from sky when sun is down.

twill (twil) n. **1.** fabric woven in parallel diagonal lines. **2.** the weave. —v. **3.** weave in twill.

T.W.I.M.C. to whom it may concern.

twin (twin) n. either of two children born at single birth.

twine (twīn) n., v., twined, twining. —n. **1.** strong thread of twisted strands. **2.** twist. —v. **3.** twist or become twisted together. **4.** encircle.

twinge (twinj) n., v., twinged, twinging. —n. **1.** sudden, sharp pain. —v. **2.** give or have twinge.

twin′kle (twing′kəl) v., -kled, -kling, n. —v. **1.** shine with light, quick gleams. —n. **2.** sly, humorous look. **3.** act of twinkling.

twin′kling, n. instant.

twirl (twûrl) v. **1.** spin; whirl. —n. **2.** a twirling.

twist (twist) v. **1.** combine by winding together. **2.** distort. **3.** combine in coil, etc. **4.** wind about. **5.** writhe. **6.** turn. —n. **7.** curve or turn. **8.** spin. **9.** wrench. **10.** spiral.

twist′er, n. **1.** person or thing that twists. **2.** Informal. whirlwind or tornado.

twit (twit) v., twitted, twitting, n. —v. **1.** taunt; tease. —n. **2.** Informal. insignificant or bothersome person.

twitch (twich) v. **1.** jerk; move with jerk. —n. **2.** quick jerky movement, as of muscle.

twit′ter (twit′ər) v. **1.** utter small, tremulous sounds, as bird. **2.** tremble with excitement. —n. **3.** twittering sound. **4.** state of tremulous excitement.

two (tōō) n., adj. one plus one.

2b Baseball. **1.** double (2-base hit). **2.** second base.

two′-bit′, adj. Informal. inferior or unimportant.

two bits, Informal. 25 cents.

two′-faced′, adj. deceitful or hypocritical.

two′-fist′ed, adj. strong and vigorous.

two′fold′ adj. (-fōld′) **1.** having two parts. **2.** twice as great. —adv. (fōld′) **3.** in twofold measure.

two′-ply′, adj. consisting of two layers, strands, etc.

two′some (-səm) n. pair.

two′-time′, v., -timed, -timing. Informal. be unfaithful to. —**two′-tim′er,** n.

two′-way′, adj. **1.** allowing movement in two directions. **2.** involving two participants.

2WD two-wheel drive.

twp., township.

twr tower.

twt traveling-wave tube.

TWU Transport Workers Union of America.

TWX (often twiks), a teletypewriter service operating in the United States and Canada. [t(eletype)w(riter) (e)x(change service)]

twy taxiway.

TX, Texas.

txtl textile.

-ty, suffix meaning state or condition, as certainty.

ty•coon′ (tī kōōn′) n. businessperson having great wealth and power.

tyke (tīk) n. small child.

tympanic membrane, membrane separating middle from external ear.

tym′pa•num (tim′pə nəm) n. **1.** middle ear. **2.** tympanic membrane. —**tym•pan′ic,** adj.

typ. 1. typical. **2.** typographer. **3.** typographic; typographical. **4.** typography.

type (tīp) *n.*, *v.*, **typed, typing.** —*n.* **1.** kind or class. **2.** representative specimen. **3.** piece bearing a letter in relief, used in printing. **4.** such pieces collectively. —*v.* **5.** typewrite. —**typ′ist,** *n.*

type′cast′, *n.*, **-cast, -casting.** cast (actor) exclusively in same kind of role.

type′script′, *n.* typewritten matter.

type′set′ter, *n.* **1.** person who sets type. **2.** machine for setting type. —**type′set′,** *v.* **-set, -setting.**

type′writ′er, *n.* machine for writing mechanically. —**type′write′,** *v.*, **-wrote** (-rōt′), **-writ•ten** (-rit′n).

ty′phoid (tī′foid) *n.* infectious disease marked by intestinal disorder. Also, **typhoid fever.**

ty•phoon′ (tī fōōn′) *n.* cyclone or hurricane of western Pacific.

ty′phus (tī′fəs) *n.* infectious disease transmitted by lice and fleas.

typ′i•cal (tip′i kəl) *adj.* **1.** serving as a representative specimen. **2.** conforming to the characteristics of a particular group. —**typ′i•cal•ly,** *adv.*

typ′i•fy′, *v.*, **-fied, -fying.** serve as typical example of.

ty′po (tī′pō) *n.*, *pl.* **-pos.** error in typography or typing.

typog. 1. typographer. **2.** typographic; typographical. **3.** typography.

ty•pog′ra•phy (tī pog′rə fē) *n.* **1.** art or process of printing. **2.** general character of printed matter. —**ty•pog′ra•pher,** *n.* —**ty′•po•graph′ic** (-pə graf′ik), **ty′po•graph′i•cal,** *adj.*

typstg typesetting.

typw. 1. typewriter. **2.** typewritten.

ty•ran′no•saur′ (ti ran′ə sôr′, tī-) *n.* large dinosaur that walked upright.

tyr′an•ny (tir′ə nē) *n.*, *pl.* **-nies. 1.** despotic abuse of authority. **2.** government or rule by tyrant. —**ty•ran′ni•cal** (ti ran′i kəl, tī-) *adj.* —**tyr′an•nize′,** *v.*, **-nized, -nizing.**

ty′rant (tī′rənt) *n.* oppressive, unjust, or absolute ruler.

ty′ro (tī′rō) *n.*, *pl.* **-ros.** novice.

tyvm thank you very much.

tzar (zär, tsär) *n.* czar.

U

U, u (yōō) *n.* twenty-first letter of English alphabet.

U.A.E. United Arab Emirates. Also, **UAE**

UAM underwater-to-air missile.

u. & l.c. *Printing.* upper and lowercase.

U.A.R. United Arab Republic.

UART (yōō´ärt), *Computers.* universal asynchronous receiver-transmitter.

UAW United Automobile Workers. Also, **U.A.W.**

U.B. United Brethren.

u·biq´ui·tous (yōō bik´wi təs) *adj.* simultaneously present everywhere. —**u·biq´ui·ty,** *n.*

ubl unbleached.

U´-boat´, *n.* German submarine.

U.C. 1. Upper Canada. **2.** under construction. **3.** undercover.

u.c. 1. *Music.* una corda: with the soft pedal depressed. **2.** *Printing.* upper case.

ucc Universal copyright convention.

UCR Uniform Crime Report.

U.C.V. United Confederate Veterans.

U/D under deed.

u.d. (in prescriptions) as directed. [from Latin *ut dictum*]

UDAG (yōō´dag), a federal program providing funds to local governments or private investors for urban redevelopment projects. [*U(rban) D(evelopment) A(ction) G(rant)*]

UDC Universal Decimal Classification.

U.D.C. United Daughters of the Confederacy.

ud´der (ud´ər) *n.* mammary gland, esp. of cow.

udtd updated.

U.F.C. United Free Church (of Scotland).

UFD user file directory.

UFO (yōō´ef´ō´; *sometimes* yōō´fō) unidentified flying object.

UFT United Federation of Teachers. Also, **U.F.T.**

UFW United Farm Workers of America.

ug´ly (ug´lē) *adj.,* **-lier, -liest. 1.** repulsive. **2.** dangerous. —**ug´li·ness,** *n.*

ugnd underground.

UHF ultrahigh frequency. Also, **uhf**

UHT ultrahigh temperature.

UI unemployment insurance.

u.i. as below. [from Latin *ut infra*]

UIT unit investment trust.

UJT unijunction transistor.

U.K. United Kingdom.

u·kase (yōō kās´, -kāz´) *n.* order by absolute authority.

u´ku·le´le (yōō´kə lā´lē) *n.* small guitar.

UL Underwriters' Laboratories (used especially on labels for electrical appliances approved by this safety-testing organization).

ULCC a supertanker with a deadweight capacity of over 250,000 tons. [*u(ltra) l(arge) c(rude) c(arrier)*]

ul´cer (ul´sər) *n.* open sore, as on stomach lining. —**ul´cer·ous,** *adj.* —**ul´cer·ate´,** *v.,* **-ated, -ating.**

ulf ultralow frequency.

ULMS underwater long-range missile system.

ul´na (ul´nə) *n.* larger bone of forearm. —**ul´nar,** *adj.*

ULSI *Computers.* ultra large-scale integration.

ult. 1. Also, **ult** ultimate. **2.** ultimately. **3.** Also, **ulto.** the last month. [from Latin *ultimo*]

ul·te´ri·or (ul tēr´ē ər) *adj.* **1.** not acknowledged; concealed. **2.** later.

ul´ti·ma (ul´tə mə) *n.* last syllable of word.

ul´ti·mate (-mit) *adj.* **1.** final; highest. **2.** basic. —**ul´ti·mate·ly,** *adv.*

ul´ti·ma´tum (-mā´təm, -mä´-) *n., pl.* **-tums, -ta** (-tə). final demand.

ultra-, prefix meaning beyond; on the far side of; extremely.

ul´tra·con·serv´a·tive (ul´trə kən sûr´və tiv) *adj.* extremely conservative, esp. in politics.

ul´tra·fiche´ (-fēsh´) *n.* form of microfiche with images greatly reduced in size.

ul´tra·high´ frequency (ul´trə hī´) radio frequency between 300 and 3000 megahertz.

ul´tra·ma·rine´, *n.* deep blue.

ul´tra·sound´, *n.* **1.** sound above limit of human hearing. **2.** application of ultrasound to medical diagnosis and therapy. —**ul´tra·son´ic,** *adj.*

ul´tra·vi·o·let, *adj.* of invisible rays beyond violet in spectrum.

umbc umbilical cord.

um´ber (um´bər) *n.* **1.** reddish brown. —*adj.* **2.** of or like umber.

umbilical cord (um bil´i kəl) cordlike structure connecting fetus with placenta, conveying nourishment and removing wastes.

um·bil´i·cus (-kəs) *n., pl.* **-ci** (-sī). navel. —**um·bil´i·cal,** *adj.*

Umbr. Umbrian.

um´brage (um´brij) *n.* resentment.

um·brel´la (um brel´ə) *n.* cloth-covered framework carried for protection from rain, etc.

u´mi·ak (ōō´mē ak´) *n.* open Eskimo boat covered with skins.

um´laut (ōōm´lout) *n.* **1.** (in Germanic languages) assimilation in which vowel is influenced by following vowel. **2.** diacritical mark (æ) used over vowel to indicate umlaut.

ump (ump) *n., v.* umpire.

um′pire (um′pīᵊr) *n., v.,* **-pired, -piring.** —*n.* **1.** judge or arbitrator. —*v.* **2.** be umpire in.

ump′teen (ump′tēn′) *adj. Informal.* innumerable. —**ump•teenth′,** *adj.*

UMT universal military training.

umus unbleached muslin.

UMW United Mine Workers.

UN, United Nations.

un-, prefix indicating negative or opposite sense, as in *unfair, unwanted,* and *unfasten.*

un•a′ble (un ā′bəl) *adj.* lacking necessary power, skill, or resources.

un′ac•count′a•ble, *adj.* **1.** inexplicable. **2.** not responsible. —**un′ac•count′a•bly,** *adv.*

un′af•fect′ed, *adj.* **1.** without affectation. **2.** not concerned or involved.

unan. unanimous.

u•nan′i•mous (yōō nan′ə məs) *adj.* completely agreed. —**u•nan′i•mous•ly,** *adv.* —**u′na•nim′i•ty** (-nə nim′i tē) *n.*

un′as•sum′ing (un′-) *adj.* modest; without vanity.

un′at•tached′, *adj.* **1.** not attached. **2.** not engaged or married.

unauth unauthorized.

un′a•vail′ing, *adj.* not effective; futile.

un′a•wares′, *adv.* not knowingly.

un•bal′anced, *adj.* **1.** out of balance. **2.** irrational; deranged.

un•bear′a•ble, *adj.* unendurable. —**un•bear′a•bly,** *adv.*

un′be•com′ing, *adj.* unattractive or unseemly.

un•bend, *v.,* **-bent, -bending. 1.** straighten. **2.** act in genial, relaxed manner.

un•bend′ing, *adj.* rigidly formal or unyielding.

un•bid′den, *adj.* **1.** not commanded. **2.** not asked.

un•blush′ing, *adj.* showing no remorse; shameless.

un•bos′om, *v.* disclose (secrets, etc.).

un•bowed′ (-boud′) *adj.* **1.** not bent. **2.** not subjugated.

un•brid′led, *adj.* unrestrained.

un•bro′ken, *adj.* **1.** not broken. **2.** undisturbed. **3.** not tamed.

un•bur′den, *v.* **1.** free from burden. **2.** relieve one′s mind, conscience, etc., by confessing.

UNC 1. Unified coarse (a thread measure). **2.** Also, **U.N.C.** United Nations Command.

unc. *Numismatics.* uncirculated.

un•called′-for′, *adj.* not warranted.

un•can′ny, *adj.* unnaturally strange or good.

un•cer′e•mo′ni•ous, *adj.* **1.** informal. **2.** rudely abrupt.

UNCF United Negro College Fund.

un•chart′ed, *adj.* not shown on map; unexplored.

un′ci•al (un′shē əl, -shəl) *adj.* of a form of writing with a rounded shape, esp. in early Greek and Latin manuscripts.

UNCIO United Nations Conference on International Organization.

un•clad′, *adj.* naked.

unclas unclassified.

un′cle (ung′kəl) *n.* brother of one′s father or mother.

Uncle Sam (sam) United States government.

un•com′pro•mis′ing, *adj.* refusing to compromise; rigid.

un′con•cern′, *n.* lack of concern; indifference.

uncond unconditional.

un′con•di′tion•al, *adj.* absolute; without conditions or reservations. —**un′con•di′-tion•al•ly,** *adv.*

un•con′scion•a•ble (-shən-) *adj.* not reasonable or honest.

un•con′scious, *adj.* **1.** lacking awareness, sensation, or cognition. **2.** not perceived at level of awareness. **3.** done without intent. —*n.* **4. the unconscious,** part of psyche rarely accessible to awareness but influencing behavior.

un•couth′ (un kōōth′) *adj.* rude; boorish.

unc′tion (ungk′shən) *n.* **1.** anointment with oil. **2.** soothing manner of speech.

unc′tu•ous (-chōō əs) *adj.* **1.** oily. **2.** overly suave.

un•cut′ (un-) *adj.* **1.** not shortened; unabridged. **2.** not yet given shape, as a gemstone.

und under.

un•daunt′ed, *adj.* not discouraged or dismayed.

undc undercurrent.

undef undefined.

un′de•mon′stra•tive, *adj.* reserved.

un′der (un′dər) *prep., adj., adv.* **1.** beneath; below. **2.** less than. **3.** lower.

under-, prefix meaning: **1.** below or beneath, as *underbrush.* **2.** lower in grade, as *understudy.* **3.** of lesser degre or amount, as *underestimate.*

un′der•a•chieve′, *v.,* **-achieved, -achieving.** perform below one′s intellectual potential. —**un′der•a•chiev′er,** *n.*

un′der•age′, *adj.* being below legal or required age.

un′der•bel′ly, *n., pl.* **-ies. 1.** lower abdomen. **2.** vulnerable area.

un′der•brush′, *n.* low shrubs, etc., in forest.

un′der•car′riage, *n.* supporting framework underneath vehicle.

un′der•clothes′, *n.pl.* underwear. Also, **un′der•cloth′ing.**

un′der•cov′er, *adj.* secret.

un′der•cur′rent, *n.* **1.** hidden tendency or feeling. **2.** current below surface or beneath another current.

un′der•cut′, *v.,* **-cut, -cutting.** sell at lower price than.

un′der•de•vel′oped, *adj.* **1.** insufficiently

developed. **2.** having relatively low living standards and industrial development.

un′der•dog′, *n.* **1.** weaker contestant, etc. **2.** victim of injustice.

un′der•done′, *adj.* not cooked enough.

un′der•es′ti•mate′ (-māt′) *v.,* **-mated, -mating.** estimate too low.

un′der•ex•pose′, *v.,* **-posed, -posing.** expose (film) to insufficient light or for too short a period.

un′der•gar′ment, *n.* item of underwear.

un′der•go′, *v.,* **-went, -gone, -going.** experience; endure.

un′der•grad′u•ate (-it) *n.* college student before receiving first degree.

un′der•ground′ *adv.* (un′dər`ground′), *adj.* (-ground′). **1.** under the ground. **2.** secret. —*n.* (-ground′) **3.** secret resistance army.

un′der•growth′, *n.* underbrush.

un′der•hand′, *adj.* sly; secret. Also, **un′der•hand′ed.**

un′der•lie′, *v.,* **-lay, -lain, -lying. 1.** lie beneath. **2.** be the cause or basis of.

un′der•line′, *v.,* **-lined, -lining. 1.** draw line under. **2.** stress; emphasize.

un′der•ling′ (-ling) *n.* subordinate.

un′der•mine′ (un′dər mīn′, un′dər mīn′) *v.,* **-mined, -mining.** weaken or destroy, esp. secretly.

un′der•neath′ (-nēth′, -nēth′) *prep., adv.* beneath.

un′der•pass′, *n.* passage running underneath.

un′der•pin′ning, *n.* **1.** system of supports. **2.** foundation; basis.

un′der•priv′i•leged, *adj.* denied normal privileges of society, esp. because poor.

un′der•score′, *v.,* **-scored, -scoring.** underline; stress.

un′der•sec′re•tar′y, *n., pl.* **-taries.** government official subordinate to principal secretary.

un′der•signed′, *n.* **the undersigned,** person signing document.

un′der-staffed′, *adj.* having insufficient number of workers.

un′der•stand′, *v.,* **-stood, -standing. 1.** know meaning of. **2.** accept as part of agreement. **3.** sympathize. —**un′der•stand′ing,** *n.*

un′der•state′, *v.,* **-stated, -stating. 1.** state less strongly than facts warrant. **2.** set forth in restrained terms. —**un′der•state′ment,** *n.*

un′der•stood′, *adj.* agreed or assumed.

un′der•stud′y, *n., pl.* **-studies.** substitute for performer.

un′der•take′, *v.,* **-took, -taken, -taking. 1.** attempt. **2.** promise. **3.** arrange funerals.

un′der•tak′er, *n.* funeral director; mortician.

un′der•tak′ing (un′dər tā′king, un′dər tā′-) *n.* enterprise; task.

un′der-the-coun′ter, *adj.* illegal; unauthorized.

un′der•tone′, *n.* **1.** low tone. **2.** underlying quality. **3.** subdued color.

un′der•tow′ (-tō′) *n.* strong subsurface current moving opposite surface current.

un′der•wear′, *n.* garments worn next to skin, under other clothing.

un′der•world′, *n.* **1.** criminal element. **2.** land of the dead.

un′der•write′ (un′dər rīt′, un′dər rīt′) *v.,* **-wrote, -written, -writing.** guarantee, esp. expense.

undetm undetermined.

undf underfrequency.

undld underload.

un•do′ (un dōō′) *v.,* **-did, -done, -doing. 1.** return to original state. **2.** untie. **3.** destroy.

un•do′ing, *n.* **1.** reversing. **2.** ruin. **3.** cause of ruin.

un′du•late′ (un′jə lāt′, -dyə-) *v.,* **-lated, -lating.** have wavy motion or form. —**un′du•lant,** *adj.* —**un′du•la′tion,** *n.*

undv undervoltage.

un•dy′ing, *adj.* eternal; unending.

un•earned′, *adj.* **1.** not earned by service. **2.** not deserved. **3.** (of income) derived from investments.

un•earth′, *v.* discover.

un•earth′ly, *adj.* **1.** not of this world. **2.** supernatural; weird. **3.** unreasonable; absurd.

un•eas′y, *adj.,* **-ier, -iest.** anxious. —**un•eas′i•ly,** *adv.* —**un•eas′i•ness,** *n.*

UNEF 1. Unified extra-fine (a thread measure). **2.** United Nations Emergency Force.

un′e•quiv′o•cal, *adj.* unambiguous.

UNESCO (yōō nes′kō), United Nations Educational, Scientific, and Cultural Organization.

un′e•vent′ful, *adj.* routine.

un′ex•cep′tion•al, *adj.* ordinary.

UNF Unified fine (a thread measure).

un•feel′ing, *adj.* lacking sympathy. —**un•feel′ing•ly,** *adv.*

unfin unfinished.

un•flap′pa•ble (un flap′ə bəl) *adj.* not easily upset.

un•fledged′ (-flejd′) *adj.* **1.** lacking sufficient feathers for flight. **2.** immature.

un•found′ed, *adj.* not supported by evidence.

un•frock′, *v.* deprive of ecclesiastical rank, authority, and function.

ung. (in prescriptions) ointment. [from Latin *unguentum*]

un•gain′ly (-gān′lē) *adj.* clumsy.

ungt. (in prescriptions) ointment. [from Latin *unguentum*]

un′guent (ung′gwənt) *n.* salve.

un′gu•late (ung′gyə lit, -lāt′) *adj.* **1.** having hoofs. —*n.* **2.** hoofed mammal.

Unh *Symbol, Chemistry, Physics.* unnilhexium.

un•hand′, *v.* release from grasp.

U

un•hinge′, v., **-hinged, -hinging. 1.** take off hinges. **2.** upset reason of; unbalance.

uni-, prefix meaning one.

UNICEF (yōō′nə sef′), United Nations Children's Fund. [U(nited) N(ations) I(nternational) C(hildren's) E(mergency) F(und) (an earlier official name)]

u′ni•corn′ (yōō′ni kôrn′) n. mythical horse-like animal with one horn.

unif uniform.

unifet unipolar field-effect transistor.

u′ni•form′ (yōō′nə fôrm′) adj. **1.** exactly alike. **2.** even. —n. **3.** distinctive clothing of specific group. —v. **4.** put in uniform. —u′ni•form′i•ty, n.

u′ni•fy′ (-fī′) v., **-fied, -fying.** make into one. —u′ni•fi•ca′tion, n.

u′ni•lat′er•al, adj. one-sided.

un′im•peach′a•ble (un′im pē′chə bəl) adj. above reproach.

un′in•hib′it•ed, adj. unrestrained by convention.

un•in′ter•est•ed, adj. not interested; indifferent.

—Usage. See DISINTERESTED.

un′ion (yōōn′yən) n. **1.** uniting; combination. **2.** labor group for mutual aid on wages, etc. —un′ion•ism, n. —un′ion•ist, n., adj. —un′ion•ize′, v.

Union Jack, British flag.

u•nique′ (yōō nēk′) adj. **1.** only. **2.** most unusual or rare. —u•nique′ly, adv.

—Usage. UNIQUE is an adjective representing an absolute state that cannot exist in degrees. Therefore, it cannot be sensibly used with a limiting or comparative adverb such as "very," "most," or "extremely": *She has a unique* (not "*very unique*" or "*most unique*") *style of singing.*

u′ni•sex′ (yōō′nə seks′) adj. of type or style used by both sexes.

u′ni•son (-sən, -zən) n. agreement.

u′nit (yōō′nit) n. one of number of identical or similar things.

U′ni•tar′i•an (yōō′ni târ′ē ən) n. **1.** member of Christian denomination asserting unity of God. —adj. **2.** concerning Unitarians or their beliefs.

u•nite′ (yōō nīt′) v., **united, uniting.** join, make, etc., into one.

United Nations, organization of nations to preserve peace and promote human welfare.

u′ni•ty (yōō′ni tē) n., pl. **-ties. 1.** state of being one. **2.** agreement. **3.** uniformity.

Univ. 1. Universalist. **2.** University.

univ. 1. universal. **2.** universally. **3.** university.

UNIVAC (yōō′ni vak′), Universal Automatic Computer.

u′ni•va′lent (yōō′nə vā′lənt, yōō niv′ə-) adj. having chemical valence of one.

u′ni•valve′, n. mollusk with single valve.

u′ni•ver′sal (yōō′nə vûr′səl) adj. **1.** of all; general. **2.** of universe. **3.** having many skills, much learning, etc. —un′i•ver′sal•ly, adv. —u′ni•ver•sal′i•ty (-sal′i tē) n.

Universal Product Code, standardized bar code.

u′ni•verse′ (-vûrs′) n. all things that exist, including heavenly bodies.

u′ni•ver′si•ty (-vûr′si tē) n., pl. **-ties.** institution composed of various specialized colleges.

unk unknown.

un•kempt′ (un kempt′) adj. untidy.

unl unloading.

un•lead′ed (-led′id) adj. (of gasoline) free of pollution-causing lead.

un•less′ (un les′, ən-) conj., prep. except that.

un•let′tered, adj. illiterate.

unlim unlimited.

unlkg unlocking.

un•mit′i•gat′ed, adj. **1.** not lessened. **2.** absolute.

unmkd unmarked.

unmtd unmounted.

un•nerve′, v., **-nerved, -nerving.** deprive of courage, strength, or determination.

Unp Symbol, Chemistry, Physics. unnilpentium.

un•par′al•leled′, adj. without equal.

un•plumbed′, adj. not explored in depth.

un•prin′ci•pled, adj. without principles or ethics.

un•print′a•ble, adj. unfit for print, esp. because obscene.

Unq Symbol, Chemistry, Physics. unnilquadium.

un•rav′el, v., **-eled, -eling. 1.** disentangle. **2.** solve.

un•read′ (-red′) adj. **1.** not read. **2.** lacking in knowledge gained by reading.

un′re•con•struct′ed, adj. stubbornly maintaining beliefs considered out of date.

un′re•mit′ting, adj. not abating; incessant.

un•rest′, n. **1.** restless state. **2.** strong, almost rebellious, dissatisfaction.

unrgltd unregulated.

UNRRA (un′rə), United Nations Relief and Rehabilitation Administration. Also, **U.N.R.R.A.**

un•ruf′fled, adj. calm.

un•ru′ly (un rōō′lē) adj., **-lier, -liest.** lawless.

UNRWA United Nations Relief and Works Agency.

uns unserviceable.

un•sa′vo•ry, adj. **1.** tasteless; insipid. **2.** unpleasant in taste or smell. **3.** morally objectionable.

UNSC United Nations Security Council.

un•sea′son•a•ble, adj. **1.** being out of season. **2.** inopportune.

un•seat′, v. **1.** dislodge from seat. **2.** remove from political office.

un•seem′ly, *adj.,* **-lier, -liest.** improper.

un•set′tle, *v.,* **-tled, -tling. 1.** cause to be unstable; disturb. **2.** agitate mind or emotions of.

un•sound′, *adj.* **1.** unhealthy. **2.** not solid. **3.** not valid. **4.** not secure.

un•spar′ing, *adj.* **1.** profuse. **2.** unmerciful.

un•speak′a•ble, *adj.* **1.** exceeding the power of speech. **2.** inexpressibly bad.

un•sta′ble, *adj.* **1.** unsteady. **2.** changeable. **3.** emotionally unsettled.

unstpd. unstamped.

un•strung′, *adj.* nervously upset; unnerved.

un•sung′, *adj.* not celebrated, as in song; unappreciated.

un•taught′, *adj.* **1.** natural. **2.** not educated.

un•ten′a•ble, *adj.* not defensible as true.

un•think′a•ble, *adj.* not to be imagined; impossible.

un•ti′dy, *adj.,* **-dier, -diest.** not tidy or neat. —**un•tid′i•ly,** *adv.*

un•tie′, *v.,* **-tied, -tying.** loosen or open (something tied).

un•til′ (un til′) *conj., prep.* **1.** up to time when. **2.** before.
—Usage. See TILL.

un′to (un′tōō; *unstressed* -tə) *prep. Archaic.* to.

un•told′, *adj.* countless.

un•touch′a•ble, *adj.* **1.** beyond control or criticism. **2.** too vile to touch. —**un•touch′a•ble,** *n.*

un•to•ward′, *adj.* unfavorable or unfortunate.

untrtd untreated.

un•well′, *adj.* ill or ailing.

un•wield′y, *adj.,* **-ier, -iest.** awkward to handle.

un•wit′ting, *adj.* not aware. —**un•wit′ting•ly,** *adv.*

un•wont′ed (un wôn′tid, -wōn′-, -wun′-) *adj.* not habitual or usual.

u/o used on.

up (up) *adv., prep., n., v.,* **upped, upping.** —*adv.* **1.** to higher place, etc. **2.** erectly. **3.** out of bed. **4.** at bat. —*prep.* **5.** to higher place, etc., on or in. —*n.* **6.** rise. —*v.* **7.** increase.

up′-and-com′ing, *adj.* likely to succeed; promising.

up•beat′, *adj.* optimistic; happy.

up•braid′ (up brād′) *v.* chide.

up′bring′ing, *n.* care and training of children.

UPC, Universal Product Code.

up′com′ing, *adj.* about to take place or appear.

up′coun′try, *adj., adv.* of, toward, or situated in the interior of a region.

up′date′ (up′dāt′, up′dāt′) *v.,* **-dated, -dating.** modernize, esp. in details.

up′draft′, *n.* upward movement of air.

updt update.

up•end′, *v.* set on end.

up′-front′, *adj.* **1.** invested or paid in advance. **2.** honest; candid.

up′grade′ *n., v.,* **-graded, -grading.** —*n.* (up′grād′) **1.** upward incline. **2.** increase, rise, or improvement. —*v.* (up grād′, up′grād′) **3.** raise in rank, position, quality, or value.

up•heav′al (up hē′vəl) *n.* sudden and great movement or change.

up′hill′, *adv.* up a slope or incline. —**up′hill′,** *adj.*

up•hold′, *v.,* **-held, -holding.** support. —**up•hold′er,** *n.*

up•hol′ster (up hōl′stər, ə pōl′-) *v.* provide (furniture) with coverings, etc. —**up•hol′ster•er,** *n.* —**up•hol′ster•y,** *n.*

UPI United Press International. Also, **U.P.I.**

up′keep′, *n.* maintenance.

up′land (up′lənd, -land′) *n.* elevated region.

up•lift′ *v.* (up lift′) **1.** improve; exalt. —*n.* (up′lift′) **2.** improvement. **3.** inspiration.

up•on′ (ə pon′, ə pôn′) *prep.* on.

up′per, *adj.* higher. —**up′per•most′,** *adj.*

up′per•case′, *adj.* **1.** (of a letter) capital. —*n.* **2.** capital letter.

upper hand, controlling position; advantage.

up′pi•ty (up′i tē) *adj. Informal.* haughty, snobbish, or arrogant.

up′right′ (up′rīt′, up rīt′) *adj.* **1.** erect. **2.** righteous. —**up′right′ness,** *n.*

up′ris′ing (up′rī′zing, up rī′-) *n.* revolt.

up′roar′, *n.* tumult; noise; din. —**up•roar′i•ous,** *adj.*

up•root′, *v.* tear up by roots.

uprt upright.

UPS 1. *Computers.* uninterruptible power supply. **2.** *Trademark.* United Parcel Service.

up′scale′, *adj.* of or for people at upper end of economic scale.

up•set′, *v.,* **-set, -setting,** *n., adj.* —*v.* (up set′) **1.** turn over. **2.** distress emotionally. **3.** defeat. —*n.* (up′set′) **4.** overturn. **5.** defeat. —*adj.* (up set′) **6.** disorderly. **7.** distressed.

up′shot′, *n.* final result.

upside down, 1. with upper part undermost. **2.** in or into complete disorder. —**up′side-down′,** *adj.*

up′stage′, *adv., v.,* **-staged, -staging.** —*adv.* **1.** at or toward back of stage. —*v.* **2.** draw attention away from by moving upstage. **3.** outdo professionally or socially.

up′stairs′, *adv., adj.* on or to upper floor.

up′start′, *n.* person newly risen to wealth or importance.

UPSW Union of Postal Service Workers.

up′-to-date′, *adj.* **1.** until now. **2.** modern; latest.

UPU Universal Postal Union.

U.P.W.A. United Packinghouse Workers of America.

up′ward (up′wərd) *adv.* to higher place. Also, **up′wards.** —**up′ward,** *adj.*

U

upwd upward.

UR unsatisfactory report.

ur urinal.

Ur. Uruguay.

u·ra′ni·um (yŏŏ rā′nē əm) *n*. white, radioactive metallic element, important in development of atomic energy.

U′ra·nus (yŏŏr′ə nəs, yŏŏ rā′-) *n*. planet seventh in order from the sun.

ur′ban (ûr′bən) *adj*. of or like a city.

ur·bane′ (ûr bān′) *adj*. polite or suave. —**ur·ban′i·ty** (-ban′i tē) *n*.

ur′chin (ûr′chin) *n*. ragged child.

URE Undergraduate Record Examination.

u·re′a (yŏŏ rē′ə, yŏŏr′ē ə) *n*. compound occurring in body fluids, esp. urine.

u·re′mi·a (yŏŏ rē′mē ə) *n*. presence in blood of products normally excreted in urine.

u·re′ter (yŏŏ rē′tər) *n*. duct that conveys urine from kidney to bladder.

u·re′thra (yŏŏ rē′thrə) *n*., *pl*. **-thrae** (-thrē), **-thras.** duct that conveys urine and, in most male animals, semen.

urge (ûrj) *v*., **urged, urging,** *n*. —*v*. **1**. force, incite, or advocate. **2**. entreat. —*n*. **3**. desire; impulse.

ur′gent (ûr′jənt) *adj*. vital; pressing. —**ur′gent·ly,** *adv*. —**ur′gen·cy,** *n*.

u′ri·nal (yŏŏr′ə nl) *n*. wall fixture used by men for urinating.

u′ri·nal′y·sis (-nal′ə sis) *n*., *pl*. **-ses.** diagnostic analysis of urine.

u′ri·nar′y (-ner′ē) *adj*. **1**. of urine. **2**. of organs that secrete and discharge urine.

u′ri·nate′ (-nāt′) *v*., **-nated, -nating.** pass urine. —**u′ri·na′tion,** *n*.

u′rine (yŏŏr′in) *n*. secretion of kidneys. —**u′ric** (yŏŏr′ik) *adj*.

urn (ûrn) *n*. vase or pot.

urol. 1. urological. **2**. urologist. **3**. urology.

u·rol′o·gy (yŏŏ rol′ə jē) *n*. medical study of urinary or genitourinary tract. —**u·rol′o·gist,** *n*.

Uru. Uruguay.

us (us) *pron*. objective case of **we.**

USA 1. United States of America. **2**. United States Army. **3**. USA Network (a cable television channel). **4**. United Steelworkers of America.

U.S.A. 1. Union of South Africa. **2**. United States of America. **3**. United States Army.

USAEC United States Atomic Energy Commission.

U.S.A.F. United States Air Force. Also, **USAF**

USAFI United States Armed Forces Institute.

U.S.A.F.R. United States Air Force Reserve. Also, **USAFR**

us′age (yŏŏ′sij, -zij) *n*. **1**. custom. **2**. treatment.

USAID United States Aid for International Development.

USAR United States Army Reserve.

usb upper sideband.

USBC United States Bureau of the Census.

USBLS United States Bureau of Labor Statistics.

USBP United States Border Patrol.

U.S.C. 1. United States Code. **2**. United States of Colombia. Also, **USC**

U.S.C.A. United States Code Annotated. Also, **USCA**

U.S.C.&G.S. United States Coast and Geodetic Survey.

USCC United States Chamber of Commerce.

USCG United States Coast Guard. Also, **U.S.C.G.**

USCRC 1. United States Citizens Radio Council. **2**. United States Civil Rights Commission.

USCS United States Civil Service.

U.S.C. Supp. United States Code Supplement.

USDA United States Department of Agriculture. Also, **U.S.D.A.**

USDE 1. United States Department of Education. **2**. United States Department of Energy.

USDHEW United States Department of Health Education and Welfare.

USDHUD United States Department of Housing and Urban Development.

USDI United States Department of the Interior.

USDJ United States Department of Justice.

USDL United States Department of Labor.

USDT United States Department of Transportation.

use, *v*., **used, using,** *n*. —*v*. (yŏŏz or, *for pt. form of* 5, yŏŏst) **1**. do something with aid of. **2**. expend. **3**. make practice of. **4**. treat. **5**. accustom. —*n*. (yŏŏs) **6**. act or way of using. **7**. service or value. —**us′a·ble,** *adj*. —**use′ful,** *adj*. —**use′ful·ness,** *n*. —**use′less,** *adj*. —**use′less·ness,** *n*. —**us′er,** *n*.

USECC United States Employees' Compensation Commission.

us′er-friend′ly, *adj*. easy to operate or understand.

USES United States Employment Service. Also, **U.S.E.S.**

USG United States Gauge.

U.S.G.A. United States Golf Association. Also, **USGA**

USGPO United States Government Printing Office.

USGS United States Geological Survey.

USHA United States Housing Authority. Also, **U.S.H.A.**

ush′er (ush′ər) *n*. person who escorts people to seats, as in theater.

USIA United States Information Agency. Also, **U.S.I.A.**

USIS United States Information Service. Also, **U.S.I.S.**

USITC United States International Trade Commission.

U.S.L.T.A. United States Lawn Tennis Association. Also, **USLTA**

USM 1. underwater-to-surface missile. **2**.

United States Mail. **3.** United States Marines. **4.** United States Mint. Also, **U.S.M.**

U.S.M.A. United States Military Academy. Also, **USMA**

USMC 1. United States Marine Corps. **2.** United States Maritime Commission. Also, **U.S.M.C.**

USMS United States Maritime Service.

USN United States Navy. Also, **U.S.N.**

USNA 1. United States National Army. **2.** United States Naval Academy. Also, **U.S.N.A.**

USNG United States National Guard. Also, **U.S.N.G.**

USNR United States Naval Reserve. Also, **U.S. N.R.**

USO United Service Organizations. Also, **U.S.O.**

USOC United States Olympic Committee.

U.S.P. United States Pharmacopeia. Also, **U.S. Pharm.**

uspd underspeed.

USPHS United States Public Health Service. Also, **U.S.P.H.S.**

USPO 1. United States Patent Office. **2.** United States Post Office. Also, **U.S.P.O.**

USPS United States Postal Service. Also, **U.S.P.S.**

USR United States Reserves. Also, **U.S.R.**

USRC United States Reserve Corps. Also, **U.S.R.C.**

U.S. RDA *Nutrition.* United States recommended daily allowance.

U.S.S. 1. United States Senate. **2.** United States Service. **3.** United States Ship. **4.** United States Steamer. **5.** United States Steamship. Also, **USS**

U.S.S.B. United States Shipping Board. Also, **USSB**

U.S.S.Ct. United States Supreme Court.

U.S.S.R. Union of Soviet Socialist Republics. Also, **USSR**

U.S.S.S. United States Steamship. Also, **USSS**

USTA United States Trademark Association.

USTC United States Tariff Commission.

USTS United States Travel Service: part of the Department of Commerce.

usu. 1. usual. **2.** usually.

u′su•al (yōō′zhōō əl) *adj.* **1.** customary. **2.** common. —**u′su•al•ly,** *adv.*

u•surp′ (yōō sûrp′, -zûrp′) *v.* seize without right. —**u•surp′er,** *n.*

u′su•ry (yōō′zhə rē) *n.* lending money at exorbitant rates of interest. —**u′sur•er,** *n.* —**u• su′ri•ous** (-zhōōr′ē-) *adj.*

U.S.V. United States Volunteers. Also, **USV**

USW ultrashort wave.

usw and so forth; etc. Also, **u.s.w.** [from German *und so weiter*]

USWAC United States Women's Army Corps.

usz undersize.

UT, Utah. Also, **Ut.**

UTC universal time coordinated.

utend. (in prescriptions) to be used. [from Latin *ūtendum*]

u•ten′sil (yōō ten′səl) *n.* device, container, etc., esp. for kitchen.

u′ter•us (yōō′tər əs) *n., pl.* **-ter•i** (-tə rī′) part of woman's body in which fertilized ovum develops. —**u′ter•ine** (-in) *adj.*

UTI urinary tract infection.

util 1. Also, **util.** utility. **2.** utilization.

u•til/i•tar′i•an (yōō til′i târ′ē ən) *adj.* of practical use.

u•til/i•ty, *n., pl.* **-ties. 1.** usefulness. **2.** public service.

u′ti•lize′ (yōōt′l īz′) *v.,* **-lized, -lizing.** use. —**u′ti•li•za′tion,** *n.*

ut′most′ (ut′mōst′) *adj.* **1.** greatest. **2.** furthest.

utn utensil.

U•to′pi•an (yōō tō′pē ən) *adj.* impossibly perfect.

ut′ter (ut′ər) *v.* **1.** speak; say. —*adj.* **2.** complete; total. —**ut′ter•ance,** *n.*

ut′ter•ly, *adv.* completely; absolutely.

U.T.W.A. United Textile Workers of America. Also, **UTWA**

UUM underwater-to-underwater missile.

UV ultraviolet. Also, **U.V.**

UV filter *Photography.* ultraviolet filter.

UVM universal vendor marking.

u′vu•la (yōō′vyə lə) *n., pl.* **-las, -lae.** small, fleshy part on soft palate.

U/W under will.

U/w underwriter. Also, **u/w**

u/w used with.

uwtr underwater.

ux. *Chiefly Law.* wife. [from Latin *uxor*]

ux•o′ri•ous (uk sôr′ē əs, ug zōr′-) *adj.* foolishly or excessively fond of one's wife.

U

V

V, v (vē) *n.* twenty-second letter of English alphabet.

VA, Virginia. Also, **Va.**

vac. 1. vacant. **2.** vacation. **3.** vacuum.

va•can•cy (vā′kən sē) *n., pl.* **-cies. 1.** state of being vacant. **2.** vacant space.

va′cant (-kənt) *adj.* **1.** empty. **2.** devoid. **3.** unintelligent. —**va′cant•ly,** *adv.*

va′cate (vā′kāt) *v.,* **-cated, -cating. 1.** empty. **2.** quit. **3.** annul.

va•ca′tion (vā kā′shən, və-) *n.* **1.** freedom from duty, business, etc. **2.** holiday. —*v.* **3.** take a vacation. —**va•ca′tion•ist,** *n.*

vacc. vaccination.

vac′ci•nate′ (vak′sə nāt′) *v.,* **-nated, -nating.** inoculate against smallpox, etc. —**vac′ci•na′tion,** *n.*

vac•cine′ (vak sēn′) *n.* substance injected into bloodstream to give immunity.

vac′il•late′ (vas′ə lāt′) *v.,* **-lated, -lating. 1.** waver; fluctuate. **2.** be irresolute. —**vac′il•la′tion,** *n.* —**vac′il•la′tor,** *n.*

va•cu′i•ty (va kyōō′i tē, və-) *n., pl.* **-ties. 1.** emptiness. **2.** lack of intelligence. —**vac′u•ous** (vak′yōō əs) *adj.* —**vac′u•ous•ly,** *adv.*

vac′u•um (vak′yōōm, -yōō əm, -yəm) *n.* space from which all matter has been removed.

vacuum bottle, bottle with double wall enclosing vacuum to retard heat transfer.

vacuum cleaner, apparatus for cleaning by suction.

vac′uum-packed′, *adj.* packed with as much air as possible evacuated before sealing.

vacuum tube, sealed bulb, formerly used in radio and electronics.

V. Adm. Vice-Admiral.

vag′a•bond′ (vag′ə bond′) *adj.* **1.** wandering; homeless. —*n.* **2.** vagrant.

va•gar′y (və gâr′ē, vā′gə rē) *n., pl.* **-garies.** capricious act or idea.

va•gi′na (və jī′nə) *n., pl.* **-nas, -nae.** passage from uterus to vulva. —**vag′i•nal** (vaj′ə nl) *adj.*

va′grant (vā′grənt) *n.* **1.** idle wanderer. —*adj.* **2.** wandering. —**va′gran•cy,** *n.*

vague (vāg) *adj.,* **vaguer, vaguest. 1.** not definite. **2.** indistinct. —**vague′ly,** *adv.* —**vague′ness,** *n.*

vain (vān) *adj.* **1.** futile. **2.** conceited. —**vain′•ly,** *adv.* —**vain′ness,** *n.*

vain′glo′ry, *n.* boastful pride. —**vain•glo′ri•ous,** *adj.*

Val *Biochemistry.* valine.

val. 1. valentine. **2.** valley. **3.** valuation. **4.** value. **5.** valued.

val′ance (val′əns, vā′ləns) *n.* drapery across top of window.

valdtn validation.

vale (vāl) *n.* valley.

val′e•dic•to′ri•an (val′i dik tôr′ē ən) *n.* graduating student who delivers valedictory.

val′e•dic′to•ry (-tə rē) *n., pl.* **-ries.** farewell address, esp. one delivered at commencement.

va′lence (vā′ləns) *n.* combining capacity of atom or radical.

val′en•tine′ (val′ən tīn′) *n.* **1.** affectionate card or gift sent on February 14 (**Saint Valentine's Day**). **2.** sweetheart chosen on that day.

val′et (va lā′, val′it, val′ā) *n.* personal manservant.

val′iant (val′yənt) *adj.* brave. —**val′iance,** *n.* —**val′iant•ly,** *adv.*

val′id (val′id) *adj.* **1.** sound; logical. **2.** legally binding. —**val′i•date′,** *v.* —**val′i•da′tion,** *n.* —**va•lid′i•ty** (və lid′i tē) *n.* —**val′id•ly,** *adv.*

va•lise′ (və lēs′) *n.* traveling bag.

val′ley (val′ē) *n.* long depression between uplands or mountains.

val′or (val′ər) *n.* bravery, esp. in battle. —**val′o•rous,** *adj.* —**val′o•rous•ly,** *adv.*

val′u•a•ble (-yōō ə bəl, -yə bəl) *adj.* **1.** of much worth, importance, etc. —*n.* **2.** (*usually pl.*) valuable articles. —**val′u•a•bly,** *adv.*

val′u•a′tion (-yōō ā′shən) *n.* estimation or estimated value.

val′ue, *n., v.,* **-ued, -uing.** —*n.* **1.** worth or importance. **2.** equivalent or estimated worth. **3.** conception of what is good. —*v.* **4.** estimate worth of. **5.** esteem. —**val′ue•less,** *adj.*

valve (valv) *n.* device controlling flow of liquids, etc. —**val′vu•lar,** *adj.*

vam voltammeter.

va•moose′ (va mōōs′) *v.,* **-moosed, -moosing.** *Slang.* leave hurriedly.

vamp (vamp) *n.* **1.** upper front part of shoe or boot. **2.** *Slang.* seductive woman. —*v.* **3.** improvise (as music).

vam′pire (vam′pīᵉr) *n.* **1.** corpse supposed to be reanimated and to suck blood of living persons. **2.** extortionist. **3.** Also, **vampire bat.** South and Central American bat.

van (van) *n.* **1.** vanguard. **2.** covered truck for moving furniture, etc. **3.** small closed trucklike vehicle.

va•na′di•um (və nā′dē əm) *n.* rare silvery metallic element, used esp. to toughen steel.

van′dal (van′dl) *n.* person who damages or destroys wantonly. —**van′dal•ism,** *n.* —**van′dal•ize′,** *v.,* **-ized, -izing.**

Van•dyke′ (van dīk′) *n.* short, pointed beard.

vane (vān) *n.* **1.** weathervane. **2.** one of set of blades set diagonally on a rotor to move or be moved by fluid.

van′guard′ (van′-) *n.* **1.** foremost part. **2.** leaders of a movement.

va•nil′la (və nil′ə; *often* -nel′ə) *n.* **1.** tropical orchid, whose fruit (**vanilla bean**) yields flavoring extract. **2.** the extract.

van′ish (van′ish) *v.* disappear. —**van′ish•er,** *n.*

van′i•ty (van′i tē) *n., pl.* **-ties. 1.** vainness. **2.** makeup table. **3.** compact (def. 4).

van′quish (vang′kwish, van′-) *v.* conquer; defeat. —**van′quish•er,** *n.*

van′tage (van′tij) *n.* superior position or situation.

vap′id (vap′id) *adj.* **1.** insipid. **2.** dull. —**va•pid′i•ty,** *n.* —**vap′id•ly,** *adv.*

va′por (vā′pər) *n.* **1.** exhalation, as fog or mist. **2.** gas. —**va′por•ous,** *adj.*

va′por•ize′, *v.,* -ized, -izing. change into vapor. —**va′por•i•za′tion,** *n.* —**va′por•iz′er,** *n.*

var. 1. variable. **2.** variant. **3.** variation. **4.** variety. **5.** variometer. **6.** various.

varhm var-hour meter.

var′i•a•ble (vâr′ē ə bəl) *adj.* **1.** changeable. **2.** inconstant. —*n.* **3.** something variable. —**var′i•a•bil′i•ty,** *n.* —**var′i•a•bly,** *adv.*

variac (vâr′ē ak′), variable-voltage transformer.

var′i•ance (-əns) *n.* **1.** divergence or discrepancy. **2.** disagreement.

var′i•ant, *adj.* **1.** varying. **2.** altered in form. —*n.* **3.** variant form, etc.

var′i•a′tion (-ā′shən) *n.* **1.** change. **2.** amount of change. **3.** variant. **4.** transformation of melody with changes in harmony, etc. —**var′i•a′tion•al,** *adj.*

var′i•col′ored (vâr′i kul′ərd) *adj.* having various colors.

var′i•cose′ (var′i kōs′) *adj.* abnormally swollen, as veins.

var′i•e•gate′ (vâr′ē i gāt′, vâr′i-) *v.,* -gated, -gating. **1.** mark with different colors, etc. **2.** vary. —**var′i•e•gat′ed,** *adj.*

va•ri′e•ty (və rī′i tē) *n., pl.* **-ties. 1.** diversity. **2.** number of different things. **3.** kind; category. **4.** variant. —**va•ri′e•tal** (-i tl) *adj.*

va•ri′o•la (və rī′ə lə) *n.* smallpox.

var′i•ous (vâr′ē əs) *adj.* **1.** of different sorts. **2.** several. —**var′i•ous•ly,** *adv.*

varistor (vâr′ə stər), voltage-variable resistor.

varitran (vâr′ə tran′), variable-voltage transformer.

var′mint (vär′mənt) *n.* **1.** undesirable, usu. verminous animal. **2.** obnoxious person.

var′nish (vär′nish) *n.* **1.** resinous solution drying in hard, glossy coat. **2.** gloss. —*v.* **3.** lay varnish on.

var′y (vâr′ē) *v.,* varied, varying. **1.** change; differ. **2.** cause to be different. **3.** deviate; diverge.

vas′cu•lar (vas′kyə lər) *adj.* of vessels that convey fluids, as blood or sap.

vase (vās, vāz, väz) *n.* tall container, esp. for flowers.

vas•ec′to•my (va sek′tə mē, və-) *n., pl.* -mies. surgery for male sterilization.

vas′sal (vas′əl) *n.* **1.** feudal holder of land who renders service to superior. **2.** subject, follower, or slave. —**vas′sal•age,** *n.*

vast (vast) *adj.* immense; huge. —**vast′ly,** *adv.* —**vast′ness,** *n.*

vat (vat) *n.* large container for liquids.

vaude′ville (vôd′vil, vōd′-, vô′də-) *n.* theatrical entertainment made up of separate acts.

vault (vôlt) *n.* **1.** arched ceiling or roof. **2.** arched space, chamber, etc. **3.** room for safekeeping of valuables. —*v.* **4.** build or cover with vault. **5.** leap. —**vault′ed,** *adj.* —**vault′er,** *n.*

vault′ing, *adj.* **1.** leaping. **2.** excessive.

vaunt (vônt, vänt) *v.* **1.** boast of. —*n.* **2.** boast.

v. aux. auxiliary verb.

vb. 1. verb. **2.** verbal.

VBE vernacular black English.

vbtm verbatim.

VC 1. venture capital. **2.** Vietcong. **3.** vital capacity.

V.C. 1. venture capital. **2.** Veterinary Corps. **3.** Vice-Chairman. **4.** Vice-Chancellor. **5.** Vice-Consul. **6.** Victoria Cross. **7.** Vietcong.

vcl vehicle centerline.

vco voltage-controlled oscillator.

VCR, videocassette recorder.

vctr vector.

VD, venereal disease.

V′-Day′, *n.* day of military victory.

V.D.M. Minister of the Word of God. [from Latin *Verbī Deī Minister*]

vdr voltage-dependent resistor: varistor.

VDT, video display terminal.

VDU *Computers.* visual display unit.

veal (vēl) *n.* flesh of calf as used for food.

vec′tor (vek′tər) *n.* **1.** quantity possessing both magnitude and direction. **2.** person or animal that transmits disease-causing organism.

V-E Day (vē′ē′), May 8, 1945, the day of victory in Europe for the Allies. [*V(ictory in) E(urope) Day*]

veep (vēp) *n. Informal.* vice president, esp. of U.S.

veer (vēr) *v.* change direction.

veg. vegetable.

veg′e•ta•ble (vej′tə bəl, vej′i tə-) *n.* **1.** plant used for food. **2.** any plant. —**veg′e•ta•ble, veg′e•tal** (-i tl) *adj.*

veg′e•tar′i•an (vej′i târ′ē ən) *n.* **1.** person who eats only vegetable food on principle (**vegetarianism**). —*adj.* **2.** of or advocating vegetarianism. **3.** suitable for vegetarians.

veg′e•tate′ (-tāt′) *v.,* -tated, -tating. **1.**

V

grow as plants do. **2.** live dull, inactive life. —**veg′e•ta′tive,** *adj.*

veg′e•ta′tion, *n.* **1.** plants collectively. **2.** act or process of vegetating.

veh vehicle.

ve′he•ment (vē′ə mənt) *adj.* **1.** impetuous or impassioned. **2.** violent. —**ve′he•mence, ve′he•men′cy,** *n.* —**ve′he•ment•ly,** *adv.*

ve′hi•cle (vē′i kəl) *n.* means of transport, etc. —**ve•hic′u•lar** (-hik′yə lər) *adj.*

veil (vāl) *n.* **1.** material concealing face. **2.** part of headdress, as of nun or bride. **3.** cover; screen. **4.** pretense. —*v.* **5.** cover with veil.

vein (vān) *n.* **1.** vessel conveying blood from body to heart. **2.** tubular riblike thickening, as in leaf or insect wing. **3.** stratum of ore, coal, etc. **4.** mood. —*v.* **5.** furnish or mark with veins.

vel. *Printing.* **1.** vellum. **2.** velocity.

Vel′cro (vel′krō) *n. Trademark.* fastening tape with opposing pieces of nylon that interlock.

veld (velt, felt) *n.* open grassy country in South Africa. Also, **veldt.**

vel′lum (vel′əm) *n.* parchment.

ve•loc′i•ty (və los′i tē) *n., pl.* **-ties.** speed.

ve•lour′ (və lŏŏr′) *n.* velvetlike fabric used for clothing and upholstery. Also, **ve•lours′.**

vel′vet (vel′vit) *n.* fabric with thick, soft pile. —**vel′vet•y,** *adj.*

vel′vet•een′ (-vi tēn′) *n.* cotton fabric resembling velvet.

Ven. **1.** Venerable. **2.** Venice.

ve′nal (vēn′l) *adj.* corrupt; mercenary. —**ve′nal•ly,** *adv.* —**ve•nal′i•ty** (-nal′i tē) *n.*

vend (vend) *v.* sell. —**ven′dor,** *n.*

ven•det′ta (ven det′ə) *n.* long, bitter feud.

vending machine, coin-operated machine for selling small articles.

ve•neer′ (və nēr′) *v.* **1.** overlay with thin sheets of fine wood, etc. —*n.* **2.** veneered layer of wood. **3.** superficial appearance.

ven′er•a•ble (ven′ər ə bəl) *adj.* worthy of reverence. —**ven′er•a•bil′i•ty,** *n.*

ven′er•ate′ (-ə rāt′) *v.,* **-ated, -ating.** revere. —**ven′er•a′tion,** *n.*

ve•ne′re•al (və nēr′ē əl) *adj.* relating to or caused by sexual intercourse.

ve•ne′tian blind (və nē′shən) window blind with horizontal slats.

Venez. Venezuela.

venge′ance (ven′jəns) *n.* revenge.

venge′ful, *adj.* seeking vengeance. —**venge′ful•ly,** *adv.*

ve′ni•al (vē′nē əl, vēn′yəl) *adj.* pardonable.

ven′i•son (ven′ə sən, -zən) *n.* flesh of deer as used for food.

ven′om (ven′əm) *n.* **1.** poisonous fluid secreted by some snakes, spiders, etc. **2.** spite; malice. —**ven′om•ous,** *adj.* —**ven′om•ous•ly,** *adv.*

ve′nous (vē′nəs) *adj.* **1.** of or having veins.

2. of or being blood carried back to heart by veins.

vent (vent) *n.* **1.** outlet, as for fluid. **2.** expression. —*v.* **3.** express freely.

ven′ti•late′ (ven′tl āt′) *v.,* **-lated, -lating. 1.** provide with fresh air. **2.** submit to discussion. —**ven′ti•la′tion,** *n.* —**ven′ti•la′tor,** *n.*

ven′tral (ven′trəl) *adj.* **1.** of or near belly; abdominal. **2.** on lower, abdominal plane of animal's body.

ven′tri•cle (ven′tri kəl) *n.* either of two lower cavities of heart. —**ven•tric′u•lar,** *adj.*

ven•tril′o•quism′ (ven tril′ə kwiz′əm) *n.* art of speaking so that voice seems to come from another source. —**ven•tril′o•quist,** *n.*

ven′ture (ven′chər) *n., v.,* **-tured, -turing.** —*n.* **1.** hazardous undertaking. —*v.* **2.** risk; dare. **3.** enter daringly. —**ven′ture•some** (-səm), **ven′tur•ous,** *adj.*

ven′ue (ven′yōō) *n.* **1.** place of crime or cause of action. **2.** place where jury is gathered and case tried. **3.** scene or locale of action or event.

Ve′nus (vē′nəs) *n.* second planet from sun.

Ven′us's-fly′trap, *n.* plant with hinged leaves that trap insects.

ver. **1.** verse; verses. **2.** version.

ve•ra′cious (və rā′shəs) *adj.* truthful. —**ve•rac′i•ty** (-ras′ə tē) *n.*

ve•ran′da (-ran′də) *n.* open porch. Also, **ve•ran′dah.**

verb (vûrb) *n.* part of speech expressing action, occurrence, existence, etc., as "saw" in the sentence "I saw Tom."

ver′bal (vûr′bəl) *adj.* **1.** of or in form of words. **2.** oral. **3.** word for word. **4.** of verbs. —*n.* **5.** word, as noun, derived from verb. —**ver′bal•ly,** *adv.*

ver′bal•ize′, *v.,* **-ized, -izing.** express in words. —**ver′bal•i•za′tion,** *n.*

ver•ba′tim (vər bā′tim) *adv.* word for word.

ver•be′na (vər bē′nə) *n.* plant with long spikes of flowers.

ver′bi•age (vûr′bē ij) *n.* **1.** wordiness. **2.** manner of verbal expression.

ver•bose′ (vər bōs′) *adj.* wordy. —**ver•bose′ness, ver•bos′i•ty** (-bos′i tē) *n.*

ver•bo′ten (vər bōt′n, fər-) *adj.* forbidden.

ver′dant (vûr′dnt) *adj.* **1.** green with vegetation. **2.** inexperienced. —**ver′dan•cy,** *n.*

ver′dict (vûr′dikt) *n.* decision.

ver′di•gris′ (vûr′di grēs′, -gris) *n.* green or bluish patina.

ver′dure (vûr′jər) *n.* **1.** greenness. **2.** green vegetation.

verge (vûrj) *n., v.,* **verged, verging.** —*n.* **1.** edge or margin. —*v.* **2.** border. **3.** incline; tend.

verif verification.

ver′i•fy′ (ver′ə fī′) *v.,* **-fied, -fying. 1.** prove to be true. **2.** ascertain correctness of. —**ver′i•fi•a•ble,** *adj.* —**ver′i•fi•ca′tion,** *n.* —**ver′i•fi′er,** *n.*

ver′i•ly (-lē) *adv. Archaic.* truly.

ver'i·si·mil'i·tude' (-si mil'i tōōd', -tyōōd') *n.* appearance of truth.

ver'i·ta·ble (-tə bəl) *adj.* genuine. —**ver'i·ta·bly,** *adv.*

ver'i·ty (-tē) *n., pl.* **-ties.** truth.

ver'mi·cel'li (vûr'mi chel'ē, -sel'ē) *n.* pasta in long threads.

ver·mil'ion (vər mil'yən) *n.* **1.** bright red. —*adj.* **2.** of or like vermilion.

ver'min (vûr'min) *n.pl. or sing.* troublesome animals collectively. —**ver'min·ous,** *adj.*

ver·mouth' (vər mōōth') *n.* white wine flavored with herbs.

ver·nac'u·lar (vər nak'yə lər, və nak'-) *adj.* **1.** (of language) used locally or in everyday speech. —*n.* **2.** native speech. **3.** language of particular group.

ver'nal (vûr'nl) *adj.* of spring. —**ver'nal·ly,** *adv.*

ve·ron'i·ca (və ron'i kə) *n.* plant with opposite leaves and clusters of small flowers.

vers. *Trigonometry.* versed sine.

ver'sa·tile (vûr'sə tl; *esp. Brit.* -tīl') *adj.* doing variety of things well. —**ver'sa·til'i·ty,** *n.*

verse (vûrs) *n.* **1.** line of poem. **2.** type of metrical line, etc. **3.** poem. **4.** poetry. **5.** division of Biblical chapter.

versed, *adj.* expert; skilled.

ver'si·fy' (vûr'sə fī') *v.,* **-fied, -fying. 1.** treat in or turn into verse. **2.** compose verses. —**ver'si·fi'er,** *n.* —**ver'si·fi·ca'tion,** *n.*

ver'sion (vûr'zhən, -shən) *n.* **1.** translation. **2.** account.

ver'so (vûr'sō) *n., pl.* **-sos.** left-hand page of book.

verst versatile.

ver'sus (vûr'səs, -səz) *prep.* in opposition or contrast to.

vert. 1. vertebra. **2.** vertebrate. **3.** vertical.

ver'te·bra (vûr'tə brə) *n., pl.* **-brae, -bras.** bone or segment of spinal column. —**ver'te·bral,** *adj.*

ver'te·brate' (-brit, -brāt') *adj.* **1.** having vertebrae. —*n.* **2.** vertebrate animal.

ver'tex (vûr'teks) *n., pl.* **-texes, -tices** (-tə-sēz') highest point.

ver'ti·cal (vûr'ti kəl) *adj.* **1.** perpendicular to plane of horizon. —*n.* **2.** something vertical. —**ver'ti·cal·ly,** *adv.*

ver·tig'i·nous (vər tij'ə nəs) *adj.* **1.** whirling. **2.** affected with or liable to cause vertigo.

ver'ti·go' (vûr'ti gō') *n., pl.* **-goes.** dizziness.

verve (vûrv) *n.* vivaciousness, energy, or enthusiasm.

ver'y (ver'ē) *adv., adj.,* **-ier, -iest.** —*adv.* **1.** extremely. —*adj.* **2.** identical. **3.** mere. **4.** actual. **5.** true.

ves'i·cle (ves'i kəl) *n.* small sac in body.

ves'per (ves'pər) *n.* **1.** *Archaic.* evening. **2.** *(pl.)* evening prayer, service, etc.

ves'sel (ves'əl) *n.* **1.** ship or boat. **2.** hollow or concave container, as dish or glass. **3.** tube or duct, as for blood.

vest (vest) *n.* **1.** sleeveless garment worn under jacket. —*v.* **2.** clothe or robe. **3.** put in someone's possession or control. **4.** endow with powers, etc.

ves'tal (ves'tl) *adj.* chaste.

vest'ed, *adj.* held completely and permanently.

vested interest, special interest in system, arrangement, or institution for personal reasons.

ves'ti·bule' (ves'tə byōōl') *n.* small room between entrance and main room. —**ves·tib'u·lar** (ve stib'yə lər) *adj.*

ves'tige (ves'tij) *n.* **1.** trace of something extinct. **2.** slight trace of something. —**ves·tig'i·al** (ve stij'ē əl, -stij'əl) *adj.*

vest'ing, *n.* the granting to an employee of the right to pension benefits despite early retirement.

vest'ment, *n.* ceremonial garment.

vest'-pock'et, *adj.* conveniently small.

ves'try (ves'trē) *n., pl.* **-tries. 1.** room in church for vestments or for meetings, etc. **2.** church committee managing temporal affairs. —**ves'try·man,** *n.*

vet (vet) *n. Informal.* **1.** veterinarian. **2.** veteran.

vetch (vech) *n.* plant used for forage and soil improvement.

vet'er·an (vet'ər ən) *n.* **1.** person who has served in armed forces. **2.** experienced person. —*adj.* **3.** experienced.

vet'er·i·nar'i·an (-ə när'ē ən) *n.* veterinary practitioner.

vet'er·i·nar'y (-ner'ē) *n., pl.* **-naries,** *adj.* —*n.* **1.** veterinarian. —*adj.* **2.** of medical and surgical treatment of animals.

vet. med. veterinary medicine.

ve'to (vē'tō) *n., pl.* **-toes,** *v.,* **-toed, -toing.** —*n.* **1.** power or right to reject or prohibit. **2.** prohibition. —*v.* **3.** reject by veto.

vet. sci. veterinary science.

vex (veks) *v.* **1.** irritate. **2.** worry. **3.** discuss vigorously. —**vex·a'tion,** *n.* —**vex·a'tious,** *adj.* —**vexed,** *adj.* —**vex'ed·ly,** *adv.*

VF 1. *Botany.* a designation applied to various plant varieties, indicating resistance to verticillium wilt and fusarium wilt. **2.** *Numismatics.* very fine. **3.** *Television.* video frequency. **4.** visual field. **5.** voice frequency.

vf 1. variable frequency. **2.** voice frequency.

vfc voice-frequency carrier.

VFD volunteer fire department.

vfo variable-frequency oscillator.

VFR visual flight rules.

V.F.W. Veterans of Foreign Wars of the United States. Also, **VFW**

VG very good.

V.G. Vicar-General.

v.g. for example. [from Latin *verbī gratiā*]

V

VGA *Computers.* video graphics adapter.

VHF very high frequency. Also, **vhf, V.H.F.**

VHS *Trademark.* Video Home System: a format for recording and playing VCR tape, incompatible with other formats.

VI Virgin Islands (for use with ZIP code).

Vi *Symbol, Chemistry.* virginium.

vi variable interval.

V.I. **1.** Vancouver Island. **2.** Virgin Islands.

v.i. **1.** intransitive verb. **2.** see below. [from Latin *vidē infrā*]

vi′a (vī′ə, vē′ə) *prep.* by way of.

vi′a·ble (vī′ə bəl) *adj.* **1.** capable of living. **2.** practicable; workable.

vi′a·duct′, *n.* long highway or railroad bridge.

vi′al (vī′əl, vīl) *n.* small glass container.

vi′and (vī′ənd) *n.* **1.** article of food. **2.** (*pl.*) dishes of food.

vib vibration.

vibes (vībz) *n.pl.* **1.** *Slang.* something, esp. an emotional aura, emitted as if by vibration. **2.** vibraphone.

vi′brant (vī′brənt) *adj.* **1.** resonant. **2.** energetic; vital. —**vi′bran·cy,** *n.* —**vi′brant·ly,** *adv.*

vi′bra·phone (vī′brə fōn′) *n.* instrument like metal xylophone, with electrically enhanced resonance.

vi′brate (vī′brāt) *v.,* **-brated, -brating. 1.** move very rapidly to and fro; oscillate. **2.** tremble. **3.** resound. **4.** thrill. —**vi·bra′tion,** *n.* —**vi′bra·tor,** *n.* —**vi′bra·to′ry** (-brə tôr′ē) *adj.* —**vi·bra′tion·al,** *adj.*

vi·bra′to (vi brä′tō) *n., pl.* **-tos.** pulsating effect produced by rapid but slight alterations in pitch.

vi·bur′num (vī bûr′nəm) *n.* shrub bearing white flower clusters.

Vic. 1. Vicar. **2.** Vicarage. **3.** Victoria.

vic. vicinity.

vic′ar (vik′ər) *n.* **1.** parish priest. **2.** representative of bishop. **3.** deputy. —**vic′ar·ship′,** *n.* —**vi·car′i·al** (vī kâr′ē əl, vi-) *adj.*

vic′ar·age (-ij) *n.* residence or position of vicar.

vi·car′i·ous (vī kâr′ē əs, vi-) *adj.* **1.** done or suffered in place of another. **2.** substitute. —**vi·car′i·ous·ly,** *adv.*

vice (vīs) *n.* **1.** evil habit or fault. **2.** immoral conduct. **3.** vise. —*prep.* **4.** instead of.

vice-, prefix meaning deputy.

vice′-ad′mi·ral (vīs′) *n.* commissioned officer ranking above rear admiral.

vice·ge′rent (-jēr′ənt) *n.* deputy to sovereign or magistrate.

vice pres. vice president. Also, **Vice Pres.**

vice president, *n.* officer next in rank to president. —**vice′ pres′i·den·cy,** *n.*

vice′roy (vīs′roi) *n.* ruler of country or province as deputy of sovereign. —**vice-re′gal** (-rē′gəl) *adj.*

vi′ce ver′sa (vī′sə vûr′sə, vīs′, vī′sē) in opposite way.

vi′chys·soise′ (vish′ē swäz′, vē′shē-) *n.* cold cream soup of potatoes and leeks.

vi·cin′i·ty (vi sin′i tē) *n., pl.* **-ties.** neighborhood; nearby area.

vi′cious (vish′əs) *adj.* **1.** immoral; depraved. **2.** evil. **3.** malicious. —**vi′cious·ly,** *adv.* —**vi′cious·ness,** *n.*

vi·cis′si·tude′ (vi sis′i tōōd′, -tyōōd′) *n.* change, esp. in condition.

Vict. 1. Victoria. **2.** Victorian.

vic′tim (vik′təm) *n.* **1.** sufferer from action or event. **2.** dupe. **3.** sacrifice. —**vic′tim·ize′,** *v.,* **-ized, -izing.**

vic′tor (vik′tər) *n.* conqueror or winner. —**vic·to′ri·ous** (-tôr′ē əs) *adj.* —**vic·to′ri·ous·ly,** *adv.*

vic′to·ry (-tə rē) *n., pl.* **-ries.** success in contest.

vict′ual (vit′l) *n.* **1.** (*pl.*) food. —*v.* **2.** supply with victuals. —**vict′ual·er,** *n.*

vid. 1. see. [from Latin *vide*] **2.** Also, **vid** video.

vid′e·o′ (vid′ē ō′) *adj.* **1.** of television. —*n.* **2.** television. **3.** the visual elements of a telecast. **4.** videotape or videocassette.

vid′e·o′cas·sette′, *n.* cassette containing videotape.

videocassette recorder, electronic device for recording and playing videocassettes.

vid′e·o·disc′, disc on which pictures and sound are recorded for playback on TV set.

video game, electronic game played on video screen or television set.

vid′e·o·tape′, *n., v.,* **-taped, -taping.** —*n.* **1.** magnetic tape on which TV program, motion picture, etc., can be recorded. —*v.* **2.** record on this.

vidf video frequency.

vie (vī) *v.,* **vied, vying.** contend for superiority.

view (vyōō) *n.* **1.** seeing or beholding. **2.** range of vision. **3.** landscape, etc., within one's sight. **4.** aspect. **5.** mental survey. **6.** purpose. **7.** notion, opinion, etc. —*v.* **8.** see; look at. **9.** regard. —**view′er,** *n.* —**view′less,** *adj.*

view′find′er, *n.* camera part for viewing what will appear in picture.

view′point′, *n.* **1.** place from which view is seen. **2.** attitude toward something.

vig′il (vij′əl) *n.* period of staying awake, esp. as watch.

vig′i·lant (-lənt) *adj.* **1.** wary. **2.** alert. —**vig′i·lance,** *n.* —**vig′i·lant·ly,** *adv.*

vig′i·lan′te (-lan′tē) *n.* person who takes law into own hands.

vi·gnette′ (vin yet′) *n., v.,* **-gnetted, -gnetting.** —*n.* **1.** small decorative design. **2.** photograph, etc., shading off at edges. **3.** literary sketch. —*v.* **4.** make vignette of.

vig′or (vig′ər) *n.* **1.** active strength. **2.** energy. **—vig′or•ous,** adj. **—vig′or•ous•ly,** adv.

Vik′ing (vī′king) n. medieval Scandinavian raider.

vil. village.

vile (vīl) adj., **viler, vilest. 1.** very bad. **2.** offensive. **3.** evil. **—vile′ly,** adv. **—vile′ness,** n.

vil′i•fy′ (vil′ə fī′) v., **-fied, -fying.** defame. **—vil′i•fi•ca′tion,** n. **—vil′i•fi•er,** n.

vil′la (vil′ə) n. luxurious country residence.

vil′lage (vil′ij) n. small town. **—vil′lag•er,** n.

vil′lain (vil′ən) n. wicked person. **—vil′lain•ous,** adj. **—vil′lain•y,** n.

vil′lein (vil′ən, -ān) n. feudal serf.

vim (vim) n. vigor.

v. imp. verb impersonal.

VIN vehicle identification number.

vin. (in prescriptions) wine. [from Latin *vīnum*]

vin/ai•grette′ (vin′ə gret′) n. dressing, esp. for salad, of oil and vinegar, usu. with herbs.

vin′ci•ble (vin′sə bəl) adj. capable of being conquered.

vin/di•cate′ (vin′di kāt′) v., **-cated, -cating. 1.** clear, as from suspicion. **2.** uphold or justify. **—vin/di•ca′tion,** n. **—vin/di•ca′tor,** n.

vin•dic′tive (vin dik′tiv) adj. holding grudge; vengeful. **—vin•dic′tive•ly,** adv. **—vin•dic′tive•ness,** n.

vine (vīn) n. creeping or climbing plant with slender stem.

vin/e•gar (vin′i gər) n. sour liquid obtained by fermentation. **—vin/e•gar•y,** adj.

vine/yard (vin′yərd) n. plantation of grapevines.

vin′tage (vin′tij) n. **1.** wine from one harvest. **2.** grape harvest.

vint/ner (vint′nər) n. person who makes wine.

vi/nyl (vīn′l) n. type of plastic.

vi/ol (vī′əl) n. stringed instrument of 16th and 17th centuries.

vi•o/la (vē ō′lə) n. *Music.* stringed instrument resembling violin but slightly larger.

vi/o•la•ble (vī′ə lə bəl) adj. capable of being violated.

vi/o•late′ (-lāt′) v., **-lated, -lating. 1.** break or transgress. **2.** break through or into. **3.** desecrate. **4.** rape. **—vi/o•la′tion,** n. **—vi/o•la′tor,** n.

vi/o•lent, adj. **1.** uncontrolled, strong, or rough. **2.** of destructive force. **3.** intense; severe. **—vi/o•lence,** n. **—vi/o•lent•ly,** adv.

vi/o•let (vī′ə lit) n. **1.** low herb bearing flowers, usually purple or blue. **2.** bluish purple.

vi/o•lin′ (vī′ə lin′) n. *Music.* stringed instrument played with bow. **—vi/o•lin′ist,** n.

vi/o•lon•cel/lo (vē′ə lən chel′ō, vī′-) n., pl. **-los.** cello. **—vi/o•lon•cel/list,** n.

VIP (vē′ī′pē′) *Informal.* very important person.

vi/per (vī′pər) n. **1.** Old World venomous snake. **2.** malicious or treacherous person. **—vi/per•ous,** adj.

vi•ra/go (vi rä′gō, -rä′-) n., pl. **-goes, -gos.** shrewish woman.

vi/ral (vī′rəl) adj. of or caused by virus.

Virg. Virginia.

vir/gin (vûr′jin) n. **1.** person who has not had sexual intercourse. **—adj. 2.** being or like virgin. **3.** untried; unused. **—vir/gin•al,** adj. **—vir•gin/i•ty,** n.

vir/gule (vûr′gyōōl) n. oblique stroke (/) used as dividing line.

vir/ile (vir′əl) adj. **1.** manly. **2.** vigorous. **3.** capable of procreation. **—vi•ril/i•ty,** n.

vi•rol/o•gy (vī rol′ə jē, vi-) n. study of viruses. **—vi•rol/o•gist,** n.

v. irr. irregular verb.

vir/tu•al (vûr′chōō əl) adj. **1.** such in effect, though not actually. **2.** simulated by computer. **—vir/tu•al•ly,** adv.

virtual reality, realistic simulation by computer system.

vir/tue (vûr′chōō) n. **1.** moral excellence. **2.** chastity. **3.** merit. **—vir/tu•ous,** adj. **—vir/tu•ous•ly,** adv. **—vir/tu•ous•ness,** n.

vir/tu•o/so (vûr′chōō ō′sō) n., pl. **-sos, -si.** person of special skill, esp. in music. **—vir/tu•os/i•ty** (-os′i tē) n.

vir/u•lent (vir′yə lənt, vir′ə-) adj. **1.** poisonous; malignant. **2.** hostile. **—vir/u•lence, vir/u•len•cy,** n. **—vir/u•lent•ly,** adv.

vi/rus (vī′rəs) n. **1.** infective agent. **2.** corrupting influence. **3.** segment of self-replicating code planted illegally in computer program.

Vis. 1. Viscount. **2.** Viscountess. **3.** vista (in addresses).

vis. 1. visibility. **2.** visual.

vi/sa (vē′zə) n. passport endorsement permitting foreign entry or immigration.

vis/age (viz′ij) n. **1.** face. **2.** aspect.

vis/-à-vis′ (vē′zə vē′) prep. **1.** in relation to; compared with. **2.** opposite.

visc viscosity

Visc. 1. Viscount. **2.** Viscountess.

vis/cer•a (vis′ər ə) n.pl. **1.** soft interior organs of body. **2.** intestines. **—vis/cer•al,** adj.

vis/cid (vis′id) adj. sticky; gluelike. Also, **vis/cous** (vis′kəs). **—vis•cos/i•ty** (vi skos′i tē) n.

vis/count (vī′kount′) n. nobleman ranking below earl or count. **—vis/count•ess,** n.fem.

Visct. 1. Viscount. **2.** Viscountess.

vise (vīs) n. device, usually with two jaws, for holding object firmly.

vis/i•ble (viz′ə bəl) adj. **1.** capable of being seen. **2.** perceptible. **3.** manifest. **—vis/i•bil•i•ty,** n. **—vis/i•bly,** adv.

vi/sion (vizh′ən) n. **1.** power or sense of sight. **2.** imagination or unusually keen per-

V

ception. **3.** mental image of something supernatural or imaginary. —**vi′sion•al,** *adj.*

vi′sion•ar′y (vizh′ə ner′ē) *adj., n., pl.* **-ies.** —*adj.* **1.** fanciful. **2.** seen in vision. **3.** unreal. —*n.* **4.** seer of visions. **5.** bold or impractical schemer.

vis′it (viz′it) *v.* **1.** go to for purposes of talking, staying, etc. **2.** afflict. —*n.* **3.** act of visiting. **4.** stay as guest. —**vis′i•tor, vis′i•tant,** *n.*

vis′it•a′tion (-i tā′shən) *n.* **1.** visit. **2.** bringing of good or evil, as by supernatural force.

vi′sor (vī′zər) *n.* front piece, as of helmet or cap.

vis′ta (vis′tə) *n.* extended view in one direction.

vis′u•al (vizh′ōō əl) *adj.* **1.** of or by means of sight. **2.** visible. —**vis′u•al•ly,** *adv.*

vis′u•al•ize′, *v.,* **-ized, -izing. 1.** make visual. **2.** form mental image of. —**vis′u•al•i•za′tion,** *n.*

vi′tal (vīt′l) *adj.* **1.** of life. **2.** living; energetic; vivid. **3.** giving or necessary to life. **4.** essential. —**vi′tal•ly,** *adv.*

vi•tal′i•ty (-tal′i tē) *n., pl.* **-ties. 1.** vital force. **2.** physical or mental vigor. **3.** power of continued existence.

vital signs, essential body functions, comprising pulse rate, body temperature, and respiration.

vital statistics, statistics concerning deaths, births, and marriages.

vi′ta•min (vī′tə min) *n.* food element essential in small quantities to maintain life. —**vi′ta•min′ic,** *adj.*

vi′ti•ate′ (vish′ē āt′) *v.,* **-ated, -ating. 1.** impair. **2.** corrupt. **3.** invalidate. —**vi′ti•a′tion,** *n.*

vit′i•cul′ture (vit′i kul′chər, vī′ti-) *n.* cultivation of grapes. —**vit′i•cul′tur•ist,** *n.*

vitr vitreous.

vit′re•ous (vi′trē əs) *adj.* of or like glass.

vitreous humor, transparent gelatinous substance that fills eyeball.

vit′ri•fy′, *v.,* **-fied, -fying.** change to glass.

vi•trine′ (vi trēn′) *n.* glass cabinet.

vit′ri•ol (vi′trē əl) *n.* **1.** glassy metallic compound. **2.** sulfuric acid. **3.** caustic criticism, etc. —**vit′ri•ol′ic** (-ol′ik) *adj.*

vi•tu′per•ate′ (vī tōō′pə rāt′, -tyōō′-, vi-) *v.,* **-ated, -ating. 1.** criticize abusively. **2.** revile. —**vi•tu′per•a′tion,** *n.* —**vi•tu′per•a•tive** (-pər ə tiv) *adj.*

vi•va′cious (vi vā′shəs, vī-) *adj.* lively; animated. —**vi•va′cious•ly,** *adv.* —**vi•va′cious•ness, vi•vac′i•ty** (-vas′i tē) *n.*

viv′id (viv′id) *adj.* **1.** bright, as color or light. **2.** full of life. **3.** intense; striking. —**viv′id•ly,** *adv.* —**viv′id•ness,** *n.*

viv′i•fy′, *v.,* **-fied, -fying.** give life to.

vi•vip′ar•ous (vī vip′ər əs, vi-) *adj.* bringing forth living young rather than eggs.

viv′i•sec′tion (viv′ə sek′shən) *n.* dissection of live animal. —**viv′i•sec′tion•ist,** *n.*

vix′en (vik′sən) *n.* **1.** female fox. **2.** ill-tempered woman.

viz. (used to introduce examples, etc.) namely. [from Latin *videlicet*]

vi•zier′ (vi zēr′, viz′yər) *n.* high official in certain Muslim countries.

VJ (vē′jā′), *Informal.* **1.** Also, **V.J.** video jockey. **2.** a video journalist.

V-J Day (vē′jā′), August 15, 1945, the day Japan accepted the Allied surrender terms. [*V(ictory over) J(apan) Day*]

VL Vulgar Latin.

v.l. variant reading. [from Latin *varia lectio*]

VLA *Astronomy.* Very Large Array.

vla very low altitude.

VLBI *Astronomy.* very long baseline interferometry.

VLCC a supertanker with a deadweight capacity of up to 250,000 tons. [*V(ery) L(arge) C(rude) C(arrier)*]

VLDL *Biochemistry.* very-low-density lipoprotein.

VLF very low frequency. Also, **vlf**

vlmtrc volumetric.

vlr very long range.

VLSI *Electronics.* very large scale integration: the technology for concentrating many thousands of semiconductor devices on a single integrated circuit.

vm velocity modulation.

V.M.D. Doctor of Veterinary Medicine. [from Latin *Veterināriae Medicīnae Doctor*]

v.n. verb neuter.

vo. *Printing.* verso.

V.O. very old (used especially to indicate the age of whiskey or brandy, usually 6 to 8 years old).

VOA 1. Also, **V.O.A.** Voice of America. **2.** Volunteers of America.

voc. *Grammar.* vocative.

vocab. vocabulary.

vo•cab′u•lar′y (vō kab′yə ler′ē) *n., pl.* **-laries. 1.** words used by people, class, or person. **2.** collection of defined words, usually in alphabetical order.

vo′cal (vō′kəl) *adj.* **1.** of the voice. **2.** of or for singing. **3.** articulate or talkative. —*n.* **4.** vocal composition or performance. —**vo′cal•ize′,** *v.,* **-ized, -izing.** —**vo′cal•i•za′tion,** *n.* —**vo′cal•ly,** *adv.*

vocal cords, membranes in larynx producing sound by vibration.

vo′cal•ist (-kə list) *n.* singer.

vo•ca′tion (vō kā′shən) *n.* occupation, business, or profession. —**vo•ca′tion•al,** *adj.*

voc′a•tive (vok′ə tiv) *adj.* of or being grammatical case used to indicate one being addressed.

voc. ed. vocational education.

vo•cif′er•ate′ (vō sif′ə rāt′) *v.,* **-ated, -ating.** cry noisily; shout. —**vo•cif′er•a′tion,** *n.* —**vo•cif′er•ous,** *adj.* —**vo•cif′er•ous•ly,** *adv.*

vodat (vō′dat), voice-operated device for automatic transmission.

vod′ka (vod′kə) *n.* colorless distilled liquor.

vogad (vō′gad), voice-operated gain-adjusting device.

vogue (vōg) *n.* **1.** fashion. **2.** popular favor.

voice (vois) *n., v.,* **voiced, voicing.** —*n.* **1.** sound uttered through mouth. **2.** speaking or singing voice. **3.** expression. **4.** choice. **5.** right to express opinion. **6.** verb inflection indicating whether subject is acting or acted upon. —*v.* **7.** express or declare. —**voice′less,** *adj.*

voice box, larynx.

voice mail, electronic system that routes voice messages to appropriate recipients.

voice′-o′ver, *n.* voice of off-screen narrator or announcer, as on television.

void (void) *adj.* **1.** without legal force. **2.** useless. **3.** empty. —*n.* **4.** empty space. —*v.* **5.** invalidate. **6.** empty out. —**void′a•ble,** *adj.* —**void′ance,** *n.*

voile (voil) *n.* lightweight, semisheer fabric.

vol., volume.

VO language *Linguistics.* a type of language that has direct objects following the verb. [V(*erb*)-O(*bject*)]

vol′a•tile (vol′ə tl) *adj.* **1.** evaporating rapidly. **2.** explosive. **3.** rapidly changeable in emotion. —**vol′a•til′i•ty,** *n.*

vol•ca′no (vol kā′nō) *n., pl.* **-noes, -nos. 1.** vent in earth from which lava, steam, etc., are expelled. **2.** mountain with such vent. —**vol•can′ic** (-kan′ik) *adj.*

vole (vōl) *n.* short-tailed stocky rodent.

vo•li′tion (vō lish′ən, və-) *n.* act or power of willing. —**vo•li′tion•al,** *adv.*

vol′ley (vol′ē) *n.* **1.** discharge of many missiles together. **2.** returning of ball before it hits ground. —*v.* **3.** hit or fire volley.

vol′ley•ball′, *n.* **1.** game in which large ball is volleyed back and forth over net. **2.** ball used in this game.

volt (vōlt) *n.* unit of electromotive force. —**volt′age,** *n.* —**volt′me′ter,** *n.*

vol•ta′ic (vol tā′ik, vōl-) *adj.* of or noting electricity produced by chemical action.

vol′u•ble (vol′yə bəl) *adj.* glibly fluent. —**vol′u•bil′i•ty,** *n.* —**vol′u•bly,** *adv.*

vol′ume (vol′yŏŏm, -yəm) *n.* **1.** book. **2.** size in three dimensions. **3.** mass or quantity. **4.** loudness or fullness of sound.

vo•lu′mi•nous (və lŏŏ′mə nəs) *adj.* **1.** filling many volumes. **2.** ample. —**vo•lu′mi•nous•ly,** *adv.*

vol′un•tar′y (vol′ən ter′ē) *adj.* **1.** done, made, etc., by free choice. **2.** controlled by will. —**vol′un•tar′i•ly,** *adv.*

vol′un•teer′, *n.* **1.** person who offers self, as for military duty. **2.** worker forgoing pay. —*v.* **3.** offer for some duty or purpose.

vo•lup′tu•ous (və lup′chŏŏ əs) *adj.* luxurious; sensuous. —**vo•lup′tu•ous•ly,** *adv.* —**vo•lup′tu•ous•ness,** *n.*

vo•lute′ (və lŏŏt′) *n.* spiral object.

vom volt-ohm-milliammeter.

vom′it (vom′it) *v.* **1.** eject from stomach through mouth. **2.** eject with force. —*n.* **3.** vomited matter.

voo′doo (vŏŏ′dŏŏ) *n.* polytheistic religion deriving chiefly from African cults.

VOR *Navigation.* omnirange. [*v*(*ery high frequency*) *o*(*mni*) *r*(*ange*)]

vo•ra′cious (vô rā′shəs) *adj.* greedy; ravenous. —**vo•ra′cious•ly,** *adv.* —**vo•rac′i•ty** (-ras′i tē) *n.*

vordme vhf omnirange distance-measuring equipment.

vor′tex (vôr′teks) *n., pl.* **-texes, -tices** (-tə-sēz′). whirling movement or mass.

vo′ta•ry (vō′tə rē) *n., pl.* **-ries. 1.** worshiper. **2.** devotee. **3.** person bound by religious vows.

vote (vōt) *n., v.,* **voted, voting.** —*n.* **1.** formal expression of wish or choice, as by ballot. **2.** right to this. **3.** votes collectively. —*v.* **4.** cast one's vote. **5.** cause to go or occur by vote. —**vot′er,** *n.*

vou. voucher.

vouch (vouch) *v.* **1.** answer for. **2.** give assurance, as surety or sponsor.

vouch′er, *n.* **1.** one that vouches. **2.** document, receipt, etc., proving expenditure.

vouch•safe′, *v.,* **-safed, -safing.** grant or permit.

vow (vou) *n.* **1.** solemn promise, pledge, or personal engagement. —*v.* **2.** make vow.

vow′el (vou′əl) *n.* **1.** speech sound made with clear channel through middle of mouth. **2.** letter representing vowel.

VOX (voks), a device in certain types of telecommunications equipment, that converts an incoming voice or sound signal into an electrical signal. [acronym from *voice-operated keying,* altered to conform to Latin *vōx* voice]

vox pop. the voice of the people. [from Latin *vox populi*]

voy′age (voi′ij) *n., v.,* **-aged, -aging.** —*n.* **1.** journey, esp. by water. —*v.* **2.** make voyage. —**voy′ag•er,** *n.*

vo•yeur′ (vwä yûr′, voi ûr′) *n.* person who obtains sexual gratification by looking at sexual objects or acts. —**vo•yeur′ism,** *n.* —**voy′eur•is′tic,** *adj.*

V.P., Vice President. Also, **VP.**

vprs voltage-regulated power supply.

vprz vaporize.

VR 1. virtual reality. **2.** voltage regulator.

vr 1. variable response. **2.** voltage regulator.

V.R. Queen Victoria. [from Latin *Victōria Rēgīna*]

v.r. reflexive verb. [from Latin *verbum reflexīvum*]

V region *Immunology.* variable region.

V. Rev. Very Reverend.

vrfy verify.

vris *Electricity.* varistor.

V

VRM variable-rate mortgage.

vs., versus.

vsb vestigial sideband.

vsbl visible.

vsd variable-speed drive.

vsm vestigial-sideband.

V. S. O. (of brandy) very superior old.

VSO language *Linguistics.* a type of language that has basic verb-subject-object word order.

V.S.O.P. very superior old pale (used especially to indicate a type of aged brandy).

VSR very special reserve (a classification of fortified wines).

vss. versions.

vstbl vestibule.

vstm valve stem.

V/STOL (vē′stôl′), *Aeronautics.* vertical and short takeoff and landing.

VSWR *Electronics.* voltage standing-wave ratio. Also, **vswr**

VT, Vermont. Also, **Vt.**

V.T.C. **1.** Volunteer Training Corps. **2.** voting trust certificate.

Vte. Vicomte.

Vtesse. Vicomtesse.

VT fuze a variable time fuze.

vtm voltage-tunable magnetron.

VTO *Aeronautics.* vertical takeoff.

VTOL (vē′tôl′), *Aeronautics.* a convertiplane capable of taking off and landing vertically, having forward speeds comparable to those of conventional aircraft. [*v(ertical) t(ake)o(ff and) l(anding)*]

VTR *Television.* videotape recorder.

vtvm vacuum-tube voltmeter.

vu *Audio.* volume unit. Also, **VU**

Vul. Vulgate (bible).

vulc vulcanize.

vul′can•ize′ (vul′kə nīz′) *v.,* **-ized, -izing.** treat rubber with sulfur and heat. —**vul′can•i•za′tion,** *n.* —**vul′can•iz′er,** *n.*

Vulg. Vulgate (bible).

vulg. **1.** vulgar. **2.** vulgarly.

vul′gar (vul′gər) *adj.* **1.** lacking good breeding or taste; unrefined. **2.** indecent; obscene. **3.** plebeian. **4.** vernacular. —**vul′gar•ly,** *adv.* —**vul•gar′i•ty** (-gar′i tē) *n.*

vul′gar•ism, *n.* **1.** vulgarity. **2.** vulgar word.

vul′ner•a•ble (vul′nər ə bəl) *adj.* **1.** liable to physical or emotional hurt. **2.** open to attack. —**vul′ner•a•bly,** *adv.* —**vul′ner•a•bil′i•ty,** *n.*

vul′ture (vul′chər) *n.* large, carrion-eating bird.

vul′va (vul′və) *n., pl.* **-vae, -vas.** external female genitals.

VU meter a meter used with sound-reproducing or recording equipment that indicates average sound levels.

vv. **1.** verses. **2.** violins.

v.v. vice versa.

V. V. O. (of brandy) very, very old.

V. V. S. (of brandy) very very superior.

V.W. Very Worshipful.

vy′ing (vī′ing) *adj.* competing.

W

W, w (dub′əl yōō′, -yōō) *n.* twenty-third letter of English alphabet.

W, west, western.

WA, Washington.

WAAC (wak), **1. a.** Women's Army Auxiliary Corps: founded during World War II. **b.** a member of the Women's Army Auxiliary Corps. **2.** *British.* **a.** Women's Army Auxiliary Corps: founded in 1917. **b.** a member of the Women's Army Auxiliary Corps. Also, **W. A.A.C.**

WAAF Women's Auxiliary Air Force.

wack′y (wak′ē) *adj.*, **-ier, -iest.** *Slang.* odd or irrational. **—wack′i•ness,** *n.*

wad (wod) *n., v.,* **wadded, wadding. —n. 1.** small soft mass. **—v. 2.** form into wad. **3.** stuff.

wad′dle (wod′l) *v.,* **-dled, -dling,** *n.* **—v. 1.** sway in walking, as duck. **—n. 2.** waddling gait.

wade (wād) *v.,* **waded, wading,** *n.* **—v. 1.** walk through water, sand, etc. **—n. 2.** act of wading. **—wad′er,** *n.*

wa′fer (wā′fər) *n.* **1.** thin crisp biscuit. **2.** small disk of bread used in Eucharist.

waf′fle (wof′əl) *n., v.,* **-fled, -fling. —n. 1.** batter cake baked in a double griddle (**waffle iron**). **—v. 2.** speak or write equivocally.

W. Afr. 1. West Africa. **2.** West African.

waft (wäft, waft) *v.* **1.** float through air or over water. **—n. 2.** sound, odor, etc., wafted.

wag (wag) *v.,* **wagged, wagging,** *n.* **—v. 1.** move rapidly back and forth. **—n. 2.** act of wagging. **3.** joker. **—wag′gish,** *adj.*

wage (wāj) *n., v.,* **waged, waging. —n. 1.** pay; salary. **2.** recompense. **—v. 3.** carry on (war, etc.).

wa′ger (wā′jər) *v., n.* bet.

wag′ger•y (wag′ə rē) *n., pl.* **-geries. 1.** roguish wit of a wag. **2.** joke.

wag′gle (wag′əl) *v.,* **-gled, -gling,** *n.* wag.

wag′on (wag′ən) *n.* four-wheeled vehicle for drawing heavy loads. Also, *Brit.,* **wag′gon.**

wagon train, train of wagons and horses.

waif (wāf) *n.* homeless child.

wail (wāl) *n.* **1.** long mournful cry. **2.** sound like this. **—v. 3.** utter wails. **—wail′er,** *n.*

wain′scot (wān′skət, -skot, -skōt) *n., v.,* **-scoted, -scoting. —n. 1.** woodwork lining wall. **—v. 2.** line with wainscot.

WAIS (wās for def. 1), **1.** Wechsler Adult Intelligence Scale. **2.** *Computers.* wide-area information server.

WAIS-R (wās′är′), Wechsler Adult Intelligence Scale-Revised.

waist (wāst) *n.* **1.** part of body between ribs and hips. **2.** garment or part of garment for upper part of body. **—waist′band′,** *n.* **—waist′line′,** *n.*

waist′coat′ (wes′kət, wāst′kōt′) *n. Brit.* vest.

wait (wāt) *v.* **1.** stay in expectation. **2.** be ready. **3.** await. **4.** wait on; serve. **—n. 5.** act of waiting. **6.** delay. **7.** ambush.

wait′er, *n.* man who waits on table. **—wait′ress,** *n.fem.*

waiting list, list of persons waiting, as for reservations or admission.

waive (wāv) *v.,* **waived, waiving.** give up; forgo.

waiv′er, *n.* statement of relinquishment.

wake (wāk) *v.,* **waked** or **woke** (wōk), **waked, waking,** *n.* **—v. 1.** stop sleeping; rouse from sleep. **—n. 2.** vigil, esp. beside corpse. **3.** track or path, esp. of vessel.

wake′ful, *adj.* awake; alert. **—wake′ful•ly,** *adv.* **—wake′ful•ness,** *n.*

wak′en, *v.* wake.

Wal. 1. Wallachian. **2.** Walloon.

wale (wāl) *n., v.,* **waled, waling. —n. 1.** mark left on skin by rod or whip. **2.** vertical rib or cord in fabric. **—v. 3.** mark with wales.

walk (wôk) *v.* **1.** go or traverse on foot. **2.** cause to walk. **—n. 3.** act, course, or manner of walking. **4.** branch of activity. **5.** sidewalk or path. **—walk′er,** *n.*

walk′a•way′, *n.* easy victory.

walk′ie-talk′ie (wô′kē tô′kē) *n.* portable radio transmitter and receiver.

walking stick, 1. stick used for support in walking. **2.** insect with long twiglike body.

walk′out′, *n.* strike in which workers leave place of work.

wall (wôl) *n.* **1.** upright structure that divides, encloses, etc. **—v. 2.** enclose, divide, etc., with wall.

wall′board′, *n.* artificial material used to make or cover walls, etc.

wal′let (wol′it) *n.* small flat case for paper money, etc.

wall′eye′ (wôl′-) *n.* **1.** condition in which eye or eyes are turned outward. **2.** N American freshwater food fish. Also, **walleyed pike.**

wall′flow′er, *n.* **1.** person who, because of shyness, remains at side of party. **2.** perennial plant with fragrant flowers.

Wal•loon′ (wo lōōn′) *n.* member of French-speaking population of S and E Belgium.

wal′lop (wol′əp) *Informal.* **—v. 1.** thrash or defeat. **—n. 2.** blow.

wal′lop•ing, *adj. Informal.* **1.** very large. **2.** impressive.

wal′low (wol′ō) *v.* **1.** lie or roll in mud, etc. **—n. 2.** place where animals wallow.

wall′pa′per, *n.* decorative paper for covering walls and ceilings.

wal'nut' (wôl'nut', -nət) *n.* northern tree valued for wood and edible nut.

wal'rus (wôl'rəs) *n.* large tusked mammal of Arctic seas.

waltz (wôlts) *n.* **1.** dance in triple rhythm. —*v.* **2.** dance a waltz. —**waltz'er,** *n.*

WAM wraparound mortgage.

wam'pum (wom'pəm) *n.* shell beads, formerly used by North American Indians as money and ornament.

wan (won) *adj.,* **wanner, wannest.** pale; worn-looking. —**wan'ly,** *adv.*

wand (wond) *n.* slender rod or shoot.

wan'der (won'dər) *v.* move aimlessly; stray. —**wan'der•er,** *n.*

Wandering Jew, trailing plant with green or variegated leaves.

wan'der•lust', *n.* desire to travel.

wane (wān) *v.,* **waned, waning,** *n.* —*v.* **1.** (of moon) decrease periodically. **2.** decline or decrease. —*n.* **3.** decline or decrease.

wan'gle (wang'gəl) *v.,* **-gled, -gling.** bring out or obtain by scheming or underhand methods.

Wan'kel engine (wäng'kəl) internal-combustion rotary engine with triangular motor that revolves in chamber.

wan'na•be' (won'ə bē') *n. Informal.* one who aspires, often vainly, to emulate another's success or status.

want (wont) *v.* **1.** feel need or desire for. **2.** lack; be deficient in. —*n.* **3.** desire or need. **4.** lack. **5.** poverty.

want'ing, *adj., prep.* lacking.

wan'ton (won'tn) *adj.* **1.** malicious; unjustifiable. **2.** lewd. —*n.* **3.** lascivious person. —*v.* **4.** act in wanton manner. —**wan'ton•ly,** *adv.* —**wan'ton•ness,** *n.*

WAP Women Against Pornography.

war (wôr) *n., v.,* **warred, warring,** *adj.* —*n.* **1.** armed conflict. —*v.* **2.** carry on war. —*adj.* **3.** of, for, or due to war.

war'ble (wôr'bəl) *v.,* **-bled, -bling,** *n.* —*v.* **1.** sing with trills, etc., as birds. —*n.* **2.** warbled song.

war'bler, *n.* small songbird.

ward (wôrd) *n.* **1.** division of city. **2.** division of hospital. **3.** person under legal care of guardian or court. **4.** custody. —*v.* **5.** ward off, repel or avert.

ward'en (wôr'dn) *n.* **1.** keeper. **2.** administrative head of prison.

ward'er, *n.* guard.

ward heeler, minor politician who does chores for political machine.

ward'robe', *n.* **1.** stock of clothes. **2.** clothes closet.

ward'room', *n.* living quarters for ship's officers other than captain.

ware (wâr) *n.* **1.** (*pl.*) goods. **2.** pottery. **3.** vessels for domestic use.

ware'house', *n., v.,* **-housed, -housing.** —*n.* (wâr'hous') **1.** storehouse for goods. —*v.* (-houz', -hous') **2.** store in warehouse.

war'fare', *n.* waging of war.

war'head', *n.* section of missile containing explosive or payload.

war'-horse', *n. Informal.* veteran of many conflicts.

war'like', *adj.* waging or prepared for war.

war'lock', *n.* male witch.

warm (wôrm) *adj.* **1.** having, giving, or feeling moderate heat. **2.** cordial. **3.** lively. **4.** kind; affectionate. —*v.* **5.** make or become warm. —**warm'er,** *n.* —**warm'ly,** *adv.* —**warm'ness, warmth,** *n.*

warm'-blood'ed, *adj.* having relatively constant body temperature that is independent of environment.

warmed'-o'ver, *adj.* **1.** reheated. **2.** stale.

warm'heart'ed, *adj.* having emotional warmth.

war'mong'er, *n.* person who advocates or incites war.

warn (wôrn) *v.* **1.** give notice of danger, evil, etc. **2.** caution. —**warn'ing,** *n., adj.* —**warn'ing•ly,** *adv.*

warp (wôrp) *v.* **1.** bend out of shape; distort. **2.** guide by ropes. —*n.* **3.** bend or twist. **4.** lengthwise threads in loom.

war'rant (wôr'ənt) *n.* **1.** justification. **2.** guarantee. **3.** document certifying or authorizing something. —*v.* **4.** authorize or justify. **5.** guarantee. —**war'rant•a•ble,** *adj.*

warrant officer, military officer between enlisted and commissioned grades.

war'ran•ty, *n., pl.* **-ties.** guarantee.

war'ren (wôr'ən) *n.* place where rabbits live.

war'ri•or (wôr'ē ər) *n.* soldier.

war'ship', *n.* ship for combat.

wart (wôrt) *n.* small hard elevation on skin. —**wart'y,** *adj.*

war'y (wâr'ē) *adj.,* **-ier, -iest. 1.** watchful. **2.** careful. —**war'i•ly,** *adv.* —**war'i•ness,** *n.*

was (wuz, woz; *unstressed* wəz) *v.* first and third pers. sing., past indicative of **be.**

wash (wosh) *v.* **1.** cleanse in or with water. **2.** flow over. **3.** carry in flowing. **4.** cover thinly. —*n.* **5.** act of washing. **6.** Also, **wash'ing.** clothes, etc., to be washed. **7.** liquid covering. **8.** rough water or air behind moving ship or plane. —**wash'a•ble,** *adj.* —**wash'board',** *n.* —**wash'bowl',** *n.* —**wash'cloth',** *n.* —**wash'stand',** *n.* —**wash'room',** *n.*

Wash., Washington.

washed'-out', *adj.* **1.** faded. **2.** *Informal.* weary or tired-looking.

washed'-up', *adj. Informal.* done for; having failed.

wash'er, *n.* **1.** machine for washing. **2.** flat ring of rubber, metal, etc., to give tightness.

wash'out', *n.* **1.** destruction from action of water. **2.** *Slang.* failure.

wasn't (wuz'ənt, woz'-) contraction of **was not.**

wasp (wosp) *n.* **1.** stinging insect. **2.** *Slang.* (*cap. or caps.*) white Anglo-Saxon Protestant.

wasp'ish, *adj.* irritable; snappish.

was'sail (wos/əl, wo sāl/) *n.* **1.** drinking party. **2.** former English toast to person's health. —*v.* **3.** drink a toast.

waste (wāst) *v.*, **wasted, wasting,** *n.*, *adj.* —*v.* **1.** squander. **2.** fail to use. **3.** destroy gradually. **4.** become wasted. —*n.* **5.** useless expenditure. **6.** neglect. **7.** gradual decay. **8.** devastation. **9.** anything left over. —*adj.* **10.** not used. **11.** left over or worthless. —**waste'ful,** *adj.* —**waste'bas'ket,** *n.* —**waste'pa'per,** *n.*

waste'land', *n.* barren land.

wast'rel (wā'strəl) *n.* **1.** spendthrift. **2.** idler.

watch (woch) *v.* **1.** look attentively. **2.** be careful. **3.** guard. —*n.* **4.** close, constant observation. **5.** guard. **6.** period of watching. **7.** *Naut.* period of duty. **8.** small timepiece. —**watch'band',** *n.* —**watch'er,** *n.* —**watch'ful,** *adj.* —**watch'man,** *n.* —**watch'tow'er,** *n.*

watch'dog', *n.* **1.** dog that guards property. **2.** guardian, as against illegal conduct.

watch'word', *n.* **1.** password. **2.** slogan.

wa'ter (wô/tər) *n.* **1.** transparent liquid forming rivers, seas, lakes, rain, etc. **2.** surface of water. **3.** liquid solution. **4.** liquid organic secretion. —*v.* **5.** moisten or supply with water. **6.** dilute. **7.** discharge water. —*adj.* **8.** of, for, or powered by water.

wa'ter•bed', *n.* water-filled plastic bag used as bed.

water buffalo, domesticated Asian buffalo with curved horns.

water chestnut, aquatic plant with edible, nutlike fruit.

water closet, room containing flush toilet.

wa'ter•col'or, *n.* **1.** pigment mixed with water. **2.** painting using such pigments.

wa'ter•course', *n.* **1.** stream of water. **2.** bed of stream.

wa'ter•craft', *n.* **1.** skill in boating and water sports. **2.** boat.

wa'ter•cress', *n.* plant that grows in streams and bears pungent leaves used in salad.

wa'ter•fall', *n.* steep fall of water.

wa'ter•fowl', *n.*, *pl.* **-fowl, -fowls.** aquatic bird.

wa'ter•front', *n.* part of city or town on edge of body of water.

water gap, transverse gap in mountain ridge.

water glass, **1.** vessel for drinking. **2.** sodium silicate.

wa'ter•ing place, resort by water or having mineral springs.

water lily, aquatic plant with showy flowers.

water line, one of series of lines on ship's hull indicating level to which it is immersed.

wa'ter•logged', *adj.* filled or soaked with water.

wa'ter•mark', *n.* **1.** mark showing height reached by river, etc. **2.** manufacturer's de-

sign impressed in paper. —*v.* **3.** put watermark in (paper).

wa'ter•mel'on, *n.* large sweet juicy fruit of a vine.

water moccasin, cottonmouth.

wa'ter•proof', *adj.* **1.** impervious to water. —*v.* **2.** make waterproof.

water rat, aquatic rodent.

wa'ter•repel'lent, *adj.* repelling water but not entirely waterproof.

wa'ter•shed', *n.* **1.** area drained by river, etc. **2.** high land dividing such areas. **3.** important point of division or transition.

water ski, short, broad ski for gliding over water while being towed by boat. —**wa'ter-ski',** *v.*, **-skied, -skiing.** —**wa'ter•ski'er,** *n.*

wa'ter•spout', *n.* tornadolike storm over lake or ocean.

water table, underground level beneath which soil and rock are saturated with water.

wa'ter•tight', *adj.* **1.** constructed or fitted to be impervious to water. **2.** incapable of being nullified or discredited.

wa'ter•way', *n.* body of water as route of travel.

water wheel, wheel turned by water to provide power.

wa'ter•works', *n.pl.* apparatus for collecting and distributing water, as for city.

wa'ter•y, *adj.* of, like, or full of water. —**wa'ter•i•ness,** *n.*

WATS (wots), a bulk-rate long-distance telephone service. [*W*(*ide*) *A*(*rea*) *T*(*elecommunications*) *S*(*ervice*)]

watt (wot) *n.* unit of electric power. —**watt'-age,** *n.*

wat'tle (wot/l) *n.* **1.** flesh hanging from throat or chin. **2.** interwoven rods and twigs.

wave (wāv) *n.*, *v.*, **waved, waving.** —*n.* **1.** ridge on surface of liquid. **2.** surge; rush. **3.** curve. **4.** vibration, as in transmission of sound, etc. **5.** sign with moving hand, flag, etc. —*v.* **6.** move with waves. **7.** curve. **8.** signal by wave. —**wav'y,** *adj.*

wave'length', *n.* distance between two successive points in wave.

wa'ver (wā'vər) *v.* **1.** sway. **2.** hesitate. **3.** fluctuate.

wax (waks) *n.* **1.** yellowish substance secreted by bees. **2.** any similar substance. —*v.* **3.** rub with wax. **4.** (esp. of moon) increase. **5.** become. —**wax'en,** *adj.* —**wax'-er,** *n.* —**wax'y,** *adj.*

wax bean, variety of string bean bearing yellowish, waxy pods.

wax museum, museum displaying wax effigies of famous persons.

wax myrtle, bayberry of southeastern U.S.

wax paper, paper made moisture-resistant by paraffin coating.

wax'wing', *n.* small crested bird.

way (wā) *n.* **1.** manner; fashion. **2.** plan;

W

means. **3.** direction. **4.** road or route. **5.** custom. **6.** (*pl.*) timbers on which ship is built.

way'bill, *n.* list of goods with shipping directions.

way'far'er, *n.* rover.

way•lay' (wā'lā', wā lā') *v.* ambush.

way'-out', *adj. Informal.* very unconventional.

ways and means, methods of raising revenue.

way'side', *n.* **1.** side of road. —*adj.* **2.** beside road.

way'ward (-wərd) *adj.* capricious. —**way'-ward•ness,** *n.*

Wb *Electricity.* weber; webers.

W/B waybill. Also, **W.B.**

w.b. 1. warehouse book. **2.** water ballast. **3.** waybill. **4.** westbound.

WBA World Boxing Association.

wba wideband amplifier.

wbfp *Real Estate.* wood-burning fireplace.

WbN west by north.

WbS west by south.

WC water closet.

W.C. 1. water closet. **2.** west central.

w.c. 1. water closet. **2.** without charge.

W.C.T.U. Women's Christian Temperance Union.

WD wiring diagram.

wd 1. *Stock Exchange.* when distributed. **2.** width. **3.** wind. **4.** wood. **5.** word.

wd. 1. ward. **2.** word.

W/D *Banking.* withdrawal.

w/d withdrawn.

W.D. War Department.

wdg winding.

wdo window.

we (wē) *pron.* nominative plural of **I.**

wea weather.

weak (wēk) *adj.* **1.** not strong; fragile; frail. **2.** deficient. —**weak'en,** *v.* —**weak'ness,** *n.*

weak'-kneed', *adj.* yielding readily to opposition, pressure, or intimidation.

weak'ling (-ling) *n.* weak creature.

weak'ly, *adj.,* **-lier, -liest,** *adv.* —*adj.* **1.** sickly. —*adv.* **2.** in weak manner.

weal (wēl) *n. Archaic.* well-being.

wealth (welth) *n.* **1.** great possessions or riches. **2.** profusion. —**wealth'y,** *adj.*

wean (wēn) *v.* **1.** accustom to food other than mother's milk. **2.** detach from obsession or vice.

weap'on (wep'ən) *n.* instrument for use in fighting.

weap'on•ry, *n.* weapons collectively.

wear (wâr) *v.,* **wore** (wôr), **worn, wearing,** *n.* —*v.* **1.** have on body for covering or ornament. **2.** impair or diminish gradually. **3.** weary. **4.** undergo wear. **5.** last under use. —*n.* **6.** use of garment. **7.** clothing. **8.** gradual impairment or diminution. —**wear'a•ble,** *adj.* —**wear'er,** *n.*

wea'ri•some (wēr'ē səm) *adj.* **1.** tiring. **2.** tedious.

wea'ry, *adj.,* **-rier, -riest,** *v.,* **-ried, -rying.** —*adj.* **1.** tired. **2.** tedious. —*v.* **3.** tire. —**wea'ri•ly,** *adv.* —**wea'ri•ness,** *n.*

wea'sel (wē'zəl) *n.* small carnivorous animal.

weath'er (weth'ər) *n.* **1.** state of atmosphere as to moisture, temperature, etc. —*v.* **2.** expose to weather. **3.** withstand. —*adj.* **4.** of or on windward side.

weath'er-beat'en, *adj.* worn or marked by weather.

weath'er•ing, *n.* action of natural agents, as wind and water, on exposed rock.

weath'er•ize', *v.,* **-ized, -izing.** make secure against cold weather.

weath'er-proof', *adj.* **1.** able to withstand all kinds of weather. —*v.* **2.** make weatherproof.

weather strip, narrow strip placed between door or window sash and frame.

weath'er•vane', *n.* device to show direction of wind.

weave (wēv) *v.,* **wove** (wōv), **woven** or **wove, weaving,** *n.* —*v.* **1.** interlace, as to form cloth. **2.** take winding course. —*n.* **3.** manner of weaving. —**weav'er,** *n.*

web (web) *n., v.,* **webbed, webbing.** —*n.* **1.** something woven. **2.** fabric spun by spiders. **3.** membrane between toes in ducks, etc. —*v.* **4.** cover with web. —**webbed',** *adj.* —**web'bing,** *n.*

web'foot', *n.* foot with webbed toes. —**web'foot'ed,** *adj.*

Web'ster (web'stər) *n. Informal.* a dictionary of the English language. Also, **Web'ster's.**

wed (wed) *v.,* **wedded, wedded** or **wed, wedding. 1.** bind or join in marriage. **2.** attach firmly.

Wed., Wednesday.

wed'ding, *n.* marriage ceremony.

wedge (wej) *n., v.,* **wedged, wedging.** —*n.* **1.** angled object for splitting. —*v.* **2.** split with wedge. **3.** thrust or force like wedge.

wed'lock, *n.* matrimony.

Wednes'day (wenz'dā, -dē) *n.* fourth day of week.

wee (wē) *adj.* tiny.

weed (wēd) *n.* **1.** useless plant growing in cultivated ground. **2.** (*pl.*) mourning garments. —*v.* **3.** free from weeds. **4.** remove as undesirable. —**weed'er,** *n.* —**weed'y,** *adj.*

weeds (wēdz) *n.pl.* black clothes for mourning.

week (wēk) *n.* **1.** seven successive days. **2.** working part of week.

week'day', *n.* any day except Sunday, or, often, Saturday and Sunday. —**week'day',** *adj.*

week'end' (-end', -end') *n.* **1.** Saturday and Sunday. —*adj.* **2.** of or for weekend.

week'ly, *adj., adv., n., pl.* **-lies.** —*adj.* **1.** happening, appearing, etc., once a week. **2.**

lasting a week. —*adv.* **3.** once a week. **4.** by the week. —*n.* **5.** weekly periodical.

weep (wēp) *v.*, **wept** (wept), **weeping. 1.** shed tears. **2.** mourn. —**weep′er,** *n.*

wee′vil (wē′vəl) *n.* beetle destructive to grain, fruit, etc. —**wee′vil•ly,** *adj.*

weft (weft) *n.* threads interlacing with warp.

weigh (wā) *v.* **1.** measure heaviness of. **2.** burden. **3.** consider. **4.** lift. **5.** have heaviness. —**weigh′er,** *n.*

weight (wāt) *n.* **1.** amount of heaviness. **2.** system of units for expressing weight. **3.** heavy mass. **4.** pressure. **5.** burden. **6.** importance. —*v.* **7.** add weight to. —**weight′y,** *adj.* —**weight′i•ly,** *adj.* —**weight′less,** *adj.*

weir (wēr) *n.* **1.** dam in a stream. **2.** fence set in stream to catch fish.

weird (wērd) *adj.* **1.** supernatural. **2.** uncannily strange. —**weird′ly,** *adv.* —**weird′ness,** *n.*

weird′o (wēr′dō) *n.* *Slang.* odd, eccentric, or abnormal person.

wel′come (wel′kəm) *n.*, *v.*, **-comed, -coming,** *adj.* —*n.* **1.** friendly reception. —*v.* **2.** receive or greet with pleasure. —*adj.* **3.** gladly received. **4.** given permission or consent.

weld (weld) *v.* **1.** unite, esp. by heating and pressing. —*n.* **2.** welded joint. —**weld′er,** *n.*

wel′fare′ (wel′fâr′) *n.* **1.** well-being. **2.** provision of benefits to poor.

well (wel) *adv.*, *compar.* **better,** *superl.* **best,** *adj.*, *n.*, *v.* —*adv.* **1.** excellently; properly. **2.** thoroughly. —*adj.* **3.** in good health. **4.** good; proper. —*n.* **5.** hole made in earth to reach water, oil, etc. **6.** source. **7.** vertical shaft. —*v.* **8.** rise or gush.

well′-advised′, *adj.* **1.** acting with care. **2.** based on wise consideration.

well′-appoint′ed, *adj.* attractively furnished.

well′-be′ing, *n.* good or prosperous condition.

well′born′, *adj.* of good family.

well′-bred′, *adj.* showing good manners.

well′-dis•posed′, *adj.* feeling favorable, sympathetic, or kind.

well′-done′, *adj.* **1.** performed accurately and skillfully. **2.** thoroughly cooked.

well′-found′ed, *adj.* having or based on good reasons, sound information, etc.

well′-ground′ed, *adj.* having good basic knowledge of a subject.

well′-heeled′, *adj.* prosperous; well-off.

well′-informed′, *adj.* having extensive knowledge.

well′-mean′ing, *adj.* intending good. —**well′-meant′,** *adj.*

well′-nigh′, *adv.* nearly.

well′-off′, *adj.* **1.** in good or favorable condition. **2.** prosperous.

well′-round′ed, *adj.* desirably varied.

well′-spo′ken, *adj.* **1.** speaking well or fittingly. **2.** spoken in a pleasing manner.

well′spring′, *n.* source.

well′-to-do′, *adj.* prosperous.

well′-worn′, *adj.* **1.** showing effects of extensive use. **2.** trite.

Welsh (welsh, welch) *n.* people or language of Wales.

welt (welt) *n.* **1.** wale from lash. **2.** strip around edge of shoe. **3.** narrow border along seam. —*v.* **4.** put welt on.

wel′ter (wel′tər) *v.* **1.** roll, as waves. **2.** wallow.

wen (wen) *n.* small cyst.

wench (wench) *n.* girl or young woman.

wend (wend) *v.*, **wended, wending.** *Archaic.* go.

went (went) *v.* pt. of **go.**

were (wûr; *unstressed* wər) *v.* past plural and pres. subjunctive of **be.**

weren't (wûrnt, wûr′ənt) contraction of **were not.**

were′wolf′ (wâr′wŏŏlf′, wēr′-, wûr′-) *n.*, *pl.* **-wolves.** (in folklore) human turned into wolf.

west (west) *n.* **1.** point of compass opposite east. **2.** direction of this point. **3.** area in this direction. —*adj.* **4.** toward, from, or in west. —*adv.* **5.** toward or from west. —**west′er•ly,** *adj.*, *adv.* —**west′ern,** *adj.* —**west′ern•er,** *n.*

west′ern•ize′ (wes′tər nīz′) *v.*, **-ized, -izing.** influence with or convert to western ideas and customs.

Westm. Westminster.

west′ward (-wərd) *adj.* **1.** moving or facing west. —*adv.* **2.** Also, **west′wards.** toward west. —*n.* **3.** westward part. —**west′ward•ly,** *adj.*, *adv.*

wet (wet) *adj.*, **wetter, wettest,** *n.*, *v.*, **wet** or **wetted, wetting.** —*adj.* **1.** covered or soaked with water. **2.** rainy. —*n.* **3.** moisture. —*v.* **4.** make or become wet. —**wet′ness,** *n.*

wet blanket, one that dampens enthusiasm.

wet′land′, *n.* low land with usu. wet soil.

wet nurse, woman hired to suckle another's infant.

wet suit, close-fitting rubber suit worn for body warmth, as by scuba divers.

WF 1. wind force. **2.** withdraw failing.

wf *Printing.* wrong font. Also, **w.f.**

wfr wafer.

WFTU World Federation of Trade Unions. Also, **W.F.T.U.**

wg 1. waveguide. **2.** wing.

W.G. 1. water gauge. **2.** *Commerce.* weight guaranteed. **3.** wire gauge. Also, **w.g.**

W. Ger. 1. West Germanic. **2.** West Germany.

WGmc West Germanic. Also, **W. Gmc.**

WH *Banking.* withholding. Also, **w/h**

Wh watt-hour; watt-hours. Also, **wh, whr**

WHA World Hockey Association.

whack (hwak, wak) *Informal,* *v.* **1.** strike sharply. —*n.* **2.** smart blow.

whale (hwāl, wāl) *n.*, *pl.* **whales** or **whale,**

v., whaled, whaling. —*n.* **1.** large fishlike marine mammal. —*v.* **2.** kill and render whales. —**whal/er,** *n.*

whale/bone/, *n.* elastic horny substance in upper jaw of some whales.

wharf (hwôrf, wôrf) *n., pl.* **wharves.** structure for mooring vessels.

wharf/age, *n.* **1.** use of wharf. **2.** charge for such use.

what (hwut, hwot, wut, wot; *unstressed* hwət, wət) *pron., pl.* **what,** *adv.* —*pron.* **1.** which one? **2.** that which. **3.** such. —*adv.* **4.** how much. **5.** partly.

what·ev/er, *pron.* **1.** anything that. **2.** no matter what. —*adj.* **3.** no matter what.

what/not/, *n.* small open cupboard, esp. for knickknacks.

what/so·ev/er, *pron., adj.* whatever.

wheal (hwēl, wēl) *n.* swelling, as from mosquito bite.

wheat (hwēt, wēt) *n.* grain of common cereal grass, used esp. for flour.

whee/dle (hwēd/l, wēd/l) *v.,* **-dled, -dling.** influence by artful persuasion.

wheel (hwēl, wēl) *n.* **1.** round object turning on axis. —*v.* **2.** turn on axis. **3.** move on wheels. **4.** turn.

wheel/bar/row, *n.* one-wheeled vehicle lifted at one end.

wheel/base/, *n.* *Auto.* distance between centers of front and rear wheel hubs.

wheel/chair/, *n.* chair mounted on wheels for use by persons who cannot walk.

wheeze (hwēz, wēz) *v.,* **wheezed, wheezing,** *n.* —*v.* **1.** whistle in breathing. —*n.* **2.** wheezing breath. **3.** trite saying.

whelm (hwelm, welm) *v.* **1.** engulf. **2.** overwhelm.

whelp (hwelp, welp) *n.* **1.** young of dog, wolf, bear, etc. —*v.* **2.** bring forth whelps.

when (hwen, wen; *unstressed* hwən, wən) *adv.* **1.** at what time. —*conj.* **2.** at time that. **3.** and then.

whence (hwens, wens) *adv., conj.* from what place.

when·ev/er, *adv.* at whatever time.

where (hwâr, wâr) *adv.* **1.** in, at, or to what place? **2.** in what respect? —*conj.* **3.** in, at, or to what place. **4.** and there.

where/a·bouts/, *adv.* **1.** where. —*n.* **2.** location.

where·as/, *conj.* **1.** while on the contrary. **2.** considering that.

where·at/, *conj.* **1.** at which. **2.** to which; whereupon.

where·by/, *conj.* by what or which; under the terms of which.

where/fore/, *adv., conj.* **1.** why; for what. —*n.* **2.** reason.

where·in/, *conj.* **1.** in what or in which. —*adv.* **2.** in what way or respect?

where·of/, *adv., conj.* of what.

where/up·on/, *conj.* **1.** upon which. **2.** at or after which.

wher·ev/er, *conj.* at or to whatever place.

where/with·al/ (-with ôl/, -with-) *n.* means.

wher/ry (hwer/ē, wer/ē) *n., pl.* **-ries.** light rowboat for one person.

whet (hwet, wet) *v.,* **whetted, whetting.** sharpen. —**whet/stone/,** *n.*

wheth/er (hweth/ər, weth/-) *conj.* (word introducing alternative.)

whey (hwā, wā) *n.* watery part that separates out when milk curdles.

whf. wharf.

which (hwich, wich) *pron.* **1.** what one? **2.** the one that. —*adj.* **3.** what one of (those mentioned).

which·ev/er, *pron.* any that.

whiff (hwif, wif) *n.* **1.** slight puff or blast. —*v.* **2.** blow in whiffs.

while (hwīl, wīl) *n., conj., v.,* **whiled, whiling.** —*n.* **1.** time. —*conj.* **2.** in time that. —*v.* **3.** pass (time) pleasantly.

whim (hwim, wim) *n.* irrational or fanciful decision or idea.

whim/per (hwim/pər, wim/-) *v.* **1.** cry softly and plaintively. —*n.* **2.** whimpering cry. —**whim/per·er,** *n.*

whim/sy (hwim/zē, wim/-) *n., pl.* **-sies.** fanciful idea; whim. —**whim/si·cal,** *adj.* —**whim/si·cal/i·ty,** *n.* —**whim/si·cal·ly,** *adv.*

whine (hwīn, wīn) *n., v.,* **whined, whining.** —*n.* **1.** low complaining sound. —*v.* **2.** utter whines. —**whin/er,** *n.* —**whin/ing·ly,** *adv.*

whin/ny (hwin/ē, win/ē) *v.,* **-nied, -nying,** *n., pl.* **-nies.** neigh.

whip (hwip, wip) *v.,* **whipped, whipping,** *n.* —*v.* **1.** strike repeatedly; flog. **2.** jerk; seize. **3.** cover with thread; overcast. **4.** beat (cream, etc.). **5.** move quickly; lash about. —*n.* **6.** instrument with lash and handle for striking. **7.** party manager in legislature. —**whip/per,** *n.*

whip/cord/, *n.* fabric with diagonal ribs.

whip/lash/, *n.* **1.** lash of whip. **2.** neck injury caused by sudden jerking of the head.

whip/per·snap/per (hwip/ər snap/ər, wip/-) *n.* insignificant, presumptuous person, esp. young one.

whip/pet (whip/it, wip/-) *n.* type of slender swift dog.

whip/poor·will/ (hwip/ər wil/, wip/-) *n.* nocturnal American bird.

whip/saw/, *n.* saw for two persons.

whir (hwûr, wûr) *v.,* **whirred, whirring,** *n.* —*v.* **1.** move with buzzing sound. —*n.* **2.** such sound. Also, **whirr.**

whirl (hwûrl, wûrl) *v.* **1.** spin or turn rapidly. **2.** move quickly. —*n.* **3.** whirling movement. **4.** round of events, etc. —**whirl/er,** *n.*

whirl/i·gig/ (hwûr/li gig/, wûr/-) *n.* toy revolving in wind.

whirl/pool/, *n.* whirling current in water.

whirl/wind/ (-wind/) *n.* whirling mass of air.

whisk (hwisk, wisk) v. **1.** sweep up. **2.** move or carry lightly. —n. **3.** act of whisking.

whisk'er, n. **1.** (pl.) hair on man's face. **2.** bristle on face of cat, etc.

whis'key (hwis'kē, wis'-) n. distilled alcoholic liquor made from grain or corn. Also, **whis'ky.**

whis'per (hwis'pər, wis'pər) v. **1.** speak very softly. —n. **2.** sound of whispering. **3.** something whispered. —**whis'per•er,** n.

whist (hwist, wist) n. card game.

whis'tle (hwis'əl, wis'-) v., -**tled, -tling,** n. —v. **1.** make clear shrill sound with breath, air, or steam. —n. **2.** device for making such sounds. **3.** sound of whistling. —**whis'tler,** n.

whis'tle-blow'er, n. person who publicly discloses corruption or wrongdoing.

whistle stop, 1. small town. **2.** short talk from rear platform of train during political campaign.

whit (hwit, wit) n. particle; bit.

white (hwīt, wīt) adj. **1.** of color of snow. **2.** having light skin. **3.** pale. —n. **4.** color without hue, opposite to black. **5.** Caucasian. **6.** white or light part. —**whit'en,** v. —**white'-ness,** n. —**whit'ish,** adj.

white blood cell, nearly colorless blood cell of immune system.

white'-bread', adj. bland; conventional.

white'cap', n. wave with foaming white crest.

white'-col'lar, adj. of professional or office workers whose jobs usu. do not involve manual labor.

white elephant, useless, expensive possession.

white'fish', n. small food fish.

white flag, all-white flag used to signal surrender or truce.

white gold, gold alloy colored white esp. by presence of nickel.

white goods, household linens.

white lie, harmless lie; fib.

white'wash', n. **1.** substance for whitening walls, etc. —v. **2.** cover with whitewash. **3.** cover up faults or errors of.

white water, frothy water, as in rapids.

whith'er (hwith'ər, with'-) adv., conj. Archaic. where; to what (which) place.

whit'ing (hwī'ting, wī'-) n. **1.** small Atlantic food fish. **2.** ground chalk used to whiten.

whit'low (hwit'lō, wit'-) n. inflammation on finger or toe.

Whit'sun•day (hwit'sun'dā, -dē, -sən dā', wit'-) n. seventh Sunday after Easter.

whit'tle (hwit'l, wit'l) v., -**tled, -tling. 1.** cut bit by bit with knife. **2.** reduce. —**whit'tler,** n.

whiz (hwiz, wiz) v., **whizzed, whizzing,** n. —v. **1.** move with hum or hiss. —n. **2.** whizzing sound. **3.** person who is very good at something. Also, **whizz.**

whl wheel.

who (hōō) pron. **1.** what person? **2.** the person that.

whoa (hwō, wō) interj. (stop!)

who•dun'it (-dun'it) n. detective story.

who•ev'er, pron. anyone that.

whole (hōl) adj. **1.** entire; undivided. **2.** undamaged. **3.** Math. not fractional. —n. **4.** entire amount or extent. **5.** complete thing. —**whol'ly,** adv. —**whole'ness,** n.

whole'-heart'ed, adj. sincere.

whole note, Music. note equivalent in value to four quarter notes.

whole'sale', n., adj., v., -**saled, -saling.** —n. **1.** sale of goods in quantity, as to retailers. —adj. **2.** of or engaged in wholesale. —v. **3.** sell by wholesale. —**whole'sal'er,** n.

whole'some (-səm) adj. beneficial; healthful. —**whole'some•ly,** adv. —**whole'some•ness,** n.

whole'-wheat', adj. prepared with complete wheat kernel.

whom (hōōm) pron. objective case of **who.**

whom•ev'er, pron. objective case of **whoever.**

whoop (hwōōp, hwŏŏp, wōōp, wŏŏp; esp. for 2 hōŏp, hŏŏp) n. **1.** loud shout or cry. **2.** gasping sound characteristic of whooping cough. —v. **3.** utter whoops.

whoop'ing cough (hōō'ping, hŏŏp'ing) infectious disease characterized by short, convulsive coughs followed by whoops.

whop'per (hwop'ər, wop'-) n. Informal. **1.** something uncommonly large. **2.** big lie.

whop'ping, adj. Informal. uncommonly large.

whore (hôr; often hŏŏr) n., v., **whored, whoring.** —n. **1.** prostitute. —v. **2.** consort with whores.

whorl (hwûrl, hwôrl, wûrl, wôrl) n. **1.** circular arrangement, as of leaves. **2.** any spiral part.

whose (hōōz) pron. possessive case of **who.**

who'so•ev'er, pron. whoever.

whr. watt-hour; watt-hours.

whse. warehouse. Also, **whs.**

whsle. wholesale.

whs. stk. warehouse stock.

wht white.

why (hwī, wī) adv., n., pl. **whys.** —adv. **1.** for what reason. —n. **2.** cause or reason.

WI, Wisconsin.

WIA Military. wounded in action.

wick (wik) n. soft threads that absorb fuel to be burned in candle, etc.

wick'ed (wik'id) adj. **1.** evil; sinful. **2.** naughty. —**wick'ed•ly,** adv. —**wick'ed•ness,** n.

wick'er, n. **1.** slender pliant twig. —adj. **2.** made of wicker. —**wick'er•work',** n.

wick'et (wik'it) n. **1.** small gate or opening. **2.** framework in cricket and croquet.

wid. 1. widow. **2.** widower.

wide (wīd) adj., **wider, widest,** adv. —adj. **1.**

W

broad. **2.** extensive. **3.** expanded. **4.** far. —*adv.* **5.** far. **6.** to farthest extent. —**wide'-ly,** *adv.* —**wid'en,** *v.* —**wide'ness,** *n.*

wide'-awake', *adj.* **1.** fully awake. **2.** alert or observant.

wide'-eyed', *adj.* having eyes open wide, as in amazement or innocence.

wide'spread', *adj.* occurring widely.

widg'eon (wij'ən) *n.* wigeon.

wid'ow (wid'ō) *n.* **1.** woman whose husband has died. —*v.* **2.** make widow of. —**wid'ow•er,** *n.masc.* —**wid'ow•hood,** *n.*

width (width, witth) *n.* **1.** breadth. **2.** piece of full wideness.

wield (wēld) *v.* **1.** exercise (power, etc.). **2.** brandish. —**wield'er,** *n.* —**wield'y,** *adj.*

wie'ner (wē'nər) *n.* small sausage; frankfurter.

wife (wīf) *n.*, *pl.* **wives** (wīvz). married woman. —**wife'ly,** *adj.*

wig (wig) *n.* artificial covering of hair for head.

wig'eon (wij'ən) *n.*, *pl.* **-eons, -eon.** freshwater duck.

wig'gle (wig'əl) *v.*, **-gled, -gling,** *n.* —*v.* **1.** twist to and fro; wriggle. —*n.* **2.** wiggling movement. —**wig'gly,** *adj.* —**wig'gler,** *n.*

wig'wag' (wig'wag') *v.*, **-wagged, -wagging,** *n.* —*v.* **1.** signal in code with flags, etc. —*n.* **2.** such signaling. **3.** message so sent.

wig'wam (-wom) *n.* American Indian dwelling.

wild (wīld) *adj.* **1.** not cultivated. **2.** uncivilized. **3.** violent. **4.** uninhabited. **5.** disorderly. —*adv.* **6.** wildly. —*n.* **7.** uncultivated or desolate tract. —**wild'ly,** *adv.* —**wild'ness,** *n.*

wild'cat', *n.*, *v.*, **-catted, -catting.** —*n.* **1.** large North American feline. —*v.* **2.** prospect independently. —*adj.* **3.** not called or sanctioned by labor union.

wil'de•beest (wil'də bēst', vil'-) *n.* gnu.

wil'der•ness (wil'dər nis) *n.* wild or desolate region.

wild'-eyed', *adj.* **1.** having a wild expression in the eyes. **2.** extreme or radical.

wild'fire', *n.* outdoor fire that spreads rapidly and is hard to extinguish.

wild'flow'er, *n.* flower of plant that grows wild.

wild'-goose' chase', senseless search for something unobtainable.

wild'life', *n.* animals living in nature.

wild rice, tall aquatic grass of N North America.

wile (wīl) *n.* cunning; artifice.

will (wil) *n.* **1.** power of conscious action or choice. **2.** wish; pleasure. **3.** attitude, either hostile or friendly. **4.** declaration of wishes for disposition of property after death. —*v.* **5.** decide to influence by act of will. **6.** consent to. **7.** give by will. —*auxiliary verb.* **8.** am (is, are) about to. **9.** am (is, are) willing to.

will'ful, *adj.* **1.** intentional. **2.** headstrong.

Also, **wil'ful.** —**will'ful•ly,** *adv.* —**will'ful•ness,** *n.*

wil'lies (wil'ēz) *n.pl.* nervousness.

will'ing, *adj.* **1.** consenting. **2.** cheerfully done, given, etc. —**will'ing•ly,** *adv.* —**will'ing•ness,** *n.*

will'-o'-the-wisp' (wil'ə ŧħə wisp') *n.* **1.** flitting, elusive light. **2.** something that fascinates and deludes.

wil'low (wil'ō) *n.* slender tree or shrub with tough, pliant branches.

wil'low•y, *adj.*, **-lowier, -lowiest.** tall and slender. —**wil'low•i•ness,** *n.*

wil'ly-nil'ly (wil'ē nil'ē) *adv.* willingly or unwillingly.

wilt (wilt) *v.* **1.** wither or droop. —*n.* **2.** wilted state.

wil'y (wī'lē) *adj.*, **-ier, -iest.** crafty; cunning. —**wil'i•ness,** *n.*

wimp (wimp) *n.* *Informal.* weak, ineffectual person. —**wimp'y,** *adj.*

win (win) *v.*, **won** (wun), **winning,** *n.* —*v.* **1.** succeed or get by effort. **2.** gain (victory). **3.** persuade. —*n.* **4.** victory.

wince (wins) *v.*, **winced, wincing,** *n.* —*v.* **1.** shrink, as from pain or blow. —*n.* **2.** wincing movement.

winch (winch) *n.* **1.** windlass. **2.** crank.

wind (wind for 1–7; wīnd for 8–11), *n.*, *v.*, **winded** (for 5–7) or **wound** (wound) (for 8–11), **winding.** —*n.* **1.** air in motion. **2.** gas in stomach or bowels. **3.** animal odor. **4.** breath. —*v.* **5.** make short of breath. **6.** let recover breath. **7.** expose to wind. **8.** change direction. **9.** encircle. **10.** roll into cylinder or ball. **11.** turn (handle, etc.). —**wind'y** (win'dē) *adj.* —**wind'er** (wīn'dər) *n.*

wind'bag' (wind'-) *n.* pompous talker.

wind'break' (wind'-) *n.* shelter from wind.

wind'chill factor (wind'chil') apparent temperature felt on exposed skin owing to combination of temperature and wind speed.

wind'ed (win'did) *adj.* **1.** having wind. **2.** out of breath.

wind'fall' (wind'-) *n.* **1.** something blown down. **2.** unexpected luck.

winding sheet (wīn'ding) shroud.

wind instrument (wind) musical instrument sounded by breath or air.

wind'jam•mer (wind'jam'ər, win'-) *n.* large sailing ship.

wind'lass (wind'ləs) *n.* drum mechanism for hoisting.

wind'mill' (wind'-) *n.* mill operated by wind.

win'dow (win'dō) *n.* opening for air and light, usually fitted with glass in frame.

window dressing, 1. art, act, or technique of decorating store display windows. **2.** something done solely to create favorable impression.

win'dow•pane', *n.* pane of glass for window.

win'dow-shop', *v.*, **-shopped, -shopping.**

look at articles in store windows without making purchases. —**window shopper.**

wind'pipe' (wind'-) *n.* trachea.

wind'shield' (wind'-, win'-) *n.* glass shield above automobile, etc., dashboard.

wind'sock' (wind'-) *n.* mounted cloth cone that catches wind to indicate wind direction.

wind'storm' (wind'-) *n.* storm with heavy wind but little or no precipitation.

wind'surf'ing (wind'-) *n.* sport of riding on surfboard mounted with a sail. —**wind'-surf',** *v.* —**wind'surf'er,** *n.*

wind'-swept' (wind'-) *adj.* exposed to or blown by wind.

wind'up' (wīnd'-) *n.* close; end.

wind'ward (wind'wərd) *n.* **1.** quarter from which wind blows. —*adj.* **2.** of, in, or to windward. —*adv.* **3.** against wind.

wine (wīn) *n., v.,* **wined, wining.** —*n.* **1.** fermented juice, esp. of grape. **2.** dark purplish red. —*v.* **3.** entertain with wine. —**win'y,** *adj.*

win'er•y, *n., pl.* **-eries.** place for making wine.

wing (wing) *n.* **1.** organ of flight in birds, insects, and bats. **2.** winglike or projecting structure. **3.** flight. **4.** supporting surface of airplane. —*v.* **5.** travel on wings. **6.** wound in wing or arm. —**wing'ed,** *adj.*

wing'ding', *n. Slang.* noisy, exciting party.

wink (wingk) *v.* **1.** close and open (eye) quickly. **2.** signal by winking. **3.** twinkle. —*n.* **4.** winking movement.

win'ner (win'ər) *n.* one that wins.

win'ning, *n.* **1.** (*pl.*) that which is won. —*adj.* **2.** charming. —**win'ning•ly,** *adv.*

win'now (win'ō) *v.* **1.** free from chaff by wind. **2.** separate.

wi'no (wī'nō) *n., pl.* **-os.** person addicted to wine.

win'some (win'səm) *adj.* sweetly or innocently charming. —**win'some•ly,** *adv.* —**win'some•ness,** *n.*

win'ter (win'tər) *n.* **1.** last season of year. —*adj.* **2.** of, like, or for winter. —*v.* **3.** pass winter. **4.** keep during winter. —**win'try, win'ter•y,** *adj.*

win'ter•green', *n.* creeping aromatic shrub.

win'ter•ize, *v.,* **-ized, -izing.** prepare to withstand cold weather.

WIP 1. work in process. **2.** work in progress. Also, **W.I.P.**

wip work in progress.

wipe (wīp) *v.,* **wiped, wiping,** *n.* —*v.* **1.** rub lightly. **2.** remove or blot. —*n.* **3.** act of wiping. —**wip'er,** *n.*

wire (wī°r) *n., adj., v.,* **wired, wiring.** —*n.* **1.** slender, flexible piece of metal. **2.** telegram or telegraph. —*adj.* **3.** made of wires. —*v.* **4.** bind with wire. **5.** *Elect.* install system of wires in. **6.** telegraph.

wire'less, *adj.* **1.** activated by electromagnetic waves rather than wires. —*n.* **2.** *Brit.* radio.

wire service, agency that sends syndicated news by wire to its subscribers.

wire'tap', *v.,* **-tapped, -tapping,** *n.* —*v.* **1.** connect secretly into telephone. —*n.* **2.** act of wiretapping.

wir'ing, *n.* system of electric wires.

wir'y, *adj.,* **-ier, -iest.** like wire; lean and strong. —**wir'i•ness,** *n.*

Wis., Wisconsin. Also, **Wisc.**

WISC (wisk), Wechsler Intelligence Scale for Children.

WISC-R (wisk'är'), Wechsler Intelligence Scale for Children-Revised.

Wisd. *Bible.* Wisdom of Solomon.

wis'dom (wiz'dəm) *n.* **1.** knowledge and judgment. **2.** wise sayings.

wisdom tooth, last tooth to erupt.

wise (wīz) *adj.* **1.** having knowledge and judgment. **2.** prudent. **3.** informed. —*n.* **4.** way; respect. —**wise'ly,** *adv.*

wise'a'cre (-ā'kər) *n.* conceited, often insolent person.

wise'crack', *n.* **1.** smart or facetious remark. —*v.* **2.** make or say as a wisecrack.

wish (wish) *v.* **1.** want; desire. **2.** bid. —*n.* **3.** desire. **4.** that desired. —**wish'er,** *n.* —**wish'ful,** *adj.* —**wish'ful•ly,** *adv.* —**wish'ful•ness,** *n.*

wish'bone', *n.* forked bone in front of breastbone in most birds.

wish'y-wash'y (wish'ē wosh'ē) *adj.* thin or weak.

wisp (wisp) *n.* small tuft. —**wisp'y,** *adj.*

wis•te'ri•a (wi stēr'ē ə) *n.* climbing shrub with purple flowers. Also, **wis•tar'i•a.**

wist'ful (wist'fəl) *adj.* **1.** pensive. **2.** longing. —**wist'ful•ly,** *adv.* —**wist'ful•ness,** *n.*

wit (wit) *n.* **1.** power of combining perception with clever expression. **2.** person having this. **3.** (*pl.*) intelligence. —*v.* **4.** *Archaic.* know. **5.** **to wit,** namely.

witch (wich) *n.* **1.** woman thought to practice magic. **2.** ugly or mean old woman. —**witch'craft',** *n.*

witch doctor, person in some cultures who uses magic esp. to cure illness.

witch'er•y, *n., pl.* **-eries. 1.** magic. **2.** charm.

witch ha'zel (hā'zəl) preparation for bruises, etc.

witch'ing, *adj.* suitable for sorcery.

with (with, with) *prep.* **1.** accompanied by. **2.** using. **3.** against.

with•draw' (with drô', with-) *v.,* **-drew, -drawn, -drawing. 1.** draw back. **2.** retract. —**with•draw'al,** *n.*

with'er (with'ər) *v.* shrivel; fade. —**with'er•ing•ly,** *adv.*

with'ers, *n.pl.* part of animal's back just behind neck.

with•hold' (with hōld', with-) *v.,* **-held, -holding.** hold or keep back.

withholding tax, that part of employee's tax liability withheld by employer from wages.

W

with•in' (wiᵺ in', with-) *adv.* **1.** inside; inwardly. —*prep.* **2.** in; inside of. **3.** at point not beyond.

with•out', *prep.* **1.** lacking. **2.** beyond. —*adv.* **3.** outside. **4.** outwardly. **5.** lacking.

with•stand' (with stand', wiᵺ-) *v.*, -stood, -standing. resist.

wit'less, *adj.* stupid. —**wit'less•ly**, *adv.* —**wit'less•ness**, *n.*

wit'ness (wit'nis) *v.* **1.** see. **2.** testify. **3.** attest by signature. —*n.* **4.** person who witnesses. **5.** testimony.

wit'ti•cism' (wit'ə siz'əm) *n.* witty remark.

wit'ting, *adj.* knowing; aware. —**wit'ting•ly**, *adv.*

wit'ty, *adj.*, -tier, -tiest. showing wit. —**wit'ti•ly**, *adv.* —**wit'ti•ness**, *n.*

wive (wīv) *v.*, wived, wiving. marry.

wiz'ard (wiz'ərd) *n.* magician. —**wiz'ard•ry**, *n.*

wiz'ened (wiz'ənd, wē'zənd) *adj.* shriveled.

wk., week.

wkg working.

wkly. weekly.

wks workshop.

wl wavelength.

WLB War Labor Board.

wlb wallboard.

WLF Women's Liberation Front.

w. long. west longitude.

Wm. William.

w/m *Commerce.* weight and/or measurement.

WMC War Manpower Commission.

wmk. watermark.

WMO World Meteorological Organization.

wnd wound.

wndr winder.

WNW west-northwest.

w/o, without.

w.o.b. *Commerce.* washed overboard.

wob'ble (wob'əl) *v.*, -bled, -bling. move unsteadily from side to side. —**wob'bly**, *adj.*

w.o.c. without compensation.

woe (wō) *n.* grief or affliction. —**woe'ful**, *adj.* —**woe'ful•ly**, *adv.* —**woe'ful•ness**, *n.*

woe'be•gone' (-bi gôn') *adj.* showing woe.

wok (wok) *n.* Chinese cooking pan.

wolf (wŏolf) *n.*, *pl.* wolves (wŏolvz), *v.* —*n.* **1.** wild carnivorous animal of dog family. —*v.* **2.** *Informal.* eat ravenously. —**wolf'ish**, *adj.* —**wolf'ish•ly**, *adv.*

wolf'hound', *n.* kind of hound.

wolfs'bane', *n.* poisonous plant.

wol'ver•ine' (wŏol'və rēn') *n.* North American mammal of weasel family.

wom'an (wŏom'ən) *n.*, *pl.* women (wim'in). adult female human being. —**wom'an•hood'**, *n.* —**wom'an•ish**, *adj.* —**wom'an•ly**, *adj.* —**wom'an•li•ness**, *n.*

womb (wŏom) *n.* uterus.

wom'bat (wom'bat) *n.* burrowing, herbivorous Australian marsupial.

won'der (wun'dər) *v.* **1.** be curious about. **2.** marvel. —*n.* **3.** something strange. **4.** Also, **won'der•ment.** amazement. —**won'der•ing•ly**, *adv.*

won'der•ful, *adj.* **1.** exciting wonder. **2.** excellent. —**won'der•ful•ly**, *adv.*

won'drous, *adj.* **1.** wonderful. —*adv.* **2.** remarkably. —**won'drous•ly**, *adv.*

wont (wônt, wŏnt, wunt) *adj.* **1.** accustomed. —*n.* **2.** habit. —**wont'ed**, *adj.*

won't (wônt) contraction of will not.

woo (wŏo) *v.* seek to win, esp. in marriage. —**woo'er**, *n.*

wood (wŏod) *n.* **1.** hard substance under bark of trees and shrubs. **2.** timber or firewood. **3.** (*often pl.*) forest. —*adj.* **4.** made of wood. **5.** living in woods. —*v.* **6.** plant with trees. —**wood'craft'**, *n.* —**woods'man**, *n.* —**wood'y**, *adj.* —**wood'ed**, *adj.*

wood'bine' (-bīn') *n.* any of various vines, as the honeysuckle.

wood'chuck', *n.* bushy-tailed burrowing rodent. Also called **ground'hog'.**

wood'cut', *n.* print made from a carved block of wood.

wood'en, *adj.* **1.** made of wood. **2.** without feeling or expression. —**wood'en•ly**, *adv.* —**wood'en•ness**, *n.*

wood'land' (-land', -lənd) *n.* forest.

wood'peck'er, *n.* bird with hard bill for boring.

wood'pile', *n.* stack of firewood.

wood'ruff (-rəf, -ruf') *n.* fragrant plant with small white flowers.

wood'shed', *n.* shed for storing firewood.

woods'y, *adj.*, -ier, -iest. of or resembling woods.

wood'wind' (-wind') *n.* musical instrument of group including flute, clarinet, oboe, and bassoon.

wood'work', *n.* wooden fittings inside building. —**wood'work'er**, *n.* —**wood'work'ing**, *n.*, *adj.*

woof (wŏof, wŏof) *n.* **1.** yarns from side to side in loom. **2.** texture or fabric. —*v.* **3.** bark like a dog.

woof'er (wŏof'ər) *n.* loudspeaker to reproduce low-frequency sounds.

wool (wŏol) *n.* **1.** soft curly hair, esp. of sheep. **2.** garments, yarn, etc., of wool. **3.** curly, fine-stranded substance. —**wool'en** or (*esp. Brit.*) **wool'len**, *adj.*, *n.* —**wool'ly**, *adj.* —**wool'li•ness**, *n.*

wool'gath'er•ing, *n.* daydreaming.

woolly bear, caterpillar with woolly hairs.

word (wûrd) *n.* **1.** group of letters or sounds that represents concept. **2.** talk or conversation. **3.** promise. **4.** tidings. **5.** (*pl.*) angry speech. —*v.* **6.** express in words. —**word'less**, *adj.*

word'age (wûr'dij) *n.* **1.** words collectively. **2.** number of words. **3.** choice of words.

word'ing, *n.* way of expressing.

word of mouth, oral communication.

word'play', *n.* witty repartee.

word processing, production of letters, reports, etc., using computers.

word processor, computer program or system for word processing.

word'y, *adj.,* **-ier, -iest.** using too many words. **—word'i•ness,** *n.*

work (wûrk) *n.* **1.** exertion; labor. **2.** task. **3.** employment. **4.** place of employment. **5.** materials on which one works. **6.** result of work. **7.** (*pl.*) industrial plant. *—adj.* **8.** of or for work. *—v.* **9.** do work. **10.** operate successfully. **11.** move or give. **12.** solve. **13.** excite. **14.** ferment. **—work'a•ble,** *adj.* **—work'er,** *n.*

work'a•day' (wûr'kə dā') *adj.* commonplace; uneventful.

work'a•hol'ic (-hô'lik) *n.* person who works compulsively.

work'book', *n.* book for students containing questions and exercises.

work'horse', *n.* **1.** horse used for heavy labor. **2.** person who works tirelessly.

work'house', *n.* penal institution for minor offenders.

working class, 1. persons working for wages, esp. in manual labor. **2.** social or economic class composed of these workers.

work'load', *n.* amount of work that machine or employee is expected to perform.

work'man, *n., pl.* **-men.** worker; laborer. Also, **work'ing•man',** *fem.* **work'ing•wom'an.** **—work'man•like',** *adj.* **—work'man•ship',** *n.*

work'out', *n.* **1.** practice or test to maintain or determine physical ability or endurance. **2.** structured regime of physical exercise.

work'shop', *n.* place where work is done.

work'sta'tion, *n.* **1.** work area for one person, as in office, usu. with electronic equipment. **2.** powerful small computer used for graphics-intensive processing.

work'up', *n.* thorough medical diagnostic examination.

world (wûrld) *n.* **1.** earth; globe. **2.** particular part of earth. **3.** things common to profession, etc.; milieu. **4.** humanity. **5.** universe. **6.** great quantity.

world'-class', *adj.* of the highest caliber.

world'ling, *n.* worldly person.

world'ly, *adj.,* **-lier, -liest. 1.** secular or earthly. **2.** devoted to affairs of this world; sophisticated; shrewd. **3.** of this world. **—world'li•ness,** *n.*

world'ly-wise', *adj.* wise as to the affairs of this world.

world'-wea'ry, *adj.* blasé.

World Wide Web, system of extensively interlinked documents: branch of the Internet.

worm (wûrm) *n.* **1.** small slender creeping animal. **2.** something suggesting worm, as screw thread. **3.** (*pl.*) intestinal disorder. *—v.* **4.** move like worm. **5.** extract (secret) craftily. **6.** free from worms. **—worm'y,** *adj.*

worm'wood', *n.* bitter aromatic herb.

worn (wôrn) *adj.* exhausted; spent.

worn'-out', *adj.* **1.** exhausted. **2.** destroyed by wear.

wor'ry (wûr'ē, wur'ē) *v.,* **-ried, -rying,** *n., pl.* **-ries.** *—v.* **1.** make or feel anxious. **2.** seize with teeth and shake. *—n.* **3.** anxiety. **4.** cause of anxiety. **—wor'ri•er,** *n.* **—wor'ri•some,** *adj.*

worse (wûrs) *adj.* **1.** less good; less favorable. *—n.* **2.** that which is worse. *—adv.* **3.** in worse way. **—wors'en,** *v.*

wor'ship (wûr'ship) *n., v.,* **-shiped, -shiping** or **-shipped, -shipping.** *—n.* **1.** homage paid to God. **2.** rendering of such homage. *—v.* **3.** render religious reverence to. **—wor'ship•er,** *n.* **—wor'ship•ful,** *adj.*

worst (wûrst) *adj.* **1.** least satisfactory; least well. *—n.* **2.** that which is worst. *—adv.* **3.** in the worst way. *—v.* **4.** defeat.

wor'sted (wŏos'tid, wûr'stid) *n.* **1.** firmly twisted wool yarn or thread. **2.** fabric made of it.

wort (wûrt, wôrt) *n.* malt infusion before fermentation.

worth (wûrth) *adj.* **1.** good enough to justify. **2.** having value of. *—n.* **3.** excellence; importance. **4.** quantity of specified value. **—worth'less,** *adj.* **—worth'less•ness,** *n.*

worth'while', *adj.* repaying time and effort spent.

wor'thy (wûr'thē) *adj.,* **-thier, -thiest,** *n., pl.* **-thies.** *—adj.* **1.** of adequate worth. **2.** deserving. *—n.* **3.** person of merit. **—wor'thi•ly,** *adv.* **—wor'thi•ness,** *n.*

would (wŏod; *unstressed* wəd) *v.* past of **will** (defs. 8, 9).

would'-be', *adj.* wishing, pretending, or intended to be.

wound (wŏond) *n.* **1.** puncture from external violence. *—v.* **2.** inflict wound. **3.** grieve with insult or reproach.

WP word processing.

wp waste pipe.

wp. *Baseball.* wild pitch; wild pitches.

W.P. 1. weather permitting. **2.** wire payment. **3.** working pressure. Also, **WP, w.p.**

WPA Work Projects Administration: a former federal agency (1935–43), originally, Works Progress Administration.

W

WPB War Production Board. Also, **W.P.B.**

WPBL Women's Professional Basketball League.

wpg waterproofing.

WPI wholesale price index.

wpm words per minute.

wpn weapon.

WPPSI (wip'sē), Wechsler Preschool and Primary Scale of Intelligence.

wps words per second.

Wr *Medicine.* Wassermann reaction.

wr 1. washroom. **2.** wrench. **3.** writer.

w.r. 1. warehouse receipt. **2.** *Insurance.* war risk.

WRA War Relocation Authority.

WRAC *British.* Women's Royal Army Corps. Also, **W.R.A.C.**

wrack (rak) *n.* ruin.

WRAF (raf), *British.* Women's Royal Air Force. Also, **W.R.A.F.**

wraith (rāth) *n.* ghost.

wran′gle (rang′gəl) *v.*, **-gled, -gling,** *n.* dispute. —**wran′gler,** *n.*

wrap (rap) *v.*, **wrapped** or **wrapt, wrapping,** *n.* —*v.* **1.** enclose; envelop. **2.** wind or fold about. —*n.* **3.** (*often pl.*) outdoor clothes.

wrap′per, *n.* **1.** one that wraps. **2.** Also, **wrapping.** outer cover. **3.** long loose garment.

wrath (rath) *n.* **1.** stern or fierce anger. **2.** vengeance. —**wrath′ful,** *adj.* —**wrath′ful·ly,** *adv.*

wrb wardrobe.

wreak (rēk) *v.* inflict.

wreath (rēth) *n.* circular band of leaves, etc.

wreathe (rēth) *v.*, **wreathed, wreathing.** encircle with wreath.

wreck (rek) *n.* **1.** anything reduced to ruins. **2.** destruction. **3.** person in poor state. —*v.* **4.** cause or suffer wreck. —**wreck′age,** *n.* —**wreck′er,** *n.*

wren (ren) *n.* small active bird.

wrench (rench) *v.* **1.** twist forcibly. **2.** injure by wrenching. —*n.* **3.** wrenching movement. **4.** tool for turning bolts, etc.

wrest (rest) *v.* **1.** twist violently. **2.** get by effort. —*n.* **3.** twist; wrench.

wres′tle (res′əl) *v.*, **-tled, -tling,** *n.* —*v.* **1.** contend with by trying to force other person down. —*n.* **2.** this sport. **3.** struggle. —**wres′tler,** *n.*

wretch (rech) *n.* **1.** pitiable person. **2.** scoundrel.

wretch′ed, *adj.* **1.** pitiable. **2.** despicable. **3.** pitiful. —**wretch′ed·ly,** *adv.* —**wretch′ed·ness,** *n.*

wrig′gle (rig′əl) *v.*, **-gled, -gling,** *n.* wiggle; squirm. —**wrig′gler,** *n.* —**wrig′gly,** *adj.*

wright (rīt) *n.* worker who builds.

wring (ring) *v.*, **wrung** (rung), **wringing,** *n.* —*v.* **1.** twist or compress. **2.** expel by wringing. **3.** clasp tightly. —*n.* **4.** twist or squeeze. —**wring′er,** *n.*

wrin′kle (ring′kəl) *n.*, *v.*, **-kled, -kling.** —*n.* **1.** ridge or furrow. —*v.* **2.** form wrinkles in. —**wrin′kly,** *adj.*

wrist (rist) *n.* joint between hand and arm.

writ (rit) *n.* **1.** formal legal order. **2.** writing.

write (rīt) *v.*, **wrote** (rōt), **written** (rit′n), **writing. 1.** form (letters, etc.) by hand. **2.** express in writing. **3.** produce, as author or composer. —**writ′er,** *n.*

write′-in′, *n.* candidate or vote for candidate not listed on ballot but written in by voter.

write′-off′, *n.* something cancelled, as a debt.

writhe (rīth) *v.*, **writhed, writhing,** *n.* —*v.* **1.** twist, as in pain. —*n.* **2.** writhing movement.

wrk work.

wrkg wrecking.

wrn warning.

wrngr wringer.

W.R.N.S. *British.* Women's Royal Naval Service.

wrnt. warrant.

wrong (rông) *adj.* **1.** not right or good. **2.** deviating from truth or fact. **3.** not suitable. **4.** under or inner (side). —*n.* **5.** evil; injury; error. —*v.* **6.** do wrong to. **7.** misjudge. —**wrong′do′er,** *n.* —**wrong′do′ing,** *n.* —**wrong′ful,** *adj.* —**wrong′ly,** *adv.*

wroth (rôth) *adj.* angry.

wrought (rôt) *adj.* **1.** worked. **2.** shaped by beating.

wrought′-up′, *adj.* perturbed.

wrpg warping.

W.R.S.S.R. White Russian Soviet Socialist Republic.

W-R star *Astronomy.* Wolf-Rayet star.

wrtr writer.

wry (rī) *adj.*, **wrier, wriest. 1.** twisted; distorted. **2.** ironic. —**wry′ly,** *adv.* —**wry′ness,** *n.*

WS weapon system.

W.S. West Saxon.

WSA War Shipping Administration.

wshg washing.

wshld windshield.

wshr washer.

WSW west-southwest.

wt. weight.

WTA 1. Women's Tennis Association. **2.** World Tennis Association.

wtd wanted.

wtg 1. waiting. **2.** weighting.

wtr water.

wtrprf waterproof.

wtrtt watertight.

wtrz winterize.

WV, West Virginia. Also, **W. Va.**

W.Va. West Virginia.

wvfm waveform.

W.V.S. *British.* Women's Voluntary Service.

WW 1. World War. **2.** *Real Estate.* wall-to-wall. Also, **W/W**

ww 1. wirewound. **2.** *Stock Exchange.* with warrants (offered to the buyer of a given stock or bond).

WWI World War I.

WWII World War II.

w/wo with or without.

WWW *Computers.* World Wide Web (part of Internet).

WY, Wyoming. Also, **Wyo., Y, Z**

Wyo. Wyoming.

WYSIWYG (wiz′ē wig′) *adj.* of or being computer display screen that shows text exactly as it will appear when printed.

X

X, x (eks) *n.* twenty-fourth letter of English alphabet.

X, motion-picture rating applied to sexually explicit films.

xan′thic (zan′thik) *adj.* yellow.

xarm crossarm.

xbar *Telephones.* crossbar.

xbra crossbracing.

xbt *Telecommunications.* crossbar tandem.

xc *Stock Exchange.* without coupon. Also, **xcp**

X-C cross-country.

X chromosome, sex chromosome that determines femaleness when paired with another X chromosome and that occurs singly in males.

xcl *Insurance.* excess current liabilities.

xconn *Telephones.* cross-connection.

xcvr transceiver.

xcy cross-country.

xd *Stock Exchange.* ex dividend. See **x** (def. 3a). Also, **xdiv.**

xdcr transducer.

Xe *Symbol, Chemistry.* xenon.

xen′o•pho′bi•a (zen′ə fō′bē ə, zē′nə-) *n.* fear or hatred of foreigners or strangers or of anything foreign or strange. **—xen′o•pho′-bic,** *adj.*

xe•rog′ra•phy (zi rog′rə fē) *n.* copying process in which resins are fused to paper electrically. **—xe′ro•graph′ic** (zēr′ə graf′ik) *adj.*

Xe′rox (zēr′oks) *n.* **1.** *Trademark.* brand name for copying machine using xerography. **2.** (*l.c.*) copy made on Xerox. **—v. 3.** (*l.c.*) print or reproduce by Xerox.

XF *Numismatics.* extra fine.

xfmr *Electronics.* transformer.

xfr transfer.

xhair crosshair.

xhd crosshead.

xhvy extra heavy.

x in *Stock Exchange.* ex interest. See **x** (def. 3b).

xing crossing.

XL 1. extra large. **2.** extra long.

Xmas (kris′məs; *often* eks′məs) *n.* Christmas.

xmsn transmission.

xmt transmit.

xmtd *Electronics.* transmitted.

xmtg *Electronics.* transmitting.

xmtr *Electronics.* transmitter.

Xn. Christian.

Xnty. Christianity.

xpl explosive.

xpndr transponder.

x pr *Stock Exchange.* without privileges.

xprt transport.

xpt *Electricity.* crosspoint.

xptn transportation.

XQ cross question. Also, **xq**

xr *Stock Exchange.* ex rights; without rights.

x′-ray′, *n.* **1.** highly penetrating type of electromagnetic ray, used esp. in medicine. **—v. 2.** photograph or treat with x-rays.

xref cross reference.

XS extra small.

xsect cross section.

xstg extra strong.

xstr transistor.

Xt. Christ.

xtal *Electronics.* crystal.

xtalk *Telephones.* crosstalk.

Xtian. Christian.

xtlo crystal oscillator.

Xty. Christianity.

xvs transverse.

XX powdered sugar.

XXL extra, extra large.

XXXX confectioners' sugar.

xya *Math.* x-y axis.

xy′lem (zī′ləm, -lem) *n.* woody tissue of plants.

xy′lo•phone′ (zī′lə fōn′) *n.* musical instrument of wooden bars, played with small hammers. **—xy′lo•phon′ist,** *n.*

xyv *Math.* x-y vector.

Y

Y, y (wī) *n.* twenty-fifth letter of English alphabet.

-y, suffix meaning: **1.** full of or like, as *cloudy.* **2.** inclined to, as *squeaky.* **3.** dear or little, as *kitty.* **4.** action of, as *inquiry.* **5.** quality or state, as *victory.*

YA young adult.

yacht (yot) *n.* **1.** pleasure ship. —*v.* **2.** sail in yacht. —**yacht'ing,** *n.* —**yachts'man,** *n.*

YAG (yag), a synthetic yttrium aluminum garnet, used for infrared lasers and as a gemstone. [y(*ttrium*) a(*luminum*) g(*arnet*)]

ya'hoo (yä'hōō) *n.* coarse stupid person.

yak (yak) *n., v.,* **yakked, yakking.** —*n.* **1.** long-haired Tibetan ox. **2.** *Slang.* incessant idle or gossipy talk. —*v.* **3.** *Slang.* gab; chatter.

yam (yam) *n.* edible potatolike root.

yam'mer (yam'ər) *v. Informal.* whine or chatter.

yank (yangk) *v.* **1.** pull suddenly; jerk. —*n.* **2.** sudden pull; jerk.

Yan'kee (yang'kē) *n.* native or inhabitant of the United States, northern U.S., or New England.

yap (yap) *v.,* **yapped, yapping,** *n.* yelp.

yard (yärd) *n.* **1.** linear unit (3 feet). **2.** long spar. **3.** enclosed outdoor area, used as a lawn, etc.

yard'age (yär'dij) *n.* amount in yards.

yard'arm', *n.* either of the yards of square sail.

yard'stick', *n.* **1.** measuring stick one yard long. **2.** criterion.

yar'mul•ke (yär'məl kə, -mə-, yä'-) *n.* cap worn by Jewish Orthodox or Conservative males, esp. during prayer.

yarn (yärn) *n.* **1.** many-stranded thread. **2.** story.

yar'row (yar'ō) *n.* plant with flat-topped clusters of white-to-yellow flowers.

yaw (yô) *v.* **1.** deviate. —*n.* **2.** deviation.

yawl (yôl) *n.* small sailboat.

yawn (yôn) *v.* **1.** open mouth wide involuntarily, as from sleepiness or boredom. —*n.* **2.** act of yawning.

yawp (yôp) *v., n. Informal.* bawl.

yaws (yôz) *n.* infectious tropical disease characterized by raspberrylike eruptions of skin.

Yb *Symbol, Chemistry.* ytterbium.

Y.B. yearbook. Also, **YB**

Y chromosome, sex chromosome present only in males and paired with X chromosome.

Y.C.L. Young Communist League.

ycw you can't win.

YD. (in the People's Democratic Republic of Yemen) dinar; dinars.

yd. yard; yards.

yd³ *Symbol.* cubic yard.

yds. yards.

ye (yē) *pron. Archaic.* **1.** you. **2.** the.

yea (yā) *adv., n.* yes.

year (yēr) *n.* period of 365 or 366 days. —**year'ly,** *adv., adj.*

year'book', *n.* **1.** book published annually with information on past year. **2.** commemorative book published as by graduating class.

year'ling (-ling) *n.* animal in its second year.

yearn (yûrn) *v.* desire strongly. —**yearn'ing,** *adj., n.*

year'-round', *adj.* **1.** continuing, available, or used throughout the year. —*adv.* **2.** throughout the year.

yeast (yēst) *n.* yellowish substance, used to leaven bread, ferment liquor, etc.

yel yellow.

yell (yel) *v.* shout loudly.

yel'low (yel'ō) *n.* **1.** color of butter, lemons, etc. —*adj.* **2.** of or like yellow. **3.** *Slang.* cowardly. —**yel'low•ish,** *adj.*

yellow fever, infectious tropical disease transmitted by certain mosquitoes. Also, **yellow jack.**

yellow jacket, yellow and black wasp.

yelp (yelp) *v.* **1.** give sharp, shrill cry. —*n.* **2.** such cry.

yen (yen) *n. Informal.* desire.

yeo. yeomanry.

yeo'man (yō'mən) *n.* **1.** petty officer in navy. **2.** independent farmer. —**yeo'man•ry,** *n.*

yes (yes) *adv., n.* expression of affirmation or assent.

ye•shi'va (yə shē'və) *n.* Orthodox Jewish school.

yes'-man', *n., pl.* **-men.** person who always agrees with superiors.

yes'ter•day (yes'tər dā', -dē) *adv., n.* day before today.

yet (yet) *adv.* **1.** so far; up to this (or that) time. **2.** moreover. **3.** still. **4.** nevertheless. —*conj.* **5.** but.

yew (yōō) *n.* evergreen coniferous tree.

YHA Youth Hostels Association.

YHVH *Judaism.* a transliteration of the Tetragrammaton, the four-letter name of God. Also, **YHWH, JHVH, JHWH** [from Hebrew *yhwh* God]

Yid'dish (yid'ish) *n.* German-based Jewish language.

yield (yēld) *v.* **1.** produce; give. **2.** surrender. **3.** give way. —*n.* **4.** that which is yielded; product. —**yield'er,** *n.*

YIG (yig), a synthetic yttrium iron garnet,

used in electronics in filters and amplifiers. [y*(ttrium) i(ron) g(arnet)*]

yip (yip) *v.*, **yipped, yipping.** *Informal.* bark sharply.

YMCA Young Men's Christian Association. Also, **Y.M.C.A.**

Y.M.Cath.A. Young Men's Catholic Association.

YMHA Young Men's Hebrew Association. Also, **Y.M.H.A.**

y.o. year old; years old.

y.o.b. year of birth. Also, **YOB**

yo′del (yōd′l) *v.*, **-eled, -eling. 1.** sing with quick changes to and from falsetto. —*n.* **2.** song yodeled.

yo′ga (yō′gə) *n.* Hindu series of postures and breathing exercises practiced to attain physical and mental control and tranquillity.

yo′gi (yō′gē) *n.* Hindu who practices yoga.

yo′gurt (yō′gərt) *n.* custardlike food made from milk fermented by bacteria. Also, **yo′-ghurt.**

yoke (yōk) *n.*, *v.*, **yoked, yoking.** —*n.* **1.** piece put across necks of oxen pulling cart, etc. **2.** pair. —*v.* **3.** couple with, or place in, yoke.

yo′kel (yō′kəl) *n.* rustic.

yolk (yōk) *n.* yellow part of egg.

yon′der (yon′dər) *adj.*, *adv.* *Archaic.* over there. Also, **yon.**

yore (yôr) *n.* time past.

you (yōō; *unstressed* yŏō, yə) *pron.* person or persons addressed.

young (yung) *adj.* **1.** in early stages of life, operation, etc. **2.** of youth. —*n.* **3.** young persons. **4.** young offspring. —**young′ish,** *adj.*

young′ster (-stər) *n.* child.

your (yŏŏr, yôr; *unstressed* yər) *pron.*, *adj.* possessive of **you;** (without noun following) **yours.**

—**Usage.** Do not confuse YOUR and YOU'RE. YOUR is the possessive form of "you": *Your book is overdue at the library.* YOU'RE is the contraction of "you are": *You're just the person we need for this job.*

you're (yŏŏr; *unstressed* yər) contraction of you are.
—**Usage.** See YOUR.

your∙self′, *pron.* emphatic or reflexive form of **you.**

youth (yōōth) *n.* **1.** young state. **2.** early life. **3.** young person or persons. —**youth′ful,** *adj.* —**youth′ful∙ly,** *adv.* —**youth′ful∙ness,** *n.*

yowl (youl) *v.*, *n.* howl.

yo′-yo (yō′yō) *n.*, *pl.* **-yos,** *v.*, **-yoed, -yoing.** —*n.* **1.** spoollike toy spun out and reeled in by string looped on finger. —*v.* **2.** move up and down or back and forth; fluctuate.

Y.P.S.C.E. Young People's Society of Christian Endeavor.

yr., year.

yrbk. yearbook.

yrs. 1. years. **2.** yours.

YT Yukon Territory, Canada (for use with ZIP code).

Y.T. Yukon Territory.

YTD *Accounting.* year to date.

yu∙an′ (yōō än′) *n.* Taiwanese dollar.

yuc′ca (yuk′ə) *n.* tropical American plant.

yuck (yuk) *interj.* *Slang.* (exclamation of disgust or repugnance). —**yuck′y,** *adj.*

Yugo. Yugoslavia.

yule (yōōl) *n.* Christmas.

yule′tide′, *n.* Christmas season.

yum′my (yum′ē) *adj.*, **-mier, -miest.** very pleasing, esp. to taste.

yup′pie (yup′ē) *n.* young, ambitious, and affluent professional who lives in or near a city. Also, **yup′py.**

yurt (yŏŏrt) *n.* tentlike dwelling of nomadic peoples of central Asia.

YWCA Young Women's Christian Association. Also, **Y.W.C.A.**

YWHA Young Women's Hebrew Association. Also, **Y.W.H.A.**

Y

Z

Z, z (zē; *esp. Brit.* zed) *n.* twenty-sixth letter of English alphabet.

za′ny (zā′nē) *n., pl.* **-nies,** *adj.* **-nier, -niest.** —*n.* **1.** clown. —*adj.* **2.** silly. —**za′ni•ness,** *n.*

zap (zap) *v.,* **zapped, zapping.** *Slang.* kill or defeat.

ZBB zero-base budgeting.

zeal (zēl) *n.* intense ardor or eagerness. —**zeal′ous** (zel′əs) *adj.* —**zeal′ous•ly,** *adv.* —**zeal′ous•ness,** *n.*

zeal′ot (zel′ət) *n.* excessively zealous person; fanatic. —**zeal′ot•ry,** *n.*

ze′bra (zē′brə) *n.* wild, striped horselike animal.

ze′bu (zē′byōō, -bōō) *n., pl.* **-bus.** domesticated ox of India.

Zech. *Bible.* Zechariah.

ZEG zero economic growth.

Zen (zen) *n.* Buddhist movement emphasizing enlightenment by meditation and direct, intuitive insight. Also, **Zen Buddhism.**

ze′nith (zē′nith) *n.* **1.** celestial point directly overhead. **2.** highest point or state.

Zeph. *Bible.* Zephaniah.

zeph′yr (zef′ər) *n.* mild breeze.

zep′pe•lin (zep′ə lin) *n.* large dirigible of early 20th century.

ze′ro (zēr′ō) *n., pl.* **-ros, -roes. 1.** symbol (0) indicating nonquantity. **2.** nothing. **3.** starting point of a scale.

zero hour, starting time.

zero population growth, condition in which population remains constant because of equal number of births and deaths.

zest (zest) *n.* something adding flavor, interest, etc. —**zest′ful,** *adj.* —**zest′ful•ly,** *adv.* —**zest′ful•ness,** *n.* —**zest′less,** *adj.*

ZI *Military.* Zone of the Interior.

ZIF (zif), *Computers.* zero insertion force.

zig′zag′ (zig′zag′) *n., adj., adv., v.,* **-zagged, -zagging.** —*n.* **1.** line going sharply from side to side. —*adj., adv.* **2.** with sharp turns back and forth. —*v.* **3.** go in zigzag.

zilch (zilch) *n. Slang.* zero; nothing.

zil′lion (zil′yən) *n. Informal.* extremely large, indeterminate number.

zinc (zingk) *n.* bluish metallic element. —**zinc′ous,** *adj.*

zinc oxide, salve made of zinc and oxygen.

zing (zing) *n.* **1.** sharp singing sound. —*v.* **2.** make such sound. —*interj.* **3.** (descriptive of such sound.)

zin′ni•a (zin′ē ə) *n.* bright, full-flowered plant.

Zi′on (zī′ən) *n.* **1.** Jewish people. **2.** Palestine as Jewish homeland. **3.** heaven as final gathering place of true believers.

Zi′on•ism, *n.* advocacy of Jewish establishment of state of Israel. —**Zi′on•ist,** *n., adj.*

zip (zip) *v.,* **zipped, zipping,** *n. Informal.* —*v.* **1.** go very speedily. —*n.* **2.** energy.

ZIP code (zip) code numbers used with address to expedite mail.

zip′per, *n.* fastener with interlocking edges.

ZIP + 4 (zip′ plus′ fôr′, fōr′), a ZIP code of nine digits.

zip′py, *adj.,* **-pier, -piest.** *Informal,* lively; smart.

zir′con (zûr′kon) *n.* mineral used as gem when transparent.

zir•co′ni•um (zûr kō′nē əm) *n.* metallic element used in metallurgy and ceramics.

zit (zit) *n. Slang.* pimple.

zith′er (zith′ər, zith′-) *n.* stringed musical instrument. Also, **zith′ern.**

zi′ti (zē′tē) *n.* short, tubular pasta.

Zn *Symbol, Chemistry.* zinc.

zn zone.

zod. zodiac.

zo′di•ac′ (zō′dē ak′) *n.* imaginary belt of heavens containing paths of all major planets, divided into twelve constellations. —**zo•di′a•cal** (-dī′i kəl), *adj.*

zof zone of fire.

zom′bie (zom′bē) *n.* reanimated corpse.

zone (zōn) *n., v.,* **zoned, zoning.** —*n.* **1.** special area, strip, etc. —*v.* **2.** mark or divide into zones. —**zon′al,** *adj.*

zonked (zongkt) *adj. Slang.* stupefied from or as if from alcohol or drugs.

zoo (zōō) *n.* place where live animals are exhibited. Also, **zoological garden.**

zoochem. zoochemistry.

zool. 1. zoological. **2.** zoologist. **3.** zoology.

zo•ol′o•gy (zō ol′ə jē) *n.* scientific study of animals. —**zo′o•log′i•cal** (-ə loj′i kəl) *adj.* —**zo•ol′o•gist,** *n.*

zoom (zōōm) *v.* speed sharply.

zoom lens, camera lens allowing continual change of magnification without loss of focus.

zo′o•pho′bi•a (zō′ə-) *n.* fear of animals.

zo′o•phyte′ (-fīt′) *n.* plantlike animal, as coral.

ZPG zero population growth.

Zr *Symbol, Chemistry.* zirconium.

zuc•chi′ni (zōō kē′nē) *n.* cucumber-shaped squash.

zwie′back′ (zwī′bak′, -bäk′, swē′-) *n.* kind of dried, twice-baked bread.

zy′gote (zī′gōt) *n.* cell produced by union of two gametes. —**zy•got′ic** (-got′ik) *adj.*

zy′mur•gy (zī′mûr jē) *n.* branch of applied chemistry dealing with fermentation.

Computer and Multimedia Glossary

access, to locate (data) for transfer from one part of a computer system to another.

acoustic coupler, a device designed to connect a telephone handset to a modem and a computer.

active-matrix, of or pertaining to a high-resolution liquid-crystal display (LCD) with high contrast, used esp. for laptop computers. Compare PASSIVE-MATRIX.

adapter, EXPANSION CARD.

add-in, a component, such as an expansion card or chip, added to a computer to expand its capabilities.

add-on, a product, as an expansion card or computer program, designed to complement another product.

address, 1. a label, as an integer or symbol, that designates the location of information stored in computer memory. **2.** to direct (data) to a specified location in an electronic computer.

addressable, (of information stored in a computer) capable of being accessed.

alpha test, an early test of new or updated computer software conducted by the developers of the program prior to beta testing by potential users.

American Standard Code for Information Interchange. See ASCII.

analog computer, a computer that represents data by measurable quantities, as voltages, rather than by numbers.

AND (and), a Boolean operator that returns a positive result when both operands are positive.

app, *Informal.* an application program; application software.

applet, a small application program that can be called up for use while working in another application.

application, 1. a specific kind of task, as database management, that can be done using an application program. **2.** APPLICATION PROGRAM.

application program, a computer program used for a specific kind of task, as word processing. Compare SYSTEM PROGRAM.

architecture, a fundamental underlying design of computer hardware, software, or both.

artificial intelligence, 1. the collective attributes of a computer, robot, or other mechanical device programmed to perform functions analogous to learning and decision making. **2.** the field of study involved with the design of such programs and devices.

ASCII (as'kē), a standardized code in which characters are represented for computer storage and transmission by the numbers 0 through 127. [A(merican) S(tandard) C(ode for) I(nformation) I(nterchange)]

assembler, a language processor that translates symbolic assembly language into equivalent machine language.

assembly language, a computer language most of whose expressions are symbolic equivalents of the machine-language instructions of a particular computer.

author, the writer of a software program, esp. a hypertext or multimedia application.

backslash, a short oblique stroke (\): used in some operating systems to mark the division between a directory and a subdirectory, as in typing a path.

backup, 1. a copy or duplicate version, esp. of a data file or program, retained for use in the event that the original becomes unusable or unavailable. **2.** a procedure for creating a backup.

back up, to make a backup of (a data file or program).

BASIC, a high-level programming language that uses English words, punctuation marks, and algebraic notation.

batch, 1. a group of jobs, data, programs, or commands treated as a unit for processing. **2.** BATCH PROCESSING.

batch processing, a form of data processing in which a number of input jobs are run as a group.

baud, a unit used to measure the speed of data transfer, usu. equal to the number of bits transmitted per second.

bay, an open compartment in the console housing a computer's CPU in which a disk drive, tape drive, etc., may be installed. Also called **drive bay.**

BBS, bulletin board system: a computerized facility, accessible by modem, for collecting and relaying electronic messages and software programs, playing games, etc. Also called **electronic bulletin board.**

beta test, a test of new or updated computer software or hardware conducted at select user sites just prior to release of the product.

binary, of or pertaining to a system of numerical notation to the base 2, in which each place of a number, expressed as 0 or 1, corresponds to a power of 2. Computers use the binary number system to store and process information.

BIOS (bī'ōs), computer firmware that directs many basic functions of the operating system, as booting and keyboard control. [B(asic) I(nput)/O(utput) S(ystem)]

bit, a single, basic unit of computer information, valued at either 0 or 1 to signal binary alternatives.

bit map, a piece of text, a drawing, etc., represented, as on a computer display, by the activation of certain dots in a rectangular matrix of dots.

block, 1. a group of computer data stored and processed as a unit. **2.** (in word processing) a portion of text or data marked off for deleting, moving, etc. **3.** to mark off (a portion of text or data) for moving, deleting, printing, etc., as in word processing.

board, 1. Also called **card.** a piece of fiberglass or other material upon which an array of computer chips is mounted. **2.** CIRCUIT BOARD (def. 1).

Boolean operation (boo'lē ən), any logical operation in which each of the operands and the result take one of two values, as "true" and "false" or "circuit on" and "circuit off."

boot, to start (a computer) by loading the operating system.

bps or **BPS,** bits per second (refers to the number of data bits sent per second between modems).

browser, an application program that allows the user to examine encoded documents in a form suitable for display, esp. such a program for use on the World Wide Web.

buffer, a temporary storage area that holds data until ready to be processed.

bulletin board. See BBS.

bus, a circuit that connects the CPU with other devices in a computer. The **data bus** transmits data to and from the CPU.

byte, a group of adjacent bits, usu. eight, processed by a computer as a unit.

C, a high-level programming language: very powerful and flexible, it is used in a wide variety of applications.

C++, a high-level programming language, a descendant of C, with the ability to manipulate object-oriented features.

cache, a piece of computer hardware or a section of RAM dedicated to selectively storing and speeding access to frequently used program commands or data.

CAD/CAM (kad'kam'), computer-aided design and computer-aided manufacturing.

capture, 1. to enter (data) into a computer for processing or storage. **2.** to record (data) in preparation for such entry.

card, BOARD (def. 1).

CD, compact disc.

CD-ROM (sē'dē'rom'), a compact disc on which a large amount of digitized read-only data can be stored. Compare ROM. [c(ompact) d(isc) r(ea-)o(nly) m(emory)]

central processing unit. See CPU.

character, any encoded unit of computer-usable data representing a symbol, as a letter, number, or punctuation mark, or a space, carriage return, etc.

character set, the numbers, letters, punctuation marks, and special symbols that can be used by a particular device, as a printer, or in a coding method, as ASCII.

chat, to engage in dialogue by exchanging electronic messages usu. in real time.

chat room, a branch of a computer system in which participants can engage in live discussions with one another.

chip, a tiny slice of semiconducting material on which a transistor or an integrated circuit is formed. Also called **microchip.**

circuit board, 1. a sheet of fiberglass or other material on which electronic components, as printed or integrated circuits, are installed. **2.** BOARD (def. 1).

CISC (sisk), complex instruction set computer: a computer whose central processing unit recognizes a relatively large number of instructions. Compare RISC

click, to depress and release a mouse button rapidly, as to select an icon.

client, a workstation on a network that gains access to central data files, programs, and peripheral devices through a server.

clock, the circuit in a digital computer that provides a common reference train of electronic pulses for all other circuits. The **clock speed,** usually measured in megahertz, indicates how fast the computer will carry out commands.

clock speed. See under CLOCK.

COBOL, a high-level computer language suited for writing programs to process large files of data. [co(mmon) b(usiness)-o(riented) l(anguage)]

code, the symbolic arrangement of statements or instructions in a computer program in which letters, digits, etc., are represented as binary numbers; the set of instructions in such a program.

color monitor. See under MONITOR.

command, a signal, as a keystroke, instructing a computer to perform a specific task.

compact disc, a small optical disc on which music, data, or images are digitally recorded for playback. *Abbr.:* CD

compatible, 1. (of software) able to run on a specified computer. **2.** (of hardware) able to work with a specified device. **3.** (of a computer system) functionally equivalent to another, usu. widely used, system.

compiler, a computer program that translates another program written in a high-level language into a form, usu. machine language, that can be executed by a computer.

compression, reduction of the size of computer data by efficient storage.

computer graphics, 1. pictorial computer output produced, through the use of software, on a display screen or printer. **2.** the technique or process used to produce such output.

configuration, 1. a computer, the equipment connected to it, plus software, set up to work together. **2.** the act of configuring a computer system.

configure, 1. to put (a computer system) together by supplying a specific computer with appropriate peripheral devices, as a monitor and disk drive, and connecting them. **2.** to insert batch files into (a program) to enable it to run with a particular computer.

console, the control unit of a computer, including the keyboard and display screen.

conversion, 1. the process of enabling software for one computer system to run on another. **2.** the transformation of data from a form compatible with one computer program to a form compatible with another.

coprocessor, a processing unit that assists the CPU in carrying out certain types of operations. A **math coprocessor** is a processing unit that performs mathematical calculations using floating-point notation.

copy protection, a method of preventing users of a computer program from making unauthorized copies, usu. through hidden instructions contained in the program code.

CPU, central processing unit: the key component of a computer system, containing the circuitry necessary to interpret and execute program instructions. Compare MICROPROCESSOR.

crash, (of a computer) to suffer a major failure because of a malfunction of hardware or software.

cursor, a movable, sometimes blinking, symbol used to indicate where data (as text, commands, etc.) may be input on a computer screen.

cyber-, a combining form representing "computer" (*cybertalk; cyberart*).

cyberpunk, 1. science fiction featuring extensive human interaction with supercomputers and a punk ambiance. **2.** *Slang.* a computer hacker.

cyberspace, 1. the realm of electronic communication. **2.** VIRTUAL REALITY.

daisy wheel, a small spoked wheel with raised numbers, letters, etc., on the tips of the spokes: used as the printing element in some computer printers. Laser and inkjet printers have almost entirely replaced daisy-wheel printers for producing high-resolution text with personal computers.

database or **data base, 1.** a collection of organized, related data in electronic form that can be accessed and manipulated by specialized computer software. **2.** a fund of information on one or more subjects, as a collection of articles or précis, accessible by computer.

data bus. See under BUS.

data highway, INFORMATION SUPERHIGHWAY.

DBMS, database management system: a set of software programs for controlling the storage, retrieval, and modification of organized data in a computerized database.

dedicated, (of a computer) designed for a specific use or an exclusive application: *a dedicated word processor.*

default, a preset value that a computer system assumes or an action that it takes unless otherwise instructed.

density, a measure of how much data can be stored in a given amount of space on a disk, tape, or other computer storage medium.

desktop computer, a computer made to fit or be used on a desk or table.

desktop publishing, the design and production of publications by means of specialized software enabling a microcomputer to generate typeset-quality text and graphics.

digerati, people skilled with or knowledgeable about computers. [DIG(ITAL) + (LIT)ERATI]

digital, involving or using numerical digits expressed in a scale of notation to represent discretely all variables occurring in a problem. Compare BINARY.

digital computer, a computer that processes information in digital form.

directory, 1. a division in a hierarchical structure that organizes the storage of computer files on a disk. **2.** a listing of such stored files.

disk, any of several types of media for storing electronic data consisting of thin round plates of plastic or metal. Compare FLOPPY DISK, HARD DISK, OPTICAL DISC.

disk drive, a device in or attached to a computer that enables the user to read data from or store data on a disk.

diskette. See under FLOPPY DISK.

display, 1. to show (computer data) on a CRT or other screen. **2. a.** the visual representation of the output of an electronic device. **b.** the portion of the device, as a screen, that shows this representation.

docking station, a small desktop cabinet, usu. containing disk drives and ports for connection to peripherals, into which a laptop may be inserted so as to give it the functionality of a desktop computer.

document, a computer data file.

documentation, instructional materials for computer software or hardware.

dongle, a hardware device attached to a computer without which a given software program will not run: used to prevent unauthorized use.

DOS (dôs, dos), an operating system for microcomputers. [*d(isk) o(perating) s(ystem)*]

dot-matrix printer, a computer printer that produces characters and graphics by pushing pins into an inked ribbon to form the appropriate pattern, or matrix, of dots.

dot pitch, a measure of the distance between each pixel on a computer screen. A lower number indicates a sharper image.

double-click, to click a mouse button twice in rapid succession, as to call up a program or select a file.

download, to transfer (software or data) from a computer to a smaller computer or a peripheral device.

dpi, dots per inch: a measure of resolution used esp. for printed text or images.

drag, to pull (a graphical image or portion of text) from one place to another on a computer screen, esp. by using a mouse.

drive bay. See BAY.

driver, software that controls the interface between a computer and a peripheral device.

DTP, desktop publishing.

dump, 1. to output (computer data), often in binary form, esp. to diagnose a failure. **2.** a copy of dumped computer data.

edit, to modify (computer data or text).

electronic bulletin board. See BBS.

electronic mail, E-MAIL.

e-mail or **email** or **E-mail, 1.** a system for sending messages via telecommunications links between computers. **2.** a message sent by e-mail. **3.** to send a message to by e-mail.

emoticon (i mō′ti kon′), an abbreviation or icon used on a computer network, as *IMHO* for "in my humble opinion" or :-), a sideways representation of a smiling face, to indicate amusement. [b. of EMOTION and ICON]

end user or **end-user,** the ultimate user of a computer or a software program.

Energy Star Program, a program of the U.S. Environmental Protection Agency encouraging the manufacture of personal computers and peripherals that can reduce their energy consumption when left idle.

enhance, to provide with more complex or sophisticated features, as a computer program.

enhanced keyboard, a keyboard having 101 keys, with 12 function keys along the top.

environment, the hardware or software configuration of a computer system.

EPROM (ē′prom′), a memory chip that can be reprogrammed by first clearing its contents with ultraviolet light: used frequently in the manufacture of personal computers and peripherals. [e(rasable) p(rogrammable) r(ead-)o(nly) m(emory)]

Ethernet, *Trademark.* a local-area network protocol featuring a bus topology (all devices are connected to a central cable) and a 10 megabit per second data transfer rate.

execute, to run (a computer program) or process (a command).

expansion card (or **board**), a circuit board that fits into an expansion slot, used to add sound capability, more memory, etc. A **sound card** is an expansion card that permits files containing music, voice, or other sounds to be played on a computer.

expansion slot, a connection to which a new circuit board can be added to expand a computer's capabilities.

export, to save (documents, data, etc.) in a format usable by another application program.

FAQ, a document that introduces newcomers to a technical topic, as in a newsgroup. [f(requently) a(sked) q(uestions)]

fax modem, a modem that can fax data, as

documents or pictures, directly from a computer.

field, a unit of information, as a person's name, that combines with related fields, as an official title, address, or company name, to form one complete record in a computerized database.

file, a collection of related computer data or program records stored by name, as on a disk.

file server, a computer that makes files available to workstations on a network. Compare SERVER.

fire wall or **firewall,** an integrated collection of security measures designed to prevent unauthorized electronic access to a networked computer system.

firmware, software stored permanently on a ROM chip.

first-generation, being the first model or version available to users: *a first-generation computer program.*

flame, *Slang.* (esp. on a computer network) **1.** an act or instance of angry criticism or disparagement. **2.** to behave in an offensive manner; rant. **3.** to insult or criticize angrily.

flash memory, a type of reprogrammable computer memory that retains information even with the power turned off.

flat-file, of or pertaining to a database system in which each database consists of a single file not linked to any other file.

floating point, a decimal point whose location is not fixed, used esp. in computer operations.

floppy disk, a thin, portable, flexible plastic disk coated with magnetic material, for storing computer data and programs. Currently, the 3½-inch disk (also called a **diskette**), housed in a square rigid envelope, is the common size used with personal computers.

flops, a measure of computer speed, equal to the number of floating-point operations the computer can perform per second (used esp. in combination with *mega-, giga-, tera-*). [fl(oating-point) op(erations per) s(econd)]

font, a set of characters that have a given shape or design. The characters in a **scalable font** can be enlarged or reduced.

footprint, the surface space occupied by a microcomputer.

format, 1. the arrangement of data for computer input or output, as the number of fields in a database record or the margins in a report. **2. a.** to set the format of (computer input or output). **b.** to prepare (a disk) for writing and reading.

FORTRAN, a high-level programming language used mainly for solving problems in science and engineering. [for(mula) tran(slator)]

freeware, computer software distributed without charge. Compare SHAREWARE.

FTP, 1. File Transfer Protocol: a software protocol for exchanging information between computers over a network. **2.** any program that implements this protocol.

function key, a key on a computer keyboard used alone or with other keys for operations.

gateway, software or hardware that links two computer networks.

gigabyte, a measure of data storage capacity equal to 1 billion (10⁹) bytes.

gigaflops, a measure of computer speed, equal to one billion floating-point operations per second.

global, (of a computer operation) operating on a group of similar strings, commands, etc., in a single step.

Gopher, 1. a protocol for a menu-based system of accessing documents on the Internet. **2.** any program that implements this protocol.

graphic, a computer-generated image.

graphical user interface, a software interface designed to standardize and simplify the use of computer programs, as by using a mouse to manipulate text and images on a display screen featuring icons, windows, and menus. Also called **GUI.**

graphics, (used with a sing. v.) COMPUTER GRAPHICS.

groupware, software enabling a group to work together on common projects, share data, and synchronize schedules, esp. through networked computers.

GUI (gōō'ē), GRAPHICAL USER INTERFACE.

hacker, Slang. **1.** a computer enthusiast who is especially proficient in programming. **2.** a computer user who attempts to gain unauthorized access to proprietary computer systems.

hard copy, computer output printed on paper; printout.

hard disk, a rigid disk coated with magnetic material, for storing computer programs and relatively large amounts of data.

hard drive, n. a disk drive containing a hard disk.

hardware, the mechanical, magnetic, electronic, and electrical devices composing a computer system. Compare SOFTWARE.

hardware platform, a group of compatible computers that can run the same software.

hard-wired or **hardwired, 1.** built into a computer's hardware and thus not readily changed. **2.** (of a terminal) connected to a computer by a direct circuit rather than through a switching network.

Help, a system for supplying documentation for a software program, accessible on-line from within the program.

high-level, (of a programming language) based on a vocabulary of Englishlike statements for writing program code rather than the more abstract instructions typical of assembly language or machine language.

hi-res (hī'rez'), high-resolution. See RESOLUTION.

hit, an instance of accessing a Web site.

home computer, a microcomputer designed for use in the home, as with game, multimedia, and educational software or electronic on-line services.

home page, the initial page of a Web site.

host computer, the main computer in a network, which controls or performs certain functions for other connected computers.

hot link, a hypertext link.

HTML, HyperText Markup Language: a set of standards, a variety of SGML, used to tag the elements of a hypertext document: the standard for documents on the World Wide Web.

http, hypertext transfer protocol: a protocol for transferring hypertext documents, the standard protocol for the World Wide Web.

hyper link, a hypertext link.

hypermedia, (usu. with a sing. v.) a system in which various forms of information, as data, text, graphics, video, and audio, are linked together by a hypertext program.

hypertext, data, as text, graphics, or sound, stored in a computer so that a user can move nonsequentially through a link from one object or document to another.

icon, a small graphic image on a computer screen representing a disk drive, a file, or a software command, as a picture of a wastebasket that can be pointed at and clicked on to delete a file.

impact printer, a computer printer, as a dot-matrix printer, that forms characters by causing a printhead to strike at paper through an inked ribbon.

import, to bring (documents, data, etc.) into one application program from another.

information superhighway, a large-scale communications network providing a variety of often interactive services, such as text databases, electronic mail, and audio and video materials, accessed through computers, television sets, etc.

information technology, the development, implementation, and maintenance of computer hardware and software systems to organize and communicate information electronically.

initialize, 1. to set (variables, counters, switches, etc.) to their starting values at the beginning of a computer program or subprogram. **2.** to prepare (a computer, printer, etc.) for reuse by clearing previous data from memory. **3.** to format (a disk).

inkjet printer, a computer printer that prints text or graphics by spraying jets of ink onto paper to form a high-quality image approaching that of a laser printer.

input, 1. a. data entered into a computer for processing. **b.** the process of introducing data into the internal storage of a computer. **2.** of or pertaining to data or equipment used for input: a computer's main input device. **3.** to enter (data) into a computer for processing.

input/output, the combination of devices, channels, and techniques controlling the transfer of information between a CPU and its peripherals. *Abbr.:* I/O

install, to put in place or connect for service or use: *to install software on a computer.*

instruction, a computer command.

interactive, (of a computer or program) characterized by or allowing immediate two-way communication between a source of information and a user, who can initiate or respond to queries.

interface, computer hardware or software designed to communicate information between hardware devices, between software programs, between devices and programs, or between a computer and a user.

interlaced, of or pertaining to technology that allows a monitor to display an image with higher resolution than it would otherwise be capable of by refreshing half the lines on the screen during one pass of an electron gun and the other half during a second pass. Interlaced monitors are more subject to flicker than **noninterlaced** ones.

interleaving, a method for making data retrieval more efficient by rearranging or renumbering the sectors on a hard disk or by splitting a computer's main memory into sections so that the sectors or sections can be read in alternating cycles.

Internet, a large computer network linking smaller computer networks worldwide (usually prec. by *the*).

interrupt, a hardware or software signal that temporarily stops program execution in a computer so that another procedure can be carried out.

intranet, a computer network with restricted access, as within a corporation, that uses software and protocols developed for the Internet.

I/O, input/output.

jaggies, a jagged, stairstep effect on curved or diagonal lines that are reproduced in low resolution, as on a printout or computer display.

Java, *Trademark.* a programming language used to create interactive applications running over the Internet.

job, a unit of work for a computer.

joystick, a lever used to control the movement of a cursor or other graphic element, as in a video game.

K, 1. the number 1024 or 2^{10}: *A binary 32K memory has 32,768 positions.* **2.** kilobyte.

KB, kilobyte.

Kb, kilobit.

keypad, a small panel of numeric and other special keys on a computer keyboard.

kilobit, 1. 1024 (2^{10}) bits. **2.** (loosely) 1000 bits. *Symbol:* Kb

kilobyte, 1. 1024 (2^{10}) bytes. **2.** (loosely) 1000 bytes. *Symbol:* K, KB

LAN (lan), LOCAL-AREA NETWORK.

language, a set of symbols and syntactic rules for their combination and use, by means of which a computer can be given directions.

laptop, a portable, usu. battery-powered microcomputer small enough to rest on the lap.

laser printer, a high-speed, high-resolution computer printer that uses a laser to form dot-matrix patterns and an electrostatic process to print a page at a time.

launch, to start (an application program).

letter-quality, designating or producing type equal in sharpness and resolution to that produced by an electric typewriter: *a letter-quality computer printer. Abbr.:* LQ

light pen, a hand-held light-sensitive input device used for drawing on a computer display screen or for pointing at characters or objects, as when choosing options from a menu.

line printer, an impact printer that produces a full line of computer output at a time.

link, an object, as text or graphics, linked through hypertext to a document, another object, etc.

LISP, a high-level programming language that processes data in the form of lists: widely used in artificial-intelligence applications. [*lis(t) p(rocessing)*]

list server, any program that distributes messages to a mailing list.

load, 1. to bring (a program or data) into a computer's RAM, as from a disk, so as to make it available for processing. **2.** to place (an input/output medium) into an appropriate device, as by inserting a disk into a disk drive.

local-area network, a computer network confined to a limited area, linking esp. personal computers so that programs, data, peripheral devices, and processing tasks can be shared. Compare MULTIUSER SYSTEM. Also called **LAN.**

log in (or **on**), to gain access to a secured computer system or on-line service by keying in personal identification information.

log off (or **out**), to terminate a session on a computer.

loop, the reiteration of a set of instructions in a computer routine or program.

lo-res (lō′rez′), low-resolution. See RESOLUTION.

lpm or **LPM,** lines per minute: a measure of the speed of an impact printer.

LQ, letter-quality.

machine language, a usu. numerical coding system specific to the hardware of a given computer model, into which any high-level or assembly program must be translated before being run.

machine-readable, (of data) in a form suitable for direct acceptance and processing by computer, as an electronic file on a magnetic disk.

macro, a single instruction, for use in a computer program, that represents a sequence of instructions or keystrokes.

mailbox, a file in a computer for the storage of electronic mail.

mailing list, a list of e-mail addresses to which messages, usu. on a specific set of topics, are sent; a discussion group whose messages are distributed through e-mail.

mainframe, a large computer, often the hub of a system serving many users. Compare MICROCOMPUTER, MINICOMPUTER.

main memory. See RAM.

management information system, a computerized information-processing force offering management support to a company. *Abbr.:* MIS

math coprocessor. See under COPROCESSOR.

MB, megabyte.

Mb, megabit.

megabit, 1. 2^{20} (1,048,576) bits. **2.** (loosely) one million bits. *Abbr.:* Mb

megabyte, 1. a measure of data storage capacity equal to 2^{20} (1,048,576) bytes. **2.** (loosely) one million bytes. *Abbr.:* MB

megaflops, a measure of computer speed, equal to one million floating-point operations per second.

megahertz, a unit of frequency equal to one million cycles per second, used to measure microprocessor speed.

memory, 1. the capacity of a computer to store information, esp. internally in RAM while electrical power is on. **2.** the components of the computer in which such information is stored.

menu, a list of options or commands from which to choose, displayed on a computer screen. A **menu bar** is a horizontal list of options near the top of a window. A **pop-up menu** appears temporarily when the user clicks on a selection. A **pull-down menu** appears beneath the option selected.

menu bar. See under MENU.

menu-driven, of or pertaining to computer software that makes extensive use of menus to enable users to choose program options.

MHz, megahertz.

microchip. See CHIP.

microcomputer, a compact computer having less capability than a minicomputer and employing a microprocessor.

microprocessor, an integrated computer circuit that performs all the functions of a CPU.

MIDI (mid/ē), Musical Instrument Digital Interface: a standard means of sending digitally encoded information about music between electronic devices, as between synthesizers and computers.

minicomputer, a computer with processing and storage capabilities smaller than those of a mainframe but larger than those of a microcomputer.

mini-tower, a vertical case, smaller than a tower and larger than a case for a desktop

computer, designed to house a computer system standing on a floor or desk.

MIPS (mips), million instructions per second: a measure of computer speed.

MIS or **M.I.S.,** management information system.

modem, 1. an electronic device that makes possible the transmission of data to or from a computer via telephone or other communication lines. **2.** to send (information, data, or the like) via a modem. [*mo(dulator)-dem(odulator)*]

monitor, a component with a display screen for viewing computer data. A **monochrome monitor** can display two colors, one for the foreground and one for the background. A **color monitor** can display from 16 to one million different colors.

monochrome monitor. See under MONITOR.

morphing, the smooth transformation of one image into another by computer, as in a motion picture.

motherboard, a rigid slotted board upon which other boards that contain the basic circuitry of a computer or of a computer component can be mounted.

mouse, a palm-sized device equipped with one or more buttons, used to point at and select items on a computer screen, with the displayed pointer controlled by means of analogous movement of the device on a nearby surface.

mouse pad, a small typically foam rubber sheet used to provide a stable surface on which a computer mouse can be moved.

MPC, Multimedia PC: a system conforming to specifications covering audio, video, and other multimedia components, and able to run multimedia software.

MPR II, a standard developed in Sweden that limits to 250 nanoteslas the electromagnetic radiation emissions from a monitor at a distance of a half meter.

MS DOS or **MS-DOS** (em/es/ dôs/, -dos/), *Trademark.* a microcomputer operating system.

multimedia, (*used with a sing. v.*) the combined use or integration of several media in computer applications, as text, sound, graphics, animation, and video.

multitasking, the concurrent execution of two or more jobs or programs by a single CPU.

multiuser system, a computer system in which multiple terminals connect to a host computer that handles processing tasks.

NC, network computer.

Net, the Internet (usually prec. by *the*).

netiquette, the etiquette of computer networks.

netizen, a user of the Internet.

network, a computer or telecommunications system linked to permit exchange of information.

network computer, a computer with minimal processing power, designed primarily to provide access to networks, as the Internet.

new media, electronic or other forms of media regarded as being experimental.

newsgroup, a discussion group on a specific set of topics, maintained on a computer network.

noninterlaced, of or pertaining to technology that refreshes all the lines on a monitor's screen at one time while maintaining screen resolution. Noninterlaced monitors are less subject to flicker than **interlaced** ones.

nonvolatile, (of computer memory) having the property of retaining data when electrical power fails or is turned off.

NOR (nôr), a Boolean operator that returns a positive result when both operands are negative.

NOT (not), a Boolean operator that returns a positive result if its operand is negative and a negative result if its operand is positive.

notebook, a small, lightweight laptop computer measuring approximately 8½

numeric keypad. See KEYPAD.

object, any item that can be individually selected or manipulated, as a picture or piece of text.

object-oriented, pertaining to or being a system, programming language, etc., that supports the use of objects, as an entire image, a routine, or a data structure.

OCR, optical character recognition.

off-line or **offline,** operating independently of, or disconnected from, an associated computer. Compare ON-LINE.

on′-line′ or **on/line/, 1.** operating under the direct control of, or connected to, a main computer. **2.** connected by computer to one or more other computers or networks, as through a commercial database service or the Internet. **3.** using a computer. **4.** with or through a computer, esp. over a network.

on-line service, a database service providing information, news, etc., accessed through a modem.

operating system, the software that directs a computer's operations, as by controlling and scheduling the execution of other programs and managing storage and input/output.

optical character recognition, the process or technology of reading printed or typed text by electronic means and converting it to digital data. Abbr.: OCR

optical disc, a grooveless disk on which digital data, as text, music, or pictures, are stored as tiny pits in the surface and read or replayed by a laser beam scanning the surface.

optical scanner. See SCANNER.

OR (ôr), a Boolean operator that returns a positive result when either or both operands are positive.

output, 1. information made available by computer, as on a printout, display screen,

or disk. **2.** the process of transferring such information from computer memory to or by means of an output device.

page, 1. a block of computer memory up to 4,096 bytes long. **2.** a portion of a program that can be moved to a computer's internal memory from external storage.

page description language, a high-level programming language for determining the output of a page printer designed to work with it, independent of the printer's internal codes. Abbr.: PDL

page printer, a high-speed, high-resolution computer printer that uses a light source, as a laser beam or electrically charged ions, to print a full page of text or graphics at a time.

palette, the complete range of colors made available by a computer graphics card, from which a user or program may choose those to be displayed.

palmtop, a battery-powered microcomputer small enough to fit in the palm.

parallel, 1. of or pertaining to operations within a computer that are performed simultaneously: parallel processing. **2.** pertaining to or supporting the transfer of electronic data several bits at a time: a parallel printer. Compare SERIAL.

Pascal, a high-level computer language designed to facilitate structured programming.

passive-matrix, of or pertaining to a relatively low-resolution liquid-crystal display (LCD) with low contrast, used esp. for laptop computers. Compare ACTIVE MATRIX.

password, a string of characters typed into a computer to identify and obtain access for an authorized user.

path, (in some computer operating systems) **1.** a listing of the route through directories and subdirectories that locates and thereby names a specific file or program on a disk drive. **2.** the currently active list of all such routes that tells the operating system where to find programs, enabling a user to run them from other directories.

PC or **P.C.,** personal computer.

PCMCIA, Personal Computer Memory Card International Association: (esp. for laptop computers) a standard for externally accessible expansion slots that accept compatible cards for enhancing the computer's functions, as by adding memory or supplying a portable modem.

PDA, personal digital assistant.

PDL, page description language.

pen-based, (of a computer) having an electronic stylus rather than a keyboard as the primary input device.

peripheral, an external hardware device, as a keyboard, printer, or tape drive, connected to a computer's CPU.

personal computer, a microcomputer designed for individual use, as for word processing, financial analysis, desktop publishing, or playing computer games. Abbr.: PC

personal digital assistant, a hand-held computer, often pen-based, that provides esp. organizational software, as an appointment calendar, and communications hardware, as a fax modem. *Abbr.:* PDA

PIM, personal information manager.

pixel, the smallest element of an image that can be individually processed in a video display system.

platform, 1. HARDWARE PLATFORM. **2.** SOFTWARE PLATFORM.

Plug and Play, (*sometimes l.c.*) a standard for the production of compatible computers, peripherals, and software that facilitates device installation and enables automatic configuration of the system.

plug-compatible, designating computers or peripherals that are compatible with another vendor's models and could replace them.

pop-up menu. See MENU.

port, 1. a data connection in a computer to which a peripheral device or a transmission line from a remote terminal can be attached. **2.** to create a new version of (an application program) to run on a different hardware platform (sometimes fol. by *over*).

portable, (of data, software, etc.) able to be used on different computer systems.

post, to send (a message) to a newsgroup.

ppm or **PPM,** pages per minute: a measure of the speed of a page printer.

printer, a computer output device that produces a paper copy of data or graphics.

printhead, the printing element on an impact printer.

printout, computer output produced by a printer.

printwheel or **print wheel.** See DAISY WHEEL.

program, 1. a sequence of instructions enabling a computer to perform a task; piece of software. **2.** to provide a program for (a computer).

programming language, a high-level language used to write computer programs, or, sometimes, an assembly language.

PROM, a memory chip whose contents can be programmed by a user or manufacturer for a specific purpose. [p(*rogrammable*) r(*ead*)-o(*nly*) m(*emory*)]

prompt, a symbol or message on a computer screen requesting more information or indicating readiness to accept instructions.

protocol, a set of rules governing the format of messages that are exchanged between computers.

pull-down menu. See under MENU.

queue (kyo͞o), a sequence of items waiting in order for electronic action in a computer system.

RAM (ram), volatile computer memory, used for creating, loading, and running programs and for manipulating and temporarily storing data; main memory. Compare ROM. [r(*andom*)-a(*ccess*) m(*emory*)]

random-access, designating an electronic storage medium that allows information to be stored and retrieved in arbitrary sequence.

random-access memory. See RAM.

raster, a set of horizontal lines composed of individual pixels, used to form an image on a CRT or other screen.

read, to obtain (data or programs) from an external storage medium and place in a computer's memory.

read-only, noting or pertaining to computer files or memory that can be read but cannot normally be changed.

read-only memory. See ROM.

readout or **read-out,** the output of information from a computer in readable form.

real-time, of or pertaining to computer applications or processes that can respond immediately to user input.

recognition, the automated conversion of words or images into a form that can be processed by a computer. Compare OPTICAL CHARACTER RECOGNITION.

record, a group of related fields treated as a unit in a database.

redlining or **red-lining,** a marking device, as underlining or boldface, used esp. in word processing to highlight suggested additional text in a document.

refresh, to redisplay the information on (a screen) so as to prevent loss or fading. A re-fresh rate of many times per second is typical for a computer's display screen.

refresh rate. See under REFRESH.

register, a high-speed storage location in a computer's CPU, used to store a related string of bits, as a word or phrase.

relational database, an electronic database comprising multiple files of related information, usu. stored in tables of rows (records) and columns (fields), and allowing a link to be established between separate files that have a matching field, as a column of invoice numbers, so that the two files can be queried simultaneously by the user.

resident, 1. encoded and permanently available to a computer user, as a font in a printer's ROM or software on a CD-ROM. **2.** (of a computer program) currently active or standing by in computer memory, as a TSR program.

resolution, the degree of sharpness of a computer-generated image as measured by the number of dots per linear inch in a hard-copy printout or the number of pixels across and down on a display screen.

response time, the time that elapses while waiting for a computer to respond to a command.

retrieve, to locate and read (data) from computer storage, as for display on a monitor.

reverse video, a mode on the display screen of a computer in which the colors normally used for characters and background are reversed.

RISC (risk), reduced instruction set computer: a computer whose central processing unit recognizes a relatively small number of instructions, which it can execute very rapidly. Compare CISC.

ROM (rom), nonvolatile, nonmodifiable computer memory, used to hold programmed instructions to the system. Compare RAM. [r(ead)-o(nly) m(emory)]

routine, a set of instructions directing a computer to perform a specific task.

run, to process (the instructions in a program) by computer.

save, to copy (computer data) onto a hard or floppy disk, a tape, etc.

scalable font. See under FONT.

scan, to read (data) for use by a computer or computerized device, esp. using an optical scanner.

scanner, a device that converts text or graphic images into a digital form that the computer can use. Also called **optical scanner.**

screen saver, 1. a computer program that blanks the screen display or puts a moving pattern on it to prevent the permanent etching of a pattern on a screen when the pattern is displayed for a long time. **2.** any of a selection of moving patterns available through this program, appearing on a screen if there has been no user input for a specified amount of time.

scroll, to move a cursor smoothly, vertically or sideways, gradually causing new data to replace old on the display screen of a computer.

SCSI (skuz′ē), a standard for computer interface ports featuring faster data transmission and greater flexibility than normal ports. [s(mall) c(omputer) s(ystem) i(nterface)]

search, 1. to command software to find specified characters or codes in (an electronic file): *to search a database for all instances of "U.S." and replace them with "United States."* **2.** to find specified characters or codes in an electronic file by means of software commands.

serial, 1. pertaining to or supporting the transfer of electronic data in a stream of sequential bits: *a serial port.* **2.** of or pertaining to the transmission or processing of each part of a whole in sequence, as each bit of a byte or each byte of a computer word. Compare PARALLEL.

server, a computer that makes services, as access to data files, programs, and peripheral devices, available to workstations on a network. Compare CLIENT, FILE SERVER.

SGML, Standard Generalized Markup Language: a set of standards enabling a user to create an appropriate scheme for tagging the elements of an electronic document, as to facilitate the production of multiple versions in various print and electronic formats.

shareware, computer software distributed without initial charge but for which the user is encouraged to pay a nominal fee to cover support for continued use.

shell, a computer program providing a menu-driven or graphical user interface designed to simplify use of the operating system, as in loading application programs.

slipstreaming, the act of updating a software program without adequately informing the public, as by failing to release it as an official new version.

slot, EXPANSION SLOT.

smiley, a sideways representation of a smiling face, :-), or similar combination of symbols, as ;-), a winking face, or :-(, a sad face, used to communicate humor, sarcasm, sadness, etc., in an electronic message.

software, 1. programs for directing the operation of a computer or processing electronic data. Compare HARDWARE. **2.** DOCUMENTATION.

software platform, a major piece of software, as an operating system, an operating environment, or a database, under which various smaller application programs can be designed to run.

sort, to place (computerized data) in order, numerically or alphabetically.

sound card (or **board**). See under EXPANSION CARD.

spam, 1. a disruptive message posted on a computer network. **2.** to send spam to.

spell (or **spelling**) **checker,** a computer program for checking the spelling of words in an electronic document.

split screen, a mode of operation on a computer that uses windows to enable simultaneous viewing of two or more displays on the same screen.

spool, to operate (an input/output device) by using buffers in main and secondary storage.

spreadsheet, an outsize ledger sheet simulated electronically by specialized computer software, used esp. for financial planning.

standalone, (of an electronic device) able to function without connection to a larger system; self-contained.

storage. See MEMORY.

store, to put or retain (data) in a computer memory unit, as a hard disk.

subdirectory, a directory hierarchically below another directory in DOS or UNIX.

subnotebook, a laptop computer smaller and lighter than a notebook, typically weighing less than 5 pounds (2.3 kg).

subroutine, a prepared instruction sequence that a programmer can insert into a computer program as needed.

suite, a group of computer software programs sold as a unit and designed to work together.

surf, to search haphazardly through (a computer network) for information or entertainment.

surge protector, a device that provides an alternative pathway for electrical energy when excessive voltage appears on the power line, shunting the energy away from computer circuits.

SVGA, super video graphics array: a high-resolution standard for displaying text, graphics, and colors on computer monitors, a higher standard than VGA.

system, a working combination of computer hardware, software, and data communications devices.

system (or **systems**) **program,** a program, as an operating system, compiler, or utility program, that controls some aspect of the operation of a computer. Compare APPLICATION PROGRAM.

systems analysis, the methodical study of the data-processing needs of a business or project.

tag, a symbol or other labeling device indicating the beginning or end of a unit of information in an electronic document.

tape drive, a program-controlled device that reads data from or writes data on a magnetic tape which moves past a read-write head.

TCP/IP, Transmission Control Protocol/Internet Protocol: a communications protocol for computer networks, the main protocol for the Internet.

telecommuting, the act or practice of working at home using a computer terminal electronically linked to one's place of employment.

Telnet, *Trademark.* **1.** a protocol for connecting to a remote computer on the Internet. **2.** any program that implements this protocol.

teraflops, a measure of computer speed, equal to one trillion floating-point operations per second.

terminal, any device for entering information into a computer or receiving information from it, as a keyboard with video display unit.

text editor, a computer program for writing and modifying documents or program code on-screen, usu. having little or no formatting ability.

toggle, to shift back and forth between two settings or modes of computer operation by means of a key or programmed keystroke.

touchscreen or **touch screen,** a computer display that can detect and respond to the presence and location of a finger or instrument on or near its surface.

tower, a vertical case designed to house a computer system standing on the floor.

track, one of a number of concentric rings on the surface of a floppy disk, or other computer storage medium, along which data are recorded.

trackball, a computer input device for con-

trolling the pointer on a display screen by rotating a ball set inside a case.

track pad, a computer input device for controlling the pointer on a display screen: used chiefly in notebook computers.

tree, a computer data structure organized like a tree whose nodes store data elements and whose branches represent pointers to other nodes in the tree.

TSR, a computer program with any of several ancillary functions, usu. held resident in RAM for instant activation while one is using another DOS program. [*t(erminate and) s(-tay) r(esident)*]

UNIX (yōō′niks), *Trademark.* a highly portable multiuser, multitasking operating system used on a variety of computers ranging from mainframes through workstations to personal computers.

upload, to transfer (software or data) from a smaller to a larger computer.

URL, Uniform Resource Locater: a protocol for specifying addresses on the Internet.

user, a person who uses a computer.

user-friendly, easy to operate, understand, etc.: *a user-friendly computer.*

user (or **user's**) **group,** a club for the exchange of information and services among computer users.

utility program, a system program used esp. to simplify standard computer operations, as sorting, copying, or deleting files. Also called **utility.**

vaporware, a product, esp. computer software, that is announced and promoted while it is still in development and that may never come to market.

VDT, video display terminal.

vector graphics, a method of electronically coding graphic images so that they are represented in lines rather than fixed bit maps, allowing an image, as on a computer display screen, to be rotated or proportionally scaled.

VGA, video graphics array: a high-resolution standard for displaying text, graphics, and colors on monitors.

video display terminal, a computer terminal consisting of a screen on which data or graphics can be displayed. *Abbr.:* VDT

virtual, 1. temporarily simulated or extended by software: *a virtual disk in RAM; virtual memory on a hard disk.* **2.** of, existing on, or by means of computers: *virtual discussions on the Internet.*

virtual reality, a realistic simulation of an environment, including three-dimensional graphics, by a computer system using interactive software and hardware.

virus, a segment of self-replicating code planted illegally in a computer program, often to damage or shut down a system or network.

visit, to access (a Web site).

volatile, (of computer storage) not retaining data when electrical power is turned off.

WAN (wan), WIDE-AREA NETWORK.

Web, (*sometimes l.c.*) World Wide Web (usually prec. by *the*).

Web page, a single, usu. hypertext document on the World Wide Web that can incorporate text, graphics, sounds, etc.

Web site, a connected group of pages on the World Wide Web regarded as a single entity, usu. maintained by one person or organization and devoted to one single topic or several closely related topics.

wide-area network, a computer network that spans a relatively large geographical area. Also called **WAN.**

wild card, a character, as an asterisk, set aside by a computer operating system to represent one or more other characters of a file name, as in the DOS command "DEL *. DOC," which would delete all files with names ending in ".DOC."

window, 1. a portion of the screen of a computer terminal on which data can be displayed independently of the rest of the screen. **2.** a view of a portion of a document bounded by the borders of a computer's display screen.

Windows, *Trademark.* any of several microcomputer operating systems or environments featuring a graphical user interface.

wired, connected electronically to one or more computer networks.

word processing, the automated production and storage of documents using computers, electronic printers, and text-editing software.

word processor, a computer program or computer system designed for word processing.

workstation or **work station, 1.** a powerful microcomputer, often with a high-resolution display, used for computer-aided design, electronic publishing, or other graphics-intensive processing. **2.** a computer terminal or microcomputer connected to a mainframe, minicomputer, or data-processing network. **3.** a work or office area assigned to one person, often one accommodating a computer terminal or other electronic equipment.

World Wide Web, a system of extensively interlinked hypertext documents: a branch of the Internet.

write, to transfer (data, text, etc.) from computer memory to an output medium.

WWW, World Wide Web.

WYSIWYG (wiz′ē wig′), of, pertaining to, or being a computer screen display that shows text exactly as it will appear when printed. [w(hat) y(ou) s(ee) i(s) w(hat) y(ou) g(et)]

XOR (eks′ôr′), a Boolean operator that returns a positive result when either but not both of its operands are positive. [(e)x(clusive) OR]

Signs

♈ Aries, the Ram.

♉ Taurus, the Bull.

♊ Gemini, the Twins.

♋ Cancer, the Crab.

♌ Leo, the Lion.

♍ Virgo, the Virgin.

♎ Libra, the Scales.

♏ Scorpio, the Scorpion.

♐ Sagittarius, the Archer.

♑ Capricorn, the Goat.

♒ Aquarius, the Water Bearer.

♓ Pisces, the Fishes.

☉ 1. the sun. 2. Sunday.

☽ ☾ ● 1. the moon. 2. Monday/

●● new moon.

))) ◐ the moon, first quarter.

○ ☺ full moon.

(((◑ the moon, last quarter.

☿ 1. Mercury. 2. Wednesday.

♀ 1. Venus. 2. Friday.

♃ 1. Jupiter. 2. Thursday.

♄ 1. Saturn. 2. Saturday.

♅ ⛢ Uranus.

♆ Neptune.

♇ Pluto.

✳✳ star.

☄ comet.

BIOLOGY

♂ male; a male organism, organ, or cell; a staminate flower or plant.

♀ female; a female organism, organ or cell; a pistillate flower or plant.

▢ a male.

○ a female.

✕ crossed with; denoting a sexual hybrid.

Avoiding Insensitive and Offensive Language

This essay is intended as a general guide to language that can, intentionally or not, cause offense or perpetuate discriminatory values and practices by emphasizing the differences between people or implying that one group is superior to another.

Several factors complicate the issue. A group may disagree within itself as to what is acceptable and what is not. Many seemingly inoffensive terms develop negative connotations over time and become dated or go out of style as awareness changes. A "within the group" rule often applies, which allows a member of a group to use terms freely that would be considered offensive if used by an outsider.

While it is true that some of the more extreme attempts to avoid offending language have resulted in ludicrous obfuscation, it is also true that heightened sensitivity in language indicates a precision of thought and is a positive move toward rectifying the unequal social status between one group and another.

Suggestions for avoiding insensitive or offensive language are given in the following pages. **The recommended terms are given on the right.** While these suggestions can reflect trends, they cannot dictate or predict the preferences of each individual.

Sexism

Sexism is the most difficult bias to avoid, in part because of the convention of using *man* or *men* and *he* or *his* to refer to people of either sex. Other, more disrespectful conventions include giving descriptions of women in terms of age and appearance while describing men in terms of accomplishment.

Replacing *man* or *men*

Man traditionally referred to a male or to a human in general. Using *man* to refer to a human is often thought to be slighting of women.

Avoid This		Use This Instead
mankind, man	→	human beings, humans, humankind, humanity, people, society, men & women
man-made	→	synthetic, artificial
man in the street	→	average person, ordinary person

Using gender-neutral terms for occupations, positions, roles, etc.

Terms that specify a particular sex can unnecessarily perpetuate certain stereotypes when used generically.

Avoid This		Use This Instead
anchorman	→	anchor

Avoid This		Use This Instead
bellman, bellboy	→	bellhop
businessman	→	businessperson, executive, manager, business owner, retailer, etc.
chairman	→	chair, chairperson
cleaning lady, girl, maid	→	housecleaner, housekeeper, cleaning person, office cleaner
clergyman	→	member of the clergy, rabbi, priest, etc.
clergymen	→	the clergy
congressman	→	representative, member of Congress, legislator
fireman	→	firefighter
forefather	→	ancestor
girl/gal Friday	→	assistant
housewife	→	homemaker
insurance man	→	insurance agent
layman	→	layperson, nonspecialist, nonprofessional
mailman, postman	→	mail or letter carrier
policeman	→	police officer law enforcement officer
salesman, saleswoman,	→	salesperson, sales representative,

Avoid This		Use This Instead
saleslady, salesgirl	→	sales associate, clerk
spokesman	→	spokesperson, representative
stewardess, steward	→	flight attendant
weatherman	→	weather reporter, weathercaster, meteorologist
workman	→	worker
actress	→	actor

Replacing the pronoun *he*

Like *man*, the generic use of *he* can be seen to exclude women.

Avoid This		Use This Instead
When a driver approaches a red light, he must prepare to stop.	→	When drivers approach a red light, they must prepare to stop.
		When a driver approaches a red light, he or she must prepare to stop.
		When approaching a red light, a driver must prepare to stop.

Referring to members of both sexes with parallel names, titles, or descriptions

Don't be inconsistent unless you are trying to make a specific point.

Avoid This		Use This Instead
men and ladies	→	men and women, ladies and gentlemen
Betty Schmidt, an attractive 49-year-old physician, and her husband, Alan Schmidt, a noted editor	→	Betty Schmidt, a physician, and her husband, Alan Schmidt, an editor
Mr. David Kim and Mrs. Betty Harrow	→	Mr. David Kim and Ms. Betty Harrow (unless *Mrs.* is her known preference)
man and wife	→	husband and wife
Dear Sir:	→	Dear Sir/Madam: Dear Madam or Sir: To whom it may concern:

Avoid This		Use This Instead
Mrs. Smith and President Jones	→	Governor Smith and President Jones

Race, Ethnicity, and National Origin

Some words and phrases that refer to racial and ethnic groups are clearly offensive. Other words (e.g., *Oriental, colored*) are outdated or inaccurate. *Hispanic* is generally accepted as a broad term for Spanish-speaking people of the Western Hemisphere, but more specific terms (*Latino, Mexican American*) are also acceptable and in some cases preferred.

Avoid This		Use This Instead
Negro, colored, Afro-American	→	black, African-American (generally preferred to Afro-American)
Oriental, Asiatic	→	Asian, or more specific designations such as Pacific Islander, Chinese American, Korean
Indian	→	*Indian* properly refers to people who live in or come from India.
		American Indian, Native American, or more specific designations (*Chinook, Hopi*), are usually preferred when referring to the native peoples of the Western hemisphere.
Eskimo	→	Inuit, Alaska Natives
native (n.)	→	native peoples, early inhabitants, aboriginal peoples (but not *aborigines*)

Age

The concept of aging is changing as people are living longer and more active lives. Be aware of word choices that reinforce stereotypes (*decrepit, senile*) and avoid mentioning age unless it is relevant.

Avoid This		Use This Instead
elderly, aged,	→	older person,

Avoid This		**Use This Instead**
old, geriatric, the elderly, the aged	→	senior citizen(s), older people, seniors

Sexual Orientation

The term *homosexual* to describe a man or woman is increasingly replaced by the terms *gay* for men and *lesbian* for women. *Homosexual* as a noun is sometimes used only in reference to a male. Among homosexuals, certain terms (such as *queer* and *dyke*) that are usually considered offensive have been gaining currency in recent years. However, it is still prudent to avoid these terms in standard contexts.

Avoiding Depersonalization of Persons with Disabilities or Illnesses

Terminology that emphasizes the person rather than the disability is generally preferred. *Handicap* is used to refer to the environmental barrier that affects the person. (Stairs handicap a person who uses a wheelchair.) While words such as *crazy*, *demented*, and *insane* are used in facetious or informal contexts, these terms are not used to describe people with clinical diagnoses of mental illness. The euphemisms *challenged*, *differently abled*, and *special* are preferred by some people, but are often ridiculed and are best avoided.

Avoid This		**Use This Instead**
Mongoloid	→	person with Down syndrome
wheelchair-bound	→	person who uses a wheelchair
AIDS sufferer, person afflicted with AIDS, AIDS victim	→	person living with AIDS, P.W.A., HIV+, (one who tests positive for HIV but does not show symptoms of AIDS)
polio victim	→	has/had polio
the handicapped, the disabled, or cripple	→	persons with disabilities, person with a disability, person who uses crutches *or* more specific description

Avoid This		**Use This Instead**
deaf-mute, deaf and dumb	→	deaf person

Avoiding Patronizing or Demeaning Expressions

Avoid This		**Use This Instead**
girls (when referring to adult women), the fair sex	→	women
sweetie, dear, dearie, honey	→	(usually not appropriate with strangers or in public situations)
old maid, bachelorette, spinster	→	single woman, woman, divorced woman (but only if one would specify "divorced man" in the same context)
the little woman, old lady, ball and chain	→	wife
boy (when referring to or addressing an adult man)	→	man, sir

Avoiding Language that Excludes or Unnecessarily Emphasizes Differences

References to age, sex, religion, race, and the like should only be included if they are relevant.

Avoid This		**Use This Instead**
lawyers and their wives	→	lawyers and their spouses
a secretary and her boss	→	a secretary and boss, a secretary and his or her boss
the male nurse	→	the nurse
Arab man denies assault charge	→	Man denies assault charge
the articulate black student	→	the articulate student
Marie Curie was A great woman scientist	→	Marie Curie was a great scientist. (unless the intent is to compare her only with other women in the sciences)

Proofreaders' Marks

The marks shown below are used in proofreading and revising printed material. The mark should be written in the margin, directly in line with the part of the text in which the change is being made, and the line of text should show the change. When more than one change is being made in the same line, slash marks are used in the margin to separate the respective marks. A slash may also be used after a single correction.

Mark in margin	Indication in text	Meaning of instruction
a/r	Peter left town in hurfy.	Insert at carets (∧)
ς or γ	Joan sent me the the book.	Delete
⌣	ma⌒ke	Close up; no space
⌣	I haven't seen the⌒m in years.	Delete and close up
stet	They phoned both Al and Jack.	Let it stand; disregard indicated deletion or change
¶	up the river. Two years	Start new paragraph
no ¶ or run in	many unnecessary additives. The most dangerous one	No new paragraph
tr	Put the book on the table. Put the table on the book.	Transpose
tr up or tr ↑	to Eva Barr, who was traveling abroad. Ms. Barr, an actress,	Transpose to place indicated above
tr down or tr ↓	in the clutch. The final score was 6–5. He pitched the last two innings.	Transpose to place indicated below
sp	He owes me 6 dollars.	Spell out
fig	There were eighteen members present.	Set in figures
#	It was a smallvillage.	Insert one letter space
##	too late.After the dance	Insert two letter spaces

451

Mark in margin	Indication in text	Meaning of instruction
hr #	jeroboam	Insert hair space (very thin space)
line #	Oscar Picks ——— # This year's Academy Awards nomination.	Insert line space
eq #	Ron ✓ got rid ✓ of the dog.	Equalize spacing between words
=	thre^e days late_r	Align horizontally
‖	the earth's surface, bounded by lines parallel to the equator	Align vertically
run over	enhance production⌡ 2. It will	Start new line
▢	▢ Rose asked the price.	Insert one em space
▢▢	▢▢ The Use of the Comma	Insert two em spaces
⊏	⊏ What's his last name?	Move left
⊐	April 2, 1945 ⊐	Move right
⌐ ¬	⌐ Please go now. ¬	Move up
⌊ ⌋	⌊Well, that's that⌋	Move down
⊐ ⊏	⊐ ATOMIC ENERGY ⊏	Center (heading, title, etc.)
fl	⊏ 2. Three (3) skirts	Flush left
fr	Total: $89.50 ⊐	Flush right
sent /?	He the copy.	Insert missing word?
⟨OK?⟩ or ⟨?⟩	by Francis Gray. ⟨She⟩wrote	Query or verify; is this correct?
⟨out: see copy⟩	the discovery of but near the hull ∧	Something missing
⊙	Anna teaches music∧	Insert period
↗	We expect Eileen Tom, and Ken. ∧	Insert comma
∧ ;	I came; I saw∧ I conquered.	Insert semicolon
⊙	Ben got up at 630 a.m. ∧	Insert colon

Mark in margin	Indication in text	Meaning of instruction
=	Douglas got a two˄ thirds majority.	Insert hyphen
$\frac{1}{m}$	Mike then left˄very reluctantly.	Insert em dash
$\frac{1}{n}$	See pages 96˄124.	Insert en dash
⌄	Don't mark the author˅s copy. Don't mark the authors˄ copy.	Insert apostrophe
!	Watch out˄	Insert exclamation point
?	Did she write to you˄.	Insert question mark
⟨⟨/⟩⟩	˄Ode on a Grecian Urn,˄ by Keats	Insert quotation marks
⟨/⟩	She said, "Read ˄The Raven˄ tonight."	Insert single quotation marks
(/⟩ or ⸨/⸩	The Nile is 3473 miles ˄5592 km˄ long.	Insert parentheses
[/] or ⸤/⸥	"He ˄Dickson˄ finished first."	Insert brackets
ital	I've seen <u>Casablanca</u> six times.	Set in *italics*
rom	(Gregory drove to Winnipeg.)	Set in roman
bf	See the definition of peace.	Set in **boldface**
lf	She repaired (the) motor easily.	Set in lightface
cap or u/c	the Italian role in Nato	Set in CAPITAL letter(s)
sc	He lived about 350 <u>B.C.</u>	Set in SMALL CAPITAL letter(s)
lc or l/c	Of Mice /And Men	Set in lowercase
u+lc or c+lc uc+lc	STOP! STOP!	Set in uppercase and lowercase
˄2	H2O	Set as subscript
2˅	A² + B2˅	Set as superscript
X	They drove to Ⓜiami	Broken (damaged) type
wf	Turn Ⓡght	Wrong font

METRIC AND
U.S. MEASUREMENTS

LINEAR MEASURE

U.S. Unit	Metric Unit	Metric Unit	U.S. Unit
1 inch (in.)	= 25.4 millimeters = 2.54 centimeters	1 millimeter (mm) 1 centimeter	= 0.03937 inch = 0.3937 inch
1 foot (12 in.)	= 304.8 millimeters = 30.48 centimeters = 0.3048 meter	1 meter (m)	= 39.37 inch = 3.2808 feet = 1.0936 yards
1 yard (36 in.; 3 ft.) 1 mile (5280 ft; 1760 yds.)	= 0.9144 meter = 1609.3 meters = 1.6093 kilometers	1 kilometer (km)	= 3280.8 feet = 1093.6 yards = 0.62137 mile

LIQUID MEASURE

U.S. Unit	Metric Unit	Metric Unit	U.S. Unit
1 teaspoon (1/6 fl. oz.)	= 4.9 milliliters	1 milliliter (ml)	= 0.033814 fl. oz.
1 tbps (1/2 fl. oz.)	= 14.8 milliliters	1 deciliter (dl)	= 3.3814 fl. oz.
1 fluid ounce (fl. oz.)	= 29.573 milliliters		= 33.814 fl. oz.
1 pint (16 fl. oz.)	= 0.473 liter	1 liter (l)	= 1.0567 quarts
1 quart (2 pints; 32 fl. oz.)	= 9.4635 deciliters = 0.94635 liter		= 0.26417 gallon
1 gallon (4 quarts)	= 3.7854 liters		

AREA MEASURE

U.S. Unit	Metric Unit	Metric Unit	U.S. Unit
1 square inch (0.007 sq. ft.)	= 6.452 square centimeters = 645.16 square millimeters	1 square millimeter (mm^2) 1 square centimeter (cm^2)	= 0.00155 square inch = 0.155 square inch
1 square foot (144 sq. in.)	= 929.03 square centimeters = 0.092903 square meter	1 square meter (m^2) 1 hectare (10,000 m^2) 1 square kilometer (km^2)	= 10.764 square = 2471 acres = 0.38608 square mile
1 square yard (9 sq. ft.)	= 0.83613 square meter		
1 acre (43,560 sq. ft.)	= 4047 square meters		
1 square mile (640 acres)	= 2.59 square kilometers		

CAPACITY

U.S. Unit	Metric Unit	Metric Unit	U.S. Unit
1 cubic inch (0.00058 cu. ft.)	= 16.387 cubic centimeters = 0.016387 liter	1 cubic centimeter (cc; cm^3) 1 cubic meter (m^3)	= 0.061023 cubic inch = 35.135 cubic feet (1.3079 cu. yd.)

1 cubic foot (1728 cu. in.)	= 0.028317 cubic meter	1 cubic kilometer (km³)	= 0.23990 cubic mile
1 cubic yard (27 cu. ft.)	= 0.76455 cubic meter		
1 cubic mile (cu. mi.)	= 4.16818 cubic kilometers		

AVOIRDUPOIS WEIGHTS

U.S. Unit	Metric Unit	Metric Unit	U.S. Unit
1 grain	= 0.064799 gram	1 gram (g)	= 15.432 grains
1 ounce (437.5 grains)	= 28.350 grams		= 0.035274 ounce
1 pound (16 oz.)	= 0.45359 kilograms	1 kilogram (kg)	= 2.2046 pounds
1 short ton (2000 lb.)	= 907.18 kilograms = 0.90718 metric ton	1 metric ton	= 0.98421 long ton = 1.1023 short tons
1 long ton (2240 lb.)	= 1016 kilograms = 1.016 metric tons		

METRIC CONVERSION TABLES

METRIC TO U.S.	U.S. TO METRIC

LENGTH

METRIC TO U.S.	U.S. TO METRIC
millimeters × 0.04 = inches	inches × 25.4 = millimeters
centimeters × 0.39 = inches	inches × 2.54 = centimeters
meters × 3.28 = feet	feet × 3.04 = meters
meters × 1.09 = yards	yards × 0.91 = meters
kilometers × 0.6 = miles	miles × 1.6 = kilometers

VOLUME

METRIC TO U.S.	U.S. TO METRIC
milliliters × 0.03 = fluid ounces	teaspoons × 5 = milliliters
milliliters × 0.06 = cubic inches	tablespoons × 15 = milliliters
deciliters × 3.38 = fluid ounces	cubic inches × 16 = milliliters
liters × 2.1 = pints	fluid ounces × 30 = milliliters
liters × 1.06 = quarts	cups × 0.24 = liters
liters × 0.26 gallons	pints × 0.47 = liters
cubic meters × 35.3 = cubic feet	quarts × 0.95 = liters
cubic meters × 1.3 = cubic yards	gallons × 3.8 = liters
	cubic feet × 0.03 = cubic meters
	cubic yards × 0.76 = cubic meters

MASS

METRIC TO U.S.	U.S. TO METRIC
grams × 0.035 = ounces	ounces × 28 = grams
kilograms × 2.2 = pounds	pounds × 0.45 = kilograms
short tons × 0.9 = metric tons	metric tons × 1.1 = short tons

AREA

METRIC TO U.S.	U.S. TO METRIC
sq. centimeters × 0.16 = sq. inches	sq. inches × 6.5 = sq. centimeters
sq. meters × 1.2 = sq. yards	sq. feet × 0.09 = sq. meters
sq. kilometers × 0.4 = sq. miles	sq. yards × 0.8 = sq. meters
hectares (ha) × 2.5 = acres	sq. miles × 2.6 = sq. kilometers
	acres × 0.4 = hectares

TEMPERATURE

degrees Fahrenheit − 32 × 5/9 = degrees Celsius
degrees Celsius × 9/5 + 32 = degrees Fahrenheit